Yearbook on

International

Communist Affairs

1971

Yearbook on International Communist Affairs 1971

HOOVER INSTITUTION PRESS
Stanford University
Stanford, California
1971

The Hoover Institution on War, Revolution and Peace, founded at Stanford University in 1919 by the late President Herbert Hoover, is a center for advanced study and research on public and international affairs in the twentieth century. The views expressed in its publications are entirely those of the authors and do not necessarily reflect the views of the Hoover Institution.

Hoover Institution Publications 105
Standard Book Number 8179-1051-4
Library of Congress Card Number 67-31024
Printed in the United States of America
© 1971 by the Board of Trustees of the
Leland Stanford Junior University

Yearbook on International Communist Affairs 1971

Advisory Board

CONTENTS

North America

Latin America and Caribbean

Asia and the Pacific

International Communist Front Organizations

PREFACE

The objective of the 1971 *Yearbook on International Communist Affairs*, the fifth volume to be published, is to provide a comprehensive survey covering the calendar year 1970 of the organizational structure, internal development, domestic and foreign policies, and activity of the communist parties throughout the world. Most of the materials are based on primary sources.

Profiles of individual communist parties include, as far as available data permit, the following information on each party: founding date; domestic conditions undder which the party operates; membership figures; electoral support and participation, if any, in government; organization and leadership; the role of auxiliary organizations; domestic political programs and activities; decisions on key problems of communist ideology, strategy, and tactics; views and positions on major international issues; orientation within the international communist movement; and principal party communications media. Pro-Chinese, Castroite, Trotskyist, and other rival communist movements are treated whenever applicable. Insofar as they affect the policies and activities of the communist parties, certain pro-communist parties and movements are noted, as are some guerrilla movements (particularly in Latin America and Africa) and heterogeneous elements of the so-called new left. In general, the organizational structure and the policies of these groups are treated only peripherally.

Communist-ruled countries present a particular problem as a result of the entwined interrelationship of government and party. In these profiles, therefore, the focus is on the position and functioning of each party, while policies pursued by the communist-ruled states are treated predominantly in the context of official party programs and attitudes.

The section on International Communist Front Organizations includes brief historical background, structure, policy lines, internal issues, and developments of the major fronts and their role within the overall world communist movement. It is followed by a Chronology, Selected Bibliography, and biographical Index. The Documents section has been dropped, but significant data contained in major documents are incorporated in the *Yearbook*'s profiles.

*   *   *

Members of the Editorial Board were responsible for most of the research and writing of the *Yearbook*. Profiles were contributed also by Dennis L. Bark, William J. Conyngham, L. A. D. Dellin, John K. Emmerson, Lewis H. Gann, H. J. M. Mennes, James F. Morrison, Nicholas C. Pano, Janos Radvanyi, Lynn Ratliff, Nelly Stromquist, Zdenek L. Suda, Witold S. Sworakowski, and M. George Zaninovich. Initials of the writer appear at the end of each profile. Ellen Leung assisted in the processing and filing of research material.

Special appreciation is due to the Curators of the Hoover Institution and to members of its Readers' Services and Serials Departments, as well as to all those organizations—government and private—which made available source material and translations. We are indebted particularly to the copy editor, Jesse M. Phillips, for putting the manuscript in its final form.

Richard F. Staar
for the Editorial Board

*   *   *

Note on Sources

Sources are cited throughout the text, with news agencies normally identified by generally accepted initials. Abbreviations are also used for the following widely quoted publications:

Yearbook on International Communist Affairs	*YICA*
World Marxist Review (Toronto, Canada, edition)	*WMR*
and its *Information Bulletin*	*IB*
International Meeting of Communist and Workers' Parties (1969)	*IMCWP*

EASTERN EUROPE AND THE SOVIET UNION

ALBANIA

The Albanian Party of Labor (Partia e Punës e Shqipërisë; APL) was founded on 8 November 1941, at which time it was called the Communist Party of Albania. The present name was assumed in 1948. As the only legal political party in Albania, the APL exercises a monopoly of power. All 264 seats in the national legislature, the People's Assembly, are held by candidates of the Democratic Front, the party-controlled political alliance of the APL and the mass organizations.

Membership. On 1 January 1970 the APL claimed 75,673 members (*Zëri i Popullit*, 28 June). The population of Albania is 2,108,000 (estimated 1970). The party claimed 64,482 full members and 11,191 candidates. It appears that the purge of the APL launched in January 1967 in conjunction with the Albanian "Ideological and Cultural Revolution"—or "revolutionization"—was halted in June 1969. During the course of the purge, party membership declined from 66,320 to approximately 50,000 (*Rruga e Partisë*, March 1969). A massive recruiting drive was apparently initiated during the summer of 1969 to replenish the ranks of the APL. At the same time several thousand expelled members were readmitted to the party.

The purge swept away many aging party careerists who had become "embourgeoised" and had developed a "new class" outlook. Also eliminated were opponents of the policies of the Ideological and Cultural Revolution. In mid-1970, the social composition of the APL was reported as laborers, 35.2 per cent; collectivized peasants, 29.0 per cent; and white-collar workers, 35.8 per cent (*Zëri i Popullit*, 28 June).

Organization and Leadership. In theory, the highest APL authority is the party congress which, according to the party statute, meets once every four years. In practice, however, the power of the APL is exercised through its Politburo (11 full members and 5 candidates), Central Committee (61 full members and 36 candidates), and Secretariat. Enver Hoxha is first secretary of the APL and the leading Politburo member. Other Politburo members are Ramiz Alia, Beqir Balluku, Adil Çarçani, Hysni Kapo, Spiro Koleka, Rita Marko, Manush Myftiu, Gogo Nushi (died 9 April), Mehmet Shehu, and Haki Toska. The Secretariat consists of Ramiz Alia, Hysni Kapo, and Xhafer Spahiu, together with Hoxha.

The leading mass organizations in the country are the Democratic Front, United Trade Unions of Albania, Union of Albanian Working Youth, Union of Albanian Women, and Albanian Writers' and Artists' Union. These all serve as transmission belts for APL policies.

The death of Politburo member Gogo Nushi at the age of fifty-seven years (Tirana radio, 9 April) marked the only significant change in the party leadership during 1970. Nushi had been a member of the Politburo since 1948 and was also president of the United Trade Unions of Albania, vice-president of the Democratic Front, and first secretary of the Berat district party organization. Politburo member Rita Marko succeeded Nushi as president of the trade union organization.

There were, however, numerous shifts in the leadership of lower and middle level party organs. These changes reflected primarily the desire of the APL to develop new cadres from among the ranks of the workers and peasants. There were also established "party groups" comprised of communists selected for their outstanding work in production and loyalty to the regime (*Zëri i Popullit*, 20 January). The members of these units were to serve as models for other workers and to ensure that the directives of the party were being carried out at the grass-roots level. This move represented another effort on the part of the APL leadership to keep the Ideological and Cultural Revolution under effective control.

In accordance with the statute of the APL, the party's Sixth Congress should have met in 1970. It was announced, however, at the 25-26 June plenum of the Central Committee that the congress would be convened in November 1971, the thirtieth anniversary of the APL (*ibid.*, 28 June).

The Ideological and Cultural Revolution. The Ideological and Cultural Revolution continued to affect major domestic policies and events in Albania during 1970. On September 8 Ramiz Alia, the APL's leading ideologist, declared that the revolution would continue indefinitely. He warned of a "continuous, protracted, and difficult struggle." Only in this way, he maintained, could the country be protected from the threat of "revisionism" (Albanian Telegraphic Agency, ATA, 8 September). Adil Çarçani, a member of the Politburo, viewed the "revolutionization" movement as an integral part of the "uninterrupted socialist revolution" in Albania (*ibid.*, 11 February). It thus appeared that the Ideological and Cultural Revolution would in some form become a permanent feature of Albanian life.

Three major revolutionary themes were emphasized: "Actions through concentrated blows," "socialist humanism," and decentralization of the political and economic administration.

The "actions through concentrated blows" movement—endorsed by Hoxha in his speech to the Central Committee at the plenum of 26-27 December 1969 (*Zëri i Popullit*, 4 January 1970)—has been likened to the Great Leap Forward of the late 1950s in China. It called for heroic efforts on the part of workers to increase productivity and efficiency and encouraged them to participate in "mass actions" during their free time to help achieve the objectives of the fourth five-year plan (1966-70), especially in the agricultural sector. In response to the party's call, it was reported, workers in one Tirana factory had produced 49 five-ton trucks in twelve hours, and in the area of Dibra 30,600 volunteers were said in one day to have dug a ten-kilometer irrigation canal, planted 110,000 saplings, and reclaimed 52 hectares of land (*Chicago Tribune*, 9 May 1970; *Christian Science Monitor*, 26 February). The "actions through concentrated blows" campaign continued throughout the year and apparently did make a positive, if somewhat disappointing, contribution to the 1970 Albanian economic effort (see below). It also seems to have aroused resentment among some workers who had grown weary of the repeated pleas for self-sacrifice (*Rruga e Partisë*, February 1970).

The theme of "socialist humanism" was enunciated by Hoxha at the same plenum, where he declared: "Socialist humanism is becoming a mass phenomenon in our country with each passing day." Although he did not dwell on this point, Hoxha attempted to rationalize the sacrifices which the working class was required to make, asserting: "The effort of each [Albanian] is directed toward the defense of the nation, the freedom of the people, and the well being of man" (*Zëri i Popullit*, 4 January). He developed this theme further and elevated it to a cardinal tenet of the revolution in his address to the 25-26 June plenum:

> People should not be asked only to work, produce, sacrifice, and fulfill the plan. These are all correct demands. They are essential and important, but they do not constitute an end in themselves. Everything that is produced in our country is for the benefit of the worker. Since this is the case, we must severely criticize and denounce the methods and practices of some cadres,

particularly in state organs and economic enterprises, who show an interest in everything from screws to cows, but who overlook man, the most important element in every kind of work. (*Ibid.*, 30 June.)

Hoxha reiterated this position in other remarks (*ibid.*, 9 November) when he urged the cadres to handle their responsibilities in a "creative" and "humane" manner, and to be always sensitive to the feelings of the people in executing party directives. The APL's emphasis on socialist humanism was intended primarily to stem the popular reaction to the demands and excesses of the "revolutionization" movement. During the first months of 1970 it was clear that the success of such mainstays of the revolution as the "workers' control" and women's emancipation movements, the educational reform program, the drive to eradicate religious influences and "backward" customs, and the campaign against "bureaucratism" were being threatened by the indifference and opposition of the masses and some cadres (see, *e.g., ibid.*, 8, 15, and 21 March; 8 and 16 April). A secondary reason for this development may have been the desire of Albania's leaders to shed their Stalinist image as they sought to expand their diplomatic and economic ties with Western and "third world" nations.

The need to decentralize decision making and administration in the nation's economic and political systems was the major theme of the June plenum of the Central Committee. Although a few halting steps in the direction of decentralization had been taken in conjunction with the Ideological and Cultural Revolution, Hysni Kapo, the party specialist for organizational matters, lashed out at the "red tape," "bureaucratic competition," "waste of resources," and "gross inefficiences" in the management of the Albanian economy (*ibid.*, 28 June). These shortcomings, he maintained, could only be corrected by granting local administrative organs and individual economic enterprises a greater voice in the decision-making process and more latitude in executing the directives of the central authorities (*ibid.*). Hoxha also strongly endorsed the concept of decentralization at the plenum and admitted that the APL's traditional policy of centralization had not been an unqualified success. "There must be," he declared, "a reversal of the idea that the center must do everything and that the districts are not equipped to undertake major projects.... We often fear that mistakes will be made at the grass-roots level, but tend to forget that we ourselves made mistakes [and] may still be making them today" (*ibid.*). He underscored his support for the decentralization program by urging that it be implemented with a minimum of delay.

As the Albanian economy has begun to mature, it has been plagued with problems in planning and administration similar to, but on a smaller scale than, those that have caused the Soviet Union and the majority of the communist party-ruled states to abandon rigid centralization and to sanction greater flexibility and experimentation in economic management. While it was clear that the APL did not intend to permit innovation in this area on the magnitude of that found in Yugoslavia, Hungary, or even the Soviet Union, it nevertheless felt constrained to retreat somewhat from its traditional Stalinism in order to promote more rapid economic growth and to weaken further the power of the bureaucracy. Sensitive to the charge that by their actions they espoused the doctrines of "revisionism" which they had repeatedly condemned, the Albanian leaders staunchly denied that "winds of liberal change" were blowing through Albania (see e.g., *ibid.*, 19 September).

The Albanian Writers' and Artists' Union celebrated its twenty-fifth anniversary in October. In a congratulatory message the APL Central Committee urged the nation's intellectuals to adhere to the cultural guidelines established by the party—that all art and literature "be rooted in the people and their socialist experience" (Tirana radio, 22 October). Kahreman Ylli, rector of the State University of Tirana since 1957, resigned his post on 8 March (*Bashkimi*, 8 March). He was replaced by Jorgji Sota, a relatively young party bureaucrat who had served as a regional party secretary in the Durres district. This move was intended to enhance the party's control over the university.

Economy. The year 1970 marked the end of the fourth five-year plan (1966-70). According to preliminary reports, with the notable exception of agriculture, plan directives were generally achieved or exceeded. Industrial production in 1970 was approximately 83 per cent greater than the 1965 level, substantially above the 50-54 per cent increase foreseen by the plan (*Bashkimi*, 23 December). Especially impressive gains were registered in petroleum, copper, electric power, chemicals, machine tool, and light industrial output. It was estimated that 1970 agricultural production would be 40 per cent above the 1965 level—considerably below the 71-76 per cent increase envisioned by the plan (*ibid.*, 24 December). One of the major objectives of the plan, the achievement of self-sufficiency in bread-grain production, was not realized. While the "actions through concentrated blows" campaign did play an important role in producing the 11 per cent increase in agricultural output during 1970, this figure was less than the 17 per cent rise decreed by the annual plan. Total collectivization of agriculture was achieved by 1970, and the APL was making an effort to consolidate the smaller collective farms, further reduce the size of private plots, and increase the level of mechanization in the countryside (*ibid.*).

One of the most impressive economic accomplishments of the year was the completion of the electrification of the country on 25 October (Tirana radio, 3 November). This goal was realized fifteen years ahead of the target date established in 1960 and thirteen months in advance of the revised plan adopted in 1967. Other noteworthy projects completed during 1970 were the glass factory in Kavaja, the plastics plant in Durrës, the copper concentration plant in Spac, and milk-processing plants in Tirana and Shkodër. An upsurge in housing construction in 1970 elicited the prediction that the nation's housing shortage would be eliminated within three or four years (*Bashkimi*, 23 December).

Albania's economic progress during the fourth five-year plan was largely attributable to Chinese loans and credits, Chinese technical assistance, and the efforts and sacrifices of the Albanian people under the slogan of "relying on one's own resources." The Albanian leadership during 1970 was very much concerned by the poor quality of production, low productivity of workers, and a breakdown of discipline among some workers—especially in the agricultural sector. In an attempt to overcome these problems the "proletarian discipline" movement was proclaimed at the December 1969 plenum of the Central Committee (*Zëri i Popullit*, 4 January 1970). According to the doctrines of "proletarian discipline," each laborer was expected to get to work on time, put in an honest day's work, strive to improve his efficiency, and increase his daily output. The problem of inefficient economic management, another grave concern of the APL, was discussed at the June plenum. The APL responded to this challenge by promulgating a series of directives concerning decentralization of planning and administrative procedures (*ibid.*, 28 June; *Christian Science Monitor*, 5 October). These proposals granted individual enterprises greater freedom in drafting budget and production plans, made them less subject to the control of the ministries, and permitted them to work more closely with local government organs. These reforms, along with the emphasis on socialist humanism, were intended to whip up popular enthusiasm for the forthcoming fifth five-year plan (1971-75).

In late November, Premier Mehmet Shehu outlined the major features of the plan, which he asserted would be the "greatest of all the five-year plans" (*Zëri i Popullit*, 22 November). He indicated that while the highest priority would be given to the development of heavy industry, "particular attention" would be accorded the task of increasing production of consumers' goods. To underscore this point Shehu revealed that, in contrast to the massive heavy industrial projects which were characteristic of the fourth five-year plan, a wide variety of new industrial plants, ranging from "very simple workshops" to "very large, complex factories," would be constructed during the fifth five-year plan. He also noted that the plan would be in part underwritten by the "substantial" credits granted Albania by China in November 1968 and October 1970. It has been estimated that these Chinese credits to Albania amount to $300 million (Radio Free Europe, *Research Report*, Munich, 3 December). Shehu stressed, however, that the ultimate responsibility for the realization of the goals of the plan lay with the Albanian people and their leaders.

Political Developments. The 1970 election campaign began on 2 July. At stake were 264 seats in the People's Assembly and some 29,000 positions in local and regional People's Councils and judicial tribunals. The main theme of the campaign was "socialist democracy"—a euphemism for infusing new blood into local and regional political bodies. It was stressed that political candidates should no longer be judged exclusively on the basis of their social origin, war record, or previous support of party policies, but rather that equal weight should be given to their attitude toward the Ideological and Cultural Revolution (*Bashkimi*, 2 July). In his campaign speech of 18 September, Hoxha declared that the Albanian people had "finally won the right and attained the political maturity to criticize all those who err, to denounce those who have done wrong, and to praise and encourage those who work well" (*Zëri i Popullit*, 19 September). Hoxha's remarks did not constitute an endorsement for Western democratic ideals, but were instead meant to express his support for the movement to expand the ranks of the nation's political activists.

The national elections were held on 20 September. According to the official returns, 100 per cent of the registered voters (1,097,123) went to the polls and voted unanimously for the Democratic Front candidates for the People's Assembly. In the local and regional balloting, 99.99 per cent were cast for the front's candidates. It was further reported that 54 per cent of the newly elected members of the People's Assembly and 60 per cent of those elected to the People's Councils had no previous political experience (*ibid.*, 20 September).

The first session of the new People's Assembly was held on 20-23 November. Mehmet Shehu was reelected premier. The other members of the Council of Ministers are Beqir Balluku (deputy premier and minister of defense), Adil Çarçani (deputy premier), Spiro Koleka (deputy premier), Xhafer Spahiu (deputy premier), Abdyl Kellezi (chairman, State Planning Commission), Kadri Hazbiu (minister of the interior), Nesti Nase (minister of foreign affairs), Koço Theodosi (minister of industry and mining), Piro Dodbiba (minister of agriculture), Thoma Deljana (minister of education and culture), Shinasi Dragoti (minister of construction), Kiço Ngjela (minister of trade), Milo Qirko (minister of communications), Aleks Verli (minister of finance), Llambi Zicishti (minister of health), and Sulejman Baholli (minister without portfolio). Haxhi Lleshi was reelected chairman of the Presidium of the People's Assembly, and Fadil Paçrami was elected president of the People's Assembly. (*Ibid.*, 22 November.)

There were three important changes in the composition of the Council of Ministers. Xhafer Spahiu, a member of the Secretariat, replaced Politburo member Haki Toska as a deputy premier. Spahiu is the APL's specialist in economic matters and a former minister of industry. Toska is an expert on agrarian problems and his removal most likely stemmed from his inability to resolve the difficulties that arose in the agricultural sector of the economy during the fourth five-year plan. Llambi Zicishti, a political unknown, was named minister of health in place of Ciril Pistolli, who was subjected to heavy criticism on the eve of the elections for alleged shortcomings in the nation's health program (*ibid.*, 21 August). Shefqet Peci was dropped as minister without portfolio in favor of Sulejman Baholli, a party functionary. Peci, who at sixty-four was the oldest member of the previous cabinet, may have been removed owing to his age in the midst of the drive to attract more young people to government and party service.

There were also two other political changes worthy of note. Behar Shtylla, a former minister of foreign affairs, was replaced by Fadil Paçrami, a journalist and writer, as president of the People's Assembly. Dhori Panariti was appointed prosecutor general in place of Lefter Goga, who was "assigned other duties."

Foreign Relations. Albania during 1970 continued to expand its diplomatic and economic ties. Diplomatic relations were established with Denmark (ATA, 29 April), Libya (*Bashkimi*, 6 May), the Central African Republic (ATA, 23 May), Switzerland (Tirana radio, 20 July), Belgium (ATA, 13 November), and the Netherlands (*ibid.*). In May (ATA, 5 May), Albania recognized Prince Sihanouk's Cambodian government in exile, based in Peking. Albania and Finland raised their diplomatic representation to the ambassadorial level in December (Tirana radio, 22 December). At the year's end, Albania maintained diplomatic relations with 48 countries, an increase of 13 since 1966 (*Zëri i Popullit*, 22 November). Furthermore, it repeatedly expressed willingness to establish diplomatic relations with virtually any nation, with the notable exceptions of the Soviet Union and the United States. Albania also continued to expand her economic ties with foreign countries. To promote international trade, the Albanians in 1970 participated in some fifteen (a record number for them) international fairs and expositions—including those at Paris, Cairo, Florence, Stockholm, Bucharest, Izmir, Leipzig, Plovdiv, Copenhagen, Budapest, Brno, Poznan, Algiers, London, and Dijon. For the first time since the end of the Second World War, Albania made a serious effort to attract foreign tourists. On this point Hoxha affirmed:

> The People's Republic of Albania is open to its friends both Marxists and non-Marxist, to progressive democrats, to honest tourists irrespective of their viewpoints who wish to come to our country to enjoy its beautiful scenery . . . without seeking to interfere in our internal affairs and engaging in subversive activity. (*Ibid.*, 19 September.)

It is interesting to note that the Albanians refused to acknowledge that their activities in the international arena constituted a modification of their long-standing "hard line" policies. Instead they sought to claim this development as a major diplomatic victory. Hoxha's analysis was typical:

> When the capitalist bourgeoisie and the modern revisionists realized that they could not defeat socialist Albania, they changed their tactics, but not their aims. They began to smile at us, to say they wanted to have diplomatic ties with our state, to expand trade, and to "swear by their gods" that they harbor no evil designs toward our country. (*Ibid.*)

Notwithstanding Hoxha's claims to the contrary, Albanian foreign policy trends during 1970 did represent an intensification of the desire, which became apparent in the aftermath of the Soviet-led invasion of Czechoslovakia in 1968, to end Albania's diplomatic isolation and almost exclusive reliance on China for political and economic aid. They also reflected the modest liberalizing tendencies that began to emerge during 1970. Despite the obvious moderation of Albania's attitude toward the outside world, the alliance with China remained the cornerstone of Albanian foreign policy.

Albanian-Chinese Relations. There appeared to be an increase during 1970 in personal exchanges between the Chinese People's Republic (CPR) and Albania. Most of these exchanges were cultural in nature. Two high-ranking Albanian delegations visited China. Between 14 May and 22 June, Minister of the Interior Kadri Hazbiu, also a candidate member of the Politburo, was in China on what seems to have been a good-will mission. More important was the visit of the delegation headed by Abdyl Kellezi, chairman of the State Planning Commission. The other members of this delegation, which was in China from 13 August to 18 October, were Kiço Ngjela (minister of trade), Shinasi Dragoti (minister of construction), Pupi Shyti (vice-chairman of the State Planning Commission), and Xhorxhi Robo (ambassador to China). After touring the provinces to emphasize Sino-Albanian solidarity and to endorse the policies of Mao Tse-tung, the delegation returned to Peking, where it was "warmly received" by Mao on 28 September (NCNA, 28 September). Following several weeks of negotiations, the Chinese and Albanians on 16 October signed an economic agreement. By the terms of this pact, China is to provide additional credits and aid for Albanian economic development during the period of the fifth five-year-plan (*ibid.*, 16 October). Most of the Chinese delegations that visited Albania were of low rank. The Chinese leaders, however, did show their esteem for the Albanians in the warm exchange of greetings on such occasions as the twenty-seventh anniversary of the Albanian army (*ibid.*, 9 July), the twenty-first anniversary of the establishment of Sino-Albanian relations (*ibid.*, 23 November), and the twenty-sixth anniversary of Albania's national liberation (*ibid.*, 28 November). In January the CPR presented Albania with a mammoth industrial exposition hall, complete with exhibits (ATA, 6 January), and in October the Chinese Academy of Sciences provided the State University of Tirana with a fully equipped nuclear radiation laboratory (*Zëri Popullit*, 2 October).

Albania strongly and consistently endorsed China's foreign and domestic policies. A *Zëri i Popullit* editorial on 31 January maintained that, contrary to Soviet allegations, the CPR's foreign policy was defensive and that it was the Soviet Union which had resorted to aggression in Czechoslovakia and was now threatening the peace and stability of the Balkan states and the nations bordering on the Indian Ocean and Mediterranean Sea. On the first anniversary of the Ninth Congress of the Chinese Communist Party, the Albanians declared that the congress had "crowned the decisive victory of the Great Proletarian Cultural Revolution" (*ibid.*, 1 April). Tirana radio (24 April) pointed to the successful launching of the first Chinese earth satellite as proof of the advanced state of China's technology. Albania again was one of the leaders in the unsuccessful movement to secure the admission of the CPR to the U.N. (*ibid.*, 15 November). During 1970 Albania continued to serve as an important base for Chinese propaganda activities in Europe, the Middle East, and Africa.

Although China in 1970 was not so blatant in her attacks on the Soviet Union as in previous years, there were were no signs of any significant problems in Sino-Albanian relations. The CPR underscored its support for Albanian foreign and domestic policies by publishing in pamphlet form the full text in Chinese of Hoxha's 18 September speech (*ibid.*, 17 October).

Albanian-Soviet Relations. During 1970, Albanian-Soviet relations showed no sign of improvement. On 6 March, *Zëri i Popullit* condemned a Warsaw Pact plan (*Kommunist*, February 1970) to establish "joint special military units." These were held to be nothing more than "mercenary units" whose function would be to keep pro-Soviet leaders in power in the Warsaw Pact states, justify the presence of Soviet troops in Eastern Europe, and prepare the way for the incorporation of Eastern Europe into the U.S.S.R. The Albanians were displeased by the continuation of economic experimentation in the U.S.S.R. (*Zëri i Popullit*, 30 March), the refusal of the Soviet government to clamp down on the activities of religious institutions (*Bashkimi*, 29 April), and the "unchecked drift" of the U.S.S.R. toward the "restoration of capitalism" (*Zëri i Popullit*, 24 May). Albania was angered by the signing of the Soviet-West German treaty on 12 August. Tirana radio (18 August) claimed that this agreement would "not serve to relax tensions, but rather to lay the foundations for a new war."

Albanian-Soviet relations were further strained by Albania's publication and broad dissemination of Hoxha's speech at the November 1960 Moscow Conference. (The text of the speech was broadcast by Tirana radio between 30 June and 5 July. It was later printed in pamphlet form in several languages and widely circulated.) While the contents of this document were largely known, its publication was intended to embarrass the Soviet leadership and to emphasize the magnitude of the differences between the U.S.S.R. and Albania. In his 18 September campaign speech, Hoxha discussed in great detail the ideological and political issues that divided the Soviets and the Albanians, and made it clear that Albania had no intention of backing down in this dispute, no matter what the consequences:

> We are neither afraid of the military threats of the treacherous Brezhnev clique nor deceived by its phony promises of reconciliation. We do not fear their fascist military adventures and are fully prepared to face them. We will neither accept their flatteries, promises, bribes, and credits, nor will we be fooled by them. They cannot penetrate our fortress either from within or without. The only course open to us is to fight, and we shall fight against them until the complete victory of socialism and communism. (*Zëri i Popullit*, 19 September.)

Undaunted by the violent Albanian rhetoric, the U.S.S.R. did make a serious overture, one of a series in recent years, to heal the breach with the Albanians. On 26 November *Izvestiia* reported that both the Soviet government and the Communist Party of the Soviet Union were eager to do "everything possible to eliminate the existing differences" with Albania. The Soviets even expressed a willingness to enter into bilateral negotiations "on the basis of equality"—a long-standing Albanian prerequisite for sitting down at the conference table. Albania did not respond favorably to this overture (Tirana radio, 29 November).

Relations with Eastern Europe. Albanian-Yugoslav cultural and economic ties were considerably strengthened during 1970. This latest phase of the Albanian-Yugoslav rapprochement began in early April when *Zëri i Popullit* (5 and 7 April) published several articles extolling the Yugoslavs for their heroic resistance to the Nazis. The Yugoslavs reciprocated (*Borba*, Belgrade, 8 April), and by the end of the summer a series of bilateral conferences dealing with such matters as film exchanges, overland transport of goods, and athletic and educational cooperation had taken place. The Albanians were most interested in developing close ties with the Kosovo-Metohija region of Yugoslavia, inhabited largely by their compatriots. In late October the State University of Tirana and the University of Prishtina agreed to exchange personnel and instructional equipment and to develop cooperative programs (ATA, 28 October). On 26 November an Albanian-Yugoslav trade agreement for 1971 was signed in Belgrade, and the groundwork was laid for the conclusion of a long-range economic treaty between the two states (Tanyug, Yugoslav press agency, 26 November).

Albania and Greece, although technically still at war, took a first step toward normalization of relations when their chambers of commerce concluded a modest trade agreement on 21 January (*Bashkimi*, 17 February). In November the two countries reestablished direct telegraphic links for the first time since 1940 (*Christian Science Monitor*, 11 November). Although the Albanians have indicated their willingness to resume diplomatic relations "on the principles of noninterference and respect of sovereignty and territorial integrity" (ATA, 21 May), the Greeks have decided not to pursue this matter until they have had the opportunity to assess the success of the economic cooperation between the two states (Tanyug, 8 November). The prospects for a complete Greek-Albanian rapprochement remain dim owing to the refusal of the Greeks to give up their claims to Northern Epirus (Athens radio, 19 December).

Albania also took the initiative to restore relations with Bulgaria. These had been suspended since July 1968, when the Albanian ambassador and his staff were expelled from Sofia for engaging in "subversive activities." Albanian-Bulgarian relations had further deteriorated in the aftermath of the Czechoslovak crisis, when Albania charged that Bulgaria had become the staging ground for a Soviet "invasion" of the Balkans. On September 8, *Bashkimi* published an article reaffirming Albania's friendship for the Bulgarian people, recalling the close cooperation between the Bulgars and the Albanians following the Second World War, and criticizing the Bulgarian leadership for its close ties with the U.S.S.R. After an absence of two years, Albania participated in the 1970 Plovdiv fair (*East Europe*, January 1971). By November it was rumored that Albania and Bulgaria were planning to resume diplomatic relations at the chargé d'affaires level (Zagreb radio, 14 November).

With the exception of Romania, Albania's ties with the East European bloc states were strained. According to the Albanians, the continuing purge of Czechoslovak communists was inspired by the Soviets and designed to eliminate those who opposed close cooperation with the U.S.S.R. (*Bashkimi*, 29 March), and Czechoslovakia had been transformed "into a full-fledged [Soviet] vassal" (*Zëri i Popullit*, 20 May). Similarly, Albania was highly critical of the Polish-West German treaty, which "represented another step on the road of rapprochement and collaboration between the West German revanchists and the Polish revisionists" (ATA, 20 November). The Albanians took particular delight in the ouster of Polish party chief Gomulka, whom they branded a "violent enemy of Albania." His downfall was viewed as "another heavy defeat for Khrushchevian revisionism." His successor, Edward Gierek, was regarded as no improvement and his tenure, the Albanians predicted, would be brief (*Zëri i Popullit*, 23 December).

International Communist Movement. Albania continued to serve as a base for the activities of pro-Chinese Marxist-leninist parties and organizations. The facilities of Tirana radio and the Albanian press were made available to both the Marxist-Leninist groups based in Albania and those which continued to operate within their homelands.

Of all the Marxist-Leninist groups which operated from Tirana, the so-called Communist Party of Poland (CPP) was among the most vocal (see *Poland*). On 6 January, Tirana radio claimed that the CPP had met in Warsaw in September 1969 and had agreed to intensify its activities against the ruling Polish United Workers' Party. The CPP Central Committee was reported to have held another meeting in Warsaw "during the first quarter of 1970" to develop its strategy for toppling the Gomulka regime and combating Soviet "social imperialism" (Tirana radio, 6 July). Surprisingly, the CPP did not take any credit for the removal of Gomulka, but it did join with the Albanians in applauding his political demise and in denouncing his successor. It was reported that Kazimierz Mijal, the founder and chief spokesman of the CPP and a resident of Albania since his flight from Poland in 1966, had been named to an important post with the Albanian-Chinese Shipping Line (*Survey*, autumn 1970).

On 18 April *Zëri i Popullit* published several letters from certain regular members of the Tirana radio audience. These correspondents praised the APL for its stand against "revisionism" and thanked the Albanians for providing them with moral and intellectual support in their struggle to promote the "ideals of Marxism-Leninism." The Albanian press also reprinted anti-Soviet and pro-Chinese materials from "Marxist-Leninist" publications (see, e.g., *Zëri i Popullit*, 12 March, 25 April, and 2 May).

Albanian contacts and exchanges with "Marxist-Leninist" and "progressive" organizations continued to increase. There was an especially significant rise in Albanian contacts with African and youth groups. Among the foreign delegations to visit Albania during 1970 were those representing the Communist Party of New Zealand, Palestine National Liberation Movement (Al-Fatah), Helsinki Marxist-Leninist Association, Federation of Black African Students in France, Madagascar Free Trade Union Association, French National Student Union, Arab Writers' Association, French National Student Union, and Union of Congolese (Brazzaville) Socialist Youth.

Publications. The central organ of the APL is the daily *Zëri i Popullit*. The party's monthly theoretical journal is *Rruga e Partisë*. Another major publication is *Bashkimi*, the daily organ of the Democratic Front. The Union of Albanian Working Youth publishes *Zëri i Rinise* twice weekly.

N. C. P.

BULGARIA

The Bulgarian Communist Party (Bulgarska Komunisticheska Partiya; BCP), although assuming this designation in 1919 and again in 1948, has existed as a separate entity since its split from the Bulgarian Social Democratic Party in 1903 under the official name of Workers' Social Democratic Party (Narrow Socialists). Occasionally, it used some modified designations, such as Workers' Party, from 1927 to 1934, and Bulgarian Workers' Party (Communist), from 1934 to 1948. It claims its "bolshevization" since 1917, the year of the Bolshevik Revolution in Russia.

While at times numerically strong and alternating between legal and illegal attempts for power, the BCP assumed the reins of government only as a consequence of the unexpected Soviet declaration of war on and armed invasion of Bulgaria during the first week of September 1944, and of a subsequent coup d'état (9 September) against an anti-Nazi Bulgarian government which was negotiating armistice terms with the Western Allies. Although officially sharing power with other political parties in the so-called Fatherland Front (Otechestven Front; FF) coalition between 1944 and 1948, the BCP assumed key positions from the beginning. Its power is now undisputed in the consolidated mass FF, which has as collective members a subservient political party—the once ruling Bulgarian Agrarian People's Union (Bulgarski Zemedelski Naroden Suyuz), the youth organization—the Dimitrov Communist Youth Union (Dimitrovski Komunisticheski Mladezhki Suyuz; DCYU), and the centralized trade union organization.

BCP membership in 1970 was given as 637,000 (*Novo Vreme*, April), the same as for 1969, which then signified an increase of about 24,000 over 1968. Whether the figure is new, or whether no count has been made in 1970, cannot be ascertained. The population of Bulgaria is about 8,500,000 (estimated 1970). The share of BCP membership is thus about 7.5 per cent.

The BCP continues to hold an absolute majority in the National Assembly (280 out of 416 seats) and controls the remaining 99 members of the Agrarian Union and 37 nonparty deputies, as all members of the parliament are nominated by the Communist-led FF and are unopposed. The central and local governments as well as all other public organizations are also clearly dominated by the BCP majority in them.

The social composition of the BCP, previously reported as consisting of 39 per cent blue-collar workers, 27 per cent peasants, and 27 per cent white-collar workers, seems to hold, which indicates an overrepresentation of white-collar workers (17 per cent of the total population) and an underrepresentation of peasants and, to some extent, blue-collar workers (37 and 42 per cent of the population, respectively). Other underrepresented groups are women, young people, and intellectuals.

Leadership and Organization. No change occurred in the top party leadership during 1970. Todor Zhivkov has been first secretary since 1954 and premier since 1956, thus holding one of the longest concurrent tenures of the two leading positions in any communist state. The eleven-member Politburo, beside Zhivkov, includes Boyan Bulgaranov, Tsola Dragoycheva, Pencho

Kubadinski, Ivan Mikhaylov, Todor Pavlov, Ivan Popov, Stanko Todorov, Tano Tsolov, Boris Velchev, and Zhivko Zhivkov (no relation to Todor Zhivkov). It has also six candidate members. The powerful Secretariat of the Central Committee consists of Zhivkov as first secretary, Venelin Kotsev, Ivan Prumov, Stanko Todorov, and Boris Velchev as secretaries, and Vladimir Bonev, Roza Koritarova, and Georgi Bokov as plain members. The Central Committee remains composed of 137 full and 87 candidate members.

As has been customary, party members continue to control the government and all important public organizations. Thus, not only the premiership, but also the only first deputy premiership (Zhivko Zhivkov) and four of the five deputy premier positions (Tsolov, Kubadinski, Mikhaylov, and Luchezar Avramov) are occupied by full or candidate members of the Politburo. Among the auxiliary mass organizations, Bulgaranov heads the Fatherland Front; Koritarova, the Central Council of the Trade Unions; Bokov, the Association of Bulgarian Journalists; and Dragoycheva, the National Committee for Bulgarian-Soviet Friendship. The youth and the women's organizations are also led by party members (Ivan Panev and Elena Ligadinova, respectively). No new membership figures for these organizations were published in 1970. In 1969 the Fatherland Front had 3,772,000 members, and among its collective members the Agrarian Union had 120,000; the youth organization, 918,000; and the trade unions, 2,417,000.

Party Internal Affairs. Provided with a leadership which has remained fundamentally unchanged since the party's Ninth Congress, in 1966, and with an organization which has continued to abide by the rules of "democratic centralism," the BCP registered no significant changes in its internal developments in the course of 1970. The 1968 reversal in the less rigid trend of the midsixties—resulting from the reverberations of the Czechoslovak "Spring" and "Summer," and crystallized in the decisions of two Central Committee plenums (July 1968 and September 1969) —continued to be felt in the party ranks and policies. Thus, greater centralization and a comprehensive party management of society as a whole in the "scientific-technical age" remained as goals of the party leadership. Some concrete steps taken in 1970 toward their implementation (see below, "Domestic Attitudes and Activities") were the establishment of the Academy for Training Cadres for Social Administration with the status of a higher educational institution (*Rabotnichesko Delo*, 18 and 22 January), several governmental agencies in the administrative and economic fields, and new experimental party organizations at the local level (*Partien Zhivot*, no. 15, 17 October) to reflect the sweeping changes in the agricultural organization of the country that were recommended by the April 1970 plenum.

The ambitious goals set in 1968 and 1969 generated, however, a host of problems which could not remain unnoticed by the party leadership. The undertaking to "harness science in the service of society" places almost impossible responsibilities on a small and technically unprepared party collective within a still technologically backward society, especially when ideological commitment is to continue to receive the highest priority. In 1968 only 9 per cent of the party members were university graduates, 70 per cent had not even completed secondary education, and the country had only 24 electronic computer centers (*Zemedelsko Zname*, 20 December 1969). High party leaders themselves, like Zhivko Zhivkov and Todorov, admitted the "lack of trained cadres" and hinted that there was cadre hostility toward the new tasks. There were also complaints about deficiencies in the ideological field, the generational gap, and party discipline in general. Todor Zhivkov himself spoke out oftentimes about "incorrect attitudes toward veteran revolutionary cadres" by the young (*Rabotnichesko Delo*, 13 February), whose share in total party membership was only 13 per cent; about improving the "scientific level of the party work" (*ibid.*, 14 January), thus alluding to the conflict between the party hacks and the professionals; and about the need for "party unity and cohesions and for ideological purity" (*ibid.*, 13 February). A most interesting inquiry among local secretariat members in the industrial Gabrovo District on the role of the party indicated that ideological work was the least desirable and most difficult of their tasks and that the economic policies of the regime were among the least understood aspects of the party line (see *ibid.*, 17 November)—a finding which, if representative, was a serious indictment of the party's failure in crucial areas of its overall goals.

Perhaps to foster the required "unity and cohesion," the party leadership rehabilitated the notorious Bulgarian "little Stalin," former party boss Vulko Chervenkov, by restoring him to membership after his expulsion from the party in 1962. (Symptomatically, the news was contained in Chervenkov's unconspicuous biographical entry in the *Short Bulgarian Encyclopedia*, published in 1969, and it seems that a May 1969 plenum of the Central Committee made the decision without ever publicizing it.) This move can be viewed both as a rather inexpensive gesture toward the seemingly still appreciable number of Chervenkov's former protégés and supporters in the party ranks (Chervenkov himself seems completely harmless because of age and health) and as an indirect signal of the harder-line policies prevailing since 1968.

A major internal event, announced and anticipated for 1970, namely the Tenth Congress of the BCP, was quietly laid to rest until, after the Communist Party of the Soviet Union (CPSU) announced the postponement of its congress to 1971, the BCP followed suit and scheduled its own for April 1971, a month after the conclusion of the CPSU's Twenty-fourth Congress. No other justification for this violation of the party statutes (which set a four-year limit between congresses) was given except that there was to be a correlation between the congresses of the two parties. As an article in *Otechestven Front* (4 December) stated:

> Convening our party congress after the CPSU congress is by no means an accidental coincidence. . . . It is an expression of the clear and consistent awareness of the BCP and the Bulgarian communists of the role and position of the Soviet Union and the CPSU. . . . Yes, we really are setting our watches by the time of the Bolshevik clock—in 1971 just as was done in 1919, in 1936, in 1956.

In light of this outspoken admission one could interpret the visit to Sofia by K. Katushev, CPSU secretary for relations with ruling communist parties, at the time of the announcement of the date of the Tenth Congress and the simultaneous visit to Moscow by V. Kotsev, the BCP secretary for ideological matters, as preparatory steps for the synchronization of the two congresses.

Perhaps to buttress the delay, the party leadership promised an ambitious agenda, including a new party program (planned since 1954 but never worked out) and discussions of a new constitution (announced in 1962, with publication promised for 1969 but not yet accomplished), alongside familiar items, such as the directives of the new "socioeconomic" five-year plan for 1971-75. Todor Zhivkov, in a speech on 23 October, heralded the expected party program as "tracing the development of [Bulgarian] society for the next twenty-five to thirty years" and characterized its role as "completing the construction of a developed socialist society" and "creating the conditions for a gradual transition to communism." Only the future will show how far the BCP will be successful in its new promises; for the time being many problems remain which cannot be solved by looking into a rosy future.

Domestic Attitudes and Activities. The year 1970 was unusually drab as to initiatives or events worth recording. It can be characterized as a petering off of the consequences of the 1968 decisions to revert to party centralization and expansion of "social management," taken as a by-product of the Czechoslovak upheavals and the reassertion of Soviet dominance of Eastern Europe. Even 1969 was more eventful in that a September plenum allegedly outlined measures to implement the decisions of the April 1968 plenum. The scheduled major event was the Tenth

Congress of the BCP, which was postponed, and the announcement of its convening for April 1971 came too late in the year to make 1970 a period of active preparation for the meeting.

Political Administration. The quest for an enhanced party role in all ranges of society had some political repercussions, but remained on the whole confined to statements rather than action, due to the well-known practical difficulties in implementing such an ambitious scheme, especially within a short span of time. Perhaps to minimize the difficulties—or put the blame elsewhere—references were made to the "experience of the U.S.S.R. [which] is of invaluable significance" (Todorov in *Rabotnichesko Delo*, 18 July).

More concretely, the party leadership began reemphasizing the need for "socialist legality" and "state discipline" on the operational level, especially in relation to the decisions of the September 1969 plenum, which foreshadowed the scandals involving primarily foreign trade irregularities on the part of officials of economic trusts and the announcement of a radical reorganization of the trusts (see below, "Economic Policies"). Reference was made to the "increased role of the public prosecutors" (*Novo Vreme*, no. 1, 1970) and to "all-embracing controls to spread out to all offices and agencies, to all leaders and executors" (*Partien Zhivot*, no. 1). The "people's councils" (local governments) were reprimanded for avoiding their duties in this regard (*Rabotnichesko Delo*, 16 February). At the end of the year, this theme of strict state discipline was reiterated at a national conference of party, state, and economic leaders with the participation of Zhivkov and Todorov. Although not much information could be derived from the published summary (*Rabotnichesko Delo*, 6 December), a prior article in *Otechestven Front* (3 December), entitled "Iron State Discipline," revealed that the blame for violations must be borne by some cabinet ministers as well, thus suggesting further measures and strengthened controls, in order to avoid further graft and corruption (see below). Restrictions against "speculative activity and non-labor income," primarily of private artisans, were decreed in October 1970, countering the liberalization policy initiated in 1965, and were another signal of the reversal to stricter administration and control (see *Ikonomicheski Zhivot*, no. 46, 11 November).

Even more ominous was the amendment to the People's Militia (Police) Act, allowing "administratively-decided surveillance of individuals for up to six months," on top of the existing prerogatives of compulsory resettlement and refusal to permit change of residence for up to six months (*Durzhaven Vestnik*, no. 24, 24 March). Renewed stress was laid also on the role of the Ministry of the Interior (Police) as "vanguard in the struggle against imperialist agents" (*Rabotnichesko Delo*, 11 September).

Other legislative acts passed by the parliament during 1970 were less clear cut. On the one hand, a law on administrative procedure which was enacted on 24 June enabled citizens to appeal administrative action to higher authority and ultimately to the court, although several such actions were explicitly exempted from appeal. On the other hand, the Presidium of the National Assembly issued a decree empowering the Council of Ministers to issue edicts which may "authorize deviations from existing laws and regulations" (*Sofia radio*, 30 November). Although limited to the application of the "new economic mechanism," this decree was in violation of the general principle that all laws should be voted by the parliament and that no decree should be in violation of such laws. Thus, party supremacy over constitutional and legal bodies and acts remained intact.

Two Central Committee plenums in 1970 came up with relatively important decisions on organizational and economic matters. The plenum of 3 March deliberated "on the territorial distribution of the production forces in the course of the next fifteen to twenty years" (*Rabotnichesko Delo*, 10 March); the other, on 27-28 April, was concerned with the "concentration and industrial development of agriculture" (*Rabotnichesko Delo*, 29 and 30 April; for details see immediately below).

Economic Policies. In line with the reversal in the economic "liberalization," signaled by the

July and November 1968 plenums and further elaborated by the September 1969 plenum, the economic policies of the regime continued in the direction of recentralization of decision making and concentration of production units. The justification for the reversal was the alleged need of the modern age for all-embracing centralized management based on cybernetics (details on the reversal in L. A. D. Dellin, "Bulgaria's Economic Reform—Advance and Retreat," *Problems of Communism*, September-October 1970, pp. 44-52).

As a result not only were conventional economic plans renamed "unified plans for socioeconomic development," but the economic system itself was restructured so as to give still greater power to the political center and at the same time provide it with technical competence and sophisticated information—despite the shortage of the necessary technicians. Thus, the primacy of politics over economics was repeatedly stressed (see "Politics and the Economy," in *Otechestven Front*, 20 January, signed by the editor in chief, Georgi Naydenov), cadre training instituted at the aforementioned academy, a Special Commission on Economic Forecasting established, concentration of economic trusts intensified in domestic and foreign trade, revamping of agriculture undertaken. While still arguing that the decentralized "new economic system," as worked out since the early sixties and allegedly implemented by 1969, was being perfected, rather than replaced by a newer (recentralized) one, the regime—through Zhivko Zhivkov—announced the approval of the "basic principles of the new economic mechanism of the new economic system" in September 1970 (Sofia radio, 4 September), thus officially contradicting the previous claim that the new system had already been applied wholesale in 1969. In fact, while the semantics may be confusing, a series of acts replaced decidedly the main features of the pre-1968 reform and the Council of Ministers was even empowered to issue regulations related to economic matters which may "deviate from existing laws and regulations," thus signaling further reversals of the decentralized model of the sixties.

One of the major specific steps toward concentration of economic power was the reorganization of the state economic trusts, announced at the end of the year. Thus, *Durzhaven Vestnik* (11 December) contained a regulation which announced the liquidation of all of the 120 such trusts as of January 1971 and their replacement by about 65 new and larger units within which the component economic enterprises would "lose their former legal and economic independence." The new supertrusts would strengthen their power also vis-à-vis the economic ministries, as they would be more directly supervised by the Council of Ministers itself, but would, on the other hand, lose the ability to plan "from below," since the plan targets would be handed down to them by the council. Thus, the original concept of establishing the trusts in the mid-sixties as links between ministries and enterprises has been modified to provide them with a new role more in agreement with the trend toward bigness, centralization, and the stifling of local autonomy, the enhancement of which was the original goal of the economic reforms.

To what an extent the serious irregularities uncovered in 1969 in the financial dealings of such economic trusts (especially the Bulgarian Merchant Marine supertrust) have motivated this rather drastic reorganization is hard to determine. But the fact that the blame was extended to heads and deputy heads of ministries, and that foreign trade units affected by the scandal were to be dissolved as of 1 April 1970 and replaced by agglomerates under the control of the Ministry of Foreign Trade, indicates that the desire to hold a tight rein over the trusts must have been one of the important determinants.

It seems that stepped-up reorganization and concentration, noticeable in many other areas of economic life, lead usually back to initial forms, or at least move in circles, and add confusion to inefficiency. Thus, a poll among the members of the Economic Association in the city of Khaskovo showed that 53.5 per cent of the economists had difficulty in understanding the directives on the new economic system and 72 per cent could not use mathematical methods (see *Ikonomicheski Zhivot*, 29 July).

The most innovative reorganizations occurred in the field of agriculture. Following the general trend toward bigness in industry and trade, the regime intensified its reorganization of agriculture, begun in 1968 and stepped up in 1969, by integrating its goal and policies at the Central Committee's April 1970 plenum, devoted exclusively to this task.

The Plenum, with Zhivkov's participation, approved the soundness of the development of agriculture "on the basis of industrial methods"—more specifically, the establishment of "agricultural-industrial complexes" as the "most suitable types of agricultural concentration, especially in crop growing"—and gave the green light to the further transformation of agriculture along these lines. These new agglomerates, primarily horizontal integrations, were to be formed by groupings among collective or state farms, or between them (the difference between these two forms is being continuously dimmed). The farms would at first preserve their relative autonomy but gradually lose it on the way to a complete merger, unless the latter should be achieved outrightly. Vertical integrations with industrial purchasing and trade enterprises would also be encouraged but the reduced enthusiasm that was initially shown for these tended to put the very meaning of the term "agricultural-industrial complex" in question. While the goal was to equalize agriculture and industry, particularly in the field of labor remuneration and social welfare benefits, typical "agro-gorods" were planned only for the grain-rich district of Tolbukhin in the Dobrudzha, at least for the time being (see *Otechestven Front*, 22 May).

The typical "agricultural-industrial complex"—according to belatedly published "temporary regulations" (*Kooperativno Selo*, 27 October)—has an average size of 20,000 to 30,000 hectares of arable land (some are as large as 50,000 hectares and others are smaller than the average-sized collective farm of 4,000 hectares). Their number grew from two or three in 1969 to about 130 by September 1970 (*Rabotnichesko Delo*, 22 September), signaling a real drive to implement the party decisions. The recentralization trend was evident also in the concentration of the control over collective-farm management in the Ministry of Agriculture. (Control had been exercised—and decentralized in 1967—by the Central Cooperative Union.

While this ambitious plan for converting the countryside into an area of huge production units could be economically appealing, serious reservations seem in order about the degree of success that may be attained not only in motivating the farmers and the farm managers to join remote entities but also in making such huge units economically viable, given the backwardness of agricultural methods and technology in today's Bulgaria. Still, these moves show that the regime is rediscovering the importance of agriculture within the Bulgarian context, although that sector remains low on the priority list in respect to the resources devoted to its modernization.

The regime's continued stress on its desire to improve living standards did not seem to be notably productive of results in 1970. The introduction of a five-day work week, promised since 1967, was again postponed (*Septemvri*, 30 December, 1969). To bolster the low income of pensioners, legislation was enacted permitting them to take gainful employment without forfeiting their pay or pension (*Otechestven Front*, 10 August). Administrative restrictions on economic activities leading to "non-labor income" and speculation affected primarily the growing number of private artisans in retail trade and services (including private lessons) who have been financially successful in meeting private needs, despite existing government limitations. The possibility of foreign employment was restricted to construction and lumber workers, and the only foreign country to which they could go was the Soviet Union (*Otechestven Zov*, 11 December). Finally, the perennial housing problem seemed as far away from solution as ever. The target of 16 square meters per person and a separate housing unit per household by 1980 continued to look like an impossibility: the current average was 10.9 square meters per person, and 15.3 per cent of the housing units were shared by two or more households. In the urban areas the figure was 12.4 square meters per person, and 27.5 per cent of the units, housing almost 50 per cent of all urban households, were shared (*Ikonomicheski Zhivot*, 12 August).

Culture, Youth, Education. The "tightening of the screws" in the intellectual and artistic area, begun in 1968, continued throughout 1970. The BCP's undisputed role in matters of the mind was unequivocally restressed. An article by the party's deputy chief of propaganda and agitation called for a "continuous and clear-cut class awareness" in all aspects of culture and education:

> This is rendered imperative by the trend toward bringing ideology into all spheres of society, to counter the changed tactics of the imperialists and their orientation toward psychological warfare and "silent" counterrevolutions, and the use of the latest achievements of science and technology in today's ideological duel. . . . We must therefore consistently implement a class line in all aspects of the educational process, increase revolutionary vigilance, and wage an uncompromising struggle against the infiltration of bourgeois ideology and morality and of antisocial views and attitudes.

> This is why it is necessary for the entire educational process to be fully in keeping with the tasks of the party at the present stage of building a developed socialist society. . . . The mastery of Marxist-Leninist theory, linked most closely with practice, means that in all cases . . . the students should be able to understand all modern processes and phenomena entirely from class positions." (*Rabotnichesko Delo*, 15 October).

In order to give substance to the emphasis on stricter and all-embracing controls (which have seemed necessary also in anticipation of the party's Tenth Congress), several reorganizations took place. The State Committee on Art and Culture was endowed with a new department on "cultural policies," charged now with a "nationwide campaign" to propagandize the congress (*Narodna Kultura*, 21 November) and the Department for Arts and Culture at the Party's Central Committee was reestablished, to symbolize and coordinate the new trend (*Rabotnichesko Delo*, 18 June).

Continuing the line set by Todor Zhivkov in March 1969, the regime's interference in the affairs of the Bulgarian writers was intensified, apparently also as a result of a Politburo decision of October 1969, mentioned only casually in *Rabotnichesko Delo* of 1 March 1970. General criticism against violations of the rules of "socialist realism" was supplemented by direct personal attacks of individual authors, the most notorious of whom was Blaga Dimitrova. Dimitrova, one of the most talented Bulgarian poets and an important communist functionary for some time, was suddenly and sharply criticized for writing "uncommitted verse" (*Puls*, 23 December 1969) and for "speaking of moral-ethical subjects without connecting them with the great ideological struggle of our nation . . . as is considered fashionable among a top clique of intellectuals" (Dimitrov prize laureate Stoyan Daskalov, in *Narodna Mladezh*, 7 January). The existence of intellectuals alienated from the party line was recognized also by the arch-dogmatist, Academician and Politburo member Todor Pavlov, and other names were added to the list in the course of the year. The leadership of the Bulgarian Writers' Union identified among the major current problems "erroneous and apathetic attitudes toward contemporary life," "indifference," "lack of partiynost," "skepticism," "passive literary criticism, deprived of class-party criteria," "the potential danger of coterie-style struggles," and the "absence of the contemporary communist as a positive and trustworthy hero" (*Literaturen Front*, 15 January, 12 March, and 15 October; *Rabotnichesko Delo*, 11 March). Among the official prescriptions for success were "a firm defense of the party positions and the creation of militant unity around the policy of the BCP"—or, as Writers' Union president Georgi Dzhagarov put it bluntly: "Talent must be subordinated to the ideological and political goals of the party. . . . If you do not agree and if you have your own personal opinion . . . then keep it to yourself and do not disseminate it among others." (*Literaturen Front*, 26 November and 3 December.)

From such pronouncements and the continuous changes in the leadership of the Writers' Union one may deduce that the conflict between values and goals of the dogmatists and those of the creative writers remained alive. In fact, many writers, even loyalists such as Chalkash, but especially young talents such as Gancho Savov, continued to warn against the "spirit of the personality cult" and refused to compromise, despite strong and increasing pressures from above—which, fortunately, have not reached the Stalinist practice of administrative persecution.

The extent to which ideological conformity was sought appeared in extreme demands such as that even musicians should wage an "irreconcilable and uncompromising struggle against the devious schemes of bourgeois ideology" and that musical criticism should be based on "class-party principles and socialist realism" (*Narodna Kultura*, 7 November). Sportsmen, such as soccer players, were blamed for their failure in world competition because of "shortcomings in a low level of ideological-educational work" (*Rabotnichesko Delo*, 13 June). Little wonder that the journalists who are spearheading indoctrination were recharged with making the mass information media "first-rate ideological weapons in the struggle for the victory of socialism and communism" and turning "the press, radio, and television into effective party instruments" (*Bulgarski Zhurnalist*, no. 5, 1970).

The regime continued also its particular attention to the indoctrination of the younger generation, with seemingly unsatisfactory results. Even within its Komsomol (DCYU), serious cadre problems were identified (*Mladezh*, July 1970). Decisions taken at the DCYU plenum in May centered upon the need to intensify indoctrination at the "Pioneer" level so that even the very young could be "made ready at the earliest possible age" (*Narodna Mladezh*, 29 May). Young persons in general were reprimanded for "excessive family influences" and "ideological vacillations," due primarily to "imperialist diversions" and the "attractiveness of the Western way of life" (see, e.g., *Partien Zhivot*, no. 11, 1970, and *Uchitelsko Delo*, 22 September and 23 October). In July, military service requirements were changed, eliminating deferment for university study. Whether this was a step to remedy ideological deficiencies or was dictated by the elimination of the shortage of skilled labor—as is the regime's claim—is unclear, but entry directly after high school into military service (where political indoctrination is conducted in an isolated milieu) was considered also as ideologically beneficial. The defense minister, General D. Dzhurov, boasted in *Narodna Armiya* (4 November), that "hatred of the enemy" was a major goal of military service. Increasing complaints about "hooliganism" and the use of alcoholic beverages and drugs among high school students (*Vecherni Novini*, 6 May and 11 July) could have contributed to the changes in the military service rules.

In the field of education proper, a national conference heard the minister of education, Stefan Vasilev, reiterate that "the schools should be transformed into powerful ideological institutions for the training of communist-minded citizens" (*Uchitelsko Delo*, 30 June). The disarray created in 1969 by Zhivkov's intervention in a Central Committee plenum on education apparently had not been cleared up. At the university level in particular—where most of the "ideological vacillations" and generational alienation, along with subject irrelevancy, have been found—signs of student reaction became noticeable. The chairman of the University Student Council at the Central Committee of the Komsomol, V. Panov, criticized (as he had done in 1969) the existing setup and demanded more meaningful student participation, even in the election of deans and presidents (*Narodna Mladezh*, 18 May). The transfer of Panov and most of his aides to different positions (*Studentska Tribuna*, 19 May) symbolized the regime's response to any form of criticism.

The traditional targets of ideological attacks, "bourgeois nationalism" and religion, continued to be assailed. An army paper declared: "Bourgeois nationalism is the most clever of all forms of imperialist ideology, [and] its main danger is that, as a rule, it skillfully camouflages its antisocialist nature behind an alleged concern for national interests" (*Narodna Armiya*, 11 June). Bulgarians of Moslem faith, the so-called Pomaks (numbering about 150,000), came under serious attacks for their "religious prejudices" and "fanaticism" and for complicity with "the reactionary role played by the Christian religion" (*Rodopski Ustrem*, 1 and 4 August).

International Views and Positions. The BCP and the Bulgarian government continued their loyal and often subservient support of the policies of the Soviet party and government on all major international issues, from Indochina to the Middle East and from Germany to the attitudes vis-á-vis the communist or the capitalist world, lacking in 1970 even the pretense of originality which has characterized some Bulgarian moves in the past.

Relations with the Soviet Union. No secret is made of the almost adoring attitude of the BCP and the Bulgarian regime toward the Soviet party and state. Todor Zhivkov, writing in the Moscow *Pravda* (21 March) stated:

> Full ideological unity and unanimity as well as close fraternal friendship exist between the BCP and the Communist Party of the Soviet Union. The eternal flame of this friendship burns deep in our people's consciousness and hearts, and the purest feelings of brotherhood and love toward the land of the Soviets live on. . . . Tomorrow as today this friendship will inspire us and open before us horizons of the future, and it will be handed down as a sacred legacy from generation to generation.

Zhivkov took also pride in the oft-quoted statement of L. I. Brezhnev: "Relations between our two countries and parties are a real example of proletarian internationalism in action."

The Bulgarian leadership renewed promptly its twenty-year treaty of friendship, cooperation, and mutual assistance with the U.S.S.R. in 1967. Commenting on this in 1970, the deputy chairman of the Council of Ministers, L. Avramov, (*Narodna Maladezh*, 11 May) said that it expressed "categorically once more the firm and unwavering determination of the BCP and the Bulgarian people to be with the Soviet Union and the Soviet people in rainy as well as sunny days, forever."

Avramov, who is also minister of foreign trade, added to the ideological, political, and military aspect of this relationship the economic and social sides, stating: "The major social and economic problems of building a developed socialist society in Bulgaria can be solved only on the basis of integrating the Bulgarian economy with the economies of the member countries of the Council for Mutual Economic Assistance and, above all, with the Soviet economy" (*Pravda*, 17 October).

Some more concrete examples of this integration, which started with the 1969 wide-ranging agreements between Bulgaria and the Soviet Union, are contained in a protocol on plan coordination for 1971-75 which was hailed as "a new moment in the history of the cooperation between the two fraternal countries" (*Rabotnichesko Delo*, 29 and 30 August). No details were provided, but the stress on specialization and of joint financing, established in 1969, is expected to be continued during the next five-year period. A subsequent trade agreement (November), implementing the goals of the protocol, revealed a rapid intensification of the trend to tie the Bulgarian economy closely to that of the Soviet Union. Not only would the value of the total trade turnover increase by about 60 per cent over the preceding five-year period, but the Soviet share alone would amount to a staggering 68 per cent of Bulgaria's total foreign trade in 1975 (*ibid.*, 5 November). (In recent years the Soviet share has usually fluctuated between 50 and 55 per cent, although in 1970 it jumped to 60 per cent.) This increase, plus the expectation that trade with the remaining communist countries will grow to about 22 per cent of the total at a minimum (the 1970 share of all communist states was already 87 per cent), would leave little for trade with the noncommunist world. Evidently the Bulgarian economy will depend even more heavily than before on Soviet equipment and plants, and will supply the Soviet Union with agricultural goods and the products of its processing industries. Integration is also to be expanded by sending additional Bulgarian construction workers and lumberjacks to the U.S.S.R., whose number would reach about 12,000 by 1975 (*Narodna Mladezh*, 22 March). All in all, while the announced "integration" does not seem to involve actual merger of Bulgarian and Soviet institutions or production units, the stepped-up cooperation ensures that the Bulgarian economy—and also its body politic—will be kept as an appendage of the Soviet Union.

Intra-Bloc and Communist Movement. In 1970, Bulgarian positions expectedly paralleled those of the Soviet Union toward other communist states and the international communist movement. The Bulgarian regime—a member of the Warsaw Pact—unreservedly supported the so-called Brezhnev doctrine of limited national sovereignty. An article in the army periodical *Narodna Armiya* (27 February), entitled "The Defense of Socialism—An International Duty of Communists," declared:

> The defense of each socialist country individually and of socialism as a whole is a natural and mandatory condition for the existence of socialism. . . . It is utopian to think that any one socialist country—excepting the U.S.S.R.—would be able to defend itself alone against the united forces of imperialism. The conditions which have emerged increase the requirements for the collective defense of socialism.

The Soviet line was backed also on the economic front—Bulgaria being also a member of the Council for Mutual Economic Assistance. Another article in the same periodical (29 January) stated:

> Bulgaria is an active participant in the socialist economic integration. . . . As a small and in the past backward country it can assure fast rates of development and an effective economy only by its participation in the international division of labor and mainly the socialist international division of labor under which the economic inter-state relations are built on the basis of fraternal cooperation and mutual aid.

On still a broader scale, Bulgaria's attachment to the Soviet-led bloc is exemplified by the continual quest for "unity of the international worker's movement within the framework of proletarian internationalism," redefined by the BCP newspaper as "loyalty to the principles of Marxism-Leninism, coordination of national and international interests, struggle against bourgeois nationalism and anti-Sovietism, combination of the independence of each Marxist-Leninist party with its international responsibilities." The paper continued: "Proletarian internationalism is today based also upon unity and unwavering friendship with the Soviet Union, the first and mightiest socialist state and the vanguard of the forces of the world revolutionary process." (*Rabotnichesko Delo*, 24 November.)

Relations with the Soviet-bloc parties and states of Eastern Europe remained as unexciting as expected. State and party visits to Czechoslovakia (February) and Poland (March) by a Bulgarian delegation, headed by Zhivkov, were aimed at reaffirming Soviet-inspired unity, deepening joint economic planning, and supporting the Soviet-led rapprochement with West Germany, based on West German recognition of the Oder-Neisse boundaries, thus consolidating postwar communist gains. A distant ally, Mongolia, sent its first secretary and premier to Sofia (June) and obtained Bulgarian condemnation of U.S. "aggression" in Indochina, together with the affirmation that the "present Chinese leadership" was inflicting serious harm on the unity of the socialist countries."

Nevertheless, there was a mellowing of the anti-Maoist stance to the point that an ambassador was appointed to occupy the long-vacant post in the Bulgarian Embassy in Peking. At the same time the Bulgarian press began raising questions as to whether the Chinese leadership may have decided to renounce extremist positions and policies (*Otechestven Front*, 17 November).

Zhivkov paid his first visit to distant Cuba (July), after a long postponement (since 1968). The significance of the visit seemed to be suggested by the speculation that Bulgaria had been assigned the task of maintaining close contacts with Fidel Castro on behalf of the Soviet bloc, since about 40 per cent of all foreign technical or economic aid to Cuba comes from Bulgaria.

Relations with Balkan Neighbors. In the Balkan area, the Bulgarian regime—reflecting most likely the plans of the Soviet leadership—tried to follow a more conciliatory policy toward both its communist and its noncommunist neighbors.

Relations with its only Warsaw Pact neighbor, Romania, which had been passing through a cooling-off period after the invasion of Czechoslovakia, experienced a turn, due probably to the realization by the Romanian leadership that some concessions to the Soviet (hence also the Bulgarian) position within the Warsaw Pact was necessary. Thus, the two party leaders, who had not met officially since 1967, headed their countries' state and party delegations for a two-day encounter on both sides of the Danube in September. Among other things, the meeting laid the groundwork for the signing of a new twenty-year treaty of friendship, cooperation, and mutual assistance, due to have been signed in 1968, on which the Romanians had stalled.

The treaty, consisting of ten articles, was signed on 19 November in Sofia (text in *Rabotnichesko Delo*, 20 November; communique, *ibid.*, 22 November), with the participation of Zhivkov and Ceauşescu. An additional agreement concerned the building of a power grid in Romania to transmit electric power from the U.S.S.R. to Bulgaria. What effect the resumption of top-level visits will have in the future was not too clear, since the Romanian side seems to have remained adamant on some basic issues. Still, the signing of the treaty and the verbal declarations accompanying it suggested a softening of the Romanian position, although each country's press has interpreted the treaty in accordance with its own prejudices.

No similar successes have been registered in Bulgaria's relations with Tito's Yugoslavia. If anything, relations seem to have deteriorated in 1970, due especially to the dispute over Macedonia. This time the "re-escalation" seems to have been undertaken by the Yugoslav leadership, in spite of conciliatory gestures by the Bulgarians. While in 1970 Bulgarian historians continued occasionally to refer to the "western provinces," including Macedonia, as having comprised part of Bulgaria, and to question the official Yugoslav position that the inhabitants of Macedonia have historically been a distinct "Macedonian nation," the official Bulgarian position accepts the existence of the Macedonian People's Republic as an integral part of the Yugoslav federation. Recent equivocations as to the ethnic character of the Macedonians seem to be as much defensive as offensive, if not more so, because a full acceptance of the Yugoslav viewpoint would raise automatically the question about the ethnic character of the population living within the Bulgarian part of Macedonia.

In his desire to side-step the issue, Zhivkov allegedly wrote to Tito, proposing a meeting and the signing of a friendship treaty. In his answer, Tito apparently sought assurances that such a meeting be thoroughly prepared and that as a precondition the Bulgarian government would unequivocally recognize the existence of a separate Macedonian nation. (The correspondence was confirmed by both sides, without details, on 19 September.) If so, such a precondition was obviously difficult to accept, especially since no tangible *quid pro quo* was offered. Western observers saw in Tito's apprehension about the future of the multi-national federation after his death a possible major reason for first pressing the Bulgarians for definitive concessions and then —if he should fail to receive them—for pressing the various Yugoslav nationalities into unity, so as to face a Bulgarian threat. Exploratory talks between delegations of the two countries were held in Sofia in November but proved fruitless.

Relations with Albania have registered little change toward improvement since the mutual expulsion of diplomats in 1968. In 1970, however, Albania participated in the Plovdiv fair in Bulgaria after an absence of two years, and resumption of diplomatic representation at the chargé d'affaires level apparently was decided upon as a result of Bulgarian initiative—perhaps to counter Yugoslav overtures toward Albania.

Bulgaria has the two NATO neighbors, Greece and Turkey. In 1970, Bulgarian-Turkish relations showed by far a greater relative progress and were highlighted by the official visit of Turkish Premier Demirel to Sofia in October. Although the visit's main practical result was the signing of a consular agreement, the entire atmosphere was very friendly and plans were laid for expanded trade, scientific, and cultural relations (communiqué in *Rabotnichesko Delo*, 10 October). Relations with Turkey assumed a notably good-neighborly character in 1969 when the main unresolved problem—the fate of the Turkish minority in Bulgaria—was tackled in a friendly spirit and resulted in the signing of a repatriation agreement which provided for the orderly emigration of qualified applicants. Of the estimated 700,000 Turkish citizens in Bulgaria, about 15,000 reportedly had been repatriated as of April 1970.

Despite the castigation of the anticommunist "Colonels' dictatorship" in Greece, normal relations were resumed after a visit by Foreign Minister Bashev to Athens in May, the first such visit since the 1967 coup in Greece. It was followed by a protocol regulating the boundaries along the Maritsa River and by visits of Greek officials to Bulgaria.

Relations with and Attitudes toward the West. In 1970, the Bulgarian government until late in the year continued its attacks on West Germany and reported an almost 40 per cent reduction in trade during 1969, as against the peak postwar year of 1966 (Bulgarian Telegraph Agency, 24 March). Only after the Brandt government's Ostpolitik was reciprocated by Moscow and Warsaw did the Bulgarian regime support the signing of treaties with West Germany by the U.S.S.R. and by Poland. But there was no indication of a Bulgarian desire to establish diplomatic relations with West Germany, unlike the late 1960s, although talks on a new, longer-term trade agreement took place.

Trade delegations visited France, Italy, and Great Britain, signing five-year agreements with the three countries. Foreign Minister Moro of Italy, which has become Bulgaria's most important noncommunist trading partner, paid a courtesy visit to Sofia and signed a five-year cultural agreement. A series of visits was exchanged with other European countries, including Todor Zhivkov's tour of Norway, Iceland, and Denmark, where he championed the need for an all-European security conference. In this year of extended personal travel, Zhivkov also visited Japan, on the occasion of the opening of EXPO 70.

Relations with the United States continued to be cool, and only minor agreements on scientific cooperation and on student exchange were reported signed in 1970. The Bulgarian press continued its vituperative campaign against "U.S. imperialism" and its "aggressive policies," and against President Nixon in person (e.g., *Otechestven Front*, 7 May; Radio Sofia, 22 July).

In sum, relations with the developed Western world have been equivocal. While with some countries, except West Germany, improvements have been noticed at least in a formal sense, regression has occurred in the economic field, where the share of the industrial countries declined from 19 to 14 per cent between 1965 and 1969 (*Ikonomicheski Zhivot*, 16 September 1970). In the special area of international tourism, foreign visitors—whose number, including passengers in transit, surpassed 2 million in 1969—were met with mixed feelings; hard currency was desired, but there were apprehensions about the spreading of "bourgeois influence," especially among the young. Together with advertisements and boasts about increased tourism there were warnings and intimidations about close contacts with foreign guests. Symptomatically, the recently inaugurated "Exhibition on Revolutionary Vigilance" in Sofia (*Narodna Kultura*, 11 April) was presented as a "warning, when the 'clock and dagger' strategists are planning new provocative campaigns," and a special "educational campaign" was conducted for families offering tourist accommodations to Western vacationeers, in order to minimize Western influence and "show the strength of socialism" (*Narodna Mladezh*, 29 June).

International Party Contacts. Aside from visits to Bulgaria by representatives of minor non-ruling communist parties, the most important contacts with ruling parties and visits of key BCP and Bulgarian government officials to noncommunist countries have already been noted above. In addition, a two-day meeting of the Warsaw Pact defense ministers was held on 21-22 May, and Zhivkov attended the communist summit meeting in Moscow on 20 August.

Main Party Publications. The daily *Rabotnichesko Delo* (Workers' Cause), edited by Secretariat member Georgi Bokov, is the central organ of the BCP. The Central Committee publishes also *Novo Vreme* (New Times), a theoretical monthly, edited by Nikolay Iribadzhakov, and *Partien Zhivot* (Party Life), a monthly journal on internal party matters, edited by Petko Rusev. More specialized nationwide publications are *Politicheska Prosveta* (Political Education) and *Ikonomicheski Zhivot* (Economic Life), biweeklies of the Central Committee, and the youth publications *Narodna Mladezh* (People's Youth) and *Mladezh* (Youth), organs of the DCYU.

L.A.D.D.

CZECHOSLOVAKIA

The Communist Party of Czechoslovakia (*Komunistická Strana Československa*; KSČ) was founded in November 1921 by left-wing secessionists from the Czechoslovak Social Democratic Party at a constituent congress in Prague. Through a coup d'état in February 1948 the party seized all power and since then has been the only significant political force in the country. Its claim to the leading role is recognized in the preamble to the 1960 constitution of the Czechoslovak Socialist Republic. It wields power through the National Front, a coalition in which a majority of votes is reserved to the KSČ representatives. The National Front also includes representatives of four other parties and of several mass organizations, which in essence are communist dominated, and has the exclusive right to nominate candidates for all electoral contests. No political activity outside the National Front is tolerated. Both top officials of the Czechoslovak government, President Ludvík Svoboda and Federal Premier Lubomír Štrougal, are members of the communist party.

Following a constitutional reform in October 1968, Czechoslovakia became a federation composed of two ethnic units: the Czech Socialist Republic and the Slovak Socialist Republic. A parallel reorganization of the communist party to correct the previous situation of "asymmetric centrism," where the separate Slovak communist party had no counterpart on the Czech side, was decided upon the same year but implementation never progressed beyond a provisional "Bureau for Party Work in the Czech Lands." Thus, a federal state continues to be ruled by a centralized communist party.

Party Organization. The highest organs of the party are the Central Committee and the Presidium. The party's Fourteenth Congress, which is also the most recent, was held during the military intervention by Warsaw Pact states in August 1968. The current leadership, anxious to satisfy the Soviet occupation authorities, does not recognize the resolutions of that meeting as valid. In its opinion, the Thirteenth Congress, held in June 1966, is the latest. Party spokesmen have indicated that the next one might take place during 1971.

Leadership. Sweeping changes in the composition of the highest governing bodies continued through 1970. Called "normalization," this process means the gradual liquidation of all reforms introduced by the former first secretary, Alexander Dubček. These were halted after April 1969, when Gustáv Husák succeeded him in the party leadership. Conspicuous changes in 1970 included the expulsion of Dubček from the party and the ouster of Oldřich Černik as federal premier and the suspension of his KSČ membership. The Presidium consists of full members Vasil Biľak, Peter Colotka, Evžen Erban, Gustáv Husák, Antonin Kapek, Josef Kempný, Josef Korčák, Jozef Lenárt, Jan Piller, Lubomír Štrougal, and Ludvík Svoboda; and candidate members Dalibor Haneš, Vaclav Hůla, and Alois Indra. The Secretariat, headed by Husák, consists of secretaries Vasil Biľak, Jan Fojtík, Miroslav Hruškovič, Alois Indra, Josef Kempný, and Oldřich Švestka, and two Secretariat members, Jozef Lenárt and Miroslav Moc. Miloš Jakeš is chairman of the Central Control and Auditing Commission. The first secretary of the Communist Party of Slovakia is Jozef Lenárt, and the chairman of the Bureau for Party Work in the Czech Lands is Josef Kempný.

Membership. The Communist Party of Czechoslovakia had 1,699,677 members in January 1968 and 44,179 primary party organizations in May 1969. By the end of 1970, membership had declined by 473,731 (or 27.8 per cent). A total of 326,817 cases (21.6 per cent) involved expulsion; among these, some 259,670 former adherents were stricken from the rolls because of indifference (e.g., failure to pay dues) and 67,147 others for violating party rules or for "ideological deviations." (*Rudé Právo*, 15 December.) Assuming that new admissions remained relatively limited during 1970 (only 4,035 in 1969), party membership at the end of the year can be estimated at slightly above 1.2 million. This represents about 8.3 per cent of the total population of Czechoslovakia, which was estimated as 14.3 million in 1968.

Domestic Affairs. A comprehensive purge dominated the party scene in 1970. It passed through several stages, gaining in intensity and severity. It began in December 1969 with "comradely interviews" involving party officials of higher levels. This phase was terminated the following spring, when party authorities claimed to have made "a fuller assessment" of the situation (*Rudé Právo*, 9 March). A much more extensive "exchange of party cards," as the purge was called officially, followed an extraordinary consultative meeting of the regional and district secretaries in Prague on 17 April. The conference gave lower-echelon officials exact instructions on how to conduct the operation. On this occasion, the party leadership voiced its discontent with what it considered past leniency in card renewals. Although suggestions as to the ideal size of party membership were lacking, it seems to have been generally assumed that a reduction of about 50 per cent would be desirable. It is possible that the subsequent "cleansing" operation was started at lower party levels with this objective in mind.

The purge continued through the summer months. At the beginning it seemed to make but little progress because of the large proportion of 1968 "liberalization" adherents at the grass-roots level. In some primary organizations there simply were no "true Marxist-Leninists"—that is, supporters of Soviet intervention—to be found who could replace liberals and carry out the investigations. The upper-level organs often had to step in and impose stricter standards of evaluation. Quite often, too, the verification commissions—or purge organs—themselves had to be reconstituted.

In October it was announced that the exchange of membership cards had been concluded, but no detailed statistics were made available. An analysis in *Život Strany* (25 October), however, indicated that termination of membership had occurred in the great majority of cases—some 80 per cent—on grounds of indifference or for failure to pay dues. Only one-fifth of the members stricken from party rosters were expelled as punishment for willful violation of party statutes. Exact figures were published in a "Report on the Course and Outcome of the Exchange of Party Cards in 1970," submitted in December to a plenary session of the Central Committee at Prague. According to this document, the KSČ had lost about 28 per cent of its members since January 1968 (*Rudé Právo*, 15 December). Although the purge had eliminated more than one-fourth of the membership, it clearly fell short of the alleged goal of 50 per cent. Despite the above, the KSČ has maintained its high position among the world's communist parties in terms of per capita membership.

Loss of a party card almost automatically involved removal from a professional position, particularly if the post carried some public influence. Thus, the purge of the party was accompanied by a large reshuffle of the political, economic, and cultural apparatus of government. The noncommunist parties represented in the National Front—mainly the Czechoslovak Socialist Party and the (Catholic) Populist Party—also undertook a "cleansing procedure" during 1970. This resulted, on the whole, in the come-back of many politicians, known for their close collaboration with "dogmatist" KSČ leaders during the "personality cult" era, who had been ousted after January 1968. More independent activity by KSČ partners in the National Front—such as the recruitment of new members and the legislative initiative which the April 1968 Action Program of the communist party explicitly encouraged—had to be abandoned. Moreover, all civil servants and personnel in executive positions who were not organized in any party were screened, and those found "unreliable" were either dismissed or transferred to minor positions. Thus the "national regeneration process" affected all components of public life.

The gradual abandonment of Dubček's policies did not depend on the success of the purge; it continued during the entire year. Meetings of the party's governing bodies could be viewed as milestones along this path. Its progress was reflected in numerous ousters from the supreme organs of party and state. The January plenum of the Central Committee deprived federal premier and Presidium member Oldřich Černík of both of these posts. Later he was expelled from the Central Committee and his party membership was suspended; finally he was ousted from the party. His replacement as premier was Lubomír Štrougal, known for conservative leanings. At the same plenum, Alexander Dubček resigned from that body. Later he was appointed ambassador to Turkey.

A similar shift toward more conservatism occurred in the Communist Party of Slovakia, where the first secretary, Štefan Sádovský (who also lost his seat on the party Presidium), was succeeded by Jozef Lenárt, a former protégé and collaborator of Antonín Novotný. The trade-union leader Karel Poláček was dismissed from the Presidium. Jozef Lenárt and the "centrist" Josef Korčák became Presidium members. Dalibor Haneš, Vaclav Hůla, and a notorious opponent of Dubček, Alois Indra, were made Presidium candidates.

The ultraconservative Antonín Kapek, who in the meantime had obtained control over the formerly very "progressive" Prague KSČ City Committee, was also coopted as a Presidium member. Important changes took place in the party Secretariat, from which the last prominent representative of the "liberalization" course, Josef Špaček, was removed, along with František Penč. Lubomír Štrougal, due to his appointment as federal prime minister, resigned both from the party Secretariat and from the chairmanship of the Bureau for Party Work in the Czech Lands, Penč, Špaček, and Štrougal were replaced by two "centrists," Miroslav Hruškovič and Oldřich Švestka, and the ultraconservative Miroslav Moc, who later became editor in chief of the party's central daily *Rudé Právo* (Prague radio, 30 January).

By June, when the Central Committee convened again, the fate of the most popular figure of the "Prague Spring" had been decided upon. Dubček had been recalled in the previous month from his diplomatic post in Ankara, and the June plenum confirmed his expulsion from the party. Among the reasons given for this measure was Dubček's "persistent refusal to recognize his errors." At the same time the ouster of other prominent figures took place: Josef Borůvka, agriculture minister in the 1968 government; Čestmír Císař, former education minister and chairman of the Czech National Council; Zdeněk Mlynář, co-author of the KSČ Action Program and former Presidium member; Josef Smrkovský, former chairman of the National Assembly and a member of the Presidium; Josef Špaček, former party secretary and Presidium member; and eight other "liberals." The Central Committee also expelled Jaroslav Kladiva, former dean of the political science faculty at Charles University in Prague and Central Committee member. (*Ibid.*, 4 July.)

The KSČ Presidium in September appeared to be absorbed by the problems resulting from the purge among the rank-and-file communists, which had almost run its course. It also decided on the appointment of the top ideologist from the Novotný era and former party secretary, Vladimír

Koucký, as ambassador to Belgium. Interpretable as a defensive move on the part of the Husák leadership, the appointment curtailed the increasingly aggressive behavior of the ultraconservative elements with whom Koucký had joined forces as soon as Warsaw Pact armies invaded Czechoslovakia. Another disciplinary measure against the group of the "ultras" appeared in the dismissal by the Czech National Council of Interior Minister Josef Groesser, a rabid dogmatist under whose instructions police organs in Bohemia and Moravia had engaged in fabricating evidence on imaginary conspiratorial activities of individuals and whole groups. He was replaced by Josef Jung (Radio Hvězda, October 23). This demotion seemed to substantiate rumors that the ultras had been preparing the overthrow of the Husák leadership. It is probable that the unusual delay in calling the next Central Committee plenum—it should have met in October but did not actually convene until early December—was caused by these internal conflicts.

The December plenum did not bring any additional expulsions or dismissals. The only spectacular decision of this kind was the final ouster of Oldřich Černík from the party. Apart from the publication of purge results, the Central Committee released additional information on immediate and future policy objectives. It appeared that the leadership had finally succeeded in formulating a coherent view on what it termed the "crisis-ridden development of the party and society after the Thirteenth Congress of the KSČ [in June 1966]." This view was contained in a document with restricted circulation, and it could be reconstructed only from more or less explicit details given by different party leaders in public speeches after the plenary session. According to these hints, the Central Committee declared for the first time that "thousands of honest communists" in August 1968 had pleaded for international aid in "defense of socialism" (Tanyug, Yugoslav press agency, 14 December). This may be viewed as an *ex post facto* attempt to legitimate the Soviet-led invasion, which almost all leading officials of 1970—including Husák, Štrougal, and Svoboda—previously had condemned. KSČ Presidium member Antonín Kapek claimed that the Central Committee at its December session "unambiguously rejected" the 1968 Action Program (Prague radio, 12 December). Although this stand would signify a major change in principle— Gustáv Husák had affirmed earlier in 1970 that the January 1968 reforms had been "necessary" and had "provided a great chance for the party" (*Rudé Právo*, 5 January)—it would not be too inconsistent with KSC policies actually pursued during the current year.

In fact the Action Program was a dead letter long before the December plenum, and the trend toward gradual liquidation of reforms introduced in 1968 appeared to be constant. In addition to mass purges, sporadic arrests of some very outspoken opponents to Soviet intervention took place. It did not seem, however, that a wholesale repressive action was planned by the group in control. In the sphere of human and civil rights, further stiffening could be observed, with closer control over mass media and additional restrictions on foreign travel. The fairly liberal issuance of passports, in agreement with stipulations of the Action Program, was abandoned. Returning to the view that unauthorized sojourn abroad constituted a crime against the security of the state, the regime started a series of legal proceedings against persons who had gone into exile after August 1968. Revision of political trials held during the 1950's (a feature of the 1968 "Prague Spring") and the rehabilitation of trial victims were not discontinued. On the other hand, legal regulations governing the rehabilitations became more complicated and rigid (*ibid.*, 8 July). The atheistic campaign, virtually abandoned in 1967 and denounced in the text of the Action Program, was resumed in the party press (*Pravda*, Bratislava, 24 January; *Rudé Právo*, 1 September) and accompanied by a drive to rally "loyalist" priests of all denominations to the cause of the communist establishment (CTK, Czechoslovak news agency, 17 September).

While it is not difficult to assess the numerical strength of the "progressivist" opposition in 1970—statistics about the purge, unlikely to eliminate it entirely, were impressive enough—it is less easy to determine the extent to which "liberals" constituted an immediate threat to the lead-

ership. Although individual cases of open defiance took place during the year, much less spontaneous mass resistance occurred than in 1969. The second anniversary of the Soviet intervention,
for example, passed by peacefully, the public restraining itself to a boycott of entertainment and
mass communications media on that day. In January 1970, the Interior Ministry claimed to have
discovered an "anti-state Trotskyite organization" which allegedly had "attempted to impair the
consolidation process." It is true that a handful of radical Marxists in the KSČ condemned the
Soviet-led invasion in equally strong terms as the "liberals," but the importance of this group
appears to have been exaggerated, perhaps in order to create an atmosphere for more severe repression (Prague radio, 12 January).

A real challenge to the wielders of power seems to have come, rather, from the opposite side.
During 1970 there were several indications that the ultraconservative elements counted on Soviet
support and believed it possible to seize control from the Husák leadership. It is difficult to identify all the adherents of this faction. Some were recruited from among dissatisfied party veterans
of the "Libeň Group," headed by Antonín Kapek. Others included younger, ambitious, adventurous or dogmatic individuals. Their platform appeared in the journal *Levá Fronta* (Left Front),
published at irregular intervals beginning in September 1970. The views of this group were occasionally found also in current party periodicals, such as *Tribuna*. Its adherents held that the whole
"regenerative process" then under way in the KSČ was doomed to failure because the leadership
had merely passed from the "rightists" into the hands of the "centrists," who were merely opportunists of another brand. Moreover, it was claimed by partisans of *Levá Fronta* that a consistent
"cleansing action" would require also elimination of the "entire opportunist clique of Antonín
Novotný, which had helped to create, carry out, and defend the disastrous policies before January
1968" (*Tribuna*, 4 February). This was a call for return to the situation during the Stalinist era.
Also, the publication by Czech Minister of Education Jaromír Hrbek of a very dogmatic interpretation of events since 1968, under the title "Manifesto of Truth," was considered a sign of determination by ultraconservatives to promote their ideas, regardless of the official KSČ line.
Husák explicitly rejected these views (Prague radio, 10 September), and the December plenum of
the Central Committee did not result in any notable concessions to the extreme conservative
wing. It was, however, difficult to decide at the end of the year whether the dogmatist threat to
the leadership had actually subsided, or whether the Husák team had been granted only a respite.

As a result of this rather opaque situation in the party, many important political issues were
left pending. For example, the only partly implemented reform of the KSČ organizational structure, intended to adapt the party to federal conditions, did not make any progress during 1970.
The Bureau for Party Work in the Czech lands, established in 1968, showed little activity. As the
year came to its close, there was little evidence that substantial change was to be expected. Certain decisions of the ruling bodies pointed, rather, to a slow return toward centralism on government as well as party levels. By a decision of the Central Committee plenum in December, the
1968 constitutional law on federation was amended practically to eliminate the powers of the two
separate ethnic republics in economic matters and to strengthen the authority of the central
government in matters of police and security (*ibid.*, 21 December). Thus, not even the one reform
carried out after the Soviet intervention was spared the impact of the general retrograde development.

Mass Organizations. The mass organizations could not escape "political normalization." The
Peace Movement, the World War Two Resistance Fighters, the Central Union of Uniform Agricultural Cooperatives, and all other such bodies had their top officials demoted or expelled. The
patriotic declarations issued during the first days of the 1968 invasion were revoked. The extent
of this purge indicated the extensive support for "liberalization" in 1968 and the intensity of anti-

Soviet feelings which the intervention precipitated. Among Czechoslovak mass organizations, the trade unions had been particularly affected by the January 1968 change in political course. Consequently, they experienced a similar upheaval after the ouster of Alexander Dubček. At the February 1970 plenum of the Central Council for Trade Unions, its chairman, Karel Poláček (elected during the post-January 1968 era), resigned from all functions. He was replaced by the conservative Jan Piller (Prague radio, 11 February). A number of personnel changes followed on all levels of the trade union movement. Policies adopted since then, while they did not signify an unqualified return to the Stalinist conception of unions as "transmission belts" for political power, definitely put an end to attempts made in 1968 and later for having these organs represent the workers vis-à-vis the state. Characteristic of trends prevailing in the unions during 1970 was the formal abolition of the Enterprise Councils, established in the spring of 1968 on the Yugoslav and Polish models. Allegedly, they had become "foci of right-wing and antisocialist strife." A new "harmonious system of directing and advisory activities" was promised (*Večerník*, Bratislava, 16 June), but no effective steps toward such a system were taken.

Culture, Education, and Youth. Cultural organizations and individuals working in the fields of science and art continued in 1970 to be subject to rigorous political control. Meanwhile, attempts to win active support from Czech and Slovak intellectuals did not make notable progress. Although the Czechoslovak Union of Writers had been dissolved (the constitutional law on federation had reserved cultural matters under jurisdiction of the two ethnic republics), the regional writers' bodies refused to recognize this decision because it violated their autonomy. A series of governmental ordinances further curbed their freedom of action, particularly by transferring the Literary Fund and royalty payments to the respective Ministries of Culture. Also announced was a ban on publication of nonperiodical items (i.e., books) without previous authorization by the government (*Rudé Právo*, 28 February; *Informace*, Prague, no. 4, 1970). In December the Ministry of Culture convened a nationwide meeting of artists and cultural workers in Prague and presented to the public the preparatory committees of new cultural organizations, composed exclusively of persons loyal to the regime (*Lidová Demokracie*, Prague, 19 December). A number of cultural and scientific periodicals were suspended or stopped on explicit order of the authorities or merged with journals and reviews of similar subject matter (CTA, 18 December). The party also carried out radical changes in the statutes of the Czechoslovak Academy of Sciences, a bulwark of "reformist" thought and one of the centers of resistance to the Soviet intervention. By reserving the right to nominate the academy president and exclude individuals from membership, the Federal Assembly put an end to the autonomy of this institution. (*Rudé Právo*, March 20.)

The educational system was another target of the regime policies in 1970. A large-scale purge took place in the schools at all levels, particularly in the universities. Official spokesmen admitted that sympathy of the Czech and Slovak professors and teachers with the reformist course of Alexander Dubček had been quasi-general. The fact that all departments of Marxism-Leninism at institutions of higher learning had to be disbanded and that among 587 members only 286 were allowed to continue their academic careers (Prague radio, 29 June) indicated to what extent the younger intellectual party elite had been permeated by the "revisionist" spirit. In order to maintain close control over the educational system, a special Pedagogic Council was established by the Czech Ministry of Education (*Učitelské Noviny*, Prague, 15 October).

In the youth movement, which had been very profoundly affected by the "Prague Spring" and which became more autonomous and diversified under its impact, the year 1970 marked a return to the principle of a single mass organization. After individual youth and student groups constituted in 1968 had been either dissolved or prevented from operating, and the loosely coordinated Association of Children's and Youth Organizations had been liquidated because of its alleged disorienting effect upon young people, the Federal Socialist Youth Union (FSYU) was founded in November at a national conference in Prague. The FSYU became the only officially approved youth organization. Its basic aim is to "integrate the socialist youth of the Czech Socialist Republic, the Slovak Socialist Republic, and the Czechoslovak People's Army." Juraj Varholík, a Slovak, became its first chairman. A branch for children under fifteen years of age, the Pioneer Organization, is a part of the FSYU. According to 1970 statistics, some 300,000 young persons above fifteen years and about a half-million Pioneers were enrolled in the FSYU, while the total eligible for membership numbered about 6 million (*Rudé Právo*, 11 November).

Armed Forces. A garrison of the Soviet army, estimated at some 70,000 to 80,000 men, continued to be stationed in Czechoslovakia during 1970 under an agreement signed at Moscow in October 1968. Czechoslovak units participated in joint military exercises with these Soviet troops during August 1970 (*Kraznaia Zvezda*, Moscow, 19 August), and a Czechoslovak delegation took part in summit talks of the Warsaw Pact countries at East Berlin in December (Prague radio, 13 December). In his Order of the Day to the army, Federal Defense Minister Martin Dzúr declared that the Warsaw Pact was different from other, similar alliances because of its "class character" and "specific military-political goals." As an example of practical implementation, Dzúr cited the "military assistance to Czechoslovakia against the counterrevolutionaries at home and the reactionaries abroad in August 1968" (*Rudé Právo*, 13 May). This interpretation of the Warsaw Pact appeared to correspond with the so-called Brezhnev Doctrine of "limited sovereignty" and to be an attempt to justify *ex post facto* the occupation of Czechoslovakia by the forces of five pact signatories.

Economy. The party leadershp searched during 1970 for policies which would be adequate for the alleviation of pressing problems, without bearing the mark of "economic revisionism." Although Gustáv Husák had indicated as early as April 1969 that the party intended to replace the New Economic Model, adopted by the Thirteenth Congress in 1966, with the concept of "planned management," it was not clear by the end of 1970 what this concept signified in practice. Spokesmen for the regime kept blaming most of the difficulties on "disruptions caused by right-wing opportunist forces" and on the "heritage of the Dubček era which had led to near anarchy" (Prague radio, 17 November). A simple return to the centralized type of management and planning did not seem to be one of the party's options. In the second half of the year it appeared that a rather rigid system of price, credit, and wage controls would be introduced, but that the enterprises would maintain a certain degree of autonomy in matters of investment and production planning (*Pravda*, Bratislava, 19, 21, 22, and 23 October). The most serious shortcomings of the Czechoslovak economy in 1970 included an unbalanced foreign trade (surplus with the East European bloc, deficit with hard-currency countries), lack of coordination in the field of capital investment and construction, a manpower shortage, high labor turnover, and low worker morale. Despite these problems, the party claimed that industrial production had increased by 8.3 per cent during the first half of the year, 1.8 per cent above planned growth. Labor productivity in industry showed an increase of 8.4 per cent, while wages rose by 4.2 per cent; the net labor productivity reached 1.3 per cent above planned growth. Gross agricultural output was expected to "fall slightly below planned targets." Capital construction during the first six months of 1970 exceeded that of the comparable period in 1969 by 9.0 per cent. Nominal per capita income increased by 3.6 per cent and reached 1,896 koruny per month. The increase in real wages did not seem to be significant, however, as the price index in the second half of 1969 rose from 3.5 to 3.9 per cent. Employment was up by 96,000 jobs, "a little above the plan." The overall foreign trade balance was negative, at the ratio of 120 to 116 (100 in 1969). (CTA, 28 July.)

Foreign Affairs. Engrossed in domestic problems and concerned about internal stability, the Husák regime developed but little initiative in international politics during 1970. Diplomatic negotiations were aimed chiefly at strengthening ties with the Soviet Union and other countries in the East European bloc. A new treaty of friendship, cooperation, and mutual assistance with the U.S.S.R. was signed in the presence of Soviet party leader Leonid Brezhnev at Prague on 6 May, the twenty-fifth anniversary of liberation. Actually, the original December 1943 pact had been extended for another twenty years in 1963. It is assumed that 1968 events rendered necessary in Soviet eyes a revision of the text, in order to create a legal basis for interference in Czechoslovak internal affairs. Comments in the KSČ press confirmed this impression, at the time when the treaty was initiated. The principle of "support for socialist achievements as well as defense and consolidation of these achievements being an international obligation of all communists" had been incorporated in the text (CTA, 4 April). The new pact also provided for more extensive cooperation in economic matters between the two countries, demonstrated later in the protocol on scientific-technical exchange in the field of nuclear energy, signed at Prague in July (*Rudé Právo*, 24 July), and the agreement on coordination of economic plans during the 1971-75 five year period, signed at Moscow in September (Prague radio, 29 September). Another commitment in relations with other socialist countries was entered upon by the Czechoslovak automobile works, "Skoda," which negotiated car production cooperation with a Bulgarian enterprise (*Hospodářské Noviny*, Prague, 20 November). In November a protocol on coordination of economic plans was signed with Poland (*Trybuna Ludu*, Warsaw, 15 November). A trade agreement with the Chinese People's Republic was concluded at Peking in June (*Rudé Právo*, 18 June). A trade pact with the German Democratic Republic, representing an increase in scheduled turnover of about 50 per cent, was concluded shortly before the end of the year (*ibid.*, 17 December).

The most important event in international relations with the noncommunist world was the five-year economic and trade agreement with the Federal Republic of Germany, signed at Zbraslav Castle near Prague in December (Prague radio, 17 December). The period covered by the protocol was the longest thus far in dealings between the two countries. It is the first document to provide for scientific and technical cooperation. This agreement might open the way to complete normalization of Czechoslovak-West German diplomatic relations, interrupted since World War II. The KSČ leadership has indicated the chief obstacle to be the unwillingness of the Federal Republic of Germany to declare null and void *ab initio* the 1938 Munich treaty (which ceded the border territories or Sudetenland to Nazi Germany and led shortly thereafter to the dismemberment of Czechoslovakia) (*Rudé Právo*, 28 August).

The only instance in which the Husák leadership seemed to put aside somewhat its reserve in foreign politics was the U.S.S.R.-sponsored campaign against international Zionism. A propaganda book by two Soviet authors entitled *Attention Zionism!* was translated into Slovak and given extensive publicity by Czechoslovak mass media. Radio and television service also carried a series of articles from the Soviet press and special commentaries by F. J. Kolar, Moscow correspondent for the Czechoslovak Broadcasting Corporation, on the alleged "Zionist conspiracy." Leading personalities of the "Prague Spring" were accused in the book and in radio and TV programs of having been "agents of Israel" and "opposed to Soviet foreign policies" (Radio Hvězda, 3 September).

International Communist Movement. It might be inferred that KSČ policy makers of 1970 would have chosen to be reserved in matters concerning world communism, should they have had complete freedom of action. Such an attitude, however, would have proven extremely difficult, as the "Czechoslovak question," concerning the legitimacy of the 1968 Soviet-led intervention, remained one of the major issues dividing the communist parties of the world. Consistent with a declaration adopted at the May 1969 Central Committee plenum, Czechoslovak leaders rejected on several occasions the views of "fraternal parties" which had criticized Soviet interference. Open polemics broke out in the KSČ press, particularly against statements and resolutions of the British, French, and Italian communists. Relations with the French Communist Party became strained when Alois Indra claimed that a French delegation to Prague in November 1969 had provided the Czechoslovak party leadership with "evidence of criminal negligence of the counter-revolutionary danger" displayed by Alexander Dubček in 1968, while the French party's Politburo explicitly denied this claim (Brno radio, 14 January; *L'Humanité*, Paris, 16 May). This difference was aggravated further by Soviet information media which picked up the story as told by Indra (TASS, 30 January). When the French party expelled the well-known publicist and Central Committee member Roger Garaudy, the Czechoslovak press indicated satisfaction. Garaudy had been one of the most vehement critics of the Soviet intervention. Even after his expulsion, however, the French communists maintained their negative attitude toward the "Brezhnev Doctrine." The British and Italian parties became in their turn targets of Czechoslovak communist attack when they indicated that they were not willing to change their position on the "Czechoslovak problem" (*Rudé Právo*, 20 January; *Mladá Fronta*, 26 March). Communist China—which Czechoslovak media kept on denouncing as "adventurist, Trotskyist, chauvinist, and dogmatist," in harmony with the general ideological line of the Soviets—was dealt a sharp rebuff when the Chinese party issued a statement of principle on the "Czechoslovak question" (NCNA, 30 January).

Participation of the KSČ in other activities of the world communist movement took the form of a series of consultations with and good-will missions to other socialist countries. These visits were in most cases reciprocated by the host parties during the year. Gustáv Husák, accompanied by three other Presidium members, met East German communist leader Walter Ulbricht at Leipzig on the occasion of the Spring Fair (Prague radio, 7 March). Later, Ulbricht came to Prague at the head of a high-ranking delegation. It is generally believed that the most important item on the agenda concerned Czechoslovak-West German contacts (*ibid.*, 21 October). The East German communists seemed anxious to make sure that the forthcoming normalization of relations between Czechoslovakia and the Federal Republic of Germany would not weaken the position or the influence of the East German state in Central Europe. Conspicuous publicity given to the visit to Prague of the secretary-general from the illegal West German communist party, Max Reimann, may have been dictated by a desire by the Husák leadership to demonstrate that the KSČ was not going to sacrifice the interests of German communism for the sake of good-neighborly relations with the Federal Republic (cf. interview with Max Reimann, Prague radio, 6 March). Gustáv Husák, with a representative party and government delegation, traveled to Budapest in the spring to participate in celebrations on the twenty-fifth anniversary of Hungary's liberation (*ibid.*, 4 April). He also took part in the congress of the Hungarian Socialist Workers' Party in the fall (*ibid.*, 22 November). A Hungarian party Secretary, György Aczél, came to Prague in the summer to discuss "experiences in ideological and political work" (Radio Czechoslovakia, 21 July). Another high-level international party meeting took place when the first secretary of the Bulgarian communist party, Todor Zhivkov, visited the Czechoslovak capital (Prague radio, 17 February).

Publications. The central press organ of the Communist Party of Czechoslovakia is the daily *Rudé Právo*. The main newspaper of the Communist Party of Slovakia is called *Pravda*. The Czech component of the KSČ, until the end of 1970 represented only by the provisional Bureau for Party Work in the Czech Lands, has no press of its own. More or less official views of the party on current political problems are reflected by the Czech weekly *Tribuna*; its Slovak counterpart is *Predvoj*. A political review, addressing a rather informed and more educated readership, is

Tvorba. The fortnightly *Nová Mysl* has developed from a purely theoretical quarterly into a more general publication dealing with important questions of domestic and world politics. Important decisions of the KSČ governing bodies and instructions to party workers at the regional and grass-roots level form the main contents of the bimonthly *Život Strany*. The Czechoslovak trade union movement publishes the daily *Práce* at Prague and its Slovak counterpart *Práca* in Bratislava. The Czech organ of the Federal Socialist Youth Union is *Mladá Fronta*, and the corresponding Slovak newspaper is called *Smena.*

Z.S.

GERMANY: GERMAN DEMOCRATIC REPUBLIC

The Socialist Unity Party of Germany (Sozialistische Einheitspartei Deutschlands; SED) was founded on 21 April 1946 in the Soviet zone of occupation when, under Soviet pressure, the Communist Party of Germany (KPD) and Social-Democratic Party of Germany (SPD) merged into a single movement. Although the communists were slightly in the minority at the time, they soon assumed control over the joint party apparatus. Late in 1947 the SED selected a "People's Congress" from among its membership. The congress, in turn, assumed the right to establish a government for East Germany and to arrange for the drafting of a constitution. The German Democratic Republic (Deutsche Demokratische Republik; GDR), was formally created in October 1949.

Government and Party Structure. In 1970 the East German communist regime continued under the long-term leadership of Walter Ulbricht, first secretary of the SED, who also functions as chairman of both the State Council and the National Defense Council. Multiple authority has given Ulbricht uncommon power, which he uses to coordinate the interests of the GDR with those of the Soviet Union.

Elections are held, but voters receive ballots of a "National Front" single list representing the SED, four subordinate parties, and a number of mass organizations. In the latest general election (2 July 1967), 11.2 million persons, or 99.93 of the electorate, voted for the National Front candidates for the People's Chamber (Volkskammer). In local elections on 22 March 1970 the vote was 99.85 per cent for the candidates on the consolidated list, causing State Council member Friedrich Ebert to call the outcome an "object lesson in true democracy for those who want to preach self-determination to the socialist GDR" (ADN, East German news agency, 24 March).

The SED normally holds a party congress every four years. Its Seventh Congress, in April 1967, elected a Central Committee of 131 full members and 50 candidates. The new committee reelected Walter Ulbricht* as first secretary and as a member of the Politburo, whose fourteen other full members were Friedrich Ebert, Paul Fröhlich, Gerhard Grüneberg,* Kurt Hager,* Erich Honecker,* Hermann Matern,* Günter Mittag,* Erich Mückenberger, Alfred Neumann, Albert Norden,* Horst Sindermann, Willi Stoph (also premier of the GDR), Paul Verner,* and Herbert Warnke. In addition Hermann Axen,* Georg Ewald, Walter Halbritter, Werner Jarowinsky,* Günter Kleiber, and Margarete Müller were chosen as candidate members. The Secretariat was composed of Werner Lamberz and the ten men whose names above are followed by an asterisk. Paul Fröhlich died in September 1970. The Central Committee in December elected Axen to full membership in the Politburo and Lamberz to candidate membership. Otherwise no changes in the party hierarchy occurred in 1970.

The Secretariat is in charge of the organizational work of the party. In addition, certain secretaries have special areas of responsibility; Hager, ideology; Norden, propaganda; Honecker, security and military problems; Grüneberg, agriculture; Jarowinsky, trade; and Mittag, industry.

Up to the time of their promotions, at least, Axen dealt with foreign relations and Lamberz was the secretary for agitation.

In 1970 Walter Ulbricht reached the age of seventy-seven years. Willi Stoph and Erich Honecker figured most prominently in speculation about his eventual successor. It is conceivable that, as the most important men in the state and party apparatus after Ulbricht, they may eventually assume collective leadership.

In April the SED announced that an exchange of party cards for all its 1.9 million full and candidate members (out of an estimated 1969 population in East Germany of 17,075,000) would take place in September and October. Walter Ulbricht in an interview (*Neues Deutschland*, 19 April) stressed that most of the party cards were due to expire in 1971 and that an exchange was a "perfectly normal procedure of inner-party life." Nevertheless he characterized it as a move "of the greatest social significance." The basic purpose of the exchange, Ulbricht explained, was to "raise the educational level of party members and of the entire working population" and to "strengthen their political-ideological firmness." It was related to the "solution of current tasks," which covered not only ideological problems, but also economic ones, including specifically the 1970 national economic plan and the long-range 1971-75 plan. In general, party members would be called upon to "conceive and explain the political, economic, scientific-technical, and spiritual-cultural problems in their complex features." Ulbricht enumerated the errors of the economists and included their restrictive, traditional thought-processes; conservative consciousness, satisfied with mediocrity; enterprise-centered egotism; lack of adherence to cooperative schedules; over-emphasis of difficulties; fruitless discussions; and overbearing behavior toward the working population. Against this background, arousing fears of pending "party purges" reminiscent of 1951 and 1960-61, Politburo member Honecker to the country's surprise revealed at the December plenum of the SED Central Committee that 1,893,594 members and candidates would receive new party documents in January 1971 and that only 8,706 would be expelled (for their "unstable, inactive relationship to the party over a prolonged period of time") (*Neues Deutschland*, 12 December).

Together with the SED, the following four parties constitute the National Front: the Christian Democratic Union of Germany (Christliche Demokratische Union Deutschlands; CDU), headed by Gerald Götting; the National Democratic Party of Germany (National-Demokratische Partei Deutschlands; NDPD), headed by Dr. Lothar Bolz; the Liberal Democratic Party of Germany (Liberal-Demokratische Partei Deutschlands; LDPD) headed by Manfred Gerlach; and the Democratic Peasant Party of Germany (Demokratische Bauernpartei Deutschlands; DBD), headed by Ernst Goldenbaum. The SED has 127 representatives and each of the other parties holds 52 seats in the Volkskammer.

A number of mass organizations also play a political role, but their views never differ from those of the SED. The most important are represented in the Volkskammer and include the Free German Trade-Union Federation (FDGB), which has 6.8 million members; the Free German Youth (FDJ), with 1.6 million; and the Democratic League of Women (DFB), with 1.3 million. Additional mass organizations serve general or specific interests. For example, the German-Soviet Friendship Society fosters friendly relations with the Soviet Union and promotes its views. The Society for Sport and Technology (GST) enrolls approximately 500,000 young people and instills "socialist soldierly virtues" to prepare them for service in the People's Army.

The SED and the Developed Socialist System. In 1967 the Seventh Congress of the SED saw its future efforts revolving around the creation of a "developed socialist system" and outlined the tasks that would "secure the dynamic and coordinated growth" of all components—economic, educational, cultural—by achieving the perfect linkage of political and technical revolutions. Progress must have been slower than anticipated, for in 1970 Walter Lamberz stated that "the task before the GDR in the 1970s will be to build a developed social system of socialism" (*WMR*, February). He added that "progress in the various spheres of society can and must proceed, within the framework of general social development, much faster than heretofore."

Adoption of a new socialist constitution in 1968 was meant to aid the development of the desired system and to provide the juridical foundation for a "socialist democracy." It was to be implemented on the basis of democratic centralism and to guarantee the sovereignty of the working people. In 1970 Politburo member Honecker, addressing a three-day international conference organized by the SED Central Committee to assess "The Growing Role of the Communist Parties in the Revolutionary Process of the Construction of Socialism and Communism," insisted that the "free development of socialist personalities" was proceeding satisfactorily, "enabling the working people to consciously shape their own existence" and "humanist ideas to become reality" (*Neues Deutschland*, 17 June).

Domestic Attitudes and Activities. The GDR operates under a "socialist economic system" of a centrally planned economy. In 1970 serious shortcomings were revealed when economics expert Günter Mittag reported to the SED Central Committee plenum of 9-10 June that the national economy had fallen behind its target goals for the early part of the year and was endangering even the long-range 1971-75 plan. Mittag called for the mobilization of all forces for a maximum increase in labor productivity and effectiveness and defined the focal points of future economic development. The prerequisites he listed included the mastery of the organization of "socialist science," preliminary research, automation of production systems, "complex socialist rationalization" through increased self-initiative, production within East Germany of the means of automation and rationalization, recognition of productivity and efficiency as an indivisible entity, and the lowering of specific investment costs and primary costs per quantity unit (ADN, 11 June). Mittag also spoke of incompetence on the part of management, such as failures to make proper cost estimates and delays in preparing research programs, and singled out the chemical, electronics, and construction industries in this respect. He also scored production shortages of such consumer goods as textiles, shoes, furniture, and household wares and the shoddy quality of many items delivered. He attributed problems of agriculture largely to adverse climatic conditions, but placed some of the blame on "slackness" in agricultural cooperatives. (*Neues Deutschland*, 11 June.)

Economic questions were again prominently treated in the major speeches to the Central Committee plenum of 9-11 December, where both successes and failures for the year and for the long-range 1966-70 plan were revealed. Politburo member Verner expressed the general view that the economic system had "proved itself wherever it was sensibly applied" and would "continue to prove itself to the degree to which the economic laws of socialism [were] consistently utilized and their effects allowed for in the plan"; it was "only necessary to correct certain excessive desires and concepts not in line with the material possibilities" (*ibid.*, 10 December). Premier Stoph presented the economic report for the year and outlined the economic goals for 1971. He listed the achievement of "extraordinarily high export targets" as the most important task, prerequisite to the "import of raw materials, foodstuffs, complete plants, and means of automation" indispensable for the economy (*ibid.*, 11 December).

Some misgivings about East Germany's part in the Council for Mutual Economic Assistance (CMEA) were revealed. Deputy Premier Gerhard Weiss, discussing the results of the CMEA meeting held in Warsaw on 12-14 May, implied East German concern over the new pressures for economic integration, which could intensify the dependence of East European economies both on one another and on the Soviet Union, and over the supply of oil from the Soviet Union, especially in view of the shortages experienced by East German industry and households during the past winter. A few weeks later the East Germans called the decision by CMEA members to set up their own investment bank a "long-debated and exceedingly important step," because an international credit policy would aid the division of labor among the socialist countries (ADN, 13 July). Toward the end of the year, the "continuous deepening" of the cooperation among CMEA countries was seen as "prerequisite for strengthening the socialist community of states and mastering the scientific-technical revolution," and the GDR pledged "increased efforts to honor fully [its] delivery obligations" (Stoph speech, *Neues Deutschland*, 11 December).

Certain groups of citizens figured prominently in the GDR's domestic planning. Extensive guidelines, for example, were issued to promote the role of women and to "involve [them] more broadly in the process of the planning and management of society and the economy and to materialize the full discharge of their shared responsibility" (*Gesetzblatt der Deutschen Demokratischen Republik*, Part II, no. 58, 9 July). Measures to assure advanced sociopolitical training for women and their development into skilled workers, subsequent utilization, and preparation for work in upper echelons, were detailed. The insufficiency of day-care facilities for children was said to be hampering women's activities, and SED organs in many cities considered the situation alarming enough to call on residents to volunteer to work without pay on the construction of kindergartens (e.g., *Freie Presse*, Chemnitz, July). The privileged position of the young and the raising of an unspoiled political elite seemed to be the basis for the development of new cities such as Halle-Neustadt (near Leipzig), where the average age of the 35,000 residents is twenty-four years, and where communist leaders talk about a "new humanity" free from the influences of the older generations.

A congress on education was held in Berlin on 5-7 May, under the slogan "Learn, Teach, and Educate in the Spirit of Lenin." A telegram of greetings from the SED Central Committee declared that socialist education had "in all spheres convincingly and emphatically proved its superiority over the capitalist system of education in West Germany." (ADN, 5 May.) The most important speech at the congress was given by Education Minister Margot Honecker, who declared that it was the task of the schools to "educate all girls and boys to become conscious, convinced socialists," to teach the young to "hate the inhumanity of imperialism" and "see through the enemy under whatever mask it may try to hide." She also revealed that the projected construction of 20,000 classrooms and the training of 90,000 teachers by 1975 would assure a tenth-grade education for all children in the GDR by 1980. (*Ibid.*) On other occasions, extension of occupational training opportunities and implementation of the previously initiated Third University Reforms were cited as important educational goals. (See *YICA*, 1970, pp. 42 f.) The estimate than in 1970 some 36 per cent of the young people of college age would be attending a university or technical school was cited as proof of the large scale of educational efforts in the GDR (*Einheit*, July).

In the field of the arts and culture, politics was never far from the surface and on occasion broke through in remarkable and unexpected fashion. In March the weekly *Volksarmee* warned East German soldiers to beware of popular music broadcasts from Western radio stations. The programs were said to have certain functions in the "psychological warfare of imperialism against the socialist countries" and to be intended to prepare listeners to "betray their republic and commit ideological desertion." Western avant-guardism and "pop" art were an "acute danger" to the socialist development of art and literature, according to the musical director of the Pedagogical Institute in Potsdam. The music of Beethoven, on the other hand, was virtually reserved for East German appreciation: "The revolutionary composer and thinker Beethoven strove in his time for a genuine humanism as we have attained it.... That is the reason why Beethoven music can no longer have any function in the state-monopolistic system of West German imperialism.... His work, like that of all progressive humanist artists of the past, comes alive only through integration into the culture of the socialist community." (Editorial, signed by the secretary of the League of Composers and Musicians, *Neues Deutschland*, 25 June.)

Relations with West Germany. In 1970 East Germany faced its toughest challenge in trying to adapt its own needs to the overtures of West Germany's *Ostpolitik* and the pressures for change exerted by the GDR's socialist bloc partners. The policies of aggressive confrontation and absolute condemnation of West Germany, which the Ulbricht regime had pursued for years, suddenly ran counter to the changing climate in Europe and at times appeared to leave the GDR in an untenable position.

As the year began, the East Germans engaged in the polemics of the past—accusing West Germany of endangering the peace of Europe, of militarism, revanchism, and tolerance for neo-Nazism—and asked for acceptance of the draft treaty that the GDR submitted to the Federal Republic in December 1969. The draft incorporated the East Germans' demand for "relations on the basis of equality," recognition of the GDR as a sovereign state under international law, acceptance of the status quo in Europe, renunciation of the use of force or threat in the mutual relationship, and affirmation that West Berlin was an "independent political unit."

The East German position was maintained through weeks of dialogue and correspondence between the two governments which eventually came to a climax in the bilateral summit meetings at Erfurt and Kassel. In the interim SED Politburo member Erich Honecker charged, at the Central Committee plenum in February, that the West German government was preparing for a new world war, and that its verbal "bridge-building" was for the purpose of "letting Bundeswehr soldiers march across at the right moment" (*Neues Deutschland*, 22 February). Foreign Minister Otto Winzer in a speech to GDR journalists (excerpted in the political weekly *Horizont*, East Berlin, no. 8, February) declared that "West German imperialism, under the slogan 'Unity of the Nation,' " was trying to "extend its power to the GDR and in the process root out socialism on German soil." When West German spokesmen referred to intra-German relations" a radio broadcast claimed that these terms meant "nothing but the transformation of the GDR from an independent socialist state into a province of the West German NATO state" (ADN, 19 February). On the eve of the Kassel meeting the semimonthly *Democratic German Report* (East Berlin, no. 10, 20 May) was allowed to come out with a headline, "Bonn Aggression Plans—We Shall Publish unless . . ."

Much speculation has ensued as to why the polemics ceased abruptly a few weeks after the Kassel meeting. Ulbricht himself initiated a conciliatory trend when he addressed the SED Central Committee plenum of 9-10 June and hinted at a possible adjustment of East German policies for the sake of East-West détente. During the celebration of "Baltic Week" at Rostock in July both Winzer and Ulbricht suggested that the successful conclusion of a treaty between West Germany and the Soviet Union would be a sign of an historical shift and recognition that a new situation had evolved in Europe. They omitted references to full recognition of the GDR as a prerequisite for fitting relations between East and West Germany into that new pattern. The new approach was in contrast to the rigidity of the East German stand displayed at Erfurt and Kassel —the "all or nothing attitude," as West German Chancellor Brandt termed it, which demanded acceptance of the draft treaty and payment of 100 billion Marks to settle alleged debts incurred before the Berlin Wall was erected in 1961, and which totally rejected the 20-point program Brandt submitted at Kassel.

After the middle of the year, however, East Germany was hard put to hide its apprehension over the activities of the Federal Republic and the changes brought about in Europe as a result of the West German *Ostpolitik*. The signing of the Soviet-West German treaty providing for the mutual renunciation of force (12 August) presented a serious dilemma for East Germany. On the day of the signing in Moscow, *Neues Deutschland* spoke of the event as "good news." The GDR Council of Ministers in its "Declaration on the Conclusion of the Treaty" evaluated the pact as a credit to the Soviet initiative for peace and security in Europe. At the same time it put major emphasis on the effect on East Germany:

> The treaty between the U.S.S.R. and the FRG determines, in binding international form, the inviolability of the state border between the GDR and the FRG and the unlimited respect of the territorial integrity also of the state of the GDR. Thereby, the normalization of the relations between the GDR and the FRG, on the basis of equality, has become a realistically soluble task. The obligations entered upon by the U.S.S.R. and the FRG in the treaty consequently require that normal diplomatic relations between the GDR and the FRG be established henceforth. (*Ausenpolitische Korrespondenz*, no. 34, 24 August.)

General acquiescence and efforts to underscore positive implications for the GDR were combined with open dissent. The youth newspaper *Junge Welt* (East Berlin, weekend supplement, 21 August) warned that vigilance was needed in spite of the treaty and that any concessions on West Berlin would be dangerous. *Neues Deutschland* (9 September) expressed East German unwillingness to participate in what the Soviet Union considered a natural consequence of the treaty—economic cooperation between all the countries directly or indirectly involved. The SED newspaper rejected this as an "attempt to penetrate into the GDR by means of so-called scientific-technological contacts, and to weaken the position of [the] country." Addressing the December plenum of the Central Committee, Ulbricht attributed "historic importance" to the Moscow treaty, and said of the Polish treaty signed by West Germany and Poland early in December: "We also believe its importance to be very great." He advocated ratification because the Moscow treaty would "open new perspectives for the establishment of peaceful coexistence between the sovereign GDR and the FRG" and stated that during the meeting of the Warsaw Pact states in East Berlin (held on 2 December) East Germany had "expressed [its] agreement that following the ratification of the [Polish] treaty, the establishment of diplomatic relations between the Peoples' Republic of Poland and the FRG should take place." (*Neues Deutschland*, 10 December.)

Even affirmative pronouncements on the treaties in many ways contradicted the warnings of the major speakers at the December plenum against "ideological subversion" and "social democratism" as the most subtle form of imperialist propaganda:

> The class enemy in Europe is counting particularly on social democratism. He hopes that bourgeois ideology, in social democratic wrapping, with its nationalism posing as "inner-German," with its "refined" anticommunism, with its "peaceful" psychological warfare against us, might be more difficult to identify than the gross cries of revanchism. (Speech by Friedrich Ebert, *ibid.*, 13 December.)

In line with these fears were the requests by other members of the Politburo for greater political, ideological, and economic delineation. Erich Honecker thus declared: "The realization that between the socialist GDR and the imperialist FRG an objective process of delineation and not of rapprochement is taking place, is of great fundamental significance." He charged that the government of West Germany was "still primarily intending to shake up the social and economic foundations of the GDR with its formulation of the so-called 'unity of the nation' and with the 'special inner-German' character of relations." (*Ibid.*, 12 December.) This argument echoed earlier East German assertions that West German offers to aid the economic development of the GDR were not made altruistically. Citing an analysis of twenty years of trade between the two states, the party organ (7 June) declared: "It turns out that it is actually the FRG which has derived substantial advantages." This was contradicted by economic experts elsewhere, who observed that it ignored a special clause in the Rome treaty for setting up the European Economic Community (EEC), which took account of the "special relationship" between East and West Germany by allowing that trade between them would not be regarded as foreign trade between outside countries (*Frankfurter Allgemeine Zeitung*, 6 April).

The status of West Berlin continued to figure prominently in East German pronouncements during 1970. The GDR for years has insisted that West Berlin is an "independent political unit, located on the territory of the GDR" and that West Germany has "no rights whatsoever" in the city. Earlier East German efforts at political and physical isolation of West Berlin from the Federal Republic became subject to review, however, because the West German government made the relaxation of tensions over Berlin a prerequisite for a vote on ratification of the Moscow and Warsaw treaties by the Bundestag. The Warsaw Pact nations at a meeting in Moscow on 20 August agreed on "concrete measures" to assure that West Berlin would "cease being a site of tension and become a site of détente." A communiqué issued at the end of the meeting claimed unanimity of agreement among those present, but before the end of the year access to the city was disrupted by the GDR and voices of dissent were heard. An editorial in *Neues Deutschland* (5 November) seemed to reserve East German "sovereign" rights to control civilian access to West Berlin with the assertion that "transportation of West Berlin's persons and goods" could be regulated only "between the GDR and the Senate of West Berlin." This could be interpreted as a virtual denial of four-power responsibility for West Berlin, which the Soviet Union continues to endorse.

Although he has objected to the intrusion of Western ideas, Walter Ulbricht met secretly with four leading members of the West German Young Socialists ("Jusos") on 18 June. When news of the talks leaked out, it was reported in the West that he had tried to impress his young visitors with the "untenable" situation in West Berlin. The German leader explained that he had initiated the meeting because of the necessity that the SED and "all peace-loving and democratic forces [in West Germany] unite against the danger of the right-wing parties." (Interview with *Junge Welt*, reported by ADN, 27 June).

The GDR and International Communism. The 1970 centenary of Lenin's birth in April was an occasion for East German discussions of his teachings on socialist internationalism. One of the major interpreters was Professor Herbert Kröger, a well-known theoretical jurist. Writing in the SED journal *Einheit* (March), he declared: "The party leadership and government of the GDR have always considered their deliberate policy for overall strengthening of the socialist German state as being a contribution toward strengthening the community of socialist countries. . . . The GDR [has] received more and more international recognition as a sovereign socialist state, as it increased closer cooperation with the Soviet Union and the other socialist countries." In a two-part article in *Horizont* (nos. 13 and 14, March and April), Kröger pointed to Article 6 of the 1968 constitution of the GDR, which makes the maintenance and development of universal cooperation and friendship with the Soviet Union and other socialist states a constitutional principle. He referred to the "Brezhnev doctrine" and commented on the interrelationship between various socialist states:

> The principle of respecting the sovereignty of other states and of noninterference in their internal affairs is augmented by the higher quality of the right and duty of all socialist states in common to protect socialist sovereignty and the independence of all members of the socialist commonwealth.

He warned against "imperialist and revisionist" ideologists who, misrepresenting Lenin's ideas on peaceful coexistence between capitalist and socialist states, tried to apply this theory to relations between socialist states, thus opening the door to "imperialist intervention and splitting efforts, as in the case of Czechoslovakia in 1968."

At ceremonies marking the twenty-first anniversary of the GDR, in October, Premier Willi Stoph spoke on the success of "socialist international action," and stressed that "the anniversary of the GDR has always been a feast of Soviet-German friendship" and that the two countries are closely linked by friendly relations in all fields (East Berlin radio, 6 October). On the occasion of the fifteenth anniversary of the Warsaw Pact, Stoph wrote that, thanks to its being based on "principles of internationalism," the pact has been able to safeguard the "territorial integrity and inviolability of the borders of all European socialist states" (*Neues Deutschland*, 14 May). When joint maneuvers of pact members were staged in the GDR in the fall, these "brotherhood in arms" exercises were said to reflect the socialist internationalism of the military coalition and to surpass in solidarity whatever the West could muster (East Berlin radio, 30 September).

Late in the year, previously "revisionist" Romania suddenly appeared in a more favorable light in the East German press. Western observers interpreted the friendly headlines as a possible tool used by the GDR to intimate its reluctance to yield to Soviet pressures for modifications of its stand on West Berlin. East Germany was more true to form in its opposition to the Chinese People's Republic. *Neues Deutschland* (22 September) complained of "deliberate misrepresentation" of historical facts by Chinese commentators who were "seeking to drive a wedge between the GDR and the U.S.S.R." The Peking *People's Daily* in particular was taken to task for its assertion that the treaty between the Soviet Union and the Federal Republic of Germany constituted "treason against the sovereignty of the GDR and against the interests of the Soviet people" and amounted to "tacit consent to West German militarism." East Germany also labeled as "slander" the Chinese insinuation that the Soviet Union concluded the treaty only to "free its hands in the East."

International Views and Positions. When Foreign Minister Otto Winzer assessed the foreign policy tasks of the GDR early in 1970, preparations for the convening of a European security conference headed the list of priorities (*Aussenpolitische Korrespondenz*, 5 January). In July, *Horizont* (no. 30) printed an article on "Joint Responsibility for Peace" in which the meaning of European security was defined: "When we speak of European security, we mean the unconditional recognition of all existing boundaries and the identical recognition of all existing states in Europe." By August the security conference was being promoted as the "requirement of the time" (*Aussenpolitische Korrespondenz*, 24 August). At the end of the year, although no concrete plans had materialized, prospects for such a conference were seen as definitely improved, largely as a result of the signing of the Moscow and Warsaw treaties. According to East Berlin radio (9 December), the only remaining obstacle to security talks were the preconditions imposed by NATO at the urging of the United States.

Throughout the year, East Germany groped for ways to enhance its role in international affairs. The most important move was the dispatch of a message by Ulbricht to some NATO countries, requesting the establishment of diplomatic relations in view of the "basically new situation" in Europe resulting from the Soviet-West German accord (*Neues Deutschland*, 10 August). The message also urged support for admitting East Germany to the U.N. and encouraging West Germany to apply for membership. Although the East German press did not name the countries addressed, reportedly they included Belgium, Canada, Denmark, France, Holland, Italy, Austria, Norway, and Sweden (*New York Times*, 11 August).

The Ulbricht message asserted that East Germany had a "legitimate claim to full-fledged participation in the work of the United Nations," since it already maintained widespread international relations. In support of this assertion the GDR in 1970 again filed applications for membership in the World Health Organization and in UNESCO, emphasizing its "humanitarian aims," its policies keyed to the "equality of all human beings," and its national objective of raising "enlightened and educated citizens" (ADN, 23 September). When the applications were turned down, the GDR accused NATO and West Germany of conspiring against it, of turning participation in the work of the world organization into a political issue, and of engaging in "insiduous activity" to persuade those in favor of the application to abstain from voting or to cast a vote against their convictions (*Neues Deutschland*, 6 October).

As in previous years, the GDR criticized the activities of the Western world and singled out the United States as the leading example of the "bankruptcy of imperialism" and as a country generally "fraught with misfortune," where the activities of the Black Panthers could be identified as virtually the sole bright spot (ADN, 17 July). On the other hand, East Germany was generous with praise for its friends. A "week of solidarity with the Arab peoples" was held in June, and various officials throughout the year pledged support to all those struggling against "Israeli aggression." East Germans continued to support a political solution to the Middle East conflict, insisted on implementation of the 1967 U.N. resolution, and accused both Israel and the United States of subverting the cease-fire by boycotting New York peace talks and intensifying the arms race or aid (*ibid.*, 9 September). In spite of the generally pro-Arab stance, the semiofficial *Berliner Zeitung* (16 September) rapped "extremist groups of the Palestinian resistance movement" and their "unsuitable methods" in highjacking airplanes. German news media also held Arab disunity—especially the fighting between Jordanian government troops and guerrillas—responsible for opening the doors to possible foreign intervention: "The gravity of the hour requires that the progressive forces of the Arab world stand united and concentrate their strength on overcoming the consequences of the Israeli-imperialist aggression" (ADN, 22 September). Credit for attempting to achieve such unity was given to Egyptian President Nasser. The day of his funeral was an official day of mourning in East Germany, with flags flying at half mast to "express the GDR citizens' great esteem for the friendly Arab people and their distinguished statesman" (*ibid.*, 1 October).

Support for the Arab cause against Israel had gained great impetus in 1969 when Iraq had become the first nonaligned country to establish diplomatic relations with the GDR. Sudan, Syria, and the U.A.R. quickly followed suit, and the Arab initiative set the example for other nations. As the list of countries granting recognition to East Germany lengthened in 1970, it became obvious that the Hallstein doctrine, embodying the West German claim to sole representation of the German people, was no longer enforceable. East Germany failed, however, to gain recognition from any Western or highly industrialized nation. Every nonaligned country that sent an ambassador to East Berlin in 1970 was a developing nation, anxious for technical and economic aid. Overtures to such countries as France, Austria, and the Netherlands proved ineffective.

International Party Contacts. Throughout 1970 the SED participated in bilateral and multilateral meetings with representatives of foreign communist parties. A few meetings were noteworthy for deviating from the established norm, such as the July visit by a party and parliamentary delegation from Czechoslovakia, during which the deputy chairman of the Czech Federal Assembly expressed to the people of the GDR the thanks of his people "for all the actions which safeguarded the security" of Czechoslovakia in 1968 (*Neues Deutschland*, 9 July). Two meetings involving the communist party of Hungary produced surprises: When János Kádár and Jenö Fock visited East Berlin in January, East German news media refrained from quoting Kádár verbatim, and when the Hungarian party held its congress in Budapest in November, Walter Ulbricht did not attend, "because his doctors had urgently advised him to take a rest"; the SED, in fact, reached down several rungs in choosing its delegation head from among the members of the Politburo. In both instances Western observers deduced that differences of opinion among the Warsaw Pact nations as to West German intentions or actions in Europe were responsible for the strange turn of events. When the Greek communist party sent a delegation headed by its chairman, Apostolos Grozos, to East Berlin in July, the most important topic discussed was the relationship of Greece to NATO. Talks with Cuban communists in April revolved around economic cooperation for the duration of East Germany's 1971-75 long-range plan. Delegations from communist parties in the West have long been traveling to East Germany, and in 1970 there was some traffic in the opposite direction. For the first time, an SED delegation went to France at the invitation of the French Communist Party; SED representatives also visited Great Britain for the purpose of "studying the problems of the struggle against the rule of state-monopolist capital." Delegations received in East Berlin included those from the communist parties of France, Finland, Austria, Japan, Sweden, and Luxembourg.

Occasions for multilateral contacts were provided by such events as the annual "Baltic Week," held at Rostock during July. SED representatives were in Budapest on 28-30 September to participate in the formulation of plans for an "anti-imperialist" world congress of 45 communist parties, and in Moscow on 20-21 October when representatives of 27 parties gathered to discuss European security.

Publications. *Neues Deutschland*, the official organ of the SED Central Committee, is the most important daily newspaper in East Germany. It has a circulation of about 800,000. The SED also publishes the *Berliner Zeitung* (circulation 500,000), and a number of dailies in major cities of the GDR; among the latter are *Freiheit* in Halle (360,000), the *Leipziger Volkszeitung* (352,000), and *Volksstimme* in Magdeburg (320,000). In addition, officially approved material appears in publications of the other National Front parties and mass organizations. Examples are *Neue Zeit* of the CDU, *Der Morgen* of the LDPD, and *Junge Welt* of the FDJ. The SED deals with party questions in the semimonthly *Neuer Weg* and with the theory and practice of scientific socialism in the monthly *Einheit*.

E.W.

HUNGARY

The Hungarian Socialist Workers' Party (Magyar Szocialista Munkáspárt; HSWP) was founded 24 November 1918 as the Communist Party of Hungary. The party gained control of Hungary in 1947. Its name was changed in 1948 to the Hungarian Workers' Party following the absorption of the Social Democrats, and then on 1 November 1956 to the Hungarian Socialist Workers' Party.

Membership, Organization, and Leadership. In a report near the end of 1970 the HSWP claimed 662,397 members (*Népszabadság*, 24 November). The population of Hungary is 10,340,000 (estimated 1970). Since its Ninth Congress, in 1966, the party has admitted 77,548 members, increasing the number by 13.3 per cent (*ibid.*). According to an analysis in the HSWP monthly *Pártélét* (November 1970), 60.6 per cent of the members are employed in the "production sector"—41.7 per cent in industry and communications, and 18.9 per cent are engaged in agriculture. The analysis noted that the number of workers within the total membership has sharply dropped by 4.5 per cent during the past four years. To defend its image as a working-class party, the leadership is seeking to recruit new members especially among manual workers employed in industry.

The HSWP has a pyramidal organization, with 21,150 basic party organizations in 1970. At the Tenth Congress, held in Budapest on 23-27 November 1970, the membership of the Central Committee was increased from 101 to 105, the Politburo from 11 to 13, and the Secretariat from 5 to 7. The first secretary of the HSWP is János Kádár, who assumed the post during the 1956 uprising. The members of the Politburo are György Aczél, Antal Apró, Valéria Benke, Béla Bisku, Lajos Fehér, Jenö Fock, Sándor Gáspár, János Kádár, Gyula Kállai, Zoltán Komócsin, Dezsö Nemes, Károly Németh, and Rezsö Nyers. The newly elected members of the Politburo are Valéria Benke (the editor in chief of the party's ideological organ *Társadalmi Szemle*) and Károly Németh (first secretary of the party organization of Budapest). The congress abolished the system of alternate membership in the Politburo; former alternate members Miklós Ajtai, Lajos Czinege, and Pál Ilku, while retaining their membership in the Central Committee and their state functions, were excluded from the Politburo. The Secretariat of the Politburo is headed by First Secretary Kádár and is composed of György Aczél, Béla Biszku, Zoltán Komócsin, Rezsö Nyers, Miklós Ovári, and Árpád Pullai.

The Tenth Congress amended the party's organizational statute. First, the minimum age for joining the party was lowered from twenty-one to eighteen years. In making this decision the leadership exhibited concern over the decrease in the number of party members under thirty and the increase in those over sixty. Second, party members were ordered to propagate actively the ideas of the party and to represent and defend party policy. The leadership presumably hopes that this explicit obligation will put an end to the passivity of the rank and file toward defending the unpopular decisions of the party. Third, it was prescribed that while party control should be exercised by the collective leadership, simultaneously individual personal responsibility should be maintained. (*Népszabadság*, 29 November.)

According to the Control Committee's report, delivered at the congress by János Brutyó, chairman of the committee, during the past four years party organs on different levels called to account 2.9 per cent of the membership for breaches of discipline. Nearly 20,000 party members had to be disciplined, and 5,000 were excluded from the party ranks. These offenses were often connected with lapses in private life and were mostly due to high living, greed, and moral laxity. (*Ibid.*, 24 November.)

Mass Organizations. The HSWP exercises much of its power through the Patriotic People's Front (PPF), a political alliance between the ruling party and representatives of various social strata. Different nationalities living in Hungary—German, South Slav, Slovak, and Romanian—also take part in PPF activities. The PPF movement has about 4,400 committees and 120,000 registered members.

The HSWP also maintains direct control over the largest mass organization, the National Trade Union Council (with 3.4 million members), and the Communist Youth League (800,000 members). Indirect party control is exercised over government bodies, collectives, and less important mass organizations, such as the Hungarian National Defense Sport Association (MHSZ), the Hungarian Partisan Association, the National Council of Hungarian Women (MNOT), and the National Peace Council, where party members hold executive posts.

The New Economic Mechanism. The HSWP's economic reform program, better known as the New Economic Mechanism (NEM), inaugurated in 1968, continued to dominate domestic affairs. The reform was designed to create a market-oriented and decentralized economy, based on managerial ability and material incentive. Characteristics of the reform include a complex price policy, wage differentiation, free movement of labor, and direct contact between Hungarian and foreign enterprises.

The economy as a whole has become more balanced since the introduction of the NEM. National income and industrial and agricultural production have increased. There are, however, debit entries in the ledger of the economy. Investment resources have been insufficient and consequently uneven. The technical standard of production has so far failed to rise to the appropriate level and often has not been competitive in the international free market. The mechanization of agriculture has remained at a low level. The party leadership attributes this inefficiency mainly to laxity in labor management and discipline. In June 1970 a new system of economic regulators was introduced to stimulate the enterprises to "use labor rationally" and to "correlate more closely higher wage levels with increased labor efficiency and productivity" (*Magyar Hirlap*, 26 June).

At the end of the year Finance Minister Péter Vályi reported to the National Assembly that labor productivity had increased to an extent greater than was envisaged. During discussion the chairman of the Central Bureau of Statistics, István Huszár, added that per capita income in the developed European countries was approximately 1.5 times that of Hungary. Since the level of employment was generally lower there than in Hungary, relatively fewer people produced this greater wealth. (*Népszabadság*, 19 December.)

Social Effects of the Economic Reform. According to official evaluation, in 1969 the per capita income of the peasantry rose by 7.4 per cent, the real wages of workers and employees by only 3.4 per cent, and the cost of living by 2.4 per cent. The party leadership realized that action should be taken against price increases before they generated uncontrollable social tension. Consequently, a stricter price control of consumers' goods was adopted. (*Magyar Hirlap*, 10 February.) Nevertheless, popular discontent over the slow improvement of living standards continued. There were numerous complaints concerning the peasantry on the grounds that its income increased at a much faster rate than that of the blue-collar worker.

During the preparatory meetings for the Tenth Congress criticism was registered over the new differentiated profit-sharing system under which a larger share went to the managerial elite than to workers. At the congress the party leadership exerted a considerable effort to quell the discontent. In this connection the secretary-general of the National Trade Union Council, Sándor Gáspár, touched upon the role of the council, which he described as being complex because of the need to "represent and defend" the interests of the individual, the various social strata, and society as a whole. On the one hand, he advocated wage differentiation as the "socialist method of income distribution." On the other, he urged the government to keep "unplanned price increases under strict control, because they were primarily the result of speculation and disregard for the interest of the workers." (*Népszava*, 27 November.)

The first secretary of the party, János Kádár, also explained that neither trade-union activity nor laws and collective agreements were sufficient guarantees for workers' rights. These were implemented by men, and there were bound to be occasional grievances and clashes of interest. He promised stronger vigilance in the future to prevent abuses. Despite these remarks, Kádár did not propose restrictive measures; rather, he called for more consistent enforcement of the existing sanctions.

While the 1970 Christmas food riots were in progress in Poland, the closest collaborator and heir apparent of Kádár, Politburo member Béla Biszku, published an article in *Népszabadság* (25 December) entitled "In the Spirit of the Congress." Biszku stated that party and government organs and individual leaders had often failed to take into account the legitimate remarks of the working people and the emergence of contradictions. He added: "If we permit these to assume serious proportions, they will retard development and impair the credit of party policy."

Contradictions within Society and the "Socialist Democracy." In a broader socioeconomic spectrum, the debate over living standards forced the party leadership to recognize the existence of "contradictions under socialist conditions" in four major fields: (*a*) between the interest of long-term planning and the daily interest of the people; (*b*) between the interests of workers and peasants; (*c*) between the general interest of society and that of groups; and (*d*) among individual interests. First Secretary Kádár stated: "The diversity of interest manifests itself in the distribution of national income; in price, wage, and market conditions; in the determination of the faster or slower equalization of the differences between town and village." (*Népszabadság*, 24 November.)

The economic reform substantially increased the independence of economic enterprises and widened the ability of economic leaders to make decisions of their own. Decentralization itself promoted limited liberalization, called by the regime "socialist democracy." The Tenth Congress stated that, after several years of preparation, the Central Committee had discussed the question of extension of democracy. It had come to the conclusion that party policy in this field needed firmness in basic principles and flexibility in execution. Béla Biszku, the party's second in command, asserted that "socialist democracy" must be viewed as a class concept. He argued that "people who set socialist democracy against the dictatorship of the proletariat" were putting forward "rightist revisionist" concepts and advocating the liquidation of the dictatorship of the proletariat. But Kádár also warned against "dogmatists" who, "in the name of defense of the dictatorship of proletariat, regard the development of socialist democracy with anxiety." (*Ibid.*, 26 November.)

In connection with this middle-of-the-road policy, the party leadership emphasized that the activity and influence of "hostile elements" in the country had steadily decreased; hence the repressive function of the state should be reduced and people holding erroneous, or even hostile, outlooks should be fought by argument and persuasion rather than by police methods. As regards the question of political opposition, Minister of the Interior András Benkei stated "so long as this [was] not hostile activity but the open clash of views—there [was] no room for administrative intervention of organs of the Ministry of the Interior." He added that the "consolidation of the mass basis" of the party and the alliance with the U.S.S.R. and the other Warsaw Pact countries had made impossible the restoration of capitalism in Hungary. But at the same time he reminded the party that "imperialism" often unsettled the "politically immature with its politic of subversion" or used the "loosening-up tactics of peaceful intrusion." (*Ibid.*, 28 November.)

Controlled Decentralization. As a result of the economic reform, the HSWP has had to face the problem of adjusting the political system to new conditions. The party leadership thus advocated a controlled decentralization of executive and administrative responsibility (see *YICA*, 1970, pp. 54-55), which Kádár described in these words: "We simultaneously strengthen central power and increase the independence of local authorities" (*Népszabadság*, 24 November 1970). In this framework the government reorganized and expanded the Department of Local Councils Affairs, attached to the Councils of Ministers, into an independent agency. (*Magyar Közlöny*, 21 July.) Simultaneously, party officials promised more power of decision for the local and regional authorities over matters which could be handled locally.

The party leadership apparently attempted also to enhance the role of the legislative body. Parliamentary subcommittees—under party supervision—prepared bills to increase activity in the scientific field, improve the social position of women, and modernize the educational system. During the fall session the Parliament modified the 1966 electoral law. Under the new dispensation, the one-party system and the leading role of the communist party continued as before. All candidates still had to accept the political program of the People's Patriotic Front (Budapest radio, 3 October). Even so, the new electoral law gave voters a choice of candidates, some of whom could be locally known citizens and not necessarily members of the communist party.

As part of the campaign to strengthen "socialist legality"—a new term introduced during the de-Stalinization campaign of Khrushchev (in 1956)—the Presidential Council issued three decrees laying down comprehensive rules for the issue of various types of passports. Most of the rules embodied in the new legal instruments reiterated regulations which were previous internal instructions of the Ministry of the Interior. The novelty of the new regulations lay in the fact that the public at large became better acquainted with the rules concerning passport matters. Another new feature of the legislation was that every citizen was stated to have the right to obtain a passport if he complied with the conditions described in the rules; the grounds for exclusion, however, were established in such a way that the Ministry of the Interior had the authority to reject practically any applicant.

The National Unity Policy. During 1970 the HSWP leadership attempted to pursue a policy of "national unity," rallying "workers, peasants, intellectuals, members of the petty bourgeoisie, people with varying philosophies, communists and non-believers" (guidelines for the Tenth Congress, in *Népszabadság*, 23 August). But along with the promise of greater opportunities and relaxation went greater emphasis on the need for more civic discipline and party guidance in all spheres of the nation's life.

On 4 April, Hungary celebrated the twenty-fifth anniversary of the country's liberation from Nazi occupation, and on 20 August the millenium of the birth of Saint Stephen, the founder of Hungary as a Christian kingdom. The party leadership used both occasions to stress the theme of national unity. On 4 April, prizes were distributed, both to doctrinaire communists such as the economist István Friss and László Hay, and to literary figures such as Gyula Illyes and Sándor Weores, who had often been subjected to party criticism. At the same time, the Presidential Council announced a partial amnesty canceling entirely all prison sentences of under one year and halving the terms of those who had been sentenced to prison terms up to five years. The 20 August celebration centered around the historical importance of St. Stephen. Representatives of the HSWP Central Committee, leading personalities of state and social life, and high-ranking church officials attended the various secular celebrations and religious ceremonies.

Problems of Youth, Ideology, and Culture. The HSWP leadership devoted particular attention to problems presented by the young generation. A plenum of the Central Committee judged that, in general, the way of thinking of young persons in Hungary was shaped largely by ideas of "socialism." "Erroneous views and incorrect attitudes," however, were found, and were attributed to "indifference, lack of a sense of responsibility, and overbearing demands" (*Népszabadság*, 20 February 1970). The first secretary of the Communist Youth League (KISZ), Lajos Méhes, added that the behavior of young people was influenced by "bourgeois demagogy" and "ultra-leftist views," but he asked the party leadership to satisfy "the demands of youth for a greater say in public and political life" (*Magyar Ifjuság*, 3 April).

Seemingly the party attempted to satisfy some of the demands. Minister of Culture Pál Ilku promised to improve the students' material conditions, the extension of university autonomy, and the creation of student "parliaments" in secondary schools. Kádár went even further. He stated that the rapid scientific-technological advance required review of the entire system of state education, including the relationship between education and social requirements. (*Népszabadság*, 24 November.)

Similarly, the regime encountered numerous difficulties in the field of ideology. Disbelief in and opposition to Marxist-Leninist ideology was spreading. The pessimism of young writers and poets and their alienation from the regime were apparently so serious that the party secretary in charge of ideology and culture, György Aczél, spoke of the menace of psychological "terror" and "pressure" against "everyone who approves of . . . the achievements of the socialist system." (*Elet és Irodalom*, literary and political weekly, 13 June.)

The party's youth organization (KISZ) criticized a small fraction of young Hungarian intellectuals for having "daydreams of a puritan 'militant communism,' a heritage of the tenets of Mao or more precisely of a mythicized Che Guevara." These "ultra-leftist" students were accused of advocating "revolutionary asceticism" and "absolute democracy." (*Magyar Ifjuság*, 30 January.)

The election at the annual meeting of the Hungarian Writers' Union also reflected the ideological ferment. The new Executive Committee included such outspoken liberal writers as László Németh, László Benjamin, and István Örkény, who were closely identified with the 1956 anti-Soviet uprising.

The party leadership also rebuffed the accusation by the left wing of the party—better known as the dogmatist opposition—that the economic reform, per se, had led to "deterioration of socialist morals." The head of the press section of the Central Committee's Agitprop Department, Imre Pozsgai, affirmed that the reform was the "biggest social venture of our time" and that its main object was to promote development of socialist conditions. He went on to state that the NEM required the "rational mobilization of human resources in the interest of more human conditions of existence." (*Társadalmi Szemle*, November).

According to an article entitled "Opposition to Ideology" (*Népszabadság*, 24 May), the theory of the gradual assimilation of the "capitalist" and "socialist" worlds (otherwise known as convergence) had created confusion among social scientists. "Bourgeois thinkers," in the party's view, were mistaken in their prediction that industrialization would overshadow all ideologies and lead to an "East-West union."

Among all the problems, nationalism seemed to be the most dangerous "ideological poison." This was admitted by the hard-liner editor in chief of *Népszabadság*, János Gosztonyi, in an article of 4 April. He pointed out:

> Nationalism in our days has an obvious anti-Soviet tendency. When we are persuaded to have the courage to be more "Magyar" this means that we should sever links with Moscow and that we too, at least occasionally, should say "No."

Under such circumstances, the call by the well-known philosopher György Lukács for a "renewal of Marxism" served the purposes of the regime, despite the fact that after 1956 Lukács had been in opposition to it. In an interview with the West German magazine *Der Spiegel* (20 April) he explained that it was essential to "introduce democracy from below" in the economic reform, and to give "the masses a say in matters that concern them."

The party's position on ideological and cultural matters was restated at the Tenth Congress. Kádár insisted on the importance of the Twentieth Congress of the Communist Party of the Soviet Union, which in his view had helped the entire international communist movement to "stand against subjectivism, dogmatism, and for the constructive application of Marxism-Leninism." He reiterated the customary doctrine concerning the need to wage an ideological struggle on two fronts—against ultra-leftist dogmatism and rightist revisionism. Kádár's main attack concentrated on sectarian, dogmatic, and other different "pseudo-revolutionary" attitudes in Hungary. People of such persuasions argued that the socialist countries, including Hungary, were nothing more than manipulated societies. He added that such views were represented by the New Left, Maoists, and Trotskyists in the capitalist countries and that they were tolerated by the "capitalist powers" because they often weakened the communist parties.

For these reasons Kádár and the party ideologue Aczél called for an intensified ideological campaign to consolidate the position and the power of the communist party. There was also declared to be a great need for a clear definition of the balance between party guidance and freedom of artistic expression in this confused ideological situation. Kádár indicated that the regime would not police artistic activity. "We regard taste as a private matter of the creative artist as long as it does not offend the interests of socialism." But, he added, the party would reserve for itself a major role in the shaping of cultural affairs, and the "worker's state" was entitled to decide which artistic creations deserved its moral and financial support. (*Népszabadság*, 24 November.)

International Relations. In 1970 much of Hungary's economic relations with both East and West centered on the development of trade relations. The economic leadership of the party pressed both for a reformed Council for Mutual Economic Assistance (CMEA) within the socialist bloc and for more extensive economic cooperation with the West. As economic and political factors in Eastern Europe cannot be compartmentalized, two-thirds of Hungary's export-import trade was conducted with CMEA countries. The construction of a second "Friendship" oil pipeline was started. According to plans, it would increase the flow of crude oil from the U.S.S.R. to Hungary from an annual 4 million tons to 6.5 million tons by 1975. For the first time in the history of the CMEA, a large part of Hungary's resources was allocated to finance the building of a huge steel plant near Kurks to "strengthen the raw material basis of the socialist bloc" (*Világgazdaság* [World Economy], Budapest, 1 September).

On 15 September, Hungary and the Soviet Union signed a "five-year plan co-ordination agreement" in Moscow. The agreement projected an expansion of trade by 50 per cent (9,000 million rubles) and called for the establishment of a uniform system of computer technology (*Népszabadság*, 16 September). Furthermore, Hungary became a member of the newly established International Investment Bank, whose purpose is to finance investments in the joint interest of the CMEA countries (*ibid.*, 16 May). In connection with Soviet integration objectives within the CMEA, the HSWP secretary in charge of economy, Rezsö Nyers, noted that important matters remained to be clarified. These included the future role of the multilateral economic regulator system, the credit and price system, and the methods of commerce and currency convertibility. (*Ibid.*, 26 November.)

Bilateral foreign trade remained the basic form of economic relations between Hungary and advanced capitalist countries. But the contacts, as Nyers pointed out, were spreading to other forms of cooperation, such as exploitation of natural resources, pursuit of joint scientific research, expansion of trade in licenses, and establishment of joint-trade associations. Development was particularly extensive with regard to Italy, Austria, and Sweden. Economic cooperation between Hungary and the Federal Republic of Germany was strengthened by a five-year agreement signed on 27 October (*Magyar Hirlap*, 28 October).

According to Nyers, the evolving system of the Common Market unfavorably affected Hungarian economic interests and particularly menaced Hungary's agricultural exports. On the other hand, the Hungarian National Bank exploited the inflationary trends of the Western currencies and redeemed its dollar debts under favorable conditions. With respect to other dollar transactions, the regime fostered technological modernization by medium-term credits in the nature of investment in Hungary. (*Népszabadság*, 26 November.)

Contrary to the 1969 positive foreign trade balance, the 1970 figures showed an adverse balance of 3,142 million foreign exchange forint, of which 1,698 million were attributed to CMEA countries and 1,444 million to "nonsocialist" ones. (*Statisztikai Havi Közlemények*, Budapest, no. 12, 1970). In the dollar area, foreign trade increased more than twice as much as in the ruble area. About 25 to 30 per cent of this increase was the result of an increase in world market prices. (*Világgazdaság*, 21 January 1971.)

In the HSWP's inter-bloc and foreign policy relations no new departures were seen and none expected. There was unequivocal support for the Soviet Union and the Warsaw Pact. Kádár's praise of the Soviet Union, at the Tenth Congress, was excessive even by standards set previously by Kádár himself. Advocating that no effort be spared on behalf of the unity of the "socialist world system," he and the party secretary in charge of international relations, Zoltán Komócsin, asserted whatever is good "for our friends and allies is good for us." Komocsin added: "If life produces situations in which Hungary's particular interests clash with the joint interest [of the socialist community], we subordinate them to joint interest, in the conviction that only this can lead to success in the long run." (*Népszabadság*, 26 November 1970.)

The party leadership repeated the well-known explanation for Hungary's participation in the 1968 invasion of Czechoslovakia. Kádár firmly stated that his party had acted according to the principle of internationalism when, together with other socialist countries, Hungary had hurried to "the assistance of Socialist Czechoslovakia." An article in the ideological journal of the party, *Társadalmi Szemle* (May 1970), criticized sharply Alexander Dubček for his role in the Czechoslovak crisis of 1968 and endorsed the Czechoslovak party purge of the Husák leadership

Following the Soviet pattern, Kádár expressed readiness to improve cooperation with every socialist country—"even with those from which we are divided by differences of opinion." In this connection, he reported to the congress that, despite numerous ideological and political differences, Hungary's interstate relations with the Chinese People's Republic had somewhat improved. (*Népszabadság*, 24 November.) The Chinese Red Cross donated 500,000 yuan ($85,000) to Hungarian flood victims (NCNA, 12 June). For the first time in years, on 26 August 1970 an ambassador of the Chinese People's Republic presented his credentials. Deputy Premier Lajos Fehér—a Politburo member—met the newly appointed ambassador, Lu Chih-hsien, at the national agriculture and food industrial exhibition in Budapest, where Lu was his country's representative. (*Ibid.*, 30 August.) On the other hand, both the Chinese and the Albanian communist parties refused to restore interparty relations with the HSWP and rejected invitations to the Tenth Congress.

As a Warsaw Pact member state and "co-author" of the March 1969 "Budapest appeal" for an all-European security conference, the Hungarian leadership echoed Soviet pronouncements on international affairs. After the signing of the Soviet-West German and Polish-West German treaties, Kádár declared that the "interest of European peace and security" called for a further step forward on the part of the West German government, which should recognize the existence of the German Democratic Republic and the "special status" of West Berlin. He added: "As soon as the situation is ripe, we are ready to develop further our relations with the Federal Republic of Germany, including, in the final resort, the regulation of diplomatic relations." (*Ibid.*, 24 November.)

At the Tenth Congress, Soviet party leader Brezhnev was full of praise for Kádár, stressing that the Hungarian party's "principled approach" to major problems met with the "full understanding and high appraisal of the communists of the Soviet Union." Brezhnev confirmed that the Soviet Union was intent on promoting the integration of the "socialist camp" in economic, political, ideological, and defense matters. He noted with satisfaction that, together with the other socialist countries, Hungary was playing an active role in giving form to the process of economic integration, and the HSWP had "made no small effort to consolidate political cooperation still further [and] strengthen the Warsaw Pact organization." (*Pravda*, 25 November.)

Publications. The central organ of the HSWP is the Budapest daily newspaper *Népszabadság*, with a circulation of 755,000 copies. The party's theoretical monthly, *Társadalmi Szemle*, has a circulation of 36,000 copies and the monthly journal dealing with party affairs, *Pártélet*, 95,000 copies. Other important newspapers are the People's Patriotic Front's *Magyar Nemzet*, the National Trade Union Council's daily *Népszava*, and the Communist Youth League's weekly *Magyar Ifuság*.

J. R.

POLAND

The communist party holding power in the Polish People's Republic goes under the official name of the Polish United Workers' Party (Polska Zjednoczona Partia Robotnicza; PUWP). Its origins date back to December 1918 and the founding of the Communist Workers' Party of Poland, which was forced to operate underground after it was outlawed by the Polish government in early 1919. It changed its name to the Communist Party of Poland in 1925. For reasons that are still not entirely clear the Comintern dissolved the party in 1938, and many of its leaders perished in the great Soviet purge. In January 1942 it reappeared under the name of the Polish Workers' Party. The newly reconstituted party quickly achieved the dominant position in the "national unity" coalition government set up to appeal to the broad mass of the population following the advance of the Red Army into Poland. After consolidating its position and undermining the remaining noncommunist parties in the coalition, the Polish Workers' Party in 1948 induced the left-wing remnants of the old Polish Socialist Party to merge with it to form the Polish United Workers' Party. Since then the PUWP has controlled elections and other formal political activities in Poland through the "National Unity Front," ostensibly a coalition of the PUWP (officially playing the leading and directing role) and two communist-controlled "independent" parties—the United Peasants' Party (Zjednoczone Stronnictwo Ludowe; UPP) and the Democratic Party (Stronnictwo Demokratyczne; DP), officially representing the peasantry and the small entrepreneurs and professionals, respectively. Also included in the coalition are representatives of "progressive" nonparty organizations and individuals. In an attempt to appear as broadly representative as possible, the party has allowed three Catholic groups to include candidates in the preferred lists of the National Unity Front: (1) "Pax," founded as the Catholic Social Club in 1945 by Bolesław Piasecki, who has argued that there is no incompatibility between Christianity and the social and economic policies of the communists though he rejects their atheism and supports the right of the Catholic church to exist; (2) the Christian Social Association, which split off from Pax in 1956 under the leadership of Jan Frankowski, after Piasecki insisted on maintaining a hard Stalinist line; and (3) "Znak," a Catholic intellectual group that is associated with the church hierarchy in Poland. The PUWP, however, clearly dominates the political life of Poland and expects all other parties and mass organizations to follow its lead and support its main policy lines.

In the 1 June 1969 elections the National Unity Front received 99.2 per cent of the valid votes for the 460 seats in the Sejm (parliament). The PUWP received 255 seats; the UPP, 117; the DP, 39; and the independents, 49 (14 for the three Catholic groups and 35 for other "independent" deputies). Although the Polish elections consist of a single list of candidates, ever since 1956 there have been more candidates than seats on the lists in each of the multimember districts. One may vote against the first choices of the National Unity Front by crossing out a name (or names) in the top part of the list, thereby automatically voting for the candidate (or candidates) immediately below the line between the preferred candidates and those in excess of the number of seats in the district. One may vote against the entire list by crossing out all the names. On the other hand, one votes for the preferred choices by leaving the ballot unmarked. It is interesting to note that Edward Gierek, the new first-secretary of the PUWP, received more votes (i.e., fewer people crossed out his name) in his district of Katowice than any other PUWP candidate in 1969.

Membership. On 4 November 1970 the PUWP daily newspaper, *Trybuna Ludu*, reported on the status of the party for the first three quarters of the year. As of 1 October the total membership stood at approximately 2,296,000 (including candidate members) as compared with not quite 2,200,000 in November 1969. The population of Poland is 32,720,000 (estimated 1970). During the first three quarters of the year 124,000 were accepted as candidates—51 per cent being workers and 47 per cent under the age of twenty-five years—and 94,000 former candidates were accepted as full members. Apparently, about 30,000 left the party or were expelled. In social composition, workers comprised 40.2 per cent of the membership; peasants, 11.6 per cent; white-collar workers, 42.5 per cent; and others, 5.7 per cent. PUWP members comprise about 7 per cent of the population.

Organization and Leadership. The PUWP is organized hierarchically, with the lower units subordinated to the next higher. The basic unit is the primary party organization, set up in factories, enterprises, cooperatives, and offices, and in territorial units (villages and small towns in the less populous areas and street or block units in the larger cities). The next level is formed by the district units, which can encompass all or part of a powiat (county) and parts of the larger cities. The third level is made up of the 19 voivodship (provincial) organizations. The highest authority of the PUWP is the party congress, which meets every four years. The congress elects the Central Committee and the Auditing Commission. The Central Committee, composed of 91 full members and an equal number of candidates, is the supreme party authority between congresses. It elects the Politburo (12 full members and 4 candidates), the Secretariat (9 members), and the Central Control Commission (36 members). The Politburo serves as the supreme policy-making body between Central Committee plenums; the Secretariat functions as the executive organ of the Central Committee and the Politburo, and supervises the work of the party bureaucracy. The Central Control Commission oversees party discipline and maintains ideological correctness. The district and provincial levels have a similar but less complex organizational structure.

The party's Fifth Congress, in November 1968, elected a Politburo and Secretariat membership which remained the same (see *YICA*, 1970, p. 62) until important changes in the leadership were ratified at the Central Committee plenum of 20 December 1970 following the riots protesting the price increases of 12 December. At that meeting the Central Committee formally elected Edward Gierek as first secretary of the PUWP, replacing Wladyslaw Gomulka, who had held that post since October 1956. Four other members of the Politburo and Secretariat were also replaced (see below.)

Mass Organizations. The PUWP relies heavily on mass membership and other smaller and more specialized organizations to (1) increase its legitimacy, (2) disseminate propaganda and mobilize support for its political and economic objectives, (3) mold socialist attitudes and control mass behavior, (4) provide a party-controlled substitute for every organization normally found in modern society and preempt the field for any potential opposition organizations, and (5) undermine existing organizations not yet under party control (e.g., the Catholic church). The publications, mass meetings, rallies, campaigns, and other activities of these organizations provide an important supplement to the direct work of the PUWP activists and press. They also provide channels through which those opposed to the PUWP can be induced to work for party objectives and can in turn be supervised by those sympathetic to the party. Moreover, they create the appearance of a more pluralistic society and provide outlets for the organizational energies of many citizens. The most important of these mass organizations are the various trade unions and the Central Council of Trade Unions (Centralna Rada Związków Zawodowych), headed by Ignacy Loga-Sowiński as chairman, which coordinates trade union activities. The trade unions play a particularly important role in mobilizing workers to fulfill the economic tasks decided on by the party and the central planning apparatus. They also perform various social welfare functions, such as administering pension funds, building homes for their workers, providing day-care centers for children and vacation homes, and carrying out work-safety campaigns. There has been an increasing tendency for unions to represent more actively the interests and demands of workers. The new party leadership seems particularly interested in increasing the degree to which the trade unions, the nearly 7,500 workers' councils, and the nearly 9,000 workers' self-government organizations (set up after 1958 in an attempt to check the spontaneous organization of workers' councils outside party control) serve as channels of feedback communication to the top levels of the party.

The two most important youth organizations are the Socialist Youth Union (Związek Młodzieży Socjalistycznej), headed by Andrzej Żabiński, with 1,216,000 members, and the Union of Village Youth (Związek Młodzieży Wiejskiej; UVY), headed by Zdzisław Kurowski, with 1,050,000 members. Providing important services to young people in the form of clubs and social organizations, summer camps, and youth magazines and newspapers, they also serve as recruitment organizations for PUWP members and as valuable training grounds for future party activists. The UVY's Fourth Congress, held on 23-25 February 1970, was addressed by several party and government officials who spoke about current agricultural policy and stressed the role of the UVY in rural modernization.

The Polish Students' Association (Zrzeszenie Studentów Polskich), headed by Stanisław Ciosek, with 180,000 members, has a low-keyed propaganda role among the more sophisticated students. The Union of Polish Scouting (Związek Harcerstwa Polskiego), with 2,000,000 members and about 70,000 leaders, is comparable to the Young Pioneers of the Soviet Union. The Women's League (Liga Kobiet) with 400,000 members, held its Fifth Congress on 17-18 November and was addressed by Council of State Chairman Marian Spychalski, who stressed the role of women in helping the government emerge from its economic predicament through education and by adapting family budgets to available food and consumers' goods.

ZBoWiD, the the Union of Fighters for Freedom and Democracy (Związek Bojowników o Wolność i Demokrację), is headed by General Mieczysław Moczar as chairman of the central board and has some 250,000 members in 3,000 circles. It is a patriotic veterans' organization. The League for the Defense of the Country (Liga Obrony Kraju), headed by Zbigniew Szydłowski, has 2,200,000 members in about 38,000 circles. It is concerned with civil defense. The Society for Ties with Poles Abroad, "Polonia," propagandizes among Polish émigrés. The Society for Secular Schools (Towarzystwo Szkoły Świeckiej), with 300,000 members, was formed in 1957 to promote the elimination of religious education in the schools; a related organization is the Society of Atheists and Freethinkers (Towarzystwo Ateistów i Wolnomyślacych).

The National Unity Front and the Democratic and United Peasant parties serve many of the same mobilization and legitimating functions as the mass organizations. According to the official view, Poland, as a people's democracy, is not yet a classless society because private enterprise is still allowed in both town and countryside. Since it is necessary that both the petty bourgeoisie and private landowning peasantry take part politically in a "people's democracy," the DP and UPP are allowed to serve the petty bourgeoisie and peasantry, while the PUWP represents the interests of the working class. The National Unity Front and the pledge of the other two parties to follow the leadership of the PUWP provides the mechanism through which the "progressive" classes cooperate in the tasks of preparing Poland for socialism. Thus the appearance of democracy remains and PUWP-controlled channels for the mobilization of mass support are created among those who would normally oppose them. The DP is headed by Zygmunt Moskwa and has 85,000 members. The UPP is headed by Czesław Wycech and has 380,000 members, of whom about 80 per cent are peasants and the rest intelligentsia.

Party Internal Affairs. Late in 1970, important changes in the leadership of the PUWP were ratified at the Central Committee plenum of 20 December following strikes and riots during the previous week. Until then the Politburo consisted of Władysław Gomułka (who as first secretary headed both the Secretariat and the Politburo), Józef Cyrankiewicz (also premier, as chairman of the Council of Ministers), Edward Gierek (first secretary of the Katowice voivodship party organization), Bolesław Jaszczuk (head of the Central Committee's Economic Department), Stefan Jędrychowski (also minister of foreign affairs), Zenon Kliszko (in charge of ideological matters and reportedly Gomułka's chief lieutenant), Stanisław Kociołek (first secretary of the Gdánsk voivodship party organization until 30 June 1970, when he was appointed a deputy premier), Władysław Kruczek (first secretary of the Rzeszów voivodship party organization), Ignacy Loga-Sowiński (chairman of the Central Council of Trade Unions and a vice-chairman of the Council of State); Marian Spychalski (chairman of the Council of State and, as such, the formal head of state); Ryszard Strzelecki (in charge of the Cadres Department, a member of the Council of State), and Józef Tejchma. Candidate members were Mieczysław Jagielski (minister of agriculture until 30 June); Piotr Jaroszewicz (Poland's permanent representative to the Council on Mutual Economic Assistance); Mieczysław Moczar (head of ZBoWiD, member of the Council of State); and Jan Szydlak (head of the Propaganda Department, with special responsibilities for youth).

The pre-20 December Secretariat consisted of Gomułka as first secretary, Jaszczuk, Kliszko, Moczar, Strzelecki, Szydlak, Tejchma, Stefan Olszowski, and Artur Starewicz.

In the reorganization of 20 December, Gomułka was replaced as first secretary by Gierek, and Jaszczuk, Kliszko, Strzelecki and Spychalski were removed from the Politburo. Three of the vacant Politburo positions were filled advancing Jaroszewicz, Moczar, and Szydlak from candidate to full membership; the other two positions went to Olszowski (heretofore only on the Secretariat) and Edward Babiuch (head of the Organization Department). Jagielski retained his candidate membership on the Politburo and was joined by Henryk Jabłoński (minister of general and higher education), Wojciech Jaruzelski (minister of defense), and Józef Kępa (first secretary of the Warsaw city party organization). Kliszko, Jaszczuk, and Strzelecki lost their positions as party secretaries along with Gomułka. They were replaced by Babiuch, Kociołek, and Kazimierz Barcikowski (first secretary of the Poznań voivodship party organization).

These events in the party were followed by changes in the government three days later at a session of the Sejm. In addition to some changes in heads of ministries, Spychalski resigned as chairman of the Council of State and was replaced by Cyrankiewicz. In turn, Cyrankiewicz gave up his position as premier, which was taken over by Jaroszewicz. Two new vice-premiers—appointed to fill the positions vacated by Jaroszewicz and Kociołek when they moved into the Secretariat—were Franciszek Kaim (who had been minister of heavy industry) and Jan Mitręga (minister of mining and the power industry, a post which he retained).

On 28 December Gierek at his request was relieved of his position as first secretary of the Katowice voivodship party organization, in which he was replaced by Zdzisław Grudzień (a member of the PUWP Central Committee and Sejm deputy). Of those ousted from the Politburo, Kliszko and Spychalski had been especially closely associated with Gomułka. Jaszczuk, a strong proponent of economic reform, reportedly had differed with Gierek on many issues, economic and otherwise. Strzelecki has been associated with more reactionary views and has been reported an ally of Moczar. Of the men closest to Gomułka, only trade union chief Loga-Sowiński remained on the Politburo (but was ousted in February 1971). Of those most associated with reform, Kociołek (also removed in February 1971), Tejchma, and Olszowski kept their positions. Two of the new Politburo members, Babiuch and Szydlak, are reportedly close to Gierek. Little is yet known about Barcikowski. Moczar seems to be the lone representative of the so-called partisan group. The new Politburo is considerably younger than the old (an average age of 51.7 years, compared with 57.3 years) and on the whole, appears to be more open-minded, pragmatic, and dynamic.

It seems clear that strong grievances against Gumułka had been building up within the party over the years since his return to power in October 1956. Advancing age and an unimaginative, bureaucratic, and sometimes petty approach to problems made him decreasingly suited for the job of leading Poland and the party through increasingly difficult economic times. There seems to have been disagreement within the party as to what economic reforms should be introduced and lack of satisfaction with the way in which Gomułka had attempted to deal with these matters. One minor consideration may have been the belief in certain party circles that Gomułka had given up too much in the agreement negotiated with West Germany (see below). Probably most important, however, was impatience with the pace of change and loss of confidence in Gomułka and those around him.

In 1970, Poland was suffering economically from a combination of excessive population growth in relation to investment, the slow pace of technological modernization, increasing difficulties in exporting to the West, rapidly rising consumer expectations, a breakdown in communications between workers and the party, low worker morale and productivity, poor management, overcentralization, and mistakes in economic planning. This condition was aggravated by two summers of poor harvests and widespread worker anxiety over an attempt to increase the efficiency of the economic system through a reform of the wage system (see below). The new wage system, which was to go into effect in January 1971, was designed to increase material incentives for productive work, but was perceived by many workers as a threat to their total incomes (because it made bonuses more difficult to earn). At the same time, the poor harvests and the need to secure money for investment led to a decision to solve the problem by the general price increase announced at the beginning of the Christmas holiday season on 12 December. Two days later a wave of protest strikes and rioting began—first among the shipyard workers of Gdańsk and later in the neighboring towns of Sopot and Gdynia, and in Szczecin and Elbląg,—in which a total of 45 were killed and 1,165 wounded. The fact that the price increases (reportedly opposed by Gierek and others in the Politburo) had been inadequately discussed in the party made the strikes and rioting all the more important in mobilizing support against Gomułka.

It was no secret that Gomułka had relatively few real supporters in the party and that he had managed to survive as long as he had in large part by skillfully balancing off the various party factions. It was also rumored that Gierek and Moczar, among others, had been carrying on secret negotiations in Silesia during the fall about the possibility of overthrowing him. Politburo candidate member Piotr Jaroszewicz and eventually Defense Minister Wojciech Jaruzelski were apparently also important members of the conspiracy. Gomułka was also reported to have suffered a nervous collapse following the outbreak of rioting, with Politburo member Zenon Kliszko temporarily taking command. After Gierek and others made an open bid for power by setting up their own alternate Politburo meeting in the old Natolin chateau near Warsaw, Gomułka and Kliszko reportedly telephoned Moscow to request the intervention of Soviet troops. Although

Gomułka had probably been the Soviet Union's closest and most important East European ally, the Soviet leadership declined to send troops—presumably because it was clear that Gomułka's authority had deteriorated too far to save him, because neither the strikes and riots nor the anti-Gomułka conspiracy had the slightest antisocialist or anti-Soviet flavor, and because Gierek and Jaroszewicz were well known and respected by the Soviet leaders and may have been perceived as the best hope for restoring order and confidence in Poland.

The new leaders have a reputation for being political realists who listen carefully to both workers and intellectuals, but who also demand discipline, hard work, and efficient economic performance. Gierek earned an excellent reputation as a good manager during his thirteen years as first secretary in the Katowice voivodship. The PUWP is stronger there than anywhere else in Poland, the workers have managed to do better economically, and the shops are reportedly fuller and the services more efficient than in most other parts of the country. Gierek has had relatively good relations with managers and the intellectuals as well as with workers. He has also been in a position to demonstrate his socialist faith and his support for the Soviet Union by playing host over the years to many hundreds of visiting Soviet delegations and tour groups. There is some evidence that Gierek favors stronger emphasis on economic ties with the West as one means of trying to solve Poland's economic problems, and that he has fewer ideological inhibitions about employing this means than his predecessor.

Domestic Attitudes and Activities. The Fifth Congress of the PUWP, meeting in November 1968, adopted a program emphasizing the rapid development and modernization of the economy through modernization of industry and modest economic reform to shape more responsible worker and management attitudes toward work, raise qualitative production standards, improve the standard of living, and raise the cultural level of the masses. (PUWP, *V ZjazdPZPR*, Warsaw, 1969). Three Central Committee plenums were held during 1970. The first, on 19-20 May, adopted a resolution outlining policy directives connected with improving the system of material incentives in the socialist sector (*Trybuna Ludu*, 25 May). The next met briefly on 14 December, two days after the announcement increasing prices, and again was concerned mainly with the economy. In his speech, Gomułka emphasized the need to insure that previously passed party resolutions were consistently carried out in practice. In regard to the price increases, he commented: "They always meet with criticism, no matter whether it is justified or unjustified." He added: "No one could possibly lack the means for fully satisfying his needs in basic food items." He emphasized the economic justification for price increases in light of the bad harvests of the previous two summers. (Warsaw radio, 14 December.) This plenum lasted only a few hours and was perhaps cut short by news from the Baltic coast about the strikes and public disturbances which began that same day. (No public announcement of the disturbances was made until the evening of 15 December, when a curfew from 6:00 p.m. to 5:00 a.m. was announced for Gdańsk.)

The final plenum, on 20 December, was devoted to formalizing the removal of Gomułka from his top party post, installing Gierek in his place, and making the other changes in party leadership noted above. That evening, following the news broadcast on the leadership changes, the new first secretary spoke to the nation over radio and TV, announcing the new directions the party planned to take and appealing "to workers, intellectuals, men of science, to all circles of society, to participate in the solution of the problems that face the country." He also appealed specifically to the workers who had been "carried away by emotions and interrupted work" to return to their duties. (Warsaw radio, 20 December.)

The Economy.   The general problems of economic reform were a major concern of the party throughout 1970. The basic problem remained one of how to improve the efficiency, quality, and profitability of Polish production so that the gap separating Poland from the Western capitalist states—and even from most of the East European socialist states—would begin to narrow rather than continue to widen. There was new emphasis on the seriousness of the situation and on the fact that other states were not standing still economically. The political importance of the economic problem was underlined by Gomułka in his 1 May speech when he stressed the importance of developing economic strength as the foundation of a strong and significant position for Poland. This theme was emphasized in a broader context by sociologist Jan Szczepański, chairman of the Department of Philosophy and Sociology at the Polish Academy of Sciences, in an important article (*Życie Warszawy*, 4 April). "Membership in blocs," he wrote, "does not solve the matter [of security] automatically. . . . The future of every state depends on its contributions to some international community, on the role it plays in a group of states, on its economic and military strength, its technical and scientific creativity, its political, intellectual, and artistic activity." He suggested that East-West talks currently under way might well lead to important shifts of forces within the blocs, and that then the "problem of the place of individual nations and states" would "arise anew." He added: "Our position in the world depends on our economic power—that is, on the level and quality of our production, on the skill of our economic organization both in production and in international trade and services." The article laid particular stress on the importance of Polish character and individual behavior in determining the strength of the country and in moving the economy forward, and was followed by a series of articles in the same paper from June to August commenting on his views. PUWP speech-makers and writers also laid particular stress throughout the year on the character, attitudes, and behavior of individual workers and managers as important keys to solving Poland's economic problems. A special economic conference, held at the Central Party School on 25-26 February, was attended by Party School workers, economists and heads of planning departments from all major academic centers, economic officials, and representatives from various industries. Władysław Zastawny, the director of the school, emphasized in his opening address the importance of breaking through certain psychological barriers created by heretofore applied methods of economic planning and management if the switch was to be made from an extensive to an intensive economy. At the same conference, Józef Pajestka, vice-chairman of the state Planning Commission, emphasized the importance of workers' initiative and the need for increasing their qualifications in achieving economic efficiency. The role of organizational efforts in support of economic reforms was stressed, particularly by Jan Szydlak in speeches at Lublin (22 September) and Wrocław (15 October).

Reforms of the economic system itself received considerable attention. The old discussion on how much decentralization of economic decision-making there should be and what form it should take continued and reflected conflict within the party between those who favored a more radical move toward market socialism and those who feared that the socially and ideologically desirable system of central planning and the foundations of the socialist state would be undermined by such reform.

Nevertheless, at the beginning of 1970 the system of financing of investments primarily by banks rather than by central allocations was introduced, along with more emphasis on the profitability of the investment. The economic reforms also called for firms to prepare their own production targets, with the Planning Commission concentrating on the coordination of individual plans and giving of advice. Higher bonuses were to be paid for cost cutting, and part of the bonus fund of each enterprise was tied to its profitability. The emphasis on increased efficiency in industry was to permit the transfer of about 2 per cent of the industrial work force to services, which were to receive additional encouragement and investment. New emphasis was placed on streamlining the economy through the introduction of new quality indices, more modern management techniques, the use of more sensitive systems for evaluating workers and managers and for paying and promoting them on the basis of their economic contribution to the enterprise, and greater emphasis on making better use in actual production of existing possibilities offered by scientific achievements at home and abroad. A new form of vertically integrated combine was introduced —following an enabling decree passed by the Council of Ministers on 23 October 1969—and new combines were established during 1970 in the machine tool and implements industries, the chemical industry, and the food industry, and were initiated in the construction industry.

The party criticized the lack of cooperation between industries and emphasized the need for greater coordination of their research and development programs. There was also considerable discussion of ways of shortening the investment cycle and criticism of the failure of the construction industry to turn over buildings for use on schedule.

In a speech at the May plenum, party economic specialist Bolesław Jaszczuk criticized the failure of the party's investment plan and noted that more had been invested than was called for. (The 1970 investment plan had been cut back to allow greater concentration on completing projects already begun.) He reviewed the current economic plans calling for modernization of the economy by concentrating investment in the most modern sectors of industry; forcing development of the transportation, raw materials, and fuel industries; increasing cooperation with capitalist companies (a type of cooperation which so far had "not been sufficiently exploited"); restructuring investment in the direction of "economic complexes" (groups of plants linked by their production processes) built around the purchase of licenses and technological concepts from abroad; the new system of industrial prices to come into effect 1 January 1971; and the 1972 plans for the downward reevaluation of capital goods and the new amortization rates.

Wage reforms, also discussed at the plenum and scheduled to go into effect at the beginning of 1971, were designed to increase the material incentives of workers to produce more goods of a higher quality. The reforms lowered many basic wages and tied total earnings more to production, quality, cost cutting, and overall enterprise profitability. An attempt was also made to tie worker bonuses more closely to those earned by managers and other white-collar workers. Theoretically, in a well-run enterprise a good worker would have been able to earn more under the new wage system, because the basic norms were to be, in effect, lowered, but it seems to have aroused widespread anxiety in many workers who felt that its effect would be to lower their total wages. There was also some expression of complaint that there were too few protections against raising work norms after production had increased in response to incentives. Considerable space was devoted in the more sophisticated Polish periodicals, most notably *Polityka*, to the economic reforms in Hungary, treating the Hungarian experiment sympathetically and with obvious interest in its potential for Poland. It is interesting that there was at least a partial rehabilitation of those economists who were attacked as "revisionists" in 1968. Stefan Kurowski, for example, was allowed to publish an article on reform of the planning system in the April 1970 issue of *Gospodarka Planowa*, the journal of the Planning Commission.

Industrial production seems to have fared reasonably well in 1969 and 1970, but the situation in agriculture was close to disastrous. Root and hay crops, although up 10 per cent from the poor 1969 levels, were not up to the 1968 figures. The grain harvest was far below the 1968 level and even farther below the target. The 1969 grain harvest amounted to 17.9 million tons. The 1970 estimate in September was for 13.9 million tons, creating an import need of 5.5 million tons (compared with just over 1.5 million tons in 1969). The Soviet Union agreed to increase its export from about 1.2 million tons to 2 million tons, but not by enough to fill the gap. At his harvest festival speech on 6 September, Gomułka painted a somber picture of the agricultural situation, confirming previous predictions of the decrease in the area sown with grain and adding that the per hectare harvest had been even less due to bad weather. He also noted a drop in the meat animal population due to bad weather and poor fodder crops in 1969 and forecast a decrease in the meat supply. Although nothing was said about solving the problem through a price increase

—let alone a general increase in prices—there were a number of other important instances when party leaders publicly emphasized the seriousness of the agricultural situation before the general price increases were announced without notice on the evening of 12 December.

In other developments in agriculture during 1970, the entire top party leadership attended the Fourth Congress of Agricultural Circles (3-4 July), together with 1,500 delegates from Poland's more than 35,000 agricultural circle cooperatives. (The circles, modeled after prewar voluntary producer cooperatives, were introduced in the late 1950's as a Polish alternative to collectivization. They are designed to increase cooperation among peasants at the village level. The state provides an incentive for working together by paying the difference between the market price and the price for compulsory agricultural deliveries into a special fund which is used to purchase farm machinery. The machines are available to those electing not to join the circle, who pay a higher rental than members. Since 1966, agricultural circle membership has increased from 2.0 to 2.5 million, and the 35,000 circles encompass 87 per cent of Poland's villages and 50 per cent of the individual farms. In his speech to the congress, Gomułka announced an additional tax relief and lower fertilizer prices to provide more incentives for increased production. He emphasized the need to increase efficiency and the role to be played by better agricultural education, more tractors and other equipment, improvements in the utilization of available equipment, land consolidation, and farming of land leased from the state land fund to agricultural circles or individual farmers. He also stressed the importance of improving rural conditions to help keep young people on the farms. (Warsaw radio, 3 July.)

The Fifth Congress of Collective Farms was held 24-25 November. Since the 1966 congress, the number of collectives has decreased from 1,214 to 1,109; some 200 were disbanded and 95 new ones started. The collectives represent 1.2 per cent of Poland's arable land. Deputy Premier Jagielski announced no new changes in policy, but noted that collectives would continue to expand through the taking over of neglected individual plots and land from the state land fund (*Trybuna Ludu*, 25 November).

Housing was a frequent topic of discussion in the Polish press during 1970, with emphasis on the need to increase the much depressed rate of construction. An article advocating higher housing prices as a means of facilitating this appeared in *Polityka* (19 September). The production and availability of most durable consumer goods continued to increase in 1970, and was in part responsible for the structure of the price changes in December. While the changes raised the price of most food products (e.g., meat by 17.6 per cent, milk by 16 per cent, fish by 11.7 per cent, jam by 36.8 per cent, coffee substitute by 92 per cent), the prices of many durables were lowered (television sets by 13.1 per cent, radios by 19.2 per cent, refrigerators by 15.8 per cent, washing machines by 17 per cent, and so on). The prices of building materials, cameras, furniture, wool and cotton textiles, foundry products, and coal were increased. The party also recognized the need to provide greater incentives for investment to expand services and handicrafts. There was considerable criticism of the old-fashioned methods of organization and technical backwardness of services and of the failure to increase the services sector as much as had been planned. The Council of Ministers in 1965 had decreed an 80 per cent increase in services by the socialist sector by 1970, but the actual increase was 35 to 55 per cent. Investments in this area were only 15 to 70 per cent realized.

The PUWP continued to pursue its policy of facilitating new private enterprise through the agency system. Under this new policy (introduced in previous years for restaurants and gas stations), state enterprises were encouraged to increase their efficiency by turning over to private agents all small shops and service enterprises under their control. A Council of State decision of 23 March held that all shops employing one or two persons, regardless of their profitability, should be put on the agency system (except for those selling ham and sausage, jewelry, and hard liquor). Those with three employees could be handed over to private agents, if they showed a loss. New uniform rules regulating the activities of the private agency system were passed by the Council of State on 5 April, giving agents employee rights of social insurance, trade union benefits, vacations, and the like, and were broadened to include all categories of restaurants and shops with up to three salesmen. Every socialist enterprise can now make agreements to lease establishments to agents for an indefinite period. Agents are to be subject to regular checkups by the enterprise with which they sign the agreement and are bound by the same regulations as apply to all socialist trade establishments, except that some requirements for professional qualifications are waived. By early April there were 4,500 eating establishments and over 20,000 retail shops operating under the agency system and accounting for 3.5 per cent of retail trade turnover.

In the area of foreign trade, the PUWP continued to stress the importance of increasing volume and planned to make the ability of an enterprise to get investment requiring foreign exchange after 1 January 1971 dependent on its ability to earn foreign exchange.

Restoring Order and the Legitimacy of the Party.   A major task facing the PUWP near the end of 1970 was the restoration of order and the popularity of the party, following the crisis created by the December food price increases and the resulting strikes and riots. The reaction of the party authorities to the strike of the Gdańsk shipyard workers, who went out onto the streets on the morning of 14 December, was a combination of appealing to reason and force. After the failure of local authorities to persuade the workers to return to work, the strike quickly got out of hand, drawing in many participants beyond the shipyards and leading to violence, looting, and the burning of several buildings, including the PUWP headquarters in Gdańsk. Protests and violence quickly spread to the neighboring cities of Sopot and Gdynia, and soon to Szczecin and Elbląg. Vice-Premier Kociołek (who was first party secretary in Gdańsk until 30 June) made an appeal for calm and a return to work, arguing that the workers' demands were largely incapable of being fulfilled (Gdańsk radio, 16 December). The government refused to give in to any of the demands and continued to emphasize the economic justification for the price increases. As the situation worsened, a state of national emergency was declared on 17 December. Premier Cyrankiewicz—repeating the role of government spokesman he played after the June 1956 events in Poznań—spoke in defense of government policies and appealed for calm and for rational discussion of the issues. He argued that the price increases were necessary if Poland was to advance technologically and economically. (Warsaw radio, 17 December.)

Following his elevation to the post of first secretary of the PUWP, Edward Gierek started off on a different tack in his speech of 20 December. While affirming that the price increases would not be rescinded (as in fact was done in February 1971 following strikes at Lodz), he said that the party would look into the possibilities of improving the lot of families in the lowest income brackets and those with many children. He also promised that an examination would be made into how the problems of working women, housing, and young people could be solved more quickly. He emphasized the importance of a reexamination of the five-year plan for 1971-75 and called on the entire nation—workers, intellectuals, men of science, people from every circle of society—to participate in the solution of these important problems, and promised to "provide political and organizational conditions, observing the norms of socialist democracy in all spheres." The blame for the economic crisis, the price increase riots and the resulting tragic deaths was placed both on "causes which resulted from real difficulties" and on "causes which resulted from badly-thought-out conceptions in the economic policy." Hinting strongly that much of the blame lay with the previous leadership, Gierek declared: "The iron rule of our economic policy and our policy in general must be always to count with reality, to consult broadly the working class and intelligentsia, to respect the principle of collective decision-making and democracy in the life of the party and the activity of its supreme authorities." He went on to reiterate Polish policy on continuing to "consolidate the friendship and alliance with the Soviet Union" and the continuation of the previous policies of normalization of relations with West Germany. Then he called on those who had stopped work to return, emphasizing that although the motives for this action were for the most part honest, it was nevertheless fraught with great danger for the country and had been "exploited by enemies of socialism, by asocial and criminal elements."

The press praised the new leadership strongly and emphasized the importance of the reestablishment of communication between the people and the party. TV political commentator Ryszard Wojna, for example, observed on 21 December that the news of Gierek's election "was received with a deep feeling of relief" because "the mechanism for dialogue between the Party and the people had become jammed." *Życie Warszawy* on 22 December noted that "the Polish community has long been waiting for the credibility gap between the nation and the party to be overcome, for the dialogue to be reestablished and the state machinery put effectively into order." The PUWP daily, *Trybuna Ludu*, stated on 23 December: "This means the reconstruction has started of the party's strong links with the working class and with the whole nation, that we are back on the road to a constructive, collective, and matter-of-fact solution of the problems arising in the conditions of a continuous flow of ideas and mutual confidence between party units, the broad aktiv, and the party masses." On 21 December the Soviet leadership, through Brezhnev, expressed congratulations to Gierek on his elections and strong support for him. The state of emergency was lifted by the Council of Ministers on 22 December, by which time the situation had largely returned to normal.

In his speech to the Sejm on 23 December, Gierek thanked Spychalski and Cyrankiewicz for their services to the country and declared that the first task was to improve the material situation of the families most greatly affected by the price increases. He announced that 7 billion złoty had been earmarked for this and that the money would be divided only after consultation with representatives of unions, the party, management, and workers in special meetings at their places of work. He also announced a freeze on food prices for at least two years, and emphasized again that there would be no change in the policy of close ties with the Soviet Union and the socialist camp and of normalization of relations with West Germany and Western Europe. (PAP, Polish news agency, 23 December.) Premier Jaroszewicz in his speech emphasized that more attention was being paid to housing and services but that no effect would be felt before 1972, that there would be no change in agricultural policy, and that the role of central planning would be strengthened while creating conditions suitable for creative initiatives by workers and managers. He also announced that the government was desirous of normalizing church-state relations and that it intended to proceed with ratification of the treaty signed earlier in the month with West Germany and establish diplomatic relations immediately thereafter. (Warsaw radio, 23 December.)

At the end of the year the party also made the decision to begin, at last, the expensive job of reconstructing the Warsaw castle, destroyed in the Second World War, in what would seem to be an attempt to cultivate popular support through an appeal to Polish national sentiment.

Party Policy Toward Socialist Attitudes and Cultural Affairs. PUWP policy with respect to the shaping of opinion continued in 1970 to be an almost unpredictable mixture of repression and relaxation. The most sensational event in this realm was the political trial and sentencing in February of five young Poles who were convicted of offenses against the good name and the political interests of Poland and "more specifically" of smuggling into the country copies of an issue of the Paris-based Polish émigré journal *Kultura* dealing with the March 1968 student unrest in Poland and copies of the Prague "2000 words" manifesto. One of the group was also convicted of furnishing information to *Kultura* about Polish student unrest. News of the trial was accompanied by long commentaries in the mass media and sharp attacks on *Kultura* as "one of the links in the system of various centers of psychological warfare directed against the Soviet camp" which were said to be connected with U.S. "imperialist centers" and the U.S. Central Intelligence Agency (Warsaw radio, 9 February). Despite the bitterness of the attacks against them, three of the five received lighter sentences than were demanded by the prosecutor and, because of the amnesty of July 1969 for offenses committed before that date, all received reduced sentences. In March, thirty university students and assistants who had been awaiting trial for as long as nine months were quietly released.

Although censorship continued to be strict, there were also signs of relaxation. Writers such as Jerzy Andrzejewski, who had been banned from print for their criticism of the invasion of Czechoslovakia, were again allowed to publish. Several who had not been allowed to travel for the same reason again received passports. Ernest Bryll's play "Kurdesz," which after its opening at Kraków in 1969 was quickly shut down because of its criticisms of present-day Polish society, reopened at Warsaw in 1970 without difficulty.

M. F. Rakowski, in the 4 April issue of *Polityka*, which he edits, argued for the necessity of recognizing that the young people of Poland have a perspective different from that of their elders, little in common with the Second World War generation, and that they are interested primarily in the future and the improvement of Polish society, adding: "Only that society which persistently breaks with old habits, which develops a sense of dignity, which is aware of the real value of its deeds and conscious of its imperfections, can be fully immune against revisionist erosion." He also emphasized the importance of developing social democracy and realizing the positive results deriving from a difference of views (within the framework of a socialist program): "Differences of views provide the propulsive power of society."

Another important set of articles relating to present and future problems appeared in *Życie Warszawy* during the summer, beginning with the 4 June article by Jan Szczepański noted above, on "The Fate of Poland and the Polish Character."

In *Kultura* (4 October), published at Warsaw, Central Committee secretary Józef Tejchma discussed the problems that he believes alienate youth: the luxuries of the rich, failure to advance people on the basis of merit, too many celebrations of trifles. He went on to emphasize the need for more attention to proper education—in the schools, mass media, and youth organizations—to provide the young with a good background and alternatives to "negative" Western influences.

It seems clear that the more sophisticated party leaders and journalists recognize that slogans, old doctrines, and simple answers are insufficient in dealing with the intellectuals and the young people and with the ideological problems of the present.

Anniversaries. The major anniversaries celebrated in 1970 were the series of twenty-fifth anniversary events commemorating the liberation from Nazi rule of cities, localities, and districts all across central and western Poland. The most important were the 9-10 May celebrations at Wrocław.

1 April, Gomułka visited Moscow for the celebration of the Lenin Centenary. On 20 April the Order of Lenin was awarded him in a Kremlin ceremony attended by the entire Politburo of the Communist Party of the Soviet Union. At the Centenary celebration he was given the honor of speaking immediately after Brezhnev as the first representative among foreign delegations.

The twentieth anniversary of the treaty between Poland and the German Democratic Republic (6 July), formalizing the relationship between the two states and recognizing the permanence of the Oder-Neisse line, was celebrated at the border by their respective premiers, Józef Cyrankiewicz and Willi Stoph. Cyrankiewicz called for Western diplomatic recognition of the GDR and its admission to the U.N.

The Polish national holiday celebrations on 22 July (the twenty-sixth anniversary of the postwar Polish state) were unusually subdued, with no parade or guests from abroad—in contrast to the celebrations of the previous year. It was billed as a "day of rest, entertainment, festivities, artistic performances, and sports events."

Relations with the Church. Despite occasional incidents, such as the 3 March riots in Chodków (Rzeszów voivodship) following government orders to tear down a shed at a Catholic church annex built without a permit, the trend toward improved church-state relations over the past two years continued during 1970. Although *Argumenty*, the organ of the Society of Atheists and Freethinkers, shifted the focus of its attacks in early 1970 from the Vatican to the Polish Catholic church and its leadership, other media critical of the church continued to attack the Vatican. Meanwhile, official government policy toward the church continued on the whole to be conciliatory.

The major concern of the Polish Episcopate during the year was over its property rights in Catholic church buildings in recovered territories and with the problem of church administration there. Immediately after the war, the Polish church was allowed to administer former German Catholic church property. In 1959, however, the Polish government claimed these properties for the state—presumably to induce the Polish church to bring more pressure on the Vatican to alter its policy of administration in the territories. The Vatican persisted in its refusal to revise the boundaries of the ecclesiastical sees in the north and west to coincide with the new Oder-Neisse boundaries and declined to place them formally under the regular Polish Catholic church administration. The Vatican's problem has been that the boundaries of the ecclesiastical sees are defined in the 1933 concordat with Germany. The sees in the recovered territories encompass not only parts of Poland but also parts of former East Prussia. Others include prewar Polish territory that has been incorporated by the Soviet Union. The Vatican does not want to break the 1933 concordat until some overall settlement can be made of the question of adjusting the boundaries of church administration between the Elbe and the former Polish-Soviet border. Moreover, the Vatican does not want to offend the German Catholic hierarchy and the powerful West German pressure groups that oppose the readjustment of boundaries. The policy of the Polish party and government has been to attack strongly the Vatican position on this matter and attempt to paint the Vatican as pro-German and as being tied in with the "Western imperialists and revisionists" that threaten the security of Polish borders. The Polish Catholic church has, nevertheless, put strong pressure on the Vatican to change its policies, particularly during 1970 when the Polish-West German negotiations to normalize relations were going on. On 8 April the Polish Episcopate formally proposed Polish-Vatican negotiations on the return of church property in the recovered territories. In the numerous personal contacts between the Vatican and the Polish Episcopate during the year, these questions probably were often discussed. Papal advisor Archbishop Sergio Pignedoli was in Warsaw on 21-25 April (ostensibly to discuss Polish missionary work in Africa). In late May, five Polish bishops and some 200 priests (former inmates of German concentration camps) went to Rome for the celebration of the Pope's fiftieth anniversary as a priest. On 1 October, Karol Cardinal Wojtyła, Archbishop of Kraków, went to Rome for ten days and had a private audience with the Pope. On 12 October, Stefan Cardinal Wyszyński, the Polish Primate, and Bolesław Kominek, the Archbishop of Wrocław, journeyed to Rome and had an audience on 17 October after the Pope met with bishops from both East and West Germany. During their stay abroad all three had extended consultations with West European church officials. These talks presumably included discussion of the Polish church's position on the administration of the recovered territories. Then in late October three other Polish bishops went to Rome and at least two remained until 20 November.

Following the initialing of the Polish-West German treaty, the Vatican press office announced that it would study the implications of the new agreement, and hinted that it preferred to await the ratification of the treaty before making any move to revise the boundaries of the ecclesiastical sees. On 29 November, Cardinal Wyszyński announced that the Pope in a letter of 9 November had given assurances that as soon as the political situation was settled the Holy See would not delay issuing proper decrees finalizing the reorganization of the dioceses in the western territories. Late in the year the Polish Episcopate and the Polish Ecumenical Council published statements warmly endorsing the Polish-West German treaty.

In another interesting development on 9 November the World Council of Churches (WCC) signed a three-year agreement with the Polish Ecumenical Council (as an agent for the Polish government) providing for cooperation in strengthening social services in Poland. During the first year the WCC is to provide $252,000 and the Poles $80,000. The agreement provides 100 more places a year for the chronically ill aged in state and church institutions, audio-visual aids for the training of nurses and social workers, medical apparatus, and deliveries of food stuffs available to the WCC.

It is also worth noting that Cardinal Wyszyński in a Christmas Eve sermon in Warsaw was very conciliatory and accepted coresponsibility for what happened during the riots and gave an implied promise of cooperation with the new government. He also made a plea to the workers: "Show understanding, forgive, feel compassion, put your hands to the plow, so that there can be more bread in your fatherland." At the same time, the new Polish party and government leaders were calling for the normalization of Church-state relations (as in the 23 December speech of the new premier, Jaroszewicz).

It is clear, however, that much still divides the Catholic church and the regime in Poland and that hard negotiations lie ahead. At the end of the year, Cardinal Wyszyński in a statement read in the Polish churches on New Year's Day listed six basic conditions for a true normalization of relations with the new government and party leadership: "(1) The right to freedom of conscience and freedom of religious life together with full normalization of relations between the church and the state; (2) the right of freely shaping the culture of one's own nation, according to the spirit of the Christian principles of coexistence of people; (3) the right to social justice expressed in fulfilling just demands; (4) the right to truth in social life, to information according with the truth, and to free expression of one's views and demands; (5) the right to material conditions which ensure decent existence of the family and of each individual citizen; (6) the right to such an attitude toward the citizens that they are not insulted, harmed, and persecuted in anything."

International Activities. Poland's most important international activities in 1970 were centered around the Soviet and Polish negotiations with the Federal Republic of Germany (FRG), and Poland's general efforts to promote East-West détente through an all-European security conference. There was frequent consultation between Poland and the Soviet Union and with other East European states in the course of the year preceding the signing of the Soviet-FRG accord on 12 August and the initialing of the Polish-FRG agreement on 18 November (signed 7 December) normalizing their relations and recognizing the Oder-Neisse boundary. Otherwise most of Poland's efforts in the international sphere were directed at expanding trade—with the other members of the Council for Mutual Economic Assistance (CMEA), with the Western capitalist states (particularly through joint agreements between enterprises), and with the "third world" (with special emphasis on Latin America).

The general international emphasis of the PUWP continued to follow the path of the past several years, stressing the importance of maintaining the closest ties with the Soviet Union and the rest of the socialist camp and of increasing the degree of economic specialization and integration in the CMEA, while at the same time working for greater East-West détente and economic cooperation in order to maximize the benefits to Poland, especially in the area of technological modernization of its economy.

The Poles continued to express concern about the West European Common Market and its potential expansion to include all of Europe, and about the growing danger that Poland and the other East European states might be squeezed out of the West European market. In a 16 April speech to the U.N. Economic Commission for Europe (ECE), Deputy Foreign Minister Józef Winiewicz praised the ECE as the only organization furthering multilateral East-West contacts and warned against present trends in West European integration as contributing toward an irreparable economic division of Europe. He emphasized the potential for greater pan-European economic cooperation and expanded trade on the basis of the solid economic development of the socialist countries.

PUWP and government organs stressed a similar theme in the political area, with repeated calls for a European security conference. Foreign Minister Jędrychowski in an interview with the Socialist Youth Union newspaper *Sztandar Młodych* (8-9 August), for example, accused NATO of "piling up artificial obstacles" on the path leading to a convocation of such a conference. He argued that the cold war is dead and that the division of Europe thwarts traditional economic and cultural bonds and hampers the development of desirable new forms of cooperation.

During 1970 by far the most space in the Polish press and in speeches by party leaders was devoted to the negotiations aiming at the normalization of relations between Poland and the FRG. The Polish position shifted somewhat in the course of the year, but the basic position at the start of the negotiations was expressed by Marian Spychalski, Politburo member and chairman of the Council of State, in a speech to the National Unity Front (20 February). He distinguished between the basic condition for agreement with the FRG—namely, West German renunciation of all territorial claims and recognition of the existing Polish western frontier— and the "prerequisites of peace and European security," which were international legal recognition of the GDR, recognition by the FRG that the 1938 Munich agreement was null and void from the beginning, recognition of the separate political status of West Berlin, and FRG ratification of the nuclear nonproliferation treaty (Warsaw radio, 20 February).

The PUWP continued its strong condemnation of Israeli policies in the Middle East and of U.S. intervention in Indochina, especially after the Cambodian invasion. Considerable attention was also given to the problem of "counteracting the psychological warfare and ideological diversion waged by the imperialists." An international symposium devoted to this subject was held in Warsaw on 21-25 April and was attended by military and civilian activists of the ideological front from Bulgaria, Czechoslovakia, the GDR, Romania, Hungary, the Soviet Union, and Poland. This was one of a series of meetings called for at a January 1970 meeting in Moscow devoted to the "problems in the struggle against anticommunism" organized by the Soviet and East European academies of science. A new book on economic diversion by Henryk Florek and Stanisław Szefler attracted attention, though it was criticized for expanding "diversion" to include virtually everything and therefore obscuring where the very real dangers of diversion lay (review by Zygmunt Szeliga in *Polityka*, 1 August). Another example of concern over Western ideological influence was the interview in *Kultura* with Politburo member and Central Committee secretary Józef Tejchma, (Warsaw, 21 January) who noted that convergence should be viewed as the most dangerous anti-Marxist and anti-socialist theory.

Warsaw Treaty Organization. A meeting of the Warsaw Pact deputy foreign ministers was held in Sofia on 26-27 January for the announced purpose of discussing the preparation of a European conference on security and cooperation called for at the March 1969 Budapest meeting of the WTO Political Consultative Committee. A meeting of the Consultative Committee was held in early December 1970 at East Berlin, apparently on initiative of the Poles, with the possible objective of persuading the GDR to be more conciliatory toward West Germany in order to speed up ratification of the treaty between Poland and the FRG.

Soviet Defense Minister Andrei Grechko visited Poland on 10-13 February for a tour and consultations with Defense Minister Wojciech Jaruzelski. He was accompanied by the political chief of the Soviet army and navy, General Alexei Yepishev, and a number of other high-ranking officers.

Council for Mutual Economic Assistance. The twenty-fourth CMEA session was held in Warsaw on 12-14 May 1970 under the chairmanship of Premier Cyrankiewicz. The most important development was a formal agreement to establish an International Investment Bank, following the recommendation of the previous session. Only Romania opposed the new bank. The rules adopted for the investment bank deviate from common CMEA practice of unanimity voting in that decisions can be made by a qualified majority vote. (The new bank is a true investment bank rather than one providing merely the clearinghouse functions of the existing CMEA International Bank for Economic Cooperation.) Recommendations were also made for broadening cooperation between ministries and their sub-units, as well as the usual discussion of economic specialization and the coordination of long-range economic plans. On 20 July Poland's CMEA representative, Vice-Premier Jaroszewicz, went to Moscow for the session of the CMEA Executive Committee.

Poland has been one of the strongest supporters of the CMEA in recent years and has advocated integration through specialization of production, taking a position almost opposite to that of the Romanians. Jaroszewicz in an article on the CMEA (*Trybuna Ludu*, 31 December 1969) called for improved international planning, a better monetary system, greater trade, and more technical cooperation. He proposed further quota reduction and trade liberalization to provide incentives to develop new lines of production and widen the range of goods exchanged. He also called for an international CMEA currency to provide a uniform standard of value.

Relations with the Soviet Union. There was every indication of close Soviet-Polish cooperation throughout 1970. Gomuľka had consistently been one of the quickest to echo the Soviet line in foreign policy in recent years and one of the most vigorous assailants of U.S. foreign policy, especially in Indochina and the Middle East. In return the Poles seem to have been accorded prestige within the socialist camp (as when Gomuľka was the first foreign delegation head to speak after Brezhnev at the Lenin Centenary), a considerable degree of autonomy in deviating from the Soviet model domestically (e.g., open Soviet support since 1960 for their policy of retaining private agriculture), more favorable terms of trade, Soviet support for their major foreign policy objective of securing protection against West Germany and permanent recognition of the Oder-Neisse boundary, greater decision-making influence in the CMEA and WTO and other affairs of the socialist camp, and a certain ability to take the initiative in foreign policy (e.g., the Rapacki plan for a nuclear-free zone in central Europe). There are important Soviet limits placed on Polish policy, to be sure, but the interests of the PUWP elites and Gomuľka's conservative and cautious brand of communism, together with more sensitivity on the Soviet Union's part toward its East European allies, have created a considerable range of common interests between the Polish and Soviet leaderships over the past few years.

The two major areas of negotiation between Poland and the Soviet Union in 1970 were in regard to relations with the West, particularly talks under way with the FRG, and trade relations for 1971-75. There were numerous consultations during the year over the German question—especially in April and May when Deputy Foreign Minister Winiewicz (chief Polish negotiator with the FRG) visited Moscow three times (2 April, 30 April, and 25 May, the third time with Foreign Minister Jędrychowski). European security matters were undoubtedly also discussed at these meetings, especially on 25 May and during discussions in Moscow on 23-25 July. It is noteworthy that the 12 August Soviet-FRG agreement on the renunciation of force included specific mention of the Oder-Neisse boundary as inviolable, to which Polish press reaction was highly favorable.

On 4 September, Poland and the Soviet Union signed a protocol for coordination of 1971-75 national economic plans and on 29 October an agreement for scientific and technical cooperation during the same period. In December, trade negotiations were held, leading to the 30 December agreement for 1971-75 under which trade between the two countries is to increase by more than 67 per cent, with particular emphasis on cooperation between industries. Under the terms of the 1971 protocol, signed the same day, Polish grain imports from the Soviet Union were to amount to 2 million tons for the year. Poland is already the Soviet Union's second most important trade partner after the GDR.

What role the Soviet Union played in the change of Polish leadership in December is still unclear, but on the day after Edward Gierek was formally elected first secretary of the PUWP a congratulatory message to him from Soviet party chief Brezhnev expressed full confidence in his leadership.

Relations with the Chinese People's Republic. Polish-Chinese relations appeared to take a turn for the better in 1970, due almost entirely to a general change in Chinese foreign policy. In July, Poland and China signed an agreement that calls for an increase in trade and, if fulfilled, will reverse a steady decrease that began in 1958. In late August a new Chinese ambassador, Yao Kuang, arrived in Warsaw, giving the Chinese ambassadorial representation for the first time since mid-1967. Poland also sent a new ambassador to Peking, after an interval of a year in which it was represented by a chargé d'affaires. Nevertheless, relations remained cool, and the Poles have sided squarely with the U.S.S.R. in its dispute with China, while opposing Soviet proposals to read the Chinese out of the international communist movement.

Relations with Other Bloc States. In Polish relations with Czechoslovakia the emphasis was on normalization and reestablishment of the ties that were strained or broken as a result of the 1968 invasion. Attempts at normalization included a visit by Czechoslovakian Premier Oldřich Černík in January 1970. An exchange of parliamentary delegations also took place, with the Czechs coming to Poland in February and the Poles to Czechoslovakia in November. Joint communiques stressed the future of Polish-Czechoslovak industrial cooperation, socialist internationalism, the need for bloc solidarity toward the FRG on the issues of the Oder-Neisse line, recognition of the GDR, recognition of the Munich agreement as invalid from the beginning, and FGR renunciation of claims to be the exclusive representative of the German nation.

A new Polish-Romanian treaty of friendship, cooperation, and mutual assistance was signed in Bucharest on 12 November, following a visit by a Polish delegation headed by PUWP First Secretary Gomułka and Premier Cyrankiewicz. Discussions were also held on matters of trade and cooperation in the course of the year. Several agreements were signed, including a protocol on economic cooperation and exchange of goods for 1971-75, calling for an increase of trade by 80 per cent over the previous five years.

Polish relations with the GDR in the economic sphere included the signing of at least eight economic cooperation agreements in the course of the year, with discussions under way on a number of other projects. Political relations appeared to be a little strained because of the Polish negotiations with the FRG. The GDR presumably wanted to make sure that its interests were not forgotten in the negotiations and hoped to get the Poles to bring pressure on the FRG to normalize relations with the GDR as well. European security problems, closer GDR-Polish-Czech military cooperation (and the reactivation of the northern tier coalition), and Berlin may also have been discussed in the consultations that took place in Poland on 18 February, 27-29 May and 25-27 September (when Premier Willi Stoph visited Poland) and in the GDR on 22-23 September. There were also other sources of strain, such as the differences in domestic policies; there was also undoubtedly Polish resentment over the lack of GDR willingness to help Poland economically and over past GDR interference with Polish shipments to the FRG. Poland also resents the GDR's ability to trade freely with the FRG (duty free and without quotas) because of a special relationship with the FRG that allows the GDR (in effect) associate membership in the European Economic Community. (GDR trade with the FRG runs over $1 billion a year, compared with about $270 million for Poland.) The two states also differ on preferences as to trade arrangements within the CMEA, with the GDR preferring bilateral arrangements to multilateral specialization agreements.

Relations with Yugoslavia. The visit to Poland by Secretary for Foreign Affairs Mirko Tepavac on 16-20 November was the first by a high-ranking Yugoslav since 1966. It followed extensive economic negotiations and the initialing of a trade agreement earlier in the month. The visit also followed a shift in Soviet and Polish policy toward greater emphasis on détente, broadening the base for security through the calling of a European conference, and expanded trade and economic cooperation with the West, thereby eliminating many of the differences that had divided the two countries.

Relations with the Federal Republic of Germany. The year 1970 marked an important turning point in Polish relations with the FRG by the signing of both an important trade agreement on 15 October and a treaty normalizing relations between the two states on 7 December. It took seven difficult rounds of negotiation lasting from February to November and considerable compromise of initial positions by both sides to reach agreement on the treaty normalizing relations. It secured for Poland what the Soviet-FRG agreement had not, namely, formal recognition of the Oder-Neisse line as the western state boundary of Poland (compared with the Soviet-FRG treaty's recognition only of the inviolability of European borders, including the Oder-Neisse). The Poles, however, failed to achieve their maximum demand for complete finalization of the boundary, which the FRG insisted must await a German peace treaty and a broader settlement of German affairs. The Poles dealt with the so-called humanitarian questions by agreeing (in a separate protocol) to facilitate emigration from Poland of certain persons of German ancestry and to allow Germans wishing to visit their relatives in Poland to do so on the same basis as other Western visitors.

In addition to affirming that the "existing border line" (as established by the Potsdam Conference) constituted the western state frontier of Poland, the treaty confirmed the "inviolability" of existing frontiers "now and in the future" and declared: " [Poland and the FRG] have no territorial claims against one another nor shall they advance such claims in the future." The treaty also included a provision that all possible disputes should be settled exclusively by peaceful means and that the parties would undertake to "refrain from the threat or the use of force." They also declared their intention to "normalize fully their relations" and agreed that expansion of cooperation in economic, cultural, and other fields was in their common interest. Finally, the treaty did not "affect bilateral or multilateral international agreements previously concluded by the parties or concerning them."

The long-term trade agreement signed on 15 October called for most-favored-nation treatment and application of GATT trade principles, gradual reduction of quotas, and the development of economic and technological cooperation and industrial coproduction. Inconclusive negotiations were also carried on in July and November with regard to possible expansion in function of the trade missions to include consular duties pending ratification of the treaty normalizing relations and establishment of formal diplomatic relations. Agreement was reached 10 October between the Polish Academy of Sciences and the Academic Exchange Service in West Germany for exchanges of scientists beginning in 1971.

In the course of the year considerable attention was given by the Poles to creating favorable conditions for eventual ratification of the Polish-FRG treaty once it had been signed. Dozens of

West German groups were invited to Poland for talks and tours of the country, including members of both the ruling and the opposition parties. Polish church groups were encouraged to invite their counterparts from the FRG.

Although the Polish-FRG treaty was signed on 7 December, its ratification remained an open question during 1970 because of the uncertainty about whether the Brandt government could muster enough support to achieve ratification and whether the agreement that had been reached on the humanitarian questions would satisfy potential opposition in the FRG. The Polish press, while enthusiastic about the agreement, expressed only cautious optimism about the future. For the Poles there was the question not only of the treaty itself, but of the long-range relationship with West Germany, the EEC, and NATO, and of the building of a new European security structure, FRG ratification of the nuclear nonproliferation treaty, recognition of the GDR, the Berlin question and West German demands for reunification, and growing West German economic power and influence in Europe.

Relations with Other States. Relations with the United States remained cool throughout 1970—in large part because of the Indochina war—but were generally good with other Western states and Japan. The Poles concentrated primarily on expanding trade and advocacy of the European security conference idea, with special Foreign Ministry delegations conferring with leaders in most West European countries and Canada in the course of the year.

Relations with France were particularly good, although the French were unwilling to agree to an early date for a European security conference. Foreign Minister Jędrychowski visited France on 4-7 May to discuss economic and cultural cooperation and political questions. In September a French parliamentary delegation visited Poland, in late October Polish-French talks were held in Paris, and on 26-28 November French Premier Jacques Chaban-Delmas and Foreign Minister Maurice Schumann paid a visit to Poland. A "Declaration of Friendship and Cooperation" was signed—with the title undoubtedly designed to stress the difference between the nature of the relations between Poland and France (friendship and cooperation) and the relationship to be formalized in the next few weeks between Poland and the FRG (only normalization). A protocol was also signed on the development of Polish-French cooperation, summing up already existing treaties.

The rapid expansion of Polish-Japanese trade since 1968 continued in 1970. On 15 August, Polish and Japanese trading firms reached agreement on an export credit of $100 million put together by a consortium of Japanese firms for the purchase of industrial plants in Japan during 1971-75. Poland is to make repayment with coking coal.

A Spanish consular and commercial office was established in Warsaw in late January pursuant to a July 1969 agreement, followed in April by the signing of a Polish-Spanish five-year trade agreement, the first at the governmental level. In July agreement was reached between Poland and Austria for compensation of Austrians for property confiscated, nationalized, or expropriated after the Second World War.

Much attention was paid by the Poles to establishing diplomatic relations and the development of trade and cooperation agreements with the Latin American countries, continuing a trend begun in 1968. In February diplomatic relations were established with Ecuador and Bolivia. An economic mission in February and March carried on talks with Venezuela, Colombia, Peru, and Ecuador. Trade talks were also carried on with Bolivia and Argentina.

There were talks or agreements with Algeria, India (including a visit to Poland by President Giri), Iraq, Turkey, Ghana, Nigeria, Afghanistan (including a visit to Poland by Premier Nur Ahmed Etemadi), Iran, Malaysia (first trade agreement), Sudan, and Pakistan.

International Party Contacts. In addition to the extensive party-government contacts between

Poland on the one hand and the Soviet Union and the GDR on the other in connection with the FRG negotiations, a Polish delegation went to Moscow for the celebration of the Lenin Centenary. Besides the decoration of Gomułka with the Order of Lenin (awarded by the Presidium of the Supreme Soviet on his birthday, 9 February), Jarosław Iwaszkiewicz, chairman of the Polish Writers' Union, received an international Lenin prize. A PUWP delegation headed by Central Committee secretary Stefan Olszowski visited Hungary on 19-23 January to discuss current ideological questions, cultural policy, and the mass media. In November an impressive Polish delegation headed by Gomułka attended the Tenth Congress of the Hungarian Socialist Workers' Party. A party-state delegation headed by Premier Cyrankiewicz visited Hungary in early April for the celebration of the twenty-fifth anniversary of Hungary's liberation. Another party-state delegation, including both Gomułka and Cyrankiewicz, visited Czechoslovakia on 6-7 May for a celebration of the twenty-fifth anniversary of the Nazi defeat. In late May a PUWP delegation headed by Zenon Kliszko visited Moscow and North Korea. A party-government delegation including Gomułka and Cyrankiewicz visited Romania in November to sign a new treaty of friendship, cooperation, and mutual assistance. The Poles played host on 16-17 March to a Bulgarian party-state delegation led by First Secretary and Premier Todor Zhivkov. In September and October a PUWP delegation led by Kliszko visited France. In late August delegations of German and French communist party leaders also came to Poland.

Publications. The daily organ of the PUWP is *Trybuna Ludu*; its monthly theoretical journal is *Nowe Drogi*. A monthly, *Życie Partii*, is directed at party activists, and a biweekly, *Chłopska Droga*, is aimed at the rural readers. Seventeen dailies are published by the voivodship party organizations. Two influential weeklies, *Polityka* and the Warsaw *Kultura*, deserve notice though they are not official PUWP publications.

* * *

The "Polish Communist Party" in Albania. Kazimierz Mijal, a former PUWP Central Committee member, left Poland in February 1966 after he came under attack for organizing a Maoist faction within the party. Since then he has been active in Tirana, Albania, broadcasting in Polish "documents" allegedly originating with the "Central Committee of the Polish Communist Party in Poland," or from its organ, *Czerwony Sztandar* (Red Banner). No information is available about the size or composition of the alleged party, but it is assumed to be primarily a diversion supported by Peking and Tirana. Mijal, who claims to be its first secretary, has taken a consistent Maoist position and has been highly critical of the PUWP as being "revisionist" and "compromised" and its leaders as "slaves to Moscow." He can be expected to continue this line of attack against the new PUWP leadership. From time to time alleged excerpts from *Czerwony Sztandar* are broadcast over Peking radio or appear in the Albanian press. A typical article (*Zëri i Popullit*, Tirana 4 December) argued that "Gomułka 'realism' in economic policy" had caused Poland to become "an appendage of the Soviet capitalist economy" and a semi-colony whose development is controlled by the interests of "Soviet social imperialism, not by the needs of the Polish people."

J. F. M.

ROMANIA

The Romanian Communist Party (Partidul Comunist Român; RCP) was founded in 1921. Declared illegal soon afterward, it went underground, to emerge only at the end of the Second World War. After coming to power in 1948 it called itself the Romanian Workers' Party; in 1965 the original name was restored. As the only political movement in Romania, the RCP exercises a monopoly of power. In November 1968 a mass organization called the "Socialist Unity Front" was formed, replacing the former "People's Democratic Front," which functioned only during elections to the Grand National Assembly or parliament. The new front, where the RCP plays the leading role and which includes representatives of major mass and civic organizations and also the national minority councils, provides a permanent organizational framework for participation by broad strata of the population in political life.

Early in 1970 the official news agency Agerpres announced that Romania had a population of 20,140,000. The majority or 58 per cent worked in agriculture, and 31 per cent were industrial workers. The remainder were office workers, teachers, and other professionals. By ethnic origin, 86 per cent were Romanians, 9 per cent Hungarians, 2 per cent Germans, and 3 per cent of other stocks.

Organization and Leadership. The supreme RCP organ is the congress, to which delegates are elected at county conferences. The party statutes require that congresses be held every four years. The Tenth Congress took place in August 1969. Between congresses, the Central Committee is the governing authority. It consists of 165 full members and 120 candidates. They come from all counties throughout the country. The last congress reelected Nicolae Ceaușescu secretary general of the party. The Central Committee elects the Standing Presidium, consisting in 1970 of Emil Bodnaraș, Nicolae Ceaușescu, Ion Gheorghe Maurer, Paul Niculescu-Mizil, Gheorghe Pană, Gheorghe Rădulescu, Virgil Trofin, and Ilie Verdeț. The Central Committee also elects the Secretariat, currently consisting of Mihail Gere, Manea Mănescu, Paul Niculescu-Mizil, Gheorghe Pană, Vasili Patilineț, Dumitru Popescu, and Virgil Trofin. In addition, there exists the Executive Committee of the Central Committee, almost identical in composition with the combined Standing Presidium and Secretariat. The real power rests with the Standing Presidium, which supervises the activities of all party agencies.

At lower levels, in each county there are party committees, headed by secretaries, and some municipalities have committees equal in rank to those of the counties. They direct and supervise the work of local units, which include factory, town, and village primary party organizations. Thus the party reaches the most remote places of the country and is able to control the economic, social, and cultural activities of the population.

In early 1970 it was announced that the party had 1,999,720 members, of whom 43.4 per cent were industrial workers, 26.6 per cent peasants, and 24 per cent office workers and intellectuals

(*Scînteia*, 20 March). As to age groups, at the time of the Tenth Congress 24 per cent of the members were under the age of thirty years, 36 per cent between thirty and forty, and the remaining 40 per cent over forty.

Although peasants comprise 58 per cent of the population, their percentage of party membership is just over one-fourth. This would seem to indicate that the RCP is not overly popular in the rural areas. During 1970, county party organizations made a special effort to enroll peasants. The press reported in general terms that this membership drive was a success, but no detailed figures were given.

Party-State Interlocking Directorate. Following the Soviet example, in Romania a person can hold simultaneously a high party position (membership on the Central Committee, Standing Presidium, Executive Committee, or Secretariat) and a high state post (on the Council of State, Council of Ministers, Supreme Court, and so on). This practically creates a personal union between party and state. Meetings of the Council of Ministers are held together with the Executive Committee of the party, with most of those in attendance belonging to both bodies. In high-level official dealings with other communist-ruled states, Romania normally is represented by Ceauşecu as RCP secretary-general and Mauer as premier, similarly to Brezhnev and Kosygin representing the Soviet Union.

Domestic Affairs. The preeminent event in Romania during 1970 was the disastrous May flood. Torrential rains in Transylvania and Eastern Moldavia suddenly swelled the rivers. The Tissa and Danube inundated large agricultural areas. More than 200 persons drowned, and almost 1,000 localities were flooded. About 300,000 persons were evacuated, and more than 80,000 had their homes completely destroyed. About two million acres of agricultural land came under water, including about 600,000 acres of crops which were a total loss. Some 40,000 head of cattle drowned. Total material losses were estimated at close to a billion dollars.

The government undertook energetic relief action, assisted also with money, medicines, supplies, and relief personnel arriving from foreign countries. Salaries to persons who had lost the possibility to work were continued, and financial help was made available for flood victims. Ceauşescu and other high-level officials visited the damaged areas, taking measures on the spot to alleviate suffering. Nevertheless, it will take years before these areas can return to normalcy.

The second concern of the population, particularly before the flood, was the fear of a Soviet invasion. This did not find its expression in the press or in public speeches. Ceauşescu's sudden trip to Moscow, during the flood disaster, and the lack of any explanation in the press as to what had occurred in Moscow during this visit, greatly increased rumors about the Russian danger. Ceauşescu's resistance to Soviet pressure has met with considerable approval. The general anti-Soviet feeling of the masses is an asset in Ceauşescu's opposition to Moscow. All Soviet attempts in past years to find a Romanian Husák (leader of Czechoslovakia), who would be willing to create a pro-Soviet faction have backfired and strengthened Ceauşescu's hand. Any Romanian communist who dared to oppose him would have to face a hostile populace. There exists a paradoxical situation in Romania, where Soviet attempts to weaken Ceauşescu's leadership have in fact strengthened it.

The three plenary meetings of the RCP Central Committee in 1970 were almost exclusively concerned with reorganization of agricultural administration, new methods for computing wages in cooperative and state farms, regulations concerning labor discipline, and finally the next five-year economic plan (1971-75). The fear of a Russian invasion and then the flood did not give the population a chance to display its grievances against the restrictions on civil liberties that have continued in Romania since the Stalin era.

The December disturbances in Poland had an echo in Romania. In his speech concluding the

16 December plenum of the Central Committee, Ceauşescu said, without mentioning the Polish events:

> I spoke about the activities and obligations of the party organs in the counties and in local councils. I would like to mention only that in keeping busy with the problems of production and other obligations, they should not forget for a moment their obligation to assure adequate supplies of commodities to the population.... I would like to inform the plenary session that we dispose of reserves and greater stocks than last year of meat, fish, fats, potatoes, rice and other alimentary products. . . . We were able to double these amounts as compared with last year. . . . The main problem is now to improve the distribution . . . and the organs which take care of providing supplies must pay the greatest attention to adequate service to the population. (*Scînteia*, 18 December.)

Ceauşescu clearly had former Polish communist leader Gomulka's mistakes in mind.

By such statements, expressing concern for the well-being of the population, with unexpected appearances on inspection trips to distant counties, to cooperative farms, market places, factories, and building sites of industrial projects—all widely publicized in the party press—Ceauşescu has been able to gain recognition and popularity among the masses. This contributed to a distinct feeling of stability and internal peace in Romania during 1970.

Cultural Affairs.   While cultivating general popularity, the Ceauşescu regime during 1970 hardened its attitude toward the previous relative liberalization in the cultural life of the country. Whereas progressive writers attempted to prevent a return to dogmatism and "social realism" in literature, by pointing to the errors of the 1950's, the RCP tried to discredit to some extent the literature of the more liberal 1960's. The principal literary review issued by the Writers' Union, *Romania Literară*, lost some of its earlier courage in tackling these controversial problems in a liberal spirit. Other, smaller reviews have overtaken it in this respect. It is highly significant that certain writers continue to voice different opinions and dare to oppose the party line. They also use the relative freedom of speech available to them to expose the strong dogmatic elements from the Stalin era which still prevail in the mass media and in education.

Religious Affairs.   The Department of Religious Cults was reorganized in October 1970, providing a certain streamlining in relations with the Orthodox and Catholic religious hierarchies.

In cooperation with the Synod of the Romanian Orthodox Church, late in 1969 the Council of State "withdrew recognition" from the Orthodox Bishop of Orades, Valerian Zaharia. No detailed reasons for this measure were given in the Romanian press. Only the decree, as published in the *Buletinul Oficial* (27 December), was reprinted subsequently.

Labor Discipline.   For almost twenty years, following the approval of the first "socialist" Labor Code, persuasion and education were used to ensure labor discipline in Romania. This was changed in 1969, when the first punitive measures for violations were introduced. Also some limitations were placed on the right to choose a place of work. Obviously these first coercive measures did not produce expected results in improving the "social behavior" of the working class, since early in 1970 three regulatory acts were adopted in order to counteract violations of labor discipline: (1) Decree no. 142 increases fines up to 10,000 lei for violations of labor contracts, (2) Decree no. 148 obliges employees to pay damages for which they are responsible, and (3) Law no. 1 on labor organization and discipline in socialist industrial and agricultural production units permits management to reduce wages when standards of behavior at work have not been met. Finally, in June, a "guideline" was issued to regulate the administration of Law no. 1, above. These new regulations introduced an important innovation: appeals from administrative decisions in labor discipline cases are now adjudicated by courts and not by higher administrative authorities, as had been the case heretofore.

In preparing the public for these new coercive measures during the first months of the year, the press published many articles on violations of labor discipline in industrial enterprises and how these affected production efficiency. The described examples were quite impressive and prepared the public for the radical steps taken later.

Agriculture. The May flood and its damages to agricultural areas destroyed all hopes for a 1970 increase in agricultural production. The considerable loss of cattle reduced meat and dairy product supplies. The government had to rely on its reserves of foodstuffs to make up for these deficiencies.

Figures published about the efficiency of the agricultural labor force during 1969 showed that productivity of cooperative and state farms was far below comparable figures for Bulgaria, Czechoslovakia, and Hungary. Although farmers in four of Romania's 39 counties worked between 206 and 271 days, in five other counties the average fell below 100 work days. The remaining time of the farm workers was spent on their own plots and on handicrafts, and as hired labor in neighboring towns and cities. These figures were published in connection with party and government measures to strengthen labor discipline. At the same time, new regulations were issued concerning wages for agricultural work. A monthly minimum wage of 300 lei (about $50 at the official exchange rate) was established for peasants on cooperative and state farms. Higher wages can be obtained by fulfilling prescribed work norms, and bonuses received for hours and work days above the norm. Also old age and disability pensions for agricultural workers were increased to 300 lei per month, additional allocations were provided for children.

The draft bill on Organization of Agricultural Production and Labor was published in the daily press (*Scînteia*, 27 June) for "public debate." It produced some critical remarks by lower-echelon party members and administrators of cooperative farms. The July plenum of the Central Committee discussed and approved the draft, and two days later the Grand National Assembly voted it into law. Only its application will show whether it meets the expectation of its initiators and at the same time fulfills the aspirations of the peasantry. It seems that the deficiencies of agricultural production in Romania were the result of low investments for production of inexpensive fertilizers, agricultural machinery, and irrigation of farmland. The press mentioned that investments in Bulgaria and Hungary for irrigation are several times higher than in Romania. Investments of state funds for industry were comparatively much higher than for agriculture. The economic plan for 1971-75 has considerably increased planned investments for agriculture and reduced the former disproportion.

Industry. Figures for industrial production in 1969 show that its value increased by 10.7 per cent over the previous year to a total of 265 billion lei (about $46 billion). Chemical and steel industries showed the best results. In general, industrial enterprises met their goals, and many of them produced more. A growing part of this industrial production is being exported. The average monthly wage in industry increased by 4.2 per cent during 1969. Participation of party organs in supervision over industrial production was broadened and strengthened by various regulations. Provisional production figures for the first six months of 1970 showed that the planned increase of production had been fulfilled, despite the negative influence of the May flood. It remains to be seen whether the considerable flood damage to highways and railroads (some 1,000 bridges were destroyed or damaged) affected production in the second half of 1970. The press dispensed much information on the progress of the construction of the iron-steel combine at Galaţi and a dam and power plant on the Danube River at the Iron Gates.

Foreign Trade. The official news agency Agerpres announced that foreign trade in 1969 increased by 8.4 per cent for exports and 6.5 per cent for imports. Later, the Romanian *Statistical Yearbook* for 1969 published the following breakdown of Romania's exports during that year:

Commodity	Percentage
Machinery and machine tools	21.7
Fuel, mineral raw materials, metals	20.6
Industrial consumers' goods	15.7
Food products	14.2
Raw materials of vegetable and animal origin	10.3
Chemical products	7.1

In 1969, exports totaled 9,799 million lei and imports 10,443 million. The trade deficit thus was 644 million lei. This showed a slight improvement over past years. Of this trade, 55.1 per cent was with communist-ruled states and 44.9 per cent with "capitalist" states.

The sales price of Romanian products abroad appeared to be profitable. Merchandise f.o.b. at the Romanian border and with an internal sales price of 100 lei was sold abroad for $5.00. Whereas the artificial exchange rate is six lei to the dollar, the sales abroad brought 20 lei for the dollar. (The black market dollar in Bucharest reaches 50 lei.)

Romania concluded trade agreements in 1970 with several noncommunist countries, showing an interest in expanding trade which produces convertible exchange values for products needed from the West.

Trade with the Soviet Union is planned to increase during 1971-75 by 35 per cent over the 1966-70 period. Despite strained political relations, agreements were concluded with the Soviet Union for the delivery to Romania of an atomic power plant and several factories.

Foreign Relations. Romania in 1970 manifested extraordinary activity in expanding and strengthening its relations with foreign countries on all continents. Corneliu Mănescu's former presidency of the U.N. General Assembly opened new avenues for Romanian diplomacy which he skillfully exploited. Not mentioning visits to the Soviet Union and other communist-ruled states, Mănescu traveled to Paris, Washington, Vienna, and several African capitals. Foreign trade minister Corneliu Burtica visited Japan, Australia, and several African countries, and state and party delegations were sent to Latin America and practically every country in Europe. Romania's peculiar relations with the U.S.S.R. and its resistance to Soviet pressure, widely publicized by the world press, probably contributed to the good will shown to Romanian emissaries and Ceauşescu himself in noncommunist capitals.

Relations with Communist-Ruled States

Soviet Union. The strained relations between the Soviet Union and Romania since the invasion of Czechoslovakia in 1968, and Romania's consistent effort to remain detached from obediently following Soviet dictates, placed the country at the beginning of 1970 in a peculiar, Yugoslav-like situation. Ceauşescu's ability to abstain from the "brotherly intervention" in Czechoslovakia, Romania's independent policy in the Council for Mutual Economic Assistance (CMEA), and its open friendly relations with Communist China were some of the characteristics of this situation. The Soviet Union, in turn, did not refrain from showing its displeasure with the behavior of the Romanians. Brezhnev's absence from the twenty-fifth anniversary celebrations of Romania's independence in August 1969 definitely had been an expression of its displeasure.

In 1970 Ceauşescu and his top associates visited Moscow on several occasions. The Romanians participated in April in the Lenin Centenary festivities, and Ceauşescu in his two speeches in Moscow skillfully used quotations from Marxist-Leninist writings to show that his demand for sovereign independence and his rejection of interference "by outsiders" in internal affairs of his country had sound foundations in these scriptures. During the catastrophic flood in May, Romanian party leaders left suddenly for Moscow and had important conversations with their

Soviet counterparts. Only later did it become known that during this visit the signing of the much delayed Romanian-Soviet friendship treaty was agreed upon for 6-7 July 1970, with Brezhnev to head the Soviet delegation.

This treaty had been negotiated and initialed in June 1968, before the Soviet-led invasion of Czechoslovakia. It renewed the 1948 treaty, concluded shortly after the communists had consolidated their domination over Romania. Although scheduled to expire in February 1968, it continued in force under an automatic five-year renewal clause. Eventually signed on 7 July 1970, without Brezhnev's participation, this is the only friendship treaty concluded by the Soviet Union in Eastern Europe that took three years from initialing to signing. After the treaty had been initialed with Romania, Brezhnev announced Soviet rights to intervene in countries of the communist bloc, if "socialist achievements" were endangered. A similar friendship agreement with Czechoslovakia, signed two months earlier, contained a clause embodying the "Brezhnev doctrine." Romania—according to some reports—refused to renegotiate the treaty and insisted that it be signed in the same form in which it had been initialed. It is noteworthy that the Soviet-Czechoslovak treaty was signed by the party leaders and the premiers of both countries, whereas the Soviet-Romanian treaty was signed only by the premiers and thus was reduced to a traditional state act by the elimination of party aspects.

In their speeches following the signing of the treaty, Premiers Maurer and Kosygin placed their emphases on different features of the document. Maurer, referring to principles of friendship and cooperation which should govern relations between both states, said: "As the treaty stipulates, the basis of relations between our countries is formed by the principles of sovereignty and national independence, equality of rights and noninterference into internal affairs, and reciprocal favors. The observation of these principles is at the present time a condition *sine qua non* for development of normal relations among all states, as well as a condition for maintaining and strengthening peace. Facts and events in international life show that any infringement on these principles creates smolderings of tension and even conflict that can seriously threaten peace." (*Scînteia*, 8 July.) This statement indicates clearly that Romania, even after signing the friendship treaty, rejected the Brezhnev doctrine.

Kosygin in his reply emphasized the need for internationalist solidarity: "The people, the communist parties, and the governments of the Soviet Union and of Romania express in this treaty their decision to consolidate and extend relations of friendship and multilateral cooperation, strengthen internationalist solidarity among socialist states, and unify their efforts toward the defense of peace in the entire world and the security of nations against aggressive forces of imperialism and reaction." He went on to elaborate on the "defense of socialist achievements" (a term borrowed from the Brezhnev doctrine) and warned against the slightest dissension in relations among communist states, since it would be exploited by adversaries seeking to spread discord throughout the "socialist community." (*Ibid.*)

The afternoon of 7 July, after signing the treaty, there took place in Bucharest a "meeting of friendship" at which Maurer and Kosygin again were the main speakers. Their remarks—dealing with the history of Soviet-Romanian relations after the Second World War and economic cooperation between both countries—were devoid of political statements. The usual receptions took place, but did not follow the "comradely" pattern of other East European capitals.

The absence of Brezhnev from the ceremony was not mentioned by the Romanian press. Kosygin in a speech apologized that the party leader could not come because of health reasons. If there is truth in the reports by Western correspondents in Moscow that Brezhnev attended a soccer match on the day the treaty was signed, his absence may have been significant. His plans to go to Bucharest were cancelled at the last moment, and Premier Maurer welcomed the Soviet delegation at the airport.

Two days after the friendship treaty was signed, Ceauşescu disclosed to a Central Committee plenum the results of conversations at Moscow in May: "I would like to mention that these discussions took place in a working atmosphere. As a result, we reached the joint conclusion to work for the continuous development of relations between our parties and countries on the basis of Marxist-Leninist principles, proletarian internationalism, equality of rights, mutual respect, and noninterference in internal affairs." Discussing the treaty, Ceauşescu stated: "[It] opens up new perspectives for the continuous development of collaboration, friendship, and alliance between our parties and countries. It promotes the principles of relations of a new type between the socialist countries, based on Marxism-Leninism, on proletarian internationalism, on equality of rights and noninterference into internal affairs, on respect for national independence and sovereignty, on mutual aid and reciprocal advantage." (*Ibid.*, 10 July.)

Ceauşescu referred three times in this speech to the same formula for relations with other states "without regard for differences in their social order." Maurer used it in his speech after signing the treaty, and before the year was over, Ceauşescu and his cohorts had repeated it on many occasions. Such reiteration, this phrasing of basic principles of Romania's relations with other states can be considered the "Ceauşescu formula," in contrast to the "Brezhnev doctrine."

The consistent use of the "Ceauşescu formula," without reaction on the part of the Soviet leadership, can be interpreted in two ways. Either the May conversations in Moscow forced the U.S.S.R. to refrain from application of the Brezhnev doctrine to Romania, or relations remained tense with the friendship treaty serving as a smoke screen to hide a new developing split between the two countries.

Communist China. On two occasions the press reported visits in 1970 by official Romanian delegations to the Democratic People's Republic of Korea and the Chinese People's Republic. North Korea consistently took precedence over China in press reports, and the Romanians visited first Pyongyang and then Peking. A delegation in early June was led by Emil Bodnăraş, member of the RCP Executive Committee, whom Ceauşescu uses often as a special envoy to foreign countries. The other delegation in mid-July was headed by Ion Ioniţa, minister of defense. In addition to these delegations, several journalists and lesser officials visited Peking. The visit to Peking of foreign trade minister Burtica in March received less publicity in the Romanian press. On this occasion a Romanian-Chinese commercial treaty was signed. Due to shipping difficulties, it has remained a dead letter.

In his address at the Lenin Centenary in Bucharest on 17 April, Ceauşescu mentioned "the particular international importance of the triumph by the people's revolution in China and the emergence of the great socialist Chinese state" (*Scînteia*, 18 April). He then recalled his strong statements concerning party unity made at the June 1969 Moscow Conference and complained that no progress in this matter had been made since that time. At the meeting of delegations from 79 communist parties held in Moscow on 22 April to celebrate the Lenin Centenary, he emphasized that Romania was determined to develop good relations with "all socialist countries," obviously alluding to China.

Ceauşescu reported to a plenum of the Central Committee about the Romanian visit to Peking: "We especially appreciated the visit by the delegation of our party and state to the Chinese People's Republic, and particularly the discussions that took place with comrades Mao Tse-tung, Lin Piao, Chou En-lai, K'ang Sheng, and other leaders of the Communist Party of China and the Chinese state. On this occasion, it became evident that the relations between our parties and countries have developed fruitfully, that both sides intend to work in this direction which corresponds with the interests, not only of our parties and countries, but also with the common cause of socialism and peace in the world." (*Ibid.*, 10 July.)

Consistently drawing attention to Romania's good relations with China, Ceauşescu probably is aware of the displeasure created in Moscow. He must realize also that this strengthens his support by other communist parties that are critical of Soviet relations with China, particularly the powerful Italian and French parties.

The Eastern Bloc.   Relations with Bulgaria, Czechoslovakia, the German Democratic Republic, Hungary, and Poland during the first half-year appeared ostentatiously cool. On several occasions the Romanian press answered attacks in Polish and East German newspapers in a tactful manner. It was obvious that the Moscow-subservient parties expected a Romanian-Soviet crisis. The atmosphere changed after the signing of the treaty in July. Ministerial-level visits from the above-mentioned countries to Bucharest started after the summer vacation period. All had friendship agreements with Romania that expired in 1968 or 1969, but none renewed them until after the Soviet Union set an example.

Treaties with Poland (12 November) and Bulgaria (19 November) were signed during visits of Gomułka and Cyrankiewicz to Bucharest and of Ceauşescu to Sofia. The Poles and Bulgarians had to accept the "Ceauşescu formula" in its exact wording, taken from Romania's treaty with the Soviet Union. Ceauşescu repeated the formula in his speeches after the signing of both agreements, and it appeared in official press releases (*Scînteia*, 13, 14, 20, and 22 November). Whereas the treaty with Poland was later discussed favorably in the Romanian press, the Bulgarian treaty produced no comments. Bulgarian leader Zhivkov's servility toward the U.S.S.R. and his critical remarks about Ceauşescu during the 1968 invasion of Czechoslovakia obviously had not been forgotten in Bucharest.

The press announced a planned December visit by East German party chief Ulbricht and Premier Stoph to Bucharest. It never took place, and no explanation appeared in Romanian newspapers.

Warsaw Pact.   Early in 1970 an article by Soviet Army General Sergei M. Shtemenko, chief of staff for the Warsaw Pact armed forces, in *Krasnaia Zvezda* (Moscow, 24 January) indicated satisfaction with the unity and cooperation among the pact allies and mentioned "combined" forces. This drew a strong reaction from Ceauşescu. Speaking on 5 February at a meeting of "basic cadres" of the Romanian armed forces ministry, the Romanian leader categorically denied that his country's armed forces were subordinated to any body other than the "Romanian party, government, and Supreme National Command." He continued: "It is impossible to conceive of ceding in any way part, no matter how small, of the right of the party and government to command and lead the armed forces. . . . Development of cooperation among our armies, in accordance with the relations between socialist countries and with the treaties in force, excludes any interference in the internal affairs of another country, or of one or another army cooperating within these treaties." (*Scînteia*, 6 February.) Ceauşescu also emphasized the defensive character of the Warsaw Pact. This statement was later discussed widely in Romanian newspapers and periodicals. The fifteenth anniversary of the pact, on 14 May, offered an occasion to describe Romania's role in the alliance. The *Scînteia* political commentator "V. Illiescu" stated that the pact would be implemented in case of an armed attack in Europe by a state or a group of states against one or several signatories to the pact. He concluded that its "sole objective" was to counter "an imperialist attack in Europe." (*Ibid.*, 14 May.)

On 21 May a meeting of the Warsaw Pact defense ministers took place in Sofia. It discussed "means of strengthening the defense potential of the Warsaw Pact member countries." Romania was represented by its deputy defense minister and chief of staff, Colonel General Ion Gheorghe.

On 21-22 June a meeting of Warsaw Pact foreign ministers took place in Budapest and was attended by Mănescu. The main subject under discussion was the Soviet-proposed conference on European security. Mănescu recommended caution in calling such a conference and demanded that it be well prepared first through diplomatic channels. This advice must have prevailed, since the calling of a conference was postponed.

The annual joint maneuvers of Warsaw Pact forces took place in October in East Germany. At first, both East German and other foreign news agencies announced that Romanian troops were participating. Later, it was made clear by Romania that only a group of staff officers had gone to these exercises as observers. Romanian troops last participated in the joint maneuvers in 1966.

On 2 December the Political Consultative Committee of the Warsaw Pact convened in East Berlin. Ceauşescu led a large Romanian delegation to this meeting, including Bodnăras, Mănescu, and several other high-ranking state officials. The one-day session issued several declarations on current international affairs. (*Scînteia*, 2 and 3 December.)

Council for Mutual Economic Assistance. In expanding its trade with noncommunist states, particularly West Germany, France, and the United States, Romania has departed from its former pattern of trading mainly with the communist-ruled countries. As foreign trade with the West has grown, commercial exchanges with its partners in the CMEA has declined presumably because the West offers Romania better possibilities to strengthen its industrial potential in accordance with real needs and not along CMEA lines. Over the past three years, this trend in Romania's economic policy has been the subject of criticism by its communist partners.

The twenty-fourth CMEA session opened in Warsaw on 12 May. Whereas the previous one in Moscow had been attended by party leaders and premiers, the Warsaw meeting drew only premiers. Romania was represented by Maurer. The main subject under discussion was the need for progressive economic integration among the member states. With the exception of a decision to create a CMEA investment bank, no other important events took place. Romania abstained from joining this bank. According to press reports, Ceauşescu had insisted that decisions should be unanimous—which would have left Romania with veto power over decisions that affected its interests. Romania, however, remained a member of the CMEA Bank for International Cooperation, which handles credits for commercial purposes. The Warsaw meeting also founded an International Association of Shipowners of Socialist Countries," which Romania refrained from joining.

Albania. Relations with Albania were limited but correct. A series of lectures on that country was offered in Bucharest and other Romanian cities. Trade union delegations and youth groups visited Albania. Unconfirmed reports ascribed the reduction of tension between Yugoslavia and Albania to a visit of Bodnaraş with Tito after the former's return from Peking. The growth of Soviet seapower in the Eastern Mediterranean was mentioned as a possible motive for the rapprochement.

Yugoslavia. Close and friendly relations were continued between Romania and Yugoslavia. Besides state and party officials traveling in both directions, Bodnăraş and Yugoslav Premier Mitja Ribičič took vacations in each other's country, conferring with Tito and Ceauşescu respectively. On 3-4 November, Ceauşescu visited Tito in his Slovenian summer residence of Brdo Kranj. The long press release mentioned practically all outstanding international problems as the subject of discussion and agreement by the two leaders. The jointly built power station at the Iron Gates on the Danube approached successful completion as the first turbines and generators began to furnish electric power to both sides. This is one of the few joint industrial projects between communist-ruled states that is being completed without friction.

Relations with Non-Communist States

United States. The highlight of 1970 was the fifteen-day visit by Ceauşescu to the United States on 12-27 October. The Romanian press contained log-type descriptions and many pictures of this sojourn, particularly of the receptions in Washington. Ceauşescu had conversations with

President Nixon and Secretary of State William Rogers. Foreign Minister Mănescu, who accompanied Ceauşescu, had separate conversations with Rogers and other high officials. During his trip to the West Coast, Ceauşescu inspected agricultural and food-processing machinery, visiting several factories and farms. The Romanian press emphasized that the conversations with Nixon and Rogers dealt with current international affairs and contributed to a better understanding of current problems.

Mănescu came to the United States in June to participate in the anniversary celebration of the United Nations at San Francisco. On this occasion, he visited President Nixon in San Clemente. He expressed thanks for American relief to the victims of the flood which was more than double the combined aid received from the Soviet Union and China.

The visit of "Apollo 12" astronauts in Romania received much attention in the press. The crowds at the airport and on Bucharest streets gave them an enthusiastic reception.

France. In January 1970 the French finance minister, Valery Giscard d'Estaing, arrived in Bucharest to sign a trade agreement for 1970-74 and to attend the second session of the mixed Romanian-French commission on economic, scientific, and technical cooperation. Also a 1970 trade protocol was signed, under which Romania will export to France products of its metallurgical industry, tractors, machine tools, and electric motors as well as foodstuffs. Ceauşescu's visit to France in June was rather of a ceremonial nature and offered him an occasion for conversations at the highest French level.

Austria. Ceauşescu was in Austria on 21-25 September to repay last year's visit by the Austrian president to Bucharest. On this occasion a long-term trade agreement for 1971-75 and a consular treaty were signed.

Turkey. The visit of Turkey's president Cevdet Sunay on 13-17 April contributed to strengthening of relations and prepared an extension of trade between both countries.

Iran. The visit of the Shah of Iran in Romania at the end of June offered an occasion to discuss the political situation in the Middle East and also to prepare for more extensive trade relations.

Africa. In 1970 Romania showed an increased interest in the underdeveloped African countries. Ceauşescu visited Morocco and had conversations with the king and his ministers. Foreign Minister Mănescu visited Congo-Brazzaville, Nigeria, Congo-Kinshasa, Burundi, Tanzania, and the Malagasy Republic during May. The minister of foreign trade, Burtica, traveled to Kenya, Tanzania, and Zambia. These Romanian visits were reciprocated by a host of African cabinet members. Among the more prominent guests in Bucharest should be mentioned Jean Bedel Bokassa, president of the Central African Republic, and Joseph Mobutu, president of Congo-Kinshasa.

In particular, Mănescu's visit to Congo-Brazzaville, the first "people's republic" in Africa, was broadly commented upon by the Romanian press. Romania's interest in expanding relations with African countries stems from their economic importance as producers of raw materials (e.g., ores, oil) and as possible markets for Romania's growing industrial productivity. Trade agreements with several African countries were signed on occasion of the visits, but appeared to have insignificant practical value because of prohibitive shipping costs.

Trying to establish broader relations with African countries in the future, the Romanian government granted stipends to more than 400 students from African countries who study the Romanian language and complete their education at Romanian universities and specialized institutes.

International Party Contacts. Top leaders from at least thirty communist parties in Western Europe, Scandinavia, Latin America, the Orient, and Africa paid visits to Romania and were lavishly received. Ceauşescu found time to see almost all of them, and the Romanian press published reports and pictures about these visits. This was another avenue for recruiting allies in the Romanian demand for party independence and noninterference with internal affairs of communist-ruled states. Particularly the visit of Enrico Berlinguer, deputy to the ailing Italian Communist Party chief Luigi Longo, and that of several French Communist Party officials received extensive attention in the press; their statements supporting the "Ceauşescu formula" were widely publicized.

The RCP eagerly reciprocated these visits, and prominent members were dispatched to practically all congresses of communist parties in noncommunist countries that took place during 1970. Romanian youth delegations were sent to several meetings of other communist youth organizations.

Publications. The official organs of the RCP Central Committee are the daily newspaper *Scînteia* and the monthly ideological review *Lupta de Clasă*, both published in Bucharest.

W. S. S.

UNION OF SOVIET SOCIALIST REPUBLICS

The Communist Party of the Soviet Union (Kommunisticheskaia Partiia Sovetskogo Soiuza; CPSU) traces its origins to the 1 March 1898 organizational meeting of the All-Russian Social Democratic Labor Party. This so-called First Congress had very little influence, because most of the participants were arrested immediately after its adjournment. More accurately, the genesis of the CPSU can be found in the split of the All-Russian Social Democratic Labor Party into Bolshevik and Menshevik factions at the Second Congress held at Brussels in July 1903. After the 1917 Revolution, the Bolsheviks, led by Lenin, declared themselves the "All-Russian Communist Party (Bolsheviks)". When the Union of Soviet Socialist Republics was adopted as the name of the country in 1925, the party became the "All-Union Communist Party (Bolsheviks)." The party adopted its present name at its Nineteenth Congress, in 1952. The CPSU is the only legal political movement in the U.S.S.R.

The structure of the CPSU parallels the administrative organization of the Soviet state. At the top of the party hierarchy, in theory, is the All-Union Congress, which according to the party statute is supposed to meet every four years. Between congresses, the highest representative organ is the Central Committee. Real power within the party remains concentrated in the Politburo, the highest policy-making organ, and in the Secretariat and the Central Committee departments which are charged with implementation of policy. Below the national level are the 14 union republic committees, followed by province committees, city committees, and urban and rural borough committees. At the grass roots are the primary party organizations.

By early 1970, party membership had passed 14 million, according to the general secretary, Leonid I. Brezhnev (*Pravda*, 22 April). A year earlier, a figure of 13,775,000 was reported (see *YICA*, 1970, p. 85). Late in 1970, during a visit to Italy, Politburo member Arvids J. Pelshe stated: "There are at present in the U.S.S.R. some 14,254,000 communists" (*L'Unità*, Rome, 24 November). Despite admonitions against excessive recruitment in the fall of 1969, pressures for recruitment apparently were high, presumably to increase representation from local party organizations at the forthcoming Twenty-fourth Congress, scheduled to open on 30 March 1971. The journal of the Central Committee (*Partiinaia zhizn*, no. 17, 1970) complained about heavy recruitment by some province committees which increased their numbers 35 to 45 per cent during the first half of 1970. The CPSU continued, however, to be an elite group, enrolling fewer than 6 per cent of the population. According to the census of 1970, the population of the U.S.S.R. is 241,748,000 (*Pravda*, 19 April).

Organization and Leadership. The formal structure of the CPSU underwent slight modification during 1970. At the top, the Central Committee and its executive organs, the Politburo and Secretariat, remained stable. In April 1966 the Twenty-third Congress elected 195 full and 165 alternate members to the Central Committee. At the end of 1970, six members had been added, while at least fourteen had died and had not been replaced. The current Central Committee is representative of the most important functional groups in Soviet society. Full-time party apparatus workers and government officials make up 85 per cent of the committee. The remaining 15 per cent is drawn from among the scientific and artistic intelligentsia, elder statesmen, industrial workers, and collective farmers. Ethnically, the party as a whole is overwhelmingly Slavic: Russians, Ukrainians, and Belorussians comprise 80 per cent of the membership. These groups furnish 87 per cent of the full and candidate members of the Central Committee.

The Politburo, the highest executive organ of the CPSU, remained unchanged in its membership during 1970. The eleven full members were Leonid I. Brezhnev, Andrei P. Kirilenko, Alexsei N. Kosygin, Kiril T. Mazurov, Arvids J. Pelshe, Nikolai V. Podgorny, Dmitri S. Polianskii, Alexander N. Shelepin, Piotr Ye. Shelest, Mikhail A. Suslov, and Gennadi I. Voronov. Candidate members were I. V. Andropov, P. N. Demichev, V. V. Grishin, D. A. Kunaev, P. M. Masherov, V. P. Mzhavanadze, S. R. Rashidov, V. V. Shcherbitskii, and D. F. Ustinov.

Half of the Politburo also belonged to the Secretariat. These were the general secretary, Brezhnev, together with Demichev, Kirilenko, Suslov, and Ustinov. The others in the 10-man Secretariat were Ivan V. Kapitonov, Konstantin F. Katushev, Fedor D. Kulakov, Boris N. Ponomarev, and Mikhail S. Solomentsev.

The Secretariat actively supervises the 25 to 30 departments of the Central Committee. These parallel the major political, economic, and cultural institutions of the Soviet government. The most significant change in department personnel in 1970 was the resignation or removal of V. I. Stepakov as head of the Propaganda Department in connection with his rumored appointment (subsequently proven false) as ambassador to China. At the end of 1970 there was no public indication as to his successor in the Central Committee apparatus. (See below, "Relations with Communist China and Asia.")

In the 14 union republics there were no changes of first secretaries of the republic parties. At the end of 1970 these were Anton I. Kochinian (Armenia), Geidar A. Aliev (Azerbaidzhan), Piotr M. Masherov* (Belorussia), Ivan G. Kabin (Estonia), Vasilii P. Mzhavanadze* (Georgia), Dinmukhamed A. Kunaev* (Kazakhstan), Turdakun U. Usubaliev (Kirghizia), Augustus E. Voss (Latvia), Antanas J. Sniechkus (Lithuania), Ivan I. Bodiul (Moldavia), Dzhabar Rasulov (Tadzhikistan), Mukhamednazar Gapurov (Turkmenistan), Piotr Ye. Shelest* (Ukraine), and Sharof R. Rashidov* (Uzbekistan). Those indicated by an asterisk were also candidate members of the Politburo.

A purge of a republic party structure occurred in Azerbaidzhan, where the secretary in charge of agriculture was dismissed in March and the chairman of the People's Control Committee in May; in the months following, the purge reached down into the city and borough committees. Another notable change at the republic level was the dismissal, in June, of the chairman of the Moldavian Council of Ministers, A. F. Diorditsa, and of the head of the republic committee's Agricultural Department for economic failures. Among the important changes at the province level were the promotions, in April, of L. N. Efremov, first secretary of Stavropol, to deputy chairman of the State Committee for Science and Technology, and T. I. Sokolov, the Orel first secretary, to first deputy chairman of the State Planning Committee. A significant change was the appointment of V. S. Tolstikov, first secretary of the Leningrad province committee, as ambassador to China.

Among CPSU auxiliary organizations, 1970 was marked by the Sixteenth Congress of the Communist Youth League (Komsomol), which opened in Moscow in May. The congress was addressed by Brezhnev, who described in familiar terms the tasks of the Komsomol in the moral upbringing and labor mobilization of Soviet youth (*Pravda*, 27 May). The report of the Komsomol's first secretary, E. Tiazhelnikov, indicated the extent to which the party continues to support its youth program. The Komsomol, for example, publishes 226 newspapers and magazines for its 27 million members, with its daily *Komsomolskaia pravda* enjoying a circulation of eight million. While the Central Committee report expressed general satisfaction with the role of the Komsomol in the CPSU's mobilization and control of the economy, Tiazhelnikov was critical of its work in higher education—reflecting the troubled relationship between the CPSU and the young intelligentsia. The congress replaced six of the nine men on the Komsomol Secretariat (*Pravda*, 31 May).

Domestic Views and Policies. During 1970 the relative stability of formal CPSU structure contrasted with evidence of diversion and conflict in the collective leadership and with the wide gamut of troublesome political, economic, and cultural issues which confronted it. Among the most important problems was that of the distribution of power within the highest levels of the party—possibly connected with the delay, within statutory limits, in convening the Twenty-fourth Congress, due to have been convened in 1970. Closely related to the policy decisions to be adopted by the next party congress, however, was the issue of the CPSU general secretary's role in the structure of power.

There were mounting indications of an effort by Brezhnev to break through the web of oligarchical restraints which has prevailed in the Soviet leadership since Khrushchev's ouster in October 1964. Brezhnev's speech of 15 December 1969 to the Central Committee plenum and the joint party, state, Komsomol, and trade union letter of January 1970 launched an intense campaign to improve economic performance during the last year of the current five-year plan. Clues appeared throughout 1970 to indicate an increase in Brezhnev's power. During the first four months of 1970, he was the only Politburo member present at military exercises in Belorussia and at the twenty-fifth anniversary of Hungary's liberation. In April he gave three major addresses on Soviet domestic and foreign policy within a week and in May a two-volume edition of his speeches since 1964 appeared—apparently as efforts toward establishing his credentials as an ideological leader. An editorial in *Voprosy istorii KPSS* (no. 7, 1970) declared that the publication of his speeches marked him as a major theoretician. In the nominations for the Supreme Soviet elections in June, Brezhnev was nominated in 33 per cent of the electoral districts, whereas the premier of the U.S.S.R., Kosygin, in second place, was nominated in only 11.8 per cent. These largely symbolic indications of ascendancy were given concrete form when Brezhnev, who does not hold any post in government, gave major speeches at meetings of the Councils of Ministers of the U.S.S.R. and the Russian republic in late May and early June (*Pravda*, 1 June).

Underlying disagreements within the Politburo appear to involve not only substantive issues but timing as well. Repeatedly Brezhnev committed himself to holding the Twenty-fourth Congress of the CPSU in 1970. In his speech on the Lenin Centenary he noted that preparations for the congress and for the ninth five-year plan were drawing to a close and that the leadership was "about to make major new decisions that [would] determine the path of development of the Soviet economy for a considerable period of time" (*ibid.*, 22 April). In early July, Brezhnev still gave the impression that the congress would be held in 1970 (*ibid.*, 3 July). A brief TASS announcement on 14 July, however, revealed that the Central Committee had postponed the congress to 1971. At the same time, the announcement appeared to restore the party-state balance by mentioning that Brezhnev would deliver the political report at the congress and that Kosygin would give the control figures for the ninth five-year plan.

The set-back in July appears only to have slowed the development of Brezhnev's cult. Laudatory references to his wartime record appeared in *Literaturnaia gazeta* (November 4) and *Pravda* (December 27). And at the end of the year, *Partiinaia zhizn* (no. 23), the only prominent CPSU journal that had not yet published a review of Brezhnev's two-volume collection of speeches, finally did so about six months after their appearance.

The problem of basic ideological definition, which has fueled divisions at high levels in the

CPSU, was tackled in a major article by Politburo candidate P. N. Demichev (*Kommunist*, no. 1, 1970) in support of "anti-revisionism"—a cardinal issue in Soviet ideological discussions since the invasion of Czechoslovakia. Demichev's denunciation of political pluralism and "de-ideologization" was echoed by Brezhnev (*Pravda*, 22 April) and Suslov (*ibid.*, 7 November) and repeatedly emphasized by Soviet commentators in a variety of contexts.

If the fundamental fear of the orthodox ideologists was the substitution of a politically neutral science for Marxism-Leninism (cf. M. Iovchuk, *Kommunist*, no. 2), there was also evident concern over the policy implications of other ideological positions. A. G. Titov in *Voprosy istorii KPSS* (no. 6) presented a vigorous attack on those who proposed a reduction in the power of the communist party. That opponents of party controls could be found in the U.S.S.R. was explicitly confirmed by O. Vasilev, who complained about the criticism by some members of the intelligentsia and in particular took note of those economic managers who declared party interference to be incompetent and held that the role of the party ended with the role of the bourgeoisie (*Ekonomicheskaia nauka*, no. 5).

The undercurrents of ideological and policy conflict were in part centered on the meaning of Stalinism. The 1969 edition of the *History of the Communist Party of the Soviet Union* (see *YICA*, 1970, pp. 90-91) not only had minimized Khrushchev's role but considerably softened the treatment of Stalin as a wartime leader. To the growing list of Soviet military men correcting adverse estimates of Stalin's abilities were added Marshal Bagramian (TASS, 28 April) and Marshal Vasilevskii (*Voprosy istorii*, no. 5). In July, without public ceremony, a granite bust of Stalin was unveiled at his Kremlin grave. This act of homage to Stalin did not, however, appear to foreshadow any new major process of rehabilitation.

The most unusual act of de-Stalinization during 1970 was the appearance in the West of a manuscript of "Krushchev's memoirs," reportedly through an intermediary in the KGB (Komitet Gosudarstvennoi Bezopastnoti; Committee of State Security). Published in the United States in serial form by *Life* magazine and as a book, *Khrushchev Remembers*, the work appeared to lack, or to have been cleansed of, any significant information on the politics of the Khrushchev period; nonetheless, it repeated much of the information in Khrushchev's "secret speech" to the Twentieth Congress of the CPSU. It was denounced as "propaganda" by *Izvestiia* (23 November) and its authenticity was challenged by a number of Western specialists on Soviet affairs. Khrushchev himself, in a signed statement, described the memoirs as a "fabrication" (*Pravda*, 17 November). Their existence and their mysterious passage to the West suggest the still Byzantine quality of politics at the highest levels of the CPSU.

Control and Dissent.   As in previous years, the struggle over ideas extended beyond the CPSU and challenged the party's intellectual and political monopoly. Disaffection within segments of the literary and scientific intelligentsia as well as a small but persistent civil rights movement continued in evidence during 1970.

The major events in the politics of Soviet literature involved the editorship of the monthly *Novy Mir* and the awarding of the 1970 Nobel prize for literature to Alexander Solzhenitsyn, the controversial author of *The Cancer Ward, The First Circle,* and *One Day in the Life of Ivan Denisovich.* The reported resignation of Alexander Tvardovskii, editor of *Novy Mir* since 1957, followed the dismissal of four editors associated with his liberal policies. The announcement of the Nobel prize was made in Stockholm on 8 October. Solzhenitsyn, who had stated that he would accept the award there, finally announced on 27 November that he would not attend the ceremony. The furor over Solzhenitsyn was broadened in mid-November by the revelation that the world-famous Soviet cellist Mstislav Rostropovich had written a letter in his defense to four major Soviet newspapers, none of which published it (*New York Times*, 17 November).

The year 1970 also witnessed a growing effort to intensify party controls over the scientific intelligentsia. The relationship of science and technology to Soviet military and economic power is a basic one, and disaffection within the scientific community has important political implications. Efforts to place in a mental asylum Dr. Jaures (Zhores) Medvedev—author of a book critical of Lysenko that was published in the West—were thwarted by the protests of several scientists, including Andrei Sakharov, the Soviet physicist who had helped to create the hydrogen bomb. Less successful was Sakharov's appearance as a witness for the defense in the trial of Pimenov, a Leningrad mathematician who was sent to Siberia for five years for possessing "underground" literature, including the Czechoslovak liberal manifesto *2,000 Words*. Sakharov continued to give evidence of his moral courage in November by his announcement that a group of Soviet scientists had established a "Committee on Human Rights" to foster the observance of legality by the Soviet government.

Details of these cases and others were transmitted to the West through the remarkable illegal "samizdat" publication, *Chronicle of Current Events (Khronika tekushchikh sobytii)*, a bimonthly account of the civil rights movement which has appeared regularly since 1968. The *Chronicle* as well as the party press gave continuing evidence during 1970 that ideological dissent and a more diffuse nationalism in the non-Russian republics would necessitate a direct response from the party apparatus. In January the ideological secretary of the Moldavian party, Dmitri Kornovan, launched a heavy attack on nationalism and the influence of Romania on intellectuals in his republic (*Sovetskaia Moldaviia*, 13 January). In October the CPSU Central Committee made a major effort to tighten controls over scientists by a resolution (*Partiinaia zhizn*, no. 21) on the Lebedev Physics Institute, the prestigious research center employing Andrei Sakharov and Igor Tamm. As 1970 closed, this resolution attacking "unscientific and idealistic concepts of bourgeois scientists" formed a central strand in the ideological campaign preceding the party's Twenty-fourth Congress (*Pravda*, 13 November; S. Pilotovich, *Sovetskaia Belorussia*, 18 November).

The growing concern of the CPSU leadership with dissent and discipline was also evident in the restoration of the Ministry of Justice (*Pravda*, 1 September). The abolition of that government agency in May 1956 had been regarded widely as a measure of de-Stalinization. Its reappearance in the early fall of 1970 indicated a further tightening of controls over the Soviet judiciary. The weaknesses of the judicial system were openly seen in the Leningrad trial of eleven alleged airplane hijackers which was the culmination of an anti-Zionist campaign against Jews seeking to emigrate to Israel. The sentencing to death of two defendants brought forth a worldwide protest organized by Jewish groups which resulted in a reduction of sentences on appeal to the supreme court of the Russian republic (*New York Times*, 31 December). The hearing, reportedly attended by Professor Sakharov, produced the first public reversal by a superior court of a lower court's decision on a matter of such significant political interest.

The Problem of the Economy.   During 1970 the Soviet leadership was required to give primary attention to the problems of economic policy and management raised by the poor economic performance of 1969 and the formulation of allocative policy for the ninth five-year plan. In the wake of the poor harvest, the Soviet growth rate for 1969 was recorded at 6 per cent by official Soviet sources and at less than 3 per cent by a number of Western analysts. The 1969 grain harvest was particularly serious, falling to approximately 160 million tons, far short of requirements. Major difficulties were experienced in the urban sector as a result of shortages in meat and dairy products—a situation which forced the Soviet Union to import large quantities of these products from Western Europe. The result of these pressures was the presentation of a plan which targeted economic growth at 6.3 per cent, the lowest since 1928. Allocations for defense, rising steadily since 1966, were held to a nominal increase and the overt share of defense actually dropped from 13.2 to 12.4 per cent of the total 1970 budget (*Pravda*, 17 December 1969).

The poor showing of the Soviet economy in 1969 could be in large part attributed to the severe winter of 1968 /69. There were, however, more complex conditions underlying the slowdown. Shortcomings in efficiency and technological development have been under discussion in the U.S.S.R. over the past decade and a half. At the beginning of 1970 it seemed clear that the expectations aroused by the historic decisions of the September 1965 Central Committee plenum had failed to materialize. The new system of incentives and operational decentralization had failed to stimulate the expected rise in labor productivity and technical growth—as Professor Birman, a foremost advocate of the reform, admitted (*Literaturnaia gazeta*, 11 February). The system of centralized planning, economic incentives, labor utilization and discipline, capital investment, and managerial efficiency came under renewed discussion.

Discussions on managerial methods ranged from proposals for further decentralization and market concessions (G. Lisichkin, *Novy Mir*, no. 12, 1969) to views of the position taken by central planning officials who argued that "complete enterprise autonomy" would undermine the regulating role of the plan as well as party control (A. Bachurin, *Planovoe khoziaistvo*, no. 11, 1969). Response by the collective leadership to problems of economic policy and growth presumably varied. It was clear that while some members of the Politburo, such as Kiril T. Mazurov, favored extension of the 1965 reform beyond the enterprise (*Pravda*, 5 June 1970), Brezhnev was not specific as to the methods for achieving it, stating that no single method of management was suitable for all conditions (*ibid.*, 22 April) but neither could there be a simple return to Stalinist methods—"past experience is a poor counselor here, and the elaboration of new things calls for persistent effort and searches" (*ibid.*, 14 April).

The situation in farming also evoked serious criticism. In a major speech, G. I. Voronov exposed "serious errors" which included continuing inefficiencies in agricultural management and the use of agricultural resources (*Leninskie znamia*, 24 March). The response of the party leadership at the December 1969 Central Committee plenum had included a sweeping campaign to reduce administrative costs and increase labor discipline as well as uncover the "hidden reserves" in industry and agriculture (V. Garbuzov, *Ekonomicheskaia gazeta*, no. 48, 1969). In respect to agriculture, Brezhnev revealed his plans for dealing with long-term problems at the July plenum of the Central Committee, where he announced plans for a 70 per cent increase in agricultural investment during the ninth new five-year plan (*Pravda*, 3 July). Subsequent postponement of the party congress and the announcement near the end of the year (*Pravda*, 12 December) that the new five-year plan had not been worked up indicated the extent of controversy in the CPSU on resource allocation. Short-term measures to boost agricultural production, adopted in July, included three decrees to raise material incentives and purchase prices (*ibid.*, 18, 19, and 21 July).

The overall economic picture in the Soviet Union improved significantly during 1970. A combination of intensive mobilization, more effective incentives, and favorable weather produced a grain crop estimated at 175 to 180 million tons in the field (*Foreign Agriculture*, U.S. Department of Agriculture, 28 September). An editorial in *Pravda* (12 December) stated: "The largest crops of grain and cotton in our country's entire farming history were grown in 1970." Economic performance showed a significant climb in industry as well, with an official growth rate of 8.3 per cent and a rise of 7.0 per cent in labor productivity (*Ekonomicheskaia gazeta*, no. 7, 1971). There were some dark spots in the generally favorable situation. Suslov, possibly for political reasons, reported in his speech on the anniversary of the revolution that the volume of agricultural produce was still insufficient to meet the country's requirements (*ibid.*, 7 November 1970). The chairman of the State Planning Committee warned that industry was still hampered by fundamental problems of efficiency (*ibid.*, 9 December).

It was clear that 1970 closed without a proper definition of the party's role in the economy. The methods of party mobilization and intervention clearly remained a source of controversy.

During the electoral campaign to the Supreme Soviet, in June, differences of opinion within the political elite were clearly present. I. V. Kapitonov, the CPSU organizational secretary, laid heavy emphasis upon the party's role (*ibid.*, 3 June) and A. J. Pelshe, the chairman of the Party Control Committee, vigorously attacked the managers (*ibid.*, 4 June). On the other hand, D. S. Polianskii affirmed the "clear delineation between party and Soviet functions and those of economic and public bodies and organizations, as Lenin demanded," was the "major requirement for the successful building of communism" (*ibid.*). As the year ended, the issue of whether the credit for the economic upsurge belonged to the CPSU apparatus or to the economic managers became part of the party-state problem. In contrast to an *Izvestiia* editorial (12 December), the main party organ claimed the major share of credit for the party: "The CPSU Central Committee mobilized party and Soviet organizations, economic cadres, and all the working people to struggle for the fulfillment of the 1970 plan, thereby assuring the successful completion of the five-year plan as a whole" (*Pravda*, 12 December).

International Views and Policies. The year 1970 produced no startling innovations in either doctrine or policy applicable to the international communist movement. In a series of speeches Brezhnev laid particular stress on its "anti-imperialist" rather than its "coexistence" aspect. In a comprehensive speech on the Lenin Centenary (*Pravda*, 22 April) he stressed the CPSU's role in world communism. In regard to Eastern Europe, he reiterated the Soviet interpretation of "proletarian internationalism"—the view that national diversity is contained within the framework of common structures and political processes. He predicted that the "general crisis of capitalism" would deepen, although his commitment to an expected world revolutionary upsurge was vague. In this respect, anti-Soviet attacks by the Chinese communists were said to be helping the enemies of socialism.

Brezhnev's general position on strategy appeared to be concensual and framed within the context of former policies. In Eastern Europe the CPSU continued its effort toward political, military, and economic integration of the organizational forms dominated by the Soviet Union. New initiatives were evident in Soviet relations with the Chinese, but with little evident change in the political and ideological dynamics evident in the past decade. A major concern of the CPSU in its relations with the nonruling parties was the control of dissent, much of it stemming from the 1968 invasion of Czechoslovakia. The Soviet approach to direct revolutionary action was highly selective and conditional, and appeared to press for the more cautious united front tactics.

A major factor in the international communist movement continued to be Soviet competition with China—and to a lesser extent, Yugoslavia—for influence in the developing countries. The strains and conflict within the international movement during 1970 were not, however, solely attributable to this competition. Deep cleavages, which the Soviets on the whole successfully contained, stemmed from nationalism, technological and social development within the various national states, and geopolitical position, and from the constraints of internal Soviet politics and pressures derived from the contradictions within U.S.S.R. foreign policy. While cautious and limited advances were evidently made, Soviet control remained far from complete. An empirical and gradualist, if optimistic, note was sounded by Mikhail Suslov in November, when he stated: "The balance of forces in the struggle between socialism and capitalism does not always change as swiftly as we would like, but it is steadily changing in favor of socialism" (*Pravda*, 7 November).

Relations with Communist Parties in Eastern Europe. In 1970 the promotion of political, military, and economic integration under Soviet hegemony remained a central element in Soviet policy toward Eastern Europe. In spite of the continuing Soviet pressure for a general conference on European security, Brezhnev reiterated his basic determination not only to sustain the status quo in Eastern Europe but also to strengthen the Warsaw Pact (*Pravda*, 2 February, 22 April, and 8 May). The themes of ideological defense and anti-imperialism were dominant in the addresses to the International Theoretical Conference, held at Moscow in mid-January, by both Soviet speakers, P. N. Demichev and B. N. Ponomarev. Demichev again enunciated the standard "antirevisionist" and "antinationalist" view that any "rationalization of socialism" in the manner of Czechoslovakia before the invasion would not be tolerated by the Soviet Union (*Pravda*, 21 January; also *Kommunist*, no. 1).

The economic sphere was the area of greatest Soviet success in multilateral integration during 1970. At Budapest, in April, Brezhnev made clear his intention of pressing for further economic integration within the framework of the Council for Mutual Economic Assistance (CMEA) (*Pravda*, 4 April). The eventual goal, according to the Soviet CMEA specialist O. Bogomolov, was a series of steps in which economic integration would lead progressively to the formation of a "world socialist economy" presided over by a "single international political structure" (*Mirovaia ekonomika i mezhdunarodnye otnosheniia*, no. 4).

In pursuit of economic integration, the Soviets took a number of important steps. On 9 January, TASS announced the formation in Moscow of an office for international exchange of information in science and technology. In July, a joint CMEA investment bank began operation, but with a number of decisions subject to the rule of unanimity (*Pravda*, 11 July). Additional steps toward longer-term integration were announced at the CMEA session in May, which approved further integration of long-term planning through coordination of member countries' 1971-75 five-year plans with Moscow. That such measures of economic integration were strongly, if quietly, resisted by some of the countries was evident in an article by the Soviet secretary for the CMEA, N. Faddeev, who specifically disavowed the intention of establishing supranational economic institutions (*Izvestiia*, 27 March).

Soviet promotion of multilateral integration was coordinated with intensive bilateral relations at both party and state levels. A new treaty of friendship and mutual assistance between the U.S.S.R. and Czechoslovakia was signed at Prague which implicitly acknowledged for the first time the validity of the so-called Brezhnev doctrine by stating that the "defense of socialist achievements" was the "common duty of socialist countries" (*Pravda*, 7 May). A similar treaty with Romania was signed at Bucharest in July, but without affirmation of the Brezhnev doctrine (*ibid.*, 8 July). The latter treaty was signed only after automatic extension of the previous treaty, and the occasion was marked by the absence of Brezhnev, who suddenly cancelled his scheduled visit to Bucharest.

An underlying conflict between the Soviets and the East Germans became evident as a result of efforts by the Soviet Union to confirm European boundaries on the basis of provisional settlements existing after the Second World War. In pressing to consolidate its hold over Eastern Europe, to secure wider diplomatic recognition of the German Democratic Republic, and to expand trade and technical assistance for its own lagging economy, the Soviet Union made approaches to West Germany which resulted in a treaty affirming present-day boundaries in Europe (*Pravda*, 13 August). The Soviet-West German treaty evidently aroused long-standing East German anxieties. Soviet and East German party-state talks "at the highest level" were reported in Moscow (*ibid.*, 16 May). The treaty appears also to have been the major topic at meetings on "urgent foreign policy problems" held in Moscow by the Political Consultative Committee (PCC) of the Warsaw Pact organization (*ibid.*, 21 and 27 August). Serious anxieties were also aroused among East German leaders because of formal recognition by West Germany of the Oder-Neisse boundary in a treaty initiated at Warsaw in November (*ibid.*, 13 November), a situation discussed by the PCC in December (*ibid.*, 4 December).

Bilateral interparty relations were still defined in 1970, as previously, by the attitude of the national party toward the CPSU (Ts. Stepanian in *Sovetskaia Rossiia*, 29 January). In Czechoslovakia, the CPSU undoubtedly supported the continuing policy of "normalization" which resulted in expulsion of Alexander Dubček on 26 June from the Central Committee of the Czechoslovak party and his loss of the ambassadorship to Turkey on the following day. TASS (6 January) reported favorably on the Husák policy of strengthening the party's leading role and conducting an exchange of party cards—that is, a purge (see *Czechoslovakia*). At the end of the year a Soviet commentator observed that the exchange of cards had been "benevolent" and "calm," and that some 326,000 of the Czechoslovak party's 1.7 million members had been either suspended or expelled (M. Tiurin in *Izvestiia*, 19 December).

Relations between the CPSU and the Hungarian Socialist Workers' Party (HSWP) took a somewhat different turn. The legitimacy of the new economic policy inaugurated in Hungary in January 1968 appears to have been endorsed by Brezhnev during his visit to Budapest in the spring (*Pravda*, 4 April). At the Tenth Congress of the HSWP, in November, Brezhnev expressed warm approval of Kádár personally, the Hungarian economic reform, and the state of interparty relations (*ibid.*, 25 November). Soviet appreciation for the political orthodoxy of Kádár's regime, however, appears to have been more limited. In reporting on the draft theses issued in advance of the congress, *Pravda* (25 August) edited out those parts of the document endorsing various forms of political liberalization, such as multiple candidacies in elections, secret ballots, and nomination of candidates without prior screening.

The rioting in Poland at Gdynia, Gdansk, and Szczecin in December was at first described as an outburst of "hooliganism and adventurism" (*ibid.*, 18 December). Replacement of the Polish party chief Gomułka by Edward Gierek, however, was speedily approved by Brezhnev (*ibid.*, 22 December).

Soviet efforts at reducing the autonomy of Romania and Yugoslavia met with little success in 1970. Both states continued in opposition to the Brezhnev doctrine and to integration into Soviet international structures. Romania's attitude was evident in her refusal to join the CEMA investment bank. While the commitment of the Romanian leadership to orthodox internal party and economic policies could be seen in party chief Ceauşescu's major speech of 6 March, tensions generated by Romanian foreign policy were evident throughout the year. The formal meeting between the CPSU and the Romanian party leadership in May was described by *Pravda* (20 May) euphemistically as a series of "comradely and candid talks."

Relations with Yugoslavia revealed a similar pattern of dissidence and maneuver. During 1970 interparty polemics were limited, and the League of Communists of Yugoslavia (LCY) was represented at both the Moscow ideological conference in January and the Lenin Centenary rites in April. The role of Yugoslavia as a center in competition with the U.S.S.R. in the "third world" was underlined by the extensive trip by Tito through the Middle East and sub-Saharan Africa in January and by his role at the Lusaka conference. Moreover, Yugoslavia expressed continued concern with Soviet integrationist policies toward Eastern Europe, particularly in the military sphere (Zagreb radio, 13 February). The common interest of Romania and Yugoslavia in maintaining their independence in relation to the U.S.S.R. continued to provide the basic stimulus to a limited rapprochement of both states with Albania and China.

The speech of Albanian leader Enver Hoxha expressing support for Romania's efforts to resist the U.S.S.R. and its political support for Yugoslavia against the Soviets was carried prominently in Chinese media (Peking radio and NCNA, 28 May) and was welcomed by LCY Executive Bureau member Miko Tripalo as a further improvement in Yugoslav-Albanian relations (Tanyug, Yugoslav press agency, 12 June). Chinese cultivation of Yugoslavia and Romania as direct counterweights to the U.S.S.R. increased during the year. On 5 June, Premier Chou En-lai received Bogdan Orešcanin, the new ambassador of Yugoslavia to China, and shortly afterward the establishment of a regular shipping service between their two countries was announced (*ibid.*, 13 June). In mid-June, during a visit to Peking, Vice-President Bodnareş of Romania received public support from Chou En-lai, who assured him that the Chinese people would "always stand together with the Romanian people" (Peking radio, 11 June). In July, after the signing of the Soviet-Romanian friendship treaty, Romanian Defense Minister Ioniţa made a formal visit to Peking.

Relations with Communist China and Asia.   The attitude of the Soviet Union toward China showed considerable variation during 1970. It was clear that the Kosygin-Chou meeting in September 1969 had resulted in subduing the tone and posture of Sino-Soviet confrontations without notably modifying the deep political and ideological conflicts which have divided the two largest communist powers for more than a decade. Major Soviet policy statements during 1970 continued the thrust of the 1969 Moscow Conference toward maintenance of the distinction between interparty and interstate relations, emphasizing the need for improved governmental relations while holding firmly to established ideological and political positions. Brezhnev made this statement at Kharkov in April: "While waging a principled struggle against splitting activity in the international communist movement and the propaganda of anti-Leninist views, we have at the same time constantly striven and are continuing to strive against the transfer of ideological disagreements to interstate relations" (*Pravda*, 15 April). Essentially the same view was expressed near the end of the year by Suslov (*ibid.*, 7 November).

The diplomatic movement at the state level was evident in the shuffling of Soviet personnel. In the spring, unofficial reports from Moscow indicated that V. I. Stepakov, relieved of his post as head of the Central Committee's Propaganda Department, had been appointed as ambassador to China, to succeed Sergei Lapin (who returned to Moscow in 1966). The appointment remained unconfirmed, however, and in September it was announced that V. S. Tolstikov, first secretary of the CPSU Leningrad province committee, would be the ambassador (*ibid.*, 16 September). The appointment of Tolstikov—presumably linked to intraparty tensions preceding the Twenty-fourth Congress—was reciprocated later by the arrival of the new Chinese ambassador (*ibid.*, 24 and 25 November). At the negotiating level, a former intimate of Khrushchev, L. F. Ilichev, replaced V. V. Kuznetsov as Soviet spokesman in the border talks with China.

The exchange of ambassadors and initialing in Peking of a Sino-Soviet trade agreement, the first since 1967 (*ibid.*, 24 November), represented the high point of interstate relationships and undoubtedly represented an upturn from the ominous situation in the spring when Brezhnev charged that China was seized by a "war psychosis" (*ibid.*, 15 April) and other Soviet commentators expressed fear that the whole Chinese population was being mobilized for war under measures which included the digging of trenches and the stockpiling of war materials (*Literaturnaia gazeta*, 14 January). Although this phase faded during the year, the movement toward diplomatic accommodation seemed, nonetheless, frozen. There was little if any prospect of the Soviet Union's assenting to Chinese allegations that disputed borderlands which Tsarist Russia acquired in 1858 and 1860 had been ceded through "unequal" (i.e., "imperialist") treaties. Similarly, the negotiations on border river use which began in July did not appear to be productive.

At the ideological and interparty levels, relations between the CPSU and the Chinese Communist Party (CCP) remained at an extremely low ebb, and their competition for influence in the international communist movement remained intense. The CPSU continued its attacks on Maoism, charging the Chinese leadership with an ongoing persecution of the CCP and its cadres and militarization of the Chinese economy and society (*Pravda*, 5 April; M. Sladovskii in *Izvestiia*, 28 April). China ignored the Lenin Centenary celebrations in the Soviet Union but quickly exploited the Soviet ideological mistake in the centennial "Theses," which attributed to Lenin a position actually held by the Austrian Otto Bauer, his bitter opponent in the Second International (NCNA, 17 April). Full-scale polemics were then resumed in the sweeping attack delivered by an editorial in *Pravda* (18 May). The CCP, during the rest of the year, continued to snipe at the CPSU and its supporters within the movement, charging, for example, that the Polish riots in December were the result of Poland's "revisionism" (*Jen-min jih-pao*, 22 December).

In 1970 the continuing Sino-Soviet antagonism reverberated throughout the international movement as it has done in the past. The CPSU, caught in the dilemma of promoting a revolutionary image in competition with the CCP while avoiding the political consequences of an extreme "adventurist" stance, reacted in various ways to widely diverse conditions. In Vietnam, for example, the CPSU offered strong support to North Vietnam and to the Vietnam Workers' Party (VWP). "No political force other than a Marxist-Leninist party," Brezhnev declared, "could have armed a fighting people with such a clear understanding of the aims of the struggle or so inspired them to a mass exploit" (*Pravda*, 22 April). This general political support was supplemented with more specific aid. During the Lenin Centenary, Brezhnev held extensive talks with Le Duan, first secretary of the VWP (*ibid.*, 25 April). In June the Soviet Union announced additional military and economic assistance to North Vietnam (TASS, 11 June).

In Southeast Asia, the Soviet position was undoubtedly complicated by the overthrow of Prince Sihanouk in Cambodia on 18 March and the subsequent operations there by U.S. and Republic of Vietnam forces. Sihanouk's trip to Moscow on the eve of his overthrow—presumably in search of Soviet support in expelling a reported 40,000 North Vietnamese and National Liberation Front of South Vietnam troops—appears to have been unproductive despite his pledge of friendship with the socialist camp and the Soviet Union (TASS, 17 March). To the overthrow of Sihanouk, coinciding with his arrival in Peking, the initial Soviet response was cautious, and Sihanouk's Chinese-supported government in exile went unrecognized by the Soviet Union and the states of Eastern Europe with the exception of Romania. The incursion into Cambodia by a common enemy did little to draw the Soviets and the Chinese together. The response of both Kosygin (*Pravda*, 5 May) and Brezhnev (*ibid.*, 8 May) to the incursion threatened no direct military action or other sanctions. Opening full-scale polemics in *Pravda* (18 May), the CPSU blamed the Chinese for the U.S. presence in Cambodia and editorially contrasted the moderate tone of Kosygin with the intensity of Chinese propaganda.

The competition of the CPSU with the Chinese communists was also evident in relation to North Korea and Japan. The extensive talks of Brezhnev and Podgorny with a North Korean party-state delegation in April were clearly designed to offset the significant visit of Chou En-lai to Pyongyang the same month (*ibid.*, 24 April). Undertones of the Chinese conflict were also evident in the prominent coverage which *Pravda* gave to the talks between the CPSU and the leaders of the Japanese Socialist Party, which revealed the Soviets' continuing search for a reliable political instrument in Japan to oppose U.S. policies throughout East Asia (*ibid.*, 19 July).

The opening of U.S.—Soviet negotiations in Helsinki on strategic arms limitations in the fall of 1969 subjected the U.S.S.R. to charges of collusion with the West against China and loss of revolutionary elan, a factor which may have contributed to the Soviets' strong "anti-imperialist" posture during the year. The quiet resumption of U.S. and Chinese talks in Warsaw, on the other hand, stimulated corresponding suspicions in Moscow, where the move was perceived as directed against the U.S.S.R. (e.g., *ibid.*, 25 January).

The Chinese resumption of broad diplomatic contacts, which began in 1969 after a three-year period of isolation, clearly pointed toward a more complex phase in the competition between Moscow and Peking. While such an expansion would probably increase Peking's leverage, in 1970 there was little evidence to suggest that the cautious diplomatic openings by China had begun to moderate the essential terms of the Sino-Soviet conflict.

Relations with Communist Parties in Western Europe. The meeting of 28 European communist parties in Moscow on 14-15 January 1970 presumably was the first conference to result from the demands of the Italian and French parties, in June 1969, for better information. Only the Albanian, Dutch, and Icelandic parties failed to attend. The meeting was designed primarily to coordinate the various parties' preparations for the Lenin Centenary and mobilize them on behalf of the Soviet Union's foreign policy objectives, particularly in reference to the proposed European security conference which has been high on the Soviet list of priorities.

The two largest communist parties in Western Europe—those of France and Italy—continued to be a source of preoccupation to the CPSU. The French Communist Party's (PCF) 1968 "reprobation" and "disapproval" of the invasion of Czechoslovakia was limited at its Nineteenth Congress, in February 1970, to "disagreement," and it was emphasized that the French party was determined to "fight uncompromisingly any show of anti-Sovietism whatever its origin" (speech of Georges Marchais, PCF deputy secretary-general, *L'Humanité*, Paris, 5 February). At the same time, however, controversy swirled around Roger Garaudy, a member of the PCF Politburo since 1956 and director of the party's Center for Marxist Study and Research. Garaudy, who has been strongly critical of the invasion of Czechoslovakia and increasingly skeptical as to the relevance of Soviet institutions to French society, was attacked prior to the Nineteenth Congress of the PCF by *Pravda* (15 January) for "breaking completely away from Leninism" and for slandering the CPSU and the Soviet Union. At the congress he was not reelected to the PCF Politburo or Central Committee, and in May he was expelled from the party. Support for Garaudy's views, however, and a certain coordination of dissident extreme left activities appeared to increase during the year. This development, combined with PCF concern to establish closer relations with France's noncommunist left-wing parties, would seem to have motivated the PCF leadership to take a somewhat more critical assessment of its approach to relations with the CPSU (see *France*).

Unlike the PCF, the Italian Communist Party (PCI) continued during 1970 to adhere to its originally expressed views of opposition to the invasion of Czechoslovakia. It also voiced its disapproval of many of the "normalization" measures undertaken by the Czechoslovak party leadership; thus, following Dubček's expulsion from the Communist Party of Czechoslovakia, the PCI secretary-general, Luigi Longo, publicly deplored the action, and Giuseppe Boffa, former Moscow correspondent of the party's newspaper *L'Unità*, paid a glowing tribute to Dubček. Like the PCF, the PCI was also faced with dissidence, the principal source being militants connected with the monthly publication *Il Manifesto* (see *Italy*) who criticized the revolutionary credentials of the PCI leadership and its "subservience" to the Soviets. CPSU spokesmen attacked the views of the *Manifesto* group, linking it with the Garaudy opposition in France (A. G. Titov, in *Voprosy istorii KPSS*, no. 1, 1970), and approved the disciplinary measures applied to its members by the PCI (Moscow radio, 17 February). The evidence of internal opposition and the PCI leadership's ambiguous position vis-à-vis CPSU policy presumably were the major reasons for the extended visit to Italy late in the year by A. J. Pelshe, chairman of the CPSU Party Control Committee (*Pravda*, 4 December).

The Austrian communist party's expulsion in 1969 of Ernst Fischer, who had denounced the "tank communism" of the Soviet-led invasion of Czechoslovakia, resulted in the exodus from the party of an important minority, thereby ending the already minor chances of the party as an electoral machine. (For the CPSU view see *Pravda*, 29 March.) In Finland, internal conflict between a pro-Soviet wing and the dominant centralist faction was in part responsible for the poor showing of the communist party front in the March parliamentary elections. Notwithstanding direct CPSU intervention throughout the year, the Finnish party leadership remained divided and weakened at both intraparty and parliamentary levels.

Among the communist parties in exile, splits over specific questions of strategy and tactics within their own countries and more general questions of the international communist movement continued in 1970. The schism in the Greek communist party on the strategy and tactics of revolution in Greece remained unhealed and engendered a further degree of division within the international movement. The CPSU continued to support the Moscow-based faction led by Secretary-General Kostas Koliyannis. The rival faction—which favors a broad united front approach and is led by Antonis Brillakis and Dimitriou Partsalides, and includes such prominent personalities as Mikis Theodorakis and Manolis Glezos—appears to be supported by the majority of communist militants in Greece and by major communist parties such as those of Italy and Romania.

The invasion of Czechoslovakia continued to figure prominently in Soviet relations with the exiled Communist Party of Spain (PCE). Maneuvering to bury this issue by discrediting the PCE leadership proved counterproductive. The decision on 30 December 1969 by the PCE leadership to expel two pro-Soviet dissidents resulted in an open conflict in which CPSU intervention backfired. During the first half of 1970 the secretary-general, Santiago Carrillo, visited Italy, Romania, and Yugoslavia in what appeared as a move to consolidate support for his views. During the Lenin Centenary celebrations, Carrillo and the Spanish party's delegation had extensive talks at Moscow with Suslov, Kirilenko, and Ponomarev in an effort to resolve this issue (*Pravda*, 3 May), but disagreements were clearly unresolved. The CPSU made a serious effort in June and July to mobilize Spanish communists behind a pro-Soviet platform. Meetings were held in Moscow on 20 June ("Independent Spain" radio, 11 July) and in Prague shortly thereafter (*ibid.*, 7 July). The Moscow meeting, led by PCE Chairman Dolores Ibárruri, fully backed the position advocated by Carrillo; the Prague meeting expressed similar support. In September the PCE expelled five other pro-Soviet dissidents, including Executive Committee member Enrique Líster, a well-known commander in the Spanish civil war. Additionally, the PCE began urging the "normalization" of relations with the Chinese Communist Party leadership (*ibid.*, 3 October).

Relations with the Middle East.   The fast-moving events in the Middle East presented a serious dilemma for the Soviet Union, revolving around such complicated issues as the activities of the commando organizations, arrangements for a cease-fire, civil war in Jordan, the changed situation in the U.A.R. following the death of President Nasser, and the treatment of local communists by the Arab governments.

Following the war in June 1967, Soviet insistence on a political solution of the Arab-Israeli conflict had run strongly counter to the views of the Palestinian Arab resistance fighters, who openly demanded the abolition of the state of Israel by military force. Originally branding the commandos as "irresponsible adventurers," the Soviet Union by 1970 recognized that the growing strength of the liberation movement and the increasing support offered it by the Chinese communists required a modification of its own approach. The new goal was to achieve a balance between support for peaceful political moves and the Soviets' professed championship of the Arab militant cause.

Late in 1969 the Soviet Union had already hinted at its willingness to support the "just struggle" of the Palestinian Arabs, but had refrained from more definite commitments. The first concrete indication of a shift in attitude occurred in February 1970 when Yasir 'Arafat, chairman of the Palestine Liberation Organization (PLO) visited the Soviet Union. His ten-day stay (10-20 February) was officially sponsored by the Soviet Afro-Asian Solidarity Committee. *Pravda* reported tersely on 21 February that the Arab delegation and members of the committee had discussed subjects of mutual interest including "cooperation in the general struggle for the liquidation of the results of Israeli-Imperialist-Zionist aggression and the defense of the legal rights and interests of the Arab people of Palestine."

In spite of the vague pronouncements in Moscow at the time of Arafat's visit, a more obvious sign of a growing Soviet involvement with the Arab guerrilla movement appeared soon after his departure. This was the announcement in March that the communist parties of Syria, Iraq, Lebanon, and Jordan had established their own all-communist commando organization, known as al-Ansar or "The Partisans." The new group—which immediately applied for admission to the unified command of the PLO, but was rejected—could not conceivably have been organized without the consent of the Soviet Union.

When civil war broke out in Jordan and there was serious fighting between government troops and guerrillas, the Soviet Union avoided partisanship and sought to contain and end the struggle, to limit splits in Arab unity, and to prevent Western or Israeli intervention or exploitation of the situation: "The fratricidal conflict in Jordan jeopardizes the vital interests of Jordan, the Palestine resistance movement, and the national liberation struggle of the Arab nations and plays into the hands of the enemies of the Arabs" (TASS, 19 September). Moscow radio saw the events in Jordan as proof of the existence of a "wide imperialist conspiracy" and *Izvestiia* (22 September) considered settlement of the problem of the Palestinian refugees the "basic condition for liquidating the crisis in the Middle East." Even in reporting on the highjackings of Western airliners the Soviet Union showed some leniency. Although *Literaturnaia gazeta* (23 September) condemned the seizure and destruction of the aircraft as terroristic acts which "provoked the just condemnation of world public opinion," a few days later *Pravda* (29 September) toned down the criticism when it questioned to what extent the actions of a comparatively small number of Palestinian partisans were "commensurate and comparable" with the "preparation of a wide military operation on foreign territory, organized by an imperialist power."

In 1970 Middle Eastern developments were most significantly affected by the relationship between the Soviet Union and the U.A.R. This relationship was highlighted by President Nasser's visit to the Soviet Union on 29 June-17 July and his acceptance of U.S. peace proposals—calling for a cease-fire and resumption of the Jarring mediation mission—within a few days after his return home. A communiqué issued at the conclusion of the Moscow talks stressed the unity of the two participant nations and pledged continued coordination of their efforts to secure a political settlement of the Middle Eastern crisis; it stated also that the Soviet Union would continue "necessary assistance" to the Arabs (TASS, 17 July). After Nasser announced acceptance of U.S. Secretary of State Rogers' proposals in a speech in Cairo (23 July) the Soviet Union acclaimed the U.A.R.'s "vital diplomatic victory" and *Pravda* editorialized (30 July) that in advancing a peaceful initiative the U.A.R. had to "overcome extremist attitudes in the Arab world" and displayed "great political courage."

After Nasser's unexpected death on 28 September the Soviet Union was confronted by the problem of safeguarding its political, military, and economic investment in the U.A.R., without appearing guilty of direct interference or offending Egyptian national sentiment. Premier Kosygin attended Nasser's funeral in Cairo, and the end of his stay was marked by a Soviet-Egyptian communiqué which described friendly relations between the two countries as a "permanent factor" unaffected by changes in the international situation or leadership. At the end of the year, efforts for the preservation of such relations were indicated by the intensification of ties between the CPSU and the ASU (the Arab Socialist Union) of the U.A.R. as Central Committee Secretary Boris Ponomarev spent ten days in Egypt to discuss "questions of the further development of interparty relations."

The coordinated Soviet and Egyptian moves in the Middle East were not acceptable to all the Arab governments of the region. When Syria, Iraq, and Algeria reacted critically to Nasser's acceding to peace proposals, the Soviet Union rallied to his support. The Iraqi Ba'th Party was said to have an "incomprehensible attitude" (*Pravda*, 1 August) which did not assist the real struggle against the aggressor. Moscow radio (4 August) condemned 'cheap extremism" among the Palestinian guerrillas for weakening Arab unity, and accused the Chinese communists of provoking and encouraging it. Other Moscow broadcasts (6 and 7 August) complained of the "poisonous weapons of fabrications" "ultrarevolutionary slogans and vituperation" that the Chinese People's Republic used against the Soviet Union in its professions of support for the Arabs, and claimed that the Chinese had rendered no concrete assistance whatsoever.

An additional complication in the Middle East was the position of the local communist parties. In Syria the illegal party was the object of a serious campaign of suppression, and the Soviet Union expressed "alarm" at reports that many party members had been tortured. In Iraq there were signs of growing dissension between the communists and the government, brought on by the Kurdish question and the part played by the communists in arranging the settlement in March (see *Iraq*). Later in the year the communists charged that a full-fledged campaign against them and all "progressives" was under way in Iraq, and demanded an investigation of the alleged murder of a prominent party member. Only in Lebanon was the position of the communists markedly improved, as the pro-Soviet Lebanese Communist Party gained legal status.

Relations with Africa. The Soviet Union continued during 1970 its efforts to bring Africa into what Brezhnev described as a "broad anti-imperialist front" (*Pravda*, 13 June). In the furtherance of this goal, however, the Soviets were confronted with competition from other communist states, in particular Yugoslavia and China.

The Yugoslav challenge, which was in the form of a militant championship of the concept of "nonalignment," included an extensive tour of Africa by President Tito in January and February, and active sponsorship and participation in the third nonaligned conference,¹ which was held in Lusaka, Zambia, on 8-10 September. The Soviet Union reacted to Tito's tour of Africa with two Moscow radio broadcasts (5 and 8 February) by Vladimir Kudriavtsev, political correspondent of *Izvestiia*, who criticized the view that "nonalignment" should lead to the creation of a "third force" between "socialism" and "capitalism." Remarking that "some seem to want to create a special camp with membership confined to nonaligned states, claiming that in doing so, they are guided by the desire to increase the influence and power of the emerging states in the international field," Kudriavtsev added that "nonalignment" should not mean "political neutrality" and that it would prove "worthwhile only when both in form and content it.is anti-imperialist."

The Soviet response to the Lusaka conference, which was attended by representatives from 54 nations (over half of which were African) was somewhat similar. A broadcast by "Radio Peace and Progress" (7 September) criticized "the doctrine being foisted upon the emerging countries about an alleged conflict between the rich and the poor nations, about dividing the world into the poor South and the rich North, that nonaligned countries should be equally distant from the East and the West." Following the conclusion of the conference, a Moscow radio commentary (11 September) claimed that while there had been disagreements on some matters, the general tone had been "anti-imperialist" and that the political platform adopted by the conference had brought the nonaligned countries closer to the "chief revolutionary force . . . the socialist countries."

Soviet competition with Communist China concentrated on the "progressive states" in Africa and on the guerrilla movements in the Portuguese colonies. China's emergence on the world diplomatic scene after its self-imposed isolation was highlighted by the Chinese agreement to build a railroad linking Tanzania and Zambia. (Negotiations for the building of the railroad had started in 1965; China finally agreed to finance the project with an interest-free loan on 12 July 1970.) Commenting on the negotiations for the railroad and on other Chinese aid, "Radio Peace and

¹The first nonaligned conference, held in Belgrade in 1961, was convened on the initiative of Presidents Tito and Nasser and attended by representatives of 24 countries. The second conference, held in Cairo in 1964 and sponsored by Yugoslavia, the U.A.R., and Ceylon, was attended by representatives of 47 countries and 11 observers.

Progress" (29 May) claimed that these moves were intended to create "a closed bloc—a kind of Afro-Asian society in which Peking would play a leading role."

Sino-Soviet rivalry was apparent in the Congo (Brazzaville), particularly following the change in name of that country from "Republic of the Congo" to the "People's Republic of the Congo" on 31 December 1969, and the establishment in early January 1970 of a ruling Congolese Labor Party (Parti Congolais du Travail; PCT) which claimed to base itself on Marxist-Leninist theory. An abortive coup on 23 March led to an extraordinary congress of the PCT, with the strengthening of its pro-Chinese faction, and throughout the year the Chinese continued to develop their relations with the Congo government and the PCT (see *China*). The extent of Chinese influence, however, was difficult to ascertain. A leading Congolese Maoist, Claude-Ernest Ndalla—first secretary of the PCT and formerly Congolese ambassador to China—headed a delegation to Moscow in June and was warmly received by Mazurov and Ponomarev. In a broadcast following the talks, Moscow radio (16 June) expressed satisfaction that China had failed to "impede the Congo's progress toward socialism."

Relations with Latin America.   During 1970 the Soviet Union showed increased interest in Latin America, and Soviet spokesmen continued to promote relatively moderate united-front tactics in most countries. Diplomatic relations were established with Venezuela and Guyana. Economic and political ties were expanded with the leftist military governments in Bolivia and Peru. The Soviet Union heralded the election of Marxist Salvador Allende as president of Chile at the end of the year and argued that events in Chile vindicated the parliamentary road for many countries in the hemisphere.

Relations with Cuba continued to thaw. Although differences regarding revolutionary strategy and tactics in Latin America may have remained, they were rarely mentioned during the year. On 22 April Fidel Castro emphasized the debt the Cuban government and all other revolutionary movements owed to the U.S.S.R. (see *Cuba*).

Communist parties in Latin America continued to struggle against "ultra-leftism" in their ranks. The major confrontation occurred within the Communist Party of Venezuela and resulted, after apparent Soviet intervention, in a split between the party's "old guard" and its centrist and reformist elements (see *Venezuela*).

International Party Contacts. For CPSU contacts with foreign communist parties and movements, in addition to those noted above, see the profiles of individual countries.

Publications. The main CPSU organs are the daily newspaper *Pravda*, the theoretical and ideological journal *Kommunist* (appearing 18 times a year), and the journal on internal party affairs and organizational party matters, *Partiinaia zhizn*, published twice a month. *Kommunist vooruzhonnykh sil* is the party theoretical journal for the armed forces, and *Agitator* is the journal for party propagandists, both published twice a month. The Komsomol publishes the newspaper *Komsomolskaia pravda* (issued six times a week), the monthly theoretical journal *Molodoi kommunist*, and the monthly literary journal *Molodaia gvardia*. Each republic of the U.S.S.R. has similar party newspapers and journals in the local language and usually also in Russian.

W. J. C.

YUGOSLAVIA

The Communist Party of Yugoslavia was founded in June 1920.[1] At the party's Sixth Congress, in November 1952, the name was changed to the League of Communists of Yugoslavia (Savez Komunista Jugoslavije; LCY). The LCY is the only political party in Yugoslavia and holds a monopoly of power through its leading role in the Socialist Alliance of Working People of Yugoslavia (Socialistički Savez Radnog Naroda Jugoslavije, SAWP) a mass political organization which includes all major mass organizations and also individuals representing various social groups.

Organization and Leadership. The Ninth Congress of the LCY, held in March 1969, eliminated the Central Committee and assigned its functions to an annual "Conference of the League of Communists." The Presidium was enlarged to consist of 52 members, including the first secretaries of the LCY organizations in the six component republics of the Yugoslav state. At the recommendation of party leader Josip Broz Tito, the congress created a 15-member "Executive Bureau of the Presidium" to strengthen the central leadership by providing a form of "collective leadership" in which there would be no chance for factionalism. It was to consist of two leaders from each republic, a leader from each of the two autonomous regions, and Tito as chairman. Those elected to the Executive Committee were, besides Tito: Edvard Kardelj, Vladimir Bakarić, Krste Crvenkovski, Nijaz Dizdarević, Stane Dolanc, Stevan Doronjski, Kiro Gligorov, Fadilj Hodža, Cvijetin Mijatović, Miroslav Pečujlić, Budislav Šoškić, Mijalko Todorović, Miko Tripalo, and Veljko Vlahović.

At the beginning of 1970 the LCY claimed a membership of 1,046,084 (Belgrade radio, 24 January). The population of Yugoslavia is 20,400,000 (estimated 1970).

Party Internal Affairs. The problem of regional-ethnic assertion continued to plague the LCY during 1970. The case of Miloš Žanko, who was replaced as the Croat party representative to the first annual LCY conference, reflected a growing struggle within the party over issues of unitarism, the status of regional-ethnic LCY components, and Soviet exploitation of Yugoslav problems (*Vjesnik*, 17 January). The Žanko case also revealed the growing fear of factionalism within the LCY, the sensitivity of Croatian party leaders to the intentions of the central leadership, and previewed the expected debates and struggles concerning the 1971-75 economic plan that reflects the liberal-conservative tension in the party. The growing focus of LCY leadership upon the problem of economic competition as reinforced by regional-ethnic rivalries meant that "the League of Communists cannot be indifferent to what sort of ideological and political atmosphere

[1] Yugoslav communists designate 1919 as the year of the party's founding, since that year saw the inception of the Socialist Workers' Party, which included both communist and noncommunist elements.

prevails in some 250 specialized, humanitarian, and similar organizations which today rally more than 5 million people." (Tanyug, 25 March). Such developments reflect the growing tendency for LCY tensions and problems to be expressed in terms of "cultural" competition and linguistic survival (e.g., Serb versus Croat), in addition to the growing awareness of top Yugoslav leaders that this has become more manifest within the party itself.

Concern has continued to persist about the composition of the LCY, which is viewed as a critical problem. According to Miko Tripalo, member of the Executive Bureau of the Presidium, "the present membership structure . . . does not adequately correspond to the trends accompanying the evolution of self-management or to changes in the social structure of society" (*Borba reflektor*, 24 January). A growing problem is the diminished proportion of peasants in the LCY —only 7.4 per cent in 1969 (*ibid.*). In recent years the LCY has been adding new members at the rate of about 150,000 annually, most under thirty years of age and a high proportion being blue-collar workers. The need to recruit workers continues to be emphasized, since most members leaving the party also fall in this category. Separations during 1969 totaled about 30,000 (*Borba*, 19 March 1970). Recruiting produced a rather appreciable gain in membership during 1970, with emphasis upon young persons, the peasantry, and workers. Recruitment policies are intended to strengthen the "grass roots" component, which is seen as consistent with the growing emphasis upon self-management. The LCY clearly seeks to avoid the stigma of the "new class" phenomenon associated with a highly and technically educated party membership.

Policy matters of primary concern were noted at a Presidium meeting on 22 April that stressed the further development of the Kosovo region, a more extensive independence of action for the federal republics, and the need for intensified LCY ideological activity (*Vjesnik*, 24 April). This pattern has prevailed for a number of years, whereby concessions tend to decentralize decision making for the regions while "ideological activity" is used as the re-centralizing instrument. At the Presidium session at Brioni on 2 July—in addition to repeating the commitment to solve the economic problems of the less developed republics and autonomous regions—the principal business was the convening of the first LCY annual conference for later in the year and the election of delegates to the conference. Continuing to show its concern with the status of the peasantry, the Presidium on 14 July adopted a draft resolution designed to buttress both the socialist and the private sectors in agriculture. This was presumably expected to help win the peasantry over to a new form of socialist cooperation. The resolution also indicated that a regional aspect might be applied to agricultural development—a view which was seen as innovative and consistent with decentralization. (*Politika*, 15 July.)

Perhaps the major policy decision by the Presidium during the year was the acceptance, in principle, of the idea of forming a "state presidency" as the authoritative "collective leadership" body of the country to ensure both external security and the degree of internal cooperation necessary to Yugoslav society (Tanyug, 4 October). (See below, "Domestic Affairs".) The proposal was on the whole well received, particularly so by the smaller nationalities within Yugoslavia. Slavko Miloslavlevski, member of the Macedonian LCY Central Committee, emphasized that a state presidency would give effect to the principle of the equality and equal responsibility of the peoples that make up the federation (*ibid.*, 23 October). Other work of the Presidium during 1970 was focused upon giving effect to the basic decisions of the Ninth Congress of the LCY, held in 1969. These involved, in general, extending self-management in industries, stabilizing the economic situation, advancing the less developed regions, and making changes in party organizational structure (*ibid.*, 25 October). Another concern was without doubt the convening of the first LCY annual conference and the questions relating to party and governmental affairs that the conference was to consider.

The providing of ideological guidelines and exemplary behavior remains the primary role of the LCY, as it has been for a number of years. In 1970 a party source stated: "The policy of the LCY is increasingly becoming an ideological-political synthesis of the creativeness, initiative, and positions of all organizations, and this is what constitutes a new quality in its work" (*ibid.*, 26 July). In addition, the Ninth Congress had stressed that LCY members should increase their ideological activity, apply with greater consistency the concept of federation in their work, and develop an atmosphere that would ensure equitable and democratic dialogue, preventing thereby the special treatment of any one class or group. There appears to be an emphasis on somewhat closer contact and activity with the "grass roots" elements of Yugoslav society, with respect both to basic local organizations and to the various republics and autonomous regions in general. A related development involves the situation and rights of party members within the LCY; in this regard, the LCY Commission for Statutory Questions stated: "In the commission's opinion, the right of a communist to retain his own opinion is of great importance for the greater democratization of the LCY, for establishing the position of LCY members as the basic factors in the creation of policies, and for achieving respect for the personal integrity of communists" (*Borba*, 16 April). Similarly, the new standing rules adopted for the Federal Assembly give deputies the right of free expression of opinion and balloting in that legislative body, and it has been increasingly suggested by some Yugoslav leaders that government officials must have the right formally to dissent from officially set government policy (*Komunist*, 16 April; *Borba*, 25 June). These developments as regards the LCY role and function suggest a further decentralizing of its operations and a weakening or "liberalizing" of its direct hold upon membership activity.

The high point of 1970 politically was the convening of the first LCY conference, which met on 29 October as an organization designed to meet annually between party congresses. At the opening, Tito stated: "This conference should . . . primarily provide an appraisal of our development since the Ninth Congress, so that we may frankly face and perceive the omissions and shortcomings in our past work, that we may present a prospect of our future development" (*Borba*, 30 October). The resolutions that came out of the conference were in no sense dramatic and merely confirmed what had already been fully discussed earlier by the LCY Presidium. Two important specific decisions reflected major topics of debate, namely, the setting up of a collective state presidency and the encouraging of individual peasants to become equal and active partners within the socialist economic sector (*ibid.*, 31 October).

Domestic Affairs. *Nationality and Regionalism.* In 1970 the issue of Kosovo continued to loom as an important problem of domestic politics. The Albanians residing in the region and comprising most of the population showed no letup in their desire for republic status, and continued to press for what they consider their economic and cultural rights. The response of the federal government has been to recognize the social, economic, and political problems of the region and to give its development a central place in the overall Yugoslav social plan covering 1971-75 (Tanyug, 22 April). Many foreign observers have remarked that deep feelings of nationalism are on the upswing among the Albanian population of Yugoslavia (e.g., *Washington Post*, 7 June).

The problem of nationalities was also reflected in discussions on the procedure for taking a census. The SAWP proposed that in the next census a citizen be allowed to refuse to declare himself as belonging to one of the established nationalities (Serb, Croat, etc.) and that anyone be allowed, if he so wished, to declare himself simply a "Yugoslav" or a "Moslem" and thereby exercise his right of "nondetermination" (Tanyug, 13 May). Over the years there has been the tendency to eliminate the "Yugoslav" self-designation completely and without prejudice; therefore, the SAWP proposal might be viewed by some more extreme nationalists of whatever persuasion as a victory for the "unitarists" and "Yugoslavists" centered in Belgrade. The nationality issue has taken on a particularly sharp form in the area of regional linguistic and cultural expression, whether this might happen to involve the Albanians and "Bosnians" or the Croats vis-á-vis the Serbs. A new policy has been instituted in this regard which is designed to speed up decentralization and to increase the power of republics by allowing them wider use of their national languages. In particular, the policy calls for a greater equity in the use of the range of national languages in federal administration and in the armed forces (*Nedeljne Informativne Novine*, Belgrade, 12 July).

If the "national language" principle is pushed to the extreme, it might raise some even more critical problems, given the increased trans-republic mobility that seems to be occurring. A recent Yugoslav study indicated that Slovenes and Macedonians are the least mobile among Yugoslavs, while both Serbs and Albanians have very large proportions of their people residing in republics or regions other than their own (*Borba*, 15 September). It is difficult to imagine a satisfactory solution in terms of fuller rights to "national languages" if such cross-regional dispersion of peoples in Yugoslavia continues to exist and even intensifies with modernization.

Free Expression. The question of free expression, at times with undertones of the nationality issue, was associated during 1970 with a number of civil disruptions, in particular those involving students. Early in the year the editorial board of the Belgrade University paper *Student* was dissolved and charged with "Stalinist" inclinations toward strengthening federal control (*Washington Post*, 27 January). Later, the arrest and sentencing of a student leader for "hostile anti-state propaganda" precipitated a massive student strike at the university (*Borba*, 21 October). Given these events, as well as intensified student activity in Zagreb concerning the autonomy of Croatian culture, it seemed clear that the issue of "free cultural expression" was associated to some extent with the nationality issue. The positive aspect of these developments would seem to be that students have taken on a major role in pressing for greater freedom in social and political expression, although this has at times become manifest in somewhat narrow regional-ethnic contexts. The status of Milovan Djilas again took a turn for the worse with the withdrawal of his passport two days prior to his intended departure for the United States. Djilas was under the restrictions of a secondary sentence that involved a conviction for disclosing state secrets and inflicting damage on the reputation of the Yugoslav state. The passport revocation resulted from his violating these restrictions by his appearing in the press and on radio and television, and making public addresses. (*Christian Science Monitor*, 7 March; *Komunist*, 11 March.) On the other hand, Mihajlo Mihajlov, after being imprisoned for insulting the Soviet Union and deriding his own government, was released on March 4, a year before the full expiration of his sentence (*New York Times*, 5 March). In cases such as those of Djilas and Mihajlov the Yugoslav authorities have seemed to continue their policy of unremitting firmness tempered with a curious form of Marxist compassion for the accused. In general, the Yugoslav government has been giving increasing attention to the problem of rules and limits upon free expression within a socialist society. In 1970 this took the specific form of extended discussion of the role of the press in an "open society," with the suggestion that some clear structure of limits or constraints would be desirable and must be officially articulated. There was also a move on the part of the SAWP to give its Serbian organ *Borba* the aspect of an all-Yugoslav newspaper by making it the organ of the SAWP Federal Conference and devoting it more to the country's overall development toward a "self-governing community of peoples and nationalities" (Tanyug, 13 May). The central aspect of the problem of free expression in Yugoslavia is that it cannot be viewed as purely an individual matter; the problems and issues raised by all forms of expression in Yugoslavia have to be considered in light of implications for existing regional, cultural, and ethnic rivalries. Coming upon the heels of the *Književne Novine* incident that highlighted 1969 (see *YICA*, 1970, p. 107) was an increasing skepticism, voiced by Tito and other Yugoslav leaders, about the content and quality of cultural expression.

Defense Strategy. Since the Soviet-led invasion of Czechoslovakia in 1968, there has been a growing attention in Yugoslavia to a regionally based "all peoples" defense system. This increased concern was reflected in the 1970 federal defense budget, which was 14 per cent higher than that of the previous year. Early in 1970 the Yugoslav National Defense Council stated: "Society as a whole has adopted the concept of nationwide defense as a powerful alternative for successful opposition to an aggressor, and, as an integral part of our self-management system, it constitutes a substantial factor in the further development of our country and of its security" (*Borba*, 16 January). In this respect, the locally based all-peoples defense systems and the institutions of self-management are judged to be compatible and, indeed, reinforcing; they also effectively tap the memory of the partisan struggle against the German invader and the locally based units employed in that effort. In this regard, Tito reportedly said: "The concept of all-people's defense represents a consistent, resolute, and creative application of the rich experience gained in the national liberation struggle" (Tanyug, 13 May). At the 3 July meeting of the National Defense Council, over which Tito presided, it was affirmed that the all-peoples defense system had been effectively developed and that it was extremely significant for its broad involvement of all social elements in a commitment to the common defense of the country (*ibid.*, 3 July). The concept of a "nationwide defense" system would require all Yugoslav citizens and organizations to fight any potential enemy whatsoever. It has gained increasing and wide support since 1968. Despite the desirability of inducing the full involvement of all citizens in their regional defense systems, this strategy still holds uncertain implications for the future relationships among various republics. For instance, there exists a possibility that republics, provinces, and work organizations may in the near future be able to purchase armaments abroad for their own use, since this is judged to be consistent with an all-peoples defense system (*Vjesnik*, 4 October). Such a regionally based defense system—stimulated by the Soviet-led invasion of Czechoslovakia and priding itself on being rooted in the partisans' national liberation effort—could have drastic implications for inter-republic relations in the event of a severe crisis over presidential succession after Tito passes from the scene.

State Reorganization.   With an obvious view to his own retirement or death and the succession crisis that might follow, Tito announced on 21 September 1970 that the LCY Presidium would discuss a reorganization of the Yugoslav state system (Tanyug, 21 September). The basic consideration was to establish a responsible, authoritative, and "collectively presiding" body which would result in a strengthening of the unity and security of the Yugoslav community (*Komunist*, 24 September). The new body, to be called the "Presidency of the Yugoslav Republic," would blend the functions of the current president with some of those of the Federal Executive Council and, comprising representatives of the various regions and the main social and political organizations, would be designed in part to try to overcome acute strains between the nationalities before Tito's final retirement. Such a state reorganization, involving a participation of the various republics on an equal basis, would have two aspects: (1) a hedge against the possibility of intense inter-national struggle, verging perhaps on civil war, in the event of a succession crisis, and, (2) an attempt to reduce the intensified hostility in recent years among various nationalities and regions. Tito and Edvard Kardelj both emphasized that the primary task of the new "collective presidency" would be to act so as to encourage the unity of the whole Yugoslav community and to overcome the differences among republics within the federal system (*Komunist*, 24 September; Tanyug, 30 September). The two critical features of the new office would be (1) its greater power to submit legislation, as contrasted with the more limited authority of the current executive organs of the Federal Assembly, and (2) its "collective" and "inter-national" composition, designed to ensure both the equality of the nationalities and the necessary unity of Yugoslav society. The thought seemed to be that leaders of all republics should be engaged in the critical task of legislative submission, a participation that must be equally accessible to all regions and nationalities of the country, given the federal structure of Yugoslavia. After the termination of the LCY conference, Tito on 14 December submitted a proposal to the Federal Assembly specifying that the constitution be changed to provide for (1) the foundation of a new collective state leadership called the State Presidency that would take effect when Tito dies and (2) the strengthening of the independent authority of the six constituent republics and the two autonomous provinces (*Borba*, 15 December). Both elements of this proposal might be interpreted as a victory for republic autonomy and further political decentralization, especially in light of the principle of balance and equality that would be expected to be maintained within the State Presidency.

Political Succession. The reorganization of Yugoslav state administration can be linked without equivocation to the problem of succession to Tito. In the common foreign interpretation, Tito is bent upon averting a major succession crisis (see, e.g., *Economist*, London, 26 September). Furthermore, aside from Tito, the man most prominent in the discussion about state reorganization has been Edvard Kardelj. The rumor that he might be the successor-designate of Tito himself seems to be supported by references to Kardelj as the "second citizen" of Yugoslavia (*Borba*, 25 January). The top Yugoslav leaders themselves recognize the dangers of a succession crisis, but still manage to view the state reorganization in much broader terms than do foreign observers. Kardelj, speaking on foreign reactions to internal Yugoslav politics, stated to the LCY Presidium on 4 October: "There have been—especially abroad but sometimes also in our own country—interpretations and attempts to reduce the entire reform of the political system and the creation of the presidency to a problem of generations or speculations that Comrade Tito intends to retire, and so on." However, he continued, ". . . we are taking steps for the future of our society which must be made today so that our peoples and our working people, or rather citizens, will be certain that the socialist, democratic, and self-managing road of our society will be as secure tomorrow as it is today." (Tanyug, 4 October.) Kardelj warned, further, that if the problem of "collective leadership" after Tito could not be resolved in a democratic way, then the forces desiring a Stalinist or semi-Stalinist system might possibly prevail, with the Yugoslav people suffering in the process (*Borba*, 5 October). Clearly, the matter of succession to Tito has very wide ramifications, not merely for averting a major internal crisis but for preserving the institutions that the Yugoslavs have developed to solve problems unique to their highly complex and diversified society.

Domestic Economy. The pervasive note of concern in Yugoslavia about the state of the economy reflects the fear that it may be growing and expanding too rapidly. The Yugoslav citizen has seen an increase in his living standard and purchasing power, but these developments have been accompanied by a rise in living costs (*Vjesnik*, 24 March; *Politika*, 28 August). Despite the fear of inflation, growth and development are seen as desirable in and of themselves, and there is a general feeling that many of the economic problems that appeared immediately following the 1965 reforms have been resolved. Mitja Ribičič, president of the Federal Executive Council, summarized conditions in this way: "The current economic situation is characterized . . . . by growing inflation and market instability, disruption of the distribution of income, and an increased deficit in the balance of payments in addition to certain positive results in economic growth and modernization of business operations" (Tanyug, 26 November 1970). Yugoslav leaders pointed out that the positive aspects of the domestic economy during 1970 included a growth in productivity, employment, and exports, which, however, must be balanced off against the instability of the market and of prices and a significant recent decline in agricultural output. The hard data that reflect the state of the economy included: a 7 per cent increase in real earnings over 1969; a 9 per cent increase in retail prices; an 11 per cent increase in living costs; a 19 per cent increase in nominal earnings; a 7 per cent drop in agricultural yields (due mainly to bad weather); a 13 per cent growth in exports, and a 33 per cent growth in imports (*ibid.*, 31 December). This pattern suggests that living costs have increased more than income and that the unfavorable trade balance is worsening. In a New Year's message anticipating the problems of 1971, Tito indicated that the major task was the stabilizing of the economy, which required in the main the avoidance of excessive investments made without adequate financial backing (*ibid.*, 30 December). The top Yugoslav leadership acknowledges that in this respect the major problem lies in finding the hard currencies and the investors willing to bring monies into Yugoslavia so that it may continue its accelerated pace of growth.

Inflation. A report by the Organization for Economic Cooperation and Development (OECD) summarized the Yugoslav situation by saying that it faced an inflationary trend aggravated by a bad balance of payments situation, although the development of the economy in recent years was judged as favorable (*OECD, Economic Surveys: Yugoslavia*, Paris, November 1969). The view has also often been expressed that while growth and modernization require a degree of inflationary pressure, the Yugoslav situation hovers on the precipice of uncontrollable eonomic problems. There is, of course, the basic recognition that the existence of a market mechanism, even that of the socialist variety, creates the basic conditions for inflationary instability. During the first nine months of 1970 wholesale prices increased by about 9 per cent and retail prices by more than 10 per cent, with costs of catering up 25 per cent and services as much as 30 per cent (Tanyug, 9 October). When compared against similar indicators for developed Western societies, these increases are found to be nearly three times higher. The retail price increase for the first 9 months in Yugoslavia represents a significantly higher rate than the previous year, while the increases in catering and services reflect in part the accelerated expansion of Yugoslav tourist trade. In view of the fear that the economy may be running out of control (with an estimated 12 per cent inflation rate), the issue of what immediate action might be taken was joined toward the end of 1970—a development that was accompanied by charges that the government was covering up important economic facts (*New York Times*, 27 November). Deputy Premier Nikola Miljanić's proposal of an economic stabilization plan that included a devaluation of the Yugoslav dinar met with strong resistance from the republics and precipitated his resignation (*Borba*, 22 November; *Vjesnik*, 18 November). What became clear was that any economic stabilization program meant a measure of control over the allocation of investment, which immediately raised the issue of republic autonomy and inter-national sensitivities. The next step was taken by Premier Mitja Ribičič, who stated that the basic aim of the 1971 socioeconomic policy was to put an economic stabilization program into effect which would halt further inflationary trends, setting 5.5 per cent as the reasonable growth rate, given the nature of the Yugoslav economy (Tanyug, 3 December). The proposal by Ribičič was not very well received, being criticized as excessively abstract and as failing to confront specific problems, and the inflationary problem was unresolved as of the end of 1970.

Agriculture. The general trend over the last few years has been toward a progressive strengthening of the Yugoslav agricultural sector. Between 1948 and 1969 the output doubled. This occurred despite such problems as the exodus of young persons from farms and the instability of the market and of prices. In addition, a Czechoslovak observer reported in 1970 that while twelve years ago 121,000 private farmers or peasants were members of the LCY, in 1969 no more than 81,000 claimed membership—a decrease that is all the more impressive in view of the increase in the total membership of the LCY over this time (*Rudé Právo*, Prague, 20 October). Once the national liberation experience became little more than a historical myth, the problems of maintaining the peasants' interest in the activity of the LCY became very difficult. The proportion of socialized agriculture in Yugoslavia has increased slowly over the years, accounting in 1969 for 14.4 per cent of total arable land and about 20 per cent of agricultural production—the latter figure reflecting the more highly mechanized and efficient nature of the socialist sector (*Borba*, 31 October). The report on agriculture at the LCY conference in October noted that agriculture had lagged behind general socioeconomic development and stated: "The starting point for equalizing and stabilizing the conditions of business operations and the earnings of income is the striving for the principle of a free formation of prices according to market conditions, for the preservation of a real parity of prices between agricultural produce and other products and services, and for the adjustment of these prices to those in the world markets" (*ibid.*). The solution to Yugoslav agriculture was felt to rest with a growth in an awareness of socialist principles, at least to the point of encouraging peasants into voluntary cooperative arrangements, and in allowing the price structures in the agricultural sector to respond to market needs.

Unemployment. Unemployment and the exodus of workers to Western Europe continued in 1970 to be important problems. Federal sources estimated that the number of Yugoslav workers employed abroad increased by 100,000 during 1969 despite a slight (3 per cent) increase in the number of employed persons within the country (*Vjesnik u srijedu*, 31 December 1969; 14 January 1970). Some of the republics, Croatia in particular, have become increasingly concerned about the movement of their native populations into foreign countries (*Borba*, 29 May). Pronouncements by the Yugoslav leadership continued to recognize that the providing of full employment remained a major problem, due in part to accelerated education in skills and professions beyond the capacity of the economy at the present stage of its development to absorb.

Private Enterprise. Growing pressure for expansion of the private enterprise sector was evident in a proposal in the Yugoslav Federal Assembly to allow craftsmen to employ a larger number of workers and to increase the permissible tonnage of trucks used by private truckers (*Borba*, 12 March 1970). In addition, there were efforts to make Yugoslav enterprises available for private capital investment by Yugoslav citizens—in part to encourage the approximately 750,000 Yugoslavs living abroad to invest their hard currencies in the Yugoslav economy (*Politika*, 4 June; *Vjesnik u srijedu*, 10 June). Similarly, the government gave attention to the possibility of establishing a "market for socialist capital" which would represent the first stock market established in a communist state (*Politika ekspres*, 18 October). These latter developments represented attempts to solve both the problem of the exodus of Yugoslav citizens and that of generating financial resources for capital investment.

Foreign Trade. The general situation of Yugoslavia's foreign trade reflected a worsening of its balance of payments. Nevertheless, the year 1969 set a record for foreign trade and showed an increase in both exports and imports, with imports somewhat greater (*Economic Review*, Belgrade, February 1970). Imports in 1969 were valued at 26.3 billion dinars and exports at 18.43 billion, with the greater part of trade being with the advanced Western countries (*Borba*, 21 December 1969). What seems significant about Yugoslav foreign trade activities is that, despite a growing unfavorable balance—due in large part to its greater trading with more advanced countries—the overall volume of foreign trade has continued to increase at a relatively high rate. In the first half of 1970 exports totaled 10 billion dinars, or about 24 per cent above the same period during the previous year, and imports reached 15.5 million dinars, or about 19.3 per cent more (Tanyug, 14 July). These figures may be indicative of a slightly changing trend toward a redressing of the balance of payments deficit.

Foreign Trade Pattern. Ever since the break with the Soviet Union, the Yugoslav leadership has been trying to maintain an open trade policy. The effect over the years has been to achieve a relative balance in quantity and value of trade between the countries of the Soviet bloc and those of the western world. During 1969, however, Yugoslav trade with the countries of Eastern Europe did not increase significantly (*Ekonomska politika*, 2 February). Meanwhile the

Yugoslavs have sought to expand trade relations with African and other less developed nations as a means of improving their balance of payments. A major development in 1970 was the concluding of a nonpreferential, nondiscriminatory trade agreement with the European Economic Community (EEC). This agreement had three significant features: (1) that Yugoslavia and the EEC will grant one another most-favored-nation treatment; (2) that the Yugoslavs gain special treatment for their baby beef exports to Common Market areas; and, (3) that a joint Yugoslav-EEC commission would seek to find additional ways for widening mutually beneficial cooperation (*Economist*, 21 March). The association with the EEC was given additional diplomatic force by the visit of Jean Rey, president of the EEC Executive Commission, to Belgrade on 1 June. Rey expressed the willingness of the EEC to expand its cooperation with the Yugoslavs. The government has also been trying to improve its trade relations with the countries of Eastern Europe—especially Czechoslovakia, which in volume of commodity exchanges ranks fourth among Yugoslavia's trading partners, following West Germany, the Soviet Union, and Italy (Tanyug, 2 April). In July 1969 the Yugoslavs concluded an agreement with the Czechoslovak government for the settlement of accounts in free currency—a development seen as an important step toward establishing the convertibility of East European currencies. Late in 1970 it was reported that an agreement was expected to be reached soon between Yugoslavia and the Soviet Union on a trade pact that would set an average growth rate of 8 per cent per annum in trade between the two countries for the 1971-75 period (Tanyug, 7 December).

Foreign Currency and Investment.   Two major ways for obtaining Western hard currencies needed by Yugoslavia are the encouraging of investment by foreign financial agencies and the importing of currencies earned by Yugoslavs working abroad. During early 1970 the International Bank of Reconstruction and Development approved a loan of $40 million to the Yugoslav Investment Bank for the purpose of modernizing the postal, telegraph, and telephone services (*Borba*, 19 February). The providing of funds through such international lending institutions has become an important source of economic investment for the Yugoslavs. The data for 1968 and 1969 show that foreign-based firms invested $43 million in the Yugoslav economy and that 157 contracts involving industrial cooperation were concluded with an assortment of foreign companies (*Privredni pregled*, 27 March 1970). In order further to encourage this type of activity, legislation was passed to allow up to one-third of foreign earnings to be repatriated to the investor's country and to make Yugoslav business taxes more attractive to the foreign investor (*Washington Post*, 31 August; *Le Monde*, Paris, 19 August). In addition, the Yugoslav Investment Bank, in conjunction with "Generalexport" of Belgrade, announced plans to invest $500,000 in a new enterprise called "Investrade," based in New York, which is to promote Yugoslav import-export capability and aid in business arrangements with U.S. enterprises (Tanyug, 16 July).

Yugoslav nationals have continued to find lucrative jobs in Western Europe, especially West Germany. They remitted about $182 million to Yugoslavia during the first half of 1970, which was $104 million more than in the same period of the previous year (Tanyug, 28 July). During 1969, total foreign exchange earnings from Yugoslavs employed abroad totaled about $250 million and, understandably, helped ease the balance of payments problem considerably (*Christian Science Monitor*, 19 August). Tourism also provided an important reservoir of hard currencies for investment purposes. The commitment of Yugoslav leaders to continued economic growth and expansion requires that such sources be developed even further so as to expand the fiscal investment pool.

Foreign Affairs.   *The Soviet Union and China.*   The uneasy relationship between Yugoslavia and the Soviet Union appeared to be aggravated during 1970. Early in the year, a Yugoslav government spokesman criticized the Soviets for "manipulating historical facts" in a new history of the Communist Party of the Soviet Union (CPSU) which placed the Yugoslavs in an unfavorable light (*New York Times*, 9 January). Other charges concerned alleged Soviet attempts to form an illegal "Communist Party of Yugoslavia" and possibly smuggle arms to anti-Tito dissidents within Yugoslavia (*Der Spiegel*, Hamburg, 14 September). There were also rumors of Soviet efforts to exploit Croatian separatist impulses—including contacts in parts of Western Europe with former elements of the Nazi-supported wartime regime in Croatia—as a way of encouraging internal dissension. The issue was joined in May 1970 when Brezhnev cancelled a planned meeting with Tito in Belgrade after Tito had allegedly demanded as a condition for the meeting that Brezhnev make assurances that any such attempts at subversive activity by the Soviet Union cease. This general level of tension between the two countries has been aggravated further by the open Soviet desire to have a deep harbor in the Mediterranean and the Yugoslav refusal to allow the Soviets to make use of Kotor on the Adriatic coast for this purpose (*Christian Science Monitor*, 17 March). Given the Soviet interest in Middle East affairs and the presence of the Soviet fleet in the Mediterranean, this need for a deep harbor has become an especially important issue due to Yugoslav fears of Soviet intent and manipulations in the wake of the invasion of Czechoslovakia and the Brezhnev doctrine, and the continued desire of the Soviets for maritime control in the Eastern Mediterranean to accompany their political engagement in the Middle East.

In June 1970 the president of the Federal Executive Council, Mitja Ribičič, visited Moscow. A measure of the continued tension between the LCY and the CPSU was reflected in the fact that Ribičič was not received by Brezhnev, but rather by Kosygin, with whom he issued a joint statement following their discussions. The only positive result that seemed to emerge from the visit was the reaffirmation that Yugoslavia and the Soviet Union would continue to honor the principles of the 1955 Belgrade declaration, a document which represented the highpoint in Yugoslav-Soviet rapprochement during the Khrushchev era (*Borba*, 2 July). Although this joint statement suggested some measure of "cautious tolerance" between the two countries, it also represented a compromise between the Soviet refusal to renounce the Brezhnev doctrine and the fervent desire of Yugoslavia to receive unequivocal assurance of Soviet intent toward herself and the eastern Mediterranean. Since the visit solved none of the important issues, it probably increased the anxiety as to Soviet designs in the event of a succession crisis.

In contrast, relations with Communist China seemed to improve considerably during the year. The two usually antagonistic communist states agreed to resume full diplomatic relations after a suspension of formal contact for nearly twelve years (*Vjesnik*, 4 March; *Observer*, London, 1 March). The Yugoslavs' appointment in May of General Bogdan Oreščanin as ambassador to China (*Vjesnik u srijedu*, 13 May) was followed in August by the designation of Tseng Tao as ambassador to Belgrade (*New York Times*, 12 August). This growing rapport can logically be traced back to mutual concern over Soviet activity during the Czechoslovak crisis and may have important bearings on the relationship of Yugoslavia to countries such as Albania as well as the Soviet Union.

Just as the Soviet Union has continued to attack the "revisionist" implications of Yugoslavia's nonalignment policies, so the Yugoslavs have continued their criticism of the Soviet Union for its state bureaucracy and, more recently, its treatment of artists such as Solzhenitsyn (*Komunist*, 22 October). A critical aspect of Yugoslav-Soviet relations appeared in the termination of a five-year agreement on arms purchases that was scheduled to expire on June 30, and the seeking by the Yugoslavs of an alternative armament supplier in both France and Great Britain (*Economist*, 30 May; *Christian Science Monitor*, 16 June). Given the evidence of Soviet intrigue as regards the internal politics of Yugoslavia, especially in relation to the problem of a possible stormy succession period, the Yugoslavs seem to be seeking to reduce their reliance upon the Soviet Union even further insofar as concerns critical strategic materials.

Eastern Europe. The clearest aspect of Yugoslav relations with other East European countries during 1970 was a generally improved cordiality, with the notable and important exception of Bulgaria.

As regards Romania, a visit by Romanian officials to Belgrade in January produced a joint communiqué that stressed the increase of mutual friendship and cooperation (Agerpres, Romanian press agency, 16 January). In addition the Romanian suggestion that the Balkans should become a nuclear-free zone was greeted with enthusiasm by the Yugoslav leadership, although some caution was expressed about the wisdom of multilateral Balkan efforts in view of Soviet anxieties (*Borba*, 12 June; *Vjesnik*, 15 July). The local border traffic controls between Romania and Yugoslavia, which have not been severe in recent years, were further liberalized in September. Talks between Tito and Romanian President Ceauşescu in Belgrade in early November were said to have been "full of understanding and friendship" and to have shown "great similarity of views" (Tanyug, 4 November). Mutual fear of implications of the Brezhnev doctrine has done much to cement friendly relations between the two countries and to set aside less immediate differences over common boundaries. The cooperation of the two countries on the Iron Gates hydroelectric project on the Danube River has also done much to establish a tradition of amity and good will.

For a number of years, and especially since the Czechoslovak crisis, relations between Yugoslavia and Albania have been improving, a trend which can also be related to a growing Yugoslav cordiality toward Communist China. The possibility of increasing trade with Albania was discussed in the Yugoslav Federal Assembly in April at considerable length (Tanyug, 2 April). Yugoslav sources have increasingly pointed to the growing friendship and rediscovery of a common interest between the people of the two countries (e.g., *Vjesnik*, 25 April). The Albanian leadership has also been reciprocating with expressions of their own "good neighborly relations" toward the Yugoslavs—a tendency that might be related to both the rediscovery of a common enemy in the Soviet Union and a more acceptable policy by the Yugoslavs as regards the Albanians in Kosovo. The overriding focus of the Albanians appears to be that of recementing a regional solidarity against the incursion of "predatory imperialists," reflected in a statement on Albanian-Yugoslav solidarity on the anniversary of the German occupation of Yugoslavia in the Albanian press, to which the Yugoslavs replied two days later with a similar proclamation on the anniversary of the Italian occupation of Albania. The immediate stimulus for renewal of friendly relations seems to be the perception of a common enemy in the Soviet Union, which is viewed as seeking to control the eastern Adriatic coast, although the renewal of friendship also provides the basis for cooperation in economic and political areas as well.

Yugoslav-Bulgarian relations, which reflected a severe rise in tension, center upon the Macedonian problem. It is surely noteworthy that Bulgarian assertiveness in relation to Macedonia has increased dramatically since the Soviet-led invasion of Czechoslovakia. Responding to the visit of the Bulgarian foreign minister early in 1970, Yugoslav officials commented that, since the initiative for the visit came from the Bulgarians, it had been hoped that something constructive would come of the meetings, which were disappointing in that the Bulgarians merely repeated their claims to Yugoslav Macedonian territory (*Economist*, 4 January). The issue became even more heated later in the year when Yugoslav authorities accused the Bulgarians of disseminating anti-Yugoslav propaganda in Yugoslav Macedonia (*Nedeljne Informativne Novine*, 9 August). In a foreign policy address to the Federal Assembly, Tito stated: "Further progress has been made in our relations with our neighbors, except with the People's Republic of Bulgaria, with which despite our efforts, regretfully, no such progress has been recorded" (*Borba*, 19 November). Three weeks later the Bulgarian government officially refused to sign three treaties with Yugoslavia because they were written in Macedonian. The refusal reflected the earlier Bulgarian position that Macedonian is a contrived language, designed as a political tool to separate Macedonian "Bulgars" from Bulgaria (*Nova Makedonija*, 5 July). The issue of the "nationality" of the Macedonians, which had lain dormant for many years, looms as a major problem for the Yugoslavs and one in which the Soviet Union can be expected to support Bulgarian positions.

Yugoslav relations with other East European Communist states—East Germany, Czechoslovakia, Hungary, and Poland—were on the whole friendly in 1970 and gave no indication of dramatic change. In March the Yugoslav party press attacked the Polish communists for what it saw as a slur of the LCY's nonalignment stance (*Komunist*, 26 March) and took the opportunity later in the year to criticize Poland's handling of strike problems, suggesting that the Polish government was not receptive to the needs of their workers. With East Germany there were signs of growing rapport. After meetings in April at Belgrade East German Foreign Minister Otto Winzer commented that the talks were "extremely fruitful," although the visit on the whole was characterized by great reserve and caution by both parties (*Frankfurter Allgemeine Zeitung*, 23 April). Relations with Hungary remained on the whole cordial and positive and with some indication of increased cooperation in economic matters. The Hungarian premier, Jenö Fock, visited Belgrade in June and held what were judged as cordial discussions with the president of the Federal Executive Council, Mitja Ribičič (Tanyug, 2 June). In November a protocol on trade for 1971 was concluded with Hungary that provides for commodity exchange valued at approximately $121 million and representing a substantial increase over the previous year (*ibid.*, 27 November). Despite the desire of the Yugoslavs to improve relations with Czechoslovakia, they have grown increasingly skeptical and concerned over what is seen as an attempt by Czechoslovak mass media to distort Yugoslav conditions and to malign the Yugoslav system, acting in this respect as the mouthpiece of the Soviets (*Borba*, 6 August). On the whole, Yugoslav relations with these northern-tier East European communist states might most accurately be described as continuing the measured hostility that has characterized them for a number of years.

The Nonaligned World.   The major event as regards the "third world" for the Yugoslavs in 1970 was the summit meeting of nonaligned countries held in Zambia during September. Early in the year Tito made a tour of a number of nonaligned African states—Tanzania, Zambia, Ethiopia, Kenya, Sudan, the United Arab Republic, and Libya—discussing the problems of nonaligned states and what might be done to give more solid effect to their attitudes on the international scene. The 6-9 April visit to Yugoslavia of the foreign minister of Algeria, Abdel Aziz Bouteflika, was interpreted as a reconciliation of strained relations resulting from the Algerian delegates' opposition to Tito's plan to convoke a nonaligned summit meeting at an earlier preparatory meeting in Belgrade (*Borba*, 10 April). The president of Sudan, Ja'far al-Numayri, visited Yugoslavia, in June, and the president of the Democratic Republic of the Congo, Joseph Mobutu, in August (*Borba*, 20 June; Tanyug, 29 August). On 28 August, the secretary-general of the U.N., U Thant, arrived in Belgrade, where he held talks with Tito on problems of peace and more specifically on the role Tito was assuming for himself as mediator in the Arab-Israeli conflict (Tanyug, 28 August).

The active and growing interest of Yugoslavia in the less-developed countries has been reflected in extensive commercial ties and efforts to expand them. During the first nine months of 1970, Yugoslavia reportedly had business transactions with nonaligned countries amounting to $100 million, and 60 Yugoslav construction-engineering companies were active in 40 places in these countries (*New York Times*, 29 November). The Yugoslavs have long been active in Africa and Asia, and in 1970 interest in Latin America was evidenced by Edvard Kardelj's visit to Chile, Peru, and Mexico. Kardelj declared that conditions favored Yugoslav cooperation with those countries (*Borba*, 25 May). Two good reasons for increased ties with the underdeveloped "third world" are: in this sector the Yugoslav regime can develop a political power-base or lever independent of either the U.S. or the Soviet power block and these countries provide outlets for Yugoslav manufactured goods that cannot be sold to West European countries because of their short-comings in quality.

The summit meeting in Zambia came about primarily through the pressure and initiative of Tito. On 13-17 April a preparatory meeting was held at Dar es Salaam to outline the basic questions to be considered—problems of world peace and state autonomy (Tanyug, 6 April). The Yugoslav foreign minister, Mirko Tepavac, following the preparatory meeting, stated that the primary goal of the summit meeting was to achieve "more efficient joint activity of the nonaligned regarding main questions of [their] political development—peace, independence, and more harmonious economic development" (*ibid.*, 29 April). The summit meeting convened in Lusaka, Zambia, on 5 September and reaffirmed the commitment to a nonaligned policy by "third world" countries attending (*Borba*, 12 September). According to a Western source, "the Lusaka conference has given the non-aligned club a new lease on life by shifting its stance. The shift is readily illustrated by the conference's statement on Cambodia, in which Cambodia's past record in defending its 'independence, sovereignty and territorial integrity' is warmly praised, implying a none too oblique censure of the Lon Nol regime now in power in Pnom Penh." (*Economist*, 19 September.) The Lusaka statement suggested an increasingly harder line toward matters of independence and state autonomy, with the implication that U.S. intervention in Southeast Asia was not compatible with the views on nonalignment held by those at the conference.

The Western World. Concurrently with their affirmations of nonalignment, the Yugoslavs showed an increasing cordiality toward the West and expressed a need for closer economic and political cooperation, particularly with the United States and West Germany. In March 1970, Karl Schiller, West Germany's minister of economics, indicated to the Yugoslavs that he envisioned closer economic cooperation between the two countries, touching upon matters such as bilateral goods exchanges, freer trade, cooperation in industrial production, credit financing, balance of payments issues, and the tourist trade (Tanyug, 5 March). In October the two governments concluded agreements that provide for extensive cooperation of West German metalworkers' unions with Yugoslav metalworkers resident in West Germany. On 25-27 November, Walter Scheel, the West German foreign minister, visited Yugoslavia and held extensive talks with Mirko Tepavac that were hailed as friendly and as promising increased cooperation in all areas of common interest between the two countries (*Komunist*, 25 November). Tepavac stated: "Yugoslavia and Federal Germany, developing friendly and fruitful cooperation, are contributing to the building of a Europe of peace, understanding, and security which all of us need" (Tanyug, 25 November). A specific economic interest of the Yugoslav government in West Germany concerns the nearly 500,000 Yugoslav workers in that country. Workers residing abroad are likely to increase in number as Yugoslavia seeks to develop its trade in new areas of Western Europe. This objective was pursued by Tito in a round of visits that began in Brussels on 6 October and was to take him eventually to all six members of the Common Market (*Christian Science Monitor*, 15 October). Despite the Yugoslavs' attempts to cultivate less developed countries, it is clear that they see their economic and political future as being intimately linked with Western Europe.

The major event involving the United States was the visit of President Nixon on 30 September-2 October. Although earlier in the year Tito sharply condemned the U.S. military incursion into Cambodia, which he saw as a violation of Cambodia's independence and neutrality (Tanyug, 6 May), it was obvious that he regarded the Nixon visit as, at the very least, signifying a serious commitment on the part of the United States as to the integrity of Yugoslavia as a state (*Borba*,

1-3 October). Nixon's visit to Yugoslavia, coupled with his earlier visit to Romania, made it clear to the Soviet Union that the United States viewed possible Soviet movement through the Balkans to achieve access to the eastern Mediterranean a matter of utmost concern. The magnitude of Tito's interest in the visit was indicated by the fact that to receive Nixon he stayed home from the funeral of President Nasser, who was a very close and long-time friend. The Yugoslav regime also was host to Premier Süleyman Demirel of Turkey, whose visit included discussion of matters of mutual interest touching upon the security of the eastern Mediterranean (Tanyug, 1 September). Over the last few years the Yugoslav position with respect to the Vatican has been improving considerably, and during 1970 the mutual diplomatic representatives of these two states were upgraded to embassy status. Also, Monsignor Agostino Casaroli, the Vatican secretary of state for public affairs, visited Yugoslavia and spoke highly of improved Yugoslav-Vatican relations (*Politika*, 27 August). Despite the fact that Italy has become the "supermarket of Yugoslavia" and has maintained for many years rather cordial relations with the Yugoslavs, a measure of tension and unease became apparent between the two countries during 1970 involving the reintroduction by the Italian government of the issue of Istria. A concrete result was a last-minute postponement by Tito of a scheduled visit to Italy, a move announced by the Yugoslavs without explanation which marked the gravity of Yugoslav concern over resurrecting the Istrian question (*New York Times*, 10 December). On the whole, the general trend in Yugoslavia as regards the West seems to suggest increasingly closer ties with West Germany, particularly in the economic sphere, and the real possibility of somewhat increased reliance politically upon the United States.

Ideology. Events relating to ideology during 1970 reflected both the growing strain in Yugoslav-Soviet relations and the internal discussion concerning the reform of political institutions. As regards the first, the Yugoslavs reacted strongly to the Soviet celebration of the Lenin Centenary, charging that in stressing the "role of Leninism in the present-day age" the Soviets were in fact making of Lenin's work a dogma opposed to the intended creative use of his principles (*Vjesnik*, 31 January). The central criticism was that they were presenting Lenin as a far more militant and rigid personality ("a bellicose Saint George brandishing his flaming sword") than the Yugoslavs would like to see, and this position was viewed by the Yugoslavs as a direct outgrowth of Soviet preoccupations with the Titoist heresy. During the year the Yugoslavs also saw fit to welcome with open arms Roger Garaudy, the French communist who was removed from the Central Committee of the French Communist Party for his criticism of the Soviet-led invasion of Czechoslovakia. This gesture had implications both as a subtle barb thrown at the Soviet Union and as an expression of the "humanistic" dimension of Yugoslav socialism (*Le Monde*, 8 April). There was also a series of articles in Yugoslav newspapers that dealt with the problem of neo-Stalinism and the threat of its reemergence in Yugoslav society, with the observation that ever larger numbers of "philosophers, political scientists, and historians" had changed from positions they held during the height of the de-Stalinization period (*Borba*, 18-20 March).

With respect to internal matters, the Yugoslavs have begun to talk increasingly about the *de facto* existence of their "open society"—with the realization, moreover, that the existence of any such open system unavoidably brings with it increased problems and more visible conflicts (*Politika*, 1 March). Given this and the concern with a possible reassertion of neo-Stalinist centralized authority, the Yugoslavs also talk increasingly about seeking out a "new ideology," one that will recognize the immediate existential relevance of self-management, proclaim the importance of having a variety of Marxist theories, and encourage LCY members to approach problems in a measured and reasonable way (*Borba*, 18-19 and 24 April). These matters touching upon ideology in Yugoslavia suggest the continuance of what have been trends existing in the country for a great many years, namely, a growing sense that pluralistic Marxism is quite proper and that one must always be on guard against bureaucratic and neo-Stalinist resurgence. The dialogues that have been going on within Yugoslav theoretical circles suggest that it has become both more difficult and more tenuous to speak of an explicit and coherent Yugoslav Marxist ideology.

Publications. The chief organs of the LCY are *Komunist*, a weekly magazine, and *Socijalizam*, a theoretical monthly. The important daily newspapers are *Borba* (Belgrade) and *Vjesnik* (Zagreb), organs of the SAWP bodies of Serbia and Croatia respectively, and *Politika* (Belgrade). The Vjesnik publishing house also puts out a weekly *Vjesnik u srijedu*. The Yugoslav communist youth organization publishes a weekly, *Mladost*. Tanyug is the official Yugoslav news agency.

M. G. Z.

WESTERN EUROPE

AUSTRIA

The Communist Party of Austria (Kommunistische Partei Österreichs; KPÖ) was founded on 3 November 1918. A pro-Chinese Marxist-Leninist party was formed in 1966 (see below).

The KPÖ enjoys legal status, but plays an insignificant role in Austrian political affairs. Since 1959 the party has been without representation in the Austrian parliament. In the general election on 1 March 1970 the KPÖ suffered a serious defeat, polling only 1.10 per cent of the total vote.

In comparison to its own estimated membership of 32,000 in 1969, the KPÖ listed 26,000 members in 1970, a figure that is only 20 per cent of its highest recorded membership, in 1953 (*Neue Zürcher Zeitung*, 3 June 1970). The population of Austria is 7,349,000 (estimated 1968). During 1970 the party was plagued with numerous defections, particularly among trade unionists (*Le Monde*, Paris, 5-6 July). The widening schism within the KPÖ (see *YICA*, 1970, pp. 120-21) continued, centering around condemnation by the "progressive" wing, under former Politburo member Franz Marek, of the Warsaw Pact invasion of Czechoslovakia, and by support by "conservatives," headed by party chairman Franz Muhri, for a course of "normalization" in the KPÖ patterned after that later instituted in Czechoslovakia. This dispute contributed not only to the decline in membership, but also to the KPÖ's election defeat. It also influenced the decision to convene the Twenty-first Congress of the party in May 1970, only sixteen months after the Twentieth Congress, and to reorganize the party's youth organization, the Free Austrian Youth (Freie Österreichische Jugend, FÖJ).

The FÖJ was replaced by the Communist Youth of Austria (Kommunistische Jugend Österreichs, KJÖ) at a constituent congress in May 1970. At a meeting of the KJÖ's Preparatory Committee, in January, a draft platform for the KJÖ was approved. It rejected the independent policies of the FÖJ—manifest in repeated criticism of the invasion of Czechoslovakia in the FÖJ's party-financed organ, *Jugend*—and supported a "joint political-ideological basis" with the KPÖ (*Volksstimme*, 25 March).

No doubt in view of the decline in party membership and the fact that 63 per cent of the KPÖ's members are over fifty years of age (*Borba*, Belgrade, 31 March), the KJÖ platform stressed the necessity for "as many of its members as possible [to] continue their political activities as members of the KPÖ" (*Volksstimme*, 25 March). This point was elaborated upon at the constituent congress by Politburo member Erwin Scharf, who defined the KJÖ's task as "developing young communists" in a "young people's organization which stands with the party" (*Volksstimme*, 9 May). Countering FÖJ rejection of identification of the goals of Austrian youth with those of the socialist states, the KJÖ's newly elected chairman, Central Committee member Otto Podolsky, stated: "[Their criticism] should be guided by the fact that we are not dealing with enemies, but with comrades who, under different conditions, are struggling on a higher level of social development for the same goal" (*ibid.*, 10 May). At this time the KJÖ announced its intention to strive "for full membership in the World Federation of Democratic Youth" (*ibid.*, 12 May).

The KPÖ-controlled Trade Union Unity organization (Gewerkschaftliche Einheit; GE) cooperates with the independent and influential Austrian Trade Union League, but has influence only in a few labor unions at the local level and is not a decisive force in national labor affairs. The "normalization" process in the GE appeared to parallel that within the KPÖ itself (see *ibid.*, 22 October; *Die Presse*, Vienna, 20 October; *Weg und Ziel*, September). Several auxiliary organizations, such as the Austrian Peace Council and the League of Democratic Women, are affiliates of international communist-front groups. There also exists an Austrian-Soviet Society (Österreichische-Sowjetische Gesellschaft).

Leadership and Organization. The KPÖ's highest organ is the congress, normally held every four years. The Twenty-first Congress, held in Vienna on May 28-31, 1970, was convened, in the words of Franz Muhri, to "create the prerequisites for overcoming the crisis in the party" (*Volksstimme*, 15 April). The congress was therefore devoted to internal matters within the party and to domestic political attitudes. The congress elected a new Politburo, Central Committee, Central Control Commission, and Arbitration Commission (*ibid.*, 2 June). Franz Muhri was re-elected party chairman, with 57 of the 319 delegates voting against him (primarily because of his moderate position on rejecting the earlier KPÖ condemnation of the invasion of Czechoslovakia). The Politburo chosen to serve under him, which because of the party schism had decreased to five members in December 1969, consisted entirely of conservatives: Franz Muhri, Friedl Fürnberg, Hans Kalt, Walter Wachs, and Erwin Scharf (previous members), and Franz Hager, Leopold Horak, Franz Karger, Franz Leitner, and Alois Peter (new members). Members of the Secretariat are Muhri, Wachs, Kalt, Scharf, and Heinrich Fritz. Scharf and Kalt were elected secretaries of the Central Committee. The Central Committee itself decreased in size from 87 to 64 members. In his analysis of the congress, Franz Muhri explained that the personnel changes were a "decisive prequisite for uniting the party and overcoming the crisis," because there could be "no united Party without a united leadership," and that the progressives, headed by Franz Marek, Egon Kodicek, Theodor Prager, and Fred Margulies, had "almost entirely incapacitated" the leadership in 1969 (*WMR*, August). None of these four progressives obtained reelection to the Central Committee, and 24 of the 27 progressives who had opposed the "normalization" within the party (see below) and unconditional alignment with the Communist Party of the Soviet Union (CPSU) were expelled. *Volksstimme* indicated on 20 November that Marek too would shortly be expelled.

Party Internal Affairs. The rift within the KPÖ, which had been growing since the Twentieth Congress, culminated at the Central Committee plenum in November 1969, at which time 27 members of the committee walked out of the meeting in protest against the expulsion of FÖJ leader Fritz Zapf from the Politburo and against the failure of the party leadership to discuss "ideological differences of opinion . . . openly and publicly" (*Volksstimme*, 27 November 1969). At a plenum in December it was decided that the Twenty-first Congress should be convened ahead of schedule, primarily because attempts to reunify the party on the basis of resolutions of the Nineteenth and Twentieth congresses had been "prevented" by the progressive wing of the party, led by Ernst Fischer and Franz Marek (*Volksstimme*, 30 May 1970). It was the first time since 1945 that a new congress had been called within a year.

In his evaluation of the Twenty-first Congress, Franz Muhri gave the reasons for convening it: (1) as a result of the party's election defeat in March "a new political situation had taken shape . . . which had to be analyzed," and (2) "the crisis within the party had been further aggravated last autumn." The purpose of the congress was to take "resolute steps to overcome the crisis." (*WMR*, August).

The election defeat influenced the reestablishment of the monolithic governance of the party at the Twenty-first Congress, and this in turn consolidated support for the party's course of "normalization." Nevertheless, the basic domestic and foreign programs of the party—as outlined by Muhri at the preelection party conference, held in Vienna in January—were not altered substantially. Muhri acknowledged then that the election would be the "most difficult" since 1945 since (1) the party was in a "difficult transition period" and (2) the election would offer a clear alternative to the Austrian Socialist Party (*Volksstimme*, 11 January).

In contrast to the KPÖ's support of the Austrian Socialist Party (Sozialistische Partei Österreichs; SPÖ) in 1966, Muhri now accused it of being "today more than ever a servant of capitalism" and a "growing threat to democracy and security." In his judgment, the SPÖ had even discarded "the socialist principles still contained in the SPÖ party program of 1958" (*ibid.*). With the intention of discrediting the Free Democratic Party (Freie Demokratische Partei; FPÖ) as fascist, he characterized it as an "antidemocratic, anti-Austrian right-wing party [which] functions primarily as an agent of the interests of large West German monopolies." This castigation was aimed at preventing the possible formation of a small coalition of the FPÖ with either the SPÖ or the Austrian People's Party (Österreichische Volkspartei, ÖVP). Thus the KPÖ demanded that both these parties reject in advance the possibility of such a coalition (*ibid.*), and sought to make this problem a central issue in the campaign (*ibid.*, 8 February).

Muhri described the KPÖ as the "only party offering a policy [of] democratic reform" and seeking to "reduce the influence of domestic and foreign capitalism and enforce methods of codetermination on the part of the workers in business, in politics, in education, and in the mass media sector" (*ibid.*, 11 January). In February, *Weg und Ziel* carried articles by Politburo member Hans Kalt urging a "real reform of democracy" and by Erwin Scharf attacking the SPÖ as "not a socialist party."

Meanwhile the *Wiener Tagebuch*, edited by Franz Marek, published three articles from the "leftist and independent" viewpoint in its January-February issue. Hannes Morschl in an article entitled "Six Reasons for Not Voting" argued that the "alternative to the prevailing system" was "not to be sought in any leaders and authoritarian organizations" but "in the solidarity of all those who are being kept dependent and powerless in the factories, in the schools, and in the universities." Kurt Urban, reelected to the Central Committee at the Twentieth Congress, saw the only alternative in voting for the SPÖ despite its policy of "social partnership," since the KPÖ, "with its silent acceptance of developments in Czechoslovakia, with the expulsion of Ernst Fischer, with its return to Stalinist positions," no longer had "any credibility among Austrian labor and among the other left-wing forces." (Urban, a Central Committee member, was not reelected at the congress in May.) Even so, the journal also included an article by conservative Politburo member Hans Kalt, who called for electoral support of the KPÖ as the "most effective weapon from the viewpoint of a genuine alternative . . . of a genuine pressure in the direction toward change of the system."

The ensuing defeat was attributed by Muhri to internal party difficulties. Indeed, he even found some positive aspects in the SPÖ victory, since the SPÖ had adopted "some important demands" of the KPÖ, such as tax reform, electoral reform, and reduction of obligatory military duty to six months. (*Ibid.*, 3 March.) Following the October by-elections in Vienna and provincial elections in the Tirol, the KPÖ acknowledged that it did not yet appear to the Austrian voters as offering an "alternative" (*ibid.*, 6 October). In November, however, the Austrian parliament passed an electoral reform law which the KPÖ Politburo viewed as providing a "real possibility" of victory for party candidates in the next parliamentary elections (*ibid.*, 28 November).

The Twenty-first Congress was held in Vienna on 28-30 May under the watchword of "stronger unity of ranks of the KPÖ and the struggle against revisionism" (TASS 31 May). Throughout May, articles in *Volksstimme* and *Weg und Ziel* espoused the cause of "normalization." Foreshadowing the line affirmed at the congress, Hans Kalt pointed to the "downward trend" in party unity for "more than a decade" and declared that anti-Soviet positions would be opposed by an "unequivocal stand" (*Weg und Ziel*, May). Central Committee member Walter Hollitscher accused Marek and Fischer of espousing a "Stalinist vulgarization of an alleged Leninist restriction of Marxism to solely Russian conditions" and pointed out that no "resolution had been made to accuse the U.S.S.R. of 'pan-communism' " (*Volksstimme*, 6 May). Bruno Furch (who was elected to the Central Committee at the congress) declared that the "anarchy of 1968-69" made it clear that the "communists of every country must come to realize that they are responsible for one another" (*ibid.*, 13 May).

The congress resolution, passed by a vote of 320 to 12, rejected a "new discussion" on developments in Czechoslovakia. It endorsed the idea of "Austria's way to socialism" as differing "in many respects from the way of the October Revolution," but rejected at the same time "theoretical conceptions which speak of different 'models' of socialism" as a contradiction of "Marxist thought." The resolution declared that "without unity in ideological principles, unity of action is also ultimately lost," and therefore called for a "clear-cut ideological separation from revisionist and also from dogmatic and sectarian views." Although the KPÖ supported "tolerant discussions on all newly arisen problems," it did so with the qualification that the "basis for this discussion must be the party, its organizations and leadership, as well as its publications." Only on the basis of fundamental principles contained in the "Theses on Future Prospects" and "Programmatic Guidelines" of the Nineteenth Congress and in the resolution of the Twentieth Congress would the reestablishment of unity be possible. Thus the resolution called on the party to place itself, "its struggle and its activities in Austria," in the center. In this connection it emphasized the importance of gaining "new, particularly young" members (*Weg und Ziel*, 7 August).

In his analysis of the congress Muhri stressed these points once again. Similar to the resolution he endorsed the "achievement of joint action" with the SPÖ and "simultaneous principled and business-like criticism of the social partnership policy and the anticommunism of the SPÖ's right-wing leaders." But it would be "a way without civil war, through an alliance of several parties." He listed two others as essential in achieving a "progressive change of the political stand taken by a sizable section of the SPO (and also of a large section of the OVP, which consists mainly of workers and peasants)." With a "firm stand on the basis of Marxism-Leninism," (1) the KPO must strengthen itself substantially, so as to lead Austria to a "profound democratic renewal" and thence to "socialism," and (2) there must be "public pressure, broad mass movements and class battles in which the working people learn from their own experience." In this connection he added: "We have failed to give a fitting rebuff to the incorrect ideas that the revolutionary party would have a chance of success only in the event of another major economic crisis." (*WMR*, August.)

The congress avoided an open break by adopting a compromise to avoid annulling the progressives' condemnation of the invasion of Czechoslovakia (see below, "International Affairs and Positions"). But Muhri's justification of the "essential personnel changes" in the party leadership as contributing to a "united party" reflected the "decisive steps" that were taken to overcome the schism (*ibid.*). According to the *Wiener Tagebuch* (July-August), the KPÖ had executed a " 'field' purge" of the Central Committee and elected a leadership which would "purposefully pursue 'normalization' on the Prague pattern." Among those removed from the Central Committee were the economist Theodor Prager, a member of the communist movement for thirty-five years; Egon Kodicek, recently elected secretary of the powerful confederation of Austrian trade unions; and Martin Gruenberg, president of the Austrian-Soviet Society. Alois Peter and Franz Leitner, ultraconservatives who had approved the intervention in Czechoslovakia, were elected to the Politburo, joining the so-called "East German" group represented by Politburo members Erwin Scharf and Hans Kalt. Prager commented that Muhri, although he had made "several serious attempts to reform and save [the] party," had "come to terms with the Soviet 'establishment' " (*Politique Aujourd'hui*, Paris, April).

On the question whether the KPÖ, under the course of "normalization," could again become a political force in Austria, progressives suggested after the congress that the elaboration of a leftist platform, as supported by Marek and Fischer, would probably be too far removed from the orthodox communist line to find a majority, but that a regrouping of the trade union forces and a rebirth of the class struggle might be effective (see *Le Monde*, 5-6 July).

Domestic Attitudes and Activities. The attack on "capitalism" in Austria was reflected in the political-ideological platforms of both the KPÖ and the KJÖ. The KJÖ regarded foreign capital and policies of "labor peace" as responsible for the absence of a "long-term education policy and a research policy" and thus for Austria's being "one of the underdeveloped countries in Europe." (*Volksstimme*, 25 March 1970). In order to more effectively participate in the "class struggle" on a "Marxist-Leninist basis in close alliance with the Austrian communist party," the KJÖ called for the organizing of "the young generation that aligns itself with the working class."

The resolution of the Twenty-first Congress indicated that, confronted with a socialist government, the KPÖ had the "job of representing the demands and interests of the working people as an independent force," leading the "broadest possible segments in unified actions" and developing their "political consciousness." Defining the party attitude toward other parties in Austria, the resolution declared that, although it was incorrect to "equate the SPÖ with the parties of big capital," within the working class the SPÖ remained the chief hindrance to the development of class consciousness and the class struggle because of its "social partnership ideology." Muhri explained the characteristic distinguishing the KPÖ from the SPÖ in terms of the "relationship between reform and revolution." The KPÖ advocated reform measures, but as a "revolutionary Marxist-Leninist party" its essential function was to "make the people aware of the struggle for economic and social improvement as part of an orientation which is aimed at curbing and eventually eliminating the power of big capital, and at implementing socialism." In sharp contrast, the "reform activity" of the SPÖ was seen as serving "not to prevent but rather to uphold capitalist rule." (*Ibid.*, 30 May.) To achieve its ends, the KPÖ would have to employ all forms of propaganda and agitation in order to "show the great masses of unionists the contradiction between their conceptions and the policy of the SPÖ government." Moreover, the KPÖ would have to give its own members spoken and written arguments to "develop their theoretical and political knowledge" and relate daily issues to "basic questions concerning the nature of capitalism and the necessity of achieving socialism." In addition, a means for the "exchange of their experiences" was needed, and since about "7,000 to 9,000" members worked in isolation in enterprises, such exchange would enable the party to "penetrate thousands of small and medium-sized enterprises." (*Weg und Ziel*, no. 7-8.)

In June a committee of former members of the communist-controlled GE formed a "Workers' Association for Trade Union Unity" which the KPÖ's *Weg und Ziel* (December) termed "incompatible with membership" in the GE and saw as having as its purpose the splitting of the GE. The Central Committee plenum in September passed a resolution reminding KPÖ functionaries that the party congress had designated the "work in enterprises and trade unions . . . as the decisive point of main stress," and that "any attempted revision, one-sided interpretation, or departure from this resolution in practice would not only conflict with congress resolutions, but would render more difficult [the party's] orientation on improvement of efforts in the enterprises." Apparently reflecting problems created by the rift in the GE membership, the resolution also specifically drew attention to the independence of the GE from the party and to the GE's purpose to join together "communist and noncommunist workers and employees in the trade union struggle." It went on to affirm that "unity of action and cooperation between the party and the GE must be strengthened and consolidated" and that "all attempts to use the GE as a platform for fractional activity in opposition to the KPÖ" would be in conflict with these principles.(*Ibid.*)

International Views and Positions. The KPÖ's prestige in the international communist movement has for many years exceeded its domestic political importance, primarily because of the party's record of staunch opposition during the Nazi era, but also because of its traditionally strong pro-Soviet orientation. The latter was shaken when the KPÖ severely censured the invasion of Czechoslovakia, but was reentrenched at the Twenty-first Congress, in May 1970, whose resolution devoted special attention to the endorsement of the Soviet practice of Marxism-Leninism. Censure of the invasion was not officially recanted, but neither was it the subject of discussion. A motion for censure was tabled by its referral to the Central Committee for consideration of "new aspects" (*Volksstimme*, 2 June).

The foreign policy position of the party was formulated in the preelection platform as follows: Austria should pursue an "active policy of neutrality" while seeking to bring about a "just peace" in Vietnam and in the Middle East, and should press for solution of the problems of European security and disarmament and the "elimination of all forms of colonialism." The policy of neutrality was defined as including recognition of the governments of the Democratic Republic of Vietnam and the Provisional Revolutionary Government of South Vietnam, acceptance of the existence of two German states, and establishment of normal diplomatic relations with the German Democratic Republic (GDR). (*Ibid.*, 11 January.) This posture was reiterated similarly at the party congress, where Franz Muhri declared the KPÖ an advocate of "active neutrality in the interests of peace, a policy of solidarity with the peoples of the third world"; criticized the United States for expanding the "Vietnam war" into an "Indochina war"; and called for negotiations between East and West Germany. Muhri also called for the defeat of those forces in the Federal Republic who sought "Anschluss" of the GDR with West Germany (*ibid.*, 30 May). But whereas the KPÖ in its preelection platform stated "we were and are against the invasion of Czechoslovakia by the troops of the five Warsaw Pact States" (*ibid.*, 11 January), the congress resolution declared: "[The party has] turned decisively against exploiting our critical position on the entry of the Warsaw Pact states for anti-Sovietism of various types." The resolution went on to include in its foreign policy goals the recognition by Austria of the Chinese People's Republic and North Korea. (*Weg und Ziel*, August.) According to Franz Muhri, the congress resolution "brushed aside every form of anti-Sovietism" and declared the party's "close unity with the Soviet Union, with the international working-class and liberation movement." Thus the congress "opposed the splitting policy of the leadership of the Communist Party of China," which was "hampering the world-wide struggle for democracy, independence, peace and socialism" at a time when the "achievement and consolidation of unity in the communist movement" was "more necessary than ever before." (*WMR*, August.)

In an article in *Pravda* (5 August), the KPÖ's support for a European security system was reiterated by Bruno Furch, elected to the Central Committee in May. He urged the convening of a European security conference and criticized the Austrian government for supporting the U.S. and West German policy of nonrecognition of the GDR. Before the plenary session of the Central Committee in September, Muhri termed the Soviet-West German treaty of August 1970 a major defeat for the "proponents of the cold war," called for diplomatic recognition of the GDR and the convening of a European security conference, and praised the "firm peace policy" of the Soviet Union (*Volksstimme*, 22 September).

Although the KPÖ congress endorsed the course of "normalization," this did not silence the opposition. In July, twenty-one former members of the Central Committee signed a written protest against the expulsion of Alexander Dubcek from the Communist Party of Czechoslovakia.

International Activities and Party Contacts. Representatives of fifteen foreign communist parties attended the KPÖ congress in May 1970. The KPÖ enjoyed the attendance of all the Eastern Europe communist-ruled states (except Albania) and not only the neighboring ones. The Soviet delegation, at the head of the visitors, was led by P. A. Rodionov, second secretary of the Georgian Communist Party and candidate-member of the CPSU Central Committee. Rodionov had also led the CPSU Central Committee delegation to Vienna for observances of the twenty-fifth anniversary of Austria's liberation on 11-19 April and for the KPÖ celebration of the Lenin Centenary. On the excuse of pressing business at home, the Italian Communist Party did not send delegates to the KPÖ congress, thus pointing up its criticism of "normalization." At the beginning of May, the KJÖ announced it was striving for full membership in the World Federation of Democratic Youth" (*Volksstimme*, 12 May).

The KPÖ was represented by Leopold Hornik at a theoretical conference sponsored by the CPSU's Institute of Marxism-Leninism, held in Moscow on 24-26 February. In January, Erwin Scharf and Franz Lang, both reelected to the Central Committee in May, visited Warsaw at the invitation of the Polish United Workers' Party. In February, Romanian Communist Party secretary Paul Niculescu-Mizil, Central Committee member Mihail Florescu, and Central Committee alternate member Stefan Andrei held talks in Vienna with Franz Muhri, Hans Kalt, and Heinrich Firsch (Buckarest Domestic Service, 13 February). At the end of July a KPÖ delegation led by Erwin Scharf visited North Korea. At the end of November a Soviet delegation visited Innsbruck for the twenty-fifth anniversary of the Austrian-Soviet Society. In late October, Politburo member Franz Hager led a KPÖ delegation to East Germany to "study socialist democracy in practice in industry and agriculture" (*Volksstimme*, 25 October). On 17 December a KPÖ delegation visited with West German communist party represenatives in Bonn.

Publications. The official organ of the KPÖ is the daily newspaper *Volksstimme*. Its circulation is estimated at 40,000 on weekdays and 70,000 on Sundays. After the resignation of the long-time editor, "progressive" Franz West, and more than twelve of his staff in the autumn of 1969, it was announced in January 1970 that Friedl Fürnberg had taken over provisional direction of the editorial board. With the 25 June 1970 issue Hans Kalt was listed as editor in chief.

The KPÖ monthly theoretical journal is *Weg und Ziel*.Franz Marek was removed as editor in November 1969 and replaced by an "editorial collective" headed by Hans Kalt. In addition to the journal's task of disseminating Marxism-Leninism, it set itself the goal in January 1970 of becoming an "aggressive political journal." After the KPÖ ended publication of the cultural and political periodical *Tagebuch* in July 1969, Franz Marek and other KPÖ "progressives" began publishing the bi-monthly "leftist and independent" *Wiener Tagebuch*, of which Marek became editor at the end of 1969. The journal is independently financed and remains the subject of KPÖ attack for its "revisionist and anarchist leanings" (*Weg und Ziel*, March and September 1970).

*   *   *

The Marxist-Leninist Party of Austria (Marxistische-Leninistische Partei Österreichs; M-LPÖ), established in May 1966, is a legal party and is pro-Chinese. The M-LPÖ is generally estimated to have fewer than 500 members, and spokesmen have acknowledged financial difficulties. The party is headed by Franz Strobl as first secretary. In December 1969, Strobl attended the twenty-fifth anniversary celebration of communist rule in Albania.

The M-LPÖ did not participate in the 1970 Austrian national elections. The party organ *Rote Fahne* (March) claimed that the reported abstention of 430,000 registered voters was an "unmistakable rejection of the ruling capitalist exploiter system" in answer to the M-LPÖ's request for an election boycott. The election defeat of the "revisionist KPÖ" was explained as attributable to its having "repulsed the masses" by betraying all revolutionary principles through its disavowal of "the proletarian revolution, the violent stripping of power from capital, and the violent expropriation of capital." Forecasting public "disappointment" in the "reformist and revisionist parties" in the elections, *Rote Fahne* urged "persistent small-scale political work" and a "tenacious and patient struggle for every individual person" whose energies could "be channeled into the development of revolutionary realization," "class consciousness," and "combat readiness."

On the international front, the M-LPÖ repeated its criticism of the "Soviet tsars," the intervention in Czechoslovakia, the "Soviet revisionist, aggressive provocations on the Chinese border," the Brezhnev doctrine, and "American imperialism." At the commencement of the Strategic Arms Limitation Talks in Vienna between the United States and the Soviet Union, both governments were called upon to "get out of Austria." The negotiations themselves were described as not serving "peace," but as having the aim of "securing and establishing the military, political, and economic ascendancy of these powers"—the talks represented, therefore, an attack against Communist China, which was termed the "decisive obstacle to the realization of plans for imperialist . . . division of the world" (*Rote Fahne*, April-May). The journal took a similar view of the conclusion of the Soviet-West German treaty in August and deplored the "threat to Austria" posed by the "close alliance of the two greatest imperialist powers of Europe" (*ibid..*, October).

D. L. B.

BELGIUM

The communist movement in Belgium is represented by three parties. The oldest and largest of these is the Communist Party of Belgium (Parti Communiste de Belgique; PCB), which was founded in 1921. The others are a second Communist Party of Belgium (hereafter referred to as PCB-II), formed in December 1963 by dissidents from the PCB, and the Marxist-Leninist Communist Party of Belgium (Parti Communiste Marxiste-Léniniste de Belgique; PCMLB), formed in November 1967 by dissidents from the PCB-II and known as the Communist Party (Marxist-Leninist) of Belgium until the current name was adopted on 28 June 1970. In addition to these three parties, there is a growing Trotskyist movement represented by the Socialist Young Guards (Jeunes Gardes Socialistes; JGS), a group aligned with the United Secretariat of the Fourth International. All four organizations enjoy legal status.

Although none of the above parties publishes membership figures, Western sources estimate that the PCB has between 11,000 and 12,500 members. The PCB-II and PCMLB are believed to have 50 and 150 members respectively; while the JGS has a growing membership, which in 1970 was estimated at more than 500. The population of Belgium is 10,000,000 (estimated 1970).

Two of the communist parties—the PCB and the PCB-II—participated in the parliamentary elections of 31 March 1968. In the elections to the Chamber of Representatives, the PCB polled 170,686 votes (3.3 per cent of the total), whereas in 1965 it had polled 236,333 votes (4.56 per cent). The party lost one seat, giving it a total of five (out of 212). In the elections to the Senate, the PCB obtained 180,156 votes (3.52 per cent), retaining its two seats (out of 106). The PCB-II, which contested the elections under four different tickets—including the United Popular Front (Front Uni Populaire)—obtained 5,358 votes for the Chamber (23,903 in 1965), and 5,271 votes for the Senate. No PCB-II candidates were elected.

The PCB was the only communist party to participate in the local elections that were held on 11 October 1970. Comparing the results with the 1964 local elections, *Le Drapeau Rouge* (16 October) noted that, with the exception of western Hainaut, the party had "suffered reversals." The PCB-II did not participate in the elections; an editorial in the party organ, *La Voix du Peuple* (September-October), declared: "[The party] has neither the strength or the necessary funds—we say this with utmost frankness—and electoral participation is not a priority for it at this time." The PCMLB declared that participation in the elections would be an "opportunist mistake" (*Clarté*, 25 September-1 October). The JGS offered its support to the PCB.

PCB. Organization and Leadership. Since 1966, the PCB has been divided into two branches, Walloon and Flemish, each of which directs in its own region the carrying out of party policy. The leaderships of the two branches meet every year to make joint decisions, with each having the right of veto. The ratio of Walloon to Flemish members in the party, however, is five to one; and all PCB parliamentary representatives are Walloons. Party policy of a national and international nature is decided at the PCB's congresses, which in recent years were held annually, with an exceptional lapse in 1969 and, once again, in 1970. The party congress elects the Central Committee. This committee, in turn, at its first meeting, elects the party's president, vice-presidents, Politburo, Secretariat, and press officials.

The leadership of the PCB during 1970 was elected at a special Central Committee plenary session which met on 20-21 December 1969. It consisted of: president, Marc Drumaux; vice-presidents, Jef Turf (president of the Flemish branch) and Jean Terfve (president of the Walloon branch); Politburo—Jean Blume, Urbain Coussement, Jan Debrouwere, Albert De Coninck, Marc Drumaux, Georges Glineur, Marcel Levaux, Gaston Moulin, Claude Renard, Jean Terfve, Jef Turf, Frans Van den Branden, and Louis Van Geyt; Secretariat—Jean Blume, Urbain Coussement, Albert De Coninck, and Jef Turf. Claude Renard was in charge of the party's publishing activities (and director of the PCB French-language weekly, *Le Drapeau Rouge*) and Jan Debrouwere was director of the party's Flemish-language weekly, *De Rode Vaan*.

The PCB directs a youth organization, the Communist Youth of Belgium (Jeunesse Communiste de Belgique; JCB), and a student group, the National Union of Communist Students (Union Nationale des Etudiants Communistes). The party does not have its own trade union, but exerts some influence in the country's largest trade union, the General Workers' Federation of Belgium (Fédération Générale du Travail de Belgique; FGTB).

Domestic Views and Policies. Aware of its limited support within the country, the PCB continued in 1970 to call for a consolidation of left-wing forces, focusing the thrust of its appeal on the Belgian Socialist Party (Parti Socialiste Belge; PSB). The latter's president, Léo Collard, had issued a call on 1 May 1969 for a regrouping of "progressive" forces (*rassemblement progressiste*), which, the PCB, despite initial scepticism, had fully endorsed (see *YICA*, 1970, p. 127). On a number of occasions at the beginning of the year, the PCB reiterated its support for the *rassemblement progressiste*, at the same time lamenting that the other potential parties and groups of the *rassemblement* were temporizing. In an editorial (*Le Drapeau Rouge*, 30 January) Marc Drumaux stressed that it was no longer possible to do nothing, and asked whether the *rassemblement* was "born or stillborn." Drumaux referred to the wildcat strikes in the Limbourg mines that were in progress at that time and added: "Discussions between progressives continue lamely at different levels or get bogged down in many a 'problem' as if nothing was happening in Limbourg." Two weeks later—in an article entitled "Will the Progressives Take Power?" (*ibid.*, 13 February)—Drumaux declined to comment on the "complicated debates and direct and indirect polemics" that had taken place in the different socialist and Christian-democratic organizations and also within the PCB, but added:

> Let us emphasize, however, once again, that the principal fault that we have noted these last weeks is the serious lagging behind of the *rassemblement* in contrast to the real class struggle which is developing in the country.

Claiming that the PCB was attempting to bridge the gap, Drumaux turned to the PSB and stated: "Whatever Léo Collard says or writes is regularly defeated by the actions of certain other socialist leaders, starting with Edmond Leburton [minister of economic affairs], boss-minister." In what appeared to be the development of a new tactical approach, Drumaux referred to a policy of taking power piecemeal "in the factories, in the communes, in the universities, in the regions," adding that such a "movement" could reach "in a growing manner all the machinery of the state, starting with the Parliament." Drumaux did not elaborate further, saying only: "These proposals do not exhaust the subject. We will have to return to it."

The new tactical approach referred to by Drumaux in February was examined at greater length a month later in a discussion forum (*ibid.*, 13 March), in preparation for a JCB national conference, in a contribution by Jacques Nagels—entitled "A Revolutionary Strategy—To Organize Nuclei of Counter-Power at All Levels." Using as one of his major premises a statement made by Santiago Carrillo, secretary-general of the Communist Party of Spain, that "the majority of today's youth tends objectively toward becoming a great revolutionary force," Nagels called for "a new political strategy for a new political generation." This new strategy, he said, could be "summarized in one phrase: to organize nuclei of counter-power at all levels." Turning to a description of the "counter-power nucleus," Nagels explained: "If there exists in a school or in a university a decision-making body, the counter-power nucleus must be formed within this body. . . . The counter-power should not be located in an organization parallel to the decision-making body, as in the case of an action committee, for example." Concerning the formation of the "nuclei" within decision-making bodies, Nagels stated:

> The strategy for the organization of counter-power nuclei is essentially a strategy of alliances. . . . In fact, the counter-power nucleus *is not* and *cannot be* formed of representatives of the vanguard of the movement alone. To be very precise: the young people who comprise the counter-power nucleus are not three communists plus three Socialist Young Guards. This democratic counter-power must in the first place be the emanation of the masses of young progressives. This implies a very flexible and broad policy of alliances. (Emphasis in text.)

During the rest of the year, the PCB repeatedly publicized its call for a strategy of "counter-power." [1] In an editorial (*ibid.*, 15 May), Marc Drumaux noted: "It is not a question of bringing down neocapitalist power 'in one fell swoop.' We want that which is possible to attain, piece by piece." The PCB also organized a special party conference on 23 May, whose two major themes were the development of "counter-power" policy and the launching of the party's campaign for the October local elections, with the latter seen as the first major attempt to further the PCB's new strategy. Although the PCB devoted what appeared to be an exceptional amount of effort to the local elections, the voting showed a marked decline in electoral support (see above), with the party's Politburo commenting: "The total result is certainly not satisfactory" (*ibid.*, 16 October). With regard to support from other groups for the PCB's call for a policy of "counter-power," reactions were either nonexistent or unfavorable. Thus—despite its support for PCB candidates in the elections (see *ibid.*, 25 September)—the Trotskyist publication *La Gauche* (28 March) commented earlier on the PCB's "counter-power" policy: "One feels stupefied by the banality of it all."

There was considerable debate in Belgium during 1970 over regional issues, with various attempts throughout the year by the government parties to amend the country's constitution so as to introduce a certain degree of regional autonomy. It was not till 18 December that legislation was finally adopted, which, among other measures, constitutionally recognized Belgians as either Flemings or Walloons, and gave both communities, plus the Brussels area, significant regional powers in cultural and economic affairs. The PCB opposed the constitutional revision, claiming that it was a maneuver by the government to "preserve the basic [unitarian] structure while giving it a 'regional' appearance" (*Le Drapeau Rouge*, 3 July). The party called for a system of "democratic federalism," in which the three regions of Flanders, Wallonia, and Brussels would be given "real political, economic, financial, fiscal, social, and cultural powers" (Politburo statement, *ibid.*, 10 July; see also Politburo statement, *ibid.*, 26 June). Following the adoption of the constitutional reform, the party paper (*ibid.*, 25 December) editorialized that all was still not set-

---

[1] Among the more extensive treatments of the subject was a second, lengthier analysis by J. Nagels in the PCB's theoretical journal, *Cahiers marxistes* (September-November 1970).

tled, and that the "political struggle" should now be directed in the context of the implementation of the constitutional changes. The paper warned that the government would attempt to create new regional bodies in a manner that would offer a favorable basis for the development of "neocapitalism" and that would, at the same time, "block the country's evolution toward democratic federalism."

International Views and Policies. The major elements of PCB foreign policy were outlined by Marc Drumaux in a speech in the Chamber of Representatives on 11 February 1970. Claiming that the "fundamental goal" of his party was the "abolition of the two military blocs in Europe," Drumaux called for a Belgian "autonomous foreign policy" of "active neutrality," which would involve "disassociation from NATO without going to the other side." Drumaux advocated a foreign policy similar to that carried out by Finland, which, he said, "is not a socialist country." Turning to questions of European integration and the European Economic Community (EEC), Drumaux warned of the dangers of supranationalism, claiming that the creation of a supranational authority within the context of the six member countries of the EEC would run the risk of giving power to the strongest member country, which he identified as West Germany. He also warned of the "special ties" between Great Britain and the United States, declaring that if Great Britain should join the EEC the "penetration of American companies" into Western Europe would "take the form of an avalanche." Drumaux stated that all proposals for European cooperation were of a "warped" nature as long as Europe remained small. Europe, he added, "is bigger, it includes capitalist and socialist countries and two German states, whether one likes it or not." Drumaux called for a revision of the Rome treaty which had set up the EEC "during the period of the cold war," arguing that a "fundamental revision" of the treaty should have as its goal "the organization of economic cooperation between all European states." (*Le Drapeau Rouge*, 13 February.)

On matters pertaining to international communist affairs, the PCB followed a line of critical support of the views and policies of the Communist Party of the Soviet Union (CPSU). The party's stand was exemplified in an article by Claude Renard (*ibid.*, 29 May) in response to the expulsion of Roger Garaudy from the French Communist Party. Renard noted that since the Soviet-led invasion of Czechoslovakia, in August 1968, there had existed "nuances, contrasts, differences in the very heart of the international communist movement." Nevertheless, he blamed "American imperialism" for the "dangerously increasing" prospect of a generalized conflict, and expressed the PCB view that, "today as before, the socialist countries and particularly the Soviet Union are the chief rampart against this danger which threatens all peoples." Renard went on to state:

> We have our own ideas concerning certain aspects of the policies of certain socialist countries and we formulate them when there is need to do so, but [the party's enemies] will never manage to stampede us into ill-considered acts capable of harming the international communist movement.

Turning to Roger Garaudy, Renard claimed that the expelled French communist had "undoubtedly moved away from the above orientation," and that while the PCB was "willing to agree heartily that this or that point in his thinking still remain[ed] valid," his recent stands had led him in effect to "put his shoulder to the wheel of the powerful propaganda and 'poisoning' apparatus manipulated by the bourgeoisie."

The PCB's reaction to the expulsion of Alexander Dubček from the Communist Party of Czechoslovakia was stronger and more precise. *Le Drapeau Rouge* (3 July) commented that the expulsion was "the result of pressure of a tendency sometimes called 'conservative' which [had] reasserted itself since the military intervention of the 'Five' [Warsaw Pact forces] in August 1968." "The political orientation which this tendency represents," the PCB newspaper went on, "can, in our opinion, under no circumstance help Czechoslovakia to overcome the difficulties which exist in that country." It added, however: "One would be wrong to interpret the expulsion of comrade Dubček, though shocking in many respects, as a return to Novotnýism." The paper noted that Gustáv Husák, first secretary of the Czechoslovak party, had declared that there would not be a return to the "artificial and very detrimental practice of political trials," and added:

> We are inclined, in fact, to believe that that period of history is forever behind us, but we believe also that international democratic opinion would be more easily convinced if there were an end to the feeding of its apprehensions by decisions of the type just taken against comrade Dubček.

The PCB expressed further disapproval of developments in Czechoslovakia following the revocation of the citizenship of Artur London, author of *The Confession* and former deputy foreign minister, who was imprisoned in 1951 and released and rehabilitated in 1956: "Many communists—including ourselves—consider that this new punishment inflicted upon one of the victims of the trials in the 1950's reminds one of procedures that the international communist movement has since condemned" (*ibid.*, 4 September).

On a number of other occasions during 1970 the PCB expressed opinions that demonstrated a certain independence from CPSU views. Thus, when Alexander Solzhenitsyn was awarded the Nobel Prize for Literature, *Le Drapeau Rouge* (16 October), while reiterating the Soviet line that the action by the Nobel prize jury had political motives, added: "Expelled or not from the [Soviet] Union of Writers, crowned or not by the Swedish jury, Solzhenitsyn remains what he is: the greatest contemporary Soviet writer." The PCB also reported favorably on the expulsion from the Communist Party of Spain of pro-Soviet dissidents such as Enrique Líster (*ibid.*); and gave considerable coverage (see, e.g., *ibid.*, 29 May) to the views of Mikis Theodorakis, a prominent member of a faction in the Communist Party of Greece which is opposed to the Soviet-supported leadership of the party's secretary-general, Kostas Koliyannis.

International Party Contacts. The PCB was represented at a meeting of European communist parties, held in Moscow in January 1970, by a relatively low-level delegation consisting only of Central Committee member Jacques Moins. In February, Jean Blume, member of the Secretariat, and Francis Delcroix, member of the Central Committee, represented the PCB at the Nineteenth Congress of the French Communist Party. Politburo members Claude Renard and Jef Turf led delegations to Yugoslavia (18-26 March) and the German Democratic Republic (5-12 April), respectively. Mikis Theodorakis, of the Communist Party of Greece, met with leaders of the PCB during a visit to Belgium on 22-23 May. Also in May, the PCB's delegation to the 15 May meeting of West European communist parties in Paris was led by Marc Drumaux, president, and Jean Terfve, vice-president. Drumaux returned to France, together with Politburo members Urbain Coussement and Frans Van den Branden, for meetings with leaders of the French Communist Party on 25-31 May. The PCB was host to an "International Conference on Indochina" in Liège on 23 June. Foreign delegates included Giorgio Amendola, member of the Political Office of the Italian Communist Party; Georges Marchais, deputy secretary-general of the French Communist Party; Kurt Erlebach, Presidium member of the German Communist Party; and two representatives of the Democratic Republic of Vietnam at the Paris peace talks —Nguyen Thanh Le and Duong Duyen. Jean Fuchs, member of the Secretariat of the JCB, represented the party's youth organization at the Sixteenth Congress of the Soviet Komsomol in May. The PCB was represented by Central Committee member Jacques Moins at an international meeting held in Rome, 27-29 June, on the issue of the Portuguese colonies in Africa (see *Italy*). At the beginning of November, the secretary-general of the Communist Party of Spain, Santiago Carrillo, met with PCB leaders in Brussels.

Publications. The PCB publishes the weekly *Le Drapeau Rouge* and three times a week the four-page bulletin *PCB Informations*. The party also publishes a weekly in Flemish, *De Rode Vaan*. Since March 1969 the party has been publishing a quarterly, *Les Cahiers marxistes*, whose purpose is reportedly to "contribute to the clarification of the nonresolved problems of socialism and the international communist movement" (*Le Drapeau Rouge*, 14 March 1969).

* * *

PCB-II. The year 1970 witnessed the near total demise of the PCB-II. Its newspaper, *La Voix du Peuple*, which in early 1968 was appearing weekly and with 20 pages, was published only six times in 1970, becoming a bimonthly in April. The last issue of the year comprised only four pages. The only two party leaders that were regularly referred to in the party's press were Jacques Grippa, PCB-II secretary-general, and Bernard Godefroid, Central Committee member and a leader of the party-sponsored committee for "Solidarity with the Palestinian Resistance and the Arab Peoples" (Solidarité avec la Résistance Palestinienne et les Peuples Arabs; SRPPA). The party continued to publicize the activities of several front organizations under its control, but it would appear that support for these organizations was minimal; they included: Solidarity Belgium-Vietnam (Solidarité Belgique-Vietnam), the United Popular Front (Front Uni Populair), and the Belgian Front against NATO (Front Belge contre l'OTAN). In addition the PCB-II had its own small Communist Youth Movement (Mouvement de la Jeunesse Communiste) and ran the Théatre Populaire de Bruxelles.

The PCB-II claimed participation in the miners' strike in Limbourg at the beginning of the year (see *Le Drapeau Rouge*, February) and in the disturbances that took place at the Free University of Brussels (*ibid.*, November-December). The main thrust of the party's activities, however, appeared to be connected with its militant support for the Arab guerrilla movement, to which it devoted considerable space in its press. During the year the PCB-II and the SRPPA sponsored several meetings and demonstrations on this subject.

In its international views, the PCB-II continued to express strong opposition to the leadership of the Chinese Communist Party, reflecting a trend first evident in 1967 (see *YICA*, 1968, pp. 37-38; 1969, p. 52; 1970, p. 131; and *Est & Ouest*, Paris, no. 439, 16-31 January 1970). At the same time, the party was seen to be realigning itself tentatively with the Communist Party of the Soviet Union and certain East European communist parties. Thus, the February issue of *La Voix du Peuple* attacked references to anti-Semitism in the Soviet Union and Poland, stating that what was practiced in those countries was "anti-Zionism and a correct policy of solidarity with the Arab peoples and the Palestinian resistance." The September-October issue of *La Voix du Peuple* carried a very favorable review of alleged achievements in the German Democratic Republic, which, the newspaper stated, had been attained through the "firm leadership" of that country's communist party.

The only contact that the PCB-II had during the year with any foreign revolutionary group was a message from the Provisional Revolutionary Government (PRG) of South Vietnam, which thanked the party for a greeting that the latter had sent on the occasion of the PRG's first anniversary (see *La Voix du Peuple*, September-October).

*   *   *

The PCMLB. During 1970 the PCMLB consolidated its position as the official, Peking-recognized communist party in Belgium. Its principal spokesmen in 1970 were Henri Glineur, Michel Graindorge, Fernand Lefebvre, and Jules Vanderlinden. The party controlled the Belgium-China Association (Association Belgique-Chine) and had what appeared to be a small youth group—the Marxist-Leninist Communist Youth of Belgium (Jeunesse Communiste Marxiste-Léniniste de Belgique; JCMLB). Support for the party appeared to originate mostly from the mining region of Borinage.

On 28 June the PCMLB held a conference of party cadres. Although the conference report (published in *Clarté*, 10-16 July) claimed that "everyone reported on successes achieved" in establishing "stronger liaison with the working class," and stated that "the year 1970 was a turning point," there was evidence during the year that the party was still experiencing difficulties of consolidation. Thus, its first congress, originally scheduled for the end of 1969 (see *YICA*, 1970, p. 132), had not taken place by the end of 1970. During the year the PCMLB also reported the breakdown of relations with another small Maoist group, centered around the weekly *L'Exploité* and led by Jacques Trifaux, with which it had entered into negotiations in 1969 (see *ibid.* and *Clarté*, 5-11 June).

In its statements on international issues the PCMLB adhered to strict Maoist interpretations, and the party's press carried numerous articles praising the views and policies of the Chinese Communist Party leadership. During the year the party's weekly organ, *Clarté*, reported on a number of meetings between PCMLB leaders and representatives of other foreign Peking-recognized communist parties. These included a meeting in Brussels with a delegation of the Communist Party of Germany (Marxist-Leninist) on 2 May (*Clarté*, 29 May-4 June); and a meeting with representatives of the Communist Party of Italy (Marxist-Leninist), at an undisclosed location, in the autumn (*ibid.*, 2-8 October).

*   *   *

The Trotskyist movement in Belgium is primarily represented by the Socialist Young Guards (Jeunes Gardes Socialistes; JGS—in Flemish, Socialistische Jonge Wacht; SJW), a student movement which in 1969 asked to be recognized by the United Secretariat of the Fourth International as a "sympathizing organization." The JGS during 1970 appeared to be increasing its support in the country. It was reportedly negotiating with several other groups of similar persuasion —including the Walloon Workers' Party (Parti Wallon des Travailleurs; PWT), the Union of the Socialist Left (Union de la Gauche Socialiste; UGS) and the Revolutionary Socialists (Revolutionaire Socialisten; RS)—for the formation of a new Revolutionary League of Workers (Ligue Révolutionnaire des Travailleurs; LRT) which would adhere to the United Secretariat as the latter's official Belgian section (*La Gauche*, 4 December). During the year, one of the most prominent leaders of the JGS was François Vercammen. The major outlet for the student group's views was the weekly Brussels publication *La Gauche*, edited by Ernest Mandel, a leader of the United Secretariat.

During the first months of the year, the JGS actively participated in the wildcat strikes in the mining area of Limbourg. While not represented in the striking miners' Permanent Committee, which comprised only miners, the JGS appears to have been the most active of the extreme-left groups involved in the dispute. (For reports on the Limbourg strike by JGS militants and sympathizers, see *Intercontinental Press*, New York, 16 February, and 2, 9, and 16 March; and *La Gauche*, 7 February.)

On international issues the JGS aligned itself most closely with the Communist League (Ligue Communiste), the French section of the United Secretariat. Together, the two organizations sponsored a conference of "revolutionary steel and automobile workers" in Belgium over the last weekend in July. The conference was reportedly attended by delegates from France, Belgium, Italy, West Germany, and Denmark. (*Intercontinental Press*, 14 September.) The major event of the year, however, was another conference sponsored by the Belgian and French organizations and the United Secretariat, which took place in Brussels on 21-22 November. Referred to as the Congress for a Red Europe, the meeting was attended by 3,500 delegates from nearly all countries in Europe and from several non-European states (see *ibid.*, 7 and 14 December).

M. P.

CYPRUS

The Reconstruction Party of the Working People of Cyprus (Anorthotikon Komma Ergazomenou Laou Tis Kiprou; AKEL) was founded as the Communist Party of Cyprus (Kommounistikon Komma Kiprou) in August 1926. Outlawed in 1933, the party was revived under the name AKEL in April 1941 and was outlawed again in 1955, when all Greek political organizations were proscribed. It became legal once again in 1959 with the proclamation of the Cyriot Republic.

AKEL is by far the strongest and best organized political party in Cyprus. Moreover, in the proportion of party members to national populace it ranks second only to its Italian counterpart among nonruling communist parties. The party membership is believed to number between 12,000 and 15,000. The population of Cyprus is 622,000 (estimated 1968). A policy of mass recruitment was begun in 1964, but the party remains almost entirely Greek Cypriot in composition.

The small adjunct to AKEL in Great Britain, the "Union of Cypriots in England," has an estimated 1,250 active members. It maintains close ties with AKEL and follows the AKEL line.

The most recent elections to the Cyprus parliament, or House of Representatives, in July 1970, gave AKEL nine of the 35 seats reserved for Greeks. (The 1960 constitution provided for a body of 50 members, 35 of whom were to be elected by the Greeks and 15 by the Turks, in separate voting. Separate Greek and Turkish "Communal Assemblies" were also provided for in the constitution to deal with religious, educational, and related matters, but have ceased to function.)

In the presidential election of February 1968, AKEL campaigned for the reelection of Archbishop Makarios, head of state since the founding of the Cypriot Republic. (The vice-presidency, which under the constitution falls to the Turkish Cypriots, was retained by the unopposed incumbent, Fazil Kucuk.)

Despite its overall strength, and Makarios's generally favorable attitude toward the party, AKEL has not held any cabinet posts in the new republic. In recent years the party has suffered embarrassment from improved Soviet-Turkish relations and has taken wavering positions on such questions as conciliation between Greek and Turkish Cypriots. The Warsaw Pact intervention in Czechoslovakia in 1968 renewed frictions with noncommunist parties in Cyprus and shook the popular base of the party. The 1970 election, however, and the particular strategy pursued by AKEL in its campaign (see below), showed conclusively that the communists wield considerable power although at the government level they have chosen, for purely tactical reasons, to understate their influence.

Leadership and Organization. Leading figures in the party are the general secretary, Ezekias Papaïoannou and his deputy, Andreas Fantis, both of whom were reelected by the Central Committee at AKEL's Twelfth Congress, held in Nicosia on 5-8 March 1970. The full election results were not published, but it is believed that the Politburo includes Pavlos Georgiou, M. Poumbouris, Andreas Ziartides, Yiannis Sofikli, and Yinnis Katsourides. The Central Committee is believed to include Michael Chambis, Yiangos Potamitis, Chrysis Demetriades, and Y. Savvidhis. AKEL members of the House of Representatives include Papaïoannou, Ziartides, Chambis, Demetriades, and Potamitis.

AKEL is particularly influential among young people, farmers, and industrial workers. It controls the island's principal trade union organization, the Pan-Cypriot Workers' Confederation (Pankipria Ergatiki Omospondia; PEO), which claims as members approximately 36,000 of the total 130,000 Cypriot wage earners (including farmers) and thus more than half of all those holding membership in labor unions. The PEO has 18 member unions and workers' organizations and is an affiliate of the World Federation of Trade Unions. The secretary-general of the PEO is Andreas Ziartides; his deputy is Mikhalikis Mikhailidis.

The AKEL-controlled United Democratic Youth Organization (Eniaia Dimokratiki Organosis Neolaias; EDON) claims to have 10,000 members, and there is believed to be a branch of EDON in Great Britain. A communist, P. Paionidis, is the president of EDON; D. Khristofinis is its secretary-general, and N. Khristodoulos its organizing secretary. EDON has an organization of secondary school students (PEOM), most of whose estimated 2,000 members are also members of EDON. EDON is a member of the communist-led World Federation of Democratic Youth and holds a seat on that body's Executive Committee. AKEL's organization for women, the Pan-Cypriot Confederation of Women's Organizations (Pankiprios Omospondia Gynekon Organosen; POGO), claims 11,000 members, but is believed, in fact, to have no more than about 2,500 members.

Other AKEL-dominated fronts include the Pan-Cypriot Peace Council (Pankiprios Epitropi Erenis; PEE), which is a member of the communist-led World Peace Council and is headed by Yiangos Potamitis; the Cypriot-Soviet Association (Kipriosovietlikos Syndesmos), headed by Panos Taliadoros; and the Cypriot-German Friendship Society, headed by M. Papapetros. There has been collaboration between the AKEL fronts and the branch of the Afro-Asian People's Solidarity Committee in Cyprus, headed by Vassos Lissaridis, a left-wing politician who formed his own party, the Democratic Center Union (EDEK), in 1969. EDEK is believed to have won some support among Turkish Cypriot student organizations, but the extent is not known. The total figure for all elements within the AKEL apparatus, including various fronts and allowing for overlapping memberships, is estimated at more than 60,000.

Domestic Attitudes and Activities. AKEL has consistently exploited anticolonialist sentiment in its protests against the restrictions placed on Cyprus by the Zurich and London agreements of 1959 and against sovereign British bases. On the other hand, because as a mass party it seeks to attract Turks as well as Greeks, AKEL has at no time more than half-heartedly supported the purely Greek objective of enosis—the union of Cyprus with Greece. Enosis was overwhelmingly popular among Greek Cypriots until the 1967 coup in Athens, and as a result AKEL's strength as a national party was for some time precariously balanced. Thereafter, AKEL began to stress its "patriotic" and "nationalist" orientation, and took credit for rising above partisan considerations to prevent an outbreak of hostilities on the island. The communists were happy to support Makarios's deemphasis of enosis and his advocacy of a "feasible" solution to the island's nationalities problem rather than a "desirable" one, envisaging a workable accommodation between Greek and Turkish Cypriots with at least a temporary abandonment of the goal of enosis. AKEL currently maintains that "the Cypriot problem can and must be solved only by peaceful means, by the people of Cyprus, without outside interference and on the basis of a fully independent, territorially integral, and demilitarized Cyprus in the interests of all Cypriots" (TASS, 25 January 1970, quoting a joint communiqué of the same date by AKEL and the Communist Party of the Soviet Union). Firmly opposed to the 1967-68 talks between Greece and Turkey, which unsuccessfully sought a settlement, AKEL has supported the inter-Cypriot discussions which began in June 1968. Because the discussions might lead to modification of the international agreements affecting Cyprus, AKEL has continually been forced to clarify to the electorate its abandonment of enosis as the "only solution" to the nationalities problem. The party now stresses, therefore, that the Turkish Cypriots are not the enemies of the Greek Cypriots, but rather that "imperialism" is the common enemy of both.

AKEL justified anew its deemphasis of enosis in a statement of 15 January 1970 which held that Turkey, until the signing of the Zurich and London agreements, had no claims on the island and did not oppose enosis. In this view, Great Britain was to be blamed for having "brought the Turkish factor into the Cyprus issue." Events since then—the violent intercommunal clashes and acts of terrorism—had forced Cypriots to admit that enosis could not be achieved under the existing conditions. The statement went on to note (despite the party's professed empathy with the Turks) that Turkish Cypriots and Turkey had meanwhile acquired "unlawful and unjust rights which they did not seem inclined to abandon." Thus, a unilateral proclamation of enosis by Greek Cypriots would be met by a Turkish thrust for partition of the island to permit the establishment of a separate Turkish state. Until conditions were suitable, therefore, the party would hold in abeyance its efforts toward enosis. The corollary to this view was that "a unified and sovereign Cyprus would never cease to be Hellenic, with the right to look toward Greece and to hope that someday the present conditions preventing enosis would change." (*Kharavyi*, 15 January.)

Warning of the "danger of a fratricidal civil split" if pro-enosis extremists were not quelled, AKEL proposed (*ibid.*, 10 January) that "all political parties issue a joint statement denouncing violence as a means of promoting political aims and objectives, denouncing the existence of underground armed groups, and appealing for the surrender of all illegally owned arms." All parties, further, "must help the state collect and control these arms" (*ibid.*, 8 January). The National Front, responsible for many terrorist incidents and outlawed by Makarios in 1969, was—according to AKEL—supported by Greek military circles, with the knowledge and sanction of the Athens government (*ibid.*, 10 January).

Relations between Greek and Turkish Cypriots were the subject of an article in the party newspaper by Yiannis Sofokli, secretary of the Paphos district of AKEL (*ibid.*, 25 January). Depicting AKEL as having made "many efforts to develop and strengthen friendship and cooperation between Greeks and Turks," Sofokli upheld the party position that resort to arms could not solve Cyprus's problems and that, were it not for interference by outside elements and the Zurich and London agreements, the two nationalities would live in harmony. AKEL, Sofokli asserted, favored increased aid to the Turkish Cypriot minority to bring housing, employment, and labor and social welfare benefits up to standards enjoyed by Greek Cypriots. On the other hand, routes through Turkish-controlled enclaves must be opened to all citizens.

Addressing AKEL's Twelfth Congress, Papaïoannou declared that though the inter-Cypriot talks had not yet produced an agreement, it would be a mistake to underestimate or overlook what had been achieved. There had, for example, been no incidents between the two communities since the talks began in June 1968. Those who criticized or sought to torpedo them had proposed no alternative. A return to talks between Greece and Turkey would mean a step toward territorial partition; a new international conference would subject Cyprus to the pressure of those who had imposed the Zurich and London agreements on the island, and the result would be a new or worse agreement of the same type. If the inter-Cypriot talks failed to solve existing differences, recourse must be not to violence, but rather to the U.N. Security Council. Should Cyprus be attacked, however, the people must defend themselves "to the utmost." (*Ibid.*, 6 March.)

AKEL, Papaïoannou continued, was unreservedly in favor of holding parliamentary elections, but was calling for a delay (from the scheduled date of 5 July) until such time as unified elections could be held, rather than the separate voting for Greek and Turkish Cypriots as provided for in the 1960 constitution. The party would continue to press for all-party discussions toward a common minimum program for a "unified, nonaligned state in which the rights of Turkish Cypriots would be clearly defined and safeguarded." An independent Cyprus, he declared, must have "absolutely no connection with the imperialist pro-war pacts of NATO, CENTO, SEATO, or any other military bloc." (*Ibid.*)

The newly elected Central Committee and Central Control Committee held their first plenum on 7 March and in secret balloting unanimously reelected Papaïoannou as general secretary and Fantis as assistant general secretary. The Central Control Committee, in separate session, elected Savvidhis as its chairman. (*Ibid.*, 8 March.)

The attempted assassination of President Makarios on 8 March, the final day of the AKEL congress, was instantly attributed by the party to "fascist agents of imperialism" (Moscow radio, 8 March). The party alleged shortly thereafter that the U.S. Central Intelligence Agency and "other NATO secret services" were attempting to conceal their duplicity, and that the Americans were playing the same role as the British in 1963—trying to gain the confidence of the Cypriot government according to the theory of "divide and rule." The U.S. warning to Makarios that an attempt might be made on his life was seen as part of that role. (*Ibid.*, 19 March.) In fact, however, the Cypriot, Soviet, and Turkish communist parties had all been predicting an assassination attempt for several weeks before the incident took place. An AKEL Politburo statement on 28 January, for example, warned that "fascist terrorist organizations" had "managed to lead astray certain patriots by exploiting national sentiments" and were planning attempts against President Makarios and other well-known political leaders (*ibid.*, 29 January).

In contrast to the communists' outspoken denunciation of the attempt on Makarios's life, AKEL made no immediate comment on the assassination, on 15 March, of Polycarpos Yiorkatzis, the former Interior minister, who had resigned in 1968 because of his alleged implication in the attempted assassination of Premier Papadopoulos of Greece in August of that year and had been accused by Makarios of a part in the attempt on his own life a week earlier. Statements by AKEL on 17 and 19 March denounced the attempt against Makarios, but made no mention of the murder of Yiorkatzis. Not until 26 March did AKEL refer to Yiorkatzis, and only then in a passing reference demanding apprehension of those responsible for both crimes. That the Cypriot people had refrained from violent manifestations in this situation was attributed by AKEL to "Soviet warnings to the imperialists and the ambitious promoters of intervention and coup d'état." Despite their failure on 8 March, the party declared, it would be naïve to believe that the "imperialists" would abandon their plans to eliminate the president, and decisive measures must be taken to "neutralize the deadly danger still hovering over Cyprus." (*Ibid.*, 27 March.)

AKEL and PEO premises in Limassol were bombed on 21 April. In an article in *Dhimokratia*, 22 April, Fantis condemned the crimes as efforts of "imperialist agents" to hinder electoral cooperation among patriotic forces. An accompanying editorial stated that, despite the government's efforts to suppress them, criminal groups continued to sow unrest and confusion so as to undermine its authority; thus the Ministerial Council's decision to schedule elections for 5 July would be proved sound only if the government took decisive measures against such groups and if all parties and political forces took a firm stand against terrorism.

AKEL went on to warn of "imperialist" attempts to exploit preelectoral tensions and thus to create conditions of anarchy and chaos. The party charged, further, that because AKEL was "a major obstacle to imperialism's divisive plan, a decisive force in the unified internal front, and a shield for Makarios and his policy," an attempt was being made to isolate it from all other parties. In its view, electoral cooperation was both possible and imperative on the basis of the existing national program declared by Makarios and approved by the people at the presidential election of February 1968, since no single party would be able to carry the burden of the "Cypriot people's liberation struggle"—this burden should be carried by the majority, if not all, of the people. Under present conditions, the self-sufficiency of any single party would mean a national weakness. (*Kharavyi*, 7 and 10 May.)

The party continued to press for postponement of the parliamentary elections, indicating that in the interests of national unity AKEL was prepared to sacrifice its prospects for at least doubling its current holding of the five seats if elections should be held as scheduled, rather than postponed. Moreover, it "would welcome with enthusiasm an agreement on the basis of which all parties were represented in parliament, even if one or more parties were given more seats than their true electoral strength." (*Cyprus Mail*, Nicosia, 19 May, reporting Papaïoannou's speech at Exo Metokhi on 16 May.)

AKEL's opposition to an election took into consideration the fact that, according to the Zurich and London agreements, the guarantor powers may intervene against a communist threat. AKEL, consequently, was reluctant to make a genuine show of strength which might precipitate outside intervention. The party entered only nine candidates, each of whom won first place in his electorate, giving it an aggregate of 39.6 per cent of the popular vote. An informal—and unannounced—agreement between AKEL and Lissaridis's EDEK party (which received two seats and 8 per cent) may have deprived the Unified Party (which received 15 seats) of a majority. The high rate of abstentions—25 per cent overall and up to 40 per cent in some electorates—favored the communists, whose campaign was organizationally superior. Glafkos Kliridhis, the leader of the Unified Party, reiterated his preelection view that if no party secured a majority, the "real arbiters of the house's work and policy" would be AKEL's deputies. AKEL countered that its representatives neither sought nor were seeking such a role, as had been underscored by the party's efforts toward multiparty collaboration. (*Kharavyi*, 7 July.)

In sum, AKEL appeared stronger as a result of developments in 1970. In a speech delivered on 30 August at a Nicosia conference of party cadres, Papaïoannou declared:

> Our party does not struggle today to establish a socialist regime in Cyprus, not because it wants to conceal the fact that it favors a socialist regime as the most just social system, but because the most immediate problem confronting the Cypriot people is not a problem of socialism, but their deliverance from the imperialist presence so they may independently determine their future without foreign intervention.

AKEL could have secured a house majority, he continued, but had refrained from doing so because the present stage of developments in Cyprus called for broad popular unity, toward which its efforts would be directed. Turkish Cypriots for their part must understand, he added, that there would be no serious obstacle to the solution of the nationalities problem if they would give up their separatist claims: other than in matters of education, religion, and cultural affairs, the state must be unified and indivisible from top to bottom. (*Ibid.*, 1 September.)

International Views and Activities. Consistently pro-Soviet in international affairs, AKEL currently professes to believe that there exists a joint U.S.-NATO design to aggravate internecine tensions in Cyprus so as to substantiate "imperialist" contentions that Cypriots are incapable of solving the island's problems and to justify an intervention. The party charged on 30 May that the session of NATO foreign ministers in Rome a few days earlier had discussed the "general principles of a plan for the settlement of the Cyprus question" in which the first step would be to establish a NATO base on the island, manned only by Greek and Turkish troops under NATO direction. Pressure on Makarios to bring Cyprus into NATO had started at the end of 1969, according to AKEL, and only a week before the assassination attempt of 8 March he had rejected a demand for the island's participation. The charges continued: "[This] proves who plotted against His Beatitude's life as well as who is responsible for the National Front terrorism." (*Kharavyi*, 30 May.) NATO affiliation, the party declared earlier, would "promote double enosis and the quartering of the island, one part going to Greece, another to Turkey, a third to Britain because of its 'sovereign' bases, and the fourth to NATO to establish its own bases" (*ibid.*, 26 February).

The alleged imperialist plans for dissolution of the Cypriot state and imposition of partition were said by AKEL to be part of "a larger scheme . . . being cooked up in the sinister wings of NATO's aggressive circles" against both Cyprus and the "progressive" Arab countries. Papaïoannou told a gathering in Yialoussa on 8 February: "[It would be] political shortsightedness and naïveté of the worst kind if we failed to see the close connection between the aggressive activities of imperialism in the Middle East and the subversive terrorist activities in our country." Cyprus was the "unsinkable aircraft and missile carrier" from which the "imperialists" wanted to "blackmail and terrorize the people of the Middle East; the base for providing arms and 'cover' to the Zionist Israeli aggressors; and the strategic point for their planned adventures in the region." Papaïoannou called for a "patriotic crusade to save Cyprus." The republic's friends, he said, were the Arabs, and the socialist and nonaligned countries, and it was to them that Cyprus must turn for support. (*Ibid.*, 10 February.)

In similar vein, the AKEL leader told delegates to the Twelfth Congress that by employing Israel as a "vanguard" the "imperialists" were trying to regain their lost positions in the Middle East (most recently Libya and Sudan), where—thanks to the presence of the Soviet fleet in the Mediterranean—a change in the balance of power had occurred in favor of the anti-imperialist forces (*ibid.*, 6 March). A congress resolution denounced Israel's continued occupation of Arab territories as a "gangsterite action contrary to the principles and aims of the U.N." and as the main cause for intensified tensions in the region. The party called for enactment of the Security Council resolution of 22 November 1967 providing for withdrawal of Israeli troops from all occupied territories as the "primary prerequisite for settlement of other related issues." (*Ibid.*, 11 March.)

Throughout the year, AKEL's attitudes to developments in the Middle East continued to reflect—and to feature in—Soviet pronouncements. The Pan-Cypriot Peace Council (see above) addressed a protest to the Israeli ambassador in Nicosia appealing for "every effort to save the lives of Arab political prisoners, including women, in the occupied Palestinian and Arab territories," allegedly the victims of "harsh ill-treatment by Israeli authorities" (*ibid.*, 7 May). Papaïoannou said in Morphou on 6 June that NATO, in essence, did not care whether the solution for the Cyprus issue was "double enosis, partition, or mutilated independence with cantons and a federal regime"—its concern was only that Cyprus should become an "imperialist springboard" (*ibid.*, 7 June). The party organ declared on 9 June that, just as the Americans could not tolerate a neutral state in Indochina, so were they opposed to a neutral Cyprus in the heart of the Middle East where the threat of a broader war was being escalated every day; just as the Americans had intervened in Cambodia to strike at the "Vietnamese people's struggle," so were they planning to intervene in Cyprus to strike from its territory at the "Arab people's struggle." In September, AKEL predicted that the "imperialists," in the wake of the crisis in Jordan, would mobilize their forces to pressure Cyprus to accede to an early intercommunal settlement "for the sake of NATO unity." The presence of the U.S. fleet around Cyprus would be used as a weapon to increase the effectiveness of their pressures. The "imperialists," further, would not hesitate to employ the tactic allegedly employed by them in Jordan—"dividing the people and even leading them to fratricide so as to provide an excuse for intervention." (*Ibid.*, 27 September.) The death of U.A.R. President Nasser, AKEL declared a week later, would further exacerbate tensions in the Middle East, and the "imperialists and international Zionism" could be expected to resort to "every plot and machination to exploit the vacuum left by the great leader" (*ibid.*, 3 October). The party subsequently spoke of an alleged U.S. "initiative" to close the Cyprus issue by the end of the year at the latest. Visits to Cyprus by U.S. diplomats late in the year, it said, represented "a special mission with instructions to determine the Cyprus government's reaction" to the American plan. (*Ibid.*, 10 October.)

Following an incident on 21 October in which a U.S. military plane apparently strayed into Soviet airspace, AKEL alleged that the plane had taken off from the British base on Cyprus—most probably without the knowledge of the Cyprus government. The government, AKEL declared, would be obliged to clarify its position immediately, and must at the same time denounce the violation of the terms of the bilateral agreement with the British, which explicitly prohibited the use of the area of the bases by other powers, and demand guarantees against further violations. The party also spoke of "confirmed reports" that the United States was sending ultramodern military aircraft to Israel via Cyprus. (*Ibid.*, 21 and 27 October.)

In European affairs, AKEL pressed for improved ties with the German Democratic Republic (GDR). Andreas Ziartides, in a speech to the Cypriot-German Friendship Society (see above), said that the nations which genuinely desired peace and wanted to prevent "imperialist" interference in the internal affairs of other nations, must "break the iron collar" created by the "revanchists" around the GDR. State relations with the GDR—a country which had repeatedly proved its friendship for Cyprus and its solidarity for the struggle of its people—must be raised from the commercial to the diplomatic level. Despite full diplomatic relations with West Germany, Ziartides contended, West German policy toward Cyprus was characterized by "duplicity and hypocrisy." (*Ibid.*, 7 May.)

The party scored the renewal of U.S. arms shipments to Greece. This event, parallel with the arming of Turkey, it declared, showed the real nature of NATO aims and pursuits: the arming of Greece bore no relation to the purportedly peaceful intentions of NATO, being intended to bolster the Greek military regime and to permit NATO use of Greece as a bridgehead against its neighbors (*ibid.*, 25 September).

Notwithstanding its general loyalty to Moscow, AKEL positions have in some instances been tempered by domestic and tactical considerations. In 1968, for example, when Warsaw Pact forces invaded Czechoslovakia, there was a considerable movement within AKEL for condemnation of the action. Eventually the AKEL leadership, with obvious reluctance, came out in support of the invasion, but only after severe internal disruptions—the effects of which have continued to be felt. AKEL also opposes the Soviets' support for Turkey's advocacy of a federative or cantonal system in Cyprus which would give local autonomy to the Turkish Cypriots. Again, since the 1967 coup in Greece, AKEL has shown stronger opposition to the Athens government than have the Soviets themselves, who have been wooing the Greeks with aid and trade.

Within the international communist movement, AKEL seldom veers from the Soviet line. The party charged in 1970 that "the damage caused to the socialist system and the communist movement by the splitting policy" of the Chinese communist leadership had, for a decade, been a "serious, detrimental phenomenon," weakening the anti-imperialist front in Asia and throughout the world, inciting "U.S. imperialism," and inviting organized aggression, conspiracies, and coups—in Vietnam, Ghana, Indonesia, and the Near East. (Article by Papaïoannou, in *Pravda*, 20 February.) Despite generally close ties with the Greek communist party (the KKE), however, there is an inconsistency in AKEL's attitude which has become particularly pronounced since the recent split in the KKE (see *Greece*); at different times during 1970, without offering explanations, AKEL expressed support for both rival factions.

Publications. AKEL's central organ is the daily newspaper *Kharavyi* (Dawn). Its theoretical organ is *Theoritikos Dimokratis* (Theoretical Democrat). AKEL also publishes a quarterly review, *Neos Dimokratis* (New Democrat); a monthly journal, *Nea Epochi (New Epoch); and a weekly, Neoi Kairoi (New Times). The PEO publishes a weekly newspaper, Ergatiki Vima* (Workers' Step). EDON publishes a monthly, *Neolaia* (Youth), and on 2 March 1970 began publication of a newspaper, *Dhimokratia.*

V. B.

DENMARK

The Communist Party of Denmark (Danmarks Kommunistiske Parti; DKP) was formed on 9 November 1919 by a left-wing splinter of the Social Democratic Party. It was originally designated the Left Socialist Party (Venstresocialistisk Parti), but upon joining the Comintern in 1920 it adopted the name "Communist Party of Denmark, Section of the Communist International." It subsequently became known simply as the Communist Party of Denmark. It has been legal at all times except during the German occupation in the Second World War. Principal support comes from among workers in Copenhagen and other major urban areas. The DKP claims 6,000 members out of Denmark's population of 4,870,000 (estimated 1968).

Since 1945, when the DKP polled 12.5 per cent of the vote and gained 18 parliamentary seats (because of its wartime resistance record), support has steadily diminished. The DKP has failed to win any parliamentary seats since 1959. In that year the Socialist People's Party (Socialistisk Folkeparti; SF) was formed by Aksel Larsen following his expulsion from the DKP for "revisionism." Larsen had been party chairman for twenty-six years. The SF succeeded in siphoning votes from both the Social Democratic Party on the right and the DKP on the left. With the former it governed Denmark for fourteen months in a coalition termed a "cooperation agreement," under which the SF held no cabinet appointments, until the special election of 23 January 1968. The election was brought about by the defection of six members of the SF parliamentary group and the consequent resignation of Jens Otto Krag's administration. Larsen was replaced as SF leader by Sigurd Ømann. The SF dissenters established a new party, the Left Socialists (Venstresocialisterne; VS), which, formed only six weeks before the election, won 2 per cent of the vote and 4 seats (although half of its parliamentary group defected shortly thereafter). The DKP failed to poll the 2.0 per cent minimum stipulated by law, the SF dropped to 6.1 per cent (from 10.9 in 1966) and lost 9 of its 20 mandates, and the Social Democrats dropped to 34.2 per cent (from 38.2) and their seats from 69 to 62. The center-right coalition formed under Radical-Liberal Hilmer Baunsgaard commanded 98 of the 179 seats.

To the left of the DKP are a number of newer, small pro-Chinese splinter groups. The oldest of these, the Communist Labor Circle (Kommunistisk Arbejdskreds; KAK), was established in June 1964 by Gotfred Appel and Benito Scocozza. Scocozza quit to join the VS. In 1968 he withdrew from the VS with a group of supporters and formed the Communist League (Marxist-Leninist)—Kommunistisk Forbund (Marxist-Leninist), or KFML. In August 1969 a youth alliance, Communist Youth (Marxist-Leninist)—Kommunistisk Ungdom (Marxist-Leninist), or KUML —was founded, apparently as a KFML affiliate and comprising principally elements of the Socialist Youth League (Socialistisk Ungdoms Forbund; SUF) excluded by the VS in May 1969. The Revolutionary Socialist (Revolutionaere Socialisten) is another offshoot of the SUF. Another Maoist youth group, the Communist Youth League (Kommunistisk Ungdoms Forbund; KUF), may have some connection with the KAK.

Leadership and Organization. The DKP chairman, Knud Jespersen, who succeeded Aksel Larsen in 1958, was reelected most recently at the party's Twenty-third Congress, in February 1969. Ib Nørlund, the secretary-general, and Jespersen, together with Poul Emanuel, Villy Fuglsang, Preben Henriksen, and Per Kristensen, comprise the Executive Committee (Politburo) of the Central Committee. The Central Committee has 39 members (of whom eight were newly elected in 1969) and 13 candidate members. There is also a five-man Control Commission.

The DKP youth organization, Communist Youth of Denmark (Danmarks Kommunistiske Ungdom; DKU), is believed to have between 1,000 and 2,000 members, although figures are not disclosed. Jørn Christensen succeeded Gunnar Kanstrup as DKU chairman in 1970. Another DKP auxiliary, the League of Women (Kvindeudvalg), concerns itself largely with domestic matters such as equal pay for women and health and welfare benefits, and has negligible political influence. Its chairman is Lilian Thomsen.

DKP strength in trade unions is insignificant. The SF, VS, and DKP control no national unions, and their combined representation in organized labor as a whole is less than 5 per cent. Kaj Buch, a member of the DKP Central Committee, sits on the International Committee of the "Workers' Conferences of the Baltic Countries, Norway, and Iceland," held annually by trade unionists in Rostock, East Germany, to which the DKP sends delegations. The 1970 meeting took place on 16-17 July.

The DKP is influential in a number of friendship organizations, the most active of which is the Denmark-Soviet Union Association, whose chairman is DKP Central Committee member Alfred Jensen.

Party Internal Affairs. An important development for the party—yet of questionable value to it—was its decision, in January 1970, to admit to its ranks Hanne Reintoft, one of the defectors from the VS parliamentary group, thereby giving the DKP its first parliamentary representative since the SF came into being in 1958. Elected to parliament in 1966 on the SF slate, she had defected in 1967 from the SF to the VS and then left the VS, with Kai Moltke, to form a two-member independent parliamentary grouping, the "Socialist Working Group" (SAG). Reintoft had sought DKP membership in late 1969 in an exchange of letters with Chairman Jespersen.

There were conflicting views within the DKP (eight Central Committee members opposed Reintoft's admission, according to *Land og Folk*, 11-12 January), as to the potential credibility or usefulness of having as its most strategically situated spokesman an absolute newcomer and—until now—not only a firm opponent and rival of the party, but also one who in the past had contributed much to the communist decline. There was no assurance, moreover, that the party would retain its single mandate in the next election—or that the votes won by a "left-socialist" Reintoft would necessarily lead to similar support for a declared communist.

Reintoft was accused by DKP critics of having sought membership in the DKP—an established party—purely as a means of political survival. This contention was as strongly rejected by Jespersen, the prime mover in her entry, as it was by Reintoft herself. Reintoft's claim, however, in an interview with *Land og Folk* (18-19 January), of having "always fought for the same objectives as those set by the Communist Party" was not borne out by the parliamentary record. She had, for instance, cast her vote in favor of an added-value levy on consumers' goods—an issue of overwhelming importance for the DKP, which had resisted the introduction, in 1966, of the new, indirect form of taxation—a decision which she now submitted was a "mistake" (*Land og Folk*, 13 January). The reasons for her latest defection, enumerated by Reintoft at a press conference held by the DKP on 12 January to mark its return to parliament, included the VS's failure to cooperate with the trade unions, its lack of effective leadership and an organized party apparatus, and its increasingly "anti-socialist" posture. In explanation of her past ideological fluctuations,

Reintoft offered that, in 1960, when she joined the SF, she was "only moderately leftist-oriented and not especially trained in socialism." As she developed into a "convinced Marxist socialist," the SF "took a turn toward the right." Her own experience—which, she implied, could be of value to the DKP—underscored the importance of paying attention to the attitudes of young people, "even when they seem awkward and confused." (*Ibid.*)

The party's failure to attract young people has been its principal problem for several years. While the DKU generally supports the DKP in both domestic and foreign policy, its members have promoted a more revolutionary and "modernized" ideology. The DKP has not always approved of this posture, and several leaders have accused the DKU of being indiscriminate in the selection of its working allies, and of frequently casting its lot with anarchist and Maoist groupings, to the detriment of the movement as a whole. The DKP, however, does not reject cooperation with such "extremists" within the mass movements.

Domestic Attitudes and Activities. Commemorating the centenary of Lenin's birth, the DKP formally reaffirmed its adherence to Lenin's teachings, to the transition from capitalism to socialism through a socialist revolution, and to internationalism (Central Committee declaration, 11 January, *Tiden*, no. 4). Leninism, in the words of Jespersen, had a "special relevance for Denmark," which had seen the failure of the "modernists" or "neo-revisionists" in the Social Democratic-Socialist coalition (1967-68) to "concoct a new ideology of which anti-Sovietism and anti-communism [were to have been] component parts." The DKP, the "biggest and best organized political force of the left," and allegedly firmly entrenched in the trade unions, was the force necessary to consolidate and activate the divided left. Jespersen assailed "certain groups" which had "sought to hamper" the DKP, alluding in particular to a small ultra-revolutionary faction of "phrasemongers"—probably the KFML (see below)—which had surfaced "with the express purpose of propagating Mao Tse-tung's ideas" and, through attacks on the Soviet party, of destroying the world communist movement. (*WMR*, May.)

DKP tactical strategy in 1970 was based upon resolutions (adopted by the Twenty-third Congress) advocating a peaceful transition to socialism through the multiparty parliamentary system, with the DKP "in the vanguard" of the quest for socialism; charging that a small privileged minority of monopolists continued to control the nation's production apparatus, its legislature, and its commerce, and that those who created the wealth—workers and functionaries—were denied any influence in policy and decision making' and calling for broad nationalization of industry and a "planned economy" to give workers more than merely a "comfortable" existence. (See *YICA*, 1970, p. 144.)

Still rebuffed by the Social Democrats, and with the VS and SF declining and in disarray, the DKP in 1970 continued to look primarily to the ranks of the trade unions for cooperative endeavors, maintaining that though the fragmentation of the labor movement had reduced its potential bargaining power, common efforts on vital issues were still feasible. In the DKP view, agitation should stress that, notwithstanding higher production and employment levels than at any previous time together with national resources and potential more than adequate to assure egalitarian prosperity, Denmark was in serious economic difficulties because of continued domination by capitalist interests. Through coordinated and decisive demands, however, the masses could bring about the collapse of the Baunsgaard government and at the same time avoid a return to the "compromise" policies of its predecessor, the Social Democratic-Socialist coalition. A "democratic" government, which must necessarily include the communist party, would: "regulate imports; control investments; intervene against tax evasion and upper-income tax shelters; curb military acquisitions; reorganize trade policies so as to eradicate the deficit in trade with West Germany; improve cost-of-living compensation; shift from commercial investment to expanded housing construction for the poor; and assure employment through expansion of the domestic market's purchasing power." (*Tiden*, no. 5, 1970.)

The Social Democratic parliamentary opposition was said to have deceived workers by acting "in words only." Using its new voice in parliament to promote a dialogue toward an offensive, both inside and outside that body, in which leftist forces would take the first step toward a confrontation with the domination of the right, the DKP would demand dynamic solutions to such problems as housing, social inequity in education, and unemployment. (*Land og Folk*, 13 January.) In a New Year's Day interview (*ibid.*, 1 January), Jespersen said that the "victorious" miners' strike in Sweden (supported by all Danish parties of the left, thereby minimizing the impact of DKP propaganda and funding) could inject new strength into the Danish labor movement. The forthcoming local election on 3 March, he said, must be made a protest against the added-value tax and other "anti-consumer" and "anti-social" government policies.

In the election, the DKP polled 1.1 per cent of the vote (up 0.1 per cent from 1966); the Social Democrats, 42.9 per cent (up 6.7); the Socialist People's Party, 3.5 per cent (down 3.8); the Left Socialists, 0.6 per cent (its first local election); and the three government coalition parties, a combined 50.5 per cent (down 1.6).

At a post-election Central Committee meeting on 14 March, Jespersen termed the results "a defeat for the right wing" and "a result of the DKP's battle against the employers' regime." The DKP's advance, he said, was "not startling," but "more like a stabilization." Social Democratic gains were attributed to opposition to the government's fiscal policies rather than to increased popularity. The SF decline, Jespersen commented, confirmed that there was "no need for two 'social democratic' parties in Denmark." (*Ibid.*, 15-16 March.)

Notwithstanding the electoral gains made by the left as a whole, the DKP leader considered the prospects for the economic future of the nation to be "gloomy." The administration was likely further to restrict consumption and tighten credit policies, gravely endangering employment and increasing Denmark's "subjugation to U.S. capitalist administrators and the infiltration of foreign capital." (*Ibid.*) Only the communists, he asserted in a speech to the Køge branch on 5 June, presented any alternative to the administration's "austerity policy." In order to alleviate the foreign exchange deficit and unemployment and in the interests of development and future planning, it was necessary to halt arms acquisitions and initiate disarmament (the "most unproductive and foreign-exchange-consuming expenditures" being those for the NATO military), effectively control investments and imports in conjunction with democratic tax reform, and remove all land from speculation and place it in the hands of the state. (*Ibid.*, 6 June.)

International Views and Positions. The DKP Labor Day (1 May) Appeal asserted that the world was "in the midst of a transition from capitalism to socialism," and that socialism would be assured once the power of monopoly capitalism was crushed. It urged that Labor Day be a day of common struggle against the "oppression and war policies" of "world imperialism" and for "peace and popular freedom, general disarmament, a European security system, and dissolution of military blocs." (*Tiden*, no. 5.)

The DKP remains firmly in the Soviet camp, maintaining frequent and close contact with Soviet and East European party leaders and rarely deviating from Soviet positions. In August 1968 it initially condemned the invasion of Czechoslovakia, but the phrasing of party statements hinted that DKP leaders might have acquiesced to the move if the Soviets had only seen fit to inform them of it in advance. Jespersen shortly thereafter made a trip to Moscow and returned with a cautiously favorable view of the invasion (see *YICA*, 1969, p. 271). Since then, the DKP has returned to virtually unquestioning loyalty. On the centenary of Lenin's birth, Jespersen declared that the Leninist foreign policy of the Soviet Union and other nations of the socialist camp showed the entire world "their desire and will for the defense of the interests of peace," notably evident in their proposal of a European security conference (*Pravda*, 10 April).

A joint communiqué by high-ranking Danish and Hungarian communist party delegations to talks in Copenhagen on 19-26 May declared that the 1969 Moscow Conference had strengthened the Marxist-Leninist unity of the communist movement, and pledged, "on the basis of the principles recognized at the Moscow meeting," to expend all efforts toward furthering international solidarity among fraternal parties and among all anti-imperialist forces. Both parties condemned the "aggressive policy" of the United States in Vietnam and stressed the importance of convening a European security conference without delay, obtaining international recognition of East Germany, and achieving a political solution in the Middle East to bring "U.S.-supported Israeli aggression" to an end. (*Tiden*, no. 6.)

The DKP has consistently opposed Denmark's bid for entry into the European Economic Community (EEC). At the same time, it has supported all initiatives toward cooperation among the Northern countries which would "assure their common and individual independence" of NATO and the Common Market—said to be "imperialism's military and economic bloc formations." Thus the "Nordek" inter-Scandinavian customs union—negotiated by Denmark, Norway, Sweden, and Finland and ratified, in January 1970, by all but the Finns, who caused the Nordek plan to collapse by withdrawing abruptly (see *Finland*)—was endorsed by the DKP but, only insofar as it meant furthering the economic independence of the North as opposed to being a "steppingstone to the EEC." The DKP was party to a joint statement released by the annual meeting of Nordic communist parties which convened at Helsinki in May, renewing their mutual condemnation of the EEC as an "economic and political alliance serving the interests of the strongest monopolies and treading underfoot the sovereign rights of the smaller countries" (Helsinki radio, 14 May).

Secretary-General Nørlund warned (in *WMR*, June) that the "imperialist" approach to "Nordicism" was not novel. The German Nazis had "exploited propaganda eulogies" of the Nordic type to gain a foothold in Scandinavia, and Western "political adventurers" had appealed to Nordicism during the 1939-40 Soviet-Finnish war in their effort to "stampede the Northern countries into an armed conflict with the Soviet Union." Similar pressures allegedly had been in evidence during the preparatory stage of erecting the NATO bloc. The current "imperialist" goal, Nørlund continued, was to buttress and extend the bloc-making policy in Europe chiefly by means of economic alliances, which, it hoped, would yield the desired political and military dividends, and it saw Nordek as a way of placing the entire North under its control. "The EEC", he asserted, "has a document which requires the Northern countries to stop their efforts for unity as a stipulation for admission to, or cooperation with, the Common Market." In the "procrastination, negotiation, and maneuver" of the Nordek talks, the focal issue had clearly been the attitude to the Common Market; through the affiliation of one or more of the Northern countries, Nordek was intended by the "imperialists" to become an arm of the Common Market.

DKP Chairman Jespersen in August called on the government to distribute "as reading matter to all Danish households" the text of the EEC's 1957 Rome treaty, "so that the people may be oriented about the facts that the treaty surrenders Danish authority to foreign powers, that it cannot be abrogated, that it favors penetration in Denmark by big capital, and that Danes are denied the right of veto." In the DKP view, the "correct" alternative to EEC affiliation would be cooperation with many countries, particularly with socialist states, which would pave the way for scientific and technological advance. In contrast to EEC affiliation, this could be done without political conditions and without a "degrading attitude" toward the people. The DKP, Jespersen pledged, was prepared to go "very far" to achieve cooperation with the Social Democrats—"as far as is necessary to keep Denmark out of the Common Market." (*Land og Folk*, 9-10 August.)

Opposition to U.S. intervention in Vietnam continued to traverse Danish party lines, and while the communists participated in several demonstrations and fund-raising initiatives in 1970, they were again unable to sponsor any major campaigns. A Central Committee declaration of 9 May accused the United States, *inter alia*, of having "arranged a coup in order to instigate aggression against Cambodia," of murdering U.S. protesters, and, with a "stream of lies which survive but a day," of "asking the world to condone its crimes." The DKP urged broad action to "overwhelm the U.S. with protests" and force the Danish government to condemn the United States and recognize the Democratic Republic of Vietnam and the Provisional Revolutionary Government of South Vietnam. The U.S. imperialists, in sum, "must be made to feel alone in a world which curses and resists their war and their crimes." Two weeks later, the Central Committee protested against the "criminal expansion of U.S. aggression against the Indochinese people," and warned the Danish public of the "consequences of Hitler methods being so openly introduced into international politics." (*Tiden*, no. 5.)

Central Committee member Ingmar Wagner was the party's representative at the special meeting of European communist parties which convened in Paris on 15 May to condemn "U.S. aggression" in Southeast Asia. Politburo member Poul Emanuel announced in August that the party had raised substantial funds in support of the "liberation struggle of the people of Southeast Asia," part of which would go toward the establishment of the new Copenhagen "information office" of the Provisional Revolutionary Government of South Vietnam (*Land og Folk*, 16-17 August).

Commenting on late-year unrest in Poland, the DKP declared that Poland's genuine friends would refrain from offering the "good advice" which the enemies of the workers, from the extreme left to the extreme right, were employing so as to exploit the situation. The DKP was confident that the measures taken by the Polish communist party would lead toward the solution of existing economic difficulties, to rectification of past errors, and to the establishment of the political line "natural to socialism." In a socialist state, demonstrations and strikes were not only "superfluous," but actually harmful to the strikers themselves and to their society. (*Ibid.*, 19 and 22 December.)

Publications. The DKP daily newspaper is *Land og Folk* (Land and People), edited by Central Committee members Villy Karlsson and Thorkild Holst. The monthly theoretical organ *Tiden* (The Times) is edited by a committee headed by Secretary-General Ib Nørlund. *Tiden* carries articles, in Danish translation, from the *World Marxist Review*, this section being supervised by Politburo member Villy Fuglsang. *Fremad* (Forward), organ of the DKU, is edited by Johan Suszkiewicz, chairman of the DKU for Copenhagen.

* * *

The Communist League (Marxist-Leninist). The KFML was established on 15 September 1968 by a group of some thirty Maoists following their withdrawal from the VS in protest against the majority's approval of the "rightist-oriented" policies of Alexander Dubček in Czechoslovakia. Benito Scocozza is the KFML chairman, and Hans Nielsen the secretary-general. Though the KFML claims to differ in principle, both ideologically and politically, from the KAK, which Scocozza co-founded and headed with Gotfred Appel, only differences of personality have manifested themselves so far.

The KFML held its third annual congress in Copenhagen on 14-15 March 1970. A resolution claimed that the party had made considerable strides in its study of Marxism-Leninism, producing an ideological and political consolidation among the membership as well as "the foundation for the solution of other tasks in the struggle."Caution was urged, however, against a theoretical rather than a "practical political" tendency in study. (*Gnistan*, Göteborg, no. 5; organ of the Swedish KFML, with which the Danish KFML is closely oriented; see *Sweden*.)

In a message praising Communist China's launching of its first earth satellite, the KFML termed the event "a great blow to U.S. imperialism . . . proof of the great strength of People's China, a magnificent victory of the triumph of Marxism-Leninism-Mao Tse-tungism during the Great Proletarian Cultural Revolution, and a victorious fruit of the great call of the Ninth National Congress to 'unite to win still greater victories.' " Through further development of its space technology, national defense, and socialist construction, China would "smash the aggressive designs of U.S. imperialism, Soviet social-imperialism, and all reaction." (NCNA, 4 May.)

The KFML publishes two organs, the monthly newspaper *Kommunist* and the irregular *Marxistisk-Leninistiske Studiebreve* (Marxist-Leninist Study Letters), in Copenhagen.

Communist Youth (Marxist-Leninist). The KUML concentrates its activities among high school students and young apprentices. The KUML organ is *Rød Front* (Red Front), issued in Copenhagen.

Communist Labor Circle. Gotfred Appel has headed the KAK since the end of 1967, when the group's co-founder, Benito Scocozza, withdrew to join the VS (from which he subsequently withdrew to form the KFML). The KAK charges the DKP with complicity with the Social Democrats, trade union leaders, and socialist parties in luring workers into cooperation with the capitalists. It also views the VS as a "petty-bourgeois reform party," but nonetheless endorsed it in the most recent (1968) parliamentary election as a "lesser evil" than the DKP.

The KAK organ, *Kommunistisk Orientering* (Communist Orientation), is a mimeographed bulletin, issued irregularly.

The Communist Youth League. The KUF, composed mainly of Copenhagen University students, was established in 1968 and endorsed by the KAK. A bulletin, *Ungkommunisten* (Young Communist), is issued by the KUF.

V. B.

FINLAND

The Communist Party of Finland (Suomen Kommunistinen Puolue; SKP) was founded in Moscow on 29 August 1918 by exiled members of the Finnish Social Democratic Party. It has been legal since 1944.

SKP membership is believed to be about 47,000 and appears to have fallen off slightly in recent years. Some 80 per cent of the membership consists of industrial laborers in the southern urban centers and agricultural workers in the less developed northern and northeastern regions. The population of Finland is 4,688,000 (estimated 1968). Despite policies which have relaxed both ideological and political requirements for new members, the party still fails to attract many semiprofessional or white-collar workers, who constitute an increasingly important segment of Finnish society. Nor has it yet won over the younger generation, the average age of party members being close to fifty years.

The SKP participates in national elections through the Finnish People's Democratic League (Suomen Kansan Demokraattinen Liitto; SKDL), an electoral front organization formed by the party on 29 October 1944. Communists are believed to comprise about a third and left-wing socialists most of the rest of the SKDL's supporters. The SKDL appears to draw a larger share of Finland's radical intellectuals than any other party and has also considerable support among the Swedish-speaking minority.

The parliamentary election of 15-16 March 1970 gave the SKDL only 36 parliamentary seats, its lowest total ever and down 5 from 1966. O this total, 33 seats are filled by SKP members. The SKDL participates in the coalition government formed by Ahti Karjalainen in July 1970, along with the Social Democratic Party, which retained first place with 52 seats (down 3), the Center Party with 36 seats (down 13), and the small Swedish People's and Liberal parties with 12 and 8 seats, respectively.

Leadership and Organization. Under a conciliation agreement reached at an extraordinary SKP congress in February 1970 between Aarne Saarinen's "reformist" majority and a "Stalinist" minority headed by Taisto Sinisalo, 35 Central Committee posts were apportioned 20 to 15 in favor of the reformists. Saarinen and Erkki Salomaa retained their posts as chairman and vice-chairman, respectively, but the agreement created a second (and equal) vice-chairmanship for Sinisalo. Arvo Aalto, a reformist, retained the post of secretary-general which he captured at the 1969 congress from the veteran "Stalinist" Ville Pessi. The Politburo, enlarged from 12 to 16 under the agreement and apportioned 10 to 6 in favor of the Saarinen forces, consists of Arvo Aulis Aalto, Arvo Hautala, Anna-Liisa Hyvönen, Olavi Hänninen, Markus Kainulainen, Erkki Kivimäki, Olavi J. Laine, Oiva Lehto, Ville Pessi, Aarne Saarinen, Erkki Salomaa, Jorma Simpura, Taisto Sinisalo, Ossian Sjöman, Leo Suonpää, and Erkki Tuominen. The eight members of the new Secretariat are Aalto, Hänninen, Kivimäki, Lehto, Pessi, Saarinen, Ossi Nurminen, and Olavi Poikolainen.

Auxiliary organizations of the SKP include the Finnish Democratic Youth League, the Finnish Defenders of Peace, and the Finnish Women's Democratic League (of which SKP Political Committee member Anna-Liisa Hyvönen is secretary-general). Of the friendship societies controlled by the SKP, by far the most important is the Finland-Soviet Union Society.

The communists continued to play an important role in the trade union movement. Following a series of amalgamations in 1969, the 260,000-member left-socialist Finnish Confederation of Trade Unions (Suomen Ammattiiydistysten Keskusliitto; SAK)—in which the SKP held 7 of 19 executive seats—united under a governing board with the Social Democrats' 107,000-member Federation of Finnish Trade Unions (Suomen Ammattijarjestö; SAJ) and various independent unions comprising some 100,000 members. On the governing board, 12 seats were allocated to the Social Democrats, 8 to the SKP, and 2 to the left-socialist Workers' and Small Farmers' Social Democratic League.

Party Internal Affairs. Negotiations for SKP reunification, initiated in April 1969 after the Stalinists walked out of the Fifteenth Congress and threatened to set up a new party and present a rival slate in the 1970 parliamentary elections, culminated at an extraordinary congress on 14 February 1970 with the ratification of a conciliation agreement. Its provisions were as follows. (1) All Central Committee members were guaranteed the right of ideological and political dissent, but adherence to majority rule would be required. (2) The party's international relations, henceforth, would be conducted by the Central Committee on the basis of an annual advance plan in which recommendations by district organizations would be considered. (3) In order to "consolidate and restore reciprocal confidence," SKDL organs would be required to follow the party line and "personal accusations which could sustain and augment differences" were not to be published. (4) The joint negotiating committee, as well as all delegates assigned to individual districts by the Central Committee, and all parallel organizations set up by the Stalinist minority were to cease their activities forthwith. (5) Dissemination of the dissidents' organ *Tiedonantaja* must, henceforth, be restricted to the Uusimaa District, from which it emanated. (6) Annual meetings of all district organizations would be held between 28 February and 1 March, under the guidance of a 12-man inspection committee appointed by the Central Committee. (*Kansan Uutiset*, 8 January.)

Leaders on both sides admitted dissatisfaction with the terms of the agreement and acknowledged that it was primarily intended as a political instrument for patching up the divisions so as to present a unified slate in the election. The fundamental ideological differences which had torn the party since 1966 when the Saarinen leadership decided to join the government, and which were brought to a head in 1968 by Saarinen's mild disapproval of the Soviet-led invasion of Czechoslovakia, were such that they could be little alleviated by the mere signing of a joint declaration. The SKP newspaper, reflecting the sentiments of both factions, commented that the agreement was a "starting point," but that discord of several years' duration, the damage to personal relationships during that time, and the resultant distrust could not be ameliorated at one congress (*ibid.*, 15 February).

The SKDL's reduced strength in the new coalition (formed only after unsuccessful attempts by various combinations of parties to form a government and followed by the interim rule of a caretaker government from May to July) was likely to exacerbate the seemingly irreconcilable viewpoints within the new SKP leadership. The Stalinists continued to insist that the ideological base of the SKP could only be compromised by participation in a coalition embracing so broad a range of political views and goals as to preclude radical change yet necessitate concessions by the communists on "nonsocialist" measures. The Saarinen forces, admitting that the SKDL's participation in the government had been less than satisfactory, countered that the advantages outweighed the drawbacks, and that to opt for opposition status would be to abandon the interests of Finnish workers. Charges by the Stalinists that the Saarinen forces were revisionist and anti-Soviet in their basic attitudes found diminishing support in Moscow. Public pronouncements by the Communist Party of the Soviet Union (CPSU) clearly favored keeping the SKDL in the government, and although resentment of the reformists' position on Czechoslovakia was still apparent, the Soviet party avoided taking sides throughout the negotiations and pressed for an early compromise.

Domestic Attitudes and Activities. Current national objectives of the SKP were elaborated in the conciliation agreement. The party seeks to dissolve the alleged concentration of Finnish production and finance and the "unification of the forces of the monopolies and of the state." In its view, productive force was being sacrificed and resources which could advance economic and social life were left untapped because of the "antithesis between interests of the top stratum of the capitalists and those of all other groups." The main party objective, therefore, was the building of a broad democratic front to promote workers' "common economic, political, and social demands." Imperative for this objective was the abandonment by the Social Democratic Party and organizations under its influence of their policy of "class collaboration" with finance capital. (*Kansan Uutiset*, 8 January 1970.)

Assessing what it judged negative aspects of the SKDL's government participation, the document noted failures in economic and tax policy. The leaders of the Social Democratic and Center parties allegedly did not yet aspire to any profound social reforms or to limitation of the power of finance capital, but were still bound to the prevailing system. Government economic measures had not been directed against private-capital monopolies, nor toward control of capital, regulation and supervision of profits, and prevention of speculation in land and residential property. No serious effort had been made to eliminate the imbalance in foreign trade—which the SKP claimed could be overcome by sufficiently increasing Finland's trade and economic cooperation with the socialist countries. The record suggested an uncalled-for appeasement of the other parties by the SKDL, in the SKP view, and even the firm opposition of the SKDL toward incorrect decisions in the cabinet and in parliament had not come to the attention of the broad popular masses; thus SKDL policy had sometimes become identified in the popular mind with that of the government as a whole (*ibid.*).

The main goals of the party for the immediate future included: annual renewal of labor contracts; a rise in real wages in at least the same proportion as the productivity of labor; sufficient government authority to control and regulate prices, rents, and interest; expansion and development of state-managed enterprises, particularly in metals and chemicals, mining, and construction; expansion of housing production and an increase in housing construction loans; support of small and medium-sized industry through low-interest loans; improved pension and insurance systems benefiting the poor, the old, the young, and the unemployed; a shift of center of gravity of taxation from medium incomes to large incomes, and to owners of property and to corporations; and democratization (i.e., nationalization) of private institutions of higher education. (*Ibid.*)

The question of a transition to socialism in an advanced capitalist country such as Finland was the topic of Saarinen's address to the Helsinki district organization on 17 January in connection with the centenary of Lenin's birth. He declared that developments in science and technology had resulted in two alternatives facing humanity: the preservation of peaceful coexistence between states or the cataclysm of a nuclear war destroying all. Although the capitalist and imperialist world system was disintegrating, he declared, the birth of the socialist world system had created in capitalism a new self-defense mechanism in whose service various fields of science, technology, and bourgeois ideology had been mobilized. This mechanism had created the so-called consumer society, in which the abundance and variety of various goods, advertising, recreational industries, and "pop" culture captivated the people, encouraged a standard-of-living competition, increased pressures at work, and isolated the people from social problems and the revolutionary struggle. Because of this self-defense mechanism, the achievement of socialism in advanced capitalist countries was highly dependent upon ideological struggle. The policy of peaceful coexistence opened new possibilities for communists and other socialist and democratic forces to increase their ideological and political influence on the superstructure of bourgeois society—the administration of the state, the communications media, the school system, and church circles. (*Ibid.*, 20 January.)

In the March election, both Saarinen and Leo Suonpaa, a member of the SKP Politburo and former vice-president of parliament, lost their parliamentary seats. Sinisalo, however, as well as all other Stalinist SKP candidates, gained reelection. Of the total 36 seats for the SKDL, 15 went to Stalinist SKP members, the remainder being divided among SKP reformists and some SKP and SKDL "centrists" neutral in the factional struggle. The Conservatives, who increased their seats by 11 to 37, were invited by President Kekkonen to form a new coalition government, but on 10 April they announced their failure because of the refusal of the Social Democrats, Centrists, and SKDL (with a combined 124 seats) to support a Conservative premier. In the maneuvering which ensued among the various parties vying for inclusion in any new government, there was considerable reluctance within the SKP and SKDL to enter into any negotiations which might include either the Conservatives or the Rural Party—a "protest" party which made spectacular gains in the election (from a single seat to 18) and was openly anticommunist. Speaking in Helsinki on May Day (1 May), Saarinen cited an alleged contradiction in the Rural Party's simultaneous opposition to monopolists and to communists—a situation which Saarinen compared to "a religiously devout person fighting both God and the Devil at the same time." Many of the protest votes captured by the Rural Party, he argued further, were a result of unemployment caused by automation—a development for which communists could not be blamed. (*Ibid.*, 3 May.) After six weeks of fruitless attempts to form a cabinet, Kekkonen on 14 May nominated a 13-member caretaker cabinet headed by Teuvo Aura, the mayor of Helsinki, and in which neither the communists nor any other members of parliament were included.

The SKP continued to maintain a firm hold over the majority of noncommunist SKDL members even though in theory the SKDL maintains an organization separate from the SKP. The divisions within the SKP, however, were clearly in evidence at the Ninth Congress of the SKDL in Helsinki on 15-18 May, and SKDL cohesion was preserved only because of the absence of any serious ideological debate. The adoption of new rules and procedures favored the moderate communists and left-wing socialists. The Stalinists secured one of the three SKDL vice-chairmanships, which went to Matti Koivunen (the others to SKP Central Committee member Anna-Liisa Tiekso and Fjalar Björkqvist). The noncommunist chairman of the SKDL, Ele Alenius, retained his post, as did secretary-general Aimo Haapanen. The new 25-member SKDL leadership included 17 communists (of whom 6 were Stalinists) and 8 noncommunists.

In general, the congress was a setback for the more liberal aspirations within the SKDL, voiced by Alenius in an opening speech which stressed the extent to which the SKDL had been handicapped by close identification with the communists. Criticizing the Stalinists' rejection of different concepts of socialism, and underscoring the importance of developing a "national" image for the SKDL, Alenius said, "Cooperation requires recognition of freedom of thought." He acknowledged, however, that the SKDL could not achieve success without the existence of the communist camp and "a strong Soviet Union." In contrast to Alenius, the Soviet delegate, Nikolai Romanov, a candidate member of the CPSU Central Committee, insisted that the communists must be the "leading political force" within the SKDL. The congress deemed the formation of the caretaker government an "artificial solution" and passed a resolution, against Stalinist opposition, calling for a return to a center-left coalition. (*Folktidningen*, 21 May.)

The opposition of the Stalinists hampered the SKP leadership in reaching a formal decision as to whether the SKDL should participate in multiparty negotiations for a new coalition government. The Saarinen forces finally pushed through a vote just in time for the talks begun on 16 June, under former Foreign Minister Ahti Karjalainen. Saarinen told the SKP Central Committee plenum on 16 June that the question of the participation of the SKDL and the Rural Party in the same government was still open. Saarinen also said that the formation of the Aura government had been based on the assumption that the SKDL, or at least trade union officials, would join. It might have been better, he said, if Koivisto's government had been allowed to continue in office until a new government had been formed. (Helsinki radio, 16 June.)

The present government under Karjalainen, announced on 14 July, comprises the Social Democrats, Centrists, SKDL, Swedish People's Party, and Liberal Party, which were apportioned 5, 3, 3, 2, and 2 cabinet portfolios, respectively. Those secured by the SKDL were Justice, Erkki Tuominen (SKP politburo); Social Affairs, Anna-Liisa Tiekso (SKP Central Committee); and Communications, Veikko Saarto. Saarinen declared on 4 September that "governments assembled from many quarters cannot carry out a policy satisfactory to all the parties that participate in them." This applied particularly to the communist party, whose long-term goals, he said, diverged "most of all" from those of its government partners. (*Kansan Uutiset*, 5 September.) Despite such statements by the SKP leadership, however, it was evident that the influence of the CPSU leadership placed the SKDL in a disproportionately strong position.

Thus, even after their election reversal the communists were able to play a major role in thwarting any "rightist" bid for inclusion in the government despite the gains of the Conservative Party. An editorial in *Pravda* on 16 July aptly illustrated the orientation of Finnish politics when it commented: "This coalition must become the *permanent basis* for the nation's development along a peaceful, democratic road" (emphasis added). Also, the award to the SKDL of the Justice post in the Karjalainen cabinet—a far more strategic ministry than was held by the communists in the previous administration, when their share of government power in terms of electoral support was substantially greater—was highly suggestive of Soviet pressure. Erkki Tuominen, the new incumbent, is a Stalinist who headed the state police from March 1948 until the end of that year, when the communists were ousted following the alleged discovery of a plot by them to overthrow the government. In his initial official statement on 18 July, Tuominen was said to have expressed the view that "all public appointments, including those in the police force, should be political" (*Helsingin Sanomat*, Helsinki, 18 July).

It was evident early in the new administration that the communists were divided among themselves. The substantial Stalinist group appeared intent upon blocking the reformists' support of the two-year-old economic stabilization program (the Liinamaa Plan, introduced in 1968). The first indication came on 14 October over a relatively minor matter, when twelve Stalinist members of the SKDL parliamentary group voted against the majority's backing of a bill on civil service contract laws. The dissidents were censured by the SKP Politburo, by a vote of 8 to 5, for having "disrupted conditions for implementing the party's general political line." Sinisalo and three other Politburo members, Oiva Lehto, Markus Kainulainen, and Erkki Tuominen, protested that communists could not support measures limiting the rights of workers, and that the opposition twelve could hardly be considered to have betrayed the SKDL's popular front policy by voting against a bill supported by the Conservative Party itself. The SKP, Saarinen rejoined, had supported the bill as "the lesser of two evils, as one is often forced to do in politics." SKDL opposition to it could have brought about the dissolution of the Karjalainen government. (*Kansan Uutiset*, 16 October.) The Stalinists argued that excessive subservience of the party in the Paasio and Koivisto governments, from 1966 to 1970, to the policies of other ruling parties, had been the main factor in the SKDL's electoral decline. Communist participation in the government, in sum, was "not an end in itself." (Sinisalo, *ibid.*, 23 October.)

International Views and Activities. The SKP conciliation agreement supported the center-left coalition government as the best suited to promote an active peace policy and to strengthen Finnish-Soviet relations. Both the proposal that Finland should be host to a European security conference and the choice of Helsinki as the site of the Strategic Arms Limitation Talks (SALT) had derived from this basic policy. Evidence of rightist aspiration to link Finland's economic life with ever stronger bonds to West European capitalism, however, was seen as manifest in Finland's joining the Organization for Economic Cooperation and Development (OECD) in 1969 and its participation in the Nordek (inter-Scandinavian customs union) negotiations. To avert this threat from the right and at the same time boost Finland's foreign trade position, the SKP advocated stepped-up imports from the Soviet Union, particularly in engines and machinery. (*Kansan Uutiset*, 8 January.)

In a May Day address Saarinen cited, as conditions for SKDL participation in a new government, adherence to a foreign policy based on the Finnish-Soviet treaty of friendship, cooperation, and mutual assistance; active promotion of a collective European security system; and support of international recognition for the German Democratic Republic (GDR) (*ibid.*, 3 May). SKP Politburo member Leo Suonpaa, in an ADN (East German news agency) interview on 30 January, stated that the German question could not be solved peacefully so long as "the Federal Republic of Germany continues obstinately to insist that it is the sole representative of the entire German people." Heralding the conclusion, in August, of the Soviet-West German treaty, the SKP (unsuccessfully) pressed for early recognition by Finland of the GDR. Speaking at Oulu on 13 September at a meeting commemorating the SKP's fifty-second anniversary, Saarinen termed the treaty a "new and eloquent demonstration of the significance and influence of the socialist world system and its leading country, the Soviet Union," and a "great stride" toward consolidating peace and security in Europe (*ibid.*, 14 September).

After having approved all moves for an inter-Scandinavian customs union through two years of government-level negotiations, the SKDL parliamentary group announced on 19 February that it would oppose any new initiatives in the negotiations—by then far advanced—until a new government was formed after the election. Saarinen's explanation as to why the SKDL had gone along with earlier Nordek decisions—as recently as 12 January, for instance, when the government as a whole had announced its readiness to conclude the talks and initiate those measures which would put the customs union into effect—was that it had gradually become evident that Nordek was to be used as a path to the European Economic Community (EEC). Finland's reservation in the proposed treaty, which provided that entry into the EEC by any party to Nordek would give Finland the automatic right to leave, was said not to be an adequate guarantee. (*Ukens Nytt*, Oslo, 20 February.)

Discussions ensued among the noncommunist government parties as to the feasibility of pressing for ratification of the Nordek treaty without the communists, but the Soviets' cooling toward the customs union virtually ruled out such a move. On 2-7 March a CPSU delegation headed by Politburo member Arvids Pelshe visited Finland. During the delegation's talks with the SKP Politburo and Secretariat and in a multilateral meeting of all government parties, the extolling of Finnish-Soviet relations (see e.g., *Pravda*, 11 March, for the text of a joint SKP-CPSU communiqué) left little room for maneuver among Nordek supporters within the government. On 24 March, only eighteen days after the Soviets' departure, the government formally announced that it would not sign the Nordek treaty because "in the prevailing circumstances" it did not "meet the requirements for an agreement of a serious and permanent nature" (*Helsingin Sanomat*, 25 March).

The Soviets continued to take steps to reinforce the influence of the SKP, whose image among the Finnish electorate had clearly suffered as a result of its internal divisions. One such measure of the importance attached by the Soviets to the unity of the SKP was the appointment, on 24 June, of Aleksei Belyakov as Soviet ambassador to Finland. Belyakov, a senior official in the CPSU Central Committee's International Section, had been sent to Finland in 1969 to attempt to reconcile the two factions; also he accompanied Pelshe to Finland in March 1970. Replacing Andrei Kovalev, who had been accused by the Saarinen forces of partiality toward the Stalinists, Belyakov was believed to be more of a neutral bent and, therefore, less likely to aggravate the ongoing schisms.

The SKP maintained its active role in Finnish-Soviet affairs. Anna-Liisa Tiekso was one of three cabinet ministers who on 17 July, only three days after installation of the Karjalainen government, accompanied President Kekkonen to Moscow for talks with top Soviet leaders including Podgorny, Kosygin, and Gromyko. A joint protocol was signed on 20 July which extended until 1990 the Finnish-Soviet treaty even though it was not due to expire until 1975. (Moscow radio, 17 July; Helsinki radio, 20 July.)

In other aspects of international affairs, the U.S. decision to "expand the war in Southeast Asia" by sending troops into Cambodia was said by the Finnish communists to mean "a prolongation of the war and a lessening of the chances for a peaceful solution" (Helsinki radio, 5 May). The SKP, represented by Saarinen and Secretariat member Olavi Poikolainen, participated in the conference of communist parties of European capitalist countries which convened in Paris on 15 May to discuss the situation in Indochina. The SKP Politburo met on 20 May in Helsinki and formally approved the decisions of the Paris conference. (TASS, 20 May.) A joint communiqué issued on 15 May following talks in Helsinki between delegations of the SKP and the (North) Korean Workers' Party condemned the United States for "extreme aggravation of tension in Korea" and "further intensification of maneuvers for aggression and war." It also denounced Japanese "militarism," which was said to have been "revived under the active patronage of U.S. imperialism for embarking upon the road of aggression against Korea and other Asian countries." (Korean Central News Agency, Pyongyang, 18 May.)

Although still critical of the 1968 intervention in Czechoslovakia, the SKP generally maintained its traditional loyalty to the Soviet Union in the international communist movement. In June, a Central Committee statement held that the policies of the Chinese Communist leaders, their verbal attacks against the Soviet Union, their "disruptive activities" within the international communist camp, and their "instigation of border incidents" had abetted the "imperialistic bourgeoisie" in all countries and obscured the concept of a united communist movement with clearly defined objectives. The statement went so far as to suggest that the posture of the Chinese leaders had been a factor in the SKDL's electoral losses. (*Kansan Uutiset*, 23 June.)

Publications. The central organ of the SKP is the daily *Kansan Uutiset* (People's News), edited by Politburo member Jorma Simpura. It has an estimated circulation of 59,000. The party's monthly theoretical journal, *Kommunisti*, is edited by Inkeri Lehtinen. Regional party organs include *Uusi Paiva* in Turku, the Kuopio party district's daily *Kansan Sana*, and the Uusimaa district's *Tiedonantaja*. *Folktidningen* (People's News) is published weekly in Swedish as the organ of the SKDL. It carries most SKP documents and is the voice of the SKP among the Swedish-speaking minority. Its editor is Mikael Romberg.

*   *   *

A small pro-Chinese splinter party, the "Finnish Association of Marxist-Leninists," is believed to have been established in 1968. It currently has cells in Helsinki, Tampere, and Turku, and includes members of the SKP and the SKDL. The main activities are education and propaganda through its study circles on Marxism-Leninism and Maoist theory. It has the endorsement of the Chinese Communist Party, whose media have carried statements of the Finnish group.

The association issues a bulletin in Helsinki, *Punakaarti* (Red Guard), edited by Tauno Olavi Huotari, assisted by Bjarne Nitovuori, Matti Puolakka, and Peter Nilsson. Other contributors have included Heikki Pihlaja and Mikko Kinnunen.

V. B.

FRANCE

The French Communist Party (Parti Communiste Français; PCF) was founded in December 1920. It is legal. Although confronted with growing dissent within its ranks and challenged by other small Marxist-Leninist organizations (see below), the PCF remained in 1970 the largest and electorally strongest left-wing party in France. Estimates of party membership, however, varied. Contrary to previous practice, which consisted of publicizing only the number of party cards sent to the PCF federations but not the total distributed by them, Georges Marchais, deputy secretary-general, claimed that the actual membership in 1970 was 400,000 (*L'Humanité*, 30 December). This total appears to have been considerably inflated. The monthly publication *Unir-Débat* (Paris, no. 49, 10 January 1971), organ of a dissident group within the PCF, estimated the membership at the end of 1970 at between 250,000 and 260,000. An estimate by the noncommunist Paris fortnightly *Est & Ouest* (no. 461, 1-15 February 1971) placed PCF membership at a maximum of 290,000. The population of France is about 50,000,000 (estimated 1970).

In the elections to the National Assembly on 23 and 30 June 1968 the PCF suffered a considerable setback. Whereas in 1967 the party had increased its representation in the 486-seat Assembly from 41 to 73 (see *YICA*, 1968, p. 208), in 1968 only 34 communist candidates were elected (including one representative from the Guadeloupe Communist Party) and votes for the party fell from 5,039,032 to 4,435,357 (i.e., from 22.46 per cent of the total to 20.03 per cent). The PCF fared somewhat better at the partial elections to the Senate on 22 September 1968. Of the 103 (out of a total of 283) renewable seats, the communists obtained 15 (including Marcel Gargar from Guadeloupe), which represented a gain of four seats over the last (1959) partial elections involving the same districts. Some qualification is necessary, however, in comparing the two years' results, since in 1968 seven new districts (all in the Paris region) were contested. As a result of the September 1968 elections the communists had a total of 18 seats in the Senate, including the one held by Gargar. In the presidential elections held in June 1969 the PCF appeared to have regained some of its electoral appeal; its candidate, Jacques Duclos, obtained 21.27 per cent of the vote—a total far greater than the combined vote of all the other left and extreme-left wing candidates (see *YICA*, 1970, 162). In the cantonal elections held on 8 and 15 March 1970 the resurgent trend was again evident. In the first ballot the PCF candidates obtained 2,014,975 votes, or nearly 24 per cent. Following the second ballot, in which the PCF advocated "the withdrawal, on a reciprocal basis, of candidates nominated by the left-wing parties in favor of the leading candidates at the first ballot" (*L'Humanité*, 9 March), the party increased its cantonal representation by 13 seats (from 131 to 144, out of 1,606 renewable seats).

Organization and Leadership. The structure of the PCF was described by the party's organizational secretary, André Vieuguet, at a conference of PCF federation secretaries in late November 1970. Vieuguet claimed that since the party's Nineteenth Congress, in February 1970 (see below), the number of party cells had increased from 19,250 to 19,500.[1] As of 31 October, the PCF was said to have 5,200 cells in factories (compared with 5,000 at the end of 1969), 5,350 rural cells (5,600 in 1969), and 8,950 other local cells (8,700 in 1969). The cells were said to be part of 2,560 sections in 97 party federations. (*L'Humanité*, 26 November).

The national leadership of the PCF was elected at the party's Nineteenth Congress, held at Nanterre on 4-9 February. The new Central Committee numbered 79 full and 28 candidate members (22 of the latter were newly elected)—for names, see *L'Humanité*, 9 February. The Central Committee, in turn, elected the following to the Politburo: Gustave Ansart, François Billoux, Guy Besse (formerly a candidate member), Jacques Duclos, Etienne Fajon, Benoît Frachon, Georges Frischmann, Raymond Guyot, Henri Krasucki, Paul Laurent, Roland Leroy, Georges Marchais, René Piquet, Gaston Plissonnier, Waldeck Rochet, Georges Séguy, and André Vieuguet (formerly candidate member). Two new candidate members were elected— Claude Poperen and Madeleine Vincent. Waldeck Rochet was reelected secretary-general of the party, with Georges Marchais as his deputy. Other members elected by the Central Committee to the Secretariat were: Etienne Fajon (newly elected), Roland Leroy, René Piquet, Gaston Plissonnier, and André Vieuguet. The election of Georges Marchais to the post of deputy secretary-general was a recognition of his *de facto* leadership of the PCF, Waldeck Rochet's health having deteriorated progressively since 1969 (see *YICA*, 1970, pp. 160-61). Another significant change in the party leadership was the failure to reelect Roger Garaudy to either Politburo or Central Committee, a decision motivated by Garaudy's repeated criticisms of PCF policy on both the international and the domestic level (see below).

Auxiliary Organizations. The PCF's primary auxiliary organization [2] is the General Confederation of Labor (Confédération Générale du Travail; CGT), the largest trade union in France. At the time of its Thirty-seventh Congress, 17-21 November 1969, the CGT claimed a membership of 2,300,000 (*L'Humanité*, 18 November). Official government estimates, however, put CGT membership at between 1,300,000 and 1,500,000. The CGT is led by PCF Politburo members Georges Séguy (secretary-general) and Benoît Frachon (president).

The other major PCF auxiliary organization is the Movement of Communist Youth (Movement de la Jeunesse Communiste; MJC), whose secretary-general is Roland Favaro. The MJC comprises four groups—the Union of Communist Students of France (Union des Etudiants Communistes de France; UECF), the Union of Young Girls of France (Union des Jeunes Filles de France; UJFF), the Union of Communist Youth of France (Union de la Jeunesse Communiste de France; UJCF), and the Union of Farm Youth of France (Union de la Jeunesse Agricole de France; UJAF). The latter groups' secretaries-general in 1970 were: Gérard Molina (UECF), Nicole Garand (UJFF), Robert Clement (UJCF), and Raymond Monteil (UJAF). The MJC held a national congress, together with its four component groups, on 4-6 December, in Paris, attended by some 1,200 delegates. The new MJC National Bureau and the respective leaderships of the four component organizations were elected at this time. The following were elected to the MJC National Bureau: Roland Favaro, secretary-general; Jean-Michel Catala (sometimes spelled Cathala), deputy secretary-general; Gérard Molina, secretary-general of UECF; Nicole Garand, secretary-general of UJFF: Gérard Lanternier, new secretary-general of UJCF; Michel Larrat, new secretary-general of UJAF; and P. Barre, Eliane Bize, G. Bras, José Fort, Jackie Hoffmann, Jeanine Jambu, Michel Jouet, Jean-Claude Le Meur, Nicolas Marchand, Michel Navarro, Mireille Riou, Georges Troubat, Alain Therouse, Dominique Vidal, and Pierre Zarka.

---

[1] The figure of 19,250 cells reported during the Nineteenth Congress was contested at that time by the dissident PCF monthly *Unir-Débat* (no. 38, 16 February), which claimed that there were only some 15,000 party cells. Another description of the PCF organizational structure, which reiterated the figures reported in November, was given by Vieugnet in October to *France Nouvelle* (no. 1302, 21 October).

[2] A considerable number of organizations in France are controlled or strongly influenced by the PCF; for a delineation and description of these groups see *Est & Ouest*, no. 433, 16-31 October 1969 (and *ibid.*, no. 435, 16-30 November, for errata).

Since the events of May 1968 (see *YICA*, 1969, pp. 325-28), which showed the importance of trade union action in the field of education (the French Ministry of Education employs some 700,000 persons), the PCF has made a special effort to consolidate itself in this area. In 1969 the PCF gained control of the leadership of the National Union of University Teachers (Syndicat Nationale de l'Enseignment Supérieure; SNE-Sup. See *YICA*, 1970, p. 161). During 1970, the UECF—operating through a group called UNEF-Renewal (UNEF-Renouveau), led by Guy Konopnicki, member of the UECF National Bureau—continued in its attempt to gain control of the National Union of Students of France (Union Nationale des Etudiants de France; UNEF), whose leadership was in the hands of the Unified Socialist Party (Parti Socialiste Unifié; PSU). At the UNEF congress in April at Orléans the four major political groups were the PSU, the Trotskyist Alliance des Jeunes pour le Socialisme (AJS—see below), Maoists aligned with *L'-Humanité Rouge* (see below), and the UNEF-Renouveau. By means of what appears to have been a somewhat dubious "invalidation" of some 10,000 membership cards out of 28,000, the four different groups' mandates to the congress were divided as follows: PSU, 34 per cent; AJS, 33 per cent; *L'Humanité Rouge*, 14 per cent; and UNEF-Renouveau, 19 per cent.[1] An attempt by the Maoists and the PSU to expel the UNEF-Renouveau group was defeated by the latter with the assistance of AJS votes. Having overcome the expulsion attempt against it, UNEF-Renouveau continued to consolidate its position within UNEF. In its June issue the PSU internal organ, *Directives*, stated: "One must realize that the bureaucratic victory of Orléans cannot be repeated next year. . . . The present situation is that the so-called reformist [i.e., UNEF-Renouveau] tendency is in the majority—the PSU, with the help of H.R. [*L'Humanité Rouge*], having temporarily prevented this tendency from taking over the leadership of UNEF." The PSU concluded that the leadership of UNEF would have to be retained "at all costs," and called for "an alliance with the AJS." The PSU leadership in the UNEF attempted by various means to retain its position, including the refusal to send out 1970-71 membership cards, followed by a second attempt on 30 November to expel UNEF-Renouveau. Partly due to the opposition of the AJS, both moves proved unsuccessful. By the end of the year the Maoists of *L'Humanité Rouge* were confronted with internal schisms; relations between the *L'Humanité Rouge* and the PSU militants had deteriorated; and the PSU faction within the UNEF was itself attacked by the PSU national leadership, which indicated a desire to abandon its interest in UNEF developments (see *Tribune Socialiste*, weekly organ of the PSU, 10 December). There were indications at the end of the year that the major confrontations in 1971 would be between UNEF-Renouveau and the AJS, the latter grouped within a tendency called Unité Syndicale (Trade Union Unity).

Other major PCF auxiliary organizations active in 1970 included the Union of French Women (Union des Femmes Françaises; UFF), the Peace Movement (Movement de la Paix), and the Movement for the Defense of Small Farmers (Movement de Défense des Exploitants Familiaux; MODEF).

Party Internal Affairs. The Soviet-led invasion of Czechoslovakia of August 1968 and the PCF's response to it and to the subsequent "normalization" in that country continued in 1970 to be a source of significant dissent within the party. Criticism of the party leadership focused on the PCF's failure to extend its 1968 condemnation of the invasion to a critical evaluation of the Soviet-imposed "normalization" in Czechoslovakia. Critics also called for greater objectivity in the party's assessment of both the domestic and the foreign policies of ruling communist parties.

---

[1] The dissident communist monthly *Politique Aujourd'hui* (November 1970) estimated that "without the various 'adjustments' " the breakdown at Orléans would have allocated 45 per cent of the votes to UNEF-Renouveau, 24 per cent to the PSU, 21 per cent to the AJS, and 10 per cent to *L'Humanité Rouge*. For another similar, although less specific, criticism of the mandate validation see *Est & Ouest*, no. 460, 16-31 January 1971.

At the same time, the issue of internal democracy within the PCF was being questioned, as was the alleged failure of the party to discuss openly and analyze its role in the political and social developments in France.

PCF dissidence was centered primarily around two monthly publications, *Unir-Débat* and *Politique Aujourd'hui*,[1] and personified in Roger Garaudy, former member of the party's Politburo and prominent author, and Charles Tillon, also a former Politburo member (until 1952), commander-in-chief of the communist Resistance forces in France during the Second World War, and a cabinet minister in the postwar government in France.

Conflict between the PCF leadership and Roger Garaudy was evident in 1967 at the time of the publication of his book *Le problème chinois* (see *YICA*, 1968, pp. 212, 217) and further exasperated in 1968 following his strong denunciation of the invasion of Czechoslovakia (see *ibid.*, 1969, p. 323). During 1969 attacks against Garaudy took on a systematic character, reaching a peak in December when he published another book, *Le grand tournant du socialisme*, which contained harsh criticism of the Soviet Union and proposed internal democratization of the PCF (see *ibid.*, 1970, p. 161). In an interview given to the Turin newspaper *La Stampa* (28 January 1970), Garaudy indicated that he expected the upcoming Nineteenth Congress of the PCF to remove him both from the Politburo and the Central Committee. To the question as to whether he thought that there was a possibility that he might be expelled from the party after the congress, he replied: "I do not think so; I do not see how they could justify this."

Garaudy was offered the opportunity to express his views in the "pre-congress discussion columns" of *L'Humanité*, although according to an editorial note his contribution (on 2 January) was shortened (with his consent) to conform to "the norms which should govern the relations between brother parties." The PCF leadership also allowed Garaudy to address the congress on 6 February. The report on his speech, however, as published in *L'Humanité* (7 February), carried only short extracts and summarized his concluding remarks with the statement: "Having expressed an obscene attack against several socialist countries, he concluded and left the podium in the total silence of the entire congress." With regard to the latter, Garaudy had stated:

> I wrote in my book and I repeat it here: anti-Sovietism is a crime against France and against peace. We have a common enemy: from Vietnam to Cuba we can only resist imperialist aggression in common struggle. But what feeds anticommunism and anti-Sovietism is not lucid and public judgment of violations of our principles, but the acts by which they are violated. When a socialist country, at the height of a miners' strike in Asturias, sends coal to Franco which helps him to break the strike, when a socialist country, having divided the party of Manolis Glezos, builds power stations for his executioners, the Greek fascists, one does not violate proletarian internationalism and feed anti-Sovietism by describing these things, but by doing them. Or by keeping silent. (*Unir-Débat*, no. 38, 16 February.)

No support was expressed for Garaudy's views at the Congress, and his major potential ally, the poet Louis Aragon, editor of the weekly *Les Lettres Françaises* and member of the Central Committee, excused himself, for reasons of ill health, from attending the congress sessions until the afternoon of 6 February, when the attacks against Garaudy and his reply had been concluded. Despite alleged ill health, Aragon was chosen by the PCF leadership to preside over the afternoon session. He was reelected to the Central Committee at the conclusion of the congress. The

[1] The dissident group within the PCF, whose open publication since 1967 has been *Unir-Débat*, dates back to 1952; *Politique Aujourd'hui* was first published in January 1969 under the editorship of Paul Noirot (former editor of the PCF monthly *Démocratie Nouvelle*). On 8 October, a new weekly *Politique Hebdo*, also under the editorship of Noirot, was initiated as a complementary publication to *Politique Aujourd'hui*. For background information on the two groups see: *YICA*, 1968, pp. 219-20, and 1969, p. 323; " 'A Communist Line for France': PCF Dissidents for Renewal of Party," Radio Free Europe, Munich, *Research Bulletin*, 5 May 1970; and " 'Politique Hebdo': New Challenge to the PCF," *ibid.*, 15 October 1970.

decision of the party leadership to give Aragon the honor of presiding at the congress session and his reelection to the Central Committee appear to have been moves by the leadership to associate Aragon—a strong critic of the invasion of Czechoslovakia—with the condemnation of Garaudy. On 5 May, Garaudy was expelled from his party cell, and on 20 May the PCF Central Committee ratified the expulsion. Charles Tillon, who aligned himself with Garaudy's views (see *Le Monde*, Paris, 3 June) by co-signing an appeal with Garaudy and two other former members of the PCF Central Committee, Maurice Kriegel-Valrimont and Jean Pronteau, was expelled later in the summer. The appeal accused the PCF of practicing a "democratic centralism, inspired by the Soviet model," which had "made it possible to remove those who posed problems and to place at the head of the party a man who [had] not participated in any of its vital struggles."

While the congress did not show any outward signs of significant disunity in the PCF, opposition among the rank-and-file to the party's policies—particularly its acceptance of "normalization" in Czechoslovakia—appeared to be growing. On 5 January—second anniversary of the deposition of Novotný by Dubček—a committee of active and former members of the PCF was formed to solicit signed support for a statement of opposition to the developments in Czechoslovakia, with signators limited to active and former PCF members. By the time the PCF congress had convened, this group—calling itself the Committee of 5 January 1970—had obtained some 200 signatures, including that of Charles Tillon. The monthly publication *Unir-Débat* (which carried the signatures as they came in) claimed (no. 38, 16 February): "This is the first time—to the best of our knowledge—that an initiative of this kind, *a communist petition*, has gathered so many signatures of members and former members of the party, of which the majority are active members of the PCF" (emphasis in text). By November the number of signators had grown reportedly to 1,200 and about half were claimed to be active members of the party (*Unir-Débat*, no. 48, 10 December). On 26 November the Committee of 5 January 1970 organized a mass rally in Paris to protest "normalization" in Czechoslovakia, which was attended by over 2,000 persons, despite alleged competition from another demonstration organized simultaneously by the PCF (*ibid.*).

Domestic Views and Policies. While continuing to be by far the strongest left-wing party in France (with more than 20 per cent of electoral support), the PCF was still not strong enough to hope to attain power on its own. During 1970 its position in French society continued to reflect a statement made by Waldeck Rochet in 1968: "We do not lull ourselves to sleep with the illusion that the majority of the workers of France has been won for the idea of socialism" (*L'Humanité*, 7 December 1968). At the end of 1970 the French Institute of Public Opinion published the results of two polls (see *France-Soir*, Paris, 29 and 30 December). The first poll indicated that two out of three Frenchmen were satisfied with the government of President Georges Pompidou and Premier Jacques Chaban-Delmas. The second poll included the question: "In the future, would you like the communist party's role in the political life of France to be more important than now? Or less important? Or to remain the same?" Answers obtained were (1) more important—16 per cent, (2) less important—24 per cent; (3) let it stay the same as now—39 per cent; and (4) no opinion—21 per cent. The percentage of those choosing the third option was seen as having increased progressively; in the summer of 1964 the figure was 32 per cent, and in January 1970 it had risen to 37 per cent.

The two-pronged approach of the PCF in its attempt to overcome the consequences of the above political context were: (1) advocacy of united action with other left-wing parties; and (2) a concerted effort to portray itself as a party committed to French democratic traditions.

Both facets of the PCF approach were reflected in an article by Central Committee member Henri Fiszbin in the party's weekly organ, *France Nouvelle* (4 November). Stating that the aim of the PCF was the advent of democracy and socialism in France, and that for this a powerful communist party was necessary, Fiszbin added: "But it is also necessary that all the groups that advocate socialism together constitute a force sufficient to carry it out." He then went on:

> The communists do not consider, they have never considered, their party's power as an end in itself. The communist party does not direct its force against the other parties on the left but against the enemies of the working class and of the people. A powerful communist party in the midst of a weak left, and regularly defeated by reaction, is not what we want.

In an endeavor to demonstrate the "sincerity of [PCF] sentiments for unity," Fiszbin claimed that the PCF had "for a long time . . . rejected the single party theory." "Plurality of parties in a country such as France," he stated, was seen by the PCF as being "necessary in the conflicts of today and in the society of tomorrow." Fiszbin noted that some people "suspect that they can see a tactical subtlety there on our part, a means of conquering power, so as then to be in a position to 'liquidate' our partners." He claimed, however, that it was "wrong to attribute intentions" to the PCF that it did not have, and added:

> A minimum of political realism is sufficient to verify that no single left-wing group can by itself carry the cause forward. Efficacity demands the union of left-wing groups. But our analysis is more fundamental and goes beyond the immediate need. Political parties in the last resort express the interests of diverse social classes and strata. In a country such as ours they are a profound and durable reality. . . . The new society, we are convinced, cannot be the work of a single party, even ours.

Finally, on the issue of whether in a socialist society the PCF would leave the government if it were put in the minority, Fiszbin stated:

> It is in no way scandalous to envisage, within the framework of socialism, changes of government and changes of political leaders. . . . We affirm our will to submit ourselves to popular judgement and we have already in the past proven our sincerity in this regard.

In its advocacy during 1970 of the unity of left-wing parties, the PCF focused its attention primarily on the Socialist Party (Parti Socialiste). In his speech at the Nineteenth Congress, Georges Marchais stated: "Our party attaches particular importance to cooperation with the Socialist Party. . . . Our two formations exert a decisive influence on the workers." Commenting on a joint declaration between the PCF and the Socialists, signed on 18 December 1969, which committed the two parties to "engage in discussions on the fundamental conditions for a political agreement" (see *YICA*, 1970, p. 164), Marchais reiterated the declaration's statement that such an agreement would constitute "the winning card of the unity of the left." The PCF deputy secretary-general added "This in no way means that we therefore intend to discard from the union of the left other democratic formations desiring to assume their responsibilities in the struggle for democracy and socialism." The PCF's attitude toward the other left-wing parties, however, was considerably less cordial, and did not reflect any significant changes from PCF statements made in 1969 (see *YICA*, 1970, p. 164). In his speech at the congress, Marchais referred to the PSU's adoption of "anti-communist and divisive positions, which played into the hands of reaction," adding: "The leftist phraseology which it is fond of adopting cannot conceal the fact that it bases its activity essentially on reformist ideology, a fact, which is particularly confirmed by the praise lavished by its secretary-general on the would-be 'Swedish socialism.' " Marchais did not offer any evaluation of the left-wing Convention of Republican Institutions (Convention des Institutions Républicains; CIR), and he described the Radical-Socialist Party (Parti Radical-Socialiste) as being led toward collaboration with "centrist politicians" and toward the adoption of a program little different from that of the government. As for the extreme-left organizations, Marchais stated: "Our party has waged a just and effective struggle against the leftists, the Maoists, and the Trotskyists. It will continue its resolute struggle, both on the national and the international level, against leftist opportunism in all its forms." (*L'Humanité*, 5 February.)

The PCF's attitude toward the other left-wing parties in France as expressed by Marchais at the congress did not change significantly during the rest of the year. Prospects for agreement on collaboration with the Socialist Party waxed and waned, and although Marchais—in a report to a PCF Central Committee meeting on 22 December—claimed that talks between the two parties had shown a "large number of convergences" (*L'Humanité*, 23 December), many differences still remained. The Socialist Party, moreover, indicated in December that more thorough discussions with the PCF would have to be postponed till after the Socialists' congress in the summer of 1971.

International Views and Policies. As indicated above, much of the dissent within the PCF and also a major source of friction between the party and potential left-wing allies centered around what appeared to be a retreat by the PCF from its disengagement from strict support for the views and policies of the Communist Party of the Soviet Union (CPSU). In his speech at the party's Nineteenth Congress, Georges Marchais referred to the PCF's "disagreement with the 21 August 1968 military intervention in Czechoslovakia," but went on to note that "subsequently" the party had "shown its understanding of the efforts aimed at finding a political solution to the crisis which [had] arisen, a line of conduct it had advocated right from the start." Marchais then added:

> At the same time our party has expressed its determination to fight uncompromisingly any show of anti-Sovietism whatever its origin, and has shown its determination in practice. Never will the French communists accept, without countering it, the least complacency with regard to anti-Soviet attitudes, which are contrary to the interests of the working class, the nation, and peace! (*L'Humanité*, 5 February.)

Politburo member Etienne Fajon took an even stronger line, referring to the "stupidity of middle-class people who had hoped that this difference of opinion [with the CPSU, over Czecho-slovakia] was the beginning of a rupture," and reasserted the "indestructible friendship" between the French and Soviet parties (*ibid.*, 7 February).

During the first part of 1970 the extent of the PCF's support for "normalization" in Czecho-slovakia was further revealed when it was confirmed that in November 1969 a French delega-tion, led by Etienne Fajon, handed over to the Czechoslovak party leadership the minutes of Waldeck Rochet's conversations with Alexander Dubček during a meeting in July 1968—an ac-tion which had contributed to Dubček's political downfall. The issue first came to broad public attention in early May through the publication of a letter by Roger Garaudy to the secretary of his cell after members had voted to recommend his expulsion. In the letter Garaudy attacked "a very limited group [which was] manipulating the party Secretariat, a group led by Georges Marchais." This group, he asserted, "carried to Prague ... elements of a dossier which made it possible to overcome Dubček." (*Le Monde*, 6 May.) The substance of Garaudy's charges, how-ever, had become known, although not broadly publicized, at the beginning of the year. On 14 January, Brno radio in Czechoslovakia broadcast a speech which Alois Indra, conservative member of the Czechoslovak communist party's Secretariat, had made the day before at a meet-ing of provincial party workers. In the speech Indra revealed that the PCF delegation to Prague in November 1969 had—to the Czechoslovak party's "great surprise"—handed over "their stenographic notes of the conversations between Waldeck Rochet and Alexander Dubček on 19 July 1968." Indra then added: "When we studied this document, it was a new shock. We had to ask ourselves: who was this Alexander Dubček? Just a man who was incapable, or something else." Czechoslovak party Politburo and Secretariat member Vasil Bil'ak used the French material to attack Dubček at the party's Central Committee plenum in Prague at the end of January. On 31 January the Soviet news agency TASS reported a press conference held that same day by the head of the International Department of the Czechoslovak Central Committee (P. Auersperg), who referred to Bil'ak's speech at the Central Committee plenum, stating:

> The French Communist Party, V. Bil'ak reported, in particular, put at the disposal of the Communist Party of Czechoslovakia a protocol on talks between the secretary-general of the French Communist Party, W. Rochet, with A. Dubček in July 1968. This protocol shows that the former First Secretary . . . informed the leaders of the French communists about the situation in Czechoslovakia in an irresponsible and incompetent way.

The issue of whether the PCF had handed over any documents to the Czechoslovak leadership was further exacerbated by Georges Marchais, who declared in a radio interview on 11 May: "I defy anyone to prove that the French Communist Party gave to the Czech Communist Party any document which could be used against any person in an eventual trial, because that is what is in question" (*Le Monde*, 13 May). On 18 May *L'Humanité* published what it alleged to be the full text of Rochet's conversations with Dubček; [1] and on 19 May the Czechoslovak party organ, *Rudé Právo*, accused Garaudy of presenting "fabricated evidence" to the French public and denied that the 1969 French party delegation to Prague had handed over any evidence against Dubček which had not already been known to them. The Czechoslovak newspaper did not comment, however, as to whether documents had been handed over by the PCF delegation.

In an apparent response to the domestic repercussions of its role in the Dubček affair, the PCF took on a somewhat more critical stand during the remainder of the year in its evaluations of developments in the Soviet Union and Eastern Europe, although the change was not immediate. Thus, in response to the expulsion of Dubček from the Communist Party of Czechoslovakia on 26 June, Georges Marchais stated: "We consider that it is not for us to take up an official position when a fraternal party adopts a disciplinary measure toward one of its members, even when this measure is inconvenient for us" (*L'Humanité*, 3 July). Some two weeks later, Marchais moved another step forward toward criticizing developments in Czechoslovakia. In a television interview, when questioned on "normalization" in that country he answered:

> It is not we who are controlling things in Czechoslovakia. Some of the measures which have been taken there do not please us. They are measures which we should not take ourselves. But we cannot meddle with the affairs of others. For our part, we are in favor of political solutions —in Czechoslovakia as everywhere else. (*Ibid.*, 22 July.)

Marchais reaffirmed the PCF's opposition to the invasion of Czechoslovakia, and added: "We have always said, and we say it again now: the policy of the French Communist Party is worked out and decided not in London, not in Washington, nor yet in Moscow, but in Paris" (*ibid.*). Following purges in the educational establishments in Czechoslovakia, the director of *L'Humanité*, René Andrieu, wrote a leading article (24 July) in which he stated: "As for the situation in Czechoslovakia, it is hardly necessary to say that it is not the answer to our prayers, and that we are not in agreement with certain measures taken there, and (as far as we are concerned) we should act differently."

[1] For a comparison of the *L'Humanité* text with the version of the conversations as reconstructed from Bil'ak's statements see *Unir-Débat*, no. 42, 10 June; see also *Est & Ouest*, no. 448, 1-15 June.

By early September, even Etienne Fajon had changed the tone of his pronouncements, qualifying tentatively his remarks on the Soviet Union. At a public meeting in Bordeaux, Fajon answered questions about what he called "certain known facts on the subject of the socialist countries," stating:

> The problem is this—even if some things are not going right, even if we are in disagreement with some things, as—it is known—we are, the problem is to know whether the establishment of socialism has been useful and progressive. . . . Every one of you, whether a communist or not, can think what he wishes to think about the Soviet Union, and criticize whatever he wishes to criticize about the Soviet Union, but he should also be aware that the future of the world depends, in part, on the fact that the Union of Soviet Socialist Republics exists. (*Ibid.*, 10 September.)

During the second half of 1970, conforming to his earlier stands, the leading PCF critic of developments in Czechoslovakia continued to be Louis Aragon. His weekly publication *Les Lettres Françaises* repeatedly published contributions on or from prominent opponents of the Czechoslovak regime. (See, e.g., the issues of 26 August, on Czech poet Jan Skacel, former editor of the liberal literary monthly *Host do Domu*, a journal discontinued by the government in the spring of 1969, and 23 September, which included the translation of a letter by Eduard Goldstucker, formerly president of the Union of Czechoslovak writers, to the Czechoslovak Minister of the Interior, protesting against the campaign of "lies, distortions, falsifications, and fantastic accusations" officially directed against him in Czechoslovakia.) Aragon also directed his criticism against Soviet policies. Thus, following the award of the Nobel prize to Alexander Solzhenitsyn and the Soviet response that the Nobel jury had played an "unworthy game" in their choice, *Les Lettres Françaises* (14 October) referred to Solzhenitsyn as "the greatest living Russian writer." On this issue, *L'Humanité* (15 October) took a more guarded stand, pleading that the debate was "complicated by distance and by the relative ignorance of the realities in question and sometimes also by the qualities or defects of editions which are offered to us." *L'Humanité* concluded:

> The finest thing for a person who loves the Soviet Union and who admires Soviet literature . . . would be to see the Stockholm decision one day turned against its ill-intentioned promoters, Alexander Solzhenitsyn's work having found its place in Russian and Soviet literature.

The extent to which the PCF had modified its pro-Soviet orientation by the end of the year was not certain. In early October, *L'Humanité* (5 October) published two communiqués—one concerning the visit to France of a CPSU delegation, led by Secretariat member Ivan Kapitonov, which had lasted twelve days; the other on conversations in Paris on 1 and 2 October between the PCF and a delegation of the Polish United Workers' Party, led by Politburo member Zenon Kliszko. The party newspaper stated that the Polish delegation was in complete agreement with the PCF "on the questions examined," while the Soviet delegation agreed with the French about "the unity of their positions on all questions discussed." On the other hand, in December, the conditions prevailing at the Leningrad trial of a number of Jews accused of conspiring to commit an airplane highjacking and the severity of the verdicts met with public disapproval in the 25 December issue of *L'Humanité*, and, with regard to the riots in Poland (see *Poland*), an editorial in the 19 December issue, signed by Etienne Fajon, placed the blame on the Polish government.

International Party Contacts. The PCF was represented at the Moscow meeting of European communist parties, 14-15 January, by a delegation led by Raymond Guyot; also, in the same month, the CGT secretary-general, Georges Séguy, led a trade union delegation to Morocco, from 18 to 26 January. The PCF's Nineteenth Congress was attended by 49 communist party delegations and nine "national parties and democratic movements" (for listing see *L'Humanité*, 5 February). In March a CGT delegation led by André Allamy, member of its Secretariat, visited Czechoslovakia. Jacques Duclos and Benoît Frachon led their respective PCF and CGT delegations to the Lenin Centenary celebrations in the Soviet Union, in April. On 15 May the PCF and the Italian Communist Party jointly sponsored, in Paris, a meeting of "solidarity with the Indochinese peoples," attended by eighteen West European communist party delegations (for listing see *ibid.*, 16 May). The PCF was represented at a follow-up meeting on the same subject, held in Naples on 25 May, by François Billoux. From 7 to 13 June the PCF was host to a delegation of the Syrian Ba'th party, led by Muslih Salim. Georges Marchais represented the PCF at another "Indochinese solidarity" meeting sponsored by the Communist Party of Belgium, and held in Liège on 23 June. A high-level PCF delegation, led by Marchais, met with the leadership of the Italian Communist Party in Rome on 25-26 June (for joint communiqué see *ibid.*, 30 June). Central Committee member Marcel Zaidner represented the PCF at a conference in Rome, on 27-29 June, of "solidarity with the peoples of the Portuguese colonies." The PCF was host to a delegation of the Democratic Party of Guinea, led by its permanent deputy secretary Mamadi Keita, on 1-10 July. From 2 to 10 July a PCF delegation led by Raymond Guyot visited Yugoslavia. The CGT was host on 18-19 July to an International Trade Union "Conference of Solidarity with the Workers and People of Indochina Struggling against U.S. Aggression," which was attended by some 300 trade union delegates from 60 countries. On 22 July PCF leaders met with a delegation of the Communist Party of Greece, led by pro-Soviet faction leaders Leonidas Gringos and Panayotis Hyphantis. Discussions were reportedly held in a "frank and fraternal atmosphere" (*ibid.*, 27 July). Late in August, PCF Politburo members Gaston Plissonnier and Paul Laurent met with the Polish communist party's First Secretary Gomułka, in Warsaw. On 1 September Georges Marchais had talks with CPSU Politburo member Andrei Kirilenko. Roland Leroy and Louis Aragon were guests of the Hungarian Socialist Workers' Party on 21-25 September. On 21 September the PCF was represented at a meeting of West European communist parties, held in London, by Central Committee member Jacques Denis. Also at the end of September, Georges Séguy led a CGT delegation to Poland. From 21 to 30 September the PCF was host to the first official delegation of the Socialist Unity Party of East Germany to visit France. The delegation was led by Politburo and Secretariat member Kurt Hager. At the end of October, René Piquet led a PCF delegation to Romania. On 2 December the PCF was host to another international meeting of "solidarity with the Indochinese peoples," which was attended by leaders of communist parties of Great Britain, Italy, the Netherlands, and Sweden. On 13 November Jacques Duclos met with Gustáv Husák, first secretary of the Communist Party of Czechoslovakia, in Prague. A high-level PCF delegation, led by Georges Marchais, visited the United Arab Republic on 7-19 December. (For joint communiqué between the PCF and the Arab Socialist Union see *ibid.*, 14 December.) Gustav Ansart represented the PCF on 22 December at a symposium held in Moscow on the fiftieth anniversary of the French Communist Party.

Publications. The main publications of the PCF in 1970 were: the daily newspaper *L'-Humanité*; a weekly, *France Nouvelle*; a monthly theoretical organ, *Cahiers du Communisme*; a popular weekend magazine, *L'Humanité Dimanche*; a peasant weekly, *La Terre*; an intellectual monthly journal, *La Nouvelle Critique*; a literary monthly, *Europe*; a bimonthly economic journal, *Economie et Politique*; a philosophically oriented bimonthly, *La Pensée*; and a historical quarterly, *Les Cahiers de l'Institut Maurice-Thorez*. In addition the party had a number of provincial newspapers. The MJC published *Nous les Garçons et les Filles*; and the UJCF's journal was *Le Nouveau Clarté*. For intraparty work the Central Committee published *La Vie du Parti*, a monthly dealing with organizational, propaganda, educational, and other problems.

* * *

Most of the communist parties and organizations independent of the PCF were banned on 12 June 1968 (see *YICA*, 1969, p. 319). In 1970 several of them had reconstituted themselves under different names or were propagating their views in renamed journals. Nearly all non-PCF Marxist-Leninist groups were either pro-Chinese or Trotskyist in orientation. (For a genealogy of the development of most of these organizations see *L'Idiot International*, Paris and London, February 1970; also *YICA*, from 1966 on.)

Pro-Chinese Groups. The views of the banned Marxist-Leninist Communist Party of France (Parti Communiste Marxiste-Léniniste de France; PCMLF) and its erstwhile weekly newspaper, *L'Humanité Nouvelle*, were propagated in 1970 by the weekly *L'Humanité Rouge*. The group centered around this publication, whose major spokesman was Jacques Jurquet, appeared to be the only one to have the support of the Chinese Communist Party leadership. Jurquet was in Peking from 7 December 1969 to 13 January 1970. On 4 June *L'Humanité Rouge* expressed its "profound joy" at learning that the daily organ of the Chinese Communist Party, *Jen-min jih-pao*, had reprinted some of its articles, claiming that this was "a great honor of a political nature." The French newspaper had a similar reaction when it was cited by the Chinese news agency NCNA on 15 September (see *L'Humanité Rouge*, 24 September).

Although at the beginning of the year the *L'Humanité Rouge* group appeared to have a relatively significant influence, particularly among students, by the autumn, following internal schisms in its ranks, this influence was no longer evident. In its issue of 1 October *L'Humanité Rouge* stated: "Division—a weapon long wished us by our enemies—has penetrated everywhere in our ranks, even to the level of our principal spokesmen." The newspaper noted that its "political and financial status" was "very serious," claiming that it had lost 5,000 student readers. Commenting on these troubles, the Trotskyist weekly *Rouge* (9 November) indicated that the *L'Humanité Rouge* supporters had split into some five to six factions, which in turn had split several times again. Some of the militants had reportedly joined the Maoist group Vive La Revolution (see below), although the majority adhered to small independent Maoist groups.

On domestic issues the *L'Humanité Rouge* advocated the formation of committees at the grass-roots level for the creation of a "revolutionary trade-union movement." In this context, one of the major actions of the group was the sponsorship on 21 June of a conference of railway men (*L'Humanité Rouge*, 21 June). Throughout the year *L'Humanité Rouge* denounced all other extreme-left organizations, concentrating its attacks primarily on the PCF and on another Maoist group, the Proletarian Left (Gauche Prolétarienne; GP), a movement centered around the monthly publication *La Cause du Peuple* (for comments on the latter group see *ibid.*, 19 March, 2, 16, and 30 April, 28 May, and special issue of July).

The Proletarian Left originated from former members of the banned Union of Communist Youths, Marxist-Leninist and other groups who joined up in late 1968 under the leadership of Alain Geismar, former secretary-general of the National Union of University Teachers. Strongly influenced by the revolutionary events in France during May 1968 (see *YICA*, 1969, pp. 325-28, 334), the GP rejected all forms of electoral participation, advocating instead violent disruption in the attainment of their goals. The organization and its newspaper were banned on 27 May, and two of the editors of *La Cause du Peuple*, Jean-Pierre Le Dantec and Michel Le Bris, arrested in April, were placed on trial. At the same time, a warrant for the arrest of Alain Geismar was issued. On 28 May, Le Dantec and Le Bris were sentenced to one year and eight months in prison respectively. Alain Geismar was arrested on 25 June, and, on 22 October, sentenced to eighteen months in prison for inciting to riot. On 24 November, Geismar was given an additional sentence of two years for continuing the activities of the banned GP. By the end of the year, support for the GP appeared to have waned considerably, with only a few hundred, mainly student, militants adhering to its views.

The only other significant Maoist group in 1970 was one called Long Live the Revolution (Vive la Révolution; VLR), whose publications were the monthly *Vive la Révolution* and the fortnightly *Tout*. The first issue of the latter publication (21 September 1970) summarized the views of the VLR: "What do we want? Everything." Estimates of the group's membership varied; *Rouge* (9 November) placed the figure at 200, stating that the organization was heterogeneous, with no control from the leadership and oriented toward "hippy-style" communal living. During the year, VLR militants participated on a number of occasions in acts of violence, often together with supporters of the GP, with whom they appeared to be most closely aligned.

Trotskyists. The two major opposing Trotskyist groupings in France originated from the Internationalist Communist Party and the Internationalist Communist Organization, both banned in 1968 and aligned respectively with the United Secretariat and the International Committee of the Fourth International. The former, since the autumn of 1968, was centered around the fortnightly (and, from mid-1969, weekly) publication *Rouge*, organ of former militants of the banned Revolutionary Communist Youth who joined up with the militants of the Internationalist Communist Party, led by Pierre Frank, to form a new party—the Communist League (Ligue Communiste)—at a convention held on 5-7 April 1969. *Rouge* became the organ of the league, whose principal spokesmen during 1970 were Pierre Frank, Daniel Bensaïd, Alain Krivine, and Henri Weber. (Krivine was the league's candidate at the presidential elections in June 1969, at which time he received 239,000 votes.) During the year the Communist League was involved in lengthy discussions with another Trotskyist-oriented group, centered around the weekly publication *Lutte Ouvrière*, in an attempt to reach agreement on the fusion of their respective organizations (see *Rouge*, 6 April, 25 May, 15 June, and 6 July). The negotiations, which had taken place also in 1969, had not been concluded by the end of the year. The Communist League was also involved in talks with the PSU to further joint participation in various activities, the most publicized of which was the creation in June of an organization called Red Help (Secours Rouge), whose alleged purpose was assistance to persons and groups faced with government "repression."

During the year, support for the Communist League appeared to be increasing, as indicated by the size of the league's delegation to the 21-22 November congress of Trotskyist militants held in Brussels (see *Belgium*), which numbered 1,100 members.

The Trotskyist followers of the International Committee of the Fourth International in 1970 included three different but interrelated groupings. (1) The Internationalist Communist Organization, banned in 1968, regained its legality on 4 July 1970. It is led by Pierre Lambert, Stéphane Just, and Charles Berg. It publishes *La Verité*, an irregular theoretical journal. (2) The Alliance of Youth for Socialism (Alliance des Jeunes pour le Socialisme; AJS) is led by Charles Berg; it publishes the monthly *Jeune Révolutionnaire.* The AJS was originally called the Federation of Revolutionary Students and was banned under that name in 1968. The federation's illegality was also lifted on 4 July 1970. (3) The Federation of Workers' Alliance Committees (Fédération des Comités d'Alliance Ouvrière) supersedes another group, banned in 1968, which was centered around the publication *Révoltes*. It is led by Stéphane Just; its principal publication in 1970 was the weekly *Informations Ouvrières*.

M. P.

GERMANY: FEDERAL REPUBLIC OF GERMANY

The Communist Party of Germany (Kommunistische Partei Deutschlands; KPD) was founded in 1918. Outlawed by the federal constitutional court in August 1956 for being in conflict with the Basic Law of West Germany, the party was ordered dissolved and membership in it was prohibited. Since that time the KPD has engaged in clandestine activities from headquarters relocated in East Berlin. Its role has been diminished by the founding, in September 1968, of a new and legal party, the German Communist Party (Deutsche Kommunistische Partei; DKP). As pro-Soviet parties, both the KPD and the DKP face some competition from the Communist Party of Germany (Marxist-Leninist)—Kommunistische Partei Deutschlands (Marxisten-Leninisten), or KPD(ML)—a pro-Chinese group which in 1970 claimed to be "in its earliest beginnings," although it has been in existence since late in 1968.

No membership figures for the KPD are available for 1970, but it is generally assumed that they are a fraction of the 7,000 estimated late in 1968, just before large-scale transfers to the DKP began. The DKP claimed 22,000 supporters within six months of its founding and membership in 1970 is estimated to have exceeded 30,000—not including the Socialist German Workers Youth (SDAJ), the communist youth organization founded in 1968. The population of West Germany is 58,015,000 (estimated 1968).

One of the immediate goals of the newly formed DKP was to participate in the national elections scheduled in West Germany for September 1969. To broaden its appeal, the communist party organized a coalition of all leftists, the Action for Democratic Progress (Aktion Demokratischer Fortschritt; ADF). Although the ADF conducted an extensive and well-financed election campaign, it polled only 197,600 votes, or 0.6 per cent of the total cast.

The DKP tested its standing as an "independent political force" for the first time in three Landtag elections in June 1970. In North Rhine-Westphalia, the most populous and most highly industrialized state, the DKP received 77,003 votes (0.9 per cent); in Lower Saxony, 15, 085 (0.4 per cent); and in the Saarland, 17,344 (2.7 per cent). It attributed its lack of voter appeal to "decades of anticommunism, the 5 per cent rule, and numerous election impediments" (DPA, West German news service, 15 June). A minimum of 5 per cent of the votes is a prerequisite for representation in the state government. When the DKP failed again to win such representation in November elections in Hesse and Bavaria, it claimed nevertheless that it had "emerged as a party of the working class and proved to be a unifying force against the nationalist and social demagogy of the right-wing circles." (ADN, East German news service, 9 November).

Communist influence in labor unions remained limited, although the DKP estimates that about two-thirds of its members also belong to organizations affiliated with the Trade Union Federation. Communists actually are represented on hundreds of factory committees, but even from this vantage point "it is hard to sell party policy," as one of the Munich DKP headquarters staff readily admitted (*Süddeutsche Zeitung*, Munich, 24 July). Factory workers are said to be willing to support DKP members if they function as individuals and represent the interests of their colleagues, but inclined to balk at efforts to advance communist party policy. In spite of the limited impact, the DKP intends to adhere to its statement of principles: "As champions of the united trade unions, which we consider one of the great achievements of the labor movement, we will oppose all trends to incorporate it in the existing power system, to divide and weaken union strength and reduce its role as a class organization, and will reject all anti-union attacks from the ruling circles." (*Ibid.*)

Leadership and Organization. The KPD in 1970 continued its close contacts with the ruling party of the East German republic, the Socialist Unity Party of Germany (SED), which for years has provided guidance and financial support for covert communist activities in West Germany. The DKP from its inception has tried to present an image of complete independence, but it appears inconceivable that a majority of former KPD leaders—including several members of the KPD Politburo—could have taken positions of importance in the DKP, soon after its founding, without approval of the SED. Moreover, the SED is the most likely source for the obvious financial affluence of the DKP.

The KPD leadership group appears to have been decimated by the transfer of many of its prominent members. Only two well-known leaders stood out in 1970—Max Reimann, for many years the KPD secretary-general, and Politburo member Erich Glückauf. Reimann has long functioned as virtually the sole spokesman for the KPD; his political activities were simplified in 1968 when he was allowed to return to the Federal Republic after fourteen years of political exile in East Berlin. Erich Jungmann has been identified as a candidate member of the KPD Politburo and as secretary of the Central Committee.

The DKP elected its leaders at its First Congress, held in Essen on 12-13 April 1969. Kurt Bachmann was chosen as party chairman and Herbert Mies as his deputy; both have histories of long-term service in the KPD. A nine-member Presidium elected by the congress included Bachmann, Mies, Kurt Erlebach, Ludwig Müller. Karl-Heinz Noetzel, Gerhard Deumlich, Hermann Gautier, Willi Gerns, and Manfred Kapluck. Karl-Heinz Schröder was named Presidium secretary, and an 85-member Parteivorstand, (party executive) was chosen. Georg Polikeit became the head of the DKP Information Service. All continued in these offices in 1970.

Party Internal Affairs. The KPD experienced a serious setback early in 1970 when the federal constitutional court in Karlsruhe on 18 February banned dissemination of the KPD draft program, originally readied for public discussion in February 1968. The KPD had hoped to use its new program to prove its desire to "achieve socialist reconstruction by peaceful democratic means." The 1970 court decision, however, contained the declaration that there was "no room for political freedom of action" for the illegal party. A KPD spokesman called it a "flagrant contradiction" of Chancellor Brandt's earlier promise to "venture more democracy" and also a "heavy blow to the credibility of a professed policy of international understanding and detente" (ADN, 18 February). Broadcasts by the clandestine "Deutscher Freiheitssender 904" declared that "the annulment of the KPD ban would not be a risk for democracy, but rather a great benefit for all socialists and democrats," and Erich Jungmann announced that "1,800 prominent persons" in the Federal Republic had appealed to the government to lift the ban.

The adverse court decision did not end the KPD's fight to achieve legalization—a technical impossibility unless the ban against distribution of its program should be reversed. The same issue came before a court in Flensburg in October, but a ruling was deferred. Meanwhile the "Initiative Committee on the Legalization of the KPD," which was organized in 1967, continues to function and the communist parties of Eastern and Western Europe have been joining the fight for reinstatement. Georges Marchais, assistant secretary-general of the French Communist Party, in a letter to Chancellor Brandt (31 July) suggested that reinstatement of the KPD "would have favorable repercussions on relations between 'democratic forces' in Western Europe and in particular communist and socialist forces" (*Le Monde*, Paris, 11 August). Additional appeals were made by the communist parties of Great Britain, Denmark, Italy, and Luxembourg. The communist-ruled countries of Eastern Europe submitted so many demands for legalization as to suggest a coordinated effort.

The DKP in 1970 tried to "strengthen and shape" the party and establish unity of action between social democrats and communists as the most important means to this end. Addressing the DKP Parteivorstand around the middle of the year, Chairman Kurt Bachmann claimed that the DKP was "successfully developing" and that new forces were finding their way to it. On the other hand, he admitted the existence of "many questions and problems" and identified "insufficient systematic and political ideological work" as a principal cause of existing shortcomings. He asked for more effective approaches to the public—"nobody comes to us by himself, we must go to the people"—but he also felt that the DKP had scored significantly, and for proof cited the rally connected with the 21 May meeting at Kassel between Chancellor Brandt and East German Premier Willi Stoph, where the party "demonstrated forcefully and convincingly for peaceful, democratic alternatives." (*Unsere Zeit*, 13 June.)

Of growing importance in 1970 was the Institute for Marxist Studies, established in Frankfurt in 1969 to "examine current social processes in line with Marxist theoretical and methodological principles" and eventually work out the "scientific rudiments of a progressive anti-monopoly alternative to various social spheres" (WMR, August). The institute is headed by Dr. Josef Schleifstein, until 1968 a candidate member of the KPD Politburo and since then a prominent member of the DKP.

Domestic Attitudes and Activities. In domestic matters, the communists—both the DKP and KPD—in 1970 transferred much of the criticism previously directed at the Kiesinger government to the new Social Democratic Party (SPD) administration of Willy Brandt, put in office in the fall of 1969. The communists for years had charged that West German military policies were catering to reactionary generals anxious to strengthen their positions of power. In 1970 they made strident accusations against Defense Minister Helmut Schmidt and the new "Bundeswehr Organization Decree" which became effective in April. The DKP accused the West German armed forces of military threats and attempted blackmail against the German Democratic Republic (GDR), of aiming to strengthen offensive power while admitting that the preservation of peace was not their primary task, and of actual war preparations and warmongering. The KPD warned against "rightist, imperialist politics," "revanchism," "reactionaries in power," and against the overall Bundeswehr strategy.

The SPD leadership was said to be "incorporated into the imperialist system" and to be governing in the interests of that system." Its refusal to repeal the emergency laws (*Notstandsgesetze*) was labeled a "most flagrant encroachment on the domestic structure in the interests of state monopoly and the centralization of power" at the expense of civil rights. The communists complained that the SPD had backed down on its promise of tax and property reforms and worker participation in management decisions, and had, in addition, ignored a wave of inflation and made plans to increase arms expenditures because of NATO needs. (*Unsere Zeit*, 13 June.) They viewed the educational system as having reached the point of "crisis" and proposed to "do away with the educational privileges of the propertied classes" (*WMR*, July).

The communist attitude toward the SPD generally alternated between severe condemnation and insistent calls for joint action. Thus the DKP sent greetings to the SPD congress, held in

Saarbrücken in May, and asked for collaboration "in the interest of democratic progress and safeguarding of the peace" and to satisfy the expectations of the "democratic public" after twenty years of governmental "aggression." The DKP also requested that the SPD congress issue an unequivocal condemnation of U.S. actions in Cambodia, Laos, and Vietnam, and that it ban the National Democratic Party (as being neo-Nazi) and "break the power of the Springer press and other monopolies of opinion." (ADN, 13 May.) When these overtures were rejected, the communists declared that the congress had dealt solely with "sweeping professions of peace." Late in the year, after the SPD had issued instructions to its members not to engage in joint efforts with communists and threatened expulsion of those ignoring the prohibition, the DKP condemned the decision as "fateful, because it [was] directed against the cooperation of all democrats," and appealed to individual Social Democrats: "Do not tolerate an anticommunist witch hunt within your party. Let us confront the right-wing cartel's dangerous activities with common actions." (*Ibid.*, 18 November.)

West German communists were strongly preoccupied with the progress of the government's *Ostpolitik*, and with the relationship between the Federal Republic and the German Democratic Republic in particular. Very early in the year, the DKP Presidium issued a statement on inter-German relations and demanded immediate acceptance of the East German draft treaty that had been submitted late in 1969. The treaty had called for negotiations on the basis of equality between the two Germanies, recognition of the GDR under international law, and acceptance of the status of an independent political unit for West Berlin.

After the "summit meeting" between Chancellor Brandt and Premier Stoph in Kassel and Erfurt the communists were disappointed at the lack of progress related to recognition of East Germany and the status quo in Europe. Kurt Bachmann vowed that the DKP would "carry on the fight for legal recognition of all European boundaries including the boundary between the German Federal Republic and the GDR and the Oder-Neisse line and for legal recognition of the GDR" (*Unsere Zeit*, 13 June). Max Reimann of the KPD phrased his views more ominously: "The refusal to recognize according to international law is connected with the intention to incorporate the GDR in some way into the Federal Republic. This, however, means war." (ADN, 12 March.)

International Views and Activities. West German communists in 1970 viewed the world as being divided into two distinct camps—one in which the forces of peace, democracy, and socialism prevailed, and the other in which the forces of imperialism, national suppression, and social reaction had the upper hand. West Germany was characterized as having a prominent place in the latter camp and was said to be "particularly dangerous" because it had "allied itself with U.S. imperialism, the most aggressive force of today" (*WMR*, February). NATO, as in previous years, was considered the evil instrument providing the necessary backing, because its "ringleaders" did not want to "put up with the present development in Europe" (*Unsere Zeit*, 16 December).

U.S. "imperialism" was said to be determined to "use force to oppose the people's desire for freedom and self-determination and for peace and progress all over the world." As evidence the DKP cited the "Nixon-ordered aggression in Cambodia" as a "clear violation of neutrality, of the Geneva Convention, and international law." It looked upon the situation in Southeast Asia and the Middle East as worsening, because "imperialism" was on the defensive and engaging in a "hopeless attempt to take the offensive again by dangerously aggravating the world situation." (*Ibid.*, 13 June.)

The DKP condemned "Israeli militarists," who in their "piratic raids" were "like the American aggressors in Vietnam," and proclaimed the solidarity of German communists with the "struggle of the Arab people for independence, freedom, and national rights." The party demanded solution of the problems of the Middle East in accordance with the United Nations decision of 1967 and the withdrawal of all Israeli troops from the occupied territories. (*Ibid.*) The DKP also objected to the Federal Republic's support of "reactionary regimes," citing as instances the provision of "Leopard" tanks to Spain and the building of submarines for the Greek government (TASS, 22 April). As a spokesman for his party, Bachmann condemned the Burgos trial of sixteen Basques (see *Spain*) and addressed a letter to Brandt asking that the West German government also publicly express displeasure with Spanish justice (*ibid.*, 16 December).

When the Federal Republic signed treaties with the Soviet Union and Poland on the renunciation of force, the West German communists characterized these moves as "a success for peace, a success for the policy of the socialist countries, and of the peace-loving democratic forces . . . throughout the world." At the end of the year Kurt Bachmann listed the most important tasks confronting his party: "To fight tirelessly for the ratification by the Bundestag of the Soviet-West German treaty, for the recognition of the German Democratic Republic by West Germany on the basis of international law, and for the earliest convocation of an all-European security conference" (*Unsere Zeit*, special year-end supplement). Max Reimann for the KPD advocated immediate ratification of the treaties as a "resolute action against revenge-seeking and neo-Fascist forces" (TASS, 15 December).

International Party Contacts. When representatives of 28 communist and workers' parties of Europe met in Moscow 14-15 January 1970, both the DKP and the KPD were represented. Late in May the West German town of Wuppertal was the setting for an international colloquium, organized by the DKP to mark the 150th anniversary of the birth of Friedrich Engels, which attracted delegates from the Soviet Union, Czechoslovakia, Hungary, Bulgaria, and East Germany. A delegation from the Communist Party of the Soviet Union also attended DKP-sponsored ceremonies in Munich on 22 April in honor of the centenary of Lenin's birth. DKP Chairman Kurt Bachmann was in Moscow late in April and was interviewed on Moscow radio.

In March, DKP delegations attended the congresses of the communist parties of Cyprus and Luxembourg. Wide publicity was given by the DKP to the reception granted to three of its leaders—Kurt Bachmann, Hermann Gautier, and Ludwig Müller—by East German Premier Willi Stoph when he traveled to Kassel to meet with Chancellor Brandt on 21 May. Questions of cooperation between the SED and the DKP were discussed in East Berlin on 25 May by SED Politburo member Albert Norden and leading representatives of the DKP. Max Reimann led a KPD delegation to Prague to discuss problems of European security on March 4-6 and was in Poland on vacation in August, during which time he was received by Polish party chief Gomułka. George Polikeit described as "more than pure coincidence" the visit of a DKP delegation to Prague early in October, "shortly before the new sounding-out efforts by the West German government in the Czechoslovak capital" (*Unsere Zeit*, 17 October).

Publications. In March 1969 the DKP began publishing a weekly newspaper, *Unsere Zeit*, in Essen. In 1970 the editorial headquarters were transferred to Düsseldorf. The publisher of *UZ* is the party chief, Kurt Bachmann; the editor is Presidium member Gerhard Deumlich. The paper, which announced that it would represent the "social, political, and national interests of the working class and all progressive forces," was instantly successful, since at the time it began distribution the existing regional communist publications in West Germany ceased publication (see *YICA*, 1970, p. 175). It maintains offices in the largest cities of the Federal Republic and has four regional editions, with an estimated total circulation close to 80,000. In addition the party issues the *DKP Pressedienst*, a general news service, and *DKP Informationen*, a publication of opinion, discussion, and documentation.

The KPD organ *Freies Volk* continued to be distributed irregularly in 1970; it was written and printed outside West Germany. The radio station "Deutscher Freiheitssender 904" broadcasting daily from its East German location, was a more important medium. Matters of interest to the KPD are also reported in the twice-weekly *Bonner Korrespondenz*, which officially is issued by the DKP; the editor is Anton Preckel, well known for his long association with the KPD and as a correspondent for the French communist newspaper *L'Humanité*.

* * *

Pro-Chinese communist activities in West Germany for several years had been fractured and confused, when Hamburg-based Maoists took the initiative for unification. Under the leadership of Ernst Aust they founded the Communist Party of Germany (Marxist-Leninist) —KPD(ML) —on 31 December 1968 and began disseminating its ideology through the publication *Roter Morgen*, a medium for revolution-minded individuals since 1967.

In 1970 the KPD(ML) published its platform in the March-April issue of *Roter Morgen*. Although the party was then more than a year old, the platform described it as being "still in its earliest beginnings" and declared that it was the "vanguard of the proletariat" in pursuit of scientific socialism. At the same time the platform revealed that the party was already encountering "revisionism" and was in danger of becoming the "rear guard of the workers' aristocracy."

The concern with "revisionist" activities apparently was justified, as later in the year splits and purges within the KPD(ML) were reported. A seceding group was headed by Willi Dickhut and G. Flatow, who had been respectively first secretary and chairman of the KPD(ML) in North Rhine-Westphalia. Disagreement, according to the *Roter Morgen* supporters, revolved around the fact that the seceding group had "replaced its absence of theory by practice lacking in theory" and that it consisted of "anarcho-Maoist grouplets," "petty-bourgeois individualists," and "SDS chieftains with Trotskyist coloring." The dissidents published their own organ, *Rote Fahne*, labeled the opposition "leftist liquidators," and attacked it in their theoretical organ *Revolutionärer Weg*, later renamed *Der Bolschewik*. The *Rote Fahne* group also caused great consternation by organizing its own youth group in opposition to the original KPD(ML)'s Red Guards, who had grown active in a number of West German cities in 1969 (*Berliner Extradienst*, West Berlin, 23 September and 28 November).

That the KPD(ML) had problems with its Red Guards was indicated by the party platform, which stated that the relationship between the two was that of cadres and mass organization. It added: "As a mass youth organization, the Red Guard must, of course, develop its own democratic centralism and be organizationally independent," but commented also that the time was not yet opportune for such "independence," because "intriguers and deviants might gain bourgeois majorities by using demagogy."

In March 1970 the Communist Party of Germany Development Organization (KPD-Aufbauorganisation; KPD-AO) was established in West Berlin (see *West Berlin*). Its proclaimed goal was to "create a revolutionary communist party on an all-German level." The KPD-AO holds that the "organizational principles of a revolutionary movement are most clearly laid down in the statutes of the Communist Party of China," and seeks to challenge the KPD(ML)'s claim that it alone applies Chinese principles in West Germany. (*Ibid.*, 14 March).

E. W.

GERMANY: WEST BERLIN

The Socialist Unity Party of West Berlin (Sozialistische Einheitspartei Westberlins; SEW) was founded on 24 November 1962 as the Socialist Unity Party of Germany-West Berlin (Sozialistische Einheitspartei Deutschlands-Westberlin; SED-W). The reference to Germany was dropped in 1969, when the name was changed because the party had come to consider itself an "independent political power" (*Die Wahrheit*, 4 February 1969).

Communist activity in West Berlin is legal, since the status of the city precludes application of the constitutional ban that outlawed the communist party in West Germany in 1956. In spite of the claim of independence, the SEW continues to look for guidance and financial support to the ruling party in East Germany, the Socialist Unity Party of Germany (SED), of which it was officially a part until 1962. It tries to present a semblance of freedom of action by participating in West Berlin's elections, distributing its own newspaper, and scheduling regular meetings or programs aimed at enlisting popular support.

Membership in the SEW in 1970 was approximately 7,000. The population of West Berlin is 2,141,000 (estimated 1968). At the Second Congress of the SEW, in May 1970, it was announced that 2,500 new members had been accepted into the party since 1966, when its First Congress was held. Declaring that there had been an influx of young members, the SEW termed itself a "party of youth and revolutionary experience." (*Ibid.*, 25 May.) Apparently the appeal to the young is regarded as offering the best chance for greater political influence in the future.

In 1970 the party's influence remained negligible—the inevitable consequence of communist lack of representation in the city government. In the latest elections to the Berlin Senate, in March 1967, the communist party received 29,934 votes, or 2 per cent of the total. Its share thus fell short of the required 5 per cent minimum and its participation in the governing body was ruled out. Looking ahead to elections scheduled for 14 March 1971, the SEW urged every party member to make contact with ten to fifteen citizens, acquaint them with the politics of the SEW, and try to win them over as sympathizers, as readers of the communist newspaper, and finally as voters for and members of the party (*ibid.*, 9 July 1970).

Leadership and Organization. The highest authority of the communist party of West Berlin is the congress. The First Congress (May 1966) elected Gerhard Danelius as party chairman and chose a 41-member "Parteivorstand" or leadership group equivalent to a central committee. Power was concentrated in the 10-member Secretariat of the Parteivorstand, whose composition remained unchanged until the Second Congress, held in Neukölln on 22-27 May 1970.

The Second Congress was attended by 381 voting delegates, 141 nonvoting delegates, and some 200 guests. It reelected Danelius as party chairman and named Erich Ziegler his deputy. The membership of the Parteivorstand was increased to 47, and this group chose a 13-member "Büro—a new body authorized by a change in the party statutes. The Büro was made up of Danelius, Ziegler, Dietmar Ahrens, Dr. Karlheinz Kniestedt, Inge Kopp, Bruno Kuster, Horst Schmitt, Gert Ellert, Harry Flichtbeil, Peter Klaar, Hans Mahle, Emil Redmann, and Heinz Thomaszik. The first seven were also named to the Secretariat of the Parteivorstand. Else Dibbern, a former Secretariat member, was elected head of the Control Commission. (*Die Wahrheit*, 24 May.)

The SEW has its own youth organization, the Free German Youth-West Berlin (Freie Deutsche Jugend-Westberlin; FDJ-W). During 1970 the FDJ-W figured prominently in May Day celebrations and in protests against what it termed the "anticommunist and revanchist" educational policies of the city government (leaflet, 6 March), and, in general, supported the Extraparliamentary Opposition (see below). Another communist auxiliary is the German-Soviet Friendship Society of West Berlin; it presents informational programs which do not appear to attract much response from the public.

Party Internal Affairs. Although the SEW held an "Extraordinary Party Day on 15 February 1969, and at that time assessed its current situation and future tasks, the party leaders in January 1970 announced the scheduling of the Second Congress. On 26 March, the editor of *Die Wahrheit* in a signed editorial called for public discussion and suggestions to aid in the preparation of a new party program, and declared that a "united struggle" of democrats and socialists, workers, and intelligentsia was a basic requirement for effecting change in West Berlin. The Parteivorstand issued a draft *Action Program of the SEW for Peace, Democracy, and Social Progress* on 16 April. In the program the party not only affirmed that the establishment of socialism was its goal, but offered to cooperate with "all opponents of capitalism and imperialism" to realize this aim.

Although as a result of the party elections several well-known names had disappeared from the list of SEW's leadership group, conflict within the party appears to have been at a minimum in 1970. The noncommunist *Kieler Nachrichten* (26 May), noting the "respectable face" of the congress proceedings and the efforts of West Berlin's communists to "play it cool," concluded that the SEW had chosen to detach itself from anarchy and violence in the streets and to seek success through infiltrating factories, trade unions, and youth groups. According to the newspaper's analysis, the SEW would like to dissuade the Extraparliamentary Opposition (Ausserparlamentarische Opposition; APO) from its more extremist or revolutionary approach and to win it over to the SEW's more subtle aims and methods.

Cooperation with the APO apparently remained elusive. The SEW, revealing that it had encountered severe criticism from "right and left opportunists" or "revisionists" who were resorting to "various tricks," declared: "[These elements] are trying vainly to compel our party to depart from Marxism-Leninism and proletarian internationalism, to bring us into collision with other Marxist-Leninist parties, and to subvert our discipline and our Leninist organizational principles." Critics were said to question the independence of the SEW and to "want to saddle [the party] with an in-between policy, a policy running between socialism and imperialism." (*WMR*, April.)

Rejecting such pressures and accusations, the SEW proclaimed its "absolute independence" and a planning strategy and tactics free from outside interference. It displayed its new emblem— the letters SEW on a red flag—at the congress and termed itself the only organized group "able to show the way out of West Berlin's deteriorating situation and point out the prospects of peace, democracy, and socialism to the city." (ADN, East German news service, 24 May.) The SEW further declared firm adherence to democratic centralism, professing an internal democracy exceeding in scope any other party, and claimed to have reached "theoretical, political, and ideological maturity." As evidence it cited inroads among Berlin workers and intellectuals, who found themselves in "increasing conflict with the system of latter-day capitalism." It also claimed credit for the "polarization of political and class forces that became evident on 1 May 1970," when trade unions for the first time in many years held meetings and organized demonstrations. (*IB*, no. 15, July.)

Domestic Attitudes and Activities. In 1970 the SEW continued to maintain that West Berlin is an independent political unit located on the territory of the German Democratic Republic. Claiming that most of the problems of the city were due to its "submission" to direction from the West German government, the communists declared that only "independent action, equality, and noninterference" could assure their solution (Danelius, speech to the Second Congress, *Die Wahrheit*, 23 May). Official visits from West Germany were labeled "dangerous provocations" or "violations of international law," and were said to be forcing the city to "function as the front line of the cold war." Much of West Berlin's "misery" was also attributed to the shortcomings of the Social Democratic city administration (the Berlin Senate), which was held responsible for the polarization of political forces and the evils resulting therefrom.

The domestic demands of the SEW in 1970 were generally not new. Prominent among them was the call for codetermination (*Mitbestimmung*), or worker participation in management decisions with regard to production, prices, profits, personnel policies, the relocation or shutdown of plants, and indeed, every facet of a company's operation. The communists defined codetermination as the "workers' struggle to overcome the system of capitalism," and not as a "stabilizing factor for the capitalist system," which allegedly was the interpretation of management (ADN, 22 May).

The draft Action Program appealed to the interests of varied groups among the Berlin population. For instance, it asked for changes in the educational system at every level to create a uniform, democratic system available to all without regard to social origin or wealth, instead of allowing the ruling circles to "shape education, research, teaching, and science to fit their striving for profits and power." The SEW's program asked for equality for women and young workers; equal pay for equal work; protection against rent increases; an "active wage policy"; and prevention of price rises or "concerted action in the interest of monopolies." It condemned "emergency laws or practice," "neofascism and revanchism," and any encroachment on the people's constitutional rights.

The SEW failed when it undertook a major campaign against the proposed "hand grenade law" (passed 11 June), which authorized equipping the police with automatic weapons and grenades for use in civil disturbances. *Die Wahrheit* (12 June) reported that a hastily organized demonstration against the law attracted 15,000 participants, but that advocates of "programs against dissenters" managed to "whip it through" the Senate.

Relations with West Germany and East Germany. The political status of West Berlin continued to be a topic of primary importance for the SEW. To assure the "viability" of the city, the party's Action Program laid down the following guidelines:

1. All sides must respect the status of West Berlin as an independent political unit.
2. West Berlin must not be treated as a *Land* of the Federal Republic, nor be governed or administered from the Federal Republic.
3. Meetings of the Federal Assembly and any committees or factions of the Bundestag must no longer take place in West Berlin.
4. The citizens of West Berlin and their elected representatives must be free to arrange their political, economic, cultural, athletic, and human relations with both East and West on a basis of equality and noninterference.
5. West Berlin must have the opportunity for unrestricted development of its economy and trade.

Regarding the relationship between East and West Germany, the SEW strongly advocated recognition of the German Democratic Republic (GDR) under international law by the Federal Republic. "All variant solutions bypassing this point will fail in view of the growing importance of the first socialist state on German soil," party chairman Danelius declared in his report to the Second Congress (*IB*, no. 12, 15 July). He saw recognition as mandatory for peace and security in Europe and for solution of the problem of Berlin. Invariably siding with East Germany, the SEW credited the GDR with having rooted out imperialism, militarism, fascism, and revanchism —all evils said to be persisting in the Federal Republic (WMR, April). To alleviate them, West Germany was asked to "put an end forever" to its claim of sole representation for all Germans and to abandon the Hallstein doctrine.

With fundamental changes becoming a distinct possibility as negotiations got under way between West Germany and the Soviet Union and Poland, criticism of the government in West Germany was toned down and directed largely at the CDU-CSU (Christian Democratic Union-Christian Social Union) coalition, although these parties had been displaced from power in the fall of 1969. The signing of the treaty of renunciation of force between West Germany and the Soviet Union was hailed by the SEW as primarily a victory for Soviet peace efforts and a "defeat" for the opposition in the Federal Republic and the Springer publishing firm (*Die Wahrheit*, 13 August). When the GDR grew alarmed at the treaty's implications for its own interests, West Berlin's communist newspaper reflected SED views in a warning that the city must not be "misused as a lever of political blackmail against the treaty," and declared that "speculation aimed at exerting pressure on the Soviet Union and the GDR" with regard to West Berlin was "completely misleading and virtually absurd" (*ibid.*, 21 August).

International Views and Activities. The Second Congress of the SEW and the Lenin Centenary provided occasions for the party to profess firm "loyalty to Marxism-Leninism and proletarian internationalism." Celebrations in honor of Lenin called for a renewed "commitment to bring his legacy home" and asserted that his theories of "imperialism as the highest and last stage of capitalism" and the "revolutionary transition from capitalism to socialism" had lost none of [their] validity or vitality. (*IB*, no. 15 July).

The SEW accused the "main imperialist powers" of providing "material, political, and military backing" for "fascist regimes and military dictatorships" in Spain, Portugal, and Greece. Singling out "U.S. imperialism" as the greatest menace to peace, the SEW described it as an "enemy of the freedom and national independence of the peoples and their right to self-determination," guilty of fomenting "racial hatred and discrimination" and "barefaced terror against dissenters" and of "unlawful interference in the affairs of other states and peoples." (*Ibid.*) Illustrating its accusations by citing the U.S. presence in Vietnam and Cambodia, the party reported at length on war protests in the United States and organized a number of events to show its solidarity with war victims in Vietnam and to collect funds for their aid; one of the most publicized events was the visit of a twelve-year-old girl who was introduced as a survivor of an alleged massacre of civilians.

While the United States was always condemned, the policies of the Soviet Union were never questioned by the SEW. Thus, firmly siding with the Arabs in the Middle Eastern conflict, West Berlin's communists credited the U.A.R. with great efforts to find a political solution. Israel, with its "destructive attitude," was said to be "intent on maintaining tension and poisoning the atmosphere." (*Die Wahrheit*, 20 August.)

The SEW is a member in good standing of the pro-Soviet faction of the international communist movement. Several communist parties of that alignment sent delegates to the Second Congress of the SEW, in May. Representatives of the Soviet, East German, West German, Polish, French, and Czechoslovak parties all addressed the delegates. Among the many that sent fraternal greetings were the communist parties of Great Britain, Belgium, Austria, Turkey, Iran, Guadeloupe, Algeria, Sweden, Japan, Greece, India, and Israel.

Publications. The central organ of the SEW, *Die Wahrheit*, is published four times a week. The editor in chief, Hans Mahle, is a member of the Büro of the Parteivorstand. Late in 1969 the party began issuing its own theoretical journal, *Konsequent*, which seems to be addressed primarily to the members of the APO and to students.

*   *   *

In March 1970 the Communist Party of Germany Development Organization (KPD-Aufbauorganisation; KPD-AO) was founded. Among the organizing members were Peter Neitzke, Christian Semler, and Jürgen Horlemann—former leaders of the Students for a Democratic Society. The new organization announced that its goal was the creation of a revolutionary communist party which would put its "claim to leadership to the test in mass struggles" and would be guided by the principles of the Chinese Communist Party. It expressed disillusionment with the Extraparliamentary Opposition, which it characterized as a combination of "leftist opportunism and rightist opposition". Obviously it also presented a challenge to the Communist Party of Germany (Marxist-Leninist) —KPD(ML) —a pro-Chinese group based in the Federal Republic.

KPD-AO plans called for the establishment of cells in factories and city districts and for indoctrination work within existing "red cells" in German universities. The group's propaganda medium is the *Rote Presse Korrespondenz* (Red Press Correspondence).

In 1970 there was little evidence of activities by the pro-Chinese youth organization "Red Guard," which in 1969 conspicuously participated in demonstrations organized by the APO in West Berlin. In the Federal Republic, the Red Guards were reported to be splintering and as increasingly dissatisfied with their relationship to the KPD(ML), which in 1970 newly defined this relationship as one of "cadres to mass organization." Chafing for more independent action, considerable numbers of Red Guards were believed to be abandoning the parent organization.

E. W.

GREAT BRITAIN

The Communist Party of Great Britain (CPGB) was founded in 1920. In 1970, while remaining the oldest and largest representative of communism in Great Britain, the CPGB continued to be faced with increasing competition from other parties and groups advocating Marxism-Leninism (see below) and from a vocal and active "new left" movement.[1]

The CPGB is a recognized political party in Great Britain. In 1970 membership in the party and in its youth group, the Young Communist League (YCL), registered a decrease from 1969. Whereas in that year the party had claimed 30,607 members for the CPGB and 3,850 for the YCL, in 1970 the figures were 30,000 (*The Economist*, London, 8 August) and 3,452 (*Comment*, 3 October), respectively. The decline in party membership reflected a trend apparent since 1964. The population of Great Britain is 56,000,000 (estimated 1970).

Communist party candidates contend in both national and local elections. In the Parliamentary general election of 1966 the party polled 62,112 votes, or 0.2 per cent of all votes cast. Although 57 candidates were nominated, none was elected and all deposits were forfeited. The 1970 elections of 18 June witnessed a marked decrease in the CPGB's electoral appeal. Fielding 58 candidates, the party obtained only 38,431 votes (0.1 per cent), with all candidates once again forfeiting their deposits. The communists also suffered heavy losses in local elections held earlier in the year. In the April elections to the Greater London Council the vote for the party dropped from 66,408 (in 1967) to 34,446; in other local elections, in May, the CPGB vote decreased from 101,000 (in 1967) to 63,000. There have been no more than two communist members at any time in the British House of Commons, and none at all since 1950.

Organization and Leadership. The National Congress is the supreme authority of the CPGB and is responsible for policy adoptions. It meets biennially when called by the Executive Committee, but a special congress can be convened under extraordinary circumstances. The National Congress elects the 42-member Executive Committee, which represents the highest authority between congresses. At its first meeting after a congress has been convened, the Executive Committee elects the party officers and the Political Committee. Whereas the Executive Committee meets every two months, the Political Committee holds sessions weekly or more frequently. Below the leadership level, the CPGB is organized into district committees, and further subdivided into area and borough committees and finally into party branches. The report of the Credentials Committee for the party's Thirty-first Congress (15-18 November 1969) noted representation from 35 district committees and 887 party branches, including 126 from factories (*Comment*, 6 December 1969).

[1] The numerous organizations and factions that are encompassed by this category are not considered Marxist-Leninist groups by officially constituted communist parties, either domestic or foreign; their review, therefore, goes beyond the limitations of the *Yearbook on International Communist Affairs*. For a relatively broad coverage of these groups, see the monthly London publications *Idiot International* and *Red Notes*, both of which are of left-radical orientation, but are not affiliated to any particular organization.

During 1970 the CPGB was run by the leadership elected early in that year (10-11 January) by the Executive Committee formed at the Thirty-first Congress. The Political Committee consisted of Tony Chater, Gerry Cohen, Reuben Falber, John Gollan, Michael McGahey, Gordon Mc-Lennan, George Matthews, Alex Murray, Bert Pearce, Bert Ramelson, James Reid, Frank Stanley, William Wainwright, George Wake, and Jack Woddis. Party officers and department heads were John Gollan (general secretary), John Tocher (chairman), Reuben Falber (assistant secretary), Tony Chater (Press and Publicity), Gordon McLennan (Organization), Bert Ramelson (Industrial), Jack Woddis (International), Margaret Hunter (Women), Betty Matthews (Education), Vic Eddisford (Electoral), and Denis Elwand (national treasurer).

The Young Communist League, affiliated to the CPGB since the latter's foundation, is the party's youth organization. In 1970 the YCL was headed by National Secretary Barney Davis until October when he was replaced by Tom Bell.

The CPGB derives its greatest strength from and exercises perceptible influence in the trade union movement. In 1970, although the party was increasingly challenged by other Marxist-Leninist groups (particularly the Socialist Labour League—SLL, a Trotskyist party), it continued to contribute actively to industrial agitation with a measure of success disproportionate to its size and electoral support (see below). During the year the party continued in its attempts to attain influence within the Amalgamated Union of Engineering and Foundry Workers (AEF), Britain's second-largest union and whose assistant divisional organizer for the Manchester area, John Tocher, was elected chairman of the CPGB in January. The party was also active in promoting its Liaison Committee for the Defence of Trade Unions (LCDTU), an "umbrella organization" for unofficial rank-and-file bodies set up in many parts of the country and in key industries, which was founded in 1966.

Party Internal Affairs. The minority dissent against the CPGB's condemnation of the 1968 Soviet-led invasion of Czechoslovakia, which had expressed itself again at the party's November 1969 Thirty-first Congress, when the CPGB reiterated its denunciation (see *YICA*, 1970, pp. 184-85), appeared to subside somewhat in 1970. The CPGB's critical evaluations of policies of the Soviet Union and other communist-ruled states, however, continued to be a source of friction within the party. According to the London *Sunday Telegraph* of 15 March, the party's Political Committee produced for the Executive Committee a draft statement attacking the Soviet Union for its "lack of democracy" in persecuting certain Soviet authors and for its hostile attitude toward Israel and the Jews. This statement reportedly provoked protests from the pro-Soviet faction within the CPGB and was accepted only when criticism of alleged growing lack of democracy in the West was included.

Domestic Views and Policies. During 1970 the CPGB, in its views and actions, continued to adhere to the guidelines set by its program *The British Road to Socialism*, a revised edition of which was published in October 1968 (see *YICA*, 1969, pp. 365-66). The party continued therefore to advocate parliamentary means toward the attainment of its goals, urging repeatedly the "unity of the left" and attempting to legitimize itself in the public eye as a party committed to British democratic traditions. At the same time, the major thrust of the CPGB's activities continued to be centered in the trade union movement.

Apart from its criticisms of malpractices in communist-ruled states (see below), one of the party's major attempts at attaining "legitimization" was seen in the publication in May in the party's theoretical monthly, *Marxism Today*, of James Klugmann's opening address at the CPGB's March Executive Committee meeting. Part of the article—entitled "Socialist Democracy"—was devoted to the party's "perspective for democracy in a Socialist Britain." Claiming that the CPGB had on many previous occasions "returned again and again to aspects of the issue of democracy," Klugmann stated:

> We envisage democratically organised political parties, including those hostile to socialism, with the right to maintain their organisation, publications, propaganda, and to contest elections under a system of proportional representation. . . .
> We stand for the maintenance of all hard-won civil liberties like Habeas Corpus and the right to be tried by Jury, for the establishment in a British socialist society of freedom to think, work, travel, to speak, dissent, act and believe, for freedom of religious worship.

The CPGB did not register notable success in its bid for unity of the left. While its attacks against what the party called "ultra-leftism" continued to tone down,[1] reflecting a trend apparent in 1969 (see *YICA*, 1970, p. 187), the CPGB's attempt to engage other extreme-left groups in dialogue and cooperation in most instances proved unsuccessful. The most consistent critic of the CPGB continued to be the Trotskyist Socialist Labour League (SLL), which repeatedly accused the communist party of remaining Stalinist in its orientation (see, e.g., the response to the Klugmann article in *Workers' Press*, 21 May), of using its influence in the trade unions to break strikes (see, e.g., Cliff Slaughter, "How the CP Broke the Miners' Strike," *ibid.*, 24 November), and of remaining despite its 1968 opposition to the invasion of Czechoslovakia, closely aligned to the Soviet Union. The CPGB registered some success in attracting left-wing segments of the Labour Party and the trade union movement to cooperate in a number of its activities, although these tended to be limited to issues relating to organized labor.

The scope and degree of success of the CPGB's activities within industry continued, as in previous years, to be disproportionate to the party's size or electoral appeal.[2] The CPGB succeeded both in electing a number of its members to executive positions in several of the country's major trade unions and in organizing several unofficial strikes, of which the biggest was the "national strike" of 8 December.

During 1970 the CPGB succeeded in having a number of members elected or reelected to executive positions in the trade union movement. In January, in the first elections to the 39-member national executive of Britain's largest union, the Transport and General Workers' Union (TGWU), in which communists have been eligible to stand, two CPGB members—Sid Easton and Jock Gibson—were elected. Another first for the CPGB in January was the election of Cyril Hopton to the Leeds district committee of the National Union of Tailors and Garment Workers, the first communist to be ever elected to this committee. On the negative side for the party, the CPGB lost three of its six representatives on the national executive of the National Union of Seamen—two were defeated, and a third did not seek reelection. In late May, CPGB member Maurice Styles was elected chairman of the 200,000-strong Union of Post Office Workers. Elections to the Scottish area of the National Union of Mineworkers in June resulted in the reelection of CPGB member David Bolton to the post of vice-president. In October, party member Jim Prendergast was elected to the 24-man executive of the National Union of Railwaymen.

The major thrust of CPGB efforts in trade union electoral activity was seen in the Amalgamated Union of Engineering and Foundry Workers. In the first part of the year several party members won executive posts in the AEF: D. Gossop was elected district secretary for Gainsborough and Lincoln; W. Hutchinson was reelected as Scottish officer; Les Dixon was elected to the

[1] One of the few CPGB comments on this subject was a "discussion contribution" on "Revolutionary Romanticism," by Willie Thompson, published in the May issue of *Marxism Today*. A comment on Thompson's article, by Marshall Harris, was published in the same journal in July.

[2] For a review of CPGB influence in organized labor see Brian Crozier, "Britain's Industrial Revolutionaries," *Interplay*, New York, January 1971.

Executive Council of the union, and Ted Scott was elected regional officer for Division 5. In June, CPGB member John Foster was reelected national organizer of the AEF. In the following month, Hugh Scanlon, a former communist who had the full support of the CPGB in his campaign, was reelected president of the AEF. At the same time, the CPGB chairman, John Tocher, formerly AEF assistant divisional organizer for the Manchester area, was elected divisional organizer. The party newspaper *Morning Star* on 23 September, following further AEF elections, claimed that "supporters of the Leftward move" within the AEF had now "a clear majority of places on the 11-man final appeals court." In November, CPGB member George Anthony was elected president of the AEF North London district; and in December party member Ken Brett was elected to one of the AEF's two posts of assistant general secretary. Commenting on the success scored by "the Left wing of the engineers' union," the *Morning Star* (6 December) noted: "The result follows the reelection last August of Mr. Ernie Roberts as the other assistant general secretary. Mr. Roberts is another Left-winger."

The CPGB made a concerted effort in 1970 to regain influence in the Electrical and Plumbing Trades Union, in which it had played a prominent role up until 1961. In this area, its endeavors failed, and in the elections to the union's executive council in December no CPGB-supported candidates were elected.

During the latter part of the year, the CPGB, operating through the LCDTU (see above), devoted much of its energies to the sponsorship of a one-day "national strike" to be held on 8 December. To further its action, the LCDTU organized a conference on 18 November, which was reportedly attended by 1,800 "elected delegates from trade union organizations," representing 300 trade union branches, 55 trades councils, 36 union district committees, four union executive councils, and 155 shop stewards' committees (*Morning Star*, 16 November). The strike was opposed by the Trades Union Congress, and the communist control of the LCDTU was publicized in the press during the first week of December (see, e.g., *Times*, London, 1 December; *Daily Telegraph*, London, 5 December). Although the CPGB had forecast a participation of one million, the number of strikers was limited to about 300,000 out of a total working population in Britain of some 26 million. It should be noted, however, that similar "national strikes" that were held on 27 February and 1 May 1969 in each case had involved no more than 90,000 participants (see *YICA*, 1970, p. 186).

International Views and Policies. The 1968 Soviet-led invasion of Czechoslovakia and the CPGB's subsequent strong condemnation of the action continued in 1970 to be a major issue affecting the British party's relations with other communist parties. During the course of the year, the CPGB took on the role of one of the major critics of the Soviet-imposed "normalization" in Czechoslovakia, extending its views on developments in that country to critical evaluations also of the policies of communist parties in other communist-ruled states. With regard to the latter, the aforementioned article by Klugmann was devoted primarily to "the great complexity of the issue of democracy in the socialist countries." Referring to "the deep aberrations from socialism, from Marxism, that have occurred at different times in different socialist countries," Klugmann indicated that such aberrations "seem to be taking place in China today," but implied that the policies of other communist states should be examined, stating:

> There is a whole series of issues in relation to socialist democracy in contemporary socialist society (some of which arose particularly sharply in relation to the question of Czechoslovakia) over which there are differences of opinion inside the international communist movement, and which we need to discuss. (*Marxism Today*, May 1970).

A similar stand was taken by John Gollan in his report to a CPGB Executive Committee meeting in September, when he stated: "I know that we can be reproached that at times we have defended things in the U.S.S.R. that, only later, we came to know as indefensible. . . . We accept this criticism." Gollan went on to add:

> We shall continue to defend the role of the Soviet Union and the Socialist world, while continuing in a fraternal way to make known any differences we may have with the actions and attitudes of the Soviet Union or other Socialist countries. (*Morning Star*, 14 September.)

During the year, the CPGB was involved in polemics primarily with the leadership of the Communist Party of Czechoslovakia. On 24 January the CPGB weekly *Comment* reprinted an article from *Rudé Právo* (Prague, 29 December 1969), organ of the Communist Party of Czechoslovakia, that had criticized the CPGB leadership's reiteration of its opposition to the invasion of Czechoslovakia; in a strongly worded editorial comment, the CPGB weekly claimed that the author of the *Rudé Právo* article had resorted to "arguments of a level not normal in a responsible exchange of views." On 23 March the CPGB daily *Morning Star* expressed its "concern" over the suspension of Alexander Dubček from the Czechoslovak party; a rebuttal by *Rudé Právo* on 26 March was reprinted, with no comment, by the CPGB organ on 28 March. Following the 26 June expulsion of Dubček by the Czechoslovak party's Central Committee, the CPGB assistant secretary, Reuben Falber, stated that the event was "bound to be received with the deepest regret and concern by many Communists" (*Morning Star*, 29 June).

Relations between the CPGB and the Communist Party of the Soviet Union (CPSU) appeared to continue to be strained, as indicated by the joint communiqué issued following a meeting in Moscow on 7 August between high-level delegations of the two parties, consisting of Gollan and Tocher for the CPGB and Kirilenko and Ponomarev for the CPSU. The communiqué failed to mention any agreement of views and referred to a "frank exchange on the problems of the world Communist movement" (*ibid.*, 8 August).

On general international affairs the CPGB tended to follow a Soviet line. The main foreign policy courses advocated included the disassociation of Great Britain from U.S. policy in Indochina, dissolution of NATO and the Warsaw Pact and their replacement by a "system of collective security," opposition to British attempts to attain membership in the European Economic Community, and the breaking off of all relations with the government of South Africa.

International Party Contacts. The CPGB was represented by Jack Woddis at a meeting of European communist parties in Moscow on 14-15 January 1970. At the beginning of February, John Gollan attended the Nineteenth Congress of the French Communist Party. Reuben Falber was the party's representative at the Twelfth Congress of the Reconstruction Party of the Working People of Cyprus (AKEL), held 5-8 March. Also during the same month, the CPGB was represented by Frank Stanley at the founding congress of the reconstituted Communist Party of Ireland, held in Belfast on 15 March, and was host to a delegation of the Romanian Communist Party, led by Executive Committee member Gheorghe Pana, which visited Great Britain during the last week of March. In April, CPGB representatives to the Lenin Centenary celebrations in the Soviet Union were Dave Bowman and Bert Ramelson. John Gollan represented the CPGB at a meeting of West European communist parties in Paris on 15 May. In mid-July the CPGB was host to the first delegation to visit Great Britain from the Socialist Unity Party (SED) of the German Democratic Republic, led by Central Committee member Kurt Seibt. In August, talks were held in Moscow between CPGB and CPSU representatives (see above), and the chairman of the Communist Party of Ireland, Andrew Barr, met with CPGB leaders in London. Also in August, Jack Woddis met in Amsterdam with leaders of the Communist Party of the Netherlands. On 21 September the CPGB was host to a meeting of representatives of nine West European communist parties—in addition to the British party, delegations were from Cyprus, France, the Federal Republic of Germany, Greece, Ireland, Italy, the Netherlands, and Spain. According to the *Morning Star* (23 September), the participants discussed "the problems arising from the development of multi-national firms" and agreed to hold a follow-up conference in London on 11-13 January 1971, to be attended by all communist parties of West Europe and to have as the sole item on its agenda "The Struggle of the Working Class of the Capitalist Countries of Europe in the Face of the Development of the Multi-National Firms." The CPGB was represented at a conference of European communist parties in Moscow on 20-21 October. A delegation of the Communist Party of Spain, led by its secretary-general, Santiago Carrillo, spent ten days in Great Britain at the beginning of December at the invitation of the CPGB; also at the beginning of the month, John Gollan addressed an international meeting in Paris of "solidarity with the people of Indochina," sponsored by the French Communist Party.

Publications. The London daily newspaper of the CPGB is the *Morning Star*. Other major party publications include *Comment*, a weekly magazine; *Marxism Today*, a monthly theoretical journal; and *Labour Monthly*, which provides commentary on political events. The YCL has an irregular monthly journal, *Challenge*, and a monthly theoretical organ, *Cogito*.

*   *   *

The SLL. Among the numerous Marxist-Leninist parties and groups that challenge the CPGB's leadership in the British communist movement, the largest and most influential (particularly in the trade union movement) appears to be the Socialist Labour League, founded in 1959; it is an affiliate of the Trotskyist International Committee of the Fourth International.

The SLL is believed to have a membership of only 1,000. Its youth movement—the Young Socialists (YS)—claims 20,000 members and apparently is the largest Marxist-Leninist youth group ever to have existed in Great Britain. Support for the YS appears to be growing. At the annual general meeting of the youth organization's monthly publication *Keep Left*, held in January 1970, it was claimed that in 1969 the newspaper "had averaged 20,668 copies a month," a circulation which showed an "average monthly rise of 1,668" (*Workers' Press*, 13 January).

The SLL is led by Gerry Healy, its national secretary. The other most prominent representatives of the SLL (which does not publish complete information on the composition of its leading bodies) are Michael Banda, editor of the SLL's daily newspaper, *Workers' Press*, and Tom Kemp and Cliff Slaughter, editors of *Fourth International*, a quarterly organ of the International Committee of the Fourth International, published in London. The YS was led by its national secretary, Sheila Torrance, until April 1970, when, at the organization's tenth annual conference, she was replaced by John Simmance. The other most prominent representative of the youth movement during the year was Aileen Jennings, editor of *Keep Left*.

The main line of SLL domestic policy in 1970 continued to be oriented toward industrial agitation. To further its influence in the trade union movement, the league participated in a number of activities sponsored by the SLL-controlled All Trade Unions Alliance (ATUA), a group similar to the CPGB-controlled LCDTU. The ATUA was formed in late October 1968 under the sponsorship of the SLL and the league's "Oxford Liaison Committee for the Defence of Trade Unions," a body which subsequently appeared to be no longer active (see *YICA*, 1969, pp. 371-72).

The SLL's approach toward organized labor was somewhat different from that of the CPGB. While the latter was making inroads in the trade union movement at a relatively high level, the SLL tended in 1970 to concentrate its activities among the rank and file and the shop stewards. Like the CPGB, the SLL focused its attention during the year on the engineering industry. In this context, the most noteworthy event in 1970 was a conference held in Sheffield on 7 February, sponsored by the ATUA. The conference was attended by some 200 delegates, most of them from the engineering industry. Geographically, the delegates came from factories in London, Scotland, the Merseyside, the North East coast, Yorkshire, the Midlands, Wales, and the South West. One of the decisions taken at the conference was to establish a special "engineering section" within the ATUA. On 19 December the ATUA held its second annual conference in Birmingham, with a reported attendance of 480 delegates and 200 observers (*Workers' Press*, 21 December). The participants reportedly represented "almost every industry." In his speech to the conference Gerry Healy claimed that the situation in Great Britain was "far more revolutionary than 1926—year of the General Strike." (*Ibid.*)

The SLL offered its support to the LCDTU-sponsored 8 December "national strike," although it repeatedly accused the CPGB of "deliberately" restricting the action "to an isolated protest by the Communist Party and 'left' trade union bureaucrats" (see, e.g., *ibid.*, 21 November).

The SLL called on its supporters to vote for the Labour Party in the June general elections. The league's policy was explained in a manifesto adopted at its twelfth national conference, held in London on 23-24 May, which stated in part:

> The Tories [Conservative Party] must be defeated in the General Election on June 18. The working class must return a Labour Party majority to parliament. This will counter the plans of the employers, who urgently want the Tories back in order to "discipline" the workers, stop wage increases, and impose unemployment. (*Ibid.*, 26 May).

As in previous years, the SLL and the YS press repeatedly attacked all other Marxist-Leninist organizations and parties. Although one of the groups consistently attacked was the International Marxist Group (the British section of the United Secretariat of the Fourth International—see below) the SLL's national secretary, Gerry Healy, one of the most prominent members of the International Committee of the Fourth International, reportedly approached the United Secretariat headquarters in Paris in April, for discussions on eventual unification of the two international bodies. By the end of the year, further signs of such a development had not become noticeable. (See *Intercontinental Press*, New York, 27 July and 5 October.)

In its reporting on international issues the SLL continued in 1970 to attack the policies of the Soviet Union. With regard to China, it appeared to side with the Chinese in the Sino-Soviet conflict (see *Workers' Press*, 8-10 January), but its support was qualified by reference to the Chinese leaders' "Stalinist" attitudes and policies. The SLL also criticized "Cuban Stalinism" (*ibid.*, 6 and 16 May). Apparently its support of ruling communist parties was limited to the Vietnam Workers' Party of North Vietnam. With regard to nonruling communist parties, the SLL's main target of criticism appeared to be the French Communist Party, to which the *Workers' Press* devoted a 14-part series of articles in May. The SLL's closest international ties appeared to be with the French affiliates of the International Committee (see *France*).

Publications. The SLL publishes a newspaper, *Workers' Press*, which appeared from Tuesday through Saturday until 12 October, when its frequency was increased to six times a week with an issue on Monday. The publication of the YS is the monthly *Keep Left*. SLL views are also carried in *Fourth International*, an irregular quarterly publication of the International Committee of the Fourth International.

* * *

In addition to the CPGB and the SLL there are numerous small Marxist-Leninist groups in

Great Britain, but none of them has been able to muster numerically significant support, with the possible exception of two groups that work closely together—the International Marxist Group (IMG) and the International Socialism Group (ISG). The IMG is the British section of the United Secretariat of the Fourth International. The main spokesmen for the IMG in 1970 appeared to be Pat Jordan, its national secretary and the editor of the group's monthly publication, *International*, Ernest Tate, and Tariq Ali. Jordan was also chairman of the Vietnam Solidarity Campaign (VSC), a coalition of numerous left-wing organizations in which the IMG and the ISG played leading roles. Whereas in 1968 the VSC succeeded in mobilizing considerable support for its demonstrations in opposition to U.S. policy in Vietnam (see *YICA*, 1969, p. 373), in 1969 this mass support was not evident, and in 1970 it declined even further, with many IMG and ISG militants orienting their activities to industrial agitation. Tariq Ali was editor of the fortnightly newspaper *Black Dwarf* until 20 February, when, together with a number of members of the editorial board, he resigned, and on 17 March published the first issue of a new fortnightly, *Red Mole*. Both newspapers continued to have a relatively wide readership throughout the year. (For details on Ali's resignation see *Intercontinental Press*, 6 April and 4 May.) The group associated with *Red Mole* founded a new organization—the Spartacus League—at a congress in London on 5-6 July. It became the youth group of the IMG.

The ISG, which originated in the Trotskyist movement but is not affiliated to the four main factions of the Fourth International, is also known as the "Cliff Group" a name derived from its chief theoretician, Tony Cliff (pseudonym of Ygael Gluckstein). The ISG publishes a weekly, the *Socialist Worker*, and a monthly theoretical journal, *International Socialism*.

The Communist Party of Britain (Marxist-Leninist), was founded at an inaugural congress in April 1968. This pro-Chinese party, led by Reg Birch, a member of the Executive Council of the AEF, claims a membership of 400. It appears to be the only pro-Chinese party in Great Britain whose activities and statements are publicized by Communist China. At the end of December, Reg Birch led a delegation of his party to Peking, where he had meetings with members of the Chinese Communist Party leadership, including Chou En-lai. The party publishes a monthly four-page newspaper, *The Worker*. A number of other contending pro-Chinese groups have been operating within an umbrella organization called the Joint Committee of Communists (JCC). At a meeting on 28 September 1969 the JCC transformed itself into the Communist Federation of Britain (Marxist-Leninist). Little information is available on this new group's leadership or on the extent of its support. Its organ is a monthly newspaper, *Struggle*. The views of the federation are also publicized in a quarterly magazine, *The Marxist*.

M. P.

GREECE

The Communist Party of Greece (Kommounistikon Komma Hellados; KKE) was founded 18-22 November 1918 in Piraeus as the Socialist Workers' Party of Greece (Socialistikon Ergatikon Komma Hellados; SEKE). In 1920 the party voted for affiliation with the Comintern, and in 1924 it assumed its present name. Outlawed during the communist insurgency in December 1947, the KKE has since maintained its leadership and cadres in the communist states of East Europe, with only a few Central Committee members in Greece to direct domestic activities. The party headquarters moved from Romania to East Germany in 1968.

Within Greece, the communists are particularly active among tobacco and factory workers, stevedores in the principal ports, and seamen. In addition, they appear to have a large following among some 100,000 persons who left Greece at the end of the civil war (1947-49) and made their homes in various countries of Europe. The KKE, with some 27,000 members in Greece and 10,000 to 15,000 in exile, split in 1968 (see *YICA*, 1970, pp. 193-95). The population of Greece is 8,803,000 (estimated 1968). It would appear that the exiled party leadership under Konstandinos (Kostas) Koliyannis commands majority support among Greek communists in the Soviet Union and East Europe, while the breakaway group under Dimitrios (Mitsos) Partsalides and Antonios Brillakis—which also calls itself the KKE and claims to represent Greek communists everywhere —holds the balance of power among cadres and fellow travelers in Greece and West Europe.

The KKE's long record of internal discord and factionalism is reflected by the existence of several Greek communist splinter groups. Followers of Nikolas Zachariadis, expelled as secretary-general under pressure from Moscow in 1956, form one group of dissidents; those of Markos Vafiadis, a commander of communist guerrillas, expelled from the party in 1958, comprise another. These factions represent the personal followings of the two rival communist leaders of the civil war period. In addition, there is the International Communist Party of Greece (Kommounistiko Diethnistiko Komma tes Ellados), which is the Greek section of the Fourth International; its organ is the monthly *Ergatike Pale*. A pro-Chinese faction also exists, with headquarters in Romania. Its leader is Polydoros Danielides, a former KKE Central Committee member; its views are made known through its bulletin, *Aganennissis*, and through Peking media.

Although an illegal party, the KKE until the coup of 1967 maintained an active political life through the United Democratic Left (Eniea Dimokratiki Aristera; EDA), a broad "progressive" electoral formation which it was instrumental in founding in 1951. In successive general elections (1951, 1956, and 1958) the EDA vote rose steadily from 10.8 to 24.4 per cent—which made it the strongest opposition party, with 79 of the 300 seats in Parliament. In the 1964 election, however, the EDA received only 11.8 per cent and 22 seats, largely due to the fact that in many districts the party abstained in favor of left-centrist candidates of George Papandreou's Center Union. The EDA, like all other political parties, was proscribed by the government on 29 April 1967, following the coup of 21 April which brought to power the current regime headed by Yeoryos Papadopoulos.

Many top leaders of both the KKE and EDA have been imprisoned by the Papadopoulos government. To avoid detection, those still at liberty in Greece have organized themselves into small groups whose members often have no knowledge of the composition or activities of other, parallel bodies. By the same token, deliberately misleading information is frequently disseminated by both KKE and EDA sources.

The national constitution drawn up by the Papadopoulos government (whose motivation for the coup was the fear that Greece would veer sharply to the left in the scheduled national elections) was approved by popular referendum in September 1968. The constitution was partly put into effect two months later, but articles providing for elections, political parties, and various civil liberties have remained in suspension. A government spokesman was quoted as saying: "Only when the government program for social reforms is completed, only when it bears fruit, will we be able to say that the communist threat has definitely and irrevocably vanished." (*Elevtheros Kosmos*, Athens, 18 January 1970.)

Leadership and Organization. The chairman of the KKE is Apostolos Grozos; the secretary-general and leading personality in the party is Konstandinos Koliyannis. The Politburo of the Central Committee includes Grigorios Faragos and Nikolaos Kaloudhis (both imprisoned in Greece), Leonidas Stringos, Panayotis Mavromatis, and (first name unknown) Hyphantis. One candidate Politburo member is Yerasimos Stefanatos. Prominent members of the Central Committee include (first names unknown) Tsolakis and Venetsanopoulos. The party's latest congress, its eighth, was held in 1961. The KKE's newly constituted youth affiliate is the "Greek Communist Youth" (KNE). The KNE is the successor of the "Communist Youth Organization" (EPON).

Leaders of the rival faction—commonly referred to as the Partsalides-Brillakis group—include also Haralambos (Bambis) Drakopoulos, Panos Dimitriou, and Zisis Zografos.

The February 1968 split within the KKE has been reflected within all organs under party control. Largest and most important of these, next to the EDA, is the mass resistance organization Patriotic Anti-Dictatorial Front (Patriotikon Metopom; PAM), of which there are pro- and anti-Koliyannis bases in Greece and branches throughout East and West Europe. In addition, there is the EDA's youth affiliate, Lambrakis Democratic Youth (Demokratike Neolaia Lambraki; DNL), as well as numerous "anti-dictatorship" or "solidarity" committees, in Europe and elsewhere, whose supporters and sympathizers are actively wooed by both rival KKE factions.

Party Internal Affairs. The history of the KKE has been marked by factional struggles and periodic purges. In more recent years, ideological differences within the international communist movement accentuated the tactical incompatability between party leaders in exile in East Europe and cadres within Greece. The Soviet-backed Koliyannis group insists on the KKE's "vanguard" role among forces opposed to the present Greek government, and is loath to dilute its ideological base or its clandestine cells with any larger number of noncommunist sympathizers or to enter into entangling alliances and tactical compromises. In contrast, the Partsalides-Brillakis faction, purged from the leadership in 1968, seeks to cooperate in a broad front with all possible allies and —at least for the time being—to subordinate questions of ideology and partisan interests to the common opposition goal of a coup d'état. Internationally, the Koliyannis faction insists on strict allegiance to the Soviet Union, while the dissidents follow the Italian party line of the independence of each communist party and its need and right to adapt to national conditions.

The dissenters have the support of most prominent Greek communist personalities, such as composer Mikis Theodorakis, a leader of both PAM and the EDA's Lambrakis Democratic

Youth, who was freed in 1970, and Manolis Glezos, a leading EDA figure still incarcerated. Each faction claims to represent the EDA abroad and each has its own EDA headquarters in West Europe. Brillakis, who headed the Executive Committee of the EDA for West Europe up to 1968, when he fled from Athens, heads the dissenting organization which has established its base in Rome. Antonis Ambatielos heads the pro-Koliyannis EDA headquarters in Paris. Similarly, there exist currently two separate and rival organizations claiming to be the PAM.

To the benefit of the Partsalides-Brillakis group, the schism in the KKE leadership brought together many elements of Koliyannis's previously scattered opposition, including not only substantial segments of the clandestine organization in Greece, but many Greek communists and fellow travelers in both East and West Europe. The Warsaw Pact invasion of Czechoslovakia in 1968 further sharpened the division. It was endorsed by Koliyannis and condemned by large proportions of the EDA and PAM, by the Partsalides-led KKE branch in Czechoslovakia (subsequently reorganized under a new leadership loyal to Koliyannis), and by many prominent communist prisoners. What seemed to be moves toward reunification at the end of 1968 were actually maneuvers for position, and the split in the party was all but sealed by January 1969 when Koliyannis convened the Thirteenth Plenum of the Central Committee in East Germany. All those opposing the secretary-general were denounced, steps were taken to purge all "antiparty" officials and functionaries, a new "Echelon of the Central Committee", responsible to the Politburo for operations inside Greece was named to replace the Bureau of the Interior headed by Brillakis, and preparations were announced for the party's Ninth Congress to deal with the "factionalist conspiracy" of the exiled rebels and their allies inside Greece.

With unofficial but open support of the Italian and Spanish communist parties and the sympathy of the Romanian and Yugoslav governments, the Partsalides-Brillakis forces stepped up their challenge to the Koliyannis leadership, holding the Thirteenth Plenum to be invalid. The split was formalized in April 1969 when the anti-Koliyannis forces met in Italy, rejected the Koliyannis purges as "antistatutory," set up their own leadership, and announced plans for an extraordinary party congress.

The Fourteenth Plenum of the (Koliyannis) Central Committee convened in mid-April 1970. The KKE's "Voice of Truth" radio reported on 1 May that, in addition to regular and alternate Central Committee members, there were also members of the Echelon of the Central Committee present. The Politburo, it was indicated, had invited those regular and alternate members who were following the revisionist splinter group and asked them to define clearly their position toward the party and its leadership, but their reply had been "negative." On the basis of a "critical examination" of party work since the Eighth Congress, the plenum adopted theses which were to constitute the basis for an open discussion within the party for the preparation of its Ninth Congress. The theses (broadcast in instalments over "Voice of Truth" radio between 6 and 21 May) noted, *inter alia*, that the party, in its Eighth Congress theses, should have better prepared the party for both the peaceful and the nonpeaceful paths to socialism in Greece and thus have prevented the one-sided stressing of the peaceful way by the "opportunists." The party leadership acknowledged that it had not fully anticipated the possibility of a second coup after the royal coup of 15 July 1965, and that it had later failed to prepare the party and the masses ideologically, politically, and organizationally for resisting the 21 April 1967 "fascist military coup." Since that time, however, the party leadership's strategy was adjudged correct, particularly with regard to the internal threat from the Partsalides-Brillakis faction.

There appear to be no immediate prospects for conciliation. Koliyannis accuses the dissidents of pursuing a policy alien to Marxism-Leninism, seeking to minimize the KKE's revolutionary character and remove it from the international communist movement, and capitalizing on positions and titles acquired through the party to subvert the EDA and PAM. The dissidents counter that the Koliyannis forces, having been in exile for some twenty years, are incapable of compre-hending—much less directing—the complex developments in Greece. Within the international communist movement, the Koliyannis group continues its policy of strict allegiance to the Soviet Union—despite differences with the Communist Party of the Soviet Union (CPSU) that have emerged since, and as a result of, the KKE schism. On the Soviet side, recent statements indicate that the CPSU, while continuing to favor Koliyannis, appears to be finding its traditional blanket endorsement of him increasingly costly in terms of popular world support.

Domestic Views and Activities. The KKE holds that the Papadopoulos "junta" was "installed by NATO plans and with the collaboration and support of the most reactionary circles of the United States," and predicts that "it will be removed from power by a mass, popular, antidicta-torial struggle supported by progressive men everywhere." Under the "junta," in the communist view, national interests are subjugated to foreign "imperialist" interests, and Greece has been turned into a "hotbed of intrigue", undermining peace and security in the region. ("Voice of Truth," 3 December 1970).

Early in 1970 a Politburo resolution declared (5 February) that government expenditures for the benefit of NATO military plans were draining the nation's economy. Despite a relative in-crease in output during 1969, the resolution asserted, there continued to be a huge trade deficit, and it was thanks only to foreign loans and to the even greater "sellout" of rich productive sources to foreigners that national bankruptcy had been avoided. (*Ibid.*, 6 February.) In the three years since the military junta had taken power, the "democratic conquests of the working class, the peasantry, the urban middle strata, of all working people, achieved after long years of strug-gle and sacrifices," had been "annihilated." The party charged that exploitation of the people's labor had taken on an unprecedented scope, and that the country's sources of wealth were being handed over to unrestrained and piratic exploitation by foreign monopoly capital and by a hand-ful of local plutocratic magnates who installed and supported the tyranny. (Politburo resolution, "Voice of Truth," 18 April.) According to the KKE, the junta was using the pretext of repelling a communist threat to conceal its real aims—to crush the rising democratic movement, link Greece more closely with NATO for the reinforcement of the latter's southeast wing, and facilitate the military plans of "imperialism" against the socialist countries and "progressive" regimes of the Near and Middle East. In the meantime, the government was trying to gain strength by disguis-ing itself under the cloak of pseudo-democratic laws. (Theses of the Fourteenth Plenum.) The reshuffle of the Greek cabinet, on 29 June, was seen by the KKE as "clearly the effort to strength the stratocracy and personal authority of Dictator Papadopoulos with a view to continuing the same policy" (Politburo statement, 1 July; "Voice of Truth," 2 July).

The KKE holds that the present government could be overthrown if all elements opposed to it were to combine forces and take advantage of the full potential of international support; each would retain its own program and ultimate objectives, but would agree to a minimum program based on points of common interests. The minimum program advocated by the KKE, as set forth in the theses of the Fourteenth Plenum, calls for: overthrow of the government; formation of a provisional government of all "antidictatorial" parties and organizations; the restoration of con-stitutional and democratic liberties; abolition of the existing constitution and all "antipopular" laws promulgated under it, along with the older emergency measures and laws, including those which prohibit the activity of the KKE; immediate release of all political prisoners; general politi-cal amnesty; free functioning and activity of all political parties; punishment of the junta leaders and purging of "fascist" elements within the army, the security forces, and all state and public bodies; measures of immediate relief for working people; restoration of the sovereign rights of the country; free elections to a constituent assembly to decide the mode of government and the constitution of the country. As unity progressed, the struggle would assume active forms, such as work stoppages, strikes, street demonstrations, fraternization between the people and the army, and general resistance to the government. The KKE, for its part, would proceed from the general Leninist principle that a revolutionary popular movement, in order to achieve victory, must assimilate and be capable of using all forms of struggle, peaceful or nonpeaceful. In a departure from positions taken in the Twelfth and Thirteenth Plenums, which appeared to favor peaceful pursuits, the KKE declared that "armed struggle" now appeared the most probable ultimate means of overthrowing the dictatorship. (*Ibid.*)

The visible reluctance of noncommunist elements to collaborate with the KKE stems both from a general wariness of identification with the communists and from the fear that an eventual civil war could lead to a complete communist takeover. They look, rather, for the army to turn against the government, and for the United States and other Western nations to exert economic and political pressures for its removal. Several non-KKE resistance groups, therefore, have joined in appeals for international economic sanctions against the government. The Koliyannis forces, in contrast, began to oppose sanctions when the Soviet Union and other socialist countries signed trade agreements with Greece, taking the position that foreign trade helped Greek peasants (according to the Australian communist party's *Tribune*, Sydney, 6 May, quoting dissident PAM representative Markos Dragoumis).

Official statements issued in 1970, in connection with mass releases of political detainees, appeared to be at variance with foreign-observer estimates. The International Red Cross (subsequently asked to abandon its operations in Greece) estimated in January 1970, for instance, that there were some 3,000 political prisoners, while government statements at that time spoke of only 1,800 to 1,900. Of a reported total, in August, of 1,096 communist prisoners, 500 were to be freed in three stages, starting immediately. The deputy minister to the premier, George Georgalas (a former leading communist named to the cabinet in July 1970), declared that the government was so consolidated that public order would not be endangered by these "concessions." (Athens radio, 10 August.) The release of 300 was authorized by a committee of judges which allegedly had examined the cases of all political prisoners; the remaining 200 were being freed "either on health grounds or because they had shown a spirit of cooperation" (*New York Times*, 11 August). Responding to this, the KKE Politburo declared that the junta, far from having made a humanitarian gesture, had been obliged to take this measure under strong pressure from Greek and international public opinion, and that the issue of political detention would remain open and become more acute after the release of the 500 ("Voice of Truth," 13 August). According to a government statement released on 8 December, there remained 600 communist and 70 noncommunist political detainees, as well as 350 serving terms for subversive or terrorist activities (*Akropolis*, Athens, 8 December). Of this combined group, 290 were said by Athens radio on 24 December to have been released by that date, at which time Papadopoulos declared that all 350 "leftists" and some 55 others still detained would be freed within four months, internal security conditions permitting (*New York Times*, 25 December).

The many arrests made during the year do not appear to have been taken into account in the government's figures. Among the prominent communists captured and convicted during 1970 were Nikolaos Kaloudhis and Zinon Zorzovilis—members, respectively, of the pro-Koliyannis Politburo and Central Committee—who were apprehended in early May while attempting to enter Greece from East Europe with forged passports and police identity cards, and Ioannis Yiannaris, also of the pro-Koliyannis Central Committee, a leading functionary in EDA and PAM who had been operating in Athens since the coup under the pseudonym Athanasios Yeoryiadhis. Security authorities announced that they had seized the archives of the group associated with Yiannaris, containing secret addresses of the Athens party organization elements, and had confiscated a printing press and a considerable sum of money in Greek and U.S. currency (Athens radio, 11 May). Kaloudhis, Zorzovilis, and Yiannaris were among eleven persons, all alleged members of the KKE Echelon, brought before a special military tribunal on charges of attempting to reestablish the underground machinery of the KKE (*Akropolis*, 7 June). Tried on 6 July, the three named were given life sentences. Seven of the others were sentenced to from two to twenty years, and one was acquitted. Kaloudhis denied the charge of sedition, declaring that the KKE program envisaged the "restoration of constitutional freedoms, the release of political prisoners, and the holding of elections to create a democratic government" (TASS, 8 July).

According to a KKE Central Committee statement of 18 December, another of its members, Stratis Tsambis, was arrested during a mass roundup of "political figures and other patriots" that took place in Athens in November. The government, allegedly, had withheld the names of Tsambis and other arrestees in order to avoid popular protests and demonstrations, both inside the country and abroad. ("Voice of Truth," 19 December.)

The composer Mikis Theodorakis featured significantly in developments in 1970. Detained by the Greek government as a security risk since the coup, his release on 13 April (negotiated by French Radical Party leader Jean-Jacques Servan-Schreiber) highlighted the division in the KKE and enabled him to play a determining role in the line-up of resisters. In the KKE split, most of the communist militants inside Greece, including Theodorakis, rebelled against the exiled leadership. Theodorakis, with other EDA leaders including Manolis Glezos, was believed to be harboring plans for a new party at the time of the coup, and though he refrained from attacking the Koliyannis group, he apparently aimed at its isolation. His release proved detrimental to the Koliyannis group, which, so long as Theodorakis was detained, had been able to benefit from his renown as a world figure in music and as a political hero among communist and other resistance forces. On 25 March, however, in a statement reportedly smuggled out of Greece, Theodorakis spoke of his failure to restore party unity and openly denounced Koliyannis's "splinter group" (*Le Monde*, Paris, 29 April). Theodorakis's positions thereafter emphasized his fundamental opposition to the Koliyannis group and to some extent compromised Koliyannis, who is totally dependent upon Soviet support.

Theodorakis held a press conference in Paris on 29 April (organized by the French "Committee for a Democratic Greece") and, speaking in the name of PAM, introduced a nine-point program looking to the formation of a "National Resistance Council," the replacement of the government, and the restoration of all constitutional and democratic freedoms on the basis of the 1952 constitution, to be followed by free elections with a view to calling a constituent assembly. He suggested that Andreas Papandreou (former cabinet minister in the Center Union government headed by his father, George Papandreou, and current leader of the "Pan-Hellenic Liberation Movement," or PAK) head the council and that former Premier Constandinos Karamanlis be included in it. As to why he thought the leadership of the CPSU and of many other communist parties continued to give full support to Koliyannis, Theodorakis said he could find no explanation for this "serious mistake," which had meant disowning the "true leaders" of the KKE— those who had proved themselves within Greece for twenty-five years and particularly since the coup. He declared: "The foreign communist parties must stop interfering in our affairs and let us work things out ourselves by democratic means. I am confident that the international communist movement will eventually revise its attitude toward us." (*Ibid.*)

The program presented by Theodorakis received the initial approval of Andreas Papandreou's PAK, with which the Partsalides-Brillakis faction of PAM had entered into a preliminary cooperative agreement in August 1968, and of the center-left "Democratic Defense," led by George Mylonas, which had subsequently become a party to the PAK-PAM plans for resistance collaboration. (The Democratic Defense may have been left without leadership in Greece, however, when its principal activists were convicted at a trial held simultaneously with the 6 July proceedings against the communists.)

The Koliyannis group declared that Theodorakis's statements "unfortunately did not justify the hopes of those who believed after recent events that he could stand on a positive and unifying basis in the interests of the antidictatorial struggle." The solution he offered was "merely a new, and even worse edition of the known agreement of the PAK-Brillakis group, aimed at isolating the KKE and recognizing the constitution of 1952 by which the KKE and various other national resistance organizations were prohibited and which is currently used by the junta's military tribunals to try and convict all patriots regardless of their political views." The group stated that they had attempted to contact Theodorakis upon his arrival in Paris, in order to "help him from following the path being offered by the splitter group," but he had not responded to their efforts, and that the KKE felt "obliged to note" that Theodorakis had "started accepting incorrect solutions long ago," with the result that now he was a "prisoner" of the splitter group of Brillakis— allegedly "behind Mr. Papandreou"—and was acting "according to [Brillakis's] indications and desires." ("Voice of Truth," 30 April.) Somewhat similarly, the pro-Koliyannis PAM Central Committee commented that the proposals and positions formulated by Theodorakis represented his personal views and were neither consistent with the PAM program nor binding upon PAM (*ibid.*, 11 May).

The KKE also reiterated (*ibid.*) that the party did not aim at monopolizing the struggle, but was ready to come to agreement for common action with other antidictatorial parties and organizations. The KKE continued, however, to insist on having a role of ideological leadership in the resistance. Its traditional inflexibility toward, and refusal to accommodate, noncommunist resisters were clearly present in an article by Politburo member Leonidas Stringos in *Pravda* on 18 April. The October Revolution and Lenin's ideas, he wrote, had opened up new prospects for the revolutionary working-class and national liberation movement in Greece where, today, the KKE was the "soul, organizer, and leader of the movement against dictatorship." The KKE was following the teaching of Lenin on the unity of the party as the most important prerequisite for the unity of all the antidictatorial forces, for the success of the party's struggle at the head of the masses, for the overthrow of the dictatorship and for ensuring democratic ways of development for Greece. This unity, Stringos concluded, must rely on principles of Marxism-Leninism and proletarian internationalism.

The Soviet report on Theodorakis's press conference, broadcast by TASS on 30 April, evidently sought to minimize the disunity between Koliyannis and the widely popular Theodorakis. It focused upon his denunciation of U.S. policy on Greece and his appeal for a united antigovernment front. The Soviets apparently chose to overlook both Theodorakis's criticism of communist-bloc countries for maintaining diplomatic relations with Greece and his concern lest continuing Soviet support of what he called the "dogmatic and less progressive elements" of the KKE could cause the KKE to become alienated from those in Greece who wished to be friends of the Soviet Union. Broadcasts from East Europe, however, hinted that Theodorakis's liberation must have been the result of some agreement with the junta, and Koliyannis supporters within the KKE and EDA attacked Theodorakis as politically inconsistent and as an opportunist bent on increasing his personal wealth.

Dissension over implementation of the PAM program soon paralyzed early prospects for collaboration. PAK issued a five-point counterprogram on 15 May which, in direct contrast to the PAM appeal, called for armed struggle. The program, specifically, urged the "rapid and energetic organization of commando units to deal a blow to the government through armed resistance." Cooperation among resistance movements, further, could be effected only among "organized groups backing political parties as such and not as individual political figures"—implying that PAK would cooperate only with movements that accepted its aims and methods. Papandreou also challenged PAM to publicly "clarify" its official position on the nature of the struggle; the response, he indicated, would determine the prospects for cooperation between PAM and PAK. In view of the fragmentation of communist and other resistance forces, it seemed that Papandreou was looking toward ultimate personal leadership of the resistance—a frequent KKE allegation. His call did not evoke the hoped-for support, however, and his program of violence appeared to alienate many within both his own organization and Democratic Defense.

Theodorakis, in an attempt to gain support following his 29 April statement, held talks in Rome with Luigi Longo of the Italian Communist Party, in Belgrade with Tito, and in Romania with Ceauşescu. (Brillakis, Drakopoulos, and Nikos Karras, a leading EDA member, had met with the Romanian leader in Bucharest on 31 March.) At a press conference in Belgrade on 17 May, Theodorakis rejected Papandreou's call for armed action, which he described as a "very serious matter, with serious responsibilities." Proposing "other means of overthrowing the colonels" without recourse to this "last resort" he advocated "mass struggle" combined with "dynamic action," which would include bombings and other acts of sabotage by organized groups to "paralyze the regime's security apparatus." Theodorakis criticized the exiled leadership under Koliyannis, and protested that only the Koliyannis faction had been invited to participate in the conference of West European communist parties which convened in Paris on 15-17 May to coordinate movements of solidarity and aid for the people of Vietnam, Cambodia, and Laos. It was "regrettable," he declared, that "the parties which the Greek people honor because they support their struggle, have accepted that Greece be represented by a group which defames our resistance and tends to divide PAM and break the unity of the antidictatorial forces." (*Le Monde*, 19 May.)

Another EDA spokesman, Markos Dragoumis, who represented the anti-Koliyannis faction of PAM on a visit to Australia in May, declared that the resistance would inevitably take the form of violent confrontation, adding: "We can see no other means left to us" (*Tribune*, 6 May). The struggle would be adapted to the situation in Greece, he explained, and would rely on a mass movement using "specific forms of violence"—especially in the cities, where it was "easier"—against the "central nervous system" of the junta. There would be no civil war as such, he said, because the "democratic forces" did not command sufficient support to evoke one. They would concentrate, rather, on violence against property and military installations, including U.S. bases.

Shortly thereafter at least one Western communist party gave signs that it was reconsidering its position. On 8 June the French Communist Party newspaper *L'Humanité*, which up to then had refrained from publishing controversial items of the conflicting groups, gave prominence to an appeal signed by Manolis Glezos and five other imprisoned EDA leaders of the anti-Koliyannis faction. Three days later *P.C.B. Informations*, the organ of the Communist Party of Belgium, followed suit. (Glezos has frequently advocated the dissolution of the KKE and its replacement by the EDA.)

PAM and PAK delegations were to have met in Stockholm in June in a bid to reconcile major differences and to arrive at an agreement for future action, but what appeared to be a power struggle between Papandreou and Theodorakis caused plans for this meeting (as well as a subsequent one between PAM, PAK, and Democratic Defense leader George Mylonas) to collapse. It was not until 6 September that the PAM-PAK meeting took place, in Paris. Various resistance leaders blamed Papandreou for the scuttling of the June meeting. He was said to have claimed that he alone had the right to represent the noncommunist left in Greece, and to have demanded the merger of the Democratic Defense with his organization as a prerequisite to the meeting with PAM. (*L Monde*, 16 September.) Theodorakis and Papandreou met again on 10 September, this time in Stockholm, where they reportedly held talks with, among others, officials of the ruling Swedish Social Democratic Party (*Sverige Nytt*, Stockholm, 15 September).

Before these meetings there were Soviet appeals to Theodorakis to reconcile his differences with Koliyannis. Theodorakis arrived with his family in the Soviet Union on 7 August, ostensibly for medical treatment at the invitation of the Soviet Composers' Union and the Soviet "Committee for Solidarity with Greek Democrats." A meeting in his honor was held in Moscow on 10 August by the Composers' Union. The next day Theodorakis reportedly told the Committee for Solidarity with Greek Democrats that the Soviet government's call for his release had played a positive role. The Komsomol presented him with a prize "for songs of courage and freedom calling youth to struggle against oppression, against fascism, for a better future." (TASS, 7, 10, 11 and 24 August.) Upon his return to Paris, Theodorakis told a press conference that in talks with CPSU and Komsomol representatives he had stressed "the needs of the Greek resistance [and] the necessity of maintaining an objective attitude and aiding, from all points of view and without discrimination, all Greek communists struggling against the military junta" (*L'Unità*, Rome, 8 September).

The honors bestowed upon Theodorakis—and the fact that he received a hearing in Moscow—suggested that the Soviets, having failed to check him, might choose to adjust their outward attitude to him and, by implication, to the many whose sentiments he appears to represent. A Soviet shift to a position of neutralism is indicated, however, rather than any disavowal of the loyal Koliyannis group. Several communist parties appeared to be looking to Moscow for signs of a possible shift—particularly in view of the increasing contrast between the Soviets' accommodation of Theodorakis and Koliyannis's intolerance of him—and in the meantime, with the notable exception of the Italian party, to be attempting to maintain an impartial stance. Some parties have not openly acknowledged the schism within the KKE, perhaps seeking in this way not only to protect their own position against any eventuality, but also to encourage reunification. This strategy was typically evident in the Australian party, which was visited during 1970 by Antonis Ambatielos, representing Koliyannis, and by Markos Dragoumis, of the rival group. Both were warmly received and given favorable coverage in the party organ.

A statement by the KKE Central Committee ("Voice of Truth," 20 September) declared that during Theodorakis's stay in the Soviet Union the KKE leadership "tried to see Theodorakis in order to convince him, even now, to discontinue his splitting activities to the detriment of the party and the unity of the antidictatorial forces," and that he initially agreed to a meeting, but subsequently "reneged . . . after direct intervention by and under the guidance of the leaders of the splitters group." Theodorakis was said also to have refused to meet with representatives of the Lambrakis Democratic Youth and the EDA, "despite his insistence upon retaining the title of president of the Lambrakis organization." Assailing Theodorakis's "pretensions" of having discussed with CPSU representatives and other Soviet personalities "topics of Greek resistance and domestic problems," the Central Committee criticized the "splitters group" for disseminating these "false reports" and charged that the group was "clinging to the composer's name, using it as a life belt."

The rivalry between the two KKE factions was vividly illustrated at the level of their youth movements, both of which were represented at the executive meeting of the World Federation of Democratic Youth (WFDY) in Katowice, Poland, on 16-21 May. The pro-Koliyannis KNE was represented by Yiannis Yiannakos, the dissidents' DNL by Theodoros Pangalos. KNE affiliation in the WFDY was unanimously adopted, with the exception of Pangalos's vote. Pangalos walked out of the meeting and issued a statement attacking the KKE and the KNE, and "even going so far as to provoke the Voice of Truth radio station by naming the place of its location." ("Voice of Truth," 4 June.)

International Views and Positions. Unreservedly pro-Soviet in foreign affairs, the KKE points to the United States as the source of every major threat to world peace. The party calls for the withdrawal of Greece from NATO and for the annulment of Greek treaties with the United States. U.S. "imperialism" and NATO are seen as being bent on destroying the independence of Cyprus, conspiring to dominate the eastern Mediterranean area, and seeking to suppress the democratic aspirations of the people of the region for the continuing benefit of U.S. and West European "monopoly capitalism." The United States is also seen by the party as being intent upon bringing about a compromise between the "junta" and King Constantine so as to "legitimize" the "fascist dictatorship."

The KKE praised the Council of Europe for allegedly bringing about the resignation of Greece from that body. (Greece, in danger of being expelled for alleged violation of human rights, had chosen to resign in December 1969.) This development, according to a Politburo resolution, reflected broad international solidarity with the Greek people, greater isolation for the government, and new opportunities for unity among "antidictatorial forces." The United States was said to have attempted to minimize the importance of the event by announcing, simultaneously, its resumption of heavy arms shipments to Greece, which was thus "increasingly entwined in the clutches of U.S. imperialism." Expelled from Libya, the United States was depicted as using Greece all the more as a transit site for conveying heavy arms to Israel and as an advance post for its "occupationist" plans against Arab socialist countries. ("Voice of Truth," 6 February.)

A later Politburo resolution (*ibid.*, 11 September) hailed the Soviet-West German treaty and praised the West German government for its "realistic evaluation of the border situation in Europe." The treaty, according to the KKE, would contribute to a relaxation of tension and create more favorable conditions for an all-European security conference. Although the signing of the agreement had not quelled the "aggressive aims of West German imperialism," it was seen as demonstrating that the Soviet Union and the whole socialist camp constituted the "bastion of world peace and security." The Middle East cease-fire agreement, between the U.A.R. and Jordan on the one hand and Israel on the other, was similarly said to be the result of persistent efforts by the Soviet Union which had "forced the U.S. to propose the cease-fire."

The visit to Greece in October by U.S. Defense Secretary Melvin Laird was said by the Politburo to have "further revealed the danger of Greece's becoming one of the first victims of the military adventurism of the U.S. and NATO." The "abundant" U.S. and British naval presence in Greek ports and U.S.-Greek maneuvers in the area together suggested that military preparations were taking place. The NATO command allegedly was to prepare Greece for a possible conflict in southeastern Europe under an arrangement in which the Americans "put down the dollars and Greece gives the blood." The junta, as a willing tool, had granted NATO new facilities for the installation of naval, air, and telecommunication bases. (*Ibid.*, 9 October.) The party subsequently charged that U.S. aircraft were taking off from Crete to carry out reconnaissance missions as far as the U.A.R., while Greek ports had become the "permanent mooring bases for vessels of the U.S. 6th Fleet" and Greek airports the "springboard bases for U.S. military aircraft" (*ibid.*, 22 October).

NATO activities in the Mediterranean were claimed by the KKE to constitute only one facet of three-pronged psychological offensive of "imperialist" forces—in the Mediterranean by a show of force directed against the U.S.S.R. and other socialist countries, in Central Europe by NATO maneuvers near the Czechoslovak border, and near the Soviet Union's far eastern borders by Japanese military exercises (*ibid.*, 23 October).

On the Cyprus issue, the KKE, like the Cypriot communist party, AKEL, has deemphasized the purely Greek goal of enosis—the union of Cyprus with Greece. Currently professing to uphold the independence of the island, the KKE sees the chief threat to Cypriot independence in the "NATO plans which served the imposition of a coup in Greece" and which "also relate to Cyprus." Thus it opposes any bid by President Makarios of Cyprus to mediate differences existing between King Constantine and the Greek government, and insists that "the way out for Cyprus, as for Greece, is to overthrow the junta, not to come to an agreement with it." (*Ibid.*, 5 January.) The attempted assassination of Makarios on 8 March was denounced by the KKE Politburo as "part of a plot woven a long time ago against the independence, integrity, and security of Cyprus." This "new provocation against the Cypriot people and against peace in the Mediterranean," it said, was inspired by the "dark espionage services of the American Pentagon and NATO," with "agents of the junta who [were] cooperating with reaction in Cyprus as their instruments"; specifically, Greek army officers and the outlawed Cypriot National Front terrorist organization were said to have been implicated in the assassination attempt. Allegedly, the U.S.-NATO aim was to aggravate the situation in Cyprus so as to provide a pretext for intervention and the ultimate transformation of the island into a "military base and springboard for their aggressive plans in the Middle and Near East." (*Ibid.*, 10 March.) It was suggested subsequently (*ibid.*, 30 April) that a number of "junta agent officers" had been dispatched to Cyprus to plan the killing of both Makarios and former Interior Minister Polycarpos Yiorkatzis. (Yiorkatzis was murdered on 15 March, and had been under suspicion in the attempt against Makarios.) A further KKE charge was that the United States was arming Turkish Cypriot terrorists to incite unrest on the island (*ibid.*, 23 October).

The Koliyannis faction, in its theses for the party's Ninth Congress, renewed its endorsement of the 1968 intervention in Czechoslovakia by Warsaw Pact forces as "an act of supreme internationalist solidarity" necessitated by "imperialist" exploitation of difficulties within the international communist camp. The 1969 Moscow Conference was termed the "most significant event in the history of the world communist and workers' movement": the basic document adopted by the conference had provided the basis for the cohesion and common action of all anti-imperialist forces for peace, and developments since the conference had affirmed the correctness of the decisions passed. The KKE condemned rightist and leftist deviations, and the "splittist and adventurist activities of the Mao Tse-tung group."

Publications. The central organs of the KKE, the newspaper *Rizospastis* and the theoretical journal *Neos Kosmos*, are published outside Greece. There are several party newspapers for Greek exiles living in socialist-bloc countries: *Elefteria* (Bulgaria), *Dimokratis* (Poland), *Laikos Agon* (Hungary), and *Neos Dromos* (Tashkent, U.S.S.R.). Clandestine publications within Greece are *Adhouloti Athina*, the organ of the Athens branch; *Rizospastis*, a domestic edition of the party's central organ; and *Odhiyiti*, issued by the KKE's youth group. The KKE operates a radio station, "Voice of Truth," thought to be located in Leipzig, East Germany. The Brillakis faction in Rome and the Ambatielos faction in Paris each publishes its own version of the EDA organ *Eleftheri Patrida*. In Greece, the pro-Koliyannis faction of PAM publishes *Lefteria*. The Partsalides group's pamphlets *Enotita* and *Alithia*, and its newspaper *Agonistis*, formerly published in Czechoslovakia, were suppressed in early 1970. Other organs of the dissidents include *O Mahitis* and *Rizospastes-Makhetes*, both issued clandestinely in Greece.

V. B.

ICELAND

The original communist party in Iceland was formed in 1930 by the secessionist left wing of the Social Democratic Party. In 1938 it absorbed a radical group of Social Democrats and became the United People's Party-Socialist Party (UPP-SP). The date of this reorganization, 24 October 1938, has since been regarded by the communists as the official founding date of their party. In 1965 the UPP-SP, some left-wing elements, and the small National Opposition Party joined in an electoral front called the Labor Alliance. In November 1968 the front became a "Marxist political party" under communist leadership, the UPP-SP was formally dissolved, and the new party was designated the Labor Alliance (LA).

With the dissolution of the front, however, the Icelandic communist movement split into three mainstreams: the LA; the Organization of Liberals and Leftists (OLL), comprising mostly noncommunist elements of the Labor Alliance front; and the Organization of Icelandic Socialists (OIS), formed in 1969 by hard-line, pro-Moscow elements who defected from the communist party in 1968. Membership figures have been closely guarded by the three new parties, each of which claims to represent Icelandic communists, but the LA is believed to have retained by far the largest share of the some 1,000 former UPP-SP members. The population of Iceland is 203,500 (estimated 1970), with 81,500 in Reykjavík.

Enjoying legal status since the inception of their party, the communists have twice been represented in the government—in the 1944-47 postwar coalition, and in 1956-58 under the front of the Labor Alliance. In the latest parliamentary elections (June 1967) the LA received 17.6 per cent of the vote—up 1.6 from 1963—and gained one seat for a total of 10 of the 60 parliamentary seats. In the 31 May 1970 municipal elections, the LA received 14.3 per cent of the total vote (compared with 16.7 per cent in 1966); the OLL received 6.2 per cent; and the OIS (which ran only in Reykjavik and gained no seats) received 0.6 per cent.

Although the LA lost some ground in the municipal elections, the combined vote of the far left parties increased from 16.7 per cent (in 1966) to 21.1 per cent, largely at the expense of the Social Democrats. A continuation of this trend in the June 1971 parliamentary elections could jeopardize the decade-old Independence Party-Social Democratic coalition government.

Leadership and Organization. *The LA.* Chairman of the Labor Alliance is Ragnar Arnalds, who was elected in November 1968 to succeed long-time UPP-SP leader Einar Olgeirsson. The party's vice-chairman is a woman, Adda Bára Sigfúsdóttir, and its secretary-general is Gudjón Jónsson, head of the Metal Workers' Union of Reykjavík. Perhaps the most powerful figure in the party is Magnus Kjartansson, member of the 30-member Central Committee and editor of the party organ, *Thjodviljinn.* Party congresses are held every third year, and party conferences in intervening years. Twenty-seven Central Committee members and 10 deputies are elected each year, while the three remaining Central Committee members—the chairman, vice-chairman, and secretary—hold three-year terms between congresses. The 1970 conference, held on 23-25 October, elected a Political Committee comprising Lúdvík Jósefsson, Magnus Kjartansson, Edvard Sigurdsson, Hulda Sigurbjornsdóttir, Olafur Jónsson, Olafur Einarsson, and Karl Sigurbergsson. The seven-man lower house parliamentary group, headed by Jósefsson, includes Kjartansson, Sigurdsson, Geir Gunnarsson, Steingrímur Pálsson, Jónas Árnason, and Sigurvin Einarsson. An eighth, Karl Gudjonsson, a thirty-year veteran of the party, defected in October 1970. Retaining his seat in the 20-member upper house despite LA attempts to replace him, Gudjonsson appeared to be wavering between the Social Democratic Party (SDP) and the OLL—whose two principal leaders, Hannibal Valdimarsson and Bjorn Jónsson, account for the remaining two seats received by the LA in the 1967 election.

The OLL. Commonly referred to as the "Hannibalists," the OLL was established 29 May 1969, two years after Hannibal Valdimarsson had first tested his personal strength by entering a rival slate in the 1967 election while still chairman of the Labor Alliance front. The slate polled 3.7 per cent but was adjudged by electoral authorities and parliament to be a component of the LA; the parliamentary mandate it won was therefore credited to the LA. Valdimarsson had resigned his chairmanship of the SDP in 1956 to head the LA front. Bjorn Jónsson, a co-founder of the OLL, holds a seat in the upper house, while Valdimarsson sits in the 40-member lower house. Afred Gislason, a third co-founder of the OLL, appeared at the end of 1970 to be in serious disagreement with Valdimarsson and Jonsson.

The OIS. Chairman of the OIS is Steingrímur Adalsteinnson. Other leading figures include Hafsteinn Einarsson, Drifa Vidar, Orn Fridriksson, Sigurjon Jónsson, Sigridur Fridriksdóttir, Gunnlaugur Einarsson, Gylfi Gudjonsson, Thorgeir Einarsson, and Edda Gudmundsdóttir—all of whom, with Adalsteinsson, constituted the OIS slate of candidates in the 1970 municipal elections (*Visir*, Reykjavík, 20 April).

On 15 January the OIS moved—by a fairly narrow margin of 50 to 37—to expel, effective 1 February, those of its members who were at the same time members of other political organizations—clearly implying the LA (*Thjodviljinn*, 17 January).

Mass Organizations. The LA continued to have a larger trade union following than any other party, although its influence at the top was considerably weakened in 1968 when Hannibal Valdimarsson and Bjorn Jónsson were reelected chairman and vice-chairman, respectively, of the powerful Icelandic Federation of Labor (IFL), which represents some 85 per cent of Iceland's 43,000 organized workers. Edvard Sigurdsson, the defeated LA condidate, continued to head the largest single union, Dagsbrún—the General Workers' Union in Reykjavík.

The schisms in the communist leadership rapidly filtered down to the party's youth elements. The main auxiliary—the Socialist Youth League of Iceland (SYLI), known also as the "Youth Battalion"—is headed by Ragnar Stefansson. It has branded the post-Olgeirsson leadership of the communist party as ideologically "soft." At its Twenty-fifth Congress, on 2-3 October 1970, the SYLI made a bid for autonomy, removing the age limit on the membership, changing the organization's name to "The Brigade, the Fighting Unit of Socialists," and declaring that only active members would be retained and that the 15-member Central Committee would henceforth comprise mainly workers (*Thjodviljinn*, 6 October). The Brigade may be ideologically closer to the OIS—which exempted members of the youth affiliate from its "purge" of LA elements—but, for the time being, appears to be pressing for independence and freedom of activity.

Those communist youths remaining loyal to the LA elected a provisional board in June, declaring that the SYLI would be reorganized. Members of the provisional board were: Agust Petursson, Eyjolfur Emilsson, Gestur Gudmundsson, Gudmundur Gudmundsson, Jon Jensson, Kristin Benediktsdóttir, Pall Halldorsson, Stefan Unnsteinsson, Tryggvy Adalsteinsson, and Orn Eliasson. (*Ibid.*, 28 June.)

Other organizations believed to be under communist control include the Iceland-U.S.S.R. Association and the Cultural and Peace Society of Icelandic Women, which in 1970 collected funds toward a health center projected by the Women's International Democratic Federation.

Domestic Views and Activities. The communists continued in 1970 their three-pronged bid to weaken the government coalition of the Independence Party (IP) and the SDP—pressing for cooperation with the SDP; exploiting IP-SDP rivalry; and, particularly on economic questions, joining with the opposition Progressive Party (PP) in assailing joint government policies.

The LA charged in January that unemployment (officially put at 2,542 persons as of the end of 1969) could no longer be blamed on external circumstances, inasmuch as the national economy had recovered during 1969 (*Thjodviljinn*, 8 January). Not only had the government economic policies led to an intolerable unemployment situation, but also to what the LA termed "forced emigration." Gudmundur Gudmundsson, vice-chairman of Dagsbrún, wrote in the union paper that were the present "low income era" prolonged, still larger numbers could be expected to emigrate (quoted, *ibid.*, 11 January). The government, it was alleged, had failed to provide incentives to avert the emigration, in 1969, of some 1,000 Icelanders—a development which, relatively, any other nation would have regarded as a "national disaster" (*ibid.*, 6 February). Magnus Kjartansson introduced a parliamentary resolution providing for financial support to Icelanders who had emigrated to Australia and were unable to return for financial reasons (*ibid.*, 25 April).

The LA alleged, further, that the government had for years tried to make the labor movement "a kind of subdepartment in the bureaucracy," and that it had been "loyally assisted in this by Hannibal Valdimarsson and Bjorn Jónsson." The four devaluations of the Icelandic kronur carried out by the present government (the latest in 1968) should be a "lesson to labor," said the LA, that victory in wage negotiations was not enough; the influence of the radical labor movement in the "power institutions" must be increased. (*Ibid.*, 24, 27 January.)

Valdimarsson and Jónsson were also attacked by the LA for supporting Iceland's entry (effective 1 March 1970) into the European Free Trade Association (EFTA). The communists had vigorously opposed EFTA affiliation, but had been unable to dissuade the PP from abstaining on the final parliamentary vote after the PP's own bill, calling for a delay on the question of EFTA membership, failed. (*Timinn*, Reykjavik, 11 January.)

A government bill that resulted in an increase in the sales tax from 8.5 to 11 per cent (on which the OLL had proposed a compromise 9.5 per cent) was said by the LA to be a "direct consequence of EFTA membership" and "only the first of an inevitable new wave of price increases" —a prospect which the labor movement was urged to take into consideration when presenting its wage demands upon the expiry in May of existing contracts (accounting for some 30,000 wage-earners, nearly two-thirds of the organized work force) (*Thjodviljinn*, 30, 31 January). As the talks became deadlocked, labor was urged not to accept any long-term contracts with clauses providing for future percentage increases, but to press for "immediate results" (*ibid.*, 16 May). Unable to reach accord with the employers' federation, the Dagsbrún executive on 15 May unanimously authorized a strike, to commence on 27 May. Other unions followed suit, and a general strike lasted through several weeks of bargaining until new wage agreements were concluded in June.

Political expediency with a view to the municipal elections prompted the divided communists to agree to cooperative talks. In the maneuvering which ensued, however, the prospects for cooperation became progressively more remote, so that three rival slates—LA, OLL, and OIS—were eventually presented. The OIS's decision to offer its own slate represented, ideologically, a far more severe blow to the communist movement in Iceland than the secession, two years earlier, of the Hannibalists, who, unlike the hard core of the OIS, had never been doctrinaire communists.

In its post-election commentary the LA charged that the IP had enhanced its electoral position by making unrealizable promises to workers, including the revaluation upward by 10 per cent of the Icelandic kronur and a simultaneous 7 per cent wage increase. Not until 4 June—after the election—had the government released data which revealed that the position of the export industries was so precarious as to be barely able to support the wage increases (15-18 per cent, compared with labor's initial demands of up to 25 per cent) already agreed upon some days earlier (*ibid.*, 6 June). Moreover, the LA charged, the false propaganda of its opponents—to the effect that the communist movement was split into three "equally large" groups—had "no doubt led to the defection of many LA supporters." The electoral victory of the LA and the success of LA labor leaders in the collective bargaining showed, the party asserted, that the LA and the labor movement were indivisible and that the LA could become the decisive force in Icelandic politics. (Editorial, *ibid.*, 26 June.)

As a result of the elections, there were eleven town councils in which no one party held a clear majority, and in which coalitions were formed. Three of these coalitions included the LA—in Akranes, with the PP, SDP, and OLL; and in Isafjordur and the Westman Islands, where the LA continued in coalition with the PP and the SDP (*Timinn*, 30 June). In Reykjavík the LA was left with only two of the 15 municipal council seats, as against four before the split. The OLL received one seat in Reykjavík.

On 4 September the LA Central Committee declared that a joint assault was being made by government and industry to undermine labor's gains, and that workers must resist all attempts by "reactionaries" to amend the labor relations act in any way which would reduce the negotiating and strike rights (*Thjodviljinn*, 8 September). Sigurdsson subsequently accused the government of answering moderate wage increases with close to 30 per cent price increases with its price-freeze bill (*ibid.*, 11 November). The bill was enacted at the end of November despite an IFL ultimatum that it would consider the June wage agreements void in that event (*ibid.*, 12 November).

At the behest of the SDP and with a view to the 1971 parliamentary elections (the date for which was not yet fixed), meetings followed between the SDP and LA, on 30 October, 27 November, and 3 December, and—apparently more frequently—between the SDP, OLL, and Karl Gudjonsson, the OLL and Gudjonsson refusing to attend any joint meeting which included the LA. The talks were hampered throughout, moreover, by the protracted parliamentary debates on the price-freeze bill—to which the LA, the OLL, and Gudjonsson, were all opposed. Finally, on 9 December, a joint meeting was held with all the negotiating parties present—in all, 19 members of parliament. SDP leader Gylfi Gislason said in a television interview after the meeting that it was the ultimate aim of his party to "join all social democrats into one large party" (*Morgunbladid*, Reykjavík, 10 December). This and other indications suggested the possibility that the OLL, and even the communist Gudjonsson, might join forces with the SDP, but there seemed little likelihood that the LA would become a party to such a merger—which would, in effect, mean the dissolution of the communist party.

At year's end the OLL was attempting to strengthen its hand by wooing the Progressive Party's Federation of Young Progressives, a substantial segment of which was believed to be dissatisfied with the parent party's policies. The PP urged its youth group to remain loyal, and declared that Valdimarsson, "in the name of leftist unity," had already split the two political parties (the SDP and Labor Alliance) which he had headed, and was now bent on "further uniting the leftists by splitting more parties." In sum, the conservative groups had "much to thank Hannibal for" (*Timinn*, 25 November).

In other developments, the LA was the only party to uphold a proliferation of student disruptions triggered by eleven Icelandic students who on 19 April temporarily occupied the Icelandic

Embassy in Stockholm, protesting "inadequate" state aid (*Althydubladid*, 20 April). Magnus Kjartansson said in parliament on 20 April that responsibility for the incident must be borne by "men in this room." The government and parliament, he said, had ignored the "just demands" of Icelandic students. (*Morgunbladid*, 21 April.) The SYLI in Reykjavík distributed to news media a statement received from the eleven, whose demands, in addition to financial aid, reflected political goals closely aligned with those of the communists. On 24 April some 100 young persons staged a sit-in at the Ministry of Education in Reykjavík, raised a red flag, and distributed a statement supporting the "Stockholm Eleven" and declaring their objective to be the seizure of power in Iceland by workers (*Thjodviljinn*, 25 April). The following day some 100 students staged simultaneous protests at Icelandic embassies in Stockholm, Oslo, Copenhagen, and Paris. The LA adjudged it a victory when, in July, appropriations to students were increased, but demanded that economic equality in higher education be assured by the establishment of an "active study-wages system" (*ibid.*, 18 July).

The LA, OLL, SYLI, OIS, Federation of Young Progressives, and Federation of Young Social Democrats all participated in a conference on "Iceland's Route to Socialism—Leftist Cooperation," sponsored by the leftist student association "Verdandi" on 18-19 July (*ibid.*, 21 July. There was reportedly little agreement at the meeting, but the participants did agree to hold another conference in the near future. The Young Progressives subsequently advocated a comprehensive leftist alliance against the "principal enemy, the conservative elements" (*Timinn*, 1 September). Despite such seeming leftist trends among Icelandic youth, however, there had been negligible support for the SYLI's proposal, in February, that the National Council of Icelandic Youth—which had just moved to resign from the World Assembly of Youth in criticism of alleged subsidies to that organization from the U.S. Central Intelligence Agency—seek affiliation in the communist-front World Federation of Democratic Youth (*Thjodviljinn*, 3 March).

International Views and Activities. The LA continued to call for Iceland's neutrality and independence, for an end to the "U.S. occupation" of Iceland, and for total withdrawal from the NATO alliance. The majority of Icelanders, the party alleged, did not know what it was to live in an unoccupied country, since the excessive influence of the United States and NATO had blunted national sentiment and encouraged Icelandic citizens to regard the occupation as a "normal situation" (*Thjodviljinn*, 10 May).

The party waged an active campaign against EFTA membership. The government's arguments in favor of affiliation were described by the party as evidence of its dedication to foreign capitalists—who, the LA insisted, must not be regarded as the "saviors of Icelandic industry" (*ibid.*, 30 January and 3 February). A party editorial (*ibid.*, 4 July) declared that Iceland's membership had proved to be only an "anteroom" to the European Economic Community (EEC). While the government had not yet revealed its intentions, the LA declared that the nation "knew from bitter experience" that the government's recent request for talks with the EEC, notwithstanding any assurances to the contrary, could ultimately lead to EEC membership.

The LA (which itself had taken no firm position on the question) criticized the administration for not having participated in the discussions with Sweden, Denmark, Norway, and Finland for a "Nordek" economic union. Lúdvik Jósefsson said while it was clear that Iceland could not join Nordek under present conditions, the government should not delay in seeking "special agreements" with it. (*Ibid.*, 6 and 7 February.) The ministers' "lack of interest" in Nordek, the party alleged, stemmed from their complacency in the role of "pawns in the chess match of the superpowers," in contrast with the "independent Swedish foreign policy" (*ibid.*, 14 February).

Another question on which the government was attacked by the communists was its alleged neglect of the question of territorial waters. The time was "long overdue," the LA asserted, for

Icelanders to oppose bids by the United States and the U.S.S.R. to impose a permanent twelve-mile international limit. The party called for a policy to extend Iceland's territorial waters to include the continental shelf and join forces with other nations seeking to defend their like interests. Such a move, it was argued, would supersede and invalidate any former "forced" agreement to submit to the arbitration of "foreign courts." (*Ibid.*, 24 September and 18 October.)

Exploiting anti-U.S. sentiment over the permanent U.S. air base at Keflavík, the party continued in 1970 to propagandize for liquidation of the installation. Iceland, it declared, had been "locked into" NATO so as to make the U.S. "occupation" permanent. Were the occupation ended, "nobody would be interested in Iceland's membership in NATO." (*Ibid.*, 18 September.) The party organized a demonstration on 10 May, marking "thirty years of occupation by foreign forces," and the SYLI sponsored a "celebration" of U.S. Independence Day (4 July) outside the Keflavík base. In most instances, anti-U.S. and antiwar activities were merged, as, for example, in the 10 May demonstration when several members of the Vietnam Movement, an antiwar group, were arrested for distributing pamphlets at the base urging servicemen to organize against the "criminal acts of the Nixon administration" and to refuse to participate in them (*ibid.*, 12 May).

Communists are active in, but do not control, the Vietnam Movement, which is the best organized antiwar group and is made up of a broad range of political elements. The LA newspaper gives prominence to the movement's activities, as, for example, when parliament member Jónas Árnason and SYLI leader Ragnar Stefansson were among the principal speakers at a meeting on 2 May in protest against the U.S. incursion into Cambodia. In its coverage of the meeting, the paper made no mention of the incidents of violence that erupted, but alleged that moral responsibility for the "crimes" in Indochina lay not only with the U.S., but with all governments that were in a military alliance. Thus, the "genocides" in Southeast Asia were also an "Icelandic domestic affair." (*Ibid.*, 5 and 6 May.)

As in previous years, the LA rarely took a position on international events that did not directly affect Iceland. This was not true of communist youth elements, however, who generally involved themselves more in developments abroad than in what they apparently saw as the isolationism of Icelandic politics. Thus, while communist youth groups were engaged in organizing opposition to the Vietnam war, the LA was much more concerned with pressing for resumption of salt-fish trading with Cuba, which had ceased with the 1961 crisis—allegedly out of "imaginary or real service to U.S. foreign policy" (*ibid.*, 28 February).

The exception was international communist affairs, in which the party until 1968 maintained an isolationist posture, avoiding important meetings and disassociating itself from ideological schisms. Under the current leadership, the party has adopted a far less impartial attitude, particularly with regard to Soviet policies. It has, for example, expressed continuing condemnation of the Soviet-led intervention in Czechoslovakia in 1968 and of Soviet activities there since. The strongest attacks appearing in *Thjodviljinn* are penned by Magnus Kjartansson—as, for example, in an editorial in the issue of 21 August, the second anniversary of the invasion. Kjartansson declared that for two years Czechoslovakia had lived under the oppression of a foreign power, its leaders had been undemocratically removed, and normal social activity and free debate had been precluded. These events, he continued, bore tragic witness to how far the superpowers (i.e., the U.S. and the U.S.S.R.) would go in order to ensure their spheres of interest, whether in Europe or Southeast Asia. Hence it was vital, finally, for small nations to end such power politics and for each to fight in its own forum. The contribution from Icelanders, for their own and other small nations' benefit, would be to eradicate foreign military bases and free Iceland from any military alliance.

Events in Czechoslovakia had constituted one of the main factors in the decision of the OIS to secede from the LA, inasmuch as the OIS accounts for the core of those with close connections to the Soviet party. The new LA leadership, in contrast, has been ignored in Moscow, although it is believed to have the sympathy of East German party leader Walter Ulbricht. In turn, the attendance by Brynolfur Bjarnason—a retired veteran leader of the Icelandic party, now identified with the OIS—at the April conference in Moscow commemorating the birth of Lenin, was not even reported by *Thjodviljinn*. The LA has been inconsistent, however, in its treatment of developments behind the Iron Curtain. Only two years after the invasion of Czechoslovakia, the party newspaper carried a series of articles from the Soviet news bureau Novosti describing the excellence of Soviet rule in the Baltic states. This prompted a member of *Thjodviljinn*'s editorial staff, Vesteinn Ludviksson, to complain in a contributed article to the paper on 7 October that too much Novosti material was carried by it. He wrote: "The objective of Novosti is to create that picture of the Soviet Union and its history which is approved by the power clique in command in the Kremlin."

Then, on 31 December, *Thjodviljinn* attacked Novosti for its "flood of foul words" in reporting the Leningrad hijacking trial. The Icelandic communists suggested that one reason why airplanes were being hijacked in the Soviet Union was "because of the absurd ruling which does not allow people to travel freely, at least not abroad. If people could buy their tickets instead of having to resort to hijacking, then the courts would have less to do."

International Party Contacts. The visit of a six-member LA delegation to Romania (5-14 September), comprising Gudmundur Gudmundsson, Gudrun Gudvardardóttir, Hulda Sigurbjornsdóttir, Ingi Helgason, Svandis Skuladóttir, and Svavar Gestsson (*Thjodviljinn*, 5 September) was a significant exception to the party's policy of avoiding formal contacts with Soviet and East European parties.

Magnus Kjartansson was one of three Icelandic members of parliament to attend the annual meeting of parliamentarians from the Baltic nations, Norway, and Iceland, in Rostock, East Germany, in July (*ibid.*, 8 July).

Publications. The central organ of the party is *Thjodviljinn*. A theoretical journal, *Ny Utsyn*, is published biweekly. A new journal, *Rettur*, commenced publication in February. The OIS paper is *Ny Dagsbrún*, edited by Hafsteinn Einarsson. *Neisti* is the organ of Brigade.

V. B.

IRELAND

The Communist Party of Ireland (CPI) was founded in 1921, but its initial existence appears to have been short lived. It was refounded in 1933—a date adopted by present Irish communists as the original year of the party's foundation. The organizational structure of the CPI was disrupted during the Second World War, partly as a result of the fact that the Republic of Ireland, in the south, declared itself neutral while Northern Ireland (a part of Great Britain) participated in the conflict. In 1948 the communists in the south founded the Irish Workers' Party (IWP) and those in the north the Communist Party of Northern Ireland (CPNI). While the two parties maintained separate organizations and held separate congresses, they had complementary programs and were united in a Joint National Council composed of representatives from their respective Executive Committees. At a special "Unity Congress" held in Belfast on 15 March 1970, the IWP and CPNI reunited, founding once again a united Communist Party of Ireland.

The CPI is estimated to have some 250 members—the total comprising about 100 in the north and 150 in the south. The population of the Republic of Ireland is nearly 3,000,000 and that of Northern Ireland about 1,500,000 (both estimated 1970).

The party has little influence in either the north or the south. In the latest elections to the national legislature in which the IWP participated (7 April 1965), it put up one candidate and polled 183 votes (0.01 per cent of the total). The IWP did not contend the elections on 18 June 1969. It has no seat in the legislature. The CPNI has not contended elections in recent years.

Leadership and Organization. The new Communist Party of Ireland's leading body—the Executive Committee—is divided into two branches representing the south and the north. At the party's founding congress in March 1970 the following were elected to the Executive Committee: northern branch—Andrew Barr, Brian Graham, James Graham, Hugh Moore, Sean Morrissey, Hugh Murphy, Edwina Stewart, James Stewart, Betty Sinclair, and Bill Somerset; southern branch—Joseph Deasy, George Jeffares, Patrick McCarthy, Sam Nolan, Sean Nolan, Michael O'Reilly, Michael O'Riordan, Sean O'Rourke, Geoffrey Palmer, and Aodh Rafferty. The Executive Committee met a week later and elected the following six-member Secretariat: Andrew Barr, Hugh Moore, Sam Nolan, Sean Nolan, Michael O'Riordan, and James Stewart. Michael O'Riordan was elected general secretary, while Andrew Barr became the party chairman. Before the reconstitution of the CPI, Michael O'Riordan and Sean Nolan were respectively general secretary and chairman of the IWP, and Hugh Moore and Andrew Barr held the same posts in the CPNI.

Views and Policies. The program of the CPI was outlined in a manifesto adopted at the March congress and entitled "For Unity and Socialism" (full text in *IB*, no. 15-16, 8 September 1970). The manifesto claims that "years of imperialist domination have stamped common fea-

207

tures on the two parts of Ireland," which is a "natural entity" and whose "people are one nation." It calls for "national unity and independence from imperialism as the essential basis for the construction of Socialism" in Ireland. In the attainment of this goal, the CPI emphasizes the "leading role of the working class," and commits the party to "develop still deeper its roots in the trade unions, the basic organizations of the working class."

In its pronouncements on international affairs, the manifesto expresses its opposition to the Irish-British Free Trade Agreement and to the European Economic Community. The party calls for a "declaration of an All-Ireland policy of independence, military neutrality and solidarity with all those fighting imperialism throughout the world." It refers to the existence of "powerful allies . . . whose interests are identical with those of the Irish people," stating that the principal ones are "the peoples of the 14 countries of Europe, Asia and Latin America who have swept capitalism aside under the leadership of Marxist-Leninist parties" and "with the Soviet Union to the fore among them."

Throughout 1970 the CPI continued to play only a very minor role in the political life of either the Republic of Ireland or Northern Ireland. In the south, according to statements made to the Trotskyist weekly *Intercontinental Press* (New York, 26 October) by John McGregor, secretary of the Trinity College Republican Club, the party had some influence in the Irish Transport and General Workers' Union, but "was not doing much with it." Mc Gregor also stated that the communists controlled the Connolly Youth Movement and an organization called the Irish Voice of Vietnam; the latter group, it was noted, had done "nothing very spectacular." In the north, the communists have played a minor role in the Civil Rights Association—a coalition of organizations supporting the rights of the Catholic minority in Northern Ireland and including in its ranks a number of "new left" and Trotskyist-oriented militants.[1] Only one communist party member, Betty Sinclair, has been active in the leadership of the association, and her participation appeared to decrease appreciably with the onset of violence in the civil strife. With regard to the conflict between Catholics and Protestants in Northern Ireland, the CPI repeatedly reiterated the contention expressed by Hugh Moore in 1969 that this was "most emphatically not a Protestant-Catholic confrontation" (see *YICA*, 1970, p. 208).

International Party Contacts. The IWP and the CPNI were represented at a meeting of communist parties in Moscow on 14-15 January. Foreign delegates at the CPI's founding congress in March came from communist parties of Bulgaria, France, Great Britain, Hungary, Romania, the Soviet Union, and Yugoslavia. The CPI was represented at the Lenin Centenary celebrations in Moscow on 21 April by Michael O'Riordan, who also represented the CPI at a meeting of West European communist parties in Paris on 15 May. The CPI was represented at a second meeting of European communist parties in Moscow on 20-21 October.

Publication. The CPI publishes an irregular journal, the *Irish Socialist*.

* * *

A very small pro-Chinese group is evident in the Republic of Ireland, called the Irish Communist Organization. In 1970 it published a weekly journal, *Communist Comment*, and a monthly theoretical review, *Irish Communist*. Membership estimates for this group in 1970 are not known. There was no evidence of a counterpart pro-Chinese group in Northern Ireland.

M. P.

---

[1] For a survey of the complex interaction of political groups active in the civil strife that has affected both northern and southern parts of Ireland since the autumn of 1968 see Iain Hamilton, "The Irish Tangle," *Conflict Studies*, London, no. 6, August 1970; see also, for the year 1970 and from a Trotskyist point of view, *Intercontinental Press*, New York, 6 and 13 April, 4 May, 22 June, 27 July, 28 September, 12 and 26 October, and 14 December 1970.

ITALY

The Italian Communist Party (Partito Comunista Italiano; PCI) was founded in 1921. In recent years the PCI has been confronted with marginal competition from a number of small parties and groups adhering to Marxism-Leninism of differing shades of interpretation. During 1970, while small groups of Maoist orientation continued to proliferate, the main challenge to the PCI's leadership within the extreme left appeared to originate from adherents to the views advocated by the monthly publication *Il Manifesto* (see below).

The PCI is the largest nonruling communist party in the world. On the last day of 1970 the party's newspaper, *L'Unità*, published the membership figures for that year, claiming 1,507,047 registered members. The PCI organ indicated that the total showed a net increase over 1969 of 3,171 members, claiming that party membership in 1969 had been 1,503,876.[1] *L'Unità* also stated that new recruits to the party in 1970 numbered 102,513. No figures were given for the PCI's youth organization—the Italian Communist Youth Federation (Federazione Giovanile Comunista Italiana; FGCI)—whose official membership has not been disclosed since 1967, when a two-thirds loss of the claimed 450,000 of 1950 was indicated. The PCI newspaper limited itself to affirming that the FGCI was showing the "beginning of a positive political recovery and organizational consolidation." The population of Italy is a little over 54,000,000 (estimated 1970).

In the May 1968 general elections for the Chamber of Deputies and the Senate, the PCI obtained 8,555,131 votes (26.9 per cent) and won 177 (out of 630) seats in the Chamber. It made an electoral alliance with the Italian Socialist Party of Proletarian Unity (Partito Socialista Italiano di Unità Proletaria; PSIUP) for the Senate elections; the combined votes totaled 8,580,813 (30 per cent), and the PCI won 87 seats (out of 322), while the PSIUP received 14. In the elections to the Chamber, the PSIUP obtained 1,414,043 votes (4.5 per cent) and obtained 14 seats. By the end of 1970 five former PCI deputies, having aligned themselves with the views of the aforementioned *Manifesto* group, had joined the "mixed group" in the Chamber, formed primarily of Alto-Adige independents and Autonomous Socialists.

The PCI and the PSIUP were the two major left-wing opposition parties to the center-left government coalition, consisting of (at the time of the 1968 elections) the Christian Democrat party (Democrazia Cristiana; DC), which obtained 266 seats in the Chamber and 135 in the Senate; the United Socialist Party (Partito Socialista Unificato; PSU), which obtained 91 seats in the Chamber and 46 in the Senate; and the Italian Republican Party (Partito Repubblicano Italiano; PRI), which obtained 9 seats in the Chamber and 2 in the Senate. In the summer of 1969 the PSU—comprising socialists from the Italian Socialist Party (Partito Socialista Italiano; PSI) and social-democrats from the Italian Social Democratic Party (Partito Socialista Democratico

---

[1] On 31 December 1969 *L'Unità* gave 1969 party membership as 1,503,181. The PCI has not offered any explanation for the differences in the end-1969 and end-1970 claims for 1969 membership. A partial explanation can possibly be found in the fact that when the 1970 membership campaign was launched in November 1969, it was stated that all new recruits would also be given the 1969 card, thus backdating their party membership. (See *L'Unità*, 14 and 16 November 1969.)

Italiano; PSDI), who had split in 1947 and united again in 1966—split again into more or less its two original components, leaving the PSI with 62 deputies and 36 senators, and the social-democrats, who retained the designation PSU, with 29 deputies and 10 senators. Following the PSU split, a minority DC government held power with parliamentary support from its erstwhile coalition partners.

On 7 February 1970 the DC government of Premier Mariano Rumor resigned. Faced with the task of forming a center-left coalition, Rumor on 28 February announced his decision to decline the attempt. He was followed by two other former premiers—Aldo Moro and Amintore Fanfani—who both attempted to form a government and failed. Rumor was requested to try again, and on 27 March he succeeded in forming a center-left government comprising the DC, PSI, PSU, and PRI. On 6 July Rumor resigned once again, and, following an unsuccessful attempt by Giulio Andreotti, another center-left government was formed by Emilio Colombo on 4 August, comprising the same four political formations.

The 1948 Italian constitution envisaged the setting up of twenty Regional Councils and Regional Juntas (the latter elected by the councils) vested with considerable legislative and executive autonomy. Four of these councils were formed in 1948 in the so-called "special statute" regions—the two islands of Sardinia and Sicily, and the two frontier regions of Val d'Aosta and Trentino-Alto Adige. Another frontier region, Friuli-Venezia Giulia, was added to the list in 1963. On 7 June 1970 elections were held for 690 Regional Council seats in the remaining fifteen "ordinary statute" regions. Of 30,915,561 registered voters, 27,225,530 participated in the elections.

The PCI registered a small loss in votes as compared with the results in these same areas during the 1968 general elections, from 7,643,705 (28 per cent) to 7,584,440 (27.9 per cent). With the exception of Piedmont, where the party received 25.9 per cent of the vote, representing a loss of 0.2 per cent, the PCI increased its vote in the industrialized regions of the north—Ligury (31.3, up 0.4), Lombardy (23.1, up 0.2), Emilia-Romagna (44.0, up 0.7), Venetia (16.8, up 0.1), and Tuscany (42.3, up 1.3)—and lost votes in the central and southern regions—Marches (31.8, down 0.4), Latium (26.5, down 1.1), Abruzzi (22.8, down 2.6), Molise (15.0, down 3.1), Campania (21.8, down 1.5), Apulia (26.3, down 0.9), Basilicata (24.0, down 2.1), and Calabria (23.3, down 0.6). In Umbria the PCI's vote of 41.8 per cent remained unchanged. The PCI's electoral ally in the 1968 Senate elections, the PSIUP, suffered a relatively large setback. Its vote went down from 4.4 to 3.2 per cent, with losses registered in all regions.

There were mixed results among the four government parties. The DC was faced with a total loss of 0.9 per cent of the vote; the highest losses were registered in Basilicata where its vote was down by 6.4 per cent. The PRI increased its vote in every region, registering a total increase of 1.1 per cent. The PSI and PSU votes taken together increased in all the regions, with an overall increase of 2.6 per cent. Compared with the 1964 provincial elections, the last time the two parties had campaigned separately, the PSU increased its vote by 0.3 per cent, while the PSI showed a loss of 0.6 per cent. The total vote for the center-left government parties increased by 2.8 per cent.

Among the right-wing parties, two registered losses and one increased its vote. The Italian Liberal Party (Partito Liberale Italiano; PLI) lost 1.2 per cent of its vote (from 5.9 to 4.7 per cent); the Italian Democratic Party of Monarchist Union (Partito Democratico Italiano di Unione Monarchica; PDIUM) lost 0.5 per cent of its vote (from 1.2 to 0.7 per cent); the neo-fascist Italian Social Movement (Movimento Sociale Italiano; MSI) increased its electoral support by 0.9 per cent (from 4.3 to 5.2 per cent).

As an outcome of the elections the center-left government parties gained control of twelve of the fifteen Regional Councils, with a total of 413 seats. The PCI was not able to obtain a straight majority on any of the Regional Councils. The party's control, therefore, of the three remaining

Regional Councils was contingent on cooperation with the PSIUP and the PSI, both of which eventually joined the PCI in the regional administrations of Emilia-Romagna (PCI, 24 seats; PSIUP, 2; PSI, 3—out of 50), Tuscany (PCI, 23; PSIUP, 1; PSI, 3—out of 50), and Umbria (PCI, 13; PSIUP, 1; PSI, 3—out of 30).

At the same time—during the period 7-8 June—elections were held for 88 Provincial Councils and 6,632 Communal Councils. In comparison with the 1964 provincial and 1968 general elections, the PCI's vote for the Provincial Councils increased by 2.6 and decreased by 0.2 respectively, the party receiving 7,620,952 votes (26.8 per cent). The center-left government parties increased their total with respect to both 1964 and 1968 elections by 2.6 and 2.2 per cent respectively, receiving 16,702,229 votes (58.6 per cent). In the elections to the Communal Councils [1] a comparison with 1964 and 1968 saw a PCI loss of votes of 0.3 and 3.4 per cent respectively, with the party receiving 4,768,511 votes (25.2 per cent). The government parties increased their combined vote by 3.1 per cent as compared with 1964, and 5.1 per cent as compared with 1968, receiving 58.8 per cent of the vote.

Organization and Leadership. The PCI is organized on the principles of democratic centralism. Its structure in 1970 was as follows: 109 federations, 18 regional committees, some 11,000 sections, and about 25,000 cells, together with a large number of youth clubs. The unpaid or part-paid directive committees of these organs numbered more than 80,000 persons; there were probably more than 1,000 full-time paid officials of the federations and sections, with some 200 to 300 at party headquarters in Rome (not including those engaged in the party press). While changes in federation and regional personnel were reported from time to time during 1970, no changes in the basic structure of the party were noted.

The directive organs of the PCI are elected at the party's congresses, the most recent being the Twelfth Congress, held in February 1969. The PCI leadership elected at that time included the Central Committee (171 members) and the Directorate (31), the latter working largely through two executive committees: the Political Office (9) and the Secretariat (7). All members of the Directorate were also members of the Central Committee. In addition there were the Central Control Commission (41 members) and a small audit board. An innovation in party machinery was the setting up, in April 1969, of five permanent commissions of the Central Committee to function in the intervals between plenum meetings. The first commission (31 members) deals with foreign affairs, including relations with other communist parties; the second (33 members), with the parliament and with regional and local authorities; the third (41 members), with economic and social questions; the fourth (35 members), with press, propaganda, and cultural matters; and the fifth (36 members), with questions of party organization.

Luigi Longo was reelected as secretary-general at the Twelfth Congress; he has held the post since Palmiro Togliatti's death in 1964. Enrico Berlinguer was elected deputy secretary-general (the post had been vacant since Longo left it to move to the top). Other leading members of the party elected at the congress were Giorgio Amendola, Pietro Ingrao, Emanuele Macaluso, Giorgio Napolitano, Agostino Novella, Gian Carlo Pajetta, and Aldo Tortorella (members of the Political Office), and Paolo Bufalini, Armando Cossutta, Fernando Di Giulio, Alessandro Natta, and Ugo Pecchioli (members of the Secretariat). Longo and Berlinguer were members of both the Political Office and the Secretariat, and Longo was chairman of the Central Committee; the chairman of the Central Control Commission was Arturo Colombi.

Changes in the party leadership since the congress have included: the resignation of Novella,

[1] Figures only available for communes with populations over 5,000 (where the proportional system was used).

secretary-general of the communist-controlled trade union CGIL (see below), from the PCI Political Office, following the adoption at the trade union's 1969 congress of the principle of "incompatibility," which dictates that trade union leaders may not also be members of parliament or hold positions in their party leadership. Novella, at the same time, resigned his seat in the Chamber of Deputies. On 18 March 1970 Novella resigned from the post of CGIL secretary-general, and, on 20 April, at a joint meeting of the PCI's Central Committee and Central Control Commission, was reelected to the Political Office. Also, at the same time, the PCI accepted the resignations from the Directorate of CGIL members Rinaldo Scheda and Luciano Lama, both having been appointed to leadership posts in the trade union organization, with Lama elected as secretary-general on 24 March. Also during the first half of the year, at an earlier meeting of the Central Committee and Central Control Commission in mid-January, thirteen workers— all of whom had played a prominent role in the industrial agitation in the autumn of 1969—were coopted into the Central Committee. At the conclusion, on 20 October, of another joint meeting of the two PCI bodies, considerable further changes in party responsibilities were announced. (1) A new Foreign Policy Commission, attached to the party's international section, was established, headed by Gian Carlo Pajetta and including Enrico Berlinguer, Umberto Cardia, Carlo Galluzzi, and Sergio Segre. (2) Aldo Tortorella was appointed director of *L'Unità*, with Luca Pavolini as co-director. (3) Alessandro Natta was appointed director of *Rinascita* and removed from the party's Secretariat, but appointed to the Political Office. (4) Carlo Galluzzi was appointed head of the party's press and propaganda section, and coopted to the Secretariat. (5) Sergio Segre was appointed head of the PCI's international section. (6) Enzo Modica relinquished his post of head of the communist group of the Lazio regional council, where he was replaced by Maurizio Ferrara. The party's local administration section, headed by Modica, was renamed the section for the regions and local administrations. These changes involved: the resignation of Pajetta as director of *L'Unità*; the resignation of Pavolini as director of *Rinascita*; the relinquishing of the leadership of the press and propaganda section by Natta; the relinquishing of the leadership of the international section by Galluzzi; and the resignations of Segre and Ferrara from their posts of co-directors of *L'Unità*. (*L'Unità*, 21 October.)

The PCI dominates the largest of the three main Italian trade union organizations, the General Confederation of Italian Labor (Confederazione Generale Italiana del Lavoro; CGIL). The CGIL contains sizable minorities of PSI and PSIUP workers, but its cadres are predominantly communist. It once claimed 3.5 million members, but has not published figures for some years. During 1970 the CGIL worked in close collaboration with the DC unions represented in the Confederazione Italiana Sindacati Lavoratori (CISL) and the PSU-PRI unions affiliated with the Unione Italiana del Lavoro (UIL). For the first time in twenty-two years, the 1 May demonstrations were jointly held with the three unions; consultations between the unions' leaderships took place throughout the year, to explore possible reunification; and on a number of occasions joint union delegations held talks with the government.

Party Internal Affairs. In the first year of the 1970's the PCI was confronted with a number of complex priorities, some of which, in view of their apparent *prima facie* incompatibility, threatened party unity. The autumn of 1969 had witnessed a massive movement of grass-roots strike action and social unrest, in which the PCI and the CGIL had tended to be followers rather than leaders. The local party organizations were to a certain extent disoriented by the circumstances, with militants in a number of localities aligning themselves with the grass-roots movement and the small groups to the left of the PCI that were rejecting the traditional policies of the Italian political parties, including those of the PCI. The communist party's difficulties in this context were compounded by the continuing and increasing activity of a group of leading former PCI members centered around the publication *Il Manifesto*,[1] three of whom had been members of the party's Central Committee. One of the major contentions of the *Manifesto* dissidents was that the PCI had reneged on its revolutionary goals, that it was pursuing reformist policies as part of a strategy to "insert" itself into government. This challenge from the left confronted the PCI at a time when the center-left government was itself faced with dissension within and between its four component parties, resulting primarily from differing views over relations with the PCI (see below). In order to further the interests of those within the center-left that called for cooperation with the communists, the PCI saw the need to disassociate itself from the disruptive activities of the aforementioned extreme left. At the same time, too great an abandonment of militancy would run the risk of compounding the disaffection among the party's rank and file. In the context of the complex options facing the PCI, a further factor—the ill health of Luigi Longo and the struggle for his succession—was an additional obstacle in the party's quest for unity.

During the course of 1970 the PCI was confronted with a number of resignations, the most notable arising in Naples, Salerno, Bergamo, Rome, and Turin. Simultaneously the PCI proceeded to expel or "radiate" several of its militants in these areas. ("Radiation" from the party is a form of expulsion that permits reentry following repentance, whereas "expulsion" is final.) While at the beginning of the year disaffection from the party or expulsionary measures tended to affect relatively small numbers of individuals, in October the PCI was faced with mass joint resignations in Rome—87 members, including Rome City Council member Pio Mancini—and in Turin—52 PCI and FGCI members, led by FGCI Central Committee member Giulio Sapelli. Among those who left the party during the year were two PCI parliamentary deputies, Liberato Bronzuto, from Naples, and Eliseo Milani, from Bergamo. Nearly all the dissidents aligned themselves with the *Manifesto* tendency.

Domestic Views and Policies. The PCI's pronouncements on domestic issues during 1970 reflected the complexity of a situation in which (1) repeated attempts to reach agreement between the four center-left parties (DC, PSI, PSU, and PRI) for the formation of a viable government floundered over the issue of relations with the PCI; (2) the regional and local elections of June further exacerbated the center-left's divisions, mainly over the question of PSI participation in PCI-dominated regional and local councils; and (3) the country was faced with growing social unrest, a deteriorating economy, and an apparent public alienation from traditional parliamentary procedures. At the same time there was a significant growth in the political power of the country's three major trade unions—the CGIL, CISL, and UIL—resulting partly from their increasing unity and disassociation (more noticeable in the CISL and UIL than in the CGIL) from their respective parliamentary parties. While expressing its opposition throughout the year to the reestablishment of a center-left government as constituted in previous administrations, the PCI appeared to waver in its choice of oppositional options—whether to commit itself to the extraparliamentary forces in the country or to offer the center-left a modicum of support, thus facilitating the enactment of social reforms and the redressment of the economy, and, in the process, legitimizing itself further with those elements in the center-left calling for closer relations with the PCI. In the context of the two options, the PCI leadership repeatedly emphasized the import of two historical developments—the party's increase in electoral support in May 1968 and what it saw as the subsequent swing to the left, particularly by the PSI and among sizable segments of the DC; and the mass strike movement of the autumn of 1969 (the "hot autumn"), which the party saw as having raised the level of labor militancy and power, with the PCI "emerging from the

[1] In its September 1970 issue, *Il Manifesto* published a "platform of discussion and political work for the unity of the revolutionary left and the construction of a new political force," which consisted of 200 theses covering both domestic and international issues.

struggles with a link with the working class that [had] probably never been as strong and on such a large scale" (Enrico Berlinguer's speech at Fifth Workers' Conference, *L'Unità*, 2 March).

In response to accusations (primarily originating from groups to its left) of indecision in selection of strategic options, PCI leaders emphasized their interrelationship, claiming that a correct approach was one which supported "struggles" at different levels. In his speech to the Fifth Workers' Conference, in March, Berlinguer attacked the " 'brilliant' cerebral solutions of those whom Marx used to call 'alchemists of revolution' "—those who claimed that their strategies could be translated into "some kind of castling of the working class within the factories, losing sight of the general political processes and thus falling into a 'closed' conception of political and social alliances." While stating that the PCI had always been "among the principal supporters and protagonists of all experiences of direct democracy and self-government," the PCI deputy secretary-general added that past experiences had shown that "no form of direct democracy, in the factory or in society, can last and develop without a struggle continually to broaden political democracy and democratic life at all levels." "Direct democracy and political democracy at all levels of society and of the state," Berlinguer stressed, "are two inseparable elements of the same process: they cannot be separated, let alone counterposed." (*Ibid.*)

During the first half of the year and within the context of what it saw to be a developing move to the left within the country, the PCI placed great importance on the holding of regional and local elections. Commenting on the party's stand, which contrasted with its strong opposition to the dissolution of the parliament and holding of general elections, Berlinguer stated that the regional and local elections would "constitute a useful and necessary check of the electorate's orientation without interrupting the present legislature and parliamentary work," and would not "interrupt the processes of unity which [were] currently taking place in the trade union and political field." Berlinguer added, moreover, that the setting up of regional administrations would encourage "new and united alignments . . . to liquidate the center-left and to create the preconditions for a shift to the left in national politics." (*Ibid.*, 22 April.)

In its concern to further a leftward shift among the political forces in the country, the PCI was careful not to antagonize potential allies within the center-left. "Our polemic," Berlinguer declared, "will be directed against all the political components of the quadripartite government, although with the necessary distinctions." With regard to the PSU, the party's view, according to Berlinguer, was "precise and clear": "The PSU has shown itself, in the eyes of the workers and all democrats, as a force of conservatism and adventure." The PSI, on the other hand, was only criticized for having accepted participation in the center-left government, and Berlinguer added, moreover, that the socialists had recently shown a "more open relationship and tendency toward the PSIUP." He emphasized that a "communist advance" in the elections would be of "decisive importance" in promoting the PSI's rejection of the quadripartite and commitment to "a democratic and leftwing alternative, proceeding from the communes, the provinces, and the regions." With regard to the DC, Berlinguer stated that "apart from the PSU and rightwing groups" the "main blow" of the PCI's electoral campaign would be directed against it. Claiming that the DC was a "party in complete crisis," Berlinguer concluded that "a communist advance [could] give greater courage and audacity to the initiative and activity of the left-wing Christian Democratic factions and afford them more room." (*Ibid.*)

In mid-year, during a time when the Italian economy appeared to be deteriorating progressively, the PCI showed itself leaning markedly toward a policy of preserving the institutional status quo in the country. Commenting on a resolution adopted by the PCI Directorate on 8 July (on the status of the economy), Berlinguer stated: "With this document we communists have given further proof that we are not only aware of the gravity of the current economic and political situation, but, above all, that we know how to assume all the responsibilities resulting from the fact that we constitute the strongest and most representative party of the working class, the party which, as such, is more capable of interpreting the defense of the interests of the national collectivity." Referring to the dangers of "production recession" and "galloping inflation," Berlinguer added:

> The only alternative which exists in order to avoid either of these prospects, both quite serious for the interests of the workers and the country's development, is a qualified production expansion. (*L'Unità*, 12 July.)

Berlinguer's call for a "qualified production expansion" was vehemently denounced by the other extreme-left groups in the country, including the supporters of *Il Manifesto* (see, e.g., Velentino Parlato, "La Virata di Berlinguer," in *Il Manifesto*, July-August 1970). The PCI, however, did not modify its new orientation, and during the rest of the year offered its support to the government in the legislature during the passage of a number of social and economic measures. At the same time, the party appeared to harden its attitudes toward the groups on its left, intimating that there was collusion between extreme right and extreme left groups. (For a discussion of this latter PCI trend, including an interview with Gian Carlo Pajetta on the subject, see *L'Espresso*, Rome, 27 December).

International Views and Policies. Within a context in which relations with the PCI was an issue of considerable controversy among Italian political forces, the nature of the PCI's independence within the international communist movement and the degree of its concern for Italian national interests continued to be questions to which the party devoted much of its attention.

On a general level, the PCI's views were summarized in a speech in the Chamber of Deputies on 11 August delivered by Enrico Berlinguer, who stated: "Our party is a component of the great communist, revolutionary, anti-imperialist, and workers' movement. Simultaneously, our party is profoundly national and completely autonomous. No objective person can deny this today." (*L'Unità*, 12 August.) In a subsequent article in *Rinascita* (21 August), Alessandro Natta further elaborated on the dual nature of the PCI's international posture:

> Let us say right now that it is unthinkable not only for us communists, but for any force that takes up the problem of socialism seriously in Italy, to seek solutions in any kind of rejection of internationalism or in any kind of break on our part with the internationalist viewpoint, connection, and commitment. By being more secure in "our" socialism, in a world in which capitalism and imperialism are world-wide realities definitely present, we would instead, in the end, do irreparable harm not only to the prospect of socialism but also to the cause of democracy and the independence of our country! In that way, rather than better guarantee the autonomy of Italian life, all we would do is reduce it to a narrowly provincial scheme completely abstract and wishful.

The degree of the PCI's commitment to the "anti-imperialist and workers' movement" continued, however, to be somewhat ambiguous. Thus, Berlinguer spoke also of the need for a "new international system based on overcoming the blocs," and Natta emphasized that the PCI's "demands for a state of real autonomy and neutrality did not and do not constitute a hypocritical premise, a disguised step in the insertion of Italy into a different politico-military bloc." "We can affirm definitely," Natta added, "that now and in the future, even in a socialist regime, we want Italy out of any and every bloc."

On matters pertaining to international communist affairs, the PCI, in its response to developments ranging from "normalization" in Czechoslovakia to the Sino-Soviet conflict, reflected its continued concern to maintain an independent posture with regard to the views and policies of other communist parties.

On the issue of the Sino-Soviet conflict, the party's views were expressed, as in the previous year (see *YICA*, 1970, pp. 216-17), primarily by Giuseppe Boffa, a former Moscow correspondent of *L'Unità*, who reiterated the PCI's equidistant approach to the problem. In an editorial in *L'Unità* (24 January), on the subject of current bilateral negotiations between China and the Soviet Union, and between each of these and the United States, Boffa stressed "the need for lucidity of analysis and cautiousness of judgment." On the issue of the Sino-Soviet talks in Peking on the frontier issue, Boffa refrained from expressing criticism of either of the protagonists, claiming only that no progress had been recorded and calling for "the ending, if only gradually, of the fratricidal conflict."

In the latter part of the year, in an article commemorating the October Revolution in Russia, Alessandro Natta wrote of the PCI's "original and positive contributions . . . toward the full affirmation of the values of independence, equality, and international solidarity based on respect for national interests and feelings." Natta claimed that the PCI's "internationalism" was "aimed beyond the forces of the communist matrix," and that its "view of socialism" did not "identify the frontiers of one's own struggle with those of the Soviet Union and the socialist nations" and did not "accord the privilege of 'model' to the one or the other experience." Natta claimed that the PCI did not "legitimize any solution through acritical indifference," but demanded "immediate judgment and confrontation." (*Rinascita*, 6 November.)

In conformity to its advocacy of critical evaluation, the PCI expressed its concern on a number of occasions during the year over developments in communist-ruled countries, particularly with regard to Czechoslovakia. On 23 January, *Rinascita* published an article by Franco Bertone analyzing an interview that Gustáv Husák, first secretary of the Communist Party of Czechoslovakia, had given to the Czechoslovak party organ *Rudé Právo*. Bertone expressed strong criticism of Husák's views, claiming that he left "no doubt as to his determination to smash to dust the political platform of the 'new direction' [taken by Alexander Dubček, from January to August 1968] which was slowly emerging, and with increasing clarity, from the party's actions during that period of turmoil," and concluded:

> The Communist Party of Czechoslovakia's rank and file, like all of Czechoslovak society, who had made too vividly clear their enthusiasm for the "new direction," are faced now with a line that flatly rejects the basic tenets of their "renewal" policy. . . . What Husák offers is a rationalized version of the old social and political model, but one endowed with a suitable set of safeguards to preserve the party and society against a repetition of the deviations of the past.

Bertone's article was attacked by *Rudé Právo* on 3 February, the Czechoslovak newspaper accusing the PCI of distorting the meaning of Husák's interview. *Rinascita*, replying to the accusation on 6 February, expressed the PCI contention that Czechoslovakia was undergoing a "profound crisis situation which does not in any way seem headed for a solution." Following the favorable review by Giuseppe Boffa (in *L'Unità*, 17 February) of the book *Three Generations*, edited by Antonin Liehm (and including a strongly worded preface by Jean-Paul Sartre, opposing the Czechoslovak government), the Czechoslovak press once again attacked the PCI (see, e.g., *Rudé Právo* 25 February). The PCI reply was in the form of an article in *L'Unità* by Political Office member Gian Carlo Pajetta. He quoted from a resolution of the PCI's Twelfth Congress (February 1969), which had stated that "faith in socialism is nourished by truth, by rigor in historical and critical research," and, recommending this maxim to the apologists of the developments in Czechoslovakia, quoted from the same congress document to justify the determination of the PCI to use its own judgment in weighing up events in Czechoslovakia:

> At our Twelfth Congress we stated the necessity "for our own complete autonomy of judgment about what is really happening in the Soviet Union and the socialist countries, and about the

policy followed by the Soviet Union, and each separate act of this policy." We also said then that "we distinguish between what to us seems positive and what seems negative, and we try to pick out the interconnections of the various elements within this reality, the contradictions and the developing tendencies.

Polemics between the PCI and the Communist Party of Czechoslovakia continued throughout the year, and on a number of occasions the Italian party reasserted its belief that the complex movement of sociopolitical reform in Czechoslovakia that had taken place under Dubček in 1968 represented not a subversive outbreak of "right-wing opportunism" but a creative and exemplary enrichment of Marxist tradition (see, e.g., *Critica Marxista*, vol. 8, no. 3, May-June 1970). The expulsion of Dubček from the Czechoslovak party on 26 June 1970 evoked an immediate response from the PCI's secretary-general, Luigi Longo, who stated: "We regret and deplore the action of the Communist Party of Czechoslovakia in expelling Comrade Dubček" (*L'Unità*, 27 June). On 29 June *L'Unità* published a statement from the CGIL describing the expulsion of Dubček as "a fact of extreme gravity" and a tribute to him by Giuseppe Boffa declaring: "Under Dubček's leadership the Communist Party of Czechoslovakia enjoyed massive popular support. . . . [His] popularity and prestige remain very high in Czechoslovakia, perhaps indeed beyond what he himself would wish."

The PCI also expressed critical views of developments in the Soviet Union. These included: a lengthy three-part analysis of Soviet economic policy (*Rinascita*, 1, 8 and 22 May), a strong indictment of Soviet opposition to the nomination of Alexander Solzhenitsyn for the Nobel Prize for Literature (*ibid.*, 16 October), and concern over the death sentences pronounced on Soviet Jews sentenced in late December for conspiring to hijack an airplane. With regard to the latter issue, *L'Unità* (27 December) published an article entitled "An Incomprehensible Sentence" which, while disclaiming that the PCI considered the severity of the sentences to have been motivated by the defendants' Jewish origin, added: "Nevertheless, we cannot shrink from pointing out facts and symptoms showing that problems relating to citizens of Jewish origin or religion— problems which have not yet been solved—exist in the Soviet Union and in other socialist countries."

During the year, the PCI on several occasions indicated its disapproval of interference by one party in the affairs of another. Thus, in an article (*L'Unità*, 19 March) on the electoral setback suffered in March by communists in Finland, Giuseppe Boffa referred to the split in the Finnish party as being "for the most part quite artificial"—an indirect comment on Soviet interference in that party's life (see *Finland*). An extensive and relatively favorable review (*ibid.*, 13 and 14 March) of the book *Toute la Vérité*, by dissident French Communist Party member Roger Garaudy, mentioned that the author had given examples of "Soviet interference in the life of other parties, the Spanish, Greek, Finnish, Italian, and Austrian," and did not contest his allegations.

A high-level delegation of the Communist Party of the Soviet Union, led by Politburo member Arvids Pelshe, visited Italy from 18 November to 3 December and held discussions with members of the PCI leadership, including Longo and Berlinguer. The joint communiqué published at the end of the visit (*L'Unità* and *Pravda*, 4 December) spoke of "frank exchanges of views on a broad range of questions." Although the two delegations "expounded to one another the positions of their parties," there was no indication that agreement had been reached.

International Party Contacts. From 2 to 7 January, the PCI leadership held discussions with a delegation of the Communist Party of Spain, led by Secretary-General Santiago Carrillo. The PCI's representative at the Moscow meeting of European communist parties on 14-15 January was Carlo Galluzzi. CPSU Central Committee member P. N. Fedoseev led a delegation to the PCI's forty-ninth anniversary celebrations, held on 21 January. Giorgio Napolitano led the PCI delegation to the Nineteenth Congress of the French Communist Party, in early February. At the same time, Gian Carlo Pajetta represented the PCI at an international conference of parliamentarians, held in Cairo and devoted to the problems of the Middle East. In conformity to its growing interest in Middle Eastern and African issues, the PCI gave extensive coverage in its press to this meeting (see *L'Unità*, 5, 6, 8, 10, and 12 February). On 6 February, PCI leaders, including Enrico Berlinguer, held talks in Rome with a delegation of the Front for the Liberation of Mozambique (FRELIMO), led by Marcelino Dos Santos. Aldo Tortorella led a PCI delegation to an international symposium on Lenin, held in Moscow during the last week of February. On 5 March a CGIL delegation, led by Luciano Lama, returned to Rome following an extensive visit to various Arab countries in the Middle East (for report see *ibid.*, 6 March).

From 12 to 22 April, the PCI was host to a delegation of the Korean Workers' Party, led by Kim Tong-kyu, Political Committee and Secretariat member. Also in April the PCI received a delegation of the Israeli Communist Party (RAKAH), led by Secretary-General Meir Vilner. The PCI was represented in a delegation, led by Gian Carlo Pajetta, at the Lenin Centenary celebrations held in Moscow on 21 April. From 27 to 30 April a PCI delegation, led by Paolo Bufalini, met with leaders of the Socialist Unity Party of East Germany, in East Berlin. A North Vietnamese delegation, led by Xuan Thuy, chief negotiator for the Democratic Republic of Vietnam at the Paris peace talks, was in Italy from 29 April to 5 May. On 5 May, PCI leaders met again with Santiago Carrillo of the Communist Party of Spain. Mikis Theodorakis, a leading member of the dissident group within the Communist Party of Greece opposing the Soviet-supported leadership, was in Italy from 12 to 14 May, during which time he met with Luigi Longo. The PCI sent a high-level delegation to the 15 May Paris meeting of West European communist parties. The delegation was led by Berlinguer, and included Giorgio Amendola and Carlo Galluzzi. On 23 May a PCI delegation, consisting of Berlinguer and Galluzzi, met with President Tito of Yugoslavia, in Belgrade. Carrillo and Theodorakis were back in Italy at the end of May, when they had further talks with the Italian party leadership.

Gian Carlo Pajetta was in Paris on 12 June to attend an international demonstration of "Solidarity with the Peoples of Indochina"; Giorgio Amendola attended a conference on the same subject in Liège, on 23 June. The PCI organized a demonstration on the subject of the Indochina conflict in Milan on 21 June. Foreign delegations included representation from the Provisional Revolutionary Government of South Vietnam, the National Liberation Front of South Vietnam, and the Arab guerrilla organization al-Fatah. At the end of June, high-level delegations of the PCI and the French Communist Party met in Rome. From 27 to 29 June, the World Peace Council and the Afro-Asian Peoples' Solidarity Organization sponsored in Rome an international conference on the "Struggle of the People of the Portuguese Colonies in Africa." The meeting attracted some 250 delegates from 64 countries; the PCI was represented by Enrico Berlinguer. The PCI was host to a delegation of the League of Communists of Yugoslavia, led by Krste Crvenkovski, from 26 June to 1 July. On 4 July, Berlinguer met with Nicolae Ceauşescu, secretary-general of the Romanian Communist Party, in Bucharest. His visit to Romania was followed, at the end of the month, by one made by Carlo Galluzzi. A PCI delegation attended a meeting of West European communist parties, held in London on 21 September. A delegation of the Romanian Communist Party, led by Executive Committee member Paul Niculescu-Mizil, met with leaders of the PCI, including Longo and Berlinguer, on 30 September in Rome. The PCI was host to a Soviet delegation, led by Sharaf Rashidov, candidate member of the CPSU Politburo, from 4 to 11 November. Also, starting in mid-November, the PCI hosted a CPSU delegation led by Arvids Pelshe (see above). A meeting between representatives of the League of Communists of Yugoslavia (delegation head, Miko Tripalo) and the PCI, led by Gerardo Chiaramonte, took place in Trieste on 16 November.

Publications. The PCI has a great number of publications. The principal ones are *L'Unità*, a daily newspaper; *Rinascita*, a weekly political journal; and *Critica Marxista*, a bimonthly theoretical organ. The party also controls a Rome daily, *Paese Sera*. The CGIL publishes a fortnightly called *Rassegna Sindacale*, and the FGCI publishes the irregular *Nuova Generazione*. *Vie Nuove* is a popular illustrated weekly published by the party.

* * *

The only pro-Chinese party in Italy acknowledged as such by the Chinese Communist Party continued to be the Communist Party of Italy-Marxist-Leninist (Partito Comunista d'Italia-Marxista-Leninista; PCI-ML), which originated from the Italian Marxist-Leninist Movement (formed in 1963),[1] founding itself as a party in October 1966. The PCI-ML is led by its secretary-general, Fosco Dinucci. The two other most prominent leaders in 1970 appeared to be Livio Risaliti and Manlio Dinucci. Osvaldo Pesce, formerly a leader of the PCI-ML, had left the party in 1970 and become a leader of a small group called the Organization of Marxist-Leninist Communists of Italy (Organizzazione dei Comunisti Marxisti-Leninisti d'Italia), whose irregular organ was *Linea Proletaria*. The PCI-ML's headquarters are in Rome; it publishes the weekly *Nuova Unità*. The party operates the Italo-Chinese Friendship Association, whose headquarters are in Milan, and the Italo-Albanian Friendship Association, centered in Rome. Both associations have branches and hold meetings in many parts of the country.

During 1970 the PCI-ML appeared to be confronted by fractional activity within its ranks. An article by Risaliti in *Nuova Unità* (20 January) referred to the activity of "some people [who] insist and insist on the supposed continuous existence of two opposing lines, seemingly with the same right of 'citizenship' within the Marxist-Leninist parties as a natural phenomenon." A week later, another article in *Nuova Unità* (27 January), by Manlio Dinucci, called for a "proletarization of the party with the greatest decisiveness, purging its ranks of petty-bourgeois self-seekers who have succeeded in infiltrating it." The extent to which the party had succeeded in consolidating itself by the end of the year was not evident. In March, however, *Nuova Unità* (10 March) published a lengthy policy document, and, in October, new party statutes were adopted (*Nuova Unità*, 15 October).

On domestic issues PCI-ML policy was characterized by continuous polemics both with the PCI and with all other extreme-left groups. With regard to the June regional elections, the party called on its supporters to "destroy electoral illusions" by writing slogans on ballot sheets (*ibid.*, 2 June). On international matters the party adhered to strict Maoist interpretations of issues. Fosco Dinucci returned from Peking in early 1970, where he had been since late 1969. Shortly thereafter he left for Albania, remaining there several weeks.

At the end of 1968 the PCI-ML was confronted with a split which resulted in the creation of a second party of the same name. The second PCI-ML, which claims to be the original one, is led by Dino Dini and Vincenzo Misefari. It is centered in Florence, and while its organ at the outset was called *Nuova Unità*, it appeared to be only publishing a monthly, *Il Partito*, during 1970. It is referred to commonly as the "red line" group to differentiate it with the Dinucci-led PCI-ML, known as the "black line." It would appear that the majority of PCI-ML militants adhered to the "black line" at the time of the split, and that by the end of 1970 support for the "red line" had practically ceased to exist.

A pro-Chinese group that continued to have significant influence during 1970 was the Union of Italian Communists (Marxist-Leninist)—Unione dei Comunisti Italiani (Marxista-Leninista)—

[1]For a history of the pro-Chinese movements in Italy see Walter Tobagi, *Storia del Movimento Studentesco e dei Marxisti-Leninisti in Italia*, Milan, Sugar Editore, 1970, 157 pp.

—founded in October 1968 from ex-PCI, student, and intellectual groups in Milan and Rome. Its principal publications were the fortnightly *Servire Il Popolo* and the irregular *Guardie Rosse*. It was led during the year by Aldo Brandirali, although his leadership was challenged successfully at the beginning of the year by one of the union's strongest federations, the one in the province of Latium. The dissident group's leader was reportedly Guglielmo Guglielmi. Brandirali, however, continued to have the support of party militants in Calabria, whose most prominent representative was Enzo Lo Giudice. At the time of the Latium group's split it was revealed that, while the union had claimed to have more than 10,000 members, actual membership was less than 1,800 (see *L'Espresso*, 8 February, and *Vie Nuove*, 8 February).

In contrast to the bohemian behavior of much of the Italian "new left," the union militants continued, as they had the previous year (see *YICA*, 1970, p. 220), to be characteristically "puritanical" both in mores and attire. The party leadership, throughout the year, repeatedly called for "criticism and self-criticism" (see, e.g., *Servire Il Popolo*, 11 April and 29 August) and opposed what it called "anarchist trade unionism." At the time of the June elections, the union called upon its supporters to vote for the PCI (*ibid.*, 2 and 30 May). Despite this, it repeatedly polemicized with the PCI, as it did with all the rest of the extreme left, including the *Il Manifesto* group (*ibid.*, 17 October).

The only other pro-Chinese group of any significance (out of at least a dozen others) was the Revolutionary Marxist-Leninist Party of Italy, which, originally a federation, became a party in 1968. It published in 1970 the monthly *Rivoluzione Proletaria* and appeared to be primarily centered in Milan. The party was led by Luciano Raimondi, Manlio Donati, Aldo Serafini, and Giuseppe Mai. With its support declining progressively, the party reiterated on several occasions its call for unification of the Italian pro-Chinese parties, placing the primary burden for this task on the "black line" PCI-ML. Thus, in August 1970, *Rivoluzione Proletaria* stated:

> The period of splinter-group fractionalism is over. There is a trend toward a reversal, but we cannot expect it to ripen spontaneously. We must encourage this trend so that it becomes an irreversible drive for unification.

The only Trotskyist group in Italy of any consequence is the Revolutionary Communist Groups (Gruppi Comunisti Rivoluzionari; GCR), which is affiliated with the United Secretariat of the Fourth International and led by Livio Maitan. The GCR publishes the monthly *Bandiera Rossa*. During 1970 support for this group appeared to be increasing, while ties were being formed with the *Il Manifesto* dissidents (see *Bandiera Rossa*, 15 October-15 November). On 19-22 March, the GCR held its Fifteenth Congress, which was attended by delegates from some fifteen cities in Italy, and by delegations of the United Secretariat and its French section, the Communist League. The GCR delegation to the Brussels Congress for a Red Europe, sponsored by the United Secretariat on 21-22 November (see *Belgium*) numbered 95 members.

M. P.

LUXEMBOURG

The Communist Party of Luxembourg (Parti Communiste de Luxembourg; PCL) was established in January 1921. It enjoys legal status and is the only communist movement in Luxembourg. The PCL does not publish membership figures. Western sources, however, place party strength at between 500 and 1,000 persons. The population of Luxembourg is 336,000 (estimated 1968). Most party support originates in the urban and mining areas of the industrial south. Pro-Chinese sympathizers are limited to the small and ineffectual Luxembourg-China Society.

At the PCL's Twentieth Congress, held on 29-30 March 1970, the party chairman, Dominique Urbany (also spelled Urbani), announced that new members had been recruited in recent months, particularly among the young, "but not in sufficient numbers" (*Zeitung vum Letzeburger Vollek*, 4 April). Although he believed that the party's influence in the national and municipal governments was significantly greater than the low party membership would indicate, he urged systematic and active recruitment of new party members and of new subscribers to the party newspaper (*ibid.*; see also *WMR*, July).

The PCL is one of several communist parties in Western Europe (among them the parties in Italy, Finland, and France) which obtain more than 15 per cent of the vote in general elections (*Est & Ouest*, Paris, 1-15 July). In the 56-member Luxembourg parliament the PCL is represented by 6 deputies. Although there was no general election in Luxembourg in 1970, the PCL did register a significant election victory during March in the municipal election at Esch-sur-Alzette, the country's most important industrial center and second largest city. The PCL became the principal electoral force by winning 27.9 per cent of the vote and 6 of the 19 seats on the town council. The left wing of the Luxembourg Socialist Workers' Party (Parti Ouvrier Socialiste Luxembourgeois; LSAP), which had formed an election alliance with the PCL, won 4 seats, and together the two groups were able to elect PCL Politburo and Central Committee member Arthur Useldinger as the city's mayor. (The anticommunist right wing of the LSAP won only 3 seats on the town council.) Thus the PCL congress, coming shortly afterward, was bolstered by what Politburo member René Urbany termed the "evidence of the people's deep trust in Communists, as well as of the general left craving for unity" (*WMR*, July, and *Est & Ouest*, Paris, 1-15 July).

Leadership and Organization. The PCL is unique among European communist parties in having always had the same team of leaders and been without splits or purges. With the party leadership concentrated in the hands of one family, it presents an image of remarkable stability. The head of the family, Dominique Urbany, was the titular as well as actual leader of the party before the Second World War and was reelected party chairman at the PCL congress. Following the death, in 1969, of Jean Kill, Urbany's brother-in-law and number two man in the party, Dominique's son René Urbany became the third member of the party Secretariat, joining his father and Arthur Useldinger (no relation to the Urbany family). In addition René Urbany inherited the editorship of the party daily, *Zeitung vum Letzeburger Vollek Z(ZVLV)*. The Urbany clan has more than ten persons in the party machinery, including Claire Urbany, the wife of Dominique, who is president of the "Alliance of Luxembourg Women." Together with her husband, René, Jacqueline Urbany heads the party's agitprop apparatus. Serge Urbany, a member of the third generation, directs communist activities among high school students. (*Est & Ouest*, 1-15 July.)

The second leading body within the PCL is the 10-member Politburo, which is elected by the 35-member Central Committee. At the party congress in March, the Central Committee was unanimously reelected, with no changes in composition (*WMR*, July). Leading figures in the party include Joseph Grandgenet, D. Meis, J. Hoffmann, Joseph Freismuth, Fernand Huebsch, and Elio Ramberti.

Outside the party, PCL members are active in the Progressive Youth Association (also known as Luxembourg Democratic Youth), the Awakening of the Resistance (an association of former antifascist militants), the National Movement for Peace, and groups such as the U.S.S.R.-Luxembourg Association.

Domestic Attitudes and Activities. The industrial city of Differdange was host to the PCL congress on 29-30 March 1970, which was attended by some 200 delegates and guests. In his speech to the congress, Dominique Urbany underscored the "ultimate" goal: "the social advancement of our people, freedom for the working man, the independence of our country and peace." This goal, he declared, could only be reached "if capitalism is abolished and replaced by socialism and if the working people of Luxembourg take political and economic power in the state into their hands." Hence, the most important task of the party was the "struggle for the everyday demands of the workers"—that is, adjustment and improvement of wages, salaries, and pensions; effective price controls; progressive social policies; protection and extension of the rights of the employee in business; democratic budgetary and educational policies; and democratic tax reform. (*ZVLV*, 31 March.)

Since the LSAP and the PCL receive more than half of the votes in Luxembourg's national elections, Dominique Urbany and Arthur Useldinger in the two major reports to the congress devoted considerable attention to "unity of action and program" with the LSAP. Urbany necessarily rejected "joint action" with the right-wing LSAP and Christian Socialist elements who espoused "anticommunism" and "anti-Sovietism." Thus unity with the socialists was far from being a fact. He emphasized that collaboration was, as exemplified in the Esch elections, "an acknowledgment of the needs of the working class and of left-wing unity and a convincing rebuttal to the government parties and the right-wing leadership of the Socialist party". (*IB*, no. 9, 1970).

Urbany declared that right-wing socialist proponents of the common market, industrial monopolies, and foreign capital were meeting with "increasingly stiff resistance among the rank and file," and appealed to leftist and liberal members of the LSAP to fight together with the PCL "for common objectives" (*ZVLV*, 31 March). In an article summing up the Twentieth congress (*WMR*, July), René Urbany reiterated the observations made by the party chairman during the congress itself, repeating almost verbatim his father's point (*ZVLV*, 4 April) that the PCL's "road to socialism leads through contact and hard social and political disputes with the reactionary forces," and that the prerequisite was the "winning of broad masses of the people." The "decisive force" in this struggle for socialism he defined as the "industrial workers," and the "prime task" as their mobilization and organization.

René Urbany also elaborated on the reasons for the successes of the party as outlined by

Dominique Urbany during a visit to Moscow in April for the Lenin Centenary celebrations: (1) tireless opposition to "capitalist exploitation" and support for "progressive municipal policies" and better wages, and (2) "constant, unremitting efforts for unity of the working-class move- ment" (*New Times*, Moscow, no. 17, 1970). Future success would not be achieved by "phrase mongering and abstract 'revolutionary romanticism.' " Only the PCL could be the "organizer and moving force [in] refashioning socialist society"—it could not be replaced by socialist-com- munist cooperation in the trade unions. Indeed, past, present, and future success was and would be dependent on the "uniform and self-sacrificing activity" of party members and militants in the large enterprises, labor unions, youth and women's groups, and the party paper, and on the "un- tiring work" of the PCL representatives in parliament and in the communities. (*WMR*, July.)

International Views and Positions. The year 1970 was proclaimed in a resolution of the PCL Central Committee as "a Leninist year, a year of reinforcing the party and improving its activity in the spirit of Marxism-Leninism" (*ZVLV*, 11 January). Subsequent eulogies on proletarian in- ternationalism and the principles of Marxism-Leninism placed the PCL firmly in the pro-Soviet camp (*ibid.*, 4 April, and *WMR*, July).

The principal foreign policy stance of the PCL (which was the first communist party in West- ern Europe to endorse the 1968 Warsaw Pact invasion of Czechoslovakia) was opposition to "all adulterations of the theories of Marx and Lenin" and "full solidarity" with the Communist Party of the Soviet Union (*ZVLV*, 4 April). Dominique Urbany chastised the "reactionaries," "oppor- tunists," and "revisionists" and their "rightist-socialist assistants," who had hoped to isolate the PCL after the Czechoslovakian crisis, and René Urbany pointed out that the party had emerged, particularly after the Esch elections, "stronger than before, capable of tackling its tasks with new vigor" (*WMR*, July).

The right-wing socialists with their convergence theories, the "preachers of humane social- ism," the Trotskyists, and the Maoists all shared in common, according to Dominique Urbany, a "hatred of the Soviet Union." He scorned their attempts to divide the PCL and the communist movement into splinter groups to "wean revolutionary intellectuals and workers" away from the party and to "distract" the working class from the struggle for socialism. Urbany also declared anew the PCL's support for the Soviet Union, in opposition to those who, seeking to weaken the socialist camp, had threatened the "Czechoslovakian working class"—the Warsaw Pact's "nec- essary act of international solidarity" had preserved "socialist gains" in Czechoslovakia and the peace of Europe. Thus he viewed the "Maoist clique" in China as facilitating the "maneuvers of American imperialism" by "casting overboard the principles of international proletarian solidar- ity" and replacing them "with chauvinism, with the leadership cult, with militaristic adventur- ism and anti-Sovietism." (*ZVLV*, 4 April.)

The party congress endorsed all those policies taken by the Soviet communist party. Urbany called for the immediate convening of a conference on collective security in Europe; introduced the congress resolution proclaiming "solidarity with the Vietnamese people against U.S. imperi- alism"; reaffirmed the need for an independent Luxembourg foreign policy based on the princi- ples of peaceful coexistence; condemned government support of the "imperialist" aims of NATO, the United States, and West Germany; criticized the Common Market for promoting industrial concentration; condemned the "militarist policy of the reactionary Israeli government"; and urged Luxembourg's recognition of the German Democratic Republic and withdrawal from NATO. (*Ibid.*, 31 March; *WMR*, July.)

International Activities and Party Contacts. Two major visits took place in 1970. Soviet Cen- tral Committee member N. V. Bannikov attended the PCL congress in March, and the PCL party chairman journeyed to Moscow for the Lenin Centenary celebrations in April. Bannikov praised the PCL as remaining "unswervingly loyal to the principles of Marxism-Leninism and proletarian internationalism" (TASS, 30 March). Praise of solidarity, calls for unity, and eulogizing of Lenin characterized the speeches at the PCL congress by representatives from the communist parties of Belgium, France, Italy, West Germany, East Germany, Czechoslovakia, Romania, Hungary, and Bulgaria (*ZVLV*, 30-31 March).

In Moscow, Dominique Urbany devoted his attention to Lenin and the "Luxembourg phenomenon," affirming that consistent support of working-class demands and of efforts for the unity of the working-class movement had given the PCL added strength (*New Times*, Moscow, no. 17). Urbany's speech was, in fact, a repetition of his declaration at the PCL congress of solidarity with the Soviet Union and the socialist countries allied with it: "In their own vital interests the working people of Luxembourg and their Communist Party must welcome everything that helps to strengthen the socialist countries and fortify their unity, and fight every manifestation of anti-Sovietism" (*ibid.*).

Publications. The PCL has published a daily newspaper since 1946, *Zeitung vum Letzeburger Vollek*. Another party periodical, *Wochenzeitung*, appears weekly.

D. L. B.

NETHERLANDS

The Communist Party of the Netherlands (Communistische Partij van Nederland; CPN) was founded in 1918 as the Communist Party of Holland. The present name was adopted in 1936. Party membership in 1970 was approximately 10,000. The population of the Netherlands is 12,900,000 (estimated 1969). Originally pro-Soviet, the CPN has in recent years pursued a policy of autonomy within the international communist movement. Several communist splinter groups of pro-Chinese tendency were also active in the country during 1970 (see below).

The CPN enjoys legal status, but its political influence has always been minor. In the latest general election, held in 1967, the CPN sent five candidates to the 150-member Lower Chamber of the Dutch Parliament (see *YICA*, 1968, p. 417). The next national elections are scheduled for 1971. In the 1970 provincial and municipal elections, the CPN achieved considerable gains, increasing the number of its seats on provincial bodies from 13 to 28 and winning 70 posts at municipal levels, including 18 aldermen's seats (as against only seven in the previous election of 1966). The significance of the election results, according to CPN Parliament member Marcus Bakker, was to be seen not in the increase in seats, but from a psychological point of view: "It evokes fear in the hearts of the bourgeois, and creates inspiration in those people who are in revolt" (*De Waarheid*, 9 February).

Leadership and Organization. The CPN held its Twenty-third Congress in Amsterdam on 6-8 February. At that time, Henk Hoekstra was reelected party chairman. On the 33-member Central Committee, four members were replaced. The nine-member Executive Committee, chosen on 23 February following the party congress, consists of Hoekstra (chairman), Roel Walraven (organizational secretary), J. IJisberg (administrative secretary, charged with supervision of propaganda), Joop F. Wolff (editor in chief of *De Waarheid*), W. Nieuwenhijse and F. Meis (responsible for CPN activities in the industrial sector), Marcus Bakker (leader of the CPN group in the Lower Chamber of Parliament), C. IJmkers (in charge of municipal council work), and Jaap Wolff (treasurer and editor in chief of *Politiek en Cultuur*) (*De Waarheid*, 9, 24 February).

The Netherlands General Youth Union (Algemeen Nederlands Jeugdverbond; ANJ) is small, but is the most important of the CPN front organizations, being the main source of future party members. During 1970 the ANJ coordinated various activities with the Netherlands Women's Movement (Nederlandse Vrouwenbeweging). Both groups were joined in their activities by the organization of former resistance fighters, United Resistance 1940-1945 (Verenigd Verzet 1940-1945). The Netherlands-U.S.S.R. Friendship Society has been an auxiliary of considerable strength and importance, but has recently severed its ties with the CPN because of the party's autonomy policy and become a center for pro-Soviet dissidents within the CPN.

Party Internal Affairs. Its successes in the 1970 elections did not noticeably strengthen the CPN as an organization. Ironically, the tasks of the party cadres were made more difficult, since the increased number of CPN members elected to representative bodies has limited the manpower normally available for ordinary party activities. Apart from the minor changes in the party leadership at the congress, the CPN in 1970 presented the picture of an internally stable party. Indeed, the election victories of the CPN in 1970 contributed to an increase in revenues from paying members and was very welcome in meeting the expense of publications, election and industrial campaigns, and the salaries of the fairly high number of paid party officials. The special financial drive, still necessary to supplement the normal revenue from membership dues and subscriptions, was reportedly not completely successful. For 1971 the target has been set at 400,000 guilders.

Domestic Attitudes and Activities. At the CPN congress in February the danger of a "concentration of the right," led by the Christian Democratic Union, was described by Chairman Hoekstra as the foremost threat to "parliamentary democracy" and a potential basis for "fascism." He appealed for the formation of a "concentration of the left"—consisting of "communists, socialists, trade union members, and progressive Christians"—that would strive for a "government of the worker's movement on a broad, progressive basis." Such a coalition could be created "within the class struggle" through cooperation, particularly during wage conflicts and strikes, with "class-conscious social democrats" and "class-conscious students." (*De Waarheid*, 7 February). In the draft program for submission to the congress, "parliamentary democracy" was hailed as "an achievement of the worker's movement" and as offering "the most favorable circumstances for the organization of the working class" within the capitalist system (*ibid.*, 4 December 1969).

In the CPN's "Action Program 1970," approved at the congress, the party's domestic and foreign policies were outlined. Major domestic demands were for higher wages and lower taxation, "democratization" of education, no interference with the right to strike, "democratization" of cultural policies, curtailment of expenditures for the Common Market (EEC), nationalization of natural gas and other natural resources, and expansion of low-rent housing (*ibid.*, 10 February 1970).

Consistent with Hoekstra's endorsement of "concentration of the left" during the congress, the CPN proposed to the Socialist Party (Partij van de Arbeid; PdA) in May that the PdA join with the CPN in "unity and cooperation in a day of protest against the American action in Indochina" throughout the Netherlands (*ibid.*, 13 May). The offer was rejected. The CPN youth group—the ANJ—took part in related protest demonstrations with students in Amsterdam, Haarlem, Utrecht, Maastricht, and other cities (*ibid.*)

In its attempts to arrive at joint actions with "other class-conscious movements," the CPN was more successful in August in its initiative to form a "Suharto Unwanted" committee against the visit to the Netherlands of President Suharto of Indonesia. Members of the CPN and its front organizations along with followers of a half-dozen other groups were on the committee (*ibid.*, 4, 5, 6 August). The result was a major opposition movement whose activities included the circulation of petitions opposing the visit, the mailing of protest telegrams to the government, the writing of anti-Suharto slogans on buildings, and the staging of a major demonstration in Amsterdam on 1 September. The committee's efforts were extensively reported in *De Waarheid* during August and September, with special emphasis on the joint nature of the various protest activities.

A third initiative for cooperation with noncommunists on the national level was contained in a CPN policy statement—"For a New Government, For a New Policy"—adopted by the party leadership on 8 October. Appealing to "all workers, technical and scientific leaders, students, farmers and horticulturists, shopkeepers—all democratic and freedom-loving Dutchmen" to support the party's "Action Program 1970," the statement reiterated some twenty demands voiced at the party congress, ranging from condemnation of NATO and the EEC to demands for increases in old-age pensions and higher taxes for the wealthy. (*Ibid.*, 10 October.)

The CPN youth group disseminated propaganda against the government's defense policies, for the National Liberation Front of South Vietnam, and for the "Suharto Unwanted" committee. It was assisted in these ventures by the Netherlands Women's Movement and the United Resistance 1940-1945.

International Views and Positions. In its "Action Program 1970" the CPN endorsed neutrality for the Netherlands, collective security in Europe, a halt to the "armaments race," an end to conflict in the Middle East, censure of the "colonels' rule" in Greece and the "generals' rule" in Indonesia, diplomatic recognition of North Vietnam, an end to the government's military intervention in the Netherlands Antilles, and abolition of all nuclear weapons (*De Waarheid*, 10 February).

An analysis of the communist movement on the international level was delivered at the CPN congress by Central Committee member Paul de Groot, formerly party chairman. His speech—entitled "Leninism and Our Time" and described by Hoekstra as the "highlight" of the congress—chastised former Soviet leader Khrushchev for "demagogical misuse" of political errors by Stalin in order to introduce a "revisionist" version of Leninism which, de Groot said, had led to "disorientation and emasculation of the communist movement in many countries" and produced election defeats for the communists in the Netherlands. He emphasized that while unity was an absolute necessity, the "cornerstone of Leninism" was the right of self-determination of nations, and that Lenin's "greatest discovery was the function of the national liberation struggle of the oppressed nations as the dynamite with which to blow up imperialism." (*Ibid.*, 9 February.)

De Groot pointed out that "unity of action" was not to be confused with "ideological conciliation." In this connection he welcomed the Soviet initiative to normalize Sino-Soviet relations as a "first step toward restoration of unity in the international communist movement." He believed that progress toward unity of action was being made, but added that it was necessary to maintain continuous opposition to efforts to transplant "controversies and conflicts between socialist states" into party ranks. He concluded by referring to the significance of Ho Chi Minh's "political testament" as a "plea to the Soviet and Chinese communists and all others to restore international unity." (*Ibid.*)

The CPN's position on NATO and the EEC was also outlined by de Groot during the party congress. Should NATO and the EEC be dissolved, de Groot believed, capitalism would be unable to survive in Europe. He considered that the struggle against these two bodies was of primary importance, and that the greatest chance for success lay in opposition to be conducted in the smaller West European countries, since opposition could more effectively be conducted under the motto of a "struggle for national liberation and national independence." (*Ibid.*)

The Warsaw Pact invasion of Czechoslovakia, in August 1968, was strongly condemned at the time by the CPN Central Committee (see *ibid.*, 26 August 1968). In 1970, however, Hoekstra expressed "regret" that the CPN was unable to form an "opinion . . . because neither the Communist Party of Czechoslovakia nor the Communist Party of the Soviet Union had rendered a clear account so far." His only direct criticism of the invasion concerned the failure to take into account the "impression . . . on the working class in the capitalist countries" created by the invasion (*ibid.*, 7 February 1970).

The CPN's tendency to seek closer relations with the Communist Party of the Soviet Union (CPSU), first apparent in 1969, was also evident in 1970. The party congress adopted a foreign policy stand similar to that of the CPSU, favoring "collective security," the nuclear nonproliferation treaty, diplomatic recognition of East Germany, and admission of the Chinese People's Republic to the United Nations (*ibid.*, 10 February). This position was expressed almost verbatim in Chairman Hoekstra's policy address to the party leadership conference on 8 October (*ibid.*, 10 October). The Soviet-West German agreement on the renunciation of force was endorsed as an "event of great significance" that would lead to a "lessening of tension in Europe" (*ibid.*, 7 August).

In regard to the December disturbances in Poland—while stating "[these events] cannot possibly be judged from the outside"—the CPN termed them a "vindication" of its own view that the leadership of the Polish communist party had "isolated" itself from the population, pursued bankrupt "revisionist policies," and placed "hopes on the illusion of profitable transactions with imperialist powers" (*ibid.*, 22 December).

International Activities and Party Contacts. The CPN congress was not attended by any foreign CP delegations, although two Soviet press representatives were present (from TASS and Novosty). The Central Committee of the CPSU sent a message to the congress appealing for unity in the international communist movement. Telegrams of greeting were sent by the communist parties of Romania, Israel, and North Vietnam. In a letter to the latter party, the congress expressed solidarity with the "heroic struggle" of the Vietnamese people (*ibid.*, 9 February).

The "practical solidarity" that Hoekstra emphasized in his speech to the congress was evident particularly with regard to the Vietnam war. On 15 May the editor in chief of *De Waarheid*, Joop F. Wolff, attended a meeting of 18 communist parties from the "capitalist countries" in Europe, held in Paris and devoted to condemnation of "American aggression in Indochina." Wolff attended as an "observer" and was not authorized to sign any declaration—primarily because the CPN had not been invited to participate in the preparations for the meeting. (*Ibid.*, 21 and 28 May.)

The EEC and the struggle against "monopolies" were the subjects of a meeting on 10 August between Joop Wolff and the head of the international section of the Communist Party of Great Britain, Jack Woddis (*ibid.*, 11 August). On 2 September, Paul de Groot attended a reception given by the North Vietnamese delegation in Paris on the occasion of the twenty-fifth anniversary of the Democratic Republic of Vietnam. With Central Committee member A. de Leeuw, de Groot also attended an international meeting in Paris on 2 December for the support of the North Vietnamese peace proposals.

The London meeting of nine West European communist parties on 21 September was attended by de Groot and Wolff. At the meeting it was announced that a conference dealing with the problems resulting from the developments of multinational enterprises (such as banks, Royal Dutch Shell, and Unilever) would be convened in January 1971. On 20 November *De Waarheid* published a communiqué dated 18 November that outlined the CPN's position on the conference. The CPN urged the coordination of all communist parties in the EEC nations to oppose the activities of the capitalist monopolies. The communiqué gave the assurance that the CPN was "fully prepared" to take part as long as measures would be taken to ensure the independence of the parties concerned.

Specifically, the CPN criticized the method of voting during such conferences, which had been responsible for its decision to discontinue participation at the conferences of the past several years. The CPN held that the approval of "collective resolutions," which allowed a numerical majority of participants to make decisions binding on all, was "not in accordance with Marxist-Leninist principles, which demand independent and creative thinking by every party." The CPN demanded, instead, that it should be the "exclusive privilege of the party leaderships to draw conclusions from the conference and to use the results of the exchange of ideas in their policies, preserving complete independence of action for every party." (*Ibid.*, 20 November.)

Publications. The most important organ of the CPN is the newspaper *De Waarheid* (The Truth), published daily in Amsterdam. It has an estimated circulation of 16,500. Deficits incurred by the CPN publications continue to be partly offset by the profits of the CPN's two commercial printing enterprises, the firms of Dijkman and Heierman. Income is also provided by the renting of conference rooms in the party-owned building in Amsterdam.

The Dijkman publishing house enjoyed an increase in commercial orders in 1970, in contrast to that of Heierman, which experienced severe financial difficulties. Heierman continued to print all party publications, including the theoretical monthly journal *Politik en Cultuur* (estimated circulation 2,500), the organ of the Netherlands Women's Movement *Vrouwen* (9,500) and the monthly journal of the Netherlands-U.S.S.R. Friendship Society (5,000). The party bookshop and publishing house, Pegasus, also experienced financial difficulties in 1970. In April, Central Committee member W. Hartog was replaced as director by committee member Jaap Wolff, brother of the editor in chief of *De Waarheid*, who subsequently announced plans to have Pegasus publish all major party publications in the future.

* * *

The Netherlands-U.S.S.R. Friendship Society serves as a center for dissident pro-Soviet communists in the Netherlands. During the Lenin Centenary celebrations in April, the society organized commemorative meetings in a number of Dutch cities. The meeting in Amsterdam was attended by diplomatic representatives from the embassies of East European countries, who also provide the society with some of its financial support. The decided pro-Soviet policy of the society presents something of an obstacle to an improvement of relations between the CPN and the CPSU, as was evident at the society's commemoration of the fifty-third anniversary of the October Revolution, attended by a delegation from the CPSU. The Soviet ambassador awarded Lenin Jubilee medals to a number of prominent society members, thus emphasizing the CPSU's approval of the activities conducted by the society.

There are four pro-Chinese political groups in the Netherlands. Their influence is small. The League of Dutch Marxists-Leninists (Bond van Nederlandse Marxisten-Leninisten; BNML), under the leadership of Chris Bischot, declined in importance in 1970. Its organ, *De Rode Vlag* (Red Flag) has appeared only once, and in stencilled form, since September 1969. BNML activities in 1970 centered on a Dutch translation of the philosophical, political, and strategic works of Mao Tse-tung.

The Marxist-Leninist Party of the Netherlands (Marxistisch-Leninistische Partij van Nederland; MLPN), under the leadership of Chris Petersen, was founded in 1969. The party's correspondence with the Chinese Communist Party and the Albanian Workers' Party is regularly published in its monthly organ, *De Kommunist*. In 1970 the MLPN sought to gain influence among industrial workers through publication of the *Centrale Bedrijfskrant* (Central Paper for Industrial Workers) and among young persons through contacts with the Rode Jeugd (Red Youth), a Maoist youth movement. The Rode Jeugd, under the leadership of Van der Valk, maintains "action groups" in Amsterdam, IJmuiden, The Hague, and Eindhoven which take part in local demonstrations and propaganda campaigns. Their main activity in 1970 was in support of the anti-Suharto protests during August and September.

The most active pro-Chinese group during 1970 was the Marxist-Leninist Communist Unity Movement of the Netherlands (Kommunistische Eenheidsbeweging Nederland—Marxistisch-

Leninistisch; KEN-ML), led by Nico Schrevel. It was formerly known as the Marxist-Leninist Center of the Netherlands (Marxistisch-Leninistisch Centrum Nederland; MLCN). The present name was adopted at the Second Congress of the MLCN, in January 1970, for the announced purpose of more effectively contributing to and emphasizing the "unity of the working class and unity of intellectuals and workers in the struggle for socialism." Membership figures were not reported, but the party is well organized and appears to be growing rather rapidly. The congress endorsed increased cooperation with the Rode Jeugd, organized joint action of students and workers, and increased courses in Marxism-Leninism and in the works of Mao Tse-tung at the party's Marxist-Leninist Center in Utrecht. The party goal was defined as "a socialist society in the Netherlands . . . based on scientific socialism as developed by Marx and Engels and as expanded by Lenin and Mao Tse-tung" (*De Rode Tribune*, no. 2).

The KEN-ML sees "the struggle against imperialism" as the most important activity of the world revolutionary movement, and includes in it the struggle against "modern revisionism," exemplified by the Soviet Union. It charges the United States and the Soviet Union with together "maintaining the existing power blocs and partitioning the countries of the third world between themselves." (*Ibid.*)

The party organ *De Rode Tribune*, published in Rotterdam, had previously had a "contemplative character" which the 1970 party congress decided to change so as to make the paper an "instrument for socialist action by people concerned with action" (*ibid.*). During the rest of the year, the paper devoted articles to criticizing the CPN congress (nos. 3 and 4), charging that CPN policies were contributing to a "direct strengthening of the existing system" (nos. 3, 4, and 5), praising the "anti-capitalist awareness" that was developing in the student movement (nos. 4, 5, and 7), criticizing Soviet foreign policy as "imperialism with a socialist label" (no. 8), and describing the KEN-ML as the "vanguard" of the Dutch working class in the West European class struggle (no. 12).

H. J. M. M. and D. L. B.

NORWAY

The Communist Party of Norway (Norges Kommunistiske Parti; NKP) was founded on 4 November 1923. It has some 3,000 members, out of a population of 3,867,000 (estimated 1969). Support for the party, which has operated legally at all times except under German occupation during the Second World War, comes primarily from unionized industrial workers in Oslo and from low-income groups in the economically disadvantaged northernmost province of Finnmark.

The NKP made its strongest showing in the 1945 election when, because of its wartime record of resistance to the Germans, the party gained 11.8 per cent of the vote. For many years, however, it has been a marginal factor in Norwegian politics. The party's decline was accelerated when the Socialist People's Party (Socialistisk Folkeparti; SF) was formed in 1961 by social democrats and nonaffiliated leftists. That same year, the SF took the last parliamentary seat held by the communists. It stands midway between the NKP and another part of the left, the social-democratic Norwegian Labor Party (Det Norsk Arbeiderparti; DNA), which was in power from 1935 to 1965 and remains the largest single party. Though itself declining rapidly, the SF continues to represent a threat to the existence of the NKP.

In the 8 September 1969 parliamentary election, the NKP polled 1.0 per cent of the popular vote, down 0.4 per cent from 1965. The SF polled only 3.4 per cent (down 2.6) and lost its two seats. Of the DNA's 3.5 per cent (and six-seat) advance, 3.0 per cent came from the SF and NKP and only 0.5 per cent from the centrist and conservative government coalition partners.

Programs of the NKP and SF espouse the same political goals—a democratic transition to socialism on the basis of Marxism, parliamentarianism, and the multiparty system. Both are anti-NATO and "anti-imperialist," and both support "third world liberation movements." Yet the SF regards the NKP as "dogmatic" and "old-Marxist" and as a minor irritation to the labor movement and the "active left." Conversely, the communists accuse the SF of splitting the labor movement by opportunistically disassociating itself from the communist label at home while "proudly espousing communist allegiance abroad." Against a backdrop of mutual polemics, electoral cooperation with the SF—the NKP's only apparent prospect for political gain—has been precluded.

Turmoil within the SF itself has further complicated the situation. A vote of confidence for the "conservative" SF majority in February 1969 led to the defection of a radical pro-Chinese youth faction and the establishment of a fourth leftist party, the Socialist Youth League (Marxist-Leninist)—Socialistisk Ungdoms Forbund (Marxist-Leninist), or SUF. The SUF gained early recognition by the Chinese Communist Party and by Maoist splinter groups throughout Scandinavia. It has drawn substantial support from the NKP youth auxiliary, Communist Youth (Kommunistisk Ungdom; KU), while those remaining in that organization have largely been polarized into radical (pro-SUF) and moderate (anti-SUF) factions.

Leadership and Organization. Reidar Larsen, who replaced the Muscovite Emil Løvlien as NKP chairman in 1965, was reelected in 1968 by the party's Twelfth Congress. (Congresses are held every third year, with national conferences in other years). Larsen heads the Political Bureau, which includes Ivar Lie, Arne Jørgensen, and Arne Pettersen as full members and Martin Gunnar Knutsen and Olav Minotti as alternates. He also heads the Secretariat, which includes Lie, Jørgensen, Pettersen, and Knutsen, together with Just Lippe, Rolf Nettum, Kolbjørn Harbu, Leif Johansen, and Leif Hammerstad. Two pro-Chinese Secretariat members were removed in 1970: Esther Bergerud was suspended by the Central Committee on 6 September by a vote of 28 to 2 (*Friheten*, 14-19 September; see also below) and Bjarne Rolstad died in February.

The KU was constituted in 1967 to replace the former NKP youth affiliate, Communist Youth of Norway (Norges Kommunistisk Ungdomsforbund; NKU), which had broken with the NKP earlier that year in sympathy with the Muscovite minority subsequently excluded from the NKP leadership in the 1968 congress elections. Elected for a two-year period by the KU's second ordinary congress in May 1969 were a seven-man Secretariat, including Georg Ovesen (chairman), Tor Olsen (organizational secretary), and Arvid Løkkeberg (secretary); and a 10-man Central Committee.

The NKU still professes to adhere to NKP principles. Since NKP and KU relations have often been strained by the KU's connections with the Maoist SUF, a "rehabilitation" of the NKU by the NKP could take place.

NKP strength in trade unions is limited. The party controls only a small number of local cells and none of the national labor unions. The party directs a "Baltic Sea Committee," which sends large delegations to the "Workers' Conferences of Baltic Nations, Norway, and Iceland," held annually by trade unionists in Rostock, East Germany. The 1970 meeting was held 16-17 July.

Friendship organizations controlled by the party include those with the Soviet Union, Czechoslovakia, and Cuba. The Norway-China Association, until 1969 under NKP control, must be considered to have fallen to the dissident camp; the association is headed by suspended NKP Secretariat member Esther Bergerud.

Party Internal Affairs. The party's internal conflict, a factor in its poor electoral performance in recent years, shifted in ideological direction during the late 1960's. The Muscovites' challenge to Larsen's self-proclaimed nationalist, left-socialist course of increased independence of Moscow and the communist camp in general has largely dissipated since the 1968 congress, when their leading protagonist, Jørgen Vogt, ousted as editor of the party organ *Friheten* in March 1967, was dropped from the party leadership. As the threat from the right wing diminished, however, that from the extreme-left Maoist element came to the fore. Larsen succeeded in concealing from the membership the extent of the disruption within the leadership until late 1969 when, apparently unable to quell the Maoists, he disclosed that "nonconformists" accounted for the majority of the *Friheten* staff and were issuing their own publication, *Røde Fane* (Red Banner), which they claimed represented dominant tendencies in one KU and three NKP districts (see also *YICA*, 1970, pp. 237-38). A comprehensive purge of the *Friheten* staff took place, and the editorial board, which since the events of 1967 had consisted of Arne Jørgensen and Reidar Larsen, was expanded to include Kåre Selnes, Martin Gunner Knutsen, Arne Pettersen, Oddbjørn Monsen, and Kolbjørn Harbu (*Friheten*, 26 January 1970), none of whom was believed to pose any threat to Larsen's rule.

Factionalism continued, however, and in August 1970 the leadership attempted a purge of 27 pro-Chinese members of the Oslo "East Side" cell who had been largely responsible for organizing opposition to the NKP leadership. According to the SUF monthly *Klassekampen* (nos. 7-8), the group received mimeographed letters from their district committee informing them that, because of their support of the "antiparty" *Røde Fane*, they were no longer regarded as members of the NKP. Most details of the action were withheld from the *Friheten* readership, but were revealed in the SUF organ by Esther Bergerud, who reported that the East Side group had sought, through *Røde Fane*, to promote discussion of the NKP's political line—which the party leadership allegedly had succeeded in barring within basic organizations. According to Bergerud, the group had voted at its annual meeting, by 27 to 12, to continue support of its publication, but the district committee had overruled the vote and convoked a new meeting. When this meeting sustained the vote of the first, the district committee chairman, Leif Hammerstad, called upon the 12-man minority to organize itself as a new East Side cell and asked the 27-man majority whether it would agree to follow the party's laws and principles. The group, headed by Dagfinn Borgen, then responded that the district committee had itself violated the party law of majority rule.

Bergerud pointed out that Larsen had declared, in connection with the Vogt challenge some years earlier, that the "practice of exclusion of members for their opinions" had been abolished by the NKP, and that the party "must accept differences of opinion in several areas of party ideology and develop along with these (see *YICA*, 1968, p. 452; *Friheten*, 20 March 1967). She commented that while the challenge from the right had been dealt with lightly, Larsen's declaration apparently was to be overlooked when a threat came from the left.

The dissidents—the East Side cell majority, together with elements of two other NKP district organizations and one KU group—formed what they called the "Marxist-Leninist Front in the NKP" (MLF) and, at a conference in June attended by some 50 persons, adopted a political platform declaring the "strategic principal enemy" to be monopoly capitalism and the "tactical principal enemy," revisionism. MLF goals were "renewal of the party's cadres . . . in cooperation with all other Marxist-Leninist groups outside the party," and, ultimately, "a party based on Mao's thought" (*Røde Fane*, July).

Larsen blamed the rift on infiltration by SUF elements seeking to take over the NKP. He denied, however, that any exclusions had taken place. The 27 dissidents, he argued, had "set themselves outside the party," but could "at any time regain their membership on certain conditions." (Quoted, *Klassekampen*, no. 9.)

Domestic Attitudes and Activities. The NKP in its 1963 program declared itself to be an "independent, democratic, and national Nordic party, based on the principles of Marxism-Leninism," having as its aim the "overthrow of capitalism in Norway through peaceful transition to a parliamentary socialist republic." The path to socialism as elaborated in its current program adopted in March 1969, promises to guarantee—"during the transition to and under socialism" —freedom of organization, assembly, and the press, and to uphold constitutional rights and principles (see *YICA*, 1970, pp. 233-34). It proposes also to implement broad nationalization of industry and investment; reduce military expenditures, curb "legal or illegal tax evasion" in the higher income brackets, and increase property taxes and capital profits.

The NKP continued to fluctuate between calls for a united front of leftist forces and allegations against the other leftist parties—and particularly the DNA—which made the prospect of such interaction remote. Representing the NKP at an SF meeting in Oslo on 12 January 1970, Arne Jørgensen reasoned that between the NKP and the SF there was much less antagonism than between both these parties and the social-democratic DNA, and that NKP and SF interests were identical on most vital issues (*Friheten*, 12-17 January). At a meeting on 14 March of the Norwegian Student Association on the theme "Gathering of the Leftist Forces," however, Reidar Larsen ruled out any organizational gathering of leftist parties until ideological differences were discussed, though he indicated that immediate cooperation was feasible on specific issues (*ibid.*, 16-21, March).

One such issue, the year's collective-bargaining agreement, drew criticism at the NKP's national conference, on 25 April. The system of collective bargaining allegedly was designed to further the interests of the employers and the bourgeoisie, and did nothing to improve the lot of workers. Thus in the current negotiations, as before, the demands of the DNA-dominated trade union federation had been far too weak, failing to take into account price rises and production growth. Socialists were warned not to harbor illusions about the DNA and to strive for united action only to the left of that party. (*Ibid.*, 27 April-2 May.)

At a Labor Day (1 May) demonstration in which the NKP, KU, SF, and SUF were represented and which an estimated 2,000 persons attended, Larsen protested official action against strikers and called upon a combined labor movement to "prepare effective plans to establish rights which will be inviolable," and to "do away with the entire concept of whether a strike is lawful or unlawful." Workers must strike, he declared "when they have a need to do so." Today, as before, he alleged, the nation's economic development was determined by a small "privileged" group in positions of power, and the worker was still regarded by the employer as "a machine to be driven to its limit." (*Ibid.*, 4-9 May.)

The settlement of a lengthy mineworkers' strike at Kiruna in northern Sweden—where the miners, according to the NKP, had to "struggle for their rights without the help of their own labor organization"—was hailed as a possible "turning point" for the entire labor movement of Scandinavia. The strike was said to have revealed that the exploitation of workers did not diminish in a "so-called" welfare state, and that the high production-growth rate in Sweden (as in Norway), on the contrary, was to be attributed to "indiscriminate rationalization" in industry, subjecting workers to "physical and psychological pressure." With an ever growing concentration of capital and centralization of power at the top labor level, workers had no real influence over their own wage and working conditions. That this could occur in Sweden, where for a generation there had been a social-democratic leadership, was proof that the social-democratic policy of class cooperation could lead only to defeat for the working class. (Resolution of the NKP Central Committee, *ibid.*, 26 January; see also *Sweden.*)

The NKP and SF held consultative talks, starting in the fall, with a view to the 1971 municipal elections. While it appeared at the year's end that agreement on joint slates might be reached in some constituencies, differences continued to be such that cooperation was likely to be limited. Similar talks in connection with the 1969 parliamentary election had collapsed (see *YICA*, 1970, p. 236).

International Views and Positions. The NKP advocates Norway's withdrawal from NATO, an all-European security system based on general disarmament, a ban on nuclear weapons, and the expansion of Norwegian economic and cultural ties with socialist states. The party holds that, through NATO, the country is directly subordinated to the "imperialist" policies of the United States and is an "outpost in NATO's nuclear strategy." The nation's military alignment with the "American power of oppression" is seen as representing a "double morality" which, although not yet recognized by many people, may eventually become a central question in Norwegian politics. No single area of the world, Reidar Larsen said in his Labor Day address, was free from "American imperialism's economic and political undermining efforts with the support of local reactionaries." (*Friheten*, 4-9 May.)

The question of economic cooperation held priority in the party's attention to international affairs. The NKP Secretariat in February unanimously declared its satisfaction with negotiations toward establishment of the "Nordek" inter-Scandinavian customs union: although "not a form of economic integration corresponding to socialist policies," Nordek would, nonetheless, contain certain economic benefits; specifically, it would contribute to preserving Nordic independence vis-à-vis the European Economic Community (EEC). In the NKP view, Nordek must be implemented according to the agreed timetable without regard for possible negotiation possibilities in the EEC, and with the goal of making the North a "peaceful and independent economic amalgamation with good economic and trade relations with all of Europe and the world." (*Ibid.*, 16 February.) The NKP national conference urged that Nordic countries view Nordek as an alternative to EEC affiliation. Should any Nordic nation enter the EEC, that nation would not only automatically subordinate itself to the EEC's "rule and common policy," but would simultaneously remove the basis for a separate economic integration policy for the North. Thus, a final break with EEC politics was necessary in order to further Nordic cooperation. (*Ibid.*, 27 April-2 May.)

Following Norway's parliamentary decision, in September, to seek EEC affiliation, a Central Committee resolution declared that it would be an illusion to look to the social democrats for resistance to the EEC or amelioration of the terms of eventual Norwegian membership. The DNA, which during its lengthy term in power had either not desired, or been unable, to further socialism, could hardly be expected at this juncture to act in the interests of socialism within the EEC—"a union which is more strongly dominated by capitalist forces than the Nordic countries, and which is founded on the basis of an agreement (the Rome treaty) which in all its main aspects presupposes a capitalist economy." (*Ibid.*, 14-19 September.)

The EEC was the major topic at the annual meeting of Norwegian, Danish, Swedish, and Finnish communist parties in Helsinki on 13-14 May. A joint communiqué stressed that initiatives for inter-Scandinavian economic cooperation must go hand in hand with efforts to establish a neutral and nuclear-free zone in the North, and emphasized the necessity of a conference of European states to "strengthen security and further economic and open cooperation in all of Europe" (*ibid.*, 18-23 May).

Remarks by NKP Secretariat member Arne Pettersen at a KU conference (16-17 May), although apparently intended to reflect the Soviet view of a European security conference, were notable in that they described a strategy seemingly at variance with official Soviet statements. Pettersen, repudiating the contention of pro-Chinese splinter elements that an all-European security system would be a "new and worse NATO," suggested that the East European bloc supported a security conference in order "not merely to unmask imperialism, or to use it as a propaganda forum, but to go a step further," using an eventual all-European security system to "create a better platform for class struggle." Therefore, while Western powers could be expected to concentrate on the question of disarmament, the bloc, according to Pettersen, would use the conference to "put imperialism on the defensive" and thereby broaden the "anti-monopolist, anti-imperialist movement." (*Ibid.*)

In 1970 the NKP continued to agitate, with no apparent effect, against Norway's NATO affiliation (which is supported by the DNA and opposed by the SF). The KU organized demonstrations held on 21-29 April in connection with NATO exercises in the Oslofjord. According to KU literature, Norway was an "ever more important link in NATO's aggressive plans," and NATO allegedly had "contingency plans which could be used against the Norwegian working class in time of crisis." West German leaders were a "decisive hindrance to lasting peace in Europe," and through continued affiliation in NATO Norway would be giving West German troops an "even bigger playground in the years to come." (*Ibid.*, 20-25 April.)

Similarly, the NKP has been frustrated by its inability to influence the antiwar movement. The two main groups, the "Norwegian Solidarity Committee for Vietnam" and the "Vietnam Movement in Norway," are themselves fragmented and mutually antagonistic. The SUF and some members of the KU support the Solidarity Committee, which collects funds for "political and material support" to the National Liberation Front of South Vietnam (NLFSV). The NKP has attempted to appear neutral, but generally supports the Vietnam Movement, which earmarks funds to the NLFSV "for humanitarian purposes only."

The NKP joined with several other leftist organizations in picketing the newly-established information office in Oslo of the Republic of South Vietnam "quislings" and urged the Norwegian government to break all forms of contact with the Saigon "junta" and recognize the Provisional Revolutionary Government (PRG) as the "sole representative of the South Vietnamese people's will" (*ibid.*, 9 March). The party maintained close ties with the information office which the PRG opened in Oslo in August.

At a meeting in Oslo on 8 May, sponsored by the Vietnam Movement and commemorating the twenty-fifth anniversary of Norway's liberation from German occupation, Reidar Larsen drew a parallel between the "Norwegian struggle against German fascism" and the "Vietnamese struggle against American imperialism." The war in Vietnam, he said, would not be settled at the Paris talks or by "meeting halfway"; rather, nothing short of total U.S. withdrawal would be acceptable as a precondition to genuine peace talks. Delegates at the meeting included Mme Nguyen Thi Binh, foreign minister of the PRG, and Le Phuong, in charge of its information office in Stockholm. (*Ibid.*, 11-16 May.)

The NKP, the Vietnam Movement, the KU, and the SF organized a "people's meeting" in Oslo on 21 May on the theme "U.S.A. Out of Indochina." The meeting, which drew some 1,000 participants, was boycotted by the SUF. (*Ibid.*, 25-30 May.)

In the wake of its surprise decision to participate in the June 1969 Moscow Conference and in its subsequent removal of pro-Chinese elements from within its ranks, the assertedly neutral NKP leadership in 1970 appeared to have shifted slightly to a midly pro-Soviet stance in the international communist camp. Even so, a return to the pre-Larsen era of subservience to the Soviets was by no means indicated.

The NKP commemorated the Lenin Centenary with a week-long theoretical seminar (14-20 March) on "Topical Questions of Leninism." The seminar was attended by party delegations from the Soviet Union, East Germany, Hungary, Italy, and Romania. (TASS, 18 March.) Ivar Lie of the NKP Political Bureau represented the party at the Centenary celebration in Moscow.

Main Party Publications. The central organ of the NKP is *Friheten* (Freedom), issued in Oslo. Formerly a daily, *Friheten* became a weekly in 1967 as a result of financial difficulties. The KU issues a bulletin called *Kommunistisk Ungdom* (Communist Youth). The NKU publishes *NKU-Informasjon* (NKU Information).

* * *

Socialist Youth League. The SUF, which has been endorsed by the most active of the other Maoist groups in Scandinavia as the party representing Norwegian Marxist-Leninists, is headed by Pål Steigan. Steigan was among those who defected from the SF in 1969. The SUF has declared its intention to create a revolutionary communist party based upon Marxism-Leninism and Mao Tse-tung's thought, taking the position that without such a party the Norwegian working class cannot overthrow monopoly capital's dictatorship and establish its own.

The "Marxist-Leninist work and study groups" (ML-gruppene) set up by the SUF in 1969 and 1970 under the direction of Torstein Haldorsen are said to have brought together revolutionary socialists who left the SF in 1969 and formerly partyless revolutionaries. The task of these groups is, by conducting basic studies in Marxism-Leninism and Mao Tse-tung's thought, to create the ideological foundation for a communist working-class party. Of a temporary nature, the groups would be disbanded with the establishment of such a party. (*Klassekampen*, no. 4, 1970, reporting on the groups' national conference, 14-15 March.)

The SUF professes to view the NKP as "anti-Leninist and revisionist" because it upholds the "recognized rules of play" in Norwegian political life, neglecting the fact that the state represents the dictatorship of the bourgeoisie over the workers and that this state must be crushed to make room for the working-class state. (*Ibid.*)

In a message to the Chinese Communist Party, the SUF Central Committee heralded China's launching of an earth satellite—an event which, according to the SUF, manifested the revolutionary progress of the Chinese people in turning China into an advanced country with a highly developed production level, armed politically and materially, and fully capable of beating off any offensive (NCNA, 4 May).

A five-member SUF delegation headed by Steigan visited China in October and was received by Mao and other Chinese party leaders. Steigan declared, upon his return, that the Norwegian people could gain victory through applying Mao's thought in existing conditions and setting Mao's philosophical thinking free from the classroom and letting it serve the people (*Klassekampen*, no. 11).

Publications. The main organs of the SUF are the monthly bulletins *Klassekampen* (Class Struggle) and *Røde Garde* (Red Guard). In addition, *Til Kamp* (To the Struggle) is issued by the SUF for dissemination among high school students.

V. B.

PORTUGAL

The Portuguese Communist Party (Partido Comunista Português; PCP) was founded in March 1921 and has been illegal since 1926. Under vigorous repression by the Portuguese government, the party clandestinely maintains a tight organization and continues to operate both at home and abroad, mainly in Romania.

Within Portugal, PCP members worked until 1970 through the underground Patriotic Front of National Liberation (Frente Patriótica de Libertação Nacional; FPLN), established in December 1962. The front, which has its coordinating center in Algiers, also attempts to rally socialists, liberals, republicans, Catholics, and liberal monarchists. During 1970, leaders of the FPLN, from headquarters in Algiers, excluded the PCP from the organization, announcing that the front would pursue a policy of armed struggle (see below, "Domestic Attitudes and Activities").

The PCP's membership comprises mainly urban workers concentrated in Lisbon and Oporto, and to a lesser degree middle-class elements including intellectuals. Although the party has enlisted a small number of farm laborers, primarily in the upper Alentejo area, it is very weak among the Portuguese agricultural proletariat. Considerable support comes from among university students, many of whom favor its legalization and the establishment of a left-wing coalition government. Western sources estimate PCP membership at 2,000. The population of Portugal is 9,505,000 (estimated 1970).

In addition to the PCP, which has a decidedly pro-Soviet orientation, there appear to exist two small pro-Chinese groups: the Portugal Action Front (Frente de Ação Popular; FAP) and the United League of Revolutionary Action (Liga Unida de Ação Revolucionaria; LUAR).

In Portugal, a country that has been led by an authoritarian government since 1926, communism has played only an insignificant role.

Leadership and Organization. The PCP maintains a closely knit apparatus and keeps its leadership within Portugal anonymous. Among the known leaders in exile are the secretary-general, Alvaro Cunhal, and two members of the Secretariat, Sergio Vilarigues and José Vitoriano.

Domestic Attitudes and Activities. The PCP goal is to overthrow the present Portuguese government, which it describes as a "fascist dictatorship," and to establish socialism. Following the pro-Soviet line, the PCP advocates mass actions, such as strikes and demonstrations, and the use of parliamentary means to achieve its objectives. A statement by the PCP Political Committee listed the following as the party's present objectives:

1. Freedom of association, speech, demonstration, strikes, and trade union activity.
2. Abolishing censorship and granting the right to information of all citizens.

3. Recognizing the legality of the democratic opposition, its organizations and propaganda media.
4. Releasing of all political prisoners, returning exiles, repealing "security measures," ending the torturing of prisoners, investigating the crimes and abuses of power committed by the fascists.
5. Really dissolving the PIDE (disguised as the General Security Department) and the Portuguese Legion.
6. Transferring the direction of mass organizations, in particular the National Trade Unions and student associations, to members of these organizations.
7. Meeting the immediate economic demands of the working class and other working people.
8. Ending the colonial war immediately. It is necessary to insist on establishing contacts and initiating negotiations with the legitimate representatives of the peoples of Angola, Guinea, and Mozambique.
9. Revising the foreign policy to establish peaceful relations with all countries. (*IB*, nos. 17-18, 1970.)

The PCP sees the current administration of Marcelo Caetano as a continuation of the Salazar government and its liberalizing policies as "confined to an insignificant softening of censorship and to a fictitious and untrue liquidation of the secret police" ("Radio Free Portugal, 12 January). Governmental economic policies, including agrarian reform, have been condemned by the PCP. It predicts that the agrarian reform project, which would create agricultural cooperatives from small and medium-sized holdings, will result in "nothing less than vast capitalist enterprise organs under capitalist control" (*ibid.*).

During 1970 the PCP continued to regard the current Portuguese military activity in Africa as a "colonial war." Cunhal, in a broadcast from Moscow ("Radio Peace and Progress," 20 May), reiterated the party's support for independence movements in Angola, Mozambique, and Guinea (Bissau), declaring that "communists regard the colonial war waged by the Portuguese fascists and colonialists, supported by the NATO powers, as a monstrous crime not only against the peoples of Angola, Guinea, and Mozambique, but also against the Portuguese people and, in particular, against the youth of Portugal." [1] Cunhal contended that each year "more than 10,000 young men fail to appear for registration and the draft," and claimed that this was an indication that they were "answering the appeal of the party."

PCP statements during 1970 made frequent reference to successes obtained the previous year, especially during the national elections (which, according to the party, permitted communists to establish wider contacts with other anti-government elements). Such feelings, however, apparently were not shared by other "antifascist" elements working with the PCP. Disagreements between the PCP and the FPLN over revolutionary strategy (possibly in existence for several years but brought to the fore by Salazar's death) culminated in 1970 with the expulsion of the communist party from the front organization. While the PCP Central Committee had criticized in June the "pseudo-revolutionary leftist verbalism of some opportunist leaders" who did not believe in the need for a firm organization (i.e., the communist party) to carry on revolution, it was not until September that the existence of an irreconcilable difference between the FPLN and the PCP became evident.

Broadcasting from Algiers, FPLN leaders accused the PCP of thwarting the revolutionary process in Portugal, where it had a "monopoly of initiative, organizational, and operational means" and preferred to "boycott them rather than have them used without its control" ("Voice of Freedom" radio, 13 September). Claiming to have the support of militants inside Portugal,

[1]The liberation movement in its African colonies has forced Portugal to maintain there between 120,000 and 150,000 troops, which absorb more than 50 per cent of the national budget. During 1969 about 1,600 Portuguese soldiers were killed in action, according to the *Washington Post* (4 July 1970).

including members of the now defunct Portuguese Revolutionary Junta, the FPLN announced that on 3 September it sent a letter to the PCP stating that "it [was] not possible, at the present stage, to allow the leadership of the PCP to have the exclusive leadership in the Portuguese anti-fascist and anticolonialist movement" and that, therefore, "organic separation" between the FPLN and the PCP had been decided upon. Explaining the reasons for this action, the broadcast further stated:

> Unity, instead of being an incentive for action, is submitted to conditions imposed by the subjective interpretation of the proper time for action. As this kind of unity can only be achieved through legal objectives and nonviolent action, it is quite possible that all verbalism about overthrowing state structures by force of arms may have had no influence whatsoever [on the masses] and the revolutionary process in Portugal may be blocked. (*Ibid.*)

Shortly thereafter, on 29 September, another FPLN broadcast from Algiers announced that a "committee for reorganization of the FPLN" had been formed and that it would set up a "revolutionary initiative of the popular masses and launching revolutionary violence against the fascist and colonialist state." The broadcast also stated that the new FPLN did not intend to be a bureaucratic organization and that there would be "hundreds of nuclei and flexible, autonomous organizations adapted to local tasks, to political circumstances and conditions." Later in the year, reaffirming its militancy, the FPLN declared: "Conditions for revolutionary action are created through revolutionary initiative and practice." In an obvious reference to the PCP, it said: "Let others remain seated in their magisterial chairs, repeating that the conditions are not yet ripe." (*Ibid.*, 1 November.)

For its part, the PCP in various radio broadcasts described the situation in the FPLN as being only the result of a coup carried out by two members of the front, Fernando Piteira Santos and Manuel Alegre. According to the PCP, Piteira Santos and Alegre—in the absence from Algeria of the two other leaders of the front, Manuel Sertorio and Pedro Soares—had taken control of the propaganda means and financial resources of the FPLN. Judging from the prolonged attack on the PCP by the "Voice of Freedom" station, it appeared that the militants in control of the Algiers-based FPLN counted on the support of a considerable number of noncommunist Portuguese oppositionists.

In October the "Voice of Freedom" reported two violent actions carried out by a group called the Armed Revolutionary Action, which allegedly works with the FLPN. On 26 and 29 October explosives were detonated on two ships in Lisbon harbor which were ready to depart for Portugal's overseas territories, causing extensive damage. The FPLN broadcast described these explosions as "acts of protest," asserting that they had been carried out to give a "concrete meaning" to solidarity with the people of Angola, Guinea, and Mozambique. The broadcast also reiterated that it was necessary to open a front of "armed revolutionary action" within Portugal.

Because of the attitudes and actions of the FPLN, the PCP was forced to defend its role as a revolutionary party. A broadcast of the PCP's "Radio Free Portugal" on 1 November emphasized that "political education, unification, and coordination of the masses" were prerequisites for revolutionary action, but conceded that "victory over fascism [would] undoubtedly be achieved through the armed struggle of the masses." Likewise, the PCP attitude toward the explosions of 26 and 29 October evinced a shift from condemnation to approval. Although "Radio Free Portugal" on 2 November condemned the bombings as "irresponsible steps" and predicted that such actions could "only lead to serious accidents involving innocent victims," a later broadcast (on 21 November) declared that bombings had "great political significance" as "an expression of the growing popular resistance against the fascist policy and of the active solidarity of the Portuguese people with the peoples of the Portuguese colonies."

A reason behind the change in the PCP attitude toward violent actions may have been the desire to prevent the FPLN from claiming credit for them. The PCP broadcast of 21 November tried to disassociate the Armed Revolutionary Action (the group which carried out these bombings) from the FPLN, contending that the group's actions had not been a "product of pseudorevolutionary verbalism" and that its "modest" communique had stated that the members of the Armed Revolutionary Action did not "pretend that individual action [could] solve the complex problems of the revolutionary process." Another PCP broadcast (24 November) firmly asserted that there was no connection between the Armed Revolutionary Action and the "Algiers adventurists."

On 20 November three more bomb explosions took place in Lisbon (at the U.S. Embassy library, the training center for political police, and dockside installations). Although no political group claimed credit for these explosions, there were striking similarities between them and the earlier bombings.

While the strength of the forces supporting the FPLN could not be determined, the expulsion of the PCP from the front constituted a heavy blow for the communist party in its quest for leadership of the revolutionary movement in Portugal. Furthermore, the FPLN claimed to have the support of several PCP members. This was denied flatly by the PCP, but if the claim is true the party might face a split in the near future.

International Views and Positions. The PCP continued to evince a staunchly pro-Soviet line. In contrast, the "reorganized" FPLN seemed to have adopted a neutralist position in the Sino-Soviet dispute.

Commenting on the second anniversary of the Warsaw Pact invasion of Czechoslovakia, the PCP reaffirmed its support for the intervention, declaring: "For all real friends of the Czechoslovak people and all real revolutionaries, the political consolidation in Czechoslovakia in these two years and above all since April 1969 . . . can only be good news" ("Radio Free Portugal," 22 August).

Expressing a different position, the "Voice of Freedom" radio stated on 5 October: "We feel that the problems of the Portuguese revolutionary movement will not be solved with unconditionally pro-Soviet and pro-Chinese attitudes. We are in solidarity with the U.S.S.R. and the People's Republic of China. . . . We feel that it is by assuming our national responsibilities and by struggling for the liberation of the Portuguese people that we will fulfill our internationalist duties."

Another opportunity for different viewpoints on international issues was provided by the Middle East conflict. While the PCP approved the Soviet government's appeal for a cease-fire in Jordan during the month of September, the FPLN called for total support of Yasir 'Arafat and the "struggle of the Palestine people." Arafat, who opposes Israel's existence, condemns the Soviet Union's recognition of Israel.

Publications. The PCP official organ is the clandestine monthly *Avante*, founded in 1931. PCP views are also printed in leaflets and pamphlets dealing with specific subjects. In addition, the party broadcasts to Portugal over "Radio Free Portugal," which is believed to be based in Romania. The FPLN transmits as "Voice of Freedom," from Algeria.

* * *

The two pro-Chinese groups in Portugal are small and apparently isolated internationally. The Popular Action Front (FAP) was founded in 1964 by former PCP Executive Committee member,

Francisco Rodrígues Campos, who has been imprisoned since 1967. As in previous years, no FAP activities came to notice during 1970. The group publishes an irregular newspaper, *Revolução Popular*.

The other pro-Chinese group, the United League of Revolutionary Action (LUAR), was founded by a group of Portuguese officials and military men in 1966. It is considered to be quite militant. On 13 February 1970, sixteen LUAR members implicated in a 1967 bank robbery were sentenced to prison terms ranging from six months to five years. The leader of the movement, Herminio da Palma Inácio, escaped to Spain in June 1969 (see *YICA*, 1970, p. 246). At the beginning of 1970 da Palma Inácio was in England, where in a television interview he announced that armed revolution would soon begin in Portugal and that plans to that end were progressing "very well" (*South China Morning Post*, Hong Kong, 8 January 1970).

N. S.

SAN MARINO

The Communist Party of San Marino (Partito Comunista di San Marino; PCS) was founded originally in 1922, then eclipsed by fascism, and refounded in 1940. Although nominally independent (and represented as such at Italian party meetings and international communist party conferences), it is in reality an offshoot of the Italian Communist Party (Partito Comunista Italiano; PCI). The party has an estimated 1,000 members. The population of San Marino is a little over 19,000 (estimated 1970).

Elections were held on 7 September 1969 for San Marino's 60-member legislative body, the Grand Council. Under San Marino law, eligibility to vote extends to anyone born in that country, although by a law passed in 1966 absentee ballots are limited to residents of Europe. In September 1969 there were 16,720 registered voters, of which 7,419 were living abroad. Owing to their inability to vote by mail, some 400 U.S. citizens flew to San Marino for the elections. While the PCS lost a small number of votes in comparison with the earlier 1964 elections, it held its 14 seats, regaining one seat which it had lost in the intervening years to a former PCS councilor who had set up his own pro-Chinese Marxist-Leninist Movement (Movimento Marxista-Leninista). The PCS received 22.76 per cent of the vote; the pro-Chinese group obtained 1.24 per cent and lost its one seat.

The PCS is the second strongest party in the republic. It stands in opposition together with the Socialist Party (7 seats, 11.90 per cent of the vote) to the coalition government of Christian Democrats (27 seats, 44.03 per cent) and Social Democrats (11 seats, 17.94 per cent). The other remaining seat is held by the Movement of Statutory Liberty, which obtained 2.10 per cent of the vote.

Organization and Leadership. The latest PCS congress (the seventh) was held in April 1968, at which time the party's Central Committee and 10-member Directorate were elected. The secretary-general since 1940 has been Ermenegildo Gasperoni, who nearly always represents the party at Italian and international communist party meetings.

Party Policy. The domestic and foreign policies of the PCS closely follow those of the PCI, but local issues naturally play a considerable part in them. The PCS campaigns against what it terms the "fascist chains" that (by an agreement unchanged since 1939) have bound the republic to the Italian state and turned it into what the party calls a "mere folklore tourist attraction." In his speech at the International Meeting of Communist and Workers' Parties, held in Moscow on 5-17 June 1969, Gasperoni stated: "Our Party has been resolutely opposing the conformist policy of the present ruling group, which subordinates our state to the intentions of the Rome government, sacrifices our rights as a sovereign state and collaborates in the strangling of our economy by big Italian monopolies which perniciously influence the entire economic life of San Marino" (*IMCWP*, pp. 627-28).

The PCS hopes to attain its goals through united action with the Socialist Party, which was praised by Gasperoni for adhering to the view that there could be "no Left unity without Communists," and for accepting a "unitary platform" (*ibid.*, p. 628).

On international issues, the PCS continued during 1970 to mirror the views expressed by the PCI (see *Italy*). The party was represented at the two conferences of European communist and workers' parties, held in Moscow on 14-15 January and on 20-21 October. The PCS also attended a conference of West European communist and workers' parties, held in Paris on 15 May. Gaston Pasolini, member of the party's Directorate, represented the PCS at a Lenin Centenary meeting in Moscow on 21 April.

Publication. The PCS publishes an irregular newspaper, *La Scintilla.*

M. P.

SPAIN

The Communist Party of Spain (Partido Comunista de España; PCE) was founded on 7 November 1921,[1] and has been illegal since 1939. Despite vigorous government enforcement of the ban and periodic arrest and imprisonment of militants, the PCE maintains an active apparatus and is considered one of the strongest anti-Franco forces.

From a claimed peak membership of 300,000 in 1937 the PCE has diminished to its current level, estimated by nonparty observers at between 5,000 and 20,000. PCE Secretary-General Carrillo, however, stated in 1970 in a public meeting at the Communist Party of Great Britain headquarters, London, 9 December, that the party had 22,000 members abroad and "two or three times" that number within Spain. The population of Spain is 32,411,000 (estimated 1970). PCE members include mainly urban intellectuals and workers, especially in Madrid, Barcelona, and Bilbao, and farm and industrial workers in Seville, Cádiz, Córdoba, and Málaga. It also derives support from exiles living in France, mainly in Paris and Toulouse.

Dissidence within the PCE over international policies led in 1970 to the expulsion of some of its leaders, who have since been trying to form another party (see below).

In addition to the PCE, there is a small splinter group calling itself the Communist Party of Spain, Marxist-Leninist (Partido Comunista de España Marxista-Leninista, PCE-ML). This party appears to be divided into two main factions, both of which are pro-Chinese and advocate violent tactics.

Organization and Leadership. The PCE is organized in all of Spain's 50 administrative provinces. At the national level are its Executive Committee and Central Committee, below which are provincial and intermediate-level committees and, finally, the party cells. The Central Committee has 111 members, 90 of whom are said to be in Spain (*Le Monde*, Paris, 4 November 1970).

Little is known about the PCE leadership within Spain. The exile PCE leadership is dispersed mainly in France and the Soviet Union, but also in Czechoslovakia, Romania, and Belgium. The PCE chairman is the seventy-five-year-old Dolores Ibárruri ("La Pasionaria" of civil war days), who lives in Moscow. She held the position of secretary-general from 1942 to January 1960, when because of age she accepted the honorary position of party chairman. The secretary-general and actual leader of the party is Santiago Carrillo, who lives in Paris but frequently visits Italy. Besides Ibárruri and Carrillo, the Executive Committee includes Gregorio López Raimundo, Horacio Fernández Inguanzo (in prison), Ramón Mendezona, Juan Gómez, José Moix, Ignacio Gallego, Santiago Alvarez, and Francisco Gutiérrez. New Executive Committee members, elected

---

[1] The PCE considers 15 April 1920 as its founding date. At that time the National Congress of Socialist Youths of Spain formed itself as the Spanish Communist Party (Partido Comunista Español). In 1921, when the latter fused with the Spanish Worker Communist Party, the PCE was created.

at a Central Committee plenum in September 1970, are Esther Blanco, Juan Calanda, José María González Jérez, V. Martín García, and Ricardo Orueta. Also elected at that meeting were 29 new Central Committee members, most of them young.

The PCE advocates strong support of rights of self-determination for Spain's three main nationalities, and therefore maintains branches (said to enjoy autonomy in adapting PCE policy to local conditions) in Catalonia, Galicia, and the Basque regions (Euzkadi). Gregorio Lopéz is secretary-general of the Unified Socialist Party of Catalonia (Partido Socialista Unificado de Cataluña: PSUC); Santiago Alvarez has the same post for the Communist Party of Galicia. Since July 1969 the PCE has cooperated with a faction of the Basque independence movement, Basque Nation and Liberty (Euzkadi ta Askatasuna; ETA)[1] and the Movement of Basque Priests in a common anti-Franco front.

The party's youth organization, the Communist Youth League (Liga Juvenil Comunista, LJC), formed in October 1961, is active in the anti-Franco Democratic Students' Union (Sindicato Democrático Estudiantil; SDE) and in the illegal labor unions called Workers' Commissions (Comisiones Obreras, or "CC OO"). The SDE operates at the university level; it maintains centers in Madrid, Barcelona, Valencia, Seville, Saragossa, and Santiago de Compostela. The communist youth movement as a whole is not considered very strong. A new mass movement, the Women's Democratic Movement, active mainly in working centers, is said to have emerged during 1970.

Within the labor movement, the communists occupy influential positions in the Workers' Commissions. Once a faction within Spain's legal, state-controlled trade union movement, the CC OO have become an independent and powerful center of anti-Franco forces that includes "progressive" Catholics (from the Acción Sindicalista de Trabajadores) and socialists (from the Unión Sindical Obrera) as well as communists. It is estimated that the CC OO provide leadership for 500,000 to one million of Spain's ten million workers (*Wall Street Journal*, New York, 21 January 1969).

Because of Spain's strong Catholic composition, the party has sought cooperation with the liberal sector of the church. Anti-Franco priests have participated in communist endeavors for democratic rights in Spain, and on occasion have supplied meeting places for organizations commonly associated with the PCE. The party, however, seeks to obtain a much greater Catholic support. Statements during 1970 by Carrillo revealed that the party considered the "socialist" section of the Catholic church its "most important ally" in Spain. The PCE has also attempted to appeal to "progressive" forces in the army. Contacts have reportedly taken place between army officers "with leftist and liberal opinions" and opposition forces, workers, and student groups.

Party Internal Affairs. Dissidence over the international views held by the party, unleashed by the PCE's condemnation of the 1968 Soviet-led invasion of Czechoslovakia, caused in 1969 the expulsion of two Central Committee members, Eduardo García and Agustín Gómez, who advocated staunch pro-Soviet positions.

García and Gómez, residing in the Soviet Union, were able to circulate during January and February 1970—in Spain as well as in European countries having Spanish communist exiles—a pamphlet entitled "On the Deformation of the Communist Party of Spain." The pamphlet accused the PCE leadership of advocating extreme anti-Sovietism in international issues and "revisionism" in domestic policies. Further, charging that the leadership used party statutes "only to

---

[1]ETA is divided into three known groups. The most militant faction advocates armed struggle and is believed to contain Maoists. The second faction, allied to the PCE, is considered small and uninfluential. The largest group, composed mostly of older Basques, is moderate.

muzzle opinion against it," the pamphlet called for the convening of a party congress to elect a new leadership—presumably more in line with policies of the Communist Party of the Soviet Union (CPSU). Secretary-General Carrillo, broadcasting over "Radio España Independiente" on 29 March, rejected charges of PCE censorship of opposing views and remarked that the dissidents, who benefited from an "excess of funds," had already managed to publish their views. Replying to the call for a new party congress, Carrillo contended that a "democratic congress" was not possible under the "repressive conditions" the PCE faced in Spain, since many party leaders within the country would be unable to attend the meeting.

Although the PCE leadership held no party congress, the vigor of dissident criticism prompted meetings of communist émigrés in Moscow and Prague. The Moscow meeting, led by Chairman Ibárruri, took place on 20 June and was reportedly attended by 250 PCE members, all of whom supported the policies of the Carrillo leadership and expressed strong condemnation of the "factional and splitting work" of a "group of irresponsible people" ("Radio España Independiente," 11 July). The Prague meeting, held in July, also expressed complete confidence in the party's leadership although it avoided any specific reference to the PCE's condemnation of the intervention in Czechoslovakia and the "normalization" process that followed. This caution was attributed to a plausible desire not to antagonize the current Czechoslovak leadership.

At an enlarged party plenum of the Central Committee in September (possibly held in Paris) five other pro-Soviet dissidents were expelled. They were Central Committee members Celestino Uriarte, José Barzana, Luis Balaguer, Jesús Sáiz, and most notably, Enríque Líster—a well-known figure in Spanish communist circles because of his military performance during the civil war. Líster also was an Executive Committee member.

In an interview late in the year, Carrillo said that the dissidents were supported only by 100 out of 1,000 party members in the Soviet Union and by 60 out of 10,000 in France (*Le Monde*, 11 November). Carrillo is believed to have the support of Spanish communists residing in Belgium and Cuba. His position, in general, appeared to be very solid despite the existence of pro-Soviet activity.

The dissidents, now led by Líster,[1] would seem to have some Soviet verbal and material support. In October they began publication of a rival version of *Mundo Obrero*, the PCE organ. According to the PCE, the rival newspaper contained "defamations of the party which Francoist propaganda itself has never surpassed." At the end of the year, the dissidents were still active in their campaign against Carrillo and apparently were seeking to form a separate party.

Domestic Attitudes and Activities. The domestic policy of the PCE has been based (since 1965 according to party claims) on specifically Spanish considerations. The party seeks to overthrow Franco and establish an "antifeudal and antimonopolistic" democracy which would lead eventually to socialism. To achieve these goals, the PCE domestic line—as elaborated by its secretary-general—maintains that "an alliance of labor and culture" is necessary. This line has been reiterated by the party, which holds that "in this era, in full scientific and technical revolution, a large part of the students and the intelligentsia are also a motive force of the revolutionary movement" (political resolution of the PCE Central Committee, September, broadcast by "Radio España Independiente" on 3 October).

Since 1969 the PCE has incorporated the concept of "an alliance of labor and culture" into a specific plan of action called the "Pact for Freedom." By this, the party seeks to ally itself with

---

[1] *Le Monde* reported on 13 March that Eduardo García had probably been arrested on 11 March by the Spanish police when he entered the country to help organize dissidence against Carrillo. This report was not verified by other sources, but may explain Garcia's absence from later dissident activities.

"all the new opposition forces in Spain, in particular with the Catholics" (Carrillo's statement, *Le Monde*, 11 November), on the basis of a three-point program: a broad coalition government, amnesty for prisoners and political exiles, and democratic liberties. Additionally, the "Pact for Freedom" would "recognize for Catalonia, Euzkadi, and Galicia a statute of autonomy on a provisional basis until a definite structure" would be given to Spain (political resolution, September).

Explaining the PCE's willingness to cooperate with any anti-Franco group, Carrillo asserted that the party's main immediate objective was to overthrow Franco and that, to this end, the PCE would ally itself "with the devil if necessary" and would "march to socialism with the hammer and sickle in one hand and a cross in the other" (public meeting, London, 9 December; see also *Frankfurter Rundschau*, Frankfurt /Main, 17 December).[1] He has also emphasized that he does not aspire a dominant role for the PCE and that he is willing to leave the leading role for "those who prove most capable of interpreting the real requirements of society" (*L'Humanité*, Paris, 6 May).

The PCE appeal for unity of anti-Franco forces did not seem to evoke any significant endorsement by noncommunist groups during 1970. The party hailed as an important step toward reaching democracy in Spain the "Document of 131"—a declaration signed by 131 leading opponents of the regime and submitted to General Franco early in the year—which asked for a number of reforms that would develop Spanish political and social institutions to a level comparable with that of other West European countries. The declaration, signed by such persons as Joaquín Ruíz Jiménez (progressive Christian democrat), Enrique Tierno Galván (socialist), and Joaquín Satrústegui (liberal monarchist), was not acknowledged by the government. The "Document of 131" was significant in that it revealed an increased concern by many respected Spaniards about the lack of basic freedoms. Although the PCE fully endorsed the "Document of 131," it is believed that communist influence on the signatories was minimal.

Another domestic event receiving special PCE attention was the trial at Burgos of sixteen ETA militants. A PCE Executive Committee statement on 11 December asked all Spaniards to participate in demonstrations and strikes to "save the lives of the six Burgos defendants facing the threat of death." When, as a result of impressive domestic and international appeals to Franco, the government commuted the death sentences to thirty-year prison terms, Carrillo held this event as "a great victory over the Franco regime" and especially as "a great victory . . . of the heroic members of ETA, who knew how to give at Burgos an example of extraordinary dignity and revolutionary courage." At the same time, Carrillo appealed for closer unity between the ETA militants and the Basque communists:

> ETA today has enormous political prestige in the Basque country, much political capital. As comrades, as brothers, we say to our ETA friends: You must not lose this political capital, and, in order not to lose this political capital, it is essential in our view—and we are ready to discuss with you as friends and comrades—that ETA should increasingly become a great revolutionary political movement in the Basque country. Otherwise, there is the danger that the heroism, the abnegation, and the sacrifice of the ETA members may be used for political capital not by ETA, but by the Basque right-wing bourgeoisie. ("Radio España Independiente," 12 January 1971.)

The Workers' Commissions. Within the labor movement, indication of PCE success was more defined, although it must be noted that the Workers' Commissions are not entirely communist-led but represent the voices of socialists and progressive Catholics as well.

---

[1] In the interview recorded by *Le Monde* (11 November) Carrillo gave a somewhat different rationale. He declared that the question of social change in post-Franco Spain posed serious problems and that the country, which could not "jump from fascism to socialism," needed a "steppingstone."

During 1970 many labor strikes organized by the CC OO took place both in the cities and in the countryside, involving approximately 300,000 workers. Although most strikes were small and scattered, they represented a challenge to the government, which though considering all strikes illegal was forced to tolerate them. Particularly important was the Asturian miners' strike, involving 33,000 coal miners. This work stoppage, which received full PCE support, began the last week of December 1969 and ended on 26 January 1971, costing the government an estimated $42,000 per day. In the end the miners' demands for higher pay and improved working conditions were not satisfied, but the CC OO were able to assert their authority since the striking workers had refused to deal with the government-controlled unions and chose the Workers' Commissions as their only representatives.

Also important was the Madrid subway strike on 29 July, affecting 1.5 million passengers. The workers nominated CC OO representatives to negotiate for them and subsequently obtained a 25 per cent wage increase (*Guardian*, New York, 21 November).

The draft law on trade unions, prepared by the cabinet in April 1969 (see *YICA*, 1970, p. 254) was still under debate during 1970.[1] A statement issued by the General Coordinating Committee of the CC OO in February announced that "coordinated and generalized action throughout the country" would be carried out to bring about a withdrawal of the government's labor law project (*España Republicana*, Havana, 15 March). On 3 November this plan of action materialized as strikes and demonstrations took place in Madrid, Barcelona, Seville, Bilbao, and several other cities. The 3 November strike, or "Amnesty Day" as it was popularly called, was possibly aided by the pervading Spanish feeling against the Burgos trial (see above). Nevertheless, it was not only the first nationwide strike organized by the CC OO, but also the first political strike organized by them against the Franco regime, since the workers demanded amnesty and independent labor unions and not wage increases. The strike was particularly successful among workers in printing, building, and metal trades. Reportedly, students also participated in the demonstrations.

The unrest in the countryside, especially in the regions of Jérez de la Frontera and Cádiz in Andalusia, was seen by the PCE as a sign of the strengthening of the Farm Workers' Commissions (Comisiones de Obreros Agrarios y Campesinos; COAC) formed in August 1969. These commissions, which were set up as the counterpart in rural areas of the industrial Workers' Commissions, are apparently also influenced by the PCE, but the exact composition of their membership is not known. In May the COAC held their first national assembly, which was attended by representatives of Andalusia, Catalonia, Aragon, Toledo, Albacete, Ciudad Real, Valencia, Legroño, and Galicia. The four objectives discussed and approved at the meeting were a worker-peasant alliance to achieve "freedom and democracy" in Spain, a profound agrarian reform with land for the tiller, agrarian security benefits, and protection against unemployment in the countryside. (*Mundo Obrero*, quoted in *España Republicana*, 1 August.)

Further indicating that the COAC had gained some strength was a meeting of their Coordinating Committee in September. The resolution issued by the committee demanded higher prices for cotton, higher wages for rural workers, and protection against unemployment. It also condemned the five-year extension of the military agreement between Spain and the United States (see below, "International Views and Positions") and announced that it would support all efforts to "solve in a peaceful way the political problems of Spain in order to reestablish freedom and democracy." (*España Republicana*, 15 November.)

The communist press made special mention of the agricultural workers' strike from 9 December 1969 to 22 February 1970 in Jérez de la Frontera, where the workers were able to achieve an

---

[1]After some relatively minor modifications to the bill drafted in 1969, the cabinet approved the bill on 12 September 1970 and sent it for approval to the Cortes. This body gave its consent on 16 February 1971.

increase of 50 pesetas on their daily wage of 102 pesetas (about $1.50). This strike was viewed by a *Mundo Obrero* editorial as "the most exemplary strike ever seen in the countryside under Francoism," not only because of the number of participating workers but also because of its long duration. Also hailed by the party was a strike in Seville on 13 October involving 20,000 cotton-farm workers and supported by Catholics in that area.

International Views and Positions. Long a supporter of Soviet policies in international affairs, the PCE had adopted, since the 1968 Soviet-led invasion of Czechoslovakia, an independent position on international issues. This has led the party to assume a critical attitude toward the Soviet Union on various occasions and a neutralist stand on the Sino-Soviet conflict.

Despite the support given by the CPSU to pro-Soviet dissidents of the PCE (see above), relations between the parties—at least publicly—continued in 1970 to be cordial. On 29 April, during the Lenin Centenary celebrations in Moscow, a meeting took place between PCE and CPSU delegates. Judging from those present, it was a meeting of considerable importance. The PCE delegation included Chairman Ibárruri, Secretary-General Carrillo, and four Executive Committee members. The CPSU was represented by Mikhail Suslov and Andrei Kirilenko—both Politburo members and Central Committee secretaries—and Boris Ponomarev, secretary in charge of relations with nonruling communist parties.

Commenting on the meeting, a PCE statement declared that the Spanish delegates "did not and could not do any political bargaining" and that they "did not modify the positions . . . defended at the International Conference [of Workers' and Communist parties, held at Moscow in June 1969], nor did the Soviet comrades ask the PCE to alter its opinions." The same statement rejected any speculation that the PCE might become anti-Soviet: "Our critical opinions will never be confused with those of the enemy camp. If the imperialists thought we Spanish communists were going to side with anti-Sovietism, they do not know us very well." ("Radio España Independiente," 24 May.)

Later in the year, however, the party's theoretical journal, *Nuestra Bandera*, carried an unusually sharp attack on Stalin and Stalinism (also broadcast by "Radio España Independiente," 18 and 25 August and 1 September). Accusing Lenin's successor of having imposed "traditions of monolithism and authoritarianism" which led to an "ideological stagnation" within the world communist movement, the article called for "revolutionary criticism" to "interpret the phenomenon of present capitalist expansion" and to "examine and explain the problems of the socialist community." It also said:

> The party's role consists not in isolating itself from what is new, but in trying to assimilate it critically. This is not only an indispensable condition for facilitating the alliance of the traditional working class with the cultural forces but also a condition for the general progress of the entire revolutionary front. . . . The communist party must establish conditions for a lively exchange of ideas within and outside its ranks. It must fight sectarianism and dogmatism. As more and more intellectuals are coming to socialism, the establishment of these conditions becomes more urgent and necessary.

A PCE Executive Committee statement on 18 April expressed "surprise" over news reports of a meeting at Moscow on 2 January between the Spanish foreign minister, Gregorio López Bravo, and various Soviet officials, including possibly the chief of the West European division of the Foreign Ministry, A. G. Kovalev. The statement pointed to the "untimeliness" of such action toward a regime which for thirty years had not been recognized by the socialist countries and was now "nearing its end." The Soviet Union nevertheless opened in April its first permanent mission in Madrid since the civil war—a merchant marine office with two of its four representatives holding diplomatic passports (*New York Times*, 13 May), and in November obtained an exchange agreement between TASS and the Spanish news service EFE.

The Soviet Union sent greetings to the PCE in March on the occasion of the party's fiftieth anniversary. According to the message, "friendly relations, militant cooperation, and mutual understanding on the fundamental problems of world communism have always existed between the CPSU and the PCE," and the CPSU has "persistently favored the consolidation and development of these relations on the basis of the principles of Marxist-Leninism and proletarian internationalism" (*Pravda*, 15 April). The CPSU also sent greetings to PCE Chairman Dolores Ibárruri on her birthday in December.

PCE statements during 1970 regarding Communist China indicated a strengthening of the party's policy of seeking both reconciliation between the CPSU and the Chinese Communist Party (CCP) and the reestablishment of relations between the PCE and the CCP. At a meeting celebrating the fifty-third anniversary of the October Revolution, PCE Executive Committee member Ignacio Gallego welcomed a Moscow statement that the CPSU and the Soviet government were "making efforts to establish normal relations" with the Chinese People's Republic. Gallego also mentioned with pleasure that the Chinese had sent a message to the Soviet government on the October Revolution anniversary expressing that differences of principle should not prevent both countries from maintaining relations. ("Radio España Independiente," 22 November.) Two months earlier, at the enlarged Central Committee plenum in September, the following resolution was adopted:

> It is our firm intention to maintain relations of friendship and collaboration with all communist parties and all socialist countries, whatever may be their positions in the present polemics, on the basis of internationalism and noninterference in the affairs of each party and each country. . . .The PCE is making the necessary efforts to normalize its relations with the CCP. In doing so, we are convinced that we are serving the cause of the Spanish revolution, the interests of the world revolution and those of the international communist and workers movement, by contributing to its unity. (*Mundo Obrero*, 30 September.)

Furthermore, Carrillo told the plenum: "Our views on the Chinese Cultural Revolution, too precipitate and superficial, should remain suspended until we have a more precise knowledge of the reality of this country" ("Radio España Independiente," 16 February 1971). He also declared that the fundamental enemy was "U.S. imperialism" and that in this respect Mao Tse-tung's declaration of 20 May (see *China*) was a "positive and valuable act."

The 1968 invasion of Czechoslovakia and the "normalization" process that ensued in that country were under constant discussion during 1970. In July the PCE protested in unequivocal terms the expulsion of Dubček from party ranks. In an article published in *Mundo Obrero* and broadcast by "Radio España Independiente" on 10 July, the party stated: "Dubček's only fault was to refuse to recognize that the intervention was right and necessary. . . . He is being tried and condemned for the crime of opinion." Remarking that Dubček had not breached party discipline, since he had accepted his party's decisions, the article added:

> According to the statutes of communist parties, it is not permissible to expel a member because he does not agree with this or that decision if he bows and submits to party discipline. If this regulation is obeyed by even clandestine communist parties, how and why can it be violated by those parties in power? By condemning those who have not been and are now in agreement with the intervention, the Czechoslovak leadership organs are condemning the overwhelming majority of the working class, the intelligentsia, and the toiling masses. Without them and against them, what is socialism?

On the second anniversary of the invasion, "Radio España Independiente" reiterated the party's criticism: "The supporters of the intervention say that it saved socialism. We who oppose it think that the intervention made a socialist people, friendly to the U.S.S.R., lose its confidence in its communist party and run the risk of being won over by anti-Sovietism." Revealing that domestic considerations (such as its self-characterization as having a predominantly Spanish rather than international allegiance) had also played a role in the PCE's repudiation of the invasion, the statement contended that the intervention "alienated some allies or potential allies in the struggle for socialism" in the countries where the communist parties endorsed the invasion.

Relations between the PCE and the communist parties of Italy, Yugoslavia, Romania, Great Britain, and Belgium appeared excellent during 1970. Both Italy and Romania registered meetings with top leaders of the PCE, and communiqués on their visits expressed complete support for the policy of the Spanish party ("Radio España Independiente," 18 January; Agerpres, Romanian news agency, 23 December).

Although both Carrillo and Ibárruri asserted in various statements that relations with the French Communist Party were "the closest and friendliest," a faction of the French party claimed that its deputy secretary-general, Georges Marchais, had covertly helped the pro-Soviet dissidents organize a meeting in France, which was attended by only 60 Spanish communists (*Unir-Débat*, Paris, 10 October). Significantly, the French Communist Party has not officially supported Líster's expulsion, as have the communist parties of Great Britain and Belgium.

A source of irritation for the PCE was Poland's decision to sell coal to Spain to offset the effects of the Asturian miners' strike, mentioned above. A declaration by the PCE Executive Committee accused Poland of betrayal and announced that it had written a letter to the Polish communist party reminding it of the need to "demonstrate its international solidarity with the fighting workers" ("Radio España Independiente," 18 January). There was no indication of a satisfactory Polish reply; furthermore, on 30 April Poland and Spain signed a five-year trade and shipping agreement and reestablished commercial relations at an official level.

The PCE, through a commentary by Virgilio Fernández, discussed Polish party chief Gomułka's replacement and the series of strikes which took place in Poland toward the end of the year. Noting that Gomułka had "failed to recognize the dissatisfaction growing in the hearts of millions of workers," Fernández concluded: "Bureaucratic forms, poor relations with the masses, and ignorance of their aspirations only lead to tragic situations for socialism, like those which have now occurred in Poland and which happened before in Czechoslovakia" (*ibid.*, 21 December).

The signing on 6 August of a five-year military and friendship accord [1] between the Spanish and U.S. governments evoked immediate repudiation by the PCE. Terming the agreement "anti-national," the party claimed that the Spanish government had "once again capitulated before U.S. imperialism" (PCE Executive Committee statement, quoted in *IB*, nos. 17-18).

International Party Contacts. A PCE delegation headed by Secretary-General Carrillo met in Rome on 2-7 January 1970 with representatives of the Italian Communist Party led by Luigi Longo. A joint communiqué emphasized the independent stand of both parties on international issues ("Radio España Independiente," 18 January). Carrillo visited Italy again early in May and met with Longo at that time.

Carrillo met with the secretary-general of the Romanian Communist Party, Nicolae Ceauşescu, during a visit to Romania on 2 September. Both men reiterated their willingness to develop "further cooperation, fraternal friendship, and solidarity." Chairman Ibárruri and a PCE delegation also visited Romania during the year. Ibárruri was awarded the country's highest order of distinction on 21 December.

Other contacts by Carrillo included meetings with Mikis Theodorakis, president of the Greek

---

[1] By this accord Spain allowed continuation of American use of four military bases, while the United States pledged to give loans, grants, and military equipment and facilities worth about $300 million (*New York Times*, 7 August).

Patriotic Front, in Paris on 2 August; with leaders of the Belgian Communist Party in early November; and with leaders of the Communist Party of Great Britain in December.

PCE delegations attended a meeting of 45 communist and workers' parties held on 28-30 September in Budapest and a meeting of 27 European communist and workers' parties in Moscow on 20-21 October.

Publications. The official organ of the PCE is *Mundo Obrero*, published semimonthly. *Nuestra Bandera* is the party's quarterly theoretical journal. Party sources claim a circulation of 60,000 to 70,000 for *Mundo Obrero* and 205,000 for *Nuestra Bandera*. Both are published abroad and distributed clandestinely in Spain. Other major PCE publications include the semimonthly *España Republicana*, published in Havana by the Cuban-Spanish Friendship Society, and *Realidad*, a monthly journal published in Rome. According to party sources, there are 32 party publications. In addition, the party directs radio programs to Spain through its station "Radio España Independiente." The station was in Prague until early 1970, when reportedly Czechoslovak authorities withdrew permission for further use of the facilities (*Christian Science Monitor*, 17 November). It now broadcasts from Bucharest.

*   *   *

The two pro-Chinese groups in Spain, in existence since 1964, are both organized under the name of the Communist Party of Spain, Marxist-Leninist. One group, which publishes *Vanguardia Obrera*, is believed to be the stronger and is recognized by Communist China. The other, which publishes *Mundo Obrero Revolucionario*, is small and seems to be isolated internationally. Very little is known about the leadership and organization of either group. Pro-Chinese communists cells are known to exist in Madrid, Asturias, Catalonia, Aragon, the Basque region, and the Canary Islands.

Neither group registered any major domestic activity during 1970. Some Maoists were said to be active within the extremist faction of ETA, but it was undetermined whether they belonged to the PCE-ML. Internationally, the PCE-ML—presumably the *Vanguardia Obrera* faction—sent a message of congratulations to the Chinese Communist Party on the orbiting of China's first satellite on 14 May. The message described this event as "a destructive blow to the policy of blackmail and monopoly pursued by U.S. imperialism as well as the Soviet revisionist clique in the field of space science" (PCE-ML Executive Committee statement, 27 April, quoted in *Peking Review*, 22 May).

A broadcast from Tirana, Albania, on 8 December announced that a meeting had taken place in October between members of pro-Chinese communist organizations operating in Spain and Colombia. Their joint statement asserted that there was a "striking parallel" between "U.S. imperialism and Soviet social imperialism" since both the United States and the U.S.S.R. were conducting a "frantic arms race" and "preparing a new world war against revolutionary peoples" (Tirana radio, 8 December). According to the same source, the PCE-ML praised "the transition from peaceful struggle to armed struggle in Colombia," holding that such a stage was very important in the formation of a proletarian party.

N. S.

SWEDEN

The Communist Party of Sweden (Sveriges Kommunistiska Parti; SKP) was founded in 1921 and renamed the Left Party Communists (Vänsterpartiet Kommunisterna; VPK) in 1967. The party is legal. Most of its 16,000 to 18,000 members are to be found among low-income workers in the urban industrial areas of Stockholm, Gävleborg, and Göteborg, and in mining communities in the northernmost province of Norrbotten. The population of Sweden is 7,912,000 (estimated 1968).

A number of Maoist organizations, formed since the Sino-Soviet rift, appear to have a greater attraction for intellectuals and students than has the VPK. Currently the most active of these is the Communist League (Marxist-Leninist)—Kommunistiska Förbundet (Marxist-Leninist), or KFML. It was founded in 1967 by extreme left-wing dissidents from the VPK in conjunction with various Maoist groups. The Swedish Clarity League (Svenska Clartéforbundet; Clarté), a student organization founded in 1924, has developed close ties with the KFML (see below).

Another Maoist organization, the Communist Workers' League of Sweden (Sveriges Kommunistiska Arbetarförbund; SKA), was formed in 1953 following a VPK purge. Although the SKA has never participated in a local or national election, and remains isolated and unimportant, it publishes a bulletin, *Revolt*, edited by Sven-Erik Holmsten. There are also two small Trotskyist organizations—"Revolutionary Marxists," which issues a bulletin called *Fourth International*, and the more independent "Bolshevik Group."

In the 20 September 1970 general election—the first combined parliamentary, county, and municipal election to be held since passage, in February 1969, of a constitutional reform marking Sweden's transition from a 384-seat bicameral to a 350-seat unicameral Parliament—the VPK polled 4.8 per cent (up 1.9 per cent from 1968), and received 17 seats. The KFML, contesting a national election for the first time, polled only 0.4 per cent and thus failed to receive the 4 per cent minimum to qualify for representation. The Social Democratic Labor Party (Socialdemokratiska Arbetarparti; SAP) failed to gain a majority, polling 45.3 per cent (down 4.8 per cent, for 163 seats), and the communists, despite their numerical weakness, were once again to play a role in the balance of power (the SAP's majority in the 1968 election having temporarily freed the SAP from relying on communist support). A proposal to the SAP by the Center Party, which made the largest gain (19.9 per cent, up 3.7, for 71 seats), that the two parties form a government coalition was rejected by Prime Minister and SAP leader Olof Palme on the grounds that such a coalition would "silence debate" and was "not appropriate in a parliamentary democracy." Announcing, instead, that his party would accept communist help to stay in power, Palme said: "We will pursue our policy for a more egalitarian society, and the communists can take it or leave it. It is up to them whether they will topple a worker's government." VPK Chairman Hermansson responded: "We will carry on an independent policy, fighting for our program, but we will never topple a socialist government to help the nonsocialist bloc gain power." (Agence France Presse, 21 September; *Sverige nytt*, Stockholm, 22 September.)

Leadership and Organization. Carl-Henrik Hermansson, VPK chairman since 1964, was last reelected by the party's Twenty-second Congress, in September 1969. Lars Werner was reappointed vice-chairman, and Tore Forsberg became party secretary. The Working Committee (Politburo) comprises Urban Karlsson, Bror Engström, Tore Forsberg, Gösta Johansson, Eivor Marklund, Lars Werner, Nils Berndtsson, and Gunvor Ryding. The Party Executive (Central Committee) has 35 members.

Because of ideological crosscurrents, formal cooperation between the VPK and its youth affiliate, the Leftist Youth League (Vänsterns Ungdomsförbund; VUF), has been at a virtual standstill since 1968 (see below).

The Socialist League (Socialistiska Förbundet; SF), established in 1967 with strong support from the VPK (see *YICA*, 1970, p. 259), became virtually defunct in 1970. *Tidsignal*, its organ, ceased publication in the summer. SF members are believed to have joined the VPK, the VUF, or the KFML.

The VPK influences no national trade unions, and controls only about 80 of the approximately 9,000 union locals, largely in building and construction, forestry, and mining. Among the friendship organizations controlled by the VPK are the Sweden-Soviet Union Association and the Swedish-East German Friendship Society.

Party Internal Affairs. The VPK leadership continued in 1970 to experience difficulty in its attempt to steer a left-socialist course between conservative and revolutionary factions, yet prevent further fragmentation on the left. Despite its condemnation of the Soviet-led invasion of Czechoslovakia in 1968, the party has been unable to avert defections to the SAP. The conservative wing seized upon this trend to intensify its attack on the Hermansson line of independence within the world communist movement. Conversely, many younger members, failing to gain Hermansson's backing against the conservatives, turned on Hermansson for his alleged collaboration with the SAP on domestic issues.

In respect to party unity and ideology, the communists' modest gain in the 1970 election—largely the result of a well-organized campaign—solved nothing, and the VPK was faced with the same internal problems as before. The fact that it qualified for parliamentary representation, however, meant that it would, for the next three years at least, influence the passage of government-sponsored legislation, while its vociferous rival, the KFML, was revealed as possessing negligible support. Thus the VPK was provided with an outward appearance of new strength.

Domestic Attitudes and Activities. The cornerstone of VPK domestic strategy continued to be the SAP's alleged betrayal of the interests of Swedish workers. A 1970 election appeal accused the SAP of having reneged on its pledges to work for improved labor conditions, for accelerated development in the northern part of the country, and against land speculation and general despoliation of the environment. Allegedly, the SAP government had done nothing to curb the concentration of industrial power or to provide adequate housing, had permitted prices and rents to soar, and, when workers were forced to strike, had joined with moneyed interests in opposing them. (See, e.g., *Ny Dag*, 18 August and 21-22 October.)

Urging party unity, increased activism, and efficient technical preparation in what for the VPK was possibly the most crucial election in its history, VPK Secretary Tore Forsberg declared in January that while "a socialist party does not stand or fall on the question of parliamentary representation" (its fundamental activity, he explained, being conducted at places of work, in residential areas, in the trade unions, and in other mass organizations), the usefulness of a voice in the legislature must not be underestimated. New organizations must be created in those electorates where the party was not represented, and new members recruited in existing organs. (*Ibid.*, 14-15 January.) The party conducted an energetic campaign, and its literature was widely disseminated. One election pamphlet stressed the need to prevent both a Center-SAP coalition government and a bourgeois majority; a handbook for voters described the new electoral system; 40,000 copies of the party program were distributed; and the party organ *Ny Dag* put out two special issues of 200,000 each, one directed to pensioners, the other to first-time voters. Hermansson and other VPK leaders traveled extensively and participated in multiparty radio and television debates.

Economic inflation and the allegedly diminished purchasing power of workers' wages were targets of VPK agitation. Party propaganda called for a general price freeze and abolition of the purchase tax on foodstuffs; total state financing of housing construction at low and permanent interest rates; and revision of the collective bargaining system (under which the National Trade Union Federation—the LO—and the Swedish Employers' Association—the SAF—meet every two or three years to determine wage scales, which then apply to most Swedish workers). The party held that by increasing corporate taxes, curbing speculative gains, and denying tax exemptions to foreign companies in Sweden, it would be possible not only to avert an increase in indirect taxation, but even to lower the direct tax on ordinary incomes. (*Ibid.*, 15-16 April; 15-21 July; 21-25 August.) The VPK claimed that its concerted agitation was largely responsible for a partial price freeze put into effect by the government shortly before the election (*ibid.*, 2-3 September).

A related VPK campaign issue was the allegedly excessive military budget. The party claimed that Swedish defenses were such that they could be penetrated with ease by an aggressor and it was, therefore, irrational to encumber the taxpayer with heavy arms expenditures. Official military-political theories, an editorial in *Ny Dag* (27-28 May) asserted, were both unrealistic and false; for Sweden—a small nation "even more vulnerable to attack of the U.S. imperialist type than Vietnam"—the most viable solution was not emulation of the defense system of a world power but "a people's defense against an occupation force." The VPK editorial recommended that proposals for a new defense system be worked out over a two-year period, during which the military expenditures should be gradually reduced to cover the maintenance of existing defenses without new investments.

The party vigorously supported a series of wildcat strikes during the year, asserting that advanced technology was subjecting workers to unprecedented physical and mental pressures for which they were not being adequately compensated. The largest, most protracted, and most controversial of the strikes occurred among mineworkers at Kiruna in northern Sweden. For several months the party press gave extensive coverage to the progress of the strike, in which VPK members played an active role. Lars Werner claimed in Parliament in January that the strikes showed that the so-called mixed economy had failed, in that contradictions within the existing economic system had multiplied and the struggle between management and labor had intensified (*ibid.*, 23-27 January). During the 1970's, Hermansson predicted in another VPK parliamentary address, 5,000 men would die in work accidents, 23,000 become disabled, another 250,000 suffer injuries, and every tenth man be physically or psychologically "broken." He added that thanks to the miners' strike, however, both industry and the bureaucracy were at last being forced to listen to workers' demands. (*Ibid.*)

As the "only party leader supporting the mineworkers," Hermansson toured northern towns, denying, however, that his presence had any party-political implications. He had come, he said, to listen and learn, not to attempt to give the miners advice on how to conduct a strike. Through unity of action, workers had themselves allegedly crossed political lines and elevated the struggle "above the level of wage demands." (*Ibid.*, 13-17 February.)

The VPK campaign was hampered throughout by a lack of support—and in some instances even overt opposition—from its youth affiliate, the VUF, which for at least a year had appeared to be hesitating between the VPK and KFML. The Maoist element, claiming 24 of the 38-member VUF leadership, formally broke with the VPK in June 1970 and formed the Marxist-Leninist Struggle League (Marxist-Leninistiska Kampförbundet; MLK). The MLK proclaimed that any differences between it and the KFML were of a "nonantagonistic character," and that the MLK would, consequently, support the KFML in the election. (*Gnistan*, organ of the KFML, no. 8.) Several MLK members including former VUF leaders Per Åke Lindblom and Martin Fahlgren subsequently joined the KFML. Those VUF cadres faithful to the VPK leadership, headed by chairman Anders Carlberg, met at Syninge on 4-5 April and Göteborg on 15-16 August, for discussions of steps to be taken to reorganize the youth party. It was agreed that groups should be formed at the local level first, and ibid that workers rather than students must form the social base. (*Ny Dag*, 10-14 April.) One such youth organization is Communist Youth (Kommunistisk Ungdom), based in Göteborg, which claims to be independent but supports the VPK program.

The extent of support for the extreme left, represented by the KFML, whose previous abstention from national elections made it an unknown political factor, evoked VPK concern throughout the 1970 electoral campaign. Although the KFML was considered to have little prospect of gaining parliamentary representation, there existed the possibility that it might draw enough votes from the VPK to prevent any communist voice in the new legislature. Thus, the VPK press charged the KFML with risking a split in the socialist vote and attacked the "bourgeois" media for their allegedly disproportionate coverage of a politically insignificant group of extremists. A typical editorial in *Ny Dag* (22-26 May) referred to the KFML as a group which sought to be taken seriously in political life, yet took no position on pragmatic political issues, and commented that, just as the KFML had been able to exist only parasitically within the VPK, so did it now lack the capacity to do anything but adopt critical and hostile attitudes toward the VPK, and thus play only a negative role in the electoral process. Finally, the editorial noted, notwithstanding its participation in the election, the KFML was issuing statements that reflected strong anti-parliamentarianism—as in the 1968 election, when the KFML tactic had been to urge broad voter boycotts. A postelection VPK statement declared that for those who had "sacrificed time and effort on fruitless sectarianism" the KFML's participation at the polls had been "a useful lesson." (*Ibid.*, 23-24 September.)

International Views and Activities. Sweden, under an SAP government, according to the VPK, is becoming ever more welded to foreign capital and to imperialist exploitation. Swedish capital investments in Latin America, Africa, and Asia allegedly have aided reactionary politicians in oppressing local workers, and imports from Greece have increased steadily despite Sweden's declared support for those opposing the Greek government. A true internationalist policy, Hermansson wrote (*Ny Dag*, 8-12 May), must embrace a struggle against capitalism and imperialism. Sweden could help to reverse the pattern of trade relations throughout the world—whereby rich countries allegedly benefit at the expense of poor ones—by agreeing to measures such as a preference system for goods from "third world" nations, and by instituting a foreign aid policy directed to support of national and social liberation movements and "third world" nations with "progressive" governments.

The VPK professed to see a radical shift to the right in government policy under Olof Palme. Addressing the VPK's national conference in Stockholm on 11-12 April, Hermansson cited as evidence the government's permission for the Republic of South Vietnam "quisling regime" to open an information office in Stockholm and its alleged plans for affiliation with the European Economic Community (EEC) (*ibid.*, 15-16 April).

Any form of affiliation with the EEC would mean a threat to Swedish independence and alliance-free policies, according to Hermansson. When monopolist concerns in different countries joined to maintain high prices and exploit consumers, that was hardly a form of integration to be encouraged, and could do more to divide, rather than unite, Europe. Any West European common market with higher customs tariffs for the rest of the world, moreover, would run counter to the basic concept of economic integration. The proposal for a Nordic economic union (Nordek), Hermansson continued, would have been of value had not "certain political forces" regarded it as a move toward an expanded common market. For this reason Finland, allegedly because of its neutral policy, had refused to sign the Nordek treaty (see *Finland*). Economic cooperation henceforth, he added, must be promoted not through any "package solution of the Nordek style" but according to interests of participants in each instance. (*Ibid.*, 8-12 May.)

The VPK subsequently attributed its success in the September election to its anti-EEC stance, and pressed for withdrawal of the government's application for entry. (*Sverige nytt*, 22 September; *Ny Dag*, 25-29 September.)

The EEC was the one major issue on which the VPK and the pro-Chinese groups cooperated in 1970. With the KFML, Clarté, and nine other organizations, including SAP and Center youth groups, the VPK formed a "No to EEC Contact Group" which sponsored a demonstration against Swedish affiliation in the EEC. The demonstration took place on 10 November, the date Swedish negotiations for entry began in Brussels. (*Ibid.*, 28-29 October.)

In other developments, the government's decision to permit South Vietnam to establish a Stockholm bureau was contrasted by the VPK with the situation prevailing during the Second World War. How would Sweden have been judged by history, Hermansson asked in a parliamentary address, if the Quisling regime in Norway had been officially endorsed by the Swedish government? This new Swedish move, he said, could only be interpreted by "the Vietnamese people" as support for those "stepping up and prolonging the dirty war." (*IB*, no. 11.) The government, Hermansson said in a campaign speech on 12 May, must take a clear position on the U.S. "expansion" of the war in Cambodia, which allegedly was to be a "new Vietnam." Palme should cancel his planned visit to the United States (July) and reduce as far as feasible all contact with the U.S. so long as it persisted in its "provocations to world peace." (*Ny Dag*, 20-21 May.)

Following a meeting with representatives from the Workers' Party of Korea in Stockholm on 10 May, a joint communiqué denounced "Japanese militarism," allegedly revived as a dangerous force of aggression directed against North Korea and other Asian nations in accordance with the "new Asian policy" of the United States (North Korean News Agency, Pyongyang, 15 May). At a different meeting, Lars Werner represented the VPK, and John Takman, a member of the Party Executive, represented the Swedish Peace Committee in talks with a delegation of the (North) Korean Peace Committee in Stockholm to coordinate activities during the "solidarity month for Korea's people" (25 June-27 July), sponsored by the World Peace Council (*Ny Dag*, 22-28 July).

In the Middle East, the VPK upheld the "struggle of Palestinians for their national right to self-determination" and condemned the "mass murders of Arab refugees and freedom fighters carried out by Jordanian reactionaries, the tools of U.S. imperialism," but declared that "the Arab and the Jewish peoples must be guaranteed equal political and cultural rights" (Party Executive resolution, *ibid.*, 23-27 October).

On the question of world peace, the VPK's foremost spokesman continued to be John Takman. As a leading member of both the VPK and the Swedish Peace Committee, he has spent much time abroad participating in "peace" initiatives sponsored by various communist, communist-front, or other self-ascribed "progressive" organizations. Takman, a physician, gained prominence among such groups as a member of the Bertrand Russell "medical fact-finding commission" that visited Hanoi in 1967.

On 4 May 1970 Takman went to Athens, purportedly at the instigation of Greek "action groups" in Sweden and Norway, for the purpose of making contact with Argyris Barros, a detained Greek communist. *Ny Dag* (8-12 May) reported that the party had withheld advance information concerning Takman's mission so as to avoid alerting Greek security authorities. Shortly after his return, Takman took part in a meeting in Göteborg in which Greek "antidictatorial committees" from 16 Swedish towns joined to establish a central organization in Malmö. (Antonis Ambatielos, a member of the Greek communist party leadership, was also at the Göteborg meeting; see *Greece.*) Takman reported his failure to contact Barris, but claimed to have met with a number of leading communists still at large—whom he declined to name, allegedly for fear of their safety.

Takman later served as Swedish Peace Committee representative to the "16th World Conference Against A & H Bombs" in Tokyo (29 July-4 August) sponsored by the World Peace Council, and as a member of an "International Commission for Investigation of U.S. War Crimes in Indochina" in Stockholm (22-25 October). The commission was headed by Gunnar Myrdal and included also Bertil Svahnström, leader of the Stockholm Conference on Vietnam, in which the World Peace Council plays a key role.

The VPK, as in previous years, did not hesitate to criticize events within the socialist world. Commenting upon the expulsion of Alexander Dubček from the Czechoslovak party, for instance, *Ny Dag* editorialized (1-7 July) that the event was of concern for communists throughout the world, and only strengthened misgivings toward a policy "that had to employ such means."

International Party Contacts. Hermansson and Forsberg represented the VPK at the annual meeting of Nordic communist parties (Sweden, Denmark, Norway, and Finland), in Helsinki on 13-14 May. Urban Karlsson was the party's representative at the 15 May meeting, in Paris, of eighteen communist parties from European capitalist countries. The VPK sent a study delegation to Romania for one week in mid-June; Lars Werner and Tore Forsberg were in Hungary at that time; and the party was represented at the "International Conference in Support of the Peoples of the Portuguese Colonies" in Rome on 27-29 June. VPK leaders received a delegation of the (North) Korean Peace Committee in Stockholm in July.

Main Party Publications. The central organ of the VKP, *Ny Dag* (New Day), edited by Per Francke, is issued twice weekly in Stockholm. In Göteborg and West Sweden, the same paper is published under the name *Arbetar-Tidningen* (Worker News). *Stormklockan* (Storm Bell), the VUF organ, is issued monthly. The voice of the VKP "old guardists" in Norrbotten (see *YICA*, 1970, pp. 261-62) is *Norrskensflamman* (Blaze of Northern Lights), the party's sole remaining daily. Despite moves by the central leadership to eliminate it, ostensibly for reasons of economy, *Norrskensflamman*, its editor Alf Lövenborg, and its leading spokesman Hilding Hagberg (former party chairman) have been able to frustrate these attempts.

* * *

Communist League (Marxist-Leninist). The Maoist KFML has its main strength in the Stockholm, Göteborg, and Uppsala areas. In addition, the party has also drawn some support from the VPK in the north.

Gunnar Bylin, who had headed the Swedish Clarity League (see below) from 1966 to 1968, became chairman of the KFML in 1969. Other KFML leaders include Bo Gustavsson, editor of *Marxistisk Forum* (Marxist Forum), the KFML's monthly theoretical journal published in Uppsala; Nils Holmberg, editor of *Gnistan* (Spark), its monthly newsletter issued in Göteborg; Kurt Lundgren, secretary; and Sigyn Meder, international secretary. Frank Baude, vice-chairman, was expelled from the party in October 1970 for alleged splitting activities and misappropriation of *Gnistan* funds (*Gnistan*, no. 11).

The KFML, which advocates a revolutionary, extraparliamentary path to socialism, entered the September 1970 election with slates headed by Gunnar Bylin in Stockholm, Frank Baude in Göteborg, Bo Gustavsson in Uppsala, and Edvin Berglund in Norrbotten. All were unsuccessful.

Baude, together with several other members of the Göteborg branch expelled with him, formed a rival group proclaiming itself the "leading proletarian center" and rejecting the KFML leadership (*ibid.*). The Baude group issues a bulletin called *Klasskampen* (Class Struggle) which advocates a Marxist-Leninist party controlled by workers rather than, as is the case with the KFML, by intellectuals.

KFML Activities in 1970. The KFML is a major force in the National Liberation Front Groups (De Förenada FNL-grupperna; DFFG), which has sponsored numerous campaigns and demonstrations protesting U.S. intervention in Vietnam and dispatched financial aid to North Vietnam and the National Liberation Front of South Vietnam. The Maoist influence within the DFFG became more conspicuous in 1970 when, at its June congress in Stockholm, attended by some 500 delegates, it was decided that in future activities the DFFG, in addition to criticizing the United States, would draw attention to the "betrayal of the people of Southeast Asia by Soviet social-imperialism" and to the "encirclement of China" (Stockholm radio, 21 June). The VPK appears to be reluctant to denounce the DFFG openly inasmuch as the organization promotes the interests of the Vietnamese communists.

In the Middle East, the KFML denounced the United States for its "criminal plot to sabotage the Palestinian people's armed struggle" and to "force the Arab nations to accept Israeli Zionism, thus making it permanently impossible for the Palestinian people to return to their homeland." The aim of the "Soviet revisionist clique"—allegedly working hand-in-glove with the United States on a spurious "peaceful settlement" in the Middle East—was said to be not the independence of the Arab nations, but the splitting of the Arab anti-imperialist front. (*Gnistan*, no. 8.)

The KFML and Clarté frequently co-sponsor "Red Front" demonstrations around common causes. The largest in 1970, on 1 May (Labor Day), was claimed to have drawn more than 16,000 participants in 25 locations throughout Sweden. On 6 May the KFML, together with Clarté, the DFFG, and the Swedish section of the U.S. Black Panther Party organized a demonstration against "American imperialism" which assertedly drew 10,000 participants. (*Ibid.*, no. 5.)

Swedish Clarity League (Clarté). Clarté, which considers itself "the communist movement's arm among student youth" (*Clarté*, no. 3, 1970), is headed by Peter Emsheimer. Peter Lorentzon edits the party's monthly journal *Clarté*. Clarté's affiliated "school clubs" also issue a journal, *Skoltidning* (School Journal).

V. B.

SWITZERLAND

Former members of the Communist Party of Switzerland (founded in 1921 and outlawed in 1940) joined with a number of socialist groups in October 1944 to found the Swiss Party of Labor (Parti Suisse du Travail /Partei der Arbeit; PdA), which operates legally. Although the PdA condemned the 1968 Warsaw Pact invasion of Czechoslovakia, its stand on foreign policy issues has been and remains pro-Soviet. Minor competition on the left comes from the Swiss People's Party (Parti Populaire Swisse; PPS—see *YICA*, 1970, p. 273), founded in September 1967, and the pro-Chinese Organization of Swiss Communists (Organization des Communistes Suisse; OCS).

PdA membership is estimated at between 4,500 and 5,000. The population of Switzerland is 6,147,000 (estimated 1968). The party polled 2.9 per cent of the vote in the latest national election, in October 1967, and has five seats in the 200-member lower house, the National Council. The PdA is not accorded "fraction" status and therefore remains without representation on legislative commissions. The party plays an insignificant role in Swiss political affairs.

In February 1970, however, the PdA successfully elected Central Committee member Roger Dafflon to the Administrative Council of the city of Geneva. He received support from Socialists in Geneva, against the advice of their own party leadership (*Neue Zürcher Zeitung*, 17 February). The party's strength remains greatest in the French-speaking cantons of western Switzerland, especially in Geneva, Vaud, and Neuchâtel. In the city of Geneva itself, the PdA is the strongest party after the Socialists. In the German-speaking industrial centers, such as Zurich and Basel, the party enjoys little support, but continues to extend its influence among the manual labor forces of foreign (largely Italian) workers. Foreign laborers in Switzerland, however, do not have the right to vote.

Leadership and Organization. Since the significant restructuring of its leadership at the party's Ninth Congress, in November 1968, no major changes have occurred within the PdA hierarchy. Jean Vincent (Geneva) continues as dominant spokesman of the three-member Secretariat (see *YICA*, 1970, p. 269); the other two secretaries are Jakob Lechleiter (Zurich) and André Muret (Lausanne). The Executive Committee includes the three Secretariat members and Frédéric Blaser, Roger Dafflon, Ernest Décosterd, Franz Dübi, Etienne Lentillon, Armand Magnin, Pietro Monetti, Karl Odermatt, Louis Sidler, Hans Stebler, Henri Trüb, and Eugénie Tüscher. The Central Committee consists of 50 members.

The party organization follows that of the Swiss Federation and its cantons. Cantonal divisions within the party receive French, German, and Italian designations. The numerous auxiliary organizations of the party appeal to various interests: Free Youth of Switzerland, Swiss Peace Movement, Swiss-Soviet Friendship Society, Swiss Committee for Aid of Vietnam, Swiss League of Women for Peace and Progress, and Society for the Defense of Tenants. These groups operate with a significant amount of autonomy in matters of strictly domestic concern, as do local party leadership committees in the cantons.

Party Internal Affairs. The PdA party program, formulated in November 1968 (see *YICA*, 1969, p. 769), remained the focal point of party attention in 1970. The PdA continued to be attacked by the pro-Chinese as a "revisionist" group for its participation in the government. This constituted, according to the OCS, a violation of Lenin's principle that participation in bourgeois governments amounted to "treason" (see *Octobre*, December 1969-January 1970). The majority membership of the PdA is composed, however, of workers and union functionaries loyal to the party principles of working within the system to establish socialism. This explains the absence of significant dissension and also accounts for Jean Vincent's view that criticism such as that of the OCS does not present a serious threat (*Neue Zürcher Zeitung*, 31 January and 24 July). Vincent did, nevertheless, take occasion to reiterate the party's interpretation of Lenin in the main speech commemorating the centenary of his birth. In this view, corresponding to the interpretation of the Italian Communist Party, Leninism was not a "dogma," but "a path of action" leading to the achievement of a socialism that is "necessarily different for every country and people." (*Vorwärts*, 18-20 April.)

Domestic Attitudes and Activities. In 1970 the PdA maintained the position endorsed in 1968 at its Ninth Congress: that socialism could be achieved in Switzerland only through existing democratic institutions and could not be imposed by a few, and that the PdA offered the only viable alternative to bourgeois domination by capitalist interests. Interest was focused on preparations for the Tenth Congress, planned for spring 1971, and parliamentary elections are scheduled for November 1971.

Near the end of 1969, party policy was elaborated upon by Central Committee member Karl Odermatt in his analysis of the tasks confronting the PdA for the year 1970. He defined the prerequisites for the achievement of the PdA's goals as the strengthening of the party organization and further dissemination of the party newspaper, *Vörwarts*. Among the party's goals, he particularly stressed the improvement of wages, working conditions, and job security; the creation of a "people's pension"; rent protection; the "right to housing and housing construction"; and the "right to education and health protection." Odermatt also called for opposition to "control by foreign capital" and urged that initiatives be taken toward solving tax and market problems. (*Vörwarts*, 24 December 1969.)

Thus the Schwarzenbach Initiative, proposed by Swiss parliament member James Schwarzenbach, that would have placed quotas on the number of foreigners working in Switzerland, was actively supported by the PdA. Shortly before the proposal was defeated at a referendum in early June, *Vörwarts* (28 May 1970) endorsed the initiative because its passage, according to the PdA, would contribute toward eliminating high rents, foreign speculation and domestic exploitation in housing and building construction, and the eviction of Swiss families from their apartments to provide living accommodations for foreigners.

Following the referendum, the program outlined by Odermatt received new approval from the Central Committee at a meeting in Lausanne on 27-28 June. Emphasizing that nothing had changed in regard to the pressing problems of housing, education, and social security, the Central Committee denounced the "class character" of the government's anti-inflation measures as favoring the concentration of capital and strengthening the bourgeoisie, who had defeated the referendum in order to protect their "profits and privileges." As expected, the party called for an intensification of the "struggle against the effects of the concentration of capital, for job security, and for true rights of co-determination." (*Ibid.*, 29 June and 2 July.) The referendum on the "right to housing," submitted to Swiss voters on 27 September, received the full support of the PdA. The referendum was narrowly defeated. (See *Voix Ouvrière*, 28 September.)

Although PdA support for the Schwarzenbach Initiative was to no avail, the party did achieve a major success with the election of Central Committee member Roger Dafflon to the Administrative Council of the city of Geneva. The campaign was particularly interesting, for in addition to the support received from the Geneva Socialists, the party waged a careful and energetic campaign accentuating those issues on which divisions could not be made according to party lines, such as problems of water and air pollution, city planning, housing, and medical care (*Neue Zürcher Zeitung*, 17 February).

International Views and Positions. In the view of the PdA, the "most decisive conflict" in 1970, as in the past, was the struggle for "peaceful coexistence." The party's basic position on international affairs, offered on Christmas Eve of 1969 by Karl Odermatt (*Vorwarts*, 24 December), was reiterated throughout the new year. Odermatt directed the PdA's attention to the traditional enemies of communism and avoided any references to the Warsaw Pact invasion of Czechoslovakia. The Middle East crisis, the Vietnam war, and American "aggression" in Southeast Asia were cited as unresolved conflicts. Together with condemnation of American "imperialist" policy in Latin America, these issues received repeated attention in the party organs throughout the year.

Odermatt's main observations, however, centered on Europe and primarily on Germany. The PdA has been the one communist party in Western Europe that has consistently and continually pressed for diplomatic recognition of the German Democratic Republic (GDR), despite the fact that privately many PdA members refer to the East German communists as "red fascists" (*Neue Zürcher Zeitung*, 13 August 1970, and *Vörwarts* editorials throughout the year). Odermatt saw the "congealed fronts" in Western Europe in a state of reactivation, for the Social Democratic Party had won the September 1969 national elections in West Germany, thereafter had signed the nuclear nonproliferation treaty, and was not averse to the proposal for a European conference on collective security: "After the significant social dissension in Great Britain, West Germany, France, and especially Italy, 1970 promises to become a year in which the working class of Western Europe will struggle not only for economic advancement but for new power positions" (*Vörwarts*, 24 December 1969).

Direct references to Czechoslovakia were avoided by the PdA. In September, Jean Vincent condemned the methods employed by the Czechoslovak communist party in its path to "normalization" (since the Dubček ouster), but did so indirectly by quoting criticism that appeared in the Spanish party organ *Mundo Obrero* (see *Neue Zürcher Zeitung*, 5 September). This attitude became particularly clear at the anniversary celebrations in Geneva for the Lenin Centenary, where the most prominent guest was Constantin Gerasimov, deputy premier of the U.S.S.R. Recalling Lenin's stay in Switzerland, Gerasimov praised especially Swiss-Soviet friendship (*Voix Ouvière*, 20 April). Vincent praised Lenin's desire for peace, and placed emphasis on Switzerland's right to pursue its own path to socialism as consistent with international unity, commenting: "Just as it is normal that there be differences in judgment and evaluation of the various roads to socialism, it is abnormal and troubling that there are differences, contradictions, and divisions in the socialist world" (*ibid.*).

The PdA's international pronouncements continued to reflect Odermatt's analysis. The PdA attacked Roger Garaudy in France for attempting to split the "unity of action" of the French Communist Party (*ibid.*, 14 February, and *Vörwarts*, 28 May) and praised the Finnish party for having reestablished party unity at its congress in February (*Voix Ouvière*, 2 March). There were attacks against the regimes in Greece and Portugal as well as against U.S. policy in Southeast Asia (see, e.g., *ibid.*, 18 April). Both the proposed European security conference and the

Soviet-West German treaty in August received enthusiastic support, and Jean Vincent urged Swiss diplomatic recognition of the GDR as a contribution to a "Europe from the Atlantic to the Urals" (*Neue Zurcher Zeitung*, 5 September, and *Voix Ouvière*, 24 July).

The PdA submitted a proposal to the upper house of the Swiss parliament on June 4 that the government accord diplomatic recognition to the GDR, North Vietnam, and North Korea. The proposal was rejected on 21 September, on the ground that "the political changes in the political situation in Europe [did] not yet justify a change" in the government's attitude. The PdA condemned this position as incompatible with the new political situation exemplified by the conclusion of the Soviet-West German treaty, and saw it as a reflection of continued support for the "bloc policy" detrimental to European security. (*Vörwarts*, 1 October.)

International Activities and Party Contacts. The Lenin Centenary celebration on 18 April marked the high point of PdA activities on the theme of international communist unity. In addition to the Soviet deputy premier (see above), nearly 600 other delegates joined in the Geneva observances, including the ambassadors to Switzerland of Bulgaria, Cuba, Hungary, Poland, Yugoslavia, and the Soviet Union. Representatives of the communist parties of Czechoslovakia, Mongolia, and France and of the migrant Spanish and Italian workers in Switzerland were also in attendance. (*Voix Ouvière*, 20 April).

The celebration, open to the press, was preceded at the beginning of April by a Lenin Centenary conference organized by the Swiss-Soviet Friendship Society. The conference unanimously adopted a resolution stressing the importance of the Leninist concept of peaceful coexistence and urging a conference of the European states on collective security. The meeting was almost marred, however, by a disagreement over the public endorsement by the Czechoslovak delegate of the Warsaw Pact invasion in 1968. The delegate of the French Communist Party moved for the endorsement's deletion from the conference protocol. The disagreement was resolved by an official statement by the conference chairman to the effect that controversial political subjects not linked to the topic of the conference were not under discussion. An open rift was thereby averted. (*Ibid.*, 3, 4, 6 April.)

As in previous years, the PdA exchanged visits with the French Communist Party. A delegation headed by Central Committee member Frédéric Blaser attended the Nineteenth Congress of the French party, held on 4-8 February in Nanterre (*ibid.*, 14 February). The visit was followed on 25-26 April by a meeting in Lausanne between delegations headed by Secretariat members Jakob Lechleiter, André Muret, and Jean Vincent of the PdA and Politburo member François Billoux of the French party. The delegations jointly endorsed the fundamental objectives of the anti-imperialist struggle as specified at the 1969 world meeting of communist and workers' parties in Moscow. In doing so they supported a European conference on collective security, ratification of the nuclear nonproliferation treaty by their countries, recognition of the GDR, and (foreshadowing the provisions of the Soviet-West German treaty) recognition of existing frontiers in Europe. (*IB*, no. 10, 1970.) The two parties also endorsed anew the posture outlined by Odermatt in December 1969, stressing the necessity "to consolidate the joint action of their countries' workers against the cosmopolitan trusts" (*L'Humanité*, Paris, 29 April 1970). The PdA accepted an invitation to make a study trip to France later in the year (*Vörwarts*, 30 April).

A PdA delegation headed by Central Committee members Jakob Lechleiter and Fernand Petit visited North Korea in August and met with Secretary-General Kim Il-song of the Korean Workers' Party. At the meeting the United States was termed the "citadel of contemporary colonialism" and its policies in Southeast Asia were censured together with Japanese and West German "militarism" (*Voix Ouvière*, 27 August). During his vacation in Romania in August, Jean Vincent met with Romanian party leader Nicolae Ceaușescu. In an exchange of views on the principal problems of the workers' and the communist movement and on international affairs, special importance was ascribed to the need for unity in the communist movement. (*Ibid.*, 28 August.)

Near the end of the year, on 27 November-6 December, a five-member delegation of the Communist Party of the Soviet Union, headed by Central Committee candidate member Boris Shcherbina, visited Switzerland at the invitation of the PdA. The communiqué issued at the conclusion of the visit outlined joint tasks facing the two parties as the struggle (1) against "imperialism" and U.S. "aggression" in Vietnam, (2) for a peaceful settlement of the Middle East conflict, (3) for peaceful coexistence, European security, and the liberation of oppressed peoples, and (4) for unity in the international communist movement. (*Pravda*, 8 December.)

Publications. The PdA publishes official organs in three languages. The daily *Voix Ouvrière* appears in Geneva and enjoys the largest circulation. *Vörwarts* is printed weekly in Basel, and *Il Lavoratore* in Locarno.

* * *

Of the two major communist splinter groups in Switzerland—the Organization of Swiss Communists and the Swiss People's Party—the OCS was the more active in 1970.

The OCS, pro-Chinese and centered in Lausanne, has few members, but it announced a significant expansion of the party organ, *Oktober*. The newspaper, which is now published in three languages, distributed its first separate German edition in a printing of 2,000 copies for January-February. The German edition was undertaken to meet the "needs of the present political situation in Switzerland" and to promote "more extensive controls" among OCS members in various cities. It was announced at the same time that the French and Italian editions would be continued.

The OCS position on international and domestic affairs was presented at the beginning of the year in *Oktober*. The "chauvinistic great-power policies" of the Soviet Union were declared to have "absolutely nothing in common with communism" and to be a total rejection of the work of Lenin and Stalin. Indeed, the Czechoslovak party's ousted leaders Novotný and Dubček and current leader Husák were termed alike "loyal disciples of Khrushchev and the degenerate revisionist U.S.S.R."—Dubček for supporting "humane socialism under American hegemony," and Novotný and Husák for wishing to establish "capitalism under the hegemony of the new tsars." Sharing the view of the Chinese and Albanian communist parties, *Oktober* declared that the U.S.S.R. and the United States were bent on dividing the world into "two spheres of power" under a "secret American-Soviet understanding at the expense of the peoples of the world."

The OCS also attacked the PdA—on the one hand for condemning the Warsaw Pact invasion of 1968, and on the other for distributing "the Soviet justification to all its members." In its French edition of *Octobre* (December 1969-January 1970) the OCS evaluated the PdA as a "reformist party" which had abandoned "all revolutionary struggle and renounced any confrontation with the bourgeoise." According to *Octobre*, the PdA, by working within the existing Swiss system, was trying to "transform rather than destroy" it, and instead of taking the class struggle to the factories, the docks, and to the streets, was preaching peaceful coexistence in "collaboration" with the "imperialists."

D. L. B.

TURKEY

The Communist Party of Turkey (Türkiye Komünist Partisi; TKP) was founded in 1920 in Istanbul. Remnants of two other early Turkish communist organizations, one formed in Anatolia, the other among émigrés in Soviet Azerbaijan, were absorbed soon thereafter. Illegal since 1925 and severely repressed within Turkey, the TKP has never been able to create a strong organization and is an insignificant political force in the country. The party is estimated to have between 1,200 and 2,000 members and 10,000 to 15,000 sympathizers. The population of Turkey is 33,539,000 (estimated 1968).

There exist a number of Turkish leftist organizations abroad which the TKP supports and appears to have infiltrated, including the Federation of Turkish Socialists in Europe and the Association for Vigilant Turks, both formed by Turks working in West Europe. Within Turkey, the TKP supports various leftist trade-union, teacher, student, and youth groups, including the Union of Progressive Forces, the Confederation of Reformist Trade Unions (DISK), the Federation of Idea Clubs (FKF), the Turkish Teachers' Union (TOS), and the 27 May Clubs.

The TKP may to some extent have infiltrated the Turkish Labor Party (TLP), an amalgamation formed in 1962 by several small groups with a wide range of socialist viewpoints, and with its greatest strength among urban intellectuals, students, and workers. The TLP, whose policies on many counts parallel those of the communists, has nonetheless shown wariness of identification with the outlawed communist party and most of its members claim to be either "national communists" or "national socialists" with no interest in the international communist movement. Even so, TLP delegations frequently participate in international meetings of communist and other leftist parties.

In the National Assembly (lower house) elections of 12 October 1969, the TLP secured only 2.7 per cent of the vote and 2 of 450 seats—down from 3.0 per cent and 15 seats in 1965. (The party holds one of 192 Senate seats.) Under an electoral amendment stipulating a minimum of 25,000 votes in a constituency to qualify a party for mandate distribution, the extremes in the political spectrum, including the TLP, lost any possibility of influencing national policy by parliamentary means, and the more radical elements (to both left and right) began to press for increased militancy. The TLP leadership for its part attempted to conceal factional struggles between those insisting that the party could achieve its socialist goals within the democratic system, and those of a growing rebel wing who saw diminishing prospects other than in extraparliamentary tactics. By the end of 1969 a series of resignations and expulsions of prominent TLP personnel had seriously threatened the party base. The TLP rebels since then have been attempting to form a rival party—an event which would be unwelcome to the exiled and isolated TKP leadership, which is opposed to further fragmentation of the left.

Leadership and Organization. Overt TKP activity is directed from abroad. Zeki Bastimar, who goes under the alias Yakub Demir, is secretary-general. Most, if not all, of the thirteen Central Committee members live in and operate from Moscow.

Party Internal Affairs. Severe cleavages between the exiled leadership and those TKP elements operating clandestinely within Turkey have resulted in occasional purges, usually supervised by a Central Committee member dispatched to Turkey for that purpose. Information on the activities or specific orientation of those purged is sparse. What is available emerges largely through TKP media, which apparently find it politically expedient to label collectively all splinter elements as "Maoists" and "proven enemies of communism," claiming in many instances that expelled party members have provided Turkish police with confidential party documents. Such charges, particularly of Maoist complicity with other "anti-nationalists," appear to be without foundation. Currently the active pro-Chinese elements in Turkey are found within the student and trade-union movements and are thought to have little use either for the TKP or for its cast-offs, whom they consider revolutionaries in words alone.

Domestic Attitudes and Activities. A TKP program is not available, but the party expresses views on the domestic situation within Turkey from time to time which serve to reveal its current interests.

The party continued in 1970 to appeal to "nationalist" sentiment and for a broad popular front which would place the general good above partisan or religious interests. In pursuing this policy the TKP has, where expedient, adjusted communist ideology to suit its ends. The party declared, for example ("Our Radio," 13 September), that interreligious antagonisms in Turkey, allegedly due only to wide misunderstanding, had prevented the masses from identifying with "reformist" movements. In fact, the party asserted, there existed no fundamental contradiction between the Islamic religion and communist ideological tenets—both were based on "social justice." In the party view, there was a prevailing misconception among Turks that socialism and communism were enemies of religion, and this was being exploited by "capitalist-imperialist agents," one of whom, Premier Süleyman Demirel, had "acquired the habit of talking on behalf of God and religion" while refusing to initiate land reform and true democracy. Whether a citizen was progressive or reactionary was contingent not upon his religious beliefs, therefore, but upon his position on the "national and social liberation struggle against imperialism." Anyone advocating progressive reform and national independence against local and foreign exploitation was, in this view, a reformist.

The defeat of the government's proposed budget, on 12 February, and Demirel's resulting resignation (he subsequently formed a new government) were cited by the TKP (*ibid.*, 14 February) as proof that the "ruling circles" of the Justice Party were incapable of solving the country's problems because they neglected popular reform to support class interests. The anti-Demirel faction of the Justice Party (26 members of its parliamentary group resigned or were ousted in 1970 and in December formed the Democratic Party) was opportunistically exploiting the national economic crisis so as to present itself to the masses as an alternative to the Demirel government, but in reality sought to uphold the same system.

On the occasion of the ninth anniversary of the TLP, in February, the TKP declared (*ibid.*, 18 February) that as a result of provocations by "imperialism" and its agents—Maoists and liquidators seeking to "blast the TLP from within"—the TLP had not been able to "fulfil completely its historic duty as a legal and overt socialist party in the national and social liberation struggle." Those in the TLP asserting that parliamentarianism alone was the correct course of struggle had also contributed to its failures.

The advocacy of multifaceted forms of struggle was a recurrent theme in the TKP's call to action. Seeking to avoid alienating any "reformist" elements—whether within the moderate left Republican People's Party, the TLP, or among student, trade union, or armed forces groupings—party propaganda preached, in general terms, broad national reform and independence. Observing a prevailing lack of coordination among existing "reformist" groupings, TKP statements stressed the necessity of a "conscious and coordinated movement for social emancipation" as a precondition to any "revolutionary liberation movement." Mere "patriotism and adherence to the principles and traditions established by Ataturk" would not achieve this. Thus, while endorsing sabotage against U.S. military bases and "spy centers" in Turkey along with "armed defense" against government forces, the TKP warned that correct tactics and strategy were paramount. A wrong step or an ill-timed counterattack could provide the "imperialists" with the chance to establish an open dictatorship or to drown the reformists in an "Indonesian-type bloody terror." (*Ibid.*, 4 and 29 April.)

Recent incidents of urban violence—ascribed by the TKP to provocations by allegedly government-sponsored "commandos" and Maoists—have been a mixed blessing for the party. With so little support within the country, the party does not want to see the activists, like its own cadres, driven underground. Having itself failed thus far to influence the ideological direction of leftist militant groups, the TKP displays a reluctance to endorse them openly yet dares not totally condemn them. Hence its current policy is to justify their cause but not always the means employed to pursue it.

The TKP Central Committee came out in full support of large-scale antigovernment demonstrations on 15-16 June, believed to have been instigated by forces within the TLP-controlled Confederation of Reformist Trade Unions, protesting a new law which had the effect of restricting DISK powers in favor of the large, moderate Confederation of Turkish Trade Unions (TURK-IS). The official response to the violence that erupted during the demonstrations was described by the TKP as "an act of aggression embarked upon by the U.S. imperialists and their domestic collaborationists" (*ibid.*, 18 June). The government's "unconstitutional" imposition of martial law, which lasted until 26 September; its decision, in August, to devaluate Turkish currency; the soaring cost of living; rising unemployment; and the new trade union law "abolishing labor rights and trade union independence"—all were said by the TKP to result from its alleged policy of "destruction and pillaging" (*ibid.*, 1 September). In order to derive foreign exchange benefits, the administration allegedly had provided some one million Turkish workers to U.S., West German, and "Common Market" monopolies and was "selling, or preparing to sell," large numbers of emigrants to Australian, Canadian, and Argentinian companies (*ibid.*, 3 September).

According to the TKP, the "enemies of the working class" fell into three main camps. These were (1) the "fascist commandos" maintained and trained by the government with funds allocated by U.S. and Turkish intelligence for the purpose of crushing liberation movements, (2) the Maoists—described as "obstructionists" and "defeatists" who were "hatching many new plots" to infiltrate and undermine the TLP and other popular groupings, and (3) the administration and the TURK-IS/employers, whose jointly devised stratagems were aimed at pitting worker against worker. (*Ibid.*, 21 September.) Singled out for particular attack were the National Democratic Reformist (MDD) groups—described as "small Maoist groups, few in number but great in noise-making," who were supported by both the U.S. Central Intelligence Agency and Communist China (the latter allegedly through banks in Switzerland, West Germany, England, and France) for the purpose of discrediting and infiltrating the workers' movement so as to divert it from social and political goals (*ibid.*, 22 November).

Professing empathy with the Kurdish population in eastern Turkey, whose rights the TKP claims to have "championed longer than any other movement," the party charged that for fifty years the bourgeoisie had "attempted to settle the Kurdish problem by bloody terror." The TKP, like the Soviet Union, subscribes to the newly revived idea of a Kurdish national state ("Kurdistan"). It calls for development of eastern Turkey "on the basis of a just settlement of political, moral, and security problems," and argues the Kurds' right to use their own language rather than "being forced to live as foreigners in their own land." The region inhabited by Kurds, in sum, must be rescued from its alleged present status as a "colony within a country." (*Ibid.*, 13 May.) The TKP subsequently alleged that the government was planning "extensive commando operations" as part of its "Ottoman-type policy" aimed at liquidating the Kurdish minority (*ibid.*, 13 October).

International Views and Activities. As a party almost completely dependent upon the U.S.S.R. for its continued existence, the TKP follows an unswervingly pro-Soviet line. The main thrust of TKP propaganda was toward undermining Turkish-U.S. relations with a view to the abrogation of bilateral agreements and the liquidation of U.S. military installations in Turkey. Government leaders were especially urged to "renounce their policy of assuming dangerous nuclear undertakings and the role of satellites," including the alleged stockpiling of nuclear warheads and permitting overflights by U.S. nuclear-armed aircraft ("Our Radio," 6 February.)

To Demirel's declaration, on 7 February, that nuclear weapons in Turkey would be deployed only for national defense, the TKP replied: "No government in the world obtains arms for display. They obtain them for a specific purpose." Moreover, the terms of the bilateral agreements allegedly stipulated that the government could use these weapons "only if allowed, and for purposes designated by the United States." Given the level of "Israeli aggression" against the Arabs, the reported disclosure that Washington had supplied tactical nuclear weapons to the Turkish armed forces for deployment under U.S. directive was to be considered a "new stab in the back of the Arab people by Turkey and its collaborators," and a new potential threat to socialist countries bordering Turkey and along the Black Sea. In the TKP's view, the only viable policy for an "underdeveloped" country such as Turkey was one based on good relations with its neighbors and support for such peace initiatives as the European security conference proposed by the socialist bloc. (*Ibid.*, 10 February.)

On the Cyprus issue, the Turkish communists continued, paradoxically, to show great empathy for the Makarios government and for AKEL, the communist party on Cyprus, which is almost completely Greek in composition. The TKP professed to view the issue as one not of a fundamentally internal origin but something engendered and perpetuated by "U.S.-NATO maneuvers." While TKP propaganda continued to capitalize on the Soviet-Turkish rapprochement and the upsurge of anti-Americanism in Turkey, it was the TLP, as a legal party operating within Turkey, that appeared to reap most of the advantage.

The TKP commented in March that the proposed supply of arms to Greece by the United States and West Germany was "closely related" to the "revival of the enosis issue" (enosis—the union of Greece and Cyprus—being the policy advocated by Makarios up to the 1967 coup in Greece, but since deemphasized). The party suggested the existence of a twofold plan by the United States and the Athens government against Turkish and Cypriot independence. It pointed out, purportedly in support of this contention, that Greek armed forces (unlike Turkish ones) were not under NATO command and thus could operate freely. (*Ibid.*, 4 March.) Despite the "lull of the past few years," the "imperialist circles" had not abandoned their plans to turn Cyprus into a NATO base, although they appeared to have made some changes in their plans. That an imperialist implementation of enosis had been averted, the TKP attributed to "efforts toward independence" by AKEL and Makarios, and to Soviet support for a Cypriot government based on equal rights for the two communities on the island. (*Ibid.*, 3 April.) Alleged imperialist support of such "reactionary and fascist organizations" on Cyprus as the outlawed right-wing militant National Front was said to be aimed at inciting enmity between Greeks and Turks to "create the necessary atmosphere" for an ultimate overthrow of Makarios and installation of a "fascist junta." There was "no doubt," in this view, that the assassination attempt against Makarios, in March, was carried out by "imperialist agents." (*Ibid.*, 10 March.)

During the visit to Turkey in October of U.S. Defense Secretary Melvin Laird, the TKP asserted that in the Jordanian crisis of mid-1970 U.S. military transport airplanes had carried weapons and equipment from Turkey to U.S. agents in Jordan. Had it not been for the "blunt and categorical" Soviet note of 20 September, the U.S. assertedly would have attacked Jordan. Deployment of the U.S. Sixth Fleet and airplanes from the Incirlik base in Turkey, at the same time, would have involved Turkey in this aggression. (*Ibid.*, 2 October.) The TKP subsequently described an agreement concluded during Laird's visit as a "new link in the chain of betrayals" by the Justice Party and a strengthening of the U.S. nuclear weapons network (*ibid.*, 7 October).

The TKP vigorously took up the Soviet protest, in connection with the hijacking to Turkey of a Soviet airliner on 15 October, against the Turkish government's refusal to comply with the Soviet demand for the immediate extradition to the U.S.S.R. of the Lithuanian father and son allegedly responsible for the hijacking, the murder of a stewardess, and injury to the pilot and navigator. The crime, the TKP declared, had been committed aboard a Soviet airplane in Soviet airspace and, according to international law, must be tried by the Soviet judiciary. The event had given the U.S. "cold war provocateurs"—alleged by the TKP to be "applying pressure" on Turkey to prevent extradition of the hijackers—a new chance to undermine Soviet-Turkish relations. Moreover, by becoming a tool of these designs, the Turkish government had once more proven its "insincerity" vis-à-vis the Soviet Union—just as the use of Incirlik and other bases on Turkish territory against Arab liberation movements had refuted Demirel's talk of friendship with Arab peoples. (*Ibid.*, 20 and 22 October.)

The forced landing on Soviet territory on 21 October of a U.S. U-8 military plane, which reportedly strayed across the Turkish-Soviet border, prompted the TKP to appeal to public opinion to protest the government's "duplicity" and willingness to "play with fire in the age of nuclear weapons and global missiles and rockets" (*ibid.*, 28 October). On the forty-seventh anniversary of the Turkish Republic, the TKP stated that Demirel's denial of the Soviet charge that the U-8 had been on a spying mission was refuted by the Soviet discovery of espionage equipment and supplies on board. Were the contents of the aircraft revealed to the world public, the Demirel administration would find itself in the same position as U.S. President Eisenhower in 1960, when he attempted to disavow the U-2's spying mission in Soviet airspace. (*Ibid.*, 29 October.)

The party subsequently professed to note an intensification in U.S. verbal attacks against the Soviet Union and alleged that these were intended as a maneuver to "camouflage" both the U-8 incident and the "warlike decisions on the use of nuclear tactical weapons by the NATO nuclear planning committee" which met in Ottawa in October. The immediate purpose of the Ottawa meeting was, according to the TKP, to undermine prospects for a European security conference. (*Ibid.*, 5 November.)

International Communist Movement. The TKP continued to echo Soviet condemnations of the Chinese Communist Party leadership. The "contradiction between the words and actual attitude" of the Chinese leaders, it declared, was apparent in their obstruction of Soviet aid to Vietnam and their attempts to disrupt the united action of socialist countries through political, ideological, and armed attacks against the Soviet Union ("Our Radio," 7 May).

Main Party Media. TKP declarations and documents appear in special supplements to *Yeni Cag* (New Age), the Turkish-language edition of the *World Marxist Review*. The party occasionally issues pamphlets which are circulated clandestinely in Turkey. The most effective medium for the dissemination of its propaganda in Turkey is a clandestine radio station, Bizim Tadvo ("Our Radio"), which pretends to broadcast from within the country but in fact transmits from

Leipzig, East Germany, under the direction of a Turkish communist, Fahri Erding. A second radio station, calling itself "The Voice of the Turkish Communist Party," began operations in September 1969. Its location, sponsorship, and specific orientation are not yet known.

V. B.

MIDDLE EAST
AND AFRICA

ALGERIA

The Algerian Communist Party (Parti Communiste Algérien, PCA) was founded in 1920 at the same time as the French Communist Party (PCF), of which it was initially a part. After October 1936 it existed independently. The party was banned in December 1962 by the new Algerian government under President Ahmed Ben Bella; in 1964 it seemingly disappeared as an autonomous organization, after party members had been instructed by the PCA leadership to join the only officially legal Algerian party, the ruling National Liberation Front (Front de Libération Nationale; FLN). When Houari Boumedienne staged a coup in June 1965 and acceded to power, communist militants joined some extremist left-wing members of the FLN in an illegal opposition group called the Popular Resistance Organization (Organisation de la Résistance Populaire; ORP). On 26 January 1966 the ORP became the Socialist Vanguard Party (Parti de l'-Avant-Garde Socialiste; PAGS).

The PAGS has always been illegal, and the initial suppression of its activities was absolute and punishment of its leaders swift and harsh. Recently a slight easing of the campaign against the communists has occurred. This may be the result either of the government's official policy of cooperation with the Soviet Union, or of the minimal effectiveness of communist efforts to exert political influence in Algeria.

In 1970 the PAGS was believed to have about 750 members. The population of Algeria is 14,000,000 (estimated 1970).

Leadership and Party Affairs. Substantial information about the leadership and structure of the PAGS is lacking, largely due to the fact that most of its support comes from Algerians living abroad. The most prominent figure is Larbi Boukhali, who was secretary-general of the PCA and now is the main spokesman and representative of the PAGS. Others frequently speaking or writing for the communists from the safety of foreign domicile in 1970 were Henri Alleg and Ahmed Karim. When an amnesty for about 100 political prisoners was announced on 1 November in celebration of Algeria's National Day, the list of beneficiaries included Bachir Hadj Ali (a former secretary of the PCA), Hocine Zahouane, and Mohammed Harbi, who were leading left-wingers before Boumedienne came to power. All three had been released from prison in 1969 and placed under house arrest; the lifting of that secondary sentence was read as a sign that the Algerian regime was growing more confident of its ability to cope with political opposition. Also granted amnesty, but barred from the cities of Algiers, Oran, Constantine and Annaba, were Paul Caballero (former secretary of the PCA in Oran), Brouzid Bouallak, and Jacques Salort. Bouallak was editor and Salort the business manager of the now defunct PCA daily *Alger Républicain*. (*Le Monde*, Paris, 6 November.)

In 1970 the National Union of Algerian Students (Union Nationale des Etudiants Algériens; UNEA)—an affiliate of the communist-front International Union of Students, and one of the few organizations to remain independent of the FLN—was repeatedly in the news and in apparent serious trouble. At the end of the year, UNEA's dissolution appeared imminent, following weeks of unrest and strikes at the University of Algiers and the arrest of a number of student activists. The government charged that the leaders behind the disturbances were agents of a clandestine party, at work according to a precise plan and carrying out their subversive activities with direction from abroad:

> This plan tends, in distorting the meaning of our revolution, to support the idea that the realization of socialism is not the objective of the FLN. This could then guarantee— in the eyes of the authors of this plan—the support of progressive forces to a grouping claiming to be Marxist-Lenist and already guided and actively supported by at least one foreign party. (*El-Moudjahid*, Algiers, 3-4 January 1971.)

The PCF newspaper *L'Humanité* (Paris, 5 January 1971) pointed out that Kaid Ahmed, leader of the FLN, had stated at a recent press conference that the subversive organization behind the student disturbances was "supported by the PAGS and given material aid by certain foreign embassies and by the French Communist Party."

Also initially autonomous, the General Union of Algerian Workers (Union Générale des Travailleurs Algériens; UGTA) came under government control in 1968; the fairly substantial influence that communists had exerted within the union was thus eliminated.

In 1970 the PAGS position in Algeria continued to be confused, because the government clearly proclaimed its adherence to socialism and was generally recognized by communist-ruled countries to be pursuing "progressive" policies. This left the Algerian communists little room to maneuver by offering truly alternative approaches to the problems facing the country. Indeed, their options were reduced to little more than repeated demands for their own legalization or criticism of the FLN interpretation of "scientific socialism" and of "reactionary" individuals in positions of influence in Algeria. This was the essence of a message to the Communist Party of Turkey on its fiftieth anniversary, in which the PAGS complained that "reactionary elements" in the Algerian government were depriving the "organizations of the working class of the most elementary democratic freedoms," that the PAGS was "obliged to operate as an illegal party," and that its militants were imprisoned without trial and without any charges against them. ("Our Radio," clandestine Turkish communist station, 1 November.)

Domestic Views and Activities. The most important PAGS statement of the year was an article by Larbi Boukhali in *World Marxist Review* (May), entitled "Lenin-Type Party and Struggle for National and Social Liberation," which clearly revealed the dilemma faced by the party and the difficulties of developing strategy for gaining greater influence.

Boukhali conceded that "Algeria has made substantial economic progress since 1962." As examples of "profound economic and social reconstruction" he cited the partial nationalization of foreign property and the formation and development of the public sector, with the objective of using industrialization for building a modern and independent national economy. The favorable assessment was balanced by the complaint that the government impeded progress through its declaration of a state of emergency to defend the privileges of the bourgeoisie and large landowners. Nevertheless, Boukhali claimed that the PAGS was extending "all possible support to progressive and social measures and all anti-imperialist actions of the government."

The most serious communist complaints, naturally, revolved around political affairs and the stated current goal of the PAGS to "democratize political life." ("Our Radio," 1 November.) Boukhali criticized the Algerian authorities for failure to create conditions favorable for an "advance of the socialist revolution." He described Algeria as being merely "in the stage of a national-democratic revolution, which it is striving to complete" and which might—with the proper changes—"produce the conditions for passing on to the socialist revolution." This type of progress, he asserted, would necessitate abandonment of official Algerian support for a "single petty-bourgeois party to the exclusion of all others." Furthermore, it would require correction of the faulty notion that "nationalist petty-bourgeois organizations are fully capable of the revolutionary remodeling of the social structure," and that in this situation, communist parties would be best advised to "fold or merge with nationalist parties."

The PAGS did not concur with such ideas in relation to its own political role. It called for a united front to replace the one-party structure, but insisted on political and organizational independence for itself. Boukhali saw the one-party principle as being used to "block independent organization of the working class" and thus to "facilitate imperialist and reactionary subversion." Nevertheless, he left some leeway for change, when he quoted from a PAGS document of 1 December 1969 (*IB*, no. 4, April 1970; see also *YICA*, 1970, p. 285) which had posed the question "Algeria: United Front or One Party?":

> We do not preclude *a priori* that, under certain conditions, a genuine socialist vanguard could emerge from the national liberation front or some other official progressive organization. In that case, the question might arise of uniting all the socialist forces in a single party, just as it had arisen in the socialist countries. Today, however, no one can say whether such a possibility will present itself [in Algeria] or when.

Whatever the eventual developments might be, the PAGS in 1969 had attempted to protect its own position: "The maintenance of a working class and socialist party operating autonomously within a united front of all progressive forces is a guarantee that the interests and aspirations of the working people will under all circumstances have a spokesman and defender." (*Ibid.*)

International Views and Party Activities. Boukhali in *World Marxist Review* (May) referred to the preamble of the constitution of the PAGS and its declarations as to national duty and proletarian internationalism. This document advocated the promotion of friendship and solidarity with all people following the road to socialism, and particularly with the Soviet Union, "that decisive force of the world anti-imperialist struggle, and our ally and supporter in building a modern and independent national economy." Boukhali also engaged in generalizations about the world at large: "The socialist world system has become the decisive international force. . . . The imperialist colonial system is crumbling to dust. . . . The national liberation movement is merging with the struggle of peoples building socialism and communism and with the revolutionary movement of workers in capitalist countries, producing a single anti-imperialist surge."

Soviet recognition of the PAGS as successor to the PCA and the contacts of the PAGS with foreign communist parties have for several years been the cause of government apprehension and consequent difficulties for Algerian communists. One of the chief problems has been the unique relationship with the French Communist Party, which gives practical support to exiled Algerian communists and allows its communications media to be used as outlets for communist propaganda from the entire Maghreb region of North Africa.

Although the Algerian government is generally willing to cultivate relations with other communist parties in Europe, it maintains almost no contact with the PCF and sometimes its bitterness toward the French party finds undisguised expression. Thus the FLN weekly *Révolution Africaine* (21-27 March 1970) took issue with an article in *L'Humanité* which reported on restrictions placed on student activities in Algeria. The FLN paper reminded French communists that "for decades, and up to the eve of our independence, [they] dared to affirm, on the basis of a doubtful and allegedly sociological analysis, that Algeria was not yet a nation," and that they had regarded the "historic uprising of the Algerian patriots on 1 November 1954 as an adventurist act with no future."

In 1970, Algerian communists attended the Nineteenth Congress of the PCF, and Larbi Boukhali in an address to the delegates declared: "The 650,000 Algerian emigrants to France, harshly exploited by their employers and housed for the most part in inferior facilities, are daily reminded that they have no better or more loyal ally than the French Communist Party and its militants in the various mass organizations" (*L'Humanité*, 7 February). Later in the year, when Bachir Hadj Ali was granted political amnesty, PCF Acting Secretary-General Georges Marchais sent a special message of greeting, expressing satisfaction with the release of the communist leader and others, and terming this event an "important success for the cause of progress and democracy" (*ibid.*, 23 November).

Normally preoccupied with its own cause, the PAGS occasionally commented on a few issues of world concern in 1970. It foresaw success for those fighting against the "colonial yoke of Portuguese fascism," spoke of "assured victory" for the people of North Vietnam, and condemned "Zionist aggression against the Arab countries." It described "U.S. imperialism" as bent on "wiping out the progressive regimes because their existence and growth [was] construed as a menace to imperialist aims." (*WMR*, May.) Although the PAGS was critical of the "adventurist methods and irresponsible acts" of some segments of the Palestinian resistance, it directed a special appeal to all Algerian progressives at the time of the civil war in Jordan, calling on them for "united action" and a show of solidarity on behalf of the fighting Palestinians (*L'Humanité*, 24 September).

Publications. The official organ of the PAGS is a clandestine, irregular newspaper, *La Voix du Peuple*; its Arabic version is called *Saout Ech Chaâb*.

E. W.

IRAN

Organized communist activity in Iran dates back to 1920, year of the founding of the Communist Party of Iran. The present communist party, called the Party of the Masses of Iran (Hizb-e Tudeh Iran), or more popularly, the Tudeh Party, was founded in October 1941, after an interval of ten years during which no organized communist party existed in the country. The Tudeh Party was banned by the government in 1949, following an assassination attempt on the Shah's life. Nevertheless, overt activities continued until the fall of Mohammed Mosadeq in August 1953. In 1954 suppression of communist activities was ordered and thousands of Tudeh Party members and collaborators were arrested. Some leaders escaped into exile in Eastern Europe, managed to regroup, and assumed direction of Iranian party affairs from headquarters in East Germany. A pro-Chinese faction split off from the pro-Soviet exiled party in 1965 and called itself the Revolutionary Organization of the Tudeh Party (ROTP). Additional splintering has occurred since then. (See below.)

Illegal, suppressed, and with most of its membership in exile, the Tudeh Party has only limited political significance in Iran. Estimates as to its total membership range from 500 to 1,000. The population of Iran is 28,400,000 (estimated 1970).

Leadership and Organization. The most important figures in Iranian communism are Reza Radmanesh, the chairman of the Tudeh Party, and Iradj Eskanderi, a Politburo member and frequent party spokesman. Others known to be influential are Ehsan Tabari and Avanessian Ardaches, who are members of the Central Committee, Ardeshir Hovanessian, and 'Abd al-Samad Kambakhsh.

Party Internal Affairs. In 1970 the Tudeh Party marked the centenary of Lenin's birth by affirming its adherence to his teachings and to Marxism-Leninism. It also vowed to apply to its own existence and activities "the experience of the brilliant victories of the Communist Party of the Soviet Union" (*WMR*, April). That this was no simple task became clear in August when the Tudeh Secretariat expressed fears for the party's survival and the physical safety of its members. Apprehension was the cause for the sudden redistribution of the party's "Organizational Procedures," equivalent to instructions, on how to "neutralize the Iranian security organization's subversive work" against communists. Emphasis was placed on adherence to the principles of "decentralization, combination of covert and overt operations, greater preference for quality than for quantity, and observance of rules governing underground organizational activity," which were termed prerequisites for a "patient, persistent, and disciplined struggle to achieve the realistic slogans of the Tudeh Party." Past deviations were held responsible for attracting the police and causing "an untold amount of disorder and trouble." Party organizers were asked, in particular, to prevent individuals from "falling into the trap of emotionalism and false revolutionism and from pursuing leftist, adventurist, and provocative actions." (Radio "Iran Courier," 5 August.)

The party criticized some members for "unrealistically appraising" conditions in Iran and advocating immediate revolution. Rather than resorting to more dramatic moves, the rank and file were asked to step up their struggle for democratic rights and freedoms, to participate in trade union activities, and to "practice patience, determination, and unity of action":

> There is a serious and basic difference between our party's view and the contention that a revolutionary situation already exists in the country and that our urgent tactical slogan should therefore be the overthrow of the regime. To overthrow the present regime and establish a national and democratic government in its place is our strategic objective at the present revolutionary stage; it would be adventurism and leftism to replace this strategic objective with tactical ones. (*Ibid.*)

Unity of action was an elusive goal for Iranian communists, to judge from an article by Reza Radmanesh (*WMR*, April), in which the Tudeh chairman declared that the party would "criticize and combat uncompromisingly all Right and 'Left' opportunism," and alluded to past expulsions of "deviationists." The party, he said, would fight "sectarianism" along with "conciliation and surrender to imperialism and the anti-popular and anti-democratic regime." Some "imposters" were said to be weakening the movement from abroad and thus helping the Shah's regime to survive.

Domestic Attitudes and Activities. The Tudeh Party was critical of almost every facet of the "White Revolution"—a term that the Iranian government applies to its program of social and economic change. Challenging the government's claims, Radmanesh (interview, *Baghdad Observer*, 2 March 1970) described the regime in Iran as being "terroristic" and "in the throes of acute crisis." He contended that all democratic activities were banned and that jails were crowded with political prisoners. Similarly, Radio "Iran Courier" (24 February) reported on "vain efforts" by the government-controlled news media to persuade the population of the Shah's sincere concern for its welfare and provided an explanation for the "failure" of such alleged propaganda: "One cannot expect anything but an increasing deterioration of the people's plight when more than a billion dollars, or 80 billion rials, is spent annually on the armed forces, the police, the gendarmerie, and the security organization's spies in a country where illiteracy, poverty, sickness, and death are playing havoc with the people's lives."

On other occasions the regime was accused of using "grotesque and disgraceful lies" in its propaganda and of disseminating them through "paid imperialist palace agents without respect for reason or conscience." As the worst example the communists cited "fabricated reports" of alleged collaboration to import arms by the Tudeh Party and a former army general, Taimur Bakhtiar, who fled the country some years ago after a falling out with the Shah and was subsequently accused of treason. The communists denied any collaboration with the comment that the Tudeh was "not naive," but a "Marxist-Leninist party that gives social revolution deep significance and never considers armed revolt as child's play," adding: "If conditions someday make it necessary to reply to arms with arms, the preparations for this will be nothing like the detective story the security organization has compiled." (Radio "Iran Courier," 14 January and 26 December.)

Much of the blame for existing economic shortcomings was put on the Iranian government's association with "world imperialism." The communists charged that "next to Israel, Iran is reckoned as imperialism's second base in the Middle East" (*Baghdad Observer*, 2 March), and that the government had practiced "great treachery" by "selling out" to imperialist interests. They objected in particular to the Shah's granting permission for foreign exploitation of large copper deposits discovered in Kerman, instead of reserving exclusive mining rights for his own country. (Radio "Iran Courier," 5 July).

The Tudeh Party not only objected to the "unscrupulous smashing" of all political opposition, but also charged that the Shah had assumed dictatorial powers and that both the Majlis (Lower House) and the Senate had become departments "for registering royal wishes"; that the courts had been made into instruments for carrying out government commands; and that, contrary to the constitution, military tribunals were set up to investigate political and press offenses. It claimed that such tribunals, operating under a decree by the Shah, had been able to "dispatch scores of patriots and freedom seekers to prison and places of execution." (*Ibid.*, 28 May.)

Early in the year the communists claimed credit for a considerable victory over the government. In February an official announcement of impending big increases in bus fares provided the spark for massive two-day (21-23 February) street demonstrations by students in Tehran. Although more than a thousand of the participants were arrested, the communists hailed the reversal of the decision to increase fares, together with the reopening of universities, as proof of the impact of the "boundless hatred" of the people for the regime (*ibid.*, 24 February). Subsequently, praising "the students who immolated themselves, the hand-to-hand battle between the students and the police, and the workers' realistic boycott action," the communists characterized the events as a "lofty, humane manifestation of the people's maturity . . . auguring final victory through unity and struggle" (*ibid.*, 15 March).

Government retreat in the face of mass demonstrations was considered a "sensation" (*Intercontinental Press*, New York, 30 March), since the last previous occurrence had been in the early 1950's, but the new-found student power was apparently short-lived. Radio "Iran Courier" broadcast on 10 December: "Tehran University is now in its fourth day of strike, because the Shah's government has again suspended classes for a week in the face of the students' legitimate demands and their just and undaunted struggle."

The February events encouraged the communists to step up their domestic demands. They protested "worker exploitation," low wages, unemployment, inadequate medical care, discriminatory educational policies, restrictions on trade union activities and on labor demonstrations on May Day, oppression of farmers, limited aid to earthquake victims, encouragement of capitalism, and a multitude of issues detailed in 1969 in the Tudeh Party's "Analysis of the Situation in the Country and Our Urgent Tasks" (*Donya*, no. 1, 1969).

The communists continued to focus attention on the status of national minorities in Iran. These groups were said to suffer from denial of education in their native languages, and thousands of Kurds and Azerbaijanis were reported to be languishing in jails under extremely bad conditions, while "many progressive young Kurd patriots [had] been brutally killed in clashes in Kurdistan" (*WMR*, April). Referring to talks between Kurds and the government of Iraq about settlement of their differences in that country, Tudeh chairman Radmanesh asserted: "The Iranian government can be relied upon to spare no endeavor to cripple the negotiations" because a solution in Iraq would "play a decisive role in escalating the national movement in Iran" (*Baghdad Observer*, 2 March).

International Views and Activities. Early in 1970 the Tudeh Party reviewed some of its ideas about the 1969 Moscow Conference, including its relations with the Soviet Union and the international communist movement:

> The Soviet Union's policy in all respects is based on correct principles and fulfillment of its internationalist duties. . . . Our party has always attached special importance to friendship and solidarity with the Soviet Union and the CPSU; this stems from its revolutionary, internationalist character, from its scientific and principled analysis of the present world. . . . Our party has always struggled against any manifestation of deviation from the proper revolutionary course, whether rightist or leftist, including Maoism in ideology or action. At the same time,

our party enthusiastically supports unity and solidarity of all communist and workers parties on the basis of principle. (Radio "Iran Courier," 6 January.)

In contrast to its praise of the Soviet Union, the Tudeh Party was always negative in its comments about the Western powers and their relations with Iran. The communists raised strong objections to NATO and to the "aggressive and colonialist" CENTO pact. They pictured the Shah as engaging in a "tooth-and-nail defense" of CENTO although in the past he had described it as a "worthless alliance" whenever it seemed opportune to stress the importance of an independent Iranian foreign policy. According to the communists, the government looked upon the pact as a "contingency measure" and had used an "obscene and incorrect" formula to prove that it did not affect Iran's daily political and military life, but would be used only in special cases and when Iran appealed to CENTO. In spite of these claims, the communists contended that "the Iranian army was not trained to meet Iran's needs, but merely to "carry out what the U.S. and British strategy has planned for Iran, either in the CENTO framework or outside it." (*Ibid.*, 8 April and 20 November.)

The communists were unhappy with British and Iranian activities in the Persian Gulf. In 1968 the Labour government had scheduled the evacuation of British forces from the area by 1971, but in 1970 the new Conservative government appeared to be ready to cancel the plans. The communists demanded that the British "colonialists" be "ousted by force." They objected to "joint maneuvers of Iranian and British commandos" south of Tehran, scheduled to begin on 4 October and last for seven weeks, and to "friendly and cordial" negotiations between Iran's foreign minister and the British. (*Ibid.*, 21 September and 14 October.)

The communists called the Shah's general policies in the Middle East an "exact copy of [those of] the Yankee imperialists." They described Iranian Embassies abroad as "centers for CIA activities," and their attaches as "agents carrying out the infernal conspiracies of this U.S. espionage organization." They spread the word that a "top secret" document described in the West German magazine *Der Stern* (29 January) had proved the existence of a nuclear manual for American pilots and that the manual listed bombing objectives that included such cities as Tehran, Tabriz, and Abadan. (*Ibid.*, 2 February.) The clandestine radio also broadcast details on a conference of U.S. diplomats, held in "total secrecy" in Tehran on 20-21 April; the alleged purpose of the meeting was to preserve "imperialist" gains by overthrowing certain governments in the Middle East and crushing incipient liberation movements. A leading role in this plot was attributed to Israel, which would be aided by Iran and Saudi Arabia. (*Ibid.*, 25 April.)

King Faisal of Saudi Arabia came in for special charges, not only as a "conspiring, despotic ruler," but for his role in the Middle East. Together with the Shah, he was held guilty of "extensive participation in the civil war in Yemen" and of involvement in the abortive coup against the Iraqi government early in 1970. (*Ibid.*, 23 January.) When the Iranian communists suggested in a statement of support for the Palestine Liberation Organization (PLO) that the time had come for "Zionist or imperialist paper tigers" to be "torn up," they presumably included Faisal in the group deserving of such a fate (Radio "Voice of PLO," Baghdad, 13 September). Some other Arabs fared better, and the Tudeh Party expressed pleasure at reestablishment of diplomatic relations between Iran and the U.A.R. (Radio "Iran Courier," 2 September).

Publications. The illegal Tudeh Party's publications are all printed abroad. They can be ordered from Sweden, but it is believed that they are prepared in Eastern Europe. The party organ, *Mardom* ("People"), and a magazine, *Donya* ("World"), both appeared irregularly in 1970. In October it was announced that the Tudeh Party would soon begin distributing a special student publication, to be called *Peykar* ("Battle"), which would defend the Iranian students' union and expose the regime's "anti-education" policy (Radio "Iran Courier," 20 October). The most important media of communications for the Tudeh Party are two clandestine radio stations operated from abroad, Radio "Iran Courier" and the "National Voice of Iran."

* * *

In 1970 the Tudeh Party repeatedly referred to problems caused by groups that were "falsifying the meaning and content of the social revolution in the spirit of leftist adventurism." These leftists were described as "petty-bourgeois, opposition-minded intellectuals of a nationalist brand," or as former party members who had "yielded to Maoist influence." Ehsan Tabari, writing in *World Marxist Review* (March), called them "Maoists of Iran, united in several groups and living almost exclusively in Europe, [where they] carry on a rabid anti-Soviet campaign and revile [the Tudeh] Party, putting various labels on it for its staunchness and consistent internationalism." The Iranian Maoists, according to Tabari, regard guerrilla war as the only form of revolution and assign the peasants a key role in it. He attributed their views to "subjectivism and voluntarism, a faulty notion of the relation between the revolutionary vanguards and the mass of the people, and misconception of Lenin's idea of the revolution as the activity of the people."

Late in the year, the Iranian government's security organization reported on the Confederation of Iranian Students Abroad, whose members live in Europe and the United States. The government agency identified several components of the confederation: adherents to the policies of the Tudeh Party's Central Committee, supporters of the "Revolutionary Organization of the Tudeh Party" (ROTP), the Marxist-Leninist Tufan ("Storm") group, and the imperialist "National Front" (Tehran radio, 28 December). Thus it appears that government officials and Tudeh Party leaders may, in fact, be opposing some of the same individuals or groups living abroad.

The security organization named Fereydun Keshavarz as the founder of the ROTP and as a former member of the Central Committee faction, and Khababa Teherani and Kurosh Lashayi as his major aides from the time when the ROTP was set up in Europe about1965. These leaders and others were said to have undergone training in the Chinese People's Republic. The security organization also alleged that the ROTP was in contact with Communist Chinese officials in France and Belgium and receiving financial support from them. It described the Tufan group as pro-Chinese Marxist-Leninist and as a major force in the Confederation of Iranian Students Abroad, and named Ahmed Qasemi, Gholamhosein Forutan, and Abbas Seghai as Tufan leaders. (*Ibid.*) These three men have been known as disgruntled former members of the Tudeh Central Committee who were instrumental in establishing the ROTP when they became "influenced by the ideological propaganda and disruptive activities of the Chinese Communist Party" (*Mardom*, December 1965-January 1966). Why they later broke away from the revolutionary faction has not been explained. The "National Front" was reported by the security organization to be a misnomer for a group basically Marxist in orientation, and a number of its leaders were said to be operating from Iraq.

Earlier in the year, the Secretariat of the Tudeh Party issued a communique (dated 3 July, with excerpts in *IB*, no. 15-16, September), announcing that a few members of the ROTP had "surrendered to the regime against which they had continuously urged an immediate armed struggle." Radio Tehran (21 June) had earlier identified Dr. Parsa Nezhad, Dr. Bizhan Qavimi, Abbas Ordibehesht, Mahmud Saleqin, Ardeshir Farid-Majtahedi, and Musa Radmanesh-Gilani as returnees from abroad who had publicly renounced their revolutionary goals. The noncommunist *Echo of Iran* (Tehran, 18 May) also had devoted much space to the "confessions" by Dr. Parsa Nezhad and reported that he had been pardoned by the Shah and was once more a "free man who can take up his medical profession in Iran."

E. W.

IRAQ

The Iraqi Communist Party (al-Hizb al-Shuyu'i al-'Iraqi; ICP) was founded in 1934. It has never enjoyed legal status, although periods of severe repression by authorities have alternated with periods of great laxity when communism was tolerated or even encouraged. The current regime of Major General Ahmad Hasan al-Bakr, of the Pan-Arab wing of the Ba'th Party, has displayed a vacillating attitude toward the communists since assuming power after a military coup in July 1968.

The ICP is believed to have about 2,000 members. There are an additional 10,000 to 20,000 supporters or sympathizers, who are selective about the communist causes they espouse, but normally back enough of them to make the ICP one of the more vigorous and influential of the Arab communist parties. The population of Iraq is 9,700,000 (estimated 1970).

Leadership and Party Internal Affairs. The ICP began the year 1970 divided into two major factions known as the "Central Committee" and the "Central Command." This division dates back to the fall of 1967, when the party split in a violent upheaval accompanied by rumors of assassination and kidnaping. The schism was engineered by a colorful revolutionary, 'Aziz al-Hajj, who set up the Central Command and advocated guerilla warfare. A few weeks after his arrest by government authorities in March 1969, al-Hajj made a radio broadcast in which he denounced the activities of his own organization and offered his support to the regime (see *YICA*, 1970, pp. 291-92).

After the party split, the Central Committee faction was generally considered the "official" ICP. It adhered to the Soviet line and to a "road of peaceful and democratic resistance." By 1969 'Aziz Muhammad had clearly emerged as its leader, although in 1968 this "orthodox" faction of the ICP reportedly was headed by 'Amir 'Abd Allah. In 1970 'Abd Allah was known to be a member of the ICP Central Committee and in retrospect it is apparent that he temporarily headed the party only because Muhammad—earlier also known as Nazim Ali—was abroad at the time of the 1968 coup and had stayed away until conditions improved for the communists in Iraq. At the party congress in September 1970, Muhammad was reelected to his post as first secretary. Others known as key members of the Central Committee faction of the ICP early in 1970 were Rahim 'Ajinah, 'Abd al-Razzaq al-Safi, Zaki Khayri, and Makram al-Talabani. Only Muhammad's reelection was announced after the congress, but it is likely that the other men also kept their posts. No new information became available in 1970 concerning Ara Khajaduri, Majid 'Abd al-Rida, Nazihah al-Dailami, Bushra Bartu, and Safa al-Hazif, all of whom were known to have been members of the Central Committee late in 1969, but 'Abd al-Razzaq Husain was mentioned by the Beirut weekly *al-Sayyad* in April as being "in charge of Palestinian affairs" and of the "Partisan Forces." There has been no word for two years concerning Baha al-Din Nuri, who in 1968 was said to have shared the leadership of the Central Committee faction with 'Abd Allah.

After al-Hajj recanted in April 1969, nothing was heard of the Central Command group for the remainder of the year, and it seemed questionable whether al-Hajj had been able to retain any of his followers. An answer was provided early in 1970, when a London-based organization supporting the Central Command—or at least a faction thereof—issued a long critical analysis of "The Situation of the Iraqi Communist Party from July 1958 to the Present" (published in *al-Hurriyah*, Beirut, 23 February and 2 and 9 March). Next it was reported from Damascus that the "Central Command wing of the ICP [was] gradually coming out into the open," and that "a number of elements which supported the former Central Command had succeeded in regrouping their forces . . . in northern Iraq . . . under the patronage of the Kurdish movement" (SANA, Syrian news agency, 22 March).

Shortly thereafter the "internal dispute" within the Iraqi Communist Party reappeared in the news. The Baghdad correspondent of SANA reported (on 2 May) that the Baghdad Area Committee and the progressive cadres [of the ICP]" had "drawn up a decision depriving the party Central Committee of its powers" and that the dispute apparently revolved around the peace agreement between the Kurds and the Iraqi government. The Central Command group put out a statement (printed in *al-Thawrah*, Baghdad, 4 May) declaring that the agreement had been reached "behind the backs of the people and in violation of the will of the progressive forces" and was a "trick to liquidate the Kurdish revolution." The Central Command also condemned a "reactionary, deviationist, and liquidating current led by the Central Committee" for endorsing the peace settlement.

The Central Committee reacted promptly with its own complaint that a "certain faction permits itself to indict a progressive political situation, using lofty words to insult while making a place for itself outside the crystallized political and class history" (*ibid.*). It termed this "childish behavior" an "unforgivable insult to the Iraqi Communist Party and the Arab and international communist movement."

The Central Committee faction, on its own behalf, had promptly expressed satisfaction with the promise of Kurdish autonomy within the boundaries of Iraq, and described the agreement as a "peaceful and democratic solution" for which it had "worked strenuously throughout the years" (Baghdad radio, 11 March). There has been speculation that the communists, in fact, served as intermediaries between the government and the Kurdish insurgents and that the pro-communist Iraqi Minister of Justice, 'Aziz Sharif, had played a major role.

That all was not well even within the ranks of the Central Committee was revealed by the Beirut weekly *al-Sayyad* (24 July), which reproduced sections of a clandestine publication called *al-Qa'idah* ("The Base"), reputedly the organ of a new splinter group. *Al-Qa'idah* charged the pro-Soviet Central Committee with "appeasement of the right, deviation from Marxism, depriving the revolution of its content and imposing an ideological reign of terror on the bases, as well as betrayal of the Palestine cause." It held the Central Committee leaders guilty of "stealing the funds of the party and spending them on pleasures of different kinds" and of "vacillating between the left and the right in accord with their personal interests."

In spite of all the internal dissension, the ICP held its second national conference or congress in September. Since there exist references to the Third Congress, held in December 1967, the 1970 event apparently was the second major convocation of the Central Committee faction. It was preceded by a series of local conferences and the selection of 102 delegates, of whom "two were martyred before the convocation . . . and some could not attend for one reason or another." The agenda of the congress included the adoption of a party program, "amendment of the internal system," and elections. (*al-Akhbar*, Beirut, 4 October.)

Domestic Attitudes and Activities. The domestic goal of the ICP is "a national-democratic revolution and the transition to a socialist revolution." (*IB*, no. 19, October 1970). The party visualizes progress toward this goal through establishment of a "national front" of progressive forces, which would act jointly and by common agreement. A national front coalition is also considered desirable by the ruling Ba'th Party, which since the military coup in July 1968 has repeatedly engaged in "dialogue" with leftist parties, including the ICP, concerning the feasibility of cooperation.

Settlement of the Kurdish problem was in the past considered a prerequisite to progress on plans for coalition rule. Therefore, the ICP Central Committee faction may have welcomed the announcement of a cease-fire on 11 March 1970, partly in expectation of its own immediate freedom for greater participation in the political life of the country. Communist joy was shortlived, because the ICP-organized demonstrations to rally mass support for the settlement and to publicize the party's contribution to the ending of hostilities served to accentuate the deep-rooted and lightly camouflaged animosity between the Ba'th and the communists. The Ba'th regime apparently interpreted such activity as a serious threat to political stability and reacted swiftly. The ICP charged that hundreds of communists were not only arrested, but "tortured, mutilated, and sometimes killed." In particular, it denounced the death of ICP Central Committee member Muhammad al-Khudari, alleging that it was murder and part of a well-organized campaign of terror related to the signing of the agreement with the Kurds (*al-Nida*, Beirut, 5 April).

Government spokesmen admitted that some communists had been arrested, but gave their possession of a large cache of arms as the reason, rather than their political beliefs, and claimed that the detainees were released when an explanation for the arms was provided (*al-Kifah*, Beirut, 7 May). The government also announced that it had named communist leader Makram al-Talabani to head a committee of investigation into the death of al-Khudari. The government abandoned all efforts at conciliation, however, following a speech by the ICP delegate, Habib Karim, to the Kurdish Democratic Party Congress early in July. It was charged that he had used the occasion to make renewed attacks against the government and had insisted on "equality" for the communists in the projected national front (*al-Thawrah*, 6 July).

The communist demand for equality clashed with the government's conditions, which stipulated that all leftist forces wanting to participate in a national front must "jointly recognize" the leadership role of the Ba'th Party, even "at the level of trade unions, people's councils, and the rest of representative institutions" (*Arab World*, Beirut, 13 May, quoting *al-Kifah*). In March the Ba'th Party had been reported ready to establish a national front based on principles to be proclaimed in a "national charter" on the 17 July anniversary of the 1968 coup. The communists submitted their own set of principles to be incorporated into the charter, but the Ba'thists rejected them and created additional disharmony by criticizing the manner of presentation.

Communist strategy for cooperation with the Ba'th Party, first detailed by the editorial staff of the communist party organ *Tariq al-Sha'b* (15 June), later figured in the proceedings of the ICP national conference (*al-Akhbar*, 4 October). In essence, it called for a "general national congress representing all parties and national blocs without exception to reach agreement in a joint and serious bid." It continued to object to the Ba'thists' "impossible conditions to make other parties subservient to it" and asked for "fixing a suitable date to hold general elections for the constituent national council." By the end of the year, however, it appeared that opposing views would be irreconcilable and result in communist refusal to participate in the newly announced "National Council" or parliament.

The ICP congress reviewed the domestic performance of the government, pointing out both positive and negative aspects. It gave the regime credit for "generally adopting an anti-imperialist policy"; for trying to develop economic independence by measures aimed at "exploiting the country's natural resources directly and with the comprehensive and unselfish assistance of the friendly socialist countries"; for progressive legislation in the field of agrarian reform, social security, and workers' pensions; and for passage of the new labor law."

Dealing with the negative aspects, the ICP considered that the regime was in essence "anti-democratic" in view of the "retention of all the reactionary laws which restrict the liberties of the citizens," the "Ba'thistizing" of the state machinery and especially the armed forces, and the application of economic policies which "exhaust and overburden the masses with taxes, fees, and increases in prices." Contradictions in the character of the regime were said to "encourage activity by imperialism" and to facilitate the "infiltration of reactionary forces into army and state posts." (*al-Akhbar*, 4 October.)

Although it held the ruling party generally responsible for any failure to rectify conditions, the conference report declared: "It is not the Ba'th which will have the decisive say in determining the country's fate, but the democratic movement, through its unity and the coalition of its parties, has the power to prevent the country from falling prey to the rule of reaction and the imperialist agents." For its own part, the ICP announced a policy toward the regime that would "continue to be based on opposing and criticizing everything that is negative and wrong . . . antidemocratic . . . and in violation of man's right and dignity," but would "back every progressive measure or firm stand against imperialism, Zionism, and reaction." (*Ibid.*)

By the end of the year, according to an editorial in the ICP monthly *Tariq al-Sha'b* (reprinted in *al-Akhbar*, 13 December), few government policies were worthy of backing. In an exclusively negative roundup the ICP condemned the government's economic policies and financial deficit, its "growing isolation from the masses," its "denial of human freedom and basic rights," its rule under a provisional constitution and without a "genuine cabinet," its "revival of the tribal system to win tribal allegiances," and the free hand granted to the national security forces, who "observe no law."

International Views and Activities. Iraq's foreign policy—and particularly its relations with the Soviet Union and the countries of the Middle East—had a strong influence on the status of the communists. The ICP, for instance, was accused of trying to embarrass the ruling Ba'th by allowing its differences with the regime to be exploited by the Syrians; this charge followed the reproduction of communist reports of persecution in the Beirut newspaper *al-Rayah*, which normally reflects the views of the Syrian Ba'th Party and had been engaging in open criticism of the Iraqi ruling party (*Arab World*, 13 April). When the Soviet press demanded an end to the suppression of communists, attacked the "strange" attitude of the Baghdad regime over its rejection of the U.S. peace plan for the Middle East, or threatened to cut off aid to the regime and demand payment for overdue debts, the ICP found itself in an unhappy position.

Regardless of the pressures, 'Aziz Muhammad and the leaders of the Central Committee faction remained unwavering in their support of the Soviet Union. In his report to the congress Muhammad stressed the "pioneering rule of the Communist Party of the Soviet Union, the importance of Leninist principles and of international proletarian solidarity in consolidating the ranks of the world communist movement." A resolution expressed gratitude to the Soviet Union and the other socialist countries for their "broad support of the Arab states in the fight against imperialism and Israeli aggression." (*al-Akhbar*, 4 October.)

The ICP congress discussed foreign policy issues in general, but focused particular attention on the "Palestine issue." It confirmed the "legitimacy of all forms of struggle against the Israeli enemy to enable the Palestinians to secure their right of self-determination on their own land after their return." It came out in favor of "moral and material" support for the Palestinian armed resistance, discussed the Rogers plan and pointed out the factors which, in its view, had prompted the United States to submit the plan: "In the forefront of these factors is the progress of the defensive capability of the states confronting Israel, the development and acquiring of a popular stamp by the resistance movement, the deepening of the social stamp of the Arab liberation movement, the threat to the imperialist and especially oil interests, the increase in the ties of co-operation, and the alliance of strength between the Arab liberation movement and the Soviet Union and socialist camp." Communist acceptance of the plan was coupled with a warning against the "intrigues of U.S. imperialism." The ICP also suggested that the Arabs end their differences and "bolster unity and solidarity in the struggle against Israeli aggression and the imperialist and reactionary forces that back it." (*Pravda*, 26 September, and *Arab World Weekly*, 17 October.)

At no time did the Iraqi communists call for destruction of the state of Israel; in accord with the Soviet Union, they opted for a political settlement of the Arab-Israeli conflict. At the end of the year they expressed their dismay at the "isolated, contradictory position" that Iraq had adopted when it refrained from supporting the resolution submitted to the U.N. General Assembly in October and when it "disregarded the candid diplomatic efforts exerted by the U.S.S.R. in support of the Arabs" (*Tariq al-Sha'b* editorial, reprinted in *Arab World*, 13 December).

The communist parties of Iraq, Syria, Lebanon, and Jordan early in 1970 announced the formation of their own commando organization, known as "The Partisans of Peace" or the "Partisan Forces." This group tried to join the Unified Command of the Palestinian Liberation Movement, but was rebuffed—probably for its lack of enthusiasm for an Arab "people's war against Israel and military action inside the occupied territory" (see *Syria*).

Outside the Middle East, the Iraqi communists showed limited concern with international issues in 1970. A congress resolution in September expressed solidarity with Vietnam, Laos, and Cambodia, but the foreign policy section of the party program resolved around such generalities as the endorsement of a "policy of coexistence between nations," a "struggle against aggressive military blocs," "defense of world peace," and "strengthening ties with the peoples of Asia, Africa and Latin America" (*IB*, no. 19, October).

Publications. The ICP Central Committee publishes a monthly organ, *Tariq al-Sha'b* (The People's Road), and a magazine *al-Thaqafah al-Jadidah* (The New Culture). Other publications identified as communist, but not attributed to any specific faction, are *al-Qa'idah* (The Base) and the weekly *Alif Ba* (AB). All of these publications are printed and distributed clandestinely in Iraq.

E. W.

ISRAEL

The first communist party in Palestine was the Socialist Workers' Party, organized in 1919 and renamed the Palestine Communist Party two years later. In 1948, after Israel became an independent state, the party changed its name to the Communist Party of Israel (Miflaga Komunistit Yisraelit; MAKI). In 1965, conflict between Arab and Israeli nationalist elements resulted in a party split, with each of the two resulting factions claiming to be *the* communist party of Israel. The basically Jewish and nationalist wing retained the party's name, while the predominantly Arab group called itself the New Communist List (Reshima Komunistit Hadasha; RAKAH), in reference to the separate "list" of candidates offered for the impending elections to the Knesset (Israel's legislative assembly).

The Soviet Union at first maintained an attitude of friendly neutrality vis-à-vis the RAKAH and MAKI, but this ended abruptly with the Arab-Israeli war of 1967, when the Soviet leaders announced that the RAKAH was truly internationalist and the only proper representative of the Israeli working class. All the countries of the Soviet bloc, with the exception of Romania, followed suit.

Both Israeli communist parties are small, each having a membership of about 1,000 in 1970. The population of Israel is 2,900,000 (estimated 1970). The two parties enjoy legal status, but play a marginal role in the politics of the country. In the national elections of October 1969, MAKI received 15,712 votes, or 1.15 per cent of the total cast, and kept its one seat in the 120-member Knesset; RAKAH received 38,827 votes, or 2.84 per cent, and kept its three seats. Municipal elections in 1969 gave RAKAH enough votes to place 35 representatives of the party on 17 municipal councils throughout the country, while MAKI failed to win a seat anywhere. RAKAH's biggest success came in 1970, in the municipal elections in Nazareth, where it polled almost 40 per cent of the vote.

Leadership and Organization. At MAKI's Sixteenth Covention, held on 30 October-2 November 1968, Moshe Sneh was elected party chairman and Shmuel Mikunis secretary-general. An eleven-member Politburo consisting of Sneh, Mikunis, Berl Balti, Eliyahu Drukman, Eliezer Failer, Shmuel Litvak, Ya'akov Zilber, Raoul Teitelbaum, Pinhas Tubin, Esther Vilenska, and Yair Tzeven was also chosen.

At RAKAH's Sixteenth Convention, held on 30 January-1 February 1969, Meir Vilner, a Jew, was reelected secretary-general and named to the mixed Arab-Jewish Politburo along with Tawfiq Tubi, Wolf Ehrlich, Uzi Burstein, Emile Habibi, David Khenin, Saliba Khamis, Emile Tuma, and Ruth Lubitsh. Tawfiq Tubi was also named secretary of a seven-man secretariat.

Both MAKI and RAKAH made serious efforts to recruit young persons. The "Alliance of Israeli Communist Youth" (BANKI), which was in existence as a youth auxiliary before the split, is now claimed by RAKAH as its own "young guard." MAKI considers BANKI an "independent youth movement," but seeks to expand its youth activities mainly through its own

"MAKI Young Generation." Both parties seek to increase their influence over what they term the "democratic organizations" in Israel, which appear to be equivalent to communist fronts. The communists' most determined efforts, however, are directed at improving their position within the powerful Israeli labor federation, the Histadrut.

Party Internal Affairs. In 1970 RAKAH repeatedly condemned the policies of MAKI. Noting a general "serious infiltration of hostile ideology," it made the following specific charges:

> . . . abandoning the proletarian class standpoint; weakening anti-imperialist positions and propaganda; sowing mistrust toward the Soviet Union and the international Communist movement; starting to infiltrate Jewish nationalist ideology; looking for and underlining mistakes made by forces within the national liberation movement of the Arab peoples and converting such mistakes into the dominant element of the movement; equating Jewish and Arab nationalism, and depicting the difference between them as the main contradiction of the region; undermining the Leninist norms of Party life; developing the theory of the higher specific weight of the Jewish party members than that of the Arab Party members; attempting to divide the Party along national lines. (*WMR*, March.)

For its part, MAKI looked upon RAKAH as suffering from the "plague of extreme Arab chauvinism" and resorting to the use of "hackneyed, one-sided, completely false" slogans about Israel and the Middle East (*Frei Yisroel*, Tel Aviv, 8 July). MAKI, however, was less intent on criticizing RAKAH than on defending its own position as an "independent party" of the international communist movement" whose "excommunication" was due to the fact that its position had been "distorted and defamed" (MAKI *Information Bulletin*, no. 2, February).

Arab-Israeli Conflict. The Arab-Israeli conflict has remained the most divisive and urgent issue confronting the two Israeli communist parties. The MAKI has continued to advocate a political solution in the Middle East, while warning that for Israel there could be "no retreat without peace." Moshe Sneh outlined the party's view in a speech to the Knesset: "We shall not accept the dictate to retreat to the lines of June 4, 1967, nor impose the dictate to confirm the lines of June 11, 1967 as permanent borders. . . . We seek borders of mutual agreement, of mutual compromise, and of security." (*Kol Ha'am*, 28 May 1970.) Efforts to dislodge Israel from the cease-fire line by force, Sneh added, would be acts of aggression demanding that Israel react in self-defense. Similar ideas received endorsement at a meeting of the MAKI Central Committee on 13 June, which praised the "heroism of Israeli soldiers and their officers," who were "preserving the security, the independence, and the very existence of Israel" (*ibid.*, 18 June).

In spite of such nationalistic pronouncements, all sides in the conflict came in for their share of MAKI criticism. Shmuel Mikunis called on the Israeli government to draw up unambiguous guidelines for a peaceful settlement "without trying to evade such facts as the question of the Palestinian Arabs and their right to self-determination." He demanded that Israel use caution to avoid a confrontation with Soviet pilots over the Suez Canal, and called for an end to "provocative anti-Soviet declarations." He expressed hope that the "Soviet leadership [would] stop on the threshhold of the abyss" and that Israel would refrain from placing its trust in the United States. Questioning the motives of both big powers, he stated: "It is not impossible that the Soviet military threat, on the one hand, and the American deferment of the Israeli government requests, on the other, are subtle moves to exert political pressure on Israel." (*Ibid.*, 28 May.)

After the American cease-fire initiative, the MAKI wondered if this was related to a "global American-Soviet accord" or to a tendency by the United States to seek such an agreement "at the expense of concessions on the part of Israel." The party nevertheless felt that Israel's lukewarm reaction to the initiative was appropriate, for it would have been "adventurism" for Israel to have replied in the negative, and "defeatism" if the government had "unconditionally and unreservedly signed the form [it was] asked to sign." (*Davar*, Tel Aviv, 4 September.) Later, when the U.N. General Assembly on 4 November adopted an Egyptian-backed resolution calling for an unconditional resumption of Arab-Israeli peace talks, MAKI argued that it distorted the content and meaning of the Security Council resolution of November 1967 and tended to increase tensions rather than promote the cause of peace in the Middle East (Jerusalem radio, 5 November).

MAKI condemnation of the activities of Arab commandos was unqualified. Politburo member Berl Balti, for instance, asserted that it was Israel's right to take defensive steps against terrorists who were seeking to establish a "democratic, secular, unified Palestine on the ruins of Israel" (*Kol Ha'am*, 16 July). Party leader Moshe Sneh was emphatic in his accusation of Arab guerrilla groups:

> For the Palestinian Arab organizations there is no other solution than the total liberation of Palestine, that is, a murderous war to liquidate an independent state and the annihilation of a people which will never accept such liquidation. A reactionary program of this kind obviously fans the feeling of hate among the peoples, intensifies chauvinistic and militaristic tendencies, and opens the door to the machinations of foreign imperialist powers. No Marxist could endorse this. (*Politique Aujourd'hui*, Paris, July-August.)

The Bureau of the MAKI Central Committee at a meeting on 9 September called upon all communist parties to denounce the "crimes of Palestinian terrorists hijacking civilian planes and holding their passengers as hostages," and stated: "This method of piracy clearly reveals the true nature of the armed Palestinian organizations that dress themselves in the garb of fighters of freedom" (MAKI, *Information Bulletin*, no. 9, September).

The RAKAH insisted that a solution to the Middle Eastern conflict would have to be based on implementation of the U.N. Security Council resolution of 1967 and complete withdrawal of Israeli forces from all occupied territory. Its Central Committee in a proclamation offered an additional solution to the impasse: "In order to halt bloodshed and to bring peace, the disbanding of the National Unity government is indispensable and it is vital to create a government of peace and national independence. The present government is one of national paralysis and national enslavement to the United States, which might result in national disaster." (*Zo Ha'derekh*, Tel Aviv, 3 June.)

The RAKAH considered the American cease-fire proposals to be in the "just and national interests of both Israel and the Arab states." But it gave most of the credit for peace initiatives to the Soviet Union and castigated the "monstrous hope of the [Israeli] government to bring about an American-Soviet confrontation and to involve NATO in the conflict." (*Ibid.*, 29 July.) Meir Vilner subsequently expressed the belief that peace could be achieved, provided the Israeli government did not succeed in "sabotage of the peace talks even before they have begun" (*ibid.*, 25 August). One of the ways to block the talks, he declared, was to "create an atmosphere of hysteria in Israel and international tensions over what the government labels 'movement of missiles toward the Canal.'" In contrast to MAKI, RAKAH termed the U.N. General Assembly resolution in November a "great contribution to peace" and proof that the nations of the world were unwilling to accept territorial annexation or continued crisis in the Middle East (Jerusalem radio, 5 November).

While supporting the views of Arab communists on the Palestinians, "whose rights and whose very existence the Israeli leaders wanted to eliminate once and for all by means of the June war," RAKAH labeled as "incorrect in principle" any plan that would abolish Israel as a sovereign state, maintaining that such a plan would only aid "imperialism and its Zionist henchmen—the common enemies of the Palestinian Arabs and the Israelis" (*Arakhim*, no. 9, July). Instead, the

RAKAH suggested, these "common enemies" should join in a broad "peace and democracy front" to assure a just peace for all (*Zo Ha'derekh*, 26 August). The party readily admitted that "anti-imperialist unity" and the cause of the Arab people were harmed by the airliner highjackings by members of the Popular Front for the Liberation of Palestine, and that these "adventurous acts . . . evoked general criticism in the world" (*WMR*, November).

Domestic Attitudes and Activities. On purely domestic issues, both RAKAH and MAKI were critical of government policies. They deplored the "reign of war budget" for 1970-71 and predicted economic stagnation and serious unemployment. They objected to alleged preferential treatment for the wealthy and "laws to stop the workers' struggle," and were particularly outraged at the implementation of the "package deal"—a complicated formula providing for wage-price-tax increases, with part of a general wage increase payable in government bonds; the "package" had been accepted by the Histadrut early in the year.

Both communist parties protested alleged religious coercion and on 9 February participated in demonstrations outside the Knesset against the decision to amend the "Who Is a Jew" law. Each party (in its *Information Bulletin*, no. 2, February) viewed the general excitement in the country over problems of religious legislation as obvious proof that the only solution would be separation of the state from religion.

Such accusations as "political terror," "persecution," "neighborhood punishment," and "arbitrary detention" figured prominently in communist complaints against the government. An article in *Der Veg* (26 August) charged that "new anti-democratic intrigues" by ruling circles testified to the "shakiness of their own security." In support of such allegations, RAKAH members of the Knesset circulated a "list of public figures" under restrictions of movement orders, house arrest, or instructions to report regularly at police stations (RAKAH *Information Bulletin*, no. 3, March). Both parties reported on a hunger strike of Arab detainees in Israeli prisons, although only RAKAH tried to substantiate claims of torture. The MAKI was more emphatic in its demands for an end to "collective punishment of the civilian population," challenging the deterrent value and contending that the practice incited the Arab population to terrorism against Israel (MAKI *Information Bulletin*, no. 1, January).

When it became known that the government had disapproved a suggested meeting between Dr. Nahum Goldmann, president of the World Jewish Congress, and President Nasser of Egypt to explore avenues for peace in the Middle East, both communist parties registered strong protests. RAKAH introduced a no confidence vote in the Knesset, but the motion was rejected overwhelmingly. MAKI abstained from voting, but declared that the government's action had adversely affected Israel's "international image as a peace-loving state" (*Kol Ha'am*, 18 June).

International Views and Activities. In 1970 MAKI grew more openly critical of the Soviet Union, accusing its leaders of "stubborn, dogmatic positions" and "contrariness in the handling of the Israeli-Arab dispute," and of "employing a strategy wherein socialist principles fall by the wayside" (*Frei Yisroel*, 11 March). Many of its charges were related to what the party called an "unprecedented poisonous anti-Israeli campaign in the Soviet Union" and pressure on Soviet Jews to participate and to vilify persons in positions of responsibility in Israel as "racist Zionists" and "inhuman fascist outcasts" (*ibid.*). Condemning "official anti-Semitism" in the Soviet Union, the MAKI urged that authorities grant permission to emigrate to Israel to all Soviet Jews, "who do not wish to or cannot assimilate."

The MAKI repeatedly demanded that the Communist Party of the Soviet Union (CPSU) "abandon the bankrupt line of identification with the warring Arabs," and "espouse a line of peaceful coexistence" in the Middle East dispute. According to Shmuel Mikunis, there were no basic conflicts of interests between Israel and the Soviet Union, and peace and friendship could have prevailed between the two countries "if the Soviet Union had not played a one-sided role at Israel's expense" (*Kol Ha'am*, 25 June). He declared also that it was "stupid to claim that the U.S.S.R. seeks Israel's destruction . . . and not logical from the Israeli point of view to turn to an hysterical anti-Soviet campaign" (*ibid.*, 23 July).

Looking beyond the borders of Israel, MAKI commented on the bloody events in Jordan and Lebanon, and warned that the "entire Arab world is stricken with agitation." It foresaw the possibility that Syria might "tear apart the upper part of Jordan, Iraq the eastern part, Saudi Arabia another section, and the Bedouins the rest." (*Ibid.*) The party referred to the "tragi-comedy" taking place in the "progressive" and anti-imperialist countries of Syria and Iraq, which were ordering mass arrests of communists while at the same time trying to "accommodate themselves to the ultra-chauvinist Arab national fronts and their terrorist anti-Israel organizations" (*Frei Yisroel*, 8 July). Ranging farther afield, the MAKI lamented the fate of Biafra—guilty only of the "crime of separatism"—which served as proof that the sovereignty of a people could be rescinded, in spite of the Leninist principle of the right to self-determination (MAKI *Information Bulletin*, no. 2, February).

In contrast to the critical attitude of MAKI, RAKAH invariably stressed the "special role of the CPSU as the leading force and the most powerful member of the socialist world system" and declared that "repelling" of anti-Soviet propaganda was a "very important and internationalist task" (*WMR*, May). In August, RAKAH credited the Soviet Union's "abundant and indefatigable efforts" with breaking the stalemate and promoting peace by achieving a cease-fire (*Zo Ha'derekh*, 26 August). Moreover, the entire Arab national liberation movement was said to have profited from Soviet assistance; in particular, such aid helped Sudan and Libya in "breaking the imperialist chain and embarking on the road of national independence and social progress" (*WMR*, November). RAKAH also seemed to consider the signing of the treaty on the renunciation of force between the Federal Republic of Germany and the Soviet Union as an achievement solely of the latter: "The FRG had to reconcile itself to the results of the Second World War and to agree to the present boundaries in Europe" (*ibid.*).

On the other hand, RAKAH condemned the United States for its actions around the world. In the Middle East, "American imperialists" were said to "operate only from the viewpoint of their exploitative interests" and to be looking upon Israel as "merely a piece on a chessboard" (*ibid.*). According to RAKAH, the Americans were also "pulling the strings behind the scenes" in the "secret coordination existing between Israel and pro-imperialist Arab countries such as Saudi Arabia." This charge was elaborated with the explanation that King Faisal of Saudi Arabia had tried to use the Rabat summit meeting in December 1969 to trap Egypt into launching an all-out war against Israel, which would have served U.S. interests by "dragging Egypt into a war and a new defeat." (*Ibid.*, 28 January.) Elsewhere the United States was allegedly working "against political solutions and the cessation of wars" and proposing more positive moves only "after its plots have been foiled and it has suffered setbacks" (*ibid.*, 26 August).

International Party Contacts. In 1970 only RAKAH was acceptable as an Israeli communist party in the pro-Soviet bloc. MAKI, however, in spite of an almost official boycott, had a few friends and contacts in the international communist movement. Romania, Cuba, and Yugoslavia and the communist parties of the Netherlands, Sweden, Norway, and Australia continued to maintain some ties with MAKI. The Netherlands communist party, on the occasion of its congress, received greetings and praise from MAKI for its "desire to restore the unity of the world communist movement on the basis of a relation of equality between all its parties, without hegemony and without excommunication, on the basis of the freedom of argument and elaboration of the issues of theory and practice" (MAKI *Information Bulletin*, no. 3, March).

When the Communist Party of Australia held its congress, MAKI's message noted common bonds between the two parties:

> We have been united in our opposition to any intervention, in particular by armed forces, of a socialist state in the affairs of another socialist state, in our opposition to the Soviet-Chinese conflict and to the occupation of Czechoslovakia, as well as to the interference of a Communist Party, or a group of communist parties, in the affairs of another communist party. . . . We are encouraged by the knowledge that communist parties abiding by their principles and independence, such as yours is, are at our side. (*Ibid.*, no. 4, April.)

The Romanian Communist Party was the recipient of a message of sympathy and solidarity in its "efforts to overcome the forces of nature and to help the victims of the floods in the cities and villages" (*ibid.*, no. 6, June). After Shmuel Mikunis spent his vacation in Romania, *Kol Ha'am* (13 October) reported that the Israeli communist leader's visit "expressed the friendly relationship" between MAKI and Romania's communist party.

Early in the year Mikunis also mentioned the existence of permanent ties with parties in Sweden, Belgium, Paraguay, and Mauritius, and of contacts with the parties in the United States, Canada, and Italy. He related details of his visit to the offices of a French Communist Party daily published in Yiddish and expressed certainty that it occurred "with the knowledge of the party leadership." (*Al Hamishmar*, Tel Aviv, 19 January.)

Publications. In 1970 the MAKI central organ *Kol Ha'am* (Voice of the People) was published weekly. Until December 1969 it had appeared daily; the cutback was due to financial difficulties. MAKI continued to publish the Yiddish *Frei Yisroel* (Free Israel) as a weekly, but turned its publications in Bulgarian and Romanian from weeklies into monthlies. English and French editions of its monthly *Information Bulletin* carried requests for prompt payment of subscriptions in view of a greatly reduced budget.

RAKAH publications include the Hebrew weekly *Zo Ha'derekh* (This is the Way), the Yiddish weekly *Der Veg* (The Way), the Arabic biweekly *al-Ittihad* (Unity), and the theoretical monthly journal *Arakhim* (Values). RAKAH also issues its own monthly *Information Bulletin*.

E. W.

JORDAN

The founding year of the Communist Party of Jordan (al-Hizb al-Shuyu'i al Urdunni; CPJ) is commonly given by noncommunist sources as 1951. Communist activity in Jordan territory on the west bank of the Jordan River can be traced back to 1943, however, and in November 1968 the CPJ received congratulatory messages on its twenty-fifth anniversary. The discrepancy is due to the fact that the territory of Jordan was limited to the east bank of the river when the country emerged as an independent entity and that the land on the west bank was acquired only after Israel was established as a nation in 1948. It was not until 1951 that a communist party for the whole of Jordan was established.

The CPJ and all other political parties in Jordan were outlawed by royal decree in 1957, after an abortive attempt was made to topple the constitutional monarchy. The CPJ has been illegal ever since, although the normally severe repressive measures have occasionally been relaxed. Under a political amnesty granted at the outbreak of war with Israel in 1967, communists were released from Jordanian jails and a period of tacit tolerance of communist activity began. The change was also due both to communist efforts to gain greater respectability and avoid provoking the government, and to the fact that the political significance of the CPJ was so slight as to cause no worry to the authorities. Party members are believed to number fewer than 1,000 and sympathizers around 5,000. The population of Jordan is 2,300,000 (estimated 1970).

Leadership and Party Affairs. The leading figure in the CPJ is Fuad Nassar, first secretary of the party since its inception. Otherwise little information is available about the party hierarchy. Two of the leading figures or public spokesmen are Fahmi Salfiti and Amin Salim; others known to have held positions of influence in recent years are Rushdi Shahin, Ahmad Sabir, 'Arabi 'Awad, Khaldun'Abd al-Hadi, Mazin Kamil, Sami Ahmad, Sami Anwar, and Farid Sa'id.

For several years the CPJ advocated the establishment of a Jordanian "National Front" or "National Charter" with the purpose of providing a coalition of such diverse political groups as the communists, the Ba'thists, the National Socialists, the Independent Socialists, and even some rightist organizations. While technically illegal, such a fledgling coalition in 1968 was able to provide some freedom of political action for the communists under a protective umbrella. By 1970, however, the front was virtually in a state of collapse and the overall situation in the country required a review of communist strategy.

To add to its problems, the CPJ in 1970 appeared to be facing serious internal dissent. This was rumored at the end of the year and confirmed when the Lebanese communist newspaper *al-Nida* (Beirut, 9 January 1971), which frequently serves as the voice of communism in the Middle East, printed the text of a CPJ Politburo appeal (dated 1 January 1971) calling for the return of defectors from the party fold. The text of the appeal showed that a group calling itself the "Leninist Cadre"—supposedly under the leadership of Fahmi Salfiti and Rushdi Shahin—had broken away and established a "Provisional Central Committee," although such an action was "in disregard of the resolutions of the [CPJ] party conference of April 1970." The conflict basically appeared to revolve around party attitudes toward the Palestinian commando movement and the creation of the communist resistance group, "al-Ansar" (see below).

The appeal seemed to indicate that there was calm in the CPJ at the time of its conference, when the "first genuine elections in the more than twenty-two years of the party's life" were held and the results met with the approval of those who later were challenging the conference's decisions and resolutions. The break was said to have occurred "after certain hostile elements published a statement, attributed to the CPJ, in the newspaper *al-Ittihad* on 4 and 7 December 1970 with the intention of harming the party's policy and positions and causing confusion within the ranks of the party on the West Bank." After presenting such rather vague information, the CPJ appeal called for party unity above any other consideration and asked for the convening of a party conference in 1971, suggesting that this would permit the exchange of views and the settlement of disputes which otherwise would benefit no one but the enemies of the communist party of Jordan.

It would be difficult to assess the effects of the dissent on the efforts of the CPJ to extend its influence among refugees, trade unionists, and women's organizations. The communist cause probably was helped, on the other hand, by the Jordanian-Soviet Friendship Society, which held its first meeting in Amman in March, with the Soviet ambassador to Jordan as the guest of honor.

Domestic Attitudes and Activities. The domestic program drafted by the CPJ in 1967 remained basically valid in 1970. This program had put heavy emphasis on the formation in Jordan of the broadest possible united front—a front capable of forming a cabinet that would ensure political freedom, nullify restrictive laws, and conduct an independent foreign policy based on Arab solidarity and on cooperation with the Soviet Union. That these communist goals were far from realization in 1970 was indicated by a CPJ statement issued on the third anniversary of the Arab-Israeli war. The statement characterized the government as a "reactionary authority, which still follows the pre-June 1967 line of total enmity for the people, maintains links with imperialism, and abandons national interests" (*al-Nida*, 6 June).

The CPJ held that misdirected governmental financial policies were responsible for the "squandering of financial aid" and for leaving the Jordanian armed forces ill-trained and without the modern weapons that the Soviet Union was willing to supply. The party also decried the work of "plotters and black forces" which were "extended like an octopus inside the army and government departments" and charged them with guilt in a "dreadful massacre" directed at the Arab liberation movement. It deplored the resulting "standstill of life," 1,000 casualties, destruction of scores of houses, and shelling of camps by artillery. (*Ibid.*)

When oil refinery workers were on strike early in the year, the party's Trade Union Committee believed that the Jordanian government of "capitalists and senior property owners" and the refinery managers were equally responsible. It declared that the government's references to "common interests and cooperation" between labor and management implied a demand for "workers' silence about exploitation," while workers were staggering under the burden of the high cost of living and owners were enjoying profits and luxuries. The government was held guilty not only as a business partner in the oil refineries, but for its past opposition to the amendment of labor laws and a delay in granting permission for the formation of new trade unions. (*Ibid.*, 13 January.)

The CPJ and the Arab-Israeli Conflict. By 1970 a new approach toward the guerrilla organizations operating within the country had become an urgent task for the CPJ. In 1968, Jordanian communists had rejected the "unrealistic political aims" of the resistance fighters as being "at variance with the objective conditions and strongly colored by extremism." By the end of 1969 the communist stance had grown more favorable, and the party advocated that all restrictions be lifted on the activities of the "patriotic fedayeen" in order to leave them free to "administer harder blows against the barbaric invaders from Israel." By early 1970 the CPJ had come full circle, as it joined the communist parties of Lebanon, Syria, and Iraq in establishing the all-communist commando organization "al-Ansar al-Silm"—the "Partisans of Peace" or the "Partisan Forces" (see below).

In accord with its new approval of guerrilla activities, the CPJ complained that on 10 February the Jordanian government had issued "eleven treacherous and conspiratorial decisions aimed at fedayeen action and the Jordanian national movement," and that the rulers of Jordan were willing to arrange a separate settlement with the "American Zionist alliance at the expense of Arabs and the Palestinians" (*al-Akhbar*, Beirut, 22 February). By June the communists had concluded that the government, with the aid of U.S. intelligence agents, was plotting to "liquidate the resistance and nationalistic movements and to plunge the people into a sea of steel, fire, and blood" and that together they were "seeking thereby to liquidate the Palestine issue, disrupt the Eastern Front, and break the ring surrounding Israel" (*al-Nida*, 24 June). When civil war raged in Jordan in September, the CPJ joined with the communists of Lebanon and Syria to urge the overthrow of King Hussein and the "fascist military regime" (Baghdad radio, 19 September).

Endorsement of guerrilla activities did not keep Jordan's communist party from defending Egyptian President Nasser's acceptance of the U.S. peace initiative. A CPJ declaration to this effect (*al-Akhbar*, 15 August) stressed that the U.A.R. had "moved from a position of strength and not weakness, especially in view of the fact that it [was] supported by a giant ally and a firm friend of the Arab peoples, the Soviet Union and the other socialist countries." Acceptance of the U.S. proposals, the communists argued, strengthened the position of the Arabs and reinforced their international standing by "increasing the sympathy of democratic world public opinion" for them. They viewed the U.A.R.'s action not as collusion with U.S. "imperialism," as some other Arabs did, but used Nasser's own words in claiming that it had the "purpose of uncovering U.S. imperialism's last cards, exposing them before public opinion, embarrassing and obstructing them." The party, furthermore, called on the commando movement to "consolidate its unity" and to coordinate efforts to develop its resistance to the occupation," and warned against falling into an imperialist trap by "turning from attacking imperialism and Israel to attacking the Soviet Union."

The CPJ remained unswervingly loyal to the Soviet Union and quietly acceded to any change of course suggested from that quarter. This was in accord with the Jordanian communists' view of the Soviet Union as the "powerful bulwark of the Arab people's fight," which was rendering "assistance of every kind to the U.A.R. so as to facilitate the repulsing of Israel's acts of aggression." "The plight in which Egypt would find itself without aid from the Soviet Union would be readily seen," editorialized the Jordanian communist party organ *al-Jamahir* (May). It substantiated the claim by citing the results of the hostile Jordanian policy toward the Soviet Union, which had left Jordan unable to defend itself against "imperialist infiltration of the country's government and economy." The communist newspaper then concluded: "Those who put out lies about Soviet domination and are hypocritically concerned about the independence and sovereignty of Egypt would like a similar lot to befall the U.A.R."

Naturally, Israel was the target of grave accusations. In a statement on the third anniversary of the "Zionist-imperialist aggression," the CPJ reviewed the situation: "The invader hordes are still occupying our Arab land and persecuting our people by all political, military, and economic means so as to force them either to submit or leave." Israel's "transgressions, barbaric methods, and criminal activities," it went on, were all perpetrated with support from "U.S. imperialism."

(*al-Nida*, 6 June.) Earlier in the year the CPJ condemned the Israelis as "neo-Nazis," when it demanded the cessation of torture and release of Arab prisoners striking against their detention and conditions in Israeli jails (*Arab World*, Beirut, 29 April).

Blame was also heaped on the United States, which through "hypocrisy and efforts by agents" was trying to "justify its support for the Israeli occupation, aggression, and goals of expansion." According to the CPJ, "the Arab people through their experience have ascertained that U.S. imperialism is [their] Enemy Number One." (*al-Nida*, 6 June.) The Jordanian communists also charged that the United States was trying to tip the balance in the Middle East in its favor by offering to guarantee the enforcement of a cease-fire and put an embargo on arms deliveries to the region after having met Israel's needs and ensured its military superiority. When this "ploy" failed, "barbarous raids on civilian objectives and children's institutions" were authorized to make Egypt accept the cease-fire proposals. (*IB*, no. 13-14, July.)

"Gaps in the Arab front" were contributing to the problems of the Middle East, according to the CPJ. The party blamed the "link of such oil-producing countries as Saudi Arabia and Kuwait with imperialism" for preventing the full mobilization of the fighting potential of the Arab masses. Morocco and Saudi Arabia were allegedly contributing to the obstruction of Arab efforts by granting exploration rights of their natural resources or permission to maintain foreign military bases on their territory and by "fabricating side battles"; an example of a side battle was the plot of al-Mahdi against national rule in Sudan. (*al-Nida*, 6 June.) Iran, Pakistan, and Turkey were charged with participating in the implementation of a "comprehensive imperialist plan covering the entire region." (*Ibid.*, 24 June.)

Publications. The CPJ publishes a monthly organ, *al-Jamahir* (The Masses). The first issue, in January 1970, contained this announcement:

> The Central Committee of our Jordanian Communist Party has decided to change the name of the party paper from *al-Taqaddum* [Progress] to *al-Jamahir*, so that the paper's name will be consistent with the conditions of our party's current struggle and with the overall situation which demands prime attention to be given to resisting aggression and liquidating it. It is changed, also, because the role of the masses and their effectiveness in resisting the invaders, both inside and outside the occupied territories, is becoming greater.

The announcement stated further that *al-Jamahir* would adopt the slogan "Workers of the World Unite!" and the emblem of the hammer and sickle in order to reflect the party's international outlook and class identity and "its future struggle at the head of the working class and the masses of peasants for the triumph of socialism and then of communism."

* * *

In 1970 the Palestinian guerrillas emerged as a crucial factor in the Middle East, as the Palestinian National Movement became more firmly structured and organized. Many of the numerous commando groups avoided identification with any political ideology and concentrated on the destruction of the "Zionist state structure" and its replacement by a Palestinian secular state where Moslems, Jews, and Christians could live together. Others promoted a distinct political view, and in this category were the "Partisans of Peace" or the "Partisan Forces" (al-Ansar al-Silm), the commando organization set up in 1970 by the communist parties of Jordan, Syria, Lebanon, and Iraq.

A statement issued in Amman on 3 March (printed in *al-Nida*, 7 March) declared that the Partisan Forces would "carry arms to resist Zionist invaders and their imperialist protectors," and emphasized that their struggle was "merged and associated, on the international level, with the struggle of the forces of freedom, progress, peace, and socialism, headed by the Soviet Union, against the forces of imperialism, international reaction and Zionism." The statement was noteworthy for its omission of any reference to the destruction of Israel and its replacement by a Palestinian state. Because of this pronounced difference from the publicized goals of other commando organizations, the request of the Partisan Forces to join the Unified Command of the guerrilla movement was rejected, pending proof of their worth by "military action inside the occupied territory." Apparently al-Ansar had failed to meet this requirement by the time the Unified Command was restructured in May and superseded by a "Central Committee" representing all units of the Palestinian Liberation Organization (PLO), for the Partisan Forces were again pointedly excluded from this "broad framework of National Unity" (*Arab World*, 7 May).

Some commando groups of the PLO are known for their left-wing extremism. The largest and most publicized is the Popular Front for the Liberation of Palestine (PFLP). The PFLP is headed by Dr. George Habash, who believes that all Palestinian Arabs should look to Communist China as their real ally and has declared that "a future state of Palestine after the liberation will be run on Marxist-Leninist principles" and will be "part of a Marxist-Leninist Arabia." In 1970 the PFLP was masterminding the hijackings and bombings of international airliners—actions that finally caused its suspension from membership in the PLO Central Committee (Radio "Voice of PLO," Baghdad, 12 September). At the time of the civil war, the Jordanian government offered a reward of $14,000 for the capture of Habash, and in November there were rumors that he had been ousted from the leadership of the PFLP. Such speculation ended after a seven-day conference of the Central Committee of the PFLP, which reelected him to another four-year term as secretary-general and recommended "new methods to revolutionize the Palestinian commando warfare against Israel" (Associated Press dispatch, Beirut, 11 November).

Habash is considered too liberal by his main leftist rival, Maoist-oriented Nayif Hawatmah, the leader of the Popular Democratic Front for the Liberation of Palestine (PDFLP), which advocates world revolution. In 1970 the PDFLP acknowledged the receipt of arms shipments from Communist China and their arrival at "Arab ports adjacent to Iraq" (*al-Hurriyah*, Beirut, 5 October). No one questions the veracity of this report, for it has long been known that Communist China provides aid to the guerrillas—particularly to al-Fatah, the large, strongly nationalistic movement headed by Yasir 'Arafat—while accusing the Soviet Union of collusion with the United States against the Arabs. The formation of the pro-Soviet "al-Ansar" may, in fact, have been aimed at counteracting the considerable Chinese influence with the guerrillas. (*An-Nahar Arab Report*, Beirut, 16 March.)

E. W.

LEBANON

The Lebanese Communist Party (al-Hizb al-Shuyu'i al-Lubnani; LCP) was established in 1924 as the Lebanese People's Party (Hizb al-Sha'b al-Lubnani). It was reconstituted in 1930 as the Lebanese Communist Party, which accepted members from both Lebanon and Syria during the period of the French mandate. In 1944, after national independence was gained by the two republics, the First Congress of the LCP decided to establish separate Lebanese and Syrian communist parties.

Banned by the French mandate authority and illegal also under the republic, the LCP operated clandestinely or semi-openly until 13 August 1970, when the Lebanese Minister of the Interior granted an official permit that made it the first communist party in the Arab countries of the Middle East to gain legal status. Presumably this has had a beneficial influence on the size of the party membership, which before formal recognition was estimated at around 2,000 members and 4,000 sympathizers. The population of Lebanon is 2,800,000 (estimated 1970). Areas of communist strength are Tripoli, Baalbek, Tyre, Sidon, and Zahle, and some sections of Beirut.

Leadership and Organization. The LCP request for formal recognition was signed by Nicola Shawi, Artine Madoyan, Yusuf Khattar al-Halu, and Mustafa Muhammad al-'Aris—all listed as "founders of the society." Shawi has been secretary-general of the party for more than thirty years; al-Halu is editor of the Beirut communist weekly *al-Akhbar*; al-'Aris is believed to be in charge of trade union activity for the party; and Madoyan headed the Armenian communists before their group merged with the LCP. Others known to have held important party posts when the LCP held its Second Congress, in July 1968, are Georges Batal, Khalil Dibs, 'Abd al-Karim Muruwwah, Khalil Na'us, and Nadim 'Abd al-Samad. Georges Hawi, who lost the editorship of the party newspaper *al-Nida* in 1967 and left for Eastern Europe as a result of internal party friction, has regained a position of importance and was a frequent spokesman for the party in 1970.

Although it continues to be dominated by intellectuals rather than labor groups, the LCP in recent years has had significant influence in the trade union movement and student organizations. The National Federation of Labor Unions, one of the nine labor organizations in the country, is communist controlled and is represented on the Supreme Labor Council of Lebanon. The LCP's influence among students dates back to its 1965 success in splitting the National Union of Lebanese Universities and subsequently gaining control over the left-wing group.

A few other Lebanese groups support the LCP or its ideology. The most important among them are the communist commandos known as the Partisans of Peace" (al-Ansar al-Silm) and the Lebanese-Soviet Friendship Society. The latter, according to a TASS report of 12 March, had recently held the first meeting of its constituent committee and elected its Executive Committee. Hashim Husain, a member of parliament, was elected president of the society, and Nicola Shawi was named to the Presidential Council.

Party Internal Affairs. Together with the request for legalization, the LCP submitted its charter and internal statutes and stated its goals:

> The ultimate and basic objective of the party is to destroy the capitalist system and the dictatorship of the bourgeoisie in order to build a socialist society in which the exploitation of man by man will be rejected. In order to attain this objective and by way of struggling for its realization, the Lebanese Communist Party is striving to cement complete national sovereignty, to realize total economic independence, to root out neo-imperialism and imperialist influence in Lebanon, to realize the urgent demands of the working classes and the other popular masses, and to bring about radical changes in the nature of Lebanese society which will bring it freedom, democracy, and social progress. (*al-Akhbar*, 23 August.)

The LCP also declared that it considered itself an "organic and inseparable part of the Arab liberation movement" and of the world communist movement "of which the Soviet Communist Party forms the vanguard."

The LCP in 1970 acknowledged that internal dissent had plagued it for several years, but claimed that the Second Congress had served to consolidate its existence. Shawi, writing in *World Marxist Review* (May), declared that the congress had "dealt a blow to the Left isolationist deviation, which had very nearly succeeded in diverting the Party from a correct assessment of Lebanese reality," and that it was equally effective in dealing with the "Right revisionist deviation, which likewise threatened to isolate the Party and hampered the reshaping of its tactics in conformity with the changed situation in Lebanon and the Arab world." Shawi referred to an "open and frenzied onslaught" by both the right and left factions, but categorically denied that they had succeeded.

Controversy revolved around the congress provision for the creation of a "mass Lebanese Communist Party." According to Shawi, the decision was subsequently proven correct by "numerical growth and closer unity," but these signs of success "infuriated" the right and left groups and caused them to step up their attacks on the party. The LCP was thus forced to contend with a combination of "dangerous conspiracies by government and reactionary forces," which were meant to "destroy the party as a prelude to destroying the popular liberation movement." (*WMR*, May.)

Domestic Attitudes and Activities. The LCP Central Committee met at the beginning of April to discuss domestic developments in the light of the "reactionary imperialist plot against the popular movement and the Palestinian resistance" and of the "feverish and suspicious American and reactionary activities in preparation for the coming presidential elections in Lebanon" (*al-Anwar*, Beirut, 12 April). Shawi, in a speech commemorating the Lenin Centenary, detailed the charges with the allegation that "reactionary quarters" ruling the country had been "subservient to international imperialism" and had "opened the country's gates to secret American and military espionage delegations" (*Arab World*, Beirut, 13 April).

After the elections in August, the LCP was dissatisfied with the "new methods" and the "so-called government of youth headed by Sa'ib Salam," and contended that merely changing faces and entrusting government responsibility to "unknown young men" could not provide the radical improvement demanded by workers and peasants. Change, according to the communists, had to begin at the bottom, and could be achieved only through a "democratic unity" government representative of all progressive and patriotic forces. Only such a unity government could be expected to safeguard the interests of the masses and properly deal with such issues as "health insurance, democratic liberties, and wage issues"; "protect fedayeen action"; and "work for a domestic, Arab, and foreign policy meeting the Lebanese people's real wishes." (*al-Nida*, 25 October.)

The LCP and the Palestine Resistance Movement. In 1969 the LCP had shown increasing support for the Palestinian guerrillas, but cautioned that advocacy of their cause should not be all-encompassing. Early in 1970 the LCP revealed an important shift when it joined the communist parties of Syria, Jordan, and Iraq in the formation of the "Partisans of Peace" or the "Partisan Forces." This all-communist commando organization applied for admission into the unified Palestinian Liberation Organization, but was refused until such time as it could prove its real worth by military action inside the Israeli occupied territories. Apparently the Partisan Forces never met this requirement; they, as well as the LCP, in fact, seem to have consciously refrained from making any call for the destruction of Israel and its replacement by a Palestinian state.

Nevertheless, LCP encouragement of the commandos increased. In May the LCP, together with the Progressive Socialist Party and the Ba'th Party, issued a statement entitled "To Possess the Capability to Stand Fast and Defeat Aggression and Plotting." The statement blamed the government of Lebanon for conditions in the south of the country, where "Israeli aggression" was said to be "striking at the unity between the Lebanese popular masses and the Palestinian resistance" in order to pave the way "for surrender and forcible solutions to liquidate the Palestine question." It went on to outline a series of steps for greater protective aid that would allow the commandos to "strike harder and deeper blows against the reckless enemy." (*al-Nida*, 27 May.)

Around the middle of October, the LCP Central Committee held an emergency meeting to review conditions prevailing in the Arab world following the cease-fire proposals by U.S. Secretary of State Rogers, the Jordanian civil war, and the death of Egyptian President Nasser. It reached the conclusion that the Arab liberation movement was passing through a "delicate and complicated stage fraught with danger," and that contradictory trends prevailed:

> All the things we feared and all the dangers we warned of have materialized. Division deepened inside the Arab liberation movement over the Rogers plan. Through this, secondary contradictions inside the movement became basic contradictions for a while. This condition covered all the Arab countries, progressive Arab regimes, national and progressive forces not in power, and the resistance movement. Even the masses were divided. Nearly all the Egyptian people supported President Abdel Nasser's acceptance of the Rogers plan. . . . The Palestinian masses stood behind the resistance movement." (*Ibid.*, 25 October.)

The LCP not only gave a status report, but detailed the "negative factors" that contributed to past developments. These included Iraq's "biased hysterical campaign . . . against the whole U.A.R. and President Nasser personally," Cairo's "hasty decision to stop the resistance radios," and Jordan's estimate that any peaceful settlement of the issue of Israeli occupation would require the liquidation of the Palestinian resistance movement. The Palestinian commandos themselves came in for criticism for "failure to mobilize the masses, to prepare a political action program, to appraise correctly Jordan's military strength," for allowing their movement to be split, and—most emphatically—for their "adventuristic hijacking of airplanes." (*Ibid.*)

Overall, the LCP concluded that the "Jordanian events" had been a "very costly experiment" and that the consequences would have been even graver except for the "intervention by Arab and external quarters—in particular Syria, the U.A.R., and the Soviet Union" (*ibid.*). The LCP sounded especially bitter about the "irresponsible behavior" of Iraq, which had earlier and consistently encouraged the resistance fighters to defy the Jordanian government and had promised Iraqi military support in any ensuing showdown. Instead of honoring these commitments, the Iraqi army withdrew when Jordan's King Hussein crushed the commando uprising in a "bloody massacre" and rejected all appeals to intervene to put an end to the slaughter. In short, the party charged, "the Iraqi government, during the whole of the fighting, gave the resistance nothing but words." (*Arab World Weekly*, 31 October.) In contrast, the LCP stated, Syria tried to make the resistance movement "avoid a battle imposed on it by the Jordanian hireling authorities," and, "when the massacre took place, Syria exposed the plot, rendered needed assistance, and denied the Jordanian reactionaries the opportunity to exploit this assistance by asking for U.S. military intervention" (*al-Nida*, 25 October). After the meeting of "Arab kings and presidents" resulted in the Cairo agreement of 27 September that ended the fighting in Jordan, the LCP gave the U.A.R. and President Nasser credit for the achievement and particularly for the prevention of U.S. military intervention (*ibid.*).

In the LCP view, the Jordanian government had "always played a role of plotting" against the Arab liberation movement. Reporting on the "second bloody phase of the massacre," *al-Nida* (11 December) claimed that Jordanian forces were attacking Palestinian camps and "indiscriminately killing women, children, and old men" while the "Amman butcher" (King Hussein) continued "friendly" talks in Washington and accepted U.S. military aid, which in turn was "intended to protect imperialist interests" and to be used against Palestinian resistance forces.

The Lebanese communists took every opportunity to confirm their friendship for the Soviet Union. In a typical expression, Shawi hailed the "tremendous all-around assistance by the socialist countries to the Arab national liberation movement in its struggle against imperialism and Zionism" (quoted by TASS, 7 November).

Other International Views and Activities. The Soviet Union was the only big power that won the approval of Lebanese communists in 1970. "Colonialism in Chad," as allegedly practiced by the French, was cited as evidence that France's ruling class wanted to become involved again in "imperialistic adventures" (*al-Nida*, 14 July). The British were said to be among the "foreign monopolies that loot the national wealth," and to have wished to invade Libya at the time the "revolution broke out there and triumphed"—a move that only the watchful presence of the Soviet fleet in the Mediterranean prevented (*ibid.*, 10 June).

The United States was accused of varied wrongdoings in Lebanon during the year. On 7 February an editorial in *al-Nida* demanded that U.S. Ambassador Dwight Porter be expelled for his "impudent interference in Lebanese affairs . . . amounting to blatant pressure and an attack on the Arab countries." The communist newspaper claimed that the United States regularly tried to exert influence on such internal matters as the composition of cabinets, parliamentary elections, and the formulation of domestic and foreign policy, all with the purpose of "serving U.S. monopolist interests and their brokers in Lebanon." Lebanese communist organs also discussed the "insolent aggression against the people of Indochina [and] the general aggressive design that the enemies of the people implement in a vast area extending from the Far East to the Arab homeland" (*ibid.*, 15 May). The U.S. peace initiative in the Middle East was allegedly a "threat of war," aimed at "stealing the Arab people's wealth and rights." Relations between the United States and Israel were described as those of an "imperialist state and its bases and lackeys" and in stark contrast to the absence of subservience in Soviet-Arab relations. President Nasser's July visit to Moscow was cited in this connection as proof that the Arabs could turn to "true friends" in the Soviet Union in time of need. (*al-Akhbar*, 5 July.)

It was noteworthy, however, that the staunchly pro-Soviet LCP issued only a brief statement at the time of Nasser's death: "The absence of this great Arab leader is a very great loss for the Arab liberation movement and will leave visible effects on the overall development of the Arab position" (*al-Nida*, 24 October).

Lebanese communists seemed uncertain as to how to interpret the political changes in Syria following the successful coup by the defense minister, Lieutenant General Hafiz al-Asad, against the leftist civilian faction of the ruling Ba'th Party on 13 November. Originally *al-Nida* was opposed to the new regime, but suddenly—and just like the Syrian Communist Party—stopped commenting. The Beirut noncommunist newspaper *al-Hayah* (23 November) reported that the

Soviet Union had exerted pressure on the Syrian Communist Party for support al-Asad, and that it could logically be assumed that similar requests not to resist the changes went out to the other communist parties of the Middle East. The LCP promptly welcomed the announcement of Syrian intent to participate in the proposed federation of the U.A.R., Libya, and Sudan, which was announced by the tripartite Arab summit meeting, held in Tripoli, Libya, in November.

An editorial in *al-Akhbar* (6 December) expressed communist concern at the situation in Sudan, where there was an "increase in hostile plotting and subversive activity aimed at sparking a collision between northern and southern Sudanese in order to preoccupy the anti-imperialist national government with side battles and enhance secessionist trends in the south." The Lebanese communists asked that the united front of all progressive forces in Sudan be preserved in order to safeguard the "national democratic" revolution of May 1969.

Publications. The principal publications of the LCP are the daily *al-Nida* (The Call) and the weekly *al-Akhbar* (The News). Both have been distributed openly for a number of years. They serve also as general information media for the illegal communist parties of the Middle East.

* * *

In 1970 the Lebanese Communist Party came under severe attack from the Organization of Lebanese Socialists (OLS), which used to be the Lebanese branch of the Arab Nationalist Movement (ANM) before it split away under the leadership of Nayif Hawatmah to establish itself as "The Marxist-Leninists." After changing its name, the OLS in December 1969 issued an "ideological manifesto" which declared that the LCP had lost its ability to function as a vanguard party and was suffering from "deviation embedded in the party roots." The OLS simultaneously offered itself as a Marxist alternative to the LCP and proposed to build "a real revolutionary Marxist-Leninist party" which would provide an organization for all revolutionaries who had to "forge their way ahead outside the framework of the Lebanese Communist Party" (*Arab World*, 28 February).

Outside this framework, fragmentation and a state of flux continued to prevail, as they have for many years. A pro-Chinese faction led by Nasib Nimr, which split off from the LCP in 1963, continued to function in 1970 as the "Marxist-Lenist Party of Lebanon" and to issue a monthly clandestine journal, *al-Shararah* (The Spark). A dispute over "undemocratic" practices and ambiguity of interpretation of the Arab problem in 1964 caused a group led by Nakhlah Mutran and Edmund 'Awn to break away from the LCP. In 1968 this faction joined with dissidents led by Samir Hamid Franjiyah to form the Union of Lebanese Communists—a group which dissolved in 1970 after a classic "Lenin versus Trotsky" dispute led to a walkout by Franjiyah and his supporters and the likelihood that they would form yet another new splinter group.

E. W.

LESOTHO

The Communist Party of Lesotho (CPL) was founded in November 1961 in close cooperation with South African communists. In February 1970 the party was banned. It now seeks to work underground.

The extent of the party's membership is unknown, but is certainly small. Lesotho has a population of 1,018,000 (estimated 1968) and is a mountainous enclave within the Republic of South Africa. Formerly it was known as British Basutoland. Since the country faces serious agrarian problems and offers minimal opportunities for employment, many men go from Lesotho to South Africa as migrant laborers. Lesotho communists argue that their country "cannot really be free and independent in the true sense unless and until the racist regime in South Africa is overthrown." (*IMCWP*, p. 634.)

Leadership and Organization. The CPL secretary-general is believed to be J. M. Kena. The party has not published any details concerning its organization.

Party Internal Affairs; Domestic Attitudes and Activities. In October 1969 the CPL held a congress and considered its draft program, "The Lesotho Road to National Democracy." Details are not known, but may be inferred from CPL statements at the Moscow Conference in June, which indicated that the party seeks to create "a united front of the progressive organizations" in Lesotho which should "replace the present neocolonialist regime, establish a national democracy and construct an economy step by step." While noting that "many members of the South African Communist Party and Liberation movement are Basotho," the CPL stated that "the conditions of the people in Lesotho are not identical with those of South Africa" and that "progress can be achieved in Lesotho independent of South Africa." (*IMCWP*, p. 634.)

In the elections held on 27 January 1970, the CPL ran one candidate in order to test its popular support. No returns were published. Instead, the prime minister, Chief Leabua Jonathan, suspended the constitution, announced a state of emergency, and banned the opposition parties, which claimed to have won the election. Jonathan claimed that the communists had played a significant part in the bloodshed that marred the elections. He added that communist contacts with the two other opposition parties were being investigated.

The electoral influence of the CPL was, even so, negligible. The party unsuccessfully attempted to form a united front with the Basutoland Congress Party (BCP), which in the communist interpretation had "spearheaded the struggle for independence." The BCP, however, "failed to mobilize all progressive forces" and "engaged in anti-left activities within Lesotho." (*The African Communist*, London, no. 41, 1970, p. 49.) The CPL seems subsequently to have attempted to form an alliance with the Marema-Tlou Freedom Party, an exceedingly conservative organization which sought increased powers for the monarchy, but its alignments have remained far from clear.

International Views and Positions. The CPL works in close association with the South African Communist Party and its ally, the African National Congress. Pro-Soviet, in its international views, the CPL condemns the activities of the "neo-colonialist" powers, especially the United States and West Germany. At the Moscow Conference in June 1969 the Lesotho delegation spoke of Communist China as a "rogue elephant charging wildly across the international scene" (*IMCWP*, p. 636).

Publications. The CPL is not known to issue any publications.

* * *

The BCP. The Basutoland Congress Party is a nationalist and Pan-Africanist party. Although there is no organized Maoist group in Lesotho, some BCP members are believed to be pro-Chinese.

L. H. G.

MOROCCO

The Moroccan Communist Party (Parti Communiste Marocain; PCM) was founded in 1943 by former members of the "Moroccan region" of the French Communist Party. Although suspended by the Moroccan government in 1959 and banned in 1960 for its incompatibility with Islam, the PCM continued to operate more or less openly, although several appeals for reversal of the ban were denied. In 1968, Ali Yata, the long-time secretary-general of the party, announced the formation of the Party of Liberation and Socialism (Parti de la Libération et du Socialisme; PLS) and named himself as head of the new group. By representing itself as a "national" political party, "strongly attached to the revolutionary traditions of the Moroccan people, the inheritance of Arab thought, and the liberal content of the Moslem religion," the PLS was able to register as a legal party. Moroccan authorities soon realized, however, that the dogma and ideology of the PLS were identical with those of the PCM. In August 1969 Ali Yata was arrested and in September was tried and sentenced to ten months in prison for reviving an illegal political party under a new name. The PLS and its newspaper, *al-Kifah al-Watani*, were banned.

PLS membership in 1970 probably fell below the 400 estimate of 1969. The population of Morocco is 15,700,000 (estimated 1970). Even during the period of legality, the party's influence was negligible and largely dependent on the prominence of a few of its members. Ali Yata tried to cope with this handicap by constant modification of his brand of communism and by soliciting support of the major opposition groups: the students of the National Union of Moroccan Students (Union Nationale des Etudiants Marocains; UNEM) and the General Union of Moroccan Students (Union Générale des Etudiants Marocains; UGEM); the members of the two main trade unions, the Moroccan Labor Union (Union Marocain du Travail; UMT) and the General Union of Moroccan Workers (Union Générale des Travailleurs Marocains; UGTM); the left-wing National Union of Popular Forces (Union Nationale des Forces Populaires; UNFP); and even the strongly nationalist Istiqlal party. Ali Yata had for years and repeatedly urged formation of a united front of all these opposition forces, but had attained only limited support from the UNFP, while the Istiqlal openly expressed strong criticism of the communists. In July 1970 the two parties the PLS had sought as partners in cooperation, did indeed sign an agreement for establishment of a national front (see below) with joint leadership, but they did not include the PLS in their plans. Ali Yata quickly expressed general approval of the union, but called for "creation of a real national front of all progressive and patriotic forces, without excluding anyone." He asserted that "this front must be openly negotiated between equal partners, with the support of the militants and the masses, and be created on the basis of an anti-imperialist and democratic program with respect for the autonomy of each of the member forces."

Leadership and Party Affairs. Ali Yata headed the PCM from 1945 until 1968, when he assumed the leadership of the PLS. Among other well-known Moroccan communists are Abdallah Hocine Layachi, Abdessalam Bourkia, Abdelaziz Belal, Simon Levy, and Dr. Hadi Messouak.

Mohamed Chouaïb Rifi was the co-signer with Ali Yaṭa of the statutes of the PLS and was also arrested in August 1969 and sentenced to prison. Both men were released in 1970.

The difficulties of the political opposition in Morocco were highlighted by King Hassan's announcement on 8 July 1970, that the country would return to constitutional rule, abrogated in 1965 when the king proclaimed a state of emergency and assumed legislative and executive power. A referendum on a new constitution was held on 24 July and approval granted by 98.7 per cent of the voters, although the UNFP and the Istiqlal had challenged the methods of the referendum and the PLS had condemned the "complete secrecy" with which the constitution had been formulated. After the referendum, the communists and the National Front called for a boycott of the legislative elections in August.

The PLS was subject to other frustrations during the year. The Istiqlal daily L'Opinion (Rabat, 13 September) reported on the methods used by the police to block the reappearance of the party newspaper al-Kifah al-Watani, of which Ali Yata was the editor. The communist publication was scheduled to reappear in the fall after a long period of interdiction, but the police unexpectedly entered the paper's printshop in Casablanca and abruptly ordered the printing halted. Both the Istiqlal and Ali Yata protested this action as censorship and as a "blow to the freedom of expression authorized and recognized in the country." Shortly thereafter, L'Opinion (28 September) reported that Ali Yata was being prevented by the Moroccan security organization from traveling abroad.

In spite of these obstacles to political activity, Ali Yata tried to sound optimistic when questioned about PLS affairs by the Italian communist daily L'Unità (Rome, 5 October). He expressed the opinion that the party ban, although confirmed by the Moroccan Court of Appeals in January, was not yet "definitive," and that there were irrefutable judicial reasons to annul it, and that the members considered recognition as a "right" they could not renounce. The communist leader attributed the ban to the judges' objection to the PLS doctrine of "scientific socialism," adding that they were not sufficiently acquainted with this ideology and that their interpretation of it was "grossly distorted."

At the end of the year Ali Yata was diplomatic in assessing the effectiveness of the UNFP-Istiqlal National Front (al-Koutla al-Watania) and the communists' attitudes and strategy toward it:

> It would be sectarian folly to maintain that Al-Koutla-Al-Watania, since formed without us, is merely a two-faction alliance temporarily concluded by the national bourgeoisie and that it should therefore be ignored. Neither should we opportunistically maintain that our fondest project is at last materializing, that the national movement is moving towards unity, that the Moroccan bourgeoisie will perform a democratic revolution and we, trailing in its wake, will support it unconditionally. . . . Though it is not the kind of alliance we have worked for over the years, Al-Koutla-Al-Watania is the next best thing and may prove a highly important element in forging that alliance. That is why we must play our part in order that this alliance should finally materialize. . . . Our joining the alliance . . . will not cause us to abandon the vanguard role of the working class, the poor peasants and the revolutionary intelligentsia; on the contrary, it should accentuate that role in the struggle for the working people's interest, stimulating the national movement with progressive ideals." (WMR, December.)

With all leftist opposition groups subject to mounting restrictions by the government, the suppressed inevitably shared an apprehension at the common danger, even though a firm political union had not been effected. This was revealed by such statements as that of UNFP member Mehdi Alaoui to the congress of the French Communist Party in February, in which he referred to "the latest wave of repression [in Morocco], which began with the kidnaping and death of our valorous comrade Mehdi Ben Barka, continued with the arrest of Majhoub Ben Seddik and Aouab, leaders of the Moroccan working class, and the arbitrary arrest and condemnation of Ali

Yata and Rifi and the dissolution of their party, the PLS, and which has intensified in recent weeks with the kidnaping of several UNFP leaders and militants" (*L'Humanité*, Paris, 7 February). The Paris daily *Le Monde* (18 February) also saw a common threat to the Moroccan opposition: "After the interdiction of the PLS and the condemnation of its leader, a certain hardening of the government [position] regarding the UNFP, and incidentally the progressive UNEM, can be observed."

That there was indeed a hardening in the official attitude toward all opposition became clear later in the year. Not only were numerous issues of *L'Opinion* confiscated, but in the fall the newspaper's editor, Mohammed Berrada, was tried and sentenced to jail for threatening the morale of the army and the maintenance of public order; this followed publication of a story charging several army officers with corruption. Not much later the UNFP found itself at a dead end trying to investigate the disappearance of Mohammed Yazghi, a member of the Central Committee and one of the most active party leaders. According to reports from France, Yazghi disappeared in November after having been the object of "close secret police surveillance" for two weeks. (*Le Monde*, 20 and 22 /23 November.)

Domestic Attitudes and Activities. Ali Yata seized every opportunity to comment on Morocco's "state of crisis"—economic, social, and political—which he attributed to "rigid conservatism" and the country's "alliance with neo-colonialism." In the economic sector he criticized the "abandonment of the national options of independence," the absence of agrarian reforms, the dependence of exports on the "good will" of Western partners, and the elimination of priority attention to industrialization. In the social sector he stressed the lack of any kind of progress, as indicated by a wage freeze, increased cost of living, higher unemployment or underemployment, and "aggravation of the material and moral poverty of the people." Lowered standards of education, he charged, were reflected in a stagnation of cultural life. (*WMR*, December, and *L'Unità*, 5 October.)

The crisis in political affairs, Ali Yata contended, was due to the government's opposition to national parties and its attempts to build up pliant pro-government political organizations. The 1970 constitution, he declared, had been imposed on the people through "falsification and fraudulence" and was "authoritarian and backward" even in comparison with the 1962 constitution. (Letter to the Swiss communist newspaper *Voix Ouvrière*, Geneva, 4 August.) Ali Yata alleged further that freedom and legality were flaunted in the legislative elections, that voters in some places had supported nonresident candidates completely unknown to them, and that more than two million young people in the age group from twenty-one to twenty-eight years were left off the registration lists and thus disenfranchised. The realization that such conditions prevailed was the reason, he said, for the boycott of the elections by all "national forces without exception." (*L'Unità*, 5 October.) After the elections, the communists looked upon the resulting "power structure" as "little short of absolutism" (*WMR*, December).

International Views and Party Contacts. As a result of the ban of the PLS and the establishment of the UNFP-Istiqlal front, Moroccan communism might well have keyed its fight for survival to closer links with the international communist movement. Nevertheless, there were no important new pronouncements forthcoming in 1970 and the opinions expressed by Ali Yata in his speech to the Moscow Conference in June 1969 presumably continued to prevail. In this address—which was bitterly attacked by the Istiqlal newspaper *L'Opinion*—Ali Yata had promised to "go on fighting against any anti-Sovietism, whatever its form and origin," and "as a matter of honor to strengthen international links with all the fraternal parties without exception," opposing "any manifestations of chauvinism" and "narrow-minded nationalism." He had called himself an "Arab Communist" with an "internationalist duty" to devote himself to the support of the cause of the Palestinian Arabs, although he added that "the Palestine resistance movement is not free from weaknesses and from the influence of harmful trends of opportunist as well as Leftist, adventurist varieties." (*IMCWP*, pp. 542-45.) Ali Yata's conference remarks confirmed a generally pro-Soviet view, although Maghreb communists have always been somewhat ambiguous in their acceptance of foreign policies of the Soviet Union, because of that country's willingness to maintain economic and political relations with Arab governments that practice anticommunism at home.

Moroccan communists expressed serious concern over the friendship and cooperation agreement between Spain and the United States, which was signed on 6 August and came into force on 26 September. Ali Yata attributed grave international repercussions to the provisions of the agreement on military bases, calling it a "reflection, in military and strategic terms, of the economic conquest of Spain by the United States" and a confirmation that Spain was an "American base of aggression against socialism." Yata looked upon the agreement as a threat to Moroccan ports on the Mediterranean and as an aid to NATO at a time when that organization was "encountering difficulties." (*L'Unità*, 5 October.)

Moroccan communists continued their close fraternal relations with the French Communist Party (PCF). In a special message on his release from prison (*L'Humanité*, 3 July), Ali Yata expressed his gratitude and solidarity to the PCF: "You have put into your support the weight of your authority and audience, the warmth of your attachment to proletarian internationalism." The PCF in turn sent greetings to Yata for his fiftieth birthday in August and hailed his "courageous activities in the service of the Moroccan people" (*ibid.*, 25 August). On the same occasion the East German ruling Socialist Unity Party (SED) dispatched congratulations over the signature of its first secretary, Walter Ulbricht.

Publications. Until the party was banned in September 1969, the PLS published a weekly, *al-Kifah al-Watani* (The Patriotic Struggle). Efforts to revive the paper in 1970, after Ali Yata's release from prison, were thwarted when police entered the publications's printshop and halted further work.

E. W.

NIGERIA

The Nigerian communist party is known as the Socialist Workers' and Farmers' Party (SWAFP). It was founded in 1963; the party's inaugural congress took place in 1965. Although the new military government in 1966 banned all political parties, the SWAFP has contined to operate through various subsidiary organizations and its trade union connections.

The extent of the SWAFP's support is difficult to determine; the party appears to be small, however, and is believed to have less than 1,000 members. The SWAFP appeals to intellectuals and to some white-collar workers in the Lagos region. It is without influence in the dominant northern part of the country. The population of Nigeria is 62,650,000 (estimated 1968).

Organization and Leadership. The SWAFP is headed by Tunji Otegbeye as secretary-general. He attended the International Meeting of Communist and Workers' Parties at Moscow in June 1969 under the designation, "Head of Delegation, Nigerian Marxist-Leninists."

The party is linked to the Nigerian Trade Union Congress (NTUC), the country's second largest trade union, which claims 400,000 members, although many of these do not actually pay dues. The NTUC's president is Wahab O. Goodluck, who also is general secretary of the Flour Mills of Nigeria Workers' Union. The NTUC general secretary is S. U. Bassey, who also is the general secretary of the Municipal and Local Authorities Workers' Union and acting editor of the NTUC newspaper, *Advance*. The NTUC is affiliated with the All-African Trade Union Federation, of which Goodluck is a vice-president, and with the Soviet-dominated World Federation of Trade Unions. In 1970 the NTUC held its Third Congress and (according to *New Times*, Moscow, 1 July) called for the creation of a single Nigerian trade union movement. The Nigerian labor movement, however, continued in 1970 to be seriously divided, and the NTUC's influence nationally remained relatively limited.

The SWAFP is also linked to the Nigerian Committee of the Afro-Asian Peoples' Solidarity Organization (NC-AAPSO). The general secretary of NC-AAPSO is Dapo Fatogun. Its "national patron" is Alhaji Aminu Kano, the federal commissioner for communications—a Northerner with radical views. Otegbeye is often referred to in *Advance* as "a prominent member of NC-AAPSO."

Other groups aligned with the SWAFP include the various "friendship societies" between Nigeria and communist-ruled states, the most prominent of which is the Nigeria-Soviet Friendship and Cultural Association, one of whose top leaders is S. O. Martins, believed to be treasurer of the SWAFP. The major youth group whose views reflect those of the SWAFP is the Nigerian Youth Thinkers' Club, founded in May 1967.

Domestic Views and Policies. The SWAFP offered its full support to the federal government during its confrontation with the secessionist state of Biafra. The suppression of the Biafran insurrection in January 1970 was thus welcomed by the party. Writing in *World Marxist Review*

(August 1970) Otegbeye referred to the leader of the Biafran secessionists, Odumegwu Ojukwu, as having been "a tool of imperialist reaction," and claimed that Nigeria had been able to "contain this imperialist conspiracy by the timely aid of the Soviet people," which had "kindled the fire of Nigerian-Soviet friendship and created a more favorable atmosphere for the spread of socialist ideas." Otegbeye concluded:

> To make permanent the gains of the Nigerian people in the struggle against imperialism, it is imperative that a National Democratic United Front of workers, peasants, soldiers, youths and students, intellectuals and other patriotic sections of our country be formed in order to consolidate the gains of the revolution and to lead the Nigerian people along the non-capitalist road of development to socialism.

"Such a victorious struggle," the SWAFP secretary-general emphasized, could "only be successfully waged under the banner of a dynamic and inspiring ideology," and added: "Such an ideology is Marxism-Leninism."

International Views and Policies. The SWAFP firmly backs the policies of the Soviet Union, and, in matters pertaining to issues within the international communist movement, aligns itself steadfastly with the Communist Party of the Soviet Union. Its stand was expressed at the Moscow Conference in June 1969 (see *YICA*, 1970, p. 315), and reiterated in 1970 in Otegbeye's aforementioned article in *World Marxist Review*, which stated: "Today Lenin and Leninism are synonymous with the birth and breath-taking growth of the Soviet Union. . . . which acts as a dependable ally of the world national liberation movements, of the struggle against colonialism and neo-colonialism."

Publications. The SWAFP has no official organ of its own. Its views, however, are reflected in the weekly newspaper of the NTUC, *Advance*. The *African Statesman*, an independent quarterly, is issued in Lagos by the "Council of Ten," a group of Nigerian intellectuals. Its chief editor is Sobo Sowemimo, who is assisted by Funmi Jibowu and Tayo Akpata. The views of the journal on subjects such as imperialism, neo-colonialism, and Zionism tend to resemble those expressed by *Advance*.

L. H. G.

RÉUNION

The Réunion Communist Party (Parti Communiste Réunionnais; PCR) was founded in 1959 by the transformation of the Réunion Federation of the French Communist Party into an autonomous organization.

The PCR is legal. In a fast-growing population of some 500,000 (estimated 1970), with a high percentage of young people, the PCR claims a membership of 3,500 (*L'Humanité*, Paris, 4 September 1967; *Tricontinental*, Havana, March-April 1969). Western sources tend to estimate PCR membership at approximately 500 (e.g., *World Strength of the Communist Party Organizations*, Washington, D.C., 1970). In an interview in 1968 the PCR secretary-general, Paul Vergès, stated: "Today the Party finds itself faced with the following alternatives: to increase its membership or, on the contrary, to freeze its numbers and increase their quality. It recently decided not to recruit new members but to make an effort toward the ideological formation of the members." (*Tricontinental*, March-April 1969.) It would appear that during 1970 the PCR's decision on this issue was still being implemented.

Although its membership is small, the PCR succeeds in mobilizing considerable electoral support, particularly among the island's sugar workers and in certain towns. The party presented three candidates in the elections to the French Assembly,[1] held on 23 and 30 June 1968: Jean-Baptiste Ponama (district of Saint-Denis), Paul Vergès (Saint-Paul), and Bruny Payet (Saint-Pierre). The PCR candidates were eliminated after the first balloting, receiving respectively 5,523 votes (out of 42,285), 14,802 (41,237), and 5,978 (25,912). In the elections of 1967 the same PCR candidates had received 10,072 votes (out of 42,288), 18,515 (39,970—in the second balloting Vergès obtained 19,765 out of 43,177), and 6,828 (29,596).

The PCR is the only party with a local organization; electoral candidates of other parties are normally Frenchmen without permanent organizations in Réunion. The party, however, in contrast to its counterparts in Guadeloupe and Martinique, has little influence in the island's municipal government, a fact which Vergès has attributed to repressive measures taken against the party after the elections of 1956 when it obtained more than 50 per cent of the vote (*ibid.*). The PCR has repeatedly accused the authorities in Réunion of perpetrating fraudulent measures during elections. The party's accusations appear to have been partly justified. In November 1969 the French Constitutional Council invalidated the local elections which had taken place in Saint-André in December 1967 and given rise to PCR claims of fraud (see *YICA*, 1968, p. 506). The subsequent elections, held on 14 and 21 December 1969, were contested by the PCR in a slate headed by Paul Vergès. In the second ballot, Vergès obtained 2,039 votes out of 4,468—a close runner-up to the Gaullist mayoral candidate, who obtained 2,329 votes. On 8 and 15 March 1970 elections were held for 19 seats on the Réunion 36-member General Council. The PCR fielded

[1] Réunion is one of France's Overseas Departments and thus an integral part of the French Republic, administered by a prefect, with an elected General Council and with elected representatives in the French National Assembly and Senate in Paris.

nineteen candidates (for names, see *Témoignages*, 20 February); all except two—Vergès, representing Saint-Pierre's first district, and Elie Hoarau, representing Saint-Pierre's third district—were eliminated in the first ballot. Following the second ballot, Vergès and Hoarau were elected. This gave the PCR a total of five positions on the General Council—the party's other three members being Evenor Lucas, Bruny Payet, and Jean-Baptiste Ponama.

The PCR controls the island's largest trade union, the General Confederation of Labor of the Réunion (Confédération Générale du Travail de la Réunion; CGTR). The CGTR held its Second Congress on 16-18 May. The congress elected a new 25-member executive committee, which, in turn, elected the following to the trade union's secretariat: Bruny Payet (secretary-general), Fabien Lanave, Raymond Hoarau, and Maurice Labenne (confederal secretaries), and Jean-Baptiste Rocheland (treasurer). The party is also influential within the Réunion Front of Autonomous Youth (Front de la Jeunesse Autonomiste de la Réunion; FJAR), whose secretary-general is André Hoareau, and in the Union of Réunion Women (Union des Femmes de la Réunion; UFR), whose secretary-general is Isnelle Amelin.

Domestic Views and Policies. During 1970 the PCR continued to advocate autonomy for Réunion within the framework of close cooperation with France, reiterating the resolutions of its 1967 congress, which had called for (1) a local legislative assembly, (2) an executive body responsible to the legislative assembly, and (3) an organization to regulate cooperation with France (see *YICA*, 1968, p. 506). Even so, estrangement from the party's strict support of autonomy in contrast to independence—already evident during 1968 (see *YICA*, 1969, p. 712)—appeared to be gaining progressively, with few PCR pronouncements in the party press criticizing Réunion independence as a goal. The party's 1968-adopted advocacy of sabotage as a tactical means (*ibid.*) was affirmed following the December 1969 local elections at Saint-André, when a meeting of the PCR Central Committee on 4 January 1970 resolved that there could be "no question of giving special priority to the electoral struggle over other forms of struggle" (*Témoignages*, 10 January).

International Views and Policies. In matters pertaining to international communist affairs the PCR has shown a tendency to adopt independent stands on various issues—divorcing itself from its erstwhile alignment with the Communist Party of the Soviet Union and the French Communist Party. This tendency—markedly evident in 1968 (see *YICA*, 1969, p. 712)—was dramatized in June 1969 at the International Meeting of Communist and Workers' Parties, held in Moscow, at which time the PCR was one of four parties that only signed one section of the conference's Main Document (see *ibid.*, 1970, p. 317). While continuing during 1970 to espouse relatively independent views, PCR leaders, as in previous years, traveled widely, maintaining contacts with other communist parties. Bruny Payet, member of the PCR Secretariat, returned to Réunion on 10 February following a trip which had included meetings with communist leaders in France, East Germany, North Korea, and the Soviet Union. Paul Vergès represented the PCR at the Nineteenth Congress of the French Communist Party, held in early February. Jean-Baptiste Ponama was the PCR delegate to the Lenin Centenary celebrations held in Moscow in April.

Publications. The daily organ of the PCR is *Témoignages*. *Jeune Réunion* is the weekly publication of the FJAR.

M. P.

SOUTH AFRICA

The Communist Party of South Africa was founded in 1921, officially outlawed in 1950, and re-constituted as the South African Communist Party (SACP) in 1953. It was the first communist movement to be established on the African continent. Although organized by Europeans, it was also the earliest multiracial party in South Africa. It now seems to appeal mainly to intellectuals and to some white-collar and other skilled workers.

Banned by the Suppression of Communism Act in 1950, the party has been unable since then to rebuild its organization. Its effective membership is small—perhaps a few hundred. The population of South Africa is 20,100,000 (estimated 1970). The SACP remains above all an organization of exiles, many of them residing in Great Britain, Tanzania, or Zambia.

Leadership and Organization. The SACP chairman is John B. Marks. In 1970 the party held an augmented meeting of the Central Committee, which discussed the "serious setbacks" suffered by the party's internal organization. It retained Marks as chairman, but appointed a new Executive Committee, whose main task was seen as the rebuilding of the party cadres. The meeting emphasized that fighting forces must be subordinate to the political movement and that cohesion should be attained by "conviction and commitment, rather than traditional bourgeois-type army discipline." At the same time, it was held that the party should be reconstructed as an "organization of professional revolutionaries, closely in touch with the working class and peasantry." (*The African Communist*, no. 43, 1970, p. 54.)

The party is closely allied to the African National Congress (ANC), which was outlawed in 1960. The ANC now operates underground and in exile. The SACP looks upon the ANC as a mass organization dedicated to the struggle for a national democratic revolution. The ANC, however, faces a similar need to rebuild its organization, and its practical importance in South Africa remains small. The ANC secretary-general is Oliver R. Tambo.

The SACP also has ties to the South African Congress of Trade Unions (SACTU), set up in 1955, which professes to be a militant, nonracial workers' association while exerting little effective influence. The SACTU has not been formally banned, but all its known officials have been either jailed or served with "banning orders" forbidding their participation in trade union activity. Steven Dhalamini, the SACTU president, is in prison. (*Ibid.*, no. 41, 1970.)

Domestic Attitudes and Activities. The SACP program, entitled "Road to South African Freedom," was adopted by the party's Sixth Congress, in 1962, and was further developed by a plenary meeting of the Central Committee in 1968. In June 1969, John Marks reiterated the party's position at the International Meeting of Communist and Workers' Parties, held in Moscow. He described the Republic of South Africa as an "imperialist state" which had designs on the sovereignty of Tanzania, Zambia, and ultimately every other African state. Owing to its economic importance and natural wealth, Marks considered South Africa to be a "strategic key-point in the global strategy of the imperialists," and declared that the South African government and its Rhodesian and Portuguese allies were being sustained by the United States, NATO, and Japan. He added that the SACP seeks a united front with all progressive elements and that under South African conditions there could be "no way to emancipation except that of a revolutionary armed struggle." Marks told the Moscow meeting that a joint campaign was being conducted by the ANC and the Zimbabwe African People's Union (ZAPU), and claimed that members of the SACP were "fighting in the front lines, side by side with [their] non-communist comrades," but added: "It is for the revolutionaries of every country to evolve their own methods, according to their own circumstances." (*IMCWP*, pp. 666-67.)

In 1970 an augmented meeting of the SACP Central Committee endorsed these positions. In addition, the meeting laid down additional guidelines on how to wage the armed struggle. The planning of operations was not to be based on a purely military approach, but must be conducted in such a way as to arouse the masses. "Any theory that localized operations of full-time guerrillas would in itself generate revolution was rejected; as also was the concept that organized armed activity should await complete political mobilization and advanced nationwide organization." (*The African Communist*, no. 43, p. 60.)

South African and Rhodesian guerrillas exist in Zambia and Tanzania but have been unable to establish permanent bases south of the Zambezi River. Meanwhile the South African government has continued to prosecute persons accused of membership in banned organizations. Among those arraigned in 1970 for various illegal activities were Benjamin Ramotse, who claimed to have been illegally arrested by Rhodesian security forces in Botswana, and Mrs. Nelson Mandela, the wife of a former ANC leader now serving a life sentence for sabotage.

International Views and Position. The party works in close liaison with the outlawed Communist Party of Lesotho. It is allied, through the ANC, with various pro-Soviet African guerrilla movements, including the Rhodesian Zimbabwe African People's Union (ZAPU), the South-West African People's Organization (SWAPO), the Frente de Libertação de Moçambique (FRELIMO), the Movimento Popular de Libertação de Angola (MPLA), and the Partido Africano da Independencia da Guiné e Cabo Verde (PAIGC).

The party's policy, as outlined at Moscow in 1969 by its chairman, is designed to support the Communist Party of the Soviet Union (CPSU) on every international issue. The party condemns the United States and its allies, denounces Israel, and supports the Arab states and North Vietnam. The SACP considers that the "external activities of the Chinese government . . . are in practice aiding and abetting [the imperialist] enemy," censures the "border provocations committed against the Soviet Union," and deplores the Maoist campaign against the CPSU. Marks stated: "Maoists subsidized a group of right-wing renegades from our struggle"—meaning the Pan-Africanist Congress of Azania (see below)—"whom documentary evidence now proves to have been started at the instance [of] the U.S. Central Intelligence Agency." As a general principle, however, he declared: "We dare not allow ourselves to be placed in a position where a few parties, or even a single party can be given a power of veto which would in effect condemn our movement to paralysis." (*IMCWP*, pp. 671-72.)

Publications. The SACP publishes the *African Communist*, a quarterly which is issued in London. A notice on its title page states: "[This journal serves as] a forum for Marxist-Leninist thought throughout our Continent."

*   *   *

The Pan-Africanist Congress of Azania. Although there is no recognized Maoist party in South Africa, the Chinese Communists are favored by the Pan-Africanist Congress (PAC). This militant black organization is an offshoot from the ANC and, like the ANC, is banned in South Africa. The PAC is allied with various exiled splinter groups, including the Zimbabwe African National Union, a Rhodesian organization. These bodies currently have little influence.

L. H. G.

SUDAN

The Sudanese Communist Party (SCP) traces its origins to 1944. It was officially founded in 1946. After independence in 1956, the SCP functioned openly for a time. It was forced underground between 1958 and 1964. Legalized temporarily, it was banned again in 1965. Since then it has continued to operate in a relatively open way. All Sudanese political parties, including the SCP, were declared illegal on 25 May 1969 following a coup d'état led by Ja'far Muhammad al-Numairi. At the outset, the ban on the SCP did not affect the party's activities unduly, and several communists were given posts in the 10-man Revolutionary Command Council and in ministerial appointments. During 1970, however, the party's relations with the government deteriorated progressively, and by mid-November most communists aligned with the SCP leadership appeared to have been removed from the Revolutionary Command Council and the cabinet (see below).

No reliable figures concerning SCP membership have been published. Most estimates range from 5,000 to 10,000. In addition there are many more supporters, whose backing makes the SCP the most influential communist party in Africa. The population of the Sudan is 15,000,000 (estimated 1970).

Leadership and Organization. The secretary-general of the SCP is 'Abd al-Khaliq Mahjub. Very little information is available on the organizational structure of the party, which does not publicize the names of its leaders. Moreover, in 1970 it continued to be beset by internal conflict, engendered primarily over the issue of relations with the government (see below).

The SCP has a sizable following among students and intellectuals, and also among urban workers, especially in Omdurman, where Mahjub managed to be elected to the legislature in April 1969 as an "undeclared candidate." The party wields influence above all within the ranks of the Sudan Workers' Trade Union Federation, an affiliate of both the All-African Federation of Trade Unions and the Soviet-dominated World Federation of Trade Unions.

Party Internal Affairs, and Domestic Views and Policies. In an interview given to the Paris daily newspaper *Le Monde* (30 July 1970), an unidentified "influential member of the Sudanese government" stated: "We have no illusions about the communists: they are cooperating with us now so as to be able to devour us later. You'd have to be simple—or quite mad—to imagine that a cat and a mouse can live together indefinitely." This statement reflected in part the complex relationship between the SCP and the al-Numairi government, which went through different phases between May 1969 and the end of 1970. The complexity of the relationship was further compounded by controversy between the SCP leadership and communist representatives within the government, some of whose affiliations with the party were unclear or apparently discontinued.

On 25 May 1969, following the coup d'état, the new Revolutionary Command Council included three communist-oriented members—Ba Bakr al-Nur, Faruq 'Uthman Hamd Allah, and Hashim al-'Atta—and the cabinet included Hamd Allah (Minister of the Interior), Joseph Garang (Minister of Supply), and Faruq Abu 'Isa (Minister of State for Prime Ministerial Affairs). The latter two, who were members of the SCP Politburo, reportedly resigned their party posts before the swearing-in ceremony took place. (*An-Nahar Arab Report*, Beirut, 27 April 1970.) Between May 1969 and the end of 1970 there occurred four additional cabinet shuffles (19 June and 28 October 1969, and 21 July and 16 November 1970) and the dismissal of three Revolutionary Command Council members (16 November 1970). The following changes affected communists or communist sympathizers. On 19 June 1969, Joseph Garang resigned his post as Minister of Supply and accepted appointment as Minister for Southern Affairs. On 28 October, Ahmad Sulaiman, a prominent member of the SCP and the only member of the party ever elected to parliament for a territorial constituency (see *YICA*, 1968, p. 537), was appointed Minister of Economics and Foreign Trade. At the same time, Amin al-Shibli (Minister of Justice), Mahjub 'Uthman (Minister of Information) and Makkawi Mustafa (Minister of Planning), all three believed to be communist sympathizers, were dropped from the cabinet, while Revolutionary Command Council member Hashim al-'Atta (see above) was appointed Minister of Animal Resources and Faruq Abu 'Isa was given additional responsibilities in the area of foreign affairs. In an analysis of the new Sudanese government, the London *Financial Times* (12 December 1969) claimed that three ministers—Garang, Abu 'Isa, and Sulaiman—were SCP members and that 'Abd al-Karim al-Mirghani (Minister of Planning) had communist leanings. On 21 July 1970, Revolutionary Command Council member Ba Bakr al-Nur (see above) was appointed Assistant Premier for Economy and Planning, Abu 'Isa became Minister of Labor (in August he was given the additional post of Minister of Foreign Affairs), 'Abd al-Karim al-Mirghani was dropped from the cabinet, and Ahmad Sulaiman's title was changed to that of Minister of Industry and Mining. On 16 November 1970 an apparent selective purge of communists and communist sympathizers took place (see below), as a result of which Ba Bakr al-Nur, Faruq 'Uthman Hamd Allah, and Hashim al-'Atta were removed from the Revolutionary Command Council and lost their cabinet posts. The dismissals appeared to be directed at persons adhering to the views of the SCP leadership rather than at individual communists. At the end of the year, however, Abu Bakr 'Awad Allah (Deputy Premier and Justice Minister) denied allegations that the Sudanese government was prompting a split in the SCP, and added that the government itself contained "dissident" communists such as Faruq Abu 'Isa and Ahmad Sulaiman, and others, like Joseph Garang, who were allegedly loyal to the party's secretary-general, 'Abd al-Khaliq Mahjub (*al-Anwar*, Beirut, 30 December).

Apart from policy differences between the SCP and the al-Numairi government, one of the major issues of conflict between the two was whether the SCP should follow the example of the Communist Party of Egypt in 1965 by voluntarily dissolving itself. Throughout the year 'Abd al-Khaliq Mahjub reiterated his opposition to a dissolution of the party, and in the autumn the SCP reportedly held a congress at an undisclosed location at which it passed a resolution, by an 80 per cent vote, rejecting all attempts to dissolve itself (*al-Kifah*, Beirut, 12 September). In addition to pressure from al-Numairi, there were indications that the SCP's dissolution was also being urged by some communist ministers in the government (*ibid.*).

In the first months of 1970 relations between the SCP and the government were relatively stable. The government was faced with a revolt led by the Imam al-Hadi 'Abd al-Rahman al-Mahdi, spiritual leader of the Ansar religious sect, whose following—primarily centered in the western provinces of Kordofan and Darfur—was estimated to number about one million persons. This first major right-wing challenge to the al-Numairi government was surmounted on 31

March, following a battle on the island of Aba, in which the insurgent forces were crushed and the Imam was killed. Although the SCP had given its full support to al-Numairi, referring to the Ansar as "right-wing reactionaries," the suppression of the revolt was followed by the arrest of Mahjub on 2 April and his deportation to Cairo the next day.

The SCP's Central Committee reacted strongly against Mahjub's deportation. On 4 April it addressed an open letter to the Revolutionary Command Council (published in *an-Nida*, Beirut, 16 April) in which it stated that "the surrender of Aba Island and the revolutionary suppression of al-Hadi 'Abd al-Rahman's sedition was a great victory for the armed forces," and claimed that "the communists were at the front of this popular battle." The Central Committee expressed itself as "surprised" by the arrest and banishment of Mahjub, a man who was said to have stood "at the fireline without hesitation" during the confrontation with the Ansar. It went on to state that his deportation, "regardless of justifications," was "a hostile action against the communist party and the communist effort to protect and develop the revolution," and added: "We have been noticing for a long time that certain quarters in the government have been persistently working against the communist party." The Central Committee demanded Mahjub's "repatriation to reoccupy his natural place at the head of those struggling for progress and socialism." Two days later, the SCP Central Committee issued a communiqué addressed to "the people of Sudan" which, reiterating much of what was stated on 4 April, added that Mahjub's deportation could not be explained as having been directed against him alone: " 'Abd al-Khaliq does not struggle alone, nor does he represent himself; he enjoys the confidence of the members of his party who elected him secretary-general." The government's action was described as "a part of a major plot aimed at liquidation of the communist party and distortion of its attitude and history," and was claimed to have "destroyed the bases of alliance, coordination, and cooperation among the revolutionary groups." The communiqué warned: "This wrong step will only benefit the reactionary circles in the country. These circles always try to engage the revolutionary force in side battles. The wishes of the rightist forces have been fulfilled." (*Ibid.*)

Following rumors that a number of communists had been arrested, Interior Minister Faruq 'Uthman Hamd Allah issued a declaration on 16 April, which stated: "The allegations that a number of communists have been arrested are unfounded; they are misleading rumors spread by known agent elements to create confusion and lack of confidence" (SANA, Syrian news agency, 16 April).

During the summer and autumn, conflict between the al-Numairi government and the SCP appeared to quiet down. During this period al-Numairi led high-level delegations to Yugoslavia (15-19 June), Bulgaria (19-22 June), Hungary (22-25 June), Czechoslovakia (25-28 June), Poland (28 June-1 July) and East Germany (1-6 July). He was also in Peking (6-13 August) and in North Korea (13-17 August), and on his way back to Sudan he stopped briefly in Moscow. Comments in Soviet and Chinese publications on developments in Sudan tended to be favorable, particularly following the extensive nationalization of foreign companies announced by al-Numairi on 25 May. The Soviet news media made few comments on relations between the Sudanese government and the SCP, although an otherwise favorable report on Sudan in *Pravda* (25 May) stated: "Reaction is striving above all to subvert by any possible method the unity of actions of the national democratic leaders against the communists and to undermine the trust between them, and to slander the communist party and attribute to it the aspiration to undivided power."

During the first half of August, Mahjub was allowed to return to the Sudan, although he was placed under house arrest. All newspapers in the Sudan were nationalized on 26 August. On 5 November, however, it was reported that two communist-oriented newspapers, the trade union organ *al-Tali'ah* and the women's union paper *al-Mar'ah*, would be allowed to publish independently.

On 16 November Mahjub was imprisoned, the aforementioned purges of communist sympathizers within the government were announced, and the businesses and property of Hamid Mah-mud Hamid al-Ansari, which allegedly belonged to the SCP, were confiscated. On 17 November, thirteen army officers described as communists were retired. In an announcement on that day the Revolutionary Command Council stated that steps had been taken against "some elements en-gaged in sabotage which pretended to be progressive and which had infiltrated trade union orga-nizations, the armed forces, and even the Revolutionary Command Council" (*L'Humanité*, Par-is, 18 November). In a speech on 23 November in Khartoum, al-Numairi—referring to "the 16 November measures"—warned that "harmful and deviationist elements" would not be allowed to do as they pleased: "They will be dealt with severely and on the spot." At a mass rally in Wad Madani on 26 November, the Minister of State for Foreign Affairs stated:

> The May revolution was not safe from disparagement by some isolated theorizing elements who wanted to impede the march of the revolution. . . . 'Abd al-Khaliq Mahjub covered him-self with false revolutionary masks and claimed to do the unprecedented. . . . Although we always tried to settle the differences with him by dialogue, he believed that he could twist life's neck to acceptance of his theory which was rejected by the people. . . . But the false mask of 'Abd al-Khaliq Mahjub was uncovered recently and the revolutionaries withdrew from him, except for a small minority to which I am appealing to reconsider their position and avoid the slippery slope of isolation from the masses. (Omdurman radio, 27 November.)

Also speaking at the rally was the new Minister of the Interior, Abu al-Qasim Muhammad Ibrahim, who claimed that the measures taken by the government were not aimed at revolution-ary groups, and stated: "The purpose of the detention of 'Abd al-Khaliq was to end the subver-sion he is carrying out by spreading division within the revolutionary forces and standing as an obstacle before the revolutionary alliance. He became an umbrella for reactionary activities." (*Ibid.*)

On 16 November the SCP Central Committee issued a statement in response to the govern-ment measures and a memorandum that the party had submitted to the Revolutionary Com-mand Council regarding the planned federation of the U.A.R., Libya, and Sudan, the latter (see below) being an issue of contention between the government and the SCP (for texts see *al-Kifah*, Beirut, 2 December). In its statement, the Central Committee reasserted the SCP's "clear record of service to the Sudanese revolution and the working masses," declaring that the party had "worked to support and protect the regime and to arouse and organize the masses in order to develop the revolution." The Central Committee termed the accusation of sabotage leveled against the SCP as "an insolent slur," and warned that it was "an invitation to traditionalist forces to continue their activities overtly and covertly against the communist party," which, in turn would help "imperialism and its helpers" to liquidate the revolution. The statement referred to the "increased activities [in the Sudan] by official Egyptian agencies, headed by their Egyptian intelligence organizations," which were directed in support of a "rightist" line and in order to "sabotage the revolutionary movement." The measures taken by the government were claimed to be part of a "trend toward the liquidation of the left." The Central Committee added: "The au-thorities have been helped in these steps by the support and blessing of secessionist elements which broke away from the communist party toward the end of September and turned the government against the party by saying the party was opposed to the government." The state-ment ended by warning: "The Sudanese revolution is exposed to unexpected internal and external dangers, and these steps are nothing but the beginning of progress along the road to the freezing of the revolution and opening the way to the return of reaction."

International Views and Policies. As a result of its own internal problems and its preoccupation with domestic developments, the SCP made few comments during 1970 on international issues, apart from its strong opposition to the planned union of the U.A.R., Libya, and Sudan. On this issue, despite the Soviet Union's support for it and the SCP's continued alignment with the Communist Party of the Soviet Union on matters pertaining to international communist affairs, the SCP recognized in the union a threat to the party's existence. The projected union planned the creation of state-controlled popular national organizations, stipulating that all political parties dissolve themselves, while the basic step in the fulfilment of the U.A.R.-Libya-Sudan federation was to be cooperation between the popular organizations of the three countries.

The SCP Central Committee made a detailed statement of their position in the aforementioned memorandum to the Revolutionary Command Council, published in *al-Kifah* (2 December). The unity of Arab peoples, the memorandum declared, was an objective necessity, but "experience [had] shown that unity cannot be imposed." It could only come through "the people's desire expressed freely and democratically." Arab unity must also be preceded by unity of the progressive forces within each Arab country and among the progressive Arab states concerned. The revolutionary movement in Sudan harbored no hostility toward similar movements in other Arab countries. Therefore, any rapprochement between the Sudan and other Arab states "should not take the form of an axis set up in the face of other Arab progressive forces." The memorandum added: "We believe that the declaration of the federation has been made without consulting any of the peoples [of the countries concerned]." This was "a grave mistake," according to the SCP, which recalled the words of the late President Nasser, speaking in Khartoum on the first anniversary of the Sudanese revolution: "Before taking any step, we must present that step to the people and its various political organizations. This is the lesson we learned after the breakup of the pioneering union of 1958"—a reference to the abortive union of Egypt and Syria.

The memorandum examined the conditions necessary for the success of the union. The "social revolutionary changes" had not been completed in the countries involved. The U.A.R. was "still lacking a revolutionary vanguard party equipped with a scientific theory capable of understanding the laws of social revolutionary development." The U.A.R. was "dominated by the bureaucracy of the state which obstructs the growth of the revolution," and was "strongly anti-Marxist." The memorandum warned against the dangers of becoming dominated by the Egyptian bureaucratic system, adding that "coordination with the Egyptian security agencies would harm the Sudanese revolution, which can proceed on a democratic road by depending on the masses without dependence on the agencies of oppression as the case is in Egypt."

Publication. The SCP publishes an illegal daily, *al-Maidan* (The Arena).

M. P.

SYRIA

The Syrian Communist Party (al-Hizb al-Shuyu'i al-Suri; SCP) is an offshoot of the Lebanese Communist Party (LCP). During the French mandate over Syria and Lebanon, membership in the LCP was open to communists from both states. Under the guidance of Khalid Bakdash, a dynamic Syrian Kurd who became first secretary of the party in 1932, Syrian elements attained dominance. When national independence was granted to Syria and Lebanon in 1944, party independence was a logical consequence and Bakdash assumed the leadership of the newly formed SCP. Separation occurred under amicable conditions, and the strong initial ties between the Lebanese and Syrian communist parties have weakened only gradually over the years. The SCP is firmly pro-Soviet in orientation.

French authorities proscribed all communist activity in 1939, and this ban continued after Syria's independence. Despite illegality, the SCP has enjoyed several periods of considerable political freedom. One began in February 1966, when a successful coup brought the extreme left-wing faction of the Ba'th (Arab Socialist) Party to power. The new Ba'th rulers were willing to grant a certain measure of tolerance for SCP activities in exchange for communist cooperation. They also provided a cabinet post, the Ministry of Communications, which without reference to party affiliation was "reserved" for a communist. This arrangement of convenience survived until 1970, in spite of factional struggles and power plays within the Ba'th Party, which invariably affected the fate of Syria's communists. The most important of these developments in 1969 and 1970 was the rivalry between the Ba'th "military" faction headed by the defense minister, Lieutenant General Hafiz al-Asad, and the "civilian" wing headed by the Ba'th Party's assistant secretary-general, Salah Jadid.

In 1970 old controversies within the Ba'th were aggravated by the Arab-Israeli conflict in general and the civil war in Jordan in particular. The "civilian" wing rejected any form of accommodation with Israel as "surrender solutions" and favored all possible Syrian assistance to the Palestine commandos in a "war of popular liberation." The "military" faction seemed to be more pragmatic and moderate in searching for solutions—al-Asad, for instance, resisted the idea of armed intervention by Syrian forces in Jordan in the first place and finally refused air cover for armored Syrian columns moving across the border. Controversy over these and other matters reached such an impasse that the Ba'th Party convened a special congress to settle the dispute. At the congress, which began on 30 October and ended on 12 November, the "civilian" faction apparently gained the upper hand at secret meetings and planned the ouster of al-Asad from his military post. Before this plan could be carried out, al-Asad assumed control of both the party and the government after a bloodless coup on 13 November. Although the SCP had clearly favored Jadid, the communists quickly came to grips with the changed realities and the implications for their own existence.

Organization and Leadership. Membership in the SCP is believed to range between 3,000 and 4,000. The population of Syria is 6,200,000 (estimated 1970). The party is headed by Khalid Bakdash, who is generally considered the most important communist in the Arab world, and has held his post—with a brief interval in 1968—since the party was established. Bakdash was re-elected to lead his party in June 1969, when the SCP's Third Congress was held in Damascus. A new Politburo, chosen at the same time, was composed of Bakdash, Ibrahim Bakri, Riyad al-Turk, 'Umar Qashshash, Yusuf Faisal, Daniel Ni'mah, and Zuhair 'Abd al-Samad. The last three and Murad Yusuf were named party secretaries. Maurice Salibi, who briefly headed the SCP in 1968 while Bakdash was in Moscow recuperating from an alleged heart attack, was dropped from the leadership rolls. No major changes appear to have occurred during 1970.

Party Internal Affairs. Khalid Bakdash, writing in *World Marxist Review* (April 1970), listed the most important tasks confronting his party at the time: "We Syrian communists are fighting together with other progressive patriotic elements to wipe out the consequences of the U.S.-supported Israeli aggression, strengthen and expand the guerrilla movement against the Zionist invaders on occupied Arab territory and, at the same time, consolidate Syria's national-democratic system."

Only a few weeks later, the SCP was completely preoccupied with its own survival and with threats to the life and freedom of its members posed by a severe anticommunist campaign. The clandestinely published party organ *Nidal al-Sha'b* reported that Syrian authorities had begun arresting party members in April, that 35 communists were detained the first day, and that arrests occurred simultaneously in seven districts. The paper alleged that the clampdown was the result of the communist party's support for the settlement of the Iraqi-Kurdish war, while the Syrian Ba'th leaders viewed an end of that conflict with serious reservations. The noncommunist newspaper *al-Hayah* (Beirut, 7 May) presented a different explanation, when it reported that the Syrian regime was "closely watching" the activities of SCP members " in the wake of campaigns launched by Khalid Bakdash against the Syrian armed forces for their conservatism and the government's refusal to cooperate with the communists in sharing power." A third version was presented by the Beirut daily *al-Kifah* (21 May), which stated that sixty-five SCP members and sympathizers had been arrested, but explained this as a reaction to the party's display of anti-government posters at the time of the Lenin Centenary.

The same issue of *al-Kifah* alluded to the possibility of a connection between the anti-communist campaign and the recent strain in Syrian-Soviet relations. It cited an incident during Lenin Centenary celebrations in Moscow, where the leader of the Syrian delegation, Interior Minister Muhammad Rabah al-Tawil, was prevented from delivering a scheduled address and was informed that the head of the Egyptian delegation would speak for all Arabs and Khalid Bakdash for all communists of the Middle East. This was interpreted by Syria as a Soviet provocation against the regime.

While it is impossible to evaluate the accuracy of such conflicting reports, there seems to have been general agreement that the Syrian authorities banned the distribution of all communist publications or propaganda and prevented SCP leaders from leaving the country. Only *Nidal al-Sha'b* (May), however, detailed "beatings and tortures." In particular, it reported such experiences for Ahmad Mustafa al-Zuhbi and Rafiq 'Abd al-Jalil Bahbuh, identified as communist leaders who had worked for the Syrian news agency SANA. According to the SCP organ (and excerpts reprinted in *Le Jour*, Beirut, 22 June), Zuhbi died in prison and his body was returned to his family in a sealed coffin with the explanation that he had succumbed to a heart attack; when the coffin was opened, it allegedly became obvious that he had been "murdered."

Khalid Bakdash later in the year offered his own explanation for the anticommunist campaign:

"The main goal was to upset and possibly even prevent cooperation between Ba'th members and the communists and to besmirch Syria's name in the eyes of the progressive world, harm our relations with the socialist countries, and ultimately weaken Syria's position vis-à-vis imperialism and Israeli aggression" (interview with *Népszabadság*, Budapest, 6 September). By that time, Bakdash obviously was no longer anxious to repeat the opinions he expressed in *Nidal al-Sha'b* in February, when he attacked the "Syrian military machine," praised the civilian or left faction of the Ba'th Party under Jadid, and criticized the right wing under al-Asad.

In spite of its earlier pronounced hostility to al-Asad, the SCP quickly reversed its stand and offered cooperation to the new regime assuming power in November. Two SCP Central Committee members accepted cabinet posts—'Umar Siba'i as minister of communications and Yusuf Faisal as minister of state—and the party apparently benefited from the reemergence of some political party life in the country, which was indicated by the formation of a "National Front" coalition composed of the al-Asad faction of the Ba'th, the Syrian Arab Socialist Union (ASU), two factions of the Socialist Unionists, the Arab Socialist Party, and the Syrian Communist Party. In view of its past, the SCP felt that an explanation for joining the coalition and the cabinet was in order:

> The communist party, when it takes part in a government, never does so with the idea that this participation is an end in itself. It rather looks at this participation as a form of struggle which it must undertake in defense of the national rights and progressive achievements of the people and in an endeavor to bring about the participation of the masses of workers and peasants, tradesmen, revolutionary intellectuals, students, soldiers, and their party and popular organizations in the direction of the affairs of the country, to achieve popular democracy and to create popular and official institutions. When the communist party feels that the presence of its representatives in the government or in one of the ministries is no longer useful to the Arab liberation movement or the national movement, or to the cause of social progress in Syria and the Arab world, it will not delay for an instant abandoning its position in that government or ministry. (*al-Nida*, Beirut, 11 December.)

Domestic Attitudes and Activities. Establishment of the National Front late in the year was a highly satisfactory development for Syrian communists, who had long advocated the "unity of all the devout and noble forces in a single progressive front." The SCP in 1970 also called for "democratic steps" as a way out of Syria's political crisis, for a permanent constitution for the country, and for the establishment of a legislature. It warned against "reactionary quarters" inside Syria and urged that "progressive gains" be maintained and that cooperation with the socialist camp and the Soviet Union in particular be strengthened. (*Arab World*, 2 November.)

Even before the change in government, the SCP was not entirely negative in its evaluation of the domestic situation. Khalid Bakdash acknowledged, for instance, that over the last four or five years significant improvements had occurred in Syria. He stressed the importance of land reforms, which had allowed many peasants to acquire farms, and the nationalization of large enterprises and factories. He pointed out with satisfaction that foreign trade had become a state monopoly and that some sectors of domestic trade had come under state management. (*Népszabadság*, 6 September.)

The Arab-Israeli Conflict. The SCP in 1970 continued its condemnation of Israel. It joined the communist parties of Lebanon and Iraq at a forum, held in Damascus on 18-19 March, which ended with an appeal to the world to aid the fight against the "criminal hand of imperialism and Zionism" (*IB*, no. 7). In May the SCP expressed its solidarity with "10,000 Arab prisoners" who reportedly staged a hunger strike in protest against maltreatment in Israeli jails in the occupied territories (TASS, 5 May). In June, the anniversary of the Arab-Israeli war of 1967 produced demands for implementation of the U.N. Security Council resolution of 22 November 1967 and for "complete liquidation of the consequences of Israeli aggression" (*ibid.*, 5 June).

Like other communist parties of the Middle East, the SCP in 1970 sought closer identification with the commandos, but without abandoning hopes for a political solution of the Arab-Israeli conflict. Early in the year it joined the communist parties of Lebanon, Jordan, and Iraq in establishing the all-communist commando organization "al-Ansar al-Silm"—the "Partisans of Peace" or the "Partisan Forces" (for details see *Jordan*). Thereafter it proclaimed support for the entire Palestine resistance movement and asked that its fighters receive protection and aid in order to continue their activities in Jordan and Lebanon and also in Syria and the other Arab countries. In discussing feasible methods of confrontation, the SCP rejected a quick "all or nothing approach" and suggested that any one objective realized in the struggle should be interpreted as a step towards the attainment of another objective. Thus the "elimination of the traces of [Israeli] aggression and the liberation of the occupied Arab territories" should be considered "complementary rather than contradictory" to the later "return of the Palestinian Arab people to their homeland." (Statement excerpted by *al-Akhbar*, Beirut, 15 August). When civil war broke out in Jordan, the communists of Syria sided with the commandos and urged the overthrow of the "fascist military regime" of King Hussein (Baghdad radio, 19 September). The party later reported that it had extensively campaigned for volunteers to fight in Jordan and had been able to send "thirty comrades who fought alongside their fedayeen brothers . . . in such organizations as the Popular Front for the Liberation of Palestine and the Popular Democratic Front for the Liberation of Palestine, [and who] displayed valor in Amman and steadfastness in Irbid" (excerpts from the SCP Politburo's September report, *al-Akhbar*, 8 November).

The SCP endorsed Egyptian President Nasser's acceptance of the U.S. peace initiative. A refusal, the party declared, would merely have served as "justification for further American arms shipments to Israel," whereas acceptance "foiled" U.S. plots to "embarrass and corner" the Arabs by making them appear to be in opposition to peace through rejection of the Rogers plan. Carrying its interpretation a step further, the SCP stated that "the liberation of the occupied Arab lands and the repatriation of the Palestinian people cannot be achieved in isolation from the U.A.R. and the Soviet Union." Implying that only those trying to weaken the Arab progressive front would create suspicions and doubts about the motives of these two countries, the SCP went on to comment: "We express regret at the negative attitude adopted by the Iraqi rulers and their information media toward the U.A.R.'s acceptance of the American peace plan." (*Ibid.*, 15 August.)

The SCP supported the proposed four-state federation of the U.A.R., Libya, Sudan, and Syria, and called it "a positive step which deserves all backing." This attitude was significant because it contrasted with that of the communists of Sudan, who bitterly opposed the projected federation. Initially, the SCP stand appeared questionable too, and the party maintained silence until the Politburo met in special session on 2 December to discuss Syrian accession to the "Tripoli charter" and the agreement reached at Cairo in November, which provided the foundation for future implementation of the union. The Politburo's statement of endorsement said in part:

> There is no doubt that rapprochement among the progressive Arab countries and steps leading to unity and military, political, and economic coordination between them could and should help not only in strengthening the position of the Arab countries in the battle against imperialism and Israeli aggression, but also in promoting social, economic, and progressive changes, developing progressive nationalist trends, bolstering the position of the progressive forces in all countries, and furthering cooperation among them. (*al-Nida*, 4 December.)

Publications. The SCP organ is *Nidal al-Sha'b*, (The People's Struggle), printed in Lebanon. The party is also able to disseminate information through two legal Lebanese communist publications, *al-Nida* and *al-Akhbar*.

*　　　*　　　*

A small pro-Chinese splinter group, calling itself the Arab Communist Marxist-Leninist Party, was reportedly gaining strength in 1970, although no figures about its membership became available. The group issued a typewritten bulletin, *Struggle of the Masses*, under the motto "Revolt is a Right."

At the time of the September civil war in Jordan, the Syrian Maoists declared that "bloody massacres" in Jordan were "instigated by American imperialism and Israel through hireling Arab rulers working as watchdogs for imperialist monopolies and Soviet revisionism." They were similarly outspoken in assessing the proposed Arab federation and charged that participation was "tantamount to letting in the back door imperialist plans of liquidation, including the Rogers plan and whatever is cooked up in the kitchen of American-Soviet revisionist collusion." The pro-Chinese also called for the destruction of Israel and for identification of all enemies of the revolution. Their domestic demands included the "liberation" of the Syrian economy from "foreign experts," an end to emergency laws and establishment of full civil liberties, and an overhaul of the armed forces to establish "genuine democracy" throughout the ranks. (*An-Nahar Arab Report*, Beirut, 14 December.)

E. W.

TUNISIA

The Tunisian Communist Party (Parti Communiste Tunisien; PCT) was founded in 1920 as part of the French Communist Party. It became independent in 1934. Banned since 1963, the party has maintained its organization clandestinely. A very small splinter group, the "Tunisian Socialist Study and Action Group" (Groupe d'Etudes et d'Action Socialiste Tunisien; GEAST), better known as the "Perspectivists," is based in France (see below). The only legal party in Tunisia is the Destourian Socialist Party (Parti Socialiste Destourian; PSD), which has been in power since 1957 under the leadership of the president of Tunisia, Habib Bourguiba. Most mass organizations, including student and labor groups, appear to follow the PSD line, and there seems to be little effective opposition from the four major leftist groups—the PCT, the Perspectivists, and the two wings of the Ba'thist Party.

The PCT is believed to have about 100 members. The population of Tunisia is 5,100,000 (estimated 1970). The party's influence in the country is negligible and seems to be confined to students and teachers; it appears to be greater among Tunisians residing abroad.

Leadership and Party Affairs. The leaders of the PCT live in Europe. The chief spokesman for the party is Mohammed en-Nafaa, who holds the office of first secretary. Mohammed Harmel serves as a secretary of the Central Committee. In addition, Khaled Ali is known as an active promoter of PCT interests. There is little information about the PCT leadership within Tunisia, since many local party militants were arrested following extensive student demonstrations centering around the University of Tunis in March 1968 and were sentenced to prison terms in mass trials held in September 1968 and February 1969.

In January 1970, President Bourguiba announced an amnesty for a large number of students who were imprisoned for participation in the March 1968 events. The students were to be released in small groups on three Tunisian national holidays: 18 January, the anniversary of the beginning of the struggle for independence in 1952; 20 March, the country's Independence Day; and 1 June, the anniversary of Bourguiba's return to Tunisia in 1955. In announcing the amnesty, the president declared: "The country, free and independent, has need of its children." He added that he expected freedom to "transform the mentality of the students and make them valuable citizens, useful to the country." (*L'Action*, Tunis, 19 January.) Shortly before, the Paris daily *Le Monde* (16 January) recalled the trials in an article which stated that the prisoners included "progressives, communists, Trotskyists, and sympathizers of the Ba'th Party."

In 1969 the PCT was characterized by complete ineffectiveness and beset by troubles, with its exiled leaders resigned to taking a conciliatory attitude toward the actions of the government. In 1970, however, the party showed some signs of renewed activity, especially in the wake of a presidential announcement in June that amendments to the constitution and a subsequent referendum were under consideration.

The first known reaction by the communists to the official pulse-taking concerning possible constitutional reforms was contained in a statement distributed to the French press on 8 July over the signature of Mohammed en-Nafaa. The communist leader declared that there remained certain prerequisites, if institutional reforms envisaged by the authorities were to assume practical meaning. Among the requirements he listed was that of a Tunisian National Assembly "really representative of all the currents that exist in the country;" this, in turn would necessitate ending the one-party system, and substituting free elections, "respect for democratic rights," and autonomy for labor and student unions. The most specific demand of the statement called for lifting the ban against the "legal activities of the Communist Party and the left-wing press."

Later in the year, in an interview with *France Nouvelle* (Paris, 28 October), en-Nafaa elaborated on the need to establish "democratic controls" in the country and to "create a new political climate." He declared that by removing the obstacles to the "exercise of freedoms," the government would be "doing nothing more than respecting its own legality." He added that the legal existence of a communist party was considered a "must" not only by workers and intellectuals who had long worked within its ranks, but also by the young who had only recently entered political life: "All of them want to be able to organize freely in order to contribute, in their way and in an alliance with all the forces of progress, to the solution of the serious problems facing the country." This necessitated the dissemination of their opinions, and en-Nafaa revealed that to meet this need he had approached the premier of Tunisia with the request that the newspaper *Dialogues*, suspended in 1965, be granted permission to publish again.

Domestic Views and Activities. The PCT in 1970 expressed serious concern about economic and social trends in Tunisia. In an article in *Jeune Afrique* (Paris, 11 August) en-Nafaa discussed domestic changes since the end of 1969. His overall judgement was that these changes represented a "complete reversal of the progressive orientation" that had previously prevailed, and that they had set the country back ten years. More specifically he criticized government policies affording "priority to private initiative, Tunisian and foreign" and to "capitalist development" while representing firm opposition to structural reforms. En-Nafaa saw official decisions as reflecting the "narrow aspirations of particular social forces," among which he identified large landowners and the business bourgeoisie anxious to exploit such immediately profitable sectors as real estate investment, trade, and services.

According to the PCT leader, the government's pro-capitalist orientation was harmful to the independent economic development of Tunisia and was opening the way to foreign capital and hence to "neo-colonialist penetration." He denounced the decision to halt the establishment of agricultural cooperatives, and asked for restrictions of large landholdings and for transfer of land to the poor peasants without compensation. Existing conditions, he alleged, meant increased worker exploitation, virtually fatal competition for small producers, and growing unemployment and underemployment. As a remedy he suggested the development of the public sector, under a capable administration that would "evolve progressively toward the social forms of management, with active participation of the workers."

Tied in with economic considerations was Tunisia's cause celèbre, the trial of Ahmed Ben Salah. Until his removal in September 1969, Ben Salah had been a sort of "super-minister" in charge of the national economy and the holder of immense political power as a member of the inner circle of the PSD. He had diligently pursued a policy of agrarian socialism which was aimed at the collectivization of all farming land by the end of 1969. In May 1970 Ben Salah was tried for "high treason"—following his removal from all government posts and expulsion from the party—on charges that he had been "juggling empty slogans borrowed from a shadowy socialism" and was guilty of "demagogy of action" (*Le Monde*, Paris, 20 May). More than fifty well-known intellectuals publicly opposed the trial as "virtually renouncing socialist principles" (*ibid.*, 10 May), and the communists asked that all the results of the trial be "squashed" and that Ben Salah's sentence of ten years at hard labor be set aside. Action by the intellectuals and communists on behalf of Ben Salah proved futile but was hardly surprising, since in his heyday he was considered the "hope of the left" and was probably one of the main representatives of the "advanced forces at the head of the PSD" for whom the communists had expressed affinity in 1969.

Education policies and the status of students represented another area of conflict. In spite of the well-publicized trials of the past, student unrest at the University of Tunis persisted and during the third week of November 1970 exploded in violent protests. The immediate impetus was provided by student exasperation at the decision to alter a bus route serving the university. Buses were attacked and tires slashed. Later police and students clashed on the campus itself, with injuries on both sides. When a number of protesters were arrested, the students organized a general strike and the government responded with threats of taking "all the steps dictated by the gravity of the situation." At the end of the year it appeared that a number of students would be tried for their part in the disturbances, and that the group of the accused was likely to be of a similar political mix as in the previous student trials.

International Views and Activities. During 1970 the PCT reaffirmed its alignment with the policies of the Soviet Union and international proletarianism. It advocated for Tunisia a consistent foreign policy that would avail itself of the advantages of assistance from the socialist countries (*France Nouvelle*, 28 October). Mohammed Harmel represented the PCT at the Lenin Centenary celebrations in Moscow in April and in a speech delivered on the occasion hailed the Soviet Union as the "principal force of the anti-imperialist struggle" and expressed gratitude for its "active support" of liberation movements and their fight for independence. Harmel voiced strong criticism of the Chinese communists, terming Maoism a "monstrous negation" of Leninism and an "exercise in adventurism and anarchism" which was aimed at the international communist movement. (*Pravda*, 26 April.)

Harmel also attended the congress of the French Communist Party in February. His somewhat cryptic statement (*L'Humanité*, 9 February) concerned itself with the Mediterranean area: "There is no power vacuum to be filled, as some people contend. There are peoples who have won their independence, who yearn to consolidate it, and who are disposed to cooperate with other countries, including France, on a just and equitable basis."

Publications. Since 1963 the PCT has published a French-language monthly, *Espoir* (Hope). Publication of an Arabic language edition, *al-Tariq* (The Way), was begun in January 1968.

*   *   *

The amnesty announced by President Bourguiba in January 1970 presumably benefited some members of the Groupe d'Etudes et d'Action Socialiste Tunisien (GEAST). This organization publishes the journal *Perspectives Tunisiennes* in Paris and is perhaps best known by the name of Perspectivists. The group is believed to have been founded in Paris in 1963 by former supporters of the Tunisian and French communist parties. Membership figures are unavailable, but probably very small. Since 1964 some Perspectivists have been returning to Tunisia. In 1968 the government arrested twelve, which may have been the entire contingent in Tunisia at the time.

A white paper prepared by the Tunisian government in advance of the September 1968 trials, described the Perspectivists as Maoists led by "about a dozen ringleaders" who were "Trotskyist-inspired and Chinese-controlled." It described the Perspectivist party hierarchy as being headed by a three-member Steering Committee and seven-member Ideological Commission, both appointed by and from the group's eleven-member Central Committee. Gilbert Naccache and Nouredine Ben Kheder were named as the main leaders of the group within Tunisia. Both received prison sentences of fourteen years as a result of the trials. Others given long sentences were Brahim Razgallah, Mohammed Rached Bellalouna, Mohammed Mahfoud, Ahmed Ben Othmane (known as "Radaoui"), and Abdel Aziz Krichene—from five to twelve years—and Abdelwahab Majdoub, Hafedh Sethom, Mohammed Charfi, and Houciene Baouendi—up to five years. Mohammed Ben Jennet, who had been sentenced to twenty years at hard labor in 1967 was given an additional four years in September 1968, even though he had been in jail at the time of the March demonstrations.

Tunisian authorities claimed that the Perspectivists recruited mainly among students and teachers and that they infiltrated various government agencies, universities, and high schools, and engaged in subversion through "endemic agitation." The trial prosecutors, to support their contention of serious danger posed by the group, quoted the stated goals of the Perspectivists from a handbill allegedly circulated by them in January 1968:

> The members of the "Perspectives" group have a mortal hatred for the bourgeois groups and exploiters as well as their front men; indeed, their objective calls for the defeat of the reactionary forces and their servants; they plan to establish the dictatorship of the proletariat, which will rid the country of all the plunderers and parasites who "govern" us now.

The 1968 arrests and trials virtually ended Perspectivist activities in Tunisia. The group's ideology, however, continued to be disseminated—though irregularly—by issues of *Perspectives Tunisiennes*. This journal and occasional pamphlets give evidence that the basic goals of the Perspectivists have remained virtually unchanged since early 1968.

E. W.

UNITED ARAB REPUBLIC

A communist party existed in Egypt and the U.A.R. from 1923 to 1965, but never enjoyed legal status or more than negligible political influence. Fragmented and subject to internal dissension, the Communist Party of Egypt (CPE) decided to dissolve itself in April 1965. It urged its members—numbering an estimated 800 to 1,000—to affiliate on an individual basis with the Arab Socialist Union (ASU), the mass political organization established by the regime of Gamal Abdel Nasser in 1962 as the only legal political group. Rationalized as a step consistent with the Soviet policy of "progressive" single-party rule, the dissolution of the CPE resulted in lessening of friction between the U.A.R. and the Soviet Union.

The influence of individual Egyptian communists was hardly diminished when the CPE ceased to exist. In fact, the new conditions permitted some party members to melt into the mainstream of Egyptian political life by becoming active in the ASU, while others continued to hold on to powerful positions in the government-controlled press. From these vantage points they are able to advocate close ties with the Soviet Union and to emphasize "socialist construction." After the Arab-Israeli war of 1967 they favored the arming of workers and peasants for a "people's war" against Israel and strongly condemned U.S. aid to Israel.

Some former CPE party members are actively associated with international communist front organizations, notably the U.A.R. branch of the World Council of Peace (WCP) and the Cairo-based Afro-Asian Peoples' Solidarity Organization (AAPSO), both of which provide a forum for attacking "imperialist-Zionist aggression." Others are engaged in efforts to get the powerful Egyptian General Trades Union Federation to affiliate with the communist-front World Federation of Trade Unions (WFTU). Ahmad Hamrush, editor of the Cairo weekly *Rose al-Yusuf*, wrote on 9 March 1970 that remaining outside of the WFTU was "not in the interest of the Egyptian working class" and would pose "a huge question for those who believe in the progressive ideology of the Egyptian Revolution." Hamrush's communist sympathies were even more clearly expressed in his attacks on French communist Roger Garaudy, who was expelled from his own party and Politburo post for failing to follow "scientific socialism."

Probably the best-known Egyptian communist is Khalid Muhyi al-Din, (the "Red Major"), a Marxist politician of long standing who is secretary-general of the U.A.R. National Peace Council and a member of the Presidential Committee of the WCP. Although often identified as a "rebel" and at odds with Nasser, Muhyi al-Din in 1968 became a member of the ASU Central Committee and in 1969 was elected to the National Assembly, the legislative body of the U.A.R. In 1968, writing in the French communist publication *Démocratie Nouvelle* (Paris, February), he advocated the formation of a "revolutionary vanguard party" that would "constitute the nervous system of the ASU and work inside it to direct the masses."

While Muhyi al-Din—who in 1970 was awarded a Lenin Peace Prize by the Soviet Union—only suggested that there should be a revolutionary vanguard party within the ASU, a Soviet publication, *The Workers' Movement in the Countries of Asia and North Africa at the Contemporary Stage* (Moscow, Science Publishing House, 1969), categorically stated that such a party was in the process of being established: "In the opinion of Egyptian communists, they could best take the ideas of scientific socialism and the ideas of Marxism-Leninism to the masses from within the ranks of the ASU - which recognizes the leading role of the working class and the principles of scientific socialism." This claim was qualified by a Soviet admission early in 1969: "Making the [Egyptian] masses conscious citizens and drawing them into the revolutionary process is a problem that has yet to be fully solved" (*New Times*, Moscow, 22 January).

In 1970 there was evidence that the problem might defy solution for a long time, because the Egyptian government was growing increasingly suspicious of communist activity. The most important sign was the reported arrest on May 12 of Lufti al-Khauli, editor of the left-leaning ideological journal *al-Tali'ah* and one of the U.A.R.'s leading communist sympathizers. There was no confirmation by Egyptian authorities, and rumors ranged widely, including one that al-Khauli was detained for alleged currency smuggling. The Associated Press reported via Amman (26 May) on an alleged "communist role in a plot" and on the arrests in the U.A.R. of al-Khauli's wife; of Nawal Nahlawi, private secretary to Muhammad Hasanain Haikal, editor in chief of the Cairo daily *al-Ahram;* and of Mrs. Nahlawi's husband, an army officer discharged after the Arab-Israeli war in June 1967. It was theorized elsewhere that Mrs. Nahlawi either was engaged in espionage or had pilfered Haikal's files to help al-Khauli prepare a communist coup in Egypt (*Arab World*, Beirut, 27 May). The only known facts are that al-Khauli expressed pro-Soviet views in *al-Tali'ah;* that in February 1970 he accompanied Yasir 'Arafat, leader of the commando organization al-Fatah, to Moscow; and that upon his return he praised the Soviet Union for its attitude toward the Palestinians (*al-Ahram*, 4 March), and its desire to see "the restoration of the legitimate Palestinian people's rights."

To determine areas of communist influence in the U.A.R. is easier than to sort out correlations and variables between Egyptian political ideology and communism. President Nasser wrestled with the latter in a Danish television interview quoted by Cairo radio on 23 May: "We hold the same views on imperialism [as the Soviet Union], but our views differ on ideology. The Soviet Union is a communist state, while we are trying to be a socialist state." Throughout the years of his rule, Nasser clearly rejected force and violence associated with communist social change, disavowed a dictatorship of the proletariat or one-class government of any kind, and termed freedom of religious belief and ritual "a sacred thing."

Nasser's concept of "Arab socialism," rather than "scientific socialism," was incorporated in the ASU National Charter, thus virtually ruling out Marxism-Leninism as a future course for Egypt. The basis of his socialism was land reform, nationalization of major industries, nonalignment in foreign relations, and official support for religion. The charter warned against the dangers of "accepting ready-made theories and dispensing with national experiences," since the "real solutions of any people cannot be adopted from the experiences of other peoples."

In contrast to Nasser, Egyptian communists point to the similarities between ASU socialism and communism. From the charter they pick references to "scientific socialism"—at one point characterized as "the suitable style for finding the right method to progress"—and try to adapt facts and terminology to Egyptian needs by opting for "national roads" to socialist achievement. They point out that in its new constitution (1968) the ASU is described as a political organization of peasants, workers, soldiers, and intellectuals and of representatives of national capital, and as equivalent to a vanguard organization of the entire people. Applying their own Marxian interpretation, they conclude that the constitution provides the basis from which to "rally the masses for the general line of the revolution." They are, on the other hand, inclined to ignore such semiofficial spokesmen as Haikal, who at the end of 1969 openly questioned the outlook for Marxism in general: "I believe that Marxism is facing modern currents and challenges that are forcing it to introduce major changes in its way of thinking. Otherwise, and no matter how hard Marxism disclaims this, it will discover that it is an obstacle to social progress." (*al-Ahram*, 12 December.) There is no reason to doubt that such views continue to prevail in the government of Anwar al-Sadat, who assumed the presidency after Nasser's death on 28 September.

E. W.

NORTH AMERICA

CANADA

The Canadian communist movement is represented by several organizations of differing orientation, of which the oldest and largest is the pro-Soviet Communist Party of Canada (CPC), founded in 1921. In addition to the CPC, in 1970 there were three Maoist groups—the Progressive Workers' Movement, the Canadian Party of Labour, and the Communist Party of Canada (Marxist-Leninist)—and a Trotskyist organization, the League for Socialist Action /Ligue Socialiste Ouvrière, aligned with the United Secretariat of the Fourth International (see below). All these have legal status.

In 1970 the membership of the CPC was estimated at about 2,500. The population of Canada is 21,089,000 (estimated 1969).

Most of the CPC's support originates from the provinces of Ontario and British Columbia, among urban laborers, white-collar workers, and students. The party has only very limited political influence. There has not been a communist in the Canadian Parliament since 1945, nor in a provincial legislature since 1948. In the last general election, held in June 1968, the party received 0.1 per cent of the vote.

The CPC's affiliated organization, the Communist Party of Quebec (Parti Communiste du Québec; PCQ) participated in the Quebec legislative elections of 29 April 1970. The party's sole candidate, Claire Dasylva-Demers, unsuccessfully contested the riding of Montreal-St. Louis, obtaining only a very small percentage of the vote. The PCQ's president, Samuel Walsh, was likewise unsuccessful in the municipal elections in Montreal, held on 25 October, in which he ran under the banner of the Association for Democracy in Montreal (Association pour la Démocratie à Montréal; ADM). Walsh was the only candidate of the ADM, which limited itself to contesting one seat in the municipal council of Montreal-St. Louis.

The CPC has a minor degree of electoral support on the municipal level, most notably in Winnipeg, where the reelection of a communist alderman in 1969 continued the unbroken pattern of limited party representation which has existed in that city government for more than forty years.

Leadership and Organization. The Twentieth Convention of the CPC, held in Toronto on 4-6 April 1969, elected the party's 51-member Central Committee, which in turn reaffirmed William Kashtan and Tim Buck as general secretary and chairman respectively. The Central Committee also chose the thirteen members of the Central Executive Committee: William Beeching, Tim Buck, Misha Cohen, Don Currie, Alfred Dewhurst, Norman Freed, George Harris, Harry Hunter (died 20 October 1969), William Kashtan, Bruce Magnuson, William Stewart, James Walsh, and Samuel Walsh. Other party officials named at this time included Bruce Magnuson, labor secretary; Charles McFadden, youth secretary; Don Currie, national organizer; Alfred Dewhurst, executive secretary; and Norman Freed, director of education. During 1970 no changes were reported in the party leadership.

The CPC maintains organizations in all but three of the ten Canadian provinces. Five provinces have their own provincial leaders: Nigel Morgan, British Columbia; Fred Schofield, Saskatchewan; William Stewart (replacing Bruce Magnuson in April 1970), Ontario; William Ross, Manitoba; and William Tuomi, Alberta. The aforementioned Parti Communiste du Québec was established in 1965 as a distinct structure within the CPC. It maintains autonomy in order to participate more effectively in the French-Canadian nationalist movement. The president of the PCQ is Samuel Walsh, who was the CPC provincial leader in Quebec from 1962 to 1965.

Following the formation in 1969 of a number of provincial communist youth organizations, the national Young Communist League (YCL) was founded at a convention in Toronto on 27-29 March 1970. The extent of the membership of the new group was not publicized, although the report on the convention claimed an attendance of 100 delegates (*Canadian Tribune*, 1 April). The two most prominent leaders of the YCL in 1970 were Charles McFadden, national secretary, and Elizabeth Hill, executive secretary.

Domestic Views and Policies. Early in 1970, addressing a Lenin centennial meeting in a speech on "The Way to Socialism in Canada," General Secretary Kashtan stated that it was "theoretically correct to advance the possibility of a peaceful path to socialism—a parliamentary path." The CPC's goals, he declared, could be attained through a "two-stage" process, of which the first phase would be the "achieving of unity of all the forces opposing the power of monopoly." Emphasizing unity, he affirmed: "The Communist Party says, I repeat and will keep on repeating, it cannot defeat monopoly by itself." In its main thrust, the speech was an appeal for cooperation with the New Democratic Party (NDP), a left-wing party which in the general elections of 1968 had received 17.3 per cent of the vote, retaining its 21 seats (out of 264) in the Canadian Parliament.

Kashtan claimed that while the NDP was not an "all-inclusive, federated farmer-labor party," it was a "significant development in Canadian political life," and the CPC's position toward it should be one of simultaneous "cooperation and competition." Cooperation was to be advocated around issues where joint agreement was feasible, such as "peace, democracy and the interests of the workers and trade union movement." CPC militants were reminded, however, that the NDP was a "reform movement within capitalism, that does not aim at bringing about a fundamental change of capitalism." Competition with the NDP—which did not "advocate or stand for socialism"—would come through the CPC's bringing of "Marxism into the working class" and fighting against "reformist ideas and attitudes which are not basically directed to change society." Kashtan justified cooperation with the reformist-oriented NDP by citing Lenin's emphasis on "determining the main enemy at a particular time." He berated the impatience of "ultra-leftists" who called for "one leap to socialism," and, emphasizing the need for "a correct strategy and correct tactics," added: "Any party that forgets that, and falls prey, instead, to super-revolutionarism, adventurism, ultra-leftism, will not be able to transform society." (*Canadian Tribune*, 18 February.)

During the year, while continuing to advocate cooperation with the NDP, the CPC devoted less space than before to reports on that party's views and activities. Apparently of greater concern to the communists was an increase in "ultra-leftist" tendencies—phenomena which the CPC perceived even within the ranks of the NDP (see W. C. Beeching, "Role and Place of NDP," *Communist Viewpoint*, January-February, and William Stewart, "Ultra-Infantile-Anarchist Left in Canada," *ibid.*, September-October). With much of its activity oriented toward supporting demonstrations of opposition to U.S. policies in Southeast Asia, the CPC was confronted on a number of occasions with what it termed "disruptive" tactics, primarily perpetrated by Maoist elements, during rallies and marches in which party militants participated. Following a "march on Ottawa to protest and to end Canadian complicity in the U.S. war in Vietnam," held on 27-28 February, an editorial in the CPC newspaper, *Canadian Tribune* (4 March), described the Maoists' "disruption and provocation" during the march as "deliberately planned and executed with militaristic precision." In its view, the Maoists were "ultra-revolutionary phrasemongers" who had "exposed themselves as enemies of peace and social progress" and were serving "the cause of counter-revolution." Similar attacks were reiterated by the party press on a number of occasions during the year, usually following "peace demonstrations"; the CPC at the same time attempted to disassociate itself from the Maoists' violence-oriented tactics (see *Canadian Tribune*, 18 March, 22 and 29 April, and 12 August).

The issue of violence took on considerably greater proportions in October as a result of two political kidnappings in Quebec. Early in the summer the *Canadian Tribune* (15 July) had published an editorial on terrorism, referring to it as "tragic infantilism" and stating: "The small groups espousing terrorism as a weapon in Canada today are mistaken. Their tactics are harmful to the movement for social change. Their 'impatience' can only retard the struggle. . . . Terrorism is impotence at best, provocation at worst." On 5 and 10 October, respectively, James Cross, British trade commissioner in Montreal, and Pierre Laporte, Quebec labor minister, were kidnaped by members of a French-Canadian separatist organization, the Front de Libération du Québec (FLQ). The CPC Central Executive Committee then issued a press release attacking the FLQ action:

> Kidnappings and other acts of terrorism are not the forms of struggle the working class and the Communist Party adopt in striving for social change. These are anarchistic methods of struggle which have nothing in common with the necessity of uniting the working class and its allies against Canadian monopoly and U.S. imperialism.

Nevertheless, while disassociating itself "from the tactics of the FLQ, tactics which do harm to the struggle for meaningful social change in Quebec and throughout Canada," the CPC committee added that "the main criticism must be leveled at monopoly and its parties, all of whom have brought this crisis about." Moreover, the party warned: "It would appear that the kidnapping incidents are being used as a pretext for an attack on democratic and civil rights, rather than on the causes that made the kidnappings possible in the first place." (*Canadian Tribune*, 14 October.)

On 16 October the Canadian government invoked the War Measures Act and, at the same time, banned the FLQ. On 17 October, the FLQ murdered Pierre Laporte. In the main, the CPC's reaction to these new developments took the form of strong opposition to the War Measures Act: "Official propaganda tries to make it appear that the action is only aimed at the FLQ in Quebec. Nothing could be further from the truth." The CPC went on to claim that the War Measures Act and the proposed Public Order (Temporary Measures) Act, which was at that time being debated in Parliament (and was finally enacted on 1 December), were "aimed against the entire Canadian working class." (*Ibid.*, 28 October.) A statement of the party's Central Executive Committee (*ibid.*, 11 November) reiterated the party's assertion that the new legislation's "main purpose" was to "crush the political opponents of the Trudeau government."

During 1970 the CPC's views on the issue of the advocacy of Quebec separatism tended to be somewhat ambiguous.[1] Party statements on Quebec concentrated primarily on the economic

---

[1]This ambiguity was partly clarified in an article by Samuel Walsh at the beginning of 1971 in which he stated: "While consistently and publicly upholding their *right* to separate, are we obliged to *advocate* that the French-Canadian people use their unquestioned sovereign right . . . even if this does not conform to the real circumstances in French Canada and to the interests of the working class? Decidedly not! For separation of Quebec under the present circumstances would do very grave harm to the economic and political interests of the working people, and *could* throw both nations into the suffocating embrace of different sectors of U.S. imperialism." (*Communist Viewpoint*, January-February 1971; emphasis in original.)

problems of that province (see, e.g., Kashtan's report to the 14-16 November meeting of the Central Committee, *ibid.*, 25 November). An editorial in the party's theoretical journal, *Communist Viewpoint* (November-December), claimed that "Communists were the first and the most consistent to recognize that Canada is a two-nation state," and added:

> We advanced the position that both the French-speaking and English-speaking nations must enjoy the democratic right of national self-determination and that each nation must possess the sovereign right to determine its destiny. We recognized that to keep Canada united a new confederation of the two nations, based on complete equality, has to be brought into being. The old unequal BNA [British North America] Act must be replaced by a new made-in-Canada constitution. It is because of this principled position that we opposed the option of separatism, advanced in the main by petty-bourgeois forces in Quebec. We urged the nationalist and separatist forces in Quebec to accept the option of a new confederation of two equal nations as the most beneficial solution to both French- and English-speaking Canadians and the only sound foundation upon which Canada could remain united.

International Views and Policies. During 1970 the CPC repeatedly reiterated its advocacy of Canadian "independence," particularly with regard to the United States. Emphasizing alleged "complicity" with U.S. policies in Southeast Asia, the party called upon the Canadian government to make a formal denunciation of those policies; it advocated Canada's withdrawal from the North Atlantic Treaty Organization and the North American Defense Command.

The CPC remained steadfastly aligned with the Communist Party of the Soviet Union (CPSU). The party press gave extensive and favorable coverage to domestic developments in the U.S.S.R. and in Soviet-aligned countries, such as the German Democratic Republic and Bulgaria. In this context, the CPC still appeared in 1970 to be preoccupied with a report published in 1967 in the party press which had criticized "Russification" policies in the Ukraine. Although the CPC had subsequently claimed that the report had been misinterpreted (see *YICA*, 1969, p. 106), the number of favorable articles on the Ukraine that appeared in its publications during the year indicated that the subject was still a source of embarrassment (see, e.g., *Canadian Tribune*, 20 and 27 May, 3 June, 9 September).

The CPC also aligned itself fully with Soviet foreign policy and supported the views of the CPSU on matters related to both inter- and intra-party affairs within the communist movement. On the anniversary of the 1968 Soviet-led invasion of Czechoslovakia, the *Canadian Tribune* (26 August 1970) referred to the "saving" of that country from "counter-revolution" by the Warsaw Pact forces, and concluded: "Spring has now really returned to Czechoslovakia. It is not at the mercy of the imperialists, but is a firm part of the socialist camp." The expulsion from the Communist Party of Czechoslovakia of its former first secretary, Alexander Dubček, was commended. Referring to "rabid redbaiters and anti-Communists" who shed "crocodile tears" over the fate of "good Communists," the *Canadian Tribune* (22 July) editorialized: "No thanks, we'll stick with the 'bad' ones who defend the cause of socialism no matter what names the enemy calls them."

In a similar vein, the CPC offered its solidarity to the leadership of the French Communist Party in its controversy with dissident Roger Garaudy, describing the latter's views as "part of a revisionist stream that has sought to undermine Marxist-Leninist views in the international Communist movement" (*ibid.*, 11 February).

In conformity with its alignment with the CPSU, the CPC continued during the year to be critical of the leadership of the Chinese Communist Party. On the occasion of the fifty-third anniversary of the October Revolution, Kashtan expressed his party's pleasure at the fact that the Chinese government had sent a message of greetings to the Soviet Union. The CPC general secretary commented that "undoubtedly second thoughts [had] now entered the minds of the leaders of the Chinese Peoples' Republic to the effect that what is necessary is not to resolve ideological differences by war but instead to work out those differences . . . through debate." At the same time, however, Kashtan compared Mao Tse-tung's views to those of Trotsky, which if carried out "could have been disastrous for the socialist system, and would have been disastrous for the cause of peace, democracy and advance on a world scale." (*Ibid.*, 11 November.)

International Party Contacts. CPC contacts with other communist parties in 1970 tended to be limited to those of a pro-Soviet orientation. Jeannette Walsh attended the Nineteenth Congress of the French Communist Party, on 4-8 February; Charles McFadden was the party's representative at the founding convention in Chicago, on 7-9 February, of the Young Workers' Liberation League, the youth movement of the Communist Party, USA. In March, Bruce Magnuson and Norman Freed attended an international theoretical conference at Moscow connected with the Lenin Centenary; that same month, the YCL's founding convention was attended by Jarvis Tyner, chairman of the aforementioned Young Workers' Liberation League. In April, William Kashtan and Samuel Walsh participated in Lenin Centenary celebrations at Moscow. In May, Herbert Aptheker, a leading theoretician of the Communist Party, USA, met with members of the CPC leadership in Winnipeg. A delegation of the YCL, led by Elizabeth Hill, attended the Sixteenth All-Union Congress of the Komsomol, in Moscow on 26-30 May, and another, led by Charles McFadden, spent two weeks in the Soviet Union in August. On 11 November the *Canadian Tribune* reported on a visit to Romania by a two-man CPC delegation, comprising Alfred Dewhurst and Norman Freed. The delegation met with leaders of the Romanian Communist Party, including Nicolae Ceauşescu, the party's secretary-general. It would appear that differences of opinion were expressed over the "main problems of the international situation and of the Communist and workers' movement," the final communiqué referring only to "an exchange of opinions" on this subject, with no mention of the attainment of any agreement.

Publications. The main organ of the CPC is the weekly newspaper, *Canadian Tribune*, published in Toronto. The party also issues a weekly newspaper in Vancouver, the *Pacific Tribune*. The theoretical journal of the party is the bimonthly *Communist Viewpoint*. The YCL started publishing in October a monthly newspaper, *Young Worker*. The Communist Party of Quebec has its own fortnightly newspaper, *Combat*.

*   *   *

The largest Maoist group in Canada during 1970 was the Communist Party of Canada (Marxist-Leninist), a group which is believed to have originated in 1967. Although it was estimated to have some 1,000 activists, and claimed members in all provinces, its influence appeared to be negligible. In Quebec the party was known as Les Intellectuels et Ouvriers Patriotes du Québec (Marxistes-Léninistes).[1] The party's principal spokesman during the year was Hardial S. Bains. The party published an irregular weekly newspaper, *Canadian Mass Line*. Its international ties appeared to be limited to a small Cleveland-based U.S. Maoist group, the American Communist Workers' Movement (Marxist-Leninist).

The Progressive Workers' Movement (PWM), whose chairman was Jack Scott, originated in 1964 from the CPC. At that time it was active only in Vancouver and Toronto. In 1968 the Toronto members of the party broke off to create the Canadian Party of Labour (CPL), a contending Maoist group. By 1970 the PWM appeared to have been reduced to less than ten members,

---

[1] The Communist Party of Canada (Marxist-Leninist) has tended to create numerous satellite organizations; for a partial listing, see *Intercontinental Press*, New York, 23 March 1970.

with no regular publication. The CPL—which was aligned with the Progressive Labor Party in the United States (see *United States of America*)—was estimated to have less than 50 members. It published the irregular monthly, *Canadian Worker*. (For further information on these two groups, see *Intercontinental Press*, 26 January and 9 March 1970.)

The only significant Trotskyist group in Canada was the League for Socialist Action (LSA), known in Quebec as the Ligue Socialiste Ouvrière (Socialist Workers' League; LSO). The LSA /LSO during the year had a growing membership estimated at about 1,000. The group had a youth movement, the Young Socialists—known in Quebec as the Ligue des Jeunes Socialistes (Young Socialist League). Manon Léger was the LSO's candidate for mayor in the municipal elections held in Montreal in October. She obtained nearly two per cent of the vote. The LSA /LSO is aligned with the United Secretariat of the Fourth International and has close ties with the Socialist Workers' Party in the United States. During 1970 its principal publication was *Labor Challenge*, a fortnightly published in Toronto.

M. P.

UNITED STATES OF AMERICA

The communist movement in the United States includes a number of rival parties, with estimated memberships ranging from fewer than 10 persons to some 13,000 and offering a broad variety of views in their domestic and foreign policies. In addition to these "orthodox" Marxist-Leninist parties are numerous groups—primarily among young persons and the country's ethnic minorities—that espouse Marxism-Leninism as a guiding ideology.[1] Mercurial in their political views and often heterogeneous organizationally, these later groups, such as the Weatherman and the Revolutionary Youth Movement II (erstwhile factions within the Students for a Democratic Society) and the Black Panther Party, continued in 1970 to represent a challenge to the regular communist parties, although, by the end of the year, support for them appeared to be diminishing (see below).

CPUSA. The oldest and largest of the orthodox communist parties in the United States is the Communist Party, USA (CPUSA), founded in 1919. In 1967 the party became federally legal, following a decision of the U.S. Court of Appeals for the District of Columbia (see *YICA*, 1968, p. 834), but electoral restrictions against it are in force in certain states.

During 1970 the CPUSA did not publicize the extent of its membership; in the previous year, however, the party's general secretary, Gus Hall, had estimated the figure at 12,000 to 13,000 (*Washington Post*, 2 May 1969). This number appears to have remained static. The CPUSA's youth movement, the Young Workers' Liberation League (YWLL), was founded in February 1970 (see below) and is believed to have a membership of 600 to 800. The population of the United States is 206,240,000 (estimated 1970).

The CPUSA is not represented politically at either national or local levels. The party's most recent major bid for elective office was made in 1968, when it sponsored the candidacies of Charlene Mitchell and Michael Zagarell for the posts of president and vice-president of the United States, respectively. This was the first time that the CPUSA had contested a presidential election since 1940, when its then general secretary, Earl Browder, received 48,579 votes, with the party on the ballot in 32 states. In 1968 the CPUSA was on the ballot only in the states of Minnesota and Washington, and received 1,075 votes out of a total of some 73 million. In the November 1970 elections the party fielded candidates in the states of New York, Illinois and Minnesota—Rasheed Storey (for governor, New York), Grace Mora Newman (lieutenant governor, New York), Arnold Johnson (U.S. senator, New York), José Stevens (U.S. House of Representatives,

---

[1]The numerous organizations and factions in this category are not considered Marxist-Leninist groups by officially constituted communist parties, either domestic or foreign; their review, therefore, goes beyond the limitations of the *Yearbook on International Communist Affairs*. For 1970 and background information, see *Anatomy of a Revolutionary Movement: Students for a Democratic Society*, Report by the Committee on Internal Security, House of Representatives, 91st Cong., 2d sess., Washington, D.C., 1970; Harold Jacobs, (ed.), *Weatherman*, n.p., Ramparts Press, Inc., 1970; and publications such as the New York weekly *Guardian*, which covers the views and activities of most of the groups.

18th Congressional District, New York), Frances Gabow (U.S. senator, Illinois), Carolyn Black (state superintendent of public instruction, Illinois), and Betty Smith (state auditor, Minnesota). None of the candidates was successful.

Organization and Leadership. The CPUSA is organized along the lines of democratic centralism. In 1969 the party's Nineteenth National Convention abolished the Secretariat section of the CPUSA. Thus, theoretically, authority is to flow from the National Convention (which should be held every two years according to the party's constitution), to the National Committee, to the National Executive Board, and then to the districts, where organizations may be set up on the level of states, counties, sections, and clubs. In some districts where membership is sparse the organizational channel runs directly from the district to the club. Clubs are set up on a variety of bases, such as electoral subdivisions, neighborhoods, areas, shops, or industries. In the months following the Nineteenth National Convention it appeared that the name of the National Executive Board had been changed to the National Political Committee and that the functions of the former Secretariat were to a certain degree being carried out by an "Organization Bureau," headed by Daniel Rubin as national organizational secretary.

The Nineteenth National Convention reelected Gus Hall as general secretary of the party and Henry Winston as chairman. It also elected an 83-member National Committee. This committee, in turn, elected the National Executive Board (or National Political Committee as it was later called). In 1970 this latter group was believed to comprise the following persons: Gus Hall, Matthew Hallinan, James Jackson, Arnold Johnson, Claude Lightfoot, Hyman Lumer, George Meyers, Charlene Mitchell, William Patterson, John Pittman, Irving Potash, Roscoe Proctor, José Ristorucci, Daniel Rubin, Rasheed Storey, Jarvis Tyner, William Weinstone, Henry Winston, Carl Winter, Helen Winter, and Michael Zagarell. Also a member of the Political Committee, until her death on 4 March, was Betty Gannett, editor of the party's theoretical monthly, *Political Affairs*. Most of the members of the National Political Committee are also party officials. In addition to the aforementioned posts held by Hall, Rubin, and Winston, the following were officials in 1970: Hallinan (educational secretary, until June when he became national education director), Jackson (international affairs secretary), Johnson (public relations secretary and chairman of the Peace Commission), Lightfoot (co-chairman of the Black Liberation Commission), Lumer (national education director, until June when he resigned to become editor of *Political Affairs*), Meyers (co-chairman of the Labor Commission), Mitchell (secretary of the Black Liberation Commission), Patterson (co-chairman of the Black Liberation Commission), Pitmann (co-editor of *Daily World*), Proctor (co-chairman of the Labor Commission), Carl Winter (co-editor of *Daily World*), and Zagarell (national youth director). Other CPUSA national officials referred to in the party press during 1970 included: Lonnie Healy (secretary of the Indian Liberation Commission), Guillermo Martínez (secretary of the Chicano Commission), and James J. Tormey (chairman of the Defense Commission).

Outside its party structure the CPUSA in 1970 had no official auxiliary bodies (such as organizations for young persons and women.) Nonetheless, the party was active in a number of organizations which, though professing independence of the CPUSA, followed the party's policy and directives and whose leaderships were composed primarily of party members. In the past one of the principal organizations falling into this pattern was the W. E. B. DuBois Clubs of America, which acted as the unofficial youth movement of the CPUSA and whose chairman was Jarvis Tyner. Following several months of preparation coordinated by a "National Organizing Committee of the Marxist-Leninist Youth Organization," a convention was held in Chicago, on 7-9 February, which founded a new youth organization to replace the DuBois Clubs and to be called the Young Workers' Liberation League.[2] Representation at the convention was reportedly limited to members of the CPUSA and the DuBois Clubs (*The Militant*, 20 February). Of the 394 registered participants at the meeting, only 275 were certified as delegates; the others were either observers or guests. The latter included Vladimir Makarov, representative of the Soviet Komsomol; Charles McFadden, youth secretary of the Communist Party of Canada; Mark Sydney, representative of the World Federation of Democratic Youth; and Federico Tomás, youth secretary of the Puerto Rican Communist Party.

In advance of the convention, a spokesman for the Organizing Committee, Carmen Ristorucci, discussed the differences between the DuBois Clubs and the new youth organization, stating that the latter would "have a more explicit commitment to the working class, to socialism and to Marxism-Leninism than the DuBois Clubs had." She stressed that "giving a working class orientation in the youth movement" would be the organization's "biggest contribution." (*Daily World*, 31 January.) In its coverage of the convention, the CPUSA repeatedly emphasized the "working class orientation" of the occasion, claiming that 52 per cent of the participants were "shopworkers" (see *ibid.*, 10-14 February). The convention established a 35-member Central Committee, to which it elected thirty-four persons, with one seat remaining vacant (for details see *Combat*, New York, 1 March). The following were elected as officers of the YWLL: Jarvis Tyner, chairman; Barry Cohen, organizational secretary; Carolyn Black, black liberation secretary; Judy Edelman, labor secretary; Roque Ristorucci, publications director; and Michael Zagarell, education secretary. The CPUSA exercised considerable control in the founding of the YWLL, a fact confirmed by Gus Hall in an interview given to the Soviet journal *Kommunist* (no. 15, October 1970), in which he referred to the party's increasing influence in the student and youth movement, and added: "We would have been unable to create a Marxist-Leninist young workers' organization if we had no influence among the best part of American youth."

The CPUSA continued to be active in a number of organizations opposing U.S. policy in Vietnam. Although the party appeared to have considerable influence on a number of local groups, it did not control any of the major national movements. The most prominent of the latter were the Student Mobilization Committee to End the War in Vietnam (SMC) and the National Peace Action Coalition (NPAC), both of which were under the control of the Trotskyist Socialist Workers' Party (SWP) and its youth movement, the Young Socialist Alliance (YSA) (see below). On the national level, the CPUSA appeared to be primarily active in a contending group, the New Mobilization Committee to End the War in Vietnam (VMC)—an "umbrella" organization comprising groups of a broad variety of political and tactical persuasions.[3] With the near demise of the NMC in mid-year and its apparent replacement by a new organization, the National Coalition Against War, Racism and Repression (NCAWRR), the CPUSA appeared to align itself with the policies of this latter organization.

The CPUSA derives its principal support from the states on the east and west coasts, primarily from the states of New York and California. Within labor organizations the party is insignificant. On 27-28 June the CPUSA-oriented publication *Labor Today* sponsored a conference in Chicago attended by some 850 union members and sympathizers. According to the New York independent radical weekly *Guardian* (4 July) the conference "was independent, with no overt evidence of

[2]According to *Combat* (New York, 1 March), convention delegates endorsed a policy by which the youth organization's local clubs could designate themselves under the alternate name of "Young Communist Liberation League."

[3]For further information on NMC, see *Subversive Involvement in the Origin, Leadership, and Activities of the New Mobilization Committee to End the War in Vietnam*, Staff Study by the Committee on Internal Security, House of Representatives, 91st Cong., 2d sess., Washington, D.C., 1970, 70 pp.; *New Mobilization Committee to End the War in Vietnam*, Parts 1 and 2, Hearings before the Committee on Internal Security, House of Representatives, 91st Cong., 2d sess., Washington, D.C., 1970, pp. 3843-4150 and 4151-4295.

the left-wing parties, but most positions adopted were those traditionally taken by the CP." The conference formed a National Coordinating Committee for Trade Union Action and Democracy with an orientation toward organizing the trade unions' rank-and-file members. Although the CPUSA's general secretary, Gus Hall, referred to the convention as "a truly historic event" (*Kommunist*, no. 15), there were no indications by the end of the year that the organization that it engendered had succeeded in attaining any appreciable support within organized labor.

Party Internal Affairs. During 1970 the CPUSA appeared to have surmounted the challenge to its unity which had followed the 1968 Soviet-led invasion of Czechoslovakia—an action that the party leadership supported despite significant opposition (see *YICA*, 1969, p. 835, and 1970, p. 481). In his aforementioned interview with *Kommunist*, Gus Hall referred to the fact that the "Czechoslovak events" had been "a subject of very sharp discussion" in the party, but maintained that the CPUSA had "inflicted a defeat on rightwing opportunism in its ranks." Commenting on the future of the party, Hall stated: "There are moments in the history of a party when it grows by waves. . . . Now, it seems to me, we are at the initial stage of a new wave of our party's growth. All that has been done up to now: the party's unification, increased influence among the working class—all this has been preparation for this very important new stage." Also in October, in an interview with the *Daily World* (6 October), the CPUSA general secretary claimed: "The Party is united now as never before."

Domestic Views and Policies. In May 1970, following five years of preparation, the CPUSA published the *New Program of the Communist Party, U.S.A.* (New York, New Outlook Publishers, 128 pp.), which the party's theoretical organ, *Political Affairs* (July 1970), described as "the product of innumerable discussions in Party bodies at all levels, of the collective thinking of the Party." The program comprises seven chapters: (1) "The United States: A Society in Crisis," (2) "The World Setting," (3) "The Forces of Progress," (4) "The Path Ahead," (5) "The Socialist Goal," (6) "The Communist Party," and (7) "Our Relations with Others."

The introduction to the program sets forth a general context in which the subsequent individual policies are elaborated, stating (pp. 7-8): "Wherever one looks, there is struggle in the United States today. . . . There is radicalization. There is a growing political Left. . . . The United States is ripe for basic social change. The goal of the Communist Party is to help our people bring about that change and to make it stick." The program analyzes (Chapter 2, pp. 39-80) the various social groups that, in the party's view, represent potential sources of support for the attainment of the CPUSA goals. Most of this chapter is devoted to the "Working Class" and to the "Black Liberation Movement" (pp. 42-54 and 54-64, respectively), with the party emphasizing:

> Only the combination of these forces possesses the power and self-interest necessary to transform our U.S. society. Any strategy for radical alternatives now or revolutionary change tomorrow that is not based on their combined strength in the struggle is impotent. Allies will come from other strata of the population oppressed by monopoly, and these are important, but by themselves they cannot successfully confront the power of monopoly. Without the engine of working class-Negro alliance, really basic progress is impossible, let alone the achievement of socialism. Even the achievement of more elementary united action is questionable. (P. 42).

In its analysis of organized labor, the CPUSA program accuses the leadership of the American Federation of Labor-Congress of Industrial Organizations (AFL-CIO) of adhering to policies of "class partnership," which, the party claims, "are based on the false proposition that labor and capital are partners, not irreconcilable foes" (pp. 45-46). On the other hand, the program views the following as favorable developments: the emergence of the Alliance for Labor Action, seen as a five-million-member group which "has taken a stand against the war in Vietnam"; the growth of black caucuses in industry and in the unions; the "increasing signs of a rank-and-file resurgence"; and union mergers and realignments, the latter exemplified by the "withdrawal of the United Auto Workers from the AFL-CIO and its association with the International Brotherhood of Teamsters in the Alliance for Labor Action" (pp. 46-47). In its view of the future of the labor movement, the program emphasizes that "the very existence of unions as effective instruments of workers rides on their determination and ability to overcome racism," and calls for the establishment and cementing of "bonds between labor and the dynamic Black liberation movement." On a more general level, the CPUSA calls on the working class to "become aware of itself as a distinct class with its own community of interests." In this context, the party attacks "professed radicals" who "echo the line that in America the class struggle has either vanished or lost its relevance," stating: "We Communists emphatically reject such concepts as the logic of surrender." (Pp. 49-50.) In the view of the party, organized labor faces a "key need" and "historic challenge" "to assert its political independence, to break out of the monopoly-controlled two-party system." "The center of gravity in the class struggle," the CPUSA claims, "is shifting more and more into the political arena" as the "conflict between labor and capital becomes more and more a political struggle." (Pp. 50-51.)

In its comments on the "Black Liberation Movement" the CPUSA program states: "The struggle for Black liberation in the United States is today the central, most crucial issue before the entire working class and its allies" (p. 54). The party proposes a number of "remedial actions" for the eradication of "racism and racial oppression," ranging from the "establishment of Black control over Black communities" to secession. With regard to the latter, the program states: "Even though Black people do not now constitute a nation, we do not place any limitations on their struggle to satisfy their aspirations up to and including their right to develop self-government and to exercise their right of self-determination" (pp. 60-61). At the same time, while claiming that the "wide range of all-Black organizations" that had developed plays "an important role" that the party supports, the program adds: "We reject the notion that Black freedom can be won without white allies." (P. 61).

In the chapter entitled "The Path Ahead" (pp. 81-95) the CPUSA program asserts that in the "rising struggles of the working class and all social strata that feel the lash of oppression of monopoly capital, lie the foundations of the country's future." The program adds, however, that "these struggles are as yet disjointed, the movements are separate and fragmented, while the power they confront is tightly centralized and highly organized" (p. 81). In response to this situation the CPUSA reiterates its call for the creation of a "new people's party," as the "concentrated political expression" of a "vast popular movement engaged in the most varied forms of struggle, from shop to campus, from ghetto to draft induction center" (p. 83). As on previous occasions when the party expressed support for the creation of a "new people's party" (see *YICA*, 1968, p. 611), the immediacy of such an eventuality is not argued. Referring to other "radical anti-war and black liberation groupings" that had in the past produced third party formations and electoral tickets, the CPUSA stresses that "if a new mass party is to be built that can seriously contest for power with the parties of monopoly, its social base must be firmly rooted in major sections of the working class and the Negro people," and adds: "As long as these decisive sectors remain substantially within the two-party orbit, that orbit remains a vital arena of struggle for political independence" (p. 84).

The CPUSA program devotes considerable attention to the issues of "reform" and "revolution" (pp. 85-91). Replying to "critics [who] will say that we contradict ourselves by trying to reform a system we claim is incurably rotten," the party states: "The struggles for day-to-day improvements are in fact basic training for the fight to take complete political power" (p. 88). In an apparent allusion to certain extremist movements to the left of the party, the CPUSA notes:

> The people display profound wisdom in being skeptical of the radical who promises to solve the fundamental ills of society in one big revolutionary sweep and yet lacks the will and competence to solve an on-the-job grievance or a community problem. (Pp. 88-89).

The program also stresses that the "profound transformation" of society that it seeks "cannot be made by a coup or conspiracy. It can only be effected through active participation of masses of people, black and white together." Emphasis is laid on the advocacy of "social change by peaceful means, through political institutions and people's organizations within the American Constitutional framework." (P. 92.) The program adds, however: "Of course, the people must be prepared to meet any eventuality. While we seek a peaceful path, as preferable to a violent one, this choice may prove to be blocked by monopolist reaction. Socialism must be sought, therefore, by whatever means circumstances may impose." (P. 93.)

In its description of the "Socialist Goal" that it advocates (pp. 96-111) the program states:

> Socialism in the United States, which will not be modeled on that in any other country, will benefit from the experiences of others in building socialism. But mainly it will reflect the distinctive features of American historical development, tradition, and environment. (P. 102.)

While claiming, however, that the "freedoms in the Bill of Rights will take on far greater meaning," the program points out that "socialism does not provide freedom for everybody and everything. . . . Nor does it provide freedom for advocacy of a return to capitalist exploitation and class society." (Pp. 103-4). The communist party, moreover, "would be the leading people's political organization in this society" (p. 104).

In the final chapter—"Our Relations With Others" (pp. 120-28)—the program emphasizes: "Communists have no interests separate and apart from the working class, from the majority of the American people. Rather, we have a special *viewpoint*." (P. 120, emphasis in original.) To confirm the point, it states: "This explains our advocacy of a new people's party, even though we have a party of our own" (*ibid.*). On the domestic level, the chapter is limited to a discussion of CPUSA relations with other left-wing groups and religious bodies. With regard to the former (pp. 121-24), the program notes that "a wide diversity of views exists on the Left," while claiming:

> Whatever the differences between ourselves and others on the Left, we concentrate on seeking areas of agreement where united action can be organized. In common action different views can be discussed most fruitfully, with the greatest hope of reaching agreement. (P. 122.)

The program lists five major ideological differences that separate other left-wing currents and "place them in conflict" with those of the CPUSA: (1) the "continuing prevalence in some circles (particularly among Right-Wing social democrats) of 'anti-Communism' "; (2) the "reformist outlook which sees reforms as ends in themselves"; (3) some "related tendencies that either deny or minimize the class struggle . . . and consequently deny or minimize the historic role of the working class"; (4) "Sectarianism, which leads people to act as if subjective desire can overcome the stubbornness of objective reality" and to "think a chosen few can substitute for millions in the process of social change"; and (5) "Ultra-Leftism, which under 'Left' banners engages in revolutionary bombast to justify adventurism and anarchism, and on occasion downright provocation actions" (p. 123).

The short section entitled "Communism and Religion" (pp. 124-25) states: "A development of vast importance is the rise of new, liberalizing currents in the world of religion" (p. 124), and adds: "We oppose all attempts to create division and antagonism among the people along religious lines. Accordingly, our Party is made up of believers and non-believers. What unites its ranks is a common social-political outlook." (P. 125.)

During 1970 CPUSA views and activities corresponded to most of the basic tenets of the party's program. Most apparent was the CPUSA's consolidation of its commitment to supporting at least one segment of the "black liberation" movement, that represented by the Black Panther Party (BPP)—a development that became noticeably apparent since July 1969 (see *YICA*, 1970, pp. 483-84). In a reflection of this commitment, the CPUSA organ *Daily World* (1 May 1970) referred to itself as "the only newspaper that fights *daily* to defend the Panthers" (emphasis in text). The party's defense of BPP members extended in August to one of the CPUSA's own members, Angela Davis, a former acting assistant professor at the University of California at Los Angeles who held membership in both parties. Davis was cited for alleged involvement in a kidnaping and fatal gun battle which occurred at a courthouse in Marin County, California, on 7 August. On 16 August a federal warrant charging unlawful flight was filed against Davis, and two days later she was named to the Federal Bureau of Investigation's list of ten most wanted fugitives (she was apprehended on 13 October in New York City).

The CPUSA's reaction to the Marin County incidents and the charges of Angela Davis's involvement in them was in the form of a statement by the party's Political Committee. After referring to "the goading realities of a bestial prison system," the committee added:

> The Communist Party has always made clear its opposition to acts of desperation or resort to gunplay on the part of individuals, no matter how awful the provocation or lofty the ideal. Communists reject the concept of revolutionary suicide or revolutionary superman-ism. (*Daily World*, 28 August).

Charges against Angela Davis were described as "an example of the exploitation of the tragedy for political frameup and the assault upon the personalities and parties of the Left" (*ibid.*). The CPUSA's criticism of the action in Marin County contrasted with that of the Black Panther Party, whose leading spokesman, Huey Newton, BPP minister of defense and supreme commander, characterized the incident as "a colossal event" and, praising the "revolutionary consciousness" of the kidnapers, stated that their actions had "changed the whole relationship between the oppressed and his oppressors" (*San Francisco Chronicle*, 12 August; see also, for similar comments by the BPP leadership, *The Black Panther*, San Francisco, 15 and 21 August).

The CPUSA made no direct comment on the BPP views; at the end of October, however, an article in the *Daily World* (30 October)—entitled "The Irresponsible 'Left' "—reported on a demonstration in support of Angela Davis that had taken place in New York City on 26 October. The party newspaper commented on the presence at that occasion of "a small band of the ultra-left," which it portrayed as "Trotskyite factions, various remnants of SDS and other Maoist splinters." These groups, reportedly, chanted slogans such as "Dare to struggle, dare to win, Jonathan Jackson—Live like him" (Jackson, a member of the BPP, was killed in the Marin County gun battle). "Implicit in the slogans of the ultra-left," the *Daily World* article continued, "is the conviction that Angela Davis is guilty (and therefore a heroine)." The article stated: "The only people who can seriously want the oppressed people of our country to imitate [Jonathan Jackson] are those who want their extermination." It concluded:

> It is essential for all progressive forces that truly want to free Angela to isolate the ultra-left. . . . In the long run the most effective way to isolate the ultra-left is to build such a mass

based defense movement that they will be exposed as the miniscule petit bourgeois sects which they are. . . . The defense movement has the possibility of mobilizing people well into the center of American politics. We must not allow these possibilities of mass struggle to be scuttled by irresponsible microfactions of the ultra-left.

Similar attacks by the CPUSA on elements of the extreme left were repeatedly expressed in the party's publications (see *Daily World*, 21 March, 9 and 22 April, 20 May, 17 September, 10 and 20 October, and 17 and 28 November; *Political Affairs*, February, May, and October). The party press also reflected a growing concern with the apparently increasing support won by the Trotskyist Socialist Workers' Party and its affiliate the Young Socialist Alliance, whose views and tactics on domestic issues were relatively similar to those of the CPUSA (see *Daily World*, 7 January, 28 February, 11, 12, and 21 March, 28 July, 2 September, and 31 December; *Political Affairs*, March, September, and November).

International Views and Policies. A steadfast supporter of the Soviet Union in all its policies, the CPUSA reaffirmed its alignment in 1970. In a report to a meeting of the party's National Committee on 16-18 January, Gus Hall described the "U.S.-Soviet relationship" as "the sharpest expression of the main class contradiction of our times on a world scale," and added:

> There is absolutely no way a socialist country or a Communist party or any other political or social force can avoid reacting to this central challenge of this historic moment. The options are limited. Either one holds to a firm revolutionary position of in no way adjusting, accommodating, flirting with or "using" this central expression of the class contradiction, or one takes an opportunistic position of accommodation, of taking momentary advantage of the situation, or of ingratiating oneself with capitalist powers by one's silence. (*Political Affairs*, March 1970.)

The CPUSA general secretary went on to analyze relations between the United States and the Chinese People's Republic, viewing increasing contacts between the two countries as being motivated by mutual "anti-Sovietism." With regard to China, he claimed that an "erroneous policy of narrow, egoistic nationalism [had] led the Maoist leadership to a position of fanatical anti-Sovietism" (*ibid.*). In the same context of total commitment to a "firm revolutionary position," Gus Hall was highly critical of the welcome extended to U.S. President Richard Nixon during his visit in September to Yugoslavia. "The roots for this action," he stated, "are in the policies of the Tito leadership. They are in the so-called policy of 'non-alignment'. The welcome was 'non alignment' in action. 'Non-alignment' is another word for opportunism." (*Daily World*, 3 October.)

In its published commentaries on developments within other communist parties, the CPUSA mirrored what it perceived to be the views of the Communist Party of the Soviet Union (CPSU). Thus, the expulsion from the French Communist Party of its leading theoretician and strong critic of the Soviet-led invasion of Czechoslovakia, Roger Garaudy, was reported with extensive citations from Soviet sources (see *ibid.*, 6 June). Also during 1970, reflecting increasingly close relations between the Soviet Union and Cuba, the CPUSA press continued its policy, initiated in 1969 concomitant to a marked Soviet-Cuban rapprochement, of giving extensive favorable reporting to developments in Cuba. As in the previous year, the CPUSA's increasing cordiality with the Cuban party leadership included a visit to Cuba by the CPUSA chairman, Henry Winston, who was present as the head of a five-man delegation for the celebrations of 26 July (see *ibid.*, 11 August).

International Party Contacts. CPUSA leaders continued to travel widely in 1970, as they had done the previous year. Political Committee members George Meyers and Roscoe Proctor attended the Nineteenth Congress of the French Communist Party in February. In April, Gus Hall and Henry Winston were in Moscow to attend the celebrations of the Lenin Centenary. Winston went to Sudan in late May as a guest of the Sudanese government, reportedly spending "several weeks" there (*Daily World*, 14 July). Political Committee member John Pittman visited the communist-controlled areas of Laos from 28 April to 5 May. The YWLL was represented at the conference of the Soviet Komsomol, in late May, by Lauren Lockshin and Tony Monteiro. Monteiro participated also in another YWLL delegation, together with Michael Zagarell and Jay Schaffner, that visited North Vietnam in July. In mid-June, the head of the CPUSA's international affairs department, James Jackson, attended an international communist party conference in East Berlin. Jackson returned to East Berlin in mid-November to attend a conference in honor of the 150th anniversary of the birth of Friedrich Engels. Political Committee member Hyman Lumer visited Israel in September, where he met with leaders of the Israeli Communist Party (RAKAH). Also in the autumn, Claude Lightfoot paid an extended visit to both East and West Germany; with regard to the latter, the *Daily World* (22 October) commented that Lightfoot was "the first U.S. Communist, since the days of Hitler and the establishment of the Federal Republic of Germany, to speak in public in that country." In mid-October, Henry Winston led a delegation to North Korea. Jarvis Tyner, YWLL chairman, led a delegation to the eighth assembly of the World Federation of Democratic Youth (WFDY), held in Budapest on 26 October-4 November. The *Daily World* (17 December) noted that "it was the first time that youth organizations from the United States were represented in the 25-year existence of the WFDY." The YWLL was elected to both the Executive Committee and the Bureau of the WFDY, and a permanent representative to the WFDY Budapest headquarters was appointed to function as secretary for North America. Gil Green was the CPUSA representative to the "World Conference on Vietnam, Laos and Cambodia," held in Stockholm on 28-30 November.

Publications. The two principal publications of the CPUSA are the *Daily World*, a newspaper published in New York five times a week (Tuesday through Saturday), and *Political Affairs*, a monthly theoretical organ. Other publications following the party's line include *People's World*, a weekly San Francisco newspaper; *Freedomways*, a quarterly review addressed to Negroes; *Labor Today*, a bimonthly trade union magazine; *American Dialogue*, a quarterly cultural magazine; and *New World Review*, a quarterly magazine on international issues. In June 1970 the CPUSA initiated the publication of *Jewish Affairs*, a bimonthly newsletter.

*   *   *

The oldest and largest of the Trotskyist parties in the United States is the Socialist Workers' Party. Founded in 1938, the SWP is aligned with the United Secretariat of the Fourth International. Following the characteristic pattern of Trotskyism, both internationally and nationally, the SWP over the years has been faced by a number of splits, defections, and reunifications. Within the United States, the three most prominent Trotskyist organizations that have split from the SWP appear to be the Workers' League, the Workers' World Party, and the Spartacist League (see below).

Owing to the fluidity of SWP membership, estimates regarding the party's strength vary considerably. In 1970 this difficulty continued to be compounded by the apparently increasing emergence of supporters of the SWP or its youth movement, the Young Socialist Alliance (YSA), who, while not holding formal membership in either organization, followed their policies and participated in activities sponsored by them. Confusion over membership figures was exemplified at the end of 1969 at the time of the YSA's Ninth National Convention, when press reports indicated that the youth movement had claimed a membership of between 5,000 and 10,000 (see *YICA*, 1970, p. 489). It would appear, however, that this figure corresponded to supporters rather than members of the YSA. In a report on the founding convention of the YWLL, the SWP newspaper, *The Militant* (20 February), commented on the YWLL's bid for 1,100 members, which the latter organization claimed would make it "the largest socialist youth organization" in the country, and added that the figure had been chosen "in obvious reference to the size of the YSA at its last convention." At the YSA's Tenth National Convention, in December 1970 (see below), no membership figures were published; it was estimated, however, that the figure had risen to between 1,200 and 1,400 (*Guardian*, New York, 9 January 1971). The SWP membership during 1970 is believed to have remained at about 1,000.

Although the SWP and the YSA continued in 1970 to have relatively few members, their influence, particularly on college campuses and within the movement of opposition to U.S. policy in Vietnam, appeared to be increasing considerably, partly through their control of the Student Mobilization Committee to End the War in Vietnam and the National Peace Action Coalition (see below). Commenting on the YSA, the director of the Federal Bureau of Investigation, J. Edgar Hoover, stated that it was "the largest and best organized youth group in left-wing radicalism" (*V.F.W. Magazine*, Kansas City, September 1970).

The SWP is a legal party and actively participates in both national and local electoral activity. In the November 1968 elections the SWP contended 45 seats in states and nationally. The party also presented Fred Halstead and Paul Boutelle as candidates, respectively, for president and vice-president. The SWP presidential ticket obtained 41,300 votes. The party's other candidatures were similarly unsuccessful. (See *YICA*, 1969, p. 483.) In 1970 the SWP presented 75 candidates at the November elections in 15 states: California (9), Colorado (3), Florida (2), Georgia (3), Illinois (7), Massachusetts (4), Michigan (9), Minnesota (3), New York (8), Ohio (6), Pennsylvania (5), Rhode Island (3), Texas (3), Washington (6), and Wisconsin (4) (for details see *The Militant*, 30 October). None of the party's candidates was successful.

Leadership and Organization. The SWP is led by a National Committee elected at the party's conventions. In 1970, leaders of the party (elected at the SWP's Twenty-third Convention, in 1969) included James P. Cannon, national chairman; Farrell Dobbs, national secretary; and Jack Barnes, national organizational secretary.

The SWP's principal auxiliary organization is the aforementioned Young Socialist Alliance, formed in October 1957 in New York City and founded as a national organization in April 1960. In 1970, the YSA was believed to comprise some fifty chapters. At the organization's Tenth National Convention, held in New York City on 27-31 December, 1,220 delegates and observers came from 34 states. The convention elected a National Committee, which, in turn, selected the YSA's three principal officers: Frank Boehm, national chairman; Cindy Jaquith, national secretary; and Norman Oliver, national organizational secretary. During 1970 the following served as YSA officers: Larry Seigle, national chairman (relinquished the post in mid-year to become editor of the SWP journal *International Socialist Review*); Susan Lamont, national secretary (replaced Seigle as chairman in September); and Nelson Blackstock, national organizational secretary. Carl Frank was elected national secretary at the time of Susan Lamont's move to the chairmanship of the organization.

Domestic Views and Policies. As in the previous year, the SWP's domestic policy and activity in 1970 continued in many respects to parallel that of the CPUSA. In its bid for broad-based tactical coalitions with dissident groups in the United States—particularly with regard to opposition to U.S. policy in Vietnam and on the issue of civil rights—the SWP's own tactics and pronouncements ranged over a broad political spectrum. The party on the one hand participated in the electoral process (see above); on the other hand its pronouncements on a number of issues—including the espousal of many Castroite revolutionary views (see below)—and its participation, together with the YSA, in violence-oriented activity, particularly on college campuses, appeared to indicate a different approach to U.S. political and social questions.

While espousing the electoral process (at least in order to attain publicity for its own views), the SWP differed from the CPUSA in limiting support to its own candidates. It repeatedly accused the Communist Party of misguidedly offering support to what it termed as "bourgeois capitalist" elements within the left-wing of the Democratic Party. In this context, and in reply to the CPUSA's own attacks (see above), the SWP press devoted considerable space to reviews of CPUSA policies, both historical and contemporary (see, e.g., *The Militant*, 19 June, 10 and 24 July, 7 August, 18 September, and 16 October).

The major thrust of SWP activity during 1970 was in the area of organizing mass demonstrations in opposition to U.S. policy in Southeast Asia. (This dominant concern of the SWP was repeatedly criticized by other left-radical groups who accused the Trotskyist organization of "single issue" orientation.) At the beginning of the year the principal vehicle available to the SWP and the YSA in the furtherance of its goal was the Student Mobilization Committee to End the War in Vietnam (SMC), an organization under Trotskyist control since mid-1968 (see *YICA*, 1969, p. 844).

On 14-15 February the SMC organized a conference in Cleveland to "plan student participation in the first phase of the 1970 offensive against the Vietnam war." The meeting was reportedly the "largest gathering of its kind" ever to be held—it was attended by some 4,000 persons, of whom 3,469 registered officially. Students came from thirty states and the District of Columbia, representing 300 colleges and universities and 100 high schools. There was also foreign representation, including anti-war activists from Canada, Australia, New Zealand, Brazil, and Argentina. The conference included a broad spectrum of political tendencies. In its report on the meeting, the Trotskyist *Intercontinental Press* (2 March) claimed:

> It became clear from the broad representation at the conference—virtually all tendencies on the student left were represented—that the SMC is now the mass expression of student radicalism in America and the place where the various political tendencies are contending for leadership of the student movement.

The main issue over which there was disagreement at the conference was whether the SMC should remain a single issue organization or involve itself in other areas of activity. The challenge that the latter political perspective presented to the SMC leadership and its SWP/YSA members was defeated. The former national executive secretary, Carol Lipman, was reelected for a second term, and a proposal was adopted to organize anti-war activities during the week of 13-18 April, with 15 April designated as the "focus of the week of action, with student strikes and mass demonstrations in towns and cities across the country" (*ibid.*; for further details on the conference see *Militant*, 27 February and 6 March, and *Guardian*, New York, 28 February).

Although the above actions were "designed to link up with, broaden, and deepen the antiwar activity proposed for the same week by the Vietnam Moratorium Committee and the New Mobilization Committee" (*Intercontinental Press*, 2 March), relations between the SMC and the other two organizations were only tenuous. By 19 April the Vietnam Moratorium Committee had decided to disband, following a relatively weakly supported three-day peace fast (13-15 April) and a series of "tax-payer rallies" on 15 April. In a letter to its supporters, the committee—which had been formed in 1969 by former volunteers from the 1968 presidential campaigns of Senator Eugene McCarthy and the late Senator Robert Kennedy (see *YICA*, 1970, pp. 482-83) —concluded that there was "little prospect of immediate change in the administration's policy in Vietnam." Other reasons given for disbanding were that the committee lacked funds, that the "political fad" of mass demonstrations had "worn off," and that President Nixon, by implementing troop withdrawals and the "Vietnamization" policy had managed to "identify himself with the cause of peace" and thereby won over much former anti-war sentiment. (Quoted in Liberation News Service, bulletin no. 250, 22 April.) Also during the first half of the year, the New Mobilization Committee was itself turning away from the advocacy of mass demonstrations. Highly heterogeneous in composition, the NMC appeared to be orienting itself to a multi-issue political perspective, and emphasizing individual acts of civil disobedience. The demonstrations organized by the NMC in mid-April were considerably smaller than those that the organization had sponsored in 1969 (see *YICA*, 1970, pp. 482-83).

In contrast to what could be seen as a demise in the mass action capabilities of the NMC, the SMC appeared to have a growing body of support during this period, although exact estimates as to the extent of participation in the organization's mid-April actions was difficult to determine.

The U.S. military intervention in Cambodia at the end of April and the subsequent reaction of opposition to the action appeared to breathe new life into the anti-war movement. Two major conferences were called for the month of June: (1) a "National Emergency Conference Against the Cambodia-Laos-Vietnam War," to be held in Cleveland, 19-21 June, and organized primarily by the SMC and the SWP /YSA; and (2) a "Strategy Action Conference," to be held in Milwaukee, 26-27 June, and sponsored by the New Mobilization Committee.

The Cleveland meeting was attended by some 1,500 persons. According to an article in the independent radical weekly *Guardian* (27 June), "all of the organized political tendencies present, except the Progressive Labor Party [see below], had their roots in the Trotskyist movement." The SWP and YSA were reported to have held together a bloc of about 1,000 votes; the Workers' League and the Spartacist League, two smaller contending Trotskyist organizations (see below), had 80 and 20 votes respectively. The Progressive Labor Party was reported as having had some 350 supporters. The conference created a new organization—the National Peace Action Coalition (NPAC)—and decided to hold three major demonstrations in the upcoming months: on 6-9 August, in Cleveland, to commemorate the 1945 bombings of Hiroshima and Nagasaki; on 29 August, in solidarity with a "Chicano [Mexican-American] Moratorium," demonstration against the war, scheduled to take place in Los Angeles; and a national anti-war demonstration on 31 October. Commenting on the meeting, the *Guardian* article noted that it "signified a deepening split in the antiwar movement. There were no representatives from the New Mobilization Committee—the major antiwar coalition. Nor any from the Communist party, Women's Strike for Peace, or traditional antiwar groups."

The meeting in Milwaukee, which was attended by some 800 persons, was characterized by the absence of any proposals for nationally coordinated mass mobilizations against the war. The outcome was inconclusive; two proposals calling for a variety of civil disobedience and mass disruption tactics were discussed, but neither was officially endorsed by the delegates. (For further details on the meeting, see *Guardian*, 4 July.) On 11-13 September some of the Milwaukee conference participants met again in that city, at which time a new organization, the National Coalition Against War, Racism, and Repression (NCAWRR) was formed. Although the NPAC was building up support for its mass demonstrations scheduled for 31 October, the NCAWRR refused to give national endorsement to these actions, leaving the question up to regional group-ings. It would appear that at this time the New Mobilization Committee ceased to exist, most of its former supporters having enlisted with the NCAWRR. The latter organization continued to reflect, however, the development that had taken place in the New Mobilization Committee, ori-enting itself to a multi-issue perspective and opposition to mass anti-war actions.

Despite the NCAWRR's failure to support the 31 October demonstrations, and the alleged low-key publicizing of the event by the radical news media (see polemic on this issue in *Militant*, 27 November, and *Guardian*, 14 November and 5 December), some 100,000 persons participated in demonstrations in more than 30 cities on that day.

The NPAC held a conference in Chicago on 4-6 December which was attended by 1,200 parti-cipants, including representatives of the NCAWRR. The major purpose of the meeting was to unite anti-war groups for a mass mobilization planned for 24 April 1971. The NCAWRR dele-gates asked the conference to delay the fixing of a specific date until other anti-war groups could be consulted and until 9 January 1971, date of the next national NCAWRR meeting. The confer-ence rejected the NCAWRR proposal, setting 24 April as the "target date for massive national antiwar demonstrations in Washington, D.C., and San Francisco" (*Militant*, 18 December).

International Views and Policies. Conforming to its ideological alignment with the United Sec-retariat of the Fourth International, the SWP repeatedly criticized the policies of the Soviet Un-ion and Communist China, both domestic and foreign. In addition to expressing complete soli-darity with North Vietnam and the National Liberation Front of South Vietnam, the SWP con-tinued in 1970—despite evidence of Cuban-Soviet rapprochement—to offer full support to Cas-troite policies (see, e.g., *Militant*, 31 July, 4 and 18 September).

The SWP carried numerous articles in its press on the activities and views of the different for-eign sections of the United Secretariat, contrasting these with what it saw as bureaucratic stultifi-cation and "reformism" in the regular communist parties (with the exception of the Cuban). The party press also reported extensively on developments in the Middle East, aligning itself stead-fastedly with the views of Palestine guerrilla organizations.

Generally, however, with an intensification in its domestic activities, the SWP and YSA, in contrast to previous years, appeared to devote less attention to international issues—with the exception of the war in Indochina. SWP and YSA members were reported as having traveled abroad on only a few occasions. Jacqueline Rice, an SWP congressional candidate, was a mem-ber of a Venceremos Brigade that went to Cuba to help in that country's sugar harvest; another congressional candidate, Andrew Pulley, took an extensive trip in Asia which included visits to India, Ceylon, Australia, New Zealand, the Philippines, and Japan. Paul Boutelle, SWP vice-presidential candidate in 1968 and congressional candidate in 1970, was in the Middle East in the autumn. Susan Lamont represented the YSA at a congress in Brussels, 21-22 November, orga-nized by the United Secretariat of the Fourth International (see *Belgium*).

Publications. During 1970 the two major publications of the SWP were the weekly newspaper, *The Militant*, and the monthly journal *International Socialist Review*. The latter first appeared as a monthly in May, having replaced the former bimonthly *International Socialist Review* and the monthly journal of the YSA, *Young Socialist*. The YSA published a fortnightly newspaper, *The Young Socialist Organizer*. The United Secretariat of the Fourth International continued publishing from New York the weekly *Intercontinental Press* under the editorship of SWP lead-er Joseph Hansen.

*   *   *

Another contending group within the communist movement in the United States, particularly among young persons, is the pro-Chinese Progressive Labor Party (PLP). Formed in 1962 following the 1961 expulsion of Milton Rosen and Mortimer Scheer from the CPUSA, the PLP was originally known as the Progressive Labor Movement. Its present name was adopted at a founding convention held in New York in April 1965.

The extent of PLP membership is difficult to ascertain, since the party does not publish any figures. Moreover, in 1969 approximately half of the delegates at the SDS National Convention in June (see *YICA*, 1970, p. 483), adhering to the views of the faction within the SDS known as the Worker-Student Alliance (WSA), formed a second SDS organization in opposition to the former SDS leadership. The WSA adherents offered full support to the views and actions of the PLP. In most instances, however, they did not hold formal membership in the pro-Chinese party, which is believed to have only some 350 members. At the SDS convention some 600 to 1,000 of the 1,500 delegates appeared to support the WSA views. While in 1969 the various factions of SDS numbered some 40,000 members in about 225 chapters, by the end of 1970, the only remaining groups calling themselves SDS were those aligned with the PLP/WSA. During the year, this remnant of SDS appeared, in turn, to be beset by internal conflict, as was also the PLP itself (see below). On a general level, support for the PLP and its student affiliate appeared to be diminishing; in view of the fluid situation, however, it was not possible by the end of the year to make any accurate assessment as to the degree of disaffection.

The PLP is not represented politically at the national or local levels. In 1968 during the U.S. presidential campaign the party appeared initially to support the Peace and Freedom Party, which was active in California. By the fall, however, the PLP was advocating abstention in the November elections (see *YICA*, 1969, p. 839). The November 1970 elections were referred to by the party and SDS as a "hoax" that only created the "illusion of change" (*Challenge /Desafío*, New York, November 1970).

Organization, Leadership, and Party Internal Affairs. The PLP does not publish details as to its organizational structure. Although the party held its second national convention in May 1968, the event remained unreported until mid-1969 and even then no details were given. In mid-1970, the Trotskyist weekly newspaper *Bulletin* (6 July) reported on dissension within the PLP leadership, dating back to November 1969, which had culminated in the expulsion from the party of William Epton, its vice-chairman, on 9 June. The PLP National Committee confirmed the report of Epton's expulsion in the September issue of its theoretical journal *Progressive Labor*, adding that he had been removed from the National Committee "many months ago." The party statement claimed that Epton and Geri Steiner—another member expelled at the same time—had "raised their warped sense of individualism above the class struggle." The National Committee used Epton's own self-criticism in its accusations against him, claiming that he had stated: "I see the Party in terms of my personal wants; I judge things by how they make me look." Geri Steiner was charged with "refusal to deal with her various 'perversions.' " The National Committee statement made no reference to the removal from leading posts or expulsion of any other members of the party, limiting itself to cautioning "those few people who might have illusions about this pair." In contrast, the aforementioned article in the *Bulletin* reported that Epton's expulsion had been coupled with that of nine other members, and that it was "part of a whole series of purges by the leadership directed against all opposition inside the party combined with forced and voluntary resignations by leading members." In November 1969, the PLP had reportedly initiated a "reorganization" of the party leadership. Following sessions of self-criticism by party leaders, three of the eight-member National Committee were removed from their posts—Jared Israel, Boston organizer; Jake Rosen, New York City organizer; and Epton, who, in addition to being party vice-chairman, was Harlem organizer. (The *Bulletin* carried excerpts of Israel, Rosen, and Epton's self-criticisms, which included such statements as the one allegedly made by Rosen, who confessed to "suffer[ing] from 'big-shot-itis.' ") Shortly thereafter, Juan and Helena Farinas, editors of the Spanish-language section of the party newspaper, *Challenge/Desafío*, were expelled. At the same time, Charles Rosen, a founding member of the party, was forced to resign, and another early and prominent member, Steve Martinot, submitted his resignation. In mid-1970, Ray Agostini, who had replaced Juan and Helena Farinas, submitted his resignation; he was then expelled.

As a result of the above developments, it would appear that the leadership of the PLP during 1970 was reduced to the remaining five members of the National Committee—Milton Rosen, national chairman; Levi Laub, West Coast organizer; Fred Jerome, San Francisco area organizer; Jeffrey Gordon, national student organizer; and Walter Linder, national trade union organizer. A three-man Steering Committee (formerly four and including Epton) composed of Rosen, Linder, and Gordon carried out the work of the National Committee between committee meetings. Early in the year, the party's theoretical journal, *Progressive Labor* (February 1970), referred to Bob Leonhardt as national student organizer; it was not stated, however, whether he had replaced Jeffrey Gordon in that post and on the National Committee.

Alignment with the views of the PLP leadership appears to have engendered significant controversy within the remnant of SDS, which in 1970 was led by its national secretary, John Pennington. At the student organization's national convention, held in Chicago on 27-30 December, a major source of opposition originated from the Columbia-Barnard SDS chapter, which denounced the leadership's criticisms of the National Liberation Front of South Vietnam and the Black Panther Party (stands that reflected the views of the PLP—see below). Although pre-convention publicity had stated that thousands of students and workers would attend the gathering, the organizers claimed a registration of only 900, and major sessions reportedly drew between 300 and 500 participants (*Militant*, 22 January 1971).

Domestic Views and Policies. The PLP continued in 1970 to believe in the revolutionary potential of the American working class and in the betrayal of this potential by all left-wing parties and groups with the exception of itself and its supporters. The party's press during the year carried extensive coverage of industrial agitation supported by the PLP and those adhering to its views. Although the party appeared to have only limited support from the Negro population—and continued to polemicize throughout the year with extreme-left groups like the Black Panther Party (see, e.g., *Challenge /Desafío*, January, August, and 5 October)—it repeatedly stressed the contention that racism was a weapon used by "bosses" to divide the workers, and that the Negro working class was a pivotal element in the attainment of revolution.

Having failed to gain any significant influence in the movement of opposition to U.S. policy in Southeast Asia, whose demonstrations resulted in a certain degree of collaboration between extreme-left groups of differing orientation, the PLP continued, as in previous years, to portray most participants in "antiwar" activity as direct or indirect "class collaborators." The party's own policy over issues such as the U.S. military intervention in Cambodia was to focus its attention on what it perceived as the underlying working class problems arising from such an action. Thus in the demonstrations in Washington that were organized in response to the Cambodian events, its participation was limited to a rally in front of the Labor Department building, where PLP speakers demanded that no campus workers be laid off during the strikes that were in progress on a number of college campuses (see *ibid.*, June).

While still adhering to the belief in the legitimacy of "mass revolutionary violence," the PLP repeatedly criticized actions of individual terror. An article in *Challenge /Desafío* (April)—entitled "Bombers Help Bosses"—claimed that "bosses use bomber-anarchists to help their campaign of lies about communists." It added that the victims of bombings and bomb threats "would be mainly working people," and "bosses desperately need workers to view communists as foolish terrorists who have no concern for working people."

International Views and Policies. One of the accusations against the PLP made by William Epton following his expulsion was that the party had adopted a policy of "U.S. chauvinism" and broken all "connections with the international movement." In this connection, Epton noted that the party had disbanded its quarterly publication, *World Revolution. (Bulletin,* 6 July.) The former vice-chairman's contentions were reflected in the appearance of considerably fewer articles in the PLP press on international developments. During the year, however, the party remained essentially Maoist in its outlook. It continued as in previous years to criticize the Vietnam Workers' Party and the National Liberation Front of South Vietnam, particularly in the light of the Vietnamese communists' agreement to participate in peace negotiations with the U.S. and South Vietnamese governments—a decision opposed by the Chinese leadership (see *Progressive Labor*, February, June, and September; and *Challenge /Desafío*, May). The party also reiterated its attacks against the Cuban party leadership (*Challenge /Desafío*, January). The PLP's alignment with Communist China in 1970 appeared, for the first time, to include a certain degree of reticence. Thus, despite the Chinese government's support for the deposed Cambodian ruler, Norodom Sihanouk, the PLP published a strongly worded criticism of his views and policies in the party's theoretical journal, *Progressive Labor* (September).

The only contact that the PLP reported during the year with other pro-Chinese parties was on the occasion of an International Solidarity Day demonstration held in New York City on 25 October and attended by delegations of the Puerto Rican Socialist League and the Canadian Party of Labour.

Publications. During 1970 the PLP issued only two publications—*Challenge /Desafío*, a monthly (from September, fortnightly) English-Spanish newspaper; and *Progressive Labor*, a bimonthly journal (in 1970 only three issues were published).

*   *   *

In addition to the CPUSA, PLP, and SWP there are a number of minor organizations in the United States advocating Marxism-Leninism of one form or another. Other pro-Chinese groups in 1970 included the following. (1) The Bay Area Revolutionary Union (also referred to as the Revolutionary Union), led by Robert Avakian, H. Bruce Franklin, and Steve Hamilton. This group irregularly published *The Red Papers*, and was active primarily around San Francisco and among college and high school students. In 1969 a number of its members participated in the June convention of SDS, with the Revolutionary Union aligning itself with the anti-PLP factions. During 1970 its membership appeared to grow from some 100 to about 300, with the organization orienting itself increasingly toward industrial agitation. Near the end of the year, the group was faced with a major split, with H. Bruce Franklin leading a break-away body to form a new organization called Venceremos, which published its own irregular newspaper by that name. The two factions appeared to divide their activities in terms of territorial jurisdiction. Venceremos concentrated on the southern part of the Bay Area, including Stanford University, where Franklin was a professor of English, while Avakian was active primarily in the north, around the city of Richmond. (2) The American Workers' Communist Party, originally founded in 1958 as the

Provisional Organizing Committee for a Marxist-Leninist Communist Party, adopted its new name in July 1968. Membership of this group was estimated at 100; its leaders included Armando Roman, general secretary; Harold Allen, national chairman; Helen Roman, national organizational secretary; and Bill Vila, education and propaganda secretary. The group published the irregular newspaper, *Vanguard*. (3) The American Communist Workers' Movement (Marxist-Leninist) was founded in 1969. Its support was primarily limited to Cleveland, where it was believed to have some 100 members. This group published an irregular newspaper, *American Mass Line*, and had close contacts with the considerably larger Communist Party of Canada (Marxist-Leninist).

Within the Trotskyist movement the major challenge to the SWP was represented by the Workers' League, an organization aligned with the International Committee of the Fourth International. This group was led by Tim Wohlforth as national secretary. It published a weekly newspaper, the *Bulletin*. Although there were no reliable estimates of its membership, the total was probably less than 200. The Workers' League's pronouncements on foreign affairs and its general approach to revolutionary tactics followed closely those of the largest section of the International Committee, the Socialist Labour League in Great Britain (see *Great Britain*).

The Workers' World Party (WWP) was another Trotskyist group which originated from the SWP. Its membership was estimated at about 90. Prominent leaders in 1970 appeared to be Dorothy Ballan, Sam Ballan, and Vincent Copeland. The youth group of the WWP was Youth Against War and Fascism (YAWF), which seemed to have a considerably larger membership than the parent party. The WWP published the fortnightly *Workers' World*. Both the WWP and the YAWF appeared to be primarily active on the East Coast of the United States.

The Spartacist League, a splinter group from the International Committee of the Fourth International, was led by James Robertson. Its membership in 1970 was estimated at less than 100 and appeared to be dwindling. This group published an irregular bimonthly, the *Spartacist*.

M. P.

LATIN AMERICA AND CARIBBEAN

ARGENTINA

The Communist Party of Argentina (Partido Comunista de Argentina; PCA) originated from the International Socialist Party (Partido Socialista Internacional), founded in 1918. Its present name was adopted in 1920.

The PCA claims to have a membership of more than 100,000 and thus to be the largest communist party in Latin America, outside of Cuba. One U.S. government source (*World Strength of the Communist Party Organizations*, 1970), however, estimates that the PCA and all the smaller communist groups together have only about 60,000 members and possibly 60,000 sympathizers. Another source (*Il Corriere della Sera*, Milan, 7 March 1971), estimates PCA membership at 30,000 active members. According to the 1970 census, the population of Argentina is 23,800,000 (*La Nación*, Buenos Aires, 6 October).

PCA membership, two-thirds of which is concentrated in Buenos Aires Province, is drawn primarily from middle and lower urban classes. Indicative of the social composition of the party was the following proportion of delegates at the Thirteenth Congress, held in March 1969: 72 workers, 4 peasants, 10 persons in the "liberal professions," 6 teachers, 2 housewives, 1 student, and 5 writers and journalists (*WMR*, August 1969). A recruiting campaign that was carried from April 1969 to April 1970 apparently added a considerable number of new members to the PCA, but did not affect the class representation. Of the newly admitted 11,650 PCA members and 5,748 youth members claimed by party sources, more than 50 per cent were workers, 25 per cent women, and 6 per cent peasants. The recruitment of university and secondary school students was said to have indicated a growth of 13 and 24 per cent respectively (*Nueva Era*, July). The PCA is believed to be financially wealthy, mainly because of its indirect participation in various commercial and banking enterprises.

The PCA is banned at present, but its illegality is not enforced by the authorities. Under the government of Arturo Illia (1963-66), the PCA was legal but did not have "juridical-political recognition," and was thus ineligible to participate in elections. Following the coup d'état of 28 June 1966, all political parties were dissolved. On 25 August 1967 a 22-article law was promulgated requiring the registration of communists in Argentina and banning them from holding public office or any official position in professional, employers', or trade union organizations. In June 1969 further anticommunist measures were adopted, establishing one to six years' imprisonment for persons who "with undoubtable communist ideological motives" should carry out activities aimed at "promoting, spreading, expanding, or upholding communism." On 3 June 1970, the death penalty was established for kidnapings, hijacking airplanes, and various acts of terrorism.

During 1967 and 1968 large membership defections within the PCA, especially in its youth sector, weakened the party considerably. Most of these dissidents joined to form another organization, the Communist Party of Revolutionary Recovery—later the Revolutionary Communist Party (Partido Comunista Revolucionario; PCR). In addition to the PCA and the PCR there are a pro-Chinese communist party—the Communist Vanguard (Vanguardia Comunista; VC) and a Trotskyist movement, now divided into several factions. (See below.)

In recent years other small leftist groups (composed of Castroite or Peronist radicals, or both) have appeared throughout the country, and while not all of them espouse communist ideologies, they share the common strategy of armed struggle to seize power. One source estimates that there are approximately 7,500 guerrillas in Argentina, distributed in about 15 leftist organizations and 750 branches (*Latinamerica Press*, Lima, 17 March 1970).

The PCA. Leadership and Organization. Victorio Codovilla, the seventy-six year-old president of the PCA and its founding father, died in Moscow on 15 April 1970 after a long illness. Gerónimo Arnedo Alvarez is the secretary-general. Important members of the Central Committee, elected in March 1969, include Rodolfo Ghioldi, Orestes Ghioldi, Vicente Marischi, Alcira de la Peña, Fernando Nadra, Héctor Agosti, Pedro Tadioli, Rubens Iscaro, Benito Marianetti, Oscar Arévalo, and Julio Laborde.

The PCA is organized pyramidally from cells, neighborhood committees, and local committees on up to provincial committees and the Central Committee. The Central Committee is composed of 21 full and eight alternate members. In addition there is the Executive Committee, with 11 members, and the Secretariat, with five.

The PCA youth movement, the Communist Youth Federation (Federación Juvenil Comunista; FJC) is organized along the same lines as the party. It was founded in 1921 and by 1967 claimed to have 35,000 card-carrying members. Defections during 1967 and 1968 affected the FJC strength considerably. Although there is believed to have been some recovery, the current membership is perhaps no more than 15,000. Héctor Santarén is the FJC secretary-general.

The PCA is weak within the labor movement despite the presence of party branches among working centers in the oil and timber industries and in sugar refineries, mines, and steel plants. The major trade union body, the General Workers' Confederation (Confederación General de Trabajadores; CGT) is controlled by Peronists, who are very powerful and reject communist support. The PCA influences the Movement for Trade-Union Unity and Coordination (Movimiento por la Unidad y la Coordinación Sindical; MUCS), which represents small regional unions, mostly those centered in Córdoba Province. PCA Central Committee member Rubens Iscaro is its secretary-general. The MUCS worked with the "Opposition CGT" (a coalition of Peronists, communists, Trostkyists, and "progressive" Christians) from 1968 until mid-1970, when it was expelled from the group (*Nueva Era*, August). Unable to work with a nationwide labor confederation, the MUCS was left in a difficult situation. (See below.)

Although peasant organizations are mostly organized under the noncommunist Argentine Agrarian Federation, the PCA claims to be an active participant in a new peasant organization, formed in 1969. This peasant group, the "Union of Agrarian Producers of Argentina" (UPARA), is said to have 50,000 members, engaged in viticulture and in the sugar cane, potato, tobacco, cotton, and tea crops.

Most PCA fronts, such as the Argentine League for the Rights of Men, the Union of Argentine Women (UMA), and the Argentine Peace Council, are illegal. There is, however, still communist participation in the Argentine Women's League, in MODENA (a group composed of civilian and military men seeking to protect national resources), and MAVIET, the "Argentine Movement of Help to Vietnam."

Domestic Attitudes and Activities. Being a pro-Soviet party, the PCA subscribes to the policy of creating a "broad democratic front"—one which would include sectors of the national bourgeoisie—as the first step toward gaining power. Under the present Argentine political situation, where a military regime holds power, the PCA essentially seeks a return to democratic rule.

The dismissal of President Juan Carlos Onganía by the military junta on 8 June prompted a statement by the PCA Executive Committee declaring that "another coup d'état" had taken place (*Nueva Era*, June). The statement called for the creation of a "coordinating center of all democratic, progressive, and democratic forces," that would fulfill the following program:

Establishment of democratic freedoms of speech, association, and press, and the right to go on strike
Amnesty for all political prisoners
Annulment of the death penalty and repressive legislation
Freedom of operation for all political parties
Salary and wage increases to meet the cost of living
Tax reductions for peasants, professionals, and small and middle-sized entrepreneurs
Defense of national resources

With the objective of creating a "broad democratic front," the PCA organized a convention of various political parties in the city of Rosario on 20 November. According to communist sources, the meeting (held in a public theater will full knowledge by the police) was attended by 4,700 delegates representing 2,000 different organizations. Delegates from the two leading political groups, the National Justicialist Movement (the political branch of Peronism) and the People's Radical Civic Union were present. Also attending the meeting were socialists, Christian democrats, and priests connected with the "Third World Priest Movement." The PCA, which had the largest representation at the meeting, reportedly set the tone for the convention.

The convention succeeded in forming a coalition representing not only communists but also elements from other five political parties. The coalition—created in an effort to emulate the Chilean Popular Unity Front that made possible the election of Salvador Allende in Chile—adopted the name of the "National Assembly of Argentines." [1]   The minimum program established at the convention was extensive, calling for 43 objectives. These included a constitutional government, freedom for all political parties, amnesty for political prisoners, nationalization of foreign trade and basic sectors of the national economy, agrarian reform, and establishment of economic, political, and cultural relation with all countries. (See *Propósitos*, Buenos Aires, 26 November, for the complete program.)

The Nacional Assembly of Argentines was considered most important by the PCA. In fact, the party stated that its "present effort and primary task" would be the "consolidating and spreading of the National Assembly of Argentines" throughout the country (*El Popular*, Montevideo, 16 December). PCA Central Committee member Héctor Agosti, in an interview published in *El Siglo* (Santiago, Chile, 18 January 1971), held that the National Assembly of Argentines was now organized in all provinces, except for Tierra del Fuego and Santa Cruz. He also stated that the PCA was "fully aware that the Assembly is not the instrument of Argentine popular unity but that it is a great initial step."

During 1970 the position of the PCA within the labor movement was further weakened. On the one hand, most of the largest Peronist unions (totaling an estimated 3.5 million workers) came together early in July to form a single CGT, the government having decided to allow the CGT to function independently after having controlled it for the past three years. The presence of this unified CGT was taken to render more difficult any attempts by the communists to infiltrate it. On the other hand, the "Opposition CGT" grew increasingly hostile of the communist-controlled

[1] Jorge Paladino, the secretary-general of the National Justicialist Movement, and Ricardo Balbin, the president of the People's Radical Civic Union, reacted to the creation of this leftist coalition by forming in December a coalition which included the Popular Conservative Party, the Progressive Democratic Party, the Argentine Socialist Party, and the Radical Civic Union. This coalition, named the Electoral Front, demanded an immediate date for nationwide general elections.

MUCS? The secretary-general of the "Opposition CGT," Raimundo Ongaro, criticized various PCA leaders and even stated that "they grow fat and rich in Argentina and then go off to Moscow to die"—a clear reference to the late PCA president, Codovilla. Ongaro convened a meeting early in July and at that time expelled the MUCS and five other unions. The MUCS was said by the PCA to have been ousted for "ideological reasons"; it seemed, however, that friction had developed because the communists insisted in working also with the unified CGT, while Ongaro advocated working only within the "Opposition CGT" (see *Nueva Era*, August). The MUCS accused Ongaro of creating "division, confusion, and frustrations among the workers" which would achieve only the formation of "powerless clandestine groupings" (*ibid.*).

PCA publications mentioned the existing labor unrest in Argentina, giving extensive coverage to the strikes which took place on 9 and 22 October (for 24 and 10 hours respectively), and on 12-13 November (36 hours) although these actions were not communist-organized. The strikes were called and carried out by workers belonging to the unified CGT, which shortly after its reorganization had adopted a "combat plan" to protest the socioeconomic policies of the government. The MUCS claimed responsibility, however, for a 20-day strike in April at El Chocón (a hydroelectric project in Neuquén Province) in which about 3,500 construction workers participated. This strike was not successful, as the workers did not achieve their demands for improved pay and living conditions, but the PCA referred to it as "one of the most beautiful pages in the history of the Argentine worker movement"—presumably because it was an instance of communist-organized labor action.

Within the student movement, the PCA performed successfully during 1970. At an extraordinary congress of the Argentine University Federation (Federación Universitaria Argentina; FUA), held early in November, the Reformist Organization Movement—the PCA-influenced student group—won 20,000 of the 25,000 votes cast to elect the new FUA leadership. The victory of the Reformist Organization Movement meant a serious setback for the PCR (see below), which had been in control of FUA for the three preceding years.

International Views and Positions. The PCA closely follows a pro-Soviet line on international issues and supports the principle of "peaceful coexistence." Writing for *World Marxist Review* (October), PCA Central Committee member Rubens Iscaro attacked "ultra leftist" groups in Argentina for maintaining that peaceful coexistence "paralyzes the will of the people" and "robs the national liberation movement of international support." He argued that "peaceful coexistence is in itself a special form of class struggle" that had given the socialist countries "extensive opportunities for invigorating their position, and that of the world socialist system as a whole."

While condemning terrorist actions within Argentina, the PCA continued to expressed support for the Cuban regime. An important development in communist Cuban-Argentine relations was the visit to Cuba of a PCA delegation, headed by Secretary-General Alvarez, on 24 December 1970-19 January 1971. A PCA communiqué, published after the visit, stated that talks were held with Fidel Castro and various members of the Politburo of the Communist Party of Cuba "in a climate of brotherhood and cordiality." According to *El Mercurio* (Santiago, Chile, 20 February 1971), Argentine communists allegedly said that a "healthy political maturity" was observed in Castro and other important Cuban communists, who were now showing "greater discretion" to the principles of "mass actions" and "peaceful coexistence." Nevertheless, Cuba has continued to maintain its extensive verbal support for Argentine extremist groups (see, e.g., *Tricontinental Bulletin*, January 1971).

[2] The "Opposition CGT," also known as the "Paseo Colón CGT" or the "Rebel CGT," seeks to "raise the economic conflicts of the workers to a political plane." It is a radical group advocating "national and social liberation," meaning the expulsion of the monopolies, destruction of the oligarchy, and the implantation of socialism. (*Marcha*, Montevideo, 10 July.) It is considered to represent about 10 per cent of the organized workers.

The PCA sent a message of congratulations to the Chilean communist leader Luis Corvalán on the success achieved by the Popular Unity coalition in the presidential elections of 4 September. The message held that the leftist victory in Chile had "continental and world-wide significance" and that it "marked a great new step in the invincible march of Latin America toward true democracy, progress, national independence, and socialism." Subsequently, the PCA organ *Nuestra Palabra* asserted that the example of Chile had shown to Marxist-Leninists in Latin America that unity could lead to victory.

International Party Contacts. During May 1970 a PCA delegation headed by Secretary-General Alvarez met in Moscow with Boris Ponomarev, secretary in the Communist Party of the Soviet Union. The joint communiqué that followed expressed "full coincidence of views of the two fraternal parties" on a number of problems of the world communist movement.

Central Committee members Orestes Ghioldi and Benito Marianetti visited Chile in September to congratulate the Communist Party of Chile on Allende's election.

A PCA delegation attended the Twentieth Congress of the Communist Party of Uruguay, held on 11-15 December.

Publications. The PCA weekly, *Nuestra Palabra*, claims a clandestine circulation of 30,000 copies. When the party was legal, it sold twice that number. The PCA also publishes *Nueva Era*, a monthly theoretical journal, and the bimonthly *Cuadernos de Cultura*, catering mainly to intellectuals. In August 1970 the party began publication of the *Boletín de Informaciones Latinoamericanas*, a fortnightly designed to "inform communist parties of the activities of fraternal parties and to cover revolutionary events in Latin American countries." The Communist Youth Federation prints a fortnightly paper, *Juventud*.

*   *   *

The PCR. The Revolutionary Communist Party, formed originally as the Communist Party of Revolutionary Recovery, was created on 6 January 1968 by dissidents from the PCA and especially its Communist Youth Federation, who rejected the PCA's attempt to create a "broad democratic front" as an attempt at "class conciliation" and "conciliation with imperialism."

The PCR leadership includes César Otto Vargas as secretary-general (he was formerly secretary of the important La Plata local committee of the PCA), Carlos Echagüe, Jorge Rocha, Miguel Rubinich, Sergio Rodríguez, Manuel Campos, Fanny Echagüea, and Lucila Irene Edelman, all of whom held important positions within the FJC prior to their expulsion from the PCA in 1967.

The PCR has links with militant, socialist-oriented Catholic organizations within Argentina, including the "Camilo Torres Command" and the "Third World Priest Movement." Internationally, the party is said to have contacts with Cuba and China.

The PCR advocates violent armed struggle to gain power, but believes that the leadership in the revolutionary struggle must be held by the party. The PCR favors only urban guerrilla struggle, contending that the "wide plains" of Argentina's interior and the "highly developed agriculture on the coast" would not permit successful operations by peasant guerrillas (*Punto Final*, Santiago, 17 June 1969).

Showing a shift in methods—from armed struggle to political work—the PCR issued on 16 June 1970 an appeal to all workers and students to "double the efforts to hit the dictatorship." The statement proposed a series of demands, calling for increased wages, credits for poor and middle class farmers, "freedom" for the student movement, freedom for political and student prisoners, nationalization of "imperialist" enterprises, and solidarity of the Argentine people with all peoples "struggling against imperialism, especially the people of Indochina."

Reporting on PCR activities, Cuban sources noted that the party was not participating in current armed actions but was concentrating instead on developing a following within the working class and student groups as a "prerequisite for organizing and applying revolutionary violence." This was reaffirmed by the PCR when its organ, *Nueva Hora* (September), reported on the first meeting of the Permanent Conference (presumably the party's coordinating body). According to the report, the fundamental task of the PCR was to "penetrate business enterprises and develop the party of the proletariat."

The defeat suffered in the FUA elections by the PCR student front, the Federation of Leftist University Groups, was considered serious by most observers, since the FUA represents about 40 per cent of the Argentine university students. The Federation of Leftist University Groups, the backbone of the party, was able to win only 3,500 of the 25,000 votes cast. Its defeat was attributed not only to a rejection of the pro-guerrilla line advocated by the PCR but also to the PCR student leaders' strong emphasis on revolutionary goals to the detriment of student demands.

On international issues the PCR hailed the election of Allende in Chile. A Central Committee statement (quoted in *Punto Final*, Santiago, Chile, 27 October) asserted that his victory was merely an initial step on the road to socialism and that the ultimate seizure of power by the communists would be achieved only by armed violence.

Publications. The PCR publishes the clandestine *Nueva Hora*.

* * *

The VC. The Communist Vanguard is a pro-Chinese communist party. It was founded by Elías Seman, probably in 1964. Although it has few militants, it is said to have some influence among student and worker groups. The current press secretary of the "Opposition CGT," Ricardo de Luca, is believed to be a VC member.

There were reports in March 1970 that the VC was preparing to hold its first national congress. In a circular addressed to its members, the party called upon them to "submit their mistakes to the strongest criticism":

> Purging ourselves of these mistaken ideas will allow us to take a significant step toward the unity of the revolutionary left under the guidance of Mao Tse-tung, the general line of the "revolutionary of the new democracy," and the strategy of the people's war as the basis and Communist Vanguard as the center. Purging ourselves of these mistaken ideas will allow us to advance in the thorough fulfillment of our role as the vanguard of the Argentine people in its progress toward a people's war.

It is not known whether the congress took place.

The party's organ, *No Transar*, published an article early in March criticizing Fidel Castro's government in the strongest terms. Condemning Cuba's participation (as an observer) at the Moscow Conference of June 1969, the Cuban support of the Soviet-led invasion of Czechoslovakia, and the visit to Havana of several ships of the Soviet navy, the article contended that the Cuban government was "increasing the concessions which chain it to the revisionist policy of the Kremlin clique." Also under attack was Castro's widely publicized goal of a 10-million-ton sugar harvest. Tying the latter campaign to the "revisionist line of converting Cuba into a new colony of the Soviet Union," the article concluded: "Whether or not this economic objective is accomplished, inspired with Soviet 'aid,' it clearly indicates the type of economy the Kremlin wants to impose on Cuba." The same article also showed special concern over Castro's verbal support of the Peruvian military government:

The Cuban government has for years defended the thesis of the Latin American socialist revolution and excluded the national bourgeoisie from revolutionary forces. Without prior explanation that same government now issues a statement to the effect that a military movement with a bourgeois base—where the national bourgeoisie does not even appear to dominate—can direct and carry through a genuinely revolutionary program.

Publications. The VC publishes a mimeographed clandestine organ, *No Transar* (No Compromise).

*   *   *

Trotskyism in Argentina is represented by two groups, the Revolutionary Workers' Party (Partido Revolucionario de los Trabajadores; PRT), aligned with the United Secretariat of the Fourth International, and Política Obrera, an apparently independent Trotskyist group. Several PRT factions and Política Obrera endorse Castroite principles and the Latin American Solidarity Organization, based in Havana.

The PRT. In 1968 the PRT divided when two-thirds of its members approved the concept of armed struggle. The views of the majority faction are expressed in its organ *El Combatiente*, and those of the minority in *La Verdad*.

The "majority PRT" is organized into an executive committee, a central committee, a military apparatus with several commando units (mostly in Rosario Province), and cells in the provinces of Salta, Tucumán, Córdoba, Rosario, and Buenos Aires. This faction believes in the formation of a "classic revolutionary party" and is willing to cooperate in armed action with other revolutionary groups. According to one source, the "majority PRT" accepts nonparty members within its ranks for direct action as combatants, and is perhaps the only revolutionary group in Argentina to do so.

The "majority PRT" was reported to have suffered serious setbacks in April and May 1970, when many of its members were arrested in Rosario and Tucumán. Nevertheless, the "majority PRT" was able to hold clandestinely its Fifth Congress on 24-27 August, publicized under the slogan "Ready for the Battle, All for War." The main outcome of the congress was the approval of a decision to "shed the old and still latent obstacles of the past and clear the path for the fulfillment of new tasks." The congress also reaffirmed the party's self-image as the leader of the revolutionary process and its belief in mass work through "agitation, revolutionary propaganda, and education in armed resistance." Further indicating the militancy of the party, the congress resolution declared: "The only justification for recognition [of the 'majority PRT'] as the unquestionable vanguard is our role in combat."

Regarding the international communist movement, the congress expressed support for the formation of a new "international" headed by the Cuban, Chinese, Vietnamese, North Korean, and Albanian communist parties and including "all combatant organizations of America and the world."

Another important result of the "majority PRT" congress was the decision to create an exclusively armed group within the party, the People's Revolutionary Army (Ejército Revolucionario Popular; ERP). According to one source, this group is led by Robi Santucho and centers in Tucumán. The leftist publication *Cristianismo y Revolución* (Buenos Aires, January-February 1971) stated, however, that the ERP operates mainly in Rosario and Córdoba and to a lesser degree in Tucumán and Buenos Aires. The ERP defines itself as a "mass organization" seeking to develop a "revolutionary civil war" against "the dictatorship and imperialism." Each ERP commando unit has a political leader assigned by the party but he is not always the military leader. (*Ibid.*)

In April, police arrested in the city of Rosario a group of 16 PRT members, who were charged with participating in attacks on police stations and a robbery on 30 March when some $117,000 was taken from a train carrying a payroll. ERP actions included the robbery of a broadcast station in Rosario ($1,500 was obtained) and an attack on a police station also in Rosario on 18 September.

Toward the end of the year a further split in the PRT was reported. A new faction, known as Milicia Obrera, was said to have rejected armed struggle and adopted instead the method of mass political work to carry out revolution. (*Confirmado*, Buenos Aires, 16 December.)

*   *   *

Castroite groups in Argentina are small and tend to have a brief existence. The Revolutionary Armed Movement, formed in 1969, seemed to have been dissolved in 1970. On the other hand, two apparently strong revolutionary groups appeared or reappeared: the Argentine Liberation Front (Frente Argentino de Liberación; FAL) and the Revolutionary Armed Front (Frente Armado Revolucionario; FAR).

The FAL. The Argentine Liberation Front, a Marxist-Leninist group advocating Castroite tactics, claims to have been formed in 1962 and to be an offshoot of various organizations, mostly Marxist. In 1970 an FAL leader, in an interview published in *Granma* (Havana, 9 December), stated: "We believe that the struggle in our country is not only one of national liberation, but of national and social liberation. In other words, in our country there will be not only an anti-imperialistic war but a civil war, too."

The FAL received national attention early in 1970 when it kidnaped a Paraguayan consul, Waldemar Sánchez, in Buenos Aires on 24 March in order to obtain the release of two FAL guerrilla members. When the government refused to accept its demands, the group issued a communiqué on 28 March declaring that since one of the guerrillas had already been "killed by the police," the consul would be released; he was freed that same day.

Other, more successful FAL actions included briefly seizing the Campo de Mayo military unit (one of Argentina's most important garrisons) on 5 April and robbing a Rosario-Buenos Aires train of some $12,000 on 24 September.

An article in *Granma* (14 December) reported that "good relations" existed between the FAL and three Peronist revolutionary groups (the Peronist Armed Forces, the Montoneros, and the Revolutionary Armed Forces), and that the forming of a "liberation front" was being studied by the four groups. Another report in *Granma* (9 December) stated that the FAL endorses Guevara's thesis of creating "two, three, many Vietnams" as the "most important contribution in recent times to the world strategy of revolution."

The FAR. The Revolutionary Armed Front, which revealed itself for the first time in July 1970, has been described as a "conglomeration of ultra-left Marxist groups with sectors of revolutionary Peronism" (*Análisis*, Buenos Aires, 4-10 August). According to a FAR leader (quoted in *Tricontinental Bulletin*, January 1971), the FAR originated as a group that "meant to join Che's guerrillas" in Bolivia. He also declared that the FAR is a Marxist-Leninist party, but that it regards Peronism as "the political expression of the great majority" of the Argentine working class and holds that revolutionary action should take this into account.

A FAR group occupied for about one hour on 30 July the small city of Garín, about twenty-six miles from the federal capital. The revolutionaries robbed a bank, seized a broadcasting station, and overpowered the local police headquarters. Upon leaving the city, the FAR militants released a communiqué which stated: "Because in Argentina fundamental rights are not granted but won, what has been taken from us by force can only be recovered, defended, and developed by force." A second communiqué reporting on the "real course of events" at Garín, claimed that the group had obtained $8,500 in cash, along with weapons, ammunition, and police badges and uniforms (*Clarín*, Buenos Aires, 2 August).

N. S.

BOLIVIA

The Communist Party of Bolivia (Partido Comunista de Bolivia; PCB) was founded in 1950. It is pro-Soviet in alignment. A pro-Chinese splinter of the PCB became the Communist Party of Bolivia, Marxist-Leninist (Partido Comunista de Bolivia, Marxista-Leninista; PCB-ML) in 1965. A Trotskyist group, the Revolutionary Workers' Party (Partido Obrero Revolucionario; POR), is currently split into three factions. A Castroite guerrilla organization, the National Liberation Army (Ejército de Liberatión Nacional; ELN), was founded in 1966.

All of these groups were illegal during 1970. The PCB, however, reportedly "engaged in public activities unhampered" (*WMR*, August 1970). The various party memberships are estimated as follows: PCB, 3,000; PCB-ML, 1,000; and the three factions of the POR, a total of 1,000. In September, the ELN was estimated to have between 80 and 100 members (*Punto Final*, Santiago, Chile, 15 September). The population of Bolivia is 4,600,000 (estimated 1970).

Recent Bolivian history has been marked by frequent shifts in political leadership and consequently by varying opportunities for communist and Castroite influence and activity. In 1964 President Víctor Paz Estenssoro of the National Revolutionary Movement (Movimiento Nacionalista Revolucionario; MNR) was exiled in the wake of a military coup which placed political power in the hands of Generals René Barrientos Ortuño and Alfredo Ovando Candia. Barrientos quickly became the dominant figure and was elected president in July 1966, only several months before Che Guevara arrived in Bolivia to begin the guerrilla campaign which was routed in October 1967. On 27 April 1969 Barrientos was killed in a helicopter crash. He was succeeded by his vice-president, Luis Adolfo Siles Salinas, who on 26 September was ousted by General Ovando.

Between September 1969 and October 1970, when he was driven from power, Ovando increased the freedom of leftist students, who took over and reorganized the universities, and of labor leaders, who called important conferences in April and May 1970. Controversy raged—encouraged by both students and workers—on many issues, among them the makeup and policies of the cabinet, the political orientation of the army, and the government's policies toward foreign investors (in particular Gulf Oil, whose properties had been nationalized in 1969). Activities of the ELN guerrillas were resumed in July 1970 and, although Ovando initiated steps to suppress them, were taken as partial justification for the seizure of power on 6 October by General Rogelio Miranda and rightists in the Bolivian armed forces. On 7 October, military leftist elements led by General Juan José Torres executed another coup! An alliance of leftist forces, called the "Political Command of the Popular Forces," which included the PCB, PCB-ML, POR, and several larger leftist parties, together with worker and student organizations, quickly threw its support behind Torres. By the end of the year, however, many students, some workers,

---

[1]In 1967 Torres was chief of staff of the armed forces and was responsible for planning the campaign which destroyed Che Guevara's guerrilla uprising. He was the Bolivian observer at the Third Non-Aligned Conference, in Lusaka, Zambia, in September 1970.

one faction of the POR, the PCB-ML, and several other groups had withdrawn their support. On 23 December the Torres government, despite some controversy within the military, released French Marxist Régis Debray, who had been sentenced in 1967 to thirty years' imprisonment for his part in Guevara's guerrilla uprising.

The PCB. Leadership and Organization. The first secretary of the PCB is Jorge Kolle Cueto. Other prominent party members are Mario Monje Molina, a former first secretary who was in prison during 1970, and Central Committee members Simón Reyes, Aldo Flores, and Luis Padilla. Party statements generally appeared in the name of the Central Committee.

The PCB's youth organization is the Communist Youth of Bolivia (Juventud Comunista de Bolivia; JCB). It is illegal and is operated clandestinely by its Executive Committee. Spokesmen for the group include Jorge Escalera and Carlos Soría Galvarro. In 1970, following the PCB lead, the JCB declared that guerrilla warfare was not the "most responsible approach" to a socialist revolution in Bolivia (*Punto Final*, 18 August.) Apparently as a result of this stand, many members dropped out of the organization, including several Executive Committee officers. According to the leader of the ELN, a considerable number of JCB members had joined his guerrillas by the end of the year (*ibid.*, 8 December).

Early in 1970, PCB leader Jorge Kolle claimed that the party was the "largest and best organized force in the organized labor movement" (*El Siglo*, Santiago, Chile, 17 March). The proceedings of the Fourteenth Congress of the Mineworkers' Federation of Bolivia (Federación Sindical de Trabajadores Mineros de Bolivia; FSTMB), in April, and of the Fourth National Workers' Congress of the Bolivian Workers' Center (Central Obrera Boliviana; COB), in May indicated that the party's role was less important. The top position in both the FSTMB and the COB was taken by Juan Lechín Oquendo, a former vice-president of Bolivia, now a leader of the Revolutionary Party of the Nationalist Left (Partido Revolutionario de Izquierda Nacionalista; PRIN). Simón Reyes was the only PCB member to win high office in the FSTMB, and the party obtained no important post in the COB. The PCB had virtually no influence in the countryside where, according to Luis Padilla, "the peasant movement remains fragmented" (*WMR*, August).

Party Internal Affairs. The intense internal conflict which weakened the PCB during the late 1960's (see *YICA*, 1970, pp. 247-48) seemed to decrease considerably during 1970. Jorge Kolle stated early in the year that "the worst of the crisis" had been overcome and that the PCB was passing through a "period of recovery" (*El Siglo*, 17 March). The party celebrated its twentieth anniversary in January. The Eighth National Conference of the PCB was held in August, and a Central Committee plenum in the latter half of November. Throughout the year reference was made to the party's forthcoming Third Congress, for which no date was specified.

Domestic Attitudes and Activities. The PCB analysis of the situation in Bolivia shifted somewhat during 1970 as the national leadership changed. Early in the year Jorge Kolle stated that the Ovando government was "bourgeois-reformist and to a certain degree anti-imperialist," and the PCB gave its support to all measures that it considered "patriotic, liberating, and anti-imperialist" (*El Siglo*, 17 March). Luis Padilla concluded that the Ovando government had "undoubtedly put some curbs on the unhindered intervention by imperialism in the country's internal affairs" by terminating or regulating the activities of U.S. investors, and by establishing diplomatic and trade relations with the Soviet Union, Romania, Poland, and Czechoslovakia (*WMR*, August). At the same time, the PCB was critical of many government policies and repeatedly warned the Bolivian people not to expect "fundamental" change from a bourgeois-democratic government. The party castigated Ovando for his removal of leftist ministers and military personnel from the government in May and July.

The PCB was more positive still in its interpretation of the Torres government, which came to power in October. At the Central Committee plenum in November the PCB reported that "the present situation was characterized by greater activity of the working people" (*IB*, no. 23-24, 1970).

Throughout the year the party called for the "incorporation of new and broader forces into the anti-imperialist and anti-oligarchic struggle" (*Unidad*, 4 February); for a "powerful anti-imperialist popular front" made up of the working class, peasantry, petty-bourgeoisie, "progressive" intelligentsia, and "progressive" sectors of the national bourgeoisie (*WMR*, August); and for the "organizational unification of all progressive forces and, first and foremost, the working people" (*IB*, no. 23-24). Although the party professed to see such unity developing early in the year, the broadest front was in evidence later, immediately following the Torres coup, when the PCB even briefly joined forces with the PCB-ML.

Luis Padilla stressed, however, that the "tasks of the anti-imperialist, democratic revolution" could be "consistently fulfilled" only if the proletariat and the communist party should "secure the *leading* role in this front and overcome the inconsistency and conciliation of the bourgeoisie" (*WMR*, August; emphasis in original). In regard to mobilizing the masses, the resolution of the Eighth National Conference declared: "It is necessary to advance clear, concrete and consistent aims modified in accordance with the level of organization and possibilities of struggle, aims that would win support of the urban and rural proletariat, as well as other strata" (*IB*, no. 17-18).

After the seizure of power by General Torres, the PCB urged all progressive forces to recognize that the "monolithic unity" of the armed forces was "nonexistent": "Behind the apparent unity of the Armed Forces, a struggle is going on between backward and progressive forces, between men who serve their country and those who serve the interests of the Pentagon" (*Unidad*, quoted in *El Popular*, Montevideo, 15 October).

Throughout the year the party alleged that U.S. citizens—in particular, members of the U.S. Central Intelligence Agency—had worked with Bolivian "right-wing" elements in order to preserve remaining U.S. "privileges" and prepare a "counterrevolutionary offensive." The PCB continued its opposition to "ultra-leftists," primarily the ELN, who persisted in the efforts to overthrow the existing government by means of guerrilla warfare. (*Ibid.* and *El Siglo*, 17 and 18 March.)

International Views and Positions. The PCB continued to align itself with the Soviet Union on matters of concern to the international communist movement. In a joint statement with the Peruvian Communist Party, dated 20 January 1970, it restated its approval of the Main Document of the Moscow Conference in June 1969, the address "Centenary of the Birth of Vladimir Ilyich Lenin," and the appeal "Independence, Freedom and Peace for Vietnam." The statement concluded with a call "to preserve the purity of the Marxist-Leninist teaching and to intensify the ideological struggle against all revisionist trends—both from the Right and the Left." (*Unidad*, 4 February, as summarized in *IB*, no. 4, 1970.)

Publications. The PCB organ is *Unidad*, reportedly published weekly during 1970 despite its illegal status since April 1967. The JCB published *Temple*.

*   *   *

The PCB-ML. Although the Communist Party of Bolivia, Marxist-Leninist, was formally established in April 1965, for several years previously pro-Chinese tendencies and even organizations existed among Bolivian communists. In October 1968 a plenum of the pro-Soviet PCB acknowledged that an "appreciable contingent of cadres and militants" had left the party to form the PCB-ML. The secretary general of the PCB-ML is Oscar Zamora Medinacelli, who is also the primary spokesman for the party.

The youth group of the PCB-ML bears the same name as its pro-Soviet counterpart, the JCB. Among its leaders are Roberto Sánchez and Raúl Gonzáles. The group plays an active role in university affairs. On 24 January 1970, in an address about the "roads of revolution" at a student forum in La Paz, Oscar Zamora asserted that "imperialism" and its "Bolivian lackeys" could be eliminated only through armed struggle. In October, Roberto Sánchez was reported to have left the university and assumed leadership of a pro-Chinese guerrilla movement, made up primarily of students, in the Chapare region of the department of Cochabamba (*Le Monde*, Paris, 7 October). At mid-year the PCB-ML had a guerrilla force of about 100, believed to be under the direction of Oscar Zamora, in the Rio Grande region of the department of Santa Cruz. The PCB-ML was active at the congress of the Bolivian Workers' Center in May.

Party Internal Affairs. In mid-1970 the PCB-ML organ *Liberacion* declared: "Parties which do not base their political line upon Marxism-Leninism are vehicles of bourgeois politics and they reduce the proletariat to tailism and the role of an instrument of the bourgeoisie." Thus party statements during the year placed great emphasis on party building, on the need for "iron discipline and democratic centralism," the elimination of "opportunist elements," strict adherence to the "universal truth of Marxism-Leninism," close ties between the party leadership and the "broad masses of the people," and self-reliance (*Peking Review*, 14 August, and Tirana radio, 20 October). Conflicts within the party, revolving in some degree around the leadership of Oscar Zamora were suggested in early 1971 when a rival PCB-ML reportedly was set up by Jorge Echazu Alvarado (*El Diario, La Paz*, 9 February).

Domestic Attitudes and Activities. According to Oscar Zamora, the "struggle of the Bolivian people" is "anti-imperialist and anti-feudal," and its immediate "principal objective" is a "national democratic" revolution. This was "aimed at the final liquidation of exploitation and imperialist domination and the freeing of the peasantry from semi-feudal exploitation." PCB-ML strategy calls for a "broad front" led by the working class, on the grounds that "there can be no alliance of classes without a well-defined vanguard and without a class capable of leading and giving the revolutionary process political and ideological content." The principal allies of the working class, in the party's view, are the poor and semi-poor peasants, followed by the urban petty-bourgeoisie, although "progressive" segments of the "national bourgeoisie" and the "peasant bourgeoisie" may participate under working-class leadership. Identified as the chief enemies are the "U.S. imperialists" and their domestic agents, the "business bourgeoisie," the "bureaucratic bourgeoisie," and the "latifundist bourgeoisie." (*Rruga e Partisë*, Tirana, September 1970.)

According to Zamora, the military government of General Ovando was "progressive and reformist in appearance," but "reactionary and pro-imperialist in content," and it held power by means of an army that was "directed by the Pentagon." In these conditions, he said, parliamentary methods—"an expression of bourgeois and revisionist pacification"—were ineffective. Instead, a "political war with class objectives," a revolutionary struggle by a "popular army," which would develop into a "war of the broad masses against the oppressors," was required. After the defeat of the imperialists and the semi-feudal remnants, a "popular democratic and anti-imperialist" government would carry out a revolutionary program and build socialism. (*Ibid.*)

International Views and Positions. During 1970 the PCB-ML condemned "U.S. imperialism and Soviet revisionist social-imperialism" and asserted that "all imperialists, revisionists and reactionaries tremble like rats" before the Chinese People's Republic (*Peking Review*, 29 May).

Publications. The organ of the PCB-ML Central Committee is *Liberación*. Party statements are also found in the *Peking Review*.

*   *   *

The ELN. The National Liberation Army, formed late in 1966, came into wide publicity during 1967 under the leadership of Che Guevara. In October of that year Guevara and all but five members of the group were killed by Bolivian military forces. The rebuilding of the ELN was carried out by Guido "Inti" Peredo, one of the survivors, until his death in September 1969. Leadership of the group was then held by Osvaldo "Chato" Peredo until his capture on 12 October 1970, and subsequently by Jorge Ruíz Paz, known as "Omar." [2]

The ELN is avowedly an international organization, incorporating within its ranks guerrillas from Bolivia, Brazil, Argentina, Colombia, Peru, Chile, and perhaps other countries (*Punto Final*, 4 August, documents). Shortly after mid-1970, "Chato" Peredo made public a letter he had written to the Uruguayan Tupamaros (an urban guerrilla organization; see *Uruguay*) expressing the ELN's thanks for "cooperation" and "aid" which had made possible an "accelerated return to the mountains" (*ibid.*, 18 August). In an open letter entitled "To the Latin American People," the foreign members of the ELN said that the Bolivian struggle was another "Vietnam," and added: "[It will spread to] all corners of our American land where Yankee and oligarchic clutches are present" (*ibid.*, 4 August, documents).

According to an official ELN statement, the Bolivian struggle was "essentially anti-imperialist" and on a continental scale, and this accounted at least in part for the high percentage of foreigners participating. Arguing that Bolivia was the "weakest link in imperialism's chain in this part of the hemisphere," the statement called for an armed struggle which would cause "Yankee imperialism and its army" to intervene in Bolivia and thus bring on the "decisive stage of the National Liberation." (*Ibid.*)

Moreover, the ELN asserted, existing conditions called for a "political organization with a fundamentally military structure," based on the guerrilla center or *foco*. The ELN described itself as the "revolutionary instrument" that would "in the end permit the taking of power for the people by means of armed struggle, the only road possible for the Socialist Revolution." (*Ibid.*) A communiqué from ELN "General Headquarters" elaborated:

> The capacity of the popular masses to take power cannot arise overnight, as if by magic, nor can it be the fruit of spontaneity, as many of those who favor a putsch would believe. Our organization maintains that the only way to achieve this in the present historical circumstances is to begin a prolonged revolutionary war, in which the fighting vanguard, through its example, makes possible the growing awareness and incorporation into the struggle of ever-broader sectors of the popular masses. (*Granma*, English, Havana, 18 October; see also *ibid.*, 1 November.)

The ELN called for the rejection of "opportunists" from the established leftist parties and of "corrupt labor-union bureaucrats" (*Punto Final*, 4 August, documents).

The ELN rejected the "pseudo-revolutionary gorilla" government of General Ovando and, in a

---

[2] "Inti" and "Chato" Peredo and their brother Roberto "Coco" Peredo (killed with Guevara in 1967) were for many years members of the PCB.

communiqué released on 10 October, declared that it did not think the Torres government would bring about "genuine change in structures," explaining: "While there can be revolutionary officers, the Armed Forces as a whole are not revolutionary" (*Granma*, English, 18 October).

The ELN, after a period of inactivity following its setbacks of 1969, resumed operations in July 1970 with 50 to 100 men in the Teoponte region about a hundred miles north of La Paz. Its first widely publicized exploit was the kidnaping of two West German technicians (ultimately released in exchange for ten imprisoned guerrillas). The ELN was joined almost immediately by a number of university student leaders, including former members of the pro-Soviet JCB. Within three months it had suffered almost complete defeat, due as much to problems among the guerrillas themselves as to clashes with the army. Nevertheless, when "Chato" Peredo was captured, a reporter for the Cuban news agency Prensa Latina commented: "Peredo's arrest should be considered no more than a setback in a long battle" (*ibid.*). From exile in Chile, Peredo claimed in an interview at the end of the year that the ELN organization had been strengthened in the cities, particularly among young people, and that its struggle would go on (*Punto Final*, 8 December.)

*   *   *

The POR. The Revolutionary Workers' Party remained divided into three factions during 1970. The first, under Hugo González Moscoso, was aligned with the Trotskyist Fourth International—United Secretariat. Its evaluation of the Bolivian situation as the year began was contained in a resolution, passed at a clandestine meeting at the end of 1969, which asserted that Bolivian "backwardness and underdevelopment" could be overcome only by a "socialist revolution led by a revolutionary army of national and social liberation arising out of guerrilla warfare." In its view, the "fundamental task for Marxist-Leninist revolutionaries" was to "*mobilize the masses in a revolutionary struggle for the seizure of power* in conjunction with, and under the leadership of, the revolutionary army!" The course to be followed in Bolivia was "that of the vicvictorious Cuban revolution!" (*Intercontinental Press*, New York, 13 April, emphasis in original.) In a statement to the Mineworkers' Federation in April, the POR Executive Committee proclaimed: "The present [Ovando] government is the government of moribund imperialist capitalism which has assumed a 'revolutionary' mask to save itself" (*ibid.*, 11 May). A similar stand was taken toward the Torres government at the end of the year (*ibid.*, 23 November). The POR repeatedly called for popular support of the ELN, and many of its members reportedly joined the guerrillas in the countryside. The organ of this POR faction is *Lucha Obrera.*

The second faction, headed by a well-known political figure and historian of the Bolivian labor movement, Guillermo Lora, had contacts with the Fourth International—International Committee. This faction believed that the Ovando government was carrying out some "positive" though "inadequate" policies. Defending the "central role of the working class and its party," this faction carried out a "consistent struggle" against "guerrillaism" and the "liquidation of the party into petty bourgeois and bourgeois political formations" (*Bulletin*, New York, 26 January 1970). During 1970 these two POR factions continued their dispute, begun the previous year in international Trotskyist organs, over ideological orthodoxy, attitudes toward the Ovando government, and support for guerrilla warfare (in particular the role of González Moscoso). The organ of this second faction is *Masas*.

The third faction, the POR-Trotskyista (PORT), is aligned with the Fourth International—International Secretariat (Posadas branch). It is led by Amadeo Vargas. In its view, a "nationalist revolutionary process" had begun under the Ovando government—a stage which it considered "almost inescapable" in the "revolutionary process in Latin America." According to this third faction, the theses adopted in April by the Mineworkers' Federation and approved in May by the

Bolivian Workers' Center, expressed the "fundamental slogans of the Fourth International [and] Posadas for the process" Latin America [was] living at this stage." (*Red Flag*, London, 25 May.) In July, Vargas was critical of the removal of liberal cabinet ministers and military leaders from positions of power in the Ovando government.

W. E. R.

BRAZIL

The original Communist Party of Brazil (Partido Comunista do Brasil) was founded in March 1922. In 1960, in an effort to give the party a more national character, the name was changed to the Brazilian Communist Party (Partido Comunista Brasileiro; PCB). In 1961 a pro-Chinese faction broke away from the traditionally pro-Soviet PCB, forming a new party in February 1962, the Communist Party of Brazil (Partido Comunista do Brasil; PCdoB). Since 1968 dissidence within the PCB ranks (one-third of its Central Committee was reportedly affected) has led to the formation of several splinter groups, predominantly of Castroite tendency, that strongly advocate subversive activities. Important among these groups are: the Revolutionary Vanguard Party (Vanguarda Popular Revolucionária; VPR), the National Liberation Action (Ação Libertadora Nacional; ALN), the Revolutionary Brazilian Communist Party (Partido Comunista Brasileiro Revolucionário; PCBR), and the Revolutionary Movement 8 (MR-8).

The communist movement has been illegal in Brazil throughout most of its existence. Although outlawed in 1947, the PCB was allowed to function and its members ran in elections under the label of other parties. During the presidency of João Goulart (1961-64) the PCB succeeded in infiltrating and controlling important labor, student, political, and bureaucratic groups. The military regime which came into power after the March 1964 coup d'état drove the party underground and banned the existing communist-influenced organizations. The military government then abolished all existing political parties, but subsequently two new parties were sanctioned: ARENA (Aliança Renovadora Nacional) and MDB (Movimento Democrático Brasileiro)! In September 1969, in an attempt to curb terrorist activities, the government issued laws providing the death penalty for subversive acts.

Estimates of recent PCB membership have dropped from 40,000 in 1964 to between 15,000 and 20,000 in 1970. Members of the pro-Chinese PCdoB are believed to number about 750. The Castroite and other groups have a membership estimated between 1,000 and 5,000. The population of Brazil is 93,305,000 (estimated 1970).

The PCB. Organization and Leadership. The PCB apparatus includes the Central Committee, various state committees, and local cells. Little is known of the party's internal affairs. The latest PCB congress (the sixth) took place in December 1967.

The PCB secretary-general is Luís Carlos Prestes. Other prominent leaders are Oto José Santos, Armando Ziller, Giocondo Días, Lucas Romão, Alfredo Castro, J. B. Tavares de Sá, Augusto Bento, Iracama Ribeiro, Olga Maranhão, Jorge Villa, Sabino Bahia, Felipe Rodrígues, María Segovia, Abel Chermont, Luís Tenório de Lima, Gentil Correa, Firmino de Lima, Marcel Braz, Luís Menesse, Valerio Konder, and Gregorio Bezerra.

The PCB formerly derived considerable support from the National Union of Students (União

---

¹Since December 1968, through Institutional Act 5, the president has assumed power to rule by decree.

Nacional dos Estudantes; UNE) and the Workers' General Command (Comando Geral dos Trabalhadores; CGT), both of which were abolished after 1964. The UNE, one of the few remaining sources of unqualified support of the PCB until 1967, was disbanded by the government in October 1968 when its most important leaders were arrested during the clandestinely convened Thirtieth National Conference of the UNE.

Domestic Attitudes and Activities. The PCB is an orthodox pro-Soviet party which upholds the role of the masses in obtaining power and opposes many of the subversive activities advocated by Castroite elements. In an article commemorating the party's forty-eighth anniversary, the PCB organ (*A Voz Operária*, February 1970), reiterated this position, stating that "it is the masses that carry out the revolution," and that the party, "sure of having elaborated a political line in keeping with the national situation," was "striving to have the masses learn and accept this line by means of agitation, propaganda, and action by the masses themselves."

The PCB holds that its primary objective under present Brazilian conditions is to "fight for democratic liberties, in particular for the right to strike and union freedom, but also for the freedom of the press and the right of assembly." To achieve this aim, the PCB seeks to create a "vast national movement," that is, a united front. (*IB*, nos. 15-16, September 1970, quoting a PCB Central Committee statement issued in April.)

During 1970 as in previous years, the PCB continued to call, without success, for the formation of a united front that would include "nationalist and democratic" elements, and also Catholics and members of the armed forces, to fight against the Brazilian military regime.

The above-mentioned statement of the PCB Central Committee indicated that the party planned to participate in the federal and state elections—scheduled for November—by supporting the MDB's platform, which demanded the abolishment of Institutional Act 5 granting the president full powers to rule by decree, the reestablishment of habeas corpus, and the defense of individual rights. By taking part in the elections, the PCB admittedly was not seeking to elect a pro-communist candidate but merely to utilize the electoral campaign to criticize the government: "We must not expect big political gains in these elections but we should not underestimate their usefulness, for they provide the masses with an opportunity to express their will, and extend the possibilities of developing new factors of resistance to the dictatorship" (*ibid.*). No significant PCB gains were discernible following the elections.

The PCB maintained its vigorous condemnation of guerrilla warfare actions in Brazil, which Prestes termed "the disease of petty-bourgeois revolutionary doctrine." In an article in the November issue of *World Marxist Review* he asserted that "guerrilla struggle must be defined in accordance with class strength and the actual potential of a mass movement at a given time," and indicated that as long as conditions were not favorable for new revolutionary methods, the PCB would continue its "modest, onerous, and painstaking" tasks of organization and propaganda. Prestes attributed the emergence of "ultra-left" groups to the "impatience" of some communists and their failure to understand "the need to retreat" after the 1964 coup destroyed all PCB mass fronts. He also spoke of a willingness for a dialogue with "Left intellectuals and young people," but made it clear that the PCB would "under no circumstances acquiesce in the erroneous and damaging conceptions of petty-bourgeois 'revolutionism.' " (*Ibid.*)

A reconciliation between the PCB and the more militant Castroite groups continued to be most unlikely. In September 1969 the ALN and the VPR made an implicit attempt to achieve unity by obtaining the release of Gregorio Bezerra, a PCB Central Committee member, who was among the 15 prisoners exchanged for kidnaped U.S. Ambassador Charles Burke Elbrick. But Bezerra himself declared in an interview:

I must say that even though I agreed to be liberated under the circumstances, I do not approve of isolated acts that do not further the revolutionary process and may, on the contrary, serve as a pretext for making the conditions of the Brazilian people still worse. . . . It is necessary to fight for principles, against regimes of force, and not against persons taken as individuals.

Bezerra also declared that "Marxist-Leninist principles of action" should be followed in the struggle and that this involved the union of the "working class, peasants, organized forces of the urban petty bourgeoisie, students, intellectuals, sections of the national bourgeoisie, and progressive elements of the army and the Catholic church." (*L'Humanité*, Paris, 6 March 1970.)

International Views and Positions. The PCB maintains a strong pro-Soviet and anti-Chinese position. This stand was reiterated during 1970 in the Prestes article in *World Marxist Review* noted above. In it, Prestes condemned the "divisive policy of the Chinese Communist Party leaders" who were bent on "discrediting the Soviet Union" and distorting "proletariat revolutionary theory."

The PCB continued to support Cuba. Its Central Committee statement asserted that the Cuban example was "winning recognition among Latin American peoples as an indication that these peoples must free themselves from imperialist domination and build a socialist society" (*IB*, 8 September). The PCB, however, carefully made a distinction between the Cuban experience and the actions carried on by the subversive groups in Brazil by saying: "The history of the Cuban revolution, not always known and often distorted in Brazil, is . . . exploited by certain elements to justify voluntarist and adventuristic theories of the revolutionary process" (*WMR*, November).

Publications. The PCB publishes an irregular clandestine newspaper, *A Voz Operária*, circulated primarily among party members. To reach wider audiences for important statements and appeals, the party distributes clandestine leaflets.

*   *   *

The PCdoB. The pro-Chinese Communist Party of Brazil, as noted earlier, has perhaps 750 members.

Organization and Leadership. Little is known of the organizational structure of the PCdoB. Leading figures are believed to be founding members Mauricio Grabois and João Amazonas. Other important members include Benedito de Carvalho, Guido Enders, Manoel Ferreira, Calil Chade, Walter Martins, Lincoln Oeste, Alcira Grabois, Ari Gonçalves, and Tarzan de Castro. The last named, who at one time organized guerrilla groups in the state of Goias and who had been living in Uruguay after the 1964 military coup, was arrested by the Brazilian police in 1971. According to *Manchete* (Rio de Janeiro, 20 February 1971), it was believed that he had established connections with the Tupamaro movement in Uruguay.

Domestic Attitudes and Activities. The PCdoB holds that "the only road for the liberation of the Brazilian people is the road of a people's war," to be taken primarily "in the countryside with the broad masses of peasants as its mainstay." Struggles of various other forms would be implemented in the cities, with the participation of workers, students, and other forces, but "in close combination with the armed action in the interior." (PCdoB Central Committee statement, reported by NCNA, 1 March 1970.)

Early in the year, the PCdoB issued an appeal for party members to go to the rural areas and work there to raise the "political consciousness of the peasants" (*ibid.*). In a subsequent Central Committee statement issued in July (*ibid.*, 23 August) the PCdoB claimed that the party had "made progress" among the peasantry and that it was "shifting the gravity center of its activities to the countryside." This assertion was then followed by an obvious criticism of the party members' behavior:

> The Central Committee has time and again emphasized the policy that the communists must organize and unfold revolutionary activities. The Central Committee once again calls on all the members of the party to pay attention to the following facts: they belong to a party which is the tool of the revolution and whose existence is chiefly for leading the masses of the people to the revolutionary stand. At all times a member of the communist party should set an example and act like a revolutionary.

Other activities of the pro-Chinese party concentrated on attacking both the PCB and the other revolutionary Marxist groups of Brazil.

The party organ, *A Classe Operária* (January), in an article entitled "Nationalism and Demagogy," condemned the PCB for having proposed intervention by "nationalist military men" to solve the country's allegedly serious political and economic situation. Terming the PCB's suggestion "a solution in the Peruvian style, applied under Brazil's specific conditions," the pro-Chinese party rejected it in the strongest manner: "If Brazil were to proceed in that direction, the clique of reactionary generals who are now in power would be replaced by another group of military men, similarly reactionary, who would feign patriotism and create the most dissolute kind of anti-American demagogy." The article concluded that the people must wage an "all-out war against the dictatorship" and must not be deceived by "reformists and nationalists."

The PCdoB continued its criticisms of actions by Castroite organizations, which it labeled "petty-bourgeois groups." The party stated that it was not opposed to "revolutionary initiative" (when utilized to mobilize and organize the masses), but it rejected the actions carried on by "some small groups" who were "isolated from the people" and who denied "the necessity of a working-class party." (NCNA, 11 March.)

International Views and Positions. The PCdoB is unequivocally pro-Chinese. A Central Committee statement, congratulating the Chinese People's Republic on launching its first man-made earth satellite, reiterated the party's "boundless faith in the revolutionary capacity of the Chinese people and in the wise leadership of Comrade Mao Tse-tung" (*Peking Review*, 29 May).

In July, a Chinese report stated that *A Classe Operária* had carried an article denouncing Soviet revisionism and, in particular, the theory of peaceful transition or the parliamentary road to socialism. The article was quoted as saying that the Soviets had "distorted, negated, and opposed the universal law of violent revolution" and were fearful of the "road of people's war as if it were a specter." The report also stated that the PCdoB Central Committee resolution adopted in July (see above) had accused the Soviet Union of "intensifying its domination" of Eastern Europe and of rendering assistance to "reactionary forces" in various Latin American countries. (NCNA, 26 July.)

The pro-Chinese party was critical of the pro-Soviet Peruvian Communist Party for supporting the new military government in Peru, which according to the PCdoB was merely posing as being "anti-Yankee." In the Peruvian case, the pro-Chinese group also attacked the Soviet Union for supporting President Juan Velasco Alvarado's government, asserting that "like any imperialist vulture," the Soviet Union had begun to "track down new markets and sources of raw materials." Likewise, the PCdoB condemned Fidel Castro, who, "with his typical hastiness and incoherence [had] crowned [President Velasco] as anti-imperialist and expressed heartfelt praise for him." (*A Classe Operária*, January 1970.)

Publications. The PCdoB publishes an irregular clandestine newspaper, *A Classe Operária*.

*   *   *

Castroite Organizations. Like some other Latin American countries, Brazil has seen the emergence of various small subversive groups which hold communist and nationalistic views and advocate "armed struggle" tactics as a means to establish a socialist system. Important among these groups are the VPR, the ALN, the PCBR, and the MR-8.

These predominantly Castroite groups function at regional and local levels, since they are not organized on a national basis. During 1970 there was an attempt to achieve unity of all the subversive groups; this was evident both in joint actions carried on by these groups and in their demands for the release of political prisoners belonging to different leftist groups (see below).

Estimates of their membership range from 1,000 to 5,000. Support is drawn mainly from students, workers, former soldiers, and to a much lesser degree, elements of the Catholic church. According to government sources, the proportion of students involved in subversive activities in high (estimates range from 35 to 56 per cent) and the average militant's age is twenty-three years.

These revolutionary groups receive verbal and possibly material support from Cuba. Through kidnapings of diplomatic representatives they have been able to obtain the release of a sizable number of comrades (115 in 1970), several of whom are now in Havana.

In addition to Carlos Marighella's death in 1969 (see *YICA*, 1970, p. 357), the Brazilian revolutionary movement suffered the loss of another major leader, Joaquim Camara Ferreira, in 1970. The level of subversive activities, however, did not decrease. Official sources revealed that from 1 January to 19 May 1970, in the state of São Paulo alone, more than 60 robberies of banks and business firms (involving about $410,000) took place. Besides, revolutionary leaders have acknowledged that political kidnapings will continue since they are "the only way of liberating" their fellow members. On the other hand, there has been no indication of increased popular support for these groups.

The most prominent guerrilla leader at present is Carlos Lamarca, a former army captain. Unlike Marighella and Ferreira, who were former members of the PCB, Lamarca does not have a history of membership in an orthodox communist party.

The VPR. Considered the largest and most active group, the Revolutionary Vanguard Party is led by Carlos Lamarca. Its membership is said to derive from a small left-wing organization of former army officers (the National Revolutionary Movement) as well as from PCB and PCdoB dissidents.

In July 1969 the VPR merged with another group, COLINA, to form a new organization called the VAR-Palmares (see *YICA*, 1970, p. 358). A split occurred two months later, as Lamarca's faction—which later adopted the name of the VPR—advocated the immediate formation of rural guerrillas, while the other group—which kept the name VAR-Palmares—favored political work to develop a "revolutionary conscience" among the masses.

The VPR is said to have its headquarters in the state of Guanabara and to have six regional commands, based in the states of São Paulo, Minas Gerais, Rio Grande do Sul, and Brasilia.

VPR activities during 1970 included three successful kidnapings of diplomatic representatives. On 11 March the VPR's "A. Raimundo de Lucena Commando" (named after Lamarca's "right hand," killed by police forces on 20 February) kidnaped the Japanese consul general in São

Paulo, Nobuo Oguchi, and forced the release of five political prisoners who went to Mexico and later to Cuba. On 11 June the West German ambassador, Ehrenfried von Holleben, was kidnaped jointly by the VPR's "Juarez Guimaraes de Brito Commando" (named after a top VPR ideologist killed in May) and the ALN. This time, the revolutionary groups obtained the release of 40 prisoners, including VPR, ALN, MR-8, COLINA, and PCBR members, who were flown to Algeria. As part of the kidnapers' demands, the Brazilian government published their manifesto. This declared that the revolutionaries sought a "people's revolutionary war" which "must be stepped up in the big urban centers and extended to the rural areas." Their objectives, as set forth in the manifesto, were:

> To overthrow the dictatorship and replace it with a popular government; to revoke all acts and decrees of the dictatorship; to promote land reform by expropriating large landholdings; to guarantee the widest freedom of organization and expression for the Brazilian people, assure the right to life and culture for all, and respect every Brazilian's individual rights strictly; and to pursue an independent foreign policy in defense of Brazil's national interests and in solidarity with the anti-imperialist struggles of all peoples. (*O Estado do São Paulo*, São Paulo, 13 June.)

The third kidnaping involved Swiss Ambassador Enrico Bucher. He was abducted on 7 December by the VPR's "Juarez Guimaraes de Brito Commando," which mounted the operation "to remind the people of Camara Ferreira" (see below). Bucher was freed after 40 days in exchange for 70 political prisoners, who were flown to Chile. The released prisoners, who belonged to the VPR, ALN, PCB, and some smaller revolutionary groups, were mostly students but among them there were also newspapermen, businessmen, and former army officers and soldiers.

On 21 April-31 May the Brazilian government carried out an intensive anti-guerrilla campaign in the Ribeira Valley, a jungle area about 120 miles south of the city of São Paulo. Army authorities announced the arrest of numerous guerrilla members and the destruction of three guerrilla training camps. Lamarca, who was in charge of the guerrillas in Ribeira Valley, denied the government's claim and held that his forces had successfully escaped the army encirclement. Lamarca declared also that the government made use of 20,000 men, together with airplanes, helicopters, and napalm bombs, while the government mentioned only the use of 2,000 soldiers.

In regard to the Ribeira Valley experience, Lamarca was quoted as having said that it had "great political value" for the revolutionaries and that it had strengthened their "determination to launch a guerrilla war in the rural regions" (document signed by Lamarca and released in Algeria, quoted in *Le Monde*, Paris, 17 July, and *Ultima Hora*, Santiago, Chile, 6 December).

Lamarca was also quoted as saying that the "comrades trained abroad" were not prepared for rural guerrilla warfare under Brazilian conditions and that they preferred to remain in the cities (*ibid.*). This comment brought speculation that Brazilian guerrillas might be undergoing training in Cuba and that differences of opinion on tactics (i.e., urban vis-à-vis rural guerrilla methods) had not been solved within the revolutionary groups. Lamarca has been described as "more capable and intelligent" than Camara Ferreira and "more cautious and elusive" than Marighella (*Manchete*, 28 March). On the other hand, he is considered a man of action and one unlikely to unite the guerrilla groups.

The VAR-Palmares was severely weakened in 1970. Important members were captured in January, and on 12 August its São Paulo regional leader, Franklin Paixo de Araujo, was arrested. Subsequent police investigations led to large arrests of VAR-Palmares militants. Government authorities claimed to have thwarted a plan this group had for undertaking rural guerrilla operations. Reportedly, the VAR-Palmares had bought 77 square miles of land in the Imperatriz region of the state of Maranhão, which had been chosen as the "main area of struggle." (*O Estado de São Paulo*, 17 October.)

The ALN. The National Liberation Action is the second-largest Castroite group. It was founded, possibly in February 1968, by dissident PCB members who became disappointed with the nonviolent "conventional models and methods" of the pro-Soviet party and decided to adopt the tactics of urban and rural guerrilla warfare associated with Castroism.

The group has suffered from the loss of its leaders Carlos Marighella and Joaquim Camara Ferreira. The latter died on 23 October 1970 during a confrontation with police forces. Authorities attributed Ferreira's death to a heart attack; the Brazilian revolutionary groups held he died after twenty-four hours of torture.

The ALN, which has a more specific ideology than the other subversive groups, believes that "the supreme duty of every revolutionary is to make the revolution." It regards the proletariat as "conformist" and "conciliatory"; hence it advocates the fusion of military and political concepts to create a "revolutionary organization." Unlike the VPR, the ALN gives priority to urban guerrilla warfare, although it regards rural guerrilla as the principal element in the establishment of an army of national liberation.

In an article published in *Granma Weekly Review* (Havana, 4 January 1970), Ferreira announced that urban guerrilla actions in Brazil would be continued and broadened until the whole urban area of the country was affected. He also said that the struggle should be spread to the countryside, which, in his opinion, constituted the backbone of guerrilla revolution.

The Cuban government has given special support to the ALN. *Pensamiento Crítico*, a Cuban ideological journal, devoted 106 of 272 pages in its February 1970 issue to Marighella. It asserted that he had "understood the meaning of the open stage [presumably, a period when revolutionary propaganda is employed to mobilize the masses] with the triumph of the Cuban Revolution and the road of the Brazilian revolution: armed struggle." In addition, *Tricontinental* (Havana), the theoretical organ of the Afro-Asian-Latin American Peoples' Solidarity Organization, printed in its January-February issue Marighella's *Mini-Manual of the Urban Guerrilla*, which by April was being distributed clandestinely in Brazil. The *Mini-Manual*, a tactical handbook for guerrillas, was also reprinted in the *Tricontinental Bulletin* (Havana, November) to commemorate the first anniversary of Marighella's death.

Shortly before his own death, Ferreira stated that unity of all revolutionary groups was possible, although he recognized "minor differences" on struggle tactics and organization between the VPR, the ALN, the MR-8, and the Tiradentes Revolutionary Movement—the latter a new group about which little is known (*Punto Final*, Santiago, Chile, 24 November). An example of guerrilla unity was provided by a manifesto on the 15 November elections issued by the above-mentioned groups. The manifesto attacked the two officially sanctioned political parties, calling the Aliança Renovadora Nacional the "government party" and the Movimento Democrático Brasileiro "an empty opposition party." The manifesto urged the people to annul their votes by writing a protest phrase on the ballot, and called for the formation of denunciation committees of the "electoral farce" throughout the country. The extent of public response to the appeal made by these revolutionary groups could not be ascertained.

The PCBR. The Revolutionary Brazilian Communist Party was founded in April 1968 by Mário Alves de Souza Vieira, Jacobo Gorender, and Apolonio Pinto de Carvalho, all of whom were expelled from the PCB in 1967.

The joint ALN-VPR manifesto at the time of the kidnaping of the West German ambassador declared that Alves de Souza Vieira had been killed while in prison. Apolonio Pinto de Carvalho, who had also been in prison, was among the prisoners exchanged for the ambassador and is now in Algeria.

In an article near the end of the year (*Punto Final*, 8 December), Apolonio Pinto de Carvalho defined the PCBR as a Marxist-Leninist party which endeavors to assimilate the characteristics of a political-military organization that sees armed struggle as the principal form of class struggle." Carvalho claimed that in combining the mobilization of the masses with armed struggle, the PCBR had developed the so-called Independent Mass Organizations—autonomous groups allegedly active in the labor movement, universities and high schools, and sugar refineries. Carvalho described the actions of the Independent Mass Organizations as "modest," although he stated that they were active in the "continual and partly planned fires at sugar cane plantations," especially those in Pernambuco, where the PCBR Central Committee reportedly is based. On the question of unity, Carvalho declared that the PCBR was willing to unite with other revolutionary groups.

On 26 July the *Diario de Pernambuco* reported that a PCBR group had attempted to kidnap the U.S. consul for Northeast Brazil. It stated also that the PCBR's main leaders were in Cuba, that Cuba had given financial backing to the movement, and that the PCBR sought to "unleash agitation in rural areas, instructing peasants in the practice of guerrilla warfare."

The MR-8. The Revolutionary Movement 8 derives its name from the date of the capture of Che Guevara in Bolivia on 8 October 1967. It is said to be a small but active group, with headquarters in Rio Grande do Sul. Like the VPR and the ALN, the MR-8 advocates armed struggle, which it seeks to develop simultaneously in the cities and the countryside.

The MR-8 suffered large arrests during 1969 and Brazilian authorities believe that the group has been disbanded. Jorge Medeiros do Vale, a banker accused in 1969 of having given $158,000 to the PCBR and $105,000 to the MR-8, was subsequently described as an MR-8 leader. Sentenced to a ten-year prison term in August 1970, Medeiros do Vale was released in January 1971 in the exchange of prisoners for the kidnaped Swiss ambassador.

N. S.

CHILE

The Communist Party of Chile (Partido Comunista de Chile; PCCh) was a direct outgrowth of the Socialist Workers' Party (Partido Obrero Socialista), founded in 1912 by Luis Emilio Recabarren. The name Communist Party of Chile was adopted in January 1922, following the party's decision in 1921 to join the Communist International. The PCCh was illegal from 1949 to 1958. It is firmly pro-Soviet.

A pro-Chinese party, the Revolutionary Communist Party of Chile (Partido Comunista Revolucionario de Chile; PCRCh), was established in May 1966, primarily as an outgrowth of the "Spartacus" group of communists which the PCCh expelled in late 1963. The Revolutionary Workers' Party—Trotskyist (Partido Obrero Revolucionario—Trotskista; PORT) was the only independent Trotskyist party in Chile in 1970. A Castroite organization, the Movement of the Revolutionary Left (Movimiento de Izquierda Revolucionaria; MIR), brought together several leftist groups in 1965.

Estimates of PCCh membership in 1970 ranged from 50,000 (*New York Times*, 23 September) to 60,000 (*ibid., Magazine*, 1 November) and 70,000 (*New Times*, Moscow, 23 September). According to the political report of the party's Fourteenth Congress, in November 1969, workers comprised 67.6 per cent of the membership, peasants 9.5 per cent, and artisans, employees, small merchants, professionals, and intellectuals the remaining 22.9 per cent. The population of Chile is 9,800,000 (estimated 1970).

During 1970 the PCCh participated in the political affairs of the nation, including the September election, primarily through the "Popular Unity" alliance (see below); the PCRCh rejected participation in the "electoral circus," as did the MIR, though the policy of the latter shifted somewhat at the end of the year (see below).

The Popular Unity Alliance. Between 1956 and 1969 the PCCh allied itself for electoral purposes with the Socialist Party (Partido Socialista de Chile; PSCh) in the Popular Action Front (Frente de Acción Popular; FRAP). On numerous occasions in 1969 PCCh leaders argued that leftist unity was necessary in order to transform Chile into a socialist state, but acknowledged that present conditions required an alliance more broadly based than the FRAP. Thus the PCCh played a leading role in founding the Popular Unity (Unidad Popular; UP) coalition at the end of the year. The UP coalition was made up of the PCCh, the PSCh, the Radical Party (Partido Radical; PR), the Social Democratic Party (Partido Social Demócrata; PSD), the Unitary Popular Action Movement (Movimiento de Acción Popular Unitaria; MAPU), a group of dissidents from the ruling Christian Democratic Party (Partido Demócrata Cristiano; PDC) of President Eduardo Frei, and the Independent Popular Alliance (Alianza Popular Independiente; API). The PCCh was the largest, best organized, and most disciplined participant even though the PR, before the recent split in its ranks, had more seats than the communists in the national Senate (9 as against 6) and Chamber of Deputies (24 as against 22).

The "Basic Program of Popular Unity" was signed on 17 December 1969, after a meeting of the seven participating organizations, and was published promptly in the PCCh organ, *El Siglo* (23 December)! This program, which the PCCh adopted as its own immediate program, rejected the "reformism" of the Frei government, pledged to rid the country of the influences of "mono-polistic capitalism" and "imperialist exploitation," and promised to "begin the construction of socialism in Chile." It called for an "assembly of the people" to replace the existing two houses of the Congress and for "democratization" of the political process on all levels. Other objectives included: nationalization of basic resources controlled by foreign capital and domestic monopo-lies, while leaving the vast majority of enterprises entirely or partly under private ownership; ac-celeration of agrarian reform, with special emphasis on the development of peasant cooperatives; and greatly increased state control of social, cultural, and educational programs. The Basic Pro-gram stated that the "popular government" would be "multi-partied" and include all "revolu-tionary" parties, movements, and trends; it would "respect the rights of opposition that is exer-cised within legal bounds."

The foreign policy objectives outlined in the Basic Program include: complete political and economic independence of Chile; maintenance of relations with all countries irrespective of their ideological and political positions; friendship and solidarity with independent or colonial peoples, "especially those developing their struggles for liberation and independence"; and promotion of "strong Latin American and anti-imperialist feelings by means of a people's international poli-cy." The program described Cuba as the "advanced post of the revolution and the construction of socialism on the Latin American continent."

UP members planned to agree on a presidential candidate before the end of December 1969, but were unable to do so. On 22 January 1970, after much bargaining and the withdrawal of indi-vidual party nominees (the PCCh had put up its famous poet and Central Committee member Pablo Neruda), it was announced that Salvador Allende would be the UP candidate. The nomi-nation of Allende, a leader of the PSCh who had been defeated in three previous presidential elec-tions (two at the head of the FRAP ticket, in 1958 and 1964), led to the first of several relatively unimportant rashes of defections from UP ranks.

On 4 September Salvador Allende narrowly defeated National Party (Partido Nacional; PN) candidate Jorge Alessandri and PDC candidate Radomiro Tomic, falling considerably below the absolute majority required for direct election to the presidency? Consequently, in accordance with the Chilean constitution, the final decision was made between the two leading candidates by the Congress. Inasmuch as the UP controlled only 80 of the 200 Congressional seats, support had to be sought among the 75 Christian Democratic congressmen. After extensive discussion be-tween UP and PDC legislators, Allende's agreement to support a constitutional amendment de-signed to guarantee the continuation of a free society in Chile, and Alessandri's withdrawal of his candidacy, the Congress voted for Allende on 24 October by a margin of 153 to 35 (with 12 ab-stentions and blank votes cast). On 30 October the president-elect announced his cabinet, which

---

[1]Also reprinted after the election in *El Siglo* (9 September 1970) and summarized in *Information Bulletin* (no. 12, 1970).
[2]The election results were:

Candidates	Men	Per cent	Women	Per cent	Total	Per cent
			Votes			
Allende	631,863	41.66	443,753	30.69	1,075,616	36.30
Alessandri	479,104	31.59	557,174	38.53	1,036,278	34.98
Tomic	392,736	25.89	432,113	29.88	824,849	27.84

Void and blank ballots came to 0.88 per cent. *Source:* Official results, released by the Ministry of the Interior, pub-lished in *El Siglo* (6 September 1970). Allende's share of the popular vote in earlier elections was 2.54 per cent in 1952, 28.85 per cent in 1958, and 38.93 per cent in 1964.

included three PCCh members in top economic positions: Américo Zorrilla (finance), Pascual Barraza (public works), and José Oyarce (labor). Allende was inaugurated on 3 November.[3]

Many UP electoral activities were carried out through the Committees of the UP (Comités de la Unidad Popular) and the Youth Commands of the UP (Comandos Juveniles de la Unidad Popular). Approximately 80 per cent of the 14,800 Committees of the UP formed during the campaign were controlled by the PCCh. The secretary-general of the Youth Commands of the UP was Omar Córdova, a militant of the PCCh's youth movement.

After the election, the Committees of the UP were directed to consolidate the UP victory and programs. On 21 December President Allende announced the establishment of the General Secretariat of Youth to coordinate the participation of persons under the age of thirty years (60 per cent of the population) in UP programs. The General Secretariat would be made up of six representatives appointed by President Allende on the basis of recommendations from leaders of the Youth Commands of the UP. Early in December Allende signed an agreement with the PCCh-controlled Single Center of Chilean Workers to coordinate labor activities (see below) and on 21 December he announced the formation of the National Peasant Council.

The PCCh. Organization and Leadership. The party's secretary-general is Luis Corvalán. The Political Commission includes Corvalán, Oscar Astudillo, Víctor Díaz, Orlando Millas, José Oyarce, Gladys Marín, Mario Zamorano, Manuel Cantero, Rodrigo Rojas, Carlos Jorquera, Volodia Teitelboim, Jorge Insunza, Bernardo Araya, Julieta Campusano, José Cademártori, and Américo Zorrilla. The Central Committee has 75 members.

The PCCh-affiliated youth movement, established in September 1932, is the Communist Youth of Chile (Juventudes Comunistas de Chile; JCCh). During 1970 the most important JCCh members were Gladys Marín (secretary-general), Omar Córdova (deputy secretary-general), David Canales, José Weibel, Jorge Caceres, Abraham Moskatblit, Juan Orellana, Luis Moya, Pedro Henríquez, Máximo Guerrero, Carlos Cerda, and Alejandro Rojas. The JCCh is estimated to have had approximately 20,000 members at mid-year.

JCCh members were among the most active campaigners for Salvador Allende, working primarily through their recently formed Ramona Parra Brigades (Brigadas Ramona Parra) and the Youth Commands of the UP (see above). Before and after the presidential election they called for the defeat of the "fascist mummies" (Chilean "reactionaries") and "Yankee imperialism" (*El Siglo*, 5 October) and for the rejection of the "ultra-leftists" who opposed the election—above all, the MIR.

The JCCh has played an increasingly active role in the University Student Federations (Federaciones de Estudiantes Universitarios; FEU) in the Chilean universities in recent years. Although some disputes arose during 1970 between members of the JCCh and other UP youth groups (e.g., at the University of Chile in April), the year was characterized mainly by their united action against non-UP groups, whether of the right or the "ultra-left." Whereas in 1964 all nine of the FEU's were controlled by the Christian Democrats, in mid-1970 the UP was dominant in seven. JCCh members were FEU presidents in four universities, including the University of Chile in Santiago. (*Ibid.*, 15 July and 21 October.) According to Alejandro Rojas, the JCCh led the three student union organizations on the secondary school level (*Ujotace*, Montevideo, 3 October, supplement), and Gladys Marín claimed that the JCCh exercised direction over the youth departments of the CUTCh and "Ranquil," the national peasant and Indian confederation which is a member of CUTCh (*El Siglo*, 2 June).

[3]In the 4 April 1971 municipal elections the PSCh won 22.38 per cent of the total vote, its strongest showing in history, and the PCCh 16.97 per cent; the total UP vote was 48.70. The Popular Socialist Union (Unión Socialista Popular), which declared its support for the UP from outside the coalition, raised Allende's support to 49.73 per cent. The PDC remained the strongest single party with 25.62 per cent; the PN drew 18.12 per cent.

JCCh relations with the MIR, which in recent years has dominated student activities at the University of Concepción, were more complex, and ultimately were crucial in altering MIR relations with the PCCh and the UP generally. MIR opposition to electoral participation as a road to socialism, and thus to UP presidential candidate Allende, resulted in open conflict with the JCCh during the campaign and even after the election. On 18 November, however, the small, MIR-dominated Revolutionary Student Front (Frente Estudiantil Revolucionario; FER) at the University of Chile agreed to support the UP slate headed by Alejandro Rojas in elections to office in the student federation at the University of Chile. The FER was given a seat on the Executive Committee of the federation after the UP gained an electoral victory in late November, in return for its support, but failed to get a UP commitment to support the MIR-led slate in the forthcoming elections to the student federation of the University of Concepción. On 2 December, members of the Ramona Parra Brigades clashed with the MIR in Concepción and killed one MIR militant, Arnoldo Rios. President Allende called upon the students to "reestablish a climate of democratic coexistence." This incident of fighting among leftists led to a greater degree of MIR cooperation with the PCCh and the UP than had existed before (see below). The JCCh and MIR agreed to join forces in the student federation election at Concepción, and a slate headed by Nelson Gutiérrez of the MIR was victorious.

The Single Center of Chilean Workers (Central Unica de Trabajadores de Chile; CUTCh), the largest confederation of unions in a country where about 35 per cent of the labor force has been unionized, is controlled by the PCCh. Luis Figueroa, a member of the PCCh Central Committee, was reelected president of the CUTCh at its Fifth Congress in November 1968. The congress expanded the CUTCh Leadership Council (Consejo Directivo)—which had previously been made up entirely of PCCh and PSCh members—to include 3 Christian Democrats, 2 Radicals, and one member of the Popular Socialist Union, along with 14 PCCh and 7 PSCh members, for a total of 27, with Víctor Díaz, of the PCCh Political Commission, as the head. At mid-year the CUTCh represented slightly over 500,000 workers, about 18 per cent of the national labor force.

Although some dissension appeared within CUTCh ranks during the year (e.g., see *Punto Final*, Santiago, 9 June), and the dissidents were denounced as "ultra-leftist" by Figueroa at the November plenary session of the PCCh, the confederation was generally a bulwark of the UP presidential campaign. On 8 July CUTCh called a nationwide strike —allegedly in defense of the people's political rights—which was supported by the student federation at the University of Chile and some other student groups and was claimed by its organizers to have the participation of some 500,000 workers. The CUTCh ordered its members to maintain a "vigilant attitude" before and after the September election in order to prevent, by force if necessary, any "reactionary attempt" to interfere with the electoral process.

According to Figueroa, the UP's "Basic Program of Popular Unity" reflected "80 to 90 per cent of the proposals elaborated by the CUTCh at its fourth and fifth congresses" (*El Siglo*, 9 October). Early in December, President Allende and three cabinet ministers signed an agreement with the CUTCh to guarantee cooperation in establishing wage policy, improving workers' living conditions, and "incorporating the workers into a body responsible for national transformation" (*La Nación*, Santiago, 8 December).

Party Internal Affairs. The PCCh held plenary sessions of its Central Committee on 6-7 February, 7-9 May, 14-15 September, and 26-30 November 1970. The February and May meetings were devoted primarily to the forthcoming presidential election; special attention was given to alleged intrigues by foreign imperialists and domestic reactionaries to prevent the election altogether or at least to assure the defeat of Salvador Allende. The September meeting discussed the electoral victory and the alleged plots to prevent Allende's inauguration. The November meeting set the first task of the PCCh as cooperating in the implementation of the UP program and warned against continued threats from "imperialists" and "reactionaries" (*IB*, no. 23-24, 1970).

Some communists have broken away from the PCCh in recent years; some others have been expelled, including some who are now members of the PCRCh and also the influential editor of the extreme leftist journal *Punto Final*; nevertheless the party seems to have gained in overall strength during 1970. At the Central Committee plenum in May, Volodia Teitelboim acknowledged that many of the new members were politically "immature," that not all of the rank and file participated actively in party affairs, and that some local leaderships were ineffective (*El Siglo*, 11 May).

Domestic Attitudes and Activities. Late in 1969 the PCCh set down its objectives for the present period in the "Political Resolution" of its Fourteenth Congress (published in *El Siglo*, 30 November 1969; abridged in *IB*, no. 1-2, 1970). According to the resolution, the "most revolutionary task in Chile today is to fight for the abolition of imperialism and the power of the monopolist and landed oligarchy," since "socialism will have no perspective unless this task is accomplished." This task was to be achieved through a "solid alliance based on a common program" of all Chilean forces, "rejecting passivity and seeking revolutionary change." The party acknowledged that the different social and political groups in the alliance would not always agree on all things and, thus, insisted on the "complete class independence" of the PCCh as "spokesman of the proletariat" (*IB*, no. 1-2, 1970) and considered the "Basic Program of Popular Unity" as its own immediate program.

An editorial by the PCCh hailed the signing of the "Basic Program" as marking a "new and higher stage in the political development" of Chile (*Principios*, June-September 1970). Another editorial (*ibid.*, February-March) argued that the political picture had changed in Chile, that not since 1938 had such a broad section of political forces and social sectors worked together. Party leaders repeatedly stated that a multi-party government was a special characteristic of the advance toward socialism (e.g., Orlando Millas, *ibid.*, June-September), and even of the consolidation of socialism in Chile (Luis Corvalán, *El Siglo*, 2 December).

Early in the year, José Oyarce wrote that the UP was not "merely an electoral combination, but rather a political alliance that proposes to change the political, economic, and social structure of the country, and to open the way for socialism"; he added that the UP intended to "put into effect a program, the most advanced in the history of the country." (*Principios*, February-March.) This program, according to Luis Corvalán, was meant to "liberate Chile from imperialist domination, to destroy the power centers of the oligarchy, to take the country out of underdevelopment, to build an independent and modern economy, to create a new condition of justice and a more advanced democracy, and to begin the construction of socialism" (*El Siglo*, 2 December).

Before and after the election in September, the PCCh warned against "open and concealed enemies, from the declared reactionaries to those who disguise themselves with ultra-leftist garb." At the end of the year, Corvalán wrote that the people had to be converted into a "truly invincible force" in order to ward off reactionary and imperialist threats: "The people of Chile and their government, on the one hand, and imperialism and the oligarchy, on the other, are entering a period of successive confrontations." He concluded:

> The possibility that the people will be forced into some kind of armed confrontation in the future cannot be discounted. In this connection, the principal task for the present consists in con-

tinuing to isolate the enemies of change, to tie their hands, to put them in straitjackets, in order to spare the country the civil war into which they would like to drag it. (*Ibid.*, 2 December.)[4]

The party was equally critical of "ultra-leftists," especially the MIR. This form of leftism was described in the Political Resolution of the Fourteenth Congress:

> [It] manifests itself as a more or less widespread trend among the new forces and among certain left-wing parties, and is the banner under which anti-Communist groups operate from ultra-revolutionary positions. It expresses itself in revolutionary phrase-mongering, in irresponsible appeals for armed struggle, in the tendency arbitrarily to restrict the range of the proletariat's alliances. (*IB*, no. 1-2, 1970.)

During the electoral campaign the PCCh characterized members of the MIR as "terrorists, adventurers, renegades, and declassed elements" (*WMR*, August) whose tactics played into the hands of the reactionaries; this evaluation did not change significantly in the months immediately following (see, e.g., *El Siglo*, 21 October). After JCCh members killed an MIR militant at the University of Concepción on 2 December (see above), however, most Chilean leftists concluded that their disputes only weakened the cause of "the people," and relations began to improve, at least on the surface for the time being. On 13 December Luis Corvalán stated: "We believe that a kind of understanding is coming between the UP and the MIR, naturally including the communists, since the MIR is closing ranks around the government headed by Comrade Salvador Allende."

According to Corvalán, there were twelve "ultra-leftist" groups in Chile. Among them was the PCRCh, which he described as a tiny "micro-group" which had "no significance in spite of the fact that the four wretches who make it up continue yapping out against the communists." (*Ibid.*, 15 December.)

International Views and Positions. The PCCh is one of the most firmly pro-Soviet parties in Latin America. During 1970, party leaders explained at great length how the life and writings of Lenin and many of the experiences of the Communist Party of the Soviet Union were relevant to contemporary Chile (see, e.g., *El Siglo*, 22 and 23 April).

As in years past, the PCCh placed great emphasis on the need for "anti-imperialist unity" among world revolutionaries. At the same time, Orlando Millas stated, "anti-imperialism" was meaningless unless it was "indissolubly connected to the struggle against opportunism of the right and of the left" (*ibid.*, 7 June). PCCh spokesman José Dickman argued that "interference by one Party in the affairs of another"—which he charged the Chinese Communist Party with practicing in recent years—could not be tolerated. On the other hand, if the "political and ideological course pursued by the leadership of a Party or country" should threaten the well-being of the socialist camp, he maintained that other communist parties had the right and duty to take corrective action as they had done in Czechoslovakia in 1968. (*WMR*, March 1970.)

According to Luis Corvalán, the PCCh experience in the UP alliance showed that "the working class and other forces fighting for socialism may be able to win power and carry out revolutionary changes without necessarily having recourse to arms." He concluded that revolutionaries in each country had to determine what road to power they should follow. (*El Siglo*, 2 December.) Although at the end of the year PCCh leaders stressed the importance of leftist unity to Uru-

---

[4]Corvalán's article was originally published in the December issue of the Soviet-controlled *Problems of Peace and Socialism* (*Revista Internacional* in Spanish; *WMR* in English, where the translation is often not faithful to the original) and, in shortened form, in *Pravda* on 1 December. The reference to "straitjackets" and several other statements drew widespread criticism from non-UP forces in Chile.

guayan communist leaders, Corvalán and others often declined to press the Chilean experience as a model for other countries to follow.

PCCh relations with Cuba were generally friendly during 1970, in particular after Fidel Castro openly endorsed Salvador Allende's candidacy in August. The party repeatedly leveled attacks at the United States ranging from condemnation of its "barbarous and brutal aggression" in Vietnam and Cambodia to allegations of interference in Chilean domestic affairs.

International Party Contacts. Orlando Millas led a delegation to the Lenin Centenary celebrations in Moscow in April; Volodia Teitelboim visited Cuba in June and Uruguay in December. Luis Corvalán visited Uruguay in September-October.

Publications. The most important of the PCCh publications are *El Siglo*, the daily official organ of the party, and the theoretical journal *Principios*.

* * *

The PCRCh. During 1963 a small but active pro-Chinese group emerged within the PCCh. Expelled from the party at the end of the year, the group chose the name "Spartacus" (Espártaco) and by mid-1964 was issuing two publications. Toward the end of 1964, PCCh Senator Jaime Barros withdrew from the pro-Soviet party. In 1965 he assumed leadership of Spartacus and, in September of that year, visited China. After returning, he led his group in the formation of the Revolutionary Communist Party of Chile in May 1966. The PCRCh was immediately recognized by the Chinese Communist Party.

The PCRCh has probably never had more than several hundred active members and seems to have decreased in size during 1970, particularly after Salvador Allende's electoral victory and immediate moves to establish contacts with the Chinese People's Republic.[5] The main unofficial spokesmen for the party line are Robinson Rojas, editor of *Causa Marxista-Leninista* and Chilean correspondent for the New China News Agency, and Galvarino Guerra; official party statements are released pseudonymously. The PCRCh has probably been most influential in land seizures by the poor; among university students in Santiago, where it has participated in the Revolutionary Student Front (see below); and in the South. The PCRCh did not soften its attitude toward the PCCh after the death of Arnoldo Rios in December, as did the MIR.

Domestic Attitudes and Activities. The PCRCh argues, claiming to follow Lenin, that there are two fundamental methods for exploiting the people—repression and deception. In its view, Chileans, unlike most Latin Americans, have been more deceived than physically repressed. (*Causa Marxista-Leninista*, no. 16, February-March 1970.) The "electoral circus," according to the PCRCh Executive Committee, was the most infamous form of deception in Chile, serving merely as an "escape valve utilized periodically by reaction in order to prevent a direct confrontation between exploiters and exploited" (*ibid.*, no. 19, August-September). Thus the party called upon the public to abstain from voting for any of the three candidates—including Allende, whom it said represented the interests of the bourgeoisie, the petty bourgeoisie, and the labor aristocracy (*ibid.*, no. 16).

According to the PCRCh, a socialist revolution could be achieved in Chile only through "people's war"; even mass struggles followed by an armed insurrection would not be sufficient. Since

[5]On 5 January 1971, China announced that an agreement to establish diplomatic relations with Chile had been signed in Paris on 15 December 1970.

the influence of "reformism" and "revisionist opportunism" was particularly great, it would be necessary first of all to extend and sharpen the class struggle. Thus PCRCh policy was directed toward "creating the conditions for the unleashing of the people's war, promoting the mass struggle, sharpening and politicizing the class struggle, while at the same time preparing for the future waging of the war." (*Ibid.*)

International Views and Positions. The PCRCh is firmly pro-Chinese. In 1970 its spokesmen devoted much effort and many pages to arguing that the thought of Mao Tse-tung constitutes "the third stage of Marxism-Leninism" and is the guide for revolutionaries in the present era (*Causa Marxista-Leninista*, no. 17, April). It condemned the "social imperialism" of the Soviet Union at great length, sometimes by reprinting important Chinese theoretical statements on the subject (e.g., *ibid.*, no. 18, June-July), and castigated the policies of the PCCh and the CUTCh (*ibid.*, no. 15, January). Fidel Castro was similarly treated—especially after his open endorsement of the candidacy of Salvador Allende in early August (*ibid.*, no. 16). PCRCh sources frequently reported and praised the guerrilla activities of the pro-Chinese People's Liberation Army (EPL) in Colombia.

Publications. The official organ of the PCRCh, issued irregularly, is *Espártaco*. Party statements, and unofficial PCRCh views, appear regularly in *Causa Marxista-Leninista*. The number of PCRCh statements in *Peking Review* decreased markedly in 1970, as compared with 1969.

*   *   *

The PORT. The Revolutionary Workers' Party, the only independent Trotskyist party remaining in Chile, is aligned with the Fourth International—International Secretariat (Posadas faction). The party apparently is small, but the extent of its membership is unknown.

The PORT stated early in 1970 that the "people's government" that would follow an electoral victory by the UP and Salvador Allende would be the beginning of the struggle for a government of the workers and peasants and for the construction of socialism in Chile (*Lucha Obrera*, April 1970). The PORT threw its full support behind Salvador Allende and the UP after the September elections. The PORT hailed the defeat of capitalism as a result of Allende's victory, but warned against the possibility of civil war arising from counterrevolutionary threats to the masses. After urging the formation of a still broader anti-imperialist, anti-capitalist united front, the PORT called for a deepening of the activities and influence of the organizations of the masses. (*Lucha Obrera*, November.)

The PORT praised developments in Cuba, Ecuador, Peru, and Bolivia (*Lucha Obrera*, November).

The organ of the PORT is *Lucha Obrera*. It is under the direction of Juan Urrutia Muñoz and appears irregularly.

*   *   *

The MIR. The Movement of the Revolutionary Left is generally said to have been formed in 1965 from militant former members of socialist, pro-Soviet, pro-Chinese, Trotskyist, and other groups.[6] In December 1967 the organization adopted a more activist line than previously, becom-

---

[6]According to *Ercilla*, Santiago, 11-17 March 1970, however, the MIR was founded in August 1961 by Oscar Waiss, Clotario Blest, Miguel Enríquez, and others; reportedly, it originally emphasized the infiltrating and influencing of labor and student organizations.

ing avowedly "Castroite" and advocating the armed road to power enunciated at the Latin American Solidarity Organization conference held in Havana in August of that year. Early in 1969 the organization went "underground" in order to facilitate confrontations and to prepare for and carry out armed actions. After Salvador Allende's inauguration as president of Chile in November 1970, the MIR surfaced once again.

MIR leaders in 1970 included Miguel Enríquez (secretary-general), Sergio Zorrilla (national director), Fernando Gutiérrez (national secretary), Jorge Fuentes (president of the student federation at the University of Concepción), Víctor Toro (leader of the settlers' movement), Luciano Cruz, and Andres Pascal Allende. Until 11 November, when President Allende announced that all political charges against MIR members had been dropped, most party leaders were either in hiding or in jail.

The MIR has been particularly active among university students. It dominates two leftist university fronts: the University Movement of the Left (Movimiento Universitario de Izquierda; MUI) at the University of Concepción, where the MIR has controlled the student federation for three years, and the Revolutionary Students' Front (Frente Estudiantil Revolucionario; FER) at the University of Chile in Santiago, where MIR influence in the university as a whole has been overshadowed by that of the Christian Democrats and the more traditional left. MIR influence is strong in the Revolutionary Peasant Movement (Movimiento Campesino Revolucionario; MCR) and in many of the peasant- and worker-oriented groups which attended the "First National Congress of the Homeless Settlers" (Pobladores sin Casa) on 10-12 October in the La Granja district of Santiago.

In the past few years several groups have broken in whole or in part from the MIR, including the People's Organized Vanguard (Vanguardia Organizada del Pueblo; VOP) and the "Manuel Rodríguez" Revolutionary Movement (Movimiento Revolucionario "Manuel Rodríguez"; MR-2).

The MIR considers itself a Marxist-Leninist organization. Its stated objectives are the uprooting of the Chilean state structure—which it charges with serving only the interests of capitalists and "imperialists"—and its replacement by a socialist state which serves the workers. The controversial position of the MIR within the Chilean left does not derive from this long-term goal, however, but from its concept of the proper road to its achievement.

In January 1969 the MIR explained its position regarding the parliamentary election of that year in a document entitled: "No to Elections—Armed Struggle the Only Road." A long statement by the National Secretariat, dated April-May 1970, on the subject of the forthcoming presidential election, described the electoral process as "nothing more than a mechanism of self-preservation for the ruling class, a more refined and subtle method than brute coercion." The MIR argued that elections were "not a road toward the conquest of power," and predicted that even if the "difficult popular electoral victory were to occur, the ruling classes [would] not hesitate to carry out a military coup." While regarding the UP program as "essentially leftist reformist," the MIR pledged: "[In the event of a military coup] we will not hesitate to place our growing armed apparatus, our forces, and all we have at the service of the defense of the workers' and peasants' conquest." Its own fundamental task during 1970 would be to carry out "armed revolutionary actions and militant mobilizations of the masses" in order to maintain and extend the high level of social struggle in the country. (*Punto Final*, 12 May, supplement.)

In October the National Secretariat released a document on the results of the election which acknowledged that the MIR had overestimated the rightist response to a leftist victory and underestimated the ability of the UP to defend its success at the polls. While maintaining that the election had merely postponed armed struggle, the MIR pledged to defend Allende's government and to intensify mass mobilization. It warned that once the "euphoria of the triumph" had passed, the UP would have to "satisfy the desires of the masses concretely and in a short time." The strategy of the bourgeoisie and "imperialism" would be to discredit the UP by keeping it from carrying out its programs, thus opening the way for a reactionary takeover with some degree of popular support. (*Ibid.*, 13 October, supplement.)

Opposition to the September election put the MIR into constant conflict with the UP, and in particular with the PCCh. Violent disputes continued until after the death of an MIR militant in Concepción in December (see above), after which a truce was reached. At the end of the year Miguel Enríquez stressed the need for joint action among leftist forces (interview, *ibid.*, 22 December).[7]

The MIR carried out a wide variety of activities during the year, some of which made a great impression on the Chilean people. Among them were seizures of public and private lands by MIR-led peasants, workers, Indians, and the unemployed, in Santiago and elsewhere. A number of self-governing squatter settlements were established, with "popular militias" for self-defense, and with these the Chilean government (especially the "people's government" of Salvador Allende) generally found it best not to interfere. The MIR also carried out a series of "expropriations," mainly bank robberies, to finance their own operations and to meet the living expenses of those in the squatter settlements. At the end of the year the MIR provided President Allende with his personal security guard.

W. E. R.

[7] Early in 1971 the MIR even urged participation in the April 1971 municipal elections.

COLOMBIA

The communist movement in Colombia began within the ranks of the Socialist Revolutionary Party (Partido Socialista Revolucionario; PSR) shortly after the party's formation in December 1926. Contacts between the PSR and the Communist International during 1929 and 1930 inspired a group of PSR members to proclaim publicly the creation of the Communist Party of Colombia (Partido Comunista de Colombia; PCC) on 17 July 1930. The party has retained this designation ever since except for a short period (1944-47) during which it was called the Social Democratic Party (Partido Social Democrático). In July 1965 a schism within the PCC between pro-Soviet and pro-Chinese factions resulted in the latter's becoming the Communist Party of Colombia, Marxist-Leninist (Partido Comunista de Colombia, Marxista-Leninista; PCC-ML). Only the PCC has legal status.

The PCC was disqualified from running its own candidates in the 1970 presidential election by the National Front agreement, implemented in 1958 and binding until 1974, which states that only a member of the Liberal or Conservative party can hold the office of president. Revisions in the agreement since 1968—when the PCC won several national congressional seats under the banner of the Liberal Revolutionary Party of the People (see below)—allowed the communists to run on their own ticket for seats in the departmental assemblies and municipal councils in 1970. PCC candidates received less than 0.5 per cent of the vote, but PCC deputies were elected in six departments (*IB*, no. 20, 1970). The PCC is estimated to have 8,000 to 10,000 members.

The three main guerrilla organizations, based in various parts of the country, are the PCC-controlled Revolutionary Armed Forces of Colombia (FARC), the pro-Chinese People's Liberation Army (EPL), and the Castroite National Liberation Army (ELN), estimated at mid-year to have 100, 150, and 80 members respectively.

The population of Colombia is 21,116,000 (estimated 1970).

The PCC exercises only marginal influence in national affairs, and the PCC-ML even less. Guerrilla warfare, although not a serious threat to the government, has been a feature of Colombian life since the late 1940's, the current wave beginning in 1964. The FARC, EPL, and ELN cause difficulties in a few areas and draw some attention away from other pressing problems. During 1970, guerrilla disruptions decreased, as in 1969, owing to the continuation of the army's "civic action programs" among the peasants and its military encounters with the guerrillas, together with policy disputes and demoralization among the guerrillas themselves and the parties that control them. After the presidential election of 19 April 1970, when National Popular Alliance (Alianza Nacional Popular; ANAPO) candidate Gustavo Rojas Pinilla claimed that his narrow loss to National Front candidate Misael Pastrana was due to election fraud, there was some fear (which proved to be unfounded) that Rojas would urge his supporters to take up arms against the government, or that some of this followers would do so on their own initiative, perhaps linking up with one or more of the existing guerrilla organizations.

The PCC: Leadership and Organization. The PCC is headed by its 12-member Executive Committee and 45-member Central Committee. The secretary-general is Gilberto Vieira. Members of the Executive Committee, besides Vieira, are: Alvaro Vásquez, Joaquín Moreno, Jesús Villegas, Roso Osorio, Hernando Hurtado, Julio Posada, Gustavo Castro, Pastor Pérez, Juan Viana, Manlio Lafont, and Manuel Cepeda Vargas. Prominent among the Central Committee members are Nelson Robles, José Cardona Hoyos, Teodosio Varela, Anteo Quimbaya, and Pedro Antonio Marín. In an article published in the Soviet journal *Kommunist* (March 1968), Gilberto Vieira referred to a clandestine party apparatus which operated when the more open hierarchy was immobilized by government pressure or arrest.

The PCC controls the Trade Union Confederation of Workers of Colombia (Confederación Sindical de Trabajadores de Colombia; CSTC), which has approximately 150,000 members and is the second-largest labor organization in a country where only a fourth of the workers are unionized. The CSTC president is Pastor Pérez, a member of the PCC Executive Committee. In line with decisions reached in 1968, the PCC expanded its labor activities in 1970, stressing the settlement of economic and social demands within the existing system (*Documentos Políticos*, Bogotá, May-June 1970). During the year, the leaders of the largest and third-largest labor organizations—the Union of Workers of Colombia (Unión de Trabajadores de Colombia; UTC) and the Confederation of Workers of Colombia (Confederación de Trabajadores de Colombia; CTC) respectively—protested that "communist infiltration" was impeding their functions and alleged that the Soviet Embassy was directly involved (*Vanguardia Liberal*, Bucaramanga, 18 September; *El Tiempo*, Bogotá, 22 November). The PCC denounced the UTC and CTC statements as the "most vulgar anti-communism" (*Voz Proletaria*, Bogotá, 19 February). As in 1969, the PCC carried on opposition to the activities of Diego Montaña Cuéllar, a prominent labor leader and intellectual who was expelled from the PCC Executive Committee in November 1967 and from the party in January 1968.

The PCC's youth organization, the Communist Youth of Colombia (Juventud Comunista de Colombia; JCC), has its own National Directorate, Executive Committee, and Central Committee. The secretary-general is Carlos Romero. Other JCC leaders include José Miller Chacón, Jaime Caicedo, Alejandro Gómez, and Eduardo Martínez. In preparation for convening a "national conference of communist students," the JCC held a meeting on 28-29 March 1970 which issued a report condemning the "pro-imperialist and anti-democratic education policies of the government," called for greater organizational efforts among students, and promised to extend the "ideological struggle against the vanguardist and sectarian tradition maintained by some sectors of the students" (*ibid.*, 9 April). Later in the year the PCC newspaper reported that a national congress of university students scheduled for October had been postponed indefinitely due to disagreements among communists regarding the National Coordinating Commission which was to make preparations for the congress (*ibid.*, 1 October). "Ultra-leftist" views have weakened the JCC and led to some opposition to the PCC line on major issues, including its participation in the 1970 departmental and municipal elections.

The Liberal Revolutionary Movement of the People (Movimiento Revolucionario Liberal del Pueblo; MRLP) is controlled by the PCC. Because it poses as a splinter of the Liberal Party, it is able to participate in elections at most levels. In 1970 the PCC used the MRLP only in seeking national Congressional seats.

The Revolutionary Armed Forces of Colombia (Fuerzas Armadas Revolucionarias de Colombia; FARC) was formed early in 1966, when a number of bandit groups led by Manuel Marulanda Vélez, alias "Tiro Fijo" (Sure Shot), came under PCC control. Marulanda remained as commander in chief of the FARC, but on several occasions in 1970 he was reported to have been killed. The second in command, until his capture in April, was Januario Valero, alias "Oscar

Reyes." According to reported disclosures by Valero, the FARC leadership included Hernando Reyes, Eduardo Pachón Prieto, Rigoberto Lozada, Noel Matta, and Luis Morantes, among others. Valero stated that the FARC worked through five fronts and one mobile group, on both legal and clandestine levels. It had been severely weakened in 1969, he said, by arrests of many of its urban leaders and as a result of allowing many university students (and some rebel priests) to come to the countryside, where they were unable to endure the hardships of guerrilla life, instead of using them in urban activities. Valero further reported a high degree of Soviet control over the training, financing, and command of the FARC. (*El Siglo*, Bogotá, 12 and 14 May 1970.)

The FARC, unlike the two other main guerrilla groups in Colombia, urged participation in the 1970 elections (*Voz Proletaria*, 9 April). Only two days after the election, however, it launched its first significant attack since 1968 against the national army. Shortly thereafter, reports circulated in Colombia (e.g., *El Tiempo*, 6 May) that the Soviet Union had instructed the FARC to turn to nonviolent propaganda activities. The group continued to engage in sporadic operations.

Party Internal Affairs. Meetings of the PCC Central Committee were held in May and July 1970. In spite of some disagreements over participation in the elections, the importance of guerrilla warfare, and other issues, the party evidently avoided any serious splits during the year.

Domestic Attitudes and Activities. According to the PCC, a "really revolutionary situation" did not exist in Colombia in 1970 and had not existed in recent years (*WMR*, February). The party sought an "anti-imperialist, anti-latifundist" revolution as a first step toward an eventual socialist revolution. Quoting Lenin, Gilberto Vieira wrote that Marxism did not "reject any form of struggle," but demanded "an absolutely *historical* examination of the forms of struggle." The PCC's current "tactical line" in Colombia, he noted, was "an amalgamation of all forms of struggle." While insisting that the PCC regarded "peasant guerrilla war as one of the highest forms of *mass struggle*," Vieira also gave a warning: "The Communist Party holds that guerrilla warfare is not at present the basic and main form of the people's struggle in Colombia. . . . [It might become the] basic form if the political situation deteriorates sharply enough and an openly despotic terrorist government comes to power." (*WMR*, May; emphasis in original.) In December, Vieira had praise for guerrilla warfare—"an important and invaluable reserve in the development of our national political crisis"—but he argued that at the present stage it was essential to form a united anti-government front in order to gain power (Prensa Latina, Cuban news agency, 16 December). In October Vieira called for a strengthening of the "'opposition front' within which groups and trends seeking radical changes in Colombian society could draw closer together on the basis of a common minimum program," and declared that such a program "would not prevent any one of the political alignments from preserving its distinctive characteristics and its theses" (*IB*, no. 21, 1970).

Early in the year, PCC attention was directed primarily toward the approaching election on 19 April. Party members campaigned actively for municipal, departmental, and national legislative positions. In February the Executive Committee declared that the party could not support any of the presidential candidates and instructed members to cast a blank ballot for that office as a form of protest (*Voz Proletaria*, 5 February). Reports circulated widely that behind the scenes the party was urging members to vote for ANAPO candidate Rojas Pinilla, though the PCC denied it. In May the Central Committee acknowledged that "concrete results" achieved by the PCC in the elections were "actually very modest," but argued that the outcome was "no gauge of the Party's real influence" (*IB*, no. 13-14).

The party interpreted the election campaign and outcome, in particular the large vote received by National Popular Alliance candidate Rojas Pinilla, as evidence of widespread popular disenchantment with the existing system. The May and July meetings of the PCC Central Committee concentrated on efforts to form an alliance with supporters of Rojas and others who expressed discontent with the National Front. Late in the year, Gilberto Vieira stated that the victory of the Popular Unity candidate Salvador Allende in the September presidential election in Chile confirmed the PCC in its belief that "the only just policy is one which unites the popular masses around a clear-cut, definite platform, without partisanship or free-lancing of any kind" (*Voz Proletaria*, 12 November). An accompanying article warned, however, that a vanguard movement required a vanguard ideology, and concluded that "ideological debate has already begun within the ANAPO" (*ibid.*).

Throughout the year the party condemned the "adventurist" tactics of such groups as the ELN, which it said lacked a clear ideology, and rejected the use of kidnaping and terrorism (e.g., *WMR*, February, and *Voz Proletaria*, 16 July).[1]

International Views and Positions. The PCC continued in 1970 to be a firm supporter of the international positions taken by the Soviet Union. Gilberto Vieira stated that the party did not want the Colombian people to "imitate everything Soviet," but to understand the significance of the Soviet Union as the "first victorious creation of the international working class, as a fortress of peace, and as the bulwark of nations struggling for their emancipation" (*Voz Proletaria*, 12 November). Party publications justified their positions by extensive reference to the writings of Lenin and the Soviet experience (e.g., *ibid.*, 9 April, and *WMR*, May).

Gilberto Vieira declared that the "nationalist movements arising in Latin America" were the PCC's "natural allies," provided they struggled against "Yankee imperialist rule" and "North American trusts" (*Voz Proletaria*, 12 November). The party assumed an increasingly friendly attitude toward Fidel Castro, though it continued to deny the applicability in Colombia of the kind of rural guerrilla warfare that is associated with "Castroism" (e.g., *WMR*, February).

The May meeting of the Central Committee adopted resolutions condemning "criminal U.S. aggression in Cambodia and Israel's policy of conquest against the peoples of the Middle East" (*IB*, no. 11, 1970).

Publications. The PCC publishes a weekly newspaper, *Voz Proletaria*; a theoretical journal, *Documentos Políticos*; and a news sheet, *Noticias de Colombia*.

* * *

The PCC-ML. The Communist Party of Colombia, Marxist-Leninist, is firmly pro-Chinese. It originated from a schism within the PCC in the early 1960's and dates as a party from 1965. Its leadership hierarchy is not clearly known, but important positions have evidently been held in recent years by Francisco Gárnica, Pedro Vásquez, Luis Carlos Miranda, Carlos Arias, Jorge Restrepo, Daniel Díaz, Humberto Salamanca Alba, Napoleón Martínez, Alejandro Soto, Víctor Julio Ramos, Pedro Lupo León Arboleda, Guillermo Ciro, and Antonio Osorio. The party's youth group, the Colombian Communist Youth (Juventud Comunista Colombiana), was formed in February 1964 by persons expelled from the pro-Soviet JCC; it has some influence in university circles. The PCC-ML controls the Bloque Independiente, a small trade union organization.

The People's Liberation Army (Ejército Popular de Liberación; EPL), established in 1967, was the first pro-Chinese rural guerrilla force to be active in Latin America. It has been described by the PCC-ML as "the armed arm of our party" and as being assigned three principal activities:

[1]On the fortieth anniversary of the founding of the PCC, in July 1970, the Executive Committee issued a 12-page booklet, *40 años de lucha por la revolución Colombiana*, which traced the strategy, goals, and activities of the party.

"fighting the army; undertaking and developing production; and mobilizing, educating, organizing, and arming the broad masses of the people" (*Peking Review*, 7 February 1969). Its main leader, until his death in early 1969, was Pedro Vásquez Rendón. During 1970 the EPL carried on sporadic operations in the Alto Sinu and Bajo Cauca regions, apparently led by Gonzalo González Mantilla, Francisco Caravello, and José Gómez.

In the view of the PCC-ML, Colombia is a semi-feudal country dependent upon and deformed by "U.S. imperialism" and its liberation from oppression can come only by means of a "people's patriotic, anti-imperialist revolution, marching toward socialism" (party statement in *World Revolution*, New York, May-June 1969).

In October 1970 the PCC-ML and the Communist Party of Spain, Marxist-Leninist, issued a joint statement which called for a denunciation and unmasking of "Soviet social imperialism," which, together with "U.S. imperialism," was seeking to dominate the world. The statement charged the United States and the Soviet Union with "conducting a frantic arms race and preparing a new world war against the revolutionary peoples." The two parties urged greater solidarity with and support for China and Albania in the "anti-imperialist struggle." They denounced the "fascist, tyrannical, bloodthirsty regimes under whose yoke the great majority of the Latin American peoples are suffering—regimes imposed by U.S. imperialism and in many instances abetted by Soviet imperialism." (Tirana radio, 8 December.)

The organ of the PCC-ML Central Committee is *Revolución*. PCC-ML statements are sometimes found in Communist Chinese publications and those of pro-Chinese parties in Europe and the Americas, particularly *Causa Marxista-Leninista*, Santiago, Chile.

* * *

The ELN. The National Liberation Army (Ejército de Liberación Nacional) was formed in Santander, northeast Colombia, in 1964. It mounted its first military action in January 1965. Up to the end of 1970, Fabio Vásquez Castaño seems always to have been its most important leader. Ricardo Lara, Juan de Dios Aguilera, and Manuel Vásquez have been in leading positions at various times. The ELN has been torn for several years by internal struggles which have resulted in executions of "traitors" and the defection of many followers. On several occasions, splits within the organization have led to the formation of rival guerrilla forces—such as the Simón Bolívar front, established by Juan de Dios Aguilera in 1968. In January 1971 it was reported that Fabio Vásquez had been tried and executed by his own men, and that Ricardo Lara had taken over the leadership of the central group of the ELN. There were reports as early as 1969 by some guerrillas who surrendered or were captured that the ELN had "degenerated into groups without any ideals, in which the only important factors are ugly emotions and egoism" (*El Tiempo*, 1 March 1969).

The ELN is reportedly "made up chiefly of peasants" (*Tricontinental Bulletin*, Havana, March 1970). One of its best-known members was the radical Roman Catholic priest Camilo Torres, who joined the guerrillas in late 1965 and was killed in February 1966. For some Latin Americans (among them, Fidel Castro), Torres has become the prototype of the "fighting Christian." Early in 1970 a Spanish priest, Domingo Lain, joined the ELN guerrillas.

The ELN argues that guerrilla warfare is the main form of struggle for the achievement of a socialist society in Colombia (*ibid.*). The group, until late 1969 a recipient of considerable verbal and material support from Cuba, financed itself during 1970 primarily by extortion. Its most spectacular exploit was the kidnaping in July of a former foreign minister, Fernando Londoño y Londoño, who was released on payment of $100,000 ransom.

W. E. R.

COSTA RICA

The Communist Party of Costa Rica (Partido Comunista de Costa Rica) was founded in 1929 and accepted as a full member of the Communist International in 1935. In 1943, following the wartime policy of many Latin American parties, the Costa Rican communists reorganized under a new name, the Popular Vanguard Party (Partido Vanguardia Popular; PVP).

Other left-wing groups in Costa Rica include the Socialist Action Party (Partido de Acción Socialista; PASO) which purports to be noncommunist but is sometimes used as a PVP front. Its chairman is Marcial Aguiluz Orellana. Another is the Authentic Revolutionary Movement (Movimiento Revolucionario Auténtico; MRA), which until 1970 was known as the Authentic Revolutionary Party (Partido Revolucionario Auténtico; PRA).

In 1948 the PVP was declared illegal and since that time has been banned from the electoral process.

The membership of the PVP, which had reached about 3,000 by 1948, was estimated to be 600 in 1969. In 1970 the PVP claimed it had admitted 600 new members during the early part of the year (*IB*, no. 12). The population of Costa Rica is 1,800,000 (estimated 1970).

On 1 February 1970 Costa Rica held a presidential and legislative election in which former President José Figueres (1948-49, 1953-58) of the left-of-center National Liberation Party won an overwhelming victory. The PASO, taking part in the elections for the first time in more than twenty years, received 1.3 per cent of the vote and obtained two seats in the 58-member Legislative Assembly. One of those seats went to PVP leader Manuel Mora Valverde, who ran as a PASO candidate.

Organization and Leadership. The secretary-general of the PVP is Manuel Mora Valverde, the party's founder and first secretary-general; the assistant secretary-general is his brother, Eduardo Mora Valverde. The organizational secretary is Arnoldo Ferreto Segura ("Oscar Vargas"). Other prominent figures include Luisa González Gutiérrez de González, Alvaro Montero Vega, Humberto Elías Carbonel, Mario Solís, and Arturo Jara.

The PVP-controlled labor organization is the General Confederation of Costa Rican Workers (Confederación General de Trabajadores Costarricenses; CGTC), which includes about 2,500 of Costa Rica's 24,000 unionized workers. Early in 1970 the CGTC sponsored a strike among the workers on the United Fruit Company's banana plantations. Although the strike was declared illegal by the courts, it spread to 20 plantations and caused unrest and some violence in the La Estrella area. In August the CGTC and the noncommunist "Costa Rican Confederation of Democratic Workers" agreed to unite in a joint struggle in behalf of the plantation workers against the United Fruit Company.

On 19-21 March the CGTC attended the second meeting of the Committee of Union Unity of the Workers of Central America and Panama (Comité de Unidad Sindical de los Trabajadores del Centro América y Panama; CUSCA) which was held in San José, Costa Rica. The meeting ratified CUSCA's constitution and established that its permanent base would be San José. The meeting also called upon all workers and labor organizations to put the interests of the working class above political, ideological, or religious "prejudices" and stressed the need for a unified struggle of "democratic and popular forces" in alliance with the working class. (*Libertad*, 4 April.)

The PVP sponsors the United Agricultural Workers' and Peasants' Federation (FUNTAC), which held a national conference on 12-14 September. A board of directors was named, with Gonzalo Sierra Cantillo as secretary-general. The meeting resolved to petition the Legislative Assembly for a "true agrarian reform law" and to hold a "large campesino march" in September 1971. (*Ibid.*, 19 September.)

The University Action Front (Frente de Acción Universitaria; FAU) is a small PVP-affiliated student organization. Its secretary-general is believed to be Oscar Madrigal Jiménez. Most university students belong to the large Federation of University Students of Costa Rica (Federación de Estudiantes Universitarios de Costa Rica; FEUCR). The FAU won 20 per cent of the vote in the FEUCR election in September and for the first time had two of its members elected to that organization's directorate.

The small Vanguard Youth of Costa Rica (Juventud Vanguardia de Costa Rica; JVCR) is the PVP youth group. Its secretary-general is José Joaquín Chacón.

On 9-12 April the "First Meeting of Central American Youth" was held in San José. It was sponsored by the World Federation of Democratic Youth (WFDY) and organized by the "Costa Rican Youth Committee." Although the communists tried to play down their direction of the meeting, it was clear from the inception of the Costa Rican Youth Committee in 1969 that various communist groups were strongly behind the movement. Delegates attended from Central America, Panama, Venezuela, the WFDY, and the International Union of Students. The meeting called for the formation of a movement to be called "Education for Youth by Youth," whose purpose would be to persuade leaders, workers, peasants, students, teachers, artists, and priests to help "oppose imperialism and the oligarchy" by an effective Central American union. (*Ibid.*, 11 April.)

Party Internal Affairs. The PVP has traditionally been and currently remains a supporter of the U.S.S.R. and the policies of the Communist Party of the Soviet Union. There is no apparent split within the party.

On 21-23 February the Central Committee of the PVP met in San José to analyze the political situation following the national election. Plans were made for celebrating the Lenin Centenary, which was said to provide an "excellent opportunity to rally all communists and other revolutionaries around Lenin's ideas and to strengthen and expand the party." (*IB*, no. 5-6.)

In early June the PVP held its First National Conference, at which it discussed party organizational and educational work to be carried on in conjunction with the Lenin Centenary. It was at this time that the party reported the admission of some 600 new members and 300 candidate members during the preceding two and a half months (*ibid.*, no. 12).

On 17 June the PVP celebrated its thirty-ninth anniversary. Assistant Secretary-General Eduardo Mora Valverde gave the main address and outlined the plans of the PVP for the coming year. These included efforts to double the party membership and enlarge the JVCR and FAU memberships; increase the circulation of the party newspaper, *Libertad*; revitalize the PVP-owned Revolution Publishing House, and publish the writings of Manuel Mora Valverde and a history of the PVP; establish a political training school; convene the party's Eleventh Congress, and "intensify the struggle on all fronts under the symbol of unity so as to give impetus to the national democratic, popular, agrarian, and anti-imperialist front" (*Libertad*, 20 June).

Domestic Attitudes and Activities. Following his election to the Legislative Assembly in February, Manuel Mora Valverde declared that the PVP was "born to fight for the economic and social transformation" of Costa Rica so as to "create conditions of real social justice." This, he said, "we call a revolution." He stressed, however, that the PVP believed that the "social order in Costa Rica [could] be changed through peaceful means." (*La República*, San José, 8 February.) The PVP has frequently and publicly repudiated terrorism, violence, and "any form of struggle which is not supported by the popular masses," citing in particular the methods of the MRA and condemning the use of kidnaping and hijacking, "regardless of the ideology of the victim" (*ibid.*, 14 April).

The secretary-general defined the objectives of the PVP's "revolution" as "consolidation and extension of the democratic system, execution of a profound agrarian reform, [encouragement of] the country's economic development in the industrial and agricultural spheres, defense of the nation's sovereignty, and the recovery of all the resources of [the] soil and subsoil so that they may be converted into well-being, culture, and civilization for the Costa Rican people." He also declared that because the PVP was Marxist, its members understood Costa Rica's "degree of development" and did not "intend at this time to establish socialism in Costa Rica, much less communism," though those would be the "goals for the future." (*Ibid.*, 8 February.)

In a speech concerning the nation's economic and diplomatic position, Eduardo Mora Valverde stressed the "great harm" done to Costa Rica's development by the "imperialistic monopolies, especially those of the United States," and declared that the United Fruit Company had long been the source of "exploitation" and intervention in the economy. In April protests were also made against the Aluminum Company of America, which had recently begun to mine bauxite. In the view of the PVP, "intervention of foreign capital" had "limited the development" of Costa Rica's industry and in effect had "liquidated" its small national industries. The solution, according to the party, would be the diversification of Costa Rica's "economic and diplomatic relations with all nations of the world," in particular the "socialist countries." (Moscow radio, domestic service, 15 October.)

In the summer Manuel Mora Valverde visited the Soviet Union and aided the Costa Rican government in arranging for the sale of surplus coffee. In return for 6,000 tons of coffee, the Soviet Union agreed to grant Costa Rica a loan valued at $10 million for the purchase of road construction machinery.

The PVP continued in 1970 to issue harsh denunciations of the MRA, with which it has been carrying on virulent ideological arguments for some time. An article by Arnoldo Ferreto called the MRA a "micro-group" of "ultra-leftists" which was trying to sow "doubt and confusion within the heart of the revolutionary movement." He warned: "We communists must wage incessant ideological warfare without truce against such ideologies." (*Libertad*, 20 June.)

International Views. In a speech commemorating the fifty-third anniversary of the October Revolution, Manuel Mora Valverde paid "fervent homage to the heroic people of the U.S.S.R.," and to Lenin as an "example and symbol of all the democratic and revolutionary forces of mankind." Although he affirmed that the PVP had learned a great lesson from the Soviet Union, Mora stressed that "revolution is not exported or imported," and that "all peoples should make their own revolution and wage their own battles." The Soviet Union, he added, was helping in the struggle for national liberation by "stopping the armed might of imperialism at every point on the planet where the revolutionary movement is threatened." (*Libertad*, 14 November.)

In contrast, referring to the Chinese communists, the PVP described the "clique of Mao" as one which "shouts much, threatens much, and uses scurrilous language," but "in practice does little or nothing in the general struggle against imperialism" (*ibid.*, 20 June). Secretary-General Mora stated in February that the PVP supported the Cuban revolution, admired its leaders, and believed that the achievements of the Cuban revolution were more important than its mistakes (*La República*, 8 February).

International Contacts. On 21 April Secretary-General Manuel Mora was present in Moscow for the celebration of the Lenin Centenary. Again, in the summer, he visited Moscow to help negotiate a Costa Rican-Soviet trade agreement (see above).

Publications. The PVP publishes a weekly newspaper, *Libertad*, which circulates openly. Enrique Mora Valverde is the TASS correspondent in Costa Rica.

*   *   *

The MRA. The Authentic Revolutionary Movement is a small Castroite group which advocates armed struggle in the "present stage of revolution" in Costa Rica. In October some MRA members hijacked a Costa Rican airliner and by holding those aboard as hostages obtained the release of Carlos Fonseca Amador, commander of the Nicaraguan FSLN, and three other guerrillas held by Costa Rican authorities (see *Nicaragua*).

L. R.

CUBA

The Communist Party of Cuba (Partido Comunista de Cuba; PCC) was founded in August 1925 and within weeks was driven underground. Some PCC members surfaced in 1937 and joined several noncommunist groups in forming the Revolutionary Union (Unión Revolucionaria). In 1939 all communists were reunited in the legal Revolutionary Communist Union (Unión Revolucionaria Comunista). In 1944 the party became the People's Socialist Party (Partido Socialista Popular; PSP), which it remained until its merger in July 1961 with Fidel Castro's 26 July Movement and the small Revolutionary Directorate (Directorio Revolucionario) to form the Integrated Revolutionary Organizations (Organizaciones Revolucionarias Integradas). This was transformed into the United Party of the Socialist Revolution (Partido Unido de la Revolución Socialista) in 1963. In October 1965 the party was reconstituted along orthodox communist lines and under the original name as the PCC.

Although the PCC has not published exact membership figures, it is generally thought to be the most elitist of all ruling communist parties, including within its ranks less than 1.5 per cent of the national population. The PCC, which was believed to have about 70,000 members in early 1969 (*Trybuna Ludu*, Warsaw, 16 April), was reported to have "more than 100,000 members" by the end of 1970 (according to Fabio Grobart, *Népszabadság,* Budapest,5 December). The U.S. State Department estimated party membership at about 120,000 in mid-1970 (*World Strength of the Communist Party Organizations*, Washington, D.C., 1970). The population of Cuba is 8,553,395 (September 1970 census).

Organization and Leadership. Political power in Cuba in 1970 was primarily in the hands of Fidel Castro Ruz and was exercised through his positions as prime minister, commander in chief of the armed forces, and first secretary of the PCC. Persons wielding varying amounts of secondary but not insignificant power are found in the party's eight-member Political Bureau, seven-member Secretariat, and 100-member Central Committee. The Political Bureau is headed by Fidel Castro; the other members are Major Raúl Castro Ruz (deputy prime minister and armed forces minister), Osvaldo Dorticós Torrado (president of Cuba), Major Sergio del Valle Jiménez (interior minister), Armando Hart Dávalos (organizing secretary), and Majors Juan Almeida Bosque, Ramiro Valdés Menéndez, and Guillermo García Frias. The Secretariat is also headed by Fidel Castro; the other members are Raúl Castro, Osvaldo Dorticós, Armando Hart, Faure Chomón Mediavilla (former Revolutionary Directorate leader), Blas Roca Calderio, and Carlos Rafael Rodríguez (the last two are former PSP leaders). Among the Central Committee members are the following ministers (in office at the end of the year—see below), Alfredo Yabur Maluf (justice), Major Belarmino Castilla Mas (education), Raúl Roa García (foreign relations), Captain Jorge Risquet Valdés (labor), and Marcelo Fernández Font (foreign trade), along with Captain José Abrahantes Fernández (deputy interior minister and head of the State Security Department), Major Manuel Piñeiro Losada (head of the General Directorate of Intelligence),

Celia Sánchez Manduley (presidential secretary), Vilma Espín Villoy (wife of Raúl Castro), and Haydée Santamaría Cuadrado (wife of Armando Hart). Approximately two-thirds of the Central Committee members are officers in the Revolutionary Armed Forces (Fuerzas Armadas Revolucionarias; FAR)—the designation of the Cuban military.

Union of Young Communists. In 1960 Fidel Castro formed the National Association of Rebel Youth. By 1962, when it changed its name to the Union of Young Communists (Unión de Jóvenes Comunistas; UJC), this organization controlled every youth group in Cuba with the exception of the University Student Federation (Federación Estudiantil Universitaria; FEU), based at the University of Havana. In November 1967 it merged with the FEU, almost all of whose leaders were by then members of the UJC, after officials in the two organizations announced that both had the same objectives in mind for the same students (*Granma*, 2 December 1967). In December 1970, however, the UJC National Committee decided that beginning in January 1971 the FEU would become the "mass organization of university students" with a separate political structure, its policies drawn up with the close cooperation of university leadership and of PCC and UJC members (*Juventud Rebelde*, 15 December 1970). In 1970 the UJC had approximately 200,000 members and remained under the direction of its first secretary, Jaime Crombet.

The UJC is responsible for carrying out the tasks of the Cuban leaders among young persons. This involves programs of study and labor—particularly in 1970 the harvesting of sugar cane. UJC members were active in the Centennial Youth Column (Columna Juvenil del Centenario), organized in 1968 to harvest cane in Camagüey Province, and in developing the Ocean Youth Column (Columna Juvenil del Mar), which trained young persons for the fishing industry. The Union of Cuban Pioneers (Unión de Pioneros de Cuba), which enrolls pre-school children and those up to the sixth grade, has long been controlled by the UJC. In December 1970 it was designated as an "autonomous organization under the leadership of the UJC," with the objective of making it a children's mass organization in 1971. It had 1,261,000 members at mid-year. Also in December the UJC established the Federation of Intermediate-Level Students (Federación de Estudiantes de la Enseñanza Media).

Other Mass Organizations. During 1970 four mass organizations were active in Cuban life: the Committees for the Defense of the Revolution (Comités de Defensa de la Revolución; CDR), the Federation of Cuban Women (Federación de Mujeres Cubanas; FMC), the Central Organization of Cuban Workers (Central de Trabajadores de Cuba; CTC), and the National Association of Small Farmers (Asociación Nacional de Agricultores Pequeños; ANAP). The CTC and ANAP are also described as workers' organizations. The party's organization for young persons, the UJC (see above), was described by Fidel Castro on 23 August as "partly a militant political organization and partly a mass organization" (*Granma*, English, 30 August).

On 1 June 1968 Miguel Martín, then secretary-general of the CTC, explained: "There are two basic reasons for the existence of the mass organizations and the trade unions: first, attainment of the economic goals of the Revolution, and, second, attainment of its ideological goals in the formation of a revolutionary consciousness" (*ibid.*, 16 June). On 20 May 1970 Fidel Castro stated that since Martín's speech "political and organizational work [had] been neglected," primarily as a result of the great emphasis placed during those two years on economic activities (*ibid.*, 31 May). During the last half of 1970 Castro elaborated on the future activities of the mass organizations. Their main responsibilities would be to mobilize workers for production, increase the quality and efficiency of labor activities, and raise the ideological level and deepen the cultural and technical education of their members.

On 23 August and on other occasions Castro stressed the need to increase the participation of the masses in solving community problems and making the decisions that affected their lives.

This, he said, called for the "development of a new society and of genuinely democratic principles" (*ibid.*, 30 August). At a CTC meeting in December he elaborated the point: "We're talking about workers' democracy, not liberal or bourgeois democracy. Liberals and the bourgeoisie have no rights, except to disappear as a class." (*Ibid.*, 20 December.)

On 7 December Castro said that revitalized mass organizations would be the basis for the creation of "a really advanced, nonbureaucratic form of social and political life." The restructuring necessary to achieve this end, however, would "have to proceed slowly, starting with the more elementary and simple tasks and working up." He vowed not to repeat the mistake, admittedly made so often in the past, of immediately implementing a new idea on a mass scale without sufficient planning, only to discredit the idea and disrupt the economy. (*Ibid.*) Since the FMC and the CDR's were felt to have performed best during 1970, the first changes were made at the end of the year in the CTC.

The Committees for the Defense of the Revolution were the largest and most active of the mass organizations during 1970. Castro reported on 28 September, the CDR's tenth anniversary, that the organization had 3,222,147 members, more than 600,000 of whom were described as "activists" (*ibid.*, 4 October). CDR national coordinator Luis González Maturelos heads the 13-member National Bureau, which is directly responsible to the PCC Central Committee and whose central office in Havana controls a substructure of provincial, district, sectional, zonal, and block committees.

According to Luis González, in 1970 more than 1.5 million CDR members were engaged in "revolutionary vigilance," the primary activity of the committees, guarding the cane fields and factories against sabotage and defending the coastline against infiltration by counterrevolutionaries (*Verde Olivo*, 27 September; Havana radio, 28 September). González also reported that a similar number were participating in "political studies" on a "continuous basis" (*Granma*, 29 September). Other CDR activities include mobilizing workers, administering programs related to public health, education, recreation, local government, and the People's Tribunals, and taking the 1970 census. During the year an organization was formed to coordinate the "many activities of the CDR's that are related to those of the Revolutionary Armed Forces" (*ibid.*, 26 September).

The Federation of Cuban Women, which celebrated its tenth anniversary in August 1970, remained under the control of its president, PCC Central Committee member Vilma Espín. In December the FMC announced that it had 1,343,098 members, comprising some 54 per cent of Cuban women over the age of fourteen. The FMC undertakes to mobilize workers for agricultural and other work, manage child-care centers throughout the country, provide general education and technological training, and organize ideological study circles. (*Ibid.*, 9 December.) On 23 August Fidel Castro declared that the FMC had "provided a magnificent example" of "what can be done with a correct method and policy" (*Granma*, English, 30 August).

The National Association of Small Farmers is headed by PCC Central Committee member José ("Pepe") Ramírez Cruz. It regulates the small farmers who retain what is called private ownership of some 30 per cent of the Cuban farmland. This land, in plots of 67 hectares or less, can be sold only to the state and some of it is under rental to the state. In an interview in December, Ramírez said that the ANAP had 225,000 members from some 180,000 small farm families. Small farmers are told what they must grow and are expected to sell their crops to the state at fixed prices. In 1970 they produced sugar cane (23 per cent of the national total), coffee (85 per cent) tobacco (90 per cent), cattle (40 per cent), and cocoa (almost 100 per cent). As Captain Antonio Núñez Jiménez, head of the National Academy of Sciences, acknowledged in 1969 (*Bohemia*, 20 June), the small farms constitute a "considerable productive force" and play an "important role in socialist construction." Fidel Castro stated on 23 August 1970 that the ANAP deserved more attention than it had received in the past few years (*Granma*, English, 30

August). The ANAP was held partly responsible for the failure to achieve the goal in sugar cane production in 1970. After its national plenum in December the ANAP announced that it had reorganized all its forces in order to provide better support for the 1971 harvest (Havana radio, 29 December).

The Central Organization of Cuban Workers is headed by its National Committee, under Héctor Ramos Latour as first secretary, and had a membership of 1.4 million in 1970 (*WMR*, August, supplement), including both state-farm laborers and urban workers. The role of the CTC in Cuban society, according to labor minister Jorge Risquet, is above all to "mobilize workers for production"; it is not to "dispute anything already established nor anything proposed by the Revolution" (*Granma*, 1 August). During the year the CTC was primarily responsible for mobilizing, training, and supervising workers for the sugar harvest, though government leaders acknowledged that they relied more on the advance guard workers, the party, and the armed forces for leadership in the cane fields.

"In the labor movement the struggle against loafers, absenteeism and parasitism has reached tremendous proportions," Castro declared on 28 September, adding that, throughout society, "loafing must be considered a crime" (*Granma*, English, 4 October). Toward the end of the year there was much official talk about a law against loafing, the draft of which, as published in *Granma* on 11 January 1971, would allow up to two years' forced labor for violators.

Another effort to overcome absenteeism and apathy at the end of the year involved the reorganization of the CTC, noted above. At a CTC meeting on 3 September Fidel Castro declared: "If socialism does not spring from the masses, it will fail. . . . We will start by making the workers' movement completely democratic. If a workers' movement isn't democratic, it is good for nothing." In accordance with this new line, he announced, local CTC officials would be chosen through "absolutely free elections." (*Granma*, English, 20 September.) This theme was reiterated in a *Granma* editorial (9 November): "Only complete trade union democracy can guarantee that comrades have the authority, morale, and confidence to put the directives of the Revolution into practice." It was estimated that some 250,000 officials would be chosen by two million workers during elections to be held between 9 November and 9 December (see *Granma*, 29 October and 11 November). Election guidelines, released by the CTC National Committee (*Granma*, 30 October), stated that any laborer could run for office if he was nominated by a comrade at his labor center. Immediately after nomination, the qualities and merits of the candidate were to be discussed by all members of the center so that his qualifications would be known to all at the time of voting. Inasmuch as the elected leaders were expected to "put the directives of the Revolution into practice" (*Granma* editorial, 9 November), Castro issued his own unofficial guidelines at the CTC meeting on 3 September:

> I am sure that a work center with a proletarian conscientiousness will not elect an absentee, liar, political hack or corrupt trade union leader from the past, because the workers know enough to see through all these people. . . . If they should elect a man who is unworthy of representing the cause and spirit of the proletariat . . . we will know that the center is in bad shape from the political point of view. (*Granma*, English, 20 September.)

On 27 November *Granma* reported that the first steps had been taken toward establishing national trade unions for each industry and electing national union officers.

Party Internal Affairs. The PCC is unlike most other ruling communist parties in several ways. First, it was created and is completely controlled by one man, Fidel Castro. The institutional structure of the party is undeveloped and does not provide either mechanisms for internal debate or guarantees against abuses by superiors. The PCC, although established in 1965, still has not held its first congress. The Political Bureau, the most influential and powerful party body, is made up entirely of former members of the 26 July Movement who are entirely subservient to

Fidel Castro. The Secretariat has little power, and the Central Committee, which has only met a couple of times in five years, is no more than a rubber stamp for decisions made at higher levels.[1] Any distinction drawn between the upper levels of the party and the government is superficial. Second, approximately two-thirds of the top party and government leaders, most of whom are members of the PCC Central Committee, are officers in the Revolutionary Armed Forces, and of these the vast majority are former 26 July fighters. Third, the party—and the government as a whole—suffers severely from a lack of trained and educated personnel at all levels. PCC Organizing Secretary Armando Hart reported in mid-1969 that 79 per cent of the party members did not have a sixth-grade education (*Granma*, English, 20 July). On 26 July 1970, Fidel Castro said that even the top national leaders often did not know what they were doing, that building socialism was much more difficult than they had anticipated, and that "the learning process [was] much longer and harder than we had imagined." (*ibid.*, 2 August).

During the late 1960's the party became increasingly involved in administering programs of all sorts on all levels, in particular those related to the sugar harvest. In early 1970 some criticism was made of ineffective party leaders at middle and lower levels; after the mid-year—when Fidel Castro announced that the sugar harvest goal would not be met—criticism of top-level leaders occurred, some efforts were made to separate party and managerial activities, and a number of ministerial changes involving party members were reported. In July, Major Belarmino Castilla Mas became education minister, replacing José Llanusa, and Marcos Lage Cuello replaced Francisco Padrón as minister for the sugar industry. In August, Captain Serafín Fernández Rodríguez was made internal trade minister, replacing Manuel Luzardo García. In October, Nora Frometa Silva replaced Manuel Enrique Escalona as light industry minister. In December, Antonio E. Lussón replaced Faure Chomón as transportation minister.

Beginning in mid-year there was much talk of the need for popular participation in the party and government. On 28 September Castro even asked: "Who could better supervise our Party than the masses, the masses themselves?" The masses, through their supervision, would "see to it that the Party is in shape to play its role as vanguard." (*Ibid.*, 4 October.) Yet the party was not to become a mass organization. In mid-1969 Armando Hart had stated: "The first thing required for Party membership is revolutionary activity, revolutionary conduct, combativeness and an understanding of the line of the Revolution" (*ibid.*, 25 May). On 20 May 1970, Castro informed the Cuban people that the party had to remain a vanguard party, "the result of a selection of the most determined" (*ibid.*, 31 May). On 28 September he touched on the same point: "It would be utopian for us to believe that everyone met the requirements of being a member of the Party." He added that mass organizations were "an excellent source of cadre material" and that party members were "elected by the masses." (*Ibid.*, 4 October.) In practice, workers may put forward candidates for party membership, but any of their nominations can be rejected by existing members, and all party officials are appointed from above.

The PCC Central Committee's Commission of Revolutionary Orientation (Comisión de Orientación Revolucionaria; COR), headed by Orlando Fundora, is responsible for "internal orientation"—primarily the "political self-improvement of the cadres and militants of the Party and mass organizations"—and for "public orientation" through "propaganda, publicity and information for the people" (statement by Fundora, *ibid.*, 29 November).[2]

---

[1] On 26 July 1970 Castro expressed interest in the formation of a "Bureau of Social Production," which would be "a political instrument of the Party to coordinate the activities of the different administrative branches" (*Granma*, English, 4 October).

[2] Four recent books on the Cuban Revolution have pointed out the concentration of power in Fidel Castro, the absence of institutional safeguards, and the lack of popular participation in many local and all national affairs. See Leo Huberman and Paul M. Sweezy, *Socialism in Cuba* (New York, 1969); K. S. Karol, *Guerrillas in Power* (New York, 1970); René Dumont, *Cuba est-il socialiste?* (Paris, 1970); Hugh Thomas, *Cuba: or The Pursuit of Freedom* (New York, 1971).

The Revolutionary Armed Forces are believed to enroll some 200,000 persons. Almost all the top officers are former members of Castro's 26 July Movement, most of them are members of the PCC, and many are on the party's Central Committee. Cuba devotes a significant part of its budget to military preparedness. On 22 April Fidel Castro revealed that in ten years Cuba had received military aid from the Soviet Union valued at $1.5 billion.

Some 100,000 members of the FAR harvested 20 per cent of the 1970 sugar crop. On 2 December 1969 (Armed Forces Day), a *Granma* editorial stated: "The discipline, organization and habits of precision and exactitude of our Revolutionary Armed Forces will be placed at the service of the sugar harvest, and their influence will be felt throughout the entire process—most especially in the cutting of the sugarcane" (*Granma*, English, 7 December).

Domestic Attitudes and Activities. Since February 1959 the Cuban people have lived under the amended Fundamental Law of the Republic of Cuba. In May 1961 they were promised a socialist constitution; on 28 September 1967 Fidel Castro said the document would be ready in 1969 or 1970. It was not forthcoming, and on 3 September and other occasions in 1970 Castro discounted the importance of such a document until after more elementary tasks, such as the democratization of the labor movement, were accomplished.

During 1958 and early 1959 Castro promised that national elections would be held within eighteen months after the fall of Fulgencio Batista. Although no such elections have taken place, Cuban leaders have continued to speak of democracy in Cuba. Originally, democracy was reportedly found in public rallies and in personal contacts between the leaders and the people. On the local level, limited participation in dispensing local justice began in 1967 with the People's Tribunals. In October 1970 there were 326 such tribunals on the regional-district level, and 2,000 on the local level. After the disappointing sugar harvest,—and perhaps partly in response to the criticisms of foreign observers[3]—a shift in concepts occurred which may be of long-term significance. On 23 August Castro declared: "We must begin to substitute democratic methods for the administrative methods that run the risk of becoming bureaucratic methods" (*Granma*, English, 30 August). Indicative of the shift were the local elections in the CTC at the end of the year (see above).

On 26 July 1968 Castro declared that the "great task of the Revolution" was "basically the task of forming the new man"—"the man of a truly revolutionary conscience, the man of a truly socialist conscience, the man of a truly communist conscience" (*ibid.*, 28 July). This "new man" in Cuba is supposed to be characterized by his devotion to the cause of revolution—the Cuban Revolution in particular—as that cause is defined by his national leaders; further, he is free of any manifestation of selfishness or materialism; he combines revolutionary thought with revolutionary action; and he gladly works or fights for the national and international goals put forward by his leaders, not expecting any payment for his efforts other than his fair share of the still limited produce of his country and the knowledge that he has done his social and moral duty. As models for all Cubans to emulate, during 1970 Cuban leaders pointed to the late Che Guevara and, during the first part of the year, to such "vanguard" labor organizations as the Advance Workers' Movement, the Centennial Youth Column, and the Cienfuegos Communist Brigade.[4]

[3]See the books by Dumont and Karol noted earlier.

[4]Guevara has been considered the model of the "new man" ever since his death in Bolivia in October 1967. In 1970, at the Third Non-Aligned Conference, held on 8-10 September in Lusaka, Zambia, Foreign Relations Minister Raul Roa characterized Guevara as "the immortal figure of the Heroic Guerrilla, commander of the dawn, the firstborn of the Third World" (*Granma*, English, 27 September). On 26 July Fidel Castro announced that Antonio Arguedas—the former Bolivian minister of the interior who gave a copy of Guerara's diary to the Cubans in 1968—had brought "Che's death mask and his hands" to Cuba, where they would be kept on public display, beginning in October, until the "peoples of America" should decide where to preserve them permanently (*ibid.*, 2 August).

Guevara wrote in 1965, in *Socialism and Man in Cuba*, that the formation of the "new man" was the responsibility of the vanguard, those who were more ideologically advanced than the masses. The masses, he said, were not fully developed; they would only "go half way and must be subjected to incentives and pressures of some intensity." One such incentive was introduced on 29 August 1969 in the form of Law 1225 (text in *Granma*, 18 September), which required the keeping of labor dossiers to record the merits and demerits of each worker (see Jorge Risquet's "Resolution on Labor Merit," *ibid.*, English, 25 October 1970) and facilitate the organization and distribution of the labor force.

During 1970, as in years past, the government generally spoke of the employment of moral rather than material incentives, the latter being in short supply and ideologically repugnant. The 1964 Labor Code allowed bonuses for overfulfillment and penalties for underfulfillment of norms, and though Jorge Risquet argued that these rewards and punishments had "lost their significance" in 1970 (*Granma*, 1 August), they were employed to some degree nonetheless. In November 1968 a "parliament of the working class" approved a law, applicable only to vanguard workers, granting full pay in case of sickness, accident, retirement, or death. In 1970, material incentives were also involved (as first suggested by Fidel Castro on 3 September after long discussions of absenteeism with members of the CTC and later set forth by the Ministry of Internal Trade), in a plan for the distribution of such scarce items as household electrical goods, bicycles, pressure cookers, and watches, only through work centers, and only to workers who "fulfill their social duties" (*ibid.*, 2 January 1971).

Sugar. After the failure of their industrialization programs during the early 1960's, Cuban leaders placed greater emphasis on sugar production as the foundation of the national economy.[5] In 1964 a decision was made to try to increase production by one million metric tons each year for the next six years—that is, from 4,474,000 tons in 1964 to 10,000,000 tons in 1970. The reasons for this effort to expand sugar production far beyond the level of pre-Castro days were discussed by Fidel Castro on 20 May 1970. (See *Granma*, English, 31 May.) Sugar, he said, was the only Cuban export whose production could be expanded rapidly enough to assure payment for a significant portion of the ever-increasing imports of oil, raw materials, foodstuffs, and equipment from the Soviet Union. Earlier, the Soviet government had agreed to increase gradually its annual imports of sugar to 5 million tons by 1970 and to pay Cuba 6.11 cents per pound, several times the current market price. On 27 October 1969 Castro went so far as to assert: "It is not a matter of reaching 10 million tons in 1970, but rather one of maintaining that production level from then on" (*Granma*, English, 2 November).

Throughout 1969 and early 1970 the attention of the Cuban people was directed almost entirely toward the 10-million-ton harvest. As early as 13 March 1968, Castro had declared: "[It is] a point of honor for this Revolution . . . a yardstick by which to judge the capability of the Revolution" (*ibid.*, 24 March). On 18 October 1969 he said that a harvest of 9,999,999 tons would be a "moral defeat" (*ibid.*, 26 October), later explaining that a successful harvest was essential so that other nations would have confidence in the Cuban economy and readily grant the credits Cuba needed for working toward its long-term objectives; on 20 December, commenting on the many foreigners who had either traveled to Cuba to cut cane or expressed their support verbally, he

[5]Statistics available from Cuba are of varying reliability. Some, such as those relating to foreign trade, are essentially accurate; most, including those dealing with social services, labor, industry, and agriculture, must be used with caution. Cuban statistics are often incomplete, usually inadequate for cross-checking, and at times contradictory; they are sometimes deliberately distorted and misleading, in particular when an effort is being made to compare Cuba after the revolution with pre-Castro Cuba. Recent indices of agricultural output, for example, often reflect great increases because they are based on 1962-63, in most respects one of the worst years since Castro's rise to power, when the momentum of pre-Castro production had been lost. These difficulties are discussed at length by Carmelo Mesa-Lago in "Availability and Reliability of Statistics in Socialist Cuba," *Latin American Research Review*, Spring 1969, pp. 53-91, and Summer 1969, pp. 47-81.

said that the harvest had become "something like a symbol of internationalism" (*ibid.*, 28 December). Sugar yields in recent years, however, have not met the goals set by the government, as is evident in the following figures:[6]

Year	Target	Actual harvest
		(In metric tons)
1966	6,000,000	4,537,000
1967	7,000,000	6,236,000
1968	8,000,000	5,164,000
1969	9,000,000	4,459,000
1970	10,000,000	8,535,281

The 1970 harvest lasted from 14 July 1969 to 23 July 1970—by many months the longest period of continuous cane-cutting in Cuban history. Some 500,000 persons, many described as "volunteers," were mobilized during the harvest, among them teachers, students, government bureaucrats, housewives, and foreign visitors, as well as rural and urban laborers and military personnel. On 19 May Castro announced that the 10 million tons would not be harvested and introduced a new slogan: "Turn the Setback into a Victory!" In the end, the harvest period had to be extended eight days beyond the originally scheduled termination date of 15 July in order to bring in 8.5 million tons (which was still an all-time record, the largest previous harvest having been 7,298,000 tons in 1952).

On 20 May Castro declared that the administrative apparatus and leaders of the revolution, not the people, were responsible for the shortfall. Over the past four years, he said, the nation's leaders, owing to their "ignorance of the problems of the sugar industry," had not detected problems in time (*Ibid.*, 31 May.) On 26 July Castro went so far as to offer to resign, though he told Chilean journalists on 1 August that to have put the offer into practice would have been "theatrical." As mentioned above, however, a number of ministers, including the minister of the sugar industry, and other leaders lost their positions during the last half of the year.

Despite Castro's blaming the leaders (as when he stated on 20 May that the people could have harvested 10 or 11 million tons under better leadership), on most occasions these men attributed the outcome to shortcomings of the people and other problems. The causes most frequently mentioned were: low labor productivity as a result of worker absenteeism, indifference, and indiscipline; inexperienced cutters who averaged at best one-sixth to one-eighth as much as the pre-1959 professionals; workers who did not properly operate or maintain new or renovated machinery; insufficient, unreliable, and improperly maintained milling, transportation, and irrigation facilities, some old and some new; sabotage; and bad weather. Throughout the harvest there was talk of a "labor shortage" in Cuba; overtime work without pay was encouraged, and time was conserved by postponing Christmas, New Year, and Easter celebrations until the following July and August, after the end of the harvest.

The goal for the 1971 harvest was put at 7 million tons. Cutting began in Camagüey Province on 20 November 1970 and production almost immediately began to fall behind schedule.

[6] Targets for 1966-70 and actual harvest yields for 1966-69 are from Fidel Castro's speech of 20 May 1970 (*Granma*, English, 31 May). The harvest figure for 1970 was given by Havana radio on 3 August 1970.

Other Production. On many occasions Cuban leaders declared that production of 10 million tons of sugar would not in itself be enough to make the 1970 harvest a success. A real success was said to require simultaneous acceleration of all other government programs in the countryside and development of the transportation and production facilities of the nation in general. Among the most important of those programs were cattle raising and the production of rice, citrus fruits, tobacco, and coffee. But Fidel Castro reported on 26 July that the nation had been "unable to wage the simultaneous battle." Quoting from a "highly secret economic report," he declared that the greatly accelerated sugar program, and in particular the 1970 harvest, had "resulted in imbalances in the economy, in diminished production in other sectors, in an increase in [Cuba's] difficulties." Decreased outputs were reported in most consumer lines, including textiles, root and other vegetables, fresh fruits, meat and poultry, beans and edible fats, and even cigars and cigarettes; increases were reported in rice,[7] fish, and eggs. (*Granma*, English, 2 August.)

Social Services. Of all the "basic social services" in Cuba, education is considered the most important.[8] At a national education seminar in December 1970, Raúl Roa stated: "In socialist society, science and technology are at the service of progress and self-improvement for man, and integral, massive, continuous, permanent and interdisciplinary education is their agent." Roa explained: "The basic objective of our education is the formation of the new man of which Major Ernesto Che Guevara was the most outstanding example, a multidimensional man in whom thought and action marched hand in hand." (*Granma*, English, 27 December.)

Elementary education is increasingly carried out in boarding and semi-boarding schools—an arrangement which facilitates efforts for the development of the "new man." Programs at the secondary and pre-university levels are designed to produce mostly technicians, teachers, scientists, and doctors, all with military training. Ultimately the university in its present form is to be eliminated, and "higher education" will be moved to the workers, in the factories or the countryside, so that they can continue their education while carrying out the duties of their occupations.

Major Belarmino Castilla told a UNESCO meeting in Paris in October that illiteracy in Cuba had been reduced in ten years from 23.6 to 3.9 per cent (*ibid.*, 1 November), though Raúl Ferrer, the national director of adult education, told a CTC meeting that in recent years illiteracy had been increasing (*Granma*, 19 September). In late September Heliodoro Martínez reported the number of students at different levels: primary (1,391,597), junior high (150,317), technological (50,181), senior high (16,779), worker-farmer education program (7,977), and university (35,046) (*Granma*, English, 11 October). Castro acknowledged in January 1971 that up to 400,000 children and adolescents between the ages of six and sixteen years were not in school "for one reason or another" (*ibid.*, 10 January); the same figure was given in January 1970. Early in 1970 José Llanusa (then minister of education) reported that more than 700,000 students were two or more years behind in their work (*ibid.*, 26 January 1970), a figure which could only have increased during the disruptions caused by the 1970 sugar harvest. The government acknowledged on several occasions that it could not properly train the number of teachers needed and was forced to allow unqualified persons to take over many classes.

The Cuban government has devoted considerable attention to national health programs. New hospitals and dispensaries, which offer free services, have been established, especially in rural

---

[7] Programs to increase rice production have been widely reported in the last few years, though harvest figures are seldom released. On 2 January 1969 Fidel Castro reported that 50,000 metric tons of rice were harvested in 1968; on 20 May 1970 he said that production had "increased several times over since 1968." According to statistics published by the United Nations, rice production averaged 206,000 tons annually during the decade before Castro's victory, reached a high of 307,000 tons in 1960, and then fell to 123,000 in 1964 and 51,000 in 1966.

[8] When evaluating Cuban claims of progress in the social services since the pre-Castro period it is necessary to understand the government's use of statistics. Figures on schools (and thus on students and teachers) and hospitals (consequently on beds, patients, etc.) in 1958 include only those run then by the state, not the significant number under private control. The private schools and hospitals of the 1950's appear for the first time in Castro's figures in the early 1960's, after they were confiscated by the state, as if they were new facilities. See Mesa-Lago, *op. cit.*, Summer 1969, pp. 68-73.

areas. At the same time the overall quality of health services seems to have declined, largely because almost half of the trained doctors in Cuba before 1959, when health conditions were high by Latin American standards, have gone into exile; their replacements, though more numerous, have not been as well trained.

Inadequate housing has become an increasingly serious problem. On 6 January 1969 Castro stated: "In the years of the Revolution we have not built more than 10,000 dwellings per year, whereas we need to build approximately 100,000 per year" (ibid., 14 January),[9] On 3 September 1970 Castro stated that housing had become a "supercritical" problem (ibid., 20 September). Castro reported on 26 July that 268,089 families paid no rent for their homes; on 7 December he announced that all families with a per capita monthly income of less than 25 pesos—of which he said there were not many—would be exempt from paying rent.

Among the hardships of the Cuban people are the rationing of most foods and other products, and the need to stand in lines for hours to try to get such items as are available. Even sympathetic foreign observers report that these conditions cause widespread grumbling and dissatisfaction. On 26 July Castro admitted:

> Our enemies say we have problems, and in reality our enemies are right. They say there is discontent, and in reality our enemies are right. They say there is irritation, and in reality our enemies are right. (Ibid., 2 August.)

For years, acknowledgments of problems were followed, especially in the speeches of Fidel Castro, by promises of a time when all people would have all their needs satisfied. In 1970, however, Castro warned the people to be prepared for more difficult times during the next decade, stating: "The road is hard. Yes. More difficult than it had seemed." (Ibid.)

The Roman Catholic church and about 30 Protestant denominations remain in Cuba, in what has been described as "coexistence" with the Marxism of the state (Punto Final, Santiago, Chile, 25 February 1969). Armando Hart made the place of Christians clear in May 1969 when discussing qualifications for membership in the PCC. The application of a highly qualified person who had participated in a wide assortment of national and internal defense activities and in agricultural work, who had a "clear political understanding," and who fully accepted "in every way the line of the Cuban Revolution" would still be given close scrutiny if he had "had a child baptized because in a moment of weakness he let his mother-in-law talk him into it." (Granma, English, 25 May.)

The official attitude toward writers and artists was given at the end of 1969 by Nicolás Guillén, a famous poet and president of the National Union of Writers and Artists of Cuba (Unión Nacional de Escritores y Artistas de Cuba; UNEAC):

> [The UNEAC is a] great family united in the common interest of the Cuban Revolution. Naturally, we are not exempt from the conflicts common to any great family—especially a literary and artistic one—but this is a family in which everyone tries to do his duty, and he who doesn't, regardless of his position, will receive the most severe revolutionary punishment for his fault. (Granma, English, 7 December.)

These guidelines were evidently observed during 1970 since there was no campaign to equal the one waged in 1969 against the "counterrevolutionary" works of two Cuban writers, Heberto Padilla and Antón Arrufat, who had been awarded prizes in a UNEAC literary contest at the end of 1968 by a specially invited jury of foreign intellectuals.[10]

[9] This yearly average falls slightly below the estimated average number of houses built during the years 1945-58 (see Mesa-Lago, op. cit., pp. 69-72).

[10] Padilla was arrested in March 1971 and released a month later after he had released a long "confession" which detailed his "counterrevolutionary" attitudes and activities.

By the end of 1970 some 600,000 persons had voluntarily left Cuba—including about 215,000 on the refugee flights which have taken place twice each week-day since 1965 between Cuba and Miami. Many were skilled professionals whose departure has complicated problems in education, medicine, and other fields. At the end of 1970 it was rumored that after persons on the present waiting list—all of whom signed up before May 1966, when applications were closed— have left Cuba, the refugee flights will be terminated by the Cuban government.

International Views and Positions. Inasmuch as the PCC has only once issued anything approaching an overall statement on foreign policy (the Central Committee statement of 18 May 1967; see *YICA 1968*, Cuba), Cuban international views and positions must be sought primarily in the speeches of Fidel Castro and other top officials, especially Foreign Minister Raúl Roa and Minister without Portfolio Carlos Rafael Rodríguez.

During 1970 Cuban leaders expressed themselves publicly on most international issues, but generally avoided the activist positions—particularly with regard to rural guerrilla warfare in Latin America—which had reached a peak in 1967. The milder manner of Cuban international relations was characterized by the absence of calls for immediate armed struggle in most Latin American countries and by closer relations with the Soviet Union and most Soviet-bloc communist parties, notably those in Latin America. This was largely the result of an overriding preoccupation with domestic issues, an apparent discouragement with immediate rural guerrilla warfare following repeated setbacks, and the need to maintain close relations with the Soviet Union in order to assure the continuation of economic and military aid.

Socialism and Underdevelopment.   On 26 July Castro stated:

> Karl Marx himself believed socialism would be a natural result of a technologically highly advanced society. But in today's world, given the presence of industrialized imperialist powers, countries such as ours have no other alternative—to overcome their cultural and technical backwardness—than socialism. (*Granma*, English, 2 August.)

This was not to mean that Marx was obsolete, for Castro emphasized on 7 December that "the essential thing in the ideas of Marx was development" (*ibid.*, 20 December). In his speech of 22 April on the Lenin Centenary he went further:

> Marxist theory was never a pattern; it was a conception .   .   . a method .   .   . an interpretation .   .   . a science. And the science is applied to each concrete case. And no two concrete cases are exactly alike.

Finally, he declared that Marx and Lenin, taken together, constituted "precisely those two human personalities that mark the transition from the prehistory to the history of mankind." (*Ibid.*, 3 May.)

According to Minister of Foreign Relations Raúl Roa (speaking on 10 September at the Third Conference of Non-Aligned Countries, in Lusaka, Zambia), the "real division in the world is that between exploited and exploiter countries," the latter being the "imperialist countries, headed by the United States." The socialist countries, he added, were the "strongest support and the most pugnacious force of the anti-imperialist front." (*Ibid.*, 27 September.)

Revolution in Latin America.   Ever since the overthrow of Fulgencio Batista in Cuba in 1959, Fidel Castro has called upon revolutionaries in Latin America to seize power in their countries by armed struggle. The urgency of this call, however, and the breadth of its applicability, has varied somewhat from one period to another, largely as a result of international conditions and pressures, or domestic conditions, or both. The advocacy of rural guerrilla warfare was strongest in two periods: the early 1960's, when it was expounded most forcefully in Castro's "Second Declaration of Havana" in 1962, and between 1966 and 1968, when it was argued best during 1967 in Régis Debray's *Revolution in the Revolution?*, Castro's speeches of 13 March and 10 August, Che Guevara's Message to the Tricontinental Conference (April), and the statements of the Latin American Solidarity Conference (July-August) in Havana, and implemented most memorably by Che Guevara in Bolivia. Advocacy of rural guerrilla warfare was most restrained immediately after the conference of Latin American communist parties at the end of 1964, and in 1969 and 1970.

On 22 April Castro stated the position he apparently held, though seldom stated, throughout the year:

> As long as imperialism exists and as long as there are fighters ready to fight for the liberation of their peoples from that imperialism, the Cuban Revolution will lend its support.... When we speak of supporting a revolutionary movement we should say that that support does not necessarily have to be expressed exclusively in favor of guerrilla movements, but includes any government which sincerely adopts a policy of economic and social development and of liberating its country from the Yankee imperialist yoke; no matter by what path that government has reached power, Cuba will support it. (*Granma*, English, 3 May.)

The two governments Cuban leaders praised most enthusiastically during the year were those of General Juan Velasco Alvarado, which came to power by a military coup in Peru in October 1968, and of Salvador Allende, which was voted into office in Chile in September 1970. In an interview with Chilean newspapermen in Havana on 1 August, Castro stated that he believed socialism could be achieved in Chile through an election victory, though not in most other Latin American countries.

Cuban leaders still anticipated eventual armed struggle in most of Latin America, but their position was more complex than in 1967. Verbal support for rural guerrilla warfare in some countries remained constant while in regard to others it declined. In December 1969 the Venezuelan Douglas Bravo, perhaps the best known "Castroite" guerrilla leader in Latin America during the 1960's, made his first of many attacks on Castro for devoting all his attention to domestic economic development and ignoring his "internationalist" obligations, namely his support of Latin American guerrillas (see Bravo interviews in *Intercontinental Press*, New York, 8 June 1970, and *Le Monde*, Paris, English edition, 12 August). Similar charges were reportedly made by the Colombian Castroite Fabio Vásquez and by lesser Castroites in other Latin American countries. Castro responded to such charges, without mentioning names, on 22 April:

> Cuba has not refused nor will she ever refuse support to the revolutionary movement. But this is not to be confused with support for just any faker [or for] destroyers of revolutions, men who had the opportunity to wage a revolutionary war, [but] instead sabotaged it and destroyed it.... That kind of pseudorevolutionary cannot count on any kind of help from Cuba, of course. Ah! But revolutionaries like Che, revolutionaries like Che who are ready to fight and die, this kind of revolutionary can always count on receiving aid from Cuba! (*Granma*, English, 3 May.)

Urban guerrilla warfare, which was discounted altogether by Cuban leaders in 1967, had become of considerable interest by 1969 and continued so in 1970. This was evident above all in Cuban support for the Uruguayan National Liberation Movement ("Tupamaros") and the Brazilian National Liberation Action (ALN). During 1970 the "Minimanual of the Urban Guerrilla," by Carlos Marighella, the founder of the ALN, was given publicity almost equal to that of Régis Debray's *Revolution in the Revolution?* in 1967.[11]

Soviet Union. Soviet-Cuban relations, which reached a low point in 1967 and early 1968, began to improve openly at the time of Fidel Castro's endorsement of the Soviet-led occupation of Czechoslovakia and continued to do so with Cuba's attendance at the International Meeting of Communist and Workers' Parties in Moscow in June 1969.[12] During 1970 relations were very close in spite of a few open and covert differences, as in attitudes toward the military government in Bolivia and moral incentives. On 22 April Castro stated: "The existence of the Soviet state is objectively .   .   . one of the most extraordinary privileges enjoyed by the revolutionary movement." He denounced "superrevolutionary theoreticians" and "superleftists," who could not "forgive the Soviet Union for existing," and concluded:

> They forgot the problems of Cuba, Vietnam, and those of the Arab world. In other words, wherever imperialism is launching its criminal attacks, there is one country, one state, that sends weapons in the amounts needed for the peoples to defend themselves from that imperialism. (*Granma*, English, 3 May.)

During the year Castro repeatedly expressed his dependence upon and gratitude to the Soviet Union (e.g., the speeches of 22 April and 26 July). On 22 April, when he revealed that the Soviet Union had given Cuba $1.5 billion in military aid, he added that Cuba was always ready to increase its military ties with them in spite of U.S. objections (*ibid.*). At the end of 1969 the Soviet armed forces newspaper *Red Star* (2 December) reported that the "newest weapons and military equipment" were being provided the Cubans. A Soviet fleet visited Cuba for the first time in July 1969; three more fleets arrived in Cuba during 1970, in May, September, and December, the last two leading to a series of exchanges between the U.S. and Soviet governments regarding the possible construction of a Soviet submarine base at Cienfuegos harbor and a violation of the 1962 Kennedy-Khrushchev understanding (*New York Times*, 15 November and 24 December; *Washington Post*, 1 October and 21 November).

Soviet economic aid to Cuba during 1970 reportedly had a value of more than $500 million; Cuban indebtedness to the Soviet Union at the end of the year, including trade deficits but not military aid, was estimated at approximately $3 billion. On 2 December TASS announced that PCC Secretariat member Carlos Rafael Rodríguez had arrived in Moscow for talks on future Soviet-Cuban economic cooperation in general and sugar purchases in particular.[13]

At the 1969 Moscow Conference, only a few weeks after the Sino-Soviet clashes on the Ussuri River, Rodríguez placed Cuba more firmly in the Soviet camp than ever before without, however, condemning Communist China by name:

> We declare from this rostrum that, in any decisive confrontation—whether concerning Soviet action in the face of the danger of the tearing off of members from the socialist system by impe-

[11]The "Minimanual" was published twice in 1970, in *Tricontinental* (January-February) and *Tricontinental Bulletin* (November). Another sharp critique of Debray's sole emphasis on rural guerrilla warfare, by two "Cuban revolutionaries," originally published in the New York *Monthly Review* in 1968 (see *YICA*, 1969, pp. 203-4), was reportedly published in Cuba in 1969 (*Tribuna Popular*, Caracas, 26 November). Nonetheless, Castro and the Cuban media welcomed the release of Debray by the Bolivian government in December and induced him to visit Cuba in early 1971.

[12]A defector from the Cuban intelligence service has stated that during late 1968 Castro signed an accord with the Soviets which committed him to muting his criticisms of the Soviet Union and of the pro-Soviet communist parties in Latin America in exchange for increases in Soviet technological assistance, shipments to Cuba of raw materials and agricultural machinery, and purchases of Cuban products. See *Christian Science Monitor*, 16 July 1969, and testimony of Orlando Castro Hidalgo before the U.S. Senate Internal Security Subcommittee on 16 October (*Communist Threat to the United States through the Caribbean*, Part 20, 91st Cong., 1st session, Washington, D.C., 1970).

[13]In late February 1971 TASS announced that the value of Soviet aid to Cuba would increase by $110 million in 1971 (*New York Times*, 28 February).

rialist maneuvers or concerning a provocation or aggression against the Soviet people, come from where it may—Cuba will unyieldingly be at the side of the USSR. (*Granma*, English, 15 June 1969.)

Deputy Prime Minister Raúl Castro repeated this pledge while attending the 1970 May Day celebrations in Moscow (Moscow radio, 8 May).

Cuban relations with most countries of Eastern Europe have improved in the past two years as ties with the Soviet Union became increasingly close.

Communist China. Cuban relations with the Chinese People's Republic (CPR), which had been very good in the early 1960's, began to deteriorate seriously after the conference of Latin American communist parties in Havana in late 1964, from which the CPR, but not the Soviet Union, had been excluded. The lowest point was reached in early 1966 when Castro accused the Chinese of carrying out a "criminal sort of economic aggression" against Cuba, of having "confused Marxism-Leninism with fascism," and other such activities; the Chinese response was only mildly inflammatory in comparison. Both countries withdrew their ambassadors in 1967, though diplomatic relations were maintained at a lower level; Cuban leaders and publications almost completely ignored events in China, and vice versa.

During 1970 a considerable improvement in Sino-Cuban relations was indicated by the resumption of delegation travel between the two countries, a revival of friendly messages between government leaders, and expanded news coverage. In November the Cuban news agency Prensa Latina opened an office in Peking and the Cuban government announced that it had agreed to the appointment of Chang Teh-chun, a senior diplomat with long service in the Soviet Union (1961-67), as ambassador to Cuba. At the end of the year Cuba still was represented in Peking by a chargé d'affaires.[14] For many years Cuba has regularly called for the admission of the CPR to the United Nations.

Although the volume of Sino-Cuban trade was reduced in 1966, commercial links between the countries remained fairly steady thereafter. Trade agreements were signed each year; Cuba received rice, soya beans, and cotton cloth from the CPR, which continued to be Cuba's second-largest communist market for sugar.

Latin America. In accord with a decision reached in 1964 by the Organization of American States (OAS), all Latin American countries (except Mexico, which refused to comply) broke diplomatic and commercial relations with Cuba.[15] In February 1970 the Chilean government of Eduardo Frei restored commercial ties with Cuba and in November the newly elected government of Salvador Allende reestablished diplomatic relations. During the year several other countries talked of "normalizing" relations with Cuba and of readmitting Cuba to its seat in the OAS.

Cuban relations with most pro-Soviet communist parties in Latin America, which had been openly hostile in 1967, were generally proper, even if not cordial, during 1970. The disputes that did arise, such as that with the Communist Party of Chile newspaper *El Siglo* in February, were not prolonged, nor carried on by top party personnel as in 1967. Even so, remarks by Cuban leaders indicated the belief that many pro-Soviet parties were incapable of leading a true anti-imperialist revolution. Pro-Chinese parties and movements were ignored altogether.

The Cubans continued to give their highest praise—while apparently giving somewhat less training and material support—to some of the guerrilla organizations in Latin America—in particular the rural National Liberation Army (ELN) in Bolivia, and the urban-based National Liberation Movement (the MLN or "Tupamaros") in Uruguay, and the National Liberation Action (ALN) in Brazil.

---

[14]The Cuban ambassador to China arrived in Peking in March 1971.
[15]The decision followed OAS confirmation of a charge by President Rómulo Betancourt of Venezuela that Cuba, in furnishing arms to Venezuelan guerrillas and terrorists, had intervened in his country's internal affairs.

Two of the best known "Castroite" guerrilla forces in South America, the National Liberation Army (ELN) in Colombia and the Armed Forces of National Liberation (FALN) in Venezuela, in particular the latter, were no longer praised in the Cuban news media and from the beginning of the year were protesting that the Cubans had abandoned them.

Aid to Revolutionaries. On 18 May 1967, after several Cubans were found taking part in a guerrilla landing on the coast of Venezuela, a statement by the PCC Central Committee declared:

> We are accused of helping the revolutionary movement, and we, quite so, are giving and will continue to give help to all revolutionary movements that struggle against imperialism in any part of the world, whenever they request it. (*Granma*, English 21 May.)

The Guevara-led insurgency in Bolivia was an effort not to aid foreign revolutionaries but to export a revolution from Cuba, as the diaries of Guevara and other Cuban participants and the comments of Bolivian communists, both pro-Soviet and pro-Chinese, clearly showed.

In the past two years, although Cuba has shown less concern for immediate armed revolution in most parts of Latin America, some training and materiel have been provided and moral support has been expressed. Training camps have been operating in Cuba since the early 1960's, the main center being at Minas del Frio in the Sierra Maestra. These camps, attended by Africans as well as Latin Americans, have begun to teach the tactics of urban in addition to rural guerrilla warfare. A defector from the Cuban General Directorate of Intelligence (DGI), Orlando Castro Hidalgo, reported that the DGI was responsible for providing money, intelligence training, false documents, travel arrangements, and contacts for the trainees, while the FAR gave military instruction. According to Castro Hidalgo, potential students were screened more carefully after the guerrilla setbacks of 1967 and 1968, and Cuban officials decided not to send Cuban military leaders to assist revolutionary groups in their own countries until after a significant level of development had been reached and the Cuban groups had been invited to come by local guerrilla leaders.[16] On 22 April 1970 Castro suggested a more careful and rigorous examination of self-proclaimed revolutionaries would be necessary now than in the past since some "fakers" had managed to get considerable Cuban assistance without deserving it.

Southeast Asia. In recent years Cuban leaders have repeatedly proclaimed their solidarity with the Democratic Republic of Vietnam, the National Liberation Front of South Vietnam (NLFSV), and the "people of Vietnam" in general. On 4 March 1969 Cuba became the first country to open an "Embassy," recognized by the NLFSV, in South Vietnam. On 11 June 1969 Cuba recognized the "Provisional Revolutionary Government of South Vietnam" (PRGSV) and on 12 June the diplomatic representation of the NLFSV in Cuba became the Embassy of the PRGSV. Raúl Roa expressed Cuban pleasure with the presence of the PRGSV, a "veritable model of a nonaligned country," at the Third Non-Aligned Conference, in Zambia, and said the delegation should have been a full participant rather than an observer. Roa told the conference delegates: "The people of Cuba have said it a thousand times: If necessary, we are ready to shed our blood for Vietnam." (*Granma*, English, 27 September.)

Fidel Castro and President Osvaldo Dorticós sent two messages to Prince Norodom Sihanouk at the end of April, one congratulating him on the formation of the Cambodian Royal Government of National Union, and the other expressing full support for and solidarity with the "program of struggle until final victory" outlined at the "Summit Conference of Indo-Chinese Peoples" held in the China-Laos-Vietnam frontier region on 24-25 April (*Granma*, English, 10

---

[16]See *Christian Science Monitor*, 16 July 1969, and the testimony of Castro Hidalgo, before the U.S. Senate Internal Security Subcommittee, (*op. cit.*).

May). According to Raúl Roa, the Cubans were disgusted that Prince Sihanouk had not been asked to participate in the Third Non-Aligned Conference. In August a "Committee of Solidarity with Vietnam, Cambodia, and Laos" was established (see *Granma*, English, 16 August).

Africa and the Middle East.   Addressing the U.N. General Assembly on 2 October, Ricardo Alarcón de Quesada, Cuban permanent representative to the U.N., said that the Cuban delegation to the Third Non-Aligned Conference would "support all efforts" to "aid the just struggle of the peoples of Guinea-Bissau, Angola, Mozambique, Zimbabwe, Namibia and South Africa" (*Granma*, English, 11 October). At the conference, Raúl Roa declared: "In South Africa, Namibia and Zimbabwe, armed aggression crouches treacherously on the borders of Zambia. The extreme seriousness of this situation calls for swift, concerted and effective action; political and moral solidarity must now be joined by effective aid." (*Ibid.*, 27 September.) There is evidence that Cuba has been providing "effective aid" for some time to the African Party for the Independence of Guinea and Cape Verde (PAIGC) and other African guerrillas. For example, the secretary-general of the PAIGC, attending the 26 July celebrations in Havana in 1970, expressed his group's appreciation for the collaboration of Cuban doctors and for "every other form of cooperation that may be of any help to our struggle" (*ibid.*, 9 August).

The Cuban position on the Arab-Israeli conflict was outlined by Ricardo Alarcón to the U.N. General Assembly:

> Cuba reaffirms her support for the Arab countries and once again calls for the withdrawal of Israeli troops from all the occupied territory of the United Arab Republic, Syria and Jordan. We also express our firm support for the people of Palestine in their heroic struggle to obtain their legitimate rights. (*Ibid.*, 11 October.)

Cuban leaders expressed their grief over the death of U.A.R. President Gamal Abdel Nasser. Close ties were maintained with Al Fatah, the Palestine guerrilla organization, whose leader Yasir 'Arafat reportedly invited Fidel Castro to visit the "bases of the Palestinian Revolution."

United States.   Cuban leaders have repeatedly declared that "U.S. imperialism" was the most serious threat to world peace and was the bulwark of exploitation and oppression throughout the world. Fidel Castro, Raúl Roa, and others charged during 1970 that the United States was planning a "new aggression" against the people of Cuba.

On 19 May Castro asserted that although capitalism and imperialism had "developed and spread without the need of repressive methods" in the U.S., this was no longer possible there:

> Perhaps the most serious problem facing imperialism is that of already having to begin to apply repressive methods so as to survive within a great nation which has none of the traditions of classical repression which other peoples have known.

He then called upon the Cuban people to "greet with emotion and optimism the struggle of our brothers the black people of the United States, the struggle of our brothers the U.S. students and the struggle of our brothers the U.S. workers." (*Granma*, English, 31 May.) Three leftist groups from the United States, calling themselves the "Venceremos Brigade," were among the volunteer helpers in the sugar harvest and other agricultural work in Cuba during 1970.[17]

Hijacking and Kidnaping.   The number of planes hijacked to Cuba during 1970 was down from 1969. Cuban leaders continued to insist that the problem could only be solved along the lines of a Cuban law which proposes reciprocity and respect of the right of asylum through bilateral agreements.[18]

---

[17] "Venceremos," Spanish for "We Will Win," is the slogan with which virtually every speech given in Cuba is concluded.
[18] See the extended comments on this subject by Ricardo Alarcón de Quesada (*Granma*, English, 11 October).

In his talk on 1 August with Chilean newspapermen, Fidel Castro declared that although Cuba did not promote the tactic of kidnaping, he would not condemn it. He declared it a product of repressive societies and concluded that it did not occur in Cuba or other countries where there was a "reign of justice." During the year prisoners from several Latin American countries, who had gained their freedom as a ransom in cases of kidnaping, were welcomed in Cuba. Among them were prisoners from the Dominican Republic (April), Brazil (June), and Nicaragua and Costa Rica (October).

The Cuban media commented only briefly on the "just executions" of West German Ambassador Count Karl von Spreti in Guatemala (April), U.S. security adviser Daniel Mitrione in Uruguay (July), and Quebec Labor Minister Pierre Laporte (October).

International Contacts. During 1970 many delegations from both communist and noncommunist countries visited Cuba to work in the sugar harvest.

High-level contacts with foreign leaders included the following.

The secretary-general of the Soviet-front International Organization of Journalists, Jiří Kubka, visited Cuba in March to discuss the organization's conference scheduled for Havana in January 1971. Konstantin F. Katushev, a member of the Central Committee of the Communist Party of the Soviet Union, was the main guest at the 26 July celebrations. Bulgarian leader Todor Zhivkov visited Cuba in July-August, Czechoslovak Foreign Minister Jan Marko in October-November, and Bulgarian Interior Minister Angel Solakov in November.

Cuban visitors to the Soviet Union included Carlos Rafael Rodríguez in January-February and December, Raúl Castro in April-May and October, and Osvaldo Dorticós, in April. Heliodoro Martínez was in Bulgaria, in June. Raúl Castro visited the German Democratic Republic to observe Warsaw Pact military maneuvers in October.

Delegations of the Laotian Patriotic Front visited Cuba in July-September and October. Visits were made to Mongolia by Raúl Castro and to North Vietnam by Vilma Espín, both in April.

Heliodoro Martínez visited Peru twice, in June and July, in connection with Cuban aid to Peruvian earthquake victims. Carlos Rafael Rodríguez in October addressed the regional conference of the U.N. Food and Agricultural Organization in Venezuela and in November led a delegation to the inauguration of President Salvador Allende in Chile. Former Bolivian Interior Minister Antonio Arguedas was in Cuba in June, and Carlos Altamirano, a leading member of the Chilean Socialist Party, in November.

A delegation from the Syrian Ba'th Party visited Cuba in January. In June, Carlos Rafael Rodríguez attended U.N. economics conferences in Geneva and New York. Raúl Roa led a Cuban delegation to the Third Non-Aligned Conference in Lusaka, Zambia, in September. Belarmino Castilla addressed the UNESCO general conference at Paris in October.

Publications. The Havana daily newspaper *Granma*, published since 1965 and named after the schooner which carried Castro and his followers to Cuba from Mexico late in 1956, is the organ of the Central Committee of the PCC. The editor is Jorge Enrique Mendoza. *Granma* appears also in weekly editions in Spanish, English, and French. The daily evening newspaper *Juventud Rebelde* is controlled by the UJC and edited by Angel Guerra Cabrera. *Verde Olivo*, the weekly organ of the FAR, under the directorship of Luis Pavón, has become an important source of authoritative statements in the continued absence of the PCC theoretical journal *Cuba Socialista*. The PCC Commission of Revolutionary Orientation publishes the monthly *El Militante Comunista*. *Casa de las Americas*, with Roberto Fernández Retamar as director, is a monthly sociopolitical and literary review. *Signos*, edited by the National Council of Culture and directed by Samuel Feijoo, began publication in November. *Bohemia*, a weekly magazine with articles on a wide variety of subjects, is under the directorship of Enrique de la Osa. A monthly political journal aimed at the "revolutionary intellectual" is *Pensamiento Crítico*, with Fernando Martínez as director. Two widely circulating publications of the Cuba-based Afro-Asian-Latin American Peoples' Solidarity Organization are *Tricontinental* (in Spanish, English, French, and Italian), which appears six times a year, and the monthly *Tricontinental Bulletin* (in Spanish, English, and French).[19]

Prensa Latina is the only Cuban news agency. The Cuban Broadcasting Institute broadcasts in Arabic, West Indian Creole, English, French, Guaraní, Quechua, Portuguese, and Spanish.

W. E. R.

[19]For information on more than 100 periodicals published in Cuba during the period 1959-1970 see *Cuban Studies Newsletter*, Vol. 1, No. 2 (May 1971), published by the Center for Latin American Studies at the University of Pittsburgh.

DOMINICAN REPUBLIC

Widespread dissension over leadership and policy questions, especially since 1965, have led to the fragmentation of the communist movement in the Dominican Republic. There are three principal organizations: the Dominican Communist Party (Partido Comunista Dominicano; PCD), which, although given recognition by the Soviet Union, has adopted an "independent" line on domestic and foreign issues; the Dominican People's Movement (Movimiento Popular Dominicano; MPD), which is pro-Chinese; and the Revolutionary Movement of 14 June (Movimiento Revolucionario 14 de Junio; MR-1J4) which is pro-Chinese and at the same time sympathetic toward the Castroites. Splits within these groups have resulted in the creation of several new factions and parties, including the People's Socialist Party (Partido Socialista Popular; PSP), the Communist Party of the Dominican Republic (Partido Comunista de la República Dominicana; PCRD or PACOREDO), and the Red Line (Línea Roja) of the MR-1J4. Only the PCD appears to enjoy recognition within the international communist movement.

Communism in the Dominican Republic is proscribed under National Laws 6, 70, and 71, which refer to propaganda and subversive activities. Although in the past the various communist groups were tolerated and their illegality, in the main, merely prevented their direct electoral participation, the present government under President Joaquín Balaguer has considerably increased its efforts, through the use of the national police and the armed forces, to curb such communist activities as terrorizing, propagandizing, and promoting strikes and violence. Nevertheless, violence has not been eliminated, and during 1970 politically motivated murders of members of the armed forces and police and especially of civilians associated with various leftist political parties occurred almost on a daily basis. [1] During the presidential election campaign held in May, an estimated 100 persons—mostly leftists—were killed (see *Le Monde*, Paris, 20 May and *New York Times*, 23 August).

The total membership of communist groups in the Dominican Republic has been estimated at about 1,100 persons, with the following breakdown: PCD, 250; MPD, 250; MR-1J4, 400; PSP, 50; PCRD, 100 (*World Strength of the Communist Party Organizations*, Washington, D.C., 1970). The population of the Dominican Republic is 4,300,000 (estimated 1970).

Sources of support for the communists, which include universities, secondary schools, and labor organizations, reflect the fragmentation of the movement. At the university level, the student movement has divided into the following organizations: "Fragua," formerly composed of PCD, MPD, and MR-1J4 adherents but led now by the Red Line of the MR-1J4; Juventud Comunista,

[1]Since the April 1965 uprising that prompted U.S. intervention, the Dominican Republic has witnessed many political murders. Responsibility for most killings has been attributed to what the government terms the "uncontrollable forces," but which are believed to be "right-wing paramilitary groups linked with the army and the police" (*Le Monde*, Paris, 20 May 1970). Leftist groups have retaliated and, as a result, killings of police and army elements have also taken place. For specific accounts of political assassinations during 1970, see the Santo Domingo daily *El Nacional de Ahora* for the entire year.

led by PCRD members; the Comité Universitario "Julio Antonio Mella," led by PCD members; and the Comité "Flavio Suero," led by MPD members. The powerful Federation of Dominican Students (Federación de Estudiantes Dominicanos; FED), which is said to enroll about 200,000 university and secondary school students, has been led since 1969 by noncommunist but left-wing students belonging to the Dominican Revolutionary Party (Partido Revolucionario Dominicano; PRD). The communist movement at the secondary school level is represented by the Union of Revolutionary Students (Unión de Estudiantes Revolucionarios; UER).

Within the labor movement, communist support is more limited. The leadership of the "Foupsa-Cesitrado" labor confederation (now weakened by internal dissent) is reportedly in hands of MPD members. The powerful "Unachosin" drivers' union includes communist party members, mostly of the MPD.[2]

The PCD. The PCD was founded clandestinely in 1942. It was reestablished openly as the Dominican People's Socialist Party (Partido Socialista Popular Dominicano) in 1946. During the military-civilian revolt in April 1965 the party identified itself once again as the Dominican Communist Party and has used this name ever since. In August 1967 it adopted (verbally but not in practice) a Castroite line by supporting the concept of armed struggle in most Latin American countries—a shift that had little effect in its relations with Moscow.

Leadership and Organization. The most prominent members of the PCD are Narciso Isa Conde (secretary-general), José Cuello, Antonio Isa Conde, Fabio Ulises García, Manuel Sánchez, Luis Gómez, Asdrúbel Domínguez, Mario Sánchez Córdoba, and Carlos Doré. Dr. Diómedes Mercedes, formerly prominent in the party, left it in May 1970 and announced that he would join the party of former Dominican President Juan Bosch, the PRD.

The PCD claims to be organized on a national scale, with cells in almost every city and in many regions of the countryside. The party has also a committee operating in New York City, where approximately 250,000 persons of Dominican origin reside.

Domestic Attitudes and Activities. The PCD declaims to have abandoned the electoral process as a means of attaining power. As to its revolutionary tactics, the party has stated that these could include "a progressive coup d'état, an urban revolt, or urban or guerrilla warfare" (statement by Isa Conde, *El Nacional de Ahora*, 24 November 1969).

Party activities during 1970 centered on the presidential elections, held in May. Continuing to endorse the "dictatorship with popular support" thesis advocated by Juan Bosch (see *YICA*, 1970, pp. 400-401), the PCD repeatedly called upon other revolutionary forces to put it into effect. In the months that preceded the election, the PCD frequently appealed for the formation of a front of revolutionary groups to demand establishment of the type of government described by Bosch. A statement by the New York-based PCD committee declared: "The new system delineated by Bosch's thesis covers fundamental aspects of the first stage of the Dominican revolution, and at the same time it sets the norms for a continuation toward socialist objectives, power to the workers, and the total collectivization of the economy" (*El Nacional de Ahora*, 23 April). Despite the appeals issued by the PCD, no positive answer came from any "progressive" political party. Bosch's party, the PRD, which ignored all PCD overtures for joint action, became the object of harsh criticism by the PCD for deciding to oppose the reelection of President Balaguer by merely boycotting the elections instead of advocating the creation of the "dictatorship with popular support." The PCD, however, continued to support the Bosch thesis. In a later statement,

[2]"Foupsa-Cesitrado" is an abbreviation for United Worker Front in Support of Autonomous Trade Unions and Trade Union Central of Dominican Workers. "Unachosin" stands for National Union of Independent Drivers.

Secretary-General Isa Conde asserted that the program advocated by the "dictatorship with popular support" thesis was appropriate to the stage of national liberation, since it would allow the establishment of a regime of "revolutionary transition." He added, however, that a revolution limited to the thesis' program would be an incomplete revolution. (*Ibid.*, 17 July.)

The elections served to increase conflict between the PCD and the pro-Chinese MPD. While the MPD proposed an "anti-reelection alliance" (which could include even rightist elements), the PCD contended that the people should fight not only against the "electoral farce" but also against the existing system of government as a whole. It also attacked the MPD's willingness to ally with all anti-Balaguer forces, not excluding sectors of the "oligarchy."

Relations between the PCD and the PCRD also seemed hostile. A PCD statement officially accused PCRD militants of "continually watching and provoking" and even "threatening to kill" PCD members (Radio Comercial, Santo Domingo, 10 November). Later in the year, the increased violence between MPD and PCRD militants (see below), prompted the PCD to issue an appeal calling upon democratic forces to "fight the acts of terrorism committed by the MPD and the PCRD."

A meeting of the Organization of American States (OAS) was scheduled to be held in Santo Domingo on 22 June. It was opposed by most liberal sectors in the country and actively condemned, through various violent demonstrations, by communist groups. The PCD asserted that the "holding of the OAS meeting in the Dominican Republic" was a "threat of repression directed at the people" (*ibid.*, 1 June). The meeting was held instead at Washington, D.C.

International Views and Positions. Since June 1969, when the PCD rejected in its totality the Main Document of the International Meeting of Communist and Workers' Parties, held at that time in Moscow, the party appears not to have made any major statements on the international communist movement.

On the occasion of the anniversary of the 26 of July Movement in Cuba, the PCD declared: "The Cuban socialist revolution delineates the essential content of the Latin American revolutionary process and teaches us that any revolutionary step which precedes socialism must be considered as an intermediate stage" (*El Nacional de Ahora*, 26 July).

Publications. The PCD publishes a clandestine weekly, *El Popular*. Its declarations also appear as paid announcements or as letter to the editor in the independent daily *El Nacional de Ahora*, which also publishes letters from the other communist groups.

*   *   *

The PSP. The adoption by the PCD of Castroite views and tactics in both domestic and international policies, although mostly limited to verbal declarations, created a split within the party in 1967. The less militant members, proclaiming their support for Moscow and "peaceful coexistence," decided to form a new party using the PCD's former name, the Popular Socialist Party (PSP). Despite its pro-Soviet stance, however, the PSP has not been recognized by the Soviet Union.

The PSP is led by Drs. Tulio H. Arvello, Félix Servio Doucoudray, and José Espaillat. It registered no activities during 1970 and may have dissolved.

*   *   *

The MPD. Formed in Havana in 1956 (by a militant wing of what was then called the Dominican People's Socialist Party) to fight "revisionist tendencies," the Dominican People's Movement became a formal party only in August 1965. It is pro-Chinese and is considered to be one of the most active and violent leftist groups.

Leadership and Organization. Leaders of the MPD include Maximiliano Gómez (the secretary-general, now in Cuba), Julio de Peña Valdés (secretary-general of "Foupsa-Cesitrado"), Jorge Puello, Agustín Moisés Blanco, Onelio Espaillat, Fernando de la Rosa, and Rafael "Fafa" Taveras. The party suffered a heavy loss during 1970 when high-ranking members Otto Morales (who, like Taveras, was considered a party ideologist) and Amín Abel Hasbún were killed by police forces on 16 July and 24 September, respectively. "Fafa" Traveras was arrested on 10 June, charged with having participated in the kidnaping of a U.S. military attaché, and was still in detention at the end of the year. Morales's death was followed by student riots in Santo Domingo.

The MPD is organized by regional committees, which include the areas of Santiago, La Romana, Barahona, Francisco de Macorís, and Santo Domingo. In the north there exist various "clandestine commandos" which reportedly belong to the MPD.

Domestic Attitudes and Activities. The MPD's stated domestic objective is the seizure of power by the proletariat, peasantry, and other "progressive" forces to install a "people's democratic dictatorship."

MPD strategy in the presidential elections called for the creation of a front of both rightist and leftist forces to oppose Balaguer's reelection. An MPD Central Committee statement (*El Nacional de Ahora*, 20 January) asked for "mass mobilization at all levels against reelection and terrorism, and integration within the movement of all sectors opposed to 'continuism' [i.e., Balaguer's reelection]." The MPD program, presented in February, advocated distribution to dispossed peasants of lands belonging to the state and the "reelectionists," reinstatement of all discharged employees, participation of workers in administration of the state enterprises, a larger education budget to improve the level of education and increase the salaries of teachers, better living standards, and respect for democratic freedoms. (*Ibid.*, 27 February.)

Answering PCD charges of opportunism for its willingness to seek an electoral alliance with rightist parties, the MPD replied that such an alliance would be a "tactical" one, and that the immediate situation called for a "democratic coalition government" as a step toward the ultimate goal of the establishment of socialism. Otto Morales, on behalf of the MPD, expressed support for Bosch's thesis but asserted that before it could be implemented there must be a "fight for a coalition government," which could only be possible through the "gathering of all opposition forces against continuism" (*ibid.*, 23 May). As in the similar appeal by the PCD, the MPD proposals for a united front never materialized. After the elections, in which Balaguer was reelected, the MPD attacked Bosch for asserting that the electoral abstention (estimated at 800,000 by *Christian Science Monitor*, 19 May) was a triumph. An MPD statement argued: "If the abstention is not taken advantage of to carry the people to power within a short time, then the PRD should have participated in the elections to win some seats and use Congress as a people's tribune" (Radio Comercial, 19 May).

The MPD attracted international attention by kidnaping a military attaché to the U.S. Embassy, Lieutenant Colonel Donald Crowley, on 24 March. The kidnaping apparently was carried out primarily to obtain the release of the party's secretary-general, Maximiliano Gómez, who had been under arrest since 16 January. Crowley was exchanged for 20 political prisoners (including Gómez and Ignacio Marte Polanco, a top MDP leader arrested in 1967). The released prisoners were flown to Mexico; shortly thereafter 19 of them were reported to be in Cuba.

The MPD did not officially claim responsibility for the kidnaping, but the "Anti-Reelectionist Commando" which carried it out was believed to consist of MPD members. One of the communiques issued by the commando referred to the examples in Brazil and Guatemala, where kidnaped diplomats had been released in exchanges for the freeing of political prisoners, and stated: "We, Dominican revolutionaries, will also live up to our word faithfully." In another incident, on 12 May, seven persons—who identified themselves as members of the "Anti-Reelectionist Commando" hijacked a plane from Santo Domingo to Cuba.

In 1970 the animosity between the MPD and the PCRD appeared to increase. Violent actions took place involving both parties. In the killing of three MPD and two PCRD members, each party accused the other. In June and again in August, the PCRD publicly demanded a nonaggression pact with the MPD, which declared that it had never been "at war" with the PCRD, and thus refused to sign any pact. An MPD Central Committee statement on 12 August accused the PCRD of "helping the Balaguerista police in the hunt against MPD and its commandos" by revealing names and addresses of MPD militants. These charges, in addition to the refusal to sign a nonaggression pact, led PCRD members to declare that the MPD had decided upon a scorched-earth policy against them.

During the year, the MPD was also accused of threatening Bosch's life because he not only criticized the party for its "adventurist policies," but went on to purge his own party in August and September of various elements said to be sympathetic to the MPD. On 31 March an MPD group attacked and wounded one of the personal secretaries of President Balaguer. The group also distributed pamphlets stating that such action was the "beginning of a plan to get rid of all Balaguer's followers."

Despite its confrontation with the PCD and the PCRD, the MPD was able to work together with the Red Line of the MR-1J4 in the student front. In elections on 7 October to choose the new FED leadership, the "Fragua" and the Comité "Flavio Suero" formed an alliance in an attempt to defeat the Social-Democratic University Front (Frente Universitario Socialista Democrático; FUSD), the student front of the PRD. The elections almost gave a victory to the communist alliance. The noncommunist FUSD retained leadership of the FED with 3,733 votes, but the "Fragua" and Comité "Flavio Suero" alliance (named "Unity of Steel") obtained 3,724. The close vote made it necessary to have the State University Council decide on the winner. The council's decision declaring the FUSD victorious was called "unjust and arbitrary" by the communist alliance. Reportedly both the "Fragua" and the Comité "Flavio Suero" declined to accept FED leadership positions which were offered to it. They hold now strong positions, however, within the co-government (comprising both students and faculty members) of the Autonomous University of Santo Domingo, which also held elections on 7 October.

Publications. The MPD publishes an irregular clandestine weekly, *Libertad*.

*   *   *

The PCRD. The Communist Party of the Dominican Republic was formed by dissidents of the MPD after the 1965 uprising. It defines itself as a Marxist-Leninist party, "created in conformity with the thoughts of Mao Tse-tung." The party's main objective seeks to install socialism and later communism, and its immediate program attempts to "defeat Yankee imperialism and all its Creole lackeys" through a democratic revolution. (Statements made by Luis "Pin" Montás, Radio Continental, Santo Domingo, 17 January 1971.)

The PCRD is considered a very extreme party. Its membership is mostly centered in the city of Santo Domingo.

Its leaders include "Pin" Montás (secretary-general), Jorge Mora Cepeda, Héctor René Montás, and Amado Robles. Gregorio Hiciano Díaz, another PCRD leader, was killed, allegedly by MPD members, on 1 June.

PCRD activities in 1970 were concentrated upon urging MPD members to sign a "public pact of nonaggression and mutual respect." In a long statement issued on 4 June over Radio Comercial, the PCRD Central Committee asked political and labor leaders, Juan Bosch, other revolutionary political groups, and directors of major newspapers and radios to mediate in the situation between the two parties.

The party continued its rejection of Bosch's thesis. A party statement in September said that Bosch's analyses and contradictions were "based on the fact that he wants to deny the proletariat their right to lead the Dominican Revolution" (Radio Comercial, 16 September). As noted earlier, Bosch's PRD in August and September expelled various persons from the party and its youth front, some of whom were charged with being PCRD members.

The PCRD condemned the kidnaping carried out by the MPD in March, asserting that such actions denied the role of the "popular masses as the moving force" and were "completely ineffective in achieving the liberation of the people in general and political freedoms in particular." The PCRD contended that the action would only justify more government repression (*ibid.*, 31 March).

In its only known international statement, the PCRD described the government of General Juan José Torres in Bolivia as "reactionary, bourgeois, and landholding." Rejecting the use of a military coup d'état to seize power, the statement asserted that one group of the military had merely replaced another in Bolivia and that the profound economic and social ills of the country would remain unchanged.

Publications. The PCRD's official organ is *El Comunista*, an irregular clandestine weekly.

*   *   *

The MR-1J4. The Revolutionary Movement of 14 June derives its name from an unsuccessful attempt to overthrow the former dictator Trujillo on that date in 1959. While the party appeared not to engage in significant activities during 1970, its Red Line faction (formed in 1968) evinced more energy.

Before the May presidential elections, the Red Line faction sent an open letter to the "progressive element" of the PRD, asking it to adopt officially the thesis of "dictatorship with popular support" and to reject the idea of participating in elections; according to the Red Line, the proper political path for the Dominican people was the "violent struggle of the masses." The open letter also mentioned that the "essential and common points" of a minimum revolutionary program should include: struggle for national independence from "repression and disappearances"; struggle for the economic and social claims of the workers, peasants, and students; and struggle for "democratic freedoms for the entire working class population." (Radio Comercial, 26 February.) A later Red Line statement (*El Nacional de Ahora*, 16 July) called for a front of all progressive forces, which would include members of the PRD, MPD and PCRD, but not the "oligarchs" or the PCD and PSP "revisionists."

Earlier (*ibid.*, 9 June), the Red Line expressed "embarrassment" over acts of violence between MPD and PCRD members. It condemned the PCRD's efforts to obtain the mediation of other parties and groups to overcome political and ideological differences, holding that such conflicts should be resolved only between revolutionaries.

On occasion of the Lenin Centenary the Red Line said that the Communist Party of the Soviet Union had fallen in the hands of "revisionists" who were "leading Russia to socio-imperialism" and that Mao Tse-tung was "the only keeper of Marxist-Leninist principles" (*ibid.*, 23 April).

N. S.

ECUADOR

The communist movement in Ecuador began in 1926 with the founding of the Socialist Party of Ecuador (Partido Socialista Ecuatoriano; PSE). In 1928 the party became a member of the Comintern. In 1931 it changed its name to the Communist Party of Ecuador (Partido Comunista del Ecuador; PCE). A pro-Chinese splinter party, the Communist Party of Ecuador, Marxist-Leninist (Partido Comunista del Ecuador, Marxista-Leninista; PCE-ML) dates from 1963.

The membership of the PCE is estimated as 700 to 800. The PCE weekly, *El Pueblo* (20 September 1969) claimed that to that date in 1969 its membership doubled, without giving figures. Most support for the communist and other left-wing groups comes from students, to a less extent from workers, and in a very limited way from peasants. The PCE-ML is believed to have between 300 and 400 members—again mostly from students with some worker support.

The Socialist Revolutionary Party (Partido Socialista Revolucionario del Ecuador; PSRE) is a Castroite organization of 500 to 600 members. The Revolutionary Workers' Party—Trotskyist (Partido Obrero Revolucionario—Trotskista; PORT) is of unknown size and leadership.

The population of Ecuador is 6,100,000 (estimated 1970).

When the military junta came to power in July 1963, the PCE was immediately declared illegal and its leaders were arrested, but the party remained intact through clandestine activities and its representation in various mass organizations. In 1966 the government returned to civilian control under Clemente Yerovi Indaburo. The anti-subversion laws of the junta were not rescinded, but the PCE regained *de facto* legality and was able to function openly, although it was not permitted to participate in the electoral process. In anticipation of the 1968 national elections, the PCE formed the Popular Democratic Union (Unión Democrática Popular; UDP) as a front organization for its candidates, who received two per cent of the popular vote. The government of José María Velasco Ibarra, who was elected president in 1968, has been faced with opposition from Congress, students, the oligarchy, and the landed gentry. The traditionally confused political climate of the country having become increasingly unstable, on 22 June 1970 Velasco Ibarra assumed supreme power, suspending the 1967 constitution, dissolving the Congress, and taking over the direction of the banks. Besides the immediate political crisis, there remained the many perennial problems of Ecuador, such as its floundering economy, high rate of population growth and unemployment, widespread illiteracy, and the large Indian population (50 per cent of the total) living at subsistence level. Within this context, the PCE and other left-wing groups add somewhat to the social turmoil but do not appear to have any significant influence in the overall political development of Ecuador.

The PCE. Organization and Leadership. In 1968 the Eighth Congress of the PCE reelected Pedro Saad as secretary-general. Important figures in the 10-member Executive Council include Elías Muñoz, Milton Jijón, Alejandro Idrovo, Alba Calderón, Efraín Alvarez, and Enrique Gil.

The party has a 21-member Central Committee. Below the national level are provincial, zonal, and cell divisions.

The Communist Youth of Ecuador (Juventud Comunista Ecuatoriana; JCE) is the youth branch of the PCE. It is a member of the World Federation of Democratic Youth. The secretary-general, elected in 1968, is Solón Guerrero. Early in February 1970 the JCE held its First National Congress, dedicated to the centenary of Lenin's birth. Pedro Saad, as the main speaker, urged the JCE to double its efforts in the "struggle to strengthen the unity of Ecuadorean youth, to preserve loyalty to proletarian internationalism, and to defend staunchly the positions of the communist party" (*El Tiempo*, Quito, 8 February). At the meeting the JCE agreed to take an active part in the coming municipal election because abstaining would mean "yielding the field to the bourgeois parties and letting their demagogy fool the people with impunity" (*ibid.*). It also resolved to double its membership by August and to increase its ideological endeavors in the name of "solidarity with principles of Marxism-Leninism" (*ibid.*). During disturbances at the University of Guayaquil in March, the JCE issued a statement denying that its members had taken part but proclaiming its intention to bring about "scientific, democratic, and nationwide university reform" through the formation of a "great National Liberation Front" which would carry out the "national, liberating, anti-imperialist, anti-feudal, and democratic revolution" (*El Comercio*, Quito, 21 March).

The most active student organization in the country, with branches in all five national universities, is the Federation of University Students of Ecuador (Federación de Estudiantes Universitarios del Ecuador; FEUE). Although traditionally PCE-controlled, the FEUE in the past few years has been an arena of dispute and struggle for leadership between pro-Soviet, pro-Chinese, Castroite, and other radical factions. The conflict between the pro-Soviet and pro-Chinese factions became especially violent during the Twenty-fifth Congress of the FEUE, held in November 1969. Since then there have been frequent encounters, with the result that during 1970 the universities were in almost constant turmoil. After considerable maneuvering and two elections the pro-Chinese candidate, Milton Alfredo Reyes and his followers took control of the FEUE (see below). President Velasco, in taking control of the government on 22 June, declared that the universities had become "fortresses of continuous unrest" and that the student organizations were communist-controlled. Velasco summarily had all universities closed down and occupied by military personnel.

The Ecuadorian Federation of Secondary Students (Federación de Estudiantes Secondarios del Ecuador; FESE), an active organization for younger students, has also traditionally been considered under the primary influence of the PCE. In 1970, however, a clear split became evident and the FESE accused the PCE leadership of being "simple-minded revisionists" for advocating participation of leftists in the June elections. The FESE called on all "workers, peasants, and students to form a unified front and to unmask those false leaders and pseudo-communists led by Pedro Saad under the banner of the UDP." (*El Tiempo*, 8 May.) (See below.)

The Confederation of Ecuadorean Workers (Confederación de Trabajadores Ecuatorianos; CTE), formed in 1944, is an affiliate of the World Federation of Trade Unions and is one of the most important PCE-dominated organizations in Ecuador. It claims some 60,000 members. The president is Leonidas Córdova, who was elected at the CTE congress of December 1968. In May 1970 the CTE expressed opposition to economic measures adopted by the government and reaffirmed its earlier decision to struggle against any attempt to increase taxes. It also called on "workers, peasants, students, and public employees to form a big action front to stop the greed of the oligarchy" (Ecuador Radio Network, Quito, 21 May). Upon the assumption of control by President Velasco in June, Dr. Bolívar Bolanos, the organization secretary of the CTE, was arrested—as were many other labor and student leaders. Bolanos was released in July. Responding to the policies of the Velasco government, the CTE demanded the "abrogation of all the decrees that harm the life of the people and the rights of the workers" and called for a 40 per cent increase in salaries and wages. It resolved, further, to "end the dictatorship" and "win a democratic and popular government." (*Ibid.*, 12 August.) In a communiqué issued in Quito on 3 October the CTE rejected the government's plan for a plebescite on the restoration of the 1946 Constitution, claiming that it could not be carried out under conditions which "restrict democratic freedoms." The CTE is a strong supporter of the extension of sovereignty over territorial waters to 200 miles and has repeatedly condemned U.S. positions on territorial limits as intended to "undermine the marine wealth of the South Pacific nations" (e.g., "La Voz de Los Andes" radio, Quito, 27 January 1971). In recent years the CTE seems to have lost some strength as workers have increasingly been influenced by more radical left-wing workers' groups.

The PCE has made considerable efforts to bring peasants and rural workers into the communist movement. The CTE has established two peasant affiliates, the Coastal Farm Workers' Federation (Federación de Trabajadores Agrícolas del Litoral; FTAL) and the Ecuadorean Federation of Indians (Federación Ecuatoriana de Indios; FEI). Luis Castro Villamar is the president of the FTAL. The president of the FEI is Dr. Bolívar Bolanos, the aforementioned CTE organization secretary. In July 1970, Colón Navaez Duque, of the CTE Executive Committee and the FEI leadership, went to Moscow at the invitation of the Union of Agricultural Workers of the Soviet Union. Although the FEI and FTAL are small and ineffectual, the PCE has declared that class struggle is developing in the countryside with "growing force" and that the agricultural wage-workers, peasants, and farm workers are day-by-day acquiring a "growing consciousness" of the necessity for a "revolutionary transformation of the country" (*El Pueblo*, Guayaquil, 23 August 1969).

The UDP has been the front party for the PCE since its formation in 1968 (see above). In an April 1969 speech, PCE Secretary-General Pedro Saad stated: "The UDP is not a front for the communist party. The communist party does not need fronts. The UDP is an independent political organization in which all types of citizens struggle for the liberation of Ecuador." (*El Pueblo*, 19 April 1969.) Nevertheless, in the 1970 municipal elections Pedro Saad headed the list of UDP candidates for the Chamber of Deputies. In his campaign he claimed that per capita income in Ecuador was the lowest in Latin America and called for greater efforts to win a "higher standard of living and greater freedoms and to end the domination of the imperialists and big landed proprietors and capitalists in Ecuador." (*IB*. no. 9, 1970.) Other policies advocated by the UDP include government control of foreign trade, trade relations with socialist countries, nationalization of the oil industry, and establishment of a 200-mile limit on the territorial waters.

Party Internal Affairs. Pedro Saad has been the PCE secretary-general since 1948. Except for a schism in 1963-64 in which pro-Chinese elements headed by Rafael Echeverría unsuccessfully tried to gain control of the Central Committee, the leadership and pro-Soviet orientation of the party have been unchallenged. The Eighth Congress of the PCE was held in August 1968.

The PCE issued a New Year's message appealing to its followers to strengthen the party's organic and ideological policy in 1970, as a tribute to the centenary of Lenin's birth. A conference on "Leninism and Agrarian Reform in Ecuador" was sponsored by the PCE Central Committee on 27 January 1970 as part of the centenary observances.

Domestic Attitudes and Activities. In a speech at the Twentieth Congress of the Communist Party of Uruguay, in December 1970, Pedro Saad referred to the Velasco government as a "dictatorship which, managed and supported by the armed forces, has established itself in the country" in an attempt to "halt the people's increasing progress toward liberation." It had, he said, "violated all democratic guarantees": "Democratic soldiers are imprisoned and tortured, students are cruelly murdered, union rights are violated, [and] municipal autonomy is trampled under foot." He pointed out that the universities had been closed, and claimed that laws "destroying the democratic process and university autonomy" had been introduced. (*El Popular*, Montevideo, 15 December.)

Concerning the economy, Pedro Saad declared that the government was following the mandate of "imperialism," the International Monetary Fund and the "oligarchy" by devaluing the currency—thereby increasing the cost of living—and refusing to raise wages. The government, he added, was conceding natural wealth in petroleum to the "Texaco-Gulf consortium" and increasing the country's indebtedness to "North American loan agencies." (*Ibid.*)

The PCE approved the government's law abolishing "outdated forms of landownership and feudal survivals in rural areas." Even though certain aspects of the law were counter to the PCE position, the party regarded it as a step forward in carrying out the land reform. (*IB.*, no. 19, 1970.)

Pedro Saad condemned the government's proposal for a plebiscite which offered the people the "insidious alternative" of reinstating the "reactionary constitution of 1946" or "continuing the dictatorship" (*El Popular*, 15 December 1970).

In spite of "attacks from the dictatorship," Saad said, the PCE was determined to continue its program of struggle for a "revolutionary answer to the Ecuadorean situation," for the "social and national liberation" of the people, for "agrarian, anti-imperialist, and democratic revolution," and for the "conquest of a popular, revolutionary, democratic and patriotic government." The party's efforts were to be directed toward bringing about "unity in the working class" and the "grouping of democratic and patriotic forces regardless of their political, union, or religious views." Finally, the PCE was determined to strengthen the "communist party front with its roots in the working class and the popular masses." On the question of means, Saad declared that the party must use "all forms of struggle depending upon the situations." He added: "We have as our basic enemy the cruelest of the imperialisms, North American imperialism, the principle enemy of humanity." (*Ibid.*)

International Views. In 1970 the PCE maintained its long-time pro-Soviet orientation and appeared to uphold Soviet international policies. The Ecuadorean people, according to Pedro Saad, were "inspired" by the "construction successes of socialist countries led by the great Soviet Union," the "victories of the Cuban revolution," and the "grandiose victory of the Chilean Popular Unity" (*El Popular*, 15 December).

On 5 April Saad spoke at the ceremonies for the opening of the Guayaquil section of the Ecuadorean-Soviet Institute for Cultural Relations.

International Contacts. On 21 April 1970 PCE Secretary-General Saad attended the Lenin Centenary celebration in Moscow. In December he was a guest at the congress of the Uruguayan Communist Party, in Montevideo.

Publications. The official organ of the PCE is *El Pueblo*, published semi-weekly in Guayaquil. Since May 1966 it has been openly distributed.

*   *   *

The PCE-ML. The Communist Party of Ecuador, Marxist-Leninist is an outgrowth of the split within the PCE which became evident in 1963. At that time a number of dissident party members led by Rafael Echeverría Flores, and including José María Roura Cevallos and César Muñoz Mantilla (both members of the Central Committee), Carlos Rodríguez, and Jorge Arellano, attempted to take over the leadership. Expelled from the PCE, they fored the pro-Chinese PCE-ML, which has claimed to be the legitimate communist party of Ecuador. Suffering from constant instability as a result of ideological disputes and personal rivalries, the party by 1968 had split into three factions, led respectively by Jorge Arellano, Rafael Echeverría, and Pedro Sorroza. In 1969 the Chinese communists recognized Echeverria as spokesman for the PCE-ML.

As noted earlier, the PCE-ML attracts support mainly from students, but it has some followers among workers. During the mid-1960's the PCE-ML was able to elect pro-Chinese officials in both the CTE and the FEUE. The PCE has since regained control of the CTE. The FEUE however, has come more than ever under the influence of pro-Chinese leaders and during 1970 was actively engaged in strikes, protests, and demonstrations leading to the closing of the universities in June. In the aftermath of a violent clash with police in April, the body of FEUE president Milton Alfredo Reyes was discovered. Reyes' family, some university officials, and FEUE leaders claimed that he was assassinated by the government (*Punto Final*, Santiago, Chile, 26 May). Other speculation suggested that his death was related to the bitter struggle among differing factions of the FEUE.

Shortly before his death, Milton Reyes gave an interview that was published in a Castroite weekly (*Mañana*, 9 April). He stated that the FEUE was "determined to broaden and make more profound the worker-farmer-student union" through extension programs in the countryside. The FEUE, as a mass organization, he declared, was "going to play a role of the first order in the struggles that the Latin American people develop for their liberation." He characterized the struggle in Ecuador as a "frontal one against the system and against Velasco."

Following the 22 June assumption of power by President Velasco, a FEUE statement charged: "Using violence, the high military command and the army—through Dr. Velasco Ibarra—have launched a new dictatorial adventure that will lead the country to dissolution." The FEUE, it added, would fight for the "hard-won rights of workers and students." (*El Tiempo*, 26 June.)

The FEUE also opposed the new higher education law which the government proposed as a basis for reopening the schools, labeling it the "black charter of slavery." The proposed law would have suspended university autonomy and reestablished entrance examinations for higher education schools.

Like the FEUE, the FESE during 1970 was notably militant. Although its affiliation following the split from the PCE (see above) was unclear, the FESE participated in many activities with the FEUE. An FESE statement of 17 June condemned the government, the armed forces, and the police, and attacked the "oligarchy and U.S. imperialism." On 24 June the government abolished the FESE. Its president, Jorge Tinoco, replied that this action would not stop the struggle. In a statement issued in Quito on 28 June he urged students to "organize a united front [and] use all legal or illegal methods with the sole goal of obtaining respect for the rights of the students and people of Ecuador."

Domestic Views. The PCE-ML maintains that revolution in Ecuador must be carried out by the broad masses under the leadership of the proletariat and must be directed against "U.S. imperialism," the "comprador bourgeoisie," and the big landlords. A united front policy, according to an article in the party organ *En Marcha* (quoted in *Peking Review*, 4 July 1969), would be of "vital importance to arouse the entire people to oppose their enemies and defeat them." The national bourgeoisie was seen as possibly helping in the struggle, but only under the leadership of the proletariat, which would adopt a flexible policy toward participation by all interested in the revolution, although "opportunists, renegades, and revisionists" would be kept out of the united front.

An *En Marcha* article of early 1970 (cited by NCNA, 6 April) denounced Ecuador's "military agreements with the United States," claiming that the agreements made it possible for "U.S. military men to run roughshod over the Ecuadorians, turned the land of the country into a military base for imperialism when it needed, made the Ecuadorean youth cannon fodder in the imperialist war of plunder, and put all the natural resources of the country in the service of imperialism."

International Views. The PCE-ML has "unbounded praise" for China and Mao Tse-tung. It has vigorously denounced the Soviet Union: "The degeneration of the Soviet revisionists is becoming more barefaced every day. The October Revolution led by Lenin has been despicably betrayed. The new tsars have pursued a fascist policy, merely paying lip service to socialism while in fact engaging in clearly imperialist undertakings" (NCNA, 7 August 1969).

The PCE-ML sent congratulations to the Central Committee of the Chinese Communist Party on China's successful launching of an earth satellite, terming this event a "triumph of the proletariat and of all the peoples of the world" (*ibid.*, 31 May 1970.)

Publications. The PCE-ML publishes a weekly organ, *En Marcha*, and an irregular weekly, *Espártaco*, both in Quito. In Guayaquil the PCE-ML publishes some materials through the Ediciones Liberación firm. Its views also appear in the *Peking Review*.

*   *   *

The PSRE. For some time the Socialist Revolutionary Party worked quite closely with the PCE, but in 1966 it declared that its relations with the pro-Soviet party were "frozen." The PSRE is militantly pro-Castro and looks to Cuba for its direction and ideology. The secretary-general is believed to be Jorge Reynolds. Arrested and later released during the June 1970 events, he claimed the Velasco government had subjected him to "inhuman interrogations" (Ecuador Radio Network, Quito, 5 August).

The PSRE disavows all elections and legal political activities, claiming that these only "confuse the masses about the true path of their liberation," which it defines as "armed struggle against the present economic-political system of exploitation" (*Granma*, Havana, 28 February 1968).

The main Castroite publication is the weekly *Mañana*, published in Quito.

*   *   *

The PORT. The Trotskyist Revolutionary Worker's Party is of unknown size and leadership. It is a part of the Posadas branch of the Fourth International. Besides the assumption of power, the PORT is dedicated to the establishment of a "Federation of Soviet Socialist Republics of Latin America." During 1970 it was reported that the PORT had begun publishing a party organ *Lucha Comunista* and a student organ entitled *Vanguardia Comunista*.

*   *   *

There are a number of small terrorist-inclined groups in Ecuador which are unstable and frequently shifting in membership. These include the movement called Victory or Death (Vencer o

Morir; VM), the Castroite Movement of the Revolutionary Left (Movimiento de la Izquierda Revolucionaria; MIR), and the Ho Chi Minh Revolutionary Command (or Auchiri).

L. R.

EL SALVADOR

The Communist Party of El Salvador (Partido Comunista de El Salvador; PCES) was organized in 1925 by communists from Mexico and Guatemala as part of a plan to establish a Communist Party of Central America. By 1930 the regional concept had been discarded and the PCES was operating as a national body. In March 1970 the PCES celebrated its fortieth anniversary.

The PCES has traditionally been pro-Soviet. Recently, divisions have surfaced within the party regarding the need for armed struggle. There are also small guerrilla groups of Castroite orientation which include the Salvadoran Revolutionary Action (Acción Revolucionaria Salvadoreña; ARS) and the Salvadoran Revolutionary Party (Partido Revolucionario Salvadoreño; PRS).

Since the early 1930's the PCES has been illegal and has functioned clandestinely. It therefore did not participate in the March 1970 legislative and municipal elections, in which President Sánchez Hernàndez's party won a decisive vote of confidence. It is believed that participation of left-wing or communist parties in the election would have made little difference in the outcome.

The most recent estimate of PCES membership is about 200. The population of El Salvador is 3,400,000 (estimated 1970).

The PCES and other left-wing parties in El Salvador are small, weak, and insignificant in the overall national political situation, due both to the laws prohibiting their activity and the increasingly successful government programs in such areas as education and agrarian reform.

Leadership and Organization. The secretary general of the PCES since 1969 is believed to be Salvador Cayetano Carpio. Other leading figures include Antonio Pineda, secretary of the Executive Committee; Schaflik Handel, member of the Political Bureau and the Secretariat; Bernardo Dominguez; Alberto Gualon; and Jorge Arias Gómez. Raúl Castellanos, a long-time member of the Central Committee, died on 30 October 1970 in Moscow. The poet Roque Dalton, a prominent spokesman for the party, is the leader of the faction which advocates armed struggle in the present situation.

The main outlet for communist activity appears to be the United Federation of Salvadoran Trade Unions (Federación Unido de Sindicatos Salvadoreños; FUSS), which is controlled by the PCES. The FUSS has about 5,500 members and its offshoot, the FESTIAVTSCES, which enrolls workers in food, textile, and related industries, has another 2,400 members. Noncommunist unions represent the vast majority of Salvadoran workers (about 26,800 members) and occasionally cooperate with the FUSS, mainly on issues involving agrarian reform. FUSS objectives include: the formation of one central union, which it would hope to control; trade and diplomatic relations with all countries, especially communist ones; and nonintervention in the affairs of other states. Hostility among the various union leaders precludes any real possibility of a merger.

On 19-21 March 1970 a FUSS delegation attended the second meeting of the communist-controlled "Committee of Union Unity of Central American and Panamanian Workers" (CUSCA) held in San José, Costa Rica, (see *Costa Rica*).

The PCES controls two very small student organizations: the Revolutionary University Students' Federation (Federación de Estudiantes Universitarios Revolucionarios) and the Vanguard of Salvadoran Youth (Vanguárdia de las Juventudes Salvadoreños). Both of these groups sent representatives to the OLAS conference in Havana in 1967. All university students in El Salvador belong to the General Association of Salvadoran University Students (Asociación General de Estudiantes Universitarios Salvadoreños; AGEUS). As recently as February 1969 AGEUS claimed to adhere to Marxist-Leninist teachings, although it is not a communist-controlled organization. All these groups appear to receive only minor support from the students and to have little practical effect.

Domestic and International Positions. Speaking at the 1969 Moscow Conference, the PCES secretary-general stated that the people of El Salvador were "engaged in an incessant fight against the economic, political, and social stranglehold of U.S. imperialism." Adding that the U.S. role was "supported by the oligarchy and the anti-democratic militarist regime," he declared: "In the conditions created by the enemies of our independent development, our people can assume power only by armed struggle closely linked with other forms of political struggle." (*IMCWP*, p. 138.)

In August 1970 Roque Dalton spoke of "imperialist and bourgeois domination of the Central American people" and claimed that a crisis had been created in the region by the Central American Common Market, which "imperialism" was using to "unify its economic interest" and "exploit the local bourgeoisie," despite the fact that the latter were "partners with the U.S. monopolies." He also charged that there was a tendency toward "state militarization" in the Central American countries which had the purpose of repressing the "democratic revolutionary movements." Dalton concluded that the answer of the people to this "organized violence" must also be violence. (Havana radio, 29 August.)

Internationally, the PCES is dedicated to "strengthening the communist movement on the basis of the immortal principles of Marxism-Leninism" and to the unification of all "progressive" forces in the struggle against their "common foe, imperialism" (*IMCWP*, p. 136). The party supports the activities of the Soviet Union and condemns the "leftist tendencies of the Mao Tsetung group" in China, which it sees as obstructing the "united action of the international communist movement and the world progressive forces" (*ibid.*, p. 139).

The PCES sent a delegation to the Lenin Centenary celebrations in Moscow on 21 April 1970.

Publications. The PCES issues a semiweekly clandestine newspaper, *La Verdad*.

L. R.

GUADELOUPE

The Guadeloupe Communist Party (Parti Communiste Guadeloupéen; PCG) originated in 1944 as the Guadeloupe Federation of the French Communist Party (Fédération de la Guadeloupe du Parti Communiste Français), which in March 1958 transformed itself into the present autonomous party. In recent years the PCG has been plagued by conflict and expulsions, and the communist left in Guadeloupe is now represented by several diffuse groups in addition to the PCG, of which the most prominent is the Guadeloupe National Organization Group (GONG).

The PCG is legal. The party was estimated in 1970 to have some 1,500 members. The population of Guadeloupe is 335,000 (estimated 1970). The PCG is an active participant in Guadeloupe's political life, on both departmental and local levels.[1] In the elections to the French National Assembly of 23 and 30 June 1968 the party ran three candidates: Hégésippe Ibéné (district of Pointe-à-Pitre), Paul Lacavé (Capesterre), and Gerty Archimède (Basse-Terre). Although each drew enough votes to participate in the second balloting on 30 June, the only one elected was Paul Lacavé, who received 12,049 votes out of 22,381. Total votes cast for the PCG candidates on the second ballot were 33,471 out of 70,736. The PCG also contended for the two Guadeloupe seats in the elections to the French Senate, held on 22 September 1968. The two candidates backed by the party were Maximilien Vrécord, a member of the PCG Central Committee, and Marcel Gargar, referred to by the PCG press as a "progressive ally." Gargar was elected, with PCG backing for Vrécord switching to him on the second ballot.

The PCG controls several municipal governments in Guadeloupe. Among the most prominent representatives of the party in this area are Henri Bangou, mayor of Pointe-à-Pitre (the largest city); Charles Edwige, mayor of Port Louis; Félix Flémin, mayor of Deshaies; and Maximilien Vrécord, mayor of Petit-Canal. The PCG presented seven candidates in elections held on 8 and 15 March 1970 for eighteen seats on Guadeloupe's 36-member General Council. Four of the party candidates—Jérôme Clery, Hermann Songeons, Maximilien Vrécord, and Félix Flémin— none of whom were previously members of the Council, were elected on the first ballot. On 11 May a number of the electoral results were declared invalid by the courts, including the elections of Songeons and Flémin. Thus, during the remainder of the year PCG representation on the General Council consisted of Clery and Vrécord together with five party members previously elected —Henri Bangou, Charles Edwige, Daniel Géniès, Paul Lacavé, and Gerty Archimède.

Leadership and Organization. The PCG held its Fourth Congress on 13-14 April 1968 and elected 38 persons to its Central Committee (*L'Etincelle*, 11 May 1968), but did not report their names except for announcing the reelection of Evremond (also spelled Euvremond) Gène as secre-

---

[1]Guadeloupe is one of France's Overseas Departments and thus an integral part of the French Republic, administered by a prefect, with an elected General Council and with elected representatives in the French National Assembly and Senate in Paris.

439

retary-general. Since the congress, the following members of the PCG Politburo have been identified in the party's press: Bernard Alexis, Gerty Archimède, Henri Bangou, R. Baron, Guy Daninthe, Daniel Géniès, Hégésippe Ibéné, Serge Pierre-Justin, Georges René, Hermann Songeons, and Pierre Tarer. Members of the party's Secretariat included: Alexis, Baron, Daninthe, and Tarer. The party's secretary-general, Gène, was killed in an air accident in Venezuela on 3 December 1969. In 1970 his functions were carried out by Guy Daninthe, who was named first secretary.

In 1967 the PCG established the Union of Communist Youth of Guadeloupe (Union de la Jeunesse Communiste de la Guadeloupe; UJCG). The party's influence among young people is, however, limited. During 1970 the PCG press reported on polemics between the party and the General Association of Guadeloupe Students (Association Générale des Etudiants Guadeloupéens; AGEG), within which the communists had wielded some influence in the past. On 5 September, L'Etincelle warned students of the AGEG's "sectarian activities" directed against "the progressive and communist forces" of Guadeloupe; and on 24 October the party newspaper referred to "perfidious actions" allegedly perpetrated by AGEG militants in the municipality of Capesterre.

The PCG has strong influence in Guadeloupe's largest trade union, the General Confederation of Labor of Guadeloupe (Confédération Générale du Travail de la Guadeloupe; CGTG), which has some 5,000 members. PCG Politburo member Hermann Songeons continued in 1970 to hold the post of CGTG secretary-general for general administration.

The party appears to have influence within the Union of Guadeloupe Women (Union des Femmes Guadeloupéennes; UFG). Prominent party members within the UFG include Gerty Archimède, Huguette Daninthe, Georgette Pierre-Justin, and George Tarer. The UFG is affiliated to the Soviet-controlled Women's International Democratic Federation.

Party Internal Affairs. The PCG continued in 1970 to be confronted by contending forces that challenged the party from a left perspective. Throughout the year the PCG press repeatedly criticized "pseudo-revolutionaries," and it would appear from the nature of the party's commentaries that opposition to the PCG's views and policies was both internal and outside the party's ranks. Early in the year, an article in L'Etincelle (7 February) commented on the activities of a dissident group centered around the publication La Verité. The party newspaper indicated that this particular source of dissidence had surfaced in 1968, although its adherents had chosen to "undermine" the party internally. L'Etincelle claimed that after "two long years of masturbation," the dissidents had finally broken from the party, adopting in the process the advocacy of a status of independence for Guadeloupe—one of the major issues of contention between the PCG and those challenging it from the left. The article accused the dissidents of having manifested "visceral racism," and a "contempt for the masses." It claimed that they had attempted to take over the leadership of the party by violent means, and had urged "suicidal" tactics, particularly among the youth. The party newspaper also stated that some of the dissidents had traveled to Communist China.

The PCG was also confronted during 1970 with problems related to the publication of its weekly newspaper L'Etincelle. In an editorial published on 14 November, the party's first secretary, Guy Daninthe, noted that many readers had complained about the "near-disappearance of [the] newspaper during the months of September and October." Daninthe apologized for this fact, explaining that the publication difficulties were due to financial restrictions.

Domestic Views and Policies. One of the major themes encompassing PCG pronouncements continued to be its advocacy of autonomy for Guadeloupe within the framework of an alliance

GUADELOUPE 441

with France. This would involve a local legislative assembly, an executive Guadeloupe organ responsible to that assembly, and a body for cooperation with France. The PCG reiterated its views on this issue in the party program published in advance of the March elections, noting that its call for autonomy did not mean advocacy of independence (*L'Etincelle*, 28 February).

Although the party on a number of occasions stressed the need for unity among "anti-colonial and progressive" movements, non-PCG overtures were not always welcomed warmly. Thus, in February the party responded guardedly to a call by Rosan Girard, mayor of Le Moule, for the formation of a "Guadeloupe Anti-Colonial and Progressive Union," placing a number of conditions on any further discussions over PCG participation. By the end of the month initial contacts between Girard and the party appeared to have broken down. (*Ibid.*, 21 and 28 February.)

In view of its opposition to the use of violence in the attainment of its goals, the PCG was often accused during the year of reformism. Replying to these charges, the party reiterated its contention that "for every stage in the struggle there is an appropriate political tactic" (see, e.g., *ibid.*, 6 June and 5 September).

International Views and Policies. During the year the PCG continued to align itself steadfastly with the views of the Communist Party of the Soviet Union and with the French Communist Party (PCF). With regard to the latter, the report on the French party's Nineteenth Congress (4-8 February) and the PCG delegate's speech at the congress (*L'Etincelle*, 21 February) offered full solidarity to the PCF leadership and emphasized the strong ties between the two parties.

International Party Contacts. In addition to being represented at the PCF congress by Gerty Archimède, the PCG sent a delegate (Henri Bangou) to a symposium held in Paris at the end of the year in commemoration of the PCF's fiftieth anniversary. The PCG was represented at the Lenin Centenary celebrations, held in Moscow on 21 April, by a delegation led by Politburo member Hégésippe Ibéné.

Publication. The PCG publishes a weekly newspaper, *L'Etincelle*.

*   *   *

The GONG. Many of the expelled members of the PCG (and, also, apparently some members of the party) have associated themselves with a small militant group, the Guadeloupe National Organization Group (Groupe d'Organisation Nationale de la Guadeloupe; GONG), created in 1963 and based in Paris. In 1964 the group espoused a pro-Chinese stand, accusing the PCG of "revisionism." It calls for independence for Guadeloupe by means of armed struggle. In 1968 a number of GONG militants were brought to trial, but most of them were acquitted (see *YICA*, 1969, p. 390).

There is very little reliable information on the leadership or organizational structure of the GONG, which, while still believed to be headquartered in Paris, has a number of activists in Guadeloupe.

The main publication of the GONG is the monthly *GONG*.

M. P.

GUATEMALA

The communist party in Guatemala, which since 1952 has been called the Guatemalan Party of Labor (Partido Guatemalteco del Trabajo; PGT), originated in the predominantly communist-controlled Socialist Labor Unification (Unificación Obrera Socialista), founded in 1921. This group became the Communist Party of Guatemala (Partido Comunista de Guatemala; PCG) in 1923 and joined the Communist International in 1924. Increasing communist activities among workers during the mid-1920's were cut off by the end of the decade and were kept at a minimum throughout the dictatorship of Jorge Ubico (1931-44). In 1947, during the presidency of Juan José Arévalo, the communists as an organized group reappeared in the clandestine Democratic Vanguard (Vanguardia Democrática). In 1949 this group took the name PCG. Communist labor leader Víctor Manuel Gutiérrez founded a second and parallel communist party in 1950, called the Revolutionary Workers' Party of Guatemala (Partido Revolucionario Obrero de Guatemala). The two groups merged in 1951 when Gutiérrez, after a trip to Moscow, dissolved his party and joined the PCG. During 1952 the party adopted the name PGT, which it continues to use. The PGT was legal between 1952 and 1954 and played an active role in the administration of President Jacobo Arbenz. It has been illegal since the overthrow of Arbenz in 1954.

Three guerrilla organizations existed in Guatemala during 1970: the military arm of the PGT, formed in 1968 and called the Revolutionary Armed Forces (Fuerzas Armadas Revolucionarias); the Rebel Armed Forces (Fuerzas Armadas Rebeldes; FAR); and the 13 November Revolutionary Movement (Movimiento Revolucionario 13 de Noviembre; MR-13). The FAR and the MR-13 (see below for both) operate independently of the PGT and of each other.

The PGT is estimated to have 750 members. At the end of 1970 the FAR and the MR-13 were each believed to have 50 to 100 members and several hundred sympathizers.

The population of Guatemala is 5,100,000 (estimated 1970).

Rural guerrilla warfare in Guatemala reached a peak during the last half of 1966 and early 1967, following a guerrilla rejection of an amnesty offer by recently elected president, Julio César Méndez Montenegro. By the end of 1967 the government response, a policy of military campaigns and army civic action programs directed by Colonel Carlos Araña Osorio, had severely weakened both the guerrillas and the PGT. Guerrilla activities were limited during 1968 (despite several spectacular but isolated acts, such as the assassination of U.S. Ambassador John Gordon Mein in August) and most of 1969, during which time the FAR reportedly reorganized its forces and adjusted its strategy (*Le Monde*, Paris, English edition, 4 March 1970). During several months preceding the presidential election in March 1970, terrorist activities were resumed, particularly the kidnaping and assassination of national and foreign officials. The government declared a "state of prevention" at the end of 1969, and reprisals from right-wing groups, such as the Organized National Anticommunist Movement (Movimiento Anticomunista Nacional Organizado; MANO) and the "Eye for an Eye" (Ojo por Ojo), followed. Widespread popular opposition to the terrorism of recent years was undoubtedly one of the main reasons the "law and order" candidate, Colonel Araña, won the election with 42.9 per cent of the vote (35.7 per cent for his closest opponent). Immediately after the election FAR kidnapings increased, reaching a high point with the abduction (31 March) and murder (5 April) of the ambassador of the Federal Republic of Germany to Guatemala, Count Karl von Spreti. Terrorist activities stopped for several months after the inauguration of Araña on 1 July, but were resumed in November, concentrating on policemen, politicians, and labor leaders. A state of siege was declared on 12 November and extended in December, during which many arrests were made.

Leadership and Organization. Little information is available on the leadership and organization of the PGT. The party is headed by its secretary-general, Bernardo Alvarado Monzón. Others prominent in the party include Central Committee members Mario Silva Jonama, José Manuel Fortuny, Julio López, Miguel Rodríguez, Huberto Alvarado, and Antonio Carrillo Giles.

The Patriotic Youth of Labor (Juventud Patriotica del Trabajo; JPT) is an auxiliary of the PGT. According to Mario Silva Jonama, "leftist views practically dominated" the JPT during the late 1960's, resulting in "subjectivist and voluntarist positions" and "petty-bourgeois 'revolutionism' " (*WMR*, March 1969). When the FAR broke with the PGT in 1968 (see below), a high percentage of JPT members allied themselves with the guerrillas. In December 1969 the PGT set up a special commission to supervise the work of the JPT, but there has been little evidence of a revitalization of the group.

The PGT has little influence among Guatemalan workers. It controls the clandestine Guatemalan Autonomous Socialist Federation (Federación Autónoma Socialista Guatemalteca; FASG), a small and relatively unimportant labor organization. The FASG participated in the meeting of the communist-controlled "Committee of Union Unity of Central American and Panamanian Workers" (CUSCA), on 19-21 March 1970 in San José, Costa Rica (see *Costa Rica*).

Party Internal Affairs. The PGT announced early in 1970 that its Fourth Congress (the Third Congress was in 1960) was held clandestinely in December 1969. Among the major issues discussed were the political, social, and economic conditions of the country, the strategy and tactics of the party in the past and in the future, and the need for greater emphasis on strict internal organization and ideological training. Considerable attention was also given to recent dissension within the party, primarily to "left adventurism." According to one report on the congress, the leftists were said to "rely entirely on spontaneity, improvisation and spectacular action, shun painstaking organizational work, underestimate the role of the Party, contact with the masses, political action and so on." The party concluded, however, that it had successfully "overcome liquidationist moods and put an end to Leftist factional activity." (*WMR*, October 1970). The congress approved a "Program of People's Revolution" and elected a new Central Committee which, according to a PGT communiqué published in the party organ *La Verdad* in January, included "young people of firm revolutionary convictions" as well as experienced party members (translated in *IB*, no. 15-16, 1970).

Domestic Attitudes and Activities. A communiqué issued by the Central Committee in January 1970, shortly after the Fourth Congress, stated that the PGT expected an "agrarian, anti-imperialist and popular" stage of revolution to precede the "building of socialism and communism" in Guatemala. According to the communiqué, the new year initiated a decade which would undoubtedly bring "strenuous battles and decisive advances and victories for the peoples." (*IB*, no. 15-16.) At the end of the year a party leader reported that, although the PGT had recently been "active in economic, political and armed struggles," the "alignment of forces [was] still unfavorable to the revolution" (*WMR*, December).

The "Program of People's Revolution" reaffirmed the PGT position that "armed struggle in the form of a people's revolutionary war is the only correct path of the Guatemalan revolution." At the same time, it stated: "The people will have to use every form of economic, social and ideological struggle . . . for the simple reason that *a correct combination of armed and political action is an indispensable factor of victory.*" (*WMR*, October, emphasis in original.) Consequently the Central Committee communiqué in January called for a "revolutionary patriotic front capable of rallying all forces" and based on a "firm alliance of the working class and the bulk of the peasantry." In order to "unite, organize and mobilize the people for advance to higher objectives," the PGT program stressed the need to "fight in united and organized fashion for [the people's] immediate economic, political and social demands and at the same time for power." (*IB*, no. 15-16.)

According to a report on the Fourth Congress, the PGT held that the expected revolution would be led by the "working class of town and country," and poor and middle peasants would make up the "main force," followed by "white-collar workers, students, professionals, etc." (*WMR*, October). At the end of the year this analysis was refined somewhat by Huberto Alvarado, who stated that "the peasant masses give in readily to the ideology of the bourgeoisie and landowners, and the party of the working class has much greater difficulty in influencing them." He then criticized "leftists" who exhibited a "neo-Narodnik petty-bourgeois idealization of the peasantry," and observed only that the peasants "may" become the "main force of the revolution." Alvarado emphasized that Indians had a revolutionary role based on class rather than racial grounds. He maintained, further, that the "national bourgeoisie" was "renouncing struggle ever more emphatically." (*WMR*, December.)

Although the PGT had urged participation in the presidential election of 1966, it called for a boycott in 1970. According to a communist quoted in the *Guardian* (London, 26 February), the party expected a victory by Araña to radicalize liberal elements in Guatemala and lead to an intensification of demands for basic change.

As in past years, the PGT showed only limited interest in international affairs during 1970. Its general orientation is pro-Soviet. It has praised the Cuban revolution and "progressive" changes in Peru (see *YICA*, 1970, p. 424). The Fourth Congress proclaimed support for "national liberation" struggles around the world, with particular reference to the war in Vietnam, and predicted the eventual triumph of socialism everywhere. (*WMR*, October.)

Publications. The PGT's national organization and its Southern Regional Committee issue the clandestine newspapers *La Verdad* and *Grito Popular*, respectively. The organ of the JPT is *Juventud*; that of the PGT's Revolutionary Armed Forces is the clandestine *FAR* (not to be confused with the Rebel Armed Forces having the same initials).

The FAR. In December 1962 the Rebel Armed Forces, or FAR, was formed by members of three guerrilla organizations: the "20 October" forces of the PGT, the "12 April" student group, and the MR-13. Many problems quickly arose within the FAR, and in March 1965 it was reorganized without the MR-13, which had come under the influence of some members of the Posadas faction of the Fourth International. In January 1968 the FAR broke formally with the PGT and merged once again with the MR-13, now purged of Trotskyist influences. Within a year the MR-13 was again separated from the FAR, and apparently it remained so throughout 1970.

The most important early leaders of the FAR were Marco Antonio Yon Sosa and Luis Augusto Turcios Lima, former Guatemalan military officers trained by the United States—Yon Sosa at Fort Gulick in the Panama Canal Zone and Turcios Lima at Fort Benning, Georgia. Turcios played an active part in the January 1966 Tricontinental Conference in Havana and died in an automobile accident several months later. He was succeeded by César Montes, his second in command. When the FAR and the MR-13 merged in 1968, Yon Sosa was made supreme commander, with Montes again as second in command. By early 1969 Montes had been demoted to private and Yon Sosa had reestablished an independent MR-13. During 1969 and the first half of 1970 the FAR was headed by Pablo Monsanto and a "National Directorate" consisting of Androcles Hernández, Feliciano Argueta, and Ramiro Díaz. On 5 September the FAR organ *Guerrillero* announced that during mid-August Ramiro Díaz and three other fighters had given notice of their separation from the FAR and taken some guerrilla funds with them. It added that they would stand trial, in person or in absentia, and receive appropriate punishment. On 16 September the four issued a statement of their own, protesting an FAR decision to reduce urban struggle and charging that the remaining FAR leaders were overly influenced by Cuban advisers.

For several years the FAR has emphasized urban activities, the most important of which were political assassinations and the kidnaping of businessmen and politicians—whose safe return was guaranteed only in exchange for the release of "political prisoners" held by the government or the payment of large ransoms, or both. In the first half of 1970 the FAR carried out a series of kidnapings, the victims including the Guatemalan foreign minister, Alberto Fuentes Mohr, and an attaché at the U.S. Embassy, Sean M. Holly (both of whom were released after FAR demands were met), as well as the aforementioned Count Karl von Spreti. A statement issued by the FAR National Directorate after the murder of the West German ambassador (*Guerrillero*, April) argued that Guatemalan conditions were such that the guerrillas had no choice but to make their demands in this manner, and that the government, having refused FAR ransom demands (for payment of $700,000 and release of twenty-two "political prisoners"), was fully responsible for his death.

The FAR boycotted the March election and regarded the low vote turnout as a victory for its policy. The election of Carlos Araña was considered unimportant by three guerrillas who received asylum in Mexico in March. They stated: "The same old rightist reactionary regime goes on existing. At least now we know we are facing the enemy. There'll be no disguises or tricks; we know him well." (*Granma*, Havana, English, 15 March.)

Publication. The official organ of the FAR is *Guerrillero*.

The MR-13. The 13 November Revolutionary Movement was formed by Marco Antonio Yon Sosa and other young military officers after an abortive uprising against the government of Miguel Ydigoras Fuentes on 13 November 1960. Yon Sosa commanded the organization until he was killed on 18 May 1970 in an encounter with Mexican troops on the Mexican-Guatemalan border. The status of the MR-13 since Yon Sosa's death is uncertain.

The most significant outside influences on the MR-13 during its decade of activity were Trotskyist (primarily between 1964 and 1966) and Communist Chinese (though not apparently as a direct result of Chinese initiatives). The MR-13 differed from the FAR primarily in its steady advocacy of a socialist revolution, its greater emphasis on political and social (in addition to military) activities, and its concentration on developing a single, secure base area in the Sierra de las Minas region (rather than maintaining a national and highly mobile guerrilla force). Unlike the FAR, the MR-13 under Yon Sosa never participated in spectacular terrorist activities or kidnapings.

Publication. The official organ of the MR-13 is *Revolución Socialista*.

W. E. R.

GUYANA

The People's Progressive Party (PPP) of Guyana was founded in 1950. At its first congress, in 1951, it declared itself a nationalist party, committed to socialism, national independence, and Caribbean unity. During the nearly two decades following, the leadership of the PPP claimed to be Marxist-Leninist, but the party was not officially affiliated with the international communist movement. During 1969 the leadership, in particular its head, Dr. Cheddi Jagan, made an unequivocal move to align the party with the Soviet Union. In turn, the PPP was recognized by Soviet leaders as a bona-fide communist party.

The Working People's Vanguard Party (WPVP) is a small pro-Chinese party recently organized in Guyana and led by Brindley Benn (see below).

The PPP is a legal party. From 1957 to 1964 it was the ruling party in British Guiana (which became independent and took the name of Guyana in 1966). In the most recent national elections, held in December 1968, the PPP won 36.9 per cent of the total vote and 36 per cent of the seats in Parliament. The People's National Congress (PNC), led by Prime Minister Forbes Burnham, won a majority, with 56 per cent of the seats. Compared with the 1964 election, when it won 43.3 per cent of the seats, the PPP showed some loss of electoral support.

It is in the nature of politics in Guyana that support for the two principal parties, the PPP and the PNC, is based not on ideology but on race. The PPP is primarily supported by the East Indian population, representing about 50 per cent of the total, and has a membership of some 20,000. Many non-member East Indians support the PPP in elections. It is estimated, however, that there are only about 100 hard-core communists within the PPP at the present time. The population of Guyana is 721,000 (estimated 1970).

In the late 1940's, Cheddi Jagan, Janet Jagan, Sidney King, and Brindley Benn began a movement to prepare for social and political reforms to be effected when independence was granted. The movement was later joined by Forbes Burnham. Early signs indicated a promising progressive nationalist movement until 1953, when ideological and ethnic divisions began to split the organization. Since that time racial issues, sectional interests, border disputes, election frauds, and the influence of British and American foreign policy have further weakened the process of national unification and development.

Leadership and Organization. In 1969 the leader of the PPP, Cheddi Jagan, announced that the party was being transformed from a loose, mass party into a Marxist-Leninist party "sharing the ideals of the international socialist-communist movement" (*Sunday Graphic*, Georgetown, 27 July). He then proceeded to reorganize the party, abolishing the posts of leader and chairman in favor of a hierarchy constructed on the pattern of the Soviet and East European parties. Jagan named himself first secretary and ordered the holding of a special conference in August 1969. The conference endorsed the reorganization and agreed to amend the party constitution to allow for the structural changes.

In line with a conference decision, a regular party congress was held in 1970 (see below) at which a 32-member General Council was elected, replacing the previous arrangement of seven officers and 15 members. The General Council in turn elected from among its members a general secretary, eight other secretaries, and a 12-member Executive Council. Although the names of those elected were not publicized, it may reasonably be assumed that controlling positions in the party are held by supporters of Cheddi Jagan, who is still first secretary. These supporters would include Janet Jagan (his wife), Ranji Chandisingh (secretary for education), Derek Jagan, Vincent Teekah, Philomena Sahoye, Harry Lall, E. M. G. Wilson (secretary for mass organizations and civil liberties), and Dr. Charles Jacob (secretary for economic affairs).

As a part of the reorganization, Cheddi Jagan created a committee within the leadership circle which was to ensure that PPP policies should conform in theory and practice to Marxist-Leninist teaching. Known as the Ideological Committee, it was headed by Jagan, his wife, and other leaders who, like the Jagans, had been trained in Moscow.

The PPP maintains a youth group, the Progressive Youth Organization (PYO), which appears to be a primary source of support for Jagan personally and for his international stance. Vincent Teekah is chairman of the PYO. During 1970 as part of the party's Lenin Centenary program the PYO organizations held three regional conferences on the subject of Lenin's teachings. The PYO sent a delegation to the Eighth Assembly of the World Federation of Democratic Youth (WFDY), held in Hungary in November. The PYO was one of twenty delegations which received the WFDY's bronze Medal of Honor, given for "long standing anti-imperialist activities" (*Mirror*, Georgetown, 22 November).

The PPP controls the Guyana Agricultural Workers' Union (GAWU), made up primarily of workers in the sugar industry. The president is Harry Lall and the vice-president is Mrs. Philomena Sahoye. For the past twenty years the GAWU has tried to gain recognition as the bargaining agent for the nation's sugar workers, and during 1970 it succeeded in bringing the sugar industry to a standstill by massive strikes. At the year's end this dispute was still unsettled, but it appeared likely that some conciliatory arrangement with the Sugar Producers' Association would eventually be made.

For many years the PPP has maintained a trading arm known as GIMPEX, which enjoyed a privileged position in communist-bloc trade and was highly profitable for the party. In July 1970, however, the government announced that it was establishing an External Trade Bureau which would handle imports exclusively from Communist countries.

The PPP also maintains a women's group, the Womens' Progressive Organization.

Party Internal Affairs. The Fourteenth Congress of the PPP was held on 5-8 September 1970 as directed by the 1969 special conference. Instead of the traditional speech by the party leader, a report prepared and approved by the General Council was circulated for discussion in advance of the congress. The report made a "concrete analysis of the situation inside Guyana against the background of the realities of international life" and stressed the "necessity in the anti-imperialist struggle of the three revolutionary streams moving closer together for concerted action" (*WMR*, December 1970).

According to the report, in Guyana the PPP is the "key to the development of the mass movement against imperialism and its puppets," and there can be "no guarantee of a peoples' victory without the vanguard role—organizationally, ideologically, politically—of the party." The "loose, mass party," the report continued, "has served its purpose. It grew up in the historical conditions of the time mainly as an electioneering party. The conditions of the struggle today and in the future demand a more effective vanguard such as can be provided only by a Marxist-Leninist party." (*Ibid.*)

Cheddi Jagan reported that the congress ended on a "high note of unity and determination—unity in the face of opponents and detractors who were sowing seeds of dissension and predicting splits, and determination to continue resolutely the struggle for national liberation and socialism" (*ibid.*). In spite of Jagan's optimism it is likely that the defections from the PPP of senior party members and religious bodies which began in 1969 as the result of his restructuring the party on communist lines has continued. How much dissension there is among the remaining members is not known, but there are some indications that mass support for the party is diminishing. The holding of the Fourteenth Congress and its procedural changes make it appear that Cheddi Jagan and his supporters are nevertheless in firm control of the party and undeterred in their intentions to establish the PPP as a member of the international communist movement.

Early in the year the PPP adopted a Lenin Centenary program which emphasized the study of Lenin's works in classes, seminars, symposiums, and regional conferences.

Domestic Attitudes and Activities. In describing the current domestic situation, Cheddi Jagan declared that Guyana was "passing through a period of mounting social, political, and economic crisis." The PNC, he said, had attained power by "blatant rigging of the 1968 election," reduced the National Assembly to a "farce," flouted parliamentary processes, and deepened the "cleavage between the two major racial groups." (*Direct from Cuba*, Havana, no. 29, 1970.) Other characteristics of the country under the government of Forbes Burnham, according to the report to the PPP's Fourteenth Congress included its "neo-colonial status," lack of economic development, collapse of the seven-year development plan, and corruption. The report called for "revolutionary change"—a "fully integrated, all-embracing program"—with all "opposition forces" united in a "broad-based anti-imperialist alliance for democracy and national liberation." (*WMR*, December.)

The PPP congress unanimously approved the program proposed in the report, which included: nationalization of foreign and local "compradore" capitalist-owned and -controlled factories, mines, plantations, banks, insurance companies, and foreign trade"; a strict system of foreign exchange control; emphasis on "simultaneous industrial and agricultural development, mainly in the public and cooperative sectors"; rent and price controls; land reform; trade with countries of both East and West; and "full democracy and workers' participation and control at all levels" (*ibid.*).

As a result of alleged fraud by the PNC in connection with the 29 June 1970 local elections—the first elections since the country attained independence—the PPP passed a resolution "not to contest" the remainder of the local elections, scheduled for December. To take part in the elections was "only to give to the PNC the excuse to pretend that Guyana is a parliamentary democracy." Moreover, the resolution concluded, the "PNC regime" had "clearly blocked the path to peaceful change" and "more and more [was] relying on violence." (*Ibid.*) In the June elections, which covered six districts (two of which were former Jagan strongholds), the PNC won 80 of the 97 seats being contested.

In October the PPP launched a campaign to expose the "erosion of civil liberties" in Guyana and sent to the U.N. Human Rights Commission a document contending that the Burnham government was destroying the democratic institutions of the country. Government ministers, it charged, were unconstitutionally arresting and detaining people, searching homes without warrants, and denying free expression, association, and assembly. (*Sunday Graphic*, 18 October.) The PPP was particularly angered by the revelation that the program for a conference of the PNC women's auxiliary contained the slogan: "The time is ripe for a one-party state" (*ibid.*, 15 November). A spokesman for the PPP commented that this slogan endorsed "political war on

the people" and represented the "attempt of a minority government to establish a fascist Du-
valier-type dictatorship in Guyana" (*ibid.*).

On 23 February Guyana officially became a republic—a procedure which the PPP had supported in principle because of the "incompatibility of a monarchy with the Socialist society"
which it envisaged (*Thunder*, October-December 1969). Cheddi Jagan and his party avoided the
Republic Day ceremonies, saying: "We do not see much cause for rejoicing . . . what we see is
merely a change in form, not content." To the Burnham government's announced plan to establish a "cooperative republic" and end the country's "exploitation by foreign capital" Jagan re-
torted: "There is no such thing as a cooperative republic. Republics are either socialist or capitalist. Marx and Engels long ago exploded the myth that socialism can be achieved by cooperatives
in peaceful competition with monopoly capitalism. The slogan of the 'cooperative republic' is a
hoax, a fraud to lull the people of Guyana into a false sense of security." (*New Times*, Moscow,
no. 10, 1970.) Jagan urged the government to look, rather, to the socialist countries for patterns
of development planning.

In two specific cases during the year the PPP advocated direct nationalization. The first was
the sugar industry, which had declined substantially, and the second the bauxite industry. The
government's plan for "significant participation" in these industries was not sufficient, Cheddi
Jagan commented. Mrs. Jagan added that the PNC, as a "pawn of big business," could not nationalize any industry, and that "nationalization can only succeed under socialism" (*Sunday
Graphic*, 22 November).

In May, "black power" leader Stokely Carmichael visited Guyana. At a press conference on 4
May he spoke on the development of black power and Pan-Africanism, which he stressed could
be applied only to Negroes and would be achieved through the most "extensive and bloody"
struggle the world has ever seen. During his visit Carmichael had separate meetings with both
Cheddi Jagan and Forbes Burnham. In recent years Jagan, himself an East Indian, has encouraged black power groups and attended conferences with designs toward developing such a movement in the Caribbean. Following Stokely Carmichael's visit he said at a news conference on 9
May that "black power in some form or the other would sooner or later come to Guyana" and
that his party was "glad Carmichael had come." The visit had made it clear, he added, that
"black power meant different things to different people."

International Views and Positions. The Fourteenth Congress of the PPP issued a resolution on
foreign affairs which

> (*a*) called for the recognition by all states of the German Democratic Republic; the seating of
> the People's Republic of China and the expulsion of Taiwan from the United Nations; the unity
> of Caribbean leaders in eradicating the vestiges of colonialism and the threat of neo-colonial-
> ism in the region; the government of Guyana to establish diplomatic relations with all socialist
> countries and pursue a genuine and meaningful policy of non-alignment;

> (*b*) condemned the continued presence of American forces in Southeast Asia; U.S. aggression
> in Vietnam, Laos, and Cambodia; continued U.S. military and economic support for Israel
> and her aggression against the Arab people;

> (*c*) expressed solidarity with and support for the national liberation movement in Southern Af-
> rica; the Cuban revolution; achievements in Libya, Sudan, Tanzania, Congo (Brassaville),
> Ceylon, Peru and Chile; the movement for the realization of Black dignity in America; and the
> popular movement in Trinidad and Tobago. (*WMR*, December 1970.)

Although the PPP has long advocated establishment of relations between Guyana and the
Soviet Union, it criticized the agreement to that effect which was reached by the Burnham

government and the Soviets in November. Cheddi Jagan called the relations only "nominal" and said that Burnham's arranging the agreement on his way to attend the Third Non-Aligned Conference in Lusaka, Zambia, looked very much like "obtaining an admission ticket to the conference" (*Direct from Cuba*, no. 29). The agreement, in fact, did not include full diplomatic relations, and neither country is to have an embassy in the other.

Jagan urged the PCN to establish relations also with Communist China, stressing the "admirable record of service the Chinese have shown in the underdeveloped countries, where they are giving assistance without any strings whatsoever." This record, the party's leader added, indicated that "China could become an excellent ally for Guyana." (*Mirror*, 29 December.) At the World Council of Peace meeting in New Delhi, in October, Cheddi Jagan sounded a noticeably different tone when he spoke about the "bitter theoretical-ideological quarrels among some ranks of the anti-imperialist peace forces." The "crude anti-communism of the rightist-reactionaries" was not so damaging, he said, as the "leftist anti-sovietism based on the false charges of Soviet imperialism and Soviet Revisionism." Jagan concluded by saying that the World Council of Peace could aid in unifying forces for peace by "publicizing the aid which the socialist countries, particularly the Soviet Union has been and is giving to the liberation movements, especially in Vietnam, West Asia and Cuba." (*Mirror*, 9 November.)

The PPP was also vocal during the year about issues related to Latin American countries. The party urged that Guyana establish complete diplomatic, commercial, and cultural relations with Cuba. The "new revolutionary, socialist Cuba," Cheddi Jagan said in a press conference, is the "country which is setting the patterns for America."

Regarding the election of Salvador Allende as president of Chile, Jagan said that the "great lesson conveyed by Chile is primarily that all forms of struggle must be taken into account and all anti-imperialist forces drawn upon, including the military." He continued: "It has been shown that left-wing united fronts, relaying on mass struggle, are able to gain electoral victories which can serve as starting points for profound revolutionary changes." (Interview, *Neues Deutschland*, East Berlin, 10 November.)

In February the PPP welcomed the government's decision to place the case of Venezuela's "violation of Guyana's territorial integrity" before the U.N. Security Countil since it was clear that the "two Anglo-Saxon imperialist powers, which have large investments," in Venezuela had "no intention of telling that country to keep its hands off Guyana." (*IB.*, nos. 5-6, 1970.) In June, when an agreement was signed creating a 12-year truce in the dispute, Jagan described the accord as "total capitulation to foreign interest."

International Contacts. During 1970 Cheddi Jagan, as in years past, traveled and spoke abroad a great deal. In October he spoke at the World Peace Council meeting in New Delhi. On the way he visited for two days in Caracas with officials of the Communist Party of Venezuela. In November, Jagan attended the Afro-Asian congress in Libya and was a guest speaker at the WFDY assembly in Budapest. Janet Jagan visited the Soviet Union and East Europe in September, reportedly for party fund-raising purposes.

Publications. The PPP publishes a quarterly theoretical journal, *Thunder*. The editor is Charles Jacob, Jr. The party also publishes a daily newspaper, the *Mirror*. In 1969 the veteran party leader H. J. B. Hubbard was dismissed as editor of *Mirror*. He was replaced by Janet Jagan.

*　　　*　　　*

The WPVP. The Working People's Vanguard Party (Marxist-Leninist) was founded in January 1969 by Brindley Benn, a former PPP member and associate of Cheddi Jagan. Benn questioned Jagan's form of Marxism and held that the PPP was following the path of "opportunism and revisionism." The WPVP is opposed to participation in elections, on the grounds that both the PNC and PPP are "racist" and thus are impeding the unification of workers in the socialist cause. Unequivocally giving his allegiance to Mao Tse-tung, Benn has applauded the Cultural Revolution in China and criticized the Soviet Union as a class-dominated society. The PPP's alignment with the Soviet Union was branded by Benn as "betrayal" of the Guyanese and others who were fighting for national liberation.

The membership of the WPVP is kept secret by Benn. Apparently the party is quite small. Although little was heard of the WPVP in 1970 it issued a statement condemning "U.S. imperialist aggression in Cambodia and Indochina" (NCNA, 12 September).

L. R.

HAITI

The Communist Party of Haiti (Parti Communiste d'Haïti), founded in 1930, disintegrated the following year when its leaders Max Hudincourt and Jacques Roumain were forced to flee the country. Roumain died later in Mexico, but Hudincourt returned to Haiti in 1946 to head the Popular Socialist Party (Parti Socialiste Populaire; PSP), established that year. The assassination of Hudincourt in 1947 ended the political life of the PSP. A second Communist Party of Haiti was formed in 1946 under the leadership of an Episcopal clergyman, Félix d'Orléans Juste Constant. Denied support by the international communist movement (which the PSP had obtained), this party dissolved itself in 1947 after complete failure in elections the preceding year.

In November 1954 a new communist movement, the People's National Liberation Party (Parti Populaire de Libération Nationale; PPLN), was formed. The PPLN broke up in July 1965, but reappeared the following year as the Party of the Union of Haitian Democrats (Parti d'Union de Démocrates Haïtiens; PUDH or PUDHA—or in Creole, Pati Union Demokrat Ayisiin, PUDA), a group that placed strong emphasis on guerrilla tactics. A second movement, the pro-Soviet People's Entente Party (Parti d'Entente Populaire; PEP), was formed in 1959. Although the PUDHA and the PEP based their activities on divergent strategic and tactical concepts—the PEP deriving support from small urban elements in and around the capital, Port-au-Prince, and the PUDHA having rural roots and claiming to be organized in eight of Haiti's nine provinces—the two parties cooperated from 1963 to 1968 in the "anti-imperialist" and "antifeudal" United Democratic Front of National Liberation. The front disbanded in April 1968, and in January 1969 the Castroite PUDHA and the pro-Soviet PEP merged to form the Unified Party of Haitian Communists (Parti Unifié des Communistes Haïtiens; PUCH). The combined PUCH is believed to have about 500 members. The population of Haiti is 5,200,000 (estimated 1970).

A pro-Chinese party, the Haitian Workers' Party (Parti de Travailleurs Haïtien; PTH), was founded in 1966 by a group of former PPLN dissidents. This group is believed to have won support among Haitian intellectuals living in exile in Europe, but it appears to have dissolved.

All political parties in Haiti were proscribed in 1949. Under the presidency of François Duvalier (1957-71), all communists have been persecuted rigorously by the government.[1] Hence, much of their activity has been carried on outside Haiti among exiles in Europe (especially the Soviet Union), Latin America, and the United States. The communist movement in Haiti is weak and has shown no better aptitude for survival than have other anti-Duvalier groups.

Leadership and Organization. According to various reports, the PUCH leadership appears to include Secretary-General Joseph Roney, Deputy Secretary Arnold Devilme, and Secretary Miklimbourg, along with Central Committee members Jacques Dorsilien (or Dorcilier), Jean

[1]On 28 April 1969 a law was passed declaring all forms of communist activity crimes against the state, the penalty for which would be both confiscation of property and death.

Pierre, Robert Cherelus, Florient Marrat, Gerard Remy, Jacques Tinois, and Ernest le Grand. Roney was reported released from prison during 1970 (according to Dorsilien in *WMR*, November). Most Central Committee members are engaged in party work from abroad. In April and June 1969 the party was seriously damaged when most of its leading militants (including six Central Committee members) were killed during confrontations with police forces.

Little is known about the party's organization inside the country. In mid-1970 Jacques Dorsilien, in a broadcast from Moscow ("Peace and Progress" radio, 16 May), claimed that "committees of patriotic resistance" had been established in the cities and that peasants were organized to struggle for agrarian reform.

Domestic Attitudes and Activities. The PUCH seeks to overthrow the "Duvalier dictatorship and the yoke of U.S. monopolies." It contends that in Haiti "peaceful and, particularly, legal methods of struggle cannot be applied under the conditions of Duvalier's tyranny." Hence, the party advocates armed struggle, to be fought by an army of national liberation. ("Peace and Progress" radio, 15 January 1970.)

The PUCH "Charter of Unity" (signed by the PUDHA and the PEP upon merging in January 1969) stated that "guerrilla war" was essential in the struggle and that the formation of urban and rural guerrilla units was the "chief task" of the party. PUCH statements during 1970, however, while reasserting the party's advocacy of armed struggle, made only scant reference to either urban or rural guerrilla actions. Thus, a PUCH statement broadcast from Havana on 22 September mentioned the need for "mobilizing the people to struggle to the end" and asserted that the communists would seek the complete support of the peasants, workers, and popular masses, which were "the only forces capable of crushing Duvalier and building a new political and social system in Haiti."

Early in the year, PUCH leaders met at an undisclosed location (probably outside the country) and emphasized party work rather than armed activities. The communiqué issued after the meeting said: "We must systematically strengthen organic party links with the working class and masses so as to assure effective participation of large popular masses in revolutionary violence" (quoted in *El Popular*, Montevideo, 11 March).

The communiqué revealed that the meeting took place to discuss the "mistakes committed in regard to tactics, organization, and party work methods which allowed [the] enemy to hit us hard during 1969." It also acknowledged some lack of consensus within the party, declaring that a "constant factor in the development of the party's political capability at the present stage" was "the struggle to obtain unity of views within the party for respect of regulations pertaining to clandestine operations, application of the collective leadership principle, and maintenance of proper security in execution of decisions."

There were no reported PUCH actions within Haiti during 1970. Party activities seemed limited to frequent broadcasts from abroad, mainly Moscow, appealing for united action against the government of Duvalier and attacking his economic policies. Various PUCH radio broadcasts called upon the army and peasants to rebel. The broadcasts also urged workers, especially public employees, to organize workers unions to fight "arbitrary dismissals, political blackmail, and administrative pressure" ("Peace and Progress" radio, 17 September).

The attempt to overthrow Duvalier on 24 April by the Haitian Coast Guard Service, although unsuccessful, was hailed by the PUCH as proof of a growing anti-Duvalier sentiment among the masses.[1] Drawing a lesson from this action, the party said:

[1]Under Colonel Octave Cayard, the commander of the Coast Guard, Haiti's only naval force, 118 men and three cutters shelled Port-au-Prince to initiate and support an uprising that was intended to be staged simultaneously by anti-Duvalier elements in the capital. A series of preventive arrests, however, thwarted the uprising. The coastguardsmen were forced to seek political asylum in the United States.

This [event] proves even more than the Haitian communists are right in saying that the revolutionary movement can only succeed when it is well prepared and carried out in unity with all patriotic forces. Even the most heroic isolated action cannot put an end to the tyranny. Haiti's future lies in the hands of closely united Haitians. (*Ibid.*, 28 April.)

International Views and Positions. There were no statements by the PUCH on international issues during 1970 except for a brief declaration indicating the party's intention to "make every effort to apply the resolutions of the International Meeting of Communist and Workers' Parties of June 1969" (*El Popular*, 23 March).

Publications. The PUCH publishes a clandestine newspaper, *Boukan* (Torch), which began appearing in March 1969. In addition, the party relies on radio broadcasts from abroad. Havana radio transmits fourteen hours per week to Haiti (eleven hours in Creole and three in French). "Peace and Progress" radio in Moscow broadcasts daily thirty-minute programs in Creole and French.

N. S.

HONDURAS

The Communist Party of Honduras (Partido Comunista de Honduras; PCH), originally organized in 1927, was shattered in 1932 by the government of Tiburcio Carías. The party reappeared in 1954, which has since been considered its official founding date. In 1961 a small group claiming to be "scientifically Marxist" split off to become the Honduran Revolutionary Party (Partido Revolucionario Hondureño; PRH), now believed to be Castroite in orientation. Since 1967, when a major dispute over tactics and strategy arose within the PCH, there have been two groups calling themselves the PCH, referred to here as the PCH (Traditional) and the PCH (Revolutionary). The former retaining the original orientation of the party, is unequivocally pro-Soviet and advocates the use of peaceful means of struggle. The latter is Castroite in ideology and advocates armed struggle as the road to power in Honduras.

There is also a small Castroite group known as the Francisco Morazán Movement (Movimiento Francisco Morazán; MFM). In 1970 the appearance of yet another revolutionary group was reported, the "Ernesto Che Guevara Revolutionary Front."

Although not formally outlawed, communist and other left-wing groups are implicitly proscribed under the 1957 Honduran constitution. The present government of Oswaldo López Arellano has been severe in its control of left-wing activities, forcing the various groups to operate clandestinely and with little effectiveness.

The membership of all factions of the PCH is believed to number between 500 and 1,500 and that of the PRH and the MFM between 150 and 300 each. The population of Honduras is 2,700,000 (estimated 1970).

The PCH (Traditional). Leadership and Organization. The first secretary of the PCH (Traditional) is Mario Morales. Others prominent in the party include Jorge Días, Carlos Aldana, Longino Becerra, and Carlos Alvarez. Because of the party's proscription, little information as to its leaders and organizational structure has been available over the past few years.

The Communist Youth of Honduras (Juventud Comunista de Honduras; JCH) is a party-affiliated organization. Since 1967 it has been allied with the MFM and under the tutelage of the PCH (Revolutionary). Most communist-oriented university students are members of the University Reform Front (Frente de Reforma Universitaria; FRU). A small number belong to the Socialist Youth (Juventud Socialista). The predominant student group, however, is the Honduras University Students' Federation, which is controlled by noncommunist students.

Communist influence in the labor movement is minor and limited to the very small Committee of Revolutionary Workers (Comité de Trabajadores Revolucionarios; CTR). Most Honduran trade unions are under the influence of the predominantly American-owned fruit companies.

Domestic and International Views. Late in 1970 the Central Committee of the PCH

(Traditional) issued a document describing the present political situation in Honduras. As a result of the recent war with El Salvador, it said, a "distinct nationalistic tendency" had arisen among the people, finding expression in the "subsequent anti-imperialist struggle of the most advanced sections of the working class and progressive intellectuals and genuine patriotism displayed by the country's armed forces." The party believed these tendencies would be developed further due to the increasing "economic and political pressure of the Central American oligarchical groups, the monopolies supporting integration, and the U.S. State Department [which was] striving to restore the broken-down mechanism of the Central American 'common market.'" The Honduran bourgeoisie, the document continued, was "conciliatory" in nature, having negotiated openly with "North American neocolonialist bodies"; being "connected with local and foreign latifundists," it considered the "growing militancy of the working class and the awakened peasants to be a threat to its class interests." (*Trabajo*, as quoted in *IB*. no. 1, 1971.)

According to the PCH document, the "greatest danger" and "topmost problem" for Honduras was its "backwardness in all fields." Honduras, it declared, must construct a "socialist society" through a "democratic, agrarian and anti-imperialist revolution" in order to solve its problems and provide the "material and moral requirements" of the people. The communists emphasized, however, that such a solution demanded a "level of organization and of popular awareness which do not exist at present." The solution for the immediate political crisis, therefore, would be the unification of all forces interested in democratization of the country, regardless of "ideological, religious and social differences." These forces would demand a new electoral law which would legalize new parties and independent candidates and would force the "ruling classes to reject their anti-popular plans." (*Ibid.*)

The government's agrarian policy, the document declared, was "reformist" in concept, attempting to modernize farming by turning "large, semi-feudal estates into capitalist-type estates and to create large, production units under the guidance of the National Agrarian Institute." This "reformism," the PCH said, infringed the rights of the peasants and failed to expropriate the large holdings of the latifundists or to return to the country the unused land owned by the banana companies. (*Ibid.*)

On international issues the PCH most recently made its views public at the Moscow Conference, where Mario Morales maintained that the present was the "epoch of the transition from capitalism to socialism on a world scale" even though "imperialism" was trying "stubbornly to retain its positions" through "reformist maneuvers" in some cases and "direct aggression" in others. Success in battle against "man's bitterest enemy," he declared, hinged on "cementing the ranks of the world proletariat" and orienting it to the "new tasks in the fight against imperialism." (*IMCWP*, p. 605.) The Soviet Union—the bastion of the working people—was in the "forefront of the forces fighting imperialism," according to Morales, who exhorted all communists to "expose with all energy and clarity the concepts of Maoism"—which had been "turned into something close to a religion" (*ibid.*, pp. 607-8).

Morales went on to describe "U.S. intervention" in the political, ideological, and cultural affairs of Latin America as a "desperate attempt by Yankee imperialism to halt the popular struggle mounting in different forms"—from parliamentary activity, where this was possible, to armed action, where the "objective and subjective preconditions" made resort to arms "acceptable as a form of struggle" (*ibid.*, p. 608).

International Party Contacts. First Secretary Morales went to Moscow in April 1970 to represent the PCH at the Lenin Centenary celebrations.

Publications. The organ of the Central Committee of the PCH (Traditional) is *Trabajo*, which appears irregularly and clandestinely. The party's information sheet, *Voz Popular*, is supposed to be issued weekly and is also circulated clandestinely.

* * *

The PCH (Revolutionary). Leadership and Organization. The first secretary of this branch is believed to be Dionisio Ramos Bejarano. Other important figures include Mario Soza Navarro ("Ricardo Moncada Zavala") and Alonzo Muñoz.

The JCH is the primary base of support for the PCH and since 1967 has been closely allied with its Castroite ideology and activities. University students apparently also often support the PCH even though they are not members.

Party Views. In 1970 a spokesman for the PCH (Revolutionary) for the first time publicly discussed the existence of two separate PCH groups when J. Valle, a member of the *Unidad* editorial staff, described the PCH (Traditional) as consisting of "rightist opportunists" who had for a long time been "conciliatory toward the military dictatorship, in open betrayal of the fundamental principles of Marxism and the interests of the Honduran people." Valle described his own party as "revolutionary and antidictatorial" and opposed to "any Western-style government." (Radio "La Voz de Honduras," Tegucigalpa, 9 November, quoting from a letter by Valle dated 5 November.)

The PCH has outlined its objective as the "destruction of the military dictatorship through mass movements and armed actions as the fundamental form of struggle." Next, it has declared, must come the "establishment of a revolutionary government" which would "carry out a program of agrarian reform," recover the "national wealth from the Yankee monopolies," give "state power to the people," make "economic independence a reality," carry out a "cultural revolution," and reestablish "full popular rights." This program was clearly in contrast to the position of the PCH (Traditional), whose objective of "democratization" of the government and the army, was branded by the PCH (Revolutionary) as a "totally unrealistic concept" which in addition to being both "false and vacuous" was "essentially reactionary." (*Tricontinental*, Havana, no. 15, November-December 1969.)

Publications. The PCH (Revolutionary) publishes a clandestine propaganda organ, *Unidad*. The party announced in November 1970 that it would soon begin publishing a journal entitled *Abril*.

L. R.

MARTINIQUE

The Martinique Communist Party (Parti Communiste Martiniquais; PCM) was founded in 1957. Communism in Martinique, however, originated as early as 1918 with the formation of a group called the "Friends of Jean Jaurès," which in 1923 became the "Jean Jaurès Communist Group." In 1925 this group joined the French Communist Party. It was disbanded in September 1939. In 1944 communists reorganized themselves as the Martinique Federation of the French Communist Party, and this group in September 1957 became the autonomous PCM.

The PCM is legal. Estimates as to its membership range from 700 to 1,300. The population of Martinique is 335,000 (estimated 1970). The PCM is an active participant in Martinique's political life, on both departmental and local levels.[1] Its following, however, has generally been declining over the past fourteen years, partly because one of its leaders, Aimé Césaire, created in 1956 the left-wing noncommunist Martinique People's Party (Parti Populaire Martiniquais; PPM), and partly as a consequence of the PCM's policy of autonomy for Martinique (see below), which does not have mass support. Whereas in 1956 the PCM had obtained 62.50 per cent of the vote, in 1967 it received only 16.24 per cent, and in the elections of June 1968 it increased its percentage to only 16.86. Neither of its two candidates was elected—the PCM did not contest the district of Fort-de-France in which Aimé Césaire ran successfully. The party also failed to win any seats in the elections to the Senate, held in September of that year. (For further details on 1968 elections, see *YICA*, 1969, p. 585.)

The PCM controls several municipal governments of Martinique. Among its most prominent representatives are Georges Gratiant, mayor of Lamentin; Sévère Cerland, mayor of Macouba; Georges Fitte-Duval, mayor of Saint-Esprit; and Edgard Nestoret, mayor of Morne-Rouge. On 8 and 15 March elections were held to eighteen of the thirty-six seats on Martinique's General Council. The PCM contested nine and won three of them. One PCM general councilor, Sévère Cerland, was not reelected; another one, Pierre Zobda-Quitman, did not run; the party's diminished presence on the General Council, however, was partly compensated by the election of Georges Gratiant, a newly elected councilor. Within the General Council the party was represented in 1970 by Georges Charles-Alfred, Georges Fitte-Duval, Georges Gratiant, and Victor Lamon.

Leadership and Organization. The PCM is led by its Politburo and Secretariat, which are elected by the Central Committee, following the latter's election at a party congress. The PCM's Fourth Congress was held on 27-29 December 1968. On 8 January 1969 the following were elected to the party's leadership: Armand Nicolas, secretary-general; Politburo—Dolor Banidol, Phi-

---

[1] Martinique is one of France's Overseas Departments and thus an integral part of the French Republic, administered by a prefect, with an elected General Council and with elected representatives in the French National Assembly and Senate in Paris.

lipbert Duféal, Georges Fitte-Duval, Mathurin Gottin, Georges Gratiant, Walter Guitteaud, Victor Lamon, Georges Mauvois, René Ménil, and Armand Nicolas; Secretariat—Philipbert Duféal (party organization), Mathurin Gottin (finances), Georges Mauvois (propaganda), Armand Nicolas (secretary-general), and Albert Platon (workers' and peasants' organizations) (*Justice*, 16 January). Dolor Banidol was killed at the beginning of December 1969 in an air accident, while on his return from attending the Fourteenth Congress of the Communist Party of Chile. On 30 April 1970, the PCM newspaper, *Justice*, referred to Edgard Nestoret as being a member of the party's Politburo, which would suggest that he may have filled Banidol's place. A meeting of the PCM Central Committee on 17 October 1970 elected Walter Guitteaud to the Secretariat, placing him in charge of party organization; at the same time Duféal was given the responsibility for propaganda. The party press did not make any reference to any new responsibilities for the former secretary for propaganda, Georges Mauvois. (*Ibid.*, 22 October.)

The PCM has its own youth organization, the Union of Communist Youth of Martinique (Union de la Jeunesse Communiste de la Martinique; UJCM). In 1969, however, the Central Committee of the UJCM was disbanded and a PCM-sponsored "Provisional Committee" was formed with the goal of reorganizing the UJCM local groups and preparing for a congress to elect a new UJCM leadership (see *YICA*, 1970, p. 441). During 1970 no further reference was made to the UJCM in the PCM's press.

The PCM obtains its primary support from the communist-controlled General Confederation of Labor of Martinique (Confédération Générale du Travail de la Martinique; CGTM), whose secretary-general is PCM Politburo member Victor Lamon. The CGTM is the largest trade union in Martinique, with some 4,000 members. Whereas in earlier years the PCM could count on considerable support from the General Association of Martinique Students (Association Générale des Etudiants Martiniquais; AGEM), which is a member of the communist-controlled International Union of Students, controversy between the party and the student group—evident in 1969 (see *ibid.*)—attained such proportions in 1970 that cooperation between the two was no longer possible (see below). It would appear that during the year a similar development took place between the PCM and another youth group—the Organization of Anticolonialist Youth of Martinique (Organisation de la Jeunesse Anticolonialiste de la Martinique; OJAM)—which, while formerly not as close ideologically to the PCM as the AGEM, had been a source of a certain amount of support to the party.

Domestic Views and Policies. The PCM's domestic policy in 1970 centered upon advocating autonomy for Martinique within a framework of close ties with France. The party called for a local legislative assembly elected by universal suffrage, an executive Martinique organ responsible to that assembly, and a body for cooperation with France comprising equal representation from Martinique and France—the latter's role to be primarily the implementation and application of financial and technical aid to Martinique.

In the furtherance of its goals, the PCM was confronted with two major issues—its relationship with the noncommunist PPM and the challenge from elements that the party termed "leftists" (*gauchistes*) and who, in contrast to the PCM's call for autonomy, advocated total independence for Martinique. Whereas in recent years the PCM had tended to be the more concerned party with regard to the question of cooperation with the PPM, in 1970 this PCM role appeared to be less evident. Considerable controversy was engendered between the two parties at the time of the March elections, when, in contrast to earlier policy, the PCM decided to contest the district of Fort-de-France, a PPM stronghold (*Justice*, 26 February, 5, 12, and 19 March, and 9

April). In its explanation of the decision before the elections, the PCM referred to the "general weakening of the democratic and anti-colonialist positions" of the PPM (*ibid.*, 5 March). Later, when the results showed a massive PPM victory in the district of Fort-de-France, the PCM focused its commentary on the fact that there had been an abstention of 58.86 per cent, and claimed that communist candidacy was a bid to win over the abstentionists and should not be interpreted as an encroachment on PPM support (*ibid.*, 19 March). The following month, in a lengthy article the PCM secretary-general, Armand Nicolas, attempted to justify the PCM action, stressing that his party had committed itself to support the PPM list in the second ballot. Stating that "the road to unity is not a straight line without obstacles," Nicolas claimed that one way to resolve possible controversy between the two parties was to conclude a "serious agreement," which would include "joint candidates" and a "joint electoral campaign." (*Ibid.*, 9 April.)

The challenge to the PCM from "leftist" groups advocating total independence for Martinique appeared to originate primarily among young people. During the year, the PCM concentrated its criticisms on the AGEM. The party reiterated its contention, expressed in a series of articles in 1969 (see *YICA*, 1970, p. 441-42), that revolutionary policy should be determined by the "objective conditions" in a country and not by "revolutionary phraseology." The PCM warned its members that "leftists," having failed to win over the masses to their cause, were attempting to "infiltrate" the meetings of the party and the CGTM in order to "sow confusion." The PCM also referred to the fact that many of the "leftist" groups called themselves "communist," and added: "The proliferation of groups calling themselves 'communist' has as its sole purpose the sowing of confusion among the masses, to the full advantage of the colonialists." (*Justice*, 16 July).

International Views and Policies. During 1970 the PCM press made relatively few references to international issues, whether of a general nature or pertaining to the international communist movement. With regard to the latter, the party reiterated its alignment with the Communist Party of the Soviet Union (CPSU), when, on the occasion of the centennial anniversary of Lenin's birth, the party's newspaper referred to the Soviet Union as "the principal force upon which relies the struggle of all peoples for liberty, peace, and socialism" (*Justice*, 16 April). The party newspaper also carried articles at the same time emphasizing the importance of "proletarian internationalism," and warning against the dangers of "nationalist tendencies" (*ibid.*). Earlier in the year, an article on Cuba underscored the "considerable aid" given that country by the Soviet Union (*ibid.*, 8 January). The PCM, however, made no comments on developments in Communist China or on the Sino-Soviet conflict.

The PCM continued to have cordial relations with the French Communist Party (PCF). It sent a delegation to the French party's Nineteenth Congress (4-8 February), led by Politburo member Georges Mauvois. In its reporting on the congress, the PCM press offered its full solidarity with the decisions taken by the PCF leadership, including the expulsion of Roger Garaudy (*ibid.*, 12 February).

International Party Contacts. In 1970, in addition to its representation at the PCF congress, the PCM sent a delegation, led by Secretary-General Armand Nicolas, to the celebrations in Moscow of the Lenin Centenary. Another high-level PCM delegation, led by Georges Mauvois, conferred in Bucharest with leaders of the Romanian Communist Party on 1-10 September. The communiqué published following the visit referred only to an exchange of opinions in a "cordial [and] friendly atmosphere" (*Justice*, 1 October), perhaps indicating that disagreements between the two parties had been expressed. The PCM was represented by Politburo member René Ménil at an international conference on the fiftieth anniversary of the PCF, held in Paris on 31 October-2 November.

Publications. The PCM publishes a weekly newspaper, *Justice*, and an irregular theoretical journal, *Action.*

M. P.

MEXICO

The Mexican Communist Party (Partido Comunista Mexicano; PCM) was founded in September 1919 with the assistance of a number of foreigners, including M. N. Roy and Mikhail Borodin. The PCM sent a delegation to the 1920 congress of the Communist International in Moscow and has on most occasions been a supporter of the Soviet Union since that time.

The main pro-Chinese party is the "Mexican Movement of Marxist-Leninist Antirevisionist Unification" (Movimiento de Unificación Marxista y Leninista Antirrevisionista; MUMAM); two smaller pro-Chinese groups are the Mexican Bolshevik Communist Party (Partido Comunista Bolchevique Mexicano; PCBM) and the Communist Spartacus League (Liga Comunista Espártaco; LCE). Two Trotskyist parties are: the People's Revolutionary Movement (Movimiento Revolucionario del Pueblo; MRP) and the Trotskyist Revolutionary Worker's Party (Partido Obrero Revolucionario Trotskista; PORT). The Socialist People's Party (Partido Popular Socialista; PPS) resulted from a split in the PCM in 1948.

All of these parties are legal, but only the PPS meets the requirement under Mexican law of a membership registration of at least 75,000 in order for a party to enter candidates in national elections. The present membership of the PCM is estimated at 5,000 and that of the other small leftist groups combined at not more than 1,000. The PPS has some 75,000 members. The communists play no significant role in the political life of the country. The population of Mexico is 50,700,000 (estimated 1970).

In July 1970 Mexico held a national election in which the candidate of the Party of Revolutionary Institutions (Partido Revolucionario Institucional; PRI), Luis Echeverria Alvarez, received some 90 per cent of the 20 million votes cast. The PCM instructed its members to abstain from voting in the election; much of the PPS membership is believed to have supported Echeverria. Thus, the prospects are for continued social and economic stability in Mexico with a minimum of political influence exercised by the communists.

Leadership and Organization. The secretary-general of the PCM is Arnoldo Martínez Verdugo. Important members of the Central Committee include Arturo Pasos, Dionisio Encinas, Román Blas Manrique, Eduardo Montes, Hugo Ponce de León, José Luna, José Luis Sustaita, Encarnación Pérez Gaytán, Juan Rejano, Ramón Ramírez, Máximo Contreras, Juan Céspedes, José Olarte, Gonzalo Villalobos, Gerardo Unzueta, Marcos Posadas, and David Alfaro Siqueiros, the well-known painter and a leading spokesman for the party.

The Communist Youth of Mexico (Juventud Comunista de México; JCM) is an auxiliary organization of the PCM. The JCM secretary-general is Celso Garza Guajardo, and the organization secretary is Marcos Leonel Posadas. The PCM also controls the National Center of Democratic Students (Centro Nacional de Estudiantes Democráticos; CNED). Both the president of the CNED, Aguilar Talamantes, and the secretary-general, Arturo Martínez reportedly are in prison.

Although the PCM cannot participate in national political events, it does use a number of front organizations to increase its influence. Among these are the People's Electoral Front and a peasant organization known as the Independent Peasants' Central (CCI) which has a small pro-communist faction.

Party Internal Affairs. The most recent PCM congress met in June 1967. An article by Blas Salinas in the PCM newspaper *La Voz de México* on 22 November 1970 (abridged in *IB*, no. 3-4, 1971) stated that for more than a decade the party has been torn by internal disputes, resulting in the expulsion of many members, the overshadowing of some former leaders, and a decline in the party's national influence and internal organizational strength. Salinas, representing the faction most closely aligned with the Soviet Union, stated that the party is composed primarily of middle-class persons and that its policies have exhibited a middle-class bias. The most dangerous tendency in the party, he said, was "sectarianism," which frequently led to "ultra-leftism" and thence to "revisionism." Thus he warned: "The enemy is constantly on the watch and is operating even in our own ranks." He called for a greater emphasis on cadre training and reliance on Leninist organizational practices, especially democratic centralism.

Certain party positions in recent years have suggested that the "revisionist" elements were exercising considerable—at times conclusive—influence, as in the PCM's condemnation of the Soviet-led occupation of Czechoslovakia in 1968. In 1970 concern over such influence was expressed in Salinas's call for the elimination of the "chauvinism and all revisionist tendencies" widely associated with Roger Garaudy, Alexander Dubček, the "Maoists," and others, and in his statement that some party members had proposed modeling PCM activities on the experience of the Communist Party of Spain (*ibid.*). Influence of "revisionists" would seem to have prompted the party's decision to support the communist party dissidents in Venezuela led by Teodoro Petkoff (see *Venezuela*).

After the July elections a conflict developed between the PCM leadership and Siqueiros when it became known that the artist had voted in spite of the decision that the party would abstain (see below). Siqueiros added to the conflict by stating that President Luis Echeverria's policies could lead Mexico toward an "advanced progressive state."

Domestic Attitudes and Activities. According to a statement of the PCM (*Voz de México*, 2 December 1969), the communist party firmly maintains that the "objective necessity for a new revolution has matured in Mexico" and that the only way to "resolve the present social and economic conflicts is to replace the ruling class by a new bloc of forces in which the workers, peasants, democratic intellectuals and other working people will play the main role." The PCM believes that "political struggle in defense of democracy" is the "pivot of the nation's political life." The party program rules out "all exclusiveness" and calls for "unity of all the democratic and anti-imperialist forces."

The most urgent domestic problems as seen by the PCM include: "(1) applying the individual rights and guarantees established by the Constitution; (2) an amnesty for all who are held in prison or otherwise persecuted for political reasons, and their reinstatement at their places of work or study; (3) repealing Article 145 of the Federal Penal Code and ending repression; (4) raising wages, salaries and pensions; (5) a democratic reform of education, and effective autonomy for all universities; (6) redistributing the land; (7) freedom of trade-union activity and respect for the right to strike; (8) a democratic electoral reform." (*Ibid.*)

In the 1970 election campaign, Secretary-General Arnoldo Martínez called on the people to "repudiate the electoral farce by abstaining and fighting for democratic demands" (*Novedades*, Mexico City, 10 July). The party program declared: "The present electoral system, the anti-democratic practices now prevailing, and the character of the registered candidates and political parties make it perfectly impossible to make any headway in the struggle for democracy by keeping the electoral rules imposed by the government" (*IB*., no. 9).

The PCM officially supported the hunger strike carried out by eighty political prisoners. This lasted forty-two days in December 1969 and January 1970 and achieved some success by drawing public attention to the allegedly unconstitutional treatment of political prisoners. In August, following its repeal of the "social dissolution" law, the government released two PCM members who had been in prison for eleven years. On 3 August, one of the two, Valentin Campa, called on "all of us" to act with "honesty and good will to change the asphyxiating situation now prevailing in Mexico."

Following the inauguration of the president, the PCM issued a document entitled "Continuism and Demagogy of the Government of Luis Echeverria" in which it declared that "no political change of significance could be expected of the replacement of one president by another," adding: "The same reactionary and anti-popular policy continues, and it generates even greater enrichment of the rich at the cost of the increased impoverishment of the poor. Echeverria did not announce a single serious measure to counteract this law of the capitalist regime which he defends." Pointing out that Echeverria was interior minister during the 1968 "popular armed student movement" the document commented:

> The persecution of the opposition, imprisonment for ideological reasons and the existence of a large number of political prisoners, are facts that contradict all the 'democratic' phraseology. A general amnesty, a political act of the government which is demanded by important democratic sectors, is the act without which the slightest mention of constitutional freedoms by the president turns out to be void of all content.

Therefore, the PCM maintained, workers must not be disarmed by talk of "progressive and democratic changes" but must, rather, "rely only on their own determination and militancy."

International Views and Positions. The PCM has traditionally followed the Moscow line, but it showed some independence by criticizing the Warsaw Pact invasion of Czechoslovakia in 1968. In a statement released in December 1969, the party declared itself "autonomous in shaping and carrying out its policies but bound with the other communist parties by profound solidarity and by common ideology, objectives and tasks." The PCM is fighting for the "unity of all communist parties and socialist countries." (*IB*., no. 9, 1970.)

In the summer of 1970 Antonio Franco, head of the PCM's International Affairs Committee, went to Cuba as a member of a cane-cutting brigade to help in the sugar harvest as an expression of "fighting solidarity with the heroic Cuban revolution." While there, Franco spoke of the "failure of North American policy in Vietnam [and of] the 'Vietnamization' of the war," adding: "This criminal action of imperialism has aroused indignation throughout the world and in the United States itself." (Radio Havana, 22 June.)

International Contacts. The PCM was represented by Central Committee member Manuel Terrazas at the Lenin Centenary celebration in Moscow during April 1970.

Publications. The official organ of the PCM is the weekly newspaper *La Voz de México*, edited during 1970 by Hugo Ponce de León.

*   *   *

The pro-Chinese communist parties and groups in Mexico are small and are splintered into several contending factions. The most active group is the Mexican Movement of Marxist-Leninist Anti-Revisionist Unification, whose leaders are former PCM members Javier Fuentes Gutiérrez and Federico Emery. In 1968 the MUMAM played an active role in the student disturbances and published a Spanish-language edition of *Chairman Mao Tse-tung on People's War*. It added a preface which praised Mao's guerrilla principles and rejected those of Che Guevara.

In June 1969 Emery and a number of his comrades were arrested for the bombing of two government buildings. At his hearing Emery stated that he was founder and leader of the MUMAM, that he had twice visited China, and that he had distributed propaganda materials sent by the Chinese.

The MUMAM issues a publication entitled *Chispa*.

Other pro-Chinese groups include the Communist Spartacus League, led by Professor Bernardo Bader Ocampo, and the Mexican Bolshevik Communist Party, led by Leonel Padilla, Arturo Velasco, Feliz González, and Antonio Farfán. The LCE organ is *El Militante*; that of the PCBM is *El Machete*.

*   *   *

There are at least two Trotskyist groups in Mexico. The leaders of the People's Revolutionary Movement, Victor Rico Galá and Raúl Ugalde, have both been in prison since 1968. The Trotskyist Revolutionary Workers' Party is led by Francisco Calmenares César. Its organ is *Voz Obrera*.

Little is known about the activities of these groups and it appears that the Mexican government is able to control them effectively by keeping most of their leaders under detention.

*   *   *

The PPS. The Socialist People's Party, which resulted from a split in the PCM in 1948, was founded and led by Vicente Lombardo Toledano until his death in November 1968. With some 75,000 members, it is one of the largest procommunist parties in Latin America. Some leaders of the PPS are communists (Lombardo Toledano considered himself an independent Marxist), but the overall membership is not. During Lombardo's leadership of the PPS there were periodic rapprochements with the PCM but no permanent alliance. Since his death the PPS has been weakened by internal leadership struggles.

L. R.

NICARAGUA

The Socialist Party of Nicaragua (Partido Socialista de Nicaragua; PSN) was formed in 1937 as the result of a split in the Party of Nicaraguan Workers, within which the communists had operated. In 1944 the government of Nicaragua permitted communists to hold a national congress, and the PSN regards that year as the date of its official founding. The party is pro-Soviet.

There is a small but active Castroite guerrilla organization in Nicaragua called the Sandinist National Liberation Front (Frente Sandinista de Liberación Nacional; FSLN) (see below). The existence of a small independent group believed to have connections with the FSLN, the Revolutionary Armed Forces (Fuerza Armadas Revolucionarias; FAR), was reported in 1969.

The PSN was outlawed in 1945 and has been illegal during most of its subsequent existence. Although it has occasionally attempted to influence the political situation through front organizations, the PSN at present is almost totally ineffective, owing both to the government's strict suppression of left-wing groups, and to its small size and weak organization.

The PSN is estimated to have about 200 members, the FSLN about 100. The population of Nicaragua is 2,000,000 (estimated 1970).

Leadership and Organization. During the past several years little information about the PSN and its structure has been released and many of its leaders are believed to be either in prison or exile. The first secretary, according to the most recent reports available (1968), is Alvaro Ramírez Gonzáles. The latest congress of the PSN was held in 1966. Plenary meetings were held in 1967 and 1969.

The PSN controls only the extreme left-wing faction of the General Confederation of Labor (Confederación General de Trabajo; CGT) which itself represents only a minor portion of the country's workers. The overall influence of the party on labor affairs is, therefore, slight. In 1970 the CGT sent a delegation to the second meeting of the "Committee of Union Unity of Central American and Panamanian Workers" (CUSCA) held in San José, Costa Rica, on 19-21 March. In a document approved by the meeting it was declared that in Nicaragua the "repression of the patriotic union movement and the workers' class continued to be ferocious" (*Libertad*, San José, 4 April). (See also *Costa Rica*.)

The PSN has attempted to maintain front groups among students and other young persons, but over the past four or five years its influence has been minimal. The continuing student unrest and violence in Nicaragua is probably carried out almost entirely by members of guerrilla-oriented Castroite groups. The PSN reportedly still maintains a small youth front called the Nicaragua Socialist Youth (Juventud Socialista Nicaraguense).

The "Confederation of Peasants and Agricultural Laborers" was founded by the PSN in 1967. To date, little is known of its program or activities (see *YICA*, 1970, pp. 449-50).

Party Internal Affairs. Although the PSN ostensibly remains a supporter of the Soviet Union, it is believed that internal dissent has weakened this alignment. At the 1969 Moscow Conference a PSN spokesman declared: "Right-wing opportunism [has] for many years distorted the Marxist-Leninist character of our organization and weakened its capacity for action, rousing distrust towards us among considerable political and social strata of our people." The party was said to lack the "benefit of the support of many fraternal parties" because of its isolation and the repression practiced by the Nicaraguan government. (*IMCWP*, pp. 564-65.)

Domestic Attitudes. In an interview in Moscow, 2 August 1969, PSN spokesman Roberto Santos described the situation in Nicaragua as characterized by a "sharp worsening of the socioeconomic and political crisis" and by the "ever increasing antipopular and antidemocratic repressive offensive" of the Somoza regime. The party, he continued, thus finds that its main task is to "attract and organize the most militant and determined popular sectors, as well as to search for unity among the popular, democratic, and revolutionary parties and organizations on the basis of action and struggle against the dictatorship, the oligarchy, and imperialism." The PSN declares that the "very nature of the [Somoza] regime"—which had "exacerbated the crisis, whipped up repressions, and relied on violence more and more"—will "inevitably spark an open struggle by the working people against the dictatorship" (*WMR*, December 1969).

International Views. The PSN's most recent declaration of its international position came at the 1969 Moscow Conference, where its delegate Roberto Santos declared that the party's "international duty" commanded it to "wage a resolute struggle against anti-Sovietism"—whether coming from the "imperialist enemy" or from within the communist movement. The "Mao Tsetung clique," he said, had betrayed the movement and could no longer be considered members of it. (*IMCWP*, p. 563.)

Santos criticized the communist and workers' parties of Latin America for not devoting "sufficient attention to the obvious need of formulating and thoroughly elaborating, through bilateral, regional and continental meetings, a general strategy of the anti-imperialist struggle." The PSN, he noted, had "fraternal revolutionary gratitude" for Cuba—the "vanguard in the Latin American revolutionary movement, the first detachment laying the foundations of socialism" in Latin America. (*Ibid.*, pp. 562-63.)

International Contacts. The PSN sent a delegation to Moscow in April to attend the Lenin Centenary celebration.

Publications. The long-standing PSN organ, *Orientación Popular*, was suppressed in 1967. Its successor, *Tribuna*, met the same fate in 1968. At present, apparently no publication is being issued by the PSN.

*   *   *

The FSLN. The Sandinist National Liberation Front is a small Castroite guerrilla organization founded by Carlos Fonseca Amador in 1961.[1] Its membership is made up primarily of students and city or rural workers, many of them former members of the PSN who became dissatis-

---

[1] The FSLN is named for Augusto César Sandino, a Nicaraguan general whose opposition to the U.S. military occupation of Nicaragua (1927-33), by means of guerrilla warfare, has made him a symbol of resistance to U.S. "imperialism."

fied with its "pacificist line." University students have participated in the violent actions carried out by the organization, and some have been jailed or killed as a result. The FSLN describes it-self as a "political-military organization whose objective is the seizure of political power through the destruction of the bureaucratic and military apparatus of the dictatorship and the establish-ment of a Revolutionary Government based on a worker-peasant alliance and the support of all the anti-imperialist patriotic forces of the country" (*Tricontinental*, Havana, No. 17, March-April, 1970). Its motto is *Patria libre o morir* ("Our Country Free or Death").

Since 1967, when Carlos Fonseca Amador attended the Latin American Solidarity Organiza-tion conference in Havana and "declared war" against the Nicaraguan government, the FSLN has been engaged in small, sporadic terrorist actions including bank robberies, bombings, attacks on factories, and assassinations of government officials. In August 1969 Fonseca Amador was arrested by the Costa Rican government. In his absence the leadership of the FSLN was assumed by a young worker, Efraín Sánchez Sancho (*OCLAE*, Havana, April 1970). On 21 October 1970 Costa Rican guerrillas hijacked a Costa Rican airliner and diverted it to Cuba; four U.S. pas-sengers (officials of the United Fruit Company) were held as hostages and then freed in ex-change for Costa Rica's release from prison of Fonseca Amador and three other Central Ameri-can guerrillas.

After his release, Fonseca Amador traveled to Cuba. In an interview he declared that the guer-rilla movement in Nicaragua had been developing "ever since the beginning of the Cuban revolu-tion" and had emerged in 1962 as a "definite military outfit—the FSLN." He claimed that the FSLN had the support of Nicaraguan peasants, who were "rebellious" in spirit but had to be in-structed in revolutionary ideology and organized by young "revolutionaries" from the cities. (*Direct From Cuba*, Havana, no. 29, November 1970.)

In commenting on the September 1970 presidential election in Chile the FSLN leader said that the conditions which made possible the election of a Marxist in Chile did not exist in Central America, especially Nicaragua, where revolutionary ideology had only recently begun to "sink into the intellectuals" (*ibid.*).

The FSLN, Fonseca Amador declared, will "continue armed struggle in Nicaragua until the country is freed of imperialist exploitation and its sovereignty and freedom are rescued from the hands of the United States and its puppet Somoza" (*Granma*, English, Havana, 1 November 1970).

The FSLN has a publication entitled *Trinchera*, whose frequency and extent of distribution are unknown.

L. R.

PANAMA

The Communist Party of Panama (Partido Comunista del Panamá) was founded in 1930. During the Second World War the party name was changed to People's Party of Panama (Partido del Pueblo de Panamá; PDP).

Other left-wing groups include the Revolutionary Unity Movement (Movimiento de Unidad Revolucionario; MUR) (see below); the pro-Cuban National Action Vanguard (Vanguardia de Acción Nacional; VAN), led by Jorge Turner, who is in exile; and the Panamanian Revolutionary Union (Unión Revolucionaria Panameña; URP), which is Castroite and pro-Chinese. The "Front of Popular Resistance" reportedly embraces both the MUR and the VAN.

The PDP has been illegal and banned from participation in Panama's political system since 1953. When the government of General Omar Torrijos Herrera took power through a coup in October 1968, all political parties were dissolved. Subsequently the suppression of communist and left-wing groups was intensified and many of their leaders and other members were either jailed or exiled. When civil liberties were officially restored in November 1969, some of those imprisoned were released, but many of them were sent into exile. In August 1970, General Torrijos issued an amnesty which effected the release of many others.

The membership of the PDP is estimated to number about 250. The party has little popular support except among some university students and has practically no effect on the political situation in Panama. The population of Panama is 1,500,000 (estimated 1970).

Leadership and Organization. Since 1951 the secretary-general of the PDP has been Rubén Darío Sousa (sometimes known by his pseudonym, "Vicente Tello"). He is in exile, presumably in Europe. Other leading figures in the party include Hugo Víctor (chairman of the Central Committee), Professor César de León, the national poet Carlos Francisco Changmarín, and Simón Vargas—members of the Central Committee, and Carlos Nuñez and the brothers Moisés and César Carrasquilla. Most or all are probably in exile.

Communists exert influence in the Federation of Students of Panama (Federación de Estudiantes de Panamá; FEP), which includes both the Union of University Students (Unión de Estudiantes Universitarios; UEU) and the Union of Secondary School Students (Unión de Estudiantes de Secundaria; UES). The FEP is a member of the communist-front International Union of Students. The PDP is believed to control the University Reform Front (Frente Reformista Universitaria; FRU). Universities were closed from December 1968 throughout most of 1969 because the Torrijos government believed them to be bases for urban guerrilla activities. Organized student activity was, therefore, minimal and the above organizations, for all practical purposes, were temporarily dissolved. During 1970 the government eased many of its restrictions and student movements began to reemerge.

Delegates from Panama reportedly attended the "First Meeting of Central American Youth," held in San José, Costa Rica on 9-12 April 1970 and sponsored by the communist-front World

Federation of Democratic Youth. The meeting called for the formation of a movement, "Education for Youth by Youth," the purpose of which would be to persuade leaders, workers, peasants, students, teachers, artists, and priests to help Central American youth "oppose imperialism and the oligarchy" by an effective Central American union. (*Libertad*, San José, 11 April.)

The PDP controls the Trade Union Federation of the Workers of the Republic of Panama (Federación Sindical de Trabajadores de la República de Panamá; FST), which is very small and has only slight influence among Panamanian workers. Its leader, Angel Gómez, has been in prison since the government closed the offices of the FST in 1968. He was last reported to be seriously ill.

Although the FST was not able to carry out any domestic programs, it did send representatives to the second meeting of the "Committee of Union Unity of Central American and Panamanaian Workers" (CUSCA), held in San José, Costa Rica on 19-21 March. The delegates passed a resolution protesting the imprisonment of union leaders in Panama. (*Ibid.*, 4 April; also see *Costa Rica*.)

Party Internal Affairs. The PDP is basically pro-Soviet in orientation. With its leadership in exile and its activities restricted, the party does not make public any significant information about its internal affairs. It is not known whether ideological dissent has developed among PDP members.

In January 1970 the Political Bureau of the Central Committee adopted a document entitled "For a Revolutionary Way Out of the Situation" which discussed the developments in Panama, especially those related to the December 1969 abortive coup against General Torrijos (see *IB*, no. 9, 1970).

In an interview of August 1970 Secretary-General Darío Sousa declared that the PDP's most pressing business was the reorganization of the "entire outlawed nucleus of the People's Party." Opposition against "suppression" by the military government must be organized, he added, in order to restore "democratic rights" in Panama, obtain the release of political prisoners, and enable exiles to return. (*Horizont*, East Berlin, no. 35, August 1970.)

Domestic and International Views. By the end of 1970 the overall political situation in Panama had improved so far as the communists were concerned. After a period of severe restrictions imposed by the military junta of General Torrijos, PDP Secretary-General Darío Sousa observed that in 1970 "repressive measures" had been halted, "political prisoners" had been released (including some communists), student groups had been allowed to reorganize and negotiations had been started for a "democratic education reform." These improvements were attributed to the "abortive 1969 coup" (against General Torrijos) which, according to Sousa, had "revealed the deepening contradiction between the oligarchy and imperialism" and the "military government." (*WMR*, February 1971.)

In the view of the PDP leader the 1968 military *coup* had begun a "process of change" in Panama which had been "gaining in scope, opening new prospects for the people." The "subjective prerequisites for accomplishing the tasks of the democratic and anti-imperialist revolution are building up," Sousa declared, and the PDP regards this "new stage" as a "period of political transition." Although the coup was "neither popular nor progressive in orientation," he added, it had thwarted "U.S. imperialist plans, demolished the old political structure on which the U.S. depended and dealt a telling blow to its faithful ally, the oligarchy." Sousa explained further that the military government expressed the interests of a "radical-minded petty bourgeoisie" and though the class composition of the government was changed, the class nature of the political system was not; the heterogeneous elements accounted for its "contradictory and vacillating character" and its "tendency to improvise." (*Ibid.*)

The economy of Panama was described by Darío Sousa as to all intents and purposes under the control of U.S. monopolies which controlled, in addition to the Panama Canal, the banking, electric power, banana plantations, and a sizable part of trade. The oligarchy, he said, has used its "political power to further its economic interests" and has "consistently channeled industrial development into an anti-national course," intensifying the "harsh exploitation of the people." Although the coup did not change the economic structure, the communists believed that the Torrijos government intended to "reform taxation, agrarian relations, education, labor-employer relations, and also limit monopoly profits," thus "stimulating the popular movement." (*Ibid.*)

The PDP supported the government's decision to allow "democratic trade unions" and its promise to "respect trade union rights and the existence of differing trends in the labor movement." The outlook for the peasant movement was also improved and, according to Darío Sousa, the government's policy now was affording "opportunities for organizing the peasants to fight for a consistent solution of the agrarian problem." The situation of the peasants was being normalized, he said, by "legalizing peasant ownership of the land with no compensation to estate owners." (*Ibid.*)

The main task of Panamanian communists in the current situation, the leader of the PDP declared, was to "heighten the revolutionary awareness of the masses and unify the forces seeking change." Although the majority of the people realized that there must be no return to the past, Darío Sousa said, their political consciousness was "still too low for them to have a clear idea of the subsequent course of events." The PDP, he explained, must (1) make clear to the people that "capitalist development" will not solve their problems, (2) develop a "general line in cooperation with all forces involved in effecting revolutionary changes, and (3) draw up a program "reflecting the interests of the people and serving as a basis for their unity and a guide to exercising power." Further, Sousa declared, the party must "expose the false contention that economic and social progress is possible without a genuinely revolutionary government," and refute the "harmful allegation that the working class cannot play the role of vanguard because of the democratic character of the Panamanian revolution and also because at this stage the petty bourgeoisie has allegedly assumed this role." (*Ibid.*)

The PDP leader warned that "U.S. imperialists' sophisticated ideological subversion" posed a "great menace" by keeping the "increasingly mature working class from bringing revolutionary consciousness into the struggle of the people," from forming an alliance with the peasants, or from winning the support of the military and civil servants. Therefore, he added, the Marxist-Leninist party of the working class—the PDP— was the "ideological and political force which U.S. imperialism will have to face first and foremost." The party's "analysis of the changes taking place in Panama" and its "theoretical substantiation of the unfolding of the popular movement" would help "foil the maneuvers of imperialism and its allies who are trying to stave off change," he concluded. (*Ibid.*)

From an international point of view the secretary-general described the present epoch as one of "transition from capitalism to socialism," characterized by the growing might of the Soviet Union and the socialist system as a whole, by the stubborn fight of the international working class against monopoly, for democracy and socialism, by the gains of the national liberation movement and the liberation of vast areas of the globe from imperialist oppression." The contradictions of the capitalist system, he explained, have been aggravated by these factors and in its state of "deep crisis" capitalism cannot solve "big social problems in any country." (*Ibid.*)

In Latin America, the PDP believed, the revolutionary process was taking more "concrete, varied and often unexpected forms," as illustrated by the experiences of Cuba, Chile, Peru, Bolivia, and Panama. (*Ibid.*)

International Contacts. Secretary-General Darío Sousa attended the Lenin Centenary celebration in Moscow on 21 April.

Publications. The organ of the PDP is *El Mazo*. It is published irregularly and clandestinely.

*   *   *

The MUR. The Revolutionary Unity Movement, a Castroite organization particularly active in Panama during the 1960's, was founded and led by Floyd Britton, who died in prison in 1969 (see *YICA*, 1970, p. 457). The MUR has advocated armed struggle as the only means for "confronting the oligarchy and imperialism in Panama" (*Granma*, Havana, English, 14 December 1969). Since Britton's death little has been reported concerning the activities or direction of the MUR.

L. R.

PARAGUAY

The Paraguayan Communist Party (Partido Comunista Paraguayo; PCP) was founded in 1928. In mid-1963 a small group split from the PCP and formed the pro-Chinese Paraguayan Leninist Communist Party (Partido Leninista Comunista Paraguayo; PLCP). By 1969, however, the PLCP had rejoined the PCP. Another, more serious split within the PCP occurred in 1965 when the Soviet Union backed the organization of a commission which expelled Secretary-General Oscar Creydt from his long-held position in the party. The National Committee for the Defense and Reorganization of the Paraguayan Communist Party (Comité Nacional de Defensa y Reorganización del Partido Comunista Paraguayo)—the name the commission assumed in 1966—accused Creydt of being too lenient with dissident pro-Chinese members of the party and of acting in a high-handed, dictatorial manner in the conduct of party affairs. Creydt, followed by many of his colleagues, then established what he claimed was the legitimate PCP. The party, however, remained securely under the control of the pro-Soviet leaders of the National Committee.

The communist party and all left-wing groups have been illegal in Paraguay since October 1936. Under the government of General Alfredo Stroessner, who has been president since 1954, enforcement of the anti-subversion laws has been strict and all opposition groups have been suppressed. The PCP operates from exile in Argentina, Brazil, and Uruguay. It is believed that fewer than ten per cent of its members actually live in Paraguay. Domestic support for the party is insignificant.

The membership of the PCP, including all factions, is estimated to be between 4,500 and 5,000. The population of Paraguay is 2,400,000 (estimated 1970).

Leadership and Organization. Since 1967 the PCP has been under the leadership of Miguel Angel Soler and Obdulio Barthe. Other prominent figures are Hugo Maciel Campos, Gustavo Colman, Augusto Canete, Efraín Morel, Victor Alonso, Antonio Mora, Enrique Martínez, and the former leaders of the PLCP, Alfonso Guerra and Sebastián Querey. It is believed that most of these PCP leaders live in Buenos Aires.

Party Internal Affairs. Since the formation of the National Committee for the Defense and Reorganization of the Paraguayan Communist Party, the attention of the leadership has been concentrated primarily on the consolidation and reorganization of the party under the committee's direction. A plenary meeting of the Central Committee on 29 June-2 July 1970 adopted new party rules and approved various documents on political theses. The plenum also made plans for the party's Third Congress which was expected to "strengthen the party politically, ideologically, and organizationally, and, by electing leading organs, conclude the process of reorganization" (*Népszabadság*, Budapest, interview with Hugo Campos, 15 September).[1]

[1] The congress was held in April 1971.

According to an article by Hugo Campos and Gustavo Colman, the party has made considerable progress since the 1967 national preparatory conference for the Third Congress, in spite of the harm done by Oscar Creydt's "insidious efforts" to subvert it. Party cadres, they claimed, had "grown numerically, with most of them possessing good theoretical grounding," and the party had "entered a new stage of unity and cohesion on all issues of principle." Experience had shown, they continued, that the party "must learn to distinguish between words and deeds, screening Party cadres from time to time irrespective of post and position to prevent enemy infiltration. It is not enough to maintain revolutionary vigilance. Vigilance must be continuously intensified." (*WMR*, June 1970.)

Hugo Campos and Gustavo Colman reported in the same article that the PCP Political Committee was concerned with the party's need to improve its work by devoting more attention to its central organ, *Adelante*, to propaganda and educational activities, and to work with the masses. It was also essential to "assure collective work in the Party's leading bodies, to better Party planning in all sectors, to tighten revolutionary discipline and combat individualism and lack of organization." (*Ibid.*)

Domestic Attitudes and Activities. Presenting the PCP's view, Hugo Campos and Gustavo Colman in the aforementioned article described Paraguay, "despite considerable power and mineral resources and millions of hectares of fertile land," as "one of the most backward Latin American countries," with a population that "languishes in extreme poverty." Because of "unemployment and the police regime of nearly thirty years," the party claims, some 600,000 Paraguayans have migrated to neighboring countries." Further, the country was seen as suffering from "intensive imperialist penetration" and from having been assigned a "special strategic place in the Pentagon's military planning," which was said to include the proposed building of a large U.S. airbase and strategic roads and the training of Paraguayan army officers in "anti-guerrilla warfare." Paraguay was said to be "ruled" by the "U.S. economic mission," which imposed its will through "economic measures that lay a heavy burden on the people." Among other interferences in Paraguay's national life the PCP article cited the "notorious CIA-sponsored Peace Corps," the "U.S. monopoly agents" serving as advisers in the ORIT (the Organización Regional Inter-Americana de Trabajadores, or Inter-American Regional Organization of Workers—the American regional group of the International Confederation of Free Trade Unions), and "West German monopoly interests." (*WMR*, June 1970.)

Campos and Colman declared that the government of General Stroessner had become "isolated and increasingly unstable": the army, "its main pillar," was "displaying symptoms of discontent"; its economic policy had produced "disastrous effects"; and its "agrarian reform" had continued to consolidate the landowners. (*Ibid.*)

As for the PCP itself, the article claimed that the party was, after its period of internal difficulty, again "making its voice heard in the nation's affairs" and "fighting heroically against the reactionary regime, working deep underground." Its main task was to "regain lost positions in the labor movement and build up the mass struggle of workers, peasants, students, intellectuals and other social groups." By gradually building its strength within popular movements, the PCP was seeking to be ready to overthrow the "venal dictatorship" when conditions should "ripen for a popular uprising." To this end the party claims to be working for the formation of a "national anti-dictatorial front." (*Ibid.*) During 1970, as in recent years, however, there was no evidence of any activity of the party in Paraguay and no arrests of party members were reported.

In an editorial in its central organ, *Adelante*, the PCP urged the formation of a "provisional government of consistent democratization" to "bury the reactionary and sell-out regime of

Stroessner." As immediate minimum measures to be adopted by such a provisional government it proposed:

> freeing of all the imprisoned patriots; lifting of the state of siege; annulling all antidemocratic repressive laws; thorough purging of the state apparatus; the calling of truly free elections for a constituent national convention; . . . putting an end to all interference by foreign officials in the activities of state organs; suppressing or reducing abusive taxes; establishing diplomatic, economic, and cultural relations with the Soviet Union and other socialist countries; increasing wages and salaries; giving outright property titles to the peasants, and establishing a genuine system of university autonomy.

During 1970 the PCP centered its activities around efforts to mobilize support for the release of political prisoners in Paraguay. In an appeal issued in August the PCP demanded the release of "hundreds of political prisoners held by the Stroessner dictatorship" and called on workers, trade unions, peasants, and members of youth and other mass organizations to "demand the liberation of their comrades" (*WMR*, November). In September, a broadcast over Moscow radio declared a "week of solidarity with Paraguayan political prisoners."

International Positions. Since the expulsion of Oscar Creydt the PCP has stressed its solidarity with the Soviet Union. At the Moscow Conference, in 1969, Hugo Campos made a notable attack on the Chinese Communist Party (see *YICA*, 1970, p. 459). In May 1970, Campos stated that the Chinese Communists were trying to find support in Latin America in order to "create groups which would allow them to develop and strengthen their influence, divide the revolutionary movement, and weaken the anti-imperialist front." Oscar Creydt was declared the leading Paraguayan Maoist. "Maoist propaganda," Campos said, was "anti-Soviet and chauvinistic, a mixture of absurd editorial pretensions and attempts [by the Chinese] to justify their hatred of the U.S.S.R. and defend the ill-named cultural revolution." Although their attempts to win over the Latin American masses had failed, Campos asserted, the Chinese had met with success in recruiting "renegades and traitors, well-known Trotskyites, certain ultra-left-wing elements of the petty bourgeoisie, [and] displaced adventurers." ("Radio Peace and Progress," Moscow, 25 May.)

International Contacts. On 21 April 1970, Efraín Morel represented the party at the Lenin Centenary celebration in Moscow. A delegation from thePCP, led by Hugo Campos, visited the Soviet Union and East Europe in the fall.

Publications. The PCP central organ is the monthly magazine *Adelante*, which is published abroad and distributed clandestinely. The PCP also makes its views known through articles and reports in the *World Marxist Review* and over radio broadcasts from Moscow.

*   *   *

The PCP-Creydt. Oscar Creydt, the long-time leader of the Paraguayan communists, has been the secretary-general of what he claims is the legitimate PCP since the split of the party in 1965 (see above). In the late 1960's Creydt was openly critical of the Soviet Union and adopted pro-Chinese and pro-Castro positions, perhaps partly as a reaction to the increasing strength of the pro-Soviet PCP and partly in an attempt to appeal to the more radical elements in the Paraguayan left wing.

Members of the Central Committee of the PCP-Creydt include Ignacio Fernández, J. Darío Quiroz, and two others known only as "Rafael" and "Blas." The PCP-Creydt is outlawed like other leftist organizations and almost all of its members reside in exile, many of them in Montevideo. The size and vigor of the Creydt faction is not known and little was heard about it during 1970.

Although the PCP-Creydt is still small, the Central Committee claimed in a March 1969 statement (*Marcha*, Montevideo, 13 June) that it nevertheless had the support of the "masses of workers and peasants" and represented the majority of communists in hiding or in prison in Paraguay. The same statement condemned the "self-styled" rival PCP—an "insignificant rightist group that is negotiating secretly for its legalization under the Stroessner military-fascist dictatorship" —and described it as "totally isolated from and disdained by the working class and by all the truly democratic forces" in Paraguay.

The Creydt faction supports the governments of North Vietnam, North Korea, the Chinese People's Republic, and Cuba. In a collection of documents published in July 1969, *Unidad con el Enemigo, Guerra con el Hermano* (Montevideo, n.d.), its Central Committee condemned the Soviet Union for carrying on, in the words of the title,"unity with the enemy and war against the brother." The Soviet attitude toward the Chinese, the document declared, was "revisionist, racist, and chauvinist." The principal threat to the communist movement, according to the Central Committee, was "opportunism of the right," though communists must also fight "left adventurists."

An irregular periodical, *Unidad Paraguaya*, is believed to be under the control of the PCP-Creydt. Apparently no issues were published in 1970.

L. R.

PERU

The Peruvian Communist Party (Partido Comunista Peruano; PCP) had its origins in the Peruvian Socialist Party, founded in 1928 by José Carlos Mariátegui. The present name dates from 1930. A national conference in January 1964 resulted in a division of the party into pro-Soviet and pro-Chinese groups. In 1969 the pro-Chinese group was split into two contending factions.

There exist in Peru also various leftist organizations more revolutionary in spirit, with Trotskyist and Castroite sympathies, such as the Movement of the Revolutionary Left (Movimiento de Izquierda Revolucionaria; MIR), the Army of National Liberation (Ejército de Liberación Nacional; ELN), the Revolutionary Leftist Front (Frente Izquierdista Revolucionario; FIR), the Revolutionary Vanguard (Vanguardia Revolucionaria; VR), and the National Liberation Front (Frente de Liberación Nacional; FLN).

The pro-Soviet and pro-Chinese groups have memberships estimated at 2,000 and 3,000 respectively (*World Strength of the Communist Party Organizations*, Washington, D.C., 1970). The pro-Soviet PCP claims that its members and affiliates (those not assigned to a cell) together number 35,000. The other communist and leftist groups are considered small, the MIR being perhaps the largest. The population of Peru is 13,600,000 (estimated 1970).

A constitutional provision prohibits communist parties from participating in Peruvian elections, but they have been allowed to operate under various degrees of police surveillance and harassment. The present military government, led by President Juan Velasco Alvarado, has not persecuted any of the communist organizations. In December 1970 it granted a total political amnesty which released from prison important leaders belonging to the MIR, ELN, and FIR.

Communist membership is predominantly urban, mainly drawn from workers, students, and professional groups. The pro-Chinese PCP seems to have the stronger hold in the universities. Communist influence within the trade union movement is exercised mainly by the pro-Soviet PCP, which influences the General Confederation of Workers of Peru (Confederacion General de Trabajadores del Perú; CGTP).

In the November 1967 by-elections held in Lima, which contains about 39 per cent of the country's electorate, 106,563 votes (13.5 per cent) were cast for the candidate of a coalition organized by the pro-Soviet PCP and known as "Unity of the Left." Plans of this coalition to participate in the 1969 national elections were cancelled when a military junta took power on 3 October 1968.

*   *   *

The Pro-Soviet PCP. Leadership and Organization. The highest organ of the pro-Soviet PCP is the national congress, which is supposed to meet every three years. The fifth such gathering was held in March 1969. The principal party leaders include Jorge del Prado Chávez, secretary-general; Raúl Acosta Salas, undersecretary-general; and Central Committee members Félix Arias Schreiber, Jorge Béjar, Alfredo Abarca, Segundo Collazos, Pompeyo Mares, Magno Falćon,and Juan Cáceres. Mario Ugarte Hurtado, the organization secretary during 1969, appeared to have been replaced by Pompeyo Mares since the beginning of 1970.

The pro-Soviet party is organized along traditional lines, from cells through local and regional committees, to the Central Committee. Known regional committees exist in the cities of Lima, Callao, Arequipa, Oroya, Cerro de Pasco, Cuzco, Huancayo, Huánuco, Chiclayo, Chimbote, Andahuaylas, Tarma, Huancavelica, Abancay, Tacna, Cajamarca, Piura, Trujillo, Ica, Ayacucho, and Puno. Lima has the largest number of local committees, concentrated in low-income neighborhoods and in the slum areas which the government now refers to as "new towns" (*pueblos jóvenes*).

The pro-Soviet youth group, the Peruvian Communist Youth (Juventud Comunista Peruana; JCP), appears to be small and operates mainly at the university level within the Student Union Movement (Movimiento de Unidad Estudiantil; MUE). Jorge Tapia continues to be the JCP secretary-general. The JCP, according to Tapia, has the following composition: university students, 45 per cent; high school students, 35 per cent; workers and employees, 16 per cent; and peasants, 4 per cent (*Unidad*, 21 January 1971).

The PCP carried out during 1970 a fund-raising campaign to help defray administrative expenses. The campaign, in effect from 1 February to 31 May, was said to have produced about $17,000 from party bonds bought by 13,000 "comrades" and contributions from 25,000 "sympathizers" (*ibid.*, 2 July).

Party Internal Affairs. As during 1969, the PCP continued to examine its organization and performance. The Central Committee, on the basis of a report presented by Pompeyo Mares, issued on 1 January 1970 a communiqué analyzing its activities since 1956. The communiqué—published in the party newspaper, *Unidad*—blamed "organizational weaknesses and inadequacies" for the difficulties encountered in trying to "solidify" the party's influence. Among the main causes of weakness was the application of an "incorrect organizational policy," which was said to have converted the party's National Organization Commission into a body which dealt with the many "administrative tasks of the Central Committee" instead of building the party. Also, according to the communiqué, party activities were concentrated on commemorating anniversaries and getting radio and newspaper publicity, rather than working with the people; there was little use of criticism and self-criticism; and the "ideological struggle" within the party was underestimated.

The subject of party organization was treated again at a Central Committee plenum held on 18-20 December. Indicating that little or no progress had been made, reference to organizational weakness continued, although this time its causes were attributed to "insufficient understanding" of the party's ideology, "failure to follow organizational by-laws," and the existence of "remnants of sectarianism and liberalism" within the party (*ibid.*, 7 January 1971).

On 16 July *Unidad* reported without comment the expulsion from the party of César Lévano, a former Central Committee member who was the paper's correspondent in Moscow during 1968 and was considered one of the most knowledgeable Peruvian communists on Soviet policy. On 29 October *Unidad* "ratified" Lévano's expulsion on the grounds of his "publicly assuming a position contrary to the party line and the interests of the working class."

Domestic Attitudes and Activities. The pro-Soviet PCP seeks the establishment of a communist society through a "democratic, agrarian, and anti-imperialist revolution." According to the party statutes (published in Lima in March 1969), the party wants to "free Peru from imperialist domination, mainly by the United States; to eliminate all feudal remnants; to end racial and national discriminations; and to liquidate the economic and political power of the large landholders and capitalists."

Given the present Peruvian situation, in which a military government has been undertaking various measures to effect social and economic changes to the benefit of the country's lower and middle sectors, the pro-Soviet PCP has adopted a policy of almost total support for the government. Explaining this position, Secretary-General del Prado held that the military government had "launched the anti-imperialistic and anti-oligarchic revolution" that his party has "worked for so unremittingly." He added, however, that the pro-Soviet PCP considered that the Peruvian "revolution" was "still in its first stage," and that the party had not forgotten the role it should play nor the need for the "hegemony of the proletariat." (*WMR*, January 1971). A more candid explanation for the almost constant communist support for the government was provided by Raúl Nuñez, a high-ranking JCP member:

> Our party is small. When it understood the direction events were taking, it decided on open, if independent, support for the revolutionary process with a fundamental aim: to contribute to changing the masses from spectators to protagonists. It was necessary and possible. (Quoted in *Rinascita*, Rome, 4 December 1970.)

PCP attitudes during 1970 were characterized by a pervading feeling of enthusiasm and confidence regarding the numerous laws passed by the government. Although the PCP played no role in the enactment of these laws, other than vigorously campaigning for them in its party organ, the new socioeconomic measures were upheld as its own personal triumphs. In addition, the PCP was also confident that the junta would maintain its "revolutionary" character.[1] In an interview granted to the *Morning Star* (organ of the Communist Party of Great Britain, London, 12 May), Secretary-General del Prado asserted: "As the conflict between the government and native reaction [the Peruvian sectors opposing change] becomes deeper, so the points of view of the government and the [communist] party draw closer."

Among the measures undertaken by the military government and receiving considerable comment and support by the PCP were regulations affecting the press, mining, the fishing industry, and foreign exchange. Deserving special attention was the General Law on Industries.

The press law, or Statute on Freedom of the Press, issued by the government on 31 December 1969, received prompt PCP endorsement in a statement by the PCP Political Commission that although the law contained provisions of a "frankly antidemocratic nature," it sought to "limit the hegemony of oligarchic and U.S. monopoly interests in controlling the press" (*Unidad*, 7 January 1970). Comments by Central Committee member Alfredo Abarca and CGTP Secretary-General Gustavo Espinoza were more specific. They lauded the "Peruvianization" features of the press law, requiring that newspaper owners and stockholders be native-born Peruvians and residents of the country for at least six months per year, as constituting a "direct blow to the foreign monopolies and the oligarchy which control the news media, press, radio, and television." Abarca and Espinoza also supported the fact that the law opened up "possibilities for transferring the newspaper companies to the trade unions and cooperatives of Peruvian journalists and printers." (*El Popular*, Montevideo, 20 February.) *Unidad* campaigned vigorously for cooperativization of the newspapers *Expreso* and *Extra*, which had been highly critical of the government and which the PCP termed "connected with [Nelson] Rockefeller, the owner of the [now nationalized] International Petroleum Company." On 4 March the government announced that both newspapers had been expropriated and would be turned into "employee-operated cooperatives."

---

[1] Both the military junta and the communist party have denied the presence of any communist party members within the government. It is generally believed, however, that the Peruvian regime receives the assistance of some Marxist-oriented advisors. The PCP sees the presence of two sectors in the military junta: a radical, anti-imperialist wing led by Velasco, and a moderate wing, inclined to "compromise, conciliation, and understanding with imperialists, reactionaries, and APRA [the reformist but noncommunist party]," led by General Ernesto Montagne, premier and defense minister. (Arias Schreiber, quoted in *El Popular*, Montevideo, 16 December 1970.)

The PCP also welcomed enactment on 14 April of the mining law, which stipulated that the refining of copper and marketing of all minerals should be managed by the state. (Mining provides an estimated 54 per cent of Peru's foreign income.) An article, "From Crisis to Revolution" (*Unidad*, 16 April), hailed the law as a "truly revolutionary decision effecting a frontal attack on foreign domination since most U.S. investment in Peru is concentrated in copper." A Central Committee plenum on 18 July further supported the law because it "diminished by a considerable degree the present power and the potential for monopolist expansion and greater imperialist plundering" (*ibid.*, 23 July).

On 27 July, after four months of public debate, the government issued the General Law on Industries, which placed basic industry under state control, regulated foreign investment in the industrial sector, and introduced planned industrial development. As part of the same legislation the government also announced (for the first time and without previous debate) the creation of "industrial communities," providing for labor participation in income and stock distribution and in running business enterprises.[2]

The "industrial communities" were opposed by many enterprise owners and strongly endorsed by the PCP, which said that the communities, instead of meaning the "end of private property," would entail "expansion of property to increasingly larger sectors of the working class, which up to now has been the owner of its working force only" (*ibid.*, 13 August). Del Prado, in an article entitled "Is There a Revolution in Peru? (*WMR*, January 1971), held that the promulgation of the industrial laws had marked a "higher stage" toward socialism because it was not possible for any length of time to "combine private and collective ownership of the means of production within one enterprise."

State marketing of fish meal and fish oil, established by the government through decree-laws issued between February and May, also received PCP support. (The fishing industry, estimated to provide a livelihood for 100,000 Peruvians, supplies a fourth of the country's foreign currency earnings.) The PCP described the legislation as an "important measure to break the hegemony of foreign, especially U.S. firms in [Peru's] economy" (*ibid.*, 28 May).

The PCP also gave support to the foreign exchange control decree-law by which the state bank, the Banco de la Nación, became the only buyer and seller of foreign currency. It described the measure as the "most advanced and well-aimed step" taken by the military junta so far (*ibid.*, 21 May).

The pro-Soviet party continued during 1970 to express concern over agrarian reform. The Central Committee plenum held on 18 July noted with satisfaction that the reform had already affected 11 of Peru's 23 departments and that a million hectares had been distributed among 34,000 families (*ibid.*, 23 July). A critical article, however, appeared a month later (*ibid.*, 21 August). It claimed that official goals for 1970 envisaged land for 100,000 families. Remarking that by June 1970 only 28,246 families had received lands, it asserted that land distribution would have to increase four times to meet the announced objective for the year. The article expressed support for an amendment (enacted on 17 May) to the law whereby distribution on "private initiative" would be prohibited, so that landholders would be prevented from dividing their holdings among relatives, technicians, and employees and thus depriving peasants of a just claim to the soil they worked. The article also emphasized that the agrarian reform undertaken by the government was not socialist but "bourgeois democratic." It added: "The Cuban agrarian reform was born bourgeois democratic and in two years it became socialist"—thus indicating hope that a

---

[2]According to this law, private industrial firms are to distribute every year 25 per cent of profit before taxes among the workers: 10 per cent as dividends and 15 per cent in shares to the "industrial community"—composed of workers and employees—until the community holds half of these shares. The General Law on Industries generated enthusiasm among the lower and middle-class sectors, and most Peruvian church officials supported it.

similar development would occur in Peru. A subsequent article, reviewing the agrarian developments during 1970 (*ibid.*, 7 January 1971), praised the "rapid pace" of the agrarian reform and noted that 65,000 peasant families had been given lands; the article did not mention that the stated goal of 100,000 families had not been reached.

While endorsing almost all measures undertaken by the military junta, the PCP criticized the government for its "two weakest points: relations with the working class and problems with the student sector." Difference as to the first point was precipitated by the government's refusal during 1970 to recognize the communist-led CGTP (see below). Criticism on the second point was probably expressed to support the objections of young PCP elements against the February 1969 university law—which banned political activities at universities, reduced student participation in their administrations, and established an organization similar to that of U.S. universities, but was presented less forcefully. On 8 November 1970 the JCP asked the government to annul this law, arguing that it "robbed the students of their principal achievements" and demanded promulgation of a new law to "allow the university to be instrumental in bringing about structural changes and at the same time fulfill the objectives of the university reform" (*Unidad*, November). The JCP's appeal was unsuccessful.

The PCP also devoted special attention to its relations with the government. A speech by President Velasco on 20 March denouncing attempts by the "enemies of the revolution" to divide the armed forces and thus stop the revolutionary changes, prompted an immediate PCP statement supporting government measures, which it regarded as "anti-imperialist, anti-oligarchic and anti-feudal changes that tend to liberate the country from foreign dependency and underdevelopment, objectives for which communists are fighting at the present stage" (*ibid.*, 25 March). Making this support more concrete, the PCP endorsed an alleged initiative by the CGTP to create "Committees for the Defense of the Revolution" (see below). An apparent reason for having the CGTP (instead of the PCP) propose the creation of these committees was the desire to make them more representative of the masses and to avoid their being linked to the PCP. President Velasco, in a speech on 21 April, declared that his government approved of the establishment of such committees throughout the country. He added, however, that the government would make sure that these organizations were not used by "small and discredited political groupings," thereby rejecting communist support. When in another speech (28 July) Velasco stated that the communist system was "inapplicable to Peru's conditions and unacceptable to the humanistic ends of the [junta's] revolution," the communist press promptly replied that his "non-acceptance of communism" was based upon "eminently subjective premises" and that "errors of concept regarding socialism and communism were evident in the presidential message" (*Unidad*, 6 August).

The CGTP. The communist-influenced General Confederation of Workers of Peru was formed in 1968, mainly by pro-Soviet PCP efforts, as a rival to the Confederation of Peruvian Workers, which claims to represent more than 70 per cent of the organized workers of country and is dominated by the noncommunist Alianza Popular Revolucionaria (APRA, or Aprista Party). The CGTP claimed in 1970 to represent between 200,000 and 300,000 workers, in 20 national federations and 8 department federations (CGTP press communiqué, 13 December). In 1969 it reported representation of 500,000 workers, in 20 national federations, but the smaller 1970 figures reflected not a decrease in membership but a less inflated claim. Its main leaders are: Isidoro Gamarra, president; Gustavo Espinoza, secretary-general; and Claudio Santa Cruz, organization secretary.

The CGTP is the most influential PCP front and it is here that the party has concentrated much of its efforts. Much of the CGTP's appeal resides in its militant position toward demanding higher wages for the workers; as a result, the communist-led confederation has been actively involved in many labor strikes, especially within the mining sector.

During 1970 the CGTP performed successfully as it grew stronger and received *de facto* acceptance by the government. (Its legal recognition did not take place until 29 January 1971.) Especially beneficial to CGTP strength was the incorporation of the powerful Federation of Bank Employees (with about 14,000 members) on 5 November. Further joining the CGTP ranks were various labor unions in fields up to then unorganized, such as the United Front of Peruvian Press Workers, which includes journalists, newspaper and magazine employees, radio and television personnel, and publicity agents (*Unidad*, 12 and 19 February); the Association of House Workers (*ibid.*, 19 March); the General Center of New Towns (*ibid.*, 6 August); the National Federation of Market Workers (*ibid.*, 28 August); and the National Federation of Garment Workers (*ibid.*, 3 December).

The most important group within the CGTP appeared to be the National Federation of Metal and Mine Workers, formed in December 1969 and which according to communist sources represented 50,000 workers by the end of 1970. During April an estimated 5,000 miners walked 120 miles from the Andean mining center of Cerro de Pasco to Lima in an appeal to President Velasco for improvement in wages and living conditions. Their success was considered a triumph for the CGTP, which organized the march. On 22 May, as a result of the above, the Cerro de Pasco Miners' and Metal Workers' Labor Union left the APRA-led Confederation of Peruvian Workers and joined the CGTP. Subsequently, on 17 August, the unions of Toquepala, Marcona, and "Metalúrgica Peruana"—three of the country's largest mining groups—signed a"pact of mutual assistance and defense" calling for unity among more than 5,000 workers in case of a labor conflict. In September, probably based on their pact, miners in Toquepala and Marcona went on strike to attain wage increases, fulfillment of existing collective labor contracts, and better treatment from the U.S. management. Cerro de Pasco miners also joined the strike, which ended successfully for the workers.

Labor unrest within the mining sector, mostly organized by the CGTP, manifested itself in a series of coordinated strikes which continued into 1971. The striking miners, who put a heavy emphasis on their demands for improved living conditions, also denounced the "abuses made by the U.S. enterprises" and called upon the government to nationalize the mines now under U.S. control—a demand which counted on full PCP support.

CGTP attention was also given to the peasant sector. The PCP organ (*ibid.*, 4 February 1971), claimed that the CGTP now represented six peasant federations at the department level (Lima, Junin, Arequipa, Cajamarca, Huancayo, and Lambayeque) and various other smaller unions. The scant coverage given to these organizations in the countryside, however, was apparently indicative of a still limited peasant hold by either the CGTP or the PCP.

As noted above, immediately after a speech on 20 March by President Velasco referring to the threat posed by the "enemies of the revolution," the CGTP issued a call upon the Peruvian people to form "Committees for the Defense of the Revolution" (Comités de Defensa de la Revolución; CDR). These committees, which were given the same name as those existing in Cuba for the purpose of closely watching any signs of political dissidence, were to fulfill a different role in Peru; namely, they were going to be informal associations to "unite and organize the people against the oligarchy and imperialist aggression" (CGTP statement, 21 March, quoted in *ibid.*, 25 March). The CDR's attained importance in April, when they were endorsed by the government through the Agrarian Reform Information and Promotion Office, which saw in them a means to mobilize popular support. But in the months that followed, the government did not appear particularly interested in these committees, possibly because of the role the communists expected to play through them. *Oiga* (Lima, 17 April) estimated that there were 1,000 committees throughout the country, of which 300 operated in the north and 95 in Lima. *Caretas* (Lima, 5 November) gave a much lower estimate, asserting that there existed only 130 in all of Peru.

Communist participation in these committees is certain, but the CDR's have remained very small groups with the vague function of allowing the people to express solidarity with the government measures.

On 28 November, Premier Ernesto Montagne, in compliance with President Velasco's call for a "united front against underdevelopment" (to be composed of businessmen and workers), met with 300 leaders from the CGTP and the noncommunist Confederation of Peruvian Workers to study possibilities for the implementation of such policy. At that time, Espinoza, the secretary-general of the CGTP, expressed support for the united front to fight underdevelopment, but charged that the industrial sector was not willing to help the country. He held as evidence the fact that although there were 12,000 industrial firms in Peru, "industrial communities" had been set up only in 2,000 of them (*Unidad*, 3 December).

International Views and Positions. The PCP continued to follow a staunchly pro-Soviet line. Illustrative of this was an article in *Unidad* (28 May), approving the expulsion of Politburo and Central Committee member Roger Garaudy from the French Communist Party. In the opinion of the PCP paper, Garaudy's statements condemning Soviet policies amounted to "pure revisionism that could not be admitted" within the French Communist Party.

Political events in Chile were closely followed by the PCP. On 12 February, *Unidad* hailed the coalition of leftist forces, known as "Popular Unity," which had been formed in Chile on 22 January after three months of negotiation. The decision by the Chilean government to establish commercial relations with Cuba was also praised and was said to be an indication of the "collapse of the [OAS] blockade against Cuba." Salvador Allende's success in the Chilean presidential elections of September was not surprising to the pro-Soviet PCP, which had repeatedly predicted it. Del Prado described the Popular Unity victory as one of the "most convincing successes in the struggle against imperialism and oligarchy in Latin America" (TASS, 14 September). Del Prado was quoted in the same source as stating that this event showed that "the imperialists and their allies" were being defeated not only on the battlefronts in Vietnam, Laos, and Cambodia but also in "the very capitalist system."

The pro-Soviet PCP also showed interest in the Cuban sugar harvest campaign. On 28 May, when it was known that Cuba would not reach the goal of 10 million tons of sugar, *Unidad* hailed as "a success without precedent" the fact that Cuba had nevertheless produced 9 million tons [the Cuban official figure was 8.5 million]—which *Unidad* said was in itself a record never before attained in the island.

Socialist help to Peru following the devastating earthquake of 31 May received ample coverage by the pro-Soviet PCP. Special mention was made in *Unidad* of contributions sent by Cuba and the Soviet Union. Cuba sent 13 field hospitals and large quantities of food, medicine, shoes (150,000 pairs), blood plasma, and field kitchens. The communist press publicized also the fact that Premier Castro and President Dorticós had donated blood.

Unidad printed lengthy articles on help from the Soviet Union, which had promised to send 65 airplanes carrying field hospitals and food (valued at $111,000). It also announced (9 July) that the Soviet Union had decided to give Peru a $30 million credit on "most favorable" conditions. Unreported by the pro-Soviet press was the fact that the Soviet Union sent only 21 airplanes and that the Chinese People's Republic made a contribution of 1.5 million yuan (about $600,000).

Both Cuba and the Soviet Union continued verbal support of the Peruvian military government. Fidel Castro was quoted as having said on 26 July, in an interview granted to a Chilean group, that "armed struggle is not a dogma." He allegedly expressed confidence that Chile would "arrive at socialism by elections" and that the military leaders in Peru were "developing a revolutionary process, with its own characteristics, different from those of Chile." (*Unidad*, 21 August.) Soviet support, as enunciated in *Pravda* (3 October) on the anniversary of the junta, asserted: "Peruvian patriots can prove undeniably and with legitimate pride that new steps were taken on the road toward realization of the twenty-year socioeconomic program adopted by the government in December 1968." *Pravda* contended, however, that socioeconomic reforms implemented by the government would "accelerate the polarization process of the class struggle simultaneously with an intensification of the political struggle."

During the year, the pro-Soviet PCP continued to criticize Communist China. *Unidad* (9 July) reprinted an article from the Soviet journal *Trud* on the "anti-worker policy of the Maoists." The article declared that a "military-bureaucratic dictatorship" was in control of China and was hostile to the working class. The article also made reference to "anti-worker" measures taken by the Chinese government, which included compulsory savings, rationing, working days of twelve to fourteen hours, and the allotment of "large amounts of financial and economic resources to develop China's nuclear-missile potential."

Other international views of the pro-Soviet PCP appeared in statements of solidarity with the struggle of the "peoples of Vietnam," repudiation of the "U.S. invasion" of Cambodia, and support for the events in Czechoslovakia during 1970, which were said to be indications of the "strengthening of socialism and the communist party as its leader" in that country.

International Party Contacts. During 1970 the pro-Soviet PCP registered more international contacts than in previous years.

A PCP delegation attended the twentieth-anniversary celebrations held by the Communist Party of Bolivia in La Paz during February. Arias Schreiber attended the Twentieth Congress of the Communist Party of Uruguay, held on 1-14 December.

Del Prado and Arias Schreiber went to the Soviet Union for the Lenin Centenary celebrations in April and the twenty-fifth anniversary of the Soviet army's "victory over fascism" in May. Both men afterward visited Bulgaria, Poland, and the German Democratic Republic. In November they visited Romania and met with leaders of the Romanian Communist Party, including Secretary-General Nicolae Ceauşescu.

The CGTP organization secretary, Claudio Santa Cruz, attended the "World Labor Conference of Solidarity with Workers and Peoples of Indochina," held on 18-19 July at Versailles, and afterward visited the Soviet Union and North Vietnam.

Publications. The pro-Soviet PCP official organ is a weekly newspaper, *Unidad*, founded on 5 October 1956. It claims a circulation of 14,000 to 15,000 copies, but actual distribution is about a third of that number. *Unidad* is currently edited by Jaime Figueroa. The party also publishes *Ensayos*, a bimonthly theoretical journal, and *Joven Guardia*, the communist youth organ. These two publications appear very irregularly.

*   *   *

The Pro-Chinese PCP. Leadership and Organization. The leadership of the pro-Chinese Peruvian Communist Party is not well known. Saturnino Paredes Macedo heads the group which is recognized by the Chinese People's Republic. Gotardo Hernán Rojas and José Carlos Vertiz head the "Patria Roja" faction, which apparently consists mostly of university students but seems to be larger than the Paredes group. The pro-Soviet PCP newspaper *Unidad* claimed on 21 August 1970 that a new splinter, known as the "Albanian Group," had appeared within pro-Chinese ranks.

Control of the universities' student governments by pro-Chinese students continued during 1970, although the political role of the universities has practically ceased since regulatory measures were taken by the junta in February 1969 (see above). Student federation elections at San Marcos University in Lima and in Arequipa—the two largest student groups—were won by a wide margin by the pro-Chinese Revolutionary Student Front (Frente Estudiantil Revolucionario; FER) which also attracts some Trotskyist and pro-Castro students. Pro-Chinese students held a special congress in Arequipa at the end of May. The conference, reportedly attended by delegates from six of the 23 units belonging to the Federation of Peruvian Students, described the present Peruvian government as "bourgeois imperialist" and termed Fidel Castro a "petty-bourgeois traitor to the revolutionary cause of Cuba and Latin America" (*Unidad*, 4 June).

A broadcast by the New China News Agency on 14 April reported that an article in *Bandera Roja*, the organ of the Paredes faction, had acclaimed the Ninth Congress of the Communist Party of China as "a great victory of Mao Tse-tung thought" and had further stated: "By pointing out that in socialist construction, in the socialist states, classes and class struggle still exist, Mao Tse-tung has developed the theory and practice of the dictatorship of the proletariat and made an outstanding contribution to Marxism-Leninism."

Publications. The Paredes group of the pro-Chinese PCP publishes *Bandera Roja*. The "Patria Roja" faction PCP publishes *Patria Roja*. Both newspapers appear irregularly.

*   *

In addition to the above-mentioned communist parties, there exist among Peru's extreme left various groups of Castroite and Trotskyist orientation, which contribute toward making that spectrum one of the most fragmented in Latin America.

The MIR. The Movement of the Revolutionary Left, originally an Aprista Party splinter group heavily influenced by the Cuban Revolution, was founded by Luis de la Puente Uceda. It reached national prominence through an active peasant guerrilla movement during 1965. This phase ended with most leaders either killed in action or imprisoned.

The extent of MIR membership is not known, but apparently the movement has some influence in the universities. Ricardo Gadea is the principal MIR leader. Imprisoned since 1965, he was set free on 22 December 1970 when the junta declared a total amnesty for all political prisoners. Also released at that time was Elio Portocarrero Ríos, another important member.

The MIR, which seeks establishment of a socialist society through a revolution based on armed struggle, holds now that the situation in Peru is characterized by a "conflict between the people on one hand and Yankee imperialism and its national intermediaries on the other" (MIR Political Declaration, June, quoted in *Intercontinental Press*, New York, 14 September). It continues to oppose the government, which is said to pursue a "capitalist reformism," and holds that the junta is not nationalist or anti-imperialist as the pro-Soviet PCP maintains. In June the MIR announced that it was preparing itself as a "political-military vanguard which will have to fight on all levels of revolutionary action against the mortal enemies of [the] people," and that its main task was to "mobilize the proletariat and the exploited classes" in a front "from below" to struggle against "imperialism and its allies" (*ibid.*).

Early in the year, in an interview, Gadea expressed disagreement with Fidel Castro's statement on 14 July 1969 to the effect that the junta might develop a "genuine revolution." Gadea argued: "The reality of the [Peruvian] government is that it is not revolutionary. Its reforms are aimed at reinforcing a monopoly capitalist development which is dominated by imperialism. This process is not conducive to the liberation of our country." (*Ibid.*, 23 February.)

In contrast with the critical position toward the government taken by the MIR, a faction that split from it in February 1969—the Revolutionary Socialist League (Liga Socialista Revolucionaria; LSR)—resolutely supports the military junta. Ismael Frías, the LSR leader (and a columnist for *Expreso* until September 1970), accused the "smaller groups" of the Peruvian left of misunderstanding the "meaning of the national revolution." He said: "The fact is that the Marxist left must choose between the imported models or a Peruvian form of socialism. It must be either national or subservient." (*Expreso*, Lima, 31 March.) In another article, Frías described the Committees for the Defense of the Revolution as "the most authentic creation of the people" so far in the revolutionary process in Peru. He claimed that there existed more than 1,000 committees with more than 50,000 members. (*Ibid.*, 23 June.)

The organ of the MIR is a clandestine newspaper, *Voz Rebelde*. The LSR publishes a newspaper, *Inkarrí*.

The ELN. The Army of National Liberation, founded in 1962 by former members of the PCP, participated also in the peasant guerrilla movement of 1965 (although its activities were not coordinated with those of the MIR). Its main leader, Héctor Béjar Rivera, was released from prison on 22 December 1970 in the government's general political amnesty.

Although, like the MIR, the ELN envisages armed struggle as the means to achieve a socialist system, there are points of disagreement between these two groups. In an interview published by *Punto Final* (Santiago, Chile, 14 April), Béjar stated that there had been no replies from other left-wing parties (including the MIR and the FIR) to his book *Peru 1965: Notes on a Guerrilla Experience*,[1] analyzing reasons for the guerrillas' failure. In the interview he reiterated his opposition to the military government: "The armed way continues to be the only way to bring about a real revolution in Peru, because it is the only one that allows the people to participate in changes. There are no revolutions from above. The Peruvian crisis is too profound to be solved with reforms, although they may be as radical as those undertaken by the government."

Béjar also paid a great deal of attention to the agrarian reform undertaken by the government, calling it the "key move in the reformist game of the military government." The agrarian reform, he contended, would merely remove "some of the power of the landowning bourgeoisie," which would continue to maintain its "industrial, commercial, and banking investments." He argued that, through agrarian reform, the government was attempting to "integrate capitalism better and make it more harmonious, developed, and modern," and that, as a consequence, the reform would not immediately benefit the large number of peasants but rather the rising middle class. Béjar was especially critical of the legal provision requiring payment for the expropriated lands; he maintained that payment would merely allow the transfer of power of the dominating classes from agriculture to industry. (*Ibid.*, 12 May.)

The FIR. The Revolutionary Leftist Front is a Trotskyist party associated with the United Secretariat faction of the Fourth International. It is led by Hugo Blanco, who in 1962 sought to radicalize peasant unions in the department of Cuzco, believing that political agitation from within would encourage peasants to claim land and would lead eventually to the larger goal of armed struggle. After seven years in prison, Blanco was released in December 1970 under the political amnesty.

[1]The original version in Spanish appeared in 1969. An English translation was published in *Intercontinental Press*, 26 January-16 March 1970.

The FIR seeks the establishment of a socialist system, but, unlike the MIR and ELN, it considers the guerrilla struggle a tactic and not a strategy. According to Blanco, the FIR also now believes that a party is necessary to organize the masses in the revolutionary process. (See *Intercontinental Press*, 23 February.)

Blanco described the pro-Soviet PCP as "interested not in revolution but in the maintenance of peaceful coexistence." Regarding the pro-Chinese PCP, he said: "Their old Stalin sectarianism has reached grotesque proportions. They are not only sectarian about the Moscow communist party but toward all other currents, including revolutionary groups, the result being that they ended up in sectarian infighting among themselves." He added, however, that there existed "self-sacrificing and dynamic revolutionaries" within the pro-Chinese groups who might overcome ideological differences and "participate in a positive way in the revolutionary process." (*Ibid.*)

As in the case of Gadea and Béjar, Blanco disagreed with Castro's verbal support of the military government, stating that it was "very sad" that Castro did so, because in Peru "all revolutionaries, including the Fidelistas," were against the government. Blanco held that the military government was not nationalist and that it was seeking a "bourgeois kind of development benefiting the new type of exploiting sectors and not the Peruvian people." In his opinion, the agrarian reform was not "crushing the old oligarchy economically but incorporating it into the developmentalist sectors." (*Ibid.*, 30 March.)

The VR. The Revolutionary Vanguard is a Marxist-Leninist party founded by former Aprista Party members in 1965. It advocates armed confrontation as a means of achieving socialism, but holds that its members should have theoretical and practical training before engaging in actual struggle.

The VR is composed primarily of intellectuals; it includes some workers as members but apparently no peasants. Reportedly, it has a significant following among university students.

During 1970 the VR continued to criticize the military junta in the strongest terms and to attack its policies, especially its industrial and agrarian reforms. The government, in its only action against left-wing leaders during the year, arrested the VR secretary-general, Ricardo Letts Colmenares, on 23 September on charges of anarchism and subversion. He was deported to Mexico but was allowed to return to Peru early in February 1971.

On 30 May 1970 a group of VR participated in demonstrations against both the Peruvian and the U.S. governments; they also attacked buildings of the conservative newspaper *La Prensa* and the Peruvian-U.S. Cultural Institute. On 26 October, some 30 students believed to belong to the VR clashed with police forces at San Marcos National University and set off two powerful bombs. This compelled authorities to suspend classes for two weeks. The students, who were demanding a repeal of the university law in effect at present, called without success for a strike in several universities.

At elections held at the Student Federation of the Catholic University in Lima, VR students won leadership positions, defeating by a substantial majority students of the Christian Democratic Party, who had been in power of the federation for the past seven years.

The FLN. The National Liberation Front was founded by PCP members in 1961. It is a small party, although it claims to have obtained more than 50,000 votes in the 1966 Lima by-elections. During January 1968 the party was weakened when it split into pro-Soviet and "independent" factions.

The pro-Soviet FLN is led by Genaro Carnero Checa and Angel Castro Lavarello. This group continues its association with the pro-Soviet PCP. The "independent" faction of the FLN is led by Salomón Bolo Hidalgo, a former priest. During 1970 both Bolo and Carnero Checa expressed support for Cuba and demanded the reestablishment of diplomatic, commercial, and cultural relations between Cuba and Peru.

N. S.

PUERTO RICO

Communism in Puerto Rico is represented by the Puerto Rican Communist Party (Partido Comunista Puertorriqueño; PCP) and the Puerto Rican Socialist League (Liga Socialista Puertorriqueña; LSP), of pro-Soviet and pro-Chinese orientation respectively. In 1970 the PCP was believed to have a membership of fewer than 20 persons, and the LSP about 30. Both parties are being increasingly eclipsed—in Puerto Rico and also in the extent of interest shown by foreign communist parties—by the considerably more influential and vocal Pro-Independence Movement (Movimiento Pro-Independencia; MPI), estimated to have from 750 to 1,500 members and 4,000 to 5,000 supporters.[1] In addition to these organizations there are three recently formed: the Socialist Workers' Party (Partido Socialista Obrero; PSO), which tends to align itself with the LSP and is believed to have 12 members; the Revolutionary Movement (Movimiento Revolucionario; MR), a splinter group from the MPI, with about 30 members; and a clandestine terrorist organization known as the Armed Liberation Commandos (Comandos Armados de Liberación; CAL), of which very little is known except that it was reportedly formed in 1967 and is led by Alfonso Beal. In late 1970 the MPI weekly organ *Claridad* (22 November) published an interview with Beal, which was subsequently reprinted by the daily newspaper of the Communist Party of Cuba, *Granma* (11 January 1971). In the interview, the CAL leader stressed that his organization was "completely independent" from all other groups in Puerto Rico. The population of Puerto Rico is 2,800,000 (estimated 1970).

The degree of popular support in Puerto Rico for parties such as the above, which advocate the severing of relations between Puerto Rico and the United States and an independent status for the island, was demonstrated in a plebiscite on 23 July 1967. Of the 1,067,349 registered voters, 66 per cent (709,293) went to the polls. Of these, 60.5 per cent voted for the existing commonwealth status, 38.9 per cent for statehood, and 0.6 per cent for independence. The PCP, LSP, and MPI (the PSO, MR, and CAL were not yet formed) advocated a boycott of the plebiscite; however, on the basis of previous electoral returns and the fact that two parties—the Independence and Statehood Republican parties—also advocated a boycott, it appears that only some 2 to 3 per cent of those who did not vote were supporters of the extreme left parties. While the demand for independence appears since to have grown—some sources place it as high as 15 per cent (see, e.g., *Christian Science Monitor*, 5 February 1970)—the support for the extreme left does not appear to have grown correspondingly.

[1] The MPI and its youth movements—the Federation of University Students for Independence (Federación de Universitarios Pro-Independencia; FUPI) and the Federation of Students for Independence (Federación Estudiantil Pro-Independencia; FEPI), the latter comprised of high school students—repeatedly claimed in the past, and again in 1970, that they were not Marxist-Leninist organizations. In late 1970, however, Juan Mari Bras, leader of the MPI, indicated in an interview with the weekly radical New York newspaper *Guardian* (14 November) that the MPI was "in the process of converting" itself into a "party . . . in the Leninist concept of a revolutionary vanguard." For further information on the MPI, see its weekly publications, *Claridad* and *Carta Semanal*.

None of the extreme left parties is represented in the legislature in Puerto Rico. All of them boycotted the 5 November 1968 elections.

The PCP. The Puerto Rican Communist Party was founded in 1934, dissolved in 1944, and founded again in 1946. Little is known of the PCP's organizational structure, except that the party appears to operate both in Puerto Rico and among the Puerto Rican population in New York City, where it works in close cooperation with the Communist Party, USA (CPUSA). The PCP's long-time secretary-general, Juan Santos Rivera, reportedly resigned from the party on 19 July 1970 (*Daily World*, New York, organ of the CPUSA, 1 August). In a speech given to the National Committee of the CPUSA, in New York City on 22 November, Félix Ojeda Ruiz, former PCP press and propaganda secretary and newly elected secretary-general, stated that Santos had attempted to "liquidate" the party and "incorporate its members" into the MPI. According to Ojeda, the former secretary-general's proposal was discussed during three consecutive meetings of the party's Central Committee, and later at a "general meeting of all the members," at which time his vote was reportedly the only one in support of such a move. Santos then "quit the party to enter the MPI." Ojeda added: "He went alone. Nobody followed him." (*Political Affairs*, theoretical organ of the CPUSA, January 1971.) As a result of Santos's resignation, it was reported (*ibid.*) that the PCP had proceeded to "reorganize all Party bodies." Information on new leading positions in the party were not available by the end of the year. (For data on party leadership in 1969, see *YICA*, 1970, p. 476.) The PCP has a youth group called the Puerto Rican Communist Party Youth (Juventud del Partido Comunista Puertorriqueño; JCPC), which has an estimated membership of nine.

The views of the PCP on matters both domestic and international mirror those of the CPUSA, with relations between the two parties, according to Ojeda, "grow[ing] ever closer" (*ibid.*). Despite the party's reported opposition to integrating into the MPI, relations between the latter and the PCP have always been cordial—in 1968 an article in the French Communist Party weekly *France Nouvelle* (11 September) claimed that "all members of the Puerto Rican Communist Party" were also affiliated to the MPI. A statement of the PCP at the time of Santos's resignation quoted the former secretary-general as justifying the party's integration in the MPI because the latter was "approaching Marxism-Leninism and in time . . . would convert itself into a Bolshevik Party of Marxism-Leninism." The PCP statement countered, however:

> Without minimizing the importance of the renown of the MPI and its ties which have always united the anti-imperialist and national liberation movement of Puerto Rico, the Central Committee tenaciously opposed the "integration" of the PCP into MPI, citing ideological grounds. (*Daily World*, 1 August.)

The PCP's small size and special relationship with the CPUSA and the MPI has tended to restrict its own development as an independent party. In his aforementioned November speech, Ojeda noted: "In the past our Party had very little fraternal relations with other parties of Latin America and gave very little attention to questions related to their principles and programs." He also admitted that for "propaganda material" the PCP "had always been depending on that sent from other countries." He claimed, however: "We are trying to create our own Marxist-Leninist literature based on the objective conditions in Puerto Rico."

The PCP publishes a monthly newspaper, *Pueblo*, and an information bulletin, *El Proletario*. Both appear irregularly.

The LSP. The pro-Chinese element in Puerto Rican communism works in close cooperation with the Progressive Labor Party (PLP) of the United States and is primarily represented by the

Puerto Rican Socialist League. This party was formed during 1964-65 by Juan Antonio Corretjer (a former member of the PCP, expelled in 1948) as a result of the splitting and dissolution of the Marxist-Leninist "Single Patriotic Action" movement (Acción Patriótica Unitaria), founded by him in 1959.

Although the LSP, like all other parties in Puerto Rico, has legal status, very little published information is available on its organizational structure. In Puerto Rico the party is represented primarily in San Juan, with a branch known as the "Area South Group" in Ponce. The LSP is also believed to have supporters in New York City. In addition to its secretary-general, Juan Antonio Corretjer, prominent members of the party in 1970 appeared to be José Marcano Romero, Milton Urbina Díaz, Alejandro Santiago Rodríguez, José Miguel Martí Barreto, Luis D. Alvarez Archilla, Gabriel Mezquida, and Manuel A. Amy Valentine.

In contrast to the PCP, the LSP does not have close ties with the MPI, which officially severed relations with the PLP in 1966 (see *YICA*, 1966, p. 252). Although in the past it had worked closely with the Puerto Rican extremist Nationalist Party (Partido Nacionalista), by 1970 the LSP appeared to have essentially severed its relations with that party. The move might have been motivated in part by the LSP's identification with the PLP's increasing opposition to the phenomenon of nationalism. This latter issue was discussed at length in an article by Corretjer published in the PLP newspaper *Challenge/Desafío* (New York, 13 December), in which he emphasized: "One is a Communist or a Nationalist—it is impossible to be both at the same time." The LSP secretary-general went on to explain:

> The struggle for independence is a specific form of class struggle. Either one struggles for an independence which benefits the workers only, by means of taking power in a revolutionary way, with the liquidation of private property and the establishment of the dictatorship of the proletariat, or one fights for a Nationalist independence, multi-class by necessity, which defeats foreign capitalist power in order to benefit a new dominant class whose power will establish private property.

In his article Corretjer reiterated that the LSP shared "completely with PLP all of the Marxist-Leninist Mao Tsetung Thought ideology," and added that his party had participated on 25 October in an International Solidarity Day march in New York with the PLP and the pro-Chinese Canadian Party of Labour.

The major LSP organs, which appear irregularly, are *Pabellón*, a bimonthly; *El Socialista*, a monthly; and *Correo de la Quincena*, a fortnightly. Most major LSP statements and reports of party activity are publicized in the monthly (from September 1970, fortnightly) organ of the Progressive Labor Party, *Challenge/Desafío*.

The PSO. Very little information is available on the Socialist Workers' Party. This small group has been described (*Challenge/Desafío*, June-July 1968) as being composed "entirely of young people." In a manifesto published in 1968, which appeared to indicate that the party was founded during that year, the PSO advocated a "new society of peace and justice under the banners of Marxist-Leninist socialism" and emphasized in its immediate goals opposition to mandatory military service. The manifesto was signed by Wilson Cortés Burgos, secretary-general; Billy Cajigas, secretary for political action; David Feliciano, organizational secretary; Néstor Velázquez Díaz, youth secretary; and Pablo González Arce, secretary for labor affairs. (*Ibid.*) While in 1968 the PSO was highly critical of the MPI and aligned itself with the LSP, the latter organization's comments on the PSO in 1969 (see *Correo de la Quincena*, no. 99, 1-15 May) indicated a certain estrangement between the two parties. Also, during the year, the leadership of the PSO appeared to be increasingly in the hands of Narciso Rabell Martínez—who was formerly the

MPI representative on the Secretariat of the Havana-based Afro-Asian Latin American Peoples' Solidarity Organization, but was removed from that post by the MPI in July 1967 for advocating street demonstrations during that year's plebiscite in Puerto Rico (see *YICA*, 1968, p. 505). By the end of 1970 the exact political orientation of the PSO, including its relations with Cuba and the MPI, was not known. The group appeared to have gone underground and to be operating the small Armed Rebel Independence Movement (Movimiento Independencia Rebelde Armada; MIRA), which during the year was reportedly involved in several terrorist incidents.

M. P.

URUGUAY

The Communist Party of Uruguay (Partido Comunista del Uruguay; PCU) dates its formation from September 1920, when the congress of the Socialist Party voted in favor of joining the Communist International. The present name was adopted in April 1921. The party has always been legal. It is firmly pro-Soviet.

The Movement of the Revolutionary Left (Movimiento de Izquierda Revolucionaria; MIR) was founded in 1963 and during 1970 was the primary pro-Chinese organization in Uruguay. The Revolutionary Workers' Party (Partido Obrero Revolucionario; POR), originally founded in 1944 as the Revolutionary Workers' League, is Trotskyist and is aligned with the International Secretariat (Posadas faction) of the Fourth International. The Revolutionary Party of the Workers (Partido Revolucionario de los Trabajadores; PRT), also Trotskyist, is aligned with the United Secretariat of the Fourth International. Numerous other leftist organizations operate in Uruguay and display Soviet, Chinese, Cuban, or nationalist leanings or combinations thereof. Among them are the Uruguayan Revolutionary Movement (Movimiento Revolucionario Oriental; MRO), the Socialist Party of Uruguay (Partido Socialista del Uruguay; PSU), the Uruguayan Revolutionary Armed Forces (Fuerzas Armadas Revolucionarias Orientales; FARO), and the National Liberation Movement (Movimiento de Liberación Nacional; MLN)—better known as the Tupamaros. The MIR, MRO, and PSU, declared illegal in December 1967, and the POR, declared illegal in March 1969, were legalized in December 1970. The PRT was legal; while the FARO and the MLN were illegal.

Except for the PCU, all these organizations are apparently small though no precise membership figures are known. PCU membership in December 1970 was estimated at between 30,000 and 35,000 persons. According to the PCU first secretary, Rodney Arismendi, workers accounted for 72.6 per cent of the members (*Komsomolskaia Pravda*, Moscow, 7 January 1971). The population of Uruguay is 2,900,000 (estimated 1970).

The electoral strength of the PCU resides in the Leftist Liberation Front (FIDEL; see below), a grouping of small leftist organizations, which it dominates. In the election of 27 November 1966 FIDEL won 5.7 per cent of the votes and emerged with five representatives (three communists) in the 99-member Chamber of Deputies and one (a communist) in the 31-member Senate.

Uruguay has long been known among Latin American countries for its democratic form of government and its far-reaching system of public welfare. By the mid-1960's, years of excessive spending, labor demands, and bureaucratization, increasingly aggravated by government inefficiency and corruption, had created a state of near national economic collapse. In foreign trade, imports far exceeded exports. Rising prices and inflation at home were partly caused by union demands for higher wages and benefits, and in turn were grounds for further demands. The cost of living rose 136 per cent in 1967 and 64 per cent in the first half of 1968. In June 1968 President Jorge Pacheco Areco promulgated "urgent security measures" and froze wages and prices of all goods and services. As a result of these measures the cost of living rose only 2 per cent in the second half of 1968, and less than 20 per cent per year during 1969 and 1970. The government authorized some wage and price increases in December 1970. Within this national setting, the PCU, with its strong position among unionized workers and students, played a leading role in opposing government efforts to stabilize the economy—in particular those policies involving assistance from the United States and the International Monetary Fund.

In comparison with the PCU, most of the other groups named above have played an insignificant role in national affairs. The Tupamaros, because of the peculiar character of their exploits, have caused considerable national tension and attracted a great deal of international notice.

The PCU. Leadership and Organization. The PCU has national and departmental structures, the latter corresponding to the country's 19 departments. Between January and November 1970, the party leaders on the national level were those elected at the Nineteenth Congress, held on 9-13 August 1966, to the 33-member Central Committee, 16-member Executive Committee, and 6-member Secretariat. The party's first secretary, who presided over all three groups, was Rodney Arismendi. The Secretariat was made up of Arismendi, Enrique Pastorino, Jaime Pérez, Rosario Pietrarroia, Enrique Rodríguez, and Alberto Suárez. The Executive Committee included the six Secretariat members and Julia Arévalo, Alberto Altesor, José Blanco, Leopoldo Bruera, Félix Díaz, José L. Massera, César Reyes Daglio, Gregorio Sapin, Eduardo Viera, and Walter Sanseviero.

At the Twentieth Congress, in December 1970, the Central Committee was increased to consist of 48 regular members and 27 alternates, while the Secretariat was reduced to five members —Arismendi, Pastorino, Pérez, Rodríguez, and Suárez—and the Executive Committee to fifteen, consisting of the five Secretariat members and Altesor, Bruera, Díaz, Massera, Pietrarroia, and Reyes Daglio, together with Gerardo Cuesta, Jorge Mazzarovich, Wladímir Turiansky, and Eduardo Viera. The congress confirmed Arismendi in his position as first secretary.

The party's youth organization, the Union of Communist Youth (Unión de la Juventud Comunista; UJC), was founded in 1955, though a communist youth group had been established as early as 1922. In December 1970 Rodney Arismendi stated that the UJC had 20,000 members (*Estudios*, no. 58, January-February 1971). The first secretary of the UJC is Walter Sanseviero; other prominent members are Jorge Mazzarovich, León Lev, and Fausto Hernández. The UJC held its Seventh Congress on 12-15 December 1969. "United action" was the main theme of the congress, and Rodney Arismendi and Walter Sanseviero called upon young communists to work with labor and youth groups in opposing the Pacheco government. In December 1970 Félix Díaz praised student support for labor demands under the slogan "Workers and Students, United and Forward" (*El Popular*, 14 December 1970).

In recent years the UJC has played an important, and sometimes dominant, role in the Federation of University Students of Uruguay (Federación de Estudiantes Universitarios del Uruguay; FEUU), an affiliate of the Soviet-front International Union of Students. The UJC controls the University Students' Committee of the Leftist Liberation Front.

The National Convention of Workers (Convención Nacional de Trabajadores; CNT) was established on 28 September-2 October 1966. In 1969 the CNT was said to represent about 400,000 workers (*El Popular*, 19 May), though PCU figures have varied widely on this (see *ibid.*, 3 December 1968 and 18 May 1969) and an increased membership during 1970 has been claimed (*ibid.*, 14 December). Individual unions in the CNT are largely noncommunist and some noncommunists hold high positions in them; the decision-making offices, however, are dominated by such communists as Enrique Pastorino, Félix Díaz, Wladímir Turiansky, and Antonio Tamayo.

The CNT held its First Congress on 15-18 May 1969, in Montevideo, and planned how it could best combat the policies of the Pacheco government. The main document of the congress (see *El Popular*, 18 May) was quoted at length by Wladímir Turiansky in 1970 to prove that "the central task of the union movement was and is to find the roads that unity can take, incorporate increasingly larger sectors of the people into the struggle, and form and organize those forces" (*ibid.*, 14 August). A substantial number of workers opposed the CNT tactics—including almost a third of the more than 500 delegates at the 1969 congress—and urged a more aggressive policy which Enrique Pastorino warned might lead to "premature total confrontations" (*Estudios*, September-December 1969). Many leftists have been critical of the CNT for sending a delegate (Antonio Tamayo) to sit on COPRIN, the government body in charge of wage and price controls.

CNT-organized strikes and demonstrations during the first half of 1970 were on a smaller scale than in 1969. Late in the year, however, these activities became larger—such as the strike on 14 October, which reportedly involved some 500,000 persons—and were all the more disruptive for being staged amid the tension caused by several spectacular actions by the Tupamaros (see below).[1] These activities undoubtedly played some part in the government's decision near the end of the year to allow a limited wage and price increase.

The Soviet Union has taken particular interest in the CNT. Four members of the Soviet Embassy staff were expelled by the Uruguayan government in October 1966, immediately after the formation of the CNT, and three more in September 1968 amid large, disruptive CNT-led strikes and demonstrations. In October 1969, CNT secretary Enrique Pastorino was made president of the Soviet-front World Federation of Trade Unions, the first Latin American to hold this high position.

The Leftist Liberation Front (Frente Izquierda de Liberación; FIDEL) was founded in 1962, pursuant to a decision reached at the Eighteenth Congress of the PCU, and since then has been the main vehicle for the party's participation in the Uruguayan political system.[2] Its limited success, in an electoral system that discourages voting for candidates on minority party tickets, was evident in the 1966 elections (see above).

FIDEL is composed of fewer than ten small political and cultural groups. Luis Pedro Bonavita serves as president. According to the General Resolution of the Twentieth Congress of thePCU, FIDEL represented an "advanced sector of the anti-imperialist and revolutionary forces which are growing in the republic, the fundamental part of the national left," and demonstrated "in actual practice the possibility and fertility of the idea of political unity without excluding any of the various forces of the left" (*ibid.*, no. 58, January-February 1971). Throughout 1970 FIDEL called for the formation of a broad front bringing together all those who sought a "new path for the republic" (*El Popular*, 16 March), though it was only after the election of the Popular Unity candidate Salvador Allende in Chile in September that an Uruguayan leftist front actually began to form (see below).

Party Internal Affairs. The PCU celebrated the fiftieth anniversary of its founding in September 1970. Its Twentieth Congress, held on 11-15 December, was attended by some 800 persons, including PCU delegates, representatives of FIDEL and several other Uruguayan organizations,

[1] The number of persons involved in the 14 October strike does not accurately reflect the degree of popular support since, according to the Cuban magazine *Bohemia* (23 October), pressure, or revolutionary compulsion, "played a critical role in determining that there should be no strikebreaking."

[2] The commonly used abbreviation is retained here even though it inaccurately suggests that the front is a Castroite organization. The PCU abbreviation, F. I. de L., is less misleading but awkward.

and foreign guests from the Soviet Union, Bulgaria, Romania, France, Italy, Chile, Peru, Argentina, Colombia, and Ecuador (*Estudios*, no. 58, January-February 1971).[3]

At the congress, Rodney Arismendi stated that the PCU was characterized by a "profound ideological and political unity," though the General Resolution of the congress warned against "non-Marxist-Leninist currents within the bosom of the labor movement" and "deviations of the right and the 'left.'" Broadly speaking, the General Resolution stated that the task of the PCU was to "win the majority of the working class politically and ideologically." More specifically, it said special attention should be directed toward: fostering the growth of the party, especially in the principal unions and factories; raising the national political role of the party; securing greater financial support; increasing support for the UJC and the women's movement; developing a front with other forces of the left; expanding agitation, propaganda, and ideological work among the masses; and extending educational activities through party publications and programs. (*Ibid.*)

During 1970 great importance was attached to the membership drive of recent years, which was said to have transformed the PCU from a vanguard into a mass party. PCU leaders generally avoided specifying membership figures, however, and were often ambiguous or contradictory in reporting the number of new members.[4] At the Twentieth Congress, Rodney Arismendi stressed that the party had great appeal for young persons (56.5 per cent of the new members "in recent years" had been between the ages of eighteen and thirty-five years) and for women (30.3 per cent of new party members since 1955). Party membership was said to have increased by 12.9 times since 1955.

Domestic Attitudes and Activities. At the Twentieth Congress, Rodney Arismendi stated that the years 1968 to 1970 had demonstrated the "depth of the crisis of the socioeconomic structure" in Uruguay, the "anti-democratic brutality of the government policy at the service of the oligarchy and imperialism," and the increasing resistance of the masses of the people. According to the General Resolution of the congress, there had been a "qualitative jump" in Uruguayan dependence on the "imperialists," while the living standards of the masses and state services had deteriorated. It charged that the "special security measures," in force during all but three months since mid-1968, were intended to speed up the "plunder" of the imperialists and others; break up the CNT and the mass movement; isolate, divide, and strike the forces of the left, especially FIDEL and the PCU; and assure a legislative power base which would support the policies of the executive branch of government. The Uruguayan people were said to be "burning with indignation" before the "lamentable spectacle of the crumbling of [the] fatherland by the eradication of public liberties and the contempt for national sovereignty." Uruguay could follow either of two roads: radical change or civil war. (*Estudios*, no. 58, January-February 1971.)

Throughout 1970 the PCU argued that those who sought to avoid civil war should band together in order to defeat the candidates of the traditional parties—the Colorados and the Nationalists (Blancos)—in the 1971 presidential and congressional election. In the words of the congress resolution, the election should be made a "great political battle of the masses, centering around the confrontation of the two programs, that of the people and that of the reactionary forces." According to Rodney Arismendi, it should be fought by means of an "advanced democratic front," which he described as follows:

[3]This issue of *Estudios* was given over to documents from the Twentieth Congress, including the General Resolution and Theses, and texts of speeches by Rodney Arismendi and sixteen other party leaders.

[4]At the Twentieth Congress, Eduardo Bleier gave a membership figure of 30,000 (*El Popular*, 13 December 1970). On 3 October Rodney Arismendi reportedly said that 20,000 persons had joined the PCU during 1968 and 1969—a figure that would seem necessary to substantiate his later claim that 26,087 new members were added between 1966 and 30 November 1970 (*Estudios*, no. 58). Alberto Suárez wrote (*ibid.*, July-August 1970) that 12,000 persons joined during 1968 and 1969, and that 20,000 joined both the PCU *and* the UJC during those years. In all probability Arismendi's 26,087 includes new PCU and UJC members.

... a political movement which has as its base of social support the alliance of the working class and of the different groups of workers with the broad strata of the middle class in the city and the country, but which will be able to pull along behind it all those directly or indirectly opposed to the oligarchy and imperialism, in particular, all those hurt by the policy that is now personified by Pacheco Areco and his court.

This "democratic front of national liberation," he declared, was the "indispensable social and political tool of the anti-imperialist and antioligarchic revolution, a necessary prologue for the triumph of socialism." (*ibid.*)

The PCU congress recommended a number of points which it felt should be on the basic program of the proposed front, including the lifting of security measures and restoration of public liberties; defense of the national economy against imperialism; a break with the International Monetary Fund and a moratorium on the foreign debt; the expulsion of "U.S. agents" and the annulment of "anti-national" impositions of loans and treaties with "imperialism"; the establishment of diplomatic and commercial relations with all countries; the nationalization of private banking, foreign trade, and the refrigeration industry; agrarian reform; autonomy for public education; salary increases and the elimination of COPRIN; effective measures for improved housing, social security, and public health; and "the formation of an advanced democratic government, with the participation of the different parties which defend the aspirations of the people" (*ibid.*).

In December, Arismendi said that the PCU had been trying to achieve a united left for some fifteen years. The PCU effort was given a significant boost by the formation of the Popular Unity (Unidad Popular; UP) front in Chile at the end of 1969. When Salvador Allende was nominated as the presidential candidate for the UP in January 1970, *El Popular* (15 January) stated editorially that the UP was a "great example that should be followed by the Uruguayan people, their leftist parties, and their popular forces." In spite of repeated calls of this nature by the PCU and FIDEL, however, other leftist parties in Uruguay were hesitant about forming an alliance with the communists. After the electoral victory of Allende on 4 September (see *Chile*), the situation in Uruguay changed rapidly. Contacts between the Christian Democratic Party (Partido Demócrata Cristiano; PDC) and FIDEL quickly led to an agreement on the front, and by the end of the year the Broad Front (Frente Amplio; FA), as it came to be called, was a reality. By January 1971 it included the PCU, FIDEL, PDC, PSU, POR, a faction of the Colorado Party led by Senator Zelmar Michelini, a faction of the National Party led by Senator Francisco Rodríguez Camusso, a group of independent citizens led by Carlos Quijano (the publisher of the weekly newspaper *Marcha*), and several other small leftist groups. It was the most far-reaching coalition in Uruguayan history. A Gallup poll at the end of the year reportedly gave 27 per cent of the popular support to the FA, as against 29 per cent for the Colorados and 20 per cent for the Nationalists (according to José Massera, *Tribuna Popular*, Caracas, 4 February 1971).[5]

International Views and Positions. The PCU is an outspoken advocate of the foreign policy positions of the Soviet Union. Following the Soviet analysis, the General Resolution of the party's Twentieth Congress described the socialist system, the international working class, and the national liberation movements as the "three great popular currents of our epoch," and designated the "principal contradiction" of the present world as that between socialism and capitalism. According to the resolution:

At the present moment, the great problem confronting the people of the world is to prevent the

[5]By the end of February 1971 the FA reportedly included or had the support of all leftist groups in Uruguay except the MIR and the Anarchist Federation (Federación Anarquista). See *Intercontinental Press*, New York, 1 March 1971.

outbreak of war, to do away with colonialism, and to develop the world revolution. It is necessary to force the imperialists to accept peaceful coexistence between states with different social
systems and this presupposes respect for sovereignty, territorial integrity, equality of rights,
and self-determination of all states and nations, large or small, the right of each people to fight
for its own national liberation and for economic, social, and political changes, using whatever
methods of struggle they may consider appropriate, including armed struggle, as well as the
right to defend themselves against the attacks of the aggressors, likewise resorting to arms, if
that is necessary.

In order to achieve these goals, the resolution held it to be essential that there be "unity of all
anti-imperialist forces, and above all the cohesion of the communist and workers parties." The
Moscow Conference of June 1969 was cited as indicating that this unity, weakened in recent
years by the "divisionist activities of the leaders of the Chinese Communist Party," was being
restored. (*Estudios*, no. 58 January-February 1971.)

In Latin America, the resolution stated, the "revolutionary process" had an "advanced and
radical character," due to the "relatively great degree of capitalist development, deformed and
fettered by the exploitation of North American imperialism and the predominance of large land
holdings." The "objective basis" of the struggle in Latin America was seen as "the aggravation
of the economic crisis," which had its origin in "outdated economic-social structures." The contradictions between the exploiting minority and the exploited majority would be resolved by an
"anti-imperialist agrarian revolution" whose essential objectives would be "to liquidate the economic and political bases of imperial domination, and to bring about advanced agrarian and
democratic transformations." The economic-social transformations in Latin America were to be
understood as "consisting of two stages, anti-imperialist and socialist," which must be differentiated from each other, but which formed part of a "single and continuous revolutionary process." (*Ibid.*)

In each country, the resolution stated, there would have to be a "hard struggle by the masses,"
united in a "democratic front of national liberation" which would include the working class, the
poor peasants, the "most aggressive sectors of the wage earners and the urban middle classes,
particularly the advanced students and intellectuals," and, under some circumstances, members
of the national and middle bourgeoisie. The front would generally be led by the working class,
though in special instances the "radical petty-bourgeoisie" might be the vanguard for certain periods of time. (*Ibid.*)

Although the resolution held that the Chilean revolutionary experience should be studied, it
judged that in most of the Latin American countries the revolutionary process would "develop by
the armed road"—an analysis expounded in great detail by Rodney Arismendi in *Lenin, la revolución y América Latina* (Ediciones Pueblos Unidos, Montevideo, 1970). The PCU did not approve of the tactics of the Tupamaros, however, and Arismendi undoubtedly had them in mind,
among others, when he pointed out that Lenin had "exposed terrorism as futile tactics, opposing
it to the Marxist revolutionary tactics of *mass* action" (*WMR*, May 1970, emphasis in original).

The PCU resolution described the Cuban Revolution as having "an impressive record of economic, social, and cultural progress, incomparably superior to that of any other Latin American
country." Recent developments in Peru, Bolivia, and Chile were also highly praised. (*Estudios*,
no. 58, January-February 1971.)

International Party Contacts. PCU members visiting abroad during 1970 included César
Reyes Daglio, in Moscow (January or February); Enrique Pastorino, in the U.S.S.R., Czecho-
slovakia, and Sudan (March and April); and Rodney Arismendi, in the U.S.S.R. for the Lenin
Centenary (April).

Important foreign communists visited Uruguay for the PCU's fiftieth anniversary celebrations in September and October and the Twentieth Congress in December. Delegates to the former included Luis Corvalán, secretary-general of the Communist Party of Chile, and to the latter: Dinmukhamed Kunaev (Soviet Union), Yivko Yivkov (Bulgaria), Dimitru Balalia (Romania), Jean Garcia (France), Sergio Cavina (Italy), Volodia Teitelboim (Chile), Félix Arias Schreiber (Peru), Athos Fava (Argentina), Gilberto Vieira (Colombia), and Pedro Saad (Ecuador).

Publications. The most important PCU publications are the daily newspaper *El Popular* and the theoretical journal *Estudios*.

* * *

The MIR. The Movement of the Revolutionary Left, founded in 1963, is the main pro-Chinese organization in Uruguay. It appears to be led in large part by young former members of the PCU and UJC, including Julio Arizaga and Washington Rodríguez. The MIR is one of the most important of the six small but active organizations which gathered around the newspaper *Epoca* and were outlawed in December 1967 for advocating the overthrow of the government. The MIR regained its legal status in December 1970. In recent years it seems to have had working relations, at least at some levels, with various movements of the left. Unlike most other leftist groups, however, it did not join the Broad Front (see above)—reportedly because it would not work alongside the PCU (*Intercontinental Press*, New York, 1 March 1971).

During 1970 the MIR organ *Voz Obrera* stated that the seizure of political power in Uruguay required a "Marxist-Leninist revolutionary party," a "people's liberation army led by this party," and a "united front of all revolutionary classes and sections." The MIR indicated that since 1968 it had been working to set up such a party, "composed of the advanced elements of the proletariat," by promoting a "unified thinking of the whole movement," establishing "close ties with the masses," studying the "national reality," and setting up a "collective leadership representative of the whole movement." This party had to be "armed with Marxism-Leninism" and "Mao Tsetung Thought, which is Leninism of our era," according to the MIR, which stressed the need to replace "bourgeois individualism and egoism, the core of the world outlook of the exploiters," with the "world outlook of the proletariat"—the latter to be achieved "in the midst of the broad masses and in the course of the class struggle." (*Voz Obrera* editorials, reprinted in *Peking Review*, 11 September and 13 November.)

A pamphlet issued by the MIR—*Tupamaros, ¿Conspiración o Revolución?: Respuesta de los Marxistas-Leninistas del Uruguay* (Montevideo, September 1970) —declared that the Tupamaros were characterized by adventurism, subjectivism, leftist opportunism, and terrorism, and were "the national expression of the *focoist* doctrine," which was "totally at odds with Marxism." According to the pamphlet, Cuba had been the main outside influence on the Tupamaros, and the *foco* doctrine was nothing more than a "deformation of the Cuban experience."

A pro-Chinese student journal, the first issue of which appeared in Montevideo in June 1970, called for opposition to "revisionism" and to the Castroite idea of the "guerrilla center," or *foco*, and stressed the need for intellectuals to mix with and learn from the workers and peasants (NCNA, 4 September).

* * *

The POR. The Revolutionary Workers' Party is a small organization aligned with the International Secretariat (Posadas faction) of the Fourth International. It is led by Luis Eduardo Naguil. During 1967 and 1968 the POR was somewhat more moderate in its revolutionary line than many other Uruguayan leftist groups. It was outlawed in March 1969 and legalized again in December 1970. The POR supported the formation of a united front during 1970 and joined the aforementioned Broad Front at the end of the year. Its official organ is *Frente Obrero*.

Two publications of the Posadas faction originate in Montevideo and are under the direction of Luis Naguil: *Cuarta Internacional*, the organ of the Executive Committee, and *Revista Marxista Latinoamericana*, the organ of the International Secretariat.

The PRT. The Revolutionary Party of the Workers, founded in 1969, is aligned with the Fourth International—United Secretariat. It believes that "only armed struggle, growing out of the mass working-class movement" can achieve revolutionary victory. It joined the Broad Front in order to advance a "revolutionary program calling on the working class to break from the bourgeoisie, both its imperialist and national sectors." (*Intercontinental Press*, 1 March 1971.) The PRT issues a newspaper, *Tendencia Revolucionario*.

*   *   *

The MRO. The Uruguayan Revolutionary Movement, created in April 1961 and one of the original members of FIDEL, was declared illegal in December 1967 for advocating the overthrow of the government. Contacts between MRO leader Ariel Collazo and FIDEL continued until November 1968 when he was repudiated by the FIDEL Executive Committee for allegedly supporting individual "terrorist" acts, a charge which he denied. Although during 1969 Collazo was critical of the "reformist" policies of the PCU and the CNT, relations improved somewhat in 1970. In December 1970 the MRO was legalized; it then joined the Broad Front. During 1970 Collazo was an increasingly outspoken advocate of a united front, although, he stated in an interview (*Marcha*, Montevideo, September) that armed and peaceful forms of struggle coexisted in Uruguay and neither had won out over the other. In December the MRO commenced publication of *Liberación*.

*   *   *

The PSU. The Socialist Party of Uruguay has existed since the early 1920's. During the early 1960's its militancy increased and its membership decreased, as a result of shifting forces within the movement. The PSU was declared illegal in December 1967 when the government charged that it had called for revolutionary violence at its Thirty-sixth Congress, held in November of that year. The party weekly newspaper *El Sol* was banned, but party leaders almost immediately began to publish an "independent" paper, *Izquierda*, which carried information from various outlawed leftist groups until it was banned in July 1969. Throughout 1970 the party published *El Oriental*. Among the leaders of the PSU are José Díaz, the party secretary-general, and José Pedro Cardoso.

The PSU regards itself as "the party of the proletariat" in Uruguay and is constantly at odds with the PCU, which also claims that class distinction. During 1969, disputes centered on the labor movement, the PSU supporting the more militant minority line at the CNT Congress in May. In 1970 the dispute regarding labor union policies continued but was overshadowed, especially at the end of the year, by conflicting attitudes toward the formation of a broad political front.

In November the PSU acknowledged that in the past it had not fully understood that "unity is one of the most important banners of the revolution." It issued a stern warning: "The working classes are essentially for unity and that banner must not be turned over to anyone, least of all to reformists and opportunists of the moment." Without announcing support for the Broad Front, then being formed, the PSU declared that such a front, if created, would have to be composed of a "centrist pole" (the Christian Democrats and others), a "reformist pole" (the PCU), and a "revolutionary pole," the last in the form of a yet-to-be-created "Revolutionary Front." (*El Oriental*, 6 November.) This "Revolutionary Front" would unite as a "permanent revolutionary axis the forces and militants of the combative left" and would "constitute a fundamental element in broader expressions of popular unity" (*ibid.*, 20 November).[6] Late in December the PSU announced its support for the Broad Front. According to José Díaz, the PSU expected the front to promote the social struggle, develop progressive ideas and popular organization, and break down the structure of the traditional parties and previous political system (*ibid.*, 15 January 1971).

*   *   *

The FARO. The Uruguayan Revolutionary Armed Forces was founded in 1969. During 1970 it was responsible for periodic bombings and armed assaults. On 15 July the FARO released the first issue of its official organ, *El Guerrillero Oriental*, which contained the group's program. It stated: "Two forms of struggle coexist in Uruguay today: the inferior forms of traditional peaceful struggle and the superior forms of increasing armed firepower. Neither should be underestimated, but it must be made clear which will predominate increasingly in the future—the armed struggle transformed into a people's war." On the "inferior" forms, the program commented: "There is still an important revisionist ideology of Marxism-Leninism in Uruguay whose tactical expression on the mass front, politically and in the trade unions, is reformism." The program called for revolutionaries to unite because only then would the "working masses, who are still held back by reformism, also begin to join in the people's war."

*   *   *

The MLN (Tupamaros). The idea of the MLN arose among Uruguayan leftists, in particular among members of the PSU, in the early 1960's.[7] It was given its first organizational form by PSU militant Raúl Sendic in 1962 among rural sugar-cane workers. The Tupamaros made their first raid in July 1963, stealing a quantity of arms from a rural rifle club. Soon the group began to direct its attention toward the cities, since 70 per cent of the population of Uruguay is urban and 45 per cent is concentrated in Montevideo alone. Marked increases in the level of MLN activities were evident in 1965, 1969, and 1970. In October 1969 the Tupamaros briefly captured the town of Pando to mark the second anniversary of the death of Che Guevara. Attacks on law enforcement personnel and kidnapings during 1969 and 1970 seriously damaged the Robin Hood image that the group had carefully cultivated during its early years.

The MLN attracted considerable international attention after mid-1970 by kidnaping foreign nationals serving in Uruguay—most importantly, Brazilian diplomat Aloysio Dias Gomide (on 31 July), U.S. security adviser Dan A. Mitrione (31 July), U.S. agricultural expert Claude Fly (7 August), and British Ambassador Geoffrey Jackson (8 January 1971). The Tupamaros obtained $7.8 million in a robbery of the Banco de la República on 12 November.

---

[6]In what José Díaz later described as a "gross tirade" against the PSU at the PCU's Twentieth Congress (*El Oriental*, 15 January 1971), Leopoldo Bruera said that PSU talk of a "combative left" was "bombastic," and Rodney Arismendi, while calling upon the socialists to reconsider their position, condemned what he regarded as almost a decade of divisive PSU policies (*Estudios*, no. 58, January-February).

[7]The name Tupamaro derives from Tupac Amarú, an Inca chieftain who led an unsuccessful rebellion against the Spanish in Peru in the 1780's.

The MLN is Marxist-Leninist (*Juventud Rebelde*, Havana, 8 June 1970). In a "Manifesto to Public Opinion," published in mid-September, it described itself as an "armed political organization of the students, workers, employees, rural workers, intellectuals, and unemployed" (*Granma*, Havana, English, 27 September). The leadership hierarchy of the MLN is unknown, though Raúl Sendic and Raúl Bidegain Greissing are known to have been among the top leaders until their capture on 7 August. A leader identified only as "Urbano" stated in a long interview later in the year (published in *ibid.*, 18 October, and *Tricontinental Bulletin*, Havana, nos. 57, December 1970, and 58, January 1971) that the loss of Sendic and Greissing had been "a hard blow." Urbano acknowledged that losses were "relatively high" in urban operations and had shown "a marked increase" during recent months. He indicated that "the replacement of the infra-structure" was the greatest problem faced by the MLN, but claimed that volunteers were many and that they provided an "easy, rapid replacement of these losses." Urbano said also that new recruits were usually trained at places outside Montevideo and that activities by armed branches went on meanwhile without any letup.

Estimates of MLN membership range from 200-400 "clandestine combatants" (*Juventud Rebelde*, 8 June) to 1500 or more (*New York Times*, 27 September), the average being about 1,000 (*Le Monde*, Paris, English, 3 February 1971). Some 200 Tupamaros were reportedly under arrest late in 1970 (*New York Times*, 27 September).

The MLN. Domestic Attitudes. The MLN has believed for some years that objective conditions for substantive revolutionary change existed in Uruguay. It proposes to define the road to revolutionary change and provide the impetus. A leader of the movement summarized its immediate objectives in an interview in 1968 with the Chilean leftist journal *Punto Final* (Santiago, Chile, 2 July):

> To create an armed force with the greatest possible haste, with the capacity to take advantage of any propitious juncture created by the crisis or other factors. To create consciousness in the population, through actions of the armed group or other means, that without revolution there will be no change. To strengthen the trade unions and to radicalize their struggles, and connect them with the revolutionary movement.

In late 1970 Urbano said the Tupamaros carried out three sometimes overlapping kinds of actions. These were: "tactical actions, aimed at obtaining supplies"; "propaganda actions," which "by themselves define the movement's objectives and conduct"; and "actions against the regime," which were "mainly aimed at undermining the foundations of the regime itself" and were particularly "directed against the forces of repression" (*Granma*, English, 18 October).

Kidnapings, according to Urbano, were originally intended both to get money or secure the release of imprisoned comrades and to "undermine the foundations of the system." He explained that the kidnaped U.S. security adviser Mitrione, who was executed on 9 August, would have been released if the government had met the MLN's demand for the release of 150 "political prisoners"; when the government refused, the "kidnaping exchange method" had to be "carried to its logical consequences in order to save it as a tool." (*Ibid.*)

The Tupamaros have always sought to avoid the conflicts which have divided leftists in Uruguay. In December 1970 they announced their support for the Broad Front, while also restating their conviction that it was impossible to achieve revolution through elections. MLN support for the front was given "in the understanding that its principal task would be the mobilization of the working masses, and that its work within these masses would neither begin nor end with the elections." (*Punto Final*, 5 January 1971.)

If the Tupamaros were in power, according to Urbano, their tasks would be "the problem of latifundism, nationalization of the banks, the expulsion of imperialism, the achievement of a higher standard of living, education, health, housing, the restoration of man's full dignity and the eradication of unemployment" (*Granma*, English 18 October).

Although the Tupamaros have acknowledged some inspiration from and sympathy toward Communist China and are thought to have received some financial aid and training from the Chinese (Antonio Mercader and Jorge de Vera, *Tupamaros: estrategía y acción*, Montevideo, 1969), they find their main source of inspiration in Che Guevara and Cuba. Even so, they apparently are not controlled by any foreign power or party.

As early as 1968 the MLN stated that one of its chief objectives was to "establish connections with other revolutionary movements of Latin America for continental action" (*Punto Final*, 2 July 1968; see also *Juventud Rebelde*, 8 June 1970). The most publicized instance of significant cooperation during 1970 was with the Bolivian National Liberation Army (ELN), as acknowledged by the ELN leader in a letter to the Tupamaros (*Punto Final*, 18 August).

W. E. R.

VENEZUELA

The Communist Party of Venezuela (Partido Comunista de Venezuela; PCV) was founded in 1931. In December 1970 the party split, one group maintaining the PCV name and the other calling itself the Movement Toward Socialism (Movimiento al Socialismo; MAS).[1] The PCV's legal status was suspended in 1962, after the party began its active policy of armed struggle, and remained so until it was legalized again on 26 March 1969. Estimates of PCV membership range from 8,000 (*World Strength of the Communist Party Organizations*, 1970) to several times that number. In social composition the PCV is largely petty-bourgeois (*Voz Proletaria*, Bogotá, 9 January 1969).

The most important guerrilla organizations in Venezuela, each split into several factions, are the Armed Forces of National Liberation (Fuerzas Armadas de Liberación Nacional; FALN) and the Movement of the Revolutionary Left (Movimiento de Izquierda Revolucionaria; MIR). The total number of guerrillas operating during 1970 is believed to have been between 100 and 250.

The population of Venezuela is 10,800,000 (estimated 1970).

The PCV, illegal at the time of the December 1968 elections and thus unable to take part under its own name, participated through the Union for Advancement (Unión para Avanzar; UPA), a political alliance formed in 1967 and kept firmly under party control. UPA candidates got slightly more than 100,000 votes (2.8 per cent of the total cast) and high-ranking PCV members—Eduardo Gallegos Mancera, Eduardo Machado, Gustavo Machado, Alonso Ojeda, Jesús Faría, and Héctor Mujica—won six of the 266 contested congressional positions.

The PCV was at a peak of power between 1958 and 1960, immediately after the overthrow of the dictatorship of Marcos Pérez Jiménez. At that time party influence on the press, labor unions, students, and some other groups was considerable. Subsequently, communist hostility toward the moderate reform government of President Rómulo Betancourt (1959-64) of the Democratic Action (Acción Democrática; AD) Party, together with the influence of the Cuban Revolution after January 1959, led the PCV to a policy of armed struggle which decreased its influence in the country, as official PCV statements during the late 1960's acknowledged. The decision to participate in the 1968 elections, reached at the Eighth Plenum of the PCV Central Committee in April 1967, made official the "tactical retreat" from armed struggle which had been emerging for several years. During 1970 all communist factions voiced their opposition to the government of President Rafael Caldera, leader of the Social Christian Party (COPEI).

Organization and Leadership. At the top level of the PCV are the Secretariat, Political Bureau, and Central Committee. Jesús Faría, who returned to Venezuela in August 1968 after

---

[1]The MAS name was actually chosen and ratified at the first congress of the group, on 14-17 January 1971. During the preceding month the group first used the PCV name and then called itself the Popular Socialist Alliance (Alianza Socialista Popular).

several years exile in Moscow, remained as secretary-general in 1970. At the Thirteenth Plenum of the Central Committee in May 1969, the Political Bureau was expanded from nine to fifteen members. Former members returned to office were Gustavo Machado, Eduardo Machado, Pompeyo Márquez, Guillermo García Ponce, Alonso Ojeda Olaechea, Pedro Ortega Díaz, Eduardo Gallegos Mancera, and Germán Lairet, while Teodoro Petkoff was dropped (see below). New members were Jesús Faría, Antonio García Ponce, Eloy Torres, Héctor Rodríguez Bauza, Freddy Muñoz, Rafael José Cortés, and Radamés Larrazábal. The Central Committee, according to the party's weekly newspaper (*Tribuna Popular*, 16 December), had 51 regular and 17 alternate members; prominent among these were Teodoro Petkoff, Héctor Marcano Coello, Argelia Laya de Martínez, Antonio José Urbina, Alexis Adam, Tirso Pinto, Juvencio Pulgar, and Eleazar Díaz Rangel.

In mid-December 1970 five members of the Political Bureau (Pompeyo Márquez, Eloy Torres, Héctor Rodríguez Bauza, Germán Lairet, and Freddy Muñoz) and 22 members of the Central Committee, withdrew from the Faría-led party and formed a separate communist party, soon named the MAS. The dissidents were quickly expelled officially from the PCV.

The MAS elected its 31-member Central Committee in January 1971. The most important PCV dissidents included on the committee were Pompeyo Márquez (with the office of secretary-general), Alexis Adam, Eleazar Díaz Rangel, Germán Lairet, Argelia Laya, Carlos Augusto León, Héctor Marcano Coello, Freddy Muñoz, Alfredo Padilla, Teodoro Petkoff, Tirso Pinto, Juvencio Pulgar, Héctor Rodríguez Bauza, Eloy Torres, Antonio José Urbina, and Luis Bayardo Sardi.

Although the majority of the PCV Political Bureau and Central Committee members remained in the original party, it was not clear which group had the support of the bulk of the party militants. In a statement published immediately after the split, Pompeyo Márquez charged that the PCV Central Committee members who remained loyal to Secretary-General Faría had "carried out a coup d'etat against the overwhelming majority of the party" (*El Nacional*, Caracas, 18 December). Early in 1971, Alonso Ojeda Olaechea declared that the "dissenters" did not have a majority of party members, and alleged that 68 per cent of the PCV National Congress (the party's "supreme authority," according to its statutes), had remained loyal after the split (*Tribuna Popular*, 14 January 1971). The only comment on party size in a short history of the PCV published by the PCV Congress was: "Some statements say that Petkoff and company constitute a majority" (*ibid.*, 4 February 1971).

The Venezuelan Communist Youth (Juventud Comunista Venezolana; JCV) has been the most active and successful PCV auxiliary organization in recent years. It has long furnished many of the nation's most active student leaders, including most of the presidents of the influential Federations of University Centers (Federaciones de Centros Universitarios; FCU). At the end of 1970 the JCV controlled the FCU's in five of the country's eight universities, among them the FCU at the University of the Andes in Mérida, previously in the hands of the MIR. The greatest JCV successes have been at the Central University of Venezuela (Universidad Central de Venezuela; UCV), in Caracas, where half of the nation's students are enrolled. The president of the FCU at the UCV during 1970 was PCV Central Committee member Alexis Adam. Other important JCV leaders were Antonio José Urbina (secretary-general), Luis Bayardo Sardi, Juvencio Pulgar, and Américo Díaz Nuñez.

The JCV was supposed to be "an auxiliary and reserve political youth organization of the Communist Party, created to apply its policies among the masses and the youth, and to incorporate young persons in general into the struggle on behalf of democracy, national liberation, and socialism" (*Tribuna Popular*, 22 April 1970). In reality, however, most JCV members sought a greater role for the JCV in determining party policies and were strongly partial to Teodoro Petkoff and Márquez rather than to Secretary-General Faría and his followers. Early in 1971 the

PCV described the JCV in 1970 as a "petty-bourgeois organization" which was "completely cut off from the party's political and ideological leadership," having become a "party struggling against the party" (*ibid.*, 15 January and 4 February 1971). Alonso Ojeda acknowledged that in December 1970 a "sizable group of JCV members—perhaps the majority—joined the dissenters" (*ibid.*, 14 January 1971). In fact, virtually every JCV leader, and apparently the vast majority of the regular members, went over to the dissenters and founded the Communist Youth of the MAS (Juventud Comunista del MAS), with Alfredo Padilla as its secretary-general in January 1971. The MAS also took over *Deslinde*, the communist bimonthly edited at the UCV.

In January 1971 the PCV—noting that the JCV during 1970 had concentrated its efforts on university students—vowed to rebuild the youth organization so that it would be "more proletarian, more aggressive, and more rooted in the masses" (*ibid.*, 19 January).

The United Workers' Federation of Venezuela (Confederación Unitaria de Trabajadores de Venezuela; CUTV), whose president is Cruz A. Villegas, is a small but active organization dominated by the PCV. In a report to the PCV Central Committee in August 1970, Eloy Torres, the party's national secretary in charge of trade union matters, stressed the need for communists to concentrate their activities on the most important unions and most strategic enterprises. He declared that the more noncommunist unions split apart due to reformist leadership, the more it was necessary to have an "open and flexible policy of alliances with all who want to champion the workers' interests and to make their organization an instrument of class struggle." (*IB*, no. 17-18 and no. 21, 1970.) Other important PCV labor leaders were Laureano Torrealba and Carlos Arturo Pardo. In the split at the end of the year, Villegas and Torrealba remained with PCV, and Torres and Pardo joined the MAS.

According to Argelia Laya, the PCV's national secretary for women's affairs, the role of the women's movement in Venezuela during 1970 was insignificant (*Deslinde*, 15 February)—an evaluation affirmed by the party in early 1971 when it described the movement as being "in a state of completely unjustified neglect" (*Tribuna Popular*, 4 February). PCV Central Committee member Eleazar Díaz Rangel was chairman of the communist-dominated Venezuelan Journalists' Association (Asociación Venezolana de Periodistas), which held its Seventh National Convention in Maracay on 24-27 September 1970. The convention called for the establishment of a Latin American Journalists' Federation. At the end of the year, Laya and Díaz were among the dissidents who formed the MAS.

The PCV has had little influence among Venezuelan peasants. Alonso Ojeda, acknowledging in mid-1969 that the PCV had underestimated the importance of activities in the countryside, attributed peasant apathy toward guerrilla forces to the successful agrarian reform policies of the AD governments of Rómulo Betancourt and Raúl Leoni (*Deslinde*, 31 July).

Party Internal Affairs. The PCV held six plenary sessions of its Central Committee during 1970: the Fifteenth Plenum, in three sessions, between February and June; the Sixteenth Plenum in late August; the Seventeenth Plenum in mid-September; the Eighteenth Plenum in early November; the Nineteenth Plenum in late November-early December; and the Twentieth Plenum on 14-16 December. The Fourth Congress, originally scheduled for mid-1970, was repeatedly postponed. The congress was finally held on 23-27 January 1971. The dissident MAS held its congress shortly before, on 14-17 January.

Since the mid-1960's the PCV has had two major internal disputes. The first dispute came as the PCV was planning and executing its "tactical retreat" from guerrilla warfare in the mid-1960's and was centered upon the person of Douglas Bravo (see below). The second culminated in the split of December 1970.

The second dispute, which occupied most of the PCV's attention during 1970, came into the open following the party's endorsement of the Soviet-led invasion of Czechoslovakia in August

1968. Although an immediate public rejection of the endorsement was voiced by only one prominent party member—Pedro Duno, a university professor who was expelled from the party in 1969 —there was disapproval on the part of many others.[2] These dissenters were led by Teodoro Petkoff, who in May 1969 was dropped from the Political Bureau for "divergence with respect to the revolutionary line." They included Germán Lairet, Manuel Caballero, Freddy Muñoz, and most of the JCV. Opposing them was a group of "old guard" conservatives (the "Stalinists," according to the dissenters), led by Guillermo García Ponce, among whom were all of the men who made up the PCV Political Bureau in January 1971. A third group, sometimes called the *renovadores* (renewers), consisted of centrists led by Pompeyo Márquez. The centrists worked to hold the party together through almost two years of increasingly vigorous and acrimonious debate and polemics. When the party split came in December 1970, most of the centrists left the party—not because they agreed with all of Petkoff's views, but because they supported free ideological debate (Petkoff interview, *Ultimas Noticias*, Caracas, 21 December).

Although the dispute came into the open as a result of the occupation of Czechoslovakia, the issues were more fundamental and on some points were the same as those raised by such dissident European communists as Roger Garaudy in France and Ernst Fischer in Austria. (Petkoff was described by the Paris newspaper *Le Monde* on 23 October 1970 as "a Venezuelan Roger Garandy.") Petkoff's two books—*Czechoslovakia: Socialism as a Problem* (*Checoeslovaquia— el socialismo como problema*, Caracas, 1969) and *Socialism for Venezuela?* (¿ *Socialismo para Venezuela?*, Caracas, 1970 —presented the main points of his argument, as follows: there was no real justification for the Soviet-led invasion of Czechoslovakia; in Czechoslovakia the Soviet Union crushed a fruitful experiment in decentralized, flexible, and nationally oriented socialism: "proletarian internationalism," for the Soviet Union and its unquestioning supporters, was merely a cloak for Soviet nationalism; the Communist Party of the Soviet Union (CPSU) and the PCV were bureaucratic and authoritarian ("Stalinist") in structure; socialism could be achieved in Venezuela only when the PCV modified or abandoned its erroneous interpretations of the stages of revolution, class alliances, the vanguard role of the communist party, freedom of discussion, and democratic centralism.

The controversy over the views expressed by Petkoff, and by those who gathered around him, was often almost indistinguishable from the ongoing dispute among PCV members as to the proper methods and content of discussion and debate. The conservatives, who had a majority in the Political Bureau and Central Committee, maintained that they approved free discussion, but added that it had to remain within the guidelines they deemed admissible (see *IB*, no. 10, 1970). Petkoff, on the other hand, insisted on greater freedom and challenged the very makeup and authority of the existing party committees and their statutes. During 1970, as before, Petkoff repeatedly made criticisms (such as his attacks on the Soviet Union) which were unacceptable to the conservatives and addressed himself, particularly in his book *Socialism for Venezuela?*, to general rather than strictly communist audiences.

Such unauthorized activities clearly threatened the unity of the PCV in 1970. Thus "party unity" became a crucial issue, urged in varying degrees by all three groups. For Petkoff and his followers, unity required the elimination of the conservatives' dominance of the PCV, and this could be achieved in part by the election of Pompeyo Márquez as secretary-general. For the conservatives, it would involve the purging, or at least silencing, of the dissenters. Petkoff never had enough support among top party leaders to eliminate the conservatives, even though the centrists also sought freer discussion. The conservatives could have marshaled the votes to expel (though not silence) his group, but they decided not to carry out a purge, realizing that it would shake up the party far more than the purge of Bravo (see below) had done.

[2]See Pedro Duno's account of party affairs in Duno, *Sobre Aparatos, Desviaciones y Dogmas* (Editorial Nueva Izquierda, Caracas, 1969).

Thus the Central Committee, in a series of meetings between February and June 1970, discussed a long report entitled "The Anti-Socialist Ideas of Petkoff," by Antonio García Ponce and Pedro Ortega Díaz, and stated that the contents of Petkoff's book on Czechoslovakia ran "counter to fundamental postulates regarding the building of socialism, the role of the Communist parties, proletarian internationalism and the international policy" of the PCV. The committee expressed its "disagreement with the contents of the book," but took no disciplinary action against Petkoff. (*IB*, no. 10.) Shortly afterward, Petkoff's *Socialism for Venezuela?* was published, and the Political Bureau rejected "all the tendentious statements and harmful suggestions" contained in the book (*Tribuna Popular*, 20 August). Guillermo García Ponce later declared that Petkoff's two books constituted "a platform aimed at the liquidation of the party and its replacement with a multi-class, shapeless, and unprincipled organization" (*ibid.*, 12 November).

The issue which finally led to the split arose over the convening of the PCV's Fourth Congress, which the Central Committee, at its plenum in early November had scheduled for 4 December, and the election of delegates. As that date approached, in some areas the regional elections of delegates appeared to show a solid base for Petkoff and the centrists. The conservatives charged that this apparent support was the result of "irregularities" at the regional level; this led to accusations that they were trying to bolster their own declining influence by interfering in local party affairs.

The committee's subsequent plenum of 23 November–4 December was marked by vitriolic charges and countercharges. Finally deciding to postpone the congress until 23 January 1971 (not indefinitely, as the conservatives had wished), the committee scheduled a further plenum for 14 December. On 7 December, however, Antonio García Ponce renewed the attack on the dissenters, and on 10 December, in an article in *Tribuna Popular*, Jesús Faría tried to minimize the strength of the dissenters, whom he labeled "enemies of the people" and "neo-anticommunists;" he also reneged on an agreement reached several days earlier with the centrists by threatening "moral and disciplinary sanctions" against party members who had practiced "deceitful maneuvers" in the delegate elections in the Caracas and Miranda regions.

At this point Pompeyo Márquez and his four supporters on the Political Bureau called a press conference and denounced the "divisionist and autocratic" conservative "old guard" leaders, charging that they were trying to defy the will of the majority of PCV members who wanted a congress immediately, that they considered Marxism a "dogma," and that they had created a party suffering from the worst of "Stalinist deformations" (*El Nacional*, 11 December). In an act which the conservatives later admitted had caught them by surprise (see *Tribuna Popular*, 4 February 1971), the centrists withdrew from the party. With Petkoff's dissidents they then announced that they were appointing themselves the "Preparatory Commission" for the Fourth Congress of the PCV, but soon afterward decided to form a separate organization, first called the Popular Socialist Alliance and then the Movement Toward Socialism.

At the end of the year the conservative PCV leaders professed to believe that the expulsion of the dissidents—who were accused of having varying degrees of Trotskyist, Marcusian, pettybourgeois leftist, and even rightist leanings—would lead to a stronger party. The MAS claimed that it could operate more effectively after the break with the "Stalinists"—the "mothball Marxists" (*Marxistas de naftalina*) who looked upon Marxism as a "catechism."[3]

---

[3] The Soviet Union played what may have been a decisive role in the split. The most important of several Soviet attacks on the dissenters, a long article by A. Mosinev in *Pravda* on 20 October, denounced Petkoff's "renegade credo" and implied that he and his followers ought to be expelled from the PCV. This article was published immediately after the arrival in Venezuela of Rudolf Shlyapnikov, assigned to the staff of the recently opened Soviet Embassy in Caracas. The presence of Shlyapnikov, who had been accused by Raúl Castro of interfering in Cuban affairs several years before, was

Domestic Attitudes and Activities. The PCV did not issue a comprehensive statement on the national situation during 1970. Such a statement was submitted to the Central Committee in June and was to have been ratified at the party's Fourth Congress—but the congress was not held until 1971. Further, as the PCV acknowledged in January 1971, the "long internal debate" revolving around Teodoro Petkoff "immobilized" and "virtually paralyzed" the party (*Tribuna Popular*, 4 February).

The dissidents and the conservative leaders agreed that the guerrilla warfare carried out by "ultra-leftists" was pointless, and that existing conditions called for a peaceful struggle against increasing "imperialist" control over the country and against the government of President Rafael Caldera through communist participation in a broad, popular front which would be based in the working class. They disagreed on some important points: the dissidents sought a socialist revolution and a "pluralistic socialist society," but denied the necessity of a communist vanguard and a dictatorship of the proletariat. The conservatives called for a "national-democratic" stage prior to the socialist revolution, and maintained the orthodox communist insistence on a communist party vanguard and a dictatorship of the proletariat. The Fifteenth Plenum, controlled by the conservative leaders called upon the party to

> contribute [its] share to working-class, democratic and anti-imperialist unity, carry forward the struggle against the Caldera government and prominent representatives of the big bourgeoisie in the service of US imperialism, as well as against the secret designs implicit in the Copei-Democratic Action alliance, help the working class and other popular forces in the fight for their economic and political demands, and uphold democratic liberties and constitutional rights (*IB*, no. 10, 1970).

International Views and Positions. The international orientation of the PCV in 1970, as in past years, was in line with the policies of the Soviet Union, though open criticism of Communist China was avoided. This orientation, the target of many of Teodoro Petkoff's attacks in 1969 and 1970, became increasingly difficult to sustain among centrists as the year progressed, in particular after the *Pravda* article of 20 October (see note 3, above).

The Central Committee declared in a plenum early in the year: "The world socialist system is the decisive force in the anti-imperialist struggle. All liberation struggles rely on the irreplaceable support of this system, above all on that of the Soviet Union." (*IB*, no. 10.) The defense of socialism was termed an "internationalist duty" for all communists, and "proletarian internationalism" was hailed as "one of the great revolutionary forces of our time." The PCV proclaimed its desire to "maintain friendly relations with all Communist and Workers' Parties and revolutionary movements operating in the world," and its determination to follow a policy of "non-interference in the internal affairs of any party." In the same statement the Central Committee reiterated the PCV's support for the Soviet-led invasion of Czechoslovakia. (*Ibid.*)

Vigorously rejecting "every form of anti-Sovietism" and declaring that there was "no room for anti-Sovietism in the ranks of the Communist Party of Venezuela," the Central Committee statement added:

> The Soviet Union is the most important material base of the world revolutionary movement. This conclusion cannot be marred by the mistakes made in building socialism and communism

widely interpreted as Soviet interference in PCV affairs. The full text of Mosinev's article was published in *Tribuna Popular* on 5 November, with supporting articles by Gustavo Machado and Radamés Larrazábal, and charges of interference by Alexis Adam, Germán Lairet, and Teodoro Petkoff. In his *How the PCV Split* (*Como se dividio el PCV*, Caracas, 1971) Eleazar Díaz Rangel—until December 1970 a member of the Central Committee of the PCV and the Executive Committee of the Soviet-front International Organization of Journalists—wrote that Guillermo García Ponce and his followers, taking the Soviet lead, had pressured Jesús Farfa into expelling Petkoff and the others for their "anti-socialist and anti-Soviet ideas."

in the Soviet Union, nor by the critical stand that may be taken on certain positions of the Soviet state and Party.... Without idealizing the Soviet Union, we must say that to defend its patrimony today is an internationalist duty that can at no moment be disregarded or neglected. (*Ibid.*)

At its 14-16 December plenum the committee totally rejected Petkoff's "lies and slander" leveled at "the Soviet Union and proletarian internationalism" (*ibid.*, no. 1, 1971).

The PCV also denounced "U.S. imperialism" for giving "political and military aid to international Zionism" in its effort to "establish domination over the Arab countries" (TASS, 1 March) and condemned the "criminal U.S. aggression in Cambodia and other areas of Indochina" (*IB*, no. 12).

Relations between the PCV and Fidel Castro, after reaching a very low point in 1967 when the PCV was the target of most Cuban attacks on pro-Soviet communists in Latin America, showed some cordiality in 1969 and continued to do so during 1970. On several occasions party leaders called for "fraternal support for socialist Cuba." Only occasionally were critical comments made, generally indirect and in reference to Cuban support for Douglas Bravo and PCV dissidents up to 1969. The PCV sent congratulations to Salvador Allende upon his inauguration as president of Chile. PCV leaders expressed their disapproval of the April kidnap-murder of the West German Ambassador to Guatemala, Count Karl von Spreti, by leftist guerrillas, but refused to endorse a resolution of the Venezuelan legislature to that effect which did not also denounce right-wing violence in Guatemala. PCV Political Bureau member Gustavo Machado criticized the August kidnap-murder of a U.S. citizen, Dan Mitrione, by urban guerrillas in Uruguay.

Teodoro Petkoff's interest in international affairs has been centered, since the Soviet-led invasion of Czechoslovakia, on what he and his growing number of followers regard as the stifling nature of Soviet policies toward and influence on the world communist movement. In *Czechoslovakia: Socialism as a Problem* he condemned bureaucratic "Stalinists" in the Soviet Union for crushing a fruitful experiment in adapting socialism to the unique national conditions of Czechoslovakia. In *Socialism in Venezuela?* he wrote that the PCV had been made a "vassal" of the Communist Party of the Soviet Union by the same "Stalinist" elements and their policies, adding that Venezuelan communists would never be the "builders of a new society" unless they broke loose from this "Stalinist mold." In fact, he argued, the world-wide crisis in the communist movement was precisely the "crisis of Stalinism, whose rigid ideological, political, organizational, and even moral standards" were being "thrown into the arena of opposing currents" that were surging up from within the movement itself—for example, from within the Italian, French, Austrian, and Venezuelan communist parties.

At the Nineteenth Plenum of the PCV Central Committee, held just before the split in the party, Petkoff declared that he did not want the PCV to be anti-Soviet, anti-Chinese, or anti-Cuban; rather, he sought an unaligned, national party (*El Nacional*, Caracas, 4 December). The additional statement to the "Venezuelan people" by the 22 Central Committee members who withdrew from the PCV stressed that their new group would be an "internationalist force," giving full support to the struggles of the Vietnamese and all others against "U.S. imperialism." The statement praised the efforts of all the leaders of "progressive humanity," whom it identified as "the Soviets, the Chinese, the Cubans, and all people who are building socialism and communism" (*El Nacional*, 18 December).

Publications. The weekly organ of the PCV is *Tribuna Popular* and the biweekly university journal is *Deslinde*. After the split in the party the main PCV organ was *Tribuna Popular*; that of the MAS was *Deslinde*.

*　　*　　*

Most of the guerrillas in Venezuela in the past decade have belonged to either the FALN or the MIR. Once united and active in several parts of the country, the guerrilla organizations began to disintegrate in the mid-1960's. The process continued in 1970. Five FALN members who surrendered to the army early in the year attributed the disintegration to difficulties in financing operations, lack of basic ideology and internal discipline, the "anarchy which reigns within the guerrilla command," and "the fact that everyone in the command is trying to take over" (*Ultimas Noticias*, Caracas, 17 January). Contributing to the internal dissension were personal rivalries, differing views on forms of armed and peaceful struggle, and varying reactions to the pacification program inaugurated by President Caldera in March 1969.

During the 1960's many Venezuelan guerrillas were trained in Cuba and, as Fidel Castro acknowledged to Venezuelan newspaper men in January 1971, received aid of all kinds from the Cuban government (*ibid.*, 20 January). In 1969 and 1970 Cuban aid to the guerrillas decreased markedly or stopped altogether (see below). Early in 1970 it was reported that the guerrillas had sent representatives to Cuba, and also to Communist China, to ask for increased support (*ibid.*, 25 January).

The FALN. The FALN was formed in 1962 as the military arm of the PCV-dominated National Liberation Front (Frente de Liberación Nacional; FLN). In April 1966 most of the guerrillas, led by then PCV Political Bureau member Douglas Bravo, rebelled against party leadership and set up the Unitary Command (Comando Único) of the FLN-FALN—often abbreviated as CUFF—in order to end control by PCV leaders living in the cities and put decision-making offices into the hands of the guerrillas themselves. The following month Bravo was removed from the PCV Political Bureau and a year later was expelled from the party, for "rebelling against the party's discipline, setting up a parallel apparatus, and working to create a split in the party" (letter by Pompeyo Márquez in *El Nacional*, 23 April 1967).

Between 1968 and 1970 some of the best-known FALN guerrillas broke with Bravo, either because they had lost faith in armed struggle or because they disagreed with Bravo's guerrilla tactics. Among these were Lunar Márquez and Luben Petkoff, brother of Teodoro Petkoff. Early in 1970 Bravo stated that all those who had broken with him had "abandoned the struggle." There had been reports, off and on for several years, that Bravo himself had left the countryside to seek medical treatment for wounds suffered in battle. Such reports became more persistent in mid-1970, and during the last half of the year Bravo was frequently alleged to be recuperating, or to have died, in Paris, Mexico City, or Caracas. Among Bravo's loyal followers at the time of his last known interview in Venezuela (April 1970) were Francisco Prada, Antonio Zamora, and Elegido Sibada.[4]

In December 1969 Bravo, for years considered one of the foremost "Castroite" guerrillas in Latin America, charged the Cuban government with devoting attention only to internal economic development and abandoning its "international revolutionary obligations," specifically its support for the Venezuelan guerrillas. In the April 1970 interviews (see note 4) Bravo proclaimed his "solidarity with the Cuban government" and said that his differences with Castro were over the tactics of guerrilla warfare and not the strategy of armed revolution, but the content of the interviews suggested strategic problems as well. An article in the July issue of the Paris journal *Les Temps Modernes*, attributed to Bravo and possibly written after Fidel Castro's 22 April condem-

[4]Confusion over Bravo's whereabouts and physical condition, as well as over his widely reported criticisms of Fidel Castro and Régis Debray, was increased by the publication between May 1970 and early 1971 of a number of "interviews," in most instances undated. All seem to derive from two interviews given in Venezuela in April 1970 to Humberto Solioni (*Marcha*, Montevideo, 15 May; *Intercontinental Press*, New York, 8 June) and Georges Mattel (excerpts in *Le Monde*, Paris, English edition, 12 August; full text in *Vea y Lea*, Caracas, 18 January 1971).

nation of guerrilla "fakers," openly charged that Cuba appeared to be changing its concept of revolutionary strategy in Latin America.[5]

In one of the interviews given in April, Bravo stated that the publication in 1967 of Régis Debray's *Revolution in the Revolution?* had increased guerrilla differences with the "leadership of the Cuban revolution," since the "thesis of the book was shared fully by the Cuban comrades." He termed Debray's book a "distortion of the Cuban experience"; it "did not formulate profound analysis," and instead offered "little recipes, interpretations which were in large part of a dogmatic variety." This "distorted version of the Cuban tactic," he said, underestimated the importance of organizing a party, a front, the peasants, and the working class, and had "unquestionably produced defeats of great magnitude in Latin America." (*Intercontinental Press*, New York, 8 June.)

According to Bravo, the guerrilla war in Venezuela was merely one part of a continental struggle. Proper tactics called for the simultaneous utilization of rural and urban forces, but with the headquarters in the mountains and the guerrilla army as the key factor. It required political-military fronts, with organizations extending into the factories, high schools, universities, and other places of work. (*Vea y Lea*, Caracas, 18 January 1971.)

The crisis that international communism was experiencing, Bravo went on to say, was due to the conflict between the "revisionist" Soviet Union and the "anti-revisionist, Marxist-Leninist" Chinese People's Republic. In this conflict the FALN, he stated, stood beside China. (*Ibid.*).

Bravo confirmed earlier reports (e.g., *El Nacional*, 9 January 1970) that a Committee for Revolutionary Integration (Comité de Integración Revolucionaria; CIR) had been formed, uniting the FALN and Carlos Betancourt's FGAJS guerrilla front (see below), with the "fundamental objective" of creating "a single army and a single party to make the revolution" (*Intercontinental Press*, 8 June). According to Bravo, the combined FGAJS and FALN consisted of three revolutionary fronts or columns (called José Leonardo Chirinos, Antonio José de Sucre, and José Antonio Páez) and various urban units, and these were the only groups waging armed struggle in Venezuela (*Vea y Lea*, 18 January 1971).

Early in 1970 it was reported that Freddy Cárquez, head of FALN "urban expropriation operations," had been expelled from the organization (*El Nacional*, 9 January). Cárquez evidently founded another guerrilla organization with other former FALN members, among them Alirio Chirinos, before availing himself of the government's pacification offers and going into exile in Chile (see *Ultimas Noticias*, 26 November, for an account by Cárquez of his abandonment of armed struggle).

By mid-1970 Alirio Chirinos had formed the Committee for People's War (El Comité de Guerra Popular; CGP). In an effort to "inject new life into the guerrilla movement," the CGP met with the Organization of Revolutionaries (see below) in August to form a new revolutionary front, apparently with a pro-Chinese orientation.

The MIR and other Guerrilla Organizations. The Movement of the Revolutionary Left was founded in July 1960 by Domingo Alberto Rangel and other left-wing dissidents from the AD party. Rangel withdrew his support for the armed struggle line of the MIR in 1963-64, but most other members did not. By 1968, however, a definite "soft line," favoring the suspension of armed struggle, had begun to appear, in opposition to the "hard line" which favored the continuation of

---

[5]On 22 April 1970, with Bravo clearly in mind though not mentioning him by name, Castro commented at length on "pseudo-revolutionaries" who had received help from Cuba and then "sabotaged" their revolutions. He promised to publish "full details" on these revolutionary "fakers" in the future. (*Granma*, English edition, Havana, 3 May). Early in 1971 Castro told Venezuelan newspaper men that the guerrillas had failed in Venezuela because their leaders had been disorganized and irresponsible (*Ultimas Noticias*, 20 January).

guerrilla warfare. By 1970 most former leaders of the MIR—including Moisés Moleiro, Américo Martín, Héctor Pérez Marcano, Simón Sáez Mérida, and Eduardo Ortíz Bucarán—had abandoned armed struggle, while Carlos Betancourt, Julio Escalona, and Fernando Soto Rojas were among those who had not.

The MIR has devoted considerable attention to winning the support of Venezuelan students, who have made up a high percentage of their guerrilla forces—often, until 1968, in alliance with the JCV at the Central University in Caracas. One indication of declining student support for the militant wing of the MIR was the JCV defeat of the MIR in the 1970 student union elections at the University of the Andes in Mérida, for several years the main MIR stronghold.

The most important MIR guerrilla front is the Antonio José de Sucre Guerrilla Front (Frente Guerrillero Antonio José de Sucre; FGAJS) in the state of Oriente, headed since its formation in March 1967 by Carlos Betancourt. By January 1970 Betancourt and Douglas Bravo had formed the Committee for Revolutionary Integration (CIR) to coordinate MIR and FALN activities (see above), though there is little evidence that the CIR achieved its objectives.

Late in 1969 Julio Escalona, Marcos Gómez, and Fernando Soto Rojas, recently separated from the FGAJS, formed the "José Félix Ribas" front and decided to maintain the MIR youth apparatus at the Central University in Caracas under the name "Marxist-Leninist MIR" (see *El Nacional*, 24 January 1970, and *Bohemia*, Caracas, 15 June). In a document circulated in late November 1969—and denounced as "anti-communist" by the PCV (*Tribuna Popular*, 11 December)—Escalona's group charged the Soviet Union with "betraying the people of the world and Marxism-Leninism," and announced its support for "the best within socialism: China, Vietnam, Korea, and Cuba."

In mid-1970 Escalona broke completely with the MIR and announced the formation of the Organization of Revolutionaries (Organización de Revolucionarios; OR), "inspired by Marxism-Leninism and the concept of people's war as the only means to achieve victory" (*El Nacional*, 7 June). The OR, evidently pro-Chinese in outlook, met in August with a group of FALN dissidents, the Committee for People's War, to form a new revolutionary front, also apparently pro-Chinese in orientation (*O Estado de São Paulo*, São Paulo, 3 September 1970).

W. E. R.

ASIA AND
THE PACIFIC

AUSTRALIA

The Communist Party of Australia (CPA) was founded in October 1920. Membership reached a high of some 20,000 during World War II, but has since declined steadily and is currently estimated at 4,000. The population of Australia is 12,031,000 (estimated 1968). The party's main strength is among organized workers in the major industrial and urban centers. The orientation of the CPA is generally pro-Soviet.

An offshoot of the CPA, the Australian Communist Party (Marxist-Leninist), or ACP(ML), was established in March 1964. It is believed to have about 250 members. The ACP(ML) supports the policies of the Chinese People's Republic.

Both parties are legal. The CPA participates, though with little success, in all national and some state elections. In the latest national election, in October 1969 (which returned the Liberal-Country Party coalition with a narrow majority over the Australian Labor Party), the CPA's seven candidates together received only 0.08 per cent of the popular vote, down from 0.4 per cent in 1966.

The CPA. Leadership and Organization. The CPA national president (chairman) is Richard Dixon, who is expected to relinquish his position in 1971 for reasons of ill health. The party's national secretary (secretary-general) and most powerful figure is Laurie Aarons. The leading body of the CPA is the 12-member National Executive (Politburo), consisting of Dixon, Aarons, Laurie Carmichael, N. Docker, Charlie Gifford, Claude Jones, Jim Moss, Joe Palmada, Alec Robertson, Mavis Robertson, John Sendy, and Bernard Taft, all of whom were elected in May 1970 by the 38-member National Committee (Central Committee), which itself was elected by the party's Twenty-second Congress, held in Sydney on 28-30 March.

The party's National Youth Committee is composed of CPA members below the age of thirty, elected by the various branch organizations. The CPA controls the Union of Australian Women, whose president is Freda Brown (currently a vice-president of the Women's International Democratic Federation and until 1970 a member of the CPA National Committee). In 1968 the CPA established the Australian Marxist Research Foundation for education and study.

The CPA's influence in organized labor was reduced in 1970 as a result of intraparty differences which removed from the CPA National Committee three leading trade unionists in key industries: E. V. Elliott, head of the Seamen's Union of Australia; Pat Clancy, secretary for New South Wales of the Building Workers' Industrial Union and member of the Interstate Executive of the Australian Council of Trade Unions; and T. Wright, secretary for New South Wales of the Sheet Metal Workers' Union. CPA leaders still holding important posts include: Laurie Carmichael, who is Victoria State and Assistant Commonwealth secretary of the Amalgamated Engineering Union, and Jack Mundey, CPA National Committee member and Sydney district president, who is secretary of the Australian Builders' Laborers' Federation in New South Wales.

Party Internal Affairs and Relations with the Soviets. Since the outbreak of the Sino-Soviet dispute in the early 1960's, there has existed severe factionalism between the "progressive" CPA leadership majority, which is bent on increasing independence of Soviet ties and the development of a national image among the electorate, and a more conservative minority, which upholds the leading role of the Soviet Union in the communist camp. Exacerbated by the 1968 Czechoslovak crisis and the party's failure to attract youth, these fundamental differences contributed to low morale at all organizational levels. Developments in 1970 produced a measure of victory for the progressives, but neither quelled the conservative challenge nor enhanced the CPA's national stature. The CPA leadership's assertion of its independence within the international communist movement, however, does appear to have evoked wide respect and empathy among parties of a similar inclination—the Italian, for example—which have not generally gone so far in their pronouncements as has the Australian party.

The text of a "1,000 Words" appeal to CPA members, signed by "100 communists and other radicals and revolutionaries, all under thirty," was published in the party's weekly newspaper, the *Tribune*, on 4 March 1970. The appeal described three main possibilities for the future of the CPA: (1) its development into a "revolutionary party relevant to Australian conditions—militant, democratic, tolerant of other groupings on the left," and affording young people a role in decision making; (2) the road of "political suicide" through "defending existing communist-ruled states rather than fighting for revolution in Australia," and thereby "becoming isolated from young radicals and Australian society as a whole"; and (3) an equally doomed "middle" course advocating "balanced positions" and "moderation" while in reality equivocating and refusing to acknowledge the existing situation.

The appeal went on to attack a draft program, "For a Socialist Australia," proposed by then National Committee member Edgar Ross, which represented an alternative from the opposition to the "Statement of Aims, Methods, and Organization" draft program approved by the 1969 national conference (see *YICA*, 1970, p. 512) and slated for consideration at the Twenty-second Congress. The Ross alternative was said to place too great an emphasis on the "duty of the communist party to popularize the achievements of the Soviet Union and systematically combat its traducers" and thus to disregard the duty of communists elsewhere to make their own revolutions. According to the appeal, Ross would find no support for his alternative among young people, and his talk of "permissiveness run mad" and declining moral standards might please some "church groups" but revealed an ignorance of the current youth revolt.

The Ross group replied to the attack by insisting that revolutions could be made only by the masses, when conditions were ripe, and not by a revolutionary minority—any premature attempt would only lead to defeat and reprisals by capitalist rulers. The group rejected the leadership majority's "isolationist trends" and pledged its continuing allegiance to what it termed "the line of the world communist movement." It proposed that the party congress should adopt neither of the drafts before it and, instead, allow at least twelve months for further study, under the guidance of a committee representing both viewpoints. (*Tribune*, 11 March.) The Soviet organ *Pravda* (29 March) commended the alternative draft program as expressing "the position of a significant number of Australian communists."

Closely related to the Ross issue was the extensive debate engendered by a visit to the Soviet Union and Czechoslovakia in late 1969 and early 1970 by National Executive member William Brown, ostensibly at the invitation of the International Organization of Journalists (IOJ) to study the mass media in socialist countries in preparation for an Australian labor conference. The party leadership had attempted to delay Brown's departure on the grounds that no official invitation had been extended by the Communist Party of the Soviet Union (CPSU), or by the IOJ, through the CPA. Brown, a leading protagonist in the Ross group, repudiated the authority of the leadership, however, and left for Moscow, claiming to have been invited not as a representative of the

CPA, but in his capacity as a member of a journalists' association. It subsequently evolved that the only "credential" Brown carried with him was a letter of introduction from an Australian union functionary. Shortly after his return, Brown complained that the CPA had refused financial aid for a report on his findings. The booklet, *Socialism and Today's Mass Media*, was published in April at his own expense. (*Tribune*, 14 January, 18 February, 25 March, and 8 April.)

The Twenty-second Congress voted 118 to 12 in favor of the "Statement of Aims, Methods, and Organization," but with various amendments, including reaffirmation of the party's right to criticize "existing socialist-based societies." It endorsed both the party leadership's condemnation of the Czechoslovak invasion as well as the CPA's independent stand at the International Meeting of Communist and Workers' Parties in June 1969. (*Ibid.*, 1 April; see *YICA*, 1970, p. 517.)

Nine National Committee members who, according to the *Tribune* (10 June), had "exercised their party rights of democratic expression to contest party policies and decisions," failed to gain reelection: Edgar Ross, William Brown, Freda Brown, E. V. Elliott, Ralph Gibson, G. Curthoys, T. Wright, J. Waten, and J. Mitchell.

On the question of tactics, National Secretary Laurie Aarons spoke of the failure of conservative dissidents to comprehend the speed of technological change and monopolist growth, and the resultant modifications in capitalist society. Stressing the necessity to adjust thought, tactics, methods of work, and organization to the new situation, he added: "Many of us still tend to think in terms of the cold war, of the defensive period following 1949, of the need to avoid isolation of the Left." (*Tribune*, 1 April.)

In an explicit reassertion of CPA independence, the congress—revealing for the first time that correspondence had passed between the CPSU and the rebel Australian party in which the Soviets sought to persuade the CPA to curb its outspoken criticism of developments within the socialist bloc—restated its rejection of interference by any other party and of any "outside efforts to influence party members or bodies in any way." In a measure designed to "remove party functionaries from the direct influence of any other party" and, at the same time, reduce expenditures, the congress moved to "terminate the system of resident posting of staff correspondents overseas." Henceforth the party would rely on "analyses of various materials from overseas, contributed articles and, in special cases, short-term visits sponsored by [the] *Tribune* to make objective investigation of particular situations." The congress also directed that a 1970-71 membership-card reissue be undertaken in conjunction with a party census to "establish beyond doubt the areas of activity of the membership, together with other information." (*Ibid.*, 8 April.)

A major congress resolution—and one which clearly angered the CPSU (see below)—called for a "full Marxist analysis" of alleged shortcomings in the development of socialism in the different socialist countries: over-centralization of the economy; a bureaucracy which had "separated itself from the people"; inadequate recognition of the fact that socialism had "more problems to solve than just building the economy"; "curtailments of political democracy and intellectual freedom which, apart from being incorrect, [were] also harmful to the further progress of society"; and dogmatic ideologies used to "justify and perpetuate" those features of society expressing a "distorted concept of socialism." In conclusion, the CPA pledged to devote attention to the further understanding of the process at work within existing socialist nations—and particularly the Soviet Union—to learn the lessons of history, and the reasons for achievements and deformations. (*Ibid.*)

Another resolution warned that disciplinary action might be taken against the Ross minority for having engaged in "slander, misrepresentation and intrigue against majority decisions." The dissenters, it was pointed out, had stated publicly their "intention of refusing to accept the decisions of this congress should they disagree with them." (*Ibid.*)

Ross and Alf Watt announced in May the establishment of Socialist Publications, which would publish "from a Marxist-Leninist standpoint ... information and appropriate comment" covering national and international affairs, and provide avenues for discussing the ideas presented (*ibid.*, 20 May). The National Committee, charging that it had not been consulted in advance of the announcement, invited Ross and Watt to "explain their intentions" to the party leadership (*ibid.*, 27 May). Aarons denounced the formation of "a factional organization" as a "dishonest and divisive" move, amounting to the "establishment of a party within the party" (*ibid.*, 10 June). On 1 July the *Tribune* published a letter from Ross and Watt denying responsibility for party disunity—which they laid to "ill-advised policies and practices instituted by the leadership." They accused *Tribune* of distorting opposition views, and reaffirmed their intention to "proceed with our plans for a new publishing center, Socialist Publications, and with an appeal for support in the venture." Ross left for the Soviet Union on 1 July for "recreation and medical treatment." The first issue of the Ross-Watt monthly, *Australian Socialist*, came out later that month. It contained a number of attacks on CPA policy and called for the establishment of organizations around the publication.

On 15 July, the Czechoslovak party organ *Rude Právo* published a strong attack upon the CPA by Pavel Negedly. It stated that upon learning that the Czechoslovak question was to be on the agenda of the CPA congress, the Czechoslovak party leadership had sent a letter to the CPA leadership asking that the question not be discussed. The CPA had proceeded to distribute copies of the Czechoslovak letter to all congress delegates, demonstrating, Negedly charged, the "frivolous and uncomradely approach of the right-wing leadership" of the CPA and its deviation from Marxism-Leninism. The *Tribune* (12 August) responded by publishing the full text of Negedly's attack together with a reply which it urged that *Rudé Právo* publish "in a similar service to freedom of information." The CPA response declared, in part: "The whole world knows that the Czechoslovak people—workers, farmers, intellectuals, youth—did not voluntarily accept, and still resent deeply, the occupation of their country." *Rudé Právo* did not print the Australian reply or acknowledge receipt of it, or mention that the *Tribune* had published the Negedly article. The Soviets reprinted the Czechoslovak attack in *New Times* (Moscow, no. 36, 9 September), but ignored the Australian reply despite a plea by Laurie Aarons to the *New Times* editorial board that it be published "in the same spirit of free and open debate as shown by *Tribune*" (*Tribune*, 7 October).

During the following months, the CPA frequently demonstrated its identification with other independent or "progressive" communist elements. Representing the CPA at the congress of the Japan Communist Party (JCP), in July, Laurie Aarons told delegates that the JCP's "concept and practice of genuine independence on vital issues of our movement" had been "a source of support and assistance for [the CPA] in making its own decisions and expressing these views" (*ibid.*, 22 July). In September, Jiri Pelikan, the ousted head of Czechoslovak television, and for many years president of the International Union of Students, sent the CPA leadership a letter thanking the Australian party for its continued solidarity with the cause of Czechoslovak reform (*ibid.*, 30 September). The CPA magazine *Australian Left Review* sponsored a series of talks by the dissident French communist Roger Garaudy in September. A Romanian party delegation held talks with CPA leaders in Sydney from 1-9 October, following Romanian-Japanese party talks in Tokyo. A joint Romanian-Australian communiqué pledged efforts for "restoring and strengthening the unity of the international communist and workers' movement, based on principles of independence, equality of rights, noninterference in internal affairs, proletarian internationalism and observance of each party's right to establish its own political line by applying Marxist-Leninist teachings to the concrete conditions in each country" (*ibid.*, 7 October). The CPA stand on Czechoslovakia was restated in a message to the 26 November meeting in Paris of dissidents within the French party adhering to the views of the publication *Unir-Débat* (no. 48, 10 December).

The CPA National Executive, meanwhile, met on 22-23 July and issued a final warning to Ross and Watt. Should they fail to assure the party leadership before the 19 August meeting of the National Executive that they had ceased their disruptive actions, action would be considered in accordance with the party constitution and the congress decisions (*Tribune*, 29 July). Formal charges—of "breaches of the Rules and Constitution"—were laid against Ross and Watt at the August meeting. Watt was suspended from party membership, pending a hearing of the charges. Ross, still in the Soviet Union, had not yet responded to the July resolution of the National Executive. (*Ibid.*, 26 August.) A four-member "investigating committee" was then appointed by the National Committee. It upheld the National Executive charges, and the National Committee on 10 October, by a vote of 32 to 3, recommended the expulsion of Ross and Watt. It was reported that the three members who voted against the report expressed their rejection of the policies and actions of Ross and Watt, but were "against expulsions" (*ibid.*, 14 October). One of the CPA's leading trade unionists, Pat Clancy, had resigned from the National Committee in August, apparently in sympathy with the Ross-Watt faction. He gave as his reason the leadership majority's alleged failure to recognize "the fundamental fact that the national and international interests of the working class are indivisible" (*ibid.*, 12 August).

The CPA subsequently chose an unorthodox forum to press its views on the international communist movement and, in practical terms, to defy the Soviets publicly by bringing these views to European communists in order to gain support for its independent posture. CPA Vice-President Eric Aarons, chief editor of the *Australian Left Review* and brother of National Secretary Laurie Aarons, published an article in the dissident Austrian communist monthly *Wiener Tagebuch* (October) entitled "Australia: An Autonomous Communist Party." Aarons traced the deterioration of relations between the CPA and CPSU, dating from the CPA's neutrality in the Sino-Soviet conflict, up to current Soviet efforts to force the CPA to withdraw its condemnation of Soviet action in Czechoslovakia. The CPA's resistance to Chinese pressures in the early 1960's (the same pressures which resulted, he observed, in the capture of the Communist Party of New Zealand by the Chinese) had been misunderstood in Moscow as "blind support" for everything the CPSU did or said—be it the dismissal of Khrushchev, the Jewish question, the infringement of artistic and intellectual freedom, or general problems of socialist democracy. Persistent and "often very clumsy" attempts directed from Moscow to encourage individual Australian communists to undermine and overthrow the leaders of the CPA and replace them by others "acceptable to the CPSU" had been decisively defeated by the congress's democratic elimination of the "Moscovite" opposition. Though the defeated pro-Soviet elements in the CPA had all but formally seceded, Aarons said, they had deferred to Soviet sentiment that the time was inopportune to promote a splinter party openly. Aarons then raised the larger question of the Soviet image within the world communist movement. The CPSU had refused to comment on "fully documented" charges of interference in CPA internal affairs and to discuss fundamental questions of principle. The Soviet attitude could only lead to further splitting and weakening of the already painfully divided and weakened world movement and was a bad omen for all those "naïve enough to think that the CPSU's relations with them rest upon socialist principles and not upon the presumed interests of the Soviet Union."

The CPSU Central Committee message to the CPA on its fiftieth anniversary (October) expressed the hope that the Australian communists would be able to overcome their difficulties on the basis of a "principled" approach, resisting attempts to distort "the purity of Marxist-Leninist teachings." (TASS, 29 October.)

Domestic Views and Activities. During most of 1970 the CPA's attention to domestic affairs was overshadowed by its preoccupation with intra-party developments. For this reason the party played only a peripheral role in the political campaign for the Victoria and South Australia state elections of 30 May, entering Elliott Johnston as candidate in South Australia and no candidate in Victoria. Similarly, the CPA decided in October against participation in the 21 November Senate elections. Instead, it pledged to "intervene actively in the campaign," urging "first preference votes" to Australian Labor Party slates. (*Tribune*, 14 October.)

The cornerstone of CPA domestic agitation was the allegedly "chronic" shortage of funds for social and other vital needs of the nation as a result of the government's "misguided priority policies." According to the CPA, taxation on incomes was distorted, defense spending disproportionately high, and genuine tax and wage justice allegedly would come about only when society itself was transformed by radical socialist change. (*Ibid.*, 4 March.)

The party continued to endorse draft resisters and to urge noncompliance with the conscription requirements of the National Service Act. The CPA National Committee on 31 May condemned an alleged government bid to introduce "forced labor camps for noncompliers," and called for wide opposition to this "desperate move to halt growing opposition to the government's aggressive policies in Vietnam and the rest of Indochina." (*Ibid.*, 3 June.)

Pursuing its efforts to "establish a dialogue between Christians and Marxists," the CPA arranged a conference with a seven-denominational delegation of the Victorian Council of Churches at Mount Martha on 6-8 February. The conference signaled no noteworthy advance for the communists vis-à-vis religious groupings. The delegates agreed, according to a vague and generalized final communiqué, that the dialogue should be continued "in similar and other forms," and noted: "We have found considerable agreement in our common concern for humanity on a world-wide basis, and have felt the urgency of encouraging Australians to share our concern." (*Ibid.*, 18 February.)

CPA agitation against the Papua-New Guinea administration of "white planter and business bosses" appeared to be merely an echo of Australian Labor Party opposition to government policy. The CPA endorsed Labor Party demands for immediate self-government in Papua-New Guinea and full independence by 1976; it accused the government of a "deliberate operation to smash militancy on the island," and exhorted the Papua-New Guinea people to wage "various forms of struggle" for early independence and a just society (*ibid.*, 14 January). On another racially toned question, the CPA professed to champion the cause of the "oppressed" Aborigine population in Australia, whose aspirations for independent development, allegedly, were being met by a "subtle modern racism called 'assimilation'" (*ibid.*, 1 April).

International Views and Positions. The CPA's current interpretation of communist "internationalism," as enunciated by Laurie Aarons at the 1970 party congress, was described as "support for all anti-imperialist forces." Despite disagreements with the Soviet party, the CPA would continue to be "all the way" in its support of the Soviet Union against "imperialism"—and of China, Albania, or any other socialist country. Similarly, while the CPA had "deep reservations" toward certain Arab nations with regard to their "anti-Jewish" posture, it identified itself with them in their stand against "Israeli aggression." (*Tribune*, 1 April.)

The external policies of the Australian government came under continued CPA attack. The government's decision, in February, to sign the nuclear non-proliferation treaty was termed by the CPA only a "marginal setback for the most hawkish elements." Australia, through the U.S. base network on its soil, was reportedly involved in the "vortex of the opposing world nuclear systems." The secrecy surrounding the Pine Gap and Woomera installations and the nuclear strike role of the F-111 aircraft which Australia had on order allegedly heightened public misgivings concerning Australia's U.S.-assigned role in its nuclear system. (*Ibid.*, 25 February.)

The party commented widely on the refusal of the government to grant a passport to the left-wing Australian journalist Wilfred Burchett, who entered Australia in March for the first time in nineteen years (having repeatedly been denied admission) and whose "anti-imperialist" writings have appeared frequently in communist and other left-wing publications in many parts of the world. Suggesting that the government's handling of the Burchett case had "at all times been masterminded in Washington," the CPA claimed (*ibid.*, 11 March) that Burchett possessed evidence showing that Australia as long ago as 1954 had been a party to U.S. plans for aggressive intervention in Vietnam, including an Australian army force about equal to the one now committed. In the party's view, the government was attempting to destroy public confidence in Burchett and thus minimize the effect of his future exposures of U.S. and Australian "rulers."

In anti-war activities, the CPA still failed to play any key role, due to the reluctance of many anti-war groups to associate openly with the communists. It did, however, secure a seat on the executive board of the major anti-war event of the year, the Vietnam Moratorium, initiated in November 1969 and including some 100 participating groups. In 1970 the Vietnam Moratorium organized nationwide demonstrations on 8-10 May and 18-20 September which did more, in the view of the CPA, to "assert the changed political climate in Australia than anything that has happened in Parliament or out, for years," and to demonstrate the low level of popular support for the government's war policy. (Editorial, *ibid.*, 20 May.)

The CPA accused the government also of conspiring with Japan to exploit the Sino-Soviet conflict so as to further "imperialist" interests throughout Southeast Asia (*ibid.*, 25 March). The *Tribune* foreign correspondent Malcolm Salmon wrote in the 27 May issue that the deliberately "low profile" struck in the communiqué of the 16-17 May Djakarta conference on Cambodia should deceive no one. The participation of Japan, he observed, represented a "historic turning point in the postwar life of Southeast Asia." As Asia's only imperialist giant, Japan was trying its hand at "regional diplomacy," having failed in its bid during the Second World War for domination by military means.

Publications. The CPA's weekly newspaper *Tribune*, its bimonthly *Australian Left Review*, and its quarterly theoretical journal *Discussion* are published in Sydney.

*   *   *

The ACP(ML). The founder and chairman of the Australian Communist Party (Marxist-Leninist) is Edward Hill, a Melbourne attorney. The vice-chairman is Clarence O'Shea (a second vice-chairman, P. Malone, died in late 1970); the secretary is Frank Johnson. The party is estimated to have about 250 members, drawn from among trade unionists and some student groups.

The ACP(ML) maintains extensive contacts with Communist China, and its statements faithfully reflect Chinese views. Praise for China's Cultural Revolution and criticism of Soviet policy appear regularly in the party's newspaper, *Vanguard*, and its monthly theoretical journal, *Australian Communist*.

The ACP(ML) heralded China's first space satellite as "a further great blow against the war threats of U.S. imperialism and Soviet revisionism" (NCNA, 28 April). A message to the Chinese Communist Party on the twenty-first anniversary of the founding of the Chinese People's Republic spoke of China's "great victories in socialist construction which are victories for all the world's toiling and oppressed people." Maoist ideology was said to be Marxism-Leninism at an entirely new and higher stage" and to point out "the path of struggle to liberation and victory over imperialism for all the world's people." (*Ibid.*, 2 October.)

V. B.

BURMA

The Burma Communist Party (BCP) was founded on 15 August 1939 under the leadership of Thakin Soe. In 1946, following a dispute over the correct strategy for achieving Burmese independence, Thakin Soe withdrew his faction of the BCP and formed the Communist Party of Burma (CPB), known as the Red Flags, and Thakin Than Tun founded a new BCP, known as the White Flags.[1] While the Red Flags went underground to initiate armed insurrection against the government, the White Flags placed primary emphasis on legal struggle until 1948, when they, too, went underground and launched armed attacks.

Between 1951 and 1963 some coordination of activities existed between the White Flags and the Red Flags. In July and August of 1963 a group of White Flag communists who had taken up residence in Communist China returned to Burma to participate in negotiations between General Ne Win's "Revolutionary Government of the Union of Burma" and members of both communist parties. In November of that year, after the breakdown of negotiations, the China-based group joined Thakin Than Tun's BCP (White Flags) in an attempt to dominate it. Subsequently, Thakin Soe's CPB (Red Flags) was labeled as Trotskyist by the other communists. While both the White Flags and the Red Flags have continued insurgent activities, the Red Flags appear to have receded into the background, with most pronouncements and terrorist activities originating from the White Flags. In December 1967 a member of the Red Flags surrendered and revealed that an underground united front of the two parties was formed in southern Burma in 1966 and was dissolved shortly thereafter.

Since the military coup led by General Ne Win on 2 March 1962, the only legal political party has been the Burma Socialist Program Party, which was established by the Ne Win government. The Revolutionary Government of the Union of Burma holds all legislative, executive, and judicial powers, which are exercised by General Ne Win as chairman of the Union Revolutionary Council.

Estimates of White Flag membership range from 400 to 5,000. As a result of government offensives, communist insurgents have shifted their activities from central and southern Burma to the northeastern border regions. The population of Burma is 27,700,000 (estimated 1970).

Little information is available regarding the socioeconomic background of the Burmese communists. The ranks of the BCP have, in general, been filled with villagers who served in the militia. During 1968 and 1969, party leaders reportedly were seeking to enroll members of the younger generation. The majority of communist leaders have come from moderately well-to-do village families, merchant families in town, or families formerly associated with the British civil service. In addition, most leaders have received at least a high school education.

---

[1]Considerable confusion exists regarding the precise names of the two groups. While the Burma Communist Party (BCP) generally refers to the White Flags and while the Communist Party of Burma (CPB) generally refers to the Red Flags, the two names have frequently been used interchangeably.

Leadership and Organization. Internal party friction has led to significant leadership and organizational changes within the White Flags (BCP). Following the assassination of the party chairman, Thakin Than Tun, on 24 September 1968, the first vice-chairman, Thakin Ba Thein Tin, announced that Thakin Zin had been elected to fill the vacant post and that together they would lead an armed revolution. A purge ensued, and by the end of 1969 only two Politburo members—Thakin Chit and Thakin Ba Thein Tin—had escaped execution at the hands of the party or the government. In the same manner the Central Committee was reduced to no more than nine members: Thakin Tin Tun, (killed 16 November 1970), "Comrade Tote", Thakin Zin, Thakin Pe Tint, Thakin Ba Thein Tin, Kyaw Mya, Thakin Chit, Thakin Pu (who may have been captured in 1968), and Naw Seng.

Intelligence reports in 1970 added Than Shwe ("Ko Kauk"), Aung Myint, and Bo Thet Tin to the list of known Central Committee members. Most of the power apparently was wielded by Thakin Chit, and Thakin Ba Thein Tin. In the fall, government troops in the Shan states killed Thakin Tin Tun, BCP Central Committee member and secretary of the National Democratic United Front (see below) (*Botataung*, Rangoon, 8 December). Thakin Tin Tun (alias "Kalagy," "Myint Maung," and "Mya Maung") had been in charge of the BCP Central Headquarters for the Kachen state, the Northern and Southern Shan states, and Upper and Central Burma since 1963.

BCP organizational structure reportedly extends from the level of the Politburo, through the Central Committee, the district committee, down to the township committee. It is estimated that BCP Central Committee members and supporters numbering about 200 resided in Peking up to the time of the 1967 anti-Chinese riots in Rangoon (*Washington Post*, 17 May 1970). BCP statements refer occasionally to the "Delegation of the Central Committee of the Communist Party of Burma in Peking," of which Thakin Ba Thein Tin is head.

The BCP has maintained a close association with the illegal National Democratic United Front (NDUF), a bloc of left-wing and pro-communist groups that was founded in 1959. The NDUF includes the Karen National Unity Party (KNUP), whose former chairman, Mah Ba Zan, is the leader of the front; the New Mon State Party, led by Naing Shwe Zin; the Kayah Progressive Party; and the Chin Supreme Committee. The NDUF is dominated by the White Flags, the only other significant element within it being the KNUP, with a membership of 1,000 to 2,500. The BCP engages in occasional joint offensives with the KNUP in the delta region. It has also collaborated with the militant Karen National Defense Organization (KNDO), which claims to have 7,000 men under arms but probably has about 5,000. During 1970, KNDO insurgent activities centered around the Salween River in the Karen state.

The BCP has also attempted to infiltrate the separatist Kachins, but with only temporary success. Nevertheless, several Kachin Independence Army (KIA) groups have received military instruction in the Chinese People's Republic. Among those thus trained was BCP Central Committee member Naw Seng, who returned to northeastern Burma with some 300 guerrillas in 1967 in order to establish a multiracial insurgent force. This "Northeast Command," is believed to be composed of ethnic minority peoples from both sides of the border and to receive material and political support from Peking. Membership estimates range from several hundred to several thousand, with 2,000 to 3,000 being the figure most commonly cited. During 1970 the "Northeast Command" engaged in widespread acts of sabotage. In March, the KIA attacked Naw Seng's headquarters near Lashio, with heavy casualties on both sides. Naw Seng is said subsequently to have moved his headquarters farther north to Bhamo.

In addition to the above insurgent groups, the Nagas in the western portion of the Burmese northeast have formed the "Eastern Naga Revolutionary Council" (ENRC), which engages in insurgent activities along the India-Burma border. During the past several years, groups of

Burmese Nagas have reportedly received training and indoctrination in China, which also supplies the ERNC with arms. There appears to be a movement, encouraged by China, toward collaboration between the ENRC and the Naga insurgents in India (*Hindustan Times*, New Delhi, 26 April).

Party Internal Affairs. The initiation of a "cultural revolution" within the BCP in 1967, with the expressed aim of eliminating the "revisionist idea of seizing political power peacefully by taking the parliamentary road," intensified the already existing split between those favoring armed struggle and those in favor of legal struggle. By the end of 1967, Chairman Thakin Than Tun and his group of "Peking returnees" (party members and followers who returned from Peking after the 1964 Central Committee meeting), who had launched the movement, had bypassed the normal party organization. On 24 September 1968 the bloody purges associated with the "cultural revolution" culminated in the assassination of Thakin Than Tun by one of his followers.

Although the purges slowed down somewhat during 1969 and 1970, captured party members reported that the BCP remained split at all levels while Central Committee members and their followers continued to execute fellow members and no criticism of Central Committee directives was tolerated. Reports indicated that in 1970, the BCP was completely controlled by Peking returnees (John Badgley, "The Union of Burma: Age Twenty-Two," *Asian Survey*, no. 2, February 1970, p. 151). The combined factors of the purges, the death of Thakin Tin Tun (1970), and hardships such as lack of food and supplies led to a decline in BCP morale, giving rise to mass surrenders during 1970 to the government, which claimed that the BCP was in "disarray," "short of supplies," and "demoralized" (Rangoon radio, domestic service, 26 June).

Domestic Attitudes and Activities. A BCP statement in 1969 outlined the "most critical questions in winning victory for the armed revolution in Burma":

> (1) [Carry out] the military line of "crushing the enemy offensives with our offensives," which was formulated with military struggle as its center; (2) [carry out] the rural class line, which was formulated for the establishment of red political power in the countryside; and (3) [carry out] the great program of "crushing revisionism," which was formulated for combating revisionism. (Thakin Ba Thein Tin, quoted by *Peking Review*, no. 13, 28 March.)

BCP statements on strategy and tactics stressed armed struggle and denied the efficacy of peaceful means:

> The Communist Party of Burma, under the guidance of Marxism-Leninism-Mao Tse-tung thought, has waged a resolute struggle against the so-called road of peaceful development of modern revisionism and has been holding aloft the victorious banner of armed revolution. (Statement of the Central Committee, 22 April 1970, quoted by NCNA, 13 May.)

Assassinated leader Thakin Than Tun was praised for integrating Marxism-Leninism and "Mao Tse-tung thought" with Burmese practice and thereby developing a "correct program, line, and policy for the liberation of the Burmese people" (*ibid.*).

Party analyses were consistently optimistic about the current situation. Popular sentiment was said to be increasingly favorable toward the communists, while dissatisfaction and distrust of the Ne Win government mounted to new heights. Claiming a solid alliance with the peasant masses, the BCP viewed its campaigns against the government as placing Ne Win's position in serious jeopardy.

Despite the BCP's optimistic reports, there were indications of possible adverse internal repercussions from the assassination of Thakin Than Tun. The continuing intraparty strife seemed to imply that no new leader capable of reunifying the shattered party leadership had yet appeared, although BCP directives called upon party members to strengthen unity in the party and its armed forces under the leadership of Chairman Thakin Zin and Vice-Chairman Thakin Ba Thein Tin.

The BCP has called for the formation of a "people's democratic federal republic," which would embrace, among other groups, the "revolutionary minority nationalities." Placing special emphasis on alliances with the Kachins, Karens, and Shans, the BCP claims to be the only political party capable of solving the country's minority problem. Nevertheless, it appears that BCP-minority relations have deteriorated markedly over the past few years. A BCP Central Committee statement specifically referred to "growing opposition and attacks by the masses of various nationalities." The *Working People's Daily* (Rangoon, 29 August 1970) reported that a group of 132 Chin nationals, former followers of a BCP member, Bo Thet Tin, had surrendered to government troops on 22 August. They claimed to be attempting to escape persecution by BCP leaders. They further averred that the communists were forcing the Chin people to give up their traditions and customs.

Unity in the NDUF apparently has been shattered. A local newspaper declared in mid-1970: "Multicolored insurgents, who have been menacing the people . . . are fighting each other because of dissension.... [A] Karen National Defense Organization (KNDO) group ... clashed with a National Democratic United Front group.... [A] White Flag communist group ... has joined the National Democratic United Front and declared war on the [KNDO] group." (*Botataung*, 24 May.)

Despite internal divisions, defections, and government "encirclement and suppression" campaigns, the BCP continued to engage in armed insurrection and sabotage. The NCNA reported (21 February): "In Pegu, Kaya State, Magwe, Irrawaddy and Tenasserim areas [of Central and South Burma] the people's armed forces hit hard at the enemy and fought many outstanding battles" as well as in Arakan. BCP activities appeared, however, to have gravitated to the Lashio area in the north, seventy-five miles from the China border. In May there was heavy fighting near Hsewi and Lashio, and in October, more than twenty clashes between communists and government forces took place, in which some 500 rebels were killed. There followed a decided lull in hostilities in November. In addition to clashing with government forces, the insurgents destroyed bridges and roads, ambushed government rice transports to seize the cargo, severed lines of communication, and, in one area, closed down twenty-three state schools. Burmese government troops claimed to have killed some 1,000 insurgents during the year (Badgley, *op. cit.*, p. 151).

Insurgent activities in the northeast have placed the Burmese government in an awkward position. Wishing to remain on peaceful terms with their gigantic neighbor, Burmese authorities have ordered government troops to avoid allowing stray bullets to hit Chinese soil during counterinsurgency campaigns. Thus the troops refrain from using their full fire power when fighting takes place close to the border. Local inhabitants add that when the guerrillas lose a battle, they simply flee to the privileged sanctuary offered by China (*Washington Post*, 17 May). Inhabitants of Kyugok (situated 100 yards from the border) claim to have witnessed Chinese troops assisting Burmese guerrillas in attacks on that town and in evacuating the wounded to China (*Washington Post*, 17 May). One correspondent claimed that Naw Seng commanded the invading forces at Kyugok. Government troops experienced three major confrontations with Chinese and insurgent forces during the month of May alone.

During the early months of 1970, the Chinese established two major military bases in the far northern frontier area north of Putao, near the junction of the Burma-China-India borders. According to a correspondent among the Karen rebel forces, the bases have radar equipment, and runways for aircraft, and hangars built in caves. He claimed that some 20,000 Chinese irregulars, primarily people's militia from tribal groups in Yunnan, appear to be operating in Shan and Kachin states of Burma (*Daily Telegraph*, London, 15 April.)

International Views and Positions. BCP pronouncements during 1970 balanced statements attributing the party's "improved situation" to international proletarian cooperation with expositions of the primary importance of self-reliance and the efficacy of armed struggle, even in isolation from other countries.

Although the BCP is firmly aligned with mainland China, the Burmese government has been attempting to improve its relations with China, which grew strained in mid-1967 as a result of the anti-Chinese riots. As a gesture of good will, in 1970 the government released all Chinese nationals who were jailed after the 1967 disturbances. During the first part of 1969, China appeared to be responding to government overtures by decreasing the intensity of its attacks and the militancy of its appeals to the communists. China subsequently abandoned this new approach although full diplomatic relations between the two countries were restored in 1970. Chinese attacks on the Ne Win government were stepped up, and the BCP was openly endorsed. Burmese communists received military training in China, and Chinese are known to be among the insurgents in the border area. While little, if any, Chinese materiel is believed to have reached communist guerrillas in southern Burma, those in the northern Shan state are reportedly dependent on China for most of their supplies.

No cordiality is wasted between the Burmese communists and the Soviets. The Ne Win government and the national army are regarded "progressive forces" in Burma by the Soviets, who have castigated the Burmese communists' fractricidal war and attacked the class basis of the party:

> Who precisely is it that makes up the ranks of the opposition [BCP and CPB] that is acting through force of arms? It is the former large landowners, the usurers and all those whom the new social structure has deprived of their former privileges. (*Pravda*, 4 January 1970.)

BCP support for China was paralleled by condemnation of the Soviet Union's "renegade clique." The BCP Central Committee statement commemorating the Lenin Centenary was a single-minded attack:

> [The renegade clique has] continued to undermine Burma's armed revolution and world revolution. [It] has turned the state of the dictatorship of the proletariat . . . into a state of the dictatorship of the bourgeoisie [and] has openly practiced social-imperialism. [Its members] have become the new tsars. Under no circumstances can the Brezhnev renegade clique, which has completely discarded the banner of Leninism and pursued 100 per cent revisionism, become Leninist. (Statement of the Central Committee of the BCP, 22 April, quoted by NCNA, 13 May.)

The BCP further accused the Soviets of carrying out "military provocations and aggression along the Sino-Soviet border in an attempt to launch a war against socialist China" (*ibid.*).

The U.S. actions against Vietnamese communist enclaves in Cambodia in the spring were regarded as "another threat to the people in Burma, Thailand, Malaya, Indonesia, and other Southeast Asian countries who are struggling for their own liberation [and] also a serious provocation against socialist China, the great rear area of world revolution" (Statement of the Central Committee, 10 May, quoted by *Peking Review*, no. 21, 22 May).

In a six-point declaration on world affairs, the BCP condemned the "coup d'état staged by the Lon Nol-Sirik Matak clique" and the U.S. action, declared support for the Joint Declaration of the "Summit Conference of the Indochinese Peoples" and for the Royal Government of National Union as the "sole legal government of the state of Cambodia," attacked the Soviet Union for failing to condemn Lon Nol and Sirik Matak by name and for not recognizing the Royal Government of National Union, and endorsed Mao's dictum calling on the people of the world to unite and defeat "U.S. imperialism" (*ibid.*).

Publications. The official organ of the BCP is *People's Power*. BCP statements are also carried in the media of the Chinese People's Republic.

* * *

During the last few years, the Red Flags (CPB) have become little more than a personality cult for their founder and chairman, Thakin Soe. In early 1968, Thakin Soe indicated to Ne Win the desire of his group to assume legal status. The following year, a number of Red Flag Central Committee members surrendered to Burmese authorities. In addition, one was killed by government troops. In 1970 there was occasional mention of Red Flag skirmishes with government troops.

On 8 November, Thakin Soe was captured by government troops along with three other Central Committee members: Khiang Tun Lwin, Ye Htut, and Min Maung, thus sharply reducing the remaining CPB leadership. The same month, CPB Central Committee member U Thaw Ka surrendered. On 14 December another CPB Central Committee member, Soe Lin, surrendered to government forces. Soe Lin claimed that many other Red Flags would like to surrender but were intimidated by communist reports of government torture and persecution of surrendered insurgents.

The *Working People's Daily* (4 September) claimed that the Arakan Communist Party, a Red Flag splinter party in southern Burma, had split further into two hostile factions during mid-1970.

S. E. Y.

CAMBODIA

The People's Revolutionary Party of Cambodia (Dang Nhan Dan Cach Mang Cao Min; PRP) was founded in 1951. Its name and statutes were originally set forth in Vietnamese and later translated into Cambodian. Following the Geneva Agreements on Indochina (1954), Cambodian communists sought to escape the label of "Vietnamese puppets" by forming the Khmer People's Party (Pracheachon Party; PP) in 1955. They have continued to operate through this front, although since the arrest of PP leaders in 1962 and the subsequent ban of the party itself, little has been heard of this organization. There have been references by Prince Sihanouk—the Cambodian chief of state until his deposition in 1970—to a "Khmer Revolutionary Front," reportedly commanded by South Vietnamese communists and based in South Vietnam near the districts of Svay Teap and Rumduol. Repeated references have also been made to the "Khmer Rouge" guerrillas, but their exact relationship with the PRP, the PP, and the "Khmer Revolutionary Front" is unknown.

The PRP is illegal and is estimated to have no more than 100 members. The PP is thought to have some 1,000 members and the support of several thousand sympathizers. According to Cambodian government sources, the Khmer Revolutionary Front has about 100 adherents. Estimates of Khmer Rouge strength range between 500 and 4,000. In addition, the Cambodian guerrillas have considerable support from South and North Vietnamese communist troops operating in the country (see below). The population of Cambodia is 7,100,000 (estimated 1970). The Khmers comprise about 85 per cent of the population. Ethnic minorities include some 450,000 Chinese (about 6.5 per cent), 250,000 to 300,000 Vietnamese (about 4.5 per cent), 80,000 Cham-Malays, 50,000 Khmer Loeu, 20,000 Thai and Lao, and 5,000 Europeans (mostly French). At least 100,000 Vietnamese have left Cambodia and gone to South Vietnam since March 1970 (*Background Notes*, U.S. Department of State, September).

During recent years Prince Sihanouk's professed neutrality had led to increasing Vietnamese communist occupation of sanctuaries along Cambodia's eastern border. Early in 1970 the government requested the North Vietnamese and the Provisional Revolutionary Government of South Vietnam (PRG) to work out a schedule for the withdrawal of their armed forces from Cambodian territory, but at a joint meeting in Phnom Penh on 16 March the Vietnamese representatives were willing to discuss only their demands for reparations for the sacking of their embassies by Cambodian mobs on 11 March—an occurrence which is thought to have been sanctioned, if not inspired, by the government. On 18 March, the National Assembly voted to depose Sihanouk, who was then in Moscow, and a triumvirate composed of Cheng Heng, Lon Nol, and Sirik Matak assumed effective control of the government. On 28 March, North Vietnam and the PRG announced the withdrawal of their representatives from Phnom Penh.

Sihanouk meanwhile went to Peking, where on 23 March he announced the formation of the "National United Front of Kampuchea" (NUFK). Although avowedly neutralist, the NUFK is headed mainly by well-known communist and ultra-left-wing elements and has been active in encouraging armed opposition in Cambodia to the new government (see below).

Leadership and Organization. Little is known of the leadership and organization of the PRP, the PP, and the Khmer Rouge (see *YICA*, 1970, p. 531).

In late 1969 it was reported that Tou Samouth was "president of the clandestine Khmer communist party"—presumably the PRP. Lon Nol has stated that Tou Samouth, who has commanded Khmer Rouge guerrillas in the field, is the head of the Khmer Rouge. According to another report, Son Ngoc Minh in 1970 was leading the PRP from Hanoi (*Far Eastern Economic Review*, 6 August). Sihanouk has repeatedly stated from Peking that Khieu Samphan, Hou Youn, and Hu Nim are the leaders of the PP; he further has maintained that the PP has supporters among Cambodian student unions in France, the Soviet Union, and East Germany.

Khmer Rouge leadership is composed mainly of former members of the Viet Minh, Khmer Viet Minh, and Khmer Issarak (Free Cambodia Organization), most of whom reportedly have been PRP members since 1954. The Khmer Rouge rank and file is largely recruited from among dissatisfied peasants and some ethnic Cambodians residing in Vietnam (referred to as Khmer Krom). One guerrilla leader mentioned by name in 1970 was Neou Pal, who commanded a sixty-man mobile armed group responsible for maintaining liaison with rebel groups and ensuring delivery of their supplies; leaders of the band reportedly were trained in North Vietnam. Other alleged Khmer Rouge leaders include Phieun Hak, Nuon Son, and Phouk Chhay.

Cambodian communists have operated through the Vietnamese and Chinese minorities in the country, with notable infiltration of the Vietnamese Community Association, the Viet Khieu.

Domestic Attitudes and Activities. Communist tactics in Cambodia have followed a pattern of propaganda and subversion stressing the Chinese communist line of violent revolution. Special emphasis has been given to propaganda efforts among students, intellectuals, and the Vietnamese and Chinese minorities.

The PRP has never published a domestic program. The Khmer Rouge, however, has denounced alleged governmental corruption and collusion with "foreign imperialism," failure to make national progress, neglect of national defense, and exploitation of the people.

On 23 April 1970 the PP, in a statement supporting Sihanouk's 23 March announcement of the NUFK, declared:

> [The PP] has consistently kept to its political stand, that of uniting the entire people . . . regardless of political tendencies, in order to wage a struggle against the U.S. imperialists and their henchmen to defend peace, independence, neutrality, sovereignty and territorial integrity and for democratic liberties and better living conditions of the people. . . . Only by uniting the entire people and using all forms of struggle, [and setting up] a patriotic, peaceful and truly neutral government . . . is it possible to achieve a truly independent, peaceful, neutral and prosperous Cambodia. (Quoted, *Vietnam Courier*, Hanoi, 9 May.)

Thus it can be seen that the PP does not wish to be regarded as openly pro-communist, but rather as nationalist and neutralist in a country which espouses a foreign policy of nonalignment.

The Cambodian communists quickly declared their support for the NUFK and the "Royal Government of National Union" (RGNU) which Sihanouk proclaimed on 5 May from Peking (see below). During the rest of the year it was difficult to distinguish between bona fide communist actions and those undertaken by Sihanouk's supporters in Cambodia. Reportedly, however, at a meeting held in Peking in July at the behest of the PRG, the Khmer Rouge refused to recognize Sihanouk's leadership of their movement, claiming that he was an opportunist. Thus, though their anti-government activities might parallel or supplement those of Sihanouk's supporters, they were not carried out under his command.

As in previous years, Cambodian and Vietnamese communists encouraged the Khmer Loeu to oppose the central government. The Khmer Loeu have been alarmed by a large ethnic Khmer influx into their territory in an attempt by the central government to settle the sparsely populated region. Their rebellion grew from minor incidents to significant proportions during 1970. About 400,000 Khmer Loeu dissidents belong to a movement known as "Fulro," which operates in Ratanakiri Province with the support of South Vietnamese communist agents who provide arms and advice.

International Views and Positions. Although there appeared to be extensive communist activity in Cambodia throughout 1970, after March it was conducted mainly in the name of the NUFK (see below). Neither the PRP or the PP as such attended the "Summit Conference of the Indochinese Peoples" (see below), where the NUFK represented Cambodia.

The Cambodian communist movement is heavily dominated by North Vietnam. Before the change of government in March, there were estimated to be from 23,000 (according to U.S. military sources) to 65,000 (according to Cambodian military sources) North Vietnamese and PRG troops stationed along Cambodia's eastern border with South Vietnam. These soldiers came into frequent conflict with the increasingly anticommunist central government. They aided domestic insurgencies, such as the aforementioned Khmer Loeu rebellion; they also furnished advisers and weapons to the Khmer Rouge. After the change in the government leadership at Phnom Penh, the Vietnamese communists threw their weight behind the pro-Sihanouk forces of the NUFK. Cambodian authorities fear that North Vietnam has not only political but also territorial designs on its neutralist neighbor.

Ideologically, the PRP and the PP have tended to favor the Chinese position in the Sino-Soviet controversy. The Khmer Rouge are reputed to be equipped with matériel of Chinese manufacture. Nevertheless, Chinese support for Cambodian communists was subordinated to the maintenance of state relations until the overthrow of Sihanouk and the establishment of the NUFK.

Publications. The official organ of the Pracheachon Party is *Somleeng Apyiakrut*, a semiweekly publication. The PP also puts out three other journals: *Mitt Pheap, Ek Peap*, and *L'-Observateur*. The official Vietnamese communist organ in Cambodia is a daily newspaper, *Trung Lap* (Neutrality).

*　　*　　*

The NUFK and the RGNU. Internal Affairs. On 18 March 1970, while he was in Moscow, Prince Sihanouk was voted out of office by the Cambodian National Assembly. Five days later, in Peking, he announced the formation of the National United Front of Kampuchea. Although Sihanouk has repeatedly stressed the neutrality of his stand, the men he chose as his ministers in the RGNU were either acknowledged communists or members of the extreme left wing. In a September interview, he described the present tendency of the RGNU as "definitely pro-communist" (*Le Monde*, Paris, 27/28 September). There was speculation that the prince was being held virtual prisoner in Peking as a figurehead for the RGNU. This possibility was strengthened by his surprising absence from the funeral of French ex-President de Gaulle in the fall, the greatly reduced publicity accorded Sihanouk in China later in the year, and the fact that despite his announced plan to reside alternately in Peking and Moscow, he did not venture outside China and its immediate periphery. Sihanouk himself told a newspaperman that he had repeatedly expressed the wish to go to the "liberated areas" of Cambodia, and that North Vietnamese Prime Minister Pham Van Dong had refused permission on the grounds that his safety could not be guaranteed (*al-Jumhuriyah*, Cairo, 21 November).

On 3 to 4 May, the NUFK held a Congress in Peking at which members of the Political Bureau were "elected," the NUFK political program was adopted, and the Royal Government of National Union was formed. Sihanouk announced the composition of the NUFK Politburo on 5 May as follows: Penn Nouth (chairman), General Duong Sam Ol, Chau Seng, Chan Youran, Chea San, Hu Nim, Khieu Samphan, Thiounn Mumm, Hou Youn, Hout Sambath, and Sarin Chhak. Three of these—PP members Hu Nim, Khieu Samphan, and Hou Youn—were allegedly carrying out revolutionary struggle in the "liberated areas" of Cambodia. The others, like Sihanouk, were in Peking.

When Sihanouk announced the composition of the NUFK leadership, he also declared the formation under the leadership of the NUFK—with himself as head of state—of the Royal Government of National Union (RGNU), composed of Penn Nouth as premier and Khieu Samphan as deputy premier (also minister of national defense and leader of the resistance inside Cambodia), with the following heads of ministries: Sarin Chhak (foreign affairs), Chau Seng (special missions), Chan Youran (popular education and youth), Dr. Ngo Hu (public health and religious and social affairs), Thiounn Mumm (economy and finance), General Duong Sam Ol (military equipment and armament), Hu Nim (information and propaganda), Hout Sambath (public works, telecommunications, and reconstruction), Hou Youn (interior, communal reforms, and cooperatives), and Chea San (justice and judicial reforms). Later Keat Chhon (minister delegate to the premier) and Thiounn Prasith (minister in charge of coordination of the effort of struggle for national liberation) were added; both became alternate members of the NUFK Politburo.

The leadership overlap between the RGNU and the NUFK is striking—eleven of the twelve original ministers being also NUFK Politburo members and both bodies being headed by Penn Nouth (although Sihanouk reserved for himself the position of head of state of the RGNU). On 20 and 21 August, the NUFK Central Committee met and established a Permanent Secretariat of three members and a Secretariat to the Politburo composed of the two alternate members, Keat Chhon and Thiounn Prasith. A joint communique issued by the NUFK and the RGNU on 17 September again lengthened the list of RGNU leaders, designating the following as vice-ministers: Poc Doeus Komar (foreign affairs), Mme Leng Thirith (popular education and youth), Chou Chet (public health and religious and social affairs), Koy Toum (economy and finance), Kong Sodip (national defense), Sor Thouk (interior and security), and Tiv Ol (information and propaganda). All of the new vice-ministers were said to be "fighting on the interior front of the country" (quoted, *Peking Review*, no. 40, 30 September). The communiqué's description of them as "resistance fighters for long years" made it probable that the new vice-ministers were members of the Khmer Rouge resistance. Chou Chet was previously a member of the PP Central Committee. Sihanouk himself was reported to have stated that it is the vice ministers and not the Peking-based leaders of the RGNU who "really govern." A circular signed by Penn Nouth formally confirmed the fact that the vice-ministers possessed the actual authority. Thus those in Peking were merely titular ministers.

The NUFK-RGNU joint communiqué of 17 September disclosed that the two bodies intended to transfer "the competence of several ministries . . . into the country in the near future," and explained: "In this way, the Political Bureau, in application of the directives of the Central Committee of the N.U.F.K., will install, step by step, the whole government there" (*ibid.*). Not only does the quoted statement show that the Cambodian revolutionaries do not wish to be considered as long-term Peking residents—an interpretation supported by Sihanouk's repeated claims that his is not a government-in-exile—but it also reveals the extreme degree to which the RGNU is subservient to the NUFK.

On 23 March, along with his proclamation of the formation of the NUFK, Sihanouk announced the creation of the Cambodian National Liberation Army (CNLA) —also known as the Cambodian National People's Liberation Armed Forces (CNPLAF) —to be directly under the command of the Ministry of Defense. In his speech, Sihanouk appealed to Cambodians at home to take up arms against Lon Nol's government and to those in Europe to join him in Peking. Two days later, RGNU Minister of Defense Khieu Samphan sent a message to Sihanouk, informing him that a CNLA command had been temporarily set up in the "liberated area" for training, organizing, and equipping soldiers and for "political and cultural education." The CNLA reportedly comprises North Vietnamese and PRG troops with Khmer Rouge, Cambodian dissident, and possibly Pathet Lao elements.[1] Sihanouk described CNLA forces as "Red Khmers and 'Sihanoukists' united as one man" (quoted, *Le Monde*, English edition, Paris, 26 August). An early estimate (*Far Eastern Economic Review*, Hong Kong, 6 August) put CNLA composition at one-third Khmer Rouge and two-thirds "Sihanoukists," and CNLA strength at 10,000 to 15,000 Cambodians, aided by some 50,000 Vietnamese communist troops. A North Vietnamese soldier, Tran Van Hong, who defected to the Cambodian government in January 1971, set maximum communist troop strength in Cambodia at 150,000 and estimated that 30 to 35 per cent were Cambodians (*ibid.*, 13 February, 1971). At a meeting in Peking in mid-July, as noted above, the Khmer Rouge refused to accept Sihanouk's leadership of their movement—presumably they operate as allied but independent forces within the NUFK. The defector Tran Van Hong stated: "The Khmer Rouge fight by themselves.... Cambodians fighting under the Viet Cong are good fighters but the Khmer Rouge fighters are lousy." (*Ibid.*) As few as 5,000 CNLA troops may engage in actual combat while the remainder work in logistics operations, although 20,000 of the associated Vietnamese troops are regulars and 30,000 are support troops (*ibid.*, 5 December 1970).

An NUFK congress, held in the "liberated areas" on 7 to 8 May, determined that three main resistance zones should be created in Cambodia. The eastern region between the Mekong River and South Vietnam, designated as Zone 1, was put under Khieu Samphan. The southwestern provinces bordering the Gulf of Siam comprise Zone 2, under Hu Nim. Zone 3, under Hou Youn, encompasses the northwestern regions bordering on Laos and Thailand.

In addition to the NUFK, the RGNU, and the CNLA, Sihanouk's position is supported by the shadowy "Cambodian People's Movement of United Resistance," which claims to be an NUFK member organization based in the "liberated areas" of Cambodia. Affiliated movements include the even more obscure Cambodian Peasants' Association, the Cambodian Trade Labor Union, the Cambodian Democratic Youths' Union, the Cambodian Democratic Women's Union, and the Association of Cambodian Patriotic Intellectuals, Professors, and Teachers. Among leaders of the Movement of United Resistance are Khieu Samphan, described as a representative of the movement in eastern Cambodia and of the various communist armed forces, and Hou Youn and Hu Nim, described as representing the movement in northwestern and southwestern Cambodia, respectively. It is unclear whether the movement is in fact synonymous with the NUFK or if it attempts to preserve a façade as an independent organization.

Domestic Positions and Activities. The political program of the NUFK, made public by Sihanouk on 5 May 1970, was a lengthy document whose major points advocated uniting the Cambodian people to oppose "imperialism" and its "flunkies" and safeguard Cambodia's independence,

---

[1]It is not known whether the Lao guerrillas are from Laos or from the Lao ethnic minority in Cambodia.

territorial integrity, and neutrality; creating a national liberation army to oppose Lon Nol; vesting all power in the hands of the "progressive working people"; guaranteeing democratic rights such as freedom of speech, press, and religion; and implementing a land reform. It described the NUFK foreign policy as "one of national independence, peace, neutrality, nonalignment, solidarity and friendship with all peace-loving and justice-loving peoples and governments," but added a declaration of "militant solidarity and cooperation" with Laos and Vietnam "according to the principle that the liberation and defense of each country are the affair of its own people and that the three peoples pledge to do their best to support one another according to the desire of the interested country on the basis of mutual respect." (Quoted, *Peking Review*, no. 20, 15 May.)

In the same press conference at which he defined the NUFK political program, Prince Sihanouk proclaimed the "Royal Government of National Union under the Leadership of the National United Front of Kampuchea" to be the "sole legal and legitimate Government of Cambodia." According to the text of the proclamation, "the essential mission of the new Government is to faithfully and entirely execute the Political Program of the N.U.F.K." (*Ibid.*) Thus the self-proclaimed government of Cambodia was formally under the leadership of the united front.

Sihanouk, as noted earlier, claimed that the RGNU was not a government-in-exile since three of its ministers (Khieu Samphan, Hou Youn, and Hu Nim) and all the vice-ministers were active in the "liberated areas" of Cambodia. Khieu Samphan, Hou Youn, and Hu Nim issued an appeal on 1 May which called upon the Cambodian people, the NUFK, and the CNLA to fulfill the following "concrete tasks":

1. To enhance the leadership, step up the armed and political struggle of the people in order to foil . . . the U.S. imperialists and to set up the people's administration at all levels.

2. To promote propaganda, training and organizational work to turn the forces of the masses into solid revolutionary organizations, enhance the people's solidarity in fighting in all fields, encourage the people to give mutual assistance, morally and materially.

3. To strengthen the building of the armed forces . . .

4. Step up the movement of developing and protecting production, the movement of savings in support of the resistance . . .

5. To strengthen the militant solidarity with the peace-loving and justice-loving countries and organizations of the world . . .

6. . . . all Buddhist dignitaries, intellectuals, students, professors, patriotic employees and all other compatriots living in areas under the temporary control of the enemy to unite and zealously take part in the patriotic organizations . . . (Quoted, *Peking Review*, no. 21, 22 May.)

Thus it can be seen that the Cambodian resistance is developing along basically Maoist lines with an emphasis on the unity of political and military activities. CNLA statements have stressed in addition the consolidating of the "liberated areas" as rear bases for the war.

On 7-8 May the Cambodian People's Movement of United Resistance held a congress in the "liberated areas" in support of the 3-4 May NUFK congress. The meeting was attended by representatives of the movement's various associated organizations: Khieu Samphan, Hou Youn, and Hu Nim as representatives of the movement; a delegate from the PP; and various minority representatives. A statement adopted at the congress declared the movement's support for the NUFK political program, the constitution of the NUFK Politburo, and the founding of the RGNU. Appealing to those who had not yet joined the ranks of resistance, it further called on the various elements of the Cambodian populace to unite more closely around the NUFK and Prince Sihanouk, to support actively the RGNU, and to implement the NUFK political program.

In November, Sihanouk claimed from Peking that NUFK committees elected by the people had been set up throughout the "liberated areas" at the village (*shum*), town (*khum*), district (*srok*), and provincial (*khet*) levels, replacing the corresponding central government organs. According to Sihanouk, the committees were addressing themselves, with "particular concern," to the "solution of all the problems affecting the daily life of [their] compatriots [and] showing the will of [the NUFK] to govern the country with the people, by the people and for the people." (*Peking Review*, no. 46, 13 November.) Earlier it was claimed that all central government taxes and "evil social practices" had been abolished, and that the property of "reactionary elements" was being confiscated and redistributed to the poor. Concurrently, it was alleged, the committees had initiated a production campaign to improve the people's livelihood and to support the resistance, classes were being held to train medical cadres and mobile medical teams to take medical assistance to the people in the countryside, and aid was being given to villages hard hit by the war. (NCNA, 9 September.)

Militias were said to have been set up under the RGNU Interior Ministry at the village, town, district, and provincial levels in the "liberated areas." Their purpose was to ensure order and security and protect the lives and property of the populace against alleged depredations of central government troops. Selected from among the villagers, militia members were expected to participate also in social and economic tasks, especially in agricultural production.

Reports of CNLA effectiveness vary. The NUFK claims to have gained control of two-thirds of the country and 2,800,000 of the population, which they estimate at 6.5 million (*Peking Review*, no. 36, 4 September and no. 46, 13 November). Phnom Penh, according to Sihanouk, was isolated from the rest of the country. Outside observers claim that while communist forces hold more than half the area of the country, including the entire northeast and most of the north, the Phnom Penh government retains control of the population centers and approximately two-thirds of the people (*Far Eastern Economic Review*, 7 November). Sihanouk claimed that between March and October 1970 the CNLA had killed, wounded, or put out of action more than 110,000 soldiers, including some 38,000 from U.S. and South Vietnamese forces. About 100 "enemy" battalions were allegedly decimated or disintegrated, and enormous quantities of materiél seized (*ibid.*). Conversely, the Phnom Penh government claimed that 5,955 communists had been killed by July 1970. At the same time, however, the official Agence Khmer de Presse daily bulletin put the figure at 11,000. Some observers estimated the number of communist dead to run as high as 40,000 (*Far Eastern Economic Review*, 16 July).

Initially, only Vietnamese dead were found following clashes with Cambodian government forces. Later, a sprinking of Cambodian bodies was evident, suggesting that Cambodian guerrillas had been integrated into North Vietnamese and PRG units. The North Vietnamese defector Tran Van Hong (see above) claimed that the main Cambodian CNLA force was used for combat. An escaped communist captive estimated that 70 per cent of the dissident soldiers were Cambodian, and stated that, at recruitment meetings in which he was forced to participate, generally 50 per cent of the village's men enlisted. Nevertheless, he said, command remained in the hands of North Vietnamese and PRG regulars. (*New York Times*, 3 November.) A report late in 1970 indicated that many local recruits were deserting rather than fight against their countrymen.

International Views and Positions. At the alleged behest of Prince Sihanouk, the Chinese People's Republic sponsored a "Summit Conference of Indochinese Peoples" on 24-25 April, rumored to have been held at a small village south of Canton (*Foreign Affairs*, July, p. 625). The conference itself was not attended by the Chinese, but Chou En-lai was host at a banquet in honor of the delegates.

The "Delegation of the Cambodian People" to the summit conference consisted of Prince Sihanouk (as head of state of Cambodia, chairman of the NUFK, and head of the delegation),

Penn Nouth (as private adviser to the head of state, NUFK representative, and deputy head of the Delegation), Huot Sambath (as ambassador extraordinary and plenipotentiary representative of the NUFK), Sarin Chhak (as the same), and Chau Seng, Thiounn Mumm, and Roeurng Mach (as representatives of the NUFK (*Peking Review*, special issue, 8 May). Evidently, all the Cambodian delegates represented the NUFK. There were none from the country's other fronts or left-wing and communist organizations. Only one delegate, Roeurng Mach, was not a high-ranking member of the NUFK and the RGNU.

The Laotian delegation was headed by Prince Souphanouvong, chairman of the Laotian Patriotic Front (NLHX). Other Laotian delegates were Khamsouk Keola (chairman of the Committee of Alliance of Patriotic Neutralist Forces and deputy head of the Delegation), Phoumi Vongvichit (secretary-general of the NLHX Central Committee), Khampheng Boupha (member of the Central Committee), and Oun Heuan Phounsavath (deputy director of the NLHX information bureau at Hanoi).

The South Vietnamese delegation comprised Nguyen Huu Tho, president of the Presidium of the Central Committee of the National Liberation Front of South Vietnam (NLF) and president of the Advisory Council of the PRG, who was the head of the delegation, and Trinh Dinh Thao, president of the Central Committee of the Vietnam Alliance of National, Democratic, and Peace Forces (VANDPF) and vice-president of the Advisory Council of the PRG, who was deputy head, together with Mme Nguyen Dinh Chi (vice-president of the Revolutionary People's Committee of Thua Thien-Hue, vice-president of the VANDPF committee of Hue, member of the VANDPF Central Committee, and PRG vice-minister of foreign affairs), Nguyen Van Hieu (NLF Central Committee member and PRG ambassador to Cambodia), and Vo Dong Giang (NLF Central Committee member).

Heading the delegation from the Democratic Republic of Vietnam (DRV) was Pham Van Dong, premier of the DRV, with Hoang Quoc Viet, member of the Presidium of the Vietnam Fatherland Front (VFF) Central Committee, as deputy head. Among others in the delegation were Hoang Minh Giam (member of the Presidium of the VFF Central Committee and DRV minister of culture), Nguyen Co Thach (vice-minister of foreign affairs), and Nguyen Thuong (ambassador to Cambodia. The high level of importance which the DRV assigned to the conference was evident in the selection of Pham Van Dong to head the delegation. The four delegations were described as representing three countries, thus indicating the assumption of the eventual dissolution of the PRG.

It is probable that the main objective of the Vietnamese communists at the time of the summit conference was to secure their sanctuaries outside Vietnam and to reestablish their supply lines. Nothing which can be considered concrete emerged from the meeting, although it was agreed among the participants in the Joint Declaration signed at the close of the conference that "meetings will take place whenever it is necessary between [the parties'] highest-level leaders or between competent representatives for exchanges of views on problems of common interest." (*Ibid.*)

The most important theme to emerge from the summit conference was the emphatic assertion of militant solidarity among the four communist movements. This solidarity was qualified by "the principle that the liberation and defense of each country is the affair of its own people" (*ibid.*), but participants nevertheless undertook to provide each other mutual support. The solidarity and unity of the Indochinese struggle became a major theme in subsequent Cambodian, Laotian, and Vietnamese statements, and in Chinese comments as well. At Chou En-lai's banquet for the conference delegates, Sihanouk hailed the "inspiring reunion of the Sino-Indochinese big family" (NCNA, 2 May).

Another theme which was considered of importance by the delegates was that of neutralism. In the joint declaration, Cambodia, Laos, and South Vietnam affirmed their struggle objectives as independence, peace, neutrality, and the prohibition of the stationing of foreign troops on their soil.

Greetings were sent to the conference by Albania, North Korea, the German Democratic Republic, the Afro-Asian Latin American Peoples' Solidarity Organization, Cuba, Hungary, Czechoslovakia, the Algerian National Council of Revolution, and the Communist Party of Malaya.

Chinese response to the conference was overwhelmingly enthusiastic. Chou En-lai announced that the launching on 24 April of China's first earth satellite was a "gift to the Summit Conference." Repeating a theme common in Chinese propaganda statements about Indochina, he declared that the people and territory of China serve as a "powerful backing" and "reliable rear area" for the three Indochinese peoples.

Mao Tse-tung, in an unusual move on 20 May, issued a statement purporting to endorse the Cambodian resistance. In its second paragraph, the document proclaimed warm support for Sihanouk "in opposing U.S. imperialism and its lackeys," for the joint declaration of the Summit Conference, and for the establishment of the RGNU (*Malayan Monitor and General News*, London, July). The paragraph concluded with a declaration of faith in an Indochinese victory. Thus the Chinese leader integrated his support for the Cambodian movement with that for the other Indochinese movements. Other paragraphs and the closing salutation of the statement condemned the United States, instead of dealing with Cambodia itself. Mao's statement was widely hailed by the communist parties in Southeast Asia as a great encouragement in their struggle against U.S. "imperialism."

Clearly, the relationship of the Peking-based NUFK and RGNU with China was extremely close. The NUFK was decidedly pro-Chinese in the context of the Sino-Soviet split. In his speech commemorating the Cambodian national day (9 November), Sihanouk described China as the "No. 1 friend of the Khmer people and the independent, non-aligned, progressive and anti-imperialist Cambodia." He further cited the "multifarious aid and complete support" which his people would "never fail to get." In May, the RGNU and the Chinese People's Republic had entered into a loan agreement, and on 17 August they had signed an agreement providing for gratuitous aid from China to the Cambodian dissidents. (*Peking Review*, no. 46, 13 November.)

China's initial response to Sihanouk, however, was far from overwhelming. Adopting in effect a policy of attrition toward him, China carried on negotiations with the Phnom Penh government for seven weeks following the change in leadership.[2] These efforts to reach an understanding with the new government continued until 5 May. Nevertheless, on 5 April in North Korea, Chou En-lai made the first official Chinese statement of "firmly supporting" Sihanouk as head of state of Cambodia. When Sihanouk announced the formation of the RGNU a month later, China became the first country to recognize the new government and severed diplomatic relations with Phnom Penh. Thereafter, China continuously upheld Sihanouk's cause, using it as a rallying point for the "three Indochinese peoples." It has been speculated that China recognized in the Cambodian situation a signal opportunity to promote and demonstrate its thesis of armed struggle and "wars of national liberation." This contention would seem to be strengthened by China's continuing insistence on its being the "reliable rear area" for revolution in Asia. As the year went on, Sihanouk increasingly appeared to be serving only a figurehead function. He was isolated inside China, and his travels seemed to be restricted. The repeated denials of his requests for per-

[2]According to Lon Nol, China let the Phnom Penh government know that: "It would consider the Sihanouk affair with the Khmer authorities an internal affair of Cambodia, forget about Sihanouk, and continue to respect [Phnom Penh's] authority provided: (1) [it] continued to permit the supply of arms and medicine to North Vietnamese and Viet Cong troops . . . so they could continue the war against South Vietnam; (2) [it] continued to allow North Vietnamese and Viet Cong troops to rest in Khmer territory; and (3) [it] continued to use [its] propaganda to support [China's] friends." (Phnom Penh radio, domestic service, 11 May.)

mission to return to his homeland carried the implication that he was no longer a free sovereign. It is likely that the longer Sihanouk is forced to remain in Peking, the less influence will he be able to exert over NUFK policies.

It is possible that Chinese aid to Cambodian "national liberation" elements may not be limited to economic, military, and moral support. Chau Seng, the RGNU minister for special missions, stated in Paris on 5 June that China could not accept the defeat of the NUFK in Cambodia and direct intervention could not be ruled out. North Vietnam's ambassador to Cairo, Tran Van So, announced on 16 April that a request from Phnom Penh for U.S. intervention in Cambodian affairs would bring China and the DRV into the struggle on behalf of Sihanouk's forces. The Hong Kong newspaper *Ming Pao* reported on 29 April that camps were being set up in South China for training Cambodians. It further stated that Chinese "volunteers" were being trained to fight in Cambodia (quoted, Djakarta radio, domestic service, 30 April). A Japanese press release dated 18 May quoted Cambodian Foreign Minister Yem Sambaur as stating that 70 to 100 Chinese had entered Cambodia recently to give strategic guidance to North Vietnamese and Chinese forces there.

Sihanouk left China only to visit North Korea and North Vietnam. An agreement on military and economic aid for the Cambodian dissidents was concluded with North Vietnam on 25 May. The joint statement which was issued on 7 June during Sihanouk's visit to Hanoi added little to the summit conference joint communiqué. The North Vietnamese people again pledged wholehearted, albeit undefined, support for Sihanouk's movement.

The DRV and the PRG were quick to condemn Sihanouk's deposition on 18 March. On 23 March, Sihanouk called for the formation of a new government, a united front, and an army of national liberation. Two days later, the DRV announced support for his stand, as did the PRG on 26 March. Although Phnom Penh attempted to continue negotiations with the DRV and the PRG for the removal of Vietnamese troops from Cambodia, on 28 March both announced the withdrawal of their diplomatic representatives from the Cambodian capital.

Most of the bodies which have been found after clashes between guerrillas and government forces in Cambodia have been Vietnamese. In late September, when government troops entered the Taing Kauk area north of Phnom Penh, villagers reported that they had been under Vietnamese communist administration for four months. A communist defector reported that after Sihanouk's deposition the PRG had sent a number of Cambodian-born Vietnamese as advisory teams to establish the Khmer Rouge organization from the hamlet level upward and to gain local support through propaganda. They were to train indigenous Cambodian communists in military tactics, propaganda, and administration. In practice, he said, the "advisers" took full control in their areas and made all decisions.

In September, a Western press source reported the presence of seven North Vietnamese divisions (theoretically 12,000 men per division, but usually between 6,000 and 8,000 in actuality) either in Cambodia or en route on the Ho Chi Minh trail to rebuild the eastern border bases which had been destroyed by U.S. actions in the spring. The troops were reported as comprising North Vietnam's First, Second, Fifth, Seventh, Ninth, Twentieth, and Twenty-fifth divisions (*Washington Post*, 5 September). Other sources, however, cited only four DRV divisions: the First, Fifth, Seventh, and Ninth, plus elements from the South Vietnamese highlands and the Bolovens Plateau in Laos and autonomous communist regiments and battalions scattered through northern Cambodia (*Far Eastern Economic Review*, 5 December).

A Japan Socialist Party delegation to Hanoi gained an implicit admission of the presence of PRG forces in Cambodia, and a Peking radio broadcast of a plea to the people of Cambodia on behalf of Sihanouk on 28 July stated for the first time that North Vietnamese troops were in the country. At an international press conference in August, Sihanouk announced that Vietnamese were serving as military instructors to the CNLA, and said: "Our chief instructor is Vo Nguyen Giap" (the DRV minister of defense). Later, however, he would only say that North Vietnamese assisted in transporting supplies from China to Cambodia. The Peking radio admission of the Vietnamese presence in Cambodia, mentioned above, has been cited as evidence of friction between the local populace and the Vietnamese troops, as have the frequent pleas by Khieu Samphan for unity, both within the NUFK and with "fraternal countries." The Vietnamese reportedly look down on their Cambodian counterparts. A Cambodian peasant who had lived in a "liberated village" under North Vietnamese military administration explained that his village turned against the Vietnamese when they stopped displaying Sihanouk's portrait and the Cambodian flag at meetings and began to expound pro-DRV propaganda.

North Korea, the other country which Sihanouk has visited since his deposition, has also come out strongly in favor of the NUFK and the RGNU. During Sihanouk's stay in North Korea, in mid-June, a new theme emerged in communist propaganda, that of an Asian united front. "Other friendly peoples" besides those of Indochina could be called upon to assist the Cambodian people against the United States. The "militant friendship and solidarity between the Korean, Chinese, Vietnamese, Lao, and Cambodian peoples" was played up to give currency to the appeal for a united front. Substance was added to the pledges of solidarity by North Korea's agreement to furnish medicine and military equipment to Sihanouk's forces. According to Cambodian field officers, North Korea also sent combat soldiers to join the CNLA.

The Laotian communist movement, which was one of the participants in the Summit Conference of Indochinese Peoples, repeatedly endorsed the NUFK. Relations between the Cambodian and Laotian dissidents are close and cordial. On 27 March, in a statement responding to Sihanouk's 23 March announcement of the NUFK, the Laotian Patriotic Front declared its full support for the new front. A Cambodian-Laotian joint communiqué was issued on 24 July. The NUFK sent a delegation to Cairo to attend the international conference on Laos.

Although at the time of his deposition Sihanouk announced plans for alternate residence in Peking and Moscow, he has yet to return to the Soviet Union. Less cordial toward the dissident regime than the Asian communist parties have been, the Soviet Union has side-stepped the issue of breaking relations with Phnom Penh and recognizing the RGNU. Both Phnom Penh and the RGNU have diplomatic missions in Moscow. The Soviet Union maintains an embassy in Cambodia, but the ambassador is not in residence. In the course of the year, the Soviets came to refer to the central government often as the "Phnom Penh authorities." In May, a lengthy Soviet government statement referred to Prince Sihanouk in passing as the "lawful head of state" of Cambodia, but the remainder was a diatribe directed against the United States for its actions against Vietnamese communist bases inside Cambodia (Moscow radio, domestic service, 4 May). Significantly, the statement refrained from condemning Lon Nol's government and referred to the Soviet Union's continuing respect for Cambodia's "neutrality and independence, its sovereignty and territorial integrity, and its borders."

The 4 May statement was fairly typical of Soviet reaction to the Cambodian situation, in which there has been much comment decrying U.S. actions and alleging Central Intelligence Agency complicity in the change of leadership, but little has been said of the actual Cambodian situation. On 5 May, TASS carried without comment a brief announcement of the formation of NUFK. On 13 May, Radio "Peace and Progress" (Moscow) broadcast an announcement that Premier Kosygin had sent a message to Sihanouk "greeting" the formation of NUFK and stating in part: "The struggle you are now waging, together with the patriotic forces of the country, against the aggressor and for Cambodia's freedom, independence, and neutrality, will continue to find sympathy and support in the Soviet Union." The message did not mention the new Royal Government.

On the Cambodian National Day (9 November) China, North Vietnam, North Korea, Albania, Romania, and Yugoslavia sent greetings to Sihanouk. The Soviet Union and its Eastern European allies failed to do so, although in 1969 messages were sent by the Soviet Union, Czechoslovakia, Poland, and East Germany. Instead, on the 1970 anniversary there was a Moscow radio broadcast to Cambodia in which no mention was made of Sihanouk or the NUFK. The commentary expressed the full support of the Soviet Union and "all other socialist countries" for the "just struggle" of the Khmer people against "interventionism." It did not condemn the Phnom Penh government, and it left unspecified the adversary, which was referred to variously as "interventionism," "imperialism," and the "enemy of liberty."

The Soviets took advantage of the Cambodian events to accuse the Chinese of "splittist" activities: "They replace the struggle against imperialism and for the solidarity of the anti-imperialist forces with that of opposing the Soviet Union, the other socialist countries, the world communist and workers' movement, and the national liberation movement" (Radio "Peace and Progress," 5 May). In a later attack, the Soviet Union accused China of "big power nationalism" which facilitated the activities of the enemies of Cambodia. On the other hand, the Soviets warmly greeted the Chinese-sponsored summit conference and expressed the belief that it would help to consolidate the "unified anti-imperialist front" in Indochina (Moscow radio, 29 April).

Sihanouk's reaction to Soviet ambivalence was more restrained than China's, although he expressed disappointment upon occasion. In a 29 September message for China's National Day, for example, Sihanouk told Chou En-lai: "China, contrary to some big powers, places its power and wealth at the service of the peoples who are struggling against exploitation and domination." In a denunciation of the U.N., he complained of the special and permanent privileges enjoyed by "certain big powers"—a clear reference to Security Council members, of which the Soviet Union is one. Although Sihanouk refrained from commenting on the failure of the Eastern European allies of the Soviet Union for failing to recognize his government, in August he openly criticized the Czechoslovak government when it thwarted a pro-NUFK diplomat who attempted to seize the Cambodian Embassy in Prague for the RGNU.

Both the RGNU and Phnom Penh sent delegations to the Nonaligned Conference held in Lusaka, Zambia, on 8-10 September. The delegations at the conference—from some fifty countries—were unable to decide upon which to recognize as representing the legal government of Cambodia. Twenty-one countries spoke in favor of the RGNU, seven backed Lon Nol, and twelve advocated leaving the seat vacant (*Washington Post*, 8 September). In the end, despite Sihanouk's well-organized publicity campaign in advance of the meeting, neither his nor Phnom Penh's delegation was admitted, and the Cambodian seat remained empty. The failure of the conference to seat the RGNU was considered a defeat for Sihanouk and a victory for Phnom Penh.

The RGNU has been recognized by the following countries: Albania, Algeria, the Chinese People's Republic, Congo (Brazzaville), North Korea, Cuba, Guinea, Iraq, Libya, Mauritania, the United Arab Republic, the Central African Republic, Romania, Somalia, Sudan, Syria, Tanzania, North Vietnam, North and South Yemen, the Provisional Revolutionary Government of South Vietnam and Yugoslavia. It is also recognized by the Laotian Patriotic Front and the al-Fatah guerrilla organization in the Middle East.

Publications. The NUFK has its own "News Agency of Kampuchea" through which it releases periodic propaganda statements. The "Voice of the NUFK" radio began broadcasting on 1 August 1970 in Khmer for three hours daily. The Cambodian Information Agency (AKI), established 10 August, also disseminates NUFK and RGNU news and statements, as do other Indochinese communist media. "Liberation Radio" in South Vietnam on 3 April added an hour to its previous half-hour Cambodian broadcasting schedule. On 5 April Hanoi radio initiated additional programs in Khmer. The Chinese media have given the NUFK and the RGNU especially intense coverage. All major NUFK and RGNU documents and events are recorded in *Peking Review* and reported by the NCNA. Peking radio has increased its wave lengths for Cambodian broadcasts since April, and its programs in French have also been expanded.

S. E. Y.

CEYLON

The first Marxist party in Ceylon was the Ceylon Equal Society Party (Lanka Sama Samaja Pakshaya; LSSP), formed in 1935. Its founders were young Western-educated intellectuals, including N. M. Perera, Colvin R. de Silva, S. A. Wickremasinghe, Philip Gunawardena, and Leslie Goonewardene. In 1939 the LSSP rejected the Stalinist line of the Third International in favor of Trotskyism, and in 1940 expelled a small Stalinist group led by Wickremasinghe. This group immediately formed the United Socialist Party, which in 1943 became the Ceylon Communist Party (Lanka Kommunist Pakshaya; LKP).

The original LSSP, now led by N. M. Perera and Leslie Goonewardene, lost much of its Trotskyist character in 1964 when it was expelled from the Fourth International. A number of small Trotskyist parties have broken from the LSSP, most of them since 1964. One such party, formerly known as the Viplavakari LSSP, is now called the People's United Front (Mahajana Eksath Peramuna; MEP) and is led by Philip Gunawardena. There are also the LSSP-Revolutionary (LSSP-R), headed by P. Bala Tampoe, and its offshoot, the Revolutionary Samasamaja Party (RSP), led by Edmond Samarkoddy. Still another splinter is the Revolutionary Communist League, formed in 1968 and led by Keerthi Balasuriya.

The predominantly pro-Soviet LKP suffered a split in 1963 when a pro-Chinese faction broke away following the expulsion of its leader, Nagalingam Sanmugathasan. In 1964 each LKP group held its own "Seventh Congress of the Ceylon Communist Party," and each has continued to use the LKP name.

At the end of 1969 an apparently new group became active. This was the Janata Vimukthi Peramuna (People's Liberation Front; JVP), popularly called the "Che Guevara movement."

The parties representing the core of the leftist forces in Ceylon are the LSSP, the pro-Soviet LKP, and the socialist Sri Lanka Freedom Party (SLFP), led by Mrs. Sirimavo Bandaranaike. The latter, except for a brief period in 1960, was the island's ruling party from 1956 to 1965, either by itself or as the dominant member of a leftist coalition. All three parties, which had formed a "United Front" in 1968, became partners in a coalition government as a result of national elections held in May 1970.

The Pro-Soviet LKP. Having a rather limited following, the pro-Soviet LKP attempts to compensate for this lack through its trade unions and by allying with the major left opposition party, the SLFP. Membership is estimated at between 1,500 and 2,000. The LKP's secretary-general, Pieter Keuneman, in June 1967 put the number at 18,000 regular and 7,000 candidate members (Justus M. van der Kroef, "The Many Faces of Ceylonese Communism," *Problems of Communism*, March-April 1968). The population of Ceylon is 12,730,000 (estimated 1971), mainly Sinhalese (about 70 per cent), with "Ceylon Tamils" and the technically stateless "Indian Tamils" (each about 10 per cent) as the next largest groups.

543

Party membership, particularly in the lower and middle ranks, is drawn mainly from clerical employees in both public and private sectors, and thus is basically of the lower middle class; some few members are of the laboring class. The top leadership is composed predominantly of middle-class intellectuals and persons in professions. Nevertheless the party has strong ties with workers through trade unions. Electoral strength is concentrated in the more literate and Westernized area of Ceylon, in and around the capital city of Colombo. The LKP's appeal among students is believed to be declining, as those students who still adhere to Marxism are becoming disenchanted with its parliamentary line and have been turning to groups that advocate violent revolution, such as the pro-Chinese LKP, the more militant of the Trotskyist parties, and, more recently, the "Guevarist" JVP.

Before the 1963 split, the LKP had since 1947 consistently won three or four of the 151 elected seats in the Lower House of Parliament (six additional seats are appointed) and received between 3 and 5 per cent of the popular vote (dropping to 2.4 per cent in 1965). In the 1970 elections the party won six seats in the Lower House.

Leadership and Organization. The top LKP leadership includes the party's general secretary, Pieter Keuneman; its president, S. A. Wickremasinghe, the Politburo (size unknown), the Central Control Commission (6 members); and the Central Committee (25 full members and 12 candidates). Prominent among these, besides the two leaders just named, are V. A. Samarawickrema the party's "national organizer" and chief disciplinarian, and L. W. Panditha, its deputy secretary and trade union trouble-shooter. Others include I. R. Ariaratnam, a member of the Politburo, C. Kumarasamy, the treasurer, and K. P. de Silva, in charge of party education. Although Wickremasinghe is the founder and current president of the party, its active leadership comes from Keuneman. Also prominent in the party is Keuneman's wife, Maude, who was born in Great Britain and was active in the British communist movement.

The party's major base of power is in the trade unions, a particularly important tool in Ceylonese politics. Shortly before the LKP split, the party led the 68,000-member Ceylon Trade Union Federation (CTUF), with its 31 affiliated unions. Following the split, the pro-Chinese faction retained control over the CTUF and the pro-Soviet group formed a rival organization, the Ceylon Federation of Trade Unions (CFTU), which in 1966 claimed 110,000 members in 22 affiliated unions. Ceylon's largest organization of public servants, the Public Service Workers' Trade Union Federation (PSWTUF), with 100,000 members, remained oriented toward the pro-Soviet faction following the split. Other important organizations oriented toward or led by the pro-Soviet LKP are the Ceylonese Women's Association (Lanka Kantha Peramuna), founded in 1961 and claiming 10,000 members, and the All-Ceylon Federation of Communist and Progressive Youth Leagues, founded in 1945 and claiming 8,000 members.

Domestic Attitudes and Activities. One of the most perplexing problems for the LKP (as well as for other Marxist parties) arises from the existence of a Tamil-speaking Hindu minority on an island where the majority are Buddhists who speak Sinhalese. Almost half the Tamil minority are stateless Indians. Until 1960 the LKP took the more orthodox communist position of defending the minority group by advocating both Sinhalese and Tamil as official languages. As this position was found to be unpopular among the Sinhalese majority, the party began to shift to an exclusively Sinhalese policy in order to hold its ground in the coalition government at the 1960 parliamentary elections. This pro-Sinhalese position grew stronger after 1965 and was reaffirmed in the 1970 elections, alienating much of the party's Tamil membership. The granting of citizenship to the million or so stateless Indian Tamils would undoubtedly be favored by the LKP were it not for the anxieties that this possibility creates among the Sinhalese. Nevertheless, the LKP has continued to seek support from radical Tamil groups such as the All-Ceylon Minority Tamil United Front (which shares the party's opposition to the caste system and other forms of social discrimination).

Elections. As a result of an alliance made in June 1968, the LKP in 1970 became one of three parties in a "United Front" government when voters in the national elections on 27 May gave the coalition 115 of the 151 elected seats in the Lower House of Parliament. Though since its inception the LKP had sought to improve its Parliamentary strength by joining such alliances, the 1970 elections provided its first opportunity to be a partner in the government. The 1970 elections were also the first in which the three parties of the current coalition—the Sri Lanka Freedom Party, the Lanka Sama Samaja Party, and the LKP—had agreed to aim at a joint government. In three previous elections (1956, July 1960, and 1965) only electoral agreements had been reached, whereby no party would contest against either of the other two in the same constituency.

The results of the elections, in comparison with those of 1965, were as follows:

	1970			1965		
	Seats contested	Seats won	Percentage of vote	Seats contested	Seats won	Percentage of vote
LKP	9	6	3.4	9	4	2.4
LSSP	22	19	8.7	24	10	7.8
SLFP	107	90	36.7	—	41	30.0
UNP	129	17	37.9	—	66	39.2

The fragmentation of the conservative parties, led by the defeated United National Party (UNP), was a significant factor in the victory of the United Front. Although the percentage of votes attained by the UNP dropped only slightly from the 1965 number, the party's failure to organize a coalition or to reach a broad electoral agreement with other parties resulted in a substantial loss in its parliamentary strength. On the other hand, the SLFP, which had slightly fewer votes than the UNP in the 1970 elections, was able to win more than five times as many seats in Parliament. Loss of support for the UNP government was frequently attributed, among other things, to a reduction in the rice subsidy, the rising cost of living, unemployment—especially among the educated, and failure to serve the interests of the Tamil minority. (the UNP had been deserted by the Tamil Federal Party, its coalition partner in government.) Some of the swing to the left was explained by the additional votes of about 800,000 young persons who voted for the first time since the voting age was lowered to eighteen years.

The three United Front parties did not challenge each other except in the three-member Colombo Central constituency, where an SLFP candidate ran against LKP General Secretary Keuneman who was, however, able to maintain his seat. S. D. Bandaranaike, a member of Parliament who left the SLFP in March 1968 and subsequently supported the pro-Chinese LKP, contested in the constituency of Gampaha as an independent. Reportedly running under an electoral agreement with the SLFP, he lost heavily when that party bowed to pressure from the pro-Soviet LKP to enter an SLFP candidate in Gampaha.

Of the 21 ministers in the new government of Prime Minister Sirimavo Bandaranaike, one was a member of the pro-Soviet LKP, three were from the LSSP, and the rest were from the SLFP. Pieter Keuneman was given the Ministry of Housing and Construction; LSSP leader N. M. Perera, the Finance Ministry (which he headed in 1964 under Mrs. Bandaranaike's government when he introduced a budget that sought strict control over banks, foreign and domestic business, and private property); deputy LSSP leader Colvin R. de Silva, the Ministry of Plantation Industries and Constitutional Affairs (a new portfolio created in anticipation of increased government control of tea, rubber, and coconut production); and LSSP Secretary-General Leslie Goonewardene, the Ministry of Communications.

The socialist content of the coalition was expected to benefit the LKP only slightly. There had been evidence of suspicion of the party by its partners (see *YICA*, 1969, pp. 113, 114), particularly from the SLFP right-wing, led by Felix Dias Bandaranaike, head of he Ministry of Public Administration. Moreover, the position of the LKP, in view of its extremely small size when measured against the SLFP, has caused some to think that it may be easily susceptible to pressure. Outside Parliament, however, the LKP and LSSP both are strong in the trade union movement and outnumber the SLFP in union membership.

The policies of the new government, set forth in the election platform, and earlier in the United Front program, aimed at correcting the apparent causes for the shortcomings of its predecessor, the UNP government of Prime Minister Dudley Senanayake. The chief problem was seen by the coalition as one of increasing economic dependency which had to be dealt with by nationalizing or otherwise controlling interests dominated by foreign capital, notably the banks and the tea industry. The election platform also promised a new administrative system to create a government more responsive to the people. This would include elected employees' councils and advisory committees in government offices. Most important, it vowed to give Ceylon the status of a sovereign and independent republic (giving up its status as an independent dominion within the Commonwealth), and to this end in July the new Parliament formed itself into a constituent assembly with the task of drafting a new constitution.

Some of the promises were fulfilled, including the important vote-getter, an extra measure of government-subsidized rice. It appeared that other programs would take a little longer to implement. After a few months in office, Finance Minister N. M. Perera (LSSP) indicated greater moderation in his outlook. Reminding impatient critics that 95 per cent of the country's foreign exchange came from tea, rubber, and coconut (of which tea alone represented two-thirds), he stated: "We have agitated for the nationalisation of the tea estates in the past 40 years. But today, after assuming office as minister of finance, I realise it is not advisable to do so now. . . . One should realise that achieving socialism is not as simple as having a meal in a tea kiosk." (*Far Eastern Economic Review*, Hong Kong, 19 September.) Emphasizing the United Front's accession to power through Parliamentary rather than revolutionary means, Perera further declared: "We have no power or mandate to act in violation of the laws of the land."

Keuneman also exhibited a mellowing after assuming his post as head of the Ministry of Housing and Construction. Because of limited funds, he said, the government would be unable to finance sufficient housing projects to meet the increasing demand. He indicated a willingness to relax his attitude toward the "capitalists": "I do not like the private sector. But if in the process of making money the private sector will help to build houses the people want, I am prepared to go with them." (*Ibid.*)

At a plenary session of the pro-Soviet LKP Central Committee, the government was challenged for not moving rapidly enough to solve certain "fundamental questions of the economy" or to implement a "democratization of state apparatus." Economic measures demanded by the party included nationalization of banks, plantations, and the Lake House (a publishing consortium which, according to the LKP, monopolizes the Ceylonese press), and a prohibition on the export of profits, dividends, and capital. In a press statement of 18 September, the party warned that the delay by the government was being exploited by the "reactionary forces and [had] begun to disorient some sections, who supported the United Front in the election struggle." While such actions as constituting an assembly to draft a constitution, providing an additional measure of rice, and extending political and trade union rights to public servants were praised by the party statement, most of the government's achievements were described as "superstructural." In December the party's labor organization, the CFTU, was reported to be demanding that the government nationalize all foreign banks and the export trade in tea and rubber in order to stop profits from leaving the country (*Ceylon Daily News*, Colombo, 6 December). Quoting from an interview with Keuneman, Moscow radio related on 6 October that the government was coping with a "very serious economic and financial crisis . . . inherited from the previous regime," although it had been "able to go forward to some extent."

International Views and Positions. The LKP is a strong supporter of the Soviet Union, though its alliance with a Trotskyist (or at least former Trotskyist) party must offend the Communist Party of the Soviet Union, which holds that Trotskyists are "doing their best to undermine the communist movement." The election results were hailed by the Soviet press as a "big victory for Ceylon's democratic forces" (*Pravda*, 29 May); also the LSSP was referred to as a "socialist" party. Other East European parties had shown some confusion as to how the LSSP should be identified, generally omitting any reference to its political character until Soviet usage indicated that the term "socialist" was acceptable. Moscow radio (30 June, in Mandarin to Southeast Asia) took advantage of the apparent success of the Soviet strategy of a united front "from above" to say to the Chinese:

> The victory won by the left-wing United Front of Ceylon shows that there is absolutely no need for the people of young countries to resort to political adventures or engage in false revolutionary war to consolidate the independence and progress of their countries. They certainly do not need to follow the Chinese leadership's wrong idea that "political power grows out of the barrel of a gun" and that there is no alternative to armed guerrilla warfare—which has already had a disastrous effect on the life of the Chinese people.

Keuneman visited India as head of a four-member government delegation, arriving on 14 September. On the next day he was given a reception at the central headquarters of the pro-Soviet Communist Party of India (CPI), where he met the party's chairman, S. A. Dange, and other leaders. Keuneman reportedly spoke of the tasks and problems facing the United Front government. Earlier, in the CPI organ *New Age* (New Delhi, 7 June), Bhupesh Gupta, editor of the paper and member of the CPI Secretariat, acclaimed the United Front as an example for left-wing forces in India, which he described as "tragically ridden by dissensions."

Following its election to power in May, the government recognized and established diplomatic relations with the governments of East Germany, North Vietnam, and North Korea, emphasizing that this was done in the context of a nonaligned foreign policy. In addition, it recognized the Provisional Revolutionary Government of South Vietnam—but did not open diplomatic relations with it—and suspended diplomatic relations with Israel. An ambassador was sent to Ceylon by Communist China after a lapse of about five years. Trips by government officials were made to China, North Korea, and the Soviet Union during the last half of the year.

*   *   *

The Pro-Chinese LKP. The pro-Chinese LKP has a following considerably smaller than that of its pro-Soviet rival. Despite their respective claims, however, the pro-Chinese party probably has greater strength in the trade-union movement than the pro-Soviet party and is more active among the Tamil peasantry. Estimates of party membership—for which figures are lacking—range from 200 to 2,000. As in the case of other Marxist parties in Ceylon, the strength of the pro-Chinese LKP is concentrated in the southwestern region, principally in the urban areas around Colombo.

Leadership and Organization. The organizational structure of the pro-Chinese LKP is much less relied upon for the actual functioning of the party and its day-to-day management than in the case of the pro-Soviet LKP. The party's leader, Nagalingam Sanmugathasan, has said that the party has no formal chairman or secretary-general; reportedly, however, he was reelected as secretary-general at the party's Ninth Congress, held in April 1968. The Seventh Congress, in 1964, elected 35 persons to the Central Committee, but it is said that committee membership actually fluctuates between 12 and 15. Among these members are Watson Fernando, president of the party and chairman of the CTUF; Ariyawansa Gunasekera, chairman of the party's All-Ceylon Peasants' Congress; and M. C. N. Shafi, assistant secretary-general of the CTUF. Other important leaders are Higgoda Dharmasena, G. K. Jinendrapala, D. N. Nadunge, and V. Seenivasagam. The names of the new Central Committee members were not published following party elections at the Ninth Congress.

Perhaps even more than for the pro-Soviet LKP, the strength of the pro-Chinese party lies primarily in its trade union affiliations. Sanmugathasan himself spent much of his adult life as a trade union organizer. The CTUF (not to be confused with the pro-Soviet LKP's CFTU) is the continuation of the original organization, the pro-Soviet party having formed the newer federation following the split in 1963. It claims 67,000 members, but is nevertheless considered to be larger than the CFTU (which claims 110,000). In addition, the pro-Chinese LKP also dominates or influences the All-Ceylon Peasants' Congress, which claims 5,000 members, and the 1,200-member Ceylonese Youth League Federation.

Domestic Attitudes and Activities. The party's program, as defined at its Ninth Congress, calls for struggles to achieve the independence of Ceylon (by freeing it from "Anglo-American imperialism"), the abolition of "feudalism," the building of an independent national economy free from "imperialist" control, the firm support of all movements of national liberation against imperialism, and the establishment of an anti-imperialist and anti-feudal unity of all nationalities in Ceylon (*Peking Review*, 21 June 1968). Regarding the correct method for achieving socialism, a resolution adopted by the Ninth Congress stated that, considering the "futility of the parliamentary path," the working class could come to power only by the "forcible overthrow of the repressive imperialist-bourgeois state machinery" (*ibid.*). A statement by Sanmugathasan in Colombo on 1 October 1970 reiterated the party's line that only a violent revolution could change the structure of society.

The party's only member of Parliament, S. D. Bandaranaike, who won his position as a member of the SLFP, lost it in 1970 when running as a pro-Chinese LKP independent. It was said that he had made an electoral agreement with the SLFP. On 7 August, the pro-Chinese LKP announced that he had been expelled as a party member for having supported Mrs. Bandaranaike as prime minister. Two days later, he countered by declaring that he supported only her "anti-imperialist and anti-capitalist" policies; his reason for contesting the elections was to expose to the masses the need for armed revolution (*Ceylon Daily News*, 10 August). He was subsequently reported to have become a supporter of the "Che Guevara movement," or JVP.

Sanmugathasan has expressed criticism of the JVP. Pro-Chinese LKP members, present at the JVP's first public rally, in Colombo on 10 August, attempted to disrupt the meeting by distributing leaflets on the superiority of Mao Tse-tung's "people's war" over the guerrilla tactics advocated by Guevara. Citing the Chinese line on guerrilla warfare, the party contended that revolution could not be made by small groups, but needed the participation of the masses.

The CTUF was reported to be conducting a campaign of meetings, seminars, and demonstrations with the object of impelling the government to nationalize foreign banks and export trade in tea and rubber (*Elanadu*, Colombo, 8 December).

International Views and Positions. The party is a staunch supporter of Communist China. In a message to the Chinese Communist Party in October, Sanmugathasan declared:

> We pledge to master Mao Tsetung Thought and apply it to the concrete revolutionary situation in Ceylon. We pledge to work to unite all forces that can be united under the leadership of the working class, to bring about the overthrow by force of foreign imperialism, feudalism and local reaction. (Quoted, NCNA, 3 October.)

China avoided making public reference to the victory of the United Front—an omission the Soviet press was quick to point out—but Premier Chou En-lai sent his congratulations to Mrs. Bandaranaike. On 30 June the New China News Agency repeated a passage of Mrs. Bandaranaike's "throne speech" of 24 June in which she told of her party's condemnation of the Soviet-led intervention in Czechoslovakia in 1968.

In September, Sanmugathasan went to Zurich to attend a trade union conference. Following the conference, he was to go to China (possibly stopping in Albania on the way) to visit with Chou En-lai and other leaders of Asian and African pro-Chinese parties, according to the *Ceylon Daily News* (19 September). There was, however, no report of such a visit in the Albanian or Chinese press.

*   *   *

The Trotskyist Parties. *The LSSP.* The LSSP is the largest Marxist party in Ceylon and had been the second largest party in opposition to the UNP. Its leaders are N. M. Perera and Leslie Goonewardene (secretary-general). Its strength lies in Sabaragamuwa, Pasdun-Korale, and the Western Province seaboard. It is the most influential party in the trade unions.

The LSSP, which represents the continuation of the original Marxist party in Ceylon, lost much of its international character (and to many, its Trotskyist character) in 1964 when, contrary to a directive of the United Secretariat faction of the Trotskyist Fourth International, it entered into a coalition government to form a government with the SLFP and was subsequently expelled from the United Secretariat.

Late in 1970 Goonewardene declared in an article entitled "New Outlook of the LSSP" (*Ceylon Daily News*, 21 December) that the reason the party had abandoned its original belief that a socialist society could be created only through the seizure of power by a mass uprising was that the "course of history" had been different in Ceylon. His statement supported a declaration made by Colvin R. de Silva (*ibid.*, 20 December) asserting that in Ceylon the "anti-imperialist struggle" had been replaced by a struggle for the "overthrow of capitalism," a position held by the Soviets but denied by the Chinese communists.

According to Goonewardene's article, the LSSP was convinced that Parliament could serve as a tool to achieve socialism, but he added: "On the question of how far the journey toward socialism can be made through Parliament and the parliamentary system, the Lanka Sama Samaja Party had not made any final judgement.... The answer to this question does not lie in our hands but in the hands of our enemies." Goonewardene's statement affirmed the party's belief in the necessity to make full use of Parliament and the government to achieve socialism, but emphasized that the LSSP still believed in the "active intervention of the masses."

The article also defended the LSSP's policy of participating in alliances (explained by its shift from "anti-imperialism" to "anti-capitalism" following the Second World War) and its policy (since 1963) calling for Sinhalese as the official language. He revealed that the latter policy was justified because the Sinhalese were the "principal mass force working in the country toward socialism." Furthermore, he stated, "the purpose of the leaders whom the Tamil people endorsed was not to promote the Tamil language but to retain the English language." The LSSP has, since it began to form coalition governments with the SLFP, adopted an increasingly strong pro-Sinhalese position.

Colvin R. de Silva, as head of the Ministry of Plantation Industries and Constitutional Affairs, has been given the task of accelerating the repatriation of stateless Tamils to India. The repatriation is being carried out on the basis of a pact between the Ceylonese government of Mrs. Bandaranaike and India in 1964 by which 525,000 stateless Tamils were to be repatriated to India; 300,000 were to receive Ceylonese citizenship, leaving the fate of the remaining 150,000 undecided. This apparent "anti-Tamil" attitude of the LSSP has caused the party to be subject to frequent verbal attacks by the breakaway LSSP-R.

De Silva has also spoken out strongly in favor of a new constitution. In attacking the defects of the present constitution, he condemned the electoral franchise regulations which allegedly make one vote in some constituencies equivalent to five votes in others. One of the motives behind the criticism was believed to be the advantage being gained by rural-based parties such as the SLFP and UNP to the detriment of the urban-based left-wing groups.

The party was attacked further by the LSSP-R when Finance Minister N. M. Perera indicated that he did not favor immediate nationalization of banks and plantations. Perera, who confronts the potential problem of an estimated 870,000 unemployed by 1973, concentrated on developing the necessary infrastructure for cooperative, private, and small-scale industry. For the time being, at least, he did not intend to nationalize that sector of industry which did not make state ownership "vital in the national interest." (Budget speech by Perera, in *Ceylon Daily News*, 26 October.)

The MEP. The People's United Front, or MEP, which broke from the LSSP in 1950 to form the Viplavakari (Revolutionary) LSSP and assumed its present name in 1959, is led by Philip Gunawardena as president and M. D. Perera as secretary. The MEP controls the Central Council of Ceylon Trade Unions, which in 1965 claimed 36,841 members in eight affiliated unions.

The LSSP-R. The LSSP-Revolutionary was formed in 1964 when its parent organization, the LSSP, was expelled from the United Secretariat. The LSSP-R, which is recognized by the United Secretariat of the Fourth International, is estimated by the rival Revolutionary Communist League to have no more than 30 to 40 members and to lack any following among young people. The party is headed by a Tamil labor leader, P. Bala Tampoe. It dominates the Ceylon Mercantile Union and the Ceylon Bank Employees' Union. The *New Left Review* (London, November-December 1970) described the LSSP-R as "the only organization free from any racism" in Ceylon, but judged it to be handicapped by a "tendency to repeat old slogans instead of analyzing new situations."

In an election manifesto issued on 16 May, the LSSP-R analyzed the United Front program:

> The Coalition Programme does not contemplate the abolition of capitalist private property. It does not even threaten any inroads upon existing capitalist property in the plantations, or in industry. All the programme really envisages is increased control by the capitalist state in the sphere of banking and commerce, and increased state enterprise in certain industries, to sustain and assist in the development of the private sector. (*Intercontinental Press*, New York, 8 June.)

The LSSP-R has been active in its Ceylon Mercantile Union, which was on strike early in the year. Government troops were used to break up the strike. Some of the workers were beaten by the troops, according to Tampoe, who stated:

> If the Government is using armed forces against us, we too will pay them back with the same coin. We too have soldiers, who are not only prepared to fight for our cause, but are ready to lay down their lives for it. (*Ceylon Daily News*, 12 February.)

At the beginning of the year Tampoe was in Paris, where on 3 January he spoke at a meeting sponsored by the Ligue Communiste, the French branch of the United Secretariat. He told the meeting: "Guerrilla war is completely unrealistic in Ceylon," but emphasized that a high revolutionary potential existed in the masses (*Intercontinental Press*, 2 February).

The RSP. During 1968 or 1969, the LSSP-R divided between the followers of P. Bala Tampoe, who remained the leader of the party, and those of Edmund Samarkoddy, who formed a new party, the Revolutionary Samasamaja Party. While the LSSP-R tends to have its strength primarily in the trade unions, the RSP apparently seeks advancement largely through Parliamentary activities. It seems to be very small.

The RCL. The Revolutionary Communist League, formed in September 1968, began in 1966 as a faction (the "Virodhaya group") of the LSSP-R and was composed largely of younger members of the parent party who were "disillusioned with the failure of the LSSP-R to qualitatively break from the politics of the LSSP and Pabloism [i.e., 'rightist revisionism']" (*Bulletin*, organ of the Workers' League, London, 14 July 1969).

The RCL is led by Keerthi Balasuriya. It is affiliated with International Committee, an extreme leftist faction of the Fourth International. The youth wing of the RCL, the Revolutionary Communist Youth, is said to have held its Second Congress in Colombo on 24 October 1969.

The JVP. In late 1969 the existence of the Janata Vimukthi Peramuna,[1] popularly called the "Che Guevara movement," became known. At that time a number of its members—mainly young dissenters from the pro-Soviet and pro-Chinese LKP's—were arrested and later released.

The JVP has been described as a "nativistic, ultra-revolutionary" party (A. Jeyaratnam Wilson, "Ceylon: A New Government Takes Office," *Asian Survey*, February 1971). It draws support from among the young people. JVP leaders include Rohan Wijeweera (a former law student), Mahinda Wijesekera, and Ven Mangala (*Ceylon Daily News*, 28 February 1971). Although the movement is particularly devoted to Che Guevara, its revolutionary models are said to include also Mao Tse-tung, Fidel Castro, and Ho Chi Minh (*Tribune*, Colombo, 16 August). It appears to be a "new left" association rather than a communist party. It is not monolithic, but consists of a number of groups, among which there is evidence of some rivalry.

The Inspector General of Police announced on 19 August that the JVP was being investigated to determine how without financial aid it could have printed 30,000 copies of a newspaper. The assumption was that the organization may have received funds from foreign sources. Some LSSP ministers have attempted to associate the JVP with the U.S. Central Intelligence Agency, and the deposed UNP has been accused of supporting it to discredit the new government.

On 8 August the three coalition parties issued a statement charging that their government was the real target of the JVP. The LSSP-led Ceylon Students' Federation and other student organizations allied to the coalition began an active campaign to counteract the JVP propaganda.

At the first open rally of the JVP, on 10 August at Colombo, Rohan Wijeweera denied that the group was opposed to the government and claimed that by spreading Marxism-Leninism among the villages his group had aided the election campaign of the present United Front. Wijeweera was said to have implied that the JVP would engage in violence should the government fail to lead the country toward socialism.

*   *   *

Publications. The pro-Soviet LKP publishes a Sinhalese daily paper, *Aththa* (Truth), which has a circulation of 22,000. It also publishes the Sinhalese weeklies *Tarunahanda* (Voice of Youth),

---

[1] Not to be confused with the 1965 election coalition partner of the MEP, the Jatika Vimukthi Peramuna (National Liberation Front; JVP).

Nava Lokaya (New World), and *Mawbima* (Motherland). The party's main Tamil publication is *Desabhimani* (Patriot), also a weekly. It has an English weekly, *Forward*. Two publications, *Kommunist Lokaya* (Communist World) and *Nava Sakthi* (New Strength), appear during campaign periods.

The pro-Chinese LKP publishes a weekly in English, *Red Flag*. It also has two "worker" dailies—*Kamkaruwa* in Sinhalese, and its Tamil counterpart, *Tolilali*, with estimated circulations of 3,000 and 2,000 respectively. The party also publishes a Tamil "cultural and general affairs" monthly, *Vasantham*.

The LSSP publishes the weeklies *Samasamajaya, Samadharmam,* and *Samasamajist* in Sinhalese, Tamil, and English respectively. The MEP publishes the weekly *Mahajana Eksath Peramuna*. The RCL has a Sinhalese publication *Virodhaya*, a Tamil publication *Ethirppu*, and since 1969 an English publication, *Asian Marxist Bulletin*, the last being dedicated to the rebuilding of the Trotskyist movement in the Indian subcontinent.

E. S.

CHINA

The First Congress of the Chinese Communist Party (Chung-kuo kung-ch'an tang; CCP) was held in Shanghai in July 1921. Mao Tse-tung, the present party chairman, was one of the twelve delegates known to have attended. The party celebrates its anniversary each 1 July.

The People's Republic of China or Chinese People's Republic (CPR) was established 1 October 1949. State organs are in all important respects dominated by the CCP, the sole legal party. The constitution adopted by the CCP in 1969 stresses the dominance of party over government in these words: "The organs of state power of the dictatorship of the proletariat . . . must all accept the leadership of the party."

The CCP is the largest communist party in the world. No membership figures, however, are available for later than 1961, when *Jen-min jih-pao* (People's Daily) reported on 1 July that there were more than 17 million CCP members. This figure was repeated by *Hung ch'i* (Red Flag) on 16 July 1962. In 1970 the party was still being reconstructed in the wake of the purges during the Great Proletarian Cultural Revolution (1966-68), making membership estimates mere guess-work. The population of mainland China is commonly estimated at about 750 million.

Organization and Leadership. According to the party constitution, the "highest leading body" of the CCP is the national party congress, which is to be convened every five years; under "special circumstances" the congress may be convened early or postponed. The Ninth Congress of the CCP—the most recent—was held in April 1969. The national congress selects the Central Committee, which in turn selects the Politburo, the Standing Committee of the Politburo, and the chairman and vice-chairman of the Central Committee. The Ninth Central Committee consists of 170 full members and 109 alternates.

Effective policy-making power within the party rests with the Central Committee and at higher levels, particularly the Standing Committee of the Politburo. The Politburo members selected by the Ninth Congress were: *Standing Committee*—Mao Tse-tung (chairman of the Central Committee), Lin Piao (vice-chairman of the Central Committee), Chou En-lai, Ch'en Po-ta, and K'ang Sheng; *other full members*—Yeh Ch'un, Yeh Chien-ying, Liu Po-ch'eng, Chiang Ch'ing, Chu Teh, Hsü Shih-yü, Ch'en Hsi-lien, Li Hsien-nien, Li Tso-p'eng, Wu Fa-hsien, Chang Ch'unch'iao, Ch'iu Hui-tso, Yao Wen-yüan, Huang Yung-sheng, Tung Pi-wu, and Hsieh Fu-chih; *alternate members*—Chi Teng-k'uei, Li Hsüeh-feng, Li Te-sheng, and Wang Tung-hsing. Of these 25 men and women, Liu Po-ch'eng, Chu Teh, and Tung Pi-wu are inactive because of age and infirmity.

The order in which the full and alternate members are normally listed is by the number of strokes in their surnames, the Chinese equivalent of alphabetical order. The grouping issued by the New China News Agency (NCNA) on 24 October 1970, in an announcement of those present at a ceremony commemorating the twentieth anniversary of the entry of the Chinese "People's

Volunteers" into the Korean War, reestablished the order of rank as follows: Chou En-lai, K'ang Sheng, Huang Yung-sheng, Chiang Ch'ing, Chang Ch'un-ch'iao, Yao Wen-yüan, Yeh Ch'un, Li Hsien-nien, Yeh Chien-ying, Wu Fa-hsien, Li Tso-p'eng, and Ch'iu Hui-tso; and alternate members Li Te-sheng, Chi Teng-k'uei, and Wang Tung-hsing. Mao Tse-tung and Lin Piao, of course, hold the highest positions, but did not attend the ceremony. Also missing from the list were Tung Pi-wu, Liu Po-ch'eng, and Chu Teh, who seldom appear in public; Hsü Shih-yü, Ch'en Hsi-lien, and Li Hsüeh-feng, chairmen of the Kiangsu, Liaoning, and Hopeh Revolutionary Committees, respectively, who are usually in the provinces; and Ch'en Po-ta and Hsieh Fu-chih, who had been absent for unexplained reasons during the last part of the year. Hsieh Fu-chih, who is also a deputy premier, minister of public security, and chairman of the Peking Revolutionary Committee, last appeared in such a list on 19 March 1970. (At a municipal party congress held on 10-15 March 1971, however, Hsieh became first secretary of the newly reestablished Peking party committee, although there were indications he may not actually have been present at the congress.) Ch'en Po-ta last appeared on 1 August 1970. Until 20 May, when his widely acclaimed "20 May Statement" was given, Mao Tse-tung himself had not appeared publicly since 14 October 1969, making this his longest recorded absence.

The executive organs of the Central Committee which existed before the Cultural Revolution —the Secretariat, with its various departments, and the Control Commission—have apparently been discontinued. Authority to create new executive organs for the party leadership was given to the Standing Committee of the Politubro by the constitution adopted in 1969. The status of the Standing Committee itself came under question at the CPR's twenty-first anniversary ceremonies on 1 October 1970, when its members were listed without distinction from the rest of the Politburo. Although reference to the committee as a separate entity has been made since then, the change at the National Day celebrations may have been an effort to concentrate greater control in the hands of Mao Tse-tung and Lin Piao. At the same ceremonies, these two, normally referred to as chairman and vice-chairman, respectively, were described by new titles: "supreme commander of the whole nation and the whole army," and "deputy supreme commander of the whole nation and the whole army." (NCNA, 10 October.)

Below the Central Committee there is a network of party committees at the provincial, special district, county, and municipal levels. There is a similar network of party committees within the People's Liberation Army (PLA), from the level of the military region down to that of the regiment.

The primary level of party organization is the branch; the party constitution says that branches are formed "in factories, mines, and other enterprises, people's communes, offices, schools, shops, neighborhoods, companies of the PLA, and other primary units."

During the Cultural Revolution, the hierarchy of party committees, excepting that of the PLA, was destroyed, and through 1970 was in the middle stages of reconstruction (see below). A hierarchy of "Revolutionary Committees," created during the Cultural Revolution from the provincial level on down, continued for the most part to exercise the authority of the former organs of both party and government. Party members acting within these committees constitute what is referred to by the official media as the "core groups" of these bodies, suggesting the leadership role that the central authority wishes them to play.

Domestic Policy Trends. The year 1970 was relatively uneventful in the internal political affairs of the CPR. The overriding concern throughout the year was the rebuilding of the organization and authority of the CCP, a process officially inaugurated at the Ninth Congress. The emphasis was on pragmatism and moderation. Within the Revolutionary Committee triumvirates, the radical "mass representatives" were losing their power bases through indoctrination or isolation, while the more stable elements improved their positions. These latter elements were the "old cadres," who, being considered necessary for their management skills, were rapidly being rehabilitated; and the PLA, which was obtaining greater representation on state and party bodies, and thereby becoming the strongest of the three Revolutionary Committee groups. The "mass representatives" found themselves also being given less representation on the new party committees, which were being formed at all levels to parallel the Revolutionary Committees.

Reconstruction of the government administration was also being carried out, but in a more secretive manner. The first State Council (or cabinet) meeting announced since 1966 was reported by Peking radio on 7 March. This was followed by the drafting and restricted circulation of a state constitution, a copy of which was obtained and distributed by the Chinese Nationalist government on Taiwan in November. The document, generally accepted as legitimate, assures leading roles to Mao Tse-tung and Lin Piao in the state government, and makes permanent the system of Revolutionary Committees, originally designated as "temporary." It was anticipated that the constitution would be approved at a fourth National People's Congress. The decision to convene such a congress, the first since 1964-65, was made at the Second Plenary Session of the Ninth Central Committee of the CCP (23 August-6 September), which called for the "necessary preparations" to hold the congress "at an appropriate time" (*Peking Review*, 11 September).

Party Building.   During 1969 only one party committee was announced at the county level (Changte County in Hunan Province) and none at the higher levels, although occasionally throughout 1970 casual references were made to the existence of county level committees which had been created the previous year. At the end of 1970, the leadership of about 160 of China's 2,100 counties and eight of the country's approximately 170 municipalities were in the hands of party committees. At the same time, China announced the establishment of the first province-level party committees (Hunan, Kiangsi, Kwangtung, and Kiangsu), and also the first committee at the provincial-capital level (Changsha, Hunan) and at the special-district (*chuan-ch'ü*) level (Ch'ao-yang, Liaoning).

Opposition to the reconstruction of an all-powerful party apparatus was still sufficiently widespread to elicit frequent warnings from Mao's more faithful followers. An article on party building appearing in the first 1970 issue of the theoretical journal *Hung ch'i* stated:

> Within our ranks there ... exists a sharp struggle between proletarian thought and the bourgeois and petty-bourgeois thought. The essence of the struggle is the question of who holds leadership. The struggle is focused on the question of whether or not the leadership of the party is needed, and on the questions on how to build the party and what kind of party we must build.

The article, attributed to the "Mao Tsetung Thought propaganda team" of a PLA unit stationed at the Peking "7 February" Locomotive and Rolling Stock plant, warned that such a struggle could be expected both from elements to the right who had succumbed to the influence of Liu Shao-ch'i, contending that party consolidation was an "inner-party business" in which the masses had "no right to interfere," and from those of the "left," who made the claim: "We old rebels are the most revolutionary and the most advanced; we must head the task of party consolidation and party building, and we must be regarded as the foundation in carrying out this task."

On 1 April, the first anniversary of the Ninth Congress of the CCP, a *Jen-min jih-pao* editorial and a commemorative article broadcast by the NCNA reaffirmed the importance of the party. They urged that the congress documents and the thoughts of Mao Tse-tung be studied to enable both CCP members and "revolutionary masses" to understand better that "without the leadership of the CCP no revolution can succeed." The CCP constitution, in particular, was to serve as an aid to party members in establishing the correct balance between radicalism and conservatism

—specifically between the contending theories of continuing and consolidating the revolution, between ideological and organizational priorities, between stringency and leniency in the treatment of erring members, and between long-term and immediate goals.

Party building is being carried out on two levels—indoctrination and organization—with the former taking first priority. An article in *Hung ch'i* (no. 7, 1970) by the worker-PLA "Mao Tsetung Thought propaganda team" at Peking University stated:

> It is necessary to pay attention to handling correctly the relationship between organizational and ideological consolidation. Giving prominence to ideological consolidation means giving prominence to the guidance and command of Mao Tsetung Thought. Only by first making a success of ideological consolidation will it be possible to lay the foundation for organizational consolidation and establish the basic orientation in this regard.

It was also made clear that ideological indoctrination was to continue to be important after the achievement of "organizational consolidation." Failure to keep this in mind led to an apparently common error: "Some comrades say at times that it is necessary to carry out ideological consolidation, but they regard it only as a means for organizational consolidation and as a step for party members to take in 'passing the test.'" In such a situation, organizational consolidation would become "equivalent to primitiveness, 'inner-party peace,' or liberalism."

The effort to build the proper ideological bases explains in part the delays in forming party committees. As the year progressed, the rate at which party committees were being formed at the various levels increased. By the end of the year, committees had been formed at the county level in most of China's 29 provinces.

The formation of county-level party committees was normally announced casually rather than as a major event, and only occasionally was it reported in the national news media. One of the few relatively detailed accounts of the party-building process (in Honan Province) revealed something of the selection of delegates to 12 county-level party congresses (Chengchow radio, 12 November). Control of the process rested with the core group of the next higher level—the special district—and the PLA party committees of military subdistricts, whose function was to "carry out overall examination and investigation" of all possible candidates among Honan cadres. Although these organizations gave "free rein to the masses," those chosen to assist in the selection of candidates were the more established cadres and "members of the Revolutionary Committees of counties, responsible persons of Revolutionary Committees of communes, secretaries of party branches of production brigades, and representatives of workers and poor and lower-middle peasants." Emphasis was placed on the ideological outlook of the candidates in order to keep power "firmly in the hands of outstanding party members loyal to Chairman Mao, Mao Tsetung Thought, and Chairman Mao's revolutionary line." The core groups and PLA committees "classified the cadres by means of the class struggle and line struggle," going "deep into the whole history and the whole record of each cadre." Senior cadres were rated on "their political and ideological standard, their standard of executing policies, and their ability to carry out their work independently," weeding out the politically impure and indecisive. At the congresses a "dual three-way alliance" principle was employed to give equal consideration to PLA personnel, cadres, and the masses—a combination established in the Revolutionary Committees—and to a new grouping of the old, the middle-aged, and the young. (*Ibid.*).

The congresses elected the party committees by means of "secret ballot." The leadership of the new committees remained generally the same military-bureaucratic groups that had exercised power since the Cultural Revolution. In most cases, the secretaries of the new committees were also chairmen of the corresponding Revolutionary Committees, and were frequently PLA representatives. (*Ibid.*).

Little was disclosed of the day-to-day role of the party committees. Their first task was, according to the Honan report, to go down to the basic levels to carry out ideological rectification and to establish a more direct chain of command. (*Ibid.*). In another case, that of the Hsiangtan County party committee, in Hunan, this meant that of the nine standing committee members and 22 ordinary members, only two of the former and three of the latter group remained in the office to handle routine work (NCNA, 3 November).

The first province level party committee appeared in Hunan, Mao's home province, following a province party congress on 24 November-4 December. The NCNA did not announce the event, however, until 14 December, suggesting that the congress may not have run smoothly and additional time was required to iron out differences. The congresses of Kiangsi, Kwangtung, and Kiangsu provinces were held simultaneously, beginning on 18 December (19 December in Kiangsu) and ending on 26 December (Mao's seventy-seventh birthday, although the NCNA report did not attach any significance to the coincidence). They were attended by an average of 1,000 delegates, who elected committees averaging about 100 members.

The establishment of party committees at the province level indicated the abandonment of what had appeared to be a policy of completing party reconstruction at lower levels before proceeding to higher levels. In some cases, the large majority of primary party organizations was said to have been reestablished before the formation of committees at the province or special district levels to which they were subordinate. At the intermediate level, which includes the counties, progress was relatively slow. Only 15 of Hunan's 82 counties had been acknowledged to have party committees at the time of the province party congress; the announcement of the formation of the province-level party committee (NCNA, 14 December) declared, however, that party congresses had been convened and county committees set up in most of the province's counties.

Attending the Hunan congress were 920 delegates representing the party membership from among the industrial workers, poor and lower-middle peasants, PLA units stationed in the province, leading revolutionary cadres, Red Guards, revolutionary intellectuals, minority nationalities, and women, presumably in declining order of importance and representation (*ibid.*). After "repeated consultation from below and above," the delegates elected a province party committee of 25 full and 15 alternate members. This was comprised exclusively of the new "three-in-one combination" of old, middle-aged, and young people, marking the abandonment of the policy of representation by background (i.e., the "three-way combination" of PLA personnel, cadres, and mass organizations).

The shift in the committees from representation by background to representation by age (including the experiment of using both forms in the counties of Honan) suggested that an attempt was being made to limit the admittance of the "proletarian revolutionaries," particularly the left extremists who had been heroes of the Cultural Revolution but were now falling into disfavor. Despite the attendance of Red Guards at the Hunan congress, the composition of the new party committee appeared to be predominantly of military and "old cadre" elements, as was the case in the three other province party committees established during the year. In all four, the leaderships were almost identical with those of the corresponding Revolutionary Committees. All four first secretaries of the new province-level committees[1] had been (and continued to be) chairmen of their respective Revolutionary Committees. All but one were military men. Of the 18 subordinate committee members identified as of February 1971, 15 simultaneously held positions of equal or nearly equal rank in the parallel Revolutionary Committees. At least 10 were active military leaders and two others had military backgrounds. Four of the new committee members were known to have been secretaries in pre-Cultural Revolution party committees of their respec-

[1]Hua Kuo-feng, Hunan; Cheng Shih-ching, Kiangsi; Liu Hsing-yüan, Kwangtung; Hsü Shih-yü, Kiangsu.

tive provinces. Eleven were members of the party's Ninth Central Committee, one as an alternate member and another (Hsü Shih-yü) as a member of the Politburo.

Leadership problems frequently developed following the formation of party committees. Just as the Revolutionary Committees were exhorted to respect the authority of the "core groups" or party activists within the committees, so they were told also to recognize the leading role of the party committees once these were formed. The proper relationship between the Revolutionary Committees and party committees was outlined by Honan radio on 13 January 1970 on the experience of the party branch committee of the Shen-ch'iu County post office. According to the report, several leaders had initially "failed to treat the relationship between the party branch and the Revolutionary Committee correctly, so that the party branch was unable to play its proper role as the core." When they understood this shift of power, the party branch worked out a plan to strengthen party leadership:

> All important problems concerning matters of principle or of policy must first be studied and decided directly by the party branch, before they are discussed, passed and implemented by the members of the Revolutionary Committee. In this way, the core leadership role of the party branch is guaranteed, the role of the Revolutionary Committee as a combat headquarters is fully played and the struggle-criticism-transformation deeply developed."

The relationship between the two committees was still a subject for debate at the end of the year. Nanking radio (28 December) reemphasized that the relative positions of "leader and led" should be enforced. This, however, was not to be done in such a way as to cause the party committee to become "tied up with routine work" by attempting to monopolize all the work of both committees. It was made clear that the party committee was to "analyze the situation, point out the direction, and hold fast to policy," leaving the Revolutionary Committee to assume executive functions.

Cadre Policy.   The policy of leniency in reinstating those cadres who had been the target of mass criticism in the Cultural Revolution continued during 1970. These were the "old cadres"—the state and party officials who had served as foremen, political organizers, and managers at every level and were now regaining positions. The "new cadres"—the heterogeneous group of militant students and peasant and worker "mass representatives" who acquired power during the Cultural Revolution—were being eased out of their positions and were not being admitted into the party automatically as their revolutionary experience had led them to expect.

In their effort to regain control from the Revolutionary Committees, party leaders encountered difficulties in encouraging non-party Revolutionary Committee members to relinquish their recently acquired positions of power and submit to the leadership of the party. The greatest resistance came from the "mass organizations," one of the three forces in the Revolutionary Committee triumvirates. An article on party building in the first 1970 issue of *Hung ch'i* explained the problem:

> [Some] comrades have desperately exaggerated the role of the former mass organizations, incorrectly handled the relations between the mass organizations and the party, and tried to put them above the party organizations to contend with the party for leadership. This is an expression of reactionary anarchism, syndicalism, and "the theory of many centers, that is, the theory of no center." To use them as the "foundation" to transform the party means to degrade party organizations from the level of the vanguard to the level of a mass organization.

Shanghai radio reported on 26 February that there were many in mass organizations who, though they had supported Mao during the Cultural Revolution, were now either tending toward extremism or attempting to consolidate their positions of authority. These people were reminded that they had "played well their revolutionary role during the Cultural Revolution ... because they were led by the party."

A *Jen-min jih-pao* article, broadcast by Peking radio on 12 June, emphasized two faults of the "new cadres": their tendency to "pay less attention to their ideological transformation since their promotion," and their lack of enthusiasm in "accepting criticism and assistance" from veteran cadres. While these faults could be eliminated only through "constant assistance on the part of the veteran cadres," those in the latter group were not free from error either. Many of them still had "insufficient understanding regarding the question of the upbringing of new cadres." According-ing to Hofei (Anhwei Province) radio (22 January), old cadres—"who have a relatively rich expe-rience in class struggle and work, and play the role of backbone"—and new cadres—"who are a new force for revolution [and] are vigorous and rich in revolutionary initiative"—were urged to "respect, learn from, help, and support one another."

The "reeducation" of cadres displaced from their positions or ideologically impure is a major preoccupation of Chinese authorities. Typically, the solution is to send these cadres "down to the countryside" (the *hsia fang* movement), where they are supposed to derive benefit from close contact with the masses. The "7 May" cadre schools were established for this purpose (see *YICA*, 1969, pp. 144-46). Originally designated (7 May 1968) as self-sufficient farms where cadres would be sent to settle down permanently or to receive training on a rotation basis after which they would return to their former position or be reassigned, the schools soon became pop-ulated by cadres who had been made redundant by administrative reorganization or were radi-cals who had fallen into disfavor at the end of the Cultural Revolution. These were not immedi-ately reassigned to administrative posts, causing the schools to become identified as places to accommodate cadres not on active duty or "questionable and erring" cadres. At the beginning of 1970, however, the schools started to conduct short-term training classes for cadres. The first such class was initiated at the original (and now the model) "7 May" school in Liu-ho (Chingan County, Heilungkiang) in November 1969. A report in *Jen-min jih-pao* on 14 June 1970 stated that nearly 800 cadres had attended the two three-month training sessions held to that time. The schools, an important element in China's administrative process, have thus become training schools for administrative officials rather than reformatories for purged or retrenched cadres.

Party-Army Relations. During the Cultural Revolution, it was the party apparatus within the PLA that was least affected by the otherwise devastating attacks on the party as a whole. The PLA became the stabilizing force that largely guaranteed the success of the Revolutionary Committees which emerged from the Cultural Revolution. It was logical, therefore, in the face of potential conflict from the newly ascended radicals—whose views were coming increasingly into conflict with the more moderate policies that followed the Cultural Revolution—that the PLA should also supply much of the leadership in the reemerging party organization. There had been reason to believe that the PLA might relax its control over general civilian administration to shift its attention to matters of a more military nature—particularly when threatened with the possi-bility of war with the Soviet Union in 1969; but in 1970 the PLA's position became even more firmly entrenched in almost all aspects of civilian administration.

The PLA's increased importance to the party, which was observed in the selection of a largely military-oriented Central Committee at the party's Ninth Congress, was confirmed in 1970 by the preponderance of military men in the newly created party committees at the lower levels. Although military men have not comprised a particularly large proportion of the Revolutionary Committees, they have occupied the most important positions. When the party committees were formed, these leaders in the majority of cases obtained corresponding leadership positions in the latter bodies. Generally, PLA representatives on the Revolutionary Committees have had the task of maintaining unity and fostering PLA standards. One of their most important functions has been to achieve a balance between established cadres—party and non-party—and representatives of the mass organizations. The political competition and frequently clashing radical and conservative values of these two groups tended to be disruptive to the committees and continued to create a problem sufficiently serious to require the PLA, as a source of ideological purity, to assume an authoritative position in the newer party committees.

At the same time, the degree of the state's dependence on the PLA continued to be a subject of disagreement. The party committee of a PLA regiment in Honan renewed a theme, dormant for about a year, of a state politically dependent on the military: "Particularly with regard to the relationship between the army and political power, the political power of the state, in the basic sense, is mainly the army. Without the army, there is no political power and the people have nothing." (Chengchow radio, 28 July.) A conflicting view was observed in Shanghai, where radical power, attained during the Cultural Revolution, remained strong under the leadership of Politburo members Chang Ch'un-ch'iao, Yao Wen-yüan, and the wife of Mao Tse-tung, Chiang Ch'ing. Though agreeing that a strong army was necessary, Shanghai radio (27 July) warned:

> The people's armed forces of a socialist country must always be placed under the leadership of the political party of the proletariat and the supervision of the masses of people. They must always preserve the glorious tradition of the People's Army, that is, unity between army and people and unity between officers and men.

In the process of party reconstruction, with current emphasis on building ideological rather than organizational foundations, greater effort was given during the year to promote the PLA as an ideological model. The Chinese news media gave considerable play to the "support-the-left" movement, by which military personnel and units were given the task of guiding ideologically the "left" local revolutionary groups. The movement forms a part of the PLA's "three supports and two militaries" campaign: supporting industry, agriculture, and the "left"; and maintaining military control of disorders and giving political and military training.

The PLA was constantly involved in indoctrinating non-military officials, and activities of military men were frequently publicized as examples of proper conduct or attitude. A Canton radio broadcast (18 July) explained how a party committee of a PLA "support-the-left" unit stationed in Tungkuan County, Kwangtung, had guided the unit to help members of the county Revolutionary Committee by conducting sessions with them to "combat self-interest and repudiate revisionism," to abolish "small-group mentality," "departmentalism," and "splittism," and to study Mao Tse-tung's teachings and eradicate such ideas advocated by Liu Shao-ch'i as "production comes first."

In Sinkiang, where the Urumchi municipal Revolutionary Committee had experienced factional difficulties, it was admitted that "in the early days" the three component groups represented on the committee (the PLA, cadres, and mass representatives) "did not entirely trust one another."

> However, after earnestly studying the relevant instructions of Chairman Mao, representatives of the army understood better the importance of trusting and relying on the masses. Since the study, they have boldly allowed other representatives to grow stronger in the teeth of the storm of class struggle, and helped them in carrying out work in all fields. In this way, representatives of the army have greatly aroused the initiative of other representatives; together they made concerted efforts to unify and exercise collective leadership. (Urumchi radio, 4 February.)

A joint editorial in *Jen-min jih-pao, Hung ch'i*, and the PLA daily *Chieh-fang chün-pao* on the forty-third anniversary of the founding of the PLA (1 August) reiterated the domestic tasks of the army, emphasizing a continuation of the "three supports and two militaries" and the strengthening of unity between the army and the masses. The editorial referred to two other slogans of current importance for the PLA: (1) the "two resolutions" (i.e., those adopted at the "Ninth Representative Conference of the Fourth Red Army" at Kutien, Fukien Province, in 1929, and at the 1960 enlarged session of the CCP Military Affairs Committee), which attacked, among other things, the "purely military viewpoint" (of separating military and political affairs and regarding them as mutually opposing) and "book learning" (or neglecting ideology and the "human factor"), and (2) the "four good's" movement, referring to model PLA units that are "good" in political and ideological work, in the "three-eight" working style, in military training, and in arranging their everyday life. (The "three-eight" working style alludes to the three concepts of a firm and correct political orientation, an industrious and simple style of work, and flexible strategy and tactics, and to the eight characters that express the concepts of unity, alertness, earnestness, and liveliness.)

It was evident that the PLA, which was providing leadership in political study for the rest of the country (much as it had done in the "Learn from the Army" campaign in 1964), was at the same time being asked to improve its own ideological standards. The thrust of the "two resolutions" and the "four good's," although intended also for emulation by civilians, was in this direction. The Macheng County People's Armed Forces Department (in the Hupeh Military District) described its experiences with the former campaign thus:

> In implementing the two resolutions, [the Department] has on the one hand struggled against erroneous inclinations from the Right and the Left, while on the other hand it has struggled against various erroneous mentalities and the selfishness in the minds of people, which have disrupted the implementation of the two resolutions. It has conducted daily repudiation of the bourgeois army-building line and constant elimination of counter-revolutionary poisonous influences and has effectively raised its awareness of the struggle between the two lines and of letting proletarian politics stand out and has guaranteed the practical implementation of the two resolutions in its various tasks. (Wuhan radio, 18 July.)

The "war preparedness" campaign continued during 1970, although in a more muted form than in the previous year when Sino-Soviet tensions were high. The movement, which has the two-fold purpose of preparing the population for a "people's war" in accordance with Maoist strategy and of stimulating production in industry and agriculture, fluctuated in intensity throughout the year, notably increasing in activity during the summer months. Many of the reports on war preparedness referred to the defense of borders other than the one with the Soviet Union; a number of them centered on the southern frontier regions of Hainan Island, Kwangsi, and Yunnan, where "political border defense" was emphasized, stressing vigilance and a correct ideological attitude. The general decline in the movement from its 1969 level was also apparent in the pronouncements of the CPR's twenty-first anniversary celebrations in October. Unlike the statements issued at the twentieth anniversary, which reflected a fear of war with the Soviet Union, they concentrated domestically on "socialist revolution and construction." Lin Piao did, however, hail the achievements of the PLA, the militia, and the people in "enhancing preparedness against war and consolidating national defense" (NCNA, 1 October).

International Views and Positions. For the CPR, the year 1970 was one of rapidly expanding international contacts. While continuing to give at least verbal support to various revolutionary movements advocating armed struggle, the CPR became increasingly concerned with establishing better relations with both communist and non-communist governments. Continuing a trend initiated in 1969, the CPR undertook to normalize its diplomatic representation by appointing ambassadors to countries where chargés d'affaires had been functioning since the Cultural Revolution. In chronological order, new ambassadors were sent to: North Korea, Finland, Mali, the Sudan, the U.A.R., Ceylon, Yugoslavia, Hungary, Poland, Somalia, East Germany, Cuba, the U.S.S.R., Iraq, South Yemen, and Switzerland. Diplomatic relations were established with Canada (13 October), Guinea (15 October), Italy (6 November), Ethiopia (24 November), and Chile (15 December).[2] The resumption of full diplomatic relations with Yugoslavia, after a break of twelve years, was a significant step for the CPR in view of the ideological differences between the two countries.

The Soviet Union.   While Sino-Soviet party relations continued to be nonexistent (as they have been since 1963), state relations between the two countries improved slightly during 1970. On 13 October the new Soviet ambassador, V. S. Tolstikov, presented his credentials in Peking, but only after months of rumors suggesting various possible appointments; subsequently, on 22 November, the Chinese reciprocated, though with a comparatively minor figure, Liu Hsin-chuan, who had not held a diplomatic position abroad before.

The status of the Sino-Soviet border—the major volatile issue between the two countries, and one that led to armed conflict in 1969—remained unresolved in 1970. The continuing negotiations helped to maintain the disagreements at the diplomatic rather than military level. Nevertheless, very little was reported on the development of the talks, and the few statements that were made indicated that little progress had been achieved. Early in the year, the Hong Kong newspaper *Ta kung pao* (9 January) reported that the CPR was seeking an "all-round solution to the border issue," meaning that it continued to press for a Soviet repudiation of the "unequal treaties" imposed upon China during the nineteenth century.

The Soviet negotiator, Vasily Kuznetsov, who had left for Moscow on 14 December 1969, ostensibly to attend a meeting of the Supreme Soviet, returned to Peking on 2 January. During his absence polemics had increased on both sides, and on his return he was not welcomed by Ch'iao Kuan-hua, leader of the Chinese delegation, who had been present at his departure. The talks presumably continued, but received little attention in the press of either side. On 10 June, Soviet Premier Alexei Kosygin stated that no progress was being made, and in November CPSU Politburo member Mikhail Suslov remarked that the talks could "not be described as easy" (TASS, 6 November). Kuznetsov returned to Moscow on 30 June for medical treatment, and was replaced by Leonid Ilichev, another deputy foreign minister, on 15 August.

The annual negotiations on navigation of the border rivers were announced the day after Kuznetsov's return to Moscow. These talks, which have been held since 1951, with the exception of 1968, took place at Heiho, Heilungkiang, beginning 10 July. The annual protocol was signed in late December. In the meantime, a Sino-Soviet trade agreement—the first since 1967—was signed in Peking on 22 November.

Despite these signs of improving state relations, there continued to exist an atmosphere of mutual criticism and distrust. The propaganda battle, which began the year with strong attacks charging "social imperialism" on the one side and "war psychosis" on the other, fluctuated slightly after a few months, then declined, remaining relatively calm for the rest of the year. A *Jen-min jih-pao* New Year editorial, for the first time since the border negotiations began in October 1969, assailed the Soviet leadership by name, denouncing "Brezhnev and company" for "enforcing fascist dictatorship at home and carrying out aggression and expansion abroad." A particularly incisive denunciation appeared in a joint editorial published by *Jen-min jih-pao*, *Hung ch'i*, and *Chieh fang chün-pao*, commemorating the centenary of Lenin's birth (22 April). It accused the Soviet leadership of betraying the October Revolution. To support this charge it

---

[2]To bypass the Taiwan issue, Canada, Italy, and Chile used a formula by which they recognized the CPR as the "sole legal government of China" and "took note" of its claim to Taiwan as an "inalienable part of the territory of the PRC." Guinea and Ethiopia recognized the CPR as the "sole legal government representing the entire Chinese people."

singled out the "Brezhnev doctrine" (which justified the 1968 Soviet intervention in Czechoslovakia) and the doctrine's implications of "social imperialism." The editorial emphasized that the Soviet people were not responsible for the "revisionist crimes" of their leaders:

> The people of our two countries have supported each other, helped each other and forged a close friendship in the course of the protracted revolutionary struggles. The handful of revisionist oligarchs are perversely trying to sow dissention and undermine the relations between the Chinese and Soviet peoples, but in the end they will be lifting a rock only to drop it on their own feet. . . . Under the great banner of Leninism, the mighty current of people's revolution is bound to break through the ice of revisionist rule, and the spring of socialism will surely return to the land of the Soviet Union! (*Peking Review*, 24 April.)

During the remainder of the year, the polemics were much milder. Although the "aggressive nature" of Soviet "social imperialism" in Czechoslovakia was attacked earlier in the year, criticism would have been expected to be most severe in August, on the second anniversary of the intervention. The Chinese press, however, was silent on the subject.

The National Day celebrations of both countries, in October, elicited unusually friendly statements. On the Chinese anniversary, the Soviet statement expressed a desire for the "normalization of state relations" and the "restoration of good neighborly relations and friendship" (TASS, 1 October). The Chinese statement answered that "differences on principle . . . should not hinder the two countries from maintaining and developing normal state relations" (NCNA, 6 November).

After April, the Chinese made only two strongly worded protests. The first was on the Soviet-West German treaty, which drew fire from the Chinese, but only on 13 September, a month after its signing. At that time, *Jen-min jih-pao* described the treaty as a "gross betrayal [of] the interests of the people of Germany, the Soviet Union, and Europe." The article charged:

> It is a monstrous fraud to cover up the aggressive features of Soviet revisionist social-imperialism and West German militarism with the cloak of "peace." It is also a component part of the monstrous "global Munich" scheme which Soviet revisionism and U.S. imperialism, collaborating and contending with each other, are energetically putting into effect to divide the spheres of influence in Europe.

The same article accused the Soviet Union of making "bigger concessions" on the West Berlin question, asserting that the current Soviet position represented a "big retreat" from its original policy of demanding that West Berlin be constituted as an independent political unit.

The second outburst was prompted by the removal of Władysław Gomułka as first secretary of the Polish United Workers' Party following workers' strikes and demonstrations in Poland in mid-December. On 22 December *Jen-min jih-pao* stated:

> For more than a decade, the Polish revisionist clique, in betrayal of the interests of the Polish people, has doggedly followed Soviet revisionism politically and become an appendage to it economically and has turned into a dependency of Soviet revisionism. It has restored capitalism in Poland and forfeited the fruits of victory reaped by the Polish people through long years of revolutionary struggle and brought increasing disasters to the broad masses of the people.

The strikes and demonstrations indicated, according to the article, that "Soviet revisionist social-imperialism in Eastern Europe" was in a critical period.

Vietnam.   During 1970 the CPR continued to favor a protracted war in Vietnam and to oppose a negotiated settlement. At the same time, it reaffirmed that the "vast expanse of China's territory" was the "reliable rear area" of the Indochinese people, signifying China's willingness to support but not become directly involved in the Indochina war. The CPR's stand was clearly manifested in a CCP Central Committee message on 2 February to the Vietnam Workers' Party (VWP) on its fortieth anniversary. The message asserted that "by persevering in a protracted war, in maintaining independence, keeping the initiative on their hands and relying on their own efforts," the Vietnamese would accomplish their objectives (*Peking Review*, 6 February).

Le Duan, first secretary of the VWP, visited Peking on 10-13 May and held talks with Mao Tse-tung, Chou En-lai, and PLA Chief of Staff Huang Yung-sheng. According to the *Economist* (London, 9 May) Le Duan requested the Chinese to allow more Soviet aid shipments to cross China. Following his visit, a new agreement offering "economic and military materials as gratuitous aid" was announced by the Chinese on 25 May. This agreement was an apparent attempt to offset the North Vietnamese loss of Cambodia as a sanctuary and the supply line through the port of Sihanoukville (now Kompong Som). On 6 October the annual nonrefundable aid agreement for the year 1971 was signed with North Vietnam. Unlike the agreement signed in 1969, it specified military as well as economic aid.

The resumption of bombing by the United States in North Vietnam was immediately condemned by the Chinese, who took the opportunity also to oppose the peace talks in Paris with the U.S. government, remarking: "The words of U.S. imperialism have never counted, particularly those of the Nixon government." A *Jen-min jih-pao* editorial on 22 November further asserted that "the U.S. imperialist new war provocations against the Vietnamese people [had] thoroughly exploded the fraud of Nixon's so-called 'new proposals for peace in Indo-China.'"

Relations with the National Liberation Front of South Vietnam (NLFSV) appeared to be maintaining a high degree of amity. On the occasion of the tenth anniversary of the founding of the NLFSV, a delegation led by NLFSV Presidium member Dang Tran Thi visited China on 18-25 December and attended a large rally in Peking on 20 December. For the same occasion Mao Tse-tung, Lin Piao, and Chou En-lai also sent their "warmest greetings" to the presidents of the NLFSV Central Committee and the Provisional Revolutionary Government of South Vietnam. The message declared that the struggle of the South Vietnamese had "greatly inspired the people of small countries with the revolutionary spirit of daring to resist aggression by big powers" and had given "power impetus" to the fight against "U.S. imperialism." It reaffirmed China's "all-out support and assistance until complete victory in the war against U.S. aggression and for national salvation." (*Peking Review*, 25 December.)

Southeast Asia and the Pacific. Indicative of the stronger leadership position enjoyed by the CPR in Indochina was the successful holding of a Chinese-supported "Indochinese summit conference" on 24-25 April. The conference—held at an undisclosed location in the frontier region of Laos, North Vietnam, and Cambodia[3]—was attended by delegations from the four major Indochinese groups opposing "American imperialism and its lackeys." Leading the delegations were: Prince Norodom Sihanouk, chairman of the National United Front of Kampuchea (NUFK; see below); Prince Souphanouvong, chairman of the Laotian Patriotic Front; Nguyen Huu Tho, president of the NLFSV; and Pham Van Dong, premier of the Democratic Republic of Vietnam. A CPR government statement on 28 April pledged China's "most resolute" support for the joint declaration issued by the conference. It also reiterated the conviction that "U.S. imperialism" would "never change its aggressive nature" and that the Nixon Administration's proposals for a "peaceful solution to the Vietnam question" and "peace and neutrality" in Laos and Cambodia were all "sheer lies." (*Peking Review*, special issue, 8 May.) Chou En-lai, who attended conference banquets on 25 and 26 April, offered "powerful backing for the three Indo-Chinese peoples," adding that China was their "reliable rear area" (*ibid.*).

[3]Some sources suggested the meeting was held in Yunnan Province; others placed it in Nanning (Kwangsi Province) or Canton.

The CPR further increased its influence in the Asian communist movement by giving official recognition and support to the "Royal Government of National Union of Cambodia under the Leadership of the National United Front of Kampuchea," headed by the deposed chief of state of Cambodia, Sihanouk (see *Cambodia*). Although this recognition was made official on 5 May, Sihanouk had been given protection and broad press coverage by the Chinese since his arrival in Peking on 19 March. His exile government was granted "free military aid" by the Chinese on 19 August. Earlier, in May, the CPR had given Sihanouk a loan, the details of which were not disclosed.

CPR relations with the Laotian communist movement appeared to be warm during 1970. Although the Chinese failed to support or mention the Pathet Lao's five-point peace plan announced on 7 March (see *Laos*), a *Jen-min jih-pao* article on 6 March offered strong encouragement to the struggle of the Laotian Patriotic Armed Forces, thus playing down proposed negotiations between the Laotian premier, Prince Souvanna Phouma, and the Pathet Lao leader, Souphanouvong.

Africa and Latin America.   CPR attitudes toward Africa were characterized by an apparent desire to consolidate an image of China as a major power.

Important among the various economic gestures to African governments was the CPR's assistance in the construction of the 1,116-mile-long Tan-Zam railway, which is to give Zambia rail access, across Tanzania, to the Indian Ocean and is expected to be completed by 1975. This major project, for which China gave a $400 million interest-free loan to Tanzania and Zambia, was officially inaugurated on 26 October 1970, although Chinese personnel had been working on it since July 1969. It appeared a possibility to Western observers that the Chinese presence in Tanzania and Zambia might help the CPR to maintain closer contacts with several African liberation movements and give China a foothold for the western end of its probable future ICBM testing range.

Contacts with Latin America were improved both by the return of an ambassador (after almost three years) to Cuba on 21 November and the establishment of diplomatic relations with Chile on 15 December. In line with its efforts for better relations with the Latin American governments, China sent $600,000 to help the Peruvian earthquake victims (NCNA, 9 June). An editorial in *Jen-min jih-pao* on 20 November expressed support for the demand by certain Latin American countries for a 200-mile limit on territorial waters. The 27 November issue of *Peking Review*, stating that fourteen Latin American countries had taken "an identical stand of principle against the plunder of their sea resources by the two super-powers," asserted that the "repeated schemes of U.S. imperialism and [U.S.S.R.] social-imperialism to divide and dominate the oceans" had thereby been frustrated.

Middle East.   Chinese support of guerrilla activities in the Middle East became more evident during 1970. Representatives of four major Arab guerrilla groups visited the CPR and held meetings with important Chinese leaders. China, which has expressed support for the demands of the Palestinian Arabs, including the dissolution of the state of Israel and the forceful takeover of its territory, continued to oppose any moves toward a negotiated settlement. This position served to benefit the Chinese in the Sino-Soviet dispute by helping to maintain a source of U.S.-Soviet friction. China was reported to have supplied limited quantities of small arms to various Arab guerrilla groups—apparently with partial reimbursement for them (see statement by Yasir 'Arafat, quoted in *New York Times*, 10 February 1970).

On 21-28 March, Yasir 'Arafat, the leader of the al-Fatah guerrilla forces and chairman of the Palestine Liberation Front (which maintains a permanent mission in Peking), visited China and met with Chou En-lai, receiving a "warm reception." Another delegation from the same group visited China in August. Considerable publicity was also given to a five-week visit in March and

April by a delegation of the "People's Front for the Liberation of the Occupied Arab Gulf," a group operating mainly in Dhofar in the Persian Gulf area.

Following an Israeli attack on Lebanese territory, Chou En-lai sent a letter to 'Arafat in what appeared to be an attempt to improve the morale of the Palestine guerrillas. It said in part:

> We highly admire you for your revolutionary spirit of fearing no sacrifice and fighting valiantly and strongly condemn the U.S.-Israeli reactionaries for their new acts of aggression....
>
> Your Excellency, your struggle is just and has the support of the revolutionary people throughout the world. The Chinese Government and people consistently and unswervingly support your struggle. We will always stand together with you. (*Peking Review*, 5 June.)

Another source of contact was provided by the visit of Dr. George Habash of the Palestine Popular Front in September. Reportedly, the Chinese expressed agreement with the group's policies of rejecting a negotiated settlement and promoting socialism in the Middle East, but criticized Habbash for relying on guerrilla activities outside Israel, for carrying out "spectacular but unwise" actions such as hijackings, for failing to concentrate on Israel as the main enemy by allowing clashes with Arab governments, and for failing to unify the Palestinian movement (*Christian Science Monitor*, 14 November).

The military confrontation between the Jordanian army and the Palestine guerrillas in September evoked an accusation that Jordan's attack had been engineered by the United States in a scheme aimed at "extermination of the guerrillas" (*Jen-min jih-pao*, 19 September). A joint communiqué following the visit of South Yemen President Salim 'Ali Rubai to Peking on 2-13 August asserted the conviction of both sides that a "protracted people's war" was the only means to achieve a Palestinian victory.

Japan. Communist Chinese attitudes toward both the Japan Communist Party (JCP) and the Japanese government were increasingly hostile in 1970.

Demonstrating the existence of a complete rupture with the JCP, the CPR augmented its coverage of pro-Chinese factions in Japan. On 2 January, *Peking Review* reported that a new "Communist Party of Japan (Left)" had been founded in November 1969, and stated that "broad masses of revolutionary people" opposed the "revisionist clique of [the JCP secretary-general] Miyamoto." The same source reported on 14 August that defections had taken place in the JCP. On 23 August, Saionji Kinkazu, a Japanese who had resided in Peking since 1958 and had served as the "unofficial" Japanese ambassador, returned to Tokyo. It was believed by most observers that Saionji (who was expelled from the JCP in 1967) would attempt to unify the various pro-Chinese groups in Japan.

On the other hand, a greater degree of cooperation between the CPR and the Japan Socialist Party was evident during the year. On 1 November the NCNA reported that delegations of both the China-Japan Friendship Association and the Japan Socialist Party, then visiting China, had signed a communiqué in which support was expressed for the most recent Chinese proposal for a "summit conference of all the countries of the world big and small ... to sign an agreement on the complete prohibition and thorough destruction of nuclear weapons and, as the first step, to reach an agreement on not using nuclear weapons."

Of special concern for the CPR was the alleged emergence of Japan as a "military power." Lashing out at the automatic and indefinite extension of the U.S.-Japan security treaty, a *Jen-min jih-pao* editorial on 23 June stated:

> Japanese militarism, which has revived under the wing of U.S. imperialism, is attempting to realize its old dream of a "Greater East Asia Co-Prosperity Sphere" by relying on the U.S.-Japan military alliance. The Japanese militarists have wildly clamoured that the vast area

from the west Pacific to the Indian Ocean is the so-called "life-line" of Japan and gone so far as to declare that they will dispatch warships to "defend the Strait of Malacca" and troops to other countries to "safeguard" Japan's economic rights and interest."

The chief of the Chinese general staff, Huang Yung-sheng, in a speech commemorating the twentieth anniversary of the CPR's entry into the Korean War, also attacked "Japanese militarism." Stating that Japanese Premier Sato, during a visit to the United States in November 1969, had referred to Taiwan as "a most important factor for the security of Japan," Huang asserted: "This is audaciously to declare [Japan's] intention of obstructing the Chinese people from liberating Taiwan and to regard Taiwan as belonging to Japan." (*Peking Review*, 3 July.)

Concern was also shown regarding the growing contacts between the Japanese government and the government of Taiwan. A *Jen-min jih-pao* article on 11 July condemned the "amity and co-operation" between Japan and the government of Chiang Kai-shek, contending that the "Japanese reactionaries [were] stepping up large-scale expansion and plunder in Taiwan."

Adding to the hostility between the CPR and Japan was the question of sovereignty over the Senkaku Islands. These eight small islands, located 100 miles northeast of Taiwan and close to a continental shelf rich in oil resources, are claimed by Japan as part of the Ryukyu chain. On 3 December, China made public its claim to the Senkakus and *Jen-min jih-pao* on 29 December asserted that "China alone has the right to explore and exploit" the seabed. The jargon-free language used in the article led observers to conclude that the CPR was treating the issue seriously.

Trade between the CPR and Japan, despite their above differences, rose to $825 million during 1970, increasing by $200 million over 1969. Nevertheless, the Chinese were quick to register their views of the Sato government when they signed the annual "Memorandum Trade Agreement" and a political communiqué with the Japanese, on 19 April. The Japanese delegation, composed of left-wing anti-Sato members of the governing Liberal Democratic Party, provided the only more or less official means of contact between the Japanese and Chinese governments. The communiqué, the culmination of forty days of talks (the trade agreement itself took only one day to negotiate), included a strong attack on Japanese policies as the price for the trade agreement. The U.S.-Japanese communiqué of 21 November 1969 (on the return of Okinawa) was sternly condemned for its alleged purpose of transforming Japan into a "military base for U.S. imperialist aggression against Asia." The communiqué further charged that Japanese "militarism" was a "harsh fact confronting the people of Asia and the whole world," and attacked the Sato government for participating in "scheming activities to create 'two Chinas' or 'one China, one Taiwan'." (*Peking Review*, 24 April.)

North Korea. A significant thaw took place in 1970 between the CPR and North Korea. During the Cultural Revolution, the Democratic People's Republic of Korea (DPRK) was accused of "revisionism," and the state and party leader, Kim Il-song, was attacked personally. In 1970, Kim was referred to by the Chinese as "the great leader of the Korean people and the close friend of the Chinese people."

The breaking of ice began in October 1969 when Choe Yong-kon, second highest-ranking member of the Korean Workers' Party (KWP), attended China's twentieth-anniversary celebrations in Peking. On 26 March 1970 the CPR ambassador to North Korea assumed his post in Pyongyang.

The most important development in the relations of the two countries was the visit of a delegation led by Chou En-lai to Pyongyang on 5-7 April. The visit was given a large amount of publicity in Chinese news media. In his two major speeches in Pyongyang (*Peking Review*, 10 April), Chou attacked Japanese "militarism" and U.S. "imperialism" as the primary common threats to both the CPR and the DPRK. He described the friendship between the two countries as one "cemented in blood," and said they were "closely related like lips and teeth"—a phrase usually reserved to describe Chinese-North Vietnamese friendship. The joint communiqué (*ibid.*) expressed support for the Laotian Patriotic Front, the Peking-based Cambodian government of Sihanouk, and the "national liberation" movements in Asia, Africa, and Latin America.

Commemorating the twentieth anniversary of the "Fatherland Liberation War of Korea" on 25 June, high-level delegations were exchanged between the CPR and North Korea. KWP Political Committee member Pak Song-chol attended activities marking the event in Peking during his visit on 24-29 June. Chinese Chief of Staff and CCP Politburo member Huang Yung-sheng at the same time visited Pyongyang, where he urged the strengthening of unity of the peoples of China, Vietnam, Cambodia, Laos, and Korea, and denounced the U.S.-Japan security treaty and U.S. "imperialism" (*ibid.*, 3 July).

In contrast, relatively minor delegations were exchanged at celebrations in October commemorating the twentieth anniversary of the entry of Chinese "People's Volunteers" into the Korean War. A speech by Huang Yung-sheng at the Peking ceremonies pledged Chinese aid in the event of a new conflict in Korea:

> If U.S. imperialism and its lackeys dare to launch another war of aggression against the Korean people, the 700 million Chinese people tempered through the Great Proletarian Cultural Revolution and armed with Marxism-Leninism Mao Tsetung Thought will as always, resolutely fulfil their internationalist duty and give all-out support and assistance in different fields to the Korean people. (*Ibid.*, 30 October.)

Support was also offered, though in more vague terms, in an editorial appearing in both *Jen-min jih-pao* and *Chieh-fang chün pao* on 25 October on the same occasion.

Two other important Korean delegations were sent to the CPR. O Chin-u, chief of staff of the Korean People's Army and a member of the KWP Political Committee, headed a group that met with Chou En-lai during its visit on 25 July-4 August. Chong Chun-taek, deputy premier and candidate member of the Political Committee, led a delegation that was in China on 14-23 October.

In the field of trade and aid, since 1967 there have been only annual CPR-DPRK protocols on the exchange of goods. On 17 October, two agreements, one on economic and technical aid and the other on the exchange of goods, were signed. The latter agreement, covering 1971-76, coincided with the CPR's new five-year plan.

United States. The CPR's attitudes toward U.S. policies remained very critical during 1970. They became most critical shortly after the U.S. intervention in Cambodia, which prompted a series of mass rallies throughout China in which 400 million persons were said to have participated. At a Peking rally on 20 May attended by Mao Tse-tung and all major party leaders, Mao issued a personal statement—read by Lin Piao—condemning "U.S. crimes of aggression against Cambodia" and the expansion of the Indochina war. The statement, which failed to mention China as a "reliable rear area," was nevertheless considered an indication that there would be a substantial increase of Chinese material aid to North Vietnam, the National Liberation Front of South Vietnam, and other Indochinese groups fighting "U.S. imperialism." Two other U.S. policies subject to severe CPR attack during the year were the support given to "Japanese militarism" and "Israeli Zionism."

Chinese-U.S. talks at Warsaw were held only on 20 January and 20 February. A meeting scheduled for 20 May was cancelled by the Chinese, following the U.S. decision to send troops into Cambodia. The Chinese communiqué implied, however, that future meetings would take place. The CPR's decision on 23 August to send an ambassador to Poland (where a chargé d'affaires had functioned since early 1967) indicated that the Chinese-U.S. talks, when reopened, would be held at the ambassadorial level.

While the U.S. government's decision in 1969 to ease restrictions on visits to China by U.S. citizens failed to produce a significant response during 1970, the decision to allow sales to China by foreign branches of U.S. business firms prompted various trade contacts between them and the Chinese.

United Nations. The increase in China's diplomatic activity extended to the United Nations, with hints that an opportunity to become a U.N. member would be welcomed. The CPR's apparent willingness to join the organization was not openly indicated in a public statement; it was observed when Chinese officials thanked various foreign delegations visiting China for advocating its admission. In addition, a *Jen-min jih-pao* editorial on 14 November, covering the Non-Aligned Conference in Lusaka, Zambia, expressed "heartful thanks for the just stand" taken by eleven countries at that conference demanding the CPR's admission into the United Nations.

The U.N. vote on the Albanian-Algerian resolution to seat CPR delegates and expell those of Nationalist China took place on 20 November. Fifty-one countries voted in favor of the resolution, 49 opposed it, and 25 abstained. *Peking Review* (27 November) hailed the majority won by the CPR as a "big defeat for the policy of U.S. imperialism." The article challenged an earlier U.S.-sponsored resolution calling for a two-thirds majority to admit the CPR, terming it an "illegal draft."

International Party Contacts. In addition to the meetings with North Korean and Vietnamese delegations referred to above, the CPR was visited by a small number of other communist leaders during the year. Considerable attention was given by the Chinese press to the visit by Emil Bodnăras, member of the Executive Committee and the Presidium of the Central Committee of the Romanian Communist Party and vice-president of Romania, who led a delegation to Peking on 9-12 June. Coincidental with this visit, during which Bodnăras reaffirmed his country's independent line and met with Mao and Lin Piao, *Peking Review* (5 June) printed an article sharply accusing the Soviet Union of attempting to subjugate Romania by "vile threats and blackmail." In a speech on 11 June, Chou En-lai expressed "support and admiration" for the Romanians, who had "consistently opposed the bullying of small countries by a big one" and "made many efforts for peace and security in Europe" (*ibid.*, 19 June). Showing a special appreciation to Romania, the Chinese pledged at that time to give $21 million in aid (raw materials and foodstuffs) to assist in reconstruction following Romania's heavy floods.

Other party contacts included visits to Peking by V. G. Wilcox, general secretary, and Ron Taylor, acting national Chairman of the Communist Party of New Zealand, on 15-22 April; Alberto Jacoviello and Maria Antonietto Macchiocchi, members of the pro-Soviet Italian Communist Party, on 27 October-4 December; and a delegation of the Communist Party of Britain (Marxist-Leninist), led by its chairman, Reg Birch, on 22 December-2 January 1971.

Publications. The official and most authoritative publication of the CCP is the newspaper *Jen-min jih-pao* (People's Daily), published in Peking. The theoretical journal of the CCP Central Committee, *Hung ch'i* (Red Flag), is published approximately once a month. The daily paper of the PLA is *Chieh-fang chün pao* (Liberation Army News). *Ta kung pao* is a national daily, which also has Chinese- and English-language editions published in Hong Kong. The *Peking Review* is a weekly published in English, French, Spanish, Japanese, and German editions; it carries translations of important articles, editorials, and documents from *Jen-min jih-pao, Hung ch'i,* and *Chieh-fang chun pao.*

The official news agency of the party and government is the New China News Agency (Hsinhua).

E. S.

INDIA

Indian communists give 26 December 1925 as the founding date of the Communist Party of India (CPI). Although Western sources usually put the founding in December 1928, there were regional Marxist groups in various parts of India earlier.

After the death of CPI Secretary-General Ajoy Ghosh, in 1962, and the Sino-Indian border conflict of the same year, the struggle between right and left factions within the party greatly intensified. This culminated in a formal split in 1964, when two separate congresses were held, each claiming to be the Seventh All-India Party Congress. Since that time, two parties have existed independently. One is commonly referred to as the "right" or pro-Soviet party, and the other as the "left" or nonaligned party. They call themselves, respectively, the Communist Party of India —the CPI, and the Communist Party of India (Marxist)—the CPI(M). In 1969 a new, Maoist communist party, the Communist Party of India (Marxist-Leninist)—the CPI(M-L), was created, largely by defectors from the CPI(M). This group derives its inspiration from the peasant revolt it instigated in 1967 in Naxalbari, West Bengal; its members, along with other numerous but smaller Maoist organizations, continue to be referred to popularly as Naxalites.

On a nationwide basis the two larger parties, the CPI and the CPI(M), are almost equal in Parliamentary strength and party membership, the CPI(M) having a slight edge over the pro-Soviet party. As a result of the most recent general elections (in 1967, with mid-term elections in four states in 1969 and in one state in 1970), the CPI obtained 145 of the total 3,573 seats in the Lower Houses of the national, state, and territorial legislatures, while the CPI(M) won 157. Active membership is probably about 80,000 in each party, despite much higher claims by the parties themselves. CPI(M-L) members are believed to number between 5,000 and 10,000. The population of India is 554,600,000 (estimated 1970).

Of the three communist parties, the CPI is the least prone to use violence. It has been able, through its relatively moderate tactics, to cooperate with the larger parties on its right to their mutual benefit and to the detriment of the CPI's most ardent rival, the CPI(M). The latter party, though it is or has been the dominant member of ruling coalitions in two states (West Bengal and Kerala), evidences less patience with the parliamentary process and is often accused of resorting to violence, particularly recently in West Bengal. The CPI(M-L), the most violent of the three organizations, opposes parliamentary methods and has refused to participate in any elections.

Geographically, the CPI tends to be rather concentrated, with 88 per cent of its membership located in six states (in decreasing size of membership: Bihar, Andhra Pradesh, Kerala, West Bengal, Uttar Pradesh, and Madras—the latter now called Tamilnadu). The strength of the CPI(M) is even more concentrated, with 70 per cent of its members in the three states of Andhra Pradesh, West Bengal, and Kerala. The members of the CPI(M-L) are active particularly in the rural areas of Andhra Pradesh, West Bengal, and Kerala.

In addition to these three parties there are a number of smaller communist parties, generally to the left of the CPI. These include the various Naxalite factions which are scattered throughout the country, and several parties, such as the Trotskyist Socialist Workers' Party, which are comparatively insignificant.

The CPI and the CPI(M) operate legally, despite occasional efforts to outlaw them. Members of both parties have been arrested from time to time; in 1970 the CPI and its followers in particular suffered mass arrests as a result of a land occupation campaign in the fall. During the year an intense governmental campaign against members and followers of the CPI(M-L)—which went underground shortly after its establishment in April 1969—severely damaged the party and other Naxalite groupings. In West Bengal, the reestablishment of the Preventive Detention Act led to numerous arrests, primarily of CPI(M-L) activists, but also of members of the more established parties, notably those of the CPI(M).

Nationally prominent parties with which the CPI and the CPI(M) compete in Parliamentary activities include the following (as described from the communist point of view and with proportional holdings in the Lower House of Parliament): the ruling National Congress Party, or Congress(R), of Prime Minister Indira Gandhi, which is seen by the CPI as sufficiently "progressive" to warrant cautious support on a rather wide range of issues, and by the CPI(M) as progressive in a very limited number of policies (44 per cent); the "Old" or "Opposition" Indian National Congress Party, popularly called the Congress(O) or Syndicate, formed when it broke away as a "reactionary" faction from the Congress(R) in 1969 (12.5 per cent); the Swatantra Party, also a "reactionary" party, representing the interests of the "monopolists" (8.5 per cent); the Bharatiya Jana Sangh, a "reactionary" anti-Moslem, Hindu nationalist party (6.7 per cent); the Samyukta (United) Socialist Party, a militant, left-nationalist party which was attacked by the communists for its shift in 1970 toward a willingness to join in coalitions with "reactionary" parties (4.4 per cent); the Praja (People's) Socialist Party, a more moderate left-nationalist party which contains some "progressive elements" (2.5 per cent); and the Dravida Munnetra Kazhagam, a Tamil party limited to the state of Tamilnadu (Madras) which has exhibited a mixture of "anti-people" and "democratic" policies and generally supports the Congress (R) (4.8 per cent).

The CPI. Estimates of the active membership of the Communist Party of India vary so much as to be of limited significance. In 1970 the party's own figure, based on the results of a renewal of memberships at the beginning of the year, was 243,238—compared with 172,902 announced at its Eighth Congress, in February 1968 (the 1970 source put the 1968 figure at 135,212). Nonsympathetic estimates of active members average about one-third of the claimed amount. The party's breakdown of current membership by states revealed that the largest numbers were in Bihar (48,580), Andhra Pradesh (37,043), Kerala (33,000), and West Bengal (28,856). Based on state population figures, the greatest concentrations were in Kerala, Andhra Pradesh, and West Bengal. The composition of the party is predominantly middle class, as was disclosed at its Eighth Congress when the party took itself to task for the low proportions of workers, peasants, and young people in its ranks.

In the Upper House (Rajya Sabha) of the national Parliament in 1970, the CPI held 10 of the 228 elected seats; in the Lower House (Lok Sabha), it had 23 out of 520 elected seats, plus one held by a CPI-supported independent. At the state level, the CPI held seats in the legislatures of almost all states and a few territories during 1970. The largest concentrations were in Kerala (12 per cent, 16 seats), West Bengal (10.7 per cent, 30 seats), and Bihar (7.9 per cent, 25 seats).

Leadership and Organization. The central leadership of the CPI includes the party chairman, Shripad Amrit Dange; the general secretary, C. Rajeshwar Rao; the Central Secretariat (chairman, general secretary, and 7 secretaries), the Central Executive Committee (25 members), the Control Commission (7 members), and the National Council (101 members). There are also party Secretariats and State Councils in each state in India. The Central Secretariat, elected in 1968 at the Eighth Congress, consists of Bhupesh Gupta, Yogindra Sharma, N. K. Krishnan, S. G. Sardesai, C. Achutha Menon, Avtar Singh Malhotra, and Bhowani Sen, in addition to Dange and Rao. (A complete list of members of the National Council and other offices was given in the party organ *New Age*, 25 February 1968.)

Chief among the CPI's major fronts is the All-India Trade Union Congress (AITUC), in which the CPI and CPI(M) exercised joint leadership until the two parties' differences led to a formal split of the AITUC in 1970. The CPI retained control of the original AITUC, leaving the CPI(M) to form a new organization. CPI Chairman S. A. Dange remained as secretary-general of the AITUC.

Differences within the organization became serious in November 1969 when a quarrel began over the site for its Twenty-eighth Annual Conference. The CPI(M) favored West Bengal because of its influence there, but the CPI, which dominated the undivided AITUC, had selected Guntur, Andhra Pradesh, and the conference was held there on 28 January-1 February. The CPI(M) boycotted the conference but the AITUC president, CPI(M) member S. S. Mirajkar, defied the directive not to attend and was subsequently expelled from the party. According to the *Times of India* (New Delhi, 5 February), many officials of CPI(M)-controlled unions in Calcutta and elsewhere also defied the boycott.

The report by the conference Credentials Committee confirmed that a majority of the organization's affiliated unions were represented at Guntur; specifically, there were delegates from 1,906 of 2,878 affiliated unions, representing 1,355,023 members out of a total of 1,860,000 as of January 1970. The state from which the largest number of unions and members were represented was West Bengal, the traditional stronghold of the CPI(M). Other states from which there was also high representation were Tamilnadu, Andhra Pradesh, and Kerala. The growth of the AITUC since 1966, when it claimed 1,100,000 members, was said to be mainly by affiliation of steel and railway unions. The congress amended the federation's constitution to facilitate the affiliation of additional unions. It was attended by delegates from trade unions of the Soviet Union, Hungary, Bulgaria, Czechoslovakia, North Korea, and Mongolia, and by two secretaries of the World Federation of Trade Unions.

The formal split occurred when a separate conference was convened by the CPI(M) on 28-31 May in Calcutta. The new organization that emerged was called the Centre of Indian Trade Unions.

Another important front, the All-India Kisan Sabha (Peasants' Association: AIKS), split in 1969 into two separate organizations—one controlled by the CPI and the other (the larger one) controlled by the CPI(M), both continuing the AIKS name. The AIKS of the CPI is led by Z. A. Ahmed, the organization's secretary-general, who is also a member of the CPI Central Executive Committee. In 1970 the twentieth session of the CPI's AIKS was held on 1-5 April in Arasat, West Bengal. At the conference a call was made for radical land reforms and for a peasant movement to occupy fallow government lands. No membership figures were given.

In his report to the Arasat session, Z. A. Ahmed made an appeal for joint action by the AIKS organizations. The CPI(M) organization responded, and on 25 April a meeting of the leaders of the two groups was held at New Delhi. According to a joint statement issued following the meeting, both felt it "absolutely essential that their committees at various levels should unite in mass struggles and action on as many issues as possible," despite the existence of "serious differences" (*New Age*, 3 May). No significant attempt to implement any specific proposals for united action was forthcoming, however, and the prospect of such attempts was made more unlikely by the refusal of the CPI(M) to support the CPI-led land occupation movement later in the year.

Other major mass organizations dominated by the CPI include the All-India Youth Federation (AIYF), led by Joginder Singh Dayal, president, and C. K. Chadrappan, general secretary; the All-India Student Federation (AISF), headed by Sudhakar Reddy, president, and Ranjit Guha, general secretary; the National Federation of Indian Women; and, for agricultural laborers, the All-India Khet Mazdoor Union.

Domestic Attitudes and Activities. The long-range goal of the CPI is the establishment in India of a "national democracy" (following Soviet guidelines) through the efforts of a united front of "progressive forces." Documents of the Eighth Congress proposed that such a front be composed of the "patriotic" faction of the national bourgeoisie, the intelligentsia, the peasants (including the rich peasants), and the workers, with the working class gradually rising to a position of leadership under the guidance of the communist party. To achieve the "national democratic state," the CPI has sought (so far unsuccessfully) to establish a coalition of "progressive" parties in the Lok Sabha. The question of whether the coalition should include the Congress (R) or its "progressive" members was subjected to a considerable amount of debate within the CPI. In answer to charges of "revisionism" by the more revolutionary groups, the CPI justified this relatively moderate strategy by pointing to the existence in the national Parliament of sufficient "democratic" elements to convert it into an instrument serving the working class. The party added, however, that to compensate for certain Parliamentary shortcomings, use must also be made of extra-Parliamentary mass struggle, including strikes and other forms of protest.

The program which the CPI has proposed for adoption by a national leftist coalition includes the following points: defense of mass struggles and minimum wages, demand for land reforms, nationalization of all banks, advancement of secularism, guaranteed rights for religious and linguistic minorities, increased state autonomy, and full autonomy within the Indian Union for Jammu and Kashmir.

Campaign for land occupation. At the beginning of July, the CPI launched a campaign throughout the country whereby peasants occupied, often forcibly, government or private lands. The first phase of the campaign, which in most areas covered the period of 1 July-9 August, was directed at government lands that were lying fallow or were "illegally occupied" by landlords. The second phase was the occupation of the big farms of former princes, former zamindars (absentee landlords), and monopolists, and of vacant building sites in the towns.

The movement, which began to die down by the end of September, resulted in the arrests of more than 20,000 agitators (including Chairman Dange), according to the Minister of Food and Agriculture on 20 August. Government reports showed that only a few thousand acres of often uncultivable land had been occupied. Certain aspects of the movement—such as the alleged failure to distribute much of the occupied land and to follow up the occupation with aid to the poor peasant who could not afford to farm the land he had acquired—generated suspicion that it had been entirely politically motivated for the purpose of weaning support away from such groups as the CPI(M) and the Naxalites. A statement of the CPI National Council, which met on 1-5 October, claimed that 334,000 acres had been occupied and that "agricultural operation" had begun "in one form or another" on 213,000 acres included in the total (*New Age*, 18 October). The same statement reported that nearly 1.5 million people participated in the struggle, which had produced 27 "martyrs" and led to the imprisonment of 62,000 "militant fighters." The role of other leftist parties was characterized by the National Council as generally disruptive. The Samyukta Socialist Party leadership was denounced for limiting its involvement to actions against small landowners and political opponents, and for terming the CPI's land struggle against big landlords and "monopolists" as a "stage-managed show." Cadres of the Praja Socialist Party, on the other hand, were praised for their cooperation in certain areas. The CPI(M) was accused of not having participated at all, except in Kerala where the government of CPI member C. Achutha Menon was already implementing radical land reform measures.

The National Council expressed satisfaction with the results of the campaign, which had not only given land to the landless, but also exerted "powerful pressure" on the government to implement land reforms. More indirectly, the campaign was described as a "great blow to the social and economic power of big landlords who today constitute a pillar of support to Right reaction including communal and other divisive forces in the countryside." (*Ibid.*, 11 October.)

Relations with the Central Government. As a result of the separation of the conservative and liberal Congress Party factions in 1969 and the legislation of various socialistic measures by Mrs. Gandhi's faction—such as the nationalization of 14 domestic banks and the abolition of privy purses and privileges for princes—there has been some speculation on the degree of cooperation that could be expected between the CPI and the Congress (R). Replying to charges that the Congress (R) and the CPI each appeared to be following the other's program, an article in *New Age* (20 September) countered that the CPI had always supported "positive steps" taken by the Congress government; most of the good points of the ruling party had, however, remained on paper, and it was only recently that more members of the Congress (R) were realizing that these should be implemented. The article contended that the program of the CPI was "one of national-democratic revolution, [which went] far beyond even the most radical items of the Congress program."

A controversy was created by what were interpreted as CPI proposals to form a united front with the Congress (R) at the national level. The aforementioned *New Age* article called for the drafting of a minimum common program which could be implemented through the joint action of "progressive" members of the Congress (R), communists, and "other democrats," concluding that this appeared to be the direction of current trends. The resolution on the political situation drawn up at the October session of the CPI National Council also contained a proposal to rally "progressive sections" of the Congress Party in the united front of West Bengal (*New Age*, 11 October). This was immediately followed by the statement: "We have correctly set the building of Left and democratic unity as the central task with the national perspective of bringing into existence a government of Left and democratic unity at the Centre.... Efforts in this direction must be more concrete and sustained." At a meeting of the All-India Congress Committee (AICC) of the Congress (R), radical member Chandrajeet Yadav proposed that the committee adopt a program of unity with the CPI and other leftist parties. The amendment was voted down, and it appeared to many observers that this amounted to a rejection of what was understood to be the CPI National Council's proposal for a CPI-Congress(R) alignment. Shortly thereafter, Chairman Dange addressed an open letter to the radical faction in the Congress(R), in which he contended: "All in all, the talk of an overall front of the Left and democratic forces to include your Congress as a whole is premature, unless vital policy changes in actual government behaviour are made" (*ibid.*, 18 October). Dange warned that, "at least on the working-class and peasant front, any talk of such overall front sounds very incongruous with reality and is in fact dangerous." Appearing in the same issue of *New Age* with Dange's letter, a commentary by General Secretary Rao attempted to smooth over the differences. Rao regretted the "unfortunate controversy" and said that the CPI did not claim that the unity it advocated was "round the corner." Addressing himself to the proposal by Yadav, Rao declared:

> Our Party would have been very happy if the main idea of appeal for all Left and democratic parties to unite to save the country from the menace of right reaction, contained in Chandrajeet Yadav's amendment, had been accepted by the AICC.

Anticipating that an advance in the date of the next general elections would find the political climate more favorable to her party, Prime Minister Gandhi dissolved Parliament on 27 December 1970, fourteen months early. The elections were scheduled for the first week in March 1971.

Activities in the States. 1. Kerala.   Since it became a state in 1957, Kerala has always given the communists their greatest parliamentary strength among India's state assemblies. In the state's first elections, the undivided CPI was able to dominate a coalition government which survived until the end of 1959. The communists again formed a ruling coalition as a result of the 1967 elections (the government in the intervening period being in the hands of other parties or the central government), though this time it was a divided party. In October 1969 the CPI(M), which had by far the most seats (49) in the 133-member assembly, was forced to withdraw from the government because of a no-confidence vote. The following month, the CPI, which had the second largest number of seats (19), was able to form a new coalition government that excluded the CPI(M) and its supporting parties. The government was composed of five parties in a coalition identified as the National Democratic Front (borrowing from the Soviet concept of "national democracy") or, more popularly, the "mini-front." The parties were the CPI (which had three ministers), the Muslim League (two ministers), the Indian Socialist Party (two ministers), and the Kerala Congress Party (one minister); the Revolutionary Socialist Party, though part of the front, was not given a portfolio. The chief minister was CPI member C. Achutha Menon.

The National Democratic Front was able to exist largely through the support of the Congress (R), which remained outside the coalition. The front was put on firmer footing when it won a vote of confidence in the Kerala Assembly on 23 March 1970 and later when it won two by-elections, in Nilambur (Calicut) and Koffarakara (Quilar). The implementation of generally effective and impartial land reforms made it difficult for the ousted CPI(M) to organize anti-government agitation.

After ruling for eight months, the National Democratic Front government was dissolved on 26 June 1970 by the state governor (an appointee of the President), who announced that elections would be held as soon as possible. The cause of the crisis, which led to the establishment of "President's rule," was an internal disagreement in the front between the Indian Socialist Party (ISP; a recent splinter of the Samyukta Socialist Party) and the Praja Socialist Party (PSP). In April, a division within the ISP was created by a demand of a section of the party that one of its members, N. K. Seshan, resign his post of finance minister. As a result, Seshan and two other ISP assemblymen left their party to join the PSP, which in turn asked for admittance to the Coordination Committee, the policy-making body of the coalition. The ISP, the only coalition party opposing the request, threatened to withdraw its remaining minister and boycott the committee if the PSP were admitted. Rather than let the dispute bring down the government, Menon sought a new mandate; elections were held on 17 September.

The elections, which with the land occupation campaign constituted one of the two most important events for the CPI during the year, reseated the National Democratic Front government, slightly reduced in size. The CPI dropped to 16 seats, the Muslim League lost 3 of its 14 seats, the Revolutionary Socialist Party retained its 6 seats, and the PSP joined the coalition, adding 3 seats (all filled by former ISP assemblymen), for a total of 36. The Kerala Congress Party left the front before the elections. The most impressive changes were the losses of the CPI(M)—despite a relatively unchanged electoral strength—which went down from 49 seats to 28, and the gains of the Congress(R), which, though polling 12 per cent fewer votes than the undivided Congress Party in 1967, jumped from 5 to 32 seats, 18 of which came from former CPI(M) constituencies. The National Democratic Front, which had the support of the Congress(R), fought against two other coalitions: the People's Democratic Front, comprised of the CPI(M), the Indian Socialist Party (which has since left the front), and three others, winning 41 seats; and the rightist Democratic

Front of the Congress (O) and the Kerala Congress Party (a local Congress splinter), which won 12 seats, all by candidates of the latter party.

The new government, formed on 4 October, consisted of four CPI members—including Menon who was reinstalled as chief minister—two Revolutionary Socialist Party members, two Muslim League members, and one member of the PSP. Menon was also given the important responsibilities of planning, law and legislation, and finance. According to an article in *New Age* (11 October) announcing the new posts, the government expected the "solid support" of the 32-member Congress(R) group in the Assembly.

2. *West Bengal.*   The CPI(M)-dominated United Front government of West Bengal, in power since February 1969, was brought down in March 1970 when its chief minister, Ajoy Mukherjee of the Bangla Congress Party (a splinter of the National Congress Party), resigned in accordance with his party's directions. The state's governor temporarily suspended the Assembly when it became apparent that no party was able to muster a new coalition on the model of the "mini-front" of Kerala. On 19 March, President's rule was imposed in West Bengal.

The government had become progressively less stable almost since its inception. Factional disputes within the front were exacerbated by a growing violence that was allowed to go unchecked by the state's Home Minister, CPI(M) member Jyoti Basu, who had control of the police. The violence originated largely with the CPI(M-L), which was held responsible for most of the numerous recent political murders in Calcutta. The CPI(M) was frequently castigated by most of the West Bengal parties for its refusal to give the police the necessary authority to deal with the situation. The party was often accused of contributing directly to the violence because of its involvement in a power struggle in the trade union movement and because of a so-called "war of extermination" between it and the CPI(M-L). (See *YICA*, 1968, pp. 301-4, for the origins of the hostility between these two parties.) Other parties (including the CPI), their mass organizations, and their supporters were also involved. The impulse to retaliate against political (or quasi-political) murders, compounded by the inability of the police to act, gave momentum to the violence. The increasing frequency of strikes and intimidation, the forcible seizure of land, and violent attacks on factory managers were described by Jyoti Basu as popular mass protests. Chief Minister Mukherjee, who in late 1969 had undertaken a fast to protest the government's inability to act, attempted to control the situation by calling in the Central Reserve Police, a decision that was condemned by Jyoti Basu (who held also the post of deputy chief minister) as an act against "democratic movements."

The CPI, which supported Mukherjee's verbal attacks on the CPI(M), was blamed by the latter party as being responsible for the "entire direction and enactment" of events which contributed to the government's fall, by providing the "ideological cover" for noncommunist parties to undermine the front, according to an article in *People's Democracy* on 19 March. The two parties formed rival coalitions, and each appeared to be attempting to form a government that excluded its opponent, as the CPI had done in Kerala.

Violence increased after the fall of the government, and the national Parliament voted to continue President's rule in the state until March 1971. During the interval each of the communist parties was active in strengthening its respective coalition: the CPI's Eight Party Combination (which included the Foward Bloc, the Socialist Unity Centre, the Samyukta Socialist Party, the PSP, the Gorkha League, and factions of the Revolutionary Communist Party of India and the Bolshevik Party), and the CPI(M)'s Six Party Front, composed of the CPI(M), Biplabi Bangla Congress, Forward Bloc (Marxist), Workers' Party, and factions of the Revolutionary Communist Party of India and the Bolshevik Party.

The example of Kerala, where a "mini-front" government could be created without the CPI(M), was considered by a number of parties—including the CPI (*New Age*, 11 October)—to be applicable to the situation in West Bengal. Using the Kerala model, the CPI and some of the other members of the Eight Party Combination apparently attempted to establish an agreement between the coalition and the Congress(R). Others, chiefly the Forward Bloc and the Socialist Unity Centre, were not prepared to cooperate with the Congress(R), and the effort was abandoned (*ibid.*, 6 December).

In the 1968 mid-term elections in West Bengal, the unexpected losses of the Congress Party encouraged the opposing leftist coalitions to cooperate in forming a government, but such a possibility appeared less likely for 1971 because of the intensity of bitterness and mistrust among the various parties. Furthermore, at the end of the year the important Bangla Congress refused to join either coalition and indicated it would oppose both in new elections.

International Views and Positions. *Relations with the U.S.S.R.* The CPI is a staunch supporter of Soviet policies with regard to the international communist movement, though on occasion it is forced to weigh the consequences of following a strictly pro-Soviet line when conflicting national interests are involved. On 28 August 1970, a New Delhi meeting of the "Parliamentarians' Committee for Peace" passed a resolution, signed by *New Age* editor Bhupesh Gupta among others, which took the Soviet Union to task for continuing to delineate the Sino-Indian border in China's favor on Soviet maps. The issue, which has emerged in Parliament at various times since 1961, concerns the borders in northern and eastern India. The committee "disapproved" what it asserted were incorrect delineations of Indian borders by the United States, the U.S.S.R., and other countries and "urged upon them to take immediate steps to rectify them." At the same time, it condemned the "reactionaries and communalists" in India who underplayed the erroneous borders in maps published in Western countries (*New Age*, 6 September).

Soviet aid projects in India, which have been attacked by many sectors—particularly the right —because of delays and expanding costs, were strongly defended by the CPI. At the huge Bokaro steel plant project, for example, increases in cost from the original estimate, delays, and failure to use Indian consultants were either denied or blamed on the Indian government.

For its part, the Soviet Union also must weigh the consequences of supporting CPI policies when they might endanger Soviet-Indian state relations. Thus the land occupation movement— the major event for the CPI during the year—was given very brief attention in the Soviet press, despite efforts by *New Age* Moscow correspondent Masood Ali Khan to show widespread support for the movement in Soviet newspapers. A contributing factor to Soviet reticence on the subject may have been the anticipated visit—announced during the heat of the land occupation movement in August—of Indian President V. V. Giri to Moscow in mid-September.

In its relations with the CPI, the Communist Party of the Soviet Union (CPSU) places considerable emphasis on the building of a broad-based leftist coalition in India. This concern was apparent in November during celebrations of the fifty-third anniversary of the October Revolution, to which the CPI sent a delegation composed of General Secretary Rao and Secretaries Bhupesh Gupta and N. K. Krishnan. According to the joint communiqué that emerged from a meeting with CPSU Secretary-General Brezhnev, the "CPSU delegation expressed its special appreciation of the important role played by the Communist Party of India and democratic forces in India." It also expressed its "understanding of the complex and difficult conditions" which the CPI faced and which were aggravated by the "insufficient cohesion of the Left and democratic forces." (*New Age*, 22 November.)

Other Areas. The election of a "progressive" coalition government in Ceylon on 27 May was welcomed by the CPI. The new government, which included the pro-Soviet Ceylon Communist Party as the smallest of the three coalition partners, sparked the appearance of numerous articles in *New Age*.

On 14 September, Pieter Keuneman, secretary-general of the Ceylon Communist Party and minister of housing and construction, arrived in India to begin a state visit. He was given a reception on 15 September at the CPI central headquarters, where he reportedly met Chairman Dange and other CPI leaders and spoke of the tasks and dangers facing the new Ceylonese united front government.

In Pakistan, the country's first direct adult-franchise election, on 7 December, was eagerly anticipated by the CPI, which has adopted the Soviet Union's concern for improved relations between India and Pakistan. Though the final outcome was dependent upon the successful drafting of a new constitution by the elected National Assembly within 120 days, *New Age* commentary viewed the immediate results as a victory of sorts. The absolute majority won by Sheik Mujibur Rahman's National Awami League was welcomed only because of the sheik's advocacy of autonomy for East Pakistan and his opposition to "imperialist diktats." The *New Age*, which has followed the activities of the clandestine pro-Soviet Communist Party of East Pakistan, expressed regret at President Yahya Khan's decision at the beginning of 1970 to continue the ban on Pakistani communists while restoring political rights to all other parties. The paper applauded the demand made early in the year by Wali Khan's pro-Soviet (but noncommunist) National Awami Party for a lifting of the ban on the communists.

The CPI has frequently demanded that the government of India recognize East Germany. The *New Age* registered disappointment, however, when that recognition finally came in July in the form of a "compromise" which extended only to the consular level. The CPI continued its demand for full diplomatic recognition.

* * *

The CPI(M). Membership figures for the Communist Party of India (Marxist) are subject to question, but it is generally estimated that the party has about 80,000 active members. The CPI(M)'s own figure, given at its Eighth Congress in December 1968, was 76,233. A decline in membership preceding the congress was chiefly the result of the breaking off of the party's extreme left in 1967-68. As in the case of the CPI, the power of the CPI(M) lies in the non-Hindi states, particularly in Kerala and West Bengal.

The 1967 general elections gave the CPI(M) 19 of the 522 seats in the Lower House of Parliament. The party's holdings in the state legislatures were concentrated in Kerala and West Bengal, where it is the largest single party. In both states—Kerala in 1969 and West Bengal in 1970—the party lost its position in the government (see above, CPI, "Activities in the States").

Leadership and Organization. The CPI(M) leadership consists of party Secretary-General P. Sundarayya, the Politburo (9 members), the Central Committee (28 members), and state secretariats and committees. Politburo members, elected at the party's Eighth Congress, are P. Sundarayya, B. T. Ranadive, M. Basavapunnaiah, E. M. S. Namboodiripad, Promode Das Gupta, Jyoti Basu, P. Ramamurti, Harkishan Singh Surjeet, and Avilliath Kutteri Gopalan. An aging founder member of the original CPI, Muzaffar Ahmad, occupies an honorary position above that of Sundarayya on the Central Committee.

The CPI(M) acquired its own trade-union federation in 1970, after having shared the leadership of the AITUC with the CPI since the parties' division in 1964. The decision to gather its trade unions into a separate organization was taken at a convention in Goa on 9-10 April, following an unsuccessful power struggle in the CPI-dominated AITUC (see above, CPI, "Leadership and Organization"). A CPI(M)-dominated "All-India Trade Union Conference" was held on 28-31 May from which the new organization, the Centre of Indian Trade Unions, emerged. B. T.

Ranadive and P. Ramamurti—both CPI(M) leaders in the undivided AITUC—were elected president and general secretary, respectively.

The Credentials Committee report claimed that the conference represented 804,637 members in 1,759 affiliated trade unions. In addition, about 200 unions in various states, with a total of 150,000 members, were said to have expressed a desire to become affiliated. (*People's Democracy*, 7 June.)

The CPI(M) is somewhat stronger than the CPI in organizing the peasantry; its AIKS claimed very close to a million members in 16 states in 1969. Activity in the CPI(M) peasant front is centered primarily in West Bengal and Kerala, with about 60 per cent of its AIKS membership located in West Bengal. Its leadership includes Politburo member A. K. Gopalan as president and Central Committee member Harekrishna Konar as general secretary.

The CPI(M), like the CPI, controls a student organization, also called the AISF. This group, however, has been, in the words of the CPI(M), "reduced to a paper organization." In the 2 August issue of *People's Democracy* a proposal was made to form a new student organization, tentatively called the Students' Federation of India. Put forth by the West Bengal branch of the AISF, the proposal included a 14-point charter of demands, the most salient of which were free universal compulsory education in the students' native languages, increased democratic rights for students, and welfare provisions for unemployed graduates. The founding conference of the Students' Federation of India was held on 27-30 December. The CPI(M) also controls an agricultural laborers' union which has a membership of about 300,000.

Domestic Attitudes and Activities. The CPI(M) was originally formed, when it broke from the CPI in 1964, as a Stalinist pro-Chinese party that favored armed revolt by workers and peasants and accepted Parliamentary participation only as a temporary means to build its base of power. Gradually, the "Parliamentary path" appeared to become a more permanent feature of the party's strategy. With the adoption in 1967 of the "Madurai line" (referring to a meeting of the Central Committee in Madurai, Tamilnadu), the CPI(M) assumed an internationally independent policy, abandoning its pro-Chinese sentiments and many of their domestic ramifications. In 1969 and 1970, however, the party exhibited a loss of patience with Parliamentary processes and, when it no longer held positions in the governments of Kerala and West Bengal, began to place even greater emphasis on its extra-parliamentary activities.

The party's long-range goal remains a dictatorship of the proletariat—a government led by the working class on the basis of a firm worker-peasant alliance. This alliance would be more exclusive than that advocated by the CPI, which party the CPI(M) has constantly criticized for its willingness to form coalitions with various "reactionary" Indian parties.

Relations with the Central Government. The CPI(M) appears to have become increasingly dissatisfied with the ruling Congress Party's failure to consolidate its initial leftward trend following the election of President Giri in 1969. A Central Committee resolution of February 1970 stated that both the Congress(O) and Congress(R) "basically represent the same landlord-bourgeois classes and therefore pursue essentially the same basic policies" (*People's Democracy*, 15 February). The same resolution emphasized, however, that "even though its leadership includes a large number of those who have become notorious for their reactionary anti-people outlook . . . the Indira Gandhi wing also contains within its fold a healthy trend which hates big landlords and monopolists." This "healthy trend" was commended "above all" for its opposition to "Hindu communal reaction."

The CPI(M) continues to challenge those—especially the CPI—who appear to be following the Congress(R) and giving it general support. The party appealed to the "democratic opposition" to consider the damage that might be done by taking this course, and to join with the CPI(M) in fighting against both Congress Party groups, with emphasis on the Syndicate and its allies. The reestablishment of the CPI-led government in Kerala in October prompted the CPI(M) Politburo to conclude that their pro-Soviet rivals had "revealed themselves as the open agents" of the Congress(R), "out to attack the advanced democratic movement" (*People's Democracy*, 27 September). The CPI(M), with the support of five pro-CPI(M) independents, claimed to have emerged as the largest single political force in the state (with 50 per cent more votes than the Congress Party and the same number of seats when party-supported independents were also included), primarily as a result of its strongly anti-Congress campaign (*ibid.*).

Hostility between the CPI(M) and the Naxalites has been a source of embarrassment for the former party and evokes frequent articles in the party organ explaining the CPI(M) position. Politburo member M. Basavapunnaiah, for example, described Naxalite activities as "left-adventurist and infantile" interpretations of Marxism-Leninism and completely unrelated to mass peasant struggles, with the possible exceptions of the original Naxalbari campaign and the tribal movement in Srikakulam, Andhra Pradesh (*People's Democracy*, 6 December 1970). The Naxalites "anarchic and terroristic raids in Robin Hood style," which created a "people's war minus people," were denounced by Basavapunnaiah as having resulted in an adverse reaction in which the "ruling classes and their stooges" were able to use the movement to discredit other communists and disrupt the entire revolutionary movement. Apparently this has particularly been the case in West Bengal, where the Preventive Detention Act was reintroduced in September. The measure was applied ostensibly to combat Naxalite activities, but in practice to extinguish all "democratic" movements, especially the CPI(M), according to its members.

International Views and Positions. The CPI(M) has strictly adhered to an independent position among the world's communist parties, refusing to align itself with either the Chinese Communist Party or the CPSU. Although in 1964 it broke from the CPI as a pro-Chinese party, it now condemns with equal intensity the "errors" of Chinese "left-sectarianism" and Soviet "revisionism."

It has not been easy, apparently, for the party to establish itself internationally among the nonaligned parties. Its first attempt was unsuccessful, when parties representing North Vietnam, North Korea, Cuba, and Romania, though reportedly invited, failed to attend its Eighth Congress in December 1968. High-level party visits to Bucharest in mid-1969 helped to improve ties with the Communist Party of Romania. In 1970, relations with the Korean Workers' Party (KWP) also improved, as attested by the numerous articles that appeared in *People's Democracy* in praise of North Korea's achievements. The high point of these latter relations was a visit by a CPI(M) delegation to Pyongyang in June and July. The delegation, which was received by Kim Il-song and other KWP leaders, was composed of Secretary-General Sundarayya and Politburo members Promode Das Gupta and E. M. S. Namboodiripad, who are also the secretaries of the West Bengal and Kerala party branches, respectively. The delegation, though warmly received, did not appear to merit the amount of publicity in the North Korean press that it might have, considering the level of representation and the mutual respect both parties have for nonalignment.

The election of a socialist government in Ceylon—a three-party coalition that included the pro-Soviet Ceylon Communist Party—was viewed by the CPI(M) as an "emphatic rejection by the overwhelming majority of the Ceylonese people" of the previously ruling party's alleged subservience to U.S. capital, rather than as a victory for the people. Though the party approved the new leftist coalition's domestic policy of nationalization and foreign policy of "dynamic neutralism," *People's Democracy* (28 June) referred to indications that "imperialist" capital might remain in the country and that the new finance minister (a Trotskyist) was reluctant to national-ize foreign banks. The *People's Democracy* article gave the following warning:

> Mrs. Bandaranaike's Government has come to office because of the massive popular discontent against the earlier Government's policies. This can be transformed into firm support for the new Government only with policies which would fight unremittingly for people's interests. Either the new Government does this or it goes the way Ghana or Indonesia went. There is no alternative path.

*　　*　　*

The Naxalites. The left-extremist movement in India derives its inspiration from the Naxal-bari, West Bengal, peasant uprising in 1967. The uprising was led by dissident CPI(M) members, who later left, or were expelled from, the party, taking with them a large number of sympathizers who subsequently formed the core of the Chinese-oriented "Naxalite" movement. The movement has suffered substantial atomization since its beginnings, particularly in 1969 and 1970, when a number of parties emerged promoting divergent tactics and strategies. Naxalites are now found in almost every state, but are most numerous in West Bengal and Andhra Pradesh.

The CPI(M-L). The largest of the Naxalite parties—and evidently the first to be established—is the Communist Party of India (Marxist-Leninist), which gives its founding date as 22 April 1969. It is recognized by the Chinese Communist Party, and articles from the CPI(M-L) monthly English-language periodical *Liberation* frequently appear in *Peking Review*. Before the forma-tion of the CPI(M-L), the loose organization from which it was derived—the All-India Coordina-tion Committee of Communist Revolutionaries—suffered a division between its West Bengal base and the important branch in the state of Andhra Pradesh. The latter group, led by Tarimela Nagi Reddy, did not join the CPI(M-L). According to the *Hindu* (Tamilnadu, 14 April 1970), there are about 10,000 hard-core followers in the CPI(M-L) and 6,000 in Nagi Reddi's Revolu-tionary Communist Centre.

The relatively young leadership of the CPI(M-L) and much of its rank and file are derived from CPI(M) dissidents at the district and branch rather than state or national levels. Kanu San-yal, the leader of the peasant revolt in Naxalbari, is reportedly the party's strategist. Charu Ma-zumdar is the secretary-general and main theoretician. Satyananda Bhattacharya appears to be another prominent figure.

The party has attracted a number of unemployed college graduates, university students, land-less peasants, and workers in tea plantations. It claims influence among peasants in the states of Orissa, Bihar, Uttar Pradesh, Assam, and Punjab, but draws its membership mainly from three states: Andhra Pradesh, Kerala, and West Bengal.

Late in 1970 it became apparent that disagreements existed within the CPI(M-L). Charu Mazumdar reportedly criticized Kanu Sanyal and other party members as "centrists" and the "ugliest form of revisionists." The differences appeared to stem from Mazumdar's inflexible ad-herence to the model of the Chinese Communist Party—not only in ideology and strategy but also in its organization. This stand reportedly has evoked broad criticism from the CPI(M-L) Central Committee (*Hindustan Standard*, 29 July). Mazumdar has also insisted that the peasants rely entirely on traditional weapons to "liquidate" the landlords, while others in the party are said to prefer more sophisticated weapons, including firearms.

Another source of conflict evident within the party involved the question of developing a mass base. In an East Pakistan weekly newspaper (*Forum*, 7 November), Mazumdar argued that a mass movement was unnecessary and, in fact, tended to be an obstacle to guerrilla warfare. On the other hand, he maintained that it was essential to inculcate the people with a revolutionary political awareness through "Mao Tsetung Thought." Mazumdar complained of "revisionism both inside and outside the party" and a "secatarian tendency" which hindered the guerrilla movement by rejecting collaboration of other revolutionaries. He also indicated the existence of discipline problems manifested by a lack of faith in the authority of the party, and particularly its leaders (*ibid.*).

Originally conceived as a rural movement, the CPI(M-L) assumed a new character when Mazumdar outlined a program for action among urban workers (*Liberation*, March 1970). The party's aim, according to Mazumdar, was to encourage the workers to abandon the obsolete conventional methods of struggle—particularly trade union activity—and to adopt more militant methods, such as "clashes with the police and capitalists, barricade fights and the annihilation of class enemies." Mazumdar warned against direct opposition to strike action by others, since it might antagonize workers who adhered to this well-tested method approved by the CPI and the CPI(M). He warned also of the dangers of seeking material gain in the struggle, stating that the urban campaign should not "degenerate into militant economic struggle" (*ibid.*). Toward the end of the year, police pressure in West Bengal forced a shift back to rural activities, according to a party directive claimed to have been obtained by the police (*Statesman*, Delhi, 18 November).

Mazumdar also proposed that the CPI(M-L) enlist students to form a "Red Guard" organization along Chinese lines. Eventually, this organization was intended to develop into a "People's Liberation Army of India."

The First Congress of the CPI(M-L) was held clandestinely on 15-16 May. Its program, published in the May-July issue of *Liberation*, stressed the necessity of guerrilla warfare. The political line, drafted by Mazumdar and adopted without substantial modifications, declared the party's aim to be the formation of a united front of peasants and workers which would create, through revolution, a dictatorship of the workers, peasants, and some of the middle class. The revolution would be achieved by first setting up small scattered militant bases which would develop into a "liberation army" and national guerrilla warfare.

The program called for "people's revolutionary committees" (like those in China) to administer at all levels of society. The conditions of the workers and peasants would be improved, and banks, foreign capital, and large landholdings would be abolished.

Other Extremist Groups. At least two groups have broken from the CPI(M-L): the National Liberation Front, composed of four splinter groups expelled from the CPI(M-L) in May 1969, led by Promode Sen Gupta; and the Revolutionary Struggle Preparation Committee. Another group, the Revolutionary Socialist Party of India (Marxist-Leninist) led by Keshava Prasad Sharma, was established in August 1969 but seems to have no connection with the CPI(M-L). These three organizations, while differing from Mazumdar in such issues as his attitude toward China, agree with the CPI(M-L) in the strategy of scattered armed uprisings.

A different point of view is held by another set of Naxalites, the major grouping of which is based in Andhra Pradesh under the leadership of T. Nagi Reddi. Reddi, whose organization is called the Revolutionary Communist Centre, stresses the building of a sound political base before launching guerrilla warfare. He proposes land distribution in rural areas and political work in the cities. Refuting charges—largely from the CPI(M-L)—that his agrarian program would encourage "economism" (a desire for material possessions), Reddi countered that it included an intensive propaganda campaign to convince the peasants that the agrarian revolution was only the first step in the seizure of political power ("Problems of People's War," a paper by Reddi carried on 2 May by the pro-Soviet Delhi weekly *Mainstream*). Reddi is critical of the CPI(M-L)'s failure to consolidate its positions and its labeling as "liberated" any area in which sporadic terrorist attacks have occurred. His own program, on the other hand, envisages the creation of "village soviets" to replace present elected village councils, and mass organizations among the urban middle-class intellectuals.

Three other organizations appear to be aligned with Reddi's Revolutionary Communist Centre: the 2,000-member Calcutta-based Maoist Communist Centre, led by CPI(M-L) defector Asit Sen, which emphasizes mass organizations in the cities and has participated in college elections; the Regional Peasants' Struggle Committee, based in Birbhum, West Bengal, and calling for implementation of an 11-point program of land redistribution; and the Communist Revolutionary Centre, led by K. P. R. Gopalan in Kerala. Gopalan contends that the present government should be brought down by a broad union of all sections of society rather than by a single narrow element. His group participated unsuccessfully in the state Assembly elections in Kerala in September.

Naxalites throughout India suffered serious setbacks in 1970. Strict security measures by Indian authorities resulted in the arrest or killing of a large number of the extremists. On 19 August, Kanu Sanyal and 29 of his followers, including Jangal Santhal, third in the party hierarchy, were arrested in the Naxalbari region of northern West Bengal. His arrest sparked violent demonstrations across West Bengal. Mazumdar, reportedly in ill health, has remained in hiding since his release from prison in early 1969.

In Andhra Pradesh, Nagi Reddi was arrested in December 1969. The state Home Minister claimed on 11 July that authorities had "broken the back" of the Naxalite movement there when two members—said to be the last of its six most important men, were killed by police. Only one of the six was a supporter of Reddi.

*   *   *

Publications. Indian communists have a network of dailies, weeklies, and monthlies throughout the country, in English and various vernacular languages. The central organization of the CPI publishes the English weekly *New Age* in New Delhi (circulation, 7,500). Bhupesh Gupta is the editor. It also publishes the weekly *Party Life* and has dailies in five states: two in Kerala, and one each in Andhra Pradesh, West Bengal, Punjab, and Manipur.

The central organ of the CPI(M) is the English weekly *People's Democracy*, published in Calcutta and edited by B. T. Ranadive (circulation 9,000 to 10,000). The CPI(M) also publishes dailies in Kerala, West Bengal, and Andhra Pradesh, and weeklies in Madras, Karnataka, West Bengal, Punjab, and Jammu and Kashmir.

The CPI(M-L) publishes a monthly in English, *Liberation*, edited by Sushital Ray Chaudhury, and a Bengali weekly, *Deshabrati*. Both were banned by the government after March 1970, but continued to appear clandestinely since then. Other extremist publications are, in Hindi, the weekly *Lok Yuddha* (People's War), issued since August 1968, and, in English, the monthly *People's Path* and biweekly *Commune*.

E. S.

INDONESIA

The Communist Party of Indonesia (Partai Komunis Indonesia; PKI) was founded on 23 May 1920 when Indonesian social-democratic associations under the leadership of Dutch radicals and Islamic nationalists, meeting at Semarang, Java, decided to join the Third International.

Declared illegal in November 1926 after an unsuccessful uprising, the PKI operated until 1945 with most of its leaders in Moscow or in Yenan, China. Upon the establishment of an independent Indonesian republic under the leadership of President Sukarno on 17 August 1945, the PKI resumed legal activity. In 1946, after an unsuccessful putsch attempt led by Tan Malaka, the head of the Trotskyist wing (the Partai Murba) which split off from the PKI in 1928, the exiled leaders returned from Moscow and Yenan and assumed direction of the party. On 18 September 1948 communist and pro-communist civilians and army officers panicked at the government's decision to demobilize many of the communist-led units and launched the Madiun rebellion in East Java. Government reaction was swift; Madiun was recaptured in two weeks, and the rebellion was completely crushed within two months.

On the night of 30 September 1965,[1] six senior generals of the Indonesian army were abducted and murdered in the course of an attempted coup mounted by a group of air force and army personnel led by Lieutenant Colonel Untung. PKI involvement in the attempt apparently was extensive. Members of the PKI and of PKI-directed front organizations, such as the People's Youth and the Women's Movement, supported the attempt, which was described as "patriotic and revolutionary" in an editorial of 2 October in *Harian Rakjat*, the party newspaper. General Abdul Haris Nasution and Major General (now General) Suharto succeeded in escaping and proceeded to crush the insurgency.

On 12 March 1966 the PKI and all its affiliate organizations were banned, and the acceptance of former PKI members into existing political organizations was declared illegal. On 5 July 1966 the Indonesian Parliament formally outlawed the studying and teaching of Marxism-Leninism. No former PKI member is to be allowed to participate in the 1971 general elections.

Before the coup attempt of September 1965, the PKI was considered to be the third in size among the communist parties of the world, with a claimed membership of 3,000,000. Also the party controlled a number of fronts. (See *YICA*, 1970, pp. 584-85.) The population of Indonesia is 121,200,000 (estimated 1970).

Leadership and Organization. The PKI has apparently split into three groups, consisting of (1) those elements who operate chiefly in Central and East Java and refer to themselves as the "Politburo of the PKI Central Committee," (2) the Peking-based "Delegation of the PKI Central Committee," and (3) the apparently Moscow-based "Marxist-Leninist Group of the PKI." An

---

[1] Actually in the early hours of 1 October, possibly with the intent of coinciding with the National Day celebrations in Communist China.

"Indonesian People's Liberation Army" (Tentara Pembebasam Rakjat Indonesia; TPRI) reportedly was formed in July 1966 from various PKI guerrilla and terrorist remnants.

A "new-style" PKI (PKI Baru) was formed from communist remnants in Indonesia after the coup attempt. It has established a more flexible organization, apparently modeled on that of the South Vietnamese guerrillas, with urban committees as well as small guerrilla bands and with regional bureaus which are responsible for small administrative units (*Washington Post*, 26 January 1970).

The number of remaining PKI members in Indonesia is unknown, but according to Southeast Asian sources there are about 169,000 at large in Central Java and 8,000 in West Borneo. Several hundred have taken refuge abroad. A U.S. government source (*World Strength of the Communist Party Organizations*, Washington, D.C., 1970, p. 91) estimates that 68,000 former party members are in jail and 47,000 under house arrest.[2] Many of those arrested are said to have been held without trial. New communist cells reportedly flourish inside the prisons and among families of detainees. Early in 1970 some 2,500 "type B" prisoners (held on suspicion of involvement in the coup attempt because of membership in front organizations) were said to have been removed to the desolate island of Buru in eastern Indonesia (*Washington Post*, 27 January). Later it was reported that another 5,000 were being transported there (*Far Eastern Economic Review*, Hong Kong, 5 September). In January, some 2,000 "type C" detainees (not classified as suspects) were officially reported to have been released in East Java (Antara, Indonesian news agency, 3 January). Those released have found it difficult to gain acceptance again in society. Citizens of the Chinese People's Republic who were detained in North Sumatra for four years or more have expressed the hope that the Indonesian government would request China to send ships for them (Djakarta radio, domestic service, 9 May).

Since 1966 the PKI leadership has passed through several hands (see *YICA*, 1970, p. 586), apparently coming to rest with Ruslan Widjajasasantra as chairman of a fifteen-member "new-style" PKI Central Committee; however, a 1970 report (*Merdeka*, Djakarta, 5 February) cited "a certain N. Hartojo, who uses many aliases" and comes from Central Java, as chairman of the "new-style" PKI. The vice-chairman, Rachmat Effendi, was arrested in Djakarta early in the year (*ibid.*). Other PKI leaders arrested during 1970 include Robert Aseng ("Richard Tuwo"), of Makassar; Siswojo ("Sardjono"), former head of the PKI Central Committee's Education Department and director of the Universitas Rakjat (People's University), who was charged with directing preparations for a communist party comeback; "S.T.," charged with formation of a national front and the development of armed struggle; "S.M.," who was mainly responsible for activities among students; and "T. Hd.," who was to set up an agitation and propaganda bureau (Djakarta radio, domestic service, 15 July; *Duta Masjarakat*, Djakarta, 13 July.) Also arrested were a number of journalists who allegedly were to attempt a PKI comeback. Pre-coup Central Committee members apparently still at large include Jusuf Adjitorop (in Peking), Anwar Dakir, Ruslan Kamaldin, Sidartojo, Sudjono, and Zaelani.

In addition to the PKI proper, communists in Indonesia work through the Indonesian People's Liberation Army; the "Police and Army Training Center" and the People's Liberation Army in Lampung, South Sumatra; the People's Youth (Pemuda Rakjat); and GEMPAR (Movement of Revolutionary Pantjasilaist University Students). The exact relationship between the PKI and guerrilla bands operating in Kalimantan (Indonesian Borneo) is unknown. The latter include the North Borneo People's Liberation Army (Pasokan Ra'ayat Kalimantan Utara; Paraku) and the Sarawak People's Guerrilla Organization (Pasokan Gerilja Rakjat Sarawak; PGRS), both of which are directed by the Sarawak Communist Organization (see *Malaysia*).

[2]Amnesty International has estimated that there are 116,000 political prisoners in 300 camps in Indonesia (*New York Times*, 28 June 1970).

Domestic Attitudes and Activities. Although little information was available, the remaining members of the "new-style" PKI Central Committee and those newly appointed reportedly have not yet solved a policy disagreement over whether to pursue armed struggles or to attempt to gain power by constitutional means. Soviet efforts to counter Chinese influence on the Indonesian communist movement may have been partly responsible for the disagreement.

In May 1970 an Indonesian army spokesman claimed that politically the PKI was following a "phased campaign." The initial phase was to exploit dissatisfaction among the people. This was followed by a phase in which issues were raised with the intention to alienate the people from the government and the Armed Forces. In the final phase, which has not been attained, they planned to instigate strikes and mass actions such as demonstrations. (*Kompas*, Djakarta, 6 May.) A plan drafted in Surabaja in January and circulated in underground publications listed the "five P's" which would weaken the Indonesian state: *penjelundupan* (smuggling), *perdjudian* (gambling), *pelatjuran* (prostitution), *pergandjaan* (marijuana), and *tukang pukul* ("protection").

Since the attempted coup, the PKI has focused its attention on implementing the "Three Banners of the Party" formulated by the PKI Politburo:

> ... to build a Marxist-Leninist Party free from subjectivism, opportunism and modern revisionism; to wage a people's armed struggle which is essentially an agrarian revolution against feudalism by the armed peasants under the leadership of the working class; and to form a revolutionary united front led by the working class and based on the worker-peasant alliance." (Statement of the Delegation of the PKI Central Committee, *Peking Review*, no. 24, 12 June.)

Confessions of captured underground PKI leaders confirmed that the party had intensified its infiltration among students and intellectuals. They had also infiltrated—"through [psychological warfare] activities or through contacts with embassies of communist countries"—among pedicab drivers, street vendors, small-scale traders, peasants, government employees, the tourist industry, and the Armed Forces (Djakarta radio, domestic service, 11 July and 13 July). An army spokesman explained:

> ... such infiltrators should be men who are power conscious and position hungry, and who can be made to feel morally obligated to the PKI. ... Such men, who are desirous of an education, are sought out and trained in schools and universities where they are taught party doctrines. Men who are fanatic in their belief or religion are made still more fanatic, and at just the right moment are used against some other religion. Men who want land, money and servants continue the struggle and are urged to commit destructive acts of sabotage, never forgetting that all such acts benefit the [communist] party and ideology. (*Duta Masjarakat*, 13 July.)

According to President Suharto's state message on the eve of National Day, "PKI remnants are still carrying out their activities underground in the form of sabotage, subversion and other activities which cause social tension. They continue to create underground groups." (Djakarta radio, domestic service, 16 August.)

PKI activities during 1970 remained limited and regional, ranging from guerrilla operations in Kalimantan to underground activities in Java, South Sumatra, and Celebes, and infiltration of already existing organizations such as the armed forces. Special emphasis was placed on the traditional communist strongholds of Central and East Java. A Western observer asserted that PKI remnants were successfully organizing a "counter government" in parts of East Java (Justus M. van der Kroef, "Indonesian Communism since the 1965 Coup," *Pacific Affairs*, XLIII, Spring 1970, p. 45). Arrested communists "confessed" that they had received instructions from leaders in Central Java. Lieutenant Colonel Jusuf Achmadi, information officer of the Central Java military command, reported that since September 1969 communists had been setting up People's

Defense Commands in Central Java (*Harian Kami*, Djakarta, 28 May 1970). Late in the year, military authorities uncovered communist plans to rebuild the party's strong base in the Wonogiri Regency of Central Java, where there were still some 169,000 communists at large (*ibid.*, 10 November). The Djakarta daily, *Pedoman* (12 May), reported that PKI remnants had divided Central Java into a "southern front" around Djokjakarta, a "central front" around Purwokerto, and a "northern front" around Purwodadi. The southern front was under "Hamim," "who speaks fluent Chinese and who has been designated by Adjitorop . . . as his representative in Java." The "central front" was said to be led by Sugijono, who was thought to favor the Soviet Union and to promote the infiltrating of legal political parties. The leader of the northern front was thought to be Subarli, who was engaged in a terrorist campaign. Such activities were said to be in accord with "PKI's belief in . . . step-by-step actions" and a strategy based on three points:

1. Try to save the cadres and evacuate Central Java, "the pacification of which has been assured."
2. Try to save the cadres within the Armed Forces.
3. Keep all administration and logistics in the hands of party sympathizers.

Under the name "Operation Sapta Marga," Indonesia continued to carry out its intensive search for PKI remnants. A number of former detainees who had been released were again arrested. A Soviet broadcast quoted a Djakarta *Times* article, based on Armed Forces information, to the effect that in Central Java alone some 4,000 communists had been arrested, and that 180 were detained in a mass raid in North Sumatra and 180 in Riao (Moscow radio, 5 July). A later broadcast (9 July, quoting the Dutch communist paper, *De Waarheid*, Amsterdam) stated that in Djokjakarta alone 4,000 persons had been arrested as communist sympathizers.

In March, a rescreening of Public Works and Electricity Department employees resulted in the alleged discovery of 8,549 communists out of the total of 20,000 investigated (Antara, 4 March). Within the Armed Forces, some 800 officers and men were accused of being implicated in the coup attempt or of remaining loyal to Sukarno. These included Commodore R. O. Sunardi, former naval commander in Java; Commodore Sjamsu Sutjipto, navy spokesman; Rear Admiral Atidjan, former communications minister under Sukarno; Major General Suadi, governor of the National Defense Institute and former ambassador to Australia; and Major General Mersid, former deputy army commander under Sukarno and former ambassador to the Philippines.

Persons who had attended universities in the Soviet Union and Eastern Europe and were holding key posts in both private firms and government offices continued to be arrested on charges of having connections with the PKI and thus of involvement in an anti-government movement. Most had belonged to communist organizations before their studies abroad.

The Partindo, a political party formed in 1959 from a merger of smaller parties, came under special attack. The government charged that nearly 80 per cent of its leadership, both central and regional, was controlled by the PKI. The newspaper *Mingguan Chas* maintained that a special bureau within Partindo had been organized by the PKI with an almost exclusively communist membership (quoted by Djakarta radio, domestic service, 13 February 1970). Its task allegedly was to enlist new members for the PKI (*ibid.*). Former Partindo Secretary-General Ali Sumarto was arrested as a leader of the attempted coup movement. In addition, 14 of the 20 members of the Partindo publication board were said to be PKI supporters (*Angkatan Bersendjata*, Djakarta, 3 August).

In the middle of the year, an underground PKI "Greater Regional Committee" was discovered in Djakarta. Communist infiltration of the capital had increased markedly during the spring, although some of the alleged infiltrators were actually released "C type" detainees. (*Ibid.*, 21

May.) Those arrested included Siswojo ("Sardjono"), former head of education on the PKI Central Committee and director of the People's University (*Djakarta Times*, 17 July). Siswojo allegedly admitted that he was to direct preparations for a PKI comeback and that the party was trying to regroup under a collective leadership (*Straits Times*, Singapore, 11 September). Three others were arrested at the same time on charges of heading an effort to establish a united front and promoting armed struggle, setting up an agitation and propaganda bureau, and propagandizing among students. Another leading communist, Lieutenant Kulup Roso Purwanto, was captured in August with four comrades. He was responsible for distributing propaganda pamphlets signed "PKI Militants" and "GEMPAR" (see above). He allegedly confessed that he had joined the party in 1969 and was connected with Siswojo. In the fall, military authorities arrested communist leader Engkos, a communist leader and former member of the banned communist railway trade union, who was the head of a sabotage ring responsible for several rail accidents in West Java. He claimed to be attempting to revive the PKI by forming "people's independence troops" along Vietnamese communist guerrilla lines.

In Central Java, the student newspaper *Harian Kami* reported that several bundles of PKI brochures had been found in a bus from Semarang in November. The pamphlets appealed to communists to remain loyal to the party and await further instructions.

Although the PKI apparently intends to disrupt the general elections scheduled for 1971, it was reported by an Indonesian newspaper (cited in *The Economist*, 7 February 1970) that communists in Central Java planned also to support senior politicians active in the former Sukarno regime in the hope that their views would be closer to PKI policy than those of the younger reformers. Former communists and others who were arrested in connection with the attempted coup have been disfranchised. Moreover, the *Djakarta Times* (26 September) reported the arrest of several former "type C" detainees for placing their names on election lists. In East Java, others have joined legal political parties, evidently in order to vote (*ibid.*, 29 September).

Occasional mention has been made of a subversive student group, identified as "CGMI," which used one of the universities in Semarang as a center for agitation. A revolutionary organization known as Gerakan Pembantu Partai PKI (Movement to Support the PKI), allegedly formed by Chinese diplomatic representatives in collaboration with the PKI, was exposed. It had been active in a number of major Indonesian cities. The organization worked to obtain equipment for PKI remnants and to indoctrinate them with the teachings of Mao Tse-tung, stressing the importance of armed struggle. (Antara, 18 April.) Mention has also been made of the Partai Nasional Merah Indonesia (Indonesian Red Nationalist Party; PNMI), uncovered by security forces. The PNMI allegedly was organized by ethnic Chinese PKI remnants. It is not clear what the relationship between the Gerakan Pembantu Partai PKI and the PNMI is, or whether in fact the two are the same.

In Kalimantan, government security operations in cooperation with Malaysia have continued against the PGRS and the Paraku (see above). Some 8,225 "coup remnants" reportedly are still at large in West Kalimantan, endangering the development of the area (*Angkatan Bersendjata*, 6 August). The Malaysia government was quoted as stating that 230 guerrillas organized by the PGRS and the Paraku were based on the Indonesian side of the Sarawak border (*Washington Post*, 11 August). A Malaysian officer indicated that some 40 communist guerrilla bands had fled toward the Indonesian border to escape Malaysian security troops (Djakarta radio, domestic service, 10 April). In the four months preceding July 1970, joint operations resulted in 65 terrorists killed and 321 captured (*Washington Post*, 25 July). After a lull during 1969, guerrilla offensives along the border increased early in the year, and recruitment activities were continued in an effort to compensate for losses inflicted by Malaysian and Indonesian anti-insurgency campaigns. Communist guerrilla operations have been aimed at undermining the region's development by stirring up animosity between the local people and the Armed Forces, and at consolidating the mostly Chinese PKI remnants. Captured documents revealed that the communists in Indonesian Borneo were attempting to incite Iban tribesmen against the Indonesian and Malaysian governments by advocating the formation of an autonomous Iban state.

International Views and Activities. Sino-Soviet rivalry for the allegiance of PKI remnants continued during 1970. The Soviet Union issued statements about Indonesia relatively frequently, while Chinese commentary was extremely sparse. The Chinese urged the PKI to eschew unrewarding parliamentary struggle in favor of the "correct" road of armed struggle, which was "in essence ... the peasants' armed agrarian revolution under the leadership of the proletariat" (*Peking Review*, no. 43, 24 October.) In a summary of anti-U.S. activities in Southeast Asia, the NCNA (25 September) made token reference to the "people's armed forces" in Indonesia which had "persevered in struggle under extremely difficult conditions," adding: "They have organized guerrilla forces and self-defense guards in the rural areas to attack the enemy repeatedly."

Throughout 1970 China disseminated statements made by the "Delegation of the PKI Central Committee" and appeared to be attempting to establish the Delegation as the rightful spokesman for Indonesian communists. In a unique move on the fiftieth anniversary of the founding of the PKI, the Chinese Communist Party delivered a message to the Delegation of the Central Committee of the PKI "to be forwarded to the Central Committee of the Communist Party of Indonesia." The message praised the PKI's historic record and deplored the "temporary setback suffered in 1965," which had "completely proved the total bankruptcy of the revisionist line of 'peaceful transition' and 'parliamentary road' advocated by the Soviet revisionist renegade clique." It expressed a deep conviction that the setback was temporary and surmountable by "unswervingly taking the road of 'political power grows out of the barrel of a gun' and adhering to the principle of self-reliance and arduous struggle ... fully relying on the masses ... particularly the peasant masses." (NCNA, 22 May.)

Soviet commentary, although profuse, was occasionally unclear whether "PKI" meant the Politburo or the Marxist-Leninist Group. The Soviets repeatedly encouraged the resurgence of a communist movement in Indonesia, but stressed that the circumstances were not suitable for the armed struggle advocated by the Chinese:

> Peking once again called on Indonesian Communists to launch an armed struggle against the reactionary military regime. They advocated forming guerrilla units in villages and persistent attacks on the enemy. However, under circumstances where a revolutionary situation does not prevail in Indonesia, the revolt advocated ... will only end in failure, and will result in new human sacrifices among Indonesian Communists and other democratic elements. It will incite the reactionary clique to step up their persecution against patriotic elements. (Moscow radio, 7 October.)

The Soviet view was that, "based on Marxist-Leninist strategy and tactics concerning class struggle and based on the actual situation in Indonesia," the primary task of the PKI at present was to "restore the rank and file ... by carrying out political activities" and forming mass organizations. The same statement also declared: "We consider the formation of an anti-imperialist united front based on democratic principles by integrating all patriotic forces as the prime and urgent task of the Indonesian Marxist-Leninists." (*Ibid.*)

On the occasion of the twenty-first anniversary of the founding of the Chinese People's Republic, the Soviets blamed the Chinese, as before, for the 1965 coup attempt:

> The leaders of the Indonesian Communist Party were pressured into agreeing to launch an adventurous military coup d'état. As a result, hundreds of thousands of Communist Party

members had to suffer at the hands of the reactionaries, and the Communist Party itself met with setbacks. (*Ibid.*, 29 September.)

This theme was also dominant in the Soviet Union's commemoration of the fiftieth anniversary of the PKI. Apparently unable to settle on a single body to congratulate, the Soviets talked about the PKI at large, although they quoted documents of the Marxist-Leninist Group. Instead of printing the customary greetings, *Pravda* (23 May) carried a long summary of PKI history, expressing confidence in the party's reemergence after the "total shipwreck" in 1965. It stated that the Soviet people were pleased with the U.S.S.R.'s increasingly close relations with Indonesia, adding that the activities of communists in Indonesia had contributed to this. It continued: "Despite everything, the staunch communists of Indonesia are continuing their fight in difficult circumstances [and] fraternal support insures fresh strength in the task ... carrying on struggle underground." (Moscow radio, 22 May.) The Indonesian communists were seen as a "progressive force" which was necessary to offset the efforts of the "anti-peoples" government in Indonesia, where the "principal feature of political life" was the "dominant influence of the military, who share power with the Right [Wing] politicians" (*New Times*, Moscow, 29 July). Soviet attempts to gain influence over the PKI have been channeled through Middle Eastern and Latin American countries as well as by more direct communication.

Elsewhere in the communist world, the Central Committee of the Albanian Workers' Party broadcast a rather lengthy greeting in English to the PKI Central Committee on its fiftieth anniversary, praising the party's historic accomplishments, including "consistent struggle ... against Soviet revisionism and its agents in the ranks of the Indonesian revolutionary movement" and the "intensification and extension of the partisan warfare and the creation of revolutionary armed forces" (Tirana radio, 23 May). The French Communist Party extended briefer "most fraternal greetings" and did not specify what it meant by the "Indonesian Communist Party Central Committee" to which it addressed them (*L'Humanité*, Paris, 23 May). The recipient of North Vietnam's lengthy greeting was likewise unspecified (Vietnam News Agency, Hanoi, 23 May).

An Indonesian Armed Forces Headquarters source disclosed a report "on the activities of foreign subversive elements and extremist groups whose activities were parallel to and in line with the strategic concept of the [attempted coup] in the past" which alleged that the PKI planned to stage a comeback in 1970 (*Angkatan Bersendjata*, 23 August). The report stressed the efforts of international communism, especially those of the Chinese People's Republic, as presenting the main threat of subversion. Foreign subversives were said to be attempting to "sharpen the conflicts and disunity found in the country," particularly through manipulation of the mass media, by exploiting regionalism, separatism, tribalism, and religious conflicts (*ibid.*). The exacerbation of rifts in the Indonesian populace may be part of the avowed communist objective of disrupting the general elections to be held in 1971. According to Indonesian army spokesmen, the embassies of socialist states served as links between the communist world and the PKI, and disseminated communist propaganda. In August 1970 two Indonesian employees of the Soviet Consulate-General in Surabaja were arrested on the charge of being members of the PKI. North Korean involvement in Indonesia came to light with the discovery in Djakarta of 5,000 books on Marxism which were about to be distributed. The books, including a biography of Kim Il-song, allegedly contained disguised directives and instructions on preparation for armed struggle and for disrupting the elections. The North Koreans were said to have switched to this tactic after attempts to disseminate propaganda through the local press had failed. (In 1969 the chief editor of a Djakarta daily was jailed for printing a speech of Kim Il-song.)

Czechoslovakia also appeared to be engaged in subversion in Indonesia. The newspaper *Mingguan Chas*, which is closely connected with the army, charged that Czechoslovak violations of

Indonesian law were "not limited to the arms smuggling." It declared that the Czechoslovak airline was known to have smuggled both arms and men into the country. These activities would possibly increase, according to the report, because "in appointing new diplomats, the Czechoslovak Foreign Ministry is giving preference to this kind of diplomat." (Quoted, Djakarta radio, domestic service, 7 March.) PKI contacts were said to be cultivated also by the various Arab diplomatic missions in Djakarta, including those of Syria and Algeria.

Publications. The PKI Politburo publishes a clandestine monthly, *Mimbar Rakjat*. Clandestine publications of the GEMPAR also express PKI positions. In addition, the *Indonesian Bulletin* apparently continues to circulate in Albania. Statements by Indonesian communists are publicized in the Chinese press and radio, as well as by East Germany, North Korea, North Vietnam, and Albania, all of which have regular broadcasts in Indonesian.

*　　*　　*

The Delegation of the PKI Central Committee. The relationship of the Peking-based "Delegation of the PKI Central Committee" with the PKI Politburo is unclear. While the two groups advocate similar strategies, tactics, and programs, the Delegation places considerably more emphasis on the thought of Mao Tse-tung.

Leadership and Organization. Headed by Jusuf Adjitorop, the Delegation of the PKI Central Committee reportedly comprises 700 persons, including former Indonesian ambassadors (mostly to communist capitals), pre-coup PKI members, and former front leaders. In Peking, the Delegation extends its influence through the Federation of Indonesian Students, the Indonesian People's Youth League, and the Indonesian Organization for Afro-Asian People's Solidarity.

In 1967, there were reports that Djawoto would replace Jusuf Adjitorop as leader of the Peking-based Delegation. Although this was substantially confirmed by the Indonesian chargé d'affaires expelled from Peking, statements have continued to be issued in the name of Adjitorop as head of the Delegation. It appears that the Peking exiles are split into two ideological factions: one headed by Djawoto; the other, labeled "revisionist," looks to Ali Hanafiah, who is thought to be in Moscow.

Domestic Attitudes and Activities. In its statement on the PKI's fiftieth anniversary (23 May 1970) the Delegation contended that the difficulties "of taking the road of armed revolution" were "only temporary" and affirmed that, "under the leadership of the Communist Party of Indonesia, the people have risen in armed struggle ever since 1967" (statement in *Peking Review*, no. 24, 12 June). Armed struggle based on the masses and specifically on the peasantry was hailed as the road the PKI should take; revolutionary bases should be established in the countryside to isolate and finally capture the cities and liberate "semi-feudal, semi-colonial" Indonesia.

The Delegation attacked President Suharto's attempts to assist Premier Lon Nol of Cambodia. It described the Indonesian administration as a "fascist regime"—the "most concentrated representative of the bureaucrat-capitalist class, the comprador class and the landlord class"—and as being "out-and-out in the service of U.S. imperialism" (*ibid.*).

International Views and Positions. The Delegation continued to endorse Chinese ideology during 1970, scoring the Soviet line of "peaceful transition" as "a road to bury the revolution and a road to ruin the Party and the revolutionary movement" (statement in Peking Review, no. 24, 12 June). The Delegation condemned "Soviet revisionism" at length, while extolling the "great red Banner of Mao Tse-tung thought."

The Delegation was no less reticent in condemning the U.S. intervention in Cambodia as an "extremely wanton atrocity." The "Lon Nol-Sirik Matak coup d'etat clique" was scored for its establishment of a "fascist military regime," as were President Suharto and Foreign Minister Adam Malik for their attempts to aid Lon Nol (*ibid.*). The Delegation endorsed Prince Sihanouk's newly formed "Royal Government of National Union" as "an important step taken by the Cambodian people in their patriotic struggle," and praised "the firm determination, mutual support and militant solidarity of the people . . . of Cambodia, Laos, and Viet Nam" (*ibid.*).

Publications. Publications issued by or carrying statements of the Delegation of the PKI Central Committee include *Suara Rakjat Indonesia*, the organ of the Indonesian Afro-Asian People's Solidarity Organization (Peking); *Voice of the Indonesian Youth*, the monthly organ of the Indonesian Students' Association (Peking); and the *Indonesian Tribune*, a monthly believed to be published by a group of Indonesians in Albania. Statements by the Delegation are also publicized by the Chinese and Albanian news media, both of which have regular broadcasts in Indonesian.

*   *   *

The Marxist-Leninist Group of the PKI. The Marxist-Leninist Group of the PKI appears to consist of exiles in Moscow led by Ali Hanafiah, former Indonesian ambassador to Ceylon. Isolated reports during 1970 indicated that members of the group were operating underground in Indonesia, but beyond that the organization has remained obscure. It is not clear whether the Marxist-Leninist Group is in opposition to the Politburo of the PKI Central Committee or whether the two are merely conflicting factions of the "Indonesian communist movement," although reports have tended to regard them as separate.

Domestic Attitudes and Activities. The Marxist-Leninist Group has defined its primary task as the "revival of the Indonesian Communist Party based on Marxism-Leninism" (*Takad Rakjat*, quoted by Moscow radio, 5 July 1970). According to a Soviet report, the group advocates the formation of a united front of "leftist democrats on the basis of the workers-peasants alliance" (Moscow radio, 13 March). It also calls for "democratization" of the government, release of all political prisoners, termination of the ban on dissemination of Marxism-Leninism, expansion of the state sector in critical branches of the national economy, supervision of foreign investments, agrarian reform, and improvement of living conditions.

A Moscow radio broadcast on 9 July referred to a "new party program document issued by the Indonesian Marxist-Leninist communists." According to the report, the program urged communists to "work tirelessly in the defense of the interests of the working people and expose the antidemocratic and anti-people nature of the new order [the Suharto government]." It also described the forthcoming elections as "another scheme to deceive the people."

Although aligned with the Soviet Union in the Sino-Soviet dispute, the Marxist-Leninist Group advocates preparation for both nonviolent and armed struggle to overthrow the "military fascist dictatorship of President Suharto," claiming that such a government could never be overthrown by legal, parliamentary measures.

International Views and Positions. Being closely aligned with the Soviet Union, the Marxist-Leninist Group has been condemned by the Chinese People's and has responded in kind. The group has expressed support for various revolutionary struggles around the world.

Publications. The Marxist-Leninist Group publishes an Indonesian-language periodical, *Takad Rakjat* (People's Will), in Moscow. Statements of the group are also publicized by news media in the Soviet Union and East Berlin and by the pro-Soviet Communist Party of India.

S. E. Y.

JAPAN

The Japan Communist Party (Nihon Kyosanto, JCP) was founded in July 1922 and was illegal until the end of the Second World War. On 4 October 1945 General Douglas MacArthur, Supreme Commander for the Allied Powers, issued a civil rights directive which provided, among other things, for the free activity of political organizations and the release of political prisoners. Leaders of the prewar JCP, some of whom had been in prison for as long as eighteen years, emerged to reestablish the party. The two most prominent were Tokuda Kyuichi and Shiga Yoshio. Nosaka Sanzo, the present chairman of the Central Committee of the JCP, returned to Japan from China in January 1946 and, with Tokuda and Shiga, formed the triumvirate which guided the JCP during its immediate postwar period. Later, Tokuda died in mainland China, and Shiga, expelled from the JCP, formed a party called the "Voice of Japan" in 1964.

The JCP, which at no time during its twenty-three years of illegal existence had more than 1,000 members, grew rapidly after the war, to 7,500 in 1946, 70,000 in 1947, and to 150,000 by 1949.

On 6 January 1950, the organ of the Cominform, *For a Lasting Peace, For a People's Democracy*, published a blistering attack on Nosaka and the JCP for advocating "peaceful revolution" and toadying to the occupying forces on the theory that they would thus help a development toward socialism in Japan. After bitter arguments within the party leadership, the Central Committee decided to bow to the Cominform's "criticism" and Nosaka abjectly apologized, accepting the accusations made against him. The party became militant; terrorist acts occurred. In June 1950 the occupation authorities banned key members of the JCP Central Committee from public life.

Membership subsequently fell off, dropping to 40,000 by 1958, and the party's appeal and influence diminished. By 1955 some JCP leaders were working for a change of policy, away from "leftist adventurism" and back to the idea of "peaceful revolution" pursued before the Cominform's rebuke. For some time a struggle ensued between factions over policy, strategy, and tactics. The Eighth Congress of the JCP, in July 1961, adopted a new program which set up the twin objectives of destroying "American imperialism" and "Japanese monopoly capitalism," and committed the party to elections, which meant that the "parliamentary system should be used to further the course of the revolution" (Robert A. Scalapino, *The Japanese Communist Movement, 1920-1966*, Berkeley, Calif., University of California Press, 1967, p. 113).

The JCP broke with the Communist Party of the Soviet Union (CPSU) in March 1964 over the partial nuclear test ban treaty and with the Chinese Communist Party (CCP) in October 1967 over ideological and policy differences. Subsequently the JCP has maintained the posture of an independent political party working within Japan's constitutional and parliamentary framework.

Party membership increased during the 1960's, to an estimated 80,000 in 1961, to 250,000 by 1966, and to 280,000 at the time of the Eleventh Congress, in July 1970. An analysis in 1970 of the members by professions revealed that 46 per cent were workers in private enterprises, 14 per cent were government employees, 6 per cent were farmers, and 6 per cent were teachers. Those between the ages of 20 and 29 years were most numerous (46 per cent) followed by those of 30-39 years (34 per cent) and 40-49 years (11 per cent).

The JCP is the largest nonruling communist party outside of Europe and the third such in the world.

The population of Japan was 103,703,522 as of 1 October 1970.

Parliamentary Strength. The JCP won five seats in Japan's first postwar elections for the House of Representatives, held in April 1946. Three years later, benefitting from disarray within the Japan Socialist Party (JSP), the party elected a record 35 candidates, all of whom lost their seats in the 1952 elections which occurred after a period of violence and purges of JCP leaders. Total votes cast for communist candidates plummeted from the 2.9 million of the 1949 elections to 895,000 in 1952. Not until twenty years after the remarkable 1949 showing was the party able to break again the "two digit barrier," when it won 14 seats in the House of Representatives (total membership, 486) in the elections of December 1969. The JCP vote then was 3,199,030 or 6.8 per cent of the total—a record number of votes and the highest percentage since 1949.

In the 250-seat Upper House (House of Councillors) the JCP holds seven seats, won in elections held in 1965 and 1968. In the latter year, the party gained 5 per cent of the popular vote in the national constituencies and 8.3 per cent in the local constituency system. As of July 1970 the JCP held 53 seats in the prefectural assemblies and 1,697 in city, town, and village councils.

An event which drew national attention in 1970 was the victory of the JCP-supported candidate for governor of Kyoto Prefecture in the election held on 12 April. The incumbent, Ninagawa Torazo, was supported by the JCP and the JSP against a candidate jointly endorsed by the Liberal Democratic Party, the Komeito (Clean Government Party) and the Democratic Socialist Party.

Leadership and Organization. Several important changes in organization and personnel were decided at the JCP's Eleventh Congress, the first in nearly four years, held on 1-7 July 1970 at Tachikawa, near Tokyo. Nosaka Sanzo was for the fifth time elected chairman of the Central Committee, now largely an honorific title, and Miyamoto Kenji, who had been secretary-general of the party, was elevated to a newly created post, chairman of the Standing Committee of the Presidium, a position equivalent to that of party chairman. A newcomer to the highest ranks of party leadership, Fuwa Tetsuzo (Ueda Kenjiro), was appointed to another position which had not existed before, director of the Central Committee Secretariat.

These personnel changes mean that Miyamoto is more strongly in control of the party than before, that Nosaka, as the "grand old man" of the JCP, is becoming somewhat of a figurehead, and that the bright, young (forty-year-old) Fuwa has been moved to a top position ahead of many older and more experienced men in the party, including his older brother (Ueda Koichiro, aged forty-three) who has long been prominent in party activities. Fuwa is a protege of Miyamoto, an elected member of the House of Representatives, and had been chairman of the JCP's Political and Foreign Policy Committee.

Other changes at the congress increased the membership of the Central Committee Presidium from 11 to 31, designated seven Standing Committee members of the Presidium, and expanded the Central Committee from 87 to 110 members. Additionally, 46 alternate members of the Central Committee were selected.

The Standing Committee of the Presidium consists of Miyamoto Kenji (chairman), Hakamada Satomi and Oka Masayoshi (vice-chairmen), Fuwa Tetsuzo, Kurahara Korehito, Matsubara Harushige, and Nishizawa Tomio. Notably, Nosaka no longer serves on the Presidium.

Two deputy directors, Ichikawa Shoichi and Kaneko Mitsuhiro, were named to the Central Committee Secretariat, headed by Fuwa Tetsuzo. Like Fuwa, both are young, in terms of Japanese politics; Ichikawa is forty-six, Kaneko forty-five. According to a statement by Miyamoto, the average age of the 10 members of the Secretariat is only forty-three years.

Party Auxiliaries and Front Organizations. *The Youth Movement.*   The JCP-supported youth movement is the Minshu Seinen Domei (Minseido), or Democratic Youth League. Its membership in July 1970 was reported to be 200,000 but in actuality was probably nearer 180,000. Its publication *Minsei Shimbun* has a circulation of 300,000.

The Minseido makes special efforts to attract young workers and therefore is particularly active in the labor unions, where it has run into direct competition with the Anti-War Youth Committee (Hansen Seinen Iinkai) (see below, "Anti-JCP Youth and Student Groups"). The Anti-War Youth Committee favors radical action, while the Minseido relies on a "soft line" and the propagation of "structural reform" directed toward the goal of a democratic coalition government. Both organizations seek members within the ranks of young laborers.

The Minseido is said to aim at increasing its membership by 50 per cent, which is regarded as difficult to achieve. Members are expected to be active in supporting JCP candidates in forthcoming elections, local and national, and to continue to work for united action with the JSP.

The Japanese student movement is split into numerous groups and factions. The "mainstream" of the principal student organization, the Zengakuren (National Federation of Students' Self-Government Associations), is controlled by the JCP. The so-called New Left includes those Zengakuren factions that are generally opposed to the established parties of the left (the JSP and the JCP) and to Sohyo (the Japan General Council of Trade Unions).

The mainstream or pro-JCP Zengakuren was reported in late 1970 to have a roster of some 551,000 affiliated students, of whom 16,000 could be considered activists. The organization continued its policy of supporting non-violence but during 1970 undertook "struggle actions" to get rid of militant factions. Violent incidents at four universities resulted. Clashes between pro-JCP and anti-JCP students numbered 58 in 1970 (as opposed to 175 in 1969). As many as 62 other disputes broke out among anti-JCP or other groups, bringing the total for 1970 to 120 (308 in 1969). In 1970 two students were killed, 325 injured, and 477 arrested in these various incidents; in 1969, two students were killed, 1,145 injured and 987 arrested. (*Koan Joho*, [Public Safety Report], a monthly magazine published by the Social Problems Research Institute, Tokyo, September 1970, p. 53.)

The pro-JCP Zengakuren held its regular nationwide congress at Nagoya in July with 3,400 members in attendance. Reports were made on the "success" of the demonstration of 23 June against the Japan-United States security treaty and on progress in the campaign to democratize educational institutions.

Peace Movement.   The JCP-sponsored Nihon Gensuikyo (Japan Council Against Atomic and Hydrogen Bombs) held its sixteenth national congress successively at Tokyo, Hiroshima, and Nagasaki from 1 through 9 August, with preparatory meetings on 30 and 31 July. Attendance by 10,000 persons was reported, including 51 foreign participants from 12 countries; six international organizations were also represented. The Japanese government refused entry to delegates from North Vietnam and the National Liberation Front of South Vietnam. Noteworthy among resolutions denouncing "U.S. imperialist aggression" and proclaiming solidarity with the peoples of Vietnam, Laos, and Cambodia was a declaration favoring the unity of (as it is popularly called) the "anti-A and -H bomb movement." This was aimed at the principal rival organization, the Gensuikin (People's Council Against Atomic and Hydrogen Bombs), which was formed in 1965 with the support of the JSP and Sohyo. The JCP's Gensuikyo had previously taken the position that there could be neither joint action nor organizational cooperation with the Gensuikin. The principle of unity was to be conditional on the prohibition of "intervention by obstructionist elements," by which was presumably meant relations with the splinter communist party, the "Voice of Japan." It seemed doubtful that Gensuikin would accept the overtures of the Gensuikyo or that unity in the movement would be restored.

During the meetings at Hiroshima, several right-wing groups staged parades and demonstrations, denouncing the "Red Gensuikyo," displaying placards, and delivering speeches and proclamations.

Labor. Japan in 1970 had 34 million employed workers, of whom some 11,605,000 (35.4 per cent) belonged to labor unions—an increase of 3.4 per cent over 1969. The largest labor federation is the Japan General Council of Trade Unions (Nihon Rodokumiai Sohyogikai, or Sohyo), which in 1970 had a membership of 4,282,000. Traditionally Soyho has been affiliated with the Japan Socialist Party to which it provided substantial political and financial support. Second to Sohyo is the Japan United Congress of Labor (Zen Nihon Rodo Sodomei—or Domei), with 2,059,000 members and affiliated with the Democratic Socialist Party. Two smaller labor organizations are the Federation of Independent Unions (Churitsu Rodokumiai Renrakukaigi—or Churitsu Roren), with 1,400,000 members, and the New Congress of Industrial Unions (Zenkoku Sangyobetsu Rodokumiai—or Shin Sanbetsu), with 75,000. Sohyo's growth has been slow in recent years—only 0.8 per cent in 1970, in contrast to 4.9 per cent for Domei. (Labor Ministry report, quoted in *Tokyo Shimbun*, 28 November 1970.)

The only labor organizations in which the JCP has been able to build any influence of consequence are unions affiliated with Sohyo. The party has also recruited members directly among factory workers and in other non-federated unions.

The Japanese labor movement was in a period of transition during the year. The elections for the House of Representatives in December 1969, in which the JSP lost 50 seats, revealed, among other things, the weakness of JSP influence within Sohyo and the resulting failure of many trade union members to vote Socialist as had been the pattern in former years.

A movement for unification of the Japanese labor movement was widely discussed during the year but no substantial progress was made toward its accomplishment.

Other Fronts. The JCP wholly or partly controls numerous organizations, including a miscellany of study circles, professional groups, labor unions based on individual memberships, cultural societies for music and literature, and groups formed for sports, peace, and friendship.

Noteworthy is the General Federation of Korean Residents in Japan (Zainichi Chosenjin Sorengokai or Chosen Soren) which is pro-North Korean and claims to represent the majority of Koreans living in Japan. It is not controlled by the JCP, but relations between the party and the Chosen Soren naturally reflect the relationship existing between the JCP and the governing party of the Democratic People's Republic of Korea (DPRK), the Korean Workers' Party (KWP). At present there is close liaison and cooperation between the Chosen Soren and the JCP, although the party did not agree with the statements included in the joint communiqué issued by Kim Il-song and Chou En-lai after their 1970 Pyongyang meetings, which claimed that Japanese militarism had *already* been revived.

The Ninth Congress of the Chosen Soren, planned for May, was postponed on short notice and new preparations instituted on the basis of decisions taken at the Fifth Congress of the KWP, which included special efforts to strengthen the organization on the basis of more thorough indoctrination of its leaders and activists in the ideology and thought of Kim Il-song. The Chosen Soren sent a delegation to the KWP congress, and there were frequent exchanges of missions during the year. Special efforts were made to receive appropriately visitors from North Korea to Japan's international exhibition—EXPO '70—and to the North Korean trade fair which opened in Japan in May.

Chosen Soren was active during the year in agitating for the facilitation of changes in the registration of Korean residents in Japan from "South Korean nationality" to "North Korean nationality." The JSP was active in these efforts and was supported by the JCP and by some of the militant factions of the New Left.

The year saw mutual efforts, through exchanges of visits and communications, to strengthen relations between the JCP and the KWP, and in turn between the JCP and the Chosen Soren.

Party Internal Affairs. *The 11th Party Congress.*   The Eleventh Congress of the JCP met in Tachikawa, near Tokyo, on 1-7 July 1970, three years and nine months after the Tenth Congress, held in October 1966. Originally scheduled for October 1969, the Eleventh Congress was twice postponed—first to May 1970 because of the elections for the House of Representatives in December 1969, and then to July, to allow more time after the Kyoto gubernatorial election on 12 April, to which party leaders attached great importance.

About 1,000 delegates attended the congress meetings. For the first time all sessions, except those concerned with financial and personnel matters, were opened to the press and public. The Japanese government announced that, as in past years, entry permits would not be granted to foreign delegates to the congress. Representatives of the Australian and Italian communist parties, Laurence Aarons and Emilio Sereni, who applied for tourist visas to visit EXPO '70, were admitted into Japan. When they spoke at the congress, the Ministry of Justice ordered them to leave the country, but they took their cases to court and obtained a ruling that the retroactive revocation of their visas was invalid. Three other parties—the Romanian, North Vietnamese, and North Korean—accepted invitations to send delegates, but only the North Koreans had a participant at the congress, their permanent representative in Japan. No invitations were extended to the Soviet or Chinese parties. The CPSU sent a telegram which was published inconspicuously in *Akahata* on 10 July, three days after the congress adjourned. Telegrams and messages of congratulations from numerous other communist parties and organizations were read to the congress during its sessions. The Chinese ignored the meetings entirely.

Submitted to the congress and approved unanimously by the delegates were: (1) the party program, "Prospects for the 1970's and Tasks for the Communist Party of Japan," and (2) the revised party rules. These had been decided upon by the Thirteenth Plenum of the Central Committee and were published on 16 and 17 May respectively. In addition, Secretary-General Miyamoto Kenji made a five-hour presentation on the first day of the Congress (1 July) of the "Report of the Central Committee" which was discussed in subsequent sessions.

The intent of the JCP to present an image of an "independent, democratic" political party, pursuing its ends exclusively through parliamentary means, emerges from these documents. The party program states that it is the "historic duty of the JCP to establish during the 1970's a democratic coalition government." This is to be achieved through forming a united front dedicated to peace, neutrality, and democracy, which would serve as the basis for winning control of a Diet majority by the JCP and "democratic forces." Repeatedly, the program emphasizes that the party must work legally through elections and actions in the Diet. Furthermore, the principle first announced in July 1969, that the coalition government envisaged by the JCP would not be a one-party dictatorship but would permit the free functioning of opposition parties, has now been included in the official party program. Asked about this point by a Japanese journalist, Miyamoto replied: "Even Marxism-Leninism recognizes the existence of opposition parties, as can be seen in the cases of the satellite political parties in Europe. In the Soviet Union, they were removed later by an armed coup d'état. The basis of the people's democracy is that it receives the support of a wide range of the general masses. It does not mean that when the communist party seizes power, the range of freedom will be narrowed." (*Yomiuri Shimbun*, Tokyo, 8 July.) The party program also stresses that if the JCP should come to power, it would respect the existing bourgeois freedoms of speech, publication, association, assembly, and religion.

Some Japanese observers described the present purpose of the JCP as the creation of a "European-style" party to cope with problems similar to those facing communist parties in the industrialized Western democracies (Kyodo, News Service, Tokyo, 1 July). Clearly the JCP wishes to expand its membership and influence, building on the considerable success achieved thus far and the broad appeal which a moderate program holds for the Japanese public.

Significantly, the party rules were amended to recognize Marxism-Leninism as the "theoretical basis" for the party's existence and not a "principle for action" as had previously been stipulated. The new rules state that the party will pursue revolutionary change in theory and in practice "independently and creatively." The principle of party direction, according to the new rules, is the unity of collective leadership based on knowledge, experience, and individual responsibility. The rules also state that the party's activities should be carried out with respect for the real interests of the people and in accord with the "morality and reason of the social classes." Apparently this is the first time a reference to "morality" has been made in the party rules. (*Ibid.*, 16 May.) The revised rules established the new position of chairman of the Presidium, to which Miyamoto Kenji was appointed. The practical effect of this change was to concentrate real power in Miyamoto's hands.

The party program, outlining prospects and tasks for the 1970's, treats in detail the special characteristics of the international and domestic situations envisaged by the party in the decade ahead. As to be expected, much attention is devoted to U.S. "imperialism and aggression" in Indochina, but the disunity in the world communist movement is likewise deplored. References are made to the "so-called Great Proletarian Cultural Revolution" carried out in China by the "Mao Tse-tung clique," the military invasion of Czechoslovakia by five communist countries led by the Soviet Union, and the Sino-Soviet border clashes—the first armed conflict between socialist countries—which "shocked the whole world and encouraged the anti-socialist propaganda of the imperialist powers." Focusing on the November 1969 joint communiqué by Premier Sato and U.S. President Nixon, the Party Program called "U.S. imperialism and Japanese militarism" the common enemies of the Japanese people, while noting, however, that because of Japan's constitutional restrictions, lack of conscription, and ban on sending troops abroad, one could not yet say that militarism in Japan had been completely revived.

On the domestic front, the party document attacked the government's policy of a high economic growth rate, contending that it was carried out at the sacrifice of the people's livelihood. Political confrontation in the 1970's was seen as centering on the Liberal Democratic Party and the JCP. Two alternatives were seen as presenting themselves: a revival of militarism and imperialism, or the overthrow of the LDP government and the establishment of a democratic coalition government based on independence, peace, democracy, and neutrality.

In a section devoted to the achievement of a democratic coalition government, attention is directed to the element of the required "mass struggle," the need for a united front, and the importance of specific groups, such as the labor unions and the farmers. The program emphasizes that Japan's parliamentary system, the rights guaranteed by the constitution, and the democratic institutions established in Japan are important accomplishments and should be defended. Consistent with the principle of seeking power through parliamentary means, the JCP places great importance on coming elections. The program urges the necessity of winning more seats, not only in the national Diet, but in prefectural and local assemblies; it notes that the JCP has seats in only about half of the 46 prefectural assemblies, none in 142 out of 564 city assemblies, and none in 1,980 out of 2,716 town and village councils.

The five "pillars" in a united front of democratic forces to achieve a democratic coalition government were described as (1) abrogation of the Japan-U.S. security treaty and the complete reversion of Okinawa, (2) peace and neutralization, (3) opposition to the retrogressive revision of the constitution and support for the establishment of a democratic administration, (4) protection of the people's livelihood and the carrying out of an independent economic policy, and (5) democratic development of education and culture.

The final section of the program was devoted to the "unity and progress" of the international communist movement. Most prominence was accorded to the recent history of the relations of the JCP with the communist parties of the Soviet Union and China, making quite clear the continuing hostility of the JCP for both. The JCP asserted, however, its desire for cooperation and friendly relations with all fraternal communist parties, including those with which there were disagreements, while continuing to oppose "Big Power-ist" intervention and to insist on the JCP's independent stand. An earlier appeal was repeated, calling for a conference of anti-imperialist nations from five continents to strengthen the unity of world action against imperialism.

Party Anniversary. The JCP celebrated the forty-eighth anniversary of its founding on 15 July with a commemorative reception in Tokyo, attended by some 1,000 persons. The foreign guests included the secretary of the Australian communist party, Laurence Aarons, who had attended the Eleventh Congress; two vice-chairmen of the General Federation of Korean Residents in Japan; the Hungarian, Polish, and Romanian ambassadors to Japan; and a representative of the Bulgarian Embassy. Speeches were made by Central Committee Chairman Nosaka, Presidium Chairman Miyamoto, and the newly elected vice-chairmen of the Presidium, Hakamada and Oka.

Domestic Attitudes and Activities. *United Front.* In 1970 the JCP continued to propagate the idea of a united front of all "anti-imperialist, democratic forces." As in 1969, however, the party was unable to establish a continuing united front with the Japan Socialist Party. The JCP and JSP cooperated only in joint one-day struggles and in the gubernatorial election in Kyoto. The party congress resolution admitted: "The fact that a united front on a nationwide scale has not yet been formed is the result of the splitting up and sectarianization of movements. . . . The democratic forces of Japan are greeting 1970 with the Security Treaty joint struggle organization, which was born as the historical outcome of the 1960 Security Treaty struggles, remaining dissolved, and with no unified joint struggle organization to take its place established." (*Akahata*, 16 May.)

Joint one-day struggles were staged on 28 April (Okinawa Day, the anniversary of the Japanese peace treaty), 23 June (date the security treaty was open to notice of termination), and 21 November (anti-war day).

The JCP and JSP combined to support the incumbent governor of Kyoto, Ninagawa Torazo, in his campaign for reelection against a former bureaucrat, Shibata Mamoru, who received the backing of the Liberal Democratic, Social Democratic, and Komei parties. Ninagawa won a sixth four-year term with more than 630,000 votes as opposed to 491,000 for his opponent. The JCP, whose young workers had been aggressively active during the campaign, was jubilant at the victory and immediately began to prepare for the elections of the governor of Tokyo Prefecture and for the House of Councillors in April and July 1971 respectively.

In spite of united action for specific purposes, relations between the JCP and JSP were not generally happy. The JCP voiced sharp criticisms after the JSP party chairman, Narita Tomomi, and a delegation visited the Soviet Union and China. Joint communiqués issued by the JSP delegation and the CPSU (18 July) and by the JSP and the CCP (1 November) were harshly criticized in lengthy articles in *Akahata*, the one concerned with the Chinese communiqué signed by the director of the Secretariat, Fuwa Tetsuzo. Analyzing "problematical points" in the JSP-CPSU joint communiqué, the JCP found no mention of U.S. "imperialist" domination of Japan, no references to China, a passive attitude toward the unity of democratic forces in Japan, and uncritical support of Soviet policy in spite of the invasion of Czechoslovakia (*Akahata*, 28 July). Fuwa was incensed at the JSP's refusal, in the joint statement with the CCP, to include the JCP in any "coalition front" unless the party self-reflected on its "criticism against China." Although the joint communiqué did not mention the "four enemy theory" (U.S. imperialism, Soviet revisionism, the Sato reactionary government, and the JCP revisionist clique), Fuwa interpreted language in the statement as in fact an implication of it. The JSP had referred to "shelving minor differences" with the Chinese while "agreeing on major points," but the Chinese designation of the JCP as one of the "four enemies," was, in Fuwa's eyes, far from a "minor difference"; he was indignant that the JSP delegation had apparently made no attempt to refute the Chinese contention that the JCP was one of the "enemies." (*Ibid.*, 7 November.)

On 17 December JSP Chairman Narita Tomomi proposed joint opposition activities against the government to include the JCP. Only the JCP welcomed the suggestion; both the Democratic Socialist Party and the Komeito refused to participate in joint action with the JCP. (*Japan Times*, 19 December.)

The Security Treaty "Crisis."   For several years the Japanese left focused on the approaching "crisis of 1970," the year in which the Japan-U.S. security treaty would become subject to notice of termination by either party. The JCP was in the vanguard of parties and groups demanding abrogation of the treaty and the removal from Japan of all U.S. military bases and personnel. A general strike was threatened, and the Japanese government and police feared demonstrations and violence which would exceed in scale and damage the riots of 1960. Fortunately for the government, however, the signatories agreed to continue the treaty "automatically," thus obviating the necessity for Diet action and the opportunity for parliamentary disruption. Moreover, the Sato-Nixon agreements of November 1969 set a date for the reversion of Okinawa (1972), and the elections which followed in December brought victory to the Liberal Democratic Party (302 out of 486 seats) and disastrous defeat for the JSP (loss of 50 seats). Thus, the defusing of the Okinawa issue and the weakening of the JSP, combined with Japan's growing economic prosperity, made the atmosphere in the country far less conducive to widespread political action than was the case in 1960. By February, Sohyo had abandoned its plan for a general strike, and the JSP renounced the "exercise of force" in the "mass struggles" planned for June.

As a result of the changed atmosphere, the aims of the JCP and the other participating parties and factions were transferred from the so-called "struggle of 1970" to the "struggle of 1972" and the "struggle of the 1970's." Observers called this a tactical retreat required by political realities in Japan.

The demonstrations took place in the ten-day period from 14 to 23 June. The so-called New Left, consisting of militant student factions, staged meetings and parades on 14 and 15 June, the latter date being the tenth anniversary of the death of a Tokyo University student, Kamba Michiko, killed during the riots of 1960. About 53,000 people were mobilized on the first day, and 28,200 on the second. Some outbreaks occurred (172 students were arrested in Tokyo on 14 June), but the level of violence was described as far below that of the previous year (*New York Times*, 16 June).

The JCP-JSP "one-day struggle" was conducted on 23 June, the actual date on which the treaty became subject to notification of termination. The JSP was reluctant to agree to joint action with the JCP, but through Sohyo intervention was persuaded at the last minute to participate. About 90,000 persons assembled for the rally in Tokyo; other joint demonstrations were held in about 300 cities and towns in 25 out of 46 prefectures.

The radical factions of the New Left held separate rallies and parades in Tokyo and other cities throughout Japan. Sporadic violence occurred, with throwing of rocks and firebombs, and the wielding of lead pipes. Strikes for brief periods by railway workers and others were called, but these caused little inconvenience to the general public. The participants in rallies and demonstrations were estimated to number 740,000 for all of Japan, exceeding those in previous years. Most observers concluded, however, that "the protests were largely symbolic" (*New York Times*, 24 June).

On 23 June, the day of the peak rallies, Nosaka Sanzo, chairman of the JCP Central Committee, appealed again for a united front of "all democratic forces, including the Communist and Socialist parties." At the same time, he denounced the Democratic Socialist Party and the Komeito, claiming that their slogans for "maintaining the treaty without the presence of U.S. troops in Japan" and for "gradual dissolution of the treaty" showed that their stand was "irreconcilable" with Japanese public opinion and would in fact "support the policy of the government and the Liberal Democratic Party to continue Japan's military alliance with the United States" (*Akahata*, 23 June).

After the 23 June demonstrations, *Akahata* (25 June) editorialized on their "enormous significance" and lauded the success of the unified action. The JCP organ admitted, however, that a weak point was the fact that a united front comparable to that of 1960 had not been formed, and speculated that, if such a front could be organized, the energies of many more people would be mobilized.

International Views and Policies. The year 1970 saw no improvement in relations between the JCP and the Soviet and Chinese communist parties. In fact, the exchange of polemics was more acrimonious than during 1969. The resolution passed by the Eleventh Congress on 1 July left no doubt as to the official attitude of the JCP toward the CPSU and the CCP. Terming the disunity in the international communist movement and the socialist camp "the most important problem in the past three years," the resolution concluded that this disunity had blocked the "effective rallying together of the anti-imperialist, international united front, thereby further expanding the room for the maneuvers of the imperialists." Singled out for special opprobrium were the Cultural Revolution—"created by the Mao Tse-tung clique," the invasion of Czechoslovakia by the military forces of five socialist nations including those of the Soviet Union, and the Sino-Soviet border conflict, the "first armed clash between two socialist nations." (*Akahata*, 16 May.)

In another lengthy section of the resolution, the Soviet and Chinese parties were denounced for "Big Power-ism," as demonstrated by their efforts to force policy lines on other nations. The example of the invasion of Czechoslovakia was again raised, and both the CPSU and the CCP were accused of "interference" through their support of splinter organizations opposed to the JCP. Lenin's warnings against Great Russian nationalism and Stalin's grab of Japan's Kurile Islands were cited to bolster the charges of "Big Power-ism." Looking toward the future, the resolution expressed a pious hope for reconciliation: "Although a certain unavoidable but necessary period of time will be required for the task, without any doubt the moment will come when our party and the Japanese people can develop truly fraternal and friendly relations with all parties and peoples of all socialist nations, including China and the Soviet Union." (*Ibid.*)

Finally, in listing international tasks, the resolution again struck out at the Soviet and Chinese parties, proclaiming that the JCP must fulfill "still more positive roles in the overcoming of Big Power interference, linked with modern revisionism and ultra-left opportunism, and for the realization of true class unity and solidarity of the international communist movement" (*ibid.*).

At the opening of the party congress on 1 July, Secretary-General Miyamoto presented the report of the Central Committee, in which he discussed at length the JCP's relations with the Soviet and Chinese parties. He dwelt in detail on Soviet "interference" in the affairs of the JCP through support of the "Voice of Japan" splinter party, including the public attention paid to this group by the Soviet Embassy in Tokyo. Miyamoto nevertheless concluded his report on a conciliatory note, expressing a hope that interference would end and that the Japanese and Soviet parties could normalize their relations. After a full discussion of the problems with the Chinese party, including Maoist support of dissident anti-JCP groups, Miyamoto also expressed hope that the CCP would "return to policy lines befitting its great glory and tradition."

JCP-CCP Relations. Nosaka Sanzo, JCP Central Committee chairman whose close wartime association and cooperation with Mao Tse-tung and the CCP leadership is well known, tried to strike a hopeful note as 1970 opened. In a New Year television interview, he stated that there was no quarrel between the Chinese and Japanese communist parties, that the JCP was on bad terms only with the "Mao Tse-tung clique." He emphasized his friendly feelings for the Chinese people and toward CCP members. He hoped that governmental relations between Japan and China could be normalized at the earliest possible opportunity. He believed, in fact, that changes in the policies of the CCP were inevitable and that the CCP would come back to the line of genuine Marxism-Leninism. He felt it would not take long to realize friendly and cooperative relations between Japan and China (JOAK-TV, Tokyo, 2 January).

The invective directed against the Chinese party reached a crescendo before the JCP congress in July and was continued through the rest of the year. At the same time an increasing flow of vituperation was broadcast from Peking. Several themes were tirelessly repeated by the JCP in its attacks on the CCP. One was the accusation that the Maoists follow an "ultra-left opportunist" line which they have tried to force the JCP to adopt. Criticizing the Cultural Revolution, the party resolution referred to the "anti-socialist essence of this attempt to deify Mao Tse-tung and establish the unlimited authority of his clique." A second theme was the contention that the "Mao clique" joined hands with Japanese monopoly capital in denouncing the JCP, particularly at the time the annual agreements for Japan-China Memorandum Trade were signed in Peking.[1] Fuwa Tetsuzo, in a press interview in February, described a "flunkyist" trend in Japanese trade circles. Obviously referring to the joint communiqués denouncing Japanese policy which the Japanese trade delegation blandly signed in Peking, Fuwa remarked that Japanese capitalists who pretended to worship Mao's thought only encouraged Chinese intervention in Japanese internal affairs. (*Asahi*, Tokyo, 14 February.)

More infuriating to the JCP was the CCP support of the pro-Maoist, anti-JCP Japanese splinter groups which continued to be active during the year. *Akahata* complained that the Peking *People's Daily* published 16 articles by these "anti-party" elements during the first three months of 1970. Likewise, the sharpest resentment was repeatedly expressed of the continuing Chinese references to the "Miyamoto revisionist clique" as one of the "four enemies of the Japanese people."

The JCP took issue with the alarm raised by the Chinese government and party over the "revival of militarism" in Japan. The joint communiqué published 9 April in Pyongyang, North Korea, after the meetings between Chou En-lai and Kim Il-song, devoted extraordinary attention to the charge that militarism had been revived in Japan. Miyamoto referred to these statements in a subsequent press conference and, noting that the JCP was in confrontation with the CCP but had the closest relations with its fraternal Korean Workers' Party, rejected the statement that

---

[1]"Memorandum Trade" refers to trade negotiated annually in Peking by a delegation of prominent members of the Liberal Democratic Party. It has represented only about 30 per cent of total Sino-Japanese trade since most trade is carried on directly by so-called Japanese "friendly firms."

militarism had been revived in Japan. He asserted that, while such a trend was discernible, militarism had not *yet* been revived, since the constitution prohibited the dispatch of military forces overseas and no conscription system was in effect. Throughout the year the theme of revived Japanese militarism emanated from Peking with growing stridency while Japanese spokesmen and publications continued to insist that the statements were false.

JCP-CPSU Relations. The participation of Soviet officials in meetings celebrating the Lenin Centenary, held in Japan by members of the splinter communist party "Voice of Japan," inspired the JCP to some of its bitterest polemics against its Russian "fraternal" party. *Akahata* revealed on 30 April that this group—headed by Shiga Yoshio, who was expelled from the JCP in 1964—had sponsored meetings in Osaka (10 April), Kyoto (21 April), and Tokyo (24 April) which were attended by I. Latishev, former *Pravda* correspondent in Tokyo, B. Posperov, member of the Far East Institute of the Soviet Academy of Sciences, and two members of the Soviet Embassy in Tokyo. Latishev and Posperov were reported to have addressed, respectively, the gatherings in Osaka and Kyoto. *Akahata* (30 April) commented that such actions by Soviet officials virtually nullified the promise made in 1968 by the CPSU in a meeting with the JCP in Tokyo that it would have nothing to do with "anti-party elements" in Japan.

On 5 May, *Akahata* published a lengthy article entitled "On New and Grave Interference in Our Party by CPSU-Controlled Agencies and Organizations" which denounced the presence of Soviet Embassy officers at the Shiga meetings as "an act of direct hostility against our party and the revolutionary movement in Japan [which constituted] intolerable intervention in the light of standards ruling the relations between communist parties." Comparing the Soviet "interference" to the "outrageous" conduct of the CPSU leadership when Khrushchev was in power in 1964, and quoting Lenin's admonitions against schism and sectarianism, the article condemned the Soviet actions as a "serious challenge" to the principles of Marxism-Leninism and as one of the "worst acts of intervention, totally incompatible with the unity of communist and workers parties," which would wreck the foundations of the international communist movement by "trampling underfoot" the fraternal parties' standards of "independence, equality, mutual nonintervention, and international solidarity." The article concluded with an expression of pessimism about the future: "The normalization of Japan-Soviet party relations can by no means be expected under a situation in which such acts of intervention are repeated without any indication of self-examination. The CPSU leadership must bear all the responsibility for whatever may result from this situation."

Meanwhile, in an unusual gesture, the JCP had sent an official delegation to the Moscow celebrations of the Lenin Centenary, held on 21-22 April. The CPSU, suspecting that a speech to be made by Tsugane Sukechika, member of the Central Committee and permanent representative in Moscow of the JCP, would contain criticisms of the Soviet party, arranged to have Tsugane address a separate local meeting instead of the international conference convened in Moscow. After protests by the JCP delegation, Tsugane was given a forum in another place in Moscow where no foreign delegates were present. His speech was later published in *Pravda* with his references to "the independence of each party and non-interference in the internal affairs of other parties" deleted, according to the CPSU, because of "space considerations." (*Tokyo Shimbun*, 1 July.)

The most significant and detailed exchange of indictments between the Japanese and Soviet parties occurring during the year started with a lengthy article which appeared in the organ of the Central Committee of the CPSU, *Party Life*, on the eve of the JCP party congress. Using the draft resolution prepared for the congress as a take-off point, the article ran the gamut of complaints against the JCP, accusing it of unfounded attacks against the CPSU, breaking the unity of the world communist movement in contravention of the teachings of Lenin, refusing to participate in the international conference of communist parties sponsored in 1969 by the CPSU, denying the existence of Japanese imperialism and trying to cover it up, encouraging the enemies of peace by opposing the non-proliferation treaty, plotting to form a third force within the international communist movement, aiding the splitting efforts of the Peking leadership, borrowing anti-Soviet fictions from the propaganda arsenal of the Mao group, and carrying on a campaign against the CPSU for two years. *Party Life* described the JCP as "fanning nationalism" and "outshining" the ruling cliques in Japan by supporting the "revanchist" claim to the Kurile Islands. The CPSU denied that it was intervening or had any intention of intervening in the affairs of the JCP. Finally, the party expressed readiness to make efforts to "restore true comradely relations with the JCP by adhering to the principle of joint struggle for peace, democracy, and socialism." (Quoted, Moscow radio, 27 June.)

The JCP reacted immediately to the challenge of *Party Life* with a brief but sharp rebuttal in *Akahata* on 29 June. The party waited until after its congress, however, to present on 5 August to the readers of *Akahata* the full text of the *Party Life* article and a comprehensive refutation which took up a page and a half of fine print. The article was entitled "New Declaration of Big Powerist Intervention" and treated, one by one, the main points in dispute between the two parties, briefly summarized as follows:

(1) CPSU intervention in the affairs of the JCP.—The charges against the CPSU for supporting the Shiga splinter party were repeated in detail, including flashbacks to the Khrushchev period and *Pravda*'s "as yet unrepudiated" 1964 praise of the Shiga dissidents as "patriots, faithful sons of the people, internationalists and self-sacrificing defenders of peace, democracy and socialism." The CPSU was again castigated for bad faith not only in breaking the 1968 agreement to cease all contacts with the Shiga group, but actually by expanding relations with its members.

(2) Imperialism.—The JCP disputed the Soviet theory of "Japanese imperialism" which implied that Japan was a powerful, independent imperialist country on an equal plane with the United States and that this "independence" had been won by Japanese monopoly capital. Such a theory, according to the JCP, ignored the subservience of Japan to U.S. imperialism, proved by the presence of U.S. military bases in Japan and by continuing U.S. controls over Okinawa. Such a theory, according to the JCP, "beautified" U.S. imperialism.

(3) Nuclear non-proliferation treaty.—The JCP contended that Soviet support of the treaty meant agreement with U.S. imperialism and disagreement with the anti-imperialist, democratic forces. The United States had favored the treaty; yet neither the Democratic Republic of Vietnam, the Democratic Republic of Korea, nor Cuba had signed it. The JCP argued that the treaty in no way hampered the nuclear powers, that it ran counter to any ban on nuclear weapons, and only encouraged U.S. imperialism, the "greatest enemy of peace."

(4) Big Power-ism.—The JCP reply reviewed at length the position on the invasion of Czechoslovakia, calling it an "act of aggression" carried out neither at the request of nor with the agreement of the Czechoslovak government. It "dealt a great blow to anti-imperialist democratic forces throughout the world."

(5) The Kurile Islands.—*Akahata* reminded the CPSU that at the soviet party's Twenty-first Congress, in January 1959, the Japanese and Soviet parties had agreed that the southern Kuriles would be returned when Japan became an independent, peaceful, and neutral state. The Soviet takeover of the Kuriles was denounced as contrary to the Leninist principle of opposition to the annexation of territory, and the "Big Power-ism" of Stalin in demanding the islands was recalled.

(6) CPSU intentions to dominate the international communist movement.—*Akahata* vehemently rejected the Soviet contentions that the JCP was trying to curry favor with Peking and that its position on national autonomy and independence signified a plot to establish a "third force" within the world communist movement. *Akahata* found this revealing of the Soviet party's own outlook, which saw international communism as a struggle between two opposing camps, one led by Moscow, the other by Peking. Thus, for the Russian party, "unification of

the communist movement" meant defeat of the CCP by the CPSU and the imposition on all communist parties of a single leadership by the Soviet party. Anyone who did not follow this line would be considered by the CPSU to be assisting the "other side," by which they meant the "Mao Tse-tung group." The JCP document concluded with an expression of assurance that the international communist movement would be able to overcome the "two wings' opportunism and Big Power-ism" and bring about unity: "Big Power-ist efforts to resist this by *Party Life* and others are no more than an attempt to turn backward the cogwheels of history, and a new failure by interveners will be unavoidable."

In late March the JCP reported that Sunama Ichiro, a candidate member of the JCP Central Committee, had called on the Soviet ambassador to protest a proposal by the Soviet government to carry out bombing exercises in waters near Japan (*Akahata*, 29 March). The Japanese government made official representations to the Soviet government requesting suspension; it was later announced by Moscow that the exercises would be cancelled.

A rare note of praise for the JCP came out of Moscow following the U.S. incursion into Cambodia. Moscow radio (6 May) cited a JCP statement condemning the U.S. action and commented: "The democratic forces in various countries are working to strengthen their unity. The JCP Central Committee statement will be a good example for their efforts."

Other International Issues.   Throughout the year the JCP kept up a continuing barrage of attacks against the United States and its policies and actions in Indochina. Among numerous statements published during the year, two released in the name of the Presidium of the Central Committee were accorded major prominence. The first appeared in *Akahata* on 4 May and was prompted by the U.S. incursion into Cambodia, which was termed an "unpardonable international crime." At the same time the Japanese government was denounced for having agreed to participate in the conference called by Indonesia on the Cambodian question and which the Central Committee termed "collective interference in Cambodia by puppet regimes and anti-communist countries in Asia under U.S. leadership." The second statement, issued by the Presidium on 23 December, began by condemning the United States for "new acts of aggression" in again bombing North Vietnam and in landing ground forces near Hanoi under the "pretext" of rescuing prisoners of war. The article enumerated the often repeated catalogue of crimes attributed to the United States in Southeast Asia and appealed for unity of the "anti-imperialist democratic forces" in meeting the challenge of aggression. Each significant foreign policy statement made in the United States and publicized action by the United States in Asia evoked a rhetorical response from the JCP. These ranged from attacks on President Nixon's "state of the union" message, his 1970 report on foreign policy, and his speeches and press conferences on the war in Indochina to critiqués of the "Nixon doctrine" and discussions of the removal of poison gas and the crimes of U.S. soldiers in Okinawa. In addition to the United States, perennial targets for attack were the Sato government for its subservience to "U.S. imperialism" and the "puppet" regimes in Indochina, especially the Lon Nol government in Cambodia.

As mentioned in the discussion of JCP-CPSU relations, the JCP opposed Japan's adherence to the nuclear non-proliferation treaty. An *Akahata* editorial of 4 February warmed that signing the treaty was making Japan a tool of U.S. "imperialist" nuclear strategy. The editorial concentrated on describing the U.S. "nuclear power buildup" and pursuit of an "atrocious intrigue of war and aggression."

The JCP continued to call for an international conference of the "anti-imperialist democratic forces of the five continents" which the party had been promoting for several years. The proposal was included in the resolution passed by the party congress on 1 July, and was reiterated in an *Akahata* article on 26 September. The JCP showed no interest in the world "anti-imperialist" conference proposed by the communist parties meeting in Moscow in 1969. *Akahata* predicted that the important anti-imperialist forces would be unlikely to participate in such an assembly, since it was "not in accordance with the present situation."

International Party Contacts. The JCP now maintains permanent representatives in Moscow, Hanoi, and Pyongyang. The latest to be assigned was Yoshida Sukeharu, member of the Presidium of the Central Committee, whose appointment to North Korea was first announced in early May, when he was reported to have visited Pyongyang on 28 April. The press later reported his departure to take up his official duties on 27 August, when he was accompanied by two other members of the Central Committee, Tashiro Fumihisa (also member of the House of Representatives) and Hirotani Shunji. The JCP representative in Hanoi, Hoshino Tsutomu, Central Committee member, returned to Hanoi on 20 March after a temporary visit in Japan, according to *Akahata* (21 March). Tsugane Sukechika, Central Committee member and permanent JCP representative in Moscow, was appointed to represent the party at the celebrations of the anniversary of Lenin's birth.

During the year the JCP had contacts with both the Romanian and East German communist parties. A JCP delegation left Tokyo for Romania at the invitation of the Romanian Communist Party on 27 August; it included two prominent members: a vice chairman of the Presidium, Hakamada Satomi, and a member of the Presidium Standing Committee, Nishizawa Tomio. In return, a four-man Romanian group spent two weeks in Japan (19 September-1 October), carrying on talks in what was described as a "warm atmosphere." Chairman Miyamoto accorded these meetings particular significance, stating at a press conference: "The talks are very important politically. The Romanian party—a European party taking an independent stand—and the Japanese party are unanimous on very many points." (*Akahata*, 26 September.)

At the invitation of the Central Committee of the East German party, a JCP delegation spent two weeks in the German Democratic Republic (25 September-10 October). It was headed by Yonehara Itaru, member of the Central Committee Presidium, and Ide Yo, deputy director of the Central Committee's International Department. No joint communiqué was issued after the meetings and the *Neues Deutschland* reported only an "exchange of opinions," pointedly omitting any reference to the usual "identity of views."

The JCP-controlled Democratic Youth League—Minseido—sent delegates to attend a meeting in Moscow on 22-23 May with members of the Soviet Komsomol. The group was headed by the Minseido chairman, Yoshimura Kinnosuke.

Publications. The circulation of *Akahata* (Red Flag), the JCP's official daily newspaper, was estimated at 420,000 at the end of 1970, with the Sunday edition reaching 1,500,000. These figures are slightly above those of 1969. The next largest JCP-affiliated publication is the organ of the Democratic Youth League, *Minsei Shimbun*, which maintained its circulation of 300,000 as in 1969. Other party publications, with estimated circulation figures, are: *Zenei* (Vanguard), a monthly theoretical magazine (100,000); *Sekai Seiji Shiryo* (World Political Documents), a bimonthly magazine (30,000); *Gekkan Gakushu* (Student Monthly) (115,000); and *Dokusho no Tomo* (Reading Friend), aimed at intellectuals (10,000). In addition, numerous local weekly newspapers are published at the prefectural, district, and city level throughout Japan by JCP units. Important semiofficial organs, in addition to *Minsei Shimbun*, are the weekly *Shinfujin Shimbun* (New Woman's News) (180,000) and the monthly *Gakushu no Tomo* (Students' Friend) (100,000).

*   *   *

Splinter Parties. The anti-JCP parties and groups fit roughly within the so-called New Left. In general, they condemn the JCP for succumbing to parliamentarianism and losing the character of a revolutionary party. On its part, the JCP denounces the splinter groups as Trotskyites embracing leftist adventurism. There are said to be approximately 10 of these anti-JCP organizations. A few merit the designation of "political party"; others are largely student and youth groups.

Kyosanshugi Rodoshato (Communist Workers' Party).—This group was started in 1961 after the JCP's Eighth Congress by a few members ejected from the party on the issue of "structural reform." They merged in 1964 with some members of the dissident "Voice of Japan" party and have cooperated with the anti-JCP "Anti-War League" and "League for Peace in Vietnam." The membership is said to be 2,000; the party publishes a weekly magazine *Toitsu* (Unity) with approximately 5,000 circulation.

Nihon no Koe (Voice of Japan).—Shiga Yoshio, one of the early leaders of the JCP, organized this party after his expulsion in 1964 following the split of the JCP with the CPSU over the partial nuclear test ban treaty. As stated earlier, Shiga's "Voice of Japan" aroused the particular ire of the JCP during 1970—including the attention of the Eleventh Congress—because of the support which meetings sponsored by it received from the Soviet government, in particular from the Soviet Embassy in Tokyo. During early May a series of six articles appearing prominently in *Akahata* denounced the Shiga group for having sold out to the Soviets, thereby winning new prosperity through "subservience to foreigners" and becoming a "tool of foreign intervention." The amount of attention and the intensity of the attacks suggested that the JCP leadership took seriously the menace of a Soviet-backed renegade party. The "Voice of Japan" remained the principal target for the JCP among all splinter groups during the year.

The party's membership is estimated at 500. Its publication, the weekly *Nihon no Koe*, is said to have a circulation of 3,000.

Nihon Kyosanto (Saha).—The group using the name of the Japan Communist Party (Left) originated after the 1966 break between the JCP and the CCP, when JCP dissidents in Yamaguchi Prefecture, led by Fukuda Masayoshi, formed the "JCP Yamaguchi Prefecture Committee (Revolutionary Left)." In 1968 the group organized a "National Council of the JCP (Left)" which held a first national congress in November 1969 and officially founded the Japan Communist Party (Left). Its professed ideology was the "Thought of Mao Tse-tung," "armed struggle," and "violent revolution." The congress was attended by 111 representatives who resolved to "break the arch criminals of United States-Japan reaction, Soviet modern revisionism and the Miyamoto revisionist traitor group." Their aim was to "seize national power by force and solve problems by war."

The JCP was quick to attack these "anti-party blind followers of the Mao Tse-tung clique," castigating the party for its "single enemy" argument against U.S. "imperialism" while ignoring Japanese monopoly capitalism, and for advocating revolution by violence (*Akahata*, 30 January 1970).

The organ of the party's Central Committee, *Jinmin no Hoshi*, is frequently quoted by the Peking press and radio. The *Peking Review*, attributing its source to *Jinmin no Hoshi*, headlined an article in August: "Over 400 Japanese Communists Jointly Quit Miyamoto Revisionist Clique's Party." This mass resignation was said to have occurred in Kyushu after one city assemblyman broke off his affiliation with the JCP. The action was called a "manifestation of the fact that the Miyamoto revisionist clique .   . has been repudiated by the Japanese working class and people and is embarking on a road of collapse." (*Peking Review*, 14 August.)

The JCP (Left) is reported to receive material assistance from China and, while the organization of the party is somewhat provincial and has shown no marked expansion of political influence, its potential, because of its staunch support for China, is not belittled by some knowledgeable observers.

Membership in the JCP (Left) is reported to be 2,000. Publications are *Choshu Shimbun*[2],

---

[2]The name "Choshu" is formed from two Chinese characters which stand for the ancient names of two provinces—Nagato (Cho) and Shubo (Shu)—which correspond to present-day Yamaguchi Prefecture, where the party originated.

twice weekly; *Jinmin no Hoshi* (People's Star), three times per month; and *Kakumei Senshi* (Warrior of the Revolution), monthly.

Nihon Marukusu-Renin Shugisha Domei, or *M-L Domei* (Japan Marxist-Leninist Alliance). —This organization, which is completely pro-Maoist, was formed 4 October 1968. It espouses the ideas of "people's war" and the "liberation front," claims to work through such organizations as the "Workers' Liberation Front," the "National Students' Liberation Front Alliance," and the "High School Students' Liberation Front Alliance." The membership is estimated at 700.

Motakuto Shiso Gakushu-kai (Society for the Study of Mao Tse-tung Thought).—This association was formed in 1968. It publishes a monthly magazine entitled *Gekkan Motakuto Shiso* (Mao Tse-tung Thought Monthly). The *Peking Review* (22 May 1970) published the text of a communication from the society, sent to the Central Committee of the CCP on 25 April, congratulating the Chinese People's Republic on the successful launching of a man-made satellite.

*　　*　　*

Anti-JCP Youth and Student Groups. Two organizations critical of the JCP and cultivating the support of young persons merit special attention. These are the Beheiren (Citizens' League for Peace in Vietnam) and Hansen Seinen Iinkai (Anti-War Youth Committee). Both have attracted widespread attention and support in recent years.

The Beheiren was founded in 1965 by a leftist writer, Oda Makoto, at the time of the first U.S. bombings of North Vietnam. It has no officers and no national organization, and maintains no regular membership. There are said to be 240 Beheiren groups throughout Japan, and while the appeal may be largely to the young, Oda boasts that the organization attracts people of all ideologies and all ages. Numerous demonstrations have been carried out against the war in Vietnam and the Japan-U.S. security treaty. Slogans indicate the purposes: "Peace for Vietnam," "Vietnam for the Vietnamese," "Stop the Japanese Government from Cooperating in the Vietnam War," and "Oppose the Security Treaty."

The Anti-War Youth Committee, with an estimated membership of 20,000 and 490 groups throughout Japan, has aimed its activities principally at young workers and has come into direct competition with the JCP's Democratic Youth League. First organized and supported by the JSP and Sohyo, the Anti-War Youth Committee has become increasingly involved with the more radical, militant elements in the youth and student movements, and the JSP and Sohyo have found that they no longer exert a controlling influence over it. The Anti-War Youth Committee has acted aggressively within the trade unions, attempting to influence union leadership, promoting strikes, and incurring the hostility of management. Outside the labor movement, it has propagandized the struggle against "public nuisances" (damage to the environment) and attempted through mass meetings and demonstrations to arouse Japanese citizens to combat pollution. Some of these activities have been conducted in concert with the Beheiren. The JCP has condemned the Anti-War Youth Committee as "Trotskyite," warned trade union members through pamphlets and articles in party publications against the trap of this "terrorist gang," and appealed for its dissolution (*Koan Joho*, November 1970).

Other Student Groups. During 1970 the numerous leftist student organizations abandoned to a large degree the violence which had characterized their actions during 1969, and concentrated increasingly on peaceful mass action. This was especially true after the demonstrations in late June against the security treaty. Although the pro-JCP youth groups regarded their June struggles against the treaty as successful, most of the opposing organizations judged these efforts as failures. Consequently, except for the few militant extremist factions, such as the "Red Army," most of the students switched their strategy to "peaceful mass action."

Continuing splits and shifts in numerical strength complicated the spectrum of the student movement in 1970. The following is an outline of the major anti-JCP student groups existing at the end of the year.

Kakukyodo (Revolutionary Communist League).—The principal factions within this grouping are the Kakumaru (Revolutionary Marxist) with 60,300 student members, of whom 1,080 are considered activists, and the Chukaku (Nucleus), with 84,600 members and 1,770 activists. Also under the general umbrella of the Kakukyodo are found two groups belonging to the Fourth International, Japan Branch: the Puroretaria Gundan (Proletarian Army Corps), and the Gakusei Inta (Student International); these have a combined membership of 6,100 with 450 activists.

Kyosando (Communist League).—This grouping includes several of the most militant groups: two factions of the Kyosando—Jokyo (Conditions) and *Hanki* (Rebel Flag); the Kyosanshugi Seinen Domei (Communist Youth League); the Sekigun (Red Army), some of whose members on 31 March hijacked a Japan Air Line plane to North Korea, where they continued to be held by the DPRK authorities; and organizations affiliated with the former Marxist Front. The total membership of the Kyosando groups is estimated at 88,500 with 1,100 activists. The violent Red Army faction is believed to have about 500 members at the most. More than 200 were reported arrested over a twelve-month period.

ML Domei (Marxist-Leninist League).—The ML League which is pro-Chinese, includes the SFL (National Student Liberation Front) and its 20,200 members, of whom 720 are activists.

Shaseido (Socialist Youth League).—The Shaseido, which is under the influence of the Japan Socialist Party, has two organizations affiliated with it. One is the Kakurokyo (Revolutionary Workers' Council), in turn connected with the Hantei Gakuhyo (National Federation of Anti-Imperialist Student Councils); the latter has 66,700 members, with 850 activists. The other group is the Kaiken Boshi Gakusei Kaigi (Student Council to Prevent Amendment of the Constitution).

Structural Reform Movement.—This includes the Kyogakudo (Communist Students' League), Purogakudo (Proletarian Students' League), and Furonto (Socialist Student Front). The anti-JCP political party Nihon no Koe (Voice of Japan) maintains an organization called Mingakudo (Democratic Students' League). The Structural Reform groups, including Shaseido and Mingakudo, have about 126,000 members, with 2,900 activists.

Non-Sect Radicals. This term refers to students who belong to no faction and also to those who have joined the Zenkyoto (National Student Federation of All-Campus Struggle Committees) to attempt to coordinate student activities of various groups and factions. Eight factions specifically support Zenkyoto: the Furonto, Purogakudo, Kyogakudo, SFL, Communist Youth League, Gakusei Inta, and Chukaku. Zenkyoto has 3,000 members in Tokyo and branches in Nihon, Tokyo, and Meiji universities. The confrontation among factions was so great that very little "coordination" was accomplished during 1970.

Two anarchist organizations, the Council of Free Socialists (or Free Federation) and the Society of the Axe, have 200 members in Tokyo.

According to Tokyo police figures, anti-JCP factions within the student movement embrace a total membership of approximately 452,400, as compared to 551,100 students who affiliate with pro-JCP groups under the aegis of Minseido; activists are estimated at 16,300 for the JCP organizations and 8,870 for the combined anti-JCP student groups.

J. K. E.

KOREA: DEMOCRATIC PEOPLE'S REPUBLIC OF KOREA

The Korean Communist Party (Choson Kongsan-dang; KCP) was organized in Seoul in 1925, during the time of Japanese rule in Korea. This original party ceased to operate in 1928. Following the defeat of Japan in the Second World War, the KCP was revived for a brief period, with its headquarters again in Seoul. The center of the communist movement soon moved to the northern part of the country, which was then occupied by Soviet forces, and under Soviet auspices the North Korean Central Bureau of the KCP was formed in October 1945. At that time, the Korean Independence League (later renamed the New People's Party) also existed, led by returnees from Yenan, China, who had received training there since 1941 from Chinese communists. In July 1946, these two groups merged, creating the North Korean Workers' Party. This fused movement absorbed the leadership of the South Korean Workers' Party (which had also been formed in 1946), and on 24 June 1949 the Korean Workers' Party (Choson Nodong-dang; KWP) was established. The KWP is the ruling party of the Democratic People's Republic of Korea (DPRK).

The size of the KWP has probably not changed greatly since October 1965, when it claimed more than 1,600,000 members. The population of North Korea is 13,900,000 (estimated 1970). KWP members comprise between 11 and 12 per cent of the population, which may be the highest ratio of party membership in the world.

Leadership and Organization. The KWP is organized along highly centralized lines under the leadership of its secretary-general, Kim Il-song. Kim's nearly absolute power is largely the result of substantial purges, beginning shortly after the defeat of the Japanese. In a series of stages, he eliminated or severely weakened the so-called domestic, Yenan, and Soviet factions, leaving himself surrounded by loyal followers, most of whom had accompanied him in anti-Japanese guerrilla operations in Manchuria and eastern Siberia before and during the Second World War. These purges—and the less sweeping ones that have continued to occur since—left the party in the hands of a predominantly military-oriented leadership.

The party's Fifth Congress was held on 2-12 November 1970. Since the party constitution provides for the convening of the congress every four years, the meeting was five years overdue, the Fourth Congress having been held in September 1961. Organizationally, the interval had witnessed the consolidation of power by a few of Kim's close subordinates, notably in 1966 when a Presidium was created within the already powerful Political Committee. The leadership list that emerged from the Fifth Congress made no mention of a Presidium, but the Political Committee was further concentrated to 11 members from the 14 or 15 holding office immediately before the congress. Candidate members of the Political Committee, which had appeared to number about 11, were drastically reduced to four. The new nine-member Secretariat also represented a slight reduction from the previous body. The size of the Central Committee, which consisted of 135 members at the Fourth Congress, was increased to 172. Eighty of the former 135 members were dropped during the intervening period or at the Fifth Congress.

The new leadership, as listed in the party organ *Nodong Sinmun* (14 November), included the following:

Political Committee	Other positions held
Kim Il-song	Secretary-general, premier, supreme commander of armed forces
Choe Yong-kon	Central Committee (CC) secretary, president of Supreme People's Assembly (SPA) Presidium
Kim Il	CC secretary, first deputy premier
Pak Song-chol	Foreign minister until June 1970, when he became second deputy premier
Choe Hyon	Minister of defense, colonel general
Kim Yong-chu	CC secretary, director of CC Organization Department
O Chin-u	CC secretary, armed forces chief of general staff, lieutenant general
Kim Tong-kyu	CC secretary, director of CC International Affairs Department
So Chol	Vice-president of SPA Presidium, lieutenant general
Kim Chung-in	CC secretary
Han Ik-su	CC secretary, director of armed forces General Political Bureau, colonel general

Candidate Members, Political Committee	
Hyon Mu-kwang	CC secretary
Chong Chun-taek	Deputy premier
Yang Hyong-sop	CC secretary
Kim Man-kum	Deputy premier

Dismissals from party leadership positions before or during the congress were extensive. The following were removed in 1969 or 1970:

Removed from KWP Political Committee	Other positions held
Kim Kwang-hyop	Member of KWP Presidium, CC secretary, deputy premier
Nam Il	Deputy premier, (retained a place in the CC ranking immediately below candidate Political Committee member Kim Man-kum)
Yi Chong-ok	Deputy premier

Pak Chong-ae	Vice-president of SPA Presidium
Kim Ik-son	Minister of State Inspection
Yi Yong-ho	Vice-president of SPA Presidium

Removed from position of KWP
Political Committee candidate member

Sok San	CC secretary
Yi Kuk-chin	
Gen. Choe Kwang	Armed forces chief of General Staff (removed in late 1968 or in 1969)
Choe Yong-chin	(Retained in CC immediately below Nam Il)
Han Sang-tu	Former minister of finance

The list reflects far-reaching changes. Six members have been dropped from the Political Committee and five have lost their positions as candidate members. Only two new members have been added to either body: Yang Hyong-sop and Kim Man-kum. Kim had been a full member of the Central Committee since the Third Congress (1956). Although not necessarily significant in this context, the common denominator of the six full members of the Political Committee who were removed (with the possible exception of Yi Yong-ho) appeared to be leaning toward the Soviet Union. Four former candidate members (Kim Yong-chu, O Chin-u, Kim Chung-in, and Han Ik-su) were elevated to full membership. Only two of the former 12 or so candidate members (Hyon Mu-kwang and Chong Chun-taek) retained their positions.

Changes occurred also in the hierarchy of those who continued in top party leadership positions. Pak Song-chol and Choe Hyon have exchanged places. Kim Yong-chu, Kim Il-song's younger brother, who had risen rather spectacularly in recent years, was moved up from about fifteenth to sixth place. The congress was guided by a "Presidium" of 39 persons—the top party leaders—apparently listed in the order of rank that existed at the opening of the congress (Pyongyang domestic radio, 1 November). Changes that were a direct result of the congress could be noted by comparing the names and rankings of the members of the congress Presidium with those on the final Central Committee roster. Pak Chong-ae and Kim Ik-son, both in the congress Presidium, were not reelected to the Central Committee. Nam Il was demoted from ninth place in the Central Committee hierarchy to sixteenth, and Choe Yong-chin from fifteenth place to seventeenth. Kim Man-kum and Yang Hyong-sop, the two new leading party members, exchanged positions during the congress.

In addition to being the ruling party, the KWP controls a number of mass organizations. A principal one is the two-million-member General Federation of Trade Unions of Korea (GFTUK), founded in November 1945 and currently led by Chon Chang-chol. Other major mass organizations are the Union of Agricultural Working People, headed by Yi Nim-su; the League of Socialist Working Youth of Korea (formerly known as the Korean Democratic Youth League), founded in January 1946 and headed by O Ki-chon; and the Korean Democratic Women's Union, founded in November 1945 and headed by Kim Ok-sun. The KWP exercises its control also through the General Federation of Korean Residents in Japan (Chongnyon;

known also by its Japanese name, Chosen Soren), which competes with the organization of the Republic of Korea residents in Japan for the loyalties of the more than 600,000 nationals who are in that country.

At least two subordinate political movements exist in North Korea: the Korean Democratic Party (Choson Minju-dang), headed by Kang Yang-uk, and the Young Friends' Party of the Chondogyo Sect (the sect being the Society of the Heavenly Way—Chondogyo Chong-u-dang), led by Pak Sin-tok. No statistics are available regarding the membership of these movements. Their function is to enhance acceptance of the United Democratic Fatherland Front (Choguk Tongil Minjujuui Chonson). The latter group, created by 71 political and social organizations in June 1949, is assigned the task of uniting "all the revolutionary forces of North and South Korea" under the leadership of the KWP, in order to implement the "peaceful unification and complete independence of the country." The KWP controls also the "Committee for the Peaceful Unification of the Fatherland," established in May 1961 and consisting of representatives from the KWP, the subordinate "democratic" parties, and the mass organizations.

The cult of Kim Il-song is becoming increasingly employed as a tool to implement general policy. Similar to "Mao Tsetung Thought" in China, the "teachings of Kim Il-song" are upheld by the KWP as having "creatively applied and further developed" Marxism-Leninism by solving fundamental questions of principle in the building of socialism and communism (speech by Kim Il at a Pyongyang meeting commemorating the Lenin Centenary, *Pyongyang Times*, 27 April 1970):

> Comrade Kim Il Sung fully clarified the tasks arising in the whole course of achieving the complete victory and final victory of socialism and going over to the high stage of communism, such as the question of the period of transition from capitalism to socialism and the dictatorship of the proletariat, the question of class struggle and ideological revolution under socialism, and the question of the final solution of the rural question and the building of material and technical bases of socialism, and indicated the concrete way for the solution of these questions. These original ideas of Comrade Kim Il Sung are a further development of Marxist-Leninist theory on the building of socialism and communism and a truly great contribution to the enrichment of its ideological and theoretical treasure-house. (*Ibid.*)

In his speech to the congress, newly elected candidate Political Committee member Yang Hyong-sop attacked those who attempted to degrade the authority of Kim Il-song, declaring that one's attitude toward the leader was the most important criterion in distinguishing a "genuine revolutionary" from an "opportunist" (Pyongyang radio, 3 November):

> An outstanding leader is the sole center of unity and cohesion which rallies the party, class, and masses as one.... Neither the guiding role of the party nor the class leadership of the working class over the popular masses in the revolutionary struggle can be realized apart from the leadership of the leader. (*Ibid.*)

Domestic Attitudes and Activities. The long-delayed Fifth Congress of the KWP was held on 2-12 November 1970. The congress focused on the country's economy, on efforts to achieve ideological purity, and to a lesser extent on national defense and international affairs. It followed the completion of a seven-year economic plan (1961-67) that was extended three additional years in 1966—which may explain why the congress was not held earlier—and announced a new six-year plan to begin in 1971.

Kim Il, a member of the Political Committee who frequently reports on economic affairs, declared in his speech to the congress that the "greatest victory" of the period of the extended seven-year plan (i.e., 1961-70) was the conversion of the country from an "industrial-agricultural state" into a "socialist industrial state" (Korean Central News Agency, 10 November). The emphasis was on heavy industry, particularly machine building, which by 1970 resulted in an annual gross industrial output value 3.3 times as great as in 1960. The new six-year plan sought an industrial increase of 200 per cent over 1970, according to Kim Il. Though these substantial increases reflect the relatively small actual amounts involved, Kim Il-song expects to keep them high throughout North Korea's industrial development. He rejects the theory—apparently held by some in his own party—that a country's rate of growth must decrease as its economy develops.

It is assumed that to maintain a high rate of growth, especially with limited outside help, the entire citizenry must adopt the "unitary ideology" of Kim Il-song. One of the major facets of this ideology, the concept of *chuche*, has been promoted constantly, indicating there are still those in society—and in the party—who do not see its merit. Essentially, the term means political independence, economic self-sufficiency, and an independent defense capability. Kim Il-song, in his speech to the congress, explained further:

> Establishing *chuche* means, in a nutshell, having the attitude of master toward revolution and construction in one's own country. This means holding fast to an independent position, refraining from dependence on others and using one's own brains, believing in one's own strength and displaying the revolutionary spirit of self-reliance, and thus solving one's own problems for oneself on his own responsibility under all circumstances. It means adhering to the creative position of opposing dogmatism and applying the universal principles of Marxism-Leninism and the experiences of other countries to suit the historical conditions and national peculiarities of one's own country. (Pyongyang domestic service, 2 November.)

Although there were apparently still some who felt that the country would profit more by depending on others for economic and military assistance and for ideological guidance, Kim added: "Now we can say that flunkeyism, national nihilism, and dogmatism as ideological trends [opposed to *chuche*] have been eliminated in the main from among our party members and people" (*ibid.*).

The practice of criticism plays an important part in the effort to achieve ideological purity. In his speech, Kim admonished all organizations to use criticism to intensify the "ideological battle against unsound ideological elements of all descriptions." He apparently did not intend that criticism should become as severe as that of the "struggle-criticism-transformation" campaign employed by the Chinese communists: "Criticism should be conducted regularly and patiently, not in a shock campaign." It was not to be used to "shift the responsibility for one's own fault onto others, to take vengeance for being criticized, to place political stigmas on others at random, or to reprimand the criticized peremptorily." (*Ibid.*)

Intensification of the practice of criticism was felt necessary because past efforts had not been entirely successful in ridding society of the remnants of the pre-communist government. Kim told the congress: "The way of life carried over from the old society is still lingering in no small measure in all domains, ranging from state activity to private life, which causes an obstacle to socialist construction and to the work of educating and remolding the working people." The major concern was for the rural areas. The peasants were said to have "small proprietor inclinations, egoism, and other obsolete ideas . . . rooted deeply in their minds." Thus, the peasantry not only lagged behind the working class technically and culturally, but also was "far behind ideologically."

Defense preparations continued to receive high priority. The finance minister's annual report on the budget to the Supreme People's Assembly in April provided an allotment of 31 per cent of the country's total expenditures for defense in 1970. This amount, compared with 30 per cent alloted for the previous year, amounted to about $746 million. (The 1970 figure for South Korea was about $333 million.)

The emphasis on developing North Korea's military capabilities, to the detriment of overall economic growth (under a policy Kim describes as "economic construction and defense building in parallel"), has created a substantial amount of dissidence within the party and has been an important factor in recent purges. While contending that the "maneuverings of the U.S. imperialists" left him no choice, Kim admitted to the congress that the nation's defense capabilities had been achieved "at a very high cost":

> Frankly speaking, our national defense expenditures, as compared with the small size of the country and its population, have proven to be too great a burden. If even a single small portion of it had been allocated to economic construction, our people's economy would have developed even faster and our people's living standards would have improved to a much higher level.

Nevertheless, Kim called for greater efforts in strengthening national defense capabilities "while simultaneously accelerating socialist construction to the maximum." He stated that there would be no change in the party line of "arming the entire people, turning the whole country into a fortress, converting the whole army into a cadre army, and modernizing the whole army." (*Ibid.*)

The congress was told by Lieutenant General O Chin-u, chief of staff of the Korean People's Army (KPA), that the army had the benefit of modern military science and techniques, and indicated it had sufficient equipment to defeat any invasion from the South (Pyongyang domestic service, 4 November). A somewhat different point of view was given to the congress by Kim Il-song:

> Frankly speaking, we are not in a position to compete with developed countries in military technical equipment, nor are we required to do so. The destiny of war is by no means decided by modern weapons or military technique. Although the imperialists have a military-technical preponderance, our people's army has on its part politico-ideological superiority over them.

Kim also called for tightening party control over the KPA, and especially over its commanders. He sought to elevate the roles of the political organs, political workers, and particularly the political commissars responsible for the execution of party political work in the KPA.

South Korea. The effort to reunite the two halves of Korea has been a primary concern pervading almost all aspects of life in the DPRK. The North Koreans approach the problem from two directions. The first comes under the often repeated slogan of "peaceful unification," by which the two halves would agree to merge without outside interference. The DPRK's specific proposals for such an event were reiterated on 3 June 1970 by the "Committee for the Peaceful Unification of the Fatherland" (*Pyongyang Times*, 8 June). Basically it called for a withdrawal of U.N. troops from South Korea and drastically reduced armed forces in both parts of Korea, as partial means for facilitating the election of a unified central government. If such elections were not immediately feasible, an interim solution, according to the proposals, could be the creation of a confederation in which both sides would retain existing social systems.

The South Koreans viewed the insistence on the withdrawal of foreign troops as a major obstacle to unification. A counter-proposal by South Korean President Pak Chong-hui on 15 August stated that his government would take "epochal and more realistic measures" for peaceful unification if the North renounced the use of force and recognized the authority of the United Nations to deal with the question. Such measures, Pak said, would include the gradual removal of "artificial barriers" between the North and South. An editorial in *Nodong Sinmum* on 23 August rejected Pak's proposal, describing it as "full of falsehood and swindle" and asserting that Pak had not suggested any practical means for solving the unification question.

The North Koreans argue that the only alternative to their proposal is revolutionary violence to eliminate the U.N. (almost entirely U.S.) forces and the South Korean government. This approach to the problem has been widely promoted by Pyongyang as offering the only realistic solution. Increasingly, the burden of this effort has been assigned to South Korean revolutionaries. This tendency was confirmed in Kim Il-song's speech to the Fifth Congress:

> The oppressed and exploited popular masses can win freedom and emancipation only through their own revolutionary struggle. Therefore, the South Korean revolution must be fulfilled primarily by the South Korean people themselves. However, the people of the northern half, as members of the same nation, have the duty and obligation to actively support the revolutionary struggle of the South Korean people. (Pyongyang domestic broadcast, 2 November.)

Kim also spoke of the past exploits of the "South Korean Revolutionary Party for Reunification," comparing its successes against the problems that beset former radical organizations in South Korea, such as the Progressive Party and the Socialist Mass Party, which he said were not "Marxist-Leninist," whereas the Revolutionary Party for Reunification had chosen the "correct" line of revolutionary violence. On 22 June, the *Pyongyang Times* carried a "manifesto" and program of the South Korean party which reportedly had first been published in the party's clandestine organ *Hyokmyong Chonson* (Revolutionary Front) (see *YICA*, 1970, p. 619).

A delegate to the Fifth Congress identified as Yi Chong-hyok, representing the Revolutionary Party for Reunification, displayed an ardent admiration for Kim Il-song and his policies. He told the congress of his party's strong devotion to Kim: "We selected revolutionary comrades with infinite fidelity to the leader [Kim] as the only absolute standard" (Pyongyang radio, 7 November).

International Views and Positions. North Korea's overriding ambition in international relations is to become so self-sufficient as not to be subject to foreign influence. This policy—which originated with Kim Il-song in 1958 and is part of the aforementioned *chuche* concept—seeks fundamentally to maintain or rebuild national identity through the achievement of self-sufficiency in the economy, in military capability, and in political and ideological leadership. *Chuche* has been given considerable international publicity by the DPRK, with the apparent aim of exporting it to the smaller, developing communist states and to non-ruling parties. Political Committee member Pak Song-chol told the Fifth Congress (to which no foreign delegations were invited) that Kim Il-song's concept of *chuche* was being praised by the people of the world as the "pinnacle of all the progressive ideas of mankind at present," and as an "ever-victorious guiding idea which should be taken as the guiding compass in the international communist movement and the anti-imperialist, anti-U.S. struggle" (Pyongyang domestic broadcast, 4 November). Pak explained the value of the concept thus:

> Today the revolution in each country is carried out by the people of that country under the leadership of its party, not by any international "center." ... It stands out as an important question as never before for each party to adhere firmly to an independent stand in its activities under conditions in which opportunism has emerged in socialist countries and in the international communist movement and complex situations have been created. (*Ibid.*)

Following this philosophy, the DPRK has attempted to present itself as a leader of the "third world," not only promoting its ideology, but also expanding its diplomatic activities, which during the past two years have been concentrated in Africa. In 1970 diplomatic relations were established at the ambassadorial level with two Asian countries: the Maldive Islands (14 June) and Ceylon (15 July). Besides the communist states of China, North Vietnam, and Mongolia, the only other Asian country which had such relations with North Korea before this time was Indonesia.

In his speech to the Fifth Congress, Kim Il-song called for the combined effort of revolutionaries in Asia, the Middle East, Africa, and Latin America to isolate U.S. and Japanese "reactionaries" and their "stooges." Specifically for Asia, he sought an anti-U.S. united front that included the peoples of Korea, China, Vietnam, Laos, and Cambodia, who were directly affected by U.S. "imperialism." The Asian united front proposal had also been made earlier, in the joint communiqué resulting from the visit to North Korea in June of Prince Norodom Sihanouk, the deposed head of state of Cambodia, who had recently announced the formation of a Peking-based Cambodian government (*Pyongyang Times*, 6 July).

Relations with the Soviet Union.   The *chuche* policy is now inspired probably more by opposition to the contagious effect of Soviet "revisionism" than by any other single factor, followed closely by similar opposition to the "left-opportunism" or "dogmatism" of the Chinese communists. Thus, while attempting to maintain a strict policy of neutrality between its two giant neighbors, the DPRK has in fact fluctuated considerably in its attitude, being influenced by such developments as the de-Stalinization policy of former Soviet Premier Khrushchev, and by the Cultural Revolution in China.

Recent relations with the Soviet Union have been warm, though overshadowed by a certain degree of distrust, and occasionally punctuated with periods of slight tension created by conflicting interests in such incidents as the capture of the U.S. intelligence ship *Pueblo* in 1968. On 16 April *Pravda* carried a statement by Kim Il-song regarding the Lenin Centenary, in which he declared:

> The Soviet people assisted our people in the cause of liberation from the fetters of Japanese imperialist colonial rule and have given great aid, both material and moral, to our people's struggle to safeguard the freedom and independence of our fatherland and build a new society.... The Korean people set great store by their friendship and solidarity with the Soviet people on the front of anti-imperialist, anti-U.S. imperialist struggle.

This expression of friendship was offset by attacks against "revisionism" which appeared to be directed toward the Soviet Union and its influence on KWP members. Kim Il-song warned in his congress speech:

> Revisionism is a trend of the counterrevolutionary opportunist ideology aimed at emasculating the revolutionary quintessence of Marxism-Leninism. The greatest harm of revisionism lies in denying the leadership of the Marxist-Leninist party and the dictatorship of the proletariat, opposing the class struggle, obscuring the line of demarcation between friend and foe, yielding to U.S. imperialism, scared by its policy of nuclear blackmail, casting sheep's eyes at the imperialists while paying lipservice to an anti-imperialist position, giving up the struggle against imperialism and compromising with it, disarming the people ideologically by spreading war phobia, bourgeois, pacifistic ideas and illusions about imperialism and reaction, and in abhorring and hindering the revolution of the oppressed peoples. (Pyongyang domestic broadcast, 2 November.)

The visit by Choe Yong-kon and Pak Song-chol to Moscow for the Lenin Centenary (22 April) was probably intended by the North Koreans to counterbalance Chou En-lai's trip to Pyongyang earlier in the month. While reaffirming North Korea's independent international position, the high-level visit was undoubtedly also reassuring to the Soviet leaders, who must have been concerned by the thawing of Sino-Korean relations. The delegation was received by Leonid Brezhnev and Nikolai Podgorny, with whom talks were said to have taken place in a "warm and comradely atmosphere."

Differences between North Korea and the Soviet Union were apparent during the visit in August of Kiril T. Mazurov, first deputy chairman of the Soviet Council of Ministers and member of the Politburo of the Communist Party of the Soviet Union, to the twenty-fifth-anniversary celebrations of Korea's liberation from Japan. Two months earlier Huang Yung-sheng, Chinese Communist Party Politburo member and armed forces chief of staff, received a warm welcome from Kim Il-song in Pyongyang during celebrations of the twentieth anniversary of the outbreak of the Korean War. The visit of Mazurov (15-19 August), on the other hand, received less publicity and he apparently did not meet with Kim Il-song. Furthermore, in comparing the Soviet and North Korean versions of Mazurov's speech on 14 August (*Pravda*, 16 August, and KCNA, 15 August), it is evident that the North Koreans did not appreciate Soviet attempts to create an Asian collective security system (see *YICA*, 1970, pp. 102-3). Mazurov's assertion that such a system "would not be in conflict with the national interests of any Asian state" did not seem to alter the North Korean attitude, as none of the relatively substantial sections on collective security in his speech was reported in the KCNA summary.

Relations with Communist China.   Relations between North Korea and China, which had cooled down considerably during the Cultural Revolution, began to thaw in October 1969, when Choe Yong-kon, president of the Presidium of the Supreme People's Assembly and second highest-ranking party member, visited Peking during China's twentieth-anniversary celebrations. This trend toward friendlier relations continued during the early part of 1970. In February, North Korean ambassador Hyon Chun-kuk returned to Peking after an absence of two and a half years. In March, Li Yun-ch'uan was appointed Chinese ambassador to North Korea, filling a post left vacant for about the same length of time.

A highly noteworthy development was the visit to North Korea by Chinese Premier Chou En-lai on 5-7 April—the first by a high-ranking Chinese official since 1963, when the now disgraced head of state Liu Shao-ch'i was there. The talks, which took place in an "atmosphere of fraternal friendship," included strong condemnation of Japanese "imperialism" and mutual support for each other's efforts in "liberating occupied territory" (i.e., South Korea and Taiwan). Significantly omitted were attacks on Soviet "revisionism" or the Soviet role in Asia.

Chou apparently had the Soviet Union in mind, however, when he said at a banquet in his honor: "At present, the attitude taken toward the U.S. and Japanese reactionaries and toward Japanese militarism constitutes an important criterion for distinguishing between genuine and sham revolution, between genuine and sham socialism and between genuine and sham Marxism-Leninism" (*Pyongyang Times*, 13 April). At the same banquet, Kim Il-song declared strong North Korean support for the "heroic struggle of the Cuban people who defend the gains of revolution and build socialism successfully" (*ibid.*), although undoubtedly aware of the rather tense relations existing between Cuba and China.

While Choe Yong-kon represented North Korea at the Chinese twentieth-anniversary celebrations (1 October 1969), only an economic delegation, led by Kim Kyong-yon, chairman of the Committee for Economic Relations with Foreign Countries, attended the anniversary observances in 1970. Two weeks later, however, a higher-level delegation, led by Chong Chun-taek, alternate member of the KWP Political Committee and vice-premier, visited China (14-23 October).

Other exchanges of high-ranking delegations occurred during the year. Pak Song-chol and Kim Chung-in were in Peking on 24-29 June. At the same time (24-28 June), Huang Yung-sheng, CCP Politburo member and armed forces chief of staff, visited Pyongyang. The latter occasion, the twentieth anniversary of the outbreak of the Korean War (25 June 1950), was attended by various other dignitaries, including Prince Norodum Sihanouk (see above). Talks with Sihanouk, who received a great amount of publicity in the North Korean press during his visit (15 June-1

July), centered on condemnation of the "U.S.-sponsored" coup which deposed him as head of state in Cambodia. Kim Il-song offered to support the "fraternal Cambodian people" by "all necessary means" (*Pyongyang Times*, 22 June), and it was even reported that he had sent North Koreans to fight in Cambodia (*New York Times*, 9 October).

On 25 July-4 August, General O Chin-u, KWP Political Committee member and KPA staff chief, led a military delegation to Peking.

International Party Contacts. North Korea continued to be very active in 1970 in establishing contacts with communist parties and movements throughout the world. In addition to those mentioned above, other high-level party visitors to North Korea during the year included the following: M.V. Zakharov, the Soviet chief of staff (24-29 April); Orlando Millas, Political Committee member of the Communist Party of Chile (12-20 May); Zenon Kliszko, Politburo member of the Polish United Workers' Party (24-30 May); Ib Nørlund, Politburo member of the Communist Party of Denmark (2-17 June); Emil Bodnăras, Presidium member of the Romanian Communist Party (7-9 June); Sándor Gáspár, Politburo member of the Hungarian Socialist Workers' Party (9-17 June); Secretary-General P. Sundarayya and Politburo members Promode Das Gupta and E. M. S. Namboodiripad of the Communist Party of India (Marxist) (16 June to about 30 June); Erwin Scharf, Politburo member of the Communist Party of Austria (29 July-5 August); Jakob Lechleiter, national secretary of the Swiss Party of Labor (11-20 August); Nicos Karas, Politburo member of the Communist Party of Greece (25 August-3 September); Pencho Kubadinski, Politburo member of the Bulgarian Communist Party (7 October to about 15 October); and Henry Winston, chairman of the National Committee of the Communist Party, USA (7-23 October).

North Korean delegations to other communist parties included the following: Choe Yong-kon and Pak Song-chol to Moscow for the Lenin Centenary (22 April); Kim Tong-kyu to Italy and San Marino (12-22 April), after visiting Syria (4-11 April); and alternate Political Committee member Hyon Mu-kwang to Norway, Sweden, and Finland during April and May.

Considerable publicity was given by the North Korean press to a visit by Major General Ja-'far Muhammad al-Numairi, chairman of the Revolution Command Council and president of Sudan, on 13-17 August. According to the joint communiqué, Kim Il-song accepted an invitation to visit Sudan at an unspecified future date.

Publications. The daily organ of the KWP is *Nodong Sinmun*. The party also publishes a journal, *Kulloja*. The government publishes *Minju Choson*, organ of the Supreme People's Assembly and the cabinet. Other newspapers are *Choson Inminkun*, organ of the KPA; *Nodongja Sinmun*, organ of the GFTUK: *Nongop Kulloja*, organ of the Union of Agricultural Working People; *Nodong Chongnyon*, organ of the League of Socialist Working Youth of Korea; and *Choguk Tongil*, organ of the Committee for the Peaceful Unification of the Fatherland. The *Pyongyang Times* and *People's Korea* are weekly English-language publications. The official news agency is the Korean Central News Agency (KCNA).

E.S.

LAOS

Founded secretly in 1946, the communist Laotian People's Party (Phak Pasason Lao; PPL), was openly founded in 1955. Although it has not been outlawed, it chooses to operate clandestinely through the Laotian Patriotic Front (Neo Lao Hak Xat; NLHX), which replaced the Free Laos Front (Neo Lao Issara) in 1954. The NLHX held its First Congress on 6 January 1956 and became a legal party as a result of the Vientiane Agreements of 1957. It is at present the communist component of the Tripartite National Union Government (often referred to by the communists as the Tripartite National Coalition Government), headed by neutralist Souvanna Phouma (half-brother of Prince Souphanouvong, chairman of the NLHX). The government was recognized by the Geneva Agreements of 23 July 1962, and previously by the Zurich Agreement of June 1961 and the Plain of Jars Agreement of June 1962.

The NLHX was initially granted four of the 19 cabinet posts in the Tripartite National Union Government (4 leftists, 4 rightists, and 11 neutralists). It has, however, refused active government participation since 1963, when it withdrew its cabinet members. The most recent national elections, held on 1 January 1967, were boycotted by the NLHX. Despite the communist boycott, the government declared that "in order to maintain internal unity" it did not want to sever relations with the NLHX, stating: "All ministerial positions are still open to them. They can return to continue their functions whenever they feel that they are also Laotians and nobody will object to them." (Vientiane radio, domestic service, 14 October 1967.)

The exact membership of the PPL is unknown. An estimate in 1964 placed the number of members at about 700. The NLHX, which is controlled by the PPL, is estimated to have between 1,500 and 3,000 members. The military arm of the NLHX, known as the Laotian People's Liberation Army (formerly and still commonly known as the Pathet Lao), was founded in 1949. It numbers between 30,000 and 40,000 and has approximately 2,500 supporters and the further support of some 2,000 to 3,000 dissident neutralists who comprise the Patriotic Neutralist Forces (see below). In addition, Pathet Lao forces are supplemented by a sizable North Vietnamese contingent (see section on "International Views and Positions). The population of Laos is 3,000,000 (estimated 1970).

Leadership and Organization. Little is known about the leadership of the Phak Pasason Lao, except that it controls and to some extent overlaps the Central Committee of the NLHX. The secretary-general of the PPL is Kaysone Phomvihan, who is also vice-chairman of the NLHX Central Committee; he appears to operate mainly from Hanoi and is apparently the most important person in the Laotian communist movement. Reports also indicate that he is a member of the Vietnam Workers' Party.

The chairman of the PPL Central Committee, Nouhak Phoumsavanh, is also NLHX Central Committee secretary and Vietnam Workers' Party high commissioner in Laos, acting as liaison between Hanoi and the NLHX. Other known PPL members include Sithon Khommandam, who is also NLHX Central Committee vice-chairman; Phoumi Vongvichit, NLHX secretary-general; General Phoume Sipraseuth, NLHX Politburo member; and Khamphouane Tounalom, NLHX Politburo member. It appears probable that General Sinkapo Chounlamany, NLHX Politburo member, belongs also to the PPL.

NLHX leadership consists of Phoumi Vongvichit, secretary-general; Prince Souphanouvong, chairman of the Central Committee; Sithon Khommandam; Kaysone Phomvihan; and Fayang, NLHX Central Committee vice-chairman. Politburo members include Kaysone Phomvihan, General Phoume Sipraseuth, Sithon Khommandam, General Sinkapo Chounlamany, Nouhak Phoumsavanh, Khamphouane Tounalom, and Phoumi Vongvichit. Additional members of the Central Committee are Maysouk Saysompheng, Tiao Souk Vongsak, Meune, Saly Vongkhamsao, Kong My, Say, Sanan Southichak, Kiao Sik Phaisomphone, Sisana Sisane, Khampheng Boupha, Pheng Phang, Lo Foung, May Chit, Apheuy Keobounheuang, Phao Phimphachanh, Chanh My, Mme Bounthay, Mme Khampheng Boupha, Mme Phaiboun Pholesna, and Nhia Vu.

The Laotian People's Liberation Army (Pathet Lao) is headed by Khamtay Siphandone as commander in chief. Other key Pathet Lao figures include generals Phoume Sipraseuth and Sinkapo Chounlamany.

Between 18 and 20 November 1970, the NLHX Central Command Labor Union held a conference to elect an administrative committee. Pathet Lao radio (25 November) described it as "the first time that Laotian workers have united and organized their official union."

In 1963, the Patriotic Neutralist Forces (PNF), commanded by Col. Deuane Sounarath (see below), broke with the Tripartite National Union government and in August 1964 unanimously adopted a resolution of complete solidarity with the NLHX, which the PNF continue to support.

Communist influence is also exercised through a number of mass organizations, the most important of which are the National Laotian Women's Federation, headed by Mme Phaiboun Pholesna; the Laotian Patriotic Teacher's Union and the Laotian Afro-Asian Solidarity Committee, both headed by Tiao Souk Vongsak; the Laotian Patriotic Cultural Workers' Union, headed by Phoumi Vongvichit; the National Patriotic Women's Association, founded and organized by Mme Khampheng Boupha; the Laotian Patriotic Workers' Union; the Laotian Youth Association; and the Laotian Buddhists' Association.

The Pathet Lao claims to have control in two-thirds of the country, comprising half of the population, and to have defended and consolidated this "liberated zone." It further asserts that the various nationalities in the zone enjoy genuine equality (Pathet Lao News Agency, 5 October 1970). According to the newspaper of the Communist Party, USA, *Daily World* (New York, 4 June), "people's power" has been established in 638 of the country's 1,078 villages and 8,620 of the 13,063 hamlets.

Internal Party Affairs. There appears to be a rift within the Laotian communist movement between pro-Chinese and pro-Soviet factions. Souphanouvong and Phoumi Vongvichit have been identified with the Soviet line, and Nouhak Phoumsavanh and Kaysone Phomvihan with the Chinese. Laotian communist statements during 1970 appeared to be designed to maintain a balance between the two positions, as in the following: "The Lao Revolution has established and consolidated a broad national united front on the basis of the worker-peasant alliance under the leadership of the party, [and has] united and promoted the tradition of heroic resistance against foreign aggressors among the nationalities" (Pathet Lao News Agency, 5 October).

Domestic Attitudes and Activities. During 1970, Laotian communist propaganda stressed Pathet Lao military victories over neutralist government forces. On 2 January, the NLHX Central

Committee predicted communist reoccupation of the Plain of Jars-Xieng Khouang area, which took place by the end of February. They claimed that between 10 February and 24 February over 1,000 opposing troops were killed, wounded, or captured (Pathet Lao News Agency, 26 February). Turning south for the first time since the 1962 Geneva Agreements, the Pathet Lao attempted to seize the government strongholds of Long Cheng and Sam Thong. After the U.S. move against Vietnamese communist enclaves in Cambodia, the Pathet Lao captured Attopeu and Saravane, southern provincial centers which had been government strongholds.

In early February, Prince Souvanna Phouma proposed neutralizing the Plain of Jars. Although this proposal was turned down by the communists, negotiations between them and the Laotian government continued throughout 1970. Souvanna Phouma expressed his willingness to travel to Hanoi, if necessary, to negotiate with North Vietnam. He also revealed that during 1969 he had told the North Vietnamese ambassador to Laos that North Vietnamese forces could use the Ho Chi Minh trail through Laos without interference if they were withdrawn from the rest of the country. This offer was denounced by North Vietnam and the Pathet Lao.

At a press conference in Hanoi on 6 March, the NLHX put forth a five-point peace plan. After condemning the U.S. presence in Laos, the plan presented basic principles for a political settlement in Laos:

1. Respect for the Kingdom of Laos and an end to U.S. "intervention and aggression" in Laos.
2. A foreign policy of "peace and neutrality" for Laos in accordance with the 1962 Geneva Agreeements.
3. Respect for the throne and holding of "free and democratic" elections.
4. During the period between the restoration of peace and the elections, the Laotian political parties should hold a consultative conference and set up a provisional coalition government. A "zone of security" should be delineated to ensure the functioning of the conference and the coalition government.
5. "The unification of Laos should be achieved through consultation between the Lao parties on the principle of equality and national accord." Pending this, neither side should encroach on the other by force. "Pro-American forces must withdraw forthwith from the areas they have illegally occupied." Both sides should eschew taking reprisals against enemy collaborators. (Pathet Lao News Agency, 7 March.)

The statement concluded with a stipulation that the United States must stop enlarging the war and cease bombings in Laos as a prior condition to negotiations.

Two points in the peace plan were new: general elections and the consultative conference. The plan overlooked the North Vietnamese involvement in Laos—an omission which Souvanna Phouma brought to Souphanouvong's attention in a telegram dated 22 March. On 9 April, while not accepting the plan, Souvanna Phouma stated that honorable agreements must be reached between the parties concerned. In a counterproposal, he called for a cease-fire under inspection by the U.N. International Control Commission—a procedure which the communists had already condemned. Exchanges between the government and the Pathet Lao continued at a halting pace during the year but never totally collapsed. On 17 July the Pathet Lao expressed willingness to participate in peace talks without a halt in U.S. bombing, but arrangements for discussions were beset by semantic obstacles. Meanwhile adulatory reference to the five-point peace plan was reiterated by the Laotian and Vietnamese communists.

During 1970, Laotian communist spokesmen again affirmed support for the NLHX twelve-point program, formulated in 1968. The main points of this program stressed strengthening and broadening the united front; unity among the peoples; protection of "democratic liberties"; equality of the sexes; establishment of a "people's democratic national union administration" to ensure national sovereignty; development of the armed forces, the economy, and education; and implementation of a "foreign policy of peace, independence, solidarity, and friendship with peoples and governments of all peace and justice-loving countries" (Text in *YICA*, 1969, *Documents.*)

On 10 April, the NLHX Central Committee instituted a campaign to increase production as part of its three-year economic plan. Armed elements as well as the peasants were ordered to step up the output of starchy foods. The campaign was described as a measure to familiarize cadres of all levels with manual labor and promote a correct attitude toward work, and to strengthen the relationship between the cadres and the people. The NLHX also called for the development of industry, cooperatives, communications, education, and health services.

Militarily, the NLHX stressed the need to strengthen its armed forces. An order issued on 20 January by the Pathet Lao Supreme Command enumerated five steps which would improve the Laotian "national liberation struggle":

1. Attack the enemy repeatedly, "regardless of conditions, circumstances, and place"; defend the people.
2. Study military, political, and other subjects; promote the revolutionary nature of the army, consolidate it, and maintain its discipline.
3. Heighten the spirit of service to the people of all nationalities; strictly implement policies; mobilize the people to expand guerrilla warfare.
4. Increase production; economize; protect public property; promote self-reliance.
5. Heighten "militant solidarity" with the Patriotic Neutralist Forces. (Pathet Lao radio, 22 January.)

On 6-8 June, a conference of the Pathet Lao and the PNF was held in a "liberated area" of Sam Neua Province to review the Laotian "struggle for liberation" and to delineate measures to be taken in the face of U.S. "adventures" and the new Indochinese developments. The immediate task of the Pathet Lao and its allies was described as pursuance of the "anti-U.S. national liberation struggle." Souphanouvong outlined a six-point program for the Pathet Lao:

1. Strengthen and widen the anti-U.S. united front.
2. Mobilize and encourage the people to perform anti-U.S. tasks and build up the "liberated areas."
3. Continue to struggle for the implementation of the five-point peace plan.
4. Heighten the spirit of self-reliance and vigilance; exercise self-defense against the enemy.
5. Enable the people of the world to understand the situation in Laos and win their support.
6. Stand side-by-side with the Vietnamese and Cambodian people against the United States; materialize the resolutions of the Indochina People's Summit Conference [see *Cambodia*]; and bring about true independence and peace in Indochina.

At the Indochina summit conference Souphanouvong promised that "the Laotian people and army" would do their share toward implementing the participants' joint declaration. Two weeks after the conference, the towns of Attopeu and Saravane were in communist hands (see above). Some observers interpreted this operation as a Laotian communist effort to assist the other Indochinese communist movements by securing the Ho Chi Minh trail.

At the Pathet Lao-PNF Conference in June, the PNF were presented as the true neutralists in Laos. With increasing frequency during 1970, Souvanna Phouma was charged with having defected to the ranks of the rightists and betrayed the neutralists, but while he and his actions were subjected to venomous attack, the Laotian throne was upheld.

In analyzing the situation, NLHX Vice-Chairman Kaysone Phomvihan declared:

The mounting military and political struggle has aroused the national spirit of the various strata of the population, especially the intermediary ones and the enemy officers and soldiers, thus creating favorable conditions for a number of revolutionary leaders to escape the enemy prison. (Pathet Lao News Agency, 5 October.)

Domestic and international conditions, he said, were favorable to the Laotian communist struggle, although the determining factor for success remained the correct leadership of a "genuine party." He claimed that the Laotian communist party was "absolutely loyal to the interests of the working class, the laboring people, and the entire nation," and was following a "correct political and military line." (*Ibid.*)

International Views and Positions. During 1970, with regard to the Sino-Soviet rift, the Laotian communist movement sought to keep a delicate balance. Its clear external allegiance was to North Vietnam, by which it is dominated. In recent years North Vietnam has maintained between 40,000 and 67,000 troops in Laos, mainly in the North Laos-Plain of Jars region and in the southern area along the Ho Chi Minh Trail. By the end of 1970 there was a decided increase in infiltration and North Vietnamese troops in Laos included special commando units and the regular 312th, 316th and 320th divisions. North Vietnamese troops evidently did a major part of the fighting in the Plain of Jars and at Xieng Khouang. Far outnumbered by them, the Pathet Lao seemed to be assuming functions of diminishing importance. In early 1970, traffic along the Ho Chi Minh trail was reported to exceed 15,000 trucks per month (*New York Times*, 25 February).

The theme of Indochinese unity against the United States was evident in Laotian communist pronouncements, although it did not receive as much emphasis as in neighboring countries. In his speech commemorating Ho Chi Minh's birthday, Souphanouvong attributed the development of regional solidarity and the Laotian revolutionary movement to the personal guidance of the late Vietnamese leader. Both the North Vietnamese government and the Provisional Revolutionary Government of South Vietnam endorsed the NLHX five-point peace program. Souvanna Phouma, on the other hand, expressed the opinion that the situation in Laos might long have been settled but for the presence of the Vietnamese forces in his country. The Pathet Lao has not acknowledged that there were North Vietnamese troops in Laos. (For Vietnamese communist use of Laos to infiltrate Thailand, see *Thailand*.)

Along with the Vietnamese communists and the Peking-based Cambodian national front proclaimed by deposed Prince Sihanouk, the Laotian communists participated in the "Summit Conference of the Indochinese Peoples," where they were represented by Souphanouvong, Phoumi Vongvichit, Khampheng Boupha, and Oun Heuan Phounsavath (the latter is deputy director of the NLHX Information Bureau in Hanoi). (See *Cambodia*.)

On the twenty-fifth anniversary of Laotian independence, the Pathet Lao hailed the "great assistance from Vietnam, the Soviet Union, China, and other socialist countries" to communist achievements in Laos (Pathet Lao News Agency, 5 October). In commemorating the Lenin Centenary, the NLHX exhorted its members to strengthen solidarity with the rest of the socialist world.

The Soviet Union displayed continuing concern for the Laotian communists during 1970. The NLHX five-point peace plan was endorsed as being in accord with aspirations of the Laotian people and the interests of peace in Indochina (*New Times*, Moscow, 17 March). On the anniversary of Laotian independence, the Soviets sent the NLHX a telegram congratulating the Laotians and condemning U.S. actions in Laos. *Pravda* noted the fourteenth anniversary of the NLHX in a laudatory editorial, and TASS published a summary of Laotian communist achievements. The Pathet Lao in turn hailed the anniversary of the Red Army, praising the Soviet military contribution to the defense of the socialist camp and of world peace.

On 19-21 May, the Soviet-supported Afro-Asian Peoples' Solidarity Organization (AAPSO) held an "International Conference of Solidarity with the Peoples of Laos" in Cairo. Phoumi Vongvichit headed the Laotian delegation to this meeting, which was attended by 72 delegates from 53 countries and 16 regions and international organizations (Hanoi radio, domestic service, 11 June) but not by China. The conference resolution condemned U.S. "intervention and aggression" in Laos, called for an international campaign to popularize the struggle of the Laotian people, and strongly supported the NLHX five-point peace plan.

Both the World Council of Peace and the AAPSO actively promoted the cause of the Laotian communists during 1970, thereby implying strong interest on the part of the Soviet Union in increasing its influence in that movement. Frequent Soviet and Laotian exchange visits suggested the same. The Soviet Union claimed that if China truly supported the "world people's struggle," it should have sent a delegation to the Cairo conference.

In contrast to the Soviet Union, the Chinese People's Republic ignored the five-point peace plan. Chinese pronouncements on Laos urged the Laotian people to continue their protracted struggle until victory should be won. The same theme was stressed by Lin Piao in his message to the Pathet Lao on its twenty-first anniversary. The Chinese press was slow to report Pathet Lao victories in the earlier part of the year. When it finally did so, its reportage was far from enthusiastic. Moreover, the Chinese linked the fighting in Laos with the Vietnam conflict—a connection which both the Laotian and the Vietnamese communists have been carefully avoiding.

Despite its apparent lack of enthusiasm about communist advances in Laos, China maintains in Laos six People's Liberation Army battalions—estimated at 20,000 men (*New Times*, Moscow, 19 March, 1970) —to guard the approximately 6,000 to 7,000 engineers and workers engaged in constructing the Lao-Chinese "friendship highway" (*Far Eastern Economic Review*, 14 November). The highway was begun in 1968 with the consent of Souvanna Phouma's government, to which it has become a major source of anxiety. The Chinese have disregarded the original road plan and have constructed side roads which the government sees as threatening to its security. (The main highway, terminating only twenty miles from the border with Thailand, is seen by the Thais as a direct threat to the northern part of their country.) In the spring of 1970, for the first time, a Laotian government airplane was fired at while flying over a road construction site. Demands for an explanation were answered by a Chinese diplomatic note denying the presence in Laos of any Chinese workers engaged in road building. A message from Souphanouvong, dated 29 September and addressed to Mao Tse-tung, Lin Piao, and Chou En-lai, expressed gratitude for China's "sincere and valuable assistance," and did not mention the Chinese construction workers or troops (*Peking Review*, no. 41, 9 October).

North Korea generally followed China's example in its dealings with Laos during 1970. A mid-May letter from the Korean National Peace Committee on the occasion of the "Week of Solidarity with the Laotian People" praised their anti-U.S. struggle but failed to mention the five-point peace plan. A speech made by a Laotian in Korea, which mentioned the proposal, was printed in *Peking Review*. Thai authorities claim that North Koreans were fighting in Laos during 1970. Dead soldiers who wore their hair in the Korean fashion were found on Laotian battlefields (*Bangkok Post*, 1 January 1971).

Elsewhere in the communist world, Laos and Cuba signed joint communiqués on 17 February and 1 October, both alleging the cause of tension in Laos to be "the North American imperialists' intervention and aggression." In the October communiqué Cuba strongly endorsed the NLHX five-point peace plan.

During 1970 the Laotian communists condemned the United States and its allies for their actions in Indochina. Included among the allies were Thailand, which has several thousand troops in Laos, and Japan, which was accused of "working hand in glove" with the United States, South Vietnam, and the Cambodian government of Lon Nol. (The Laotian communists were prompt to support Sihanouk's Royal Government of National Union.) Also linked with the United States for condemnation was Israel.

Publications. NLHX directives and policy statements are disseminated by the Pathet Lao's clandestine radio station, believed to be in Sam Neua Province, and by the Pathet Lao News Agency (Khaosan Pathet Lao). The NLHX publishes two newspapers, *Kongthap Potpoi Passon* (organ of the Pathet Lao) and *Lao Hak Xat*. The Laotian Information Service of the NLHX began publishing *Laotian News* in January 1970. In Hanoi, the NLHX has set up an information bureau which is affiliated with the Vietnam Fatherland Front.

*   *   *

The PNF. Founded in 1960, the Patriotic Neutralist Forces openly broke with the Laotian government in 1963 and allied themselves with the NLHX, which had withdrawn from the Tripartite National Union government that year. NLHX statements have sought to present the PNF as the organization of "authentic neutralists" in Laos and thus to reduce Souvama Phouma's neutralist following.

Leadership and Organization. The 2,000 to 3,000 PNF members are headed by Colonel Deuane Sounarath. The PNF appears, however, to be divided into two groups: one under Deuane Sounarath, commander in chief and also PNF supreme commander in the Plain of Jars; the other under General Khampheng Boupha, PNF supreme commander in northern Laos. At its First National Conference, in April 1969, the PNF set up the "Alliance Committee of the Laotian Patriotic Neutralist Forces," headed by Khamsouk Keola, to consolidate the PNF organization and take charge of short-term tasks.

Domestic Attitudes and Activities. In 1969 the PNF adopted a five-point program calling for neutrality, peace, national unity, an elected government, respect for the king and Buddhism, prosperity, and so on. In order to realize these objectives, the PNF declared a policy of alliance with all forces seeking the same goals.

In April 1970 the PNF was represented at the Summit Conference of the Indochinese Peoples by Khamsouk Keola. (See *Cambodia.*) On 6-8 June the PNF and the Pathet Lao held a meeting to review their struggle and outline future tasks (see above).

On 21 April the PNF radio station broadcast a New Year's greeting from the Central Committee of the Neutralist Peace Party (NPP) to the NLHX Central Committee. In what proved to be the only mention of this new party during 1970, the message urged the Laotian people to enhance their solidarity, defend and improve the "liberated areas," and implement NLHX directives. The message affirmed the NPP's loyalty to the revolutionary process, its solidarity with all "patriotic" forces, and its "confidence in the NLHX Central Committee's clear-sighted leadership, the power of the masses, and the revolution's final victory." In conclusion, the broadcast demanded that the United States and the Souvanna Phouma government unconditionally accept the NLHX five-point peace plan and halt U.S. bombing in Laos. It seems probable that the NPP has been set up as the political arm of the PNF, paralleling the relationship between the NLHX and the Pathet Lao. No substantial information concerning the new party has become available.

International Views and Positions. The PNF has declared its intention to establish diplomatic relations with all countries of the world, regardless of their political ideologies, on a basis of mutual respect, and to welcome all aid without political ties as a contribution to the development of Laos. It has also declared its support for the "Vietnamese people's struggle against U.S. aggression" and its opposition to U.S. actions in Laos.

Publications. PNF statements are broadcast by the clandestine PNF radio station. Its directives are also disseminated by the Pathet Lao News Agency and the Pathet Lao radio station.

S. E. Y.

MALAYSIA

The communist movement in Malaysia is divided into two virtually independent groups: the Communist Party of Malaya (CPM), which operates in West Malaysia and Singapore,[1] and the terrorist groups organized within the Sarawak Communist Organization (SCO) in East Malaysia. Both have a predominantly Chinese ethnic composition and maintain a pro-Chinese stance, which is reflected in their domestic activities.

The CPM originated in 1928 as the South Seas Communist Party (Nang-yang kung-ch'an tang), composed exclusively of overseas Chinese, with headquarters in Singapore. The South Seas Communist Party, whose mission was to direct activities in most of Southeast Asia, was transformed into the Communist Party of Malaya in 1930. By 1945 it had attained a strong position through its anti-Japanese actions during the Second World War. In 1948, when the CPM initiated a campaign of armed struggle against British rule, the government outlawed the party and declared a state of emergency, which was not terminated until July 1960 —three years after the independent Federation of Malaysia was established. As a result of government measures during this long period, the CPM was reduced to small, scattered underground groups on the Malay Peninsula and along the Thai-Malaysian border. The party has its headquarters in the border area, where it continues to exercise varying degrees of territorial control.

The CPM is estimated to have between 2,000 and 2,500 members, including 500 in West Malaysia (centered chiefly around the urban centers in the states of Penang, Johore, and Negri Sembilan) and 1,200 to 2,000 operating as insurgents on the 361-mile-long Thai-Malaysian border. The communist militants of East Malaysia are estimated to number about 500 in Sarawak, including about 230 on the Indonesian side of the border; no communist activity has been reported in Sabah. The CPM is also believed to have some 2,000 active sympathizers. The population of Malaysia is 10,800,000 (estimated 1970).

The CPM remains illegal, and in recent years the government has carried out intensive nationwide anticommunist campaigns which have led to the arrest of many persons accused of being communists. In an attempt to facilitate capture of terrorists operating along the Thai border, the governments of Malaysia and Thailand have made a number of agreements for coordinated anticommunist military and police efforts. A combined headquarters is maintained at Songkhla, Thailand. On 7 March 1970 the two countries extended mutual rights of pursuit and permitted mutual territorial penetration up to five miles and for as long as seventy-two hours. The latest accord (30 September) called for intensified joint operations, coordinated sea patrols, new and attractive surrender terms for insurgents, and reinforcement of psychological warfare units operating along the border. An agreement with Indonesia on similar arrangements in East Malaysia and Indonesian Borneo was signed in November 1969.

[1]Singapore's communists nominally belong to the CPM, which regards Singapore as an integral part of Malaya (meaning all of the Malay Peninsula formerly part of the British empire).

Organization and Leadership. Very little information is available on the organizational structure of the CPM. Regional party control in West Malaysia is apparently shared by two border committees: the Penang-Kedah committee on the western extremity of the border, and the Kelantan-Perak committee on the eastern extremity.

The party's secretary-general is Chin Peng, one of the most senior surviving guerrilla leaders in Southeast Asia. The party chairman is Musa Ahmad. Abdul Rashid Bin Maidin, now under detention in Perak, is said to be the third ranking CPM member. The Central Committee is believed to have about ten members. The Politburo probably consists of four members, including Chin Peng and Li On Tung. Propaganda functions are led by Chen Tien. Other prominent members include Lam Fung Sing, Liew Yit Fun, Chiam Chung Him, Eu Chooi Yip, Lu Cheng, and Siew Chong, all of whom are probably in exile in mainland China, and Wu Tien Wang, who is believed to be with the Twelfth Regiment of the Malayan National Liberation Army (MNLA). Although Chin Peng himself is said to be operating along the Thai-Malaysian border, it is not known whether the majority of the Central Committee or Politburo members are also in that area.

The CPM carries out military operations through the MNLA, founded on 1 February 1949. This force is referred to by the Malaysian government as the Communist Terrorist Organization. The MNLA is actively involved in terrorist actions which according to various observers show many characteristics of communist tactics in South Vietnam. Although the MNLA originally consisted of twelve regiments, it has at present only three: the Eighth (or Western), the Twelfth (or Central), and the Tenth (or Eastern), none of which maintains full regimental strength. The supreme commander of the MNLA is believed to be Chin Peng.

The CPM operates also through two fronts: the Malayan National Liberation League (MNLL) and the Partai Persaudaraan Islam (Islamic Brotherhood; Paperi). The MNLL, allegedly founded in 1949 as a successor to the PUTERA/AMCJA front (a left-wing coalition set up in 1947 to oppose the establishment of a federation of Malaya), is the united front organization of the CPM. The Malaysian government has described it as being responsible for the constitutional struggle and certain aspects of the illegal or "militant" struggle of the party (*The Militant Communist Threat to West Malaysia*, Ministry of Home Affairs, Kuala Lumpur, October 1966, p. 4). There are MNLL missions in Peking and Hanoi. The other communist front, the Paperi, was founded in April 1965 and was probably established by the CPM's Central Department of Malay Work. No activities of the Paperi were reported during 1970.

Although the CPM firmly advocates the use of violent struggle for the seizure of power, it has also pursued a policy of infiltrating left-wing opposition parties—primarily the Labour Party of Malaya (LP) which has a predominantly Chinese membership, and the Partai Sosialis Rakyat Malaya (Socialist People's Party of Malaya; PSR),[1] which is largely Malay. Premier Tunku Abdul Rahman threatened to proscribe both political movements in early 1970, but the government failed to follow through. Many of the LP and PSR branches in Malaya have ceased to function, and it is possible that former LP and PSR members are being encouraged to join cells of the illegal MNLL.

The LP, whose objectives include "common ownership of the means of production, distribution, and exchange," was expelled from the Socialist International in 1966 when it was found to be "90 per cent communist-penetrated" and "indistinguishable from a communist organization." It did not participate in the May 1969 national elections because of alleged government repression and was partly successful in urging a voter boycott. Possibly 3 per cent of the electorate in the western and southern areas of mainland Malaysia followed LP instructions and ab-

[1] Formerly the Partai Rakyat Malaya (People's Party of Malaya—PR).

stained from voting (see Stuart Drummond and David Hawkins, "The Malaysian Elections of 1969," *Asian Survey*, April 1970).

The PSR is basically a party of extreme nationalists advocating the concept of a "Greater Indonesia," whether by peaceful or violent means. It participated in the May 1969 elections, contesting a few seats in the states of Malacca (where it polled 13.6 per cent of the votes), Pahang (14.7 per cent), and Perlis (6.7 per cent), and obtained a victory with two State Assembly seats (both in Pahang) out of a total of 282.

Domestic Attitudes and Activities. In an extensive analysis marking the fortieth anniversary of the CPM (30 April 1970), Radio "Voice of the Malayan Revolution" (VMR) on 26 April declared a "new democratic revolution" to be the present objective of the party. The broadcast enunciated a party program designed to accomplish that goal, declaring it to be in the interests of the working class, farmers, petty bourgeoisie, national bourgeoisie, and the "anti-imperialist patriotic class" to:

> Overthrow the power of British imperialism and its puppets and establish the People's Republic of Malaya.
> Protect the people's democratic rights and respect freedom of religion.
> Nationalize the industries of the imperialists and their lackeys; protect the national bourgeoisie's commercial and trade industries.
> Abolish the semifeudalist and feudalist system and implement the agrarian system "land for the (landless)"; nullify all debts with usurers.
> Improve the livelihood of the workers and the lower paid workers; implement equal pay for both sexes.
> Implement equal rights for all races in all fields.
> Establish a strong people's armed forces.
> Develop a new culture of all nationalities [and] combat the old culture of imperialism and feudalism.
> Support the North Kalimantan people's struggle to determine the fate of the country and nation; support the liberation struggle of all oppressed people and nations.

The VMR said later (4 October) that the "people's republic" was to be "led by the working class and based on the worker-peasant federation and the affiliated bourgeois and national bourgeois classes."

Since 1967 the CPM has repeatedly affirmed its commitment to armed struggle. A broadcast in 1970 declared: "The integration of the universal truth of Mao Tse-tung's thought with the concrete practice of our country's revolution is the only guarantee for victory in our country's revolutionary struggle" (*ibid.*, 26 April). Although the party's frequent warnings against revisionist or capitulationist policies might indicate that some members favored a policy of seeking power through constitutional means, there were no signs of a split or of the emergence of a pro-Soviet faction.

The MNLA is the chief vehicle through which the CPM executes its policy of armed struggle. It has been described as "an armed organization . . . conducting propaganda among the masses, organizing and arming the masses, and assisting them in setting up revolutionary rule" (*ibid.*, 4 October). A broadcast on the twenty-first anniversary of the founding of the MNLA contained the following resume of tasks facing that force:

> All the commanders and fighters of the National Liberation Army must rally closely around the Central Committee of the Communist Party of Malaya, assiduously study and apply Mao Tse-tung thought in a living way, improve their fighting skill, strengthen their sense of organization and discipline, consolidate the unity between the armed forces and the people, give full

play to the spirit of revolutionary heroism of fearing neither hardship nor death, launch a vigorous offensive against the enemy and make new contributions to the development of the people's war. (*Ibid.*, 3 February.)

In September, Peking claimed that between February and June the MNLA had killed 250
Malaysian and Thai troops and police (NCNA, 22 September).

During 1969-70, the CPM increased its membership through the recruitment of villagers in the
three southern provinces of Thailand (Songkhla, Yala, and Narathiwat). In 1969, guerrillas
along the border were estimated at 800 to 1,000 (*YICA*, 1970, p. 639), compared with the present
1,200, to 2,000. Despite the increase in membership, the CPM is not strong enough to mount a
major offensive (see, e.g., *Far Eastern Economic Review*, Hong Kong, 21 May). Nevertheless the
CPM moves with impunity in the border towns, which regularly pay protection money. Joint
Thai-Malaysian counterinsurgency campaigns in mid-1970 uncovered three major communist
camps in southern Thailand which together could accommodate about 600 persons. The guerrillas, deprived of their bases, subsequently moved south across the border into Malaysia, with the
Eighth Regiment operating in the state of Kedah, the Tenth in Kelantan as well as in the Waeng
District of Narathiwat Province, Thailand, and the Twelfth Regiment in Perak (NCNA, 12 July
and 23 August). Communist propaganda work further extended into Perlis.

The CPM celebrated the fortieth anniversary of the party (30 April) and the twenty-second
anniversary of its armed insurgency (20 June) by setting off a number of explosive devices in
West Malaysia and also in Singapore. In their boldest attempt, a bomb was exploded on 23 June
under a bridge near the Parliament building in Kuala Lumpur. Although the explosion caused little damage, it was highly praised in CPM propaganda.

In conjunction with the anniversary of the insurgency, the MNLL Central Committee and
MNLA General Headquarters issued their first joint statement. It declared that both were "determined to wage unyielding struggle under the leadership of the CPM to establish the People's
Republic of Malaya and win national liberation" (VMR, 20 June). The two organizations also
endorsed the goals set forth in the CPM fortieth anniversary declaration.

One of the topics which the CPM touched upon repeatedly was the racial situation in Malaysia. The fortieth-anniversary statement devoted considerable attention to the subject, declaring:

> The hidden traitor [Lai Tek, former CPM secretary-general] dished up the fallacy that the
> Chinese and Indian nationalities in Malaya were overseas residents, and the Malays were na-
> tives. Between the Chinese and Malay[s], the development of the revolutionary movement was
> uneven. . . . Therefore, armed struggle could not be continued before a so-called national unity
> with the Malays as the core was formed. . . . The question of nationalities is, in the final analy-
> sis, one of classes. (VMR, 26 April.)

Captured communists have asserted that the CPM intends to exploit racial tension to spark incidents leading to nationwide racial conflict (*Far Eastern Economic Review*, 21 May). Despite
CPM emphasis on racial unity and its attempts to broaden the party's ethnic base, membership
remains overwhelmingly Chinese.

The PSR was also concerned about race. It maintained that "racialism" is a blind created by
Chinese capitalists and Malay aristocrats to disguise exploitation of their own people.

Along with its cross-ethnic appeal, the CPM has been making special efforts at recruitment in
various religious groups. It has shown special interest in the Malay Moslems, but has gained
very few adherents among them. Communist propagandists were said to be disguising themselves as religious teachers. The CPM circulated extracts from the Koran which were construed
to prove that Islam favors the "national liberation struggle," and party members assisted Malays in southern Thailand in building a mosque.

In response to Malaysian and Singapore government efforts to "jam" VMR programs, the CPM began to broadcast in the fall from transmitters in the border area which employed a variety of frequencies and were therefore difficult to counter.

In the middle of the year, Malaysian Home Affairs Minister Tun Ismail stated that communist activities in schools and universities had been increasing (*Straits Times*, Singapore, 4 July). Subsequent government statements indicated that the institutions affected might be closed to counter CPM influence.

International Views and Positions. The CPM ardently supports the strategy and policies of the Chinese Communist Party (CCP), terms Mao Tse-tung "the Lenin of the current era," and regards China as "the center of world revolution." In turn, the CCP has praised the CPM for upholding revolutionary principles in the face of "revisionist" opposition. Malaysian officials maintain that the border terrorists receive aid from China and that their leader, Chin Peng, makes frequent trips there.

In January 1970 the CPM publications department announced the translation and printing of various writings by Mao, including his *Selected Works* (*Peking Review*, no. 3, 16 January). According to the VMR, the CPM and the MNLA had drawn up the curriculum for a "mass movement" to study Mao's thoughts.

The CPM condemned the Soviet Union, denouncing it, along with the United States, Great Britain, and the governments of Malaysia and Singapore, for the establishment and perpetuation of Malaysia. The CPM also charged that the Soviet Union had been accelerating its "infiltration" of Malaya in an effort to undermine the revolutionary struggle there. A VMR broadcast (19 January) declared: "The Soviet revisionist clique is hated by and scared to death of the Malayan people who, under the leadership of the Communist Party of Malaya, are holding aloft the great Mao's thought, anti-imperialism, anti-revisionism, and are persistently following the path of seizing political power by armed force."

The CPM statement on the Lenin Centenary briefly praised the founder of the Soviet Union before launching into a lengthly diatribe against that country. It concluded, "We should study and apply in a living way Mao Tse-tung thought, Marxism-Leninism of our era, hold still higher the great red banner of Mao Tse-tung thought, [and] unite with the genuine Marxist-Leninists of all countries" (NCNA, 29 April).

Thailand, as an ally of the United States, was attacked by the CPM: "The reactionaries of Thailand who rely on U.S. 'aid' to linger out their own life can never save the Rahman-Razak clique from its doom" (NCNA, 23 January). Western intelligence reports indicate that some insurgents from northeastern Thailand have been trained by the CPM forces along the border.

Another object of CPM criticism was Indonesia. President Suharto's "fascist militarist regime" was viewed as interfering in the internal affairs of Malaysia and "exploiting language, religion, and cultural similarities between the two countries" to spread "the extremely reactionary chauvinistic theory that the Malay people must unite to cope with China" (VMR, 20 February).

On its fortieth anniversary, the CPM received congratulations from the CCP, the Vietnam Workers' Party of North Vietnam, the Communist Party of Thailand, and the Albanian Party of Labor, among others. The Soviet Union apparently did not take note of the occasion.

Publications. The CPM has no regular official publication. Its statements are circulated through numerous pamphlets and by the Communist Chinese press and radio, and since October 1969 through the Yunnan-based "Voice of the Malayan Revolution" radio. The VMR broadcasts in Chinese, Malay, and Tamil. Programs in all three languages were increased in March 1970. The *Malayan Monitor and General News* (founded in 1947 as the *Malayan Monitor*; name changed at the end of 1966) is a mimeographed monthly issued in London. Although not an official CPM publication, it prints CPM policy statements. Choong Wai Koh of West Malaysia is the news editor.

Party views and positions are publicized also in two Singapore dailies, *Barisan* and *People's Tribune*; in the *Malayan Bulletin*, the organ of the MNLL mission in Peking; and in various minor publications, copies of which have been recovered along the Thai-Malaysian border. Border activities are also reported by Radio "Voice of the People of Thailand," the clandestine radio station of the Communist Party of Thailand.

* * *

The SCO. The communist movement in East Malaysia is concentrated in Sarawak. All clandestine groups in the state are organized within a multifront organization, generally known as the Sarawak Communist Organization, which works for the establishment of a communist state in Sarawak, Sabah, and Brunei and is believed to be directed by the somewhat nebulous Borneo Communist Party. Although the SCO operates along the border between Sarawak and Kalimantan (the Indonesian part of the island of Borneo), it has no known official ties with either the Communist Party of Malaya or the Communist Party of Indonesia. Estimates of SCO membership vary, but there appeared to be some 270 guerrillas operating in Sarawak and some 230 based in Indonesian Kalimantan at the beginning of 1970. By the close of the year, the Indonesian side of the border had been largely cleared of guerrillas, while the number in Sarawak had grown to 500. Most of the Sarawak insurgents are concentrated in the Second, Third, and, to a lesser degree, the First Division of that state. Some 156 guerrillas reportedly were killed or captured by October, while an additional 23 surrendered. The guerrillas appear to be operating in small bands, continually on the move. Communist sympathizers in Sarawak are thought to number between 10,000 and 20,000.

The SCO has been described by the government as "100 per cent Chinese." It recruits especially among disenchanted urban youths. While Malays represent only 17 per cent of the population of Sarawak, the ethnic Chinese constitute more than 30 per cent. The fact that the Chinese are the largest single racial group in the state probably accounts for a certain sympathy toward communist "anti-Malaysia" campaigns.

Organization and Leadership. The SCO consists of a Central Committee, area and town committees, district committees, and branches and cells. The Central Committee operates through four work departments: labor movement, peasantry, students, and political party. Very little is known of the leadership of the movement, although it is generally believed that some members of the Sarawak United People's Party (see below) are associated with it.

The military arms of the SCO, referred to collectively in Chinese reports as the Sarawak People's Armed Forces, are said to be the Sarawak People's Guerrilla Army (Pertahanan, or Pasokan-Gerilja Rakjat Sarawak; PGRS), under a leader known as Jahaj, and the North Kalimantan People's Armed Force (Pasokan Ra'ayat Kalimantan Utara; Paraku) which is thought to number 160 to 170 men. Both are based on the Indonesian side of the border. The Paraku is headed by Wong Kee Chok. The PGRS and the Paraku possibly include some Indonesian soldiers who deserted after the abortive communist-inspired coup in 1965 and fugitive members of the now banned Communist Party of Indonesia.

The SCO has sought to influence several legal labor and political organizations, the most important of which is the Sarawak United People's Party (SUPP), founded in 1959. The SUPP is identified with Chinese urban interests, although it is believed that about 10,000 of the 24,000 members of the party are non-Chinese. Communist infiltration of the SUPP has apparently been extensive enough to split it into a moderate "social-democratic" right wing and a communist-influenced, China-oriented left wing. The SUPP secretary-general, Stephen Yong, and the chairman, Ong Kee Hui, are not identified as communists, but the party program and activities closely parallel those of the SCO in rejecting the Federation of Malaysia as a "colonialist plot" and advocating the establishment of separate political states on the Malay Peninsula and in Borneo, and also in calling for improved labor conditions, trade relations with Communist China, and the lifting of government controls on Chinese businessmen.

In March 1970 the Communist Party of North Kalimantan (CPNK), announced its formation. At present, this new party operates only in Sarawak. Its relationship to the SCO is not clear, but the CPNK may have replaced the former "Sarawak Liberation League," which had been the principal body within the SCO. Wong Kee Chok, the head of the Paraku, is designated as the "Secretary, (Eastern) Bureau of the Central Committee of the Communist Party of North Kalimantan." Little else is known of the composition of CPNK leadership, which may in fact be split. The manifesto, which announced the formation of the party (see below), was signed only by the secretary and not by the Central Committee as a whole.

Elections were scheduled to take place in Sarawak in 1969 between 10 May and 7 June 1969, but were halted when violence erupted in West Malaysia on 13 May, and eventually were held in 1970 from 4 June to 3 July. The SUPP polled the largest number of votes (28.6 per cent), but won only 11 of the 47 state constituencies, obtaining five seats in the national Parliament. In a surprise move on 7 July, the SUPP agreed to form a coalition with two other parties to achieve a ruling majority in the state legislature of Sawarak.

There were reports in 1970 of a split within the SCO as a result of government counterinsurgency measures. One faction, centered around Kuching, supported participation in the elections in an effort to infiltrate the administration through the SUPP. The rival group called for an election boycott and attempted to disrupt polling through intimidation of the populace.

Domestic Attitudes and Activities. Like the CPM in West Malaysia, the SCO accepts the Maoist doctrine of armed struggle. It apparently relies heavily on its two guerrilla arms, the Paraku and the PGRS, which are described as political, production, and fighting forces. An editorial in the Sarawak communist *Liberation News* has identified three major tasks necessary to achieve the "complete emancipation of North Kalimantan": "building a party, an army, and a broad national united front" (quoted, NCNA, 14 January). After paying respects to the Maoist doctrine of armed struggle, the editorial described the plan for the realization of this aim: "On the basis of running study classes on a big scale to study Mao Tse-tung thought and of consolidating our ranks organizationally, we will energetically develop mass work and at the same time strive to arm the masses and gradually establish a powerful people's army" (*ibid.*) The article's restrained tone and tacit acknowledgement that armed struggle would be premature at present would seem to reinforce the claims of the Indonesian and Malaysian governments that the PGRS and the Paraku have been significantly weakened, despite continual Chinese assertions of communist victories. An article in *Afro-Asian Journalist* (Peking, no. 1, 1970), ostensibly by a member of the Kalimantan movement, declared that the present stage was that of a "national-democratic revolution," the task of which was to unite all "revolutionary forces, including the petty bourgeoisie and national bourgeoisie, with the proletariat assuming the leadership and the workers and peasants constituting the main force, to direct their spearhead against imperialism, revisionism, the Malay feudal comprador clique and the comprador clique within the country." Elsewhere in the article, however, "the central task and the highest form of revolution" were identified as the seizure of power through armed force, and the present offensive was described as a peasant war waged under the leadership of a revolutionary organization.

The guerrilla forces in East Malaysia appear to lack supplies as well as manpower because of being unable to replace the automatic weapons they gained during and immediately after the "Confrontation" with Indonesia. Almost three-quarters of their weapons captured recently have been homemade (*Far Eastern Economic Review*, 22 January). The physical condition of prisoners often revealed extreme deprivation and there were frequent reports of starvation. A government counterinsurgency campaign in early 1970 uncovered a terrorist training center near Kuching which could accommodate 100 to 150 persons (Kuala Lumpur radio, 2 March). By mid-June, 70 per cent of the guerrillas in the First Division reportedly had been killed or captured, or had surrendered (*Straits Times*, Singapore, 16 June). The Indonesian and Malaysian governments agreed, however, that the danger was not over. The chief of staff of the Malaysian armed forces warned that the Sarawak communists were embarking on a propaganda campaign to reactivate their contacts in urban areas (Kuala Lumpur radio, domestic service, 25 September), and propaganda was apparently introduced into the schools, in a tactic which has been effective in winning followers and obtaining recruits to replace casualties.

In an attempt to hinder the first general elections in Sarawak and retaliate for anticommunist campaigns, the SCO undertook a wave of terrorism, chiefly through its Third Division. Terrorist incidents again rose in numbers in November after an apparent lull.

The SCO opposed the recent government census in East Malaysia through leaflets which claimed the survey to be a "criminal plot" to "gather counterrevolutionary intelligence" (NCNA, 4 September).

The CPNK, in the manifesto announcing its foundation in March, outlined the "maximum" objectives of the party as to "overthrow completely the bourgeoisie and all exploiting classes, replace bourgeois dictatorship with proletarian dictatorship . . . and finally bring about the realization of communism." Its "minimum" program called for carrying out the "national democratic revolution in North Kalimantan," smashing the "'Malaysian' feudal-bureaucratic comprador clique [which was] ruling North Kalimantan," and establishing a "new North Kalimantan guided by the principles of new democracy." The CPNK dedicated itself to leading the "broad masses of people . . . to seize power by armed force; to carry out other forms of class struggle; to seize victory in the national democratic revolution in North Kalimantan and to create the necessary conditions for carrying out a socialist revolution in North Kalimantan." These goals, it indicated, would be achieved through a combination of legal and illegal methods. The manifesto further declared that since North Kalimantan was a multiracial entity, it was suitable for the dissemination of communism and for carrying out armed struggle. The workers and peasants, according to the document, would "inevitably become the task force of the revolution."

International Views and Positions. The communist movement in Sarawak is basically pro-Chinese and it is believed to receive both verbal and material assistance from China, despite the reported internal split over the issue of armed struggle. Chinese interest in the SCO is reflected in the many references in Chinese broadcasts to victories of the "North Kalimantan revolutionaries." Sharing the CPM's anti-Indonesia and anti-Malaysia stance, the Sarawak guerrillas receive verbal endorsement from that party.

With Marxism-Leninism and the thought of Mao Tse-tung as "the theoretical basis," the CPNK claims to adhere "persistently to the principles of proletarian internationalism and [to be] resolute in uniting with the truly Marxist-Leninist political parties and organizations in the whole world." It has condemned "modern revisionism with the Soviet revisionist renegade clique as its center." It has not, however, been publicly acknowledged by China. Neither has the China-based "Voice of the Malayan Revolution," the CPM radio station, acknowledged its existence despite the CPNK's announced intention to establish "the closest contact with the Communist Party of

Malaya" in order to coordinate efforts toward destroying the "military dictatorial role of the 'Malaysian' feudal-bureaucratic-comprador class over North Kalimantan."

Publications. Sarawak communist groups have at least two publications, *Liberation News* and *News Bulletin*. Other communist or communist-oriented newspapers known to circulate in Sarawak include the *Workers' and Farmers' News, National Independence,* and the *Masses News*.

S. E. Y.

MONGOLIA

The Mongolian People's Party was founded in 1921 as an amalgamation of two revolutionary groups led by Damdiny Sukhe-Bator and Horloogiyn Choybalsan. Its First Congress was held in March of that year under the protection of the Soviet Red Army. Since the Third Congress (1924), the party has been known as the Mongolian People's Revolutionary Party (Mongol Ardyn Huuvisgalt Nam; MPRP). The MPRP holds a monopoly of power in the Mongolian People's Republic (MPR). In 1970, First Secretary Yumzhagiin Tsedenbal claimed a party membership of 71,000[1] (*Népsabadság*, Budapest, 23 December 1970). The population of the MPR is 1,300,000 (estimated 1970).

Organization and Leadership. The MPRP is organized approximately on the same pattern as the Communist Party of the Soviet Union (CPSU). In contrast with the separation of the highest offices of the party and the state in the Soviet Union, however, in the MPR the posts of premier and first secretary of the MPRP are held by one person—Tsedenbal. The party congress is in theory the supreme body, but more important are the Central Committee (with 75 full and 51 candidate members), the Politburo (7 full and 2 candidate members), and the Secretariat (5 members). The government is dominated by the party. The chairman (Tsedenbal) and the seven deputy chairmen of the highest state body, the Council of Ministers, all belong to the party's Central Committee and half of them are members of the Politburo.

The following members of the Secretariat were elected at the Fifteenth Congress of the MPRP, in June 1966: Nyamyn Jagvaral, Demchigiyn Molomjamts, Badamyn Lhamsuren, Tsaganlamyn Dugersuren, and First Secretary Tsedenbal. Full members of the Politburo are Tsedenbal, Jagvaral, Dugersuren, Molomjamts, Damdinjavyn Maydar, Sonomyn Lubsan, and Jamsrangiyn Sambuu; candidate members are Namsrayn Lubsanrabdan (also chairman of the Control Commission) and Lhamsuren.

Auxiliary organizations of the party include the Mongolian Revolutionary Youth League (MRYL, also referred to as Revsomol), which has a membership of more than 80,000. Its secretary is Choyjiljavyn Purevjav. For younger persons there is a "Young Pioneers" organization, which has 90,000 members. Both are modeled after the Komsomol and Young Pioneer organizations in the Soviet Union. Also important is the Central Council of Trade Unions (CCTU). The chairman is Dovchingiyn Yadamsuren. The CCTU claimed a membership of 170,000 in 1969/70 (*WMR*, supplement, August 1970). It includes unions for agricultural, industrial, trade and transport, construction, and cultural-education workers.

The social composition of the MPRP has been reported by Tsedenbal as 26 per cent workers, 24 per cent peasants and farmers, and 50 per cent intellectuals (*Népszabadság*, 23 December). Twenty per cent of the party members are said to be women. According to party statements,

---

[1] A membership of "almost 50,000" was reported by Ulan Bator radio on 1 March 1968. A total of 58,048 members and candidates as of April 1971 was reported at the party's Sixteenth Congress (Montsame, 7 June 1971).

more than 50 per cent of the members are under forty years of age and 45 per cent have either higher education or specialized secondary education.

Domestic Attitudes and Activities. Judging by reports in *Unen* (the official MPRP daily organ), the overriding subject of domestic interest is the country's economic activity. At a plenum of the MPRP Central Committee on 26 January 1970, discussion appeared to be limited to economic matters. First Secretary Tsedenbal presented a report on "certain tasks aimed at increasing the responsibility of party and state organs for improving the qualitative indices of the national economy" (Ulan Bator radio, 26 January). The broadcast report on the plenum stated that the need for such improvement was indeed urgent, since the MPR was "developing at a much slower pace than other fraternal countries." More to the point, it noted:

> We make no secret of the fact that in our state certain vitally important indices of the national economy, in particular the pace of raising the efficiency of social productivity, have slowed down somewhat. The plenum of the party Central Committee has therefore set the party and state organizations the tasks of launching a large-scale drive to eliminate these shortcomings in the very near future.

Specific mention was made that the economic plan for the grain harvest of 1969 had not been fulfilled. (*Ibid.*)

In industry, an increase in the gross industrial output of 11.2 per cent was planned for 1970. The official MPR press agency, Montsame (30 January), noted that if this plan were fulfilled, industry would account for nearly 26 per cent of the total national income. Tsedenbal acknowledged toward the end of the year that industry had successfully completed its five-year plan (1966-70) but that agriculture had not. He gave as reasons for the shortcomings in agriculture the severe winter of 1967-68 and the drought of the 1968 summer which together had caused 45 million head of livestock to perish (*Népszabadság*, 23 December 1970).

International Views and Positions. *Relations with the Soviet Union.*   In a series of purges between the fourteenth and fifteenth MPRP congresses (1961 and 1966), Tsedenbal ensured his hold over the party and gave it a strongly pro-Soviet stance in the Sino-Soviet conflict. This alignment was further strengthened by the occurrence of armed clashes along the Sino-Soviet border during 1969. Military and economic assistance from the Soviet Union has been considerable. Mongolia's military defenses against China are vastly augmented by the presence of Soviet troops and, reportedly, tank and antiaircraft missile units and possibly IRBM's on Mongolian territory.

A Soviet-Mongolian joint communiqué, resulting from a visit to Moscow by Tsedenbal on 26-31 October 1970, declared that the exchange of opinions on subjects of foreign policy and the world situation "again confirmed the full coincidence of positions on all questions discussed" (Moscow domestic service, 1 November). The communiqué indicated Mongolia's support for European collective security, and its agreement with the Soviet-West German treaty of August 1970. Tsedenbal expected the treaty to "promote the normalization of the situation in Europe and the creation of an atmosphere of peaceful cooperation between all European states (*ibid.*). In the communiqué he also offered the MPR's backing for the Asian collective security system proposed by the Soviet Union in 1969—the only enthusiastic support for the proposal thus far among Asian countries.

Eighty per cent of the MPR's foreign trade is with the Soviet Union, with other member countries of the Council for Mutual Economic Assistance (CMEA) accounting for approximately 12 per cent. Mongolia is also heavily dependent upon the Soviet Union for economic assistance. The purpose of Tsedenbal's October visit to the Soviet Union was to secure Soviet assistance for the

1971-75 economic plan. The protocol, signed on 28 October, covered a wide range of economic topics.

The Soviet Union continued to make use of the MPR in its attacks on the Chinese leadership. Soviet broadcasts to China frequently stated that the Chinese ruling elements had been responsible for the deterioration in Sino-Mongolian relations and that military relations between the Soviet Union and Mongolia were strong. An article in the Soviet army newspaper *Krasnaya zvezda* (Moscow, 15 January) stated: "Ties of combat brotherhood, sealed in blood, bind our countries' soldiers. Thanks to the Soviet Union's disinterested assistance, the Mongolian People's Army has well-trained cadres and modern equipment at its disposal. Any encroachment on the inviolability of its frontiers will meet a worthy rebuff."

Relations with China. The significance of the sizable Soviet defense assistance to the MPR was not lost on the Chinese, who have also built up defenses on their side of the border. A broadcast on the occasion of the forty-third anniversary of the Chinese People's Liberation Army (Nanning radio, 4 August) charged that Soviet "social imperialists" had "moved troops" into Mongolia and were "plotting to launch a large-scale war of aggression against China."

While actively expanding their international contacts during the year, the Chinese continued to remain cool to the MPR. On the other hand, the two countries are not completely isolated from each other. Diplomatic relations are carried on by chargés d'affaires, who give receptions on various occasions. When the Mongolian chargé d'affaires invited Chinese guests (at the deputy-minister level) to celebrate the forty-ninth anniversary of the MPR, that event was perfunctorily reported by NCNA on 11 July. The two countries continued to engage in trade with each other. During a visit to Japan, Deputy Premier D. Gombojav stated at a press conference that the MPR intended to develop trade with China, though it had no plans to request Chinese economic aid (*Japan Times*, Tokyo, 21 August). On 14 July a trade protocol between Mongolia and China was signed in Peking.

The Chinese have somewhat lessened their attacks against the Mongolians, but polemics continued in 1970 and were particularly strong from the latter side. Tsedenbal took the occasion of the Lenin Centenary celebrations to accuse the "Peking national chauvinists" of "rendering service to international and imperialist reaction," stating that the "Mao group" had entered a "new, more dangerous phase," marked by a "complete break from Marxism-Leninism," "rabid anti-Sovietism," and "calls for war against the homeland of Lenin and Leninism . . . and against other socialist countries" (TASS, 19 April, and *Unen*, 22 April). On 27 March, Ulan Bator radio carried a speech by Politburo candidate member B. Lhamsuren in which he attacked the Chinese leaders as "bourgeois ideologists and latter-day revisionists," and added: "[They attempt to] belittle the importance of Mongolian-Soviet friendship, to undermine our country's international prestige, and to drive a wedge . . . between our two people. . . . The imperialists' campaign of misrepresentation against our country is closely linked with the hostile great power chauvinist activities of the present rulers of China toward the MPR."

Not only is Mongolia in complete sympathy with the Soviet Union's position regarding China, but it has also its own unique problems with that country. These stem both from the historic struggles between the Mongol and Han (Chinese) peoples and from the current situation which finds Mongols divided by the border. There are more Mongols in China (mainly in Inner Mongolia) than in the MPR. Fearing a "Pan-Mongol" movement, the Chinese have attempted to blunt the nationalism of these Mongols and consequently have been accused by the MPR of trying to eliminate Mongolian culture in China. On 27 August, Ulan Bator radio complained:

> Everyone knows that each nationality has its own culture and that if that culture is destroyed the nationality in effect no longer exists. . . . Attempts have been made [by the Chinese leader-

ship] to replace Mongolian culture with Han culture, including the settlement in Inner Mongolia of Hans from other provinces. . . . This makes it doubtful whether the Mongolian spoken and written languages, customs and ways can long be preserved.

Other Countries. In addition to numerous cultural, scientific, and trade agreements made during recent years, the MPR has also been active in establishing diplomatic relations. In 1970 it had diplomatic relations with 50 countries, though five years earlier it had relations with only 31. During 1970 the MPR agreed to establish relations at the ambassadorial level with Senegal (10 June), Singapore (11 June), Italy (27 June), Sudan (6 July), and Morocco (13 July).

International Party Contacts. Important visitors to Mongolia from communist countries during 1970 included President Ludvík Svoboda of Czechoslovakia (26-29 March); the Cuban minister of defense, Raúl Castro (25-30 April); the secretary of the Central Control Committee of the Hungarian Socialist Workers' Party, Ozkar Barinkai (17-25 June); and Hungarian President Pal Losonczi (29 June-3 July).

Mongolian visitors abroad included a delegation, led by MPRP Secretary Dugersuren, which attended the Nineteenth Congress of the French Communist Party in February. Secretary Lhamsuren led party representatives to the Soviet Union on 11-20 March to study the CPSU's organization in "ideological work." Another delegation headed by Secretary D. Molomjamts visited Czechoslovakia on 4-12 May. MPR President Sambuu led a delegation to Poland on 8-12 June, paying an official visit to the Soviet Union to attend the Lenin Centenary celebration (22 April), returning to the MPR two days later. He was again in the Soviet Union, on 15-20 May, after having attended a CMEA meeting in Warsaw. A party-government delegation led by him visited Bulgaria on 3-6 June and stopped briefly in the Soviet Union on its return to the MPR.

Publications. The MPRP daily newspaper *Unen* (Truth) is edited by Tsendijn Namsray and has a circulation of about 82,000. The party's monthly, *Namyn Andral* (Party Life), is also edited by Namsray. Other newspapers include *Zaluchuudyn Unen* (Young People's Truth), the semiweekly organ of the MRYL (circulation 60,000); *Khudulmur* (Labor), the semiweekly of the CCTU; and *Ulan Od* (Red Star), organ of the Mongolian People's Army, appearing three times a week, which is edited by Colonel J. Yadma. The official MPR news agency is Montsame.

E. S.

NEPAL

The Communist Party of Nepal (CPN) was founded during September 1949 in West Bengal, India, by a small number of Nepali members of the Indian Communist Party. In 1952 the CPN was banned. In 1955 the party softened its politically unrewarding anti-monarchial policy and the following year, in exchange for its temporary acceptance of constitutional monarchy, the ban was lifted. In 1960 King Mahendra proscribed all political parties, dissolved the short-lived Parliament, and assumed all governmental powers. Though the ban on political parties continues, limited legislative powers are held by a "panchayat" (or assembly) system, established in 1962, that extends from the village level to the national level and in which a few CPN members (technically, former members) participate.

As a consequence of the CPN Central Committee's decision in 1955 to drop its strongly anti-monarchial stance, the party split between the "moderate" supporters of the new line under the general secretary, Keshar Jang Rayamajhi, and dissident "extremists," led by Pushpa Lal Shrestha. Following a number of crises within the party, during which time the leadership of the Pushpa Lal group moved to India, in 1962 each group "expelled" the other's leaders. The Sino-Indian conflict of October 1962 contributed to a split among the extremists, with Pushpa Lal's group adopting an attitude critical of China, and a minority faction led by Tulsi Lal Amatya giving China its support. Disagreements over policy led to further minor divisions within the party.

Though it is more accurate to label Nepali communists simply as moderates or extremists, the former are often designated "pro-Soviet" and the latter "pro-Chinese."[1] The moderates, most of whom remain in Nepal, advocate a temporary accommodation with the existing political system in order to improve the communist position. The extremists contend that only by working toward a revolutionary overthrow of the king can they adhere to the true principles of communism.

Although the ban on political parties continues, the moderate faction of the CPN has been able to function more or less openly. In 1959, in Nepal's first parliamentary election, the CPN won 7.5 per cent of the votes and four seats in Parliament. In 1963, CPN members (technically, former members, since political parties continued to be proscribed) were said to have won 18 seats in the newly instituted 125-member National Panchayat. It is not known how many of the party's members currently participate in the National Panchayat, but it is estimated that 10 to 15 per cent of the deputies are CPN sympathizers (*World Strength of the Communist Party Organizations*, Washington, D.C., 1970).

Before the 1960 ban on parties the CPN claimed to have 6,000 full members and 2,000 cadets or candidates (*Samiksha*, 11 June 1963). Current estimates of CPN membership vary widely. A U.S. government source (*World Strength of the Communist Party Organizations*, Washington, D.C., 1970), puts the total membership at 8,000 and adds that the party's own claim is nearly

---

[1]An important exception among the extremists is Pushpa Lal. Although often accused of being pro-Chinese, he has never made such a claim and in fact maintains close ties with the pro-Soviet Communist Party of India.

twice this figure. Other unofficial estimates are in the range of 1,000 to 2,000 members. In any case, the number of those active in party work is small. The relative strength of the factions cannot be ascertained accurately, but it is believed that the extremists are the more numerous and that the majority of them support the pro-Chinese policies of Tulsi Lal. The population of Nepal is 11,200,000 (estimated 1970).

Regionally, communist strength in Nepal is concentrated in the Kathmandu Valley and in the eastern portion of the Terai, a narrow plain adjoining India. In the hill areas communist influence is limited to a few towns, such as Palpa and Dharan. The extremist faction residing in India enjoys the support in Nepal of a rather large "Maoist" student population and of some sections of the peasantry.

Leadership and Organization. Little is known of the leadership of the moderate CPN faction. A report on its "Third Congress" (appearing in the Indian communist newspaper *New Age*, New Delhi, 12 January 1969; see *YICA*, 1969, p. 614) gave no information other than to state that a Central Committee of 15 full and 7 alternate members had been elected. Rayamajhi is known to be the secretary-general; another leader, and member of the Politburo of the Central Committee, is Kamar Shah. Though officially disbanded, the faction's organizational structure includes, in addition to the aforementioned central bodies, regional committees and local cells.

The left faction, in India, although itself divided geographically as well as ideologically into groupings around Pushpa Lal (in Benares) and Tulsi Lal (in Darbhanga), maintained a unified party structure during 1970. As in the case of the moderate faction, little is known of the current leadership. Tulsi Lal is the general secretary. A nine-member Politburo, elected at the faction's "Third Congress" in 1962, consisted of Tulsi Lal, Pushpa Lal, Hikmat Singh, Devendra Ray Shrestha, Bharat Mohan Adhikari, Jai Govind Shah, Bharat Roy Joshi, Punne Prataya Rana, and Mahesh Kumar Upadhyaya. Kamal Koriala was identified as a member of the faction's Politburo when he was released from prison in early 1970, after having served a two-year sentence for participation in subversive activities during 1961-62.

Other prominent members (or "former members") of the CPN representing various shades of the party's political spectrum, and who may or may not be associated with the three leaderships mentioned above, include the following: Shailendra Kumar Upadhyaya, a "moderate" who was appointed Home and Panchayat minister in June 1970; D. P. Adhikari, reportedly back from residence in India; and Shambu Ram Shrestha and Man Mohan Adhikari (one of the most popular communist leaders), both released in 1969 after long prison terms.

A significant CPN weakness is that nearly all the top leaders come from the three most prosperous high-caste communities in Nepal: (1) the Brahmans of the Terai and Kathmandu, (2) the Vaisya (commercial) castes of the Newar community in the Kathmandu Valley, and (3) the Chettri (Kshatriya or warrior, now mostly landowning) castes of the Terai and lower hill areas (Leo E. Rose, "Communism under High Atmospheric Conditions," in *The Communist Revolution in Asia*, ed. Robert A. Scalapino, 2d ed., Englewood Cliffs, N.J., 1969). Caste antagonisms clearly influence and accentuate rivalries within the party. Rayamajhi is a Brahman, while both Tulsi Lal and Pushpa Lal are Newars.

Domestic Attitudes and Activities. The political system in Nepal is dominated by King Mahendra. The panchayats constitute the legislative assemblies, extending from the town to the national level. These have become increasingly subordinate to royal influence since their establishment in 1962. They continue, however, to receive tentative support from CPN moderates. Potentially lending themselves to CPN infiltration, in view of party experience up to 1960 in organizing social front groups, are the four-tiered "class organizations." They elect their own representatives to the parallel four-tiered panchayats at each level, with a specified number of members from each of six classes: peasants, labor, women, graduates, youth, and former servicemen.[2]

The CPN, whose organization was not completely destroyed by the 1960 proscription of political parties, initially benefited from what amounted to preferential treatment as compared with other "former" political movements—notably the Nepali Congress Party, which until 1960 was the major anti-monarchy force in Nepal. In an effort to create a balance, King Mahendra granted pardons in 1968 to imprisoned and exiled leaders of the Nepali Congress Party. After one of these men (B. P. Koirala) made statements critical of the monarchy, communist leaders Man Mohan Adhikari and Shambu Ram Shrestha were released from prison, apparently to create a balance of political forces.

Home Minister (and former CPN member) S. K. Upadhyaya was reported to have suggested in mid-1970 that King Mahendra modify the panchayat system. Among other changes he recommended enlarging the franchise for elections to the National Panchayat, allowing the public and the press to attend sessions of that body, and amending the Press Act, which currently permits the government to take legal action against any journal. Certain advisers to the king voiced opposition against the universal franchise as being tantamount to revival of the party system. King Mahendra did agree to allow application of the Press Act to become subject to judicial review (*Far Eastern Economic Review*, 9 July).

Supporters of Pushpa Lal, referred to as Maoists, received attention in the Nepali press on various occasions. In February a number of persons were arrested and large quantities of propaganda materials seized at Bhaktapur, adjacent to the district of Kathmandu. In Biratnagar, southeastern Nepal, the chairman of the Baklauri village panchayat, who was secretary of the local CPN unit before 1960, was arrested early in the year. The Bartung model village panchayat area in the district of Palpa, west of Kathmandu, was described by one paper as a "center for Maoist propaganda." The weekly *Arati* (Kathmandu, 2 February) reported that the panchayat's chairman was calling upon the people to "teach Maoism to their children." The paper also indicated that the chairman had received money from a certain embassy for distributing "Maoist propaganda."

District panchayat elections held during April and May throughout the country were said to have allowed Maoist elements to come to power in the Terhathum district of northeastern Nepal. The pro-Soviet weekly *Samiksha* stated on 11 September that these elements were "not only propagating Maoism, but also collecting subscriptions forcibly, conducting raids on the houses of anti-social and feudal elements and beating them."

According to the same source, Maoist "Naxalites" from India (see *India*) had infiltrated Terhathum and the adjacent Taplejung districts. Portraits of Mao Tse-tung could be found in most primary and secondary schools there. Earlier in the year, there were reports that the Indian Naxalite leader Kanu Sanyal had entered eastern Nepal with more than 100 followers and made contact with the Chinese Embassy in Kathmandu (*Pratidhwani* weekly, Kathmandu, 1 May). Another report stated that Sanyal had visited Dharan in eastern Nepal during 24-26 April and held secret consultations with former communists and students, having decided to foment disturbances within educational and industrial centers from Dharan and Biratnagar as bases (*Arati*, 23 May).

Toward the end of 1969 and during 1970 there were indications that CPN elements might align themselves with sections of the Nepali Congress Party. CPN leader Shambu Ram Shrestha, however, revealed an attitude critical of that party. In an interview with the weekly *Asiali Awaz* (Kathmandu, 17 July), he asserted that B. P. Koirala and his followers had been attempting

---

[2]Of the 125 members of the National Panchayat, only 15 are elected from the class organizations.

since 1961 to capture power in Nepal through the political cooperation and facilities provided by the Indian government. Because of this, he said, they "remain silent on or oppose issues which are in the interests of Nepal."

A meeting of Nepali Congress leaders, held at Bombay in March, was attended by various high-ranking party members such as B. P. Koirala, Subarna Shamsher, Ganesh Man Singh, and included CPN representatives. Subarna Shamsher and another leader were reported to have proposed unsuccessfully that the Nepali Congress adopt a policy of striving for increased participation within the panchayat system. The party reportedly split over the issue, but Koirala was said to have remained uncommitted. The position of the CPN members attending the meeting was not determined, although the communists, too, have been sharply divided over pro- and anti-monarchical opinions.

Centers for the most active political forces are Tribhuvan University in Kathmandu and the various colleges throughout the country. Students, disenchanted with the Nepalese government and concerned about the high number of unemployed graduates, began agitating on a large scale in 1969. In 1970 their activities increased substantially.

Nepali students generally identify themselves as followers either of the Maoist "progressives," supporting Pushpa Lal, or of the "democratic" faction which aligns itself with the Nepali Congress Party. A minor third force is avowedly "nationalist." "Non-communist" students in 1969 displaced "progressives" in control over the Tribhuvan University Students' Union, the country's major student organization, but lost this position in the annual election of 14 August 1970, when "progressives" won back four of the five executive posts in a close contest where they had a majority of eleven votes among 600 cast. The only non-communist winner was a Nepali Congress sympathizer, who was elected treasurer.

Before the elections, the university's dominant pro-Nepali Congress students in April 1970 had organized the "first national democratic student conference," with the purpose of forming a national student organization to seek the establishment of a "freely elected government." About 150 students met on 22 April. On the following day, police broke up the conference, and arrested 70. They were charged with delivering highly objectionable political speeches." A second meeting was held clandestinely on 27 April, at which time the Nepal Students' Union, with Bipin Koirala as chairman, was founded. This new grouping presents a challenge to the smaller, pro-government Nationalist Independent Union (the only officially registered national students' union) and particularly to the pro-Chinese All-Nepal Free Student Union. Arrests of activists in the Nepal Students' Union were frequent during the year. Members complained that, although 80 per cent of Nepali students were not communist sympathizers, the government by contrast had permitted a small number of Maoists in 1969 illegally to form the All-Nepal Free Student Union and subsequently done little to curb their activities.

International Views and Positions. Nepal's geographic position has caused the country's political interests to focus internationally on India and China. Sandwiched between these two mutually hostile giant neighbors, Nepal had adopted an official position of neutrality between them. China and India are either criticized or praised by political forces in Nepal. India, which is by far the largest source of Nepal's trade and aid, has been criticized vehemently by many local groups. Demands from communists and non-communists alike that India withdraw its 250-man military mission were successful in 1970. Also in 1970, tensions began to develop following unsuccessful attempts to renegotiate a trade and transit treaty between the two countries. The situation was given wide publicity by the Chinese.

In his interview with *Asiali Awaz* (17 July), Shambu Ram Shrestha was highly critical of India's policies toward Nepal. Calling upon Indian leaders to "renounce the policy followed by the

British imperialists" and to develop Nepal-India relations on the basis of equality, he said: "[The Indians] regard Nepal's northern border as their defense line. They baselessly maintain that our other friendly neighbor, the People's Republic of China, will commit aggression."

Also indicating an attitude favorable toward China was the popular CPN leader Man Mohan Adhikari, who, since his release from prison in 1969, apparently has not committed himself to either the moderate or extremist groups. *Samiksha* (24 July) reported Adhikari as having declared: "We shall be guided by the brilliant light of the thoughts of Mao Tse-tung." Adhikari has expressed anti-Indian, anti-Soviet, and pro-Chinese sentiments since his release from prison, but within the context of a nonaligned foreign policy.

Publications. The pro-Soviet weekly *Samiksha* (Analysis) is published in Kathmandu and edited by "former communist" Madan Dixit, a close associate of S. K. Upadhyaya. Until parties were declared illegal in 1960, the CPN had an official organ called *Navayug* (New Age).

E. S.

NEW ZEALAND

The Communist Party of New Zealand (CPNZ) was founded in December 1920. Since 1963 the party has followed a pro-Chinese line. A pro-Soviet splinter group, the Socialist Unity Party (SUP), is headed by a former CPNZ chairman, George Jackson, who resigned from the parent party in 1966. The Socialist Action League (SAL), a Trotskyist group organized in late 1969, is headed by George Fyson. All have legal status.

The combined membership of the three parties is not more than 500—about 300 for the CPNZ, 100 for the SUP, and perhaps fewer than 100 for the SAL. The population of New Zealand is 2,786,000 (estimated 1969). CPNZ membership has declined steadily from a high of about 2,000 at the end of the Second World War, and the party has played a negligible role in the country's political life. No communist candidate has ever been elected to political office. In the November 1969 Parliamentary election the CPNZ received 364 votes, compared with 1,207 in 1966 and 2,868 in 1963. Some 30 communists in all—estimated at 15 each for the CPNZ and SUP—are believed to hold executive positions in the trade union movement.

The CPNZ accuses the Labour Party of having helped make New Zealand a stronghold of social democracy by failing to adopt the revolutionary posture needed to develop in workers the proletarian consciousness which could bring about social change through radical demands. Preempting worker support, the Labour Party has effectively robbed the CPNZ of any real hopes for electoral success. In response to this situation, the CPNZ, instead of watering down its revolutionary goals, as many communist parties elsewhere have done, has chosen to break completely with social-democratic movements and to disavow any expectation of a possible transition to socialism through electoral processes.

The CPNZ. Leadership and Organization. The leading organs of the CPNZ are the National Committee and its Political Committee and Secretariat; below this level are district committees in the major cities. The general secretary and leading figure is Victor Wilcox. The National Committee includes also Ron Taylor (acting CPNZ chairman), John Foulds, Ralph Hegman, William McAra, Hugh McLeod, Ray Nunes, A. Rait, and Rita Smith. Nunes is a member of both the Political Committee and the Secretariat; McAra and Hegman are members of the Political Committee. Rait is the party's Auckland district secretary. The party press provides only fragmentary information concerning the CPNZ leadership, and contributors are seldom identified.

Party Internal Affairs. Throughout its existence, the CPNZ has been torn by factional strife between those determined to maintain an ideologically "pure" and elite core of revolutionaries— even at the expense of possible electoral gain—and those bent on pragmatic political advance. Frequent purges have failed to consolidate the party, whose continuing divisions demonstrate the frustration of a tiny party relegated to the outermost fringe of the nation's political arena and unable to relate Marxist-Leninist theory to the context of day-to-day activity.

CPNZ consolidation and recruitment have been hampered continuously by the occasional emergence, either within or outside the party, of Trotskyist and other factional groupings. The formation in late 1969 of a "Revolutionary Committee within the CPNZ" by an Auckland district group led to the expulsion of its leader, S. W. Taylor, and a number of his adherents. The party leadership claimed a year later that the Taylor group had no following, having been exposed as a "ludicrous religious form of Trotskyism" (*People's Voice*, 16 September 1970). A new purge was undertaken in 1970, this time in the Wellington district, but affecting also the national base of the CPNZ. The first indication of this came in a National Committee statement in February which declared that the principle of democratic centralism had been "breached in practice by many in [the] party including leading members." The statement urged: "[Members should] accept the duty individually and collectively to study the Thought of Mao Tse-tung, the Lenin of our era, providing as it does the ideological, political, and organizational guide to resolving the many problems and differences which still exist at all levels in our party." General Secretary Wilcox urged that "temporarily antagonistic" contradictions within the party be "reduced to non-antagonistic ones," and condemned those who, "under the cloak of revolutionary phrases," adopted "the usual approach of the petty bourgeoisie in [CPNZ] ranks during periods of inner party struggle." (*Ibid.*, 4 March.)

In August, Wilcox announced that efforts to overcome differences between the central leadership in Auckland and the Wellington district leadership had met with total failure. On this basis the Wellington district committee was to be dissolved and reorganized, in accordance with a Political Committee ruling. Wilcox charged that for the previous eighteen months the Wellington leadership, headed by Jack Manson (a member of both the National Committee and the Political Committee) and R. Bailey had worked to develop an anti-party group taking an opportunist approach to class struggle and supporting actions of reformist trade union leaders. The group, moreover, allegedly had a negative attitude toward, and failed to recognize the importance of, the revolutionary youth movement. (*Ibid.*, 26 August.) The party justified the action as a necessity in the "revolutionary struggle that separates the bourgeois ideological chaff from the proletarian ideological grain"—the more revolutionary a proletarian party became, the more the opportunists were forced to expose themselves—and cited the example of the Russian Bolshevik minority's seizure of state power: "It is not the size of the communist party that determines its influence but the purity of its ideology." (*Ibid.*, 2 September.)

The opposition leaders appeared to retain control of the majority in the Wellington party district. The Secretariat convened in special session on 12 September and noted that the group had continued to disseminate propaganda in the name of the Wellington district CPNZ despite their having "refused to sign a reaffirmation of the ideological, political, and organizational principles of the CPNZ and Marxism-Leninism," and had thus "placed themselves outside the party" (*ibid.*, 16 September.) The formal expulsion of the six-member Wellington leadership was announced on 21 October in the *People's Voice*, which stated that the Political Committee, on the grounds that "the progressive movement must be able to identify those who menace it while posing as members of it," had agreed to make the expulsions public. Those expelled were Jack Manson, R. Bailey, P. Kelly, G. Goddard, K. Stanton, and R. I. Smith. According to the announcement, reenrollment in the Wellington district branch (excluding those expelled) would continue until 11 November. The decision to expel the six leaders had been taken because of the "complete rejection by them of the decision by the National and Political Committees to reorganize the Wellington district." The "bourgeois line of class collaboration" propagated by them within the unions was said to have been an anti-party line which, by restricting struggle to levels acceptable to the trade union hierarchy, amounted to maintaining industrial peace and perpetuating the existing system of exploitation of the working class.

Domestic Attitudes and Activities. In practice, the CPNZ has virtually no coherent political program. Acknowledging that "revolutionary potentialities" in New Zealand are practically nonexistent, the party agitates over specific grievances against "class enemies" and the government, while maintaining that the capitalist system in New Zealand is heading for inevitable collapse. (Ironically, the party's most active role is in its Chinese trade concession in black tea, the sale of which is regularly advertised in the party press.) The party leadership stresses that it is not trying to build the CPNZ into a mass party, lest it suffer corruption by "trade unionism" and abandon revolutionary objectives. This lack of direction and an accompanying low morale within the party are more or less constant problems and are frequently the subjects of reports and criticisms by party leaders. Reflecting the party's limitations, both the *People's Voice* and the *New Zealand Communist Review* draw heavily from Chinese news agency materials and frequently resort to reprinting articles from their own earlier issues. With a dearth of party theoreticians, they are obliged openly to solicit written material.

The cornerstone of CPNZ ideology is Lenin's "mass-line" method as embodied in Maoist theory. Thus, the party seeks to "discover and train a network of people capable of recognizing and analyzing important political developments and to give the benefit of that analysis to the progressive movement, stressing the necessity, as Mao taught, of seeking truth from facts." The "scattered and unsystematic ideas of the masses must be concentrated through study, then propagated and explained to the masses until the masses embrace them as their own and translate them into action and test the correctness of these ideas in such action." (*People's Voice*, 17 June 1970).

The party saw New Zealand society as being "in the era of the final defeat of capitalism," dominated by local and U.S. monopolists. The trade unions— "a far cry from Marx's schools of revolution"—were merely "schools of reformism and a bulwark of social democracy." The "Establishment," by maintaining strong bonds with the trade union hierarchy, had succeeded in maintaining a docile, nonrevolutionary working class—a "gilt-edged guarantee to 'political stability'" and inroads by foreign capital. Thus a major party task must be to expose the contradiction between revolutionary class struggle and class collaboration, or reformism, so as to transform the unions into militant organizations of class struggle. A clear distinction was to be made, however, between the party's attitude toward the union leadership and the potentially revolutionary but presently misled rank and file. Basic party strategy, therefore, would be to work within the unions while at the same time attacking their policies. (*New Zealand Communist Review*, January-February.)

The party professed to see three stages of exploitation of workers under the capitalist redistribution of worker-created wealth: (1) monopolist seizure of worker-created wealth, of which only a portion was returned to workers as wages; (2) direct and indirect taxation to maintain an ever-growing nonproductive state apparatus; and (3) state and local levies. Thus, worker demands must not be confined to "a fair day's wage" and lower taxes, but extended to a struggle for the abolition of the entire capitalist "wage-swindle system." (*People's Voice*, 10 June.)

The party continued to have little success in drawing young persons to its ranks, although it does appear to have substantial influence within one left-radical group, the anti-Vietnam war, anti-U.S. Progressive Youth Movement (PYM), headed by Chris Lind. The CPNZ press regularly carries reports on PYM protests and demonstrations and has defended the PYM against attacks by the pro-Soviet Socialist Unity Party. A *People's Voice* article (25 February) insinuated that the government was condoning police brutality and acts of violence against the PYM by "'undetectable' fascist gangs." Unable to take control of the PYM or any other youth organization, however, the CPNZ has appealed to anti-imperialist youths to recognize that for their protest to become a potent force for social change, the communist party must occupy "a vital place" among young revolutionaries. The "Establishment" could be overcome only by "organization, based on Marxism-Leninism and Maoist thought." Rather than merely expressing contempt for trade unions, young persons were urged to work within them so as to aid in shattering "reformist illusions." (Wilcox, in *New Zealand Communist Review*, July.) CPNZ National Committee member Ray Nunes represented the party at a "Radical Activist Congress" in Wellington on 16 August which was attended by radical youth leaders and by all leftist parties. Nunes debated Socialist Action League representative Keith Locke on "Mao or Trotsky: Which Way for the Revolution in New Zealand?"

The CPNZ's traditional attacks on the British monarchy and on New Zealand's role as a Commonwealth member were renewed in connection with the March visit of Queen Elizabeth. The visit—a "non-event" in the eyes of the party, and "a circus whose only effect can be to distract attention from real issues"—was said to be "based on hypocrisy and illusion." Royalty, the CPNZ asserted, had been "stranded on the shores of history" and no longer had any useful function, while the Commonwealth itself was a "legal fiction" which the New Zealand government used as a platform when it suited its interests. New Zealand had participated in "England's wars," but had been "just as quick to jump into the wars of the U.S."—in Korea and in Vietnam. The one remaining bond between England and New Zealand—the fact that England was a good market for New Zealand's primary produce—would be destroyed should Britain join the EEC (European Economic Community). (*People's Voice*, 11 March.)

The party continued to present itself as the only New Zealand political entity seeking to further the interests of the Maori minority. *People's Voice* (4 February) claimed that, notwithstanding the 1840 Waitangi Treaty on the safeguarding of Maori rights, the Maoris had been "systematically robbed of their heritage by war, by forcible seizure, by swindling, by economic pressure, and by tricky legislation" in a bid by the authorities to assimilate them into New Zealand capitalist society and to corrupt their traditional form of communal life. Once assimilated, Maoris were severely limited in the choice of jobs because of the inferior education provided them; when employed, they earned less than whites, and they suffered more unemployment.

International Views and Positions. The CPNZ frequently asserts that it is "the sole party in the Capitalist West to remain true to the spirit of October." In its Russian Revolution anniversary issue (November 1970), *New Zealand Communist Review's* editorial board asserted that the party, "attacked from within and without," had "clung firmly to the inviolable truth of Marxism-Leninism." It had "defeated its external enemies and repeatedly strengthened itself by purging the opportunists and scabs within its ranks."

CPNZ international positions faithfully reflect those of the Chinese Communist Party, which in turn gives prominence to the pro-Chinese articles and statements of the CPNZ and never fails to give New Zealand communists a cordial reception in Peking. In 1970, Wilcox and Taylor were in Peking from 15 to 20 April. They met with Chou En-lai, K'ang Sheng, Chang Ch'un-ch'iao, and other Chinese leaders, and a banquet was given in their honor the day after their arrival. In a typical demonstration of mutual CPNZ-CCP admiration, an article on Lenin first published in the April issue of the *New Zealand Communist Review* was later released by the NCNA in abbreviated form, and the text of the NCNA release then reproduced in *People's Voice* (24 June). The article hailed Lenin as "the great continuer and developer of Marxism in the era of imperialism," and also praised Stalin, under whose leadership the Russian people had "unfolded miracles of achievement" and, "out of chaos," fashioned the world's first working-class state and nation.

It condemned the "traitors" who had concealed themselves within the Soviet party and who, after Stalin's death, had set about to destroy its Marxist-Leninist foundation. Then, the article proceeded, it had become the lot of Mao to rescue Marxism-Leninism from the revisionist stranglehold of Khrushchev and his cohorts and to solve the problem of how to prevent the socialist revolution from being turned back along the capitalist path.

Commemorating the centenary of Lenin's birth, the CPNZ noted that the occasion was being observed "for ulterior motives" by the "Red Czars," who had twisted Lenin's principles to suit their own ends and who, out of opportunism, ignored Lenin's tenet on the necessity of arming the proletariat against the bourgeoisie. CPNZ members were urged to dedicate the centenary to renewing the study and practice of Mao's teachings on continual struggle against those who would revise and distort Leninism. (*People's Voice*, 22 April.) Two companion articles in the party newspaper (*ibid.*, 15 and 22 April) purported to reveal a "severe, deepening crisis" in Soviet industry and agriculture. Soviet leaders allegedly had undermined the dictatorship of the proletariat and restored capitalism, with the result that the people were impoverished and the economy was ruined.

An alleged "Red Czar" nuclear buildup along the Chinese border was cited as evidence that the Soviets' professed advocacy of peaceful coexistence applied only to their "collaboration and appeasement with [U.S.] imperialism," and that their talk of banning nuclear weapons was a "confidence trick" to limit the "nuclear club." All of which, according to the CPNZ, reaffirmed Mao's edict that "reactionary forces on the verge of extinction invariably conduct desperate struggles" and "are bound to resort to military adventure and political deception in all their forms in order to save themselves from extinction." (*Ibid.*, 12 August.)

The launching, in April, of China's first satellite was heralded by the CPNZ as a "mighty victory for the world's revolutionary people," and a "sickening poke in the eye for all those who have military ambitions towards the heart of socialism, People's China." The achievement "made a mockery of the Soviet revisionists who had been telling their people that China was technically in the stone age," and it "put in their place the petty puppets like [New Zealand Premier Keith] Holyoake who had been prattling about China being in chaos as a result of the cultural revolution." (*Ibid.*, 29 April.)

For the CPNZ, however, it is not the Soviet Union, but the United States, that is "Enemy No. 1." An article in *People's Voice* (4 March) declared that recent United Nations voting revealed clearly the extent to which New Zealand was "under the U.S. imperialist thumb." New Zealand had voted against China's taking its "rightful place" in the U.N., in favor of the continued "occupation" of South Korea, and against the rights of West Irians in "fascist" Indonesia. It had abstained from voting on the "violation of human rights" in Israeli-occupied Arab territories and, to its "everlasting disgrace," on the resolution condemning South Africa's policy of apartheid and mistreatment of political prisoners. This record, the party contended, showed that government representatives had opposed or abstained from voting on every resolution to support "the rights or welfare of non-white peoples."

CPNZ pronouncements on the Vietnam war did not deviate from Chinese statements. The party alleged in April that the "grave danger of New Zealand being led into an escalated war in Indochina and ultimately with China" required "urgent intensification of the pressure to withdraw New Zealand troops from Vietnam." Holyoake, as a "willing stooge" for the United States, was prepared to involve New Zealand forces in any SEATO intervention to "help tottering tyrannies fight their own peoples." The government's "forward defense" policy, applied as an excuse to send troops overseas, allegedly was intended to bolster a U.S.-British bid to "plunder Asian lands by force." (*Ibid.*, 8 April.)

U.S. Vice-President Spiro Agnew's visit to New Zealand, in January, was seen by the CPNZ as part of the "fraudulent de-Americanization policy" in Southeast Asia, described by the party as a device for "increasing the direct participation of the Vietnamese puppet regime and the satellite governments like New Zealand, Australia, Thailand, the Philippines, and Taiwan." As for the "Vietnamization" policy, this was "designed to appease public opinion and gain at lower cost the U.S. aim to conquer Vietnam." (*Ibid.*, 28 January.) The CPNZ Secretariat in April predicted that the "desperate extension of aggression by the U.S. administration" into Cambodia would be used to "justify further aggression by the SEATO powers under the guise of combating communist aggression." Faced with military defeat, world-wide protest, severe internal rebellion, and economic problems, the United States was resorting to multifaceted tactics to achieve global dominance. (*Ibid.*, 15 April.)

The CPNZ accused the Soviets of supporting U.S. "aggression" in Indochina by (1) Sino-Soviet border provocations, (2) "openly supplying the U.S. with raw materials necessary for the continuance of the war," and (3) "bringing pressure to bear on the Vietnamese to force them to make a deal with the U.S. aggressors." Kosygin's "junta" was said to have employed "exactly the same tactics before, and failed," in efforts "to establish a Russian 'presence' in Southeast Asia and to exclude Chinese influence." The Soviets, further, had not hesitated to "wave a threat of war over People's China in an effort to distract its attention from that part of the world," and, the CPNZ concluded, were "prepared to see the national liberation struggle in Southeast Asia go down to defeat if it would give their influence in the area a foothold." (*Ibid.*, 3 June.)

The CPNZ maintains close relations with the pro-Chinese splinter Australian Communist Party (Marxist-Leninist). A joint communiqué issued during a visit to New Zealand from 3 to 6 September by E. F. Hill, the chairman of that party, repudiated "revisionism, right opportunism, left sectarianism, parliamentarianism, and trade union politics," and declared that world revolution would be achieved only by armed struggle (*ibid.*, 9 September).

The CPNZ frequently issues reports on the social and economic achievements of Albania. A series of articles on that country appeared in the *People's Voice* following a visit there in September by a CPNZ youth delegation which Len Parker headed.

Publications. The CPNZ's weekly newspaper, *People's Voice*, and its monthly journal, *New Zealand Communist Review*, are published in Auckland. In addition, Ron Taylor broadcasts to New Zealand regularly in a "Letter from Albania" over Tirana radio.

*   *   *

The SUP. Socialist Unity Party leaders include, besides chairman George Jackson, F. E. McNulty (general secretary of the New Zealand Freezing Workers' Union), G. H. Andersen (secretary of the Northern Drivers' Union), and Alex Drennan. The party's principal role continues to be within organized labor. The SUP has negligible influence within the international communist movement and is not recognized, even in pro-Soviet quarters, as the official communist party of New Zealand. The party continues to act as a mouthpiece for Soviet policies, and indications are that it may be receiving some financial support from Moscow. The average age of SUP members is high, and the party appears to hold little appeal for youth.

The SUP monthly newspaper, the *New Zealand Tribune*, is published in Wellington.

*   *   *

The SAL. The first national conference of the Socialist Action League, held in Wellington on 22-24 August 1970, elected George Fyson as national secretary and Hugh Fyson as editor of the SAL biweekly newspaper *Socialist Action*. The conference endorsed the main document of the

1969 World Congress of the Fourth International, "The New Rise of the World Revolution." A political report, by Keith Locke, noted that of the leftist movements in New Zealand, only the SAL had "a clear orientation towards the Labour Party." Uncompromising in its opposition to Labour's right-wing leadership and program, the SAL supported the party because it was based on the union movement and retained the support of the overwhelming majority of the working class. Any significant working-class radicalization, Locke declared, would inevitably be expressed within the Labour Party. (*Intercontinental Press*, New York, 21 September.)

Condemning "ultra-leftism," Hugh Fyson wrote in *Socialist Action* (5 June) that there could be no short cut to socialist transformation, no substitute for the gradual building of a mass revolutionary movement. No mass revolutionary movement existed in New Zealand at the present time, nor any immediate fascist danger. Thus, ultra-leftist tactics could not hope to arouse ordinary New Zealanders to revolution but, on the contrary, gave the impression that the revolutionary movement was "at odds with reality."

V. B.

PAKISTAN

The Communist Party of Pakistan (CPP) was founded in 1948 from the sections of the Communist Party of India that had been functioning in those areas of the subcontinent from which Pakistan was created by partition in the previous year. The party's origins go back to the early 1920's, when a predominantly Moslem group of political activists, based in Calcutta, was operating in Bengal. By 1947 the movement in Bengal had lost almost completely its Moslem character and had come under control of Hindu politicians. Eastern Bengal became East Pakistan through the partition, and in the early 1950's the strength of the CPP in that area was severely reduced by governmental suppression and communal hostilities that forced large numbers of Hindus to seek refuge in India, taking with them an estimated two-thirds of the party membership.[1] Leaders who opted for East Pakistan at the time of partition include Moni Singh, who was imprisoned for most of the next twenty years,[2] and Ila Mitra, who became an exile in India.

The CPP has been proscribed since 1954 and at present is numerically and organizationally very weak, particularly in West Pakistan. Its membership is estimated at 500 in West Pakistan and 2,500 in East Pakistan,[3] where there is generally considered to be a higher degree of political awareness, largely the result of grievances over economic and political inequalities between the two wings of the country. The population of Pakistan is 136,900,000 (estimated 1970), of which more than half live in East Pakistan. Although CPP members pay dues and keep informed, generally they have not been active and there seems to be little coordination among them. No national or regional meeting is known to have been held since 1953.

The CPP has been involved only to a limited degree in the trade union movement. Professionally, most of its members are teachers, representing all levels of education. Since students are one of the most active leftist forces, it is probably among them that the communists exercise their greatest influence.

Although the CPP is the traditional communist party in Pakistan, recent communist activities appear to be limited to organizations identified as the Communist Party of East Pakistan (a pro-Soviet party that attended the International Meeting of Communist and Workers' Parties in Moscow in June 1969) and the Communist Party of East Pakistan (Marxist-Leninist), a Maoist party formed in mid-1970.

In one of the rare public statements by Pakistani communists, the unidentified general secretary of the Communist Party of East Pakistan contributed an article to the Lenin Centenary issue of the *World Marxist Review* (May 1970), in which he gave his party's view on a number of do-

---

[1]Marcus F. Franda, "Communism and Regional Politics in East Pakistan," *Asian Survey*, Berkeley, July 1970.

[2]On 18 December 1970, President Yahya Khan decreed that "all" political prisoners (estimated at 1,700) be released. Moni Singh was presumably included.

[3]Franda, *op. cit.* In *World Strength of the Communist Party Organizations*, Washington, D.C., 1970, much lower figures are given: 700 in East Pakistan and 750 in West Pakistan.

mestic developments. He suggested that the party to a large extent had been responsible for the change in government in 1969: "As a result of our united front policy the people of East and West Pakistan fought heroically and unitedly and the reactionary authoritarian Ayub regime was toppled." He condemned the pro-Chinese party, which had broken away in 1968 and since become divided into three or four splinter groups, for advocating an election boycott and armed struggle. Particularly singled out for attack was the Awami (People's) League, the most powerful East Pakistan party. The Awami League, he said, was justified in demanding full autonomy for East Pakistan, and declared that his own party's program included recognition of the right to self-determination and secession for all Pakistani nationalities; but he denounced the Awami League's efforts to arouse Bengali chauvinism and its calling all non-Bengalis "exploiters of East Pakistan." The main election slogan of the Communist Party of East Pakistan, according to the general secretary, was "unity of all the democratic forces of Pakistan against the Right-reactionary and communal forces . . . a democratic constitution [and] a patriotic democratic government."

Owing to the ban on communist activities, many communists have sought to gain influence by working within the National Awami Party (or National People's Party; NAP—see below), which itself has been divided along Sino-Soviet lines since 1966, with a formal split occurring in mid-1968.

The NAP. The National Awami Party was founded in 1957 by the union of a breakway faction of the Awami League and the Ganatantri Dal (Democratic Party) in East Pakistan with the Azad Pakistan Party (or Free Pakistan Party) and several regional groupings in West Pakistan. After the CPP was banned in 1954, communists joined or cooperated with the above organizations and continued to support the NAP when it was formed. Now divided into two organizations, the NAP has always been a small party operating in both East and West Pakistan, although more active in the former wing.

Two main leadership groups of the NAP have been functioning as separate parties since the beginning of 1968. One, commonly called "pro-Soviet," has Khan Abdul Wali Khan as president. The other, "pro-Chinese" party is led by Maulana Abdul Hamid Bhashani, founder of the NAP in East Pakistan. Wali Khan's NAP operates in both wings of the country, but is stronger in West Pakistan, particularly in the Peshawar plain of the Northwest Frontier Province, the base of the pre-independence "Red Shirts," or Khudai Khitmatgars (Servants of God), of Abdul Ghaffar Khan, Wali Khan's father. Bhashani's party, which has been weakened by the appearance of three dissenting factions since 1969, is almost exclusively a party of East Pakistan. Although termed "pro-Soviet" and "pro-Chinese," both parties are concerned internationally more with eliminating or limiting the influence of the countries of the West than with trying to function within the framework of an international ideology. Both have appealed to the government to remove the ban on communist organizations.

The Pro-Soviet NAP. Wali Khan's party, which has retained the Soviet recognition accorded the united NAP as the most "progressive" legal party in the country, is led in East Pakistan by Professor Muzaffar Ahmed, who had precipitated the formal break in the NAP. Mahumdul Huq Usmani is the secretary-general of the party's West Pakistan branch. The president of the latter branch was Mian Mahmud Qasuri until 28 July 1970 when he resigned from the party in opposition to Wali Khan's emphasis on full regional autonomy.

The main point in Wali Khan's program was that West Pakistan, instead of being a single unit, should return to its pre-1955 division into four provinces (Punjab, Sind, Baluchistan, and the Northwest Frontier). This demand, pressed by many opposition parties, was met by President Yahya Khan toward the end of 1969, before the start of campaigning for the December general elections. Also high among the party's priorities was a demand for full regional autonomy of the provinces, conceding to the central government only the power to control defense, foreign affairs, and currency matters. Economically, its program called for democratic socialism. Internationally it sought a neutral foreign policy.

Wali Khan's "pro-Soviet" NAP has had little overt association with the CPP. At a January conference of active NAP members in Lahore, the party appealed (unsuccessfully) to the government for withdrawal of the ban on activities of the communist party (Moscow radio, 14 January). According to the organ of the pro-Soviet Communist Party of India, *New Age* (New Delhi, 15 February), the conference adopted a program similar to that of the pro-Soviet Communist Party of East Pakistan. The program was also said to advocate unity between both factions of the NAP and cooperation between them and the Awami League—the popular Bengali party of Sheik Mujibur Rahman, who is the primary figure in the East Pakistan autonomy movement. Such an alliance with the Awami League has been sought most actively by Muzaffar Ahmed in East Pakistan, with the result that some differences have arisen between the western and eastern branches of Wali Khan's party. An alignment with the relatively rightist Awami League would not be favored by party members in West Pakistan, where the league has almost no following.[4] Muzaffar Ahmed and Wali Khan also diverged in their reactions to the Legal Framework Order of March 1970, a decree providing for the drafting of a national constitution for Pakistan by the newly elected National Assembly. The order, which gave the president the authority to dissolve the Assembly if he refused to authenticate the draft constitution or if no draft was produced within 120 days of the elction, was welcomed by Wali Khan, but was opposed by Muzaffar Ahmed as an infringement on the sovereignty of the National Assembly.

The Pro-Chinese NAP. Although the Soviet press indicates approval of Wali Khan's organization, no such recognition has been given by the Chinese Communist Party to the more militant NAP of Maulana Bhashani. Eager to maintain their good relations with the Pakistani government, the Chinese have ignored Bhashani and the pro-Chinese factions and have not supported the autonomy movement in East Pakistan, though they have continued to encourage the pro-Chinese extremists in the neighboring Indian province of West Bengal. At the same time, the Soviet press has attacked Bhashani for propagating the "ultra-left Naxalite line" of the Maoists in India (see *India*, section on "The Naxalites").

Bhashani, an 87-year-old peasant leader, has denied being pro-Chinese; nevertheless, many of his statements reveal pro-Chinese sentiments. He defines the NAP as a broad-based social-democratic party and accepts the cooperation of CPP members within the party. He rejects, however, the concept of a communist Pakistan, advocating instead "Islamic socialism"—a stand that contributed to the divisions within his formerly secularly-oriented party. Bhashani, who has not adopted a Marxist ideology, acknowledges having worked for a long time with many "honest, idealistic, and self-denying" communists, but is critical of a number of "so-called communists" in Pakistan who "speak only of revolution, [but] play the role of opportunists and non-revolutionaries" (*Dainik Pakistan*, Dacca, 2 October). Other leaders of the party, in addition to Bhashani, include Secretary-General Masihur Rahman, elected on 2 August 1970 to replace Mohammed Toaha, and C. R. Aslam, president of the small West Pakistani branch. Much of the party's following comes from the peasants, among whom Bhashani has been active, but it enjoys also some support from students and industrial workers. Its peasant organization, the East Pakistan Krishak Samity (Peasants' Society) is led by Bhashani. It controls also the East Pakistan Students Union and the East Pakistan Sramik Federation (Labor Federation).

The pro-Chinese NAP, which provides the only legal means of political expression for those on the extreme left, has been weakened by the appearance of at least three dissenting factions. Ac-

---

[4]M. Rashiduzzaman, "The National Awami Party of Pakistan: Leftist Politics in Crisis," *Pacific Affairs*, Fall 1970.

cording to the *Far Eastern Economic Review* (Hong Kong, 16 January 1971), the splitting was so serious that the party may have ceased to be the "front organization of all pro-Peking left elements." The largest of the three factions, led by Mohammad Toaha and Abdul Huq (trade union and peasant leaders, respectively), severed ties with the NAP during 1970. Toaha, who was secretary-general of the party, resigned on 31 May. Huq, who served as vice-president of the NAP and secretary-general of the Krishak Samity, resigned in June.

Toaha and Huq's disagreement with Bhashani emerged in late 1969 over opposition to the party leader's concept of "Islamic socialism" and his willingness to participate in the December elections instead of unleashing a peasants' revolution.[5] In mid-1970, both men reportedly formed the Communist Party of East Pakistan (Marxist-Leninist), adopting a policy opposing parliamentary tactics and advocating armed revolution. According to *Ananda Bazar Patrika* (Calcutta, 2 October), the dissidents, led by Toaha and Huq, decided to create the new Maoist party at a joint meeting with persons identified as Indian "Naxalites" at an undisclosed location on the Indian-Pakistani border near Sikkim. This new party was said to include former student leaders (believed by government authorities to have been members of the banned Communist Party of East Pakistan) and to have close links with Dacca intellectuals.

Domestically, the new party was reported to be engaged in "considerable field work" in certain districts (*Far Eastern Economic Review*, 16 January 1971). Internationally, it was said to have contacts with Naxalite organizations in West Bengal. A letter sent by the party to its Indian counterpart, the Communist Party of India (Marxist-Leninist), and printed in the latter party's Bengali organ *Deshabrati*, reportedly expressed a desire to establish "closer collaboration" between the two groups to carry out peasant guerrilla activities (*Times of India*, New Delhi, 3 June). The letter was said to have stated: "Like you, our slogans also are: 'China's Chairman is our Chairman' and 'China's path is our path.'" Because China's state relations are friendly with Pakistan and hostile with India, however, the Chinese Communist Party has not given public recognition to the party of Toaha and Huq, as it has to the Indian Maoist party.

Two other dissenting groups remain within the pro-Chinese NAP, both limited to sections of East Pakistan. One, led by Abdul Matin, proclaimed itself to be Maoist and called for direct armed revolution along the lines advocated by the Indian Maoist movement. It has considerable support in Pabna, Abdul Matin's home town, and is involved to some extent in trade union activity in Chittagong. The other, led by Masihur Rahman and Anwar Zahid, is the most moderate in the party. It has indicated a willingness to use the parliamentary system but has made no mention of attempts to form a coalition with other parties.

The splintering of Bhashani's party has had repercussions among students. The pro-Chinese section of the East Pakistan Students' Union has been divided into three groups: one, led by Jamal Haider, calls itself the East Bengal Revolutionary Students' Union and is said to follow Bhashani; another, named the East Bengal Students' Union, supports Abdul Matin's faction; and the third, headed by Dilip Barua, follows Mohammed Toaha (*Pakistan Observer*, Dacca, 3 May).

The Elections. Pakistan's national elections, held on 7 December 1970,[6] were the first since 1947 to be conducted on a direct-vote basis. The provincial elections, held ten days later, were the first since the early 1950's and the first ever in Baluchistan. Other innovations—in addition to the

---

[5] Toaha's views had apparently reversed from those he held in 1969, when he attacked and expelled from the NAP a group of Maoists led by Abdul Matin (see *YICA*, 1970, p. 664).

[6] The national elections, originally scheduled for 5 October, were postponed to December because of flooding in East Pakistan. The cyclone and tidal wave that devastated parts of the same province in November delayed elections only in those areas directly affected.

direct vote, which replaced an electoral college system—included the restoration of West Pakistan's four former provinces and thereby National Assembly representation on the basis of population rather than on a parity between East Pakistan and the former "one unit" of West Pakistan. Instead of controlling half of the 300 National Assembly seats, East Pakistanis could elect 162 legislators, leaving the four western provinces to divide the remaining 138 seats.

Although the Awami League was expected to win easily in East Pakistan, the extent of its gains surpassed all expectations when it won all but two of the province's 162 seats—a majority in the full Assembly, even though it won no seats in the western provinces. The party was also given seven of the 13 Assembly seats reserved for women. In West Pakistan, a surprise came in the form of defeat for many of the traditional "old guard" leaders and victories for candidates of the three-year-old Pakistan People's Party of Zulfiqar Ali Bhutto, which won 81 of the western wing's 138 seats. In the provincial assemblies, the Awami League won 288 of East Pakistan's 300 seats. Bhutto's party won a majority in Punjab and a plurality in Sind.

The NAP of Wali Khan, which campaigned actively in the elections, could fill only six seats in the National Assembly—three from the Northwest Frontier and three from Baluchistan (which has only four representatives in the Assembly). The party won 13 out of 40 seats in the Northwest Frontier provincial assembly, eight out of 20 in the Baluchistan assembly, and one of the 300 seats in East Pakistan.

Bhashani's position regarding the elections remained ambiguous during most of the year, probably reflecting the strains of the pro- and anti-election factions within his party. Bhashani, whose anti-election slogan had been "food before votes," put down more specific conditions at a tea garden workers' rally at Shamsernagar, Sylhet (East Pakistan), in February 1970. These included the granting of provincial autonomy, reservation of seats for peasant and worker representatives in the National Assembly, and government recognition of basic rights for peasants and workers. On 27 June, a party council meeting (from which Bhashani was absent) reportedly decided to contest the elections, and its working committee set up an eight-member parliamentary committee to nominate candidates.[7] On 2 August, the council approved participation, but only provided the Legal Framework Order was amended. At a Dacca rally on 20 October, Bhashani appeared to be more favorably disposed toward his party's entering the elections when he declared that this would be done "as part of the struggle for the realization of the people's demands" (*Far Eastern Economic Review*, 17 October). The party presented 13 candidates from East Pakistan only. Following the cyclone and tidal wave in the province, Bhashani on 24 November asked the candidates to withdraw. Their names remained on the ballots but none of them won.

The main immediate task of the newly elected National Assembly was to be the drafting of a constitution for Pakistan. By his Legal Framework Order, President Yahya Khan allowed 120 days after the elections for this purpose. Responsibility for the drafting of the document fell to the Awami League and the Pakistan People's Party, which together controlled 241 of the 300 elected seats. Their divergent stands on various issues—notably on autonomy for East Pakistan, but also on the economy and on foreign relations, particularly with India, China, and the West—threatened to make the negotiations for the draft unproductive.[8]

---

[7]Rashiduzzaman, *op. cit.*

[8]President Yahya Khan's effort to establish a civilian government were frustrated by events in early 1971. Negotiations by the two parties failed to produce a new constitution within the allotted time and the National Assembly was not allowed to convene—a development which added momentum to the growing Bengali separatist movement. On 25 March 1971, the Pakistan army, dominated by West Pakistanis, moved into the eastern province. The Awami League was banned and Sheik Mujib was arrested. The Bengalis resisted the troops and a running battle broke out between the two forces. The secessionists renamed East Pakistan "Bangla Desh" (Bengal Nation) and established an exile government in India.

Publications. The Communist Party of East Pakistan reportedly has an organ, *Shikha*. Otherwise, the communist organizations do not appear to have any publications of their own. The NAP of Bhashani controls a Bengali weekly, *Janata*, and Wali Khan's party has a Bengali daily, *Sangbad*. Both are printed in Dacca.

E. S.

PHILIPPINES

The Philippine Communist Party (Partido Komunista ng Pilipinas; PKP) was organized in 1930 on 26 August and officially proclaimed on 7 November. In 1932 it was declared illegal. Efforts by the PKP to expand and consolidate its power were relatively unsuccessful until the Second World War and the Japanese occupation of the Philippines. On 29 March 1942 the PKP assumed the leading role in the formation of a "broad coalition of guerrilla resistance organizations" known as the People's Anti-Japanese Army (Hukbong Bayan Laban sa Hapan), commonly known as the Huks and later renamed the People's Liberation Army (Hukbong Mapagagpalaya ng Bayan). In December 1968 a pro-Chinese faction broke with the PKP and formed a Maoist-oriented PKP—here designated the PKP(M)—which in some reports is called the PKP, Marxist-Leninist. The following year, the Huk organization split along parallel lines.

Although outlawed by the 1957 Anti-Subversion Act (Republic Act 1700), the PKP has continued to operate clandestinely. While no precise statistics are available, reports generally indicate that there are some 1,500 to 2,000 party members, whose activities include forming front organizations, infiltrating already existing noncommunist organizations, and supporting the Huk movement. According to the Philippine government, however, the PKP has a mass base of 37,000 sympathizers, backed by 100 armed men and 100 combat support troops. In a June 1966 interview, Jesús Lava, secretary-general of the PKP, stated that the Philippine branch of the Chinese Communist Party (CCP), also founded in 1930, was still active and was engaged in the development of front organizations among Chinese residents and citizens and in liaison operations with the Huks. Lava specifically denied any formal connection between the PKP and the Philippine branch of the CCP, but expressed his party's appreciation for the latter's assistance in the "common struggle." He placed the membership of the Philippine branch of the CCP at 1,500 to 2,000. Western sources have placed it at 300 to 500. The population of the Philippines is 38,000,000 (estimated 1970).

An additional Marxist organization, the Democratic Union of Filipino Youth (Malayang Pagkakaisang Kabataan Philipino; MPKP), was founded by former leaders of the Nationalist Youth Movement (see PKP(M) below) who were expelled from that body in 1967 because of ideological differences. The best-known founding member of the MPKP is Francisco Nemenzo, Jr., a political scientist at the University of the Philippines. Nemenzo denies charges that the MPKP is Soviet-oriented, but also rejects the thought of Mao Tse-tung as the key to revolution in the Philippines. Instead, he insists that revolution must conform with the local situation and not with a borrowed model.

Leadership and Organization. Little information is available regarding the current leadership and organization of the PKP. Jesús Lava is the secretary-general. In January 1970 the government released several communist leaders who had served sentences for rebellion, murder, and arson (see *YICA*, 1970, p. 670). Those freed included José Lava (brother of Jesús Lava and former secretary-general), Simeon Rodriguez (former treasurer), Angel Baking (former chief of special warfare), Federico Bautista (former head of intelligence), Salome Cruz, and Cesareo Torres. Upon release, José Lava declared that he remained a communist (*South China Morning Post*, Hong Kong, 6 January). Although the other men reportedly shared his sentiments, former Politburo member Salome Cruz stated that she was leaving the party and returning to Catholicism. Remaining imprisoned were Federico Maclang (former organizational secretary) and Ramón Espiritu (former finance secretary).

Although the PKP has often endorsed the Huks, during 1970 it began to criticize them as bandits who lacked ideological motivation. The military strength of the Huks has been put at 300 in a recent estimate, which stated that 150 were in Central Luzon. The same estimate put "combat support" at 3,600 and the "mass base" of support at 32,000. (H. A. Averch, F. H. Denton, and J. E. Koehler, *A Crisis of Ambiguity: Political and Economic Development in the Philippines*, Santa Monica, Calif., RAND Corporation, January 1970, p. 204.) Sympathizers actively cooperating with the movement have been put recently at 3,000 to 5,000 (*Far Eastern Economic Review*, Hong Kong, 2 April). A report by the Philippine Department of Defense differs from these estimates, placing Huk strength at 256 armed men and 200 combat support troops, and the mass base at 43,000. Figures for the "mass base," however, usually refer to the total number of inhabitants in Huk-controlled regions, and estimates differ as to the extent. Huk activities primarily focus on the rural areas of Central Luzon, particularly in the provinces of Pampanga, Bulacan, Nueva Ecija, and Tarlac. Reports indicate that they exercise varying degrees of control over approximately 176 villages—roughly one out of every twelve—in the poorest parts of Central Luzon. The chief of the Philippines Constabulary described Central Luzon in 1970 as being in a "virtual state of anarchy" (*ibid.*, 9 July). The Huks are said to have established a sound financial base; government estimates place their annual collections at $400,000 to $500,000. The money comes mainly from "sympathizers," whose contributions may be voluntary or forced.

Leadership of the Huks rested until late 1970 in the hands of Secretary-General Pedro Taruc (a cousin of the founder of the movement Luis Taruc), who was killed on 17 October (in a clash with army troops near Angeles City, Luzon), and of Faustino del Mundo (alias "Commander Sumulong"), who was captured on 16 September. Local and foreign observers suspected that the capture of del Mundo was arranged in a political deal between him and President Marcos. Philippine Army reports indicate that del Mundo, officially second in command, was the real authority in the Huk movement. With the death of Taruc and the capture of del Mundo, the Huks lost their only remaining leaders of stature, and mass surrenders followed. Del Mundo was succeeded by George Ocampo ("Commander Tony"), and Fortunato Salak ("Commander Fonting") reportedly became second in command. Both were killed by the Philippine Constabulary in early November, and their successors have not been identified.

Although Taruc and del Mundo were often referred to by the government as communists, they informed a select group of five members of the Philippine Congress at a secret meeting in the summer of 1970 that they resented the label and were not attempting to overthrow the government. They claimed to be socialists. whose objective was to "obtain social justice for the downtrodden masses, especially the tenants" (*Philippine Free Press*, Manila, 25 July). Congressman José Lingad conveyed to President Marcos an offer from the two leaders to cooperate with the government in restoring peace to Central Luzon (*ibid.*, 1 August). One of their conditions for cooperation was the disbanding of paramilitary organizations which allegedly had been terrorizing the people.

According to the Pampanga Philippine Constabulary commander, del Mundo was merely a bandit—a judgment also reached by some others (Averch, Denton, and Koehler, *op. cit.*), who further claimed that the Huks worked through local politicians. Statements from such varied sources as the Communist Party, USA and the Chinese Communist Party preferred similar charges.

Although ties between the Huks and the PKP are obscure and probably tenuous, the PKP apparently has endorsed the Huks' activities and sought to capitalize on their successes whenever possible.

Party Internal Affairs. During 1967 a split in the PKP became apparent between those advocating armed struggle as the sole path of "national and social liberation" and those favoring both illegal and legal action. The two factions also differed on the correct stance to adopt within the international communist movement. While non-Maoist elements in the PKP refrained from taking a stand on the Sino-Soviet split, the pro-Chinese faction came out unequivocally against the "revisionist clique ruling in the Soviet Union." In December 1968, Maoist elements in the PKP held a "Congress of Reestablishment," which proclaimed the formation of an independent, Maoist PKP—the PKP(M). A captured issue of their journal, *Ang Bayan*, claimed that there were two factions in the original PKP—the one that insisted on the "road of peaceful and parliamentary struggle" being under the leadership of Jesús Lava, and the other under Taruc and del Mundo (see above). The journal accused the "Lava clique" of attempting to establish a united front in which the national bourgeoisie would be in command instead of carrying out party development and organizing a PKP army. It charged also that Faustino del Mundo was trying to "amass wealth privately," "seek safety by making secret pacts with individual bourgeois politicians," and "carry out the line of mediation between landlords and peasantry." According to the PKP(M), the Lava faction decided in April 1968 to eschew armed struggle and to compromise with the administration on the land reform issue.

Upon his release from prison in January 1970, José Lava in effect confirmed the PKP(M) allegations against the "Lava faction" by declaring that he "intended to exhaust all legal and peaceful means in the struggle for reforms in the country's political, economic, and social systems." He added: "In a developing country like the Philippines one cannot be a real communist without at the same time being a nationalist." (*Far Eastern Economic Review*, 12 March.) Lava's group is sometimes labeled "Stalinist," although there is no apparent documentary support for this terminology.

Domestic Attitudes and Activities. Although supporting the "protracted struggle" of the Huks, the PKP has placed primary emphasis on "legal" and "parliamentary" forms of struggle in an effort to form a broad united front. No PKP program has been made public in recent years, but a Soviet commentary in late 1969 described the party as shifting to "peaceful propagation of its ideas among the workers, peasants, and intellectuals so as to ensure concerted action of anti-imperialist, anti-feudal forces working for authentic independence and democracy" (Moscow radio, domestic service, 3 December).

The government has responded to terrorism with military operations and attempts at intensified socioeconomic reform. In response to the anti-government, anti-U.S. mass rallies during the first months of 1970—in which the Nationalist Youth Movement of the PKP(M) was active (see below)—anti-insurgency military campaigns were stepped up while the reform program largely fell into neglect. Huk activity nevertheless appears to have continued throughout the Central Luzon stronghold.

The Huks, without seeming to have any set program, stress nationalist sentiments and oppose the U.S. military presence in the Philippines (*Philippine Free Press*, Manila, 25 July). At the aforementioned secret conference with five members of Congress, Taruc and del Mundo stressed a desire for peace and the rule of law, and an antipathy to bloodshed. They advocated land reform whereby the government would resettle landless farmers and provide them with necessary credits and material support. Del Mundo claimed that both leaders supported President Marcos in the 1969 election. The Huk leaders denounced alleged abuses by locally formed paramilitary units in Central Luzon, stating that these units, which were supposed to protect the villages, were instead spreading terror among the peasants. The leaders claimed that members of the paramilitary units were responsible for terrorist killings which the government attributed to the Huks. They claimed to have no alternative but to fight back in order to protect the "downtrodden peasants." (*Ibid.*)

International Views and Positions. Party statements warning of the dangers of both "left adventurism and infantilism" and "right opportunism" indicated that the PKP was attempting to maintain neutrality in the Sino-Soviet split. The formation of the PKP(M), however, may have caused the PKP to shift or appear to shift somewhat toward a pro-Soviet position.

In 1970 the Chinese communists for the first time took official note of the PKP(M) as the true communist party in the Philippines (NCNA, 4 August), but the emphasis in Chinese statements was on urban unrest and the "reawakening of the broad masses" in the islands. Virtually ignoring the role of the PKP, the Chinese hailed vociferously the anti-government demonstrations throughout the first quarter of the year in which the pro-Chinese Nationalist Youth Movement (see below) participated actively (NCNA, 29 January).

Soviet comments on developments in the Philippines, few and far between, emphasized anti-American themes. While condemning the "brutal repression" of the communists in the islands, the Soviet Union has sought to normalize its relations with the Philippine government as part of its diplomatic offensive in Southeast Asia against the Chinese People's Republic.

Late in the year, the newspaper of the Communist Party, USA, *Daily World* (29 October), carried an article by William Pomeroy in which the captured Huk leader "Sumulong" was portrayed as a bandit who had cut his links with the PKP and had ruled parts of Pampanga Province by terror. Hinting at an "understanding" between "Sumulong" and "American . . . intelligence and security forces" in the Philippines, the correspondent asserted that the Huk leader killed communists who sought to enter his area and that he prevented the formation of mass organizations. The article also alleged that Pedro Taruc's position in the Huk organization was that of a "'political adviser' whose role was to give a false social justice character to the Sumulong gang." The article referred to the PKP(M) as a "small extremist group" that had "no mass base to speak of."

Publications. Although the PKP has no regular publication, its positions are frequently in the *Chinese Commercial News*, a Chinese-language daily (Manila), and *The Graphic*, a weekly publication in English.

* * *

The PKP(M). The Maoist-oriented PKP(M) is headed by Jose Maria Sison ("Amado Guerrero"), a former University of the Philippines lecturer who is chairman of the Central Committee. Little else is known about the leadership of this "revitalized" party. For Sison's role in labor and youth organizations, see below.

The armed wing of the PKP(M) was formed in March 1969 when the Huk organization split along ideological lines paralleling the rift in the PKP. Several Huk units operating primarily in Tarlac Province broke away and formed the New People's Army (NPA), under Bernabé Buscayno ("Commander Danté,") a self-educated peasant. The NPA, described as not only a fighting unit but also a propaganda and organizing force, is estimated to have 400 to 500 hard-core guerrillas and 400 combat support troops, and a "mass base" of 20,000 to 41,000 sympathizers.

There has been serious rivalry within the NPA between military commanders and ideological leaders. Arthur Garcia, who was reportedly the second highest in rank among the leaders and the NPA's ideological adviser, was assassinated in January 1970 along with five of his field officers. It was rumored that they had been killed by followers of "Commander Danté." Before his death, reports circulated that Garcia had taken over control of the NPA from "Danté," who allegedly had been relieved of all power in a conflict over tactics. Garcia, trained in China during 1967 in guerrilla warfare and agitation and propaganda techniques, served as a direct link between the PKP(M) and the militant student groups. He was a former vice-chairman of the Nationalist Youth Movement (see below). "Commander Bakal," NPA leader in Zambales Province, was killed by government troops on 16 November 1970.

Domestic Activities and Attitudes. At its first plenum in 1969, the PKP(M) Central Committee made preliminary preparations for an "agrarian revolution," strengthened the Central Committee by including "proletarian revolutionary cadres" from the NPA and the peasant movement, formed a military commission, ratified the basic rules of the NPA, and discussed ways to improve party education, finances, and organization. It described the measures as a comprehensive program to "integrate Marxism-Leninism-Mao Tse-tung Thought with the concrete practice of the Philippine Revolution" (*Far Eastern Economic Review*, 12 March). The PKP(M) long-range objective is to establish a strong rural revolutionary base through the formation of a broad united front with all "nationalist" forces and use the countryside to isolate the cities.

With the NPA, the PKP(M) is determined to overthrow the Philippine government through armed struggle. At present, its efforts toward this goal take the form of terrorism. Strongly Maoist in orientation, all PKP(M) members are supposed to have copies of *Quotations from Chairman Mao Tse-tung*. NPA units, according to captured documents, are required to have a political commissar and every NPA soldier must study the thought of Mao Tse-tung, particularly the "three main rules of discipline and eight points of attention." According to an NCNA broadcast (24 August, 1970), the NPA soldiers actively propagandize, organize, and arm the masses, including the Igorots of Central Luzon. After impoverished peasants study the thought of Mao Tse-tung at nightly two-hour propaganda sessions which stress the inequities of the present regime, their class consciousness is allegedly enhanced and many join the guerrillas. The NPA assists in setting up militia units in villages where it had helped implement rent reduction and the "punishment" of "despotic landlords, local tyrants, and enemy agents" (*ibid.*).

The PKP(M) in 1970 was active primarily in Central Luzon, but was reportedly expanding into North and South Luzon, the Visayas (particularly Negros), and Mindanao. The NCNA claimed that "guerrilla zones" had been established in the provinces of Tarlac, Pampanga, Nueva Ecija, Zambales, Bulacan, Bataan, and Pangasinan.

The PKP(M) has established a "Maoist university" where poor peasants study the thought of Mao Tse-tung. Instruction stresses peasant-worker unity to overthrow the government, which is to be replaced by one modeled on that of the Chinese People's Republic.

In the fall, "Commander Danté" appeared to be trying to strengthen his organization by calling for a merger with followers of the captured Huk leader Faustino del Mundo. Reportedly, he also called for the liquidation of all Huks who did not join his force (*Straits Times*, Singapore, 21 September). The attempt to strengthen the NPA apparently did not meet with success.

On 29 December, in an incident which shocked the Philippine armed forces, Lieutenant Victor N. Corpus, a graduate of the Philippine Military Academy (PMA), raided the PMA armory with the assistance of ten NPA members. He then deserted to join "Commander Danté's" force, leaving behind a statement which read, "I am resigning as an officer of the PMA to join the real army—which is the New People's Army." (*Philippine Free Press*, 9 January 1971.) According to the PKP(M) organ *Ang Bayan*, Corpus was immediately "integrated" into the NPA. Philippine intelligence reported that Buscayo had been sick and that Corpus was expected to assume control of the NPA.

The PKP(M) has endorsed two major front organizations, the former Labor Party (Lapiang Manggagawa; LM) and the Nationalist Youth Movement (Kabataang Makabayan; KM). Founded in 1962 by a group of radical trade union leaders, the LM merged with three other organizations in 1967 to form the Socialist Party of the Philippines (SPP), in which LM secretary-general Ignacio Lascina and vice-chairman José Sison apparently retained their positions. The new party has 2,300 members, 70 per cent of whom reside in Manila (*Far Eastern Economic Review*, 17 October 1970). The SPP continued a precarious existence in 1970, attempting to politicize workers and peasants while maintaining its legal status. Lascina has been much less radical in his political statements than the KM leaders.

The KM was founded in 1964 by José Lansang and José Sison. The party's chief of propaganda, José Lapuz, has claimed that the KM has 6,000 members; Western observers put the number at 3,000 to 5,000 (*Washington Post*, 12 July 1970). Its Women's Bureau reportedly has 200 hard-core members (*Liberation*, New York, November). The leadership has gone underground due to government measures taken against the organization.

On 9 December 1969 the KM hierarchy was reorganized. The leaders who emerged, in order of rank, included Nilo Tayag,[1] national chairman (arrested 11 June 1970 and charged with subversion) and Dr. Escalante, national vice-chairman, followed by Antonio Tayco, (relieved of office in mid-1970 and subsequently arrested), Eugene Gray, Monico Atienza, Carlos Jacinto, and Raquel Edralín. The real power in the organization, however, is believed by Western observers to remain in the hands of Sison, who went underground in the spring to work with the PKP(M). Former secretary-general Leoncio Co was captured on 4 March while allegedly lecturing at the "Maoist university" in Tarlac.

Early in 1970, the Movement for a Democratic Philippines (MDP), an umbrella organization, was formed to coordinate radical movements among students, workers, and peasants. The KM and its offshoot, the Democratic Youth Association (Samahang Domekratikong Kabataan; SDK) soon came to dominate the new body. Their influence was clearly evident in the MDP four-point program, which is aimed at consolidating the "progressive left" and isolating reactionaries; winning over "middle" elements; mobilizing the masses in an "anti-imperialist, anti-feudal" struggle; and engaging in political activity. After some initial success, the MDP appears to have fallen into disorder caused by wide divergences of goals among member organizations.

The KM, declaring its "national democratic mission" to be to complete the "Philippine revolution"—which had been "frustrated by a new type of colonialism, American imperialism"—has called for unity of "all national classes" to struggle for "national liberation." It also advocates land reform on the Chinese model, "nationalist industrialization" and more diversified economic development, and endorses armed insurrection aimed at overthrowing the government (*Philippine Free Press*, 30 October). Such an insurrection, according to the KM, can come only if the students unite with the masses and the NPA (*ibid.*). A KM informer alleged that the organization was building up an arsenal in Mindoro, whence it planned to engage in armed struggle (*ibid.*).

The KM has described itself as the "vanguard of the Filipino youth in seeking full national

---

[1]Tayag is said to have acted as liaison man between the KM and the NPA in Angeles City, Pampanga.

freedom and democratic reforms and in combating imperialism, feudalism, and bureaucratic capitalism." It has launched a "learn from the people" campaign, in accordance with their policy of learning the problems of the peasants and workers from the people instead of from books. The KM, however, also includes indoctrination of the peasantry among its activities.

The KM was very active in the student demonstrations against the government during the first part of the year. During the height of the disturbances in Manila, President Marcos stated that a plot had been discovered whereby students would be utilized for an attempt to assassinate himself and the three officials next in the line of succession to the presidency, with the intention of creating chaos in the country. He further charged that the student movement was being manipulated by the NPA.

In addition to the KM and the LM, numerous smaller communist-oriented organizations are active in the Philippines. Shortly after the founding of the LM in 1962, the Free Association of Peasants (Malayang Samahan ng Magsasaka, commonly known as the Masaka) was formed. This rural organization enlists agricultural workers and small farmers and is reported to have some 30,000 members. It is headed by Felix Olalia, a former Huk commander and labor organizer. The Masaka is reportedly active in the communist indoctrination of peasants and in the printing and distribution of pro-Chinese documents and pamphlets.

A number of small front organizations are controlled by the KM and LM, such as the "Committee for Freedom in South Vietnam" and the "Bertrand Russell Peace Committee of the Philippines." Although KM officials have repeatedly denied that there are any Chinese in their organization, two former KM members asserted that the movement maintained close contact with pro-Peking elements among the Chinese population and that an "informal Chinese section" participated in anti-U.S. demonstrations (see *YICA*, 1970, p. 670).

International Views and Positions. The PKP(M) is vigorously pro-Peking and correspondingly hostile toward Moscow. It has designated "American imperialism" as the "number one enemy of the Philippine people." As stated above, China for the first time recognized the existence of the PKP(M) in 1970, and complimentary reporting on the "revitalized" party was especially frequent during August, when it was praised for "vigorously [leading] the masses . . . in waging revolutionary struggles" (NCNA, 4 August). NPA activities were mentioned sporadically.

China was enthusiastic about student activism during the first part of the year:

> The Philippine progressive student movement has played a vanguard role in the vigorously developing mass movement. . . . The scale, duration, swiftness and fierceness of their struggle [were such as had] not been seen for many years. . . . In the course of struggle over the past year, the Philippine people have raised their political consciousness and strengthened their unity. More and more revolutionary workers, peasants and students are diligently studying Marxism-Leninism-Mao Tse-tung Thought with a view to obtaining revolutionary truth to guide their revolutionary practice. (*Peking Review*, no. 4, 23 January.)

The anti-U.S. nature of the demonstrations was stressed repeatedly.

The Soviet press apparently did not mention either the PKP(M) or the NPA during 1970. In February it commented briefly on rising anti-U.S. sentiments, without reporting the violent demonstrations in which the KM was active (Moscow radio, 25 February).

KM objectives in 1970 focused primarily on the U.S. role in Vietnam and the U.S. economic influence and military presence in the Philippines. Philippine Air Force intelligence reports claimed that the KM received financial support for its demonstrations not only from the PKP(M) but also from the Communist Party, USA.

Publications. The clandestine organ of the PKP(M), *Ang Bayan*, appears sporadically in English, Tagalog, and Pampanga. The irregular *Progressive Review*, published in English, is the organ of the KM. It frequently reflects PKP(M) positions and was originally edited by Sison.

S. E. Y.

SINGAPORE

The communist movement in Singapore is theoretically an integral part of the Communist Party of Malaya (CPM), whose headquarters and leaders are based along the Thai-Malaysian border (see *Malaysia*). The movement has, however, a certain degree of independence, which has been considerably enhanced in recent years by the reduction of the CPM to a guerrilla movement and the separation of Singapore from the Federation of Malaysia in 1965. In view of Singapore's predominantly Chinese population (some 75 per cent), which in many respects identifies itself with the achievement of mainland China, distinction between communist groups and others with similar aims and sympathies is blurred. Hard-core communist party membership in Singapore is estimated at 200. The population of Singapore is 2,000,000 (estimated 1970).

Leadership and Organization. Because of its illegal status, communist activity in Singapore has been of a two fold nature: underground, and through front organizations and parties. The clandestine organization is difficult to delineate, owing to the communists' strict adherence to a policy of virtual elimination of all records and files and the replacement of party organs by "front publications."

The leadership of the Singapore communist movement appears to be split into two major contending factions: those tending to favor a nonviolent approach to communist goals and those advocating armed struggle. The principal front organization, the Barisan Sosialis (Socialist Front), appears to be split similarly. There is a small, extreme left-wing party in Singapore, the Partai Rakyat (People's Party; PR), which was founded in December 1956 as the Singapore branch of the former Partai Rakyat Malaya (People's Party of Malaya—see *Malaysia*).

The Barisan Sosialis was founded on 26 July 1961 by former members of the People's Action Party (PAP) under the leadership of Lim Chin Siong. The PAP is the ruling party in Singapore. The Barisan Sosialis—composed of communists, sympathizers, and dissident extremists from the PAP—receives support from the 29 trade unions that are associated with it and has also the occasional cooperation of the PR, which has been described as a satellite of the Barisan with a Malay appeal.

The current Barisan Sosialis Central Committee, elected in 1967, includes Lee Siew Choh (chairman), See Cheng Kiong (vice-chairman), Koo Yung (assistant secretary-general),* Tay-cheng Kang (treasurer), Chai Kuen Fak (assistant treasurer), Fong Swee Suan,* Poh Soo Kai,* Yang Ya Wu, Liang Li Ing,* Chang Tek Suen, Li Chen Min, Chen Ru Pen, and Hsieh Chin Chen. (Those designated by an asterisk were under arrest and in detention during 1970). Lim Chin Siong retired from his post as secretary-general upon release from detention in August 1969 and apparently has not been replaced.

In general, the Barisan Sosialis is China-oriented.

Domestic Attitudes and Activities. Present communist policy in Singapore is difficult to ascertain both because of splits within the clandestine organization and its fronts and because of the Singapore government's overtures to the Soviet Union, North Korea, and Eastern Europe.

The Barisan Sosialis regards struggle for the reunification of Singapore and Malaysia as its main task—thus differing with the Communist Party of Malaya, which has declared its present objective to be the instigation of a "new democratic revolution." Although the Barisan Sosialis is internally divided over this difference, it affirmed its stand for reunification early in 1970 in a circular calling for "retaliation" against the "counterrevolutionary plot of divide-and-rule." Chairman Lee Siew Choh has indicated that his party would be willing to accept any proposal for reunification, even if it came from the present government. The CPM has ignored reunification, simply calling on all the people of the former territory of Malaya, not the present governments, to unite.

The Barisan Sosialis boycotted the most recent Singapore election (April 1968), and the PAP won all 58 Parliament seats.

During 1970 communist activities in Singapore apparently remained limited to demonstrations, sporadic violence, and verbal attacks against the government. The Barisan Sosialis and the PR condemned the government for its alleged connection with "U.S. and British imperialism," for "fraudulent reforms" and "military suppression," and for allegedly failing to meet the needs of the broad masses. As in previous years, the PR advocated armed struggle.

During April, May, and June, Singapore communists, and Barisan Sosialis members exploded a number of bombs (killing one child and injuring another) and encouraged the burning of a bus. On 30 May, several windows in a British-owned bank were broken by a crowd of leftists. Some of the incidents appeared to be linked with the fortieth anniversary of the CPM on 30 April. The government arrested 15 suspects, all of whom were Barisan Sosialis functionaries, including a female member of the Central Committee, Liang Li Ing. Altogether, 27 Barisan Sosialis officials were arrested during the first half of the year.

Although the Barisan Sosialis apparently followed CPM directives in perpetrating the bombings, it disclaimed credit for them, stating that the "series of indiscriminate bomb explosions and bomb plots allegedly let loose to 'commemorate the anniversary of the founding of the Malayan Communist Party'" were really part of an "imperialist plot to discredit the communist party, the Liberation movement, and the people's patriotic movement as a whole" and that the work was "done by agents provocateurs and slanderously publicized in the imperialist press as 'Maoist'" (*Malayan Monitor and General News*, May). In contrast, a CPM broadcast ("Voice of the Malayan Revolution" radio, quoted by NCNA, 28 May) praised the bombings as the work of "revolutionary masses" who were "combining propaganda activities with combat actions."

Foreign Minister Sinnathamby Rajaratnam declared that the Singapore communists had turned to urban terrorism in an effort to undermine the country's stability. He attributed the change to the failure of their efforts to use peaceful persuasion in gaining public support. After his arrest, Liang Li Ing stated that current Barisan Sosialis activities were dictated by the CPM and the violence stemmed from the leftists' dismay at the people's enthusiastic preparations for Singapore's national day (9 August).

On 15 November *Barisan*, organ of the Barisan Sosialis, called upon workers to set up clandestine unions. Earlier, a broadcast by the CPM's "Voice of the Malayan Revolution" radio had praised Singapore workers for their struggle against foreign vested interests and advocated the formation of secret factions within existing trade unions.

Reportedly, the Barisan Sosialis conducts kindergartens which politically indoctrinate children between the ages of three and six years. The *Sun* (Singapore, 5 July) reported that police had confirmed the existence of rural communist indoctrination centers for pre-school children. Young children have been found circulating communist propaganda.

International Views and Positions. Since Singapore is claimed by the CPM to be within the area of its "jurisdiction," no representative of the Singapore communist movement as such attended international meetings or party congresses. Traveling communist-front leaders designated themselves as representatives of a "Malayan organization."

The Singapore communists support the pro-Chinese position of the CPM in the Sino-Soviet dispute and link the Soviet Union and the United States as collaborators bent on "betraying the struggles of all the heroic peoples."

The Barisan Sosialis opposes Malaysia as a political entity, calling it a "neocolonialist creation of the U.S.-British imperialists." It has denounced Indonesia's anticommunist campaign, and has expressed support for the Vietnamese people in their "heroic struggle against U.S. imperialist aggression and for national salvation" and for the "just struggle against U.S. imperialism and its lackeys" in Cambodia (*Barisan*, quoted by NCNA, 22 April). The Barisan Sosialis attacked the Japanese government, accusing it of attempting to annex Southeast Asia (*Barisan*, quoted by NCNA, 23 March).

Publications. The Singapore communists have no official publications. *Barisan* (or *Chern Sian Pau*) is published weekly by the Barisan Sosialis. Pro-communist publications include the *Plebian, News Bulletin* and *Rakyat*, together with *Mimbar Rakyat*, issued by the PR, and *People's Tribune*, the organ of the PR. The *Malayan Monitor and General News*, a mimeographed monthly published in London, carries CPM policy statements.

S. E. Y.

THAILAND

Although a communist party was formed in Thailand as early as 1929 by the Siam Special Committee of the South Seas Communist Party (Nan-yang kung-ch'an tang), which had been founded in 1928, the Communist Party of Thailand (CPT) was not founded until 1 December 1942. The party is illegal. The new Thai constitution promulgated in June 1968 provided for the legal existence of political parties for the first time since 1958, but the Communist Party of Thailand and all communist front organizations were excluded.

Noncommunist observers have estimated the CPT to have between 200 and 500 active members, some 3,000 to 5,000 full-time guerrillas, and up to 25,000 sympathizers or supporters (*Le Monde*, Paris, English edition, 25 March 1970; *New York Times*, 9 July). The population of Thailand is 36,200,000 (estimated 1970).

Leadership and Organization. A number of CPT leaders apparently reside in Peking, where the party has been represented by CPT Central Committee member (Miss) Nit Phuongdaphet. CPT leaders under detention since 1969 include Politburo members Thong Jamsri ("Thavorn Vongsuma") and Bim Buaorn ("Chin Buaprasert"),Vichai Tuampancharden, and Chaiwat Tanyapras. Central Committee member Prasert Eiewchai ("Erb"), who had been the chief organizer and treasurer of the communist movement in Thailand, was arrested on 3 July 1970 after a three-year man hunt. At his home, police seized propaganda, instruction manuals, a considerable amount of money in cash and gold (allegedly for paying CPT agents), a radio transmitter, an arsenal of Chinese-made grenades and other weapons, lists of Thai naval vessels, maps showing police stations and government offices, and letters from provincial guerrilla leaders asking for weapons. A number of other admitted communists were also arrested. According to Thai government reports, leaders of the terrorists operating in the northeast include Yod Phatisawat, Choy Latisingh, and Kasem, all of whom were trained in North Vietnam.

There are at least 1,000 communist guerrillas in northern Thailand, particularly in Chieng Rai, Loei, Nan Phitsanulok, Tak, and Muang Petchabun provinces. They mainly comprise alienated Meo hill tribesmen led by Chinese-trained Thai or Sino-Thai cadres. Their supplies are furnished to a degree through Chinese channels and also by some 5,000 supporters among the hill tribes (*Far Eastern Economic Review*, Hong Kong, 2 July 1970). The guerrillas reportedly maintain twelve training camps along the northern Thai border (*Le Monde*, English edition, 25 March).

The northeast, with a population of 11 million, formerly a sheltered 2,000 armed terrorists. By 1970, government campaigns had reduced the number to 1,000 or 1,500 (*Economist*, 14 March; *Far Eastern Economic Review*, 14 May), and some 13,000 sympathizers (*Le Monde*, English edition, 4 November). Roughly 4 per cent of those who surrendered or were captured in the northeastern insurgency area had been trained in North Vietnam.

In the south, the Communist Party of Malaya (CPM) operates a number of bases along the

Thai-Malaysian border, where the predominantly ethnic Chinese communists are winning recruits among the 800,000 Moslem minority (*Le Monde*, 25 March). About 200 CPT terrorists in the south are in regular contact with the CPM guerrillas in the area. On 22 October, Thai authorities captured a training and liaison center in Nakhon Si Thanmaeat Province. It is the first camp in southern Thailand known to have been constructed by indigenous Thais. There are about 500 insurgents in North-Central Thailand (*Washington Post*, 3 May) and some 100 along the border with Burma.

The communist movement in Thailand attracts mainly persons of non-Thai ethnic minority groups. The highest positions in the CPT are thought to be held by Chinese, Sino-Thais, and Vietnamese, while pure Thais generally occupy subordinate posts.

The CPT has operated through the Thailand Independence Movement (TIM), established 1 November 1964, and the Thailand Patriotic Front (TPF), set up on 1 January 1965, both of which are based in Peking. The TPF, represented in Peking by Phayom Chulanont, is a "member organization" of the TIM and thus under its political leadership. Both bodies appear to be of little consequence at present, and neither received much mention in Chinese pronouncements during 1970. On 1 January 1969, the guerrillas of the former Thai People's Armed Forces were reorganized into the Thai People's Liberation Armed Forces (TPLAF), to serve as the military arm of the CPT. Apparently the CPT also has a militia.

Major communist front organizations include the Thailand Federation of Patriotic Workers and the Thailand Patriotic Youth Organization (both of which have declared adherence to the TFF), and the Thai Afro-Asian Solidarity Committee. Other mass organizations include the Association of Liberated Farmers and Planters, the Patriotic Teachers' Group, the Thai Monks' Group, the Patriotic Combatants' Group, and the Lawyers' Group.

Domestic Attitudes and Activities. The division within the CPT leadership, evident first during 1967, appeared to continue throughout 1970. Appeals for unity were frequent and were intensified particularly after the arrest of Prasert Eiewchai in July. In a key broadcast on 17 July, the clandestine communist "Voice of the People of Thailand" (VPT) radio issued a summary of communist activity during the first half of the year, praising the terrorists and condemning Thai-U.S. anticommunist campaigns. The main thrust of the broadcast came in the conclusion:

> The Communist Party of Thailand calls on . . . the People's Liberation Army, guerrillas and militiamen to develop people's war and launch more and systematic attacks on the enemy troops so as to wipe out more of them, expand and consolidate the base areas and people's regional administrations. . . . Members of the Communist Party of Thailand [should] hold higher the great Red Banner of Mao Tse-tung Thought, strengthen their unity and unite more closely and extensively with the patriotic and democratic-minded people throughout the country so as to resolutely carry people's war through to the end. (Quoted, NCNA, 18 July.)

The CPT was calling for a united front of all anti-U.S. forces to wage armed struggle and for greater unity within the party. In December the VPT statement on the twenty-eighth anniversary of the CPT again called for close unity under the party.

On 1 January, a New's Year's broadcast over the VPT repeated the ten-point program announced by the CPT in 1969 (see *YICA*, 1970, pp. 681-82). Key points were as follows:

> (1) Resolutely carry out people's war, drive U.S. imperialism out of Thailand, overthrow [the] government of the Thanom clique [and] establish a people's government [which] consists of representatives of the working class, peasants, petty bourgeoisie, national bourgeoisie, and of the patriotic and democratic personages, and which genuinely carries out an independent and democratic policy.

(2) Abolish all laws, notices, orders, and regulations detrimental to the people and the country. . . .

(3) Confiscate all property and land of the U.S. imperialists, the Thanom clique, the counterrevolutionaries, and tyrannical landlords and distribute them for the benefit of the people and the nation. . . .

(4) Abolish all traitorous and unjust agreements and treaties; unite with all the countries which support the Thai people's revolution. . . .

(5) The various nationalities shall enjoy the right of autonomy within the big family of Thailand. . . .

(6) Abolish the feudal system of exploitation step-by-step. . . .

(7) Promote and develop state industrial and commercial enterprises; protect private industrial and commercial enterprises which are not detrimental to the national economy. . . .

(8) Ensure the workers' employment, wages, and security. . . .

(9) Women shall enjoy equal rights with men. . . .

(10) Weed out the reactionary and corrosive U.S. imperialist and feudal culture [and] promote and develop revolutionary culture. . . .

The New Year's message also urged that special attention be given to the study, comprehension and constant application of Maoism. It concluded with an appeal for unity throughout the country against the United States and the Thanom (Kittikachorn) government, and for support and expansion of armed struggle by the TPLAF.

The CPT officially supports the road of armed struggle, of "surrounding the cities from the countryside and forcibly seizing state power" (VPT, 1 January). The repeated calls in 1970 for increased armed struggle may indicate some disagreement within party leadership as to the appropriate degree of struggle.

The TPLAF is both a fighting organ and a production force. The VPT (11 May) claimed that the guerrillas were successfully coordinating fighting and crop raising:

> With a gun in one hand and a spade in the other, they have courageously fought the U.S.-Thanom clique. . . . In achieving cooperation between the labor force and the armed forces, in holding that fighting and producing are of equal importance, and by using arms to protect this production, the liberation soldiers and other armed forces of the people have strengthened their militant spirit, are protecting the people's crops, and are encouraging production. They strengthened the already close unity between the people's soldiers and the people.

The TPLAF also sent "armed propaganda teams" into the countryside to arouse the masses through talking, displaying slogans, distributing handbills, and giving theatrical performances.

The CPT called on the peasants to join in the struggle to overthrow the "feudal exploitation system," charging that "negligence of the rulers in maintaining conservation projects had led to frequent floods and droughts from which agricultural production was suffering," and that what meager harvest the peasants reaped was absorbed "by landlords and usurers through cruel exploitation" under various pretexts (NCNA, 15 April). Unity, organization, and persistence in armed struggle under the CPT were advocated as the only solution to the peasants' plight.

The CPT maintained that although the government was attempting to discredit the communists by claiming that they extorted food and property from the people, the opposite was true: government troops "brought oppression and misery everywhere" by robbing the people of their livestock, and burning crops and homes, while "liberation soldiers" invariably paid for supplies, even in the owner's absence. According to the CPT, people recognized the honesty of the communists and were "sharing their crops and pork with the liberation soldiers," and were "not only doing their best to supply the guerrillas but even joining the bands." (VPT, 7 January.) Villagers also were said to be furnishing the communists with vital information.

In mid-1970 the Thai government found it necessary to raise the taxes on certain commodities, mainly luxury goods. The new taxes were designed to be borne by the rich, but the real burden was swiftly passed on to the poor through raised prices. The CPT condemned the measure as making life even harder for the people and called on them to resist it, further claiming that additional government revenues thus obtained would be channeled into increased military expenditures to finance "suppression of the people" both in Thailand and in Indochina (*ibid.*, 13 July).

The insurgents in the north and northeast have slowly begun to expand from their previously limited bases into predominantly Thai areas. Late in the year some were reportedly within 270 kilometers of Bangkok (*Bangkok Post*, 6 November).

The communists are attempting to secure bases in the hill tribe areas along the Laos border from which to exert pressure on the lowland Thais, among whom they have won little support. In December 1969, the CPT announced that it had "liberated a village" about eight kilometers from the northern border and thirty kilometers from the projected terminus of the Chinese road under construction through Laos (VPT, 6 December). Late in 1970 a major guerrilla base, supplied by mainland China, was discovered in the northeast. Its presence may indicate plans for further expansion.

The scale of communist terrorism during the year increased to the point where the government announced that the TPLAF had shifted from guerrilla tactics to conventional warfare. Deputy Prime Minister Praphas Charusatiara claimed that the terrorists had moved from village to district-level operations and were planning to kidnap and assassinate high-ranking officials in order to frighten the inhabitants into cooperating with the communists (*Bangkok Post*, 29 October). The new orientation involved attacks by groups of 100 terrorists against government posts or tribal welfare settlements—targets which previously had been avoided. Villagers reported acts of torture, mutilation, and murder, and said that school children were kidnaped to force their parents to support the dissidents. In addition to terrorizing the populace, CPT guerrillas further pursued the policy of armed struggle by demolishing bridges and ambushing patrols. Possibly exaggerated figures were reported by the NCNA (10 April):

> According to incomplete statistics, the People's Liberation Army and people of Thailand fought 150 battles with the reactionary troops and police of the U.S.-Thanom clique throughout the country in the first three months of this year, killing or wounding more than 300 enemies, shooting down or damaging eight enemy helicopters, destroying a number of enemy military vehicles and 11 bridges of military importance, and capturing large numbers of weapons and war material.

On 20 September, the governor of Chiang Rai Province, an army colonel, and a police colonel were captured and executed by guerrillas as they traveled to a rendezvous with a terrorist leader who allegedly wished to surrender. This attack initiated a new wave of communist terrorism in Thailand.

Activity of the CPM guerrillas along the southern border of Thailand also increased during the year (see *Malaysia*). The communists of Malaysia apparently were stepping up recruitment in the Thai border villages, appealing in particular to the Moslem population in that area. The NCNA (23 January) linked the activities of the border guerrillas with Thailand rather than Malaysia:

> Victories and development of the people's armed struggle in south Thailand have given great encouragement to the people's armed struggle in other parts of the country. The patriotic army and people in various places of Thailand will also support the people's armed struggle in the south with their own fighting. Supported by the people of the whole country, the People's Liberation Army and people in the south will win still greater victories.

On the other hand, the capture of several large communist bases forced the southern terrorists to flee into Malaysia during the mid-year.

The CPT was vociferous in condemnation of the government's plan, later dropped, to send aid to the new Lon Nol regime in Cambodia for support of its struggle against Vietnamese communist invaders. The party also loudly denounced the alleged dispatch of Thai troops to Laos to "serve U.S. imperialism in expanding the war of aggression" against that country (VPT, quoted by NCNA, 31 March.)

International Views and Positions. During 1970 the CPT continued to praise the Chinese People's Republic and the Maoist doctrine of armed struggle. Nevertheless, it it did not devote much energy to denouncing the Soviet Union. Alleged CPT victories were attributed to the "greatness and correctness of the brilliant teachings of the great teacher of the revolutionary people of the world, Chairman Mao Tse-tung" (VPT, quoted by NCNA, 18 September). Thai communists welcomed Mao Tse-tung's 20 May statement on U.S. actions against Vietnamese encampments in Cambodia by pledging to "strengthen [CPT] unity with the fraternal Cambodian, Laotian, and Vietnamese peoples [and to] persist in fighting and violently defeating the U.S.-Thanom clique [by] waging the protracted peoples' war" (VPT, 25 May).

Chinese reports, in turn, frequently endorsed the CPT claiming that over the past five years the revolutionary forces in Thailand had made great advances in their struggle against the Thai government and the United States. An NCNA report (6 August) claimed that armed struggle had spread to 130 districts in 36 provinces (five more provinces than the CPT claims) out of the 528 districts and 71 provinces. Describing the guerrillas' study of Maoism and its application to their attitudes and actions, *Peking Review* (no. 7, 13 February) praised the TPLAF for its efforts at building a "new-type people's army on a political basis," and, quoting a passage in which Mao Tse-tung described the Chinese Red Army before the Second World War, stated that the TPLAF was doing exactly the same things under the CPT.

China gave wide publicity to the "fifth anniversary of the Thai people's armed struggle" on 7 August, declaring that the struggle had now developed into a "people's war." Chinese enthusiasm in commemorating the anniversary was attributed by some observers to anxiety about CPT morale in the face of setbacks experienced during 1970. Albania and North Vietnam also congratulated the CPT.

China continually played upon the CPT's 25 May call—repreated at intervals throughout the year—for greater unity among the people of Indochina. This became one of the main themes of the Thai communist movement, along with the promotion of armed struggle. On 18 July the NCNA quoted a CPT Central Committee statement:

> The Communist Party of Thailand calls on ... the People's Liberation Army, guerrillas and militiamen to develop people's war and launch more and systematic attacks on the enemy troops so as to wipe out more of them, expand and consolidate the base areas and people's regional administrations and fight in coordination with the three Indo-Chinese peoples and other Asian people.

In February, a Meo refugee stated that as far back as 1964 about twenty men and women from "the land of Mao Tse-tung" had come to his village to persuade the inhabitants to oppose the government. The *Bangkok Post* (16 January) reported that Meo rebels were receiving guerrilla warfare training in China and North Vietnam, and that on returning to North Thailand they brought with them Chinese and Vietnamese cadres and some Chinese weapons of the newest types, though most of them carried weapons that were obtained or made locally. It was feared in Bangkok that the Meo dissidents would become a substantial threat to the government if they succeeded in strengthening their existing ties with China, North Vietnam, and Pathet Lao territory.

Seven insurgency centers in North Vietnam which formerly accepted Thais for training were reported to have been converted to other purposes. Thai communists are now trained by veteran CPM guerrillas along the Thai-Malaysian border. There remain, however, 15 known training camps for Thais in Yunnan Province, China, within seventy-five miles of Thailand, and schools which Thai communists attend are operated in Canton and Anoy. There are also 25 known training centers in Laos, mostly along the infiltration trails. Thirteen of the centers are less than two years old. An elite CPT group is reportedly being groomed for leadership in Canton, while the camps in Laos are mainly for "intermediate" training of Thais who are to return to their home areas as workers and fighters. Because of linguistic similarities, the Thais are trained mainly by Pathet Lao instructors, although the schools are under Chinese and North Vietnamese supervision. (*Washington Post*, 3 May.)

Prime Minister Souvanna Phouma of Laos admitted late in 1969 that small groups of North Vietnamese guerrillas were passing through the country each month to infiltrate Thailand and that his government was powerless to stop the flow (*Hindustan Times*, New Delhi, 15 December). Late in 1970 the Thai government reported that some 150 Pathet Lao and North Vietnamese troops entered Thailand through Laos, armed with modern carbines and rifles (*Working People's Daily*, Rangoon, 15 December).

A North Vietnamese defector to the Laotian government reportedly admitted that under orders from Hanoi he had introduced a propaganda battalion of 1,000 hill tribesmen into Thailand (*ibid.*, 1 February). Thai Prime Minister Thanom announced in the fall that according to captured documents some 57,000 communist troops were massing near the southern border of Laos and preparing for attacks on Thailand. He stated that although some of the troops were Thai communists, the bulk were Pathet Lao and North Vietnamese (*Bangkok World*, 3 September). In addition, a Laotian minister disclosed that North Vietnamese troops were studying the Thai language in Laos (*ibid.*).

Communist infiltration also occurred in East Thailand, In June, Under-Secretary of the Interior Puang Suwanrath reported indications that South Vietnamese and Cambodian communists had infiltrated every Thailand-Cambodia border province (*Bangkok Post*, 20 June). A subversive underground movement among Vietnamese refugees was discovered in the Cambodian border area in Ubon Province. The underground appeared to be acting in support of communists inside Cambodia. South Vietnamese communist guerrillas were reported to have entered Thailand briefly from Cambodia and inquired about border patrols from villagers.

In CPT opinion, Prince Sihanouk's "Royal Government of National Union" was the legitimate government of Cambodia. The VPT maintained that "the people of Thailand, who always regard the Cambodian people as their dearest brothers, stand firmly by the side of the fraternal Cambodian people and resolutely support their struggle against U.S. imperialism and its lackeys and for the defense of Cambodia's independence, peace, democracy, neutrality, national sovereignty and territorial integrity" (quoted, NCNA, 17 April). The mutually reinforcing relationship between the "wars of national liberation" being fought in Indochina and Thailand was repeatedly expounded.

One of the main objectives of the CPT is to "drive U.S. imperialism from Thailand" (VPT, 7 August). According to the party, "through the collusion of the traitorous Thanom-Praphas clique, the U.S. imperialists have increasingly encroached on Thailand's independence and sovereignty" (*ibid.*, 4 September). President Nixon's five-point proposal for an Indochina settlement, announced in mid-1970, was greeted by the CPT as "another foolish political maneuver aimed at deceiving the people and masking the U.S. imperialist vicious scheme to expand the war throughout Indochina" (*ibid.*, 12 October). The Thai government was condemned for aiding the United States, the Republic of Vietnam and Lon Nol in Cambodia. President Suharto of Indonesia was censured for his efforts to preserve Cambodian neutrality.

CPT anger in 1970 was also directed against Malaysia, for its cooperation with Thailand against CPM guerrillas in the south. The VPT (24 February) charged that Malaysian soldiers "arrogantly searched, plundered, arrested, and maltreated the people."

Publications. The CPT publishes an irregular clandestine journal, *Ekkarat* (Independence). CPT policy statements are broadcast by "Voice of the People of Thailand" (Siang Pracheachon), a clandestine radio station operating from the China-Laos-North Vietnam border area. The broadcasts are in the various hill tribe dialects as well as in Thai. CPT views are also disseminated by Chinese and North Vietnamese media and by *Siang Phee Rak Chart*, a monthly Thai periodical, and *Malayan Monitor and General News*, a monthly published in London.

S. E. Y.

VIETNAM: DEMOCRATIC REPUBLIC OF VIETNAM

The Vietnam Workers' Party (Dang Lao Dong Viet Nam, often referred to as the Lao Dong Party; VWP) is an outgrowth of the Indochinese Communist Party founded in 1930. In May 1941, party members organized the nationalistic anti-French, anti-Japanese "League for Vietnamese Independence" (Viet Nam Doc Lap Dong Minh), known as the Viet Minh. After the Indochinese Communist Party was nominally dissolved in November 1945, party functions were carried on clandestinely by the "Association for Marxist Studies," under the leadership of Truong Chinh. In February 1951, the supposedly nonexistent Indochinese Communist Party held its Eleventh Congress and the Viet Minh was absorbed into the "United Vietnam Nationalist Front" (Mat Tran Lien Hiep Quoc Dan Viet Nam), better known as the Lien Viet, a front organization created in 1946, in which the communist component was consolidated under the name of the Vietnam Workers' Party. In September 1955 the Lien Viet was absorbed by the Vietnam Fatherland Front (Mat Tran To Quoc Viet Nam).

On 18 January 1962, Hanoi radio announced the formation on 1 January 1962 of the People's Revolutionary Party (Dang Nhan Dan Cach Mang; PRP), which was formed from the covert network of communist cadres left behind by the Viet Minh when it regrouped north of the 17th parallel in 1954. The establishment of the PRP was the outcome of the need to provide more effective leadership and organization to the National Liberation Front of South Vietnam (Mat Tran Dan Toc Giai Phong Mien Nam Viet Nam; NLFSV), founded on 20 December 1960. Despite attempts by both North and South Vietnamese communists to present the PRP as an "indigenous southern proletarian party," it is in fact the southern branch of the Vietnam Workers' Party. (See *Vietnam: Republic of Vietnam.*)

According to the 1960 constitution of the Democratic Republic of Vietnam (DRV), the highest organ of state power is the National Assembly, which enacts laws, supervises the enforcement of the provisions of the constitution, and elects the president and vice-president. The National Assembly is headed by a permanent president, Truong Chinh, and is composed of 455 deputies, of whom 366 were elected on 26 April 1964 and ran as candidates of the Vietnam Fatherland Front. The remaining 89, representing South Vietnam, were reportedly elected in 1946. Although a number of these deputies presumably are no longer living, no replacements or new members have been announced.

As outlined in the 1960 constitution, the formal government structure of the DRV is distinct from that of the ruling Vietnam Workers' Party. In practice, however, the VWP dictates and supervises the administrative, legislative, judicial, military, cultural, and economic aspects of the government through parallel but separate hierarchial organizations extending to the lowest territorial units.

The latest official estimate of party strength was an April 1966 statement by Ho Chi Minh in which he put the VWP membership at 760,000. This indicated an increase of 300,000 members since the party congress in 1960. There are no later official figures, but party membership presumably has increased since 1966. The population of North Vietnam is 21,200,000 (est. 1970).

Leadership and Organization. The VWP is a highly centralized, hierarchial party, with committees at all levels of administration. The basic party organization is the *chi bo* (branch or chapter), officially described as the unit responsible for the "task of linking the party with masses, implementing the party line and policy among the masses, and reflecting the opinions, aspirations, and desires of the masses to the leading bodies of the party." A *chi bo* is established wherever there are more than three regular party members; it is responsible to the party committee of the area. A *chi bo* may be divided into cells (*tieu-to*), which have no administrative authority. At the apex of the hierarchy is the party congress, normally held every four years and most recently held in September 1960. Between congresses, the party Central Committee directs the activities of the VWP, but plenary sessions of the party Central Committee are held only occasionally; it is the Politburo which actually determines VWP policy and supervises its implementation on behalf of the Central Committee.

Although reports indicate that the VWP Central Committee consists of approximately 100 members, apparently only 43 full members and 30 alternate members have been officially referred to as Central Committee members. Since the death of Ho Chi Minh, in 1969, the Central Committee has been without a chairman. The party is at present under "collective leadership" whose key figures are Le Duan, Truong Chinh, Pham Van Dong, and Vo Nguyen Giap. Le Duan is first secretary of the Central Committee.

The Politburo of the VWP apparently consists of nine full members and two alternate members (alphabetical order): Hoang Van Hoan, Le Duan, Le Duc Tho, Le Thanh Nghi, Nguyen Duy Trinh, Pham Hung, Pham Van Dong, Truong Chinh, and Vo Vguyen Giap, and alternates Tran Quoc Hoan and Van Tien Dung. A report in the *New York Times* (12 October 1969) referred to the possibility of a tenth "covert" Politburo member known as Nguyen Van Muoi, believed to be the second-ranking member of the NLFSV Central Committee and reportedly working with Pham Hung in South Vietnam and directing the Central Office for South Vietnam (COSVN—see *Vietnam: Republic of Vietnam*). Although Ton Duc Thang—vice-president of the DRV, member of the VWP Central Committee, and president of the Presidium of the Vietnam Fatherland Front—was elected by the National Assembly to succeed Ho Chi Minh as president of the DRV (see below), Ho Chi Minh's position in the VWP Politburo was not filled and the position of party chairman has remained vacant.

The most important mass organization is the Vietnam Fatherland Front, of which the VWP is the leading component. Founded in September 1955, the front has continued to advance a program maintaining that Vietnam is indivisible but allowing for different conditions in the North and South. Communist elements still in South Vietnam have been instructed not to identify themselves with the Vietnam Fatherland Front, but to create separate movements with the same objectives. The chairman of the Vietnam Fatherland Front is Ton Duc Thang (current president of the DRV). Presidium members include Hoang Quoc Viet, Le Dinh Tham, Mme Nguyen Thi Thap, Nguyen Van Hoang, Tran Dang Khoa, Truong Chinh, and Xuan Thuy. Tran Huu Duc is secretary-general and Nguyen Thi Luu is deputy secretary-general. (For Front objectives see *YICA 1970*, p. 688.)

Important mass organizations affiliated under the Vietnam Fatherland Front are the Vietnam General Federation of Trade Unions, headed by Hoang Quoc Viet; the Vietnam Labor Youth Union, headed by Vu Quang; and the Vietnam Women's Union, headed by Mme Nguyen Thi Thap.

Party Internal Affairs. Two factions exist within the VWP leadership. One group, led by Le Duan, Pham Van Dong, Pham Hung, and Vo Nguyen Giap, is generally characterized as less dogmatic in its Marxist orientation. It is apparently willing to take expedient measures even if they might be inconsistent with Marxism. This group calls for subordinating socialist construction, ideological indoctrination, and party discipline in the North to winning the war in the South. In the context of Sino-Soviet rivalry, Le Duan favors a selective combination of both pro-Chinese and pro-Soviet policies. The second faction, led by Truong Chinh, Le Duc Tho, Nguyen Duy Trinh, and possibly Hoang Van Hoan (see *YICA*, 1970 pp. 689-90), contends that communist orthodoxy is of prime importance. While also committed to a victory in the South, it advocates a return to guerrilla tactics and the subordination of the war in the South to the political and economic tasks of the North. Truong Chinh, president of the National Assembly and the leading party theoretician, is an outspoken proponent of pro-Chinese policies.

The post of VWP chairman apparently remains unfilled because of the opposing claims of Le Duan and Truong Chinh. Other contenders for the post include Pham Van Dong and Vo Nguyen Giap. A history of the VWP which came out in January 1970, cited only Le Duan and Truong Chinh among the living VWP members as having made important contributions to basic policy. By quoting Le Duan at greater length than Truong Chinh and by linking him more directly with present policy, the history seemed to suggest that he had achieved the greater eminence.

On 14 February, Le Duan published a long article in *Nhan Dan*, the VWP newspaper, entitled "Under the Glorious Banner, for Independence, Freedom, and Socialism, Let Us Advance and Achieve New Victories." It purported to be in commemoration of the fortieth anniversary (3 February) of the Indochinese Communist Party. The extensive discussion and publicity it received in Hanoi renewed speculation that Le Duan had achieved an edge over Truong Chinh. *Nhan Dan* devoted an entire issue to a review of the article and in a subsequent editorial called for serious study of the text to raise political consciousness and work efficiency. The article was thus recognized as a theoretical contribution to Vietnamese communism. Heretofore, Le Duan had been recognized as an organizational leader and economic administrator but not as a theoretician. The publication of the lengthy article over his signature instead of that of recognized theoretician Truong Chinh was interpretable as indicating a shift in the Hanoi leadership in Le Duan's favor or possibly at least a move designed to create such a shift. Although Le Duan has no constitutional power, as first secretary he personally controls the party apparatus.

In his will, Ho Chi Minh called for party unity, thus forestalling open rivalry within the Politburo. In December 1970, sixteen months after his death, the position of chairman still was vacant. Since his death, Ho has become virtually deified; his name is invoked in connection with every government or party edict. In a speech broadcast by Hanoi radio on 18 May, Pham Van Dong expressed a typical sentiment:

> In the most painful days of our nation when President Ho Chi Minh departed from us, the entire Vietnamese people shared the same feeling, the same thought: Our Uncle Ho is not dead, he will live forever with our mountains and our rivers, in our revolutionary cause, and in the hearts of our people.

In the same speech, Ho was described as "the incarnation of the independence, freedom, happiness, and deep aspirations of the Vietnamese people." Ho Chi Minh emulation campaigns have been initiated, and a new class of exemplary cadres has been designated "Ho Chi Minh cadres."

In discussing the role of the party in his *Nhan Dan* article, Le Duan stressed organization. He accused some cadres of separating ideological and political tasks from organizational responsibilities, to the detriment of the latter. To counter this development, he advocated reorganizing the party and the government, including the removal of "degraded elements who are detested by the masses and are unworthy of a revolutionary vanguard party." (Quoted by Hanoi radio, domestic service, 21 February.) Although such party members were described as "not numerous," they were viewed as very harmful to the party. Le Duan thus set the stage for a purge which could conceivably remove his rivals from power. Concurrently, he called for the admission of new "Ho Chi Minh" party members, particularly young people. By constantly being replenished, he indicated the party would reflect the ever changing revolutionary movement.

In late March, the theoretical journal *Hoc Tap* carried an order for a purge. On 25 April, Hanoi radio announced a Politburo resolution, signed by Le Duan, which declared that most cadres and party members were below standard. Charges included inferior character, inferior political standards, working poorly, failure to do one's duty, "sagging determination to fight," low ethical standards, corruption, bullying, indiscipline, and infringing on the rights of others. All those unworthy of party membership, regardless of rank, it was disclosed, would be expelled from the VWP in a purge lasting from 19 May 1970 to 19 May 1971 in commemoration of the eightieth year of Ho Chi Minh's birth. They would be replaced by the new Ho Chi Minh cadres, who must be introduced into the party by the Vietnam Labor Youth Union. All party organs were required to submit plans for implementing the purge to the Central Committee Secretariat; a guiding committee was established to supervise the campaign. Party members were reminded that differing opinions could be expressed during debate, but that once a decision was reached, all must abide by it.

A broadcast of 19 June by the Vietnam News Agency (VNA) explained that the membership drive was being carried out under the guideline, "Relying on the masses to build the party, control the work and quality of all party organizations, cadres, and members [and] create good opportunities for the people to make criticism of party cadres and members and to recommend qualified people for party membership." Although details were kept secret, press reports indicated that the progress of the drive was not smooth. "Hundreds" of cadres were reported to have been sent to the countryside to help local committees. An additional Politburo resolution (VNA, 19 June) dealt with "heightening the standard of party members" and revealed that 75 per cent of the new cadres had been Vietnam Labor Youth Union members.

A 6 July *Nhan Dan* editorial admitted recruitment difficulties, claiming that although the majority of the people were enthusiastic, many were "at a loss in carrying out the campaign." A plethora of meetings and discussion had obscured its correct aim and direction. The central task, at which most localities had failed, was to "hold firmly to the political tasks of the revolution." Thus, limited results were common, especially in the provinces which were "still tinged with the backwardness of small-scale production and therefore unable to concentrate on the correct issues."

In addition to membership quality, the VWP faces the problem of maintaining its claim that it is a proletarian party while in actuality it is largely divorced from the working class and the peasantry. In 1968 Le Duc Tho disclosed that workers comprised only 18.5 per cent of the membership. Furthermore, the party appears to be underrepresented in some military units. An article by Lieutenant General Song Hao (December 1969) served as the basis for a drive which was instituted in February 1970 to increase party control in the armed forces.

Domestic Attitudes and Activities. Le Duan, in the aforementioned article of 14 February 1970, devoted considerable attention to the economic problems and policy of the DRV. He indicated that industrial development of the country was a crucial need: "If we think that we can build socialism with proletarian dictatorship and our enthusiasm alone and if we disregard all objective laws and economic facts, which are sometimes hard and cruel, we are grossly mistaken" (Hanoi radio, domestic service, 20 February). Attacking the doctrinaire approach to economic policy, Le Duan argued the case for flexibility in management and concentration on a technological revolution as the means for building a prosperous economy. (Two other "revolutions" were proposed by Le Duan. A "revolution in production relations" would put an end to "capitalist dictatorship" and private production and collectivize all production into a system of socialist public ownership, paving the way for the technological revolution; and a "revolution in ideology and culture" would transform the peasant into a "socialist man" by teaching him to accept collectivization and to master mechanization, thereby eliminating the remnants of small-scale production, indiscipline, and irresponsibility.) Le Duan asserted that in order to build the economy it would be necessary to rebuild the country's education system and increase the number of trained experts who could contribute to technological development. Citing Lenin's "new economic policy" as a precedent for his flexible approach, he advocated encouraging production through "material means"—which could mean offering profit incentives—as well as by political education. Better planning was also said to be necessary. Labor should be redistributed from farm to factory, and control should be decentralized. Developing of regional economy (e.g., in agricultural food processing, small industries, and handicrafts) should be stressed—a measure advocated also by Pham Van Dong in his mid-year address to the National Assembly. In short, the development from an agricultural economy to one based on heavy industry would involve full realization of collective ownership, mechanization, and education of peasants and workers to persuade them to accept the necessary changes.

As Le Duan admitted in his signal article, economic progress in North Vietnam has been slow. Production in heavy industry, chemical industry, and coal mining is insufficient; and light industry has failed to contribute adequately to the mechanization of handicrafts and to raising the admittedly low standard of living. Agriculture, too, has remained backward, although it occupies 75 per cent of the labor force. (To counter these conditions, a "productive labor movement" was launched on 12 February.)

Le Duan insisted that party control should encompass key enterprises and "basic standards," but he criticized the prevalence of bureaucracy. A balance had to be achieved between regional and central development, between industry and agriculture, between production and consumption—all with an eye to raising the standard of living.

The DRV press admitted that food shortages were plaguing the country. A communiqué of the Council of Ministers, dated 20 December, disclosed that the October rice crop was harvested so slowly that many fields would not be plowed in time for the winter-spring and spring crops. Since no mention was made of natural disasters, this failure probably was due to poor discipline and lack of motivation among the farmers.

On 13 August, Central Committee member and deputy premier Do Muoi spoke about economic problems. As reported in the August issue of *Cong Tac Ke Hoach* (Hanoi), he announced that the organization and utilization of labor forces was still quite inefficient: the planning carried on by cadres was ineffectual, and workers were idle, while the country's resources remained undeveloped; rice-field acreage was not fully used, the raising of livestock and poultry had not been pursued, fish breeding had been overlooked, and there were no plans for cultivating fruit and timber trees. As a result, Do Muoi declared, the people still lacked consumers' goods, and many handicraftsmen were unemployed. To correct these conditions, labor efficiency had to be increased, including the "rational reassignment of the labor forces" from the delta area, where there was a population surplus to the highlands area, where there was a deficit. Moreover, manufacturing costs had to be cut.

A productive labor movement was officially inaugurated on 12 February. Its purpose was to raise production and offset the habit of "late to work, early to leave," which afflicted North

Vietnam's industry. Although the mobilization of all labor forces and the consequent increase in efficiency and output were to be achieved by expanding party control over labor, increasing discipline and "socialist laws," and intensifying political and ideological education, it appears that, in practice, reliance was put upon material incentives in the form of such measures as the "piece-work payment system" (Hanoi radio, 17 February) and bonuses (*Nhan Dan*, 17 March). A decree of 3 March laid down a new policy of setting rice and grain quotas for cooperatives for a five-year period. Surpluses were to be retained by cooperative members to utilize, barter, or sell to the state at a price higher than that paid for quota production. In an attempt to curb the black market, a new drive against speculators was instituted. According to Pham Van Dong's report to the legislature early in 1971 (VNA, 5 March), quotas were fulfilled for "many main products" in agriculture and other areas of production.

North Vietnam has experienced an increase in theft, corruption, black marketeering, and pilfering during recent years. In January 1970 the police and the VWP municipal committee in Hanoi launched a campaign to maintain law, order, and discipline. In addition to the apparent goals of the movement, it appears that firm ideological control over the populace and the exclusion of external influences were among the objectives. There seemed also to be an intention to stem a decline in morale occasioned by the continuing war and the death of Ho Chi Minh. In April, a report on the campaign indicated that such offenses as violations of security, illegal trading, robbery, juvenile delinquency, and disturbing the peace remained prevalent. Destructive counter-revolutionaries, it was announced, could be identified "by such actions as loud singing, the wearing of outlandish clothes and hair styles, and the reading of decadent books and novels." (*Nhan Dan*, 12 April.)

Those who were lax in their work were to be forced to produce. Undesirables were to be sent to industrial and agricultural camps outside Hanoi, according to a resolution of the Hanoi Municipal People's Council (12 February). Law and order were also enforced through people's courts, which are noted for their severity. Teams of youths were said to have been organized into a "street administration" to patrol the city and report violations.

By mid-year it was apparent that the authorities were dissatisfied with the results of the campaign and had decided to expand it. On 21 October, the National Assembly passed decrees dealing with offenses against state and private property and providing for punishment ranging from three months' to life imprisonment or even death. The heavier sentences were for professional and organized criminals and for those who used force or weapons to seize important property. The decree concerning state property was designed to instill in the people the concept of collective ownership; in the past, state property apparently was considered fair game by the people. The decree concerning private property had a specific article prohibiting the "abuse of power or high office" to appropriate another's property—indicating that the relatively well-off as well as the poor had been involved in offenses. An article by Tran Nieu, deputy head of the People's Supreme Control Authority, confirmed this impression (*ibid.*, 1 November). Abuses involving "corruption, waste, speculation, hoarding, and tax evasion" were revealed by Trinh Van Binh, deputy finance minister (Hanoi radio, 5 November).

According to communist defectors from the DRV, low morale is a military as well as a civilian problem and was exacerbated in late April by reports of impending U.S. and South Vietnamese actions against communist bases in Cambodia. Lieutenant Colonel Nguyen Van Nang, deputy commander of the communist Subregion 2 (on the Cambodian border), surrendered on 20 May. He stated that some 800 North Vietnamese soldiers, including six battalion commanders and other officers, had been sent to the rear for "rehabilitation" because of reluctance to go to battle. He further stated that 30 per cent of the troops in eight battalions (probably 400 men) had resisted orders to fight and requested permission to return home. Other defectors noted a reluctance to enlist in the military services. To offset such problems, "Ho Chi Minh emulation drives" have been started, with results that so far have remained obscure.

The development which obviously exerts a major influence over the VWP and the DRV, and which causes many of their problems, is the war in the South. North Vietnamese statements have regularly alleged that the Republic of Vietnam government in Saigon is on the verge of collapse, that the U.S.-backed Vietnamization and pacification programs are doomed to failure, and that the "anti-imperialist struggle" in the cities and among the students of the South is growing stronger. The U.S. forces are depicted as isolated in the masses of the South Vietnamese. Concurrently, Vietnamese communist leaders caution the people that the Americans are tricky and that heightened vigilance is necessary. An article in the Vietnamese People's Army daily, *Quan Doi Nhan Dan* (11 August), declared that it was imperative to defeat the pacification program and that, to this end, it was most important to maintain the offensive. "Reactionary" agents and informants were to be eliminated, and the occupation and domination of villages and hamlets— "the foundation for the development of the entire revolutionary war"—was considered more crucial than ever before.

During the year, great military successes over the United States were alleged and acclaimed, while DRV leaders vowed to pursue the struggle in the South to victory. While claiming that the Paris peace talks had been forced upon the United States by its military failures, statements from Hanoi offered no prospects of a negotiated settlement to the war. The communists' war strategy apparently reverted to the postulate of long-term, low-level hostilities which would be more bearable to them than to the enemy. This course was presaged in a December 1969 article by General Vo Nguyen Giap, which emphasized U.S. power and mobility and called for appropriate new tactics to cope with this. Le Duan's aforementioned article emphasized that a combination of political campaigns, local uprisings, guerrilla tactics, and conventional warfare offered the best way to offset the preponderant strength of the opponent. Stress was placed on protracted struggle, which was seen as gradually weakening the enemy while strengthening the communists' forces politically and militarily.

Concomitant with the return to a low level of hostilities, the DRV launched an army recruitment drive, apparently designed to strengthen the People's Liberation Armed Forces in South Vietnam. North Vietnamese soldiers constitute an estimated 80 per cent of that body. In Laos, North Vietnamese troop involvement in the latter half of 1970 appeared greatly reduced,[1] but the expanding struggle in Cambodia probably necessitated additional recruitment. Vo Nguyen Giap informed the Central Military Affairs Committee that increased conscription and recruitment was necessary in order to meet the requirements of communist forces in South Vietnam and other parts of Indochina.

International Views and Positions. Failure to attain self-sufficiency in agriculture and industry has forced the DRV to depend on the U.S.S.R. and China for its vital supplies. During 1970 the North Vietnamese government and party continued to steer an independent course in respect to Sino-Soviet rivalry. Some observers claimed to detect a tendency to favor the U.S.S.R., basing their contentions on such evidence as the fact that Le Duan led the VWP delegation to the Moscow celebration of the Lenin Centenary, North Vietnam's ranking the U.S.S.R. first and China second when expressing thanks to socialist nations for support and praising their achievements, and Le Duan's frequent mention of Lenin, Stalin, and the Soviet Union in presenting precedents and sanctions for the policies in his 14 February *Nhan Dan* article (in which he did not mention

---

[1]North Vietnamese troops in the Plain of Jars—previously set at 16,000 — were estimated by U.S. intelligence sources at the beginning of the rainy season at little over 2,000, mostly in defensive positions (*Far Eastern Economic Review*, 31 October 1970).

Mao Tse-tung and only once cited China). On the other hand, Le Duan's attendance at the Moscow celebration was counterbalanced by his stopping over in Peking and meeting with Chou En-lai on his way there; and North Vietnam's blunt rejection of U.S. President Nixon's five-point peace plan at the Paris peace talks and new trade and aid agreement with China could be interpreted as indicating a growing cordiality.

Hanoi radio on 26 May announced the signing (on 25 May) of a military and economic aid agreement with the Chinese People's Republic. Although the amount was not specified, the protocol provided supplementary nonrefundable aid in addition to that granted for 1970 in an agreement signed on 26 September 1969. U.S. officials have estimated that the Chinese furnished some $200 million in aid in 1970 (*New York Times*, 18 January 1971). Further agreements on economic and technical aid and on military aid were signed in Peking on 6 October to cover the year 1971. Again, the aid was described as nonrefundable. According to the *Far Eastern Economic Review* (7 November 1970), the new protocols gave North Vietnam access to China's markets and included complete industrial projects to be constructed by Chinese technicians. This orientation of Chinese aid to the DRV was possibly related to Le Duan's call for national industrial reconstruction. In any case, Chinese interest in military developments in Vietnam continued unabated. In an unusual move, on 21 and 22 December NLFSV and North Vietnamese military men reported on the current situation in Vietnam to Chinese Foreign Ministry meetings during the week of celebration of the tenth anniversary of the NLFSV and the twenty-sixth anniversary of the People's Army of North Vietnam. At the meetings, Li Te-sheng, alternate member of the Politburo of the Chinese Communist Party and head of the General Political Department of the People's Liberation Army, gave a major speech in which he referred to assisting the people of Indochina "with concrete actions" and "deeds" (*ibid.*, 2 January 1971, p. 8).

Chinese statements about Vietnam during 1970 characteristically emphasized mutual opposition to the United States and referred to the "reliable rear area" and "powerful backing" that China and its people were providing to the Vietnamese in their resistance against U.S. forces. Repeated Chinese stress on persistence in protracted struggle indicated continuing Chinese disapproval of the Paris peace talks and any attempts at negotiated peace short of a complete military victory.

In contrast to the Chinese, the Soviets have supported North Vietnam's participation in the Paris peace talks as well as its military struggle against the United States, claiming that "the DRV fights consistently for a political settlement in Vietnam" (*Pravda*, 2 September.) Lengthy excerpts from Le Duan's 14 February article, emphasizing party organization and rejuvenation and international proletarian solidarity against imperialism, were published in *Pravda*.

On 11 June the DRV and the U.S.S.R. signed an agreement providing supplementary aid for 1970. The Hanoi announcement of the pact specified that the aid was for the purpose of domestic economic development and for national defense. The Soviet deputy minister of foreign trade was quoted as stating that Soviet aid to Vietnam would continue until U.S. withdrawal from that country. The amount of the aid was not disclosed, but U.S. sources estimated it at $500 million in 1970, of which only 30 per cent was military (*New York Times*, 18 January 1971). According to Moscow radio (22 January), Soviet exports to Vietnam in 1970 were to increase by 50 per cent; the VNA (28 February), however, set the increase at 30 per cent. On 20 January, Moscow radio claimed that machinery and equipment for a number of new factories was en route to North Vietnam. A later report (TASS, 4 February) indicated that Soviet engineers were rebuilding the port at Haiphong and increasing its capacity by eight to ten times. Some 1,000 Soviet technicians are believed to be in North Vietnam, helping to install and operate Soviet equipment. Intelligence reports claim that 2,000 North Vietnamese are trained in the Soviet Union annually.

Indochinese solidarity, as in recent years, was one of the main themes in North Vietnamese statements on international affairs in 1970 and was echoed by communist parties throughout the region. Events in Cambodia in the late spring gave it added currency and substance. Prince Sihanouk's loss of office; the open hostility between the new Cambodian government and the Vietnamese communist troops which used the country as a privileged sanctuary, base, and supply route; and the "Summit Conference of the Indochinese Peoples" on 24-25 April[2]—all these developments served to bring into the open North Vietnamese activities throughout Indochina and to strengthen the bonds existing between parties in the area. (See *Cambodia*.) On 21 April, Le Duan announced an Indochinese united front policy in Moscow at the Lenin Centenary. The Summit Conference, in effect, laid the foundations for realizing that policy. In an unusually open statement on 1 June, General Vo Nguyen Giap declared: "We pledge to fight shoulder to shoulder with the fraternal peoples of Laos and Cambodia for genuine independence and freedom and to lead the national liberation undertaking of the Indochinese peoples to complete victory" (*Nhan Dan*, 1 June). This was the first DRV admission of its leadership role in the various Indochinese communist insurgencies.

The DRV has troops stationed in Laos and Cambodia as well as in South Vietnam, and the communist parties in those countries are subservient to the VWP. The insurgencies in Cambodia and, to a lesser extent in southern Laos, have received frequent and vigorous declarations of support from the Vietnamese communists as parts of a common struggle against the United States. Statements from Hanoi protesting the apparent massacre of Vietnamese in Cambodia in mid-1970 were especially numerous. A North Vietnamese delegation attended the "International Conference of Solidarity with the Peoples of Laos," held in Cairo on 19-21 May by the Afro-Asian Peoples' Solidarity Organization.

Prince Sihanouk and a large entourage from Peking visited Hanoi from 25 May to 8 June. While there, he was accompanied everywhere by Prime Minister Pham Van Dong, and all his meetings were chaired by the DRV president, Ton Duc Thang. Apparently, however, he met with the two most powerful VWP figures, Le Duan and Truong Chinh, only on formal occasions. A joint statement at the conclusion of the visit merely reiterated the principles endorsed by the Summit Conference of the Indochinese Peoples and analyzed U.S. weaknesses. North Vietnam expressed no material commitment to the Cambodian leader.

Elsewhere in Asia, the DRV continued its friendly relations with North Korea. The customary visits and greetings were exchanged between the VWP and communist parties in the region. The labor strikes in the Philippines were praised in the Hanoi press, and the U.S.-Japan security treaty was condemned. Diplomatic recognition between the DRV and Ceylon was established.

The DRV reportedly has given training in guerrilla warfare to Meo hill tribesmen from northern Thailand, Naga dissidents from northeastern India, and Palestinian commandos. On 15 May 1970, the DRV observed what was termed its "annual international day of solidarity with the Palestinian people." On 9 September, a trade treaty between North Vietnam and Syria was ratified.

Beyond Southeast Asia, during 1970 the DRV and the VWP sent friendly messages also to various communist regimes and revolutionary movements around the world, according special attention to Cuba and Mongolia. In July the DRV signed a cultural exchange agreement with Cuba. Both a cultural cooperation plan and a consular agreement were signed with the Mongolian People's Republic. Vietnamese support for "anti-imperialist, anti-colonialist" movements in Africa was affirmed in a "week of solidarity," observed on 22-28 May. At mid-year, Somalia agreed to establish diplomatic relations with the DRV.

---

[2]Attended by delegations of the DRV, the Vietnam Fatherland Front, Sihanouk's National United Front of Kampuchea, the NLFSV, the Vietnam Alliance of National, Democratic, and Peace Forces (VANDPF), and the Laotian Neo Lao Hak Xat (NLHX) and Patriotic Neutralist Forces (PNF). It was held in southern China.

In Western Europe, relations with the French Communist Party were particularly cordial. A DRV delegation headed by Le Duc Tho attended the Nineteenth Congress of the French party; the report of the congress expressed grief for the death of Ho Chi Minh and support for the Vietnamese struggle. As in previous years, French communists gave some $200,000 to the Vietnamese cause (VNA, 9 June).[3] Further monetary support was received from the French Peace Movement.

North Vietnam maintained fraternal relations with the communist countries of Eastern Europe. It signed aid agreements with the German Democratic Republic (supplementary aid; VNA, 16 July), Czechoslovakia (*Nhan Dan*, 9 November), and Romania (VNA, 19 November). On 27 August, a cultural cooperation plan with Bulgaria was concluded.

In the Western Hemisphere, the DRV was a vocal supporter of the anti-war movement in the United States. In conjunction with its view of the United States as its prime enemy, it endorsed the "struggle of the black people . . . a colonial people pent up in imperialist America," whom they regarded as allies and "companions-in-arms" (*Nhan Dan*, 18 August). Special mention was made of the Black Panther Party, whose minister of information, Eldridge Cleaver, headed an "anti-imperialist" delegation that visited the DRV during a week of solidarity with the black people of the United States.

Elsewhere in the hemisphere, the Vietnamese communists had praise for the people of Venezuela, Colombia, Guatemala, Peru, Bolivia, and Ecuador as well as Cuba, with whom they claimed to share a common enemy, the United States.

Almost all communist parties and states expressed support for the Vietnamese communists against the "U.S. imperialists." One exception was the Progressive Labor Party of the United States, which condemned the Vietnamese for entering into peace negotiations.

Publications. VWP policy statements and directives are carried primarily in the daily organ of its Central Committee, *Nhan Dan* (People's Daily), whose editor in chief is Hoang Tung; in *Hoc Tap* (Studies), the monthly theoretical organ of the Central Committee; and in *Quan Doi Nhan Dan* (People's Army), the daily organ of the Vietnamese People's Army. Other major publications include *Tien Phong* (Vanguard), the organ of the Central Committee of the Vietnam Labor Youth Union; *Lao Dong* (Labor), the organ of the Vietnam General Federation of Trade Unions; *Cuu Quoc* (National Salvation), the weekly organ of the Central Committee of the Vietnam Fatherland Front; *Doc Lap* (Independence), the weekly organ of the Central Committee of the Vietnam Democratic Party; and *To Quoc* (Motherland), the bimonthly organ of the Vietnam Socialist Party. International publications include *Vietnam Courier*, a political weekly published in English and French by the Committee for Cultural Relations with Foreign Countries, and *Vietnam*, an illustrated monthly published in English, French, Russian, Chinese, and Vietnamese.

Party statements are also broadcast by the Vietnam News Agency, which is headed by Dat Tung.

S. E. Y.

[3]Previously given to the DRV and the NLFSV, the contribution in 1970 was for the DRV and the Provisional Revolutionary Government of South Vietnam (PRG).

VIETNAM:
REPUBLIC OF VIETNAM

Formed from the covert network of communist cadres left behind by the Viet Minh when it re-grouped north of the 17th parallel in 1954, the People's Revolutionary Party (Dang Nhan Dan Cach Mang; PRP) was formally established on 1 January 1962. Its formation was not announced, however, until 18 January, when the Vietnam News Agency in North Vietnam reported that the new party had been formed as a result of a "conference of Marxist-Leninists meeting in South Vietnam in late December [1961] under the guidance of veteran revolutionaries." According to the North Vietnamese agency, the PRP was to be "a vanguard, thoroughly revolutionary political party," whose immediate tasks were "to unite and lead the working class, peasants, and other laboring people ... in South Vietnam" to overthrow the government. The PRP is illegal.

The establishment of the PRP was the outcome of the need to provide more effective leadership and organization to the National Liberation Front of South Vietnam (Mat Tran Dan Toc Giai Phong Mien Nam Viet Nam; NLFSV), founded on 20 December 1960. A statement circulated among NLFSV cadres (quoted in Douglas Pike, *Viet Cong*, Cambridge, Mass., M.I.T. Press, 1966, p. 140) declared that although the revolutionary movement had become stronger, it lacked organization and leadership and for this reason it was necessary that the "revolution in the South" be placed under a "unified leadership system." No doubt was left that the PRP was to be the "paramount organization" which would be responsible for the leadership of all other organizations within the NLFSV.

Despite attempts by both North and South Vietnamese communists to present the PRP as an "indigenous southern proletarian revolutionary party," it is in fact the southern branch of the Vietnam Workers' Party (Dang Lao Dong Viet Nam; VWP) of the Hanoi-based Democratic Republic of Vietnam (DRV). (See *YICA*, 1970, pp. 714-15.) The international communist movement does not recognize the independent existence of the PRP, since it deals directly with the North Vietnamese regime and party in matters concerning material aid and supplies. The PRP has denied, however, that it has any official ties with the DRV and the VWP beyond the normal "fraternal ties of communism."

Since its formation in 1962, the PRP has made no effort to deny its communist nature or its paramount role as a member of the NLFSV, whose activities it controls—along with those of the People's Liberation Armed Forces (PLAF), commonly referred to as Viet Cong[1]—through an elaborate structure within the NLFSV comprising parallel committees and subcommittees from the top down to the village level. It maintains that the use of "revolutionary violence" is necessary in its efforts to overthrow the Saigon-based government of the Republic of Vietnam. (See *YICA*, 1970, p. 715.)

[1]The term Viet Cong is condensed from Viet Nam Cong San, meaning "Vietnamese communists."

The PRP was estimated in 1962 to have not more than 35,000 members; more recent estimates have placed the membership between 85,000 and 100,000. Reports during 1968 and a document captured during 1969 seemed to indicate that party recruitment had suffered as a result of the demands of the war. Qualifications for PRP membership reportedly were then modified, with emphasis being placed on the recruitment of youths. The population of South Vietnam is 18,000,000 (estimated 1970).

The PRP. Leadership and Organization. The highest authority in the PRP is the party congress, which theoretically elects the "central level" or Central Committee (Ban Chap Hanh Trung Uong Dang), which in turn elects from among its members the Presidium, Secretariat, and Central Control Section, as well as its own officers, including a chairman and an assistant. The number of members of the Central Committee is unknown, and reports indicate that no nationwide meeting of PRP members has ever been convened. Under the Central Committee and its executive agency, the Central Office for South Vietnam (COSVN), comes the Central Committee of the interzone (*xu* or *bo*), which is basically a liaison and administrative echelon necessitated by the fact that geography and security needs prevented the complete concentration of leadership within the "central level." In 1966, the interzone committee had 21 members, with a presidium consisting of a chairman, secretary-general, and assistant secretary-general. Although the precise relationship between the interzone Central Committee and the higher echelon of the central-level Central Committee is not known, the central level appears to give directives which are implemented by the interzone body. In 1969 the COSVN was situated in Tay Ninh Province, but in 1970 it was broken into small units scattered through South Vietnam, Laos, and Cambodia. Regional committees elaborate COSVN directives, support (but do not command) PLAF main forces, and administer all subordinate PRP organizations.

Below the interzone Central Committee there is a split along rural and urban lines. The rural chain of command consists of the zone (*khu*), province (*tinh bo*), district (*quan*), village (*xa*), and hamlet branch (*chi bo*), while the urban chain consists of the special zone (*dac khu*), city (*tanh bo*), town or part of a city (*khu pho*), street zone (*kha pho*), and street branch (*chi bo*). At the bottom in both rural and urban areas is a three-man cell structure (*tien to*). In addition there exists what is called a "single-contact member" (*dang vien don tuyen*), who is found at all levels from the zone to the branch. He is appointed by the central-level Central Committee, which alone knows his identity. The various levels of the party appear to be well integrated through the use of overlapping committee membership, with the Central Committee at each level composed in part of top-ranking leaders from the level immediately below. (See Pike, *op. cit.*, pp. 145-50.)

The entire PRP apparatus, however, is controlled by the COSVN, which is the executive field agency of the PRP Central Committee and thus virtually coterminous with it. Some COSVN personnel are believed to be secret members of the VWP Central Committee.

Very little is known about the leadership of the PRP. The chairman of the Central Committee is Vo Chi Cong. Although references have been made to a "Nguyen Van Cuc," reports indicate that Vo Chi Cong is the same person. The secretary-general is Tran Nam Trung, whose name is believed to be the pseudonym of Lieutenant General Tran Van Tra, deputy chief of staff of the Vietnamese People's Army of North Vietnam and alternate member of the VWP Central Committee; Tran Nam Trung has also been identified as vice-chairman of the NLFSV Central Committee and chairman of that committee's Military Committee. Other members of the PRP leadership reportedly include Nguyen Van Lien (as deputy secretary-general), Vo Han Hau (secretary), Nguyen Van Chi (chairman of the Saigon-Cholon-Gia Dink committee of the PRP), Huynh Van Ngi and Pham Thi Yen (members of the just-mentioned committee), Tran Do (believed to be a North Vietnamese army general), Pham Xuan Thai, Pham Trong Dan, Ibeh

Aleo, Tran Bach Dang, Dang Tran Thi, Rochom Thep, Le Thanh Nam, Huynh Van Tam, Tran Van Tranh, Tran Hoai Nam, and Tran Van Binh. Huynh Tan Phat, president of the Provisional Revolutionary Government of the Republic of South Vietnam (PRG—see below), reportedly also is a member of the PRP leadership.

The PRP controls two major mass organizations, the People's Revolutionary Party Youth League (Doan Thanh Nien Nhan Dan Cach Mang; PRPYL) and the Vanguard Youth League (Thanh Nien Xung Phong), both formed in 1962.

Domestic and Foreign Policies. Initial policy statements issued by the PRP deemphasized the communist element of the party, and PRP cadres were instructed to minimize the socialist-communist theme when necessary. At the same time, however, instructions to PRP cadres stressed: "Our party does not conceal its ultimate objective, which is to achieve socialism and communism."

In January 1962, PRP policy was outlined in the "Ten-Point Platform," which proposed the formation of a "national, democratic coalition government" to carry out a democratic reform program, economic reforms, anti-American measures, "reestablishment" of "normal relations" between the North and the South, and a foreign policy of peace. (Full program in *YICA*, 1970, pp. 716-17.)

In a broadcast letter greeting the PLAF on the occasion of the lunar New Year 1970, the PRP Central Committee claimed that there was a continuing need to "make vigorous changes in the action and higher determination of party chapters in various areas, among the armed forces, and among the masses in order to meet the requirements of the forthcoming tasks" (Liberation Radio, 6 February). Apparently it did not specify the changes and did not outline the anticipated tasks. Earlier in the year (*ibid.*, 22 January, quoting *Tien Phong*, no. 8) the PRP called for "proper attention ... to the economic and financial front," which was closely associated with the military and political struggle: "Only by stepping up [production] can we strengthen the economic potentials of resistance." To this end, production was to be accelerated, thriftiness increased, savings encouraged, and usury combated. Supplies, transportation, and the exchange of goods in liberated areas were to be organized. The spirit of mutual assistance was to be developed, and savings bank activities were to be associated with manpower exchange activities. Local conditions should determine the crops raised in a given area. At the same time, the party cautioned:

> ... not to strengthen political education and awareness in mobilizing financial contributions for the revolution while the masses are financially able, shows a lack of the working class stand and reflects the standpoint of the peasantry and the bourgeoisie. Revolutionary cadres must be exemplary and vanguard in contributing to the revolution and not squander the money or property of the revolution. Financial management must firmly grasp the principles of democratic centralism.

Troop proselytizing was also emphasized in PRP statements during 1970. The "troop proselytizing" movement was supposed to be closely linked with all "political and armed offensive tasks," thus forming the "three offensive spearheads." The movement was described as essentially a civilian task, which had as its objective winning over of "the backward puppet [i.e., Saigon] troops." Communist forces in South Vietnam experienced a severe manpower shortage during the year, prompting the PRP to declare: "Only by overcoming the tendency of belittling the troop proselytizing task can we develop its effect and satisfactorily meet the demands of the revolution." (*Ibid.*, 20 January.)

Little information is available regarding the international views and positions of the PRP. In

April 1962 the PRP issued a statement declaring its support for NLFSV goals of "peace, neutralism, independence, and unification"; denounced U.S. "aggression" in South Vietnam; thanked the Soviet Union, Communist China, and other communist states for their support; urged international support for the "Vietnamese people's struggle"; called for implementation of the 1954 Geneva Agreements; and hinted that it would call on the Soviet Union for aid unless the U.S. forces left Vietnam. During 1970 the PRP continued to refrain from international activity. It issued no public statements on the Sino-Soviet dispute and the Chinese Cultural Revolution.

Publications. The PRP publishes a number of clandestine newspapers and periodicals. Its main publications include *Nhan Dan* (People's Daily), the weekly newspaper of the party, patterned after the North Vietnamese daily of the same name, and *Tien Phong* (Vanguard), a monthly political and theoretical journal.

*   *   *

The establishment of the National Liberation Front of South Vietnam on 20 December 1960 was formally announced by Hanoi radio following the adoption of a VWP Central Committee resolution calling for the establishment of a national united front in the South to rally "all patriotic forces" to overthrow the then Diem government and thereby guarantee the necessary "conditions for the peaceful reunification of the Fatherland."

The NLFSV consists of a network of organizations whose leadership is provided at all levels by corresponding PRP bodies. NLFSV organization was elaborated in a series of resolutions adopted at the Third Congress of the VWP, on 5-10 September 1960, which pointed out that the NLFSV was to "unite all patriotic parties and religious movements, as well as all political organizations that struggle against the U.S.-Diem clique." On 10 June 1969 the NLFSV's Liberation Radio announced the establishment of the Provisional Revolutionary Government of the Republic of South Vietnam (PRG).

The NLFSV. Leadership and Organization. Although separate from the NLFSV, the PRP leadership structure exists within and controls all the activities of both the NLFSV and the PLAF (see below). The NLFSV began its organizational phase in mid-1959, at least a year before its formal establishment in December 1960. Basing itself on the villages, the NLFSV created a large number of nationwide sociopolitical organizations in a context where mass organizations were virtually nonexistent. The NLFSV is represented at the hamlet and village level by the "administrative liberation associations," which themselves are composed of "functional liberation associations" and political parties. Abroad, it is supported and in part represented by other fronts.

(1) The "administrative liberation association" structure resembles that of a layered government organization. Nominally, authority runs from the NLFSV Central Committee down through a number of administrative levels to the village administrative liberation associations, but in fact all command authority and reporting passes vertically through PRP channels. The NLFSV Central Committee is supposed to have 64 members, but several seats and positions are apparently unfilled. The leadership consists of a chairman, Nguyen Huu Tho, and five vice-chairmen: Ibeh Aleo, Vo Chi Cong, Dr. Phung Van Cung (also known as Tran Van Cung), Huynh Tan Phat (also secretary-general of the NLFSV Central Committee), and Tran Nam Trung (whose name is believed to be an alias for the North Vietnamese Army general Tran Van

Tra). The NLFSV Presidium includes the above mentioned chairman and vice-chairmen, together with Tran Bach Dang, Mme Nguyen Thi Binh, Thich Thien Hao, Tran Buu Kiem, Nguyen Van Ngoi, Pham Xuan Thai, Nguyen Huu The, and Dang Tran Thi. The Secretariat consists of Huynh Tan Phat as secretary-general, Le Van Huan and Ho Thu as deputy secretary-generals, Ung Ngoc Ky, and Ho Xuan Son. On 23 January 1970 the NLFSV announced the death of Central Committee member Huynh Thien Tu, said to be a representative to the front of the Hoa Hao compatriots.

Below the NLFSV Central Committee are the following: three interzone headquarters; seven zones, or suboffices for the interzones; approximately 30 provincial committees; and the lower echelons comprising the district, town, and village committees and organizations. The village and hamlet committees are the chief operational units of the NLFSV. Reports during 1967 suggested that the interzone level might have been eliminated.

(2) The "functional liberation associations" are mass organizations of sociopolitical nature, organized horizontally at the village level. They consist of the following: the Farmers' Liberation Association (Hoi Nong Dan Giai Phong), headed by Nguyen Huu The; the Liberation Federation of Trade Unions (Hoi Lao Dong Giai Phong), headed by Pham Xuan Thai; the Women's Liberation Association (Hoi Phu Nu Giai Phong), headed by Mme Nguyen Thi Binh; the Youth Liberation Association (Hoi Thanh Nien Giai Phong), headed by Tran Bach Dang; the Student Liberation Association, or "Association for the Union of Students and Schoolboys for the Liberation of South Vietnam" (Hoi Lien Hiep Sinh Vien Va Hoc Sinh Giai Phong Mien Nam Viet Nam), headed by Tran Buu Kiem; and the Cultural Liberation Association, or "Association of Arts and Letters for the Liberation" (Hoi Van Nghe Giai Phong), headed by Tran Huu Trang.

As far as can be determined, there is no actual public participation in any of these groups. All of them, however, serve a common objective by enhancing horizontally the vertical control of the NLFSV command structure, and all of them are affiliated with corresponding international communist front organizations.

(3) In addition to the "administrative liberation associations" and the "functional liberation associations," the NLFSV is composed of a number of organizations such as political parties, special interest groups, and externally oriented organizations.

Two political parties in addition to the PRP are represented in the NLFSV; the Radical Socialist Party (Dang Xa Hoi Cap Tien) and the Democratic Party of South Vietnam (Dang Dan Chu Mien Nam Viet Nam). The Radical Socialist Party was founded in July 1962 and is headed by Nguyen Van Thieu, secretary-general, and Nguyen Ngoc Thuong, deputy secretary-general. Its chairman is unknown. Oriented toward intellectuals, particularly teachers and university students, it claims to represent a noncommunist social element within the framework of the NLFSV. The Democratic Party of South Vietnam was formed on 30 June 1944 and is headed by Tran Buu Kiem, chairman, and Huynh Tan Phat, secretary-general. It has described itself as the "party of patriotic capitalists and the petty bourgeoisie," and also as the "party of intellectuals, industrialists, and tradesmen"; it appeals primarily to the urban population. Both parties are represented by their leaders in the overall leadership of the NLFSV.

Special-interest groups include professional associations (*van hoi*), the most important of which is the Patriotic and Democratic Journalists' Association (Hoi Nha Bao Yeu Nuoc Van Dan Chu), together with religious and ethnic minority associations and a broad range of minor groups such as the Association of Families of Patriotic Soldiers (Hoi Gia Dinh Binh Si Yeu Nuoc) and the Leagues of Soldiers Returned to the People (Nhom Binh Si Tro Ve Voi Nhan Dan), among many others.

The NLFSV also is supported by a number of international organizations concerned with projecting the front's image abroad. The most important is the Afro-Asian Peoples' Solidarity Organization (Uy Ban Doan Ket Nhan Dan A Phi; AAPSO).

Also included in the NLFSV are the headquarters of the PLAF—formerly known as the South Vietnam Armed Forces of Liberation and in early October 1967 renamed the South Vietnam People's Liberation Armed Forces. Although operating within the framework of the NLFSV, the PLAF is in fact controlled by the Military Affairs Committee of the COSVN (which, as noted earlier, is the executive agency of the PRP Central Committee). North Vietnamese generals reportedly directing the PLAF include Chy Huy Man, Le Trong Tan, Hoang Van Thai, Le Chuong, Ha Ke Tan, Van Tien Dung, Tran Do, Hoang Quoc Viet, Bay Dung, Ba Tran, Nguyen Don, To Ky, and Pham Hung. It is believed that Pham Hung is the head of the COSVN.

In April 1968, Vietnamese communist sources announced the formation of the Vietnam Alliance of National, Democratic, and Peace Forces (Lien Mien Dan Toc Dan Cav va Hoa Binh a Viet Nam; VANDPF), which is headed by Trinh Dinh Thao and described as an alliance of "intellectuals, students, civil servants, and others who despite their different political leanings and religious colors are identified with one another in their hatred for the unbearable rule of the U.S. puppets." On 5 November 1968, the VANDPF signed a joint communiqué with the NLFSV declaring its "unanimity with the NLFSV on all subjects." (See also *YICA*, 1969, pp. 907-9.)

Although exact figures for the total membership of the NLFSV are not available, the Hanoi Domestic Service has claimed that the NLFSV comprises 30 organizations and some 7,000,000 members. Western sources at the beginning of 1970 estimated that the organized communist movement in South Vietnam consisted of some 40,000 main force or regular armed personnel and 100,000 guerrilla troops and administrative support cadre (*World Strength of the Communist Party Organizations*, Washington, D.C., 1970, p. 110). An infrastructure, consisting of some 75,000 to 85,000 political cadres, tax collectors, province and hamlet chiefs, party members, and intelligence agents is thought by some to exist (*Far Eastern Economic Review*, 7 May). As in 1969, the NLFSV claimed to have liberated four-fifths of the country and 11,000,000 people. It further asserted that "revolutionary power" had been established in 44 towns and cities—including Saigon, Hue, Da Nang, Can Tho, and Da Lat—in 150 of the 260 district and provincial capitals, and in 1,500 of the 2,700 villages in South Vietnam (Liberation Press Agency, 22 May 1970). According to Western estimates, however, in mid-1970 less than 8.0 per cent of the population lived in areas controlled by the NLFSV and only 6.5 per cent of the hamlets were in these areas (Charles A. Joiner, "Political Processes in the Two Vietnams," *Current History*, December 1970, p. 357).

Domestic Attitudes and Activities. Since the mid-1950's all communist activities have been outlawed in the Republic of Vietnam. The present constitution, adopted 1 April 1967, prohibits all activity aimed at furthering communism. In addition, earlier security and antisubversion legislation still remains in force. The NLFSV has, in turn, attacked the Saigon government as a "reactionary, belligerent, and corrupt puppet regime," a "lackey of the U.S. imperialists."

The NLFSV's domestic program was first formulated in a 10-point program broadcast from Hanoi on 4 February 1961. On 31 August 1967, Liberation Radio announced that the NLFSV had adopted a new 14-point political program which was hailed as the "only correct path to complete the democratic revolution in South Vietnam." It is primarily an expanded and updated version of the 1961 program. While continuing to designate the NLFSV as the "sole genuine representative of the heroic South Vietnamese people," the political program stated in its introduction that the "NLFSV warmly welcomes all political parties, mass organizations, and patriotic and progressive personalities who broadly rally within and outside the front," but omitted any mention of the PRP, and, while offering "equal treatment" to "those functionaries of the puppet administration" and "puppet army" willing to serve in the "state machine after the liberation of South Vietnam," it excluded any form of cooperation with the existing Republic of Vietnam administration.

Domestically, the main goals announced in the program were:

(1) To achieve a broad and progressive democratic regime; to abolish the disguised colonial regime established by the U.S. imperialists in South Vietnam.... To hold free general elections [in] accordance with the principle of universal, equal, direct suffrage and secret ballot.
(2) To build an independent and self-supporting economy, to improve the people's living conditions.
(3) [To] carry out the slogan "Land to the Tiller."

It further advocated a number of social reforms and the strengthening of the PLAF (see *YICA*, 1970, p. 721). The program placed emphasis on step-by-step "reunification of Vietnam," which would be realized through "peaceful negotiations between the two zones without either side using pressure against the other and without foreign interference." Pending reunification, the people in both zones would "jointly resist foreign invasion and defend the fatherland," and at the same time strive to expand economic and cultural exchanges.

On 8 June 1969, a "Congress of People's Representatives" held under the joint chairmanship of Nguyen Huu Tho, chairman of the NLFSV, and Trinh Dinh Thao, chairman of the VANDPF, adopted a resolution announcing the establishment of the "Provisional Revolutionary Government of the Republic of South Vietnam" (see *YICA*, 1970, pp. 721-22). Following the establishment of the PRG, the NLFSV transferred to it all state functions both internal and external, including its position at the Paris peace talks. The leadership or cabinet of the PRG included: Huynh Tan Phat, chairman; Phung Van Cung, Nguyen Van Kiet, and Nguyen Don, vice-chairmen; Tran Buu Kiem, minister to the chairman's office; Tran Nam Trung, minister of defense; Mme Nguyen Thi Binh, minister of foreign affairs; Phung Van Cung, minister of the interior; Cao Van Bon, minister of economy and finance; Luu Huu Phuoc, minister of information and culture; Nguyen Van Kiet, minister of education and youth; Duong Quynh Hoa, minister of health, social action, and disabled soldiers; and Truong Nhu Tang, minister of justice.

Despite the PRG's claiming to represent a broad section of opinion in South Vietnam, 20 of the 38 members of its cabinet and advisory council hold currently or have held positions in the NLFSV or in the PLAF, and 12 others are members of the VANDPF. Two additional members of the PRG leadership are North Vietnamese generals: Tran Nam Trung, who was named minister of defense, and Dong Van Cong, a vice-minister of defense. In addition, all important PRG cabinet positions are held by NLFSV members. The chairmanship and vice-chairmanship of the Advisory Council are allocated to Nguyen Huu Tho and Trinh Dinh Thao, chairmen of the NLFSV and VANDPF respectively.

The PRG adopted a 12-point action program (for complete text see *YICA*, 1970, *Documents*) which stressed unity in the struggle against the United States; abolition of the Saigon government; consultations with "the political forces ... in South Vietnam that stand for peace, independence, and neutrality ... with a view to setting up a provisional coalition government"; a number of domestic reforms; and normalization of relations between North and South Vietnam.

Communist forces in South Vietnam defined as three major targets for attack in 1970 the U.S. and Republic of Vietnam "clear-and-hold strategy," pacification program, and "Vietnamization" plan (Liberation Radio, 31 January). Throughout the year, NLFSV radio broadcasts contended that both the pacification and the Vietnamization programs were being defeated. Special efforts were made to encourage the youth and students of South Vietnam to continue their resistance against the U.S. "schemes." As part of their strategy, the communists sought to disrupt the senatorial elections (30 August), attempting to persuade people to boycott the polls and harassing the candidates. On election day, they perpetrated some seventy terrorist incidents, which resulted in the deaths of 55 civilians, with an additional 140 wounded. Nevertheless, an estimated 70 per cent of those eligible voted. Liberation Radio subsequently denounced the newly elected officials as representing no one.

In accordance with decisions made in North Vietnam (see *Vietnam: Democratic Republic of Vietnam*), South Vietnamese communist military leaders placed increased emphasis on the role of guerrilla warfare, particularly the role of urban guerrilla warfare. Terrorism, which Hanoi radio (26 November) described as the "punishment of stubborn and cruel agents," was a common tactic for opposing pacification during 1970. The targets of the attacks, according to the communists, included hamlet, village, and military post chiefs and deputy chiefs, police chiefs, chiefs of intelligence organizations, and such urban leaders as chairmen of municipal councils and mayors. Often, however, terrorism was vented against the families of government soldiers. Individuals and platoon-sized squads perpetrated thousands of abductions and assassinations during the year. It appears that toward the middle of 1970, the South Vietnamese communist leadership found that the terrorism was marring their popular image. A captured document deplored the acts of petty guerrilla functionaries, who had "damaged the prestige of the revolution and lowered the revolutionary spirit of the people." Nevertheless, it condoned "authorized and cleared terrorism." A directive issued in the summer called on each armed reconnaissance cell to kill "at least" one chief or deputy chief in each of five categories, plus district leaders, and to warn thirty other enemy personnel that they, too, would be punished if they did not become cooperative. The "punishment" of the reactionary elements was intended to encourage "people's uprisings."

A captured PLAF document dated 8 September revealed that special "anti-pacification groups" had been formed. In addition to anti-pacification activities, these groups were to consolidate village revolutionary organizations and incite the peasants to kill the local officials.

Communist forces in South Vietnam faced serious problems during 1970. The Saigon government had instituted a number of organizations down to the local level, compelling the peasantry to participate in self-defense and reconstruction programs. Government security forces were stationed permanently in most areas, making collaboration risky. The government's land reform program, implemented in the fall of 1970, served further to weaken the appeal of the communists by offsetting one of the major grievances against the central government. Previously, the NLFSV had been strongest in local level organization, but in 1970 the people were tired of the war, and government reform and aid programs were finally reaching them. The population, according to Western observers, was alienated from the communist guerrillas (Allen E. Goodman, Randolph Harris, and John C. Wood, "South Vietnam and the Politics of Self-Support," *Asian Survey*, January 1971, p. 1). A document captured in February declared: "The people's confidence concerning the revolution [has become] weaker."

U.S. sources generally agreed that the communist infrastructure in South Vietnam had been virtually shattered. Nevertheless, other observers claimed that a "shadow government" of some 75,000 to 85,000 functionaries was prepared to assume responsibilities in the event that the present government should collapse or be forced out of office (*Far Eastern Economic Review*, Hong Kong, 7 May).

During 1969, the NLFSV had set up Revolutionary Committees to serve as the governing bodies at the local levels. The committees originally provided such services as medical and education programs, but by 1970 they had ceased to operate. Local party units failed to establish a new network, leaving an administrative vacuum at the local level. Thus communist control in the countryside was weakening just at the time when the government began to increase its influence. A document addressed to the PLAF commanders of the delta region, captured in February 1970 and believed to have been written by North Vietnamese General Hoang Van Thai, a PLAF executive officer, asserted: "It is clear that enemy forces on the battlefield of the Mekong Delta are having the upper hand. . . . Our activities have left much to be desired. [The enemy] has realized part of his scheme of pacification in the delta by extending his control over both territory and people."

Where government power was strongest, the PLAF turned to subversion and infiltration with a measure of success. Communist personnel may have successfully penetrated all levels of the government apparatus in 1970 (*ibid.*). According to a U.S. Central Intelligence Agency report made in May 1970 (*New York Times*, 19 October), more than 30,000 communist agents had infiltrated the Saigon government agencies, including the police, the armed forces, and the intelligence agency. Their apparatus was, according to the report, virtually indestructible, greatly reducing chances of the government's long-range survival, and penetration was continuing to grow, with a goal set at 50,000 infiltrators. Thousands of trained military personnel had been shifted to the work of infiltrating government organs. These agents were organized under three separate PLAF sections. The largest number, some 20,000 full-time operatives, were under the Military Proselytizing Section, whose mission was to undermine the morale and effectiveness of government troops and police. Many of these operatives were officers and noncommissioned officers in the Republic of Vietnam forces who recruited PLAF soldiers and fostered disunity, disloyalty, and violence in their own units. They were backed up by a network of couriers and keepers of hideouts. (*Ibid.*)

A second group of about 7,000 was under the PLAF Military Intelligence Section. These agents primarily engaged in espionage at all levels in the police, the armed forces, and the civilian administration. Some of the high-level agents attempted to influence government policy. This section also intercepted top secret army and police communications. (*Ibid.*)

The third group, about 3,000 agents, was the PLAF security service, which thoroughly infiltrated the police, army, and military intelligence services and also the central intelligence office, political parties, and religious sects. The main task of this group was to keep the communists informed of how much the government knew about them and to prevent government penetration of communist organizations. (*Ibid.*)

The NLFSV has formulated a "three-pronged attack": armed struggle, political struggle, and troop proselytizing (see above). Armed struggle, in this context, emphasized mainly guerrilla and terrorist tactics. Political struggle included a continuous stream of propaganda plus encouragement of such movements as strikes and anti-U.S. demonstrations. As in previous years, political struggle was considered of more importance than armed struggle. The PLAF was reminded of Ho Chi Minh's statement that "each soldier must be a propagandist." The political and military aspects, however, were both necessary: "Indeed, the need to combine armed forces with political forces, armed struggle and armed uprisings with revolutionary offensives is a basic rule for winning victory in the revolutionary war in the southern part of our country" (Liberation Radio, 16 April).

The third "prong," troop proselytizing, received great emphasis during 1970. Reports indicate that the pacification program had reduced the number of communist guerrillas in South Vietnam to a significant degree. A document captured in February 1970 stated that "local force units were unable to replace their personnel losses, then their combat effectiveness was lowered." According to Western counts, 8,000 to 10,000 men were being lost by the communists monthly, a figure which was confirmed by captured PLAF documents (*Washington Post*, 13 August). Thus the NLFSV felt it imperative to attempt to reconstitute its forces through recruitment.

In previous years, PLAF elements remained in the particular villages in which they were conducting propaganda and recruitment sessions, but in 1970 conditions in the countryside were too hostile for this. Instead, villagers were removed to "liberated areas" for proselytizing—a procedure which accounted in part for the numerous abductions of peasants during 1970 and furthermore served to offset apparent growing agrarian indifference to communist directives in the absence of continual influence from NLFSV cadres. "Agit-prop" teams, used by the communists during the late 1950's and early 1960's, were again employed to revive waning revolutionary fervor in the delta region.

Not only were PLAF forces weakened numerically, but also the U.S. and government moves against communist sanctuaries in Cambodia in the spring of 1970 (see *Cambodia*) disrupted the flow of supplies from North Vietnam to forces in the South. PLAF members were encouraged to practice austerity. Communist leaders called for accelerated food production and rational use of manpower.

At a "grand meeting" on 19 December in a "liberated area," the NLFSV celebrated its tenth anniversary (20 December). The occasion was observed by the issuance of much propaganda concerning the accomplishments of the revolutionary forces. Further to honor the anniversary, the PLAF launched a series of military offensives throughout the country, commencing in late November. The occasion was observed with greater fervor than previous anniversaries, presumably in an effort to demonstrate the NLFSV's continuing popular support and effectiveness.

Despite apparent reverses, the NLFSV continued to call for a "total victory" in the war. The communist news media continually cited alleged U.S. weaknesses and defeats, but cautioned the people that nevertheless the United States was "very stubborn and shrewd" and must be dealt with accordingly. The South had yet to be liberated although NLFSV forces were now in a "victorious and offensive position" (Liberation Radio, 20 August). The NLFSV 10-point peace plan of May 1969 was repeatedly invoked as the correct solution to the war (see *YICA*, 1970, p. 727).

Relations with North Vietnam. Communist forces in South Vietnam were faced with a number of problems which paralleled and partly resulted from those problems facing the North (see *Vietnam: Democratic Republic of Vietnam*). The emphasis on proselytizing, increasing peasant class consciousness and revolutionary élan, and the calls for economy and mobilization of resources were sounded in Hanoi as well as in the South. Similarly, counterrevolutionary agents and influences were fervently condemned.

Despite continuous declarations of solidarity, there were indications of friction between North and South Vietnamese communist forces over issues involving command functions, supplies, and combat assignments. The North Vietnamese reportedly tended to regard themselves as superior to the Southern communists in training and discipline, and neither liked to be placed under the command of the other. South Vietnamese communist troops apparently also failed to respect their Northern counterparts, who were not as severely punished for infringements of rules. Inadequate supplies of food and matériel increased the friction, as PLAF troops resented the arrival of North Vietnamese forces, which were better equipped than the local forces. The North Vietnamese, in turn, resented being assigned to dangerous reconnaissance missions and having PLAF soldiers promoted ahead of them. They further resented the fact that the populace favored local troops when supplying food and medicine. Upon arrival in the South, the Northern troops became disillusioned: They had been informed that the United States and the Republic of

Vietnam had been defeated; the actual situation in the South contradicted this and exacerbated the existing friction.

Although in 1970 infiltration into South Vietnam from the North was down to an average of 5,000 to 6,000 per month, or half the 1969 rate, there continued to be a higher percentage of North Vietnamese troops than of locally recruited guerrillas (*Washington Post*, 13 August). According to U.S. Department of Defense estimates in June, between 117,000 and 119,000 North Vietnamese troops were fighting in the South, of whom 17,000 to 19,000 were active in PLAF units. Sir Robert Thomson, head of the British Advisory Mission to Vietnam, stated that in some regions PLAF units were as much as 70 or 80 per cent North Vietnamese.

The local populace also resented the Northern troops. When a Northern unit moved into a new region, the peasants reportedly urged them to return to their homes. To counter this tendency, the officers commanded their troops to assist the villagers, particularly with medical aid. The results, however, were limited because of the shortage of medicines.

Although the PRG denies that its policies emanate from Hanoi, its members have repeatedly stated that they are inspired by Ho Chi Minh: For instance, PRG Chairman Huynh Tan Phat declared: "In a quarter of a century, led by President Ho and tightening their ranks in a broad united front, our people have overcome countless dangers and trials" (quoted by Liberation Radio, 27 August). In two lengthy articles in the Hanoi daily *Nhan Dan* (31 May and 1 June) the North Vietnamese minister of defense, General Vo Nguyen Giap, pledged that the North would lead "the national liberation undertakings of Indochinese peoples to complete victory." While the Southern communists continued to deny the presence of North Vietnamese forces in South Vietnam, the Hanoi regime admitted its control of the NLFSV, which dominates the PRG. Southern communist leaders regularly used the name of "venerated and beloved President Ho" to encourage the people's revolutionary spirit. Western observers speculated that the PRG intended to separate Ho Chi Minh the anti-colonialist and nationalist fighter from Ho Chi Minh the founder and leader of a communist state, thus qualifying him to serve as an inspiration to the "neutralist" PRG and the NLFSV.

International Views and Positions. In its 1967 political program the NLFSV outlined a foreign policy of "peace and neutrality" to guarantee the "independence, sovereignty, unity, and territorial integrity of the country and help safeguard world peace." The 12-point action program of the PRG reaffirmed the correctness of such a policy and emphasized the same points outlined in the NLFSV political program. Specifically, the PRG action program referred to the need to "support actively the national independence movement of the Asian, American, and Latin American people struggling against imperialism, colonialism, and neocolonialism." It further stated that the PRG would seek "to establish diplomatic and cultural relations with all countries, irrespective of political and social regime, including the United States." Also stressed were good relations with neighboring Cambodia and Laos.

In Cambodia, the replacement of Prince Sihanouk as head of the government by General Lon Nol, in March, radically altered conditions in Indochina (see *Cambodia*). Sihanouk immediately set up the "National United Front of Kampuchea," to which the PRG and the NLFSV promptly pledged support. At the time, the PLAF and North Vietnam had some 40,000 troops stationed in sanctuaries inside the Cambodian border. These forces soon began to engage in open conflicts with Cambodian government troops. Shortly thereafter, U.S. and Republic of Vietnam forces moved against the communist enclaves in Cambodia.

At the behest of Sihanouk, a "Summit Conference of Indochinese Peoples" (see *Cambodia*) was held in the southern China border area on 24-25 April. It was attended by the major communist fronts and governments of Indochina, including the PRG, the NLFSV, and the

VANDPF. The conference issued a joint statement calling for militant solidarity of the Vietnamese, Cambodian, and Laotian revolutionary movements. It was speculated that the primary objective of the Vietnamese communists at the time of the conference was to secure their sanctuaries outside Vietnam and to reestablish their supply lines which had been disrupted.

Following the conference, Vietnamese communist declarations of solidarity with the "brotherly Khmer people" and the Laotian people, which had been made before, became increasingly frequent. Concurrently, the struggle in Cambodia between local and Vietnamese communists and government troops grew in scope and bitterness. By the end of the year, there were believed to be some 50,000 North Vietnamese and PLAF regulars in Cambodia. The PRG and the NLFSV were particularly persistent and vociferous in their condemnation of alleged massacres of local Vietnamese civilians at the hands of Cambodian government forces. According to a communist defector there are Laotian and Thai communists in South Vietnam, and North Koreans serve as advisers to the COSVN (*Far Eastern Economic Review*, 3 February 1971).

Within the context of the international communist movement, the NLFSV and PRG continued to refrain from commenting on the Sino-Soviet dispute. Nevertheless, the rivalry between the two most powerful communist countries affected Vietnam. The Soviet Union was enthusiastic in its support of the NLFSV and the PRG at the Paris peace talks, while Communist China persisted in opposing their participation in negotiations. The Chinese called for a total victory in the "people's war" in South Vietnam and repeatedly emphasized China's role as the "reliable rear area" for the Indochina struggle. The Soviets consequently charged them with wanting the war to continue for China's own benefit.

The NLFSV sent a delegation led by Ho Xuan Son, member of the Secretariat of the NLFSV Central Committee, to the Lenin Centenary celebrations in Moscow. In his address, Ho Xuan Son praised the Soviet Union as Lenin's creation. He also stated that the Vietnamese people would always remember Brezhnev's offer to render aid to his people's struggle and expressed their gratitude for Soviet support.

On 19 December, as noted earlier, the NLFSV observed the tenth anniversary of its founding (20 December) at a meeting held in a "liberated area." In honor of the occasion, the Vietnamese communists sent a number of delegations to various communist and noncommunist countries, including China and the Soviet Union. North Vietnam observed the anniversary more extensively than in previous years, demonstrating the greater significance of the tenth anniversary.

China and the Soviet Union used the occasion to restate their views on the Vietnamese conflict. A message from Mao Tse-tung, Lin Piao, and Chou En-lai, dated 20 December, declared that the United States had already been defeated in the armed struggle, adding:

> The peoples of Vietnam, Laos, and Cambodia have already formed a powerful united front against U.S. imperialism. Filled with hatred against the common enemy and fighting shoulder to shoulder, they have brought about an excellent situation through battle. *We believe that the three peoples of Indochina, persevering in protracted people's war, will certainly drive the U.S. aggressors out of Indo-china.* (Quoted, *Peking Review*, no. 52, 25 December; emphasis in source.)

In contrast, the message from the Soviet Union expressed "full approval" for the eight-point peace plan which was introduced by Mme Nguyen Thi Binh at the Paris peace talks in September (see below). The Soviets observed the anniversary in conjunction with a "week of solidarity with the people of Vietnam," as did the other Eastern European countries and North Korea and Mongolia. Messages similar to that of the Chinese leaders were sent by pro-Chinese governments and parties, including Albania, Sihanouk's "Royal Government of National Union" (Cambodia), and the communist parties of Indonesia, Malaya, and Thailand. For example, the message from the Central Committee of the Communist Party of Malaya declared: "The great victory won by the people of South Vietnam through persisting in a protracted people's war has once again eloquently verified the truth that by waging a people's war, any imperialism which outwardly looks strong can be defeated." Radio "Voice of Malayan Revolution," 20 December).

Toward the end of December, Vietnamese communist relations with China grew noticeably more cordial. For the first time, China officially came out in support of the NLFSV ten-point and "supplemental" eight-point peace proposals, calling them "the correct way for the settlement of the Vietnam question" (*Far Eastern Economic Review*, 2 January 1971, p. 8). On 21 and 22 December, NLFSV and North Vietnamese military men outlined the situation in Vietnam to meetings of the Chinese Ministry of Defense in Peking. During the course of the week there were long celebrations of the NLFSV's tenth anniversary and the twenty-sixth anniversary of the North Vietnamese army, and Li Teh-sheng, alternate member of the Politburo of the Chinese Communist Party and head of the General Political Department of the People's Liberation Army, gave a major address in which he referred to "concrete actions" and "deeds" to help the people of Indochina achieve victory. The Vietnamese people's struggle, according to Li, was also the Chinese people's struggle (*ibid.*).

During 1970, considerable emphasis was placed on developing the international prestige of the NLFSV and the PRG in an effort to obtain international respectability as viable political entities. The NLFSV and the PRG exchanged messages with various communist movements around the world on appropriate occasions. Trips by delegations were frequent, and the PRG foreign minister, Mme Nguyen Thi Binh, traveled extensively. Notable developments for the PRG were its recognition by Ceylon (14 July) and the raising to embassy level of diplomatic relations with the United Arab Republic.

The NLFSV and the PRG continued to praise the anti-war movement in the United States. They also came out in support of the "seething struggle of the black people in the U.S. against oppression, exploitation, and racial discrimination" (Liberation Press Agency, 18 August). In the fall, they received a letter from Huey P. Newton, the Black Panther Party's minister of defense, informing South Vietnamese insurgents that the party was prepared to send volunteers to fight with them "in the spirit of international revolutionary solidarity" (*ibid.*, 9 October).

The South Vietnamese communists continued to claim that they had forced the United States to enter into peace negotiations; also they accused it of insincerity in its proposals. Nevertheless, on 17 September Mme Nguyen Thi Binh put forth an eight-point classification of the "10-point overall solution." The main items were:

(1) The United States should stop the war and the Vietnamization program and totally withdraw from South Vietnam by 30 June 1971.

(2) The problem of the Vietnamese armed forces should be resolved by the Vietnamese parties.

(3) A new Saigon government, without the present heads, should be formed, dedicated to "peace, independence, and neutrality."

(4) Free and general elections should be held in South Vietnam to select a national assembly and work out a democratic national constitution. For this, a provisional coalition government would be essential.

(5) The provisional coalition government should consist of "persons of the Saigon administration who really stand for peace, independence, neutrality, and democracy," representatives of various political and religious groups, and members of the PRG.

(6) The peaceful reunification of Vietnam ultimately should be achieved.

U.S. counter-proposals were offered on 7 October. No apparent progress was made at Paris toward a political settlement of the Vietnam conflict.

Publications. The NLFSV publishes a number of clandestine newspapers and periodicals. In 1970 it was decided that *South Viet Nam in Struggle*, an English- and French-language newspaper, would, as of 20 December, become the "official mouthpiece" of the NLFSV, "directly placed under its Central Committee." The paper claimed circulation in 17 countries in Asia, 40 in Africa, 26 in the Americas, 27 in Europe, 12 in the Middle East, and two in Oceania.

The Liberation Press Agency, founded in 1961 as the official press agency of the NLFSV and directed by Vo Nhon Ly, claims that it issues 40 publications, all clandestine. The major ones include *Giai Phong* (Liberation), the organ of the NLFSV Central Committee; *Trung Lap* (Neutrality), ostensibly published by a group affiliated with the NLFSV and dedicated to a "neutral solution to the Vietnam problem"; *Quan Giai Phong* (Liberation Troops), the army newspaper; *Phu Nu* (Women); and two irregular NLFSV journals, *Co Giai Phong* (Miss Liberation) and *Thoi Su Pho Thong* (News Review). The VANDPF publishes its own organ, *Lien Minh* (Alliance). NLFSV-PRG policy statements are also broadcast over Liberation Radio, founded in 1962, and are frequently carried by the Vietnam News Agency in Hanoi. Both the Liberation Press Agency and Liberation Radio are believed to be based in Tay Ninh Province. Reports indicate that the actual writing, translation, and publication of NLFSV propaganda is done in North Vietnam by the Foreign Languages Publishing House.

S. E. Y.

INTERNATIONAL COMMUNIST FRONT ORGANIZATIONS

INTRODUCTION

In 1921, the year in which Lenin undertook to modify political strategy both within the Soviet Union and in the context of international communism, he devised the formula of "front organizations," which became an integral part of both tactics and the organization of the communist movement. In view of Lenin's publicly proclaimed realization that communist revolution was not imminent in the West and that the majority of the working class was not won over to the communist cause, it became necessary to find means to modify this situation. One of the prerequisites was that there should be "transmission belts" between parties and the masses. Whereas in 1920 this function was served only by the International Veterans' Union and two rather limited organizations, the International Trade Union Council and the International Women's Secretariat, during 1921 the two latter were enhanced by a definite structure, and a number of additional front organizations were founded. The new fronts included the International Committee of Aid to Soviet Russia, the International Workers' Aid Organization, and the Red Sport International (Sportintern). In 1922 the International Revolutionary Aid Organization (MOPR) was created, followed in 1923 by the International Peasants' Union (Krestintern). In 1927, Willi Münzenberg, who had directed the International Committee of Aid to Soviet Russia, sponsored the creation of the Anti-Imperialist League (later known as the Congress Against War and Fascism).

Outwardly these organizations did not appear to be of a communist character; emphasis was placed on their humanitarian, cultural, pacifist, or other roles. In practice, communist action within them was dominant. Their foundation was initiated by communists, key positions were held by communists, and the financial resources of the organizations originated from communist sources. Linked to the Comintern, they faced the same vicissitudes and, in some instances, even preceded it in official dissolution.

The "grand alliance" between communist and democratic forces, in·existence on national and international levels during the Second World War and in its immediate aftermath, favored the renewal, under a somewhat modified form, of front organization strategy. Some of the postwar front organizations were created by the reactivation of earlier fronts (the World Federation of Trade Unions, the Women's International Democratic Federation, the World Peace Council), while others were new (such as the International Association of Democratic Lawyers and the World Federation of Scientific Workers).

During their existence of now more than twenty years, these organizations have undergone transformations and been faced by varied problems—the cold war, the Stalin-Tito schism, the 1956 events, the consequences of the Sino-Soviet conflict, differing views as to revolutionary tactics, and the consequences of the invasion of Czechoslovakia by Warsaw Pact forces in 1968. The purpose of the surveys that follow is to outline the origins, organizational structures, official aims, modes of operation, and current activities of the major international communist front organizations in existence at this time.

WORLD PEACE COUNCIL

The "world peace" movement headed by the World Peace Council (WPC) dates from August 1948, when a "World Congress of Intellectuals for Peace" in Wroclaw, Poland, set up an organization called the "International Liaison Committee of Intellectuals." This committee in April 1949 convened a "First World Peace Congress" in Paris. (Part of the meeting was held in Prague because the French government refused visas to delegates from communist countries.) The congress launched a "World Committee of Partisans of Peace," which in November 1950 was renamed the "World Peace Council." Originally based in Paris, it was expelled in 1951 by the French government, moving first to Prague and then, in 1954, to Vienna—where it adopted the name "World Council of Peace." Although outlawed by Austria in 1957, the World Council of Peace continued its operations in Vienna under the cover of an ostensibly new organization, the "International Institute for Peace" (IIP). In September 1968, World Council of Peace headquarters were transferred to Helsinki, while the IIP remained in Vienna. Although no formal announcement has been made, the World Council of Peace appears to have been renamed the World Peace Council (WPC). Publications from its new headquarters bear the designation "World Peace Council," as do organization documents.

Structure. The WPC embraces "national peace committees" in some 80 countries. The highest authorities of the WPC are the Council of the World Peace Council and its Presidential Committee and Secretariat.

The Council of the WPC, with 460 members, comprises representatives of national peace committees and also of national, regional, and international organizations and movements agreeing with WPC aims and principles. Council sessions are expected to meet at least every two years. Because of events in Czechoslovakia in 1968, however, the latest meeting, scheduled for that year, was not held until June 1969 (in East Berlin).

The Presidential Committee, which is elected by the Council and normally meets twice a year, controls the WPC between sessions of the Council. Authorized to have 50 members and to co-opt new members from time to time, subject to Council approval, the committee elects its highest officer, a coordinating chairman, as well as members of the Secretariat, presided over by a secretary-general.

Isabelle Blume (of Belgium) is the coordinating chairman of the Presidential Committee, which had 45 members in 1970. The other members were: Georgi Andreev (Bulgaria), Richard Andriamanjato (Malagasy Republic), Herbert Aptheker (United States), Damantang Camara (Guinea), Alberto Casella (Argentina), Romesh Chandra (India), Alfred Dickie (Australia), James Endicott (Canada), Guido Fanti (Italy), Evgeny Federov (Soviet Union), Carlton Goodlett (United States), Raymond Guyot (France), Yoshitaro Hirano (Japan), Jaroslaw Iwaszkiewicz (Poland), Cheddi Jagan (Guyana), Kang Yang-uk (North Korea), Matti Kekkonen (Finland),

Alexandr Korneichuk (Soviet Union), Hertta Kuusinen (Finland), Murad Kuwatli (Syria), Enrique Lister (Spain), Lucio Luzzatto (Italy), H. D. Malaviya (India), Juan Marinello (Cuba), Faruq Masarini (Lebanon), Khalid Muhyi al-Din (U.A.R.), Ivor Montagu (Great Britain), Agostinho Neto (Angola), Nguyen Van Hieu (South Vietnam), Oscar Niemeyer (Brazil), Martin Niemöller (West Germany), Albert Norden (East Germany), Olga Poblete de Espinosa (Chile), Gordon Schaffer (Great Britain), 'Aziz Sharif (Iraq), Endre Šik (Hungary), Tikiri Subasinghe (Ceylon), Oliver Tambo (South Africa), Haddam Tidjani (Algeria), Marcelino dos Santos (Mozambique), chairman of the Front for the Liberation of Mozambique (FRELIMO), Yusuf al-Seba'i (U.A.R.), secretary-general of the Afro-Asian Peoples' Solidarity Organization (AAPSO), Pierre Gensous (France), secretary-general of the World Federation of Trade Unions (WFTU), Dr. Samba Gueye (Senegal), and Josef Lukaš (Czechoslovakia). The last five have been co-opted to the Presidential Committee since the 1969 Council meeting. The rank of Honorary President, created in 1969, is held by two former committee members, John Bernal (Great Britain) and Louis Saillant (France)—a third, Lázaro Cárdenas (Mexico), died in October 1970 —and by Pablo Picasso (Spain) and Krishna Menon (India).

The Secretariat, headed by Romesh Chandra (India), includes also Alexandr Berkov (Soviet Union), Marta Buschmann (West Germany), James Forest (United States), Gabor Göbölyös (Hungary), Manuel Lafuente (Spain), H. D. Malaviya (India), Jerzy Markiewicz (Poland), Luciano Mencaraglia (Italy), Ardito Pellizzari (Italy), Raymond Perinetti (France), Emilson Randriamihasinoro (Malagasy Republic), David Rummelsburg (East Germany), Varoujan Salatian (Syria), Alfredo Varela (Argentina), and Nikolai Voshinen (Soviet Union).

The executive bodies of the International Institute for Peace—ostensibly independent of those of the WPC but, in fact, elected by the WPC Council—are the 7-member Presidium and the 30-member Executive Committee. IIP Presidium members elected by the 1969 Council meeting are (with WPC members indicated by asterisks): James Endicott* (Canada), president; J. Dobretsberger* (Austria) and Nikolai Polyanov* (Soviet Union), vice-presidents; J. Lukaš (Czechoslovakia), director; Gregorz Sokolowski (Poland), deputy director; Georg Fuchs (Austria), treasurer; and Herman Mitteräcker (Austria), assistant treasurer. The Executive Committee consists of two executive members: S. Doernberg (East Germany) and R. Riemeck (East Germany); and 28 ordinary members: Ismail Abdin* (Sudan), G. Arilie (Italy), Alexandr Berkov* (Soviet Union), Göran von Bonsdorff* (Finland), Isabelle Blume* (Belgium), M. Buenzod (Switzerland), Alberto Casella* (Argentina), Romesh Chandra* (India), Yves Cholière* (France), Walter Diehl* (West Germany), G. Favilli (Italy), R. Frisch (Norway), Ibrahim Garba-Jahumpa (Gambia), G. Harosti (Hungary), Yoshitaro Hirano* (Japan), W. Hollitscher (Austria), Nikolai Inozemtsev (Soviet Union), G. Kade (West Germany), Manuel Lafuente* (Spain), Maurice Lambilliotte (Belgium), G. Nadzhakov* (Bulgaria), Olga Poblete de Espinosa* (Chile), Varoujan Salatian* (Syria), T. Schonfeld (Austria), Anne Synge (Great Britain), Alfredo Varela* (Argentina), Ernest Vollaire (France), and Ernst von Wedel (West Germany).

Membership. The WPC is organized on a national basis. No figure of the total number of members has ever been disclosed, but the WPC has members from more than 100 countries, most of them representing national peace committees. New affiliates accepted into the WPC in 1970 included the Committee for International Peace Action (United States), of which Carlton Goodlett, a WPC Presidential Committee member, is chairman, and the Nicaragua Committee for World Peace.

Principles and Aims. The principles and aims of the WPC include: the prohibition of all weapons of mass destruction and the halting of the arms race, the abolition of foreign military bases,

and a general, simultaneous, and controlled disarmament; the elimination of all forms of colonialism and racial discrimination; respect for the right of popular sovereignty and independence, as
being essential for the establishment of peace; respect for the territorial integrity of states; and
noninterference in the internal affairs of nations.

From its inception the WPC has defended the policies of the Soviet Union and has attacked
those of the Western powers. In recent years, WPC activities have focused primarily upon "U.S.
aggression" in Southeast Asia and support of the Soviet call for a new European security system.
Increasingly, it is attempting to broaden and coordinate the efforts of its members and affiliates
in various parts of the world by linking, as joint objects of attack, what it characterizes as (1)
"racism" and "neocolonialism"—from the U.S. to the Portuguese colonies and to South Africa
and Rhodesia; (2) "imperialism"—the U.S., West Germany, and Israel; and (3) "fascism"—
Greece, Portugal, and Spain. Although a broad segment within the WPC disapproved of the
1968 Soviet-led invasion of Czechoslovakia, the WPC as an organization has remained firm in its
support of the Soviet Union. The Chinese People's Republic has not participated in WPC activities for several years.

Views and Activities in 1970. Delegates from 50 countries attended a meeting of the Presidential Committee in Moscow on 2-6 April, during the celebrations of the Lenin Centenary. Sessions
were devoted to "Lenin and the struggle for peace, against imperialism and the danger of world
war; Lenin and the question of peaceful coexistence and disarmament; and Lenin and the questions of unity in the struggle for peace and national independence" (WPC *Information Bulletin*,
no. 5, 17 March). Resolutions were adopted on: (1) disarmament, warning that recent advances
in rocket technology harbored the danger of a new stage in the nuclear arms race, and announcing a campaign for general and complete disarmament under efficient control, for extension of
the test ban treaty to include underground explosions, for measures to ban chemical and bacter-
iological weapons, and for outer space and the sea bed to be declared nuclear-free zones; (2)
Southeast Asia, condemning the U.S. extension of the war into Laos and Cambodia, and supporting the Stockholm Conference appeal (see below) for the immediate and unconditional withdrawal of all U.S. and allied troops from South Vietnam; (3) the Middle East, demanding a cessation of Israeli bombing raids against the Arabs, the withdrawal of Israeli troops from occupied
Arab territories, and recognition of the rights of the Palestinian people; and (4) calling for an all-
European conference without preconditions. A "Message to the Soviet Government and People"
stated that the WPC was inspired by the "resolute and tireless struggle of the Soviet government
and people for peace, against the threat of a new world war, and for the settlement of all international problems by negotiations." (TASS, 2 April.)

Some 100 representatives from 50 countries attended a second meeting of the Presidential
Committee, in New Delhi on 16-18 October. A message from U.N. Secretary-General U Thant
thanked WPC members for their "loyalty to the cause of peace" (*Neues Deutschland*, East Berlin, 10 October). Messages of support were received also from the prime minister of Ceylon and
the president of Sudan (*New Age*, New Delhi, 25 October). Chandra spoke of the need for "political and geographic expansion" of the WPC, prompted primarily, he said, by the growth of liberation movements in Africa and the independence of a large number of African nations. Within
the past year, he stated, "every liberation movement in Africa has joined the WPC" (ADN, East
German news agency, 17 October). The WPC's highest honor, the Joliot-Curie Peace Medal,
was awarded posthumously to Jawaharlal Nehru, whose daughter, Indian Prime Minister Indira
Gandhi, received the medal and paid tribute to the WPC (*New Age*, 25 October).

The meeting declared that the West German-Soviet treaty concluded in August had "opened
up a new stage in the political life of Europe," and was "an example for the normalization of rela-

tions between all European states." A resolution on Indochina, which claimed that the United States was seeking to perpetuate the war, called on peace-loving forces and democratic organizations to support the Stockholm Conference on Vietnam, Laos, and Cambodia (28-30 November). The Soviet Union was praised for its assistance to the Arab people, and the Organization of African Unity (OAU) was urged to "consider means of cooperation with the WPC in their common struggle." A message to the United Nations on its twenty-fifth anniversary expressed the hope that the U.N. would be freed from its "limitations" so as to make it "a genuinely effective institution capable of the speedy removal of the hotbeds of war." (*Patriot*, New Delhi, 17 and 20 October; TASS, 20 October; *Pravda*, 20 October.)

Having finally acquired UNESCO Consultative Status, Category C, in April 1969, the WPC has been campaigning for a higher association. At the Presidential Committee meeting in Moscow in April, Chandra spoke of the development of WPC contacts with the United Nations and its different agencies during the period since the World Assembly for Peace (East Berlin, June 1969). The WPC had been co-opted into three "special committees" of the Non-governmental Organizations' Conference attached to the U.N.: Human Rights, Disarmament, and the Second Development Decade. Thanks to the participation of the WPC at the meetings of these special committees in Geneva in February, it had been able to establish "very useful contacts with the organizations with which [it] used not to have relations." At the WPC's proposal, a subcommittee of the Special Committee on Human Rights, consisting of the WPC, the World Federation of United Nations' Associations, and the International Commission of Jurists was to prepare a program for Anti-Racial Discrimination Year (1971). (*Conference Documents.*)

The IIP sponsored a colloquium on the twenty-fifth anniversary of the United Nations in Vienna on 20-21 June, at which the chairman (James Endicott) and several speakers were WPC members. Ernst Winter represented UNESCO.

In the *Letter to National Committees* (no. 46, 12 June), the WPC claimed that its relations with UNESCO had been strengthened, and that those UNESCO officials with whom the WPC had contacts were "favorably disposed towards the good attitudes and activities of the WPC." Purportedly in response to a request by UNESCO leaders, the WPC was "trying to interest national movements in supporting the setting up or development of Friends of UNESCO Clubs in different countries." Following the WPC's Presidential Committee meeting in New Delhi (16-18 October), the WPC and its affiliated All-India Peace Council co-sponsored a "Symposium on Education and Peace," in connection with the UNESCO Education Year.

As one of several groups comprising the ostensibly nonaligned "Stockholm Conference on Vietnam," initiated in 1967 by the non-communist Swedish Peace and Arbitration Society, the WPC has succeeded in assuming a key role in, and working increasingly through, the International Liaison Committee (ILC) that was constituted as a permanent body by the conference in 1969. Alexandr Berkov and James Forest were members of an ILC delegation that visited Hanoi on 3-14 January 1970, led by ILC Chairman Bertil Svahnström (Sweden), to study North Vietnam's reconstruction needs and to report their findings to an ILC meeting in Stockholm on 17-18 January which was to prepare for the fifth Stockholm Conference on Vietnam on 28-30 March (Vietnam News Agency, 3, 9, and 14 January). WPC delegates to the conference included Isabelle Blume, Grudi Atanasov (Bulgaria), Damantang Camara, Lucio Luzzatto, Krishna Menon, Yoshitaro Hirano, Jerzy Bukowski, Pauline Rosen (United States), and Xuan Thuy (North Vietnam). Other international organizations represented included the communist front International Association of Democratic Lawyers (IADL), International Federation of Resistance Fighters (FIR), and Women's International Democratic Federation (WIDF); also the All-African Trade Union Federation (AATUF), and, for the first time, the Pathet Lao. (*Letter to National Committees*, no. 20, 3 March; *Neues Deutschland*, 28-29 March.) The conference moved to appoint an international commission to "collect, study, and publish evidence concerning crimes committed by U.S. troops in Vietnam," and a secretariat in Stockholm to coordinate aid to Vietnam (*L'Humanité*, Paris, 2 April).

Radio "Peace and Progress" (Moscow), broadcasting in Chinese on 31 March, criticized China for its absence from the conference. The Chinese leadership, allegedly, had "openly shown its unwillingness to participate in any political activity aimed at terminating the Vietnam war." China, in this view, hoped not only that the war would continue but that, ultimately, it would "turn into a world war"; were it not for Peking's "harmful attitude," the Vietnamese "would have achieved much more in their heroic struggle against the U.S. aggressors." Finally, the "anti-people, adventurous, and incorrect policy" of the Chinese leaders was "aimed at alienating the Vietnamese people from their main loyal ally, the Soviet Union, in the struggle against U.S. imperialism."

The Stockholm meeting saw only the latest in a series of attempts by the WPC to set up a "U.S. war crimes" commission. Earlier in 1970, Chandra, Menon, and Niemöller had made a strong bid at a broad-based meeting of U.S. and Canadian anti-war groups in Montreal (31 January-1 February) to set up such a commission there (*L'Humanité*, 3 February). Unable to organize the commission in Montreal, the WPC turned, with more success, to Stockholm and the ILC. The ILC's 17-member International Commission of Inquiry into U.S. War Crimes in Vietnam, announced by the ILC on 14 April (*Information Letter*), was headed by the Swedish pacifist Gunnar Myrdal and included five WPC members—Melba Hernandez (Cuba), Krishna Menon, Martin Niemöller, Jöe Nordmann (France; IADL secretary-general), and László Reczei (Hungary)—and, among others, Lev Smirnov (Soviet Union; IADL Council member) and John Takman (a leading member of the Communist Party of Sweden). The first session of the commission convened in Stockholm on 22-25 October, examined "documents, witnesses, films, photographs, and legal studies," and determined that "the nature and extent of crimes committed by American troops and their allies in Indochina over a long period are equivalent to genocide." It decided to draft rules of procedure for the commission, and to improve contacts with "similar" organizations "such as the IADL." The second session of the commission was set for mid-1971, Canada and West Germany being provisionally considered as possible sites. (*Conference Documents*; TASS, 21 October; *L'Humanité*, 26 October.)

The WPC on 9 March called on national committees to launch a campaign for Laotian independence and neutrality, and asked for support for AAPSO's "International Conference of Solidarity with the People of Laos" (Cairo, 19-21 May). (Pathet Lao News Agency, 6 March; *Egyptian Gazette*, Cairo, 23 March.) Chandra led the WPC delegation to the conference, which planned two weeks of international solidarity with the Laotian people: 23-30 July, commemorating the signing of the Geneva Agreements on Laos in 1962, and 12-19 October, the anniversary of Laotian independence (*Egyptian Gazette*, 20, 21, and 22 May; *Le Progrès Egyptien*, Cairo, 20 May.) At a ceremony held in connection with the conference, Khalid Muhyi al-Din was presented with the Lenin International Peace Prize (*Izvestiia*, 21 May).

The WFTU, World Federation of Democratic Youth (WFDY), WIDF, and AAPSO were among twenty organizations invited to join the ILC Executive Committee at its 23-24 May meeting. The committee had previously been limited to the founding organizations: the WPC, the International Confederation for Disarmament and Peace (ICDP); the War Resisters' International (WRI); the Christian Peace Conference (CPC); and the Swedish Peace and Arbitration Society.

The first financial contribution to the new ILC Secretariat was made in June by Martin Niemöller on behalf of the "Aid for Vietnam Committee" in West Germany. (*Stockholm Conference Information Letter*, no. 3, 10 June.) The WPC subsequently told its national committees that it was "responsible for organizing the major part of the preparatory work" for a proposed enlarged meeting of the ILC (originally planned for June or July but not held until 28-30 November), which would include newly co-opted organizations (*Letter to National Committees*, no. 47, 23 June). The WPC was heavily represented at the 28-30 November meeting, the sixth "Stockholm Conference on Vietnam, Laos, and Cambodia" (renamed after the U.S. "expansion" of the war). Delegates agreed to organize mass protests on 20 December 1970 and 6 March, 3-4 April, and 1 May 1971; to charter a ship to collect medical goods for Vietnam from European ports; to organize an international parliamentary petition to the U.S. Congress; to boycott U.S. firms supplying war materials; and to campaign for the granting of political asylum in any country for U.S. military deserters. (TASS, 3 December 1970; *Morning Star*, London, 3 December.)

The WPC continued to campaign for international recognition of East Germany, asserting also that "normalization of relations between the two German states would have positive effects in creating a lasting collective security system" (*Neues Deutschland*, 30 January). It organized a "Seminar on Fascism, Neo-Fascism, and Neo-Nazism" in Frankfurt-Main on 2-3 May to commemorate the twenty-fifth anniversary of the "defeat of Hitlerite Fascism and the end of the Second World War in Europe." The seminar, in which other communist front organizations also took part, was divided into three commissions, on fascism and the threat to peace, the socioeconomic bases of fascism, and the problems of neo-Nazism in the Federal Republic of Germany. A final communique condemned "reactionary and neo-Fascist forces in Federal Germany," and called for recognition of the European frontiers resulting from the Second World War, and of the German Democratic Republic under international law. (*Letter to National Committees*, no. 35, 19 May; *Neues Deutschland*, 4 May.)

Among participants at a round-table conference on European security, held in the *Izvestiia* offices in Moscow in early July, were, from the WPC, Maurice Lambilliotte and Raymond Goor, Belgian chairmen of the "Vienna Conference on European Security and Cooperation," and Presidential Committee members Albert Norden and Josef Lukaš (*Izvestiia*, 10 July).

The WPC and the East German Peace Council staged an international seminar on "the topical importance of the Potsdam Agreements and the requirements for peace and security in Europe," in Potsdam on 1-2 September. The participants—95 from 25 countries—declared that the Potsdam Agreements were "still the foundation for establishing a reliable European security system." They welcomed the signing of the Soviet-West German treaty on 12 August, affirming that the cold war must be overcome and peaceful coexistence be the rule in relations between all European states, regardless of differences in their socioeconomic order. (ADN, 2 September.)

A meeting of European WPC-affiliated national peace movements, attended by 46 representatives from 21 countries, convened in Sofia on 23-24 November. Their proposals for action in 1971 included: (1) seminars on European security in Warsaw in February, in Czechoslovakia in the second half of June, and in East Germany in early September; (2) a "European Hearing" on the theme "What Does European Security and Cooperation Mean for Us?" to be organized by West German organizations in March; (3) meetings in the spring of representatives of peace committees in NATO countries, in Baltic countries, and in East European countries, and in September, in West Germany, of all European peace committees; (4) a European Peace, Security, and Cooperation Week in May; and (5) visits by high-level WCP delegations to various European countries to meet representatives of the political forces and of mass organizations. (*Conference Documents*.)

In Middle East and African affairs, the WCP continued to cultivate its influence within such organizations as the International Confederation of Arab Trade Unions (ICATU), AAPSO, and other "progressive" movements in the region. The International Committee of Support for the Arab Peoples, of which Krishna Menon is chairman and Khalid Muhyi al-Din secretary-general, organized a meeting (originally planned for Cairo in December 1969) in Rome on 21 January

1970 in preparation for an "International Conference for Peace and Justice in the Middle East." The participants agreed to devote more attention to the Palestine resistance movement; as a first step, 21 March was designated "International Day of Solidarity with the Palestinian People." (*Egyptian Gazette*, 13 January; *L'Humanité*, 30 January; *Letter to National Committees*, no. 12, 3 February.) A meeting of international organizations, convened by the WPC and including the IADL, WFTU, WFDY, International Union of Students (IUS), International Organization of Journalists, ICATU, AAPSO, AATUF, Pan-African Youth Movement (PAYM), and Arab Lawyers' Federation, was held in Cairo on 14-15 April. The participants moved to establish a commission to examine "Israeli war crimes in Arab territories," and to make every effort to hold the peace and justice conference before the end of November. (*Le Progrès Egyptien*, 10 April; *Letter to National Committees*, no. 31, 11 May.) Despite continued efforts by the WPC, however, the conference was not held in 1970. At year's end, it was decided that the conference should be convened in Europe, but a site had not been found.

Some 80 delegates attended the "First Conference of Arab and Asian Peace Committees" in Baghdad on 9-10 April. Sixty of the delegates arrived from Moscow, where they had attended the WPC Presidential Committee meeting. President Bakr of Iraq paid tribute to the "positive development" of relations between Iraq and the WPC; other major speakers included 'Aziz Sharif, Iraqi minister of justice and member of the WPC and the Iraqi Communist Party, and Romesh Chandra. The WPC's Joliot-Curie Gold Medal was awarded to the Iraqi National Council for Peace and Solidarity. (Baghdad radio, 8 and 9 April; *Le Monde*, Paris, 12-13 April.) Few details emerged concerning the conference; its main thrust, apparently, was in favor of a convocation of all "anti-imperialist" forces. Shortly before the conference, the WPC and AAPSO had officially welcomed the agreement of 11 March between the Iraqi government and Iraqi Kurds as a strengthening of the struggle against "Zionism."

The WPC expressed satisfaction with the cease-fire agreement on the Middle East, but held that the Arab states would be "fully entitled to liberate their lands if the political endeavors at present under way fail." (*al-Akhbar*, Cairo, 12 August; WPC press release, no. 21.) A WPC delegation led by Chandra met with U.A.R. President Nasser in Cairo on 30 August. The WPC described Nasser's death, in September, as a "staggering blow for the Arab peoples and the world." The Arab leader was said to have been "deeply aware" that the "cause of the Arab people would prevail only in close friendship with the Soviet Union, the socialist countries, and the progressive forces of peace and national independence all over the world." (WPC press release, no. 32, 30 September.)

Together with the AAPSO, the WPC held a "Conference in Support of the Peoples of the Portuguese Colonies" in Rome on 27-29 June. A "permanent secretariat" was set up at the Casa della Cultura, Via Corso 267, including members of the Italian preparatory committee for the conference, the WPC-AAPSO Joint Mobilization Committee, and the Rome-based Conference of Nationalist Organizations of the Portuguese Colonies (CONCP). Delegates to the conference, from 177 national and international organizations in 64 countries, included the Popular Movement for the Liberation of Angola (MPLA), the African Independence Party of Guinea and the Cape Verde Islands (PAIGC), the FRELIMO, and the Palestine guerrilla organization al-Fatah. The U.N. "Committee of 24" against racialism and colonialism sent an 8-member observer delegation. (*Le Monde*, 26 June; *L'Unità*, Rome, 27 and 29 June.) The pro-Chinese National Union for the Total Independence of Angola (UNITA) attacked the participating groups because, it said, they refused to admit any organizations—including itself—which did not have the blessing of the Soviet Union (*Guardian*, London, 29 June).

The conference participants condemned all military aid to Portugal and agreed to increase material aid to liberation movements. International organizations, in particular the United Nations, were urged to exclude Portugal; the "positive decision" of UNESCO no longer to invite Portugal to international meetings was commended. (*L'Unità*, 30 June; "Radio Free Portugal," 4 July.)

The WPC proclaimed 3 August as an "International Day of Solidarity with Peoples of Guinea-Bissau and the Cape Verde Islands." On 30 November the invasion of Guinea was the subject of a joint meeting of WPC and other delegates to the Stockholm Conference on Vietnam, Laos, and Cambodia (*Letter to National Committees*, no. 70, 3 December).

Seeking to link racism in the United States and Africa, the WPC's *Letter to National Committees* (no. 6, 29 January, and no. 13, 6 February, respectively) published a memorandum by Angie Dickerson (United States), a WPC member, on the "repression of the Black Panthers in the U.S.A." and an unsigned letter describing the suffering of "Namibian and Zimbabwean patriots in South African and Rhodesian prisons." Special days designated by the WPC in 1970 to protest racism included: 14 February, "International Day Against Racism"; 26 June, "Freedom For South Africa Day"; 22 August, "No Arms For Racialist South Africa Day"; and 26 August, "Day of International Solidarity with the People of Namibia" (South-West Africa). An "International Conference on Racism and War," one of the organizers of which was the WPC, and which was to have been held in Toronto in October, apparently did not take place, although it was to have been a prelude to world-wide activities for the U.N.'s Anti-Racial Discrimination Year (1971). The main speakers were to have included Black Panther Huey Newton ("if the authorities let him leave California") and Oliver Tambo, acting president of the African National Congress and a WPC Presidential Committee member. (*Peace Courier*, no. 2, 30 September.)

Representatives from the WPC, AATUF, and the South Vietnam Liberation Youth Union were among the 300 delegates at the third PAYM Conference in Dakar, on 26-31 December. The PAYM Secretariat-General's report to the conference expressed "satisfaction with the fruitful relations existing between PAYM and such international organizations as the WFDY, IUS, and WPC." (Tunis radio, 26 December; TASS, 27 and 30 December.)

In regard to Latin America, the WPC called for a campaign on 19-26 July against the blockade of Cuba and for the reopening of diplomatic and commercial relations between Cuba and Latin American countries; pledged solidarity with Puerto Rico, allegedly a nation which had been "turned into a colony bristling with North American bases and whose sons were being used as cannon fodder for aggression" (*El Popular*, Montevideo, 7 August); proclaimed 9-14 October as an "International Week of Solidarity with the Latin American Peoples"; declared the promotion of international cooperation with Peru as one of its main objectives (*L'Expresso*, Lima, 5 July); and expressed its satisfaction with the elections in Chile, whose new president, Salvador Allende, had "always given the WPC valuable cooperation" (*Press Release*, no. 29, 25 September).

Publications. The WPC periodical *Information Bulletin* was replaced by *Peace Courier*, a semimonthly, in September 1970. It was to appear in English, French, and Spanish. The WPC also distributes a *Letter to National Committees*, of which there were some 75 issues in 1970. Published on an irregular or *ad hoc* basis are *Conference Documents* (issued in connection with WPC convocations), *Letter to Members*, and *WPC Statement*. WPC campaigns are publicized in occasional press releases, of which there were some 40 in 1970.

V. B.

WORLD FEDERATION
OF TRADE UNIONS

The World Federation of Trade Unions (WFTU) was set up at the initiative of the British Trade Union Congress (TUC). After a preparatory conference in February 1945, in London, the founding congress was held in October of that year in Paris, where the first headquarters of the organization was established. Since then the WFTU has moved its base of operations twice after expulsion for subsersive activities—to Vienna in 1951 and to Prague in 1956.

In recognition of Britain's leadership in establishing the WFTU, Sir Walter Citrine was elected the first president of the WFTU. At the U.S.S.R.'s insistence, Louis Saillant of France was elected secretary-general. Saillant is generally considered responsible for bringing the Secretariat and other ruling bodies of the federation under communist control, causing a leading spokesman of the TUC to claim in 1948 that the WFTU was "rapidly becoming nothing more than another platform and instrument for furtherance of Soviet policy." Rebelling against political control, some non-communist affiliates in 1949 gave up their membership to found an alternative organization, the International Conference of Free Trade Unions (ICFTU).

Organization and Leadership. The highest authority of the WFTU is the Congress, which meets every four years. Each affiliate body sends delegates to these meetings in proportion to the number of its members. The latest Congress was held in Budapest in October 1969 and was attended by 461 delegates, observers, and guests from 97 countries, said to be representative of "153 million workers, organized in 51 affiliated organizations and 46 non-affiliated organizations." (*World Trade Union Movement*, no. 11, 1969).

The Congresses have no policy-making function and are too large to transact much specific business. They elect the federation's General Council, Executive Bureau (newly established in 1969), and Secretariat. The 1969 meeting elected a General Council of 66 regular and 68 deputy members—representing 55 national affiliates and 11 "Trade Union Internationals" (TUIs)—an Executive Bureau of 23 members and their deputies, and a Secretariat of four. The greatest power within the WFTU is concentrated in the officers of the Executive Bureau. The following were chosen to fill these posts in 1969: honorary president, Louis Saillant (France); president, Enrique Pastorino (Uruguay); secretary-general, Pierre Gensous (France); vice-presidents, Benoît Frachon (France), al-Shaf'i Ahmad al-Shaikh (Sudan), and Shripat Amrit Dange (India). Elected to full membership in the Executive Bureau were: R. Iscaro (Argentina), B. Cerqueira (Brazil), R. Koritarova (Bulgaria), Roso Osorio (Colombia), L. Peña (Cuba), A. Ziartides (Cyprus), K. Poláček[1] (Czechoslovakia), R. Vilon-Guezo (Dahomey), G. Séguy (France), H. Warnke (East Germany), S. Gáspár (Hungary), S. A. Dange (India), A. Novella (Italy), Chon Chang-chol (North Korea), Elias Habr (Lebanon), D. Yadamsuren (Mongolia), W. O. Goodluck (Nigeria), I. Loga-Sowinski (Poland), F. Danalache (Romania), S. A. al-Shaikh (Sudan), A. N. Shelepin

[1]Replaced in 1970 by Jan Piller.

(U.S.S.R.), C. Villegas (Venezuela), and Hoang Quoc Viet (North Vietnam). Positions were reserved for China and Indonesia. Named members of the Secretariat were the secretary-general and Mahendra Sen (India), Ibrahim Zakaria (Sudan), Evgeny Cherednichenko (U.S.S.R.), and Sandro Stimilli[2] (Italy). One seat was reserved to be filled by a Chilean and subsequently Mario Navarro was appointed.

The Trade Union Internationals (TUIs) represent workers of particular trades or crafts. One of the main purposes of the TUIs is to recruit local unions which do not, through their national centers, belong to the WFTU itself. Though the TUIs are in theory independent—each TUI has its own offices and officials, holds its own meetings, and publishes its own bulletin—their policies and finances are controlled by the WFTU department having supervision over their particular areas. The General Council meeting of the WFTU in December 1966 decided that each TUI should have its own constitution; this move for bolstering the appearance of independence had the purpose of allowing the TUIs to join international bodies as individual organizations.

In the past the WFTU has set up a number of subsidiary organizations to deal with specific problems and to achieve collaboration with non-communist trade unionists in solving them. Subsidiaries have concerned themselves with such issues as the Vietnam war, monopolies, the European Common Market, and tourism (see *YICA*, 1969, pp. 949-50). One of the most important subsidiaries is the "Special Commission on U.N. Agencies," which was set up in 1967 to try to expand WFTU activities in the United Nations. The WFTU has Category A status with a number of U.N. agencies, including the Economic and Social Council, the International Labor Organization, the Food and Agriculture Organization, and UNESCO (see *YICA* 1970, p. 750).

Aims and Policies. The WFTU constitution states that the federation exists "to improve the living and working conditions of the people of all lands." It also details the prime purposes of the WFTU: (1) to organize and unite within its ranks the trade unions of the whole world irrespective of considerations of race, nationality, religion, or political opinion; (2) to assist, whenever necessary, the workers of socially or industrially less developed countries in setting up their trade unions; (3) to carry on the struggle for the extermination of all fascist forms of government and every manifestation of fascism, under whatever form it operates and by whatever name it may be known; and (4) to combat war and the causes of war and work for a stable and enduring peace.

The constitution clearly endorses political activity by the WFTU, but this has at times led to serious friction. Non-communist unions have complained that the WFTU is subservient to the Soviet Union and that it supports Soviet causes around the world, while reserving criticism for the Western nations or those politically at odds with the Soviet Union. Political controversy is at the root of the inactivity of the Chinese trade unions in the WFTU since 1966, and of the Yugoslavs' refusal to reaffiliate after their expulsion in 1950 at the height of the Stalin-Tito antagonism. Only in 1968, when Warsaw Pact forces occupied Czechoslovakia, have the actions of the Soviet Union ever been seriously questioned or criticized by the WFTU (see *YICA*, 1970, pp. 750-51).

Views and Activities in 1970. In 1970 the WFTU marked its twenty-fifth anniversary with a series of international meetings in various parts of the world and a special jubilee session on 16-19 October at the conclusion of a General Council meeting in Moscow. In addition, it continued with its normally extensive program of conferences dealing with trade union problems and international political issues.

The first important meeting was held on 30 January-1 February in Prague, in honor of the twenty-fifth anniversary of the WFTU's inauguration in London in 1945. The Australian com-

[2]Replaced in 1970 by Albertino Mazetti.

munist newspaper *Tribune* (Sydney, 18 February) reported that the meeting decided to "take all possible measures to heal the 21-year old split" between the WFTU and the International Confederation of Free Trade Unions (ICFTU), "be ready to change the name and organizational structure of the WFTU if it were shown such steps would assist contacts with the ICFTU," and "make more active use of the two organizations' common connection with the UN and the ILO."

An Executive Bureau meeting held in Khartoum on 24-26 February was noteworthy as marking the first time that an administrative organ of the WFTU had met in Africa and also as the first such event to be held outside Europe since 1960. Those in attendance heard a report on the Middle East situation and discussed the possibility of convening a "Solidarity Conference with the Workers and People of Palestine." After the conclusion of the meeting Pierre Gensous stopped in Cairo for talks with officials of the International Confederation of Arab Trade Unions (ICATU). While there, he assured his hosts of WFTU support for the Arabs' "just and legitimate struggle for both the liberation of their land and the restoration of Palestine" (*Egyptian Gazette*, Cairo, 2 and 4 March). These pronouncements presumably served to alleviate Arab suspicions dating back to the 1969 Congress, where Gensous declared that the WFTU favored a Middle Eastern settlement that "did not endanger the rights of the Israeli people and the Israeli state to exist." The Arabs could derive additional satisfaction from a joint meeting of the WFTU, the ICATU, the Permanent Congress of Trade Union Unity for the Workers of Latin America (CPUSTAL), and the Palestinian General Trade Union Federation, in Prague on 8-9 April, which set up an "International Committee of Solidarity with Palestine." This move occurred shortly after an editorial in the Albanian trade union paper *Puña* (24 March) had accused the WFTU of giving only sham support to the Arab liberation struggle, because the federation's "revisionist leaders" were "obedient puppets of Soviet diplomacy."

A number of leading members of the WFTU attended a meeting in Ulyanovsk, U.S.S.R., on 15-18 April which was organized by the Soviet trade unions to mark the Lenin Centenary. Speakers praised Lenin's international proletarianism and the achievement of the socialist countries, and stressed the need to strengthen the unity of action of working people and trade unions in the fight against capitalist exploitation.

The French General Confederation of Labor (CGT) was the organizing force behind an "International Trade Union Conference of Solidarity with the Workers and People of Indochina Struggling Against U.S. Aggression." It met in Versailles on 18-19 July and attracted 300 delegates from 60 countries, who listened to Secretary General Gensous's exhortation that the WFTU deal with the "urgent task" of condemning U.S. policies in Indochina, and to his appeal for all trade unions to exert pressure on their governments to isolate the United States and force it to withdraw its troops (*L'Humanité*, Paris, 18 and 20 July). The conference was most noteworthy for the fact that it was the first time that the WFTU was permitted to make a public appearance in France since 1951, when the organization was expelled from the country.

A second "World Conference on the Problems of Working Youth" (the first dated back to 1958) was held in Varna, Bulgaria, on 28 September-1 October. It was attended by 200 delegates from 50 countries. Three main documents were adopted at the conclusion of the deliberations: (1) a "Charter of the Demands of Working Youth," which set forth what it termed the aspirations of young people in the capitalist world for better pay and for the establishment of better conditions for work, education, vocational training, and cultural leisure; (2) an appeal for young working people to be in the front rank of "revolutionary struggles for social progress"; (3) a statement on promoting more active participation of young working people in trade unions (Bulgarian Telegraphic Agency, 1 October).

The Executive Bureau held its second meeting of the year in Ulan Bator, Mongolia, on 8-10

October, to discuss preparations for the General Council meeting and the development of WFTU activities in Asia. The twentieth meeting of the General Council took place in Moscow on 13-16 October and adopted resolutions that ran the gamut of the WFTU's interests around the world. There were separate documents dealing with Vietnam and the Middle East. A resolution on South Africa denounced apartheid and supported the idea of making 1971 an international year against racism and racial discrimination. It also suggested that under the aegis of the United Nations and under the motto of "No Arms for South Africa," trade unions and women's and youth organizations should reach an international agreement to protest the breakdown of a complete boycott of arms to South Africa (TASS, 16 October). A statement on Cuba denounced "U.S. imperialist provocations" against that country. It alleged that the U.S. Central Intelligence Agency was planning an armed invasion with the aim of committing sabotage, assassinations, and other crimes against the Cuban people. The Council also adopted a resolution on celebrating the centenary of the proclamation of the Paris Commune on 18 March 1971, since "the Paris Commune was a prototype of a new society of social justice, a society free from exploitation of man by man," and its "great significance" lay in its "deep internationalist nature and the aspiration for brotherhood among the working people of all countries and peace among nations." (TASS, 15 October.)

In spite of these geographically targeted resolutions, international trade union unity was the keynote of the General Council meeting. Aleksandr Shelepin of the U.S.S.R. was one of a number of speakers who forcefully pointed out the "necessity of ensuring unity of action both on a national and international scale" and the "development of cooperation on a class basis with all trade unions irrespective of their orientation." To achieve progress, Shelepin advocated stepping up talks between the WFTU on the one hand and the ICFTU and the World Federation of Labor and autonomous trade unions on the other; he further recommended greater cooperation with the ICATU, the All-Africa Trade Union Federation (AATUF), and the Permanent Congress for Trade Union Unity of Latin American Workers (CPUSTAL) so as to promote consolidation of trade union interests in the developing countries. He stressed the growing need for the previously suggested all-European trade union conference on social and economic problems. (*Trud*, Moscow, 15 October.)

The insistent call for unity was somewhat counterbalanced by Shelepin's emphasis on the "necessity of exposing resolutely the ignoble role of reformism." He identified the trade unions of the United States as the "main striking and guiding force of the reformist trade union movement," and drew attention to the "unprecedented upheavals" and the "severe organizational, moral, and political defeats suffered by the AFL-CIO [American Federation of Labor-Congress of Industrial Organizations] both on the international scene and in its own country" because of its unorthodox attitudes. (*Ibid.*)

The WFTU repeatedly discussed the relationship between the United Nations and the trade union movement. On the occasion of the twenty-fifth anniversary of the U.N., the *World Trade Union Movement* (December) verbalized the WFTU belief in the value of the U.N. as the "principal standing organization for consultation and action among States for peace and progress." Nevertheless, it could not forget that the U.N. "is an arena of struggle between the forces which advocate an anti-imperialist conception of world development and those which advocate a reactionary conception and defend the privileges of the monopolies and the positions of strength imposed by military or economic power." In the future, the article stated, the WFTU would press for the U.N. to pay more sustained attention to the specific problems of women and youth. It would continue to center its own activities within the U.N. on questions of "peace and disarmament, economic and social development, the fight against colonialism and apartheid."

The WFTU issued a number of statements on major international developments. On 26

March, Laos, Cambodia, and Korea and the "imminent danger of the spreading of U.S. aggression in Vietnam to other countries of Southeast Asia" were the topics of a protest (CTK, Czechoslovak news agency, 26 March). A May statement condemned "new acts of barbarous aggression by Israeli troops against Lebanese territory" and the "adventurous expansionist policy of the Israeli leaders" (*Le Peuple*, France, 15-30 May). In August the WFTU secretariat commented on the Soviet-West German treaty on the renunciation of force: "The Soviet-West German treaty signed in Moscow is a document of great importance for the European peoples. It is a great contribution, in fact, to the detente in Europe." (*L'Humanité*, 21 August). There were statements on the "dictatorial Greek regime" which impeded the freedom of trade unions (TASS, 20 November), and on the "aggression which has victimized Guinea and was carried out by mercenaries in the service of the imperialists" (*PCB Informations*, Belgium, 1 December).

Relations among Affiliates. The General Federation of Labor Trade Unions of Jordan and the Federation of the Workers of the Arab Republic of Yemen became affiliates of the WFTU in 1970.

While newcomers were welcomed, there was also recrimination directed at former friends. Moscow radio, for instance, criticized China on 4 October for ignoring the WFTU anniversary and asserted these reasons for the omission: (1) the trade union movement had ceased to exist in China, although such a state of affairs was contradictory to the WFTU's charter of trade union rights; (2) WFTU policy continuously sought to raise workers' salaries and their social welfare and had nothing in common with such Chinese slogans as "Poverty is a Good Thing" and "Preparations for Famine"; (3) the WFTU had always favored the solidarity of anti-imperialist and progressive forces with the Soviet Union and the "socialist community," while the Chinese leaders had demonstrated contempt for the desire of the revolutionary forces for solidarity and had attempted to divide and isolate the ranks of the anti-imperialist front.

The Soviet Union came in for criticism for practicing "McCarthyism in Prague" as an aftermath of the Soviet-led invasion of Czechoslovakia in 1968. An article in the British *Voice of the Unions* (December) recalled that in August 1968 the Czechoslovakian staff at the WFTU had voted unanimously to condemn the Soviet invasion of Czechoslovakia and reaffirmed its support for the Dubček government. In 1970, it charged: "The Czech employees at the WFTU are now being asked to withdraw their support for these resolutions. Seven of the sixty-odd native-born staff were fired at the beginning of November as a result of their refusal. . . . The Russian-inspired purge of the WFTU comes at a time when the WFTU is seeking to establish further contact with unions in the West."

The Italian affiliates also expressed dissatisfaction and sought to reform WFTU policy. At the time of the 1969 Congress they had complained about the "Budapest fog," declaring that "what might have been a Congress of a new type, fresh and alive, remained blanketed by the grey fog of incomprehensible anxieties and fears." In October 1970, the Italian General Confederation of Labor (CGIL) at a meeting in Rome reemphasized the value of the "political struggle" conducted by the CGIL in the WFTU, and in defense of the autonomy of trade unions in all countries irrespective of the political orientation of the government. CGIL Secretary, Mario Didò, expressed the general international views of the Italians he represented: "Our international policy is based on the principles of respect for national independence and sovereignty, on the right of the people to self-determination and against any concept of 'limited sovereignty' imposed on other nations." (*L'Unità*, Rome, 23 October).

Publications. The most important publication of the WFTU is the illustrated magazine *World Trade Union Movement*. In 1970 there were eleven issues, circulated in some 70 countries through editions in all major languages. The *Trade Union Press* is an international bulletin, published monthly in English, French, Russian, Spanish, German, and Polish; the monthly *News in Brief* is available in the first four of these languages. The WFTU also issues special pamphlets whenever its activities or interests warrant it. In 1970, for instance, a special booklet detailed the "Decisions of the 7th World Trade Union Congress." The first issue of a quarterly publication entitled *WFTU and Vietnam* was released in April; later in the year it was renamed *WFTU and Indochina.*

The WFTU broadcasts in several languages from various locations in Eastern Europe.

E. W.

WORLD FEDERATION OF DEMOCRATIC YOUTH

The World Federation of Democratic Youth (WFDY) was founded in November 1945 at a "World Youth Conference" convened in London by the World Youth Council. At first the WFDY appeared to represent a variety of shades of political opinion, but the key positions were taken by communists. By 1950 most of the noncommunists had left to found their own organization, the World Assembly of Youth (WAY). The WFDY has been based in Budapest since its expulsion by the French government in 1951. It holds category C status with UNESCO and is on the register of ECOSOC.

According to the WFDY constitution, all youth organizations and other bodies that contribute to the safeguarding of the activities of young persons are eligible for membership. A total membership of some 100 million persons in 200 organizations in 98 countries is claimed (TASS, 12 October 1970); the vast majority of WFDY members live in communist-ruled countries. The WFDY claims to be financed entirely by affiliation fees; no details are published.

Structure. The highest governing body of the WFDY is the Assembly, which is supposed to convene every three years, and to which all affiliated organizations may send representatives. The Eighth Assembly was held in Budapest from 26 October to 4 November 1970. The Executive Committee is elected by the Assembly and is supposed to meet at least twice a year, while day-to-day work at the headquarters is conducted by the Bureau of the Executive Committee, which meets as necessary and controls the WFDY Secretariat, its various departments, and its regional commissions.

The Eighth Assembly elected to the Executive Committee 57 representatives, comprising one person from each of the following countries (two where indicated): Angola, Argentina, Bolivia, Bulgaria, Brazil, Burundi, Canada, Ceylon (2), Chile, Colombia, Costa Rica, Cuba, Cyprus, Czechoslovakia, Denmark, Dominican Republic, Ecuador, Finland, France, East Germany, West Germany, Britain, Greece (2), Guatemala, Guyana, Hungary, India, Iran, Iraq, Italy (2), Japan (2), North Korea, Lebanon, Madagascar, Mexico, Mongolia, Panama, Poland, Romania, Senegal, Sierra Leone, Somalia, South Africa, Spain, Sudan, Syria, Soviet Union (2), United States, Uruguay, Venezuela, North Vietnam, and South Vietnam. Places were reserved for an additional representative from Chile, and for one representative each from China and Peru, to provide for a total of 60 members. The new 26-member Bureau consists of the president (Angelo Oliva; Italy), seven vice-presidents (one each from Chile, North Korea, Cuba, Hungary, India, Sudan, Soviet Union), the secretary-general (Michel Jouet, France), two deputy secretaries-general (Sierra Leone, Venezuela), the treasurer (Argentina), and 13 secretaries (Bulgaria, Colombia, Czechoslovakia, Dominican Republic, East Germany, Finland, Iraq, Japan, Lebanon, Poland, Romania, South Africa, United States). A place was reserved for China. The Auditing Commission has a chairman (Belgium) and three members (Australia, Puerto Rico, and Zanzibar). (*WFDY News*, November-December.)

WFDY subsidiaries include: the International Committee of Children's and Adolescents' Movements (CIMEA), which organizes international camps and film festivals; the International Bureau of Tourism and Exchanges of Youth (BITEJ), charged with planning and supervising work camps, meetings, and conferences for young tourists (BITEJ is an associate member of the Coordinating Committee for International Voluntary Service, which works under the aegis of UNESCO); the International Sports Committee for Youth, which arranges special events in connection with WFDY-IUS World Youth Festivals; the International Voluntary Service for Friendship and Solidarity of Youth (SIVSAJ), geared to increasing WFDY influence in developing countries by sending "young volunteers" to work with the people of these countries; and various "International Committees of Solidarity."

Aims and Policies. The avowed aims of the WFDY are to contribute to the education of young persons in the spirit of freedom and democracy; to raise the living standard of the young; to end colonialism; to ensure peace and security in the world; to promote the active participation of young persons in economic, social, cultural, and political life; to ensure in all countries and for all young persons full freedom of speech, the press, religious belief, assembly, and organization; and to further the spirit of international friendship and support the principles of the United Nations. In practice, unquestioned support of the Soviet Union has been evident at all times in WFDY pronouncements and actions. The 1968 Warsaw Pact invasion of Czechoslovakia and its aftermath created considerable disharmony among WFDY affiliates, but at no juncture was Soviet control threatened. Because of the Sino-Soviet dispute, the Chinese have not participated in WFDY activities for several years.

Views and Activities in 1970. In an open letter to its affiliated national organizations in commemoration of the twenty-fifth anniversary of the WFDY, Angelo Oliva called for a "greater commitment" to the "struggles of the peoples and youth." Specific goals in connection with this commitment included U.S. withdrawal from Vietnam, international recognition of the German Democratic Republic (GDR), a political solution in the Middle East, and efforts to thwart fascism in Spain, Portugal and Greece, and colonialism and racism everywhere. The WFDY called for 24 April to be celebrated both as "World Youth Day against Colonialism, Neo-Colonialism, Imperialism, and for Peace" and in commemoration of the centenary of Lenin's birth. A special committee was formed to coordinate Lenin festivities in different continents. The event, Oliva said at a press conference in Budapest on 20 April, was of particular significance for the WFDY, whose activities, throughout its existence, had been "guided by Leninist ideals and Leninist teachings." (MTI, Hungarian News Agency, 20 April; *L'Unità*, Rome, 21 April.)

A joint WFDY-Komsomol "World Youth Meeting" was held in Leningrad from 31 May to 5 June, following the Sixteenth Congress of the Komsomol. The meeting had the theme of "Leninism and the Struggle of Youth for Peace, National Independence, Democracy, and Social Progress" and was attended by representatives of 142 organizations in 96 countries. Michel Jouet asserted at the meeting that the current level of youth revolt around the world evidenced a "deep crisis in imperialism"; but he urged young people to realize that they could be ultimately effective, "according to Leninist tenets," only "as part of the general struggle of revolutionary and democratic forces." Final resolutions pledged, among other objectives, to make 1971 "a year of world-wide action of youth against imperialism" and to increase "moral and material support for the peoples of Angola, Guinea (Bissau), South Africa, Zimbabwe (Rhodesia), Zambia, and Mozambique in their struggle for independence." (Moscow radio, 4 June; TASS, 1-4 June.)

An international seminar on "The Relevance of Leninism in the Struggle of Young People and Students against Imperialism and for Democracy and Socialism," organized jointly by the

WFDY and the youth organization of the French Communist Party was held in Paris on 27 February-1 March. Delegations attended from Italy, Japan, Senegal, the Dominican Republic, the Soviet Union, South Vietnam, West Berlin, West Germany, Bulgaria, Spain, Hungary, Luxembourg, Poland, Romania, Switzerland, Czechoslovakia, and Yugoslavia. East German representatives were refused entry into France. Seminar discussions concluded that "the struggle for the construction of socialism" was "linked to the struggle of young people and students against imperialism." (*L'Humanité*, Paris, 28 February and 2 March.)

A similar seminar, for young people of Central America, was sponsored by the WFDY and held in San José, Costa Rica, on 9-12 April. Described by the WFDY as "the first Central American youth meeting for the rights of youth," this seminar, according to *Libertad* (San José, 11 April), gathered representatives from "all the Central American countries, from Panama, Venezuela, the WFDY, and the IUS . . . despite government opposition."

The Executive Committee met in Katowice, Poland on 16-21 May. Some 100 delegates from 54 countries attended the meeting, "to mark the Lenin Centenary and the twenty-fifth anniversary of the victory over fascism." The main discussions concerned preparations for the WFDY's Eighth Assembly. At a rally in Katowice on 18 May, Jouet appealed to "youth of the world" to "fight for the setting up of a militant alliance aimed against all militarist and neo-fascist forces, for peace in the world." (PAP, Polish News Agency, 18 and 21 May.) A telegram to West German Chancellor Willy Brandt appealed for an end to the alleged "policy of discrimination against the GDR" and for acceptance of "political and territorial realities in Europe." (ADN, East German News Agency, 21 May).

It was reported at Katowice that the WFDY had admitted to membership 14 of 29 organizations which had applied. Those accepted were the Communist Youth of Austria, Communist Youth of Greece, Young Workers' Liberation League (new youth movement of the Communist Party, USA), Dahomey Youth Movement, Democratic Youth of Togo, National Union of Togo Youth, Revolutionary Rwangasor Youth (Burundi), Argentinian Confederation of Secondary School Students, Revolutionary Youth of Chile, Social-Democratic Youth of Finland, Socialist Students' Union of Finland, Youth Action Council of Great Britain, Communist Youth of Norway, and (West) German Socialist Working Youth. It was announced, further, that in accordance with the Seventh Assembly's decision to reserve one place each in the Executive Committee for West German and U.S. organizations, the new affiliates from these countries would immediately take their places in the committee. (*WFDY News*, June.)

At a pre-Assembly press conference in Budapest on 21 October, Jouet described the WFDY's attempt to rally "youth organizations of the most varied kinds" in a "broad-based anti-imperialist bloc." For this reason, several organizations not affiliated with the WFDY had been invited to attend. (Budapest radio, 21 October.) The Assembly, convened on 26 October, was attended by 540 delegates from 95 countries, representing 292 organizations (MTI, 3 November). The major document adopted was a "Declaration of Principles," which stated that the general theme of WFDY activities would be "Youth Accuses Imperialism." The Assembly decided to organize a "world meeting of working youth" and a European meeting on collective security in 1971, and also to hold a tenth World Youth Festival in August 1971 (the ninth was in Sofia in August 1968). Participants agreed that the posts of president and secretary-general of the WFDY should remain, respectively, with members of the youth organizations of the Italian and French communist parties. (*L'Humanité*, 6 November.)

Jouet addressed himself to the "need to adjust to local conditions"—the same "formulas" might not bind the youth movement in all countries, and Oliva expressed regret that the WFDY had "lost contact" with Chinese youth (MTI, 27 October). Evgeni Tiazhelnikov, the chief Soviet delegate and a member of the Komsomol Central Committee, went farther, charging the

Chinese with having "kept aloof" in recent years from the activities of "Socialist" countries—in contrast, he said, to "the tremendous role played by Chinese youth and the stance taken by their organizations when the Chinese people were first stirred to revolution" (TASS, 28 October). Apparently in response to this criticism, the Union of Working Youth of Albania attacked the WFDY on Tirana radio a week later (11 November). The WFDY, it charged, had embarked upon a "retrograde line" immediately after the Soviet party's Twentieth Congress; the WFDY thus reflected and supported the "traitorous activity and policy pursued by the Soviet revisionists"—as when, at the time of the invasion of Czechoslovakia, WFDY leaders "closed their ears and shut their eyes and mouths as if nothing was happening." The Albanian broadcast charged also that the WFDY leadership had sought cooperation with organizations allegedly financed by the U.S. Central Intelligence Agency, such as the World Assembly of Youth, and that WFDY actions on the European security issue would bring the United States and the Soviet Union closer together, thereby threatening China.

Although the choice of Executive Committee members had been decided in advance of the Assembly (at the Executive Committee meeting in Katowice), approval of the choice at the Assembly plenary session did not pass without discussion. Objections were raised by speakers from Greece and Austria, where in each instance, rival organizations exist side by side, both of which are members of the WFDY. The Lambrakis Democratic Youth (Greece) objected to the co-opting into the committee of the newly organized Greek Communist Youth (KNE), and a Free Austrian Youth representative protested that his organization was not included. Reflective of Soviet influence in the WFDY, the Assembly applauded the KNE delegate, but in the Austrian case Oliva declared that the Assembly was not a "suitable forum for solving problems of an internal political character." (*Mlada Fronta*, Prague, 5 November; see also Greece and Austria).

During the course of the Assembly, the third CIMEA and fourth BITEJ conferences were held in Budapest on 27 October and 28-29 October, respectively (*ibid.*, 29 October). The CIMEA elected a nine-member Presidium including a president (from France), vice-presidents (Soviet Union and Sudan), general secretary (Hungary), and ordinary members (Cyprus, Cuba, Finland, Mongolia, and Poland). The new BITEJ Council comprised a president (Czechoslovakia), vice-president (Hungary), and five members (East Germany, Finland, France, Algeria, and the Soviet Union). Three organizations—from Poland, Iceland, and Sudan—were accepted as full members of BITEJ and four others—two from Dahomey and one each from Mexico and Nigeria—became associate members. (*WFDY News*, November-December).

The WFDY criticized preparations for the "World Youth Assembly" held by the U.N. (New York, 9-18 July), declaring: "The subject matter and the trend of the discussion which the organizers of the assembly are trying to impose on it are far from those which could provide for a real discussion of problems concerning youth." The WFDY, it indicated, would put forward at the meeting a political platform "aimed at rallying into a united anti-imperialist front the actions and struggle of youth against the policy of aggression, repression, and exploitation." (TASS, 6 July.) The WFDY delegation, however, headed by Jouet and including Mikis Theodorakis (Greece), was unable to influence either the direction of the proceedings or the shaping of final communiqués.

The WFDY Bureau designated 2-8 May a "Week of Action for the Recognition of the GDR," and called for signature campaigns, appeals to parliamentarians, letters to newspapers, and the distribution of leaflets, declaring that 8 May, the twenty-fifth anniversary of the "victory over Hitler's Fascism," provided an opportunity for "democratic" forces to launch new initiatives in the struggle for European security, recognition of the GDR, and against "revanchism and neo-Nazism" in West Germany. Jouet led a WFDY delegation to the broad-based "International Conference of Youth on European Security," which convened in Helsinki on 27-31 August. Both the WFDY and the World Peace Council, a prime mover in organizing the conference, helped shape the final communiqué, which included declarations that both Germanies should be accepted as full members of the U.N. and its specialized agencies, and that the time had come for the creation of a European security system which would result in effective measures to promote disarmament, the withdrawal of troops, and the liquidation of military bases and equipment on territories of foreign states and, ultimately, of blocs altogether. (WFDY Conference Documents.)

The WFDY Bureau convened in extraordinary session during the third week of February to condemn Israel for its bombing raids on the U.A.R. The meeting, attended by representatives of the Palestinian Liberation Organization, designated 2 March a "Day of International Protest against the Crimes Committed by the Israeli Aggressors, Supported by the American Imperialists" (*Komsomolskaya Pravda*, Moscow, 21 February; *al-Ahram*, Cairo, 23 February; *Le Progrès Egyptien*, Cairo, 28 February). A WFDY delegation led by vice-president Andrei Grachev (Soviet Union) arrived in Cairo on 18 April for talks with the Arab Students' Union. At a press conference on 21 April, Grachev announced plans for an international symposium on "imperialist monopolies and machinations in the Middle East" and for an international camp in Amman, Jordan, to "express solidarity with the Palestinian people in their just struggle against the imperialist-Israeli aggression." (*Egyptian Gazette*, Cairo, 22 April.)

In the WFDY's monthly newssheet *Solidarity* (subtitled "The WFDY in Solidarity with the Arab Peoples, the Peoples of the Portuguese Colonies and Southern Africa"; no. 1-2), various solidarity days were announced with different African "national liberation movements." A supplement described the "tasks ahead" for the Popular Movement for the Liberation of Angola (MPLA). A WFDY seminar on "The Role of Youth in the Development and Building of the Nation" was held in Cotonou, Dahomey, on 18-23 April and was attended by representatives from 15 West African countries and the Soviet Union. The seminar condemned apartheid in Rhodesia and NATO support for Portugal and South Africa, and reaffirmed "moral and material support for the fighting youth" in Angola, Mozambique, Guinea (Bissau), South Africa, Zimbabwe, and Namibia. (TASS, 18 April; Cotonou radio, 24 April.) At the invitation of the African Party of Independence of Guinea and the Cape Verde Islands (PAIGC), a WFDY delegation led by Sindiso Mfenyana (South Africa), head of the WFDY's Regional Commission for Africa, and including Renzo Imbeni, a member of the Italian Communist Youth Federation (FGCI) visited the "liberated zones" of Guinea (Bissau) in early March. They went on to Conakry for the first National Cultural and Arts Festival, which began there on 9 March. (*WFDY News*, April.)

In agitation against U.S. involvement in the Vietnam war, the WFDY sponsored a "European tour" by twelve-year-old Vo Thi Lien, a purported witness to "American crimes" at My Lai. The tour group started from Budapest on 12 January and visited Bulgaria, Norway, Sweden, Denmark, Finland, England (as guests of the Young Communist League), Belgium, East Berlin, and West Berlin (as guests of the West Berlin Free Youth League). (MTI, 12 January; ADN, 28 February; *Morning Star*, London, 14 February.) A booklet, produced by the WFDY in collaboration with the International Union of Students and entitled *With Vietnam to the Final Victory*, urged increased demands for the recognition of the Provisional Revolutionary Government of the Republic of South Vietnam (PRGSV), for support of the International Liaison Committee of the Stockholm Conference on Vietnam (see *World Peace Council*), and for the "unmasking" of U.S. President Nixon's "Vietnamization stunt." On 8 May the WFDY issued a statement condemning the U.S. military offensive in "neutral" Cambodia, and declaring its full support for the joint statement adopted by the Indochinese summit conference. A WFDY delegation was in Paris on 23-25 November for multilateral talks with representatives of the youth organization of the French Communist Party, the PRGSV, and North Vietnam (*L'Humanité*, 26 November).

A month-long WFDY international work camp opened at Lake Seliger (Soviet Union) on 5

July, with students from 33 countries studying at Moscow institutes. Participants were required to work on the construction of schools, clubs, and tourist centers (TASS, 5 July). The June issue of *WFDY News* announced plans for some 100 international volunteer work camps in several countries, under BITEJ-SIVSAJ sponsorship.

The WFDY engaged in a number of bilateral and multilateral meetings with communist parties or movements to chart future joint activities. A Bolivian delegation, including Eduardo Campero of the Communist Youth of Bolivia, was at WFDY headquarters on 22-26 January to discuss WFDY aid for a "National Literacy Campaign" (*WFDY News*, no. 1-2). Oliva headed a WFDY delegation to Belgrade in February for talks with the Yugoslav Youth Union (Tanyug, Yugoslav news agency, 10 February). The WFDY sent a delegation to the 15 March Conference of the Belgian communist youth auxiliary (*Le Soir*, Brussels, 17 March). WFDY representatives, together with representatives of the Hungarian Communist Youth and the Dimitrov Communist Youth League (of Bulgaria) met in March-April with Yiannis Yiannakos, member of the Central Council of the Lambrakis Democratic Youth, and Iakovos Papadopoulos, president of the Coordinating Committee of Anti-Dictatorial Action of Greek Youth Abroad ("Voice of Truth" radio, of the Communist Party of Greece, 2 April). A WFDY delegate attended the congress, in Vienna, of the reconstituted Communist Youth of Austria on 9-10 May (TASS, 10 May). Tibor Lakatos (Hungary; CIMEA secretary-general) represented the WFDY at a meeting in Pautin, France, at which the communist-controlled Union of Valiant Youth became the "Pioneers of France" (*L'Humanité*, 26 May). Oliva was among WFDY representatives to the Sixteenth Congress of the Komsomol, held in Moscow during May (TASS, 26 May).

Publications. The WFDY publishes a bimonthly magazine, *World Youth*, in English, French, and "in a number of national editions," and a monthly newssheet, *WFDY News*, in English, French, and Spanish editions. Other publications are issued by the WFDY which are directed to specific areas of interest; in addition, special magazines and pamphlets commemorate congresses, festivals, and other events.

V. B.

INTERNATIONAL UNION
OF STUDENTS

The International Union of Students (IUS) was established in August 1946 at a congress in Prague attended by students of varying political and religious persuasions. According to its constitution, the union was founded as a "representative organization of the democratic students of the whole world who work for progress." By 1951 most non-communists had left the IUS because of its domination by pro-Soviet elements. The IUS has headquarters at Vocelova 3, Prague.

Full or associate membership in the IUS is open to national student unions and to other student organizations in countries where no national union exists. The IUS claims a total membership of approximately 10 million in 88 organizations (*Mlada Fronta*, Prague, 29 October 1970). The Chinese communists have boycotted the IUS since 1966.

The IUS has consultative Category C status with UNESCO; applications for Category B status have been repeatedly deferred.

Structure and Leadership. The highest governing body of the IUS is its Congress, which is supposed to meet every two years and to which affiliated and associated organizations send delegates. The Tenth Congress, originally scheduled for early 1970, was postponed until February 1971, with Bratislava as the site. The Congress elects the Executive Committee, comprising the Secretariat, Finance Committee, and individual members. National student organizations to be represented on the Executive Committee are chosen by the Congress, but each designated organization selects its own representative. The Executive Committee usually meets at least twice a year. (See *YICA*, 1970, pp. 761-62 for a list of organizations elected to the Executive Committee at the 1967 Congress, which is believed to have remained virtually unchanged through 1970.)

The two top IUS posts and their incumbents are: president, Dušan Ulčák (Czechoslovakia), named on 2 February 1970 to succeed Zbyněk Vokrouhlický (Czechoslovakia), who had been removed from office in September 1969 because of his disapproval of events in Czechoslovakia; and Secretary-General, Mehdi al-Hafid (Iraq).

Aims and Policies. The official aims of the IUS as incorporated in its constitution are to: defend the interests of students; promote national culture; eradicate all forms of discrimination and, in particular, of racial discrimination; and achieve "realization of the aspirations of students in colonial, semi-colonial, and dependent countries struggling against colonialism and imperialism." IUS protests and criticisms are invariably directed against the West; even under considerable pressure of external events, the organization has never seriously criticized the Soviet Union. The IUS claims to be financed solely by affiliation fees and the sale of its publications, but no details are published.

Views and Activities in 1970. Extensive efforts were made by the IUS in 1970 to consolidate its ranks in the aftermath of the 1968 Soviet-led invasion of Czechoslovakia. This was no more than a formality in the case of Czechoslovakia itself, however, where the invasion had been strongly condemned among student unions. A new national body, the Czechoslovak University Students' Center (CUSC), was set up in 1969; loyal to the policies of the new regime, the CUSC is therefore acceptable to the IUS. An IUS delegation, led by President Dušan Ulčák and including three Secretariat members—Mazen al-Husaini (Jordan), Krzysztov Opalski (Poland), and Martín Quiroda (Argentina)—toured Czechoslovak university centers on 12-18 May. Jan Procházka, CUSC chairman, said the purpose of the visit was to observe the "present state of consolidation" at Czechoslovak universities, demonstrate the "renewed cooperation of the representative organization of the Czech university students with the IUS which two years ago was rudely disturbed by the then Union of University Students by its hazardous repudiation of cooperation," and "clarify" the "aims and intentions of the IUS." Ulčák was able to attest, at the close of the visit, that the Czechoslovak student movement had successfully "overcome its recent crisis." (*Mlada Fronta*, 13, 16, and 19 May; Czechoslovak news agency, CTK, 18 May.)

There were indications, however, that the new Czechoslovak student leaders were having problems in their relations with European and other student organizations, and an article in *Predvoj*, the weekly organ of the CUSC, on 18 June referred to "a very negative attitude" encountered among some European students' unions. At least two initiatives were taken by the IUS leadership to overcome this disharmony among its affiliates. An international seminar for university students, organized jointly by the CUSC and IUS, was held in Bratislava on 27-29 November, the main topic being the "development of international students' solidarity" (CTK, 29 November.) Earlier, representatives of IUS member organizations met in Prague on 17 April to celebrate the centenary of Lenin's birth, and pledged themselves to support "Lenin's heritage" as "the only revolutionary tradition." (*Mlada Fronta*, 18 April.)

The IUS Secretariat issued a statement in February declaring its readiness to assist in preparations for the United Nation's twenty-fifth anniversary World Youth Assembly (New York, 9-18 July). "Being wary of the governmental nature of the UN," the IUS argued that the meeting should be "entirely a youth project, prepared and conducted by youth without governmental interference," that delegates should be selected by student and youth organizations themselves, and that U.N. membership of the country of origin should not be the criterion for an invitation to participate. It demanded equal representation in the meeting of the "youth suffering under the yoke of the Portuguese colonialists in Africa, under the yoke of apartheid and racial discrimination in the Republic of South Africa and in Rhodesia, the youth of the heroic Palestinian nation, and the youth suffering under Fascist oppression in Spain, Portugal, and Greece." (*IUS News Service*, no. 6.)

A subsequent IUS report (*ibid.*, supplement, August) complained that at the meeting there had been "feverish maneuvers to bar condemnation of U.S. imperialism and other imperialist powers for their aggression" and that many governments had "directly interfered in the formation of national delegations." In sum, though, the IUS stated, the World Youth Assembly meeting could "never be regarded as truly representative of the youth and students of the world," but nevertheless the voices of liberation movements of the Portuguese colonies, South Africa, Palestine, Greece, Spain, Puerto Rico and others were heard there for the first time in the history of the U.N.

The bid by the IUS to extend its domain in the world student movement was challenged by two British student unions, the Scottish Union of Students (SUS) and the National Union of Students of England, Wales, and Northern Ireland (NUSEWNI). The SUS and NUSEWNI were accused by the IUS in October of trying to paralyze preparations for a tenth "European Meeting of National Unions of Students," planned to be held in Sweden. The preparatory committee for the European meeting included four IUS member organizations—from Ireland (the Union of Students of Ireland; USI), Yugoslavia, Poland, and Hungary. It warned that "these maneuvers" by the SUS and NUSEWNI were "supported by the same forces which split the international student movement twenty years ago," when non-communist unions which left the IUS formed the Coordinating Secretariat of National Unions of Students (COSEC). (*Mlada Fronta*, 17 October.) The USI and IUS co-sponsored the third "European Seminar on Education" near Dublin on 22-25 September, dealing with themes of higher education and social change, change in university government, and the role of student organizations in achieving educational change. (*IUS News Service*, no. 19; Prague radio, 16 November.)

The IUS hailed the East-West German talks, declaring that the recognition in international law of the German Democratic Republic (GDR) and by all states of the boundaries arising from the Second World War were "decisive prerequisites to peace and security in Europe" (*Neues Deutschland*, East Berlin, 9 January.) It exhorted "progressive" students to organize signature and other campaigns during "European Week for the Recognition of the German Democratic Republic" (2-9 May) so as to emphasize the "positive role of the GDR in the struggle for peace and against the danger represented by imperialists, neo-Nazis and revanchists" (CTK, 31 March).

On 4 April, the twenty-first anniversary of the establishment of NATO, the IUS issued a statement warning that this "spearhead of world imperialism" was "as active as ever in threatening to plunge the peoples of the world into a new conflict whose outcome could hardly be grasped." NATO, it said, was "far from being merely an Atlantic organization"; its "tentacles" had reached into Vietnam and the Middle East (where NATO powers were backing Israeli "aggression"), and it supported the "vassal regime" in Portugal. The IUS appealed to all national student unions to intensify their protest activities against NATO and to support the security conference proposed by the Warsaw Pact states—"in the interests of everlasting peace in the world." (*IUS News Service*, no. 8.)

Protesting the prosecution of political opponents of the Greek government, the IUS declared on 21 April, the third anniversary of the coup, that Greece was "once again the center of provocations against its neighbors, especially Cyprus." Student unions were called upon to organize "Free Greece" campaigns, and meetings and rallies in support of the IUS-affiliated National Union of Greek Students (EFEE). (*Ibid.*, no. 9.)

The IUS continued to experience strains in its relations with student unions in the Arab world, whose chief interest appears to be in using the IUS to foment international sentiment against Israel. The IUS went to some length to avoid conflicts with its Arab associates and to win their favor. At a press conference at IUS headquarters on 2 March, Dušan Ulčák announced that a new monthly magazine, *The Arab Struggle*, would be published by the IUS, first in English and later in French and Arabic editions, whose aim, he said, was to "acquaint a wide student public with the situation and political aims of the governments of Arab countries and liberation movements." The IUS would also publish a pamphlet on "crimes committed by the Israeli occupiers of Arab territory," using "facts and arguments exclusively from Israeli sources." (*Mlada Fronta*, 3 March.) An IUS delegation attended the second "World Conference on Palestine," held in Amman, Jordan, on 2-6 September by the General Union of Palestinian Students (GUPS); the first conference, in Cairo in 1965, had set up a permanent secretariat comprised of representatives of the GUPS, IUS, and WFDY. A final communiqué supported Palestinians "in their efforts to reestablish a nonsectarian state in Palestine" and rejected "in all its forms" the 1967

U.N. Security Council resolution on the Middle East. (*Fatah*, organ of the Palestinian Liberation Organization, 17 September.)

Addressing delegates to the congress of the Kurdish Students' Society in Europe (KSSE), held in Stockholm on 1-5 August, Mehdi al-Hafid reiterated the IUS's support for the struggle of the Kurdish students and people for their national rights, and called for the deepening of the relations between the IUS and the KSSE (an IUS member organization). (*IUS News Service*, no. 19.)

IUS activities in Africa focused principally upon the "liberation struggle" in Portuguese colonies. IUS officials in March met in Konakry with leaders of the African Party of Independence of Guinea and the Cape Verde Islands (PAIGC) and the Youth of the African Democratic Revolution (TASS, 31 March). The IUS celebrated 4 February as "International Day of Solidarity with the Angolan People and Students Struggling for National Independence" and as the ninth anniversary of the start of the armed struggle by the Popular Movement for the Liberation of Angola (MPLA), "convinced of the final victory of the Angolan people and of the fact that as a national liberation movement it surpasses the framework of Angola alone, constituting an intrinsic part of the liberation movement of all peoples struggling against colonialism, neo-colonialism, and imperialism." (*IUS News Service*, no. 3-4.)

On the occasion of the tenth anniversary of the founding of the Lumumba University in Moscow, the IUS Secretariat sent a message expressing "appreciation of the contribution of the Soviet government, people, and students in extending moral and material support to the international liberation movement in general and to the African liberation movement in particular." Declaring its support for "all anti-racist forces," the IUS condemned the "notorious South African apartheid regime and British imperialism, for extending their racial policies even into sport." (*Ibid.*) The Ian Smith government's declaration of Rhodesia as a republic on 1 March, was said by the IUS to have been made "on the advice and with the support of Britain, the U.S., South Africa, and Portugal . . . buttressed by their military organization, NATO" (*ibid.*, no. 6). The IUS scored the repression of its affiliate, the National Union of Moroccan Students (UNEM), and other "progressives" by the "feudal, pro-imperialist regime" in Morocco, and protested to Spain its extradition to Morocco of Moroccan "progressives" (*ibid.*, nos. 5 and 6). The IUS appeal was reiterated in May following the arrest of nine UNEM leaders during a student strike (*ibid.*, nos. 11 and 12). The IUS and its affiliated National Union of Nigerian Students (NUNS) co-sponsored a seminar on "The Students' Role in National Reconstruction" at the Ahmadu Bello University in Nigeria in October, following a visit by a NUNS delegation to IUS headquarters some months earlier (*ibid.*, nos. 18 and 19).

In regard to Southeast Asia, the IUS and WFDY, as co-sponsors of a continuing "Campaign of Action of Youth and Students for the Final Victory of the Vietnamese People, for Freedom, Independence, and Peace," announced in *IUS News Service*, no. 9, a broad fund-raising initiative for material aid for North Vietnam under the slogan "For a Hospital for Vietnam." Expressing "alarm and indignation" at American bombing in Laos, the IUS demanded "a speedy end to U.S. interference in the Laotian peoples' affairs," and "strict compliance with the Geneva Agreements of 1962." It voiced "firm confidence," nonetheless, in the "victory of the progressive democratic forces in Laos, rallied behind the leadership of the Patriotic Front." (TASS, 25 March.) The IUS denounced alleged massacres of Vietnamese living in Cambodia (CTK, 24 April), and urged broad support for the week of international protest to be held from 26 October to 1 November (organized by the Stockholm Conference on Vietnam; see *World Peace Council*) (*IUS News Service*, no. 18; *Mlada Fronta*, 26 October). Mahdi al-Hafid, Siegfried Katzschmann, and Luis Corchado (Puerto Rico) arrived in Hanoi on 20 November at the invitation of the Vietnam Students' Union (Vietnam News Agency, 20 November).

The IUS called on member organizations to condemn the "massacre of South Korean patriots and actively to support the South Korean people's and students' "supreme national task" of overthrowing "American imperialism's colonial domination," so as to "hasten the day of the unification of their homeland" and "eliminate all miseries and unbearable sufferings of the South Korean people" (*IUS News Service*, no. 7). The IUS condemned the "U.S. imperialist provocation" of 5 June in allegedly "sending a reconnaissance espionage ship into the coastal waters of North Korea," and declared that it was "in self-defense" that the vessel had been sunk by North Korea (*ibid.*, nos. 13 and 14). An IUS delegation including Dušan Ulčák, Adelino Nuñez (vice-president) and Martín Quiroda arrived in Pyongyang on 14 October (NCNA, 14 October). The IUS demanded that the Japanese government "cease immediately its nationalist, systematic persecution and repression of Korean residents in Japan, in connivance with the American imperialists"; condemned alleged attacks by Japanese "fascist" students on Korean students and other citizens residing in Japan; and proclaimed its solidarity with the General Association of Koreans Residing in Japan (*IUS News Service*, no. 19).

The first issue in 1970 of the *IUS Information Bulletin*, edited by the Latin American Committee of the IUS, was dedicated to the eleventh anniversary of the Cuban Revolution. It included photographs of Cuban Premier Fidel Castro working in the cane fields, and denounced the U.S. blockade of Cuba. In Chile, the IUS and the State Technical University Students' Federation (FEUT) jointly organized an "International School of Student Leaders" in Santiago, conducted on 3-8 August, as "an expression of solidarity with Cuba, Vietnam, and the peoples fighting for liberation." At this "school," representatives from the IUS, WFDY, and FEUT and from Bolivia, Venezuela, Cuba, Peru, Argentina, and Uruguay discussed the "anti-imperialist and anti-oligarchist struggle of youth and students in Latin America and throughout the world," students and the revolutionary process, and students and political power. (*El Siglo*, Santiago, 20 July and 4 August.) The IUS sent a delegate to Chile for the first "National Meeting of Youth," held on 1-3 May and organized by the Single Center of Chilean Workers; the meeting was attended also by delegates from Argentina, Uruguay, Bolivia, and Peru (*ibid.*, 3 May). Later a two-member IUS Secretariat delegation attended the inauguration of Chilean President Salvador Allende and met with leaders of FEUT and the Federation of University Students of Chile (*IUS News Service*, no. 24, December). Numerous appeals issued by the IUS called for the release of political prisoners and an end to the repression of "progressive" students in Nicaragua, Venezuela, Argentina, Mexico, Panama, Ecuador, and Colombia. An IUS delegation attended the "first Central American youth meeting for the rights of youth," sponsored by the WFDY in San José, Costa Rica, on 9-12 April (*Libertad*, San José, 11 April).

László Kovács (Hungary), head of the IUS Student Needs and Welfare Department, stated in *World Student News* (no. 7/8) that since 1955, when the IUS scholarship program was introduced, some 2,500 students, mostly from IUS-affiliated unions, had commenced higher studies in the Soviet Union and East Europe. Though the project still concentrated on colonial and newly independent countries, it had been extended to Greece, Portugal, and Spain, "as an expression of solidarity with students struggling against imperialism, colonialism, neo-colonialism, and Fascist dictatorship throughout the world." On the negative side, some of the approved candidates, "for unknown reasons," did not arrive in the donor country, discrediting the project. Had the IUS done "more to maintain regular contacts with its scholarship holders," Kovács concluded, it "probably would have resulted in more of these students successfully completing their studies."

Publications. The principal IUS publications are the monthly magazine, *World Student News*, edited by Mazen al-Husaini and published in English, French, German, and Spanish editions, and a fortnightly bulletin, *IUS News Service*, issued in English, French, and Spanish editions.

V. B.

WOMEN'S INTERNATIONAL DEMOCRATIC FEDERATION

The Women's International Democratic Federation (WIDF) was founded in Paris in December 1945 at a "Congress of Women" organized by a communist-dominated organization, the "Union des Femmes Françaises." The WIDF headquarters was in Paris until January 1951, when the organization was expelled by the French government. Since then it has operated from East Germany; the address is Unter den Linden 13, Berlin.

Structure. The highest organ of the WIDF is its Congress, which is supposed to meet every four years. Comprised of representatives of affiliated organizations, plus some individual members, it examines the work of the federation, plans its future activities, selects the president and the WIDF Council, and ratifies Council decisions. The Sixth Congress was held in Helsinki on 14-18 June 1969.

The WIDF Council meets annually and controls activities between congresses. The composition of the Council was altered by the 1969 Congress, which ruled that each country should be represented by three members and three alternates, irrespective of the number of its affiliated organizations. The Council elects the WIDF Bureau and the Secretariat, and appoints the Finance Control Commission.

The Bureau consists of the WIDF president, 10 vice-presidents, the secretary-general, and additional members elected by the Council. It meets at least twice a year and implements decisions taken by the Congress and the Council. The Bureau is assisted by the Secretariat, consisting of the secretary-general, the secretaries, and a treasurer.

The Sixth Congress elected Hertta Kuusinen (Finland) as WIDF president, to succeed Eugénie Cotton (France), who held the post from the organization's founding in 1945 until her death in 1967. The new president is a member of the Politburo of the Finnish Communist Party. Cécile Hugel (France) was reelected to the position of secretary-general, which she had held since 1967. The Congress also named six honorary vice-presidents to acknowledge their "outstanding contribution to the formation, development, and prestige of the WIDF": Dr. Andrea Andreen (Sweden), Dolores Ibárruri (Spain), Ceza Nabarouri (U.A.R.), Rada Todorova (Bulgaria), Marie Pritt (Britain), and Margarita de Ponce (Argentina). The vice-presidents are Ilse Thiele (East Germany), Vilma Espín de Castro (Cuba), Funmilayo Ransome-Kuti (Nigeria), Miluse Fischerova (Czechoslovakia), Marie-Claude Vaillant-Couturier (France), Aruna Asaf Ali (India), Hiratsika Raicho (Japan), Freda Brown (Australia), Julia Arévalo (Uruguay), and Soviet cosmonaut Valentina Nikolayeva-Tereshkova. Countries represented among the Bureau members are Algeria, Angola, Argentina, Canada, Chile, Great Britain, Iraq, Korea, Mexico, Mongolia, South Africa, and Sudan. The Sixth Congress determined that the Secretariat should consist of the secretary-general and secretaries from the national organizations of West Germany, Britain, India, Iraq, Japan, Mexico, Romania, Spain, South Africa, the U.S.S.R., and Chile, and a treasurer from Bulgaria. Permanent "guests" of the Secretariat were to be the editor-in-chief of *Women of the Whole World* (Poland) and the secretary of the Secretariat (East Germany). The Auditing Committee was to be chaired by Edith Erdei (Hungary) and to include members from Austria, Lebanon, Luxembourg, and Venezuela. That some changes may have taken place since the time of the 1969 Congress is likely in view of the signatures on a circular letter, dated 20 May 1970, which asked members to contribute to the WIDF Fund before the Council meeting in October. The letters were signed by Maria Taneva as treasurer and Dilshad Chari as secretary.

Membership in the WIDF is open to women's organizations and groups of women anywhere in the world, and in exceptional cases to individuals. Total membership is estimated to be in excess of 200 million and in 1970 consisted of 99 affiliated and associated organizations in 90 countries (*Women of the Whole World*, no. 1, 1970). Although Chinese organizations were heavily represented in the past, China has long been inactive as a result of the Sino-Soviet dispute and in protest of the pro-Soviet orientation of the federation; neither China nor Albania participated in the Sixth Congress. The WIDF tries to maintain contact with nonaffiliated women's groups through its International Liaison Bureau, which has headquarters in Copenhagen and a secretariat based in Brussels.

The WIDF maintains close relations with other communist front organizations that share its ideology and interests, such as the World Peace Council (WPC), the World Federation of Trade Unions (WFTU), and the World Federation of Democratic Youth (WFDY). It continually aims to expand its contacts with agencies of the United Nations, where it has ties with the International Labor Organization and the World Health Organization, and since May 1969 has enjoyed Category A consultative status with UNESCO.

Aims and Policies. According to its charter, the WIDF aims to unite all the women of the world regardless of race, nationality, religion, or political belief, so that they may work together to defend their rights as citizens, mothers, and workers; protect children; ensure peace, democracy, and national independence; and establish bonds of friendship and solidarity among themselves.

Views and Activities in 1970. In 1970 the WIDF not only engaged in its normal pursuits, but also celebrated its twenty-fifth anniversary and began to implement plans for the future that were laid down by the Sixth Congress in 1969.

Official activities began with a Bureau meeting held in East Berlin on 21-24 January. Resolutions were adopted condemning Israeli "aggression," "colonialism" in Angola and Mozambique, and "fascism" in Spain, Portugal, Greece, and South Africa; other resolutions supported an all-European security conference, the recognition of East Germany under international law, and the struggles of the people of Cuba and Latin America against U.S. "imperialism." It was announced that the Lenin Centenary would be celebrated at the upcoming Council meeting scheduled for October.

A circular letter dated 13 August reminded affiliated organizations that the Bureau meeting had decided to "collect information on (1) the nature of imperialism in our epoch and its effect on the lives of women and children, and (2) the development of democratic women's organizations throughout the world, which will form the basis of a book on the history of the democratic women's movement." The letter requested that any material of value to the compilation of this history of democratic women's organizations be submitted to the Secretariat.

The next important meeting was a "Seminar on Illiteracy among African Women," held in Khartoum on 1-6 February and jointly organized by the WIDF, UNESCO, and the Sudanese Women's Federation. Even before the seminar opened, it was announced that the WIDF was planning to establish a center in Khartoum to train teachers and to help with a literacy campaign.

International Women's Day—one of several annual celebrations of the WIDF—was held on 8 March. It was highlighted by declarations of support for the Arab people, a protest against the continued detention of Greek women political prisoners, and announcements of the success of a campaign by the Union of French Women to raise funds for the establishment of an "Institute for the Protection of Mother and Child" in North Vietnam.

As in previous years, WIDF expressions of solidarity with North Vietnam and condemnation of U.S. activities in Indochina were frequent. In April, President Hertta Kuusinen headed a delegation to Hanoi to discuss plans for the proposed research center and in September a more specialized group was sent to help with the design. After U.S. troops entered Cambodia, a special statement by the WIDF protested the action as a "flagrant violation of international law" and accused the United States of taking the world to the brink of a new global war and using aggression to "hush up its defeats and weaknesses" (TASS, 5 May). Labeling the "indescribable tortures" inflicted on South Vietnamese prisoners detained in "tiger cages" as a "brutal illustration" of the "very nature of U.S. aggression against the Vietnamese people," the WIDF also pledged to "put the culprit to the people's justice" (South Vietnam Liberation Press Agency, 13 August). *Women of the Whole World* (no. 1, 1970) expressed its solidarity with the women of Vietnam in a special section entitled "To Hasten Their Victory," in which the WIDF detailed the "savage crimes" of the U.S. government and called on the women of the world to "stop the criminal hand of the US aggressors" and "ensure that the right of the people, the women and children of Viet Nam to live in independence, peace and happiness emerges triumphant in the not-too-distant future."

The WIDF turned its attention to Europe at an "International Women's Conference on the Problems of European Security and Cooperation," held in Ystad, Sweden, on 16 June. Delegates from twenty countries attended, and the formation of committees in Poland, West Berlin, East Germany, Czechoslovakia, and the Netherlands in support of calling an all-European security conference was reported. The Greek delegate stressed the dangers from the "revival of fascism" in Greece, and telegrams were sent to the United Nations, the Council of Europe, and the Greek government protesting that trend. In December the WIDF appealed for solidarity with the women of Portugal in opposing that country's "colonial wars" ("Radio Free Portugal," 2 December). At a meeting of international peace organizations in Potsdam, East Germany, in September the WIDF announced plans for a meeting of women from Africa and the NATO countries to examine action against apartheid.

No part of the world or continent was omitted from the deliberations of the Council, which met in Budapest on 5-9 October. With about 260 delegates from 91 countries in attendance—including Romesh Chandra (India), WPC secretary-general, and Hanna Szego (Hungary), chairman of the U.N. Commission on the Status of Women—the Council adopted statements supporting a European security conference, aid to Vietnamese women, and assistance to the victims of "Israeli aggression." The Council made a general appeal for solidarity with women fighting for national independence, progress, and peace, and championed the fight against racial discrimination and illiteracy, and for women's and children's rights.

The Council adopted a special twenty-fifth anniversary declaration, discussed the role of the federation and its future activities, and commemorated the centenary of the birth of Lenin. At a press conference following the conclusion of the Council meeting, it was announced that women's organizations from Dahomey, Nigeria, Venezuela, Peru, and the Malagasy Republic had been newly accepted as members of the WIDF.

In addition to the meetings organized by the WIDF, leaders or representatives of the federation traveled extensively to ascertain facts about the conditions of women and children around the world and to participate in activities arranged by other groups. Among the more important events that attracted WIDF representatives was a symposium on Lenin and women's emancipation in Moscow on 17-21 February, where Secretary-General Cécile Hugel spoke of the importance of the WIDF and Vice-President Valentina Nikolayeva-Tereshkova described the role of women in the Soviet Union as the embodiment of Lenin's teaching. On 26 April, President Hertta Kuusinen was presented with the Lenin Centenary Medal in Moscow, which she accepted with the comment that she considered it an honor given to the WIDF. A delegate from the WIDF attended the second Uruguayan Working Women's National Conference in Montevideo in May. Hertta Kuusinen visited in North Korea in July and was the guest of honor at a luncheon given by Premier Kim Il-song.

Publications. For twenty years the WIDF has published *Women of the Whole World*, originally a monthly and then a quarterly magazine in English, French, Russian, German, and Spanish editions. In 1970 there was another cutback, due to financial difficulties. A special issue of the magazine was distributed in time to commemorate the sixtieth anniversary of International Women's Day on 8 March. The first regular issue was delayed until October, and enclosed with it was an explanation from the Editorial Board that it was timed "for the twenty-fifth anniversary of the victory over fascism and the foundation of the WIDF" and that the "material situation" prevented the production of another issue during the year. Apparently the WIDF was forced to cut back on publications of all kinds, since the normal variety of pamphlets and brochures was lacking in 1970. Topics of unusual interest—Greece and the problems of political prisoners, for example—were treated in special issues of an *Information Bulletin*.

E. W.

INTERNATIONAL ORGANIZATION OF JOURNALISTS

The International Organization of Journalists (IOJ) was founded in June 1946 in Copenhagen. The International Federation of Journalists (IFJ) and the International Federation of Journalists of Allied and Free Countries were both formally disbanded and merged with the IOJ, so that for a time it was representative of journalists over the world. By 1950, all non-communist unions had withdrawn from the IOJ in order to refound, in 1952, the IFJ. Since 1955 the IOJ has made unsuccessful overtures to the IFJ for cooperation and for eventually forming a new world organization of journalists. It was for the purpose of bridging differences with the IFJ that the IOJ in that year founded the International Committee for Cooperation of Journalists (ICCJ). No IFJ member is known to have affiliated with the ICCJ, however, and most ICCJ officers are also leading members of the parent IOJ. The IOJ headquarters, originally in London, moved to Prague in 1947.

Structure. National unions and groups of journalists are eligible for membership in the IOJ, as are also individual journalists. The IOJ claims 150,000 members (CTK, Czechoslovak news agency, 16 April 1970), the majority of whom are in communist-controlled countries.

The highest body of the IOJ is the Congress, which is supposed to meet every four years. So far there have been six meetings, the last in Berlin in 1966. The Seventh Congress, the first to be held outside Europe and originally planned for Havana in December 1970, was rescheduled to convene there on 4-9 January 1971.

The Congress elects the Executive Committee, which includes officers, or vice-presidents, who are collectively referred to as the Presidium, and ordinary members. The committee meets at least once a year. Jean-Maurice Hermann (France) has been Presidium president since 1950. The roster of 15 vice-presidents and some 25 ordinary members of the Executive Committee was assumed in 1970 to be little changed from 1966 (see *YICA*, 1970, p. 770, and *ibid.*, 1969, p. 975). The IOJ's five-man Secretariat is headed by Secretary-General Jiří Kubka (Czechoslovakia), who has held this post since 1946. Norbert Siklosi (Hungary) is treasurer. The IOJ claims to be financed entirely by affiliation fees; no accounts are published.

The IOJ was awarded consultative and informational Category B status with UNESCO in 1969, "in appreciation of its comprehensive training activities for journalists from young nations," after having held consultative Category C status since 1962. The IOJ also holds consultative status, Category II, with UNESCO's Economic and Social Council (ECOSOC).

Aims and Policies. Although the avowed aims of the IOJ include "defense of the right of every journalist to write according to his conscience and conviction," its activities and pronouncements suggest a political orientation clearly attuned to Soviet interests and critical of Western policies. Typically, for example, the IOJ publicizes and denounces alleged instances of persecution of journalists in Western nations, while generally overlooking similar developments within the communist world.

A principal activity of the IOJ is its schools for training journalists. Drawing mostly on journalists from developing countries, such schools have been set up in Hungary, East Germany, Guinea, and Mali.

Communist China has not participated in IOJ activities for several years. A rival organization, the Afro-Asian Journalists' Association (AAJA) was founded by the Chinese in 1963 (see below).

Views and Activities in 1970. The IOJ's main endeavors in 1970 were with a view to its Seventh Congress, and, specifically, toward achieving as wide a representation and as great a degree of unanimity as possible. For this reason, the organization appeared bent upon avoiding positions or pronouncements that could evoke controversy or even any serious debate among its associates with regard to IOJ general policies.

Discussion at a joint Secretariat-Presidium meeting, in Potsdam on 7-9 June, focused upon "the tasks of the IOJ in the struggle for peace and social progress in all parts of the world." At a press conference following the meeting, Hermann enumerated foremost IOJ efforts: on behalf of "fighting Vietnam," where it planned to "assist in improving the material-technological basis for the work of Vietnamese journalists"; for the release of detained "democratic" Greek journalists; and for the recognition in international law and admission to the U.N. of East Germany. Delegates to the meeting also attended an "international conference on the significance of the Potsdam Agreements," organized by the West German Journalists' Association on 7 June. (ADN, East German news agency, 7-9 June.)

There was considerable travel by IOJ officers during the year to gain support for the congress, particular emphasis being placed on Latin America and Cuba. Leopoldo Vargas, IOJ secretary from Colombia, was dispatched to Peru, Chile, and Uruguay in January-February (*Unidad*, Lima, 15 January). At the seventh "Venezuelan National Assembly of Journalists," held in Maracay on 24-27 September, an IOJ delegation including Eleazar Diaz Rangel (Venezuela), Juan Campbell Montesino (Chile), Emilio Herasme Pena (Dominican Republic), and Edda Cavarico (Colombia) was a signatory to a statement supporting the amalgamation of Latin American journalists in a single organization. (*Tribuna Popular*, Caracas, 1 October.)

An IOJ delegation arrived in Havana on 19 March to take part in a meeting of the Union of Cuban Journalists (UPEC), which discussed preparations for the IOJ Congress. The delegation, led by Jiří Kubka, included: secretaries Nestor Aurelian (Romania), Leopoldo Vargas, and Bohumil Svoboda (Czechoslovakia), and members Norbert Siklosi, Josef Valenta (president of the union of Czechoslovak Journalists), Osmund Schwab (secretary-general of the [East] German Journalists' Union), and Viacheslav Chernishev (secretary-general of the Soviet Union of Journalists). The UPEC meeting drew up a protocol establishing the organizational basis of the IOJ Congress, signed by IOJ vice-president Ernesto Vera, for UPEC (of which he is president), and Kubka for the IOJ. (*Granma*, Havana, 20 and 25 March; *El Siglo*, Santiago, 26 March.) In a Havana radio interview on 6 July, Vera indicated that a major topic on the Congress agenda would be "North American penetration and control of the information media in Latin America." He spoke also of the opportunity that delegates would have of seeing "the achievements and the victories of Socialism" in Cuba.

On 1 July, *Granma* published the text of an IOJ Presidium appeal for publicity for the congress, which, it declared, would be "the start of a new era of growth, of strengthening [the IOJ's unity] and its role in the struggle for the dignity of its profession, against imperialism and at the service for a peaceful world, free and united, from which would be expelled for ever the forces of slander, hatred and exploitation." The appeal also accused "North American imperialism" of preparing "large-scale aggression" against Cuba with "the complicity of Latin American puppet governments and counterrevolutionary groups."

Preparations for the congress were discussed further at an expanded Secretariat meeting in Sofia on 16-17 November, attended by journalists from Bulgaria, East Germany, Cuba, Mongolia, Poland, Romania, the Soviet Union, Hungary, and Czechoslovakia, and presided over by IOJ Vice-President Georgi Bokov (Bulgaria). (*Rabotnichesko Delo*, Sofia, 18 November.)

By 31 December about 160 delegates and observers of the 350 expected had arrived in Havana. Leopoldo Vargas complained of an "imperialist provocation against the Congress"—the aircraft which had taken him to Cuba (from Colombia) had been "unjustifiably held for three hours" at "imperialism's fortified air base in the Bermuda islands." Representatives from Laos, North Korea, and North Vietnam were to spend two days in Moscow before traveling to Havana. South Vietnamese representatives were to be drawn from the Provisional Revolutionary Government's delegation to the Paris talks. On 28 December the Association of Journalists of Korean Citizens Resident in Japan protested against the Japanese government's refusal to grant reentry permits to its three-member delegation, thereby preventing its attendance. (Havana radio, 31 December; *Granma*, 28 and 29 December.)

The IOJ protested the U.S. intervention in Cambodia, demanding that "occupation units" be withdrawn and "Cambodia's neutrality respected," and appealing to "all progressive and honest journalists throughout the world to do everything in their power to reveal in the press, radio, and television the aggressive policies of the USA in Southeast Asia, and to mobilize nations to fight for an end to US imperialism's dirty war in Indochina." (CTK, 5 May.)

An IOJ appeal issued in connection with its International Journalists' Day, 8 September, declared that this date, the anniversary of the Nazi execution of Julius Fučik, a Czechoslovak journalist, would henceforth be commemorated as "the day of international solidarity of journalists with all their persecuted colleagues" (CTK, 5 September). A related appeal urged "journalists of the world" to "protest through the press, radio, and television so as to obtain the release of the leading functionaries of the Greek communist party and patriotic front arrested by the military regime," to "fight tirelessly against the dictatorship in Greece," and to "support the patriotic forces there in building a new regime" (*Neues Deutschland*, East Berlin, 29 May). An IOJ statement noted that at a time when the "progressive world" was recalling the anniversary of the U.N. Declaration of Human Rights, "fascist Spain" was "trying 16 Basque patriots for their part in the people's struggle for freedom and democracy" (CTK, 15 December).

With regard to IOJ training programs, Endre Borbely (Hungary), an IOJ "deputy secretary" —apparently a new IOJ office—was in Lagos in April where, after talks on future cooperation with leading members of the Nigerian Journalists Union, he announced plans for the IOJ's first seminar for Nigerian journalists (*Nigerian Observer*, Lagos, 13 April; *The New Nigerian*, Lagos, 13 April). One group of journalists, from the U.A.R., India, Burma, Iraq, Tanzania, and Ghana, completed an IOJ course in Budapest in August (CTK, 25 August); another, from North Vietnam, arrived there on 31 October for a four-month IOJ course (MTI, Hungarian news agency, 31 October).

In July it announced that the English writer, James Aldridge, a holder of the World Peace Council's International Peace Prize, had been awarded the IOJ International Press Prize, awarded annually to "prominent progressive journalists" (CTK, 24 July).

Publications. The IOJ issues a monthly journal, *The Democratic Journalist*, in English, French, Russian, and Spanish editions, edited by Oldrich Bures, and a fortnightly *Information Bulletin*.

Kubka announced (*Democratic Journalist*, no. 7-8) that the IOJ Secretariat was to publish, in cooperation with several national unions, "an extensive work entitled *Lenin—The Journalist*," containing "all the ideas from Lenin's work concerning the press and journalism," and to be issued in several languages. The "entire activity of our international organization," he declared, "has always been inspired by the great work of the revolutionary thinker, V. I. Lenin."

*   *   *

The AAJA. The Afro-Asian Journalists' Association was set up in Djakarta in April 1963, with an Afro-Asian press bureau and a permanent Secretariat. Until the attempted communist coup in Indonesia (1965), the AAJA appeared to represent a possibly serious rival to the pro-Soviet IOJ, particularly in developing countries. At that juncture, AAJA headquarters were "temporarily" moved to Peking. Djawoto, the AAJA's Indonesian secretary-general, who was dismissed from his post as Indonesia's ambassador to China, has since headed the Secretariat in Peking, which has become the permanent seat of AAJA operations.

The AAJA Secretariat, in addition to Djawoto, includes Supeno and Umar Said (both of Indonesia), Yang I (China), Sugiyama Ichihei (Japan), Said Salim Abdullah (Tanzania), Ahmed Gora Ebrahim (South Africa), and D. Manuweera (Ceylon). The AAJA claims members in 53 countries, but this distribution would seem to reflect individual memberships as well as formal participating organizations.

There is no indication that the AAJA has succeeded in winning over the allegiance of IOJ members or member organizations. Few journalists' organizations and governments have expressed open support for the AAJA or indicated that they would send delegates to an eventual AAJA conference. Unable to make pragmatic headway, the AAJA's energies are devoted mainly to propagating the Chinese line in international political affairs.

Views and Activities in 1970. The AAJA Secretariat called upon its member organizations of "progressive and revolutionary journalists and liberation fighters in Asia and Africa" to celebrate with "militant action" the AAJA's seventh "Afro-Asian Journalists' Day," 24 April 1970. The occasion was to promote the "consolidating [of] militant solidarity among the people and progressive and revolutionary journalists who fight against U.S.-led imperialism, Soviet social-imperialism and all reaction." Djawoto was the main speaker at a ceremony in Peking, attended by "members of the Executive Secretariat of the Afro-Asian Writers' Permanent Bureau, journalists from Afro-Asian countries and other regions, and leading members of Chinese journalistic and other organizations." (NCNA, 15 and 24 April.)

The United States was "vehemently denounced" by the AAJA for "instigating Cambodia's extreme right-wing clique to stage, in Phnom Penh on 18 March, a coup d'état against Prince Norodom Sihanouk, head of state of Cambodia." The Secretariat called upon member organizations and individual Afro-Asian journalists to render "resolute support, through various activities, for the Cambodian people in their valiant struggle against U.S. imperialism and its lackeys, and for the five-point declaration issued by Cambodian head of state, Prince Norodom Sihanouk." (*Ibid.*, 16 April.) Subsequent statements extended "sincere congratulations" on the founding of the "Royal Government of National Union of Kampuchea" and declared full support for the joint declaration of the "summit conference of the Indochinese people" (*ibid.*, 1 and 8 May). On 17 August, Sihanouk met with Djawoto and AAJA Secretariat members Manuweera, Yang I, Sugiyama, Sa'id Salim 'Abd Allah, Supeno, and Umar Said (*Ibid.*, 17 August.)

In April, the *Afro-Asian Journalist* (no. 1) carried an article by W. Linang of "North Kalimantan" (that is, Sabah, Sarawak, and Brunei) acclaiming the "victorious development" of the "people's armed struggle" there. Adhering to Mao Tse-tung's teaching that "the seizure of power by armed force and the settlement of issues by war is the central task and the highest form of revolution," the North Kalimantan people, under the leadership of their revolutionary organization, were "sure to win." (*Ibid.*, 11 April.) In a later issue, an article by Gunawan, of Indonesia, portrayed the "fascist military regime" in that country as an "instrument of imperialism" and asserted that the Indonesian people had now seen the "delusive nature" of the "peaceful road" (*ibid.*, 14 September).

The AAJA contended that any military intervention by the United States in the Middle East would considerably accelerate unity among "anti-imperialist" forces and result in a broad "people's war" throughout the Arab world. The "frenzied attacks against the Palestinian guerrillas engineered by U.S. imperialism in Jordan, the U.S. aid to Israeli Zionists, and the reinforcement of the U.S. Sixth Fleet in the Mediterranean and U.S. air force stationed in Turkey" were all described as "part and parcel of a U.S. imperialist scheme vainly attempting to stamp out the flames of the armed struggle of the Palestinian people." (*Ibid.*, 23 September.)

"People's war" was the general policy promoted by the AAJA in Africa also. In a statement marking the tenth anniversary of the Sharpeville uprising in South Africa, the AAJA declared that "the only answer to the counterrevolutionary violence by which the South African regime maintains itself is organized armed revolution," conditions for which were "becoming excellent" (*ibid.*, 21 March).

The AAJA conducts journalism courses in Peking for "aspiring young people of the Afro-Asian nations." These have included journalists from South Africa, South-West Africa, Mozambique, Lesotho, Zimbabwe (Rhodesia), and Ceylon.

The AAJA's main publication, *Afro-Asian Journalist*, appears irregularly. Pamphlets on specific issues are published from time to time.

V. B.

WORLD FEDERATION OF SCIENTIFIC WORKERS

The World Federation of Scientific Workers (WFSW) was founded in London in 1946 at the initiative of the British Association of Scientific Workers. Eighteen organizations of scientists from 14 countries were represented at the inaugural meeting. Although the WFSW purported to be a scientific rather than a political organization, communists succeeded in obtaining most of the official posts at the start, and have retained control ever since. The WFSW headquarters is in London, but the office of the secretary-general is in Paris.

Membership in the WFSW is open to organizations of scientific workers everywhere and to individual scientists from countries where no affiliated groups are active. The WFSW claims to represent 300,000 scientists in 30 countries; most of the membership is derived from 14 groups in communist-ruled countries. The only large non-communist affiliate is the British Association of Scientific Workers, which has 21,000 members. Scientists of distinction who do not belong to an affiliated organization may be nominated for "corresponding membership"; selection is made by the Executive Council, which has the authority to nominate up to 25 corresponding members from any country. Corresponding members in 1970 were residents of 27 countries.

Structure. The governing body of the WFSW is the General Assembly, in which all affiliated organizations are represented. It is supposed to meet biennially, but has not always done so. Nine meetings have been held to date; the last—originally scheduled for September 1968 but postponed because of the Warsaw Pact invasion of Czechoslovakia in August of that year—was held in April 1969, in Paris.

The Executive Council is theoretically responsible for controlling the activities of the WFSW between assemblies. According to the WFSW constitution, the council should consist of 27 members—17 chosen on an individual basis and 10 regional representatives. Council meetings are supposed to be held at least once a year, but at times have been hard to arrange. As a consequence, much of the day-to-day work and a large measure of authority have been delegated to the Bureau, which meets frequently. The Bureau consists of the WFSW president, vice-presidents, and treasurer, the Executive Council chairman and vice-chairman, the chairman of the Editorial Board, and the heads of regional centers.

Leadership. The president of the WFSW is Professor Eric Burhop (Great Britain). Following the death of President Cecil Power in August 1969, Burhop was appointed as acting president by the Bureau in January 1970 and was confirmed by the Executive Council in September as full president until the 1972 General Assembly; he had been named chairman of the Executive Council in 1969. The vice-chairman of the Executive Council is Academician A. Y. Ishlinski (Soviet Union). There are three vice-presidents: Professor Hermann Budzislawski (East Germany), Academician I. I. Artobolevsky (Soviet Union), and Dr. S. H. Zaheer (India). Professor Pierre

Biquard (France) is secretary-general; assistants to the secretary-general are Dr. Grigori Kotov-sky (Soviet Union), Dr. Muhammad al-Lakani (U.A.R.), Miss Anita Rimel (Great Britain), and P. L. Marger (France; appointed in September 1970 and possibly replacing Dr. Theodore Nemec, also of France). John K. Dutton (Great Britain) is organizing secretary and Dr. William A. Wooster (Great Britain) is treasurer.

The WFSW has regional centers in New Delhi, Cairo, and Prague, headed respectively by Dr. N. P. Gupta, Dr. S. Hedayat, and Academician I. Málik.

The WFSW has consultative Category B status with UNESCO. It exchanges information with such U.N. groups as the International Labor Organization (ILO) and the World Health Organization.

Aims and Policies. The WFSW has a constitution and a "Charter for Scientific Workers," to which its affiliates must subscribe (see *YICA*, 1968, p. 736). Although the avowed aims of the WFSW are exclusively scientific, the organization has engaged in activities of a political nature. Restraint is, where expedient, exercised in WFSW pronouncements so as to avoid alienating Western affiliates—notably the British and French—which have at times taken exception to the WFSW's campaigning against Western policies while never criticizing the Soviet Union. The Chinese affiliates have maintained only nominal membership since the Sino-Soviet rift. In 1963, China inaugurated an "Asian regional branch" of the WFSW, which operates as a rival of the WFSW. It organized international symposiums in 1964 and 1966, but in recent years has been almost totally inactive.

Views and Activities in 1970. The thirty-second meeting of the WFSW Bureau was held in East Berlin on 10-11 January 1970. Resolutions were adopted against the use of nuclear, biological, and chemical weapons, and in support of holding a governmental European security conference which "could result in the creation of zones free of nuclear weapons and turn the frontiers between the NATO Pact and Warsaw Treaty countries into a peace frontier, assuring the security of all European countries." The WFSW called for the reactivation of the WFSW Committee for European Security, and for an examination by it of means by which scientists could contribute to a policy of disengagement and disarmament in conventional as well as nuclear, biological, and chemical weapons. (ADN, East German news agency, 12 January; *Scientific World*, no. 2.)

WFSW Acting President Burhop and Secretary-General Biquard warned that unless the Strategic Arms Limitation Talks, opening in Vienna on 14 April, were successful, "the future of mankind will be precarious." Recent nuclear weapon developments, and the possibility that "some desperate military men might advise 'strike first, or we go under,'" could mean that the nuclear deterrent would cease to deter. They welcomed the ratification, in London, Moscow, and Washington, of the nuclear non-proliferation treaty, and called on governments which had not signed to do so. They pointed out, however, that the treaty involved no reduction in nuclear arms, and that its value would "be judged by the extent to which it contributes to further agreements on measures involving real disarmament." In the meantime, the dangers represented by nuclear weapons were said to be escalating, not least by virtue of the alleged fact that "the NATO military doctrine still envisages the first use of nuclear weapons." The statement suggested, however, that responsibility for halting the arms race lay not only with the United States, but also with the Soviet Union. Multiple-warhead, independently orbited reentry vehicles (MIRV), for example, were apparently being developed by both countries, raising to a "new stage of nuclear arms competition" the previous nuclear arms balance which for seven years, assertedly, had "made possible a minor abatement in the worst excesses of the cold war." (*Morning Star*, London, 19 March.)

The Executive Council met in Belgrade on 23-27 September. An "appeal to scientists of the whole world and to public opinion in general" declared that both "Vietnamese and American sources" had supplied evidence to show that for ten years the United States had conducted large-scale chemical warfare against "the Vietnamese people." Defoliation was said to have had "disastrous effects upon men and animals" and to be a threat to all of Southeast Asia. The herbicides and toxic gases employed in Vietnam, moreover, had been banned by international law in 1925. As scientists, therefore, "whose noble mission is for the well-being of mankind," the Council declared that the time had come for "scientists of the whole world, of all political views, to take on the responsibility of studying the problem exhaustively." On this basis, it proposed an "international meeting of men of science to examine the different aspects of the chemical war in Vietnam." Lord Boyd-Orr (Great Britain), a former director-general of the U.N. Food and Agricultural Organization, called for support for the conference, which was scheduled to be held in Paris in November (but was convened on 12-13 December; see below). (*Morning Star*, 12 October; *L'Humanité*, Paris, 14 October.)

Other resolutions—of a political rather than a scientific orientation—called for an end to "discrimination" against the German Democratic Republic, and for its admission to UNESCO; and for a Middle East settlement based on "negotiation and agreement with the participation of all parties, including the Palestinian Arabs" (*Scientific World*, no. 6).

Future planning discussed by the Council included: a symposium on "Young Scientific Workers and Contemporary Society," in Enschede, Netherlands, on 14-16 July 1971 and to be attended by about 100 scientists; a conference, in East Germany, on the dangers of nuclear, biological, and chemical weapons in Europe, possibly toward the end of 1970 (not yet held); a symposium on "The Scientist and Society" in 1972; a delegation to North Vietnam (see below); and a request to Dr. S. H. Zaheer (India), WFSW vice-president, to draw up a document containing proposals for future activity concerning "the problem of the application of science and technology to serve the needs of developing countries," to be presented to the next Bureau meeting. (*Ibid.*)

Some 100 scientists and researchers from 14 countries attended the WFSW's "Conference on Chemical Warfare in Vietnam." Huynh Tan Phat, president of the Provisional Revolutionary Government of the Republic of South Vietnam, and Phan Van Dong, premier of North Vietnam, sent a message to the meeting denouncing the "widespread chemical warfare carried out by the United States." Professors Nguyen Han Hieu (National Liberation Front of South Vietnam), Pfeiffer (United States), and Pham Van Bach (North Vietnam) read reports on the allegedly serious consequences, "many not yet calculable," of the U.S. use of chemical weapons in Vietnam. A final resolution condemned the use there of poisonous chemical agents, which allegedly brought "general famine and immense suffering to civilians," the long-term effects of which would bring about a "complete upheaval, perhaps irreversible, of the ecology, the soil, and the climate of great areas of Vietnam." The use of poison gases was denounced, further, as "a violation of the rules laid down by the 1925 Geneva Convention and reconfirmed by the 16 December 1969 UN resolution." The document noted that, notwithstanding certain reservations that had been expressed on the relation between cause and effect concerning genetic anomalies which defoliants could produce, the absence of proof did not make the process tolerable. It concluded by demanding the withdrawal of U.S. and allied troops from Vietnam, Laos, and Cambodia, and called upon all scientists to "intensify their activities to support the Indochinese people's just and heroic struggle." (*Ibid.*)

International Contacts. A "Declaration on the Rights of Scientists," prepared by a WFSW subcommittee, formed the basis of a three-day meeting in Paris (apparently in August) between members of the subcommittee and UNESCO and ILO representatives. They reportedly discussed "further steps stemming from the Declaration," but no details were released. (*Scientific World*, no. 6.) Pierre Biquard and his wife arrived in Pyongyang on 2 September for a two-week stay as guests of the North Korean Democratic Scientists' Association (Korean Central News Agency, 2 and 17 September). Eric Burhop led a six-man WFSW delegation to Hanoi at the end of December to "show support for Vietnamese colleagues fighting U.S. aggression." The delegation included also Professors R. Levins (United States), S. Rose (Great Britain), and J. H. de Haas (Netherlands). Copies of the resolution on chemical warfare in Vietnam adopted by the Paris conference were handed out at a press conference in Hanoi on 23 December. (*Morning Star*, 21 December; Vietnam News Agency, 31 December.)

Publications. The official publication of the WFSW is *Scientific World*, issued bimonthly in English, French, Russian, German, Spanish, and Czechoslovak editions and edited by David Pavett (Great Britain). The WFSW *Bulletin*, which appears irregularly and is issued only to members, is published in English, French, German, and Russian editions. "Science and Mankind" is the general title of a series of WFSW booklets that have appeared in several languages. The WFSW also publishes pamphlets on particular subjects from time to time.

V. B.

INTERNATIONAL FEDERATION OF RESISTANCE FIGHTERS

The International Federation of Resistance Fighters (Fédération Internationale des Résistants; FIR) was founded in 1951 in Vienna by its predecessor, the International Federation of Former Political Prisoners (Fédération Internationale des Anciens Prisonniers Politiques; FIAPP). The FIAPP, founded in 1946, did not include resistance fighters. Organizations of former partisans and resistance fighers, and of political prisoners and victims of Naziism and fascism, are eligible for FIR membership, while individuals are admitted as "associated members." Fifty-four national organizations from 21 European countries and Israel currently make up the FIR membership. Since its founding, the FIR has been mainly composed of communist groups. The FIR headquarters is in Vienna, while a small secretariat is maintained in Paris. Although no details are published, the FIR claims to be financed by affiliation fees, gifts, legacies, and other subventions.

The avowed aims of the FIR are to keep alive the memory of those who died in "underground" fighting against Naziism and fascism, to protect the rights of those resistance fighters who survived, to prevent a reemergence of Naziism and fascism, and to ensure world peace. Its actual policies, however, have been primarily in support of Soviet policy directed against the Federal Republic of Germany and alleged West German "revanchism." Soviet policy in other matters as well seems to have its passive support. The FIR has been unable to establish a strong organizational base due to the many internecine divergences belying its claim to represent the interests of all victims of Naziism and fascism. Most conspicuous examples of this discrepancy between word and deed are the disregard for Polish-Jewish survivors of Nazi concentration camps shown by the Polish affiliate (ZBoWiD) and the discrimination shown by the FIR leadership toward Israeli FIR members. Other elements which have adversely affected the FIR's popular base include the long-standing criticism by the Yugoslav organization of resistance fighters (SUBNOR) of the Soviet domination of the FIR; and, more recently, "purges" by the Czechoslovak Association of Anti-Fascist Fighters (SPB) of many veteran resistance fighters for their support of the reform policies of the deposed Czechoslovak leader Alexander Dubček.

FIR activities include the organization of annual rallies at former Nazi concentration camps, medical conferences on the effects of imprisonment and maltreatment in the camps, and seminars on resistance history, designed to emphasize the role of communist-led resistance groups. The FIR is not represented in the United Nations and has generally made little headway in its continuing attempts to establish working relationships with non-communist organizations.

Structure and Leadership. The highest governing body of the FIR is its Congress, which convenes every four years (every three until 1969). The Sixth Congress—the most recent—was held in Venice in November 1969. The Congress elects the FIR Bureau and ratifies members, nominated by national associations, to serve together with the Bureau on the General Council of the FIR. The General Council is supposed to meet at least once a year, between congresses. In 1970 there were 119 members of the General Council, of whom 49 were members of the Bureau.

Arialdo Banfi (Italy) has been Bureau president since 1965. There are currently 15 vice-presidents: Jacques Debu-Bridel (France), Dimo Dichev (Bulgaria), Petr Dudáš (Czechoslovakia), Albert Forcinal (France), Istvan Gabor (Hungary), Nicolae Guina (Romania), Helge Theil Kierulff (Denmark), Włodimierz Lechowicz (Poland), Alexei Petrovich Maresiev (Soviet Union), André de Raet (Belgium), Josef Rossaint (West Germany), Georg Spielmann (East Germany), Ludwig Soswinski (Austria), Umberto Terracini (Italy), and Pierre Villon (pseudonym for Roger Ginsberger; France).

Bureau members elect the Secretariat from among themselves. It is headed by the secretary-general, Jean Toujas (France). Other officers are the deputy secretary-general, Gustav Alef-Bolkowiak (Poland); two secretaries, Giuseppe Gaddi (Italy) and Wolfgang Bergold (East Germany), and the treasurer, Theodor Heinisch (Austria). The Bureau president also serves on the Secretariat.

Views and Activities in 1970. Unable to reconcile differences among its associates arising from the 1968 Soviet-led invasion of Czechoslovakia, the FIR has gradually adopted the strategy of openly acknowledging the continuing existence of divergent views on Czechoslovakia while pointing to the FIR's unanimity on all other major questions of concern to the organization and stressing the need to concentrate on the pursuit of "common tasks." Internally, this strategy may have paid dividends, for in 1970 the issue of Czechoslovakia no longer appeared to represent a disruptive factor in FIR planning. Externally, however, the FIR's seemingly tacit approval of Soviet involvement in Czechoslovak affairs may have reduced further the FIR's already weak prospects for alignments with non-communist resistance groups.

The dominant theme in FIR agitation continued, in 1970—the twenty-fifth anniversary of the defeat of Nazi Germany—to be alleged neo-fascism in West Germany. The FIR protested to the mayor of Wertheim the holding there, by "former and modern-day Nazis," of the Nationaldemokratische Partei Deutschlands (NPD) party conference. The Bureau, while convening in Vienna on 19-20 April with FIR representatives from 18 countries, issued an "urgent warning" on the alleged resurgence of militaristic and revanchist forces in West Germany and declared the "main task" of the 1970's to be the convocation of a European security conference. (*Informationsdienst der FIR*, no. 2, 12 February; *Volksstimme*, Vienna, 22 April; *Neues Deutschland*, East Berlin, 22 April.) Following the fall riots in Würzburg, the FIR Secretariat proclaimed that the "neo-Nazi and other right-wing extremists" responsible for the disturbances would leave "no stone unturned to hinder a detente in Europe." It pledged the continuing alertness to this danger of its members, together with other "democratic forces" in the Federal Republic. (*Informationsdienst der FIR*, no. 17, November.) In similar vein, the shooting, in November, of a Soviet soldier at the Soviet war memorial in West Berlin "deeply shocked all former resistance fighters and victims of fascism," according to the FIR, which declared that the recent strengthening and coalescing of right-wing extremist elements foretold an upsurge in "the methods of terror and assault which were also used by the NSDAP [Nazi party]" (*Volksstimme*, 11 November).

The FIR was represented at various events in commemoration of the defeat of Nazi Germany. Wolfgang Bergold was the representative at ceremonies at the former Mauthausen concentration camp, and Theodor Heinisch at the unveiling of a memorial at Gmünd. Ceremonies at Terezin in Czechoslovakia were attended by Bergold, and at Copenhagen by Gustav Alef-Bolkowiak. Charles Bossi (France), Bureau member, and Géo Van Den Eynde (Belgium), Council member, were representatives at meetings in London and Birmingham of the British Defence Committee for the Victims of Nazi Persecution. Marcel Paul (France), Bureau member and president of the National Federation of Deportees and Internees, Resistance Fighters and Patriots, and Jean Toujas were representatives at ceremonies in France (the latter at the anniversary congress of the

National Association of Former Combatants of the French Resistance, in Sallanches). André de Raet was the delegate to a meeting of the Association of Victims of the Nazi Regime (VVN) in West Germany. Ceremonies in Hungary were attended by Jean Toujas and Giuseppe Gaddi; in Israel, by Giulio Mazzon (Italy) and Abraham Neumann (Israel), Bureau members; in Italy, by Umberto Terracini, FIR vice-president and president of the National Association of Politically Persecuted Anti-Fascists; and in the Soviet Union, by Jean Toujas. (*Informationsdienst der FIR*, no. 9, 8 June.) The FIR, adhering to the view that "war crimes must be punished," and calling for the pursuit and prosecution of the many Nazi criminals allegedly still at liberty in West Germany, claimed a victory when, in November, the U.N. adopted a convention on non-limitation for war crimes, for which the FIR had agitated for many years (*ibid.*, no. 17, November).

An FIR communiqué issued following a General Council meeting in Vienna on 10-11 October welcomed as "an important contribution to a detente in Europe" the Soviet-West German agreement on the renunciation of force. Delegates expressed the hope that the treaty would be ratified without delay, "in spite of the efforts of neo-Nazi and other elements to prevent it," and that it would advance prospects for the convening of a European security conference. Also the communiqué again raised the FIR's proposal for the convening of a meeting of European resistance fighters and war veterans on the subject of European security. (FIR press release, no. 15, 12 October.) The FIR has long been attempting to organize such a meeting, but all efforts to date to persuade non-communist groups to join in the venture have proved unsuccessful. In letters to its affiliates in West Germany (the VVN) and Poland (ZBoWiD), Jean Toujas expressed gratification at the agreement on a West German-Polish treaty which, like the West German-Soviet agreement that preceded it, was "a significant step toward European security." The FIR also paid tribute to the memory of Charles de Gaulle, who, it said, had "refused to bow his head to the Nazi aggressor," "led the French people out of defeat to victory," and desired that "the two halves of Europe should be brought together."(*Informationsdienst der FIR*, no. 17, November.)

The FIR continued to draw attention to the Greek government's imprisonment of national "patriots"—including some of those who had previously suffered under "fascist domination" in the Second World War—by publishing lists of alleged executions, torture, and arrests under the Papadopoulos regime (*ibid.*, no. 3, 25 February). In July the FIR sent a message of solidarity to Gerasimos Priphtes (Greece), Bureau member detained since shortly after the 1967 coup, and a protest to the Greek premier against the trial, which began on 6 July, of Greek "resistance fighters and patriots" (see *Greece*) (*ibid.*, no. 11, 9 July).

The FIR's Fifth Medical Congress, first planned for Warsaw in September 1968 and then for Paris in April 1970, was finally held in Paris on 21-24 September. More than 100 doctors and scientists from 22 European countries, Israel, and the United States were expected to take part in the congress—"more than double the number of experts" in the first FIR medical congress, in Copenhagen in 1954. The agenda included discussion of diseases of metabolism and psycho-physiological investigations of exhaustion and premature aging. (*Ibid.*, no. 12, September.) Notwithstanding its optimistic projections, the FIR was apparently unable to establish the international documentation and study center, specializing in former resisters' medical-social problems, for which for years it has solicited support.

Also still in future planning is a meeting of journalists and editors of all publications concerning the resistance movement, which the FIR Cultural Commission seeks to convene in order to "improve and coordinate" their material.

Publications. The FIR publishes a journal in French and German, *Résistance Unie/Der Wiederstandskämpfer*, issued ten times a year, and an irregular fortnightly in French and German,

Service d'Information de la FIR/Informationsdienst der FIR. It also issues occasional press releases, of which there were some 20 in 1970, and pamphlets on problems relating to its movement.

V. B.

INTERNATIONAL
ASSOCIATION
OF DEMOCRATIC LAWYERS

The International Association of Democratic Lawyers (IADL) was founded at an "International Congress of Jurists" held in Paris in October 1946 under the auspices of a paracommunist organization, the Mouvement National Judiciaire, and attended by lawyers from 25 countries. Although the movement originally included elements of various political orientations, the leading role was played by leftist French lawyers, and by 1949 most non-communists had resigned.

The IADL was originally based in Paris but was expelled by the French government in 1950. It then moved to Brussels, where it remains; some organizational work has also been carried out from Warsaw.

Membership is open to lawyers' organizations or groups and to individual lawyers, and may be on a "corresponding," "donation," or "permanent" basis. Lawyers holding membership through organizations or individually are estimated to number about 25,000. The IADL claims to be supported by membership fees and donations; no details of its finances are published.

The IADL's consultative status, Category C, with the U.N.'s Economic and Social Council (ECOSOC) was rescinded in 1950 but reinstated in 1967.

Structure and Leadership. The highest organ of the IADL is the Congress, in which each member organization is represented. First held yearly, the Congress is now supposed to meet every three years. Because of reverberations following the 1968 Czechoslovak crisis, the Ninth Congress—first planned for that year—was not held until 15-19 July 1970 (see below). The Congress elects the IADL Council, which is supposed to meet yearly and consists of the Bureau, the Secretariat, and a representative of each member organization and of the co-opted members.

The key officers of the IADL are: the president, Pierre Cot (France); the honorary president, Dennis Nowell Pritt (Great Britain); and the secretary-general, Joë Nordmann (France). All three were reelected at the 1970 Congress. Few other results of the elections have been released. There are believed to be between 15 and 20 vice-presidents, from Bulgaria, Czechoslovakia, Hungary, North Korea, Poland, Romania, the Soviet Union, North and South Vietnam, and four Arab nations including Jordan. Several Greek lawyers in political detention were made honorary members of the Bureau. (TASS, 20 July; "Voice of Truth," Greek communist radio, 27 July.)

Aims and Policies. The principal avowed aims of the IADL are: to develop mutual understanding among the lawyers of the world; to support the aims of the United Nations, especially through common action for the defense of democratic liberties; to encourage the study and application, in the field of law, of democratic principles conducive to the maintenance of peace; and to promote the independence of all peoples and prevent the placing of any restrictions on this independence through legislation or in practice. Consistently following the Soviet line in both national and international matters, however, the IADL has denounced as a "violation of human rights"

748

any persecution of communists or communist parties in countries outside the Soviet orbit, while denying or ignoring the existence of any violation of human rights in communist-ruled countries.

Chinese members no longer attend IADL meetings. Since the Sino-Soviet rift, Chinese and pro-Chinese elements of the IADL have been attempting to activate the rival Afro-Asian Lawyers' Conference (AALC), which they founded at a conference of Afro-Asian lawyers in Conakry in October 1962. Efforts to organize a second conference have been unsuccessful, and AALC activities have been confined to propaganda in support of Chinese positions.

Views and Activities in 1970. The IADL continued in 1970 to turn its attention outward, rather than attempt to reconcile internal divergences engendered or exacerbated by the 1968 Soviet-led invasion of Czechoslovakia. Pressure from Soviet and East European affiliates notwithstanding, the IADL leadership has refused to rescind its official disapproval of the invasion. While the fact that the three key officers in the IADL continue to be representatives from non-communist countries clearly lends credibility to IADL pronouncements on international affairs, at the same time it permits these officers publicly to express views ostensibly representative of the organization but —as in the case of Czechoslovakia—sometimes at variance with those of Soviet and East European associates. A recent case in point was the telegram sent by Pierre Cot and Joë Nordmann to the Soviet government protesting the verdict in the December 1970 hijacking conspiracy trial. Stating that they were "Deeply concerned, both as lawyers and friends of the Soviet Union, by the sentence of death passed on the accused for a simple attempt not followed by effects," Cot and Nordmann called for "a new, public hearing." (*L'Humanité*, Paris, 28 December.) Such strains between the IADL leadership and the Soviet Union have reduced IADL activities essentially to protests and denunciations of purported legal injustices in non-communist countries around the world.

The IADL's Ninth Congress, held in Helsinki on 15-19 July 1970, was attended by some 350 delegates from 55 countries. The International Commission of Jurists (ICJ) and Amnesty International were represented by observers. The tone of the meeting appeared to have been set in advance, indicating a common agreement to avoid further disruption of IADL internal affairs by airing differences. Czechoslovakia was not discussed, and Cot and Nordmann were returned to office. The opening day was devoted to a "study of the situation in Indochina," followed on the next by a ceremony, in cooperation with the Finland-Soviet Union Society, marking the Lenin Centenary, at which the main speaker was Alexander Gorkin, chairman of the Soviet Supreme Court. In a final communiqué the Congress appealed to "lawyers of the whole world" to rally support on "as wide a basis as possible" for an IADL-sponsored international conference on "Torture as a System of Repression of Political and Social Activities." With a view to organizing a conference of European lawyers (to gain support for an all-European security conference), the IADL Bureau was to publish a series of articles on "the legal aspects of European security and cooperation."

The congress, further, acclaimed the purported success of the "Conference in Support of the Peoples of the Portuguese Colonies" (held in Rome on 27-29 June under the joint sponsorship of the World Peace Council and the Afro-Asian Peoples' Solidarity Organization), called on "all lawyers" to work for "the recognition in international law of the struggle of these people," and proposed that the IADL secretariat send observer missions to the "liberated territories" so that they could "see for themselves the reality of new life." Other resolutions called for abrogation of the United States-Japan security treaty and the unconditional return of Okinawa to Japan, announced the decision to organize each year from 25 June to 27 July a world-wide "month of common struggle to force the aggressive troops of U.S. imperialism to withdraw from South Korea" (a theme already adopted by most other communist-front organizations and by many communist parties), and called for withdrawal of U.S. troops from Indochina and implementation of the 1967 U.N. resolution on the Middle East. (TASS, 14, 17, 20 and 21 July; Helsinki radio, 15 July; *Le Monde*, Paris, 24 July; *L'Humanité*, 29 July; Vietnam News Agency, 30 July.)

The IADL made several thrusts during the year directed to U.S. policy in Southeast Asia: Igor Karpets (Soviet Union), an IADL vice-president, attended a commemorative meeting in Moscow to mark the second anniversary of the Son My massacre in South Vietnam (TASS, 16 March); the U.S. was declared responsible for massacres of Vietnamese civilians in Cambodia (*L'Humanité*, 18 April); a joint communiqué issued by the IADL, Amnesty International, the ICJ, the International Federation of Human Rights, and the International Secretariat of Catholic Lawyers judged U.S. "persecution" of Vietnamese civilians to be a violation of the 1949 Geneva Convention (*ibid.*, 6 May); an IADL delegation, composed of Joë Nordmann, Eduardo Warshaver (Argentina), and Yonosuke Inamoto (Japan), delivered to the U.S. Embassy in Paris the IADL congress resolution demanding the withdrawal of troops from Vietnam (*L'Humanité*, 29 July; Vietnam News Agency, 30 July); and an IADL communiqué of 12 August spoke of "grave facts about the repression exercised against the Indochinese peoples by the Saigon and Phnom Penh puppets"—the alleged return by the Lon Nol administration to Saigon, for incarceration at Con Son, of 700 Vietnamese residing in Cambodia (*PCB Informations*, Brussels, 20 August).

Current IADL views on the question of European security were enunciated by Pierre Cot in an interview published in *Scînteia* (Bucharest) on 9 April. An all-European security conference, Cot declared, would be "an important stage toward the liquidation of the division of Europe." It was significant, further, that West European governments "which in the past spoke against the abolition of the two blocs set up during the cold war period, accept now, for the first time, the principle of a European conference focusing on the problems of achieving European security." For the time being it would be "proper to discuss the points of convergence and then, in a new and improved climate, also the divergences . . ." While such a conference required careful preparation, Cot added, this must not be a "pretext for delay."

In April the IADL issued an appeal to all lawyers "to intervene urgently, via humanitarian, political, and religious societies, in order to save the lives of the Greek democrats who are now in danger" (*L'Humanité*, 11 April). This followed the debarment of Roger Lallemand (Belgium), representing the IADL, the International Federation of Human Rights, and the Belgian League of Human Rights, and seven other foreign observer lawyers from further attendance at a trial in Athens of 34 political detainees. They were reportedly told that their presence constituted an "insult to Greek justice." (*The Guardian*, London, 31 March; *The Times*, London, 31 March.) Nevertheless, two French lawyers—Roland Rappaport and Jean-Claude Chauveaud—represented IADL interests at a subsequent political mass trial in Athens in early July (*L'Humanité*, 10 July).

Protesting alleged violence by the Spanish government against striking workers, the IADL denounced the "lack of political liberty and trade union rights in Spain," calling, specifically, for the formation of a commission of inquiry into shootings and arrests of workers in Granada (*PCB Informations*, 4 August). Jacqueline Portelle (France), an observer for the IADL at the Basque trial in Burgos, reported on the opening days of the trial at a press conference in Paris on 8 December (*L'Humanité*, 10 December). Protesting the death sentence passed on six of the accused, the IADL, in a press release from Brussels on 29 December, demanded a new trial because of alleged legal "irregularities" in the first.

IADL activities in the Middle East continued to reflect firm support of Soviet policies, including increasing empathy with guerrilla movements. Roland Weyl (France) visited a Palestinian refugee camp in Lebanon and then, together with other IADL representatives from fifteen countries, a refugee camp near Cairo (*France Nouvelle*, Paris, 14 January). Israeli air attacks were said, subsequently, to have underlined the "growing danger of a further conflagration" in the Middle East, and the IADL renewed its appeal to all lawyers for continued efforts "with a view to gaining respect for the decisions of the U.N., especially those which concern the complete withdrawal of Israeli forces from all the Arab territories which have been occupied for nearly three years" (*L'Humanité*, 16 May). In September, in a statement on the Jordanian crisis, the IADL demanded "an immediate cease-fire to end the massacre of the peoples and an urgent search for political solutions taking into account the aspirations of the national liberation movements of the Arab peoples in respect of the fundamental national rights of these peoples" (*ibid.*, 24 September). In similar vein, the IADL demanded that the trial, in Teheran, of 17 Irani youths accused of connections with the Palestinian al-Fatah organization be conducted "according to the conditions laid down in the U.N. Declaration of Human Rights" (*PCB Informations*, 1 December). The IADL was represented at the trial by French lawyer Michel Hanotiau (*Le Monde*, 26 December).

In African affairs, the IADL drew attention to the alleged "repression against democrats" in Congo (Kinshasa), Angola, and Cameroun (*ibid.*, 20 February and 8 September). It protested the conviction, for illegal reconstitution of the dissolved Moroccan Communist Party, of Ali Yata and Mohamed Chouaïb Rifi. Bernard Andreu (France), the IADL's legal observer at the appeal hearing, judged that the Party of Liberation and Socialism had been legally constituted, and denied the existence of "any material or intentional element against the accused proving that there was an illegal reconstitution of the Moroccan Communist Party." (*PCB Informations*, no. 16, 7 February; *L'Humanité*, 10 February.) The French government was scored by the IADL for having provided "military as well as moral" support to South Africa. In a statement occasioned by South African Prime Minister Vorster's visit to France in June, the IADL claimed that the "international community" denounced as a "flagrant violation of the United Nations Charter" the policy of apartheid, of which Vorster was "one of the chief protagonists," and the "economic oppression of African populations and disregard of the rights of man." (*Ibid.*, 13 June.)

The question of political prisoners was the main focus of IADL agitation in Latin America. The IADL, the International Federation of Human Rights, the International Secretariat of Catholic Journalists, and Amnesty International collectively dispatched French lawyers Jean-Louis Weil and L.-E. Pettiti to Brazil in February-March to "inquire into the new laws and conditions of political prisoners there." Their findings were that torture was "systematic and widespread" in Brazil, and that it was "no longer a question of isolated incidents, but of a political instrument aimed at terrorizing the opposition of the extreme left." (*Le Monde*, 8-9 March; *L'Humanité*, 9 March.) Similarly, Nicole Dreyfus (France) reported at a press conference organized in Paris on 14 December by the IADL and the French section of Amnesty International on her "mission of inquiry into the situation of political prisoners in Mexico." This followed an appeal by Pierre Cot to the Mexican president for an amnesty for political prisoners. (*Le Monde*, 13-14 December.)

Publications. The IADL's two principal publications, both in English and French editions, are the *Review of Contemporary Law*, edited by Pierre Cot, which is supposed to appear semiannually but does not always do so, and the *Information Bulletin*, issues of which appear irregularly and are frequently devoted to a single topic. The IADL also issues pamphlets on questions of topical interest.

V. B.

AFRO-ASIAN WRITERS' PERMANENT BUREAU

The Afro-Asian Writers' Permanent Bureau (AAWPB) was originally set up by the Soviets at an "Afro-Asian Writers' Conference" in Tashkent in October 1958. Following a second conference, in Cairo in February 1962, a permanent bureau was established with headquarters in Colombo, Ceylon. The Chinese communists gained control of the organization at a meeting of its Executive Committee in Bali, Indonesia, in July 1963, and established a new Executive Secretariat in Peking on 15 August 1966. Thus, while the organization is still officially based in Colombo, it operates exclusively from Peking. The AAWPB's failure, to date, to organize a third Afro-Asian Writers' Conference indicates that the kind of consensus required by the Chinese for a successful conference is still lacking. (In contrast, the pro-Soviet faction—the AAWPB-Cairo—which broke away from the original AAWPB when the Chinese took control of it, has held a third and also a fourth conference; see below.) AAWPB membership strength is difficult to determine; its claim to have affiliates in some 40 countries probably takes into account individual as well as organizational memberships.

AAWPB Secretary-General Rathe Deshapriya Senanayake (Ceylon) returned to Ceylon from Peking in mid-1968. On 2 April 1970 the New China News Agency reported that Saionji Kinkazu (Japan) was "acting head ad interim of the AAWPB Secretariat" in Senanayake's absence, but there was apparently a shift later in the year; F. L. Risakotta (Indonesia) was described as "acting head ad interim" by the same source on 18 August.

Views and Activities in 1970. In the spring of 1970 an editorial entitled "Great Era, Noble Mission" appeared in the AAWPB journal, *The Call* (quoted, NCNA, 27 May). It urged "progressive Afro-Asian writers" to "plunge themselves into the heat of the Afro-Asian peoples' revolutionary struggle," following the example of "many enthusiastic songsters, talented painters and poets, who are at the same time inspiring political agitators" in Africa and Asia, and in whose hands "literature and art serve as bugles arousing the masses to fight." Western colonialism, allegedly, had "subjected the masses not only to political oppression and economic exploitation but also to cultural enslavement." The masses had received no recognition in literary and artistic works, while the "colonialist butchers, adventurers, plantation owners and missionaries" were portrayed as heroes in the making of history. It was the "duty" of Afro-Asian writers and artists, therefore, to "correct this reversal of history and restore historical truth."

Notwithstanding such exhortations to action, the AAWPB apparently has had little success in gaining new support. Unable to organize major meetings or campaigns, it has restricted its activity largely to verbal attacks, echoing Chinese pronouncements, which are directed primarily against the U.S. presence in Asia as military and cultural "aggression." A typical declaration by the Executive Secretariat, on 15 April, affirmed full support for the "Cambodian people" in their "just struggle against U.S. imperialism and the Lon Nol clique," and expressed the "firm belief" that the "heroic peoples of Vietnam, Laos, and Cambodia" would win "final victory in their struggle against "U.S. imperialism and its lackeys throughout Indochina" (*ibid.*, 16 April). Subsequent statements lauded the joint declaration issued by "the Indochinese people's summit conference" and "Chairman Mao's solemn statement" in support of "the world people's struggle against U.S. imperialism" (*ibid.*, 1 and 28 May).

An appeal issued on 4 July by the AAWPB, together with the Ceylon-China Friendship Association and "various associations of solidarity with the countries of Indochina," urged recognition by Ceylon of the "Royal Government of National Union of Kampuchea" under the leadership of Prince Norodom Sihanouk. On 7 July a rally was held by the same organizations in Colombo, at which the main speaker was Senanayake. (*Ibid.*, 9 July.)

The AAWPB bulletin, *The Call*, is issued from Peking at irregular intervals in English, French, and Arabic.

*   *   *

The AAWPB-Cairo. The pro-Soviet faction of the Afro-Asian Writers' Permanent Bureau, based in Cairo, was founded there on 19-21 June 1966 at an "extraordinary meeting" attended by delegations from Cameroun, Ceylon, India, Sudan, the Soviet Union, and the U.A.R. Its relatively successful "Third Afro-Asian Writers' Conference" in Beirut in 1967, with some 150 delegates from 42 countries, represented the first serious blow to the pro-Chinese AAWPB. Since then, the pro-Soviet organization appears to have consolidated and augmented its base of support.

The secretary-general of the AAWPB is Yusuf el-Sebai (U.A.R.), who is also Secretary-General of the Afro-Asian People's Solidarity Organization (AAPSO) and a Presidential Committee member of the World Peace Council (WPC). The assistant secretary-general is Edward al-Kharat (U.A.R.). The AAWPB has a ten-member Permanent Bureau, with members from India, Japan, Lebanon, Mongolia, the Portuguese colonies, Senegal, South Africa, the Soviet Union, Sudan, and the U.A.R. There is also a 30-member Executive Committee.

Views and Activities in 1970. The Indian Preparatory Committee (IPC) for the fourth Afro-Asian Writers' Conference, in New Delhi, convened there on 23 February. Dr. Mulk Raj Anand (a WPC member) and Sajad Zahir were IPC secretary-general and chairman, respectively. In addition, there were three delegates from Cairo headquarters, including Edward el-Kharat and 'Abd al-Rahman al-Shargawi (U.A.R.), and three Soviet writers, including A. V. Sofronov, deputy chairman of the Soviet Afro-Asian Solidarity Committee. (*Patriot*, New Delhi, 24 February; *New Age*, New Delhi, 1 March.) Subsequent preparatory sessions were held in Moscow in June, attended by Yusuf el-Sebai and representatives from ten countries (TASS, 23 June; Moscow radio, 25 June) and in Cairo in September (*al-Ahram*, Cairo, 25 September). The WPC *Letter to National Committees* (no. 46) urged support for the conference.

The fourth Afro-Asian Writers' Conference was held in New Delhi on 17-20 November, with some "150 foreigners and 200 Indians" in attendance, among them Indian Prime Minister Indira Gandhi, Yusuf al-Siba'i, Sajad Zahir, Mulk Raj Anand, Suniti Kumar Chatterjee (India), S. Idris (Lebanon), J. Kariari (Kenya), G. Musperov (Soviet Union), Shimao Toshio (Japan), Haldun Taner (Turkey), Orlin Vasilev (Bulgaria), and Kamil Yashen (Soviet Union). Other countries represented were: Algeria, Bahrein, Ceylon, Congo (Brazzaville), Czechoslovakia, Dahomey, Gambia, East Germany, Guinea, Ghana, Hungary, the Malagasy Republic, Mali, Mauritius, Mongolia, Morocco, Mozambique, Poland, Senegal, Sudan, Syria, Tanzania, Upper Volta, and South Vietnam. Mira Alečković and Ćiril Kosmac represented Yugoslavia as observers.

Indira Gandhi presented the AAWPB's "Lotus Prize" to To Hoai (North Vietnam), Alex La Guma (South Africa, in exile; WPC member), Zulfia Khanum (Soviet Union), Mahmoud Darwish ("Palestine"), and H. R. Bachbach (India). The sixth recipient, Agostinho Neto (head of the Popular Movement for the Liberation of Angola—(MPLA), was prevented by illness from attending. Mrs. Gandhi also accepted a medal presented posthumously to her father, Jawaharlal Nehru. She noted, in a brief address, that "in India, writers are not accountable to Government," and that "writers have often been pioneers of protest; they have raised their voice against foreign rule and domestic social injustice." (*Thought*, New Delhi, 28 November.)

According to a Soviet broadcast ("Radio Peace and Progress," Moscow, 17 November, in Chinese) there were no delegates from China at the conference "because all internationally known literary figures there have been persecuted" and because the present Chinese leaders "altogether disapproved of the basic principles of the Afro-Asian solidarity movement."

Four working groups discussed: (1) imperialism in Indochina and the Middle East, and racism and colonialism in South Africa; (2) cultural links between African and Asian countries; (3) new forms and content in the work of Afro-Asian writers; and (4) organizational questions. A "general statement" declared that the creative activity of Afro-Asian writers was inseparable from the struggle for freedom and social equality, and expressed "unequivocal solidarity with people fighting imperialism, wherever they may be." Among proposals for future action it was suggested that: the fifth AAWPB conference should be held in Alma-Ata, Soviet Union, in the second half of September 1973; a poetry symposium be held in Dakar, Senegal; the *Lotus* be published regularly "with the resolve to increase the international circulation of the magazine and to focus on literary works in countries where the Afro-Asian peoples are waging national liberation battles"; delegations be sent to the fighting zones of Asia and Africa to examine the situations there; an Afro-Asian news agency and a documentation center be set up to give news of the political struggles of the two continents; scholarships be awarded for exchanges among Afro-Asian writers; and exhibitions and cultural festivals be organized every two years. (*Patriot*, 19 and 21 November.)

There was substantial criticism among the large Indian contingent of Soviet domination of the conference. One group charged, for instance, that the IPC had been "constituted in an arbitrary way" and was not representative inasmuch as many important writers had been excluded. The leader of the Indian delegation was criticized by some for presenting a report "which had nothing to do with the problems of Indian writings, literature, and people." (*Times of India*, New Delhi, 21 November; *Indian Express*, New Delhi, 23 November.) It was presumably because of the dissension heard at the New Delhi conference that the suggestion was made (and adopted) that the next one, the fifth, should be held in the Soviet Union.

The main organ of the AAWPB is the "literature/arts and sociopolitical quarterly" *Lotus* (until September 1969 named *Afro-Asian Literature*). In addition, books by various "Afro-Asian men of letters" have been published by the AAWPB in the Soviet Union—some 700 of which were reportedly displayed at the 1970 conference.

V. B.

CHRONOLOGY

JANUARY

12 Czechoslovakia	Discovery of an "anti-state Trotskyist organization" is announced by the Interior Ministry of the Czech Socialist Republic.
12 Denmark	Communist Party of Denmark acquires its first parliamentary seat since 1958 through affiliation of a former independent deputy.
14 Czechoslovakia	Party Secretary Alois Indra states that deposed First Secretary Dubček "deliberately ignored the serious warning about the danger of counter-revolution which had been given to him by the French Communists in the spring of 1968." Central Committee meeting in Prague replaces Premier Černík, last top governmental official of Dubček era, with conservative centrist Štrougal.
14-15 U.S.S.R.	A meeting of European communist parties is held in Moscow.
16 Bulgaria	Zhivkov addresses national conference of party, state, and economic leaders.
18 Tunisia	The first group of students imprisoned for their participation in demonstrations in 1968 is released from prison under an amnesty, announced by President Bourguiba early in the year, to be carried out in stages.
21-24 Women's International Democratic Federation	Meeting in East Berlin, the WIDF Bureau adopts resolutions condemning Israeli "aggression," and supports a European security conference and recognition of the German Democratic Republic.
26-27 February Yugoslavia	President Tito makes official visits to several African countries in preparation for the Lusaka meeting of non-aligned states.
28-1 February India	The non-aligned Communist Party of India (Marxist) boycotts a communist labor federation conference, signaling a formal split in the federation.

30
Philippines

The Nationalist Youth Movement, an affiliate of the Maoist-oriented Philippine Communist Party, leads demonstrations which storm the presidential palace. Five demonstrators are killed, 157 wounded, and several hundred arrested.

FEBRUARY

4-9 France	The French Communist Party holds its Nineteenth Congress.
5 Indonesia	Arrest of Rachmat Effendi, vice-chairman of the Communist Party of Indonesia, is reported.
6-8 Netherlands	The Communist Party of the Netherlands holds its Twenty-third Congress.
7-9 United States	The Young Workers' Liberation League is founded at a convention in Chicago. It replaces the former W. E. B. DuBois Clubs of America, the unofficial youth organization of the Communist Party, USA.
14 Finland	Extraordinary congress of the Communist Party of Finland accords 20 Central Committee posts to "reformist" majority and remaining 15 to "Stalinist" minority, under conciliation agreement. Politburo posts are apportioned 10 to 6 in favor of reformists. Reformists retain chairman and vice-chairmanships, but a second vice-chairmanship is created for minority leader.
18 Germany: Federal Republic of Germany	The constitutional court in Karlsruhe bans dissemination of the draft program of the illegal Communist Party of Germany; the program had been readied in 1968 in the hope that it would aid in the party's fight for legalization.
19 Finland	Opposition by Finnish People's Democratic League and the U.S.S.R. results in government's refusal to ratify treaty for "Nordek" inter-Scandinavian customs union.
21-23 Iran	Tudeh Party members and sympathizers play an important part in large-scale street demonstrations in Tehran; the government rescinds bus fare increases that set off the disturbances.
24-25 Bulgaria	Ideological conference of Soviet-bloc countries meets in Sofia.
24-26 World Federation of Trade Unions	The Executive Bureau meets in Khartoum; it is the first time that an administrative organ of the WFTU has convened in Africa.

MARCH

Germany: West Berlin	The Communist Party of Germany Development Organization is founded. The organization announces that it will be guided by the principles of the Chinese Communist Party.
March-April Germany: Federal Republic of Germany	The platform of the pro-Chinese Communist Party of Germany (Marxist-Leninist) is published in the party organ *Roter Morgen*, more than a year after the party was established.
1 Austria	Austrian general election is held. The Communist Party of Austria polls 1.1 per cent of the vote.
1 Yugoslavia/ China	Resumption of full diplomatic relations is reported; (the Yugoslav ambassador arrives in Peking in May, and the Chinese send their ambassador to Belgrade in August).
3 Jordan/Syria/ Lebanon/Iraq	In Amman the communist parties of Jordan, Syria, Lebanon, and Iraq announce the establishment of an all-communist commando organization.
3 Yugoslavia	Milovan Djilas's passport is revoked two days before his scheduled departure for the United States.
4 Yugoslavia	Mihajlo Mihajlov is released a year early from prison on sentence of four and a half years for insulting the Soviet Union.
7 China	The holding of the first State Council meeting since 1966 is announced. Shortly afterward, a state constitution is drafted and given limited circulation.
11 Brazil	The Japanese consul-general in Sao Paulo is kidnaped by members of the Revolutionary Vanguard Party and later ransomed by release of five political prisoners belonging to various leftist groups.
11 Cambodia/ Vietnam: Democratic Republic of Vietnam/ Vietnam: Republic of Vietnam	Embassies, in Phnom Penh, of North Vietnam and the Provisional Revolutionary Government of the Republic of South Vietnam are sacked by anti-communist groups.

11 Iraq	An agreement ends fighting between government troops and Kurds and leads Iraqi communists to celebrate and publicize their contribution to ending hostilities. The government considers the demonstrations a threat and many communists are arrested.
12 Cambodia/Vietnam: Republic of Vietnam	The Cambodian government announces that it has suspended the trade agreement signed with the Provisional Revolutionary Government of the Republic of South Vietnam in September 1969.
13 Cambodia/Vietnam: Republic of Vietnam	The Cambodian government announces that it has requested the Provisional Government of the Republic of South Vietnam to withdraw its troops from Cambodia by 15 March.
15 Ireland/ Northern Ireland	At a special "Unity Congress" held in Belfast, the Irish Workers' Party and the Communist Party of Northern Ireland reunite, founding once again a united Communist Party of Ireland.
15-16 Finland	Finnish People's Dmocratic League wins 36 seats in parliamentary election; 33 seats go to communist members of the front.
18 Cambodia	Cambodian Parliament votes Prince Sihanouk out of office. Cheng Heng becomes head of state, assisted by General Lon Nol and Sirik Matak.
18 Italy	Agostino Novella resigns from the post of secretary-general of the communist-controlled CGIL, Italy's largest trade union. He is replaced on 24 March by Luciano Lama.
19 Cambodia/China	Prince Norodom Sihanouk arrives in Peking.
19 India	The government of West Bengal, dominated by the non-aligned Communist Party of India (Marxist), is dissolved. Violence in the state increases.
19-22 Italy	The Revolutionary Communist Groups, the Italian section of the United Secretariat of the Fourth International, holds its Fifteenth Congress.
22 Germany: German Democratic Republic	In local elections, 99.85 per cent of East German voters approve the candidates of the "National Front."
22 Luxembourg	The Communist Party of Luxembourg becomes principal electoral force in municipal elections with six seats on the town council of Esch-sur-Alzette, Luxembourg's most important industrial center. Politburo and Central Committee member Arthur Useldinger becomes mayor of Esch.
23 Cambodia	Prince Sihanouk calls for the formation of a National United Front of Kampuchea. It is officially recognized by the Chinese People's Republic on 5 May.

24
Dominican Republic

A revolutionary group believed to be associated with the pro-Chinese Dominican People's Movement kidnaps a U.S. military attaché, subsequently obtaining the release of 20 political prisoners as ransom.

28
Cambodia/
Vietnam: Democratic
Republic of Vietnam/
Vietnam: Republic
of Vietnam

North Vietnam and the Provisional Revolutionary Government of the Republic of South Vietnam announced the withdrawal of their representatives from Phnom Penh.

28-30
World Peace Council

WPC co-sponsors fifth Stockholm Conference on Vietnam. Participants from 62 countries and 30 international organizations agree to set up a commission for investigation of "U.S. war crimes" in Vietnam.

29-30

The Communist Party of Luxembourg holds its Twentieth Congress.

APRIL

Greece	Fourteenth Plenum of Central Committee, Communist Party of Greece, attended only by members loyal to pro-Soviet leadership, adopts theses, in preparation for Ninth Congress, which defend post-coup party policies, denounce internal opposition faction, and chart an all-opposition common minimum program for the overthrow of Papadopoulos government.
Jordan	The Communist Party of Jordan holds a conference, which, according to a party statement, includes the "first genuine elections in more than twenty-two years."
2 Sudan	The secretary-general of the Sudanese Communist Party, 'Abd al-Khaliq Mahjub, is arrested, and, the following day, deported to Cairo. In early August he is allowed to return, but is placed under house arrest.
5 Guatemala	The ambassador of the Federal Republic of Germany to Guatemala, Count Karl von Spreti, is murdered by the Guatemalan Rebel Armed Forces.
5-7 China/ Korea: Democratic People's Republic of Korea	Chinese Premier Chou En-lai visits North Korea. This is the first visit by a high-ranking Chinese official to Korea since 1963.
8-9 World Federation of Trade Unions	An International Committee of Solidarity with Palestine is set up at a trade union meeting held in Prague.
12 Japan	Ninagawa Torazo, candidate supported by the Japan Communist Party, is elected governor of Kyoto Prefecture.
13 Greece	Composer and communist leader Mikis Theodorakis, detained as a security risk since the 1967 coup, is released, largely through the efforts of French Radical Party leader J.-J. Servan-Schreiber.

14-15
World Peace
Council

Meeting of international organizations, convened in Cairo by the World Peace Council, decides to establish a commission to investigate "Israeli war crimes in Arab territories."

15
Argentina

Victorio Codovilla, president of the Communist Party of Argentina and one of its founding members, dies in Moscow after long illness.

16
Germany:
West Berlin

The draft *Action Program of the SEW for Peace, Democracy, and Social Progress* is published by West Berlin's communist party, which adopts the program at its Second Congress in May.

19
Germany: German
Democratic Republic

After the announcement by the ruling SED of an impending exchange of party cards for all members, Walter Ulbricht states that this move is of "greatest social significance."

21-22
Japan

The Japan Communist Party sends a delegation to attend the Lenin Centenary celebrations in Moscow.

22
Yugoslavia

The eighth session of the LCY Presidium deals with key problems of the changing role of the party, its internal democratization, and the new state reorganization.

24-25
Cambodia/Laos/
Vietnam: Democratic
Republic of Vietnam/
Vietnam: Republic
of Vietnam

"Summit Conference of the Indochinese Peoples" is held in the Chinese People's Republic.

29
Greece

Mikis Theodorakis introduces nine-point program envisaging formation of National Resistance Council, possibly headed by Andreas Papandreou, leader of Pan-Hellenic Liberation Movement, and including former Premier Constandinos Karamanlis. He urges foreign communist parties to "stop interfering" in Greek party affairs.

30
Cambodia

United States and Republic of Vietnam troops move into Cambodia in an effort to eliminate Vietnamese communist enclaves there.

MAY

Germany: Federal Republic of Germany	The German Communist Party sends greetings to the congress of the Social Democratic Party and asks that the two parties collaborate in the interest of democracy and peace. Later in the year the latter prohibits its members from engaging in joint efforts with communists and threatens expulsion for violators.
Greece	Nikolaos Kaloudhis and Zinon Zorzovilis, members, respectively, of the Politburo and Central Committee, Communist Party of Greece, are apprehended while attempting to enter Greece from East Europe with forged passports and police identity cards. A third major arrest is that of Ioannis Yiannaris, also a Central Committee member, who had been operating under cover in Athens.
Sweden	Left Party Communists leading member John Takman attempts to visit Greek communists detained or operating clandestinely. Advance information of his mission is withheld by Swedish party so as to avoid alerting Greek security authorities.
United States	Following five years of preparation, the *New Program of the Communist Party, U.S.A.* is published.
2-9 Bulgaria	Foreign Minister Bashev visits Turkey (May 3), Egypt (May 3-7), Lebanon (May 7) and Greece (May 8-9); the stay in Athens was not announced beforehand and signaled a rapprochement between the two countries.
2-3 World Peace Council	Seminar in Frankfurt-Main commemorates the twenty-fifth anniversary of "defeat of Hitlerite Fascism" and is attended by 70 representatives from 19 European countries.
5 France	Leading French Communist Party theoretician Roger Garaudy is expelled from his party cell. On 20 May the party's Central Committee ratifies the expulsion.
5-7 Germany: German Democratic Republic	At a congress on education, East German Education Minister Margot Honecker declares that the schools must educate children to become "conscious, convinced socialists" and to "hate the inhumanity of imperialism."

6 Czechoslovakia/ U.S.S.R.	A new treaty on friendship, cooperation, and mutual assistance is signed at Prague.
6 France/ Czechoslovakia	The Paris daily *Le Monde* publishes a letter from Roger Garaudy to his party cell, which brings to broad public attention the French Communist party's role in the deposition of Alexander Dubček, former first secretary of the Communist Party of Czechoslovakia.
9-10 Austria	Constituent congress of the Austrian communist party's new youth organization, the Communist Youth of Austria (KJO) meets in Vienna. Chairman Otto Podolsky rejects independent policies of the predecessor group, the Free Austrian Youth, dissolved by the party in October 1969.
12-14 Council for Mutual Economic Assistance	Twenty-fourth CMEA session held in Warsaw.
13 Council for Mutual Economic Assistance	CMEA Investment Bank founded.
13-14 Scandinavia	Annual meeting of Norwegian, Danish, Swedish, and Finnish communist parties, in Helsinki, proclaims that initiatives for inter-Scandinavian economic cooperation must go hand in hand with efforts to establish neutral and nuclear-free zone in the North, and stresses necessity of a conference of European states to "strengthen security and further economic and open cooperation in all of Europe."
15 France	A meeting of "solidarity with the Indochinese peoples" is held in Paris and is attended by 18 West European communist party delegations.
19 Cuba	Fidel Castro announces that the 1970 sugar harvest will fall at least one million tons below the target of 10 million tons.
19-21 Afro-Asian People's Solidarity Organization/Laos	AAPSO sponsors an "International Conference of Solidarity with the Peoples of Laos" in Cairo.
20 China	Mao Tse-tung's "20 May statement" is read to a Peking rally. It calls for unity of the "people of the world" to defeat U.S. "imperialism" and becomes a popular document in China and among pro-Chinese groups abroad. Mao's appearance at the rally is his first since 14 October 1969.
22-27 Germany: West Berlin	The Socialist Unity Party of Germany-West Berlin holds its Second Congress and reelects Gerhard Danelius as party chairman.

27 Ceylon	General elections replace the United National Party with a strongly socialist coalition of three parties: the pro-Soviet Ceylon Communist Party, which wins six out of 151 elected seats in the Lower House of Parliament; the Trotskyist Lanka Sama Samaja Party, which wins 19; and the socialist Sri Lanka Freedom Party, which wins 90.
27 France	The pro-Chinese organization Proletarian Left and its publication *La Cause du Peuple* are banned, and the editors of the letter, Jean-Pierre Le Dantec and Michel Le Bris, are placed on trial.
28-31 Austria	The Twenty-first Congress of the Communist Party of Austria is held in Vienna, with the purpose of ending the split between "progressives" and "conservatives" within the party. Dominated by the "conservative" faction, the congress endorses a "path of normalization" similar to that instituted in Czechoslovakia following the 1968 invasion.
28-31 India	The non-aligned Communist Party of India (Marxist) establishes a new trade union federation, the Centre of Indian Trade Unions, thus completing a split in the All-India Trade Union Congress, which remains in the hands of the rival pro-Soviet Communist Party of India.
30 Pakistan	Mohammed Toaha resigns as secretary-general of Maulana Bhashani's National Awami Party. Shortly thereafter, he and the former vice-president of that party, Abdul Huq, reportedly form the Communist Party of East Pakistan (Marxist-Leninist).

JUNE

Germany: Federal Republic of Germany	For the first time since its establishment, the German Communist party participates in elections as an "independent political force." It fails to win representation in the governments of three states, because it falls far short of receiving the prerequisite 5 per cent of all votes cast.
Sweden	Leftist Youth League's pro-Chinese leadership majority breaks with parent Left Party Communists and forms Marxist-Leninist Struggle League. Youth elements remaining faithful to Left Party Communists attempt to reorganize Leftist Youth League cells.
6-8 Laos	Joint conference of the Pathet Lao and the Patriotic Neutralist Forces is held in Sam Neua Province to map out military tasks against the United States and its allies.
7 Italy	Elections are held for the first time to 15 Regional Councils, as a result of which the Italian Communist Party succeeds in forming coalition regional administrations, together with two socialist parties, in three regions.
9 United States	William Epton, vice-chairman of the pro-Chinese Progressive Labor Party, is expelled from the party.
9-10 Germany: German Democratic Republic	Serious economic shortcomings are reported to the thirteenth plenum of the Socialist Unity Party of Germany.
11 Brazil	Members of the Revolutionary Vanguard Party and the National Liberation Action kidnap the German ambassador and subsequently obtain as ransom the release of 40 political prisoners belonging to various leftist groups.
11 Germany: West Berlin	An estimated 15,000 people participate in communist-organized demonstrations against the proposed "hand-grenade law" which authorizes equipping police with automatic weapons and grenades for use in civil disturbances. The law is passed nevertheless.

768

13
Israel

In a display of nationalism, the Israeli Communist Party (MAKI) Central Committee praises Israel's fighting men and resistance to efforts to dislodge them from the cease-fire lines.

15
Iraq

The Iraqi Communist Party organ *Tariq al-Sha'b* outlines communist strategy for cooperation with the ruling Ba'th Party.

15-16
Turkey

Communist Party of Turkey declares full support for anti-government demonstrations, ascribes official response to incidents of violence as aggression by "U.S. imperialists and their domestic collaborationists."

16
Czechoslovakia

Enterprise councils, nuclei of workers' self-government dating from spring 1968, are disbanded.

16
Women's International
Democratic Federation

The WIDF holds an "International Conference on the Problems of European Security and Cooperation" in Ystad, Sweden.

18
Germany: German
Democratic Republic/
Federal Republic
of Germany

Walter Ulbricht meets secretly with four members of the West German Young Socialists ("Jusos"), the youth wing of the Social Democratic Party.

18
Great Britain

The Communist Party of Great Britain registers a marked decline in electoral support in the general election, its vote falling from 0.2 per cent (in 1966) to 0.1 per cent.

19-21
United States

At a "National Emergency Conference Against the Cambodia-Laos-Vietnam War," held in Cleveland, the National Peace Action Coalition is formed under the leadership of the Socialist Workers' Party, a Trotskyist group aligned with the United Secretariat of the Fourth International.

20-21
World Peace Council/
International
Institute for Peace

Colloquium is held in Vienna to mark the twenty-fifth anniversary of the United Nations, attended by a UNESCO representative.

23
Belgium

The Communist Party of Belgium is host to an "International Conference on Indochina," held in Liège. Delegates include leaders from the communist parties of Italy, France, the Federal Republic of Germany, and the Democratic Republic of Vietnam.

23
Japan

The Japan Communist Party joins the Japan Socialist Party in a "one-day joint struggle" to oppose the security treaty with the United States on the day the treaty became subject to notice of termination by either party. Including representatives of all factions and leftist parties, an estimated 740,000 persons take part in rallies and demonstrations throughout Japan.

25-26
Albania

The tenth plenum of the Central Committee of the Albanian Party of Labor is held. The plenum strongly endorses decentralization in economic and state organs.

25-26
Czechoslovakia

The Central Committee expels former First Secretary Dubček and other prominent representatives of the 1968 "liberalization" course.

25-30
Yugoslavia

Premier Mitja Ribičić visits the Soviet Union, receives a proper but lukewarm reception, and obtains Soviet reaffirmation of the 1955 Belgrade Declaration.

26
India

The Kerala state "mini front" government of the pro-Soviet Communist Party of India is dissolved.

27-29
World Peace Council/
Afro-Asian Peoples'
Solidarity
Organization

Conference in Support of the Peoples of the Portuguese Colonies, co-sponsored by the WPC and the Afro-Asian Peoples' Solidarity Organization, is held in Rome, attended by 350 delegates from 177 organizations in 64 countries. A permanent secretariat is set up in Rome.

29
Czechoslovakia

All departments of Marxism-Leninism at institutions of higher education are closed and two-thirds of the scientific personnel expelled.

30
Yugoslavia

The Yugoslav long-term arms purchase agreement with the Soviet Union expires without any indication of renewal.

JULY

1 India	The pro-Soviet Communist Party of India launches a massive nationwide land-occupation movement. The campaign begins to die down by the end of September.
1-7 Japan	The Eleventh Congress of the Japan Communist Party is held at Tachikawa near Tokyo with 1,000 delegates present, including representation from the Australian, Italian, and North Korean communist parties.
5 Cyprus	In parliamentary elections, the nine candidates of the Reconstruction Party of the Working People of Cyprus, all successful, secure an aggregate 39.6 per cent of popular vote.
5-6 Great Britain	At a congress held in London, a new youth organization—the Spartacus League—is formed. It aligns itself with the International Marxist Group, the British section of the United Secretariat of the Fourth International.
6 Greece	Communist party leaders Nikolaos Kaloudhis, Zinon Zorzovilis, and Ioannis Yiannaris, arrested in May, receive life sentences.
8 Czechoslovakia	Restrictions are imposed upon rehabilitation of victims from the "personality cult" period.
14 Finland	Finnish People's Democratic League receives 3 of 15 cabinet posts in coalition government announced by new Premier Ahti Karjalainen. Justice Ministry goes to communist party Politburo member.
15 Indonesia	Arrest of Siswojo (alias Sarjono), former head of the Communist Party of Indonesia Central Committee education department, is reported.
16 Dominican Republic	Otto Morales, an important leader of the pro-Chinese Dominican People's Movement, is killed by police forces.

15-19
International
Association of
Democratic Lawyers

Ninth Congress convenes in Helsinki, attended by 350 lawyers from 55 countries.

18-19
France

The communist-controlled General Confederation of Labor hosts an "International Trade Union Conference of Solidarity with the Workers and People of Indochina Struggling Against U.S. Aggression."

19
Puerto Rico

Following an unsuccessful attempt to disband the Puerto Rican Communist Party (PCP) and integrate its membership into the Pro-Independence Movement, the party's secretary-general, Juan Santos Rivera, resigns his post and leaves the PCP.

20
Council for Mutual
Economic Assistance

Forty-seventh CMEA Executive Committee meeting is held in Moscow.

30
Argentina

A small group representing both Marxists and revolutionary Peronists occupies for about one hour the small town of Garin, about 26 miles from Buenos Aires.

AUGUST

Greece	In bid to reunite the Communist Party of Greece, the Soviets invite Mikis Theodorakis to Moscow. He is honored by Soviet groups, but refuses to hold talks with secretary-general or other leaders of Greek party.
Norway	Communist Party of Norway attempts purge of an Oslo cell's pro-Chinese majority following dissidents' formation of an opposition group, the Marxist-Leninist Front, within the party.
1 China	The Chinese People's Republic celebrates the forty-third anniversary of the founding of the People's Liberation Army. This marks the last appearance during the year of Ch'en Po-ta, one of five members of the Chinese Communist Party's Politburo Standing Committee. Speculation arises that Ch'en has been removed from that body.
1-9 Japan	The Gensuikyo (Council against Atomic and Hydrogen Bombs) holds its sixteenth national congress successively in Tokyo, Hiroshima, and Nagasaki, with a reported total attendance of 10,000 including 51 participants from 12 countries.
9 Uruguay	Murder of U.S. Security Adviser in Montevideo by the National Liberation Movement (the Tupamaros).
10 Ceylon	A relatively new political grouping, the Janata Vimikthi Peramuna, or "Che Guevara movement" as it is popularly called, holds its first open rally. The leader of the group, which is described as "ultra-revolutionary," denies that it is opposed to the government.
12 U.S.S.R./Germany: Federal Republic of Germany	U.S.S.R. and FRG sign renunciation of force agreement.
13 Lebanon	A permit issued by the Minister of the Interior grants legal status to the Lebanese Communist Party.

15 China/U.S.S.R.	A new Soviet representative at the Sino-Soviet border negotiations, Leonid Ilichev, arrives in Peking, replacing Vasily Kuznetsov, who returned to Moscow on 30 June for medical treatment.
16 United States	A federal warrant charging unlawful flight is filed against Angela Davis, member of the Communist Party, USA and the Black Panther Party, in connection with a citation against her for alleged involvement in a kidnaping and fatal gun battle which had occurred at a courthouse in Marin County, California, on 7 August. (Davis is apprehended on 13 October in New York City).
17 Cambodia/China	Agreement is signed in Peking providing the National United Front of Kampuchea with free military aid for 1970 from China.
19 India	Kanu Sanyal, a leader of the Communist Party of India (Marxist-Leninist), is arrested along with 29 of his followers, sparking violent demonstrations throughout West Bengal.
21 Germany: German Democratic Republic	The East German youth newspaper *Junge Welt* warns against Soviet concessions on West Berlin following the signing of the Moscow treaty on renunciation of force between the U.S.S.R. and the Federal Republic of Germany.
27 Japan/Korea: Democratic Republic of Korea	Yoshida Sukeharu, member of the Presidium of the Central Committee of the Japan Communist Party, takes up his duties in Pyongyang as official party representative in North Korea.

SEPTEMBER

Iraq	The Central Committee faction of the Iraqi Communist Party holds its Second Congress and reelects 'Aziz Muhammad as first secretary.
Jordan	While civil war rages in Jordan, the Jordanian communist party joins the communists of Lebanon and Syria in urging the overthrow of King Hussein and his "fascist military regime."
Italy	The monthly publication *Il Manifesto*, whose supporters represent the major extreme-left challenge to the Italian Communist Party, publishes a "platform of discussion and political work for the unity of the revolutionary left and the construction of a new political force."
1 Czechoslovakia	The ultra-conservative wing of the communist party begins to publish a new review *Leva fronta* (The Left Front).
1-2 World Peace Council/ East German Peace Council	International seminar is held in Potsdam on "the topical importance of the Potsdam Agreements and the requirements for peace and security in Europe." The 95 participants from 25 countries uphold the agreements and laud the Soviet-West German treaty signed on 12 August.
3 Portugal	The Patriotic Front of National Liberation, an underground group against "fascism," expels the Portuguese Communist Party from the organization, accusing it of blocking the revolutionary process.
4 Chile	Salvador Allende, at the head of the Popular Unity Alliance, receives too few votes for direct election to the presidency. He is elected by the Congress on 24 October and inaugurated on 3 November.
5-8 Guyana	The Fourteenth Congress of the People's Progressive Party is held in Georgetown.
8-10 Yugoslavia/Zambia	Tito attends the third summit conference of non-aligned countries in Lusaka, Zambia.

9 Israel	The Israeli Communist Party (MAKI) Central Committee calls upon communist parties everywhere to denounce the hijacking of civilian airliners by the Palestinian resistance.
10 Czechoslovakia	First Secretary Husák rejects in a public speech the call by extreme conservatives for continuation of the purge and urges "understanding for those who now have lost their party membership."
14 Yugoslavia	An article in *Der Spiegel* highlights espionage and subversive activity of the Soviet Union in trying to stir up dissident forces within Yugoslavia and among Yugoslav expatriates in Western Europe.
17 India	Elections in Kerala state reseat the "mini front" government of the pro-Soviet Communist Party of India. The Communist Party of India (Marxist) remains outside the coalition.
18 Czechoslovakia	A meeting of the communist party Presidium evaluates results of the "exchange of party cards."
20 Albania	Albanian national elections. Democratic Front candidates for the People's Assembly receive 100 per cent of votes cast.
20 Sweden	In Sweden's first combined parliamentary, county, and municipal election, Left Party Communists poll 4.8 per cent and receive 17 of 350 seats. Failing to gain majority, Social Democratic Labor Party accepts communist support to stay in power. The pro-Chinese splinter, Communist League (Marxist-Leninist), participating in its first election, polls 0.4 per cent and fails to qualify for parliamentary representation.
21 Great Britain	The Communist Party of Great Britain is host to a meeting of nine West European communist parties held in London.
21-24 International Federation of Resistance Fighters	Fifth Medical Congress, first planned for 1968, is held in Paris. Some 100 participants from 21 countries decide to intensify "research into resistance pathology and retarded after-effects" of U.S. chemical warfare in Vietnam.
23-27 World Federation of Scientific Workers	Executive Committee confirms Professor Eric Burhop (Britain) as president, succeeding Cecil Power, who died in 1969. Preparations are announced for an anti-nuclear, -chemical, and -biological weapons conference.
23 Peru	Ricardo Letts Colmenares, the leader of a Marxist-Leninist group sharply critical of the Peruvian government, is arrested on charges of anarchism and subversion, and later deported to Mexico. He is allowed to return to Peru in February 1971.

Late September
Spain

A Central Committee Plenum of the Communist Party of Spain expels five pro-Soviet dissidents, including Enrique Lister, a member of the party's Executive Committee.

OCTOBER

Spain	Pro-Soviet dissidents expelled from the Communist Party of Spain the previous month begin publication of a rival party newspaper, using the same name as that of the parent party organ, *Mundo Obrero*.
4 Austria	By-elections in Vienna and provincial elections in the Tirol are held. The Communist Party of Austria suffers an election defeat comparable to that of March 1970.
5-9 Women's International Democratic Federation	The WIDF Council meeting is held in Budapest with 260 delegates from 91 countries in attendance. Special ceremonies mark the twenty-fifth anniversary of the WIDF.
13 Canada/China	Diplomatic relations are established between the Chinese People's Republic and Canada.
13 China/U.S.S.R.	V. S. Tolstikov, the first Soviet ambassador to China since 1966, presents his credentials in Peking. The Chinese reciprocate on 22 November by sending Liu Hsin-chuan to Moscow.
14 Finland	Finnish People's Democratic League parliamentary group splits on minor bill. Twelve Stalinist members who vote against majority backing of bill are censured by communist party Politburo for having "disrupted conditions for implementing the party's general political line."
16-19 World Federation of Trade Unions	The WFTU marks its twenty-fifth anniversary at a meeting of its General Council in Moscow.
20 Italy	At the conclusion of a joint meeting of the Italian Communist Party's Central Committee and Central Control Commission a number of major changes in the party leadership are announced.
22-25 World Peace Council	WPC is strongly represented at initial session of "International Commission of Inquiry into U.S. War Crimes in Vietnam," in Stockholm, which accuses the United States of crimes "equivalent to genocide."

23
Brazil

Joaquim Camara Ferreira, leader of the National Liberation Action, is reported to be dead. Police authorities attribute his death to a heart failure but members of Camara's leftist group claim that he died as a result of torture.

23
Czechoslovakia

Radio Hvezda (formerly Radio Czechoslovakia) announces dismissal of ultra-conservative Czech Interior Minister Josef Groesser.

26 and 29
Portugal

Two ships are extensively damaged by explosions set by a group called the Armed Revolutionary Action, which is believed to work with the underground Patriotic Front of National Liberation.

NOVEMBER

Algeria	Several well-known leaders of the communist Socialist Vanguard Party (PAGS) gain their freedom after an amnesty in celebration of Algeria's National Day.

2-12
Korea: Democratic
People's Republic
of Korea

The Korean Workers' Party holds its long overdue Fifth Congress in conjunction with the completion of a seven-year economic plan, itself extended three years. With the exception of a representative from South Korea, no foreign delegations are invited.

3
Spain

The illegal Workers' Commissions, in which members of the Communist Party of Spain have an active role, hold their first nation-wide political strike.

6
China/Italy

Diplomatic relations are established between China and Italy.

11
Czechoslovakia

A Federal Socialist Youth Union of Czechoslovakia, including a junior branch of Pioneers, is organized as successor to the Czechoslovak Youth Union (which disintegrated in 1968).

13
Syria

Defense Minister Hafiz al-Asad assumes power in a bloodless coup. In spite of their earlier hostility to al-Asad and the Ba'th Party faction he represents, the communists offer their cooperation.

Two members of the Syrian Communist Party Central Committee accept cabinet posts.

16
Sudan

The Sudanese government carries out a purge of elements within the government aligned with the Sudanese Communist Party. At the same time, the party's secretary-general, 'Abd al-Khaliq Mahjub, is imprisoned.

17-20
Afro-Asian Writers'
Permanent Bureau

Fourth Afro-Asian Writers' Conference convenes in New Delhi with some 350 delegates from some 50 countries. It is decided that the fifth conference shall be held in 1973 in Alma Ata, Soviet Union.

20-23 Albania	The first session of the Seventh Legislature of the People's Assembly meets. Mehmet Shehu is reelected premier.
20 Argentina	In an apparent attempt to emulate the Chilean coalition Popular Unity, the Communist Party of Argentina organizes a national political convention, which forms the National Assembly of Argentines. This coalition adopts as its main objective the overthrow of the military government by mass actions.
21-22 Belgium	A meeting attended by 3,500 delegates from nearly all countries in Europe and from several non-European states is held in Brussels. Referred to as the "Congress for a Red Europe," it is sponsored by the United Secretariat of the Fourth International, the latter's French section (the Communist League), and the Belgian Socialist Young Guards.
20 China/United Nations	For the first time, there is a simple majority in the United Nations General Assembly for a resolution to recognize the credentials of the government of the Chinese mainland rather than that of Taiwan. The vote is 51 to 48 with 25 abstentions; a two-thirds majority vote was required by the earlier passing of a procedural motion.
22 China/U.S.S.R.	The first Sino-Soviet trade agreement since 1967 is signed in Peking.
23-27 Hungary	Tenth Congress of the Hungarian Socialist Workers Party is held.
24-4 December China	A party congress in Hunan re-establishes the first province-level party committee in China since these bodies were disbanded during the Cultural Revolution. This is followed by the forming of three more province-level committees at the end of December.

DECEMBER

Jordan	Rumors of a serious party split in the communist Party of Jordan are confirmed when a Politburo appeal (dated 1 January 1971) asks defectors to return pending a search for solutions.
Syria	The Syrian Communist Party joins a national front coalition.
2 France	The French Communist Party is host to a meeting of "solidarity with the Indochinese peoples" which is attended by leaders of communist parties of Great Britain, Italy, the Netherlands, and Sweden.
2 Syria/Sudan	A special session of the Syrian Communist Party's Politburo approves the proposed four-state federation of the U.A.R., Libya, Sudan, and Syria; Sudanese communists, however, voice strong opposition.
7 Brazil	Members of the Revolutionary Vanguard Party kidnap the Swiss ambassador and subsequently obtain the release of 70 political prisoners as ransom.
7 Pakistan	Elections are held for the National Assembly. The pro-Soviet (but non-communist) National Awami Party of Wali Khan wins 6 out of 300 seats, all in West Pakistan. Provincial assembly elections on 17 December give Wali Khan's Party 13 out of 40 seats in the Northwest Frontier Province, 8 out of 20 in Baluchistan, and one out of 300 in East Pakistan. The pro-Chinese National Awami Party of Maulana Bhashani withdrew from the contests on 24 November.
7 Poland/Germany: Federal Republic of Germany	Polish-FRG treaty normalizing relations between the two states and recognizing the Oder-Neisse boundary is signed in Warsaw.
8 Great Britain	The Liaison Committee for the Defense of Trade Unions, an organization controlled by the Communist Party of Great Britain, sponsors a one-day national strike, in which an estimated 300,000 persons participate.

10-11 Czechoslovakia	A Central Committee meeting endorses the report on the concluded "exchange of party cards" which did not renew 473,731 memberships, or a decrease of 27.8 per cent. It confirms expulsion of former Premier Černik.
11-15 Uruguay	The Communist Party of Uruguay holds its Fifteenth Congress in Montevideo.
12 Poland	Price increases announced in the evening over Polish radio.
12-13 World Federation of Scientific Workers	Conference on Chemical Warfare in Vietnam, convening in Paris, finds U.S. use of chemical weapons the cause of "perhaps irreversible" damage to the Vietnamese ecology and climate and its use of poison gases a violation of the 1925 Geneva Convention.
14 Poland	Strikes and rioting over food price increases begin in Gdańsk; soon spread to Sopot, Gdynia, Szczecin, and Elbląg.
14 Yugoslavia	President Tito formally submits his proposal to the Federal Assembly for constitutional changes relating to the establishment of a collective State Presidency.
Mid-December Venezuela	The Communist Party of Venezuela splits after two years of internal conflict, the dissidents forming the "Movement toward Socialism."
15 Chile/China	Diplomatic relations are established between the Chinese People's Republic and Chile.
18 Czechoslovakia	It is announced that about twenty cultural and scientific periodicals are suspended or merged with other journals.
20 Poland	Seventh Central Committee plenum. Gomułka is removed from power as first party secretary. Edward Gierek replaces him. Also removed from the Politburo and Secretariat: Zenon Kliszko, Marian Spychalski, Ryszard Strzelecki, Bolesław Jaszczuk.
22 Peru	In accordance with a presidential decree granting political amnesty, Ricardo Gadea, Héctor Béjar, and Hugo Blanco, leaders of the Movement of the Revolutionary Left, the Army of National Liberation, and the Revolutionary Leftist Front respectively, are released from prison.
23 Bolivia	Régis Debray is released from prison after serving less than four years of a thirty-year sentence.
23 Poland	Józef Cyrankiewicz replaces Marian Spychalski as chairman of the Council of State. Piotr Jaroszewicz becomes premier; Franciszek Kaim and Jan Mitręga become new deputy premiers.

27-30   The founding conference of the Students' Federation of India is held
India   in Kerala. The federation is the new student front of the non-aligned
               Communist Party of India (Marxist).

27-31   The Trotskyist Young Socialist Alliance holds its Tenth National
United States Convention in New York City.

BIBLIOGRAPHY

GENERAL ON COMMUNISM

Ader, Emile B. *Communism: Classic and Contemporary.* Woodbury, N.Y., Barron's Educational Series, 1970. 307 pp.

Althusser, Louis. *For Marx.* New York, Pantheon, 1970. 272 pp.

Aptheker, Herbert. *The Urgency of Marxist-Christian Dialogue.* New York, Harper & Row, 1970. 196 pp.

Astrada, Carlos. *El marxismo y las escatologías.* Buenos Aires, Juárez Editor, 1970. 304 pp.

Balinky, Alexander. *Marx's Economics: Origin and Development.* Lexington, Mass., Heath, 1970. 178 pp.

Banks, Joseph Ambrose. *Marxist Sociology in Action: A Sociological Critique of the Marxist Approach to Industrial Relations.* Harrisburg, Pa., Stackpole Books, 1970. 324 pp.

Berger, Peter L., and Neuhaus, Richard J. *Movement and Revolution.* New York, Doubleday, 1970. 240 pp.

Birnbaum, Karl. *Peace in Europe: East-West Relations.* Oxford University Press, 1970. 159 pp.

Breines, Paul (ed.). *Critical Interruptions: New Left Perspectives on Herbert Marcuse.* New York, Herder and Herder, 1970. 188 pp.

Burns, Emile (ed.). *A Handbook of Marxism.* 2 volumes. New York, Haskell House, 1970.

Cogniot, Georges. *Présence de Lénine.* 2 volumes. Paris, Editions sociales, 1970.

Crozier, Brian. *Since Stalin: An Assessment of Communist Power.* New York, Coward-Mc-Cann, Inc., 1970. 247 pp.

Curtis, Michael (ed.). *Marxism.* New York, Atherton, 1970. 336 pp.

Dallin, Alexander, and Breslauer, George W. *Political Terror in Communist Systems.* Stanford, Stanford University Press, 1970. 172 pp.

Deutscher, Isaac. *Russia, China and the West: A Contemporary Chronicle, 1953-1966.* New York, Oxford University Press, 1970. 360 pp.

Ebenstein, William. *Today's Isms: Communism, Fascism, Capitalism, Socialism.* Englewood Cliffs, N.J., Prentice-Hall, Inc., 1970. 302 pp.

Eliot-Bateman, Michael (ed.). *The Fourth Dimension of Warfare, Volume I - Intelligence, Subversion, Resistance.* New York, Praeger, 1970. 181 pp.

Fischer, Ernst. *The Essential Marx.* New York, Herder and Herder, 1970. 187 pp.

Freedman, Robert Owen. *Economic Warfare in the Communist Bloc.* New York, Praeger, 1970. 210 pp.

Garaudy, Roger. *Marxism in the Twentieth Century.* New York, Scribner's, 1970. 224 pp.

Gollwitzer, Helmut. *The Christian Faith and the Marxist Criticism of Religion.* New York, Scribner's, 1970. 173 pp.

Gunder Frank, Andre. *Lumpenburguesía; lumpendesarrollo.* Medellín, La Oveja Negra, 1970. 158 pp.

Hazard, John. *Communists and Their Law: A Search for the Common Core of the Legal Systems of the Marxian Socialist States*. Chicago, University of Chicago Press, 1970. 560 pp.

Hoffmann, Gerhard, and Wille, Wilhelm. *World Mission and World Communism*. Richmond, Va., Knox, 1970. 142 pp.

Huntington, Samuel P., and Moore, Clement H. (eds.). *Authoritarian Policies in Modern Society: The Dynamics of Established One-Party Systems*. New York, Basic Books, 1970. 533 pp.

Institut für Internationale Solidarität der Konrad Adenauer Stiftung. *Kommunistische Herrschaftssysteme in Theorie und Wirklichkeit*. Mainz, Hase & Köhler Verlag, 1970. 230 pp.

Jackson, W. Douglas (ed.). *Agrarian Policies and Problems in Communist and Non-Communist Countries*. Seattle, University of Washington Press, 1970.

Johnson, Chalmers (ed.). *Change in Communist Systems*. Stanford, Stanford University Press, 1970. 368 pp.

Kanet, Roger E. *The Behavioral Revolution and Communist Studies*. New York, Free Press Macmillan, 1970. 350 pp.

Leff, Gordon. *The Tyranny of Concepts: A Critique of Marxism*. University of Alabama Press, 1970. 256 pp.

Lenin Y Mariategui. Lima, Librería Juan Mejía Baca, 1970. 255 pp.

Leonhard, Wolfgang. *Die Dreispaltung des Marxismus: Ursprung und Entwicklung des Sowjetmarxismus, Maoismus und Reformkommunismus*. Düsseldorf, Econ-Verlag, 1970. 575 pp.

Lerner, Warren. *Karl Radek: The Last Internationalist*. Stanford, Stanford University Press, 1970. 240 pp.

Lichtheim, George. *Georg Lukacs*. New York, Viking, 1970. 146 pp.

Lipschutz, Alejandro. *Seis ensayos filosóficos marxistas 1959-1968*. Santiago, Editorial Andrés Bello, 1970. 208 pp.

Lunacharskii, Anatoli. *Semblanzas de revolucionarias*. Montevideo, Biblioteca de Marcha, 1970. 180 pp.

Luxemburg, Rosa. *Gesammelte Werke*. 2 volumes. Berlin, Dietz Verlag, 1970.

————. *Schriften zur Theorie der Spontaneität*. Reinbek, Rororo-Klassiker, 1970. 251 pp.

MacIntyre, Alasdair Chalmers. *Herbert Marcuse: An Exposition and a Polemic*. New York, Viking, 1970. 114 pp.

Magana Contreras, Manuel. *Poder laico*. México, Ediciones de Foro Político, 1970. 190 pp.

Mallin, Jay (ed.). *Strategy for Conquest: Communist Documents on Guerilla Warfare*. Coral Gables, Florida, University of Miami Press, 1970. 381 pp.

Mészáros, István. *Marx's Theory of Alienation*. London, Merlin, 1970. 352 pp.

Nataf, André. *Le Marxisme et son ombre ou Rosa Luxembourg*. Paris, André Balland, 1970. 204 pp.

Parenti, Michael. *The Anti-Communist Impulse*. New York, Random House, 1970. 333 pp.

Parkinson, George (ed.). *Georg Lukacs: The Man, His Work and His Ideas*. New York, Random House, 1970. 254 pp.

Poretsky, Elisabeth K. *Our Own People: A Memoir of 'Ignace Reiss' and His Friends*. Ann Arbor, University of Michigan Press, 1970. 278 pp.

Rumiantsev, Aleksei Matveevich. *Categories and Laws of the Political Economy of Communism*. Moscow, Progress, 1970. 388 pp.

Sánchez Azcona, Jorge. *Derecho, poder y marxismo*. Mexico City, Editorial Porrúa, 1970. 222 pp.

Schaff, Adam. *Marxism and the Human Individual*. New York, McGraw-Hill, 1970. 268 pp.

Selsam, Howard, Goldway, David, and Martel, Harry (eds.). *Dynamics of Social Change: A Reader in Marxist Social Change*. New York, International Publishers, 1970. 416 pp.

Shimoniak, Wasyl. *Communist Education: Its History, Philosophy and Politics*. Chicago, Rand-McNally, 1970. 383 pp.

Sweezy, Paul M., and Magdoff, Harry (eds.). *Lenin Today: Eight Essays on the Hundredth Anniversary of Lenin's Birth*. New York, Monthly Review Press, 1970. 125 pp.

Thompson, Sir Robert. *Revolutionary War in World Strategy, 1945-1969*. New York, Taplinger Publishing Company, 1970. 171 pp.

Trotskii, Leon. *My Life: An Attempt at an Autobiography*. New York, Pathfinder Press, 1970. 602 pp.

U.S. Department of State. Bureau of Intelligence and Research. *World Strength of the Communist Party Organizations*. Washington, D.C., U.S. Government Printing Office, 1970. 223 pp.

Waters, Mary-Alice (ed.). *Rosa Luxembourg Speaks*. New York, Pathfinder, 1970. 473 pp.

Wilde, Harry. *Leo Trotzki in Selbstzeugnissen und Bilddokumenten*. Reinbek, Rororo-Bildmonographien, 1970. 190 pp.

————— . *Rosa Luxemburg: Ich war—ich bin—ich werde sein*. Vienna, Verlag Fritz Molden, 1970. 264 pp.

Zhukov, Yurii, et al. (eds.). *The Third World: Problems and Prospects*. Moscow, Progress, 1970. 280 pp.

EAST EUROPE AND
THE SOVIET UNION

General

Bannan, Alfred J., and Edelenyi, Achilles. *Documentary History of Eastern Europe*. New York, Twayne, 1970. 392 pp.

Bykov, Aleksandr Naumovich. *Nauchno-tekhnicheskie svyazi stran sotsializma*. Moscow, Izdatelstvo "Mysl," 1970. 224 pp.

Daim, Wilfried. *The Vatican and Eastern Europe*. New York, Ungar, 1970. 189 pp.

Duncan, Raymond W. (ed.). *Soviet Policy in Developing Countries*. Waltham, Mass., Ginn-Blaisdell, 1970. 350 pp.

Ebel, Robert E. *Communist Trade in Oil and Gas: An Evaluation of the Future Export Capability of the Soviet Bloc*. New York, Praeger, 1970. 449 pp.

Farrell, R. Barry (ed.). *Political Leadership in Eastern Europe and the Soviet Union*. Chicago, Aldine, 1970. 359 pp.

Fischer-Galati, Stephen (ed.). *Man, State and Society in East European History*. New York, Praeger, 1970. 343 pp.

Gross, Hermann (ed.). *Osteuropa—Wirtschaftsreformen: Dokumente und Kommentare zu Ost-Europa-Fragen*. Bonn, Edition Atlantic Forum, 1970. 125 pp.

Il'nitskaya, G. P. (ed.). *Spravochnik Partiinogo Rabotnika*. Moscow, Politizdat, 1970. 487 pp.

Lavigne, Marie. *Les Economies socialistes soviétique et européenes*. Paris, Librairie Armand Colin, 1970. 511 pp.

Levesque, Jacques. *Le Conflit sino-soviétique et l'Europe de l'Est*. Montreal, Les Presses de l'Université de Montréal, 1970. 387 pp.

Mazanov, Gennadii Grigor'evich. *Mezhdunarodnye raschety stran chlenov SEV*. Moscow, Izdatelstvo "Finansy," 1970. 112 pp.

McSherry, James E. *Stalin, Hitler, and Europe: The Imbalance of Power, 1939-1941*. Cleveland, World Publishing Company, 1970. 357 pp.

Palmer, Alan. *The Lands Between: A History of East-Central Europe Since the Congress of Vienna*. New York, Macmillan, 1970. 405 pp.

Raupach, Hans, Fels, Eberhard, and Böttcher, Erik (eds.). *Jahrbuch der Wirtschaft Osteuropas*. München, Günter Olzog Verlag, 1970. 506 pp.

Roberts, Henry L. *Eastern Europe: Politics, Revolution and Diplomacy*. New York, Knopf, 1970. 334 pp.

Schopflin, George (ed.). *The Soviet Union and Eastern Europe: A Handbook*. New York, Praeger, 1970. 614 pp.

Toma, Peter A. (ed.). *The Changing Face of Communism in Eastern Europe*. Tucson, University of Arizona Press, 1970. 413 pp.

Völgyes, Iván and Mary. *Czechoslovakia, Hungary and Poland*. Camden, N.J., Nelson, 1970. 223 pp.

Wagner, Francis S. (ed.). *Toward a New Central Europe: A Symposium on the Problems of the Danubian Nations.* Astor Park, Fla., Danubian Press, 1970. 392 pp.

Wasowski, Stanislaw (ed.). *East-West Trade and the Technology Gap: A Political and Economic Appraisal.* New York, Praeger, 1970. 214 pp.

Albania

Dodic, Lazar. *Historischer Rückblick auf die Stellung Albaniens im Weltkommunismus.* Trittau/Holstein, Verlag Jürgen Scherbarth, 1970. 142 pp.

Prifti, Peter. *Albania Since the Fall of Khruschchev.* Cambridge, Mass., Center for International Studies, M.I.T., 1970. 35 pp.

Bulgaria

Brown, James F. *Bulgaria Under Communist Rule.* New York, Praeger, 1970. 339 pp.

Czechoslovakia

Borin, Max, and Plogen, Vera. *Management und Selbstverwaltung in der CSSR: Bürokratie und Widerstand.* Berlin, Klaus Wagenbach Verlag, 1970. 143 pp.

Lochman, Jan Milic. *Church in a Marxist Society: A Czechoslovak View.* New York, Harper & Row, 1970. 198 pp.

Loebl, Eugen. *Stalinism in Prague: The Loebl Story.* New York, Grove Press, 1970. 330 pp.

London, Arthur. *The Confession.* New York, William Morrow, 1970. 442 pp.

Maxa, Josef. *A Year is Eight Months.* Garden City, N.Y., Doubleday, 1970. 201 pp.

Rodnick, David. *The Strangled Democracy: Czechoslovakia, 1948-1969.* Lubbock, Texas, Caprock Press, 1970. 214 pp.

Shawcross, William. *Dubcek.* New York, Simon and Schuster, 1970. 317 pp.

Souckova, Milada. *A Literary Satellite: Czechoslovak-Russian Literary Relations.* Chicago, University of Chicago Press, 1970. 179 pp.

Szulc, Tad. *Czechoslovakia Since World War II.* New York, Viking Press, 1970. 640 pp.

Weeraratne, Victor. *Springs of Freedom in Czechoslovakia.* North Quincy, Mass., Christopher Publishing House, 1970. 162 pp.

Zartman, I. William (ed.). *Czechoslovakia: Intervention and Impact.* New York, University Press, 1970. 119 pp.

Germany: Democratic Republic of Germany

Akademie der Wissenschaften. Zentral Institut für Geschichte. *Marxismus und die deutsche Arbeiterbewegung.* Berlin, Dietz, 1970. 600 pp.

Bröll, Werner. *Die Wirtschaft der DDR: Lage und Aussichten.* München, Olzog, 1970. 151 pp.

Friedrich, Walter von (ed.). *Methoden der marxistisch-leninistischen Sozialforschung.* Berlin, VEB Dt. Vlg. der Wissenschaftler, 1970. 365 pp.

Havemann, Robert. *Fragen, Antworten, Fragen: Aus der Biographie eines deutschen Marxisten.* München, Piper, 1970. 301 pp.

Herrmann, Elizabeth M. *Zur Theorie und Praxis der Presse in der Sowjetischen Besatzungszone Deutschlands.* Düsseldorf, Droste Verlag, 1970. 160 pp.

Holm, Hans Axel. *The Other Germans: Report From an East German Town.* New York, Pantheon Books, 1970. 314 pp.

Honecker, Erich. *Mit dem Blick auf das Jahr 2000 die Aufgaben von heute lösen.* Berlin, Dietz, 1970. 120 pp.

Huebner, Theodore. *The Literature of East Germany.* New York, Ungar, 1970. 134 pp.

Ludz, Peter Christian. *Soziologie und Marxismus in der DDR.* Neuwied, Luchterhand, 1970. 896 pp.

Hungary

Braham, Randolph L. *Education in the Hungarian People's Republic.* Washington, D.C., U.S. Department of Health, Education, and Welfare, 1970. 227 pp.

Kovrig, Bennet. *The Hungarian People's Republic.* Baltimore, Johns Hopkins Press, 1970. 206 pp.

Pryce-Jones, David. *The Hungarian Revolution.* New York, Horizon Press, 1970. 127 pp.

Volgyes, Iván. *The Hungarian Soviet Republic, 1919: An Evaluation and a Bibliography.* Stanford, Hoover Institution Press, 1970. 90 pp.

Poland

Benes, Václav, and Pounds, Norman J.G. *Poland.* New York, Praeger, 1970. 416 pp.

Raina, Peter. *Gomulka: Politische Biographie.* Köln, Verlag Wissenschaft und Politik, 1970. 192 pp.

Szczepanski, Jan. *Polish Society.* New York, Random House, 1970. 214 pp.

Vierheller, Viktoria. *Polen und die Deutschlandfrage, 1939-1949.* Köln, Verlag Wissenschaft und Politik, 1970. 184 pp.

Wagner, Wenceslas J. (ed.). *Polish Law Throughout the Ages.* Stanford, Hoover Institution Press, 1970. 476 pp.

Wandycz, Piotr Stefan. *Soviet-Polish Relations, 1917-1921.* Cambridge, Mass., Harvard University Press, 1970. 403 pp.

Romania

Fischer-Galati, Stephen. *Twentieth Century Rumania.* New York, Columbia University Press, 1970. 248 pp.

Matley, Ian M. *Romania: A Profile.* New York, Praeger, 1970. 292 pp.

U.S.S.R.

Allard, Sven. *Russia and the Austrian State Treaty: A Case Study of Soviet Policy in Europe.* University Park, Pennsylvania State University Press, 1970. 248 pp.

Amal'rik, Andrei. *Involuntary Journey to Siberia.* New York, Harcourt-Brace-Jovanovich, 1970. 297 pp.

———. *Will the Soviet Union Survive Until 1984?* New York, Harper & Row, 1970. 93 pp.

Blackwell, William L. *The Industrialization of Russia: An Historical Perspective.* New York, Thomas Y. Crowell, 1970. 198 pp.

Bordeaux, Michael. *Patriarch and Prophets: Persecution of the Russian Orthodox Church Today.* New York, Praeger, 1970. 359 pp.

Bornstein, Morris, and Fusfield, Daniel R. (eds.). *The Soviet Economy: A Book of Readings.* Homewood, Ill., Dorsey, 1970. 467 pp. 2nd ed.

Brezhnev, Leonid I. *Leninskim kursom.* 2 volumes. Moscow, Politizdat, 1970.

Brumberg, Abraham (ed.). *In Quest of Justice: Protest and Dissent in the Soviet Union Today.* New York, Praeger, 1970. 477 pp.

Centre de Recherches sur L'U.R.S.S. et les Pays de L'Est. *Annuaire de L'U.R.S.S.: Droit, Economie, Sociologie, Politique, Culture, 1969.* Paris, Centre National de la Recherche Scientifique, 1970. 820 pp.

Chernenko, K.U., and Smirtiukov, M.S. (eds.). *Resheniia partii i pravitel'stva po khoziaistvennym voprosam.* Moscow, Politizdat, 1970. 686 pp.

Cohn, Stanley H. *Economic Development in the Soviet Union.* Lexington, Mass., Heath, 1970. 135 pp.

Cornell, Richard (ed.). *The Soviet Political System: A Book of Readings.* Englewood Cliffs, N.J., Prentice-Hall, Inc., 1970. 392 pp.

Crowley, Edward L. (ed.). *The Soviet Diplomatic Corps, 1917-1967.* Metuchen, N.J., Scarecrow Press, 1970. 240 pp.

Duncan, W. Raymond (ed.). *Soviet Policy in Developing Countries.* Waltham, Mass., Ginn-Blaisdell, 1970. 350 pp.

Eriksen, John G., and Farrell, Robert (eds.). *The Development of Soviet Society: Plan and Performance.* Munich, Institute for Study of the USSR, 1970. 365 pp.

Friedberg, Maurice. *The Jew in Post-Stalin Soviet Literature.* Washington, D.C., B'nai B'rith, 1970. 59 pp.

Gómez, Eugenio. *Stalin.* Montevideo, Elite, 1970. 108 pp.

Groshev, I.I. *Voprosy partiinoi propagandy v usloviiakh stroitel'stva kommunizma.* Moscow, "Mysl," 1970. 192 pp.

Grzybowski, Kazimierz. *Soviet Public International Law: Doctrines and Diplomatic Practice.* Leyden, A.W. Sijthoff, 1970. 544 pp.

Hayter, Sir William. *Russia and the World: A Study in Soviet Foreign Policy.* New York, Taplinger, 1970. 133 pp.

Hopkins, Mark W. *Mass Media in the Soviet Union.* New York, Pegasus, 1970. 384 pp.

Joravsky, David. *The Lysenko Affair.* Cambridge, Mass., Harvard University Press, 1970. 459 pp.

Kaser, Michael. *Soviet Economics.* New York, McGraw-Hill, 1970. 248 pp.

Khrushchev, Nikita S. *Khrushchev Remembers.* Boston, Little, Brown and Company, 1970. 639 pp.

Kochan, Lionel (ed.). *The Jews in Soviet Russia Since 1917.* New York, Oxford University Press, 1970. 357 pp.

Kohler, Foy D. *Understanding the Russians.* New York, Harper and Row, 1970. 441 pp.

Kolkowicz, Roman (ed.). *The Soviet Union and Arms Control.* Baltimore, Johns Hopkins Press, 1970. 212 pp.

Korolev, A., Nazarov, M., and Tulenbaev, B. (eds.). *Sovershenstvovat stil' i metody partiinoi raboty.* Moscow, Politizdat, 1970. 230 pp.

Kucherov, Samuel. *The Organs of Soviet Administration of Justice: Their History and Operation.* Leiden, E.J. Brill, 1970. 754 pp.

Kuhn, Delia and Ferdinand. *Russia on our Minds: Reflections on Another World.* Garden City, N.Y., Doubleday, 1970. 299 pp.

Laird, Roy D. *The Soviet Paradigm.* New York, Free Press, 1970. 272 pp.

Laird, Roy D. and Betty A. *Soviet Communism and Agrarian Revolution.* London, Penguin Books, 1970. 158 pp.

Liebman, Marcel. *The Russian Revolution.* New York, Random House, 1970. 389 pp.

Meissner, Boris, and Rhode, Gotthold (eds.). *Grundfragen sowjetischer Aussenpolitik.* Stuttgart, Verlag W. Kohlhammer, 1970. 175 pp.

Miller, Robert F. *One Hundred Thousand Tractors: The MTS and the Development of Controls in Soviet Agriculture.* Cambridge, Mass., Harvard University Press, 1970. 423 pp.

Narkiewicz, Olga A. *The Making of the Soviet State Apparatus.* Manchester, Manchester University Press, 1970. 238 pp.

Niemeyer, Gerhart. *Deceitful Peace: A New Look at the Soviet Threat.* New Rochelle, N.Y., Arlington House, 1970. 201 pp.

Osborn, Robert J. *Soviet Social Policies: Welfare, Equality and Community.* Homewood, Ill., Dorsey, 1970. 294 pp.

Oswald, J. Gregory (comp. and tr.). *Soviet Image of Contemporary Latin America: A Documentary History, 1960-1968.* Austin, University of Texas Press, 1970. 365 pp.

Parrish, Michael. *The Soviet Armed Forces: Books in English, 1950-1967.* Stanford, Hoover Institution Press, 1970. 128 pp.

Pedosov, A.D. (chief ed.). *Politicheskaia i organizatorskaia rabota v sovremennykh usloviakh.* Moscow, "Mysl," 1970. 192 pp.

Petrovich, N.A., Lomakin, N.A., and Kravchenko, A.S. *Partiinoe stroitel'stvo.* Moscow, Politizdat, 1970. 430 pp.

Pinkus, B., and Greenbaum, A.A. (comps.). *Russian Publications on Jews and Judaism in the Soviet Union, 1917-1967: A Bibliography.* Jerusalem, The Historical Society of Israel, 1970. 275 pp.

Pospelov, P.N. (ed.). *Istoriia kommunisticheskoi partii sovetskogo soiuza.* Volume IV. Moscow, Politizdat, 1970. 663 pp.

Rakowska-Harmstone, Teresa. *Russia and Nationalism in Central Asia: The Case of Tadzhikistan.* Baltimore, Johns Hopkins Press, 1970. 325 pp.

Revesz, Laszlo. *Ideologie und Praxis in der sowjetischen Innen- und Aussenpolitik.* Mainz, Hase & Koehler Verlag, 1970. 129 pp.

Salomon, Michel. *Méditerranée Rouge: Un Nouvel Empire Sovietique?* Paris, Laffont, 1970. 399 pp.

Skilling, H. Gordon, and Griffiths, Franklyn (eds.). *Interest groups in Soviet Politics.* Princeton, N.J., Princeton University Press, 1970. 433 pp.

Slepov, L.A. *Leninskaia partiia—partiia proletarskogo internatsionalizma.* Moscow, Politizdat, 1970. 294 pp.

Volin, Lazar. *A Century of Russian Agriculture: From Alexander II to Khrushchev.* Cambridge, Mass., Harvard University Press, 1970. 476 pp.

Wagenlehner, Günther. *Staat oder Kommunismus: Lenin's Entscheidung gegen die kommunistische Gesellschaft.* Stuttgart, Seewald Verlag, 1970. 260 pp.

Walters, Robert S. *American and Soviet Aid: A Comparative Analysis.* Pittsburgh, University of Pittsburgh Press, 1970. 299 pp.

Weeks, Albert L. *The Other Side of Coexistence: An Analysis of Russian Foreign Policy.* New York, Pitmann, 1970. 304 pp.

Welch, William. *American Images of Soviet Foreign Policy: An Inquiry into Recent Appraisals from the Academic Community.* New Haven, Yale University Press, 1970. 316 pp.

Wolfe, Thomas W. *Soviet Power and Europe: 1945-1970.* Baltimore, Johns Hopkins Press, 1970. 534 pp.

Zaluzhnyi, V.I. *Narodnyi kontrol' v sovremennykh usloviiakh.* Moscow, "Mysl," 1970. 182 pp.

Yugoslovia

Auty, Phyllis. *Tito: A Biography.* New York, McGraw-Hill, 1970. 343 pp.

Broekmeyer, M.J. (ed.). *Yugoslav Workers' Self-Management.* Dordrecht, D. Reidel, 1970. 259 pp.

Chloros, A.G. *Yugoslav Civil Law: History, Family and Property.* Oxford, Clarendon Press, 1970. 436 pp.

Christman, Henry M. (ed.). *The Essential Tito.* New York, St. Martin's Press, 1970. 197 pp.

Dedijer, Vladimir. *The Battle Stalin Lost: Memoirs of Yugoslavia, 1948-1953.* New York, Viking Press, 1970. 341 pp.

Horvat, Branko. *An Essay on Yugoslav Society.* White Plains, N.Y., International Arts and Sciences Press, 1970. 245 pp.

Prcela, John, and Guldescu, Stanko (eds.). *Operation Slaughterhouse: Eyewitness Accounts of Postwar Massacres in Yugoslavia.* Philadelphia, Dorrance & Co., 1970. 557 pp.

Roggemann, Herwig. *Das Modell der Arbeiterselbstverwaltung in Jugoslawien: Theorie und Praxis der Gewerkschaften.* Frankfurt/Main, Europäische Verlagsanstalt, 1970. 263 pp.

Rubenstein, Alvin Z. *Yugoslavia and the Nonaligned World.* Princeton, N.J., Princeton University Press, 1970. 353 pp.

WEST EUROPE

General

Schlomann, Friedrich-Wilhelm, and Friedlingstein, Paulette. *Die Maoisten: Pekings Filialen in Westeuropa*. Frankfurt/Main, Sozietäts-Verlag, 1970. 300 pp.

Austria

Hautman, Hans. *Die Anfänge der linksradikalen Bewegung und der kommunistischen Partei Deutsch-Österreichs, 1916-1919*. Wien, Europa Verlag, 1970. 176 pp.

Finland

Wagner, Ulrich. *Finnlands Kommunisten: Volksfront-Experiment und Parteispaltung*. Stuttgart, Kohlhammer Verlag, 1970. 200 pp.

France

Aaron, Raymond. *The Elusive Revolution: Anatomy of a Student Revolt*. New York, Praeger, 1970. 200 pp.

Angeli, Claude, and Gillet, Paul. *Debout, Partisans!* Paris, Fayard, 1970. 386 pp.

Delbrel, Madeleine. *Ville marxiste, terre de missions*. Paris, Editions du Cerf, 1970. 280 pp.

Duclos, Jacques. *Memoires, 1968-1970*. 4 volumes. Paris, Fayard, 1970.

Garaudy, Roger. *Toute la vérité*. Paris, Grasset, 1970. 196 pp.

Guerin, Daniel. *Front populaire, révolution manquée*. Paris, Maspero, 1970. 317 pp.

Kriegel, Annie. *Aux origines du communisme français*. Paris, Flammarion, 1970. 448 pp.

Monnerot, Jules. *Demarxiser l'université*. Paris, La Table Ronde, 1970. 184 pp.

Oelgart, Bernd. *Idéologues et idéologies de la nouvelle gauche*. Paris, Union générale d'éditions, 1970. 192 pp.

Parti communiste français. *Congrès 19., Nanterre, 1970: Rapports, interventions et documents, salutations et messages*. Paris, Comité Central du Parti communiste français, 1970. 593 pp.

Germany: Federal Republic of Germany

Baerwald, Helmut. *Deutsche Kommunistische Partei: Die kommunistische Bündnispolitik in Deutschland*. Köln, Verlag Wissenchaft & Politik, 1970. 128 pp.

Buber-Neumann, Margarete. *Der kommunistische Untergrund*. Kreuzlingen, Neptun Verlag, 1970. 112 pp.

Deutsche Kommunistische Partei. *5. Tagung, 1970: An der Schwelle der 70er Jahre*. Düsseldorf, Parteivorstand der DKP, 1970. 34 pp.

Dulles, Eleanor Lansing. *One Germany or Two*. Stanford, Hoover Institution Press, 1970. 315 pp.

Kool, Fritz (ed.). *Die Linke gegen die Parteiherrschaft.* Olten, Walter-Verlag, 1970. 639 pp.

Meissner, Boris. *Die deutsche Ostpolitik 1961-1970: Kontinuität und Wandel.* Köln, Verlag Wissenschaft und Politik, 1970. 448 pp.

Ridder, Winfried. *Die DKP: Programm und Politik.* Bonn, Verlag Neue Gesellschaft GmbH, 1970. 78 pp.

Sandoz, Gerard. *La gauche allemande.* Paris, Julliard, 1970. 256 pp.

Great Britain

Hulse, James W. *Revolutionists in London: A Study of Five Unorthodox Socialists.* London, Oxford University Press, 1970. 246 pp.

Newton, Kenneth. *The Sociology of British Communism.* New York, Fernhill House, 1970. 214 pp.

Italy

Alcara, Rosa. *La formazione e i primi anni del Partito Comunista Italiano nella storiografia marxista.* Milano, Cooperativa Edz. Jaca Book, 1970. 188 pp.

Chiaromonte, Gerardo. *I comunisti e i contadini.* Roma, Editori Riuniti, 1970. 128 pp.

Lucini, Marcello. *L'imperialismo comunista.* Milano, Vita e Pensiero, 1970. 250 pp.

Secchia, Pietro. *L'azione svolta dal Partito Comunista in Italia durante il fascismo (1927-1932).* Milano, Feltrinelli, 1970. 530 pp.

Tobagi, Walter. *Storia del movimento studentesco e dei marxisti-leninisti in Italia.* Milano, Sugar, 1970. 157 pp.

Spain

Lorenzo, Cesar M. *Les anarchistes espagnols et le pouvoir.* Paris, Le Seuil, 1970. 430 pp.

Nuñez de Arenas, Manuel. *Historia del movimento obrero espanõl.* Barcelona, Edit. Nova Terra, 1970. 264 pp.

Switzerland

Hardmeier, Benno. *Aus der Geschichte der schweizerischen Arbeiterbewegung.* Bern, Lang, 1970. 156 pp.

Hass, Leonhard. *Carl Vital Moor, 1852-1932: Ein Leben fur Marx und Lenin.* Köln, Benzig, 1970. 380 pp.

MIDDLE EAST AND AFRICA

Beeri, Eliezer. *Army Officers in Arab Politics and Society.* New York, Praeger, 1970. 514 pp.

Cohen, Aharon. *Israel and the Arab World.* New York, Funk and Wagnalls, 1970. 704 pp.

Dagan, Avigdor. *Moscow and Jerusalem: Twenty Years of Relations Between Israel and the Soviet Union.* London, Abelard-Schuman, 1970. 255 pp.

Guild, William B. *Communist Influence in Sub-Saharan Africa.* Maxwell AFB, Alabama, 1970. 62 pp.

Ismael, Tarez Y. *Governments and Politics of the Contemporary Middle East.* Homewood, Ill., Dorsey Press, 1970. 450 pp.

Khadduri, Majid. *Political Trends in the Arab World: The Role of Ideas and Ideals in Politics.* Baltimore, Johns Hopkins Press, 1970. 298 pp.

———. *Republican Iraq: A Study of Iraqi Politics Since the Revolution of 1958.* New York, Oxford University Press, 1970. 318 pp.

Khalili, Joseph E. *Communist China's Interaction With the Arab Nationalists Since the Bandung Conference.* New York, Exposition Press, 1970. 121 pp.

Kimche, Jon. *The Second Arab Awakening.* New York, Holt, Rinehart and Winston, 1970. 288 pp.

Klieman, Aaron S. *Soviet Russia and the Middle East.* Baltimore, Johns Hopkins Press, 1970. 107 pp.

Lefever, Ernest W. *Spear and Scepter: Army, Police, and Politics in Tropical Africa.* Washington, Brookings Institution, 1970. 251 pp.

Legvold, Robert. *Soviet Policy in West Africa.* Cambridge, Mass., Harvard University Press, 1970. 372 pp.

Lenczowski, George (ed.). *The Political Awakening in the Middle East.* New York, Prentice Hall, 1970. 180 pp.

Middle East Institute. *The Soviet Union and the Middle East: A Summary Record.* Washington, D.C., Middle East Institute, 1970. 51 pp.

Moore, Clement Henry. *Politics in North Africa: Algeria, Morocco, and Tunisia.* Boston, Little, Brown and Company, 1970. 360 pp.

Pajetta, Gian Carlo. *Socialismo e Mondo Arabo.* Roma, Editori Riuniti, 1970. 115 pp.

Nkrumah, Kwame. *Class Struggle in Africa.* New York, International Publishers, 1970. 96 pp.

Ottaway, David. *Algeria: The Politics of a Socialist Revolution.* Berkeley, University of California Press, 1970. 336 pp.

Solodovnikov, V.G., Letnev, A.B., and Manchkha, P.I. *Politicheskiye Partii Afriki.* Moscow, Nauka, 1970. 343 pp.

Trevelyan, Lord Humphrey. *The Middle East in Revolution.* London, Macmillan, 1970. 275 pp.

Weyl, Nathaniel. *Traitors' End: The Rise and Fall of the Communist Movement in Southern Africa.* New Rochelle, N.Y., Arlington House, 1970. 261 pp.

Yaari, Ehud. *Strike Terror: The Story of Fatah.* New York, Sabra Books, 1970. 388 pp.

NORTH AMERICA

Communist Party, U.S.A. *New Program of the Communist Party, U.S.A.* New York, New Outlook Publishers, 1970. 128 pp.

————— . *Of The People, For The People.* New York, New Outlook Publishers, 1970. 32 pp.

Foster, Julian, and Long, Durward. *Protest: Student Activism in America.* New York, William Morrow & Co., 1970. 596 pp.

Green, Gil. *Terrorism—Is it Revolutionary?* New York, New Outlook Publishers, 1970. 40 pp.

Howe, Irving (ed.). *Beyond the New Left.* New York, McCall, 1970. 249 pp.

Jacobs, Harold (ed.). *Weatherman.* Berkeley, Cal., Ramparts Press, Inc., 1970. 519 pp.

Lightfoot, Claude. *Black America and the World Revolution.* New York, New Outlook Publishers, 1970. 96 pp.

Lothstein, Arthur (ed.). *"All We Are Saying ...": The Philosophy of the New Left.* New York, G.P. Putnam's Sons, 1970. 381 pp.

Lyons, Eugene. *The Red Decade.* New Rochelle, N.Y., Arlington House, 1970. 423 pp.

Methvin, Eugene H. *The Riot Makers.* New Rochelle, N.Y., Arlington House, 1970. 586 pp.

Morris, Leslie. *Look on Canada Now.* Toronto, Progress, 1970. 216 pp.

Myerson, Michael. *These Are the Good Old Days: Coming of Age as a Radical in America's Late, Late Years.* New York, Grossman, 1970. 178 pp.

LATIN AMERICA

General

Adler, Gerhard. *Revolutionäres Lateinamerika*. Paderborn, Schoningh, 1970. 220 pp.

Arismendi, Rodney. *Lenin, la revolución y América Latina*. Montevideo, Editorial EPU, 1970. 480 pp.

Bahne, Siegfried (ed.). *Archives de Jules Humbert Droz*. Dodrecht, Holland, D. Reidel, 1970. 655 pp.

Carlton, Robert G. (ed.). *Soviet Image of Contemporary Latin America: A Documentary History, 1960-1968*. Austin, University of Texas Press, 1970. 365 pp.

Clissold, Stephen. *Soviet Relations with Latin America, 1918-1968: A Documentary Survey*. New York, Oxford University Press, 1970. 313 pp.

Debray, Régis. *Strategy for Revolution: Essays on Latin America*. New York, Monthly Review Press, 1970. 256 pp.

Ferla, Salvador. *Cristianos y marxistas*. Buenos Aires, Peña Lillo, 1970. 360 pp.

Gott, Richard. *Guerrilla Movements in Latin America*. London, Nelson, 1970. 452 pp.

Instituto Marx-Engels-Lenin. *La lucha de guerrillas a la luz de los clásicos del marxismo-leninismo*. Caracas, Librería Politécnica Moulines, 1970. 130 pp.

Johnson, Cecil. *Communist China and Latin America, 1959-1967*. New York, Columbia University Press, 1970. 324 pp.

Larteguy, Jean. *The Guerrillas*. New York, World Publishing Company, 1970. 267 pp.

Max, Alphonse. *Guerrillas in Latein Amerika*. Zürich, Schweizerische Handelszeitung, 1970. 62 pp.

Oswald, Joseph Gregory, and Strover, Anthony J. (eds.). *The Soviet Union and Latin America*. New York, Praeger, 1970. 190 pp.

Torres, Camilo. *Dos rebeldes; vida y textos pro Camilo Torres y Carlos Marighella*. Lima, Editorial Machu Picchu, 1970. 105 pp.

————— . *Revolutionary Writings*. New York, Herder and Herder, 1970. 207 pp.

Argentina

Ghioldi, Rodolfo, *et al. Vigencia del leninismo hoy en la Argentina*. Buenos Aires, Editorial Anteo, 1970. 264 pp.

Melo, Carlos R. *Los partidos políticos argentinos*. Córdoba, Universidad Nacional, 1970. 313 pp.

Partido Comunista de la Argentina. *Estatuto del Partido Comunista de la Argentina, aprobado en el XIII Congreso Nacional celebrado entre los días 25 y 29 de marzo de 1969*. Buenos Aires, Editorial Anteo, 1970. 31 pp.

Ratzer, José. *Los marxistas argentinos de 90*. Buenos Aires, Ediciones Signos, 1970. 193 pp.

Rosales, Juan. *Los cristianos, los marxistas y la revolución*. Buenos Aires, Ediciones Silaba, 1970. 449 pp.

Bolivia

Alcazar, José Luís. *Nancahuasú: La guerrilla del Ché en Bolivia*. Mexico City, Ediciones Era, 1970. 297 pp.

Harris, Richard. *Death of a Revolutionary: Ché Guevara's Last Mission*. New York, Norton, 1970. 219 pp.

James, Daniel (comp.). *The Complete Bolivian Diaries of Ché Guevara and Other Captured Documents*. New York, Stein and Day, 1970. 330 pp.

Malloy, James M. *Bolivia: The Uncompleted Revolution*. Pittsburgh, University of Pittsburgh Press, 1970. 396 pp.

Lara, Jesús. *Nancahuasú*. Cochabamba, Los Amigos del Libro, 1970. 168 pp.

Partido Comunista de Bolivia. *Vladimir Ilich Lenin*. Cochabamba, Los Amigos del Libro, 1970. 189 pp.

Reyes Rodríguez, Eliseo. *Diarios de Bolivia por Rolando [pseud.] Pombo [pseud.] Braulio [pseud.]*. Caracas, Ediciones Barbara, 1970. 163 pp.

Ruíz, Jaime Gabriel. *El Ché no murió en Bolivia*. Lima, Santa Magdalena, S.A., 1970. 237 pp.

Selser, Gregorio. *La C.I.A. en Bolivia*. Buenos Aires, Editorial Hernández, 1970. 400 pp.

Brazil

Partido Comunista do Brasil. *La guerra popular en el Brasil*. Montevideo, Nativa Libros, 1970. 57 pp.

Chile

Nuñez, Carlos. *Chile ¿La ultima opción electoral?* Santiago, Editorial Prensa latinoamericana, 1970. 116 pp.

Programa básico de gobierno de la unidad popular. Santiago, Imprenta Horizonte, 1970. 48 pp.

Colombia

Rojas, Robinson. *Colombia: surge el primer Vietnam en América Latina*. Santiago de Chile, PLA, 1970. 64 pp.

Partido Comunista de Colombia. *40 [i.e. Cuarenta] años de lucha por la revolucíon colombiana*. Bogotá, Comisión Nacional de Propaganda, 1970. 13 pp.

Cuba

Bonachea, Rolando, and Valdés, Nelson (eds.). *Selected Works of Fidel Castro: 1952-1958*. Vol. I. Cambridge, Mass., M.I.T. Press, 1970.

Castro, Fidel. *The Making of a Revolution*. Cambridge, Mass., M.I.T. Press, 1970. 350 pp.

————. *Socialismo y comunismo, un proceso único*. Montevideo, Editorial Aportes, 1970. 188 pp.

Clytus, John, with Rieker, Jane. *Black Man in Red Cuba*. Coral Gables, Fla., University of Miami Press, 1970. 158 pp.

Dalton, Roque. *¿Revolución en la Revolución y la Critica de Derecha*. Havana, Casa de las Americas, 1970. 204 pp.

Dumont, René. *Cuba ¿Es socialista?* Caracas, Editorial Tiempo Nuevo, 1970. 261 pp.

García Montes, Jorge. *Historia del Partido Comunista de Cuba*. Miami, Ediciones Universal, 1970. 559 pp.

Green, Gil. *Revolution, Cuban Style: Impressions of a Recent Visit.* New York, International Publishers, 1970. 125 pp.

Guevara, Ernesto. *Obras 1957-1967.* 2 volumes. Havana, Casa de las Américas, 1970.

Horowitz, Irving Louis (comp.). *Cuba: diez años después.* Buenos Aires, Editorial Tiempo contemporáneo, 1970. 172 pp.

Karol, K.S. *Guerrillas in Power: The Course of the Cuban Revolution.* New York, Hill and Wang, 1970. 624 pp.

Lamore, Jean. *Cuba; que sais-je?* Paris, Presses Universitaires de France, 1970. 125 pp.

Macaulay, Neill. *A Rebel in Cuba: An American's Memoir.* Chicago, Quadrangle Books, 1970. 199 pp.

O'Connor, James R. *The Origins of Socialism in Cuba.* Ithaca, Cornell University Press, 1970. 338 pp.

Ortega, Luis. *¡Yo soy el Ché!* México, Ediciones Monroy Padilla, 1970. 314 pp.

Pardo Llada, José. *El "Ché" que yo conocí.* Medellín Editorial Bedout, 1970. 142 pp.

Peraza, Fermín. *Revolutionary Cuba: A Bibliographical Guide, 1968.* Coral Gables, Fla., University of Miami Press, 1970. 262 pp.

Seiglie Ferrer, Carlos. *Siete diálogos. Cuba: pasado y presente.* Miami, Libreria y Distribuidora Universal, 1970. 302 pp.

Sinclair, Andrew. *Che Guevara.* New York, The Viking Press, 1970. 114 pp.

Toirac, Inciano D. *Cuba, el comunismo y la política norteamericana.* Miami, AIP Publications Center, 1970. 132 pp.

Widmann, Carlos. *Report aus Kuba.* München, List, 1970. 150 pp.

Peru

Asociacíon Cultural Peruano-Soviética. *1917-1969; Homenaje peruano a la Unión Soviética.* Lima, Librería Juan Mejía Baca, 1970. 62 pp.

Basadro, Jorge. *Lenin en escritos peruanos.* Lima, Jorge Falcón, 1970. 144 pp.

Béjar, Héctor. *Peru 1965: Notes on a Guerrilla Experience.* New York, Monthly Review Press, 1970. 144 pp.

Partido Comunista Peruano. *La clase obrera ante la ley de industrias; una nueva etapa en el proceso revolutionario.* Lima, 1970. 55 pp.

Uruguay

Arismendi, Rodney. *La izquierda uruguaya ante la hora de America Latina.* Lima, Ediciones Unidad, 1970. 57 pp.

Anon. *Tupamaros, ¿conspiración o revolución?* Montevideo, Editorial "Voz Rebelde," 1970. 44 pp.

ASIA

General
Allen, Sir Richard. *A Short Introduction to the History and Politics of Southeast Asia.* New York, Oxford University Press, 1970. 306 pp.

Bloodworth, Dennis. *An Eye for the Dragon: Southeast Asia Observed, 1954-1970.* New York, Farrar, Straus & Giroux, 1970. 414 pp.

Burchett, Wilfred G. *The Second Indochina War: Cambodia and Laos.* New York, International Publishers, 1970. 204 pp.

Ch'en, Jerome, and Tarling, Nicholas (eds.). *Studies in the Social History of China and South-East Asia.* Cambridge, Cambridge University Press, 1970. 424 pp.

Chomsky, Noam. *At War with Asia.* New York, Pantheon Books, 1970. 313 pp.

Gettelman, M. and S., and Kaplan, L. and C. *Conflict in Indochina.* New York, Random House, 1970. 461 pp.

Gurtov, Melvin. *Southeast Asia Tomorrow: Problems and Prospects for U.S. Policy.* Baltimore, Johns Hopkins Press, 1970. 114 pp.

Kolevzon, Edward R. *East Asia: China, Japan, Korea.* Rockleigh, N.J., Allyn & Bacon, 1970. 147 pp.

Lifton, Robert Jay (ed.). *America and the Asian Revolutions.* Chicago, Aldine, 1970. 178 pp.

Pirovano-Wang, N. *L'Asie orientale de 1840 à nos jours.* Paris, Fernand Nathan, 1970. 265 pp.

Sen Gupta, Bhabani. *The Fulcrum of Asia: Relations Among China, India, Pakistan, and the USSR.* New York, Pegasus, 1970. 383 pp.

Wilson, Richard. *Asia Awakes: A Continent in Transition.* New York, Weybright & Talley, 1970. 460 pp.

Burma
Bröker, Hans. *Burma 1969, die gegenwärtige politische Lage und einige ihrer Hintergrundsprobleme.* Köln, Bundesinstitut für Ostwissenschaftliche und Internationale Studien, 1970. 29 pp.

Donnison, F.S.V. *Burma.* New York, Praeger, 1970. 263 pp.

China
Barnett, A. Doak, and Reischauer, Edwin O. (eds.). *The United States and China: The Next Decade.* New York, Praeger, 1970. 250 pp.

Beal, John Robinson. *Marshall in China.* Garden City, N.Y., Doubleday, 1970. 385 pp.

Belden, Jack. *China Shakes the World.* New York, Monthly Review Press, 1970. 524 pp.

Boorman, Howard L. (ed.). *Biographical Dictionary of Republican China.* 3 volumes. New York, Columbia University Press, 1970.

Buchanan, Keith McPherson. *The Transformation of the Chinese Earth: Aspects of the Evaluation of the Earliest Times to Mao Tse-tung.* New York, Praeger, 1970. 336 pp.

Buck, Pearl S. *China As I See It.* New York, John Day, 1970. 305 pp.

Bush, Richard Clarence. *Religion in Communist China.* Nashville, Abingdon Press, 1970. 432 pp.

Chai, Winberg (ed.). *Essential Works of Chinese Communism.* New York, Pica Press, 1970. 464 pp.

Chen, Yung Ping. *Chinese Political Thought: Mao Tse-tung and Liu Shao-chi.* The Hague, Martinus Nijhoff, 1970. 129 pp.

Ch'en, Jerome (ed.). *Mao Papers: Anthology and Bibliography.* New York, Oxford University Press, 1970. 221 pp.

China After the Cultural Revolution: A Selection from the Bulletin of Atomic Scientists. New York, Vintage Books, 1970. 247 pp.

Cohen, Jerome Alan (ed.). *The Dynamics of China's Foreign Relations.* Cambridge, Mass., Harvard University Press, 1970. 139 pp.

Croizier, Ralph C. (comp.). *China's Cultural Legacy and Communism.* New York, Praeger, 1970. 313 pp.

Dawson, Owen Lafayette. *Communist China's Agriculture: Its Development and Future Potential.* New York, Praeger, 1970. 326 pp.

Douglass, Bruce, and Terrill, Ross (ed.). *China and Ourselves: Explorations and Revisions by a New Generation.* Boston, Beacon Press, 1970. 259 pp.

Dutt, Gargi and V.P. *China's Cultural Revolution.* New York, Asia Publishing House, 1970. 260 pp.

Dyson, Antony, and Towers, Bernard (eds.). *China and the West: Mankind Evolving.* London, Garnstone Press, 1970. 141 pp.

Ebon, Martin. *Lin Piao: The Life and Writings of China's New Ruler.* New York, Stein & Day, 1970. 378 pp.

Esmein, Jean. *La Revolution Culturelle Chinoise.* Paris, Editions du Seuil, 1970. 347 pp.

Franke, Wolfgang. *A Century of Chinese Revolution, 1851-1949.* Columbia, University of South Carolina Press, 1970. 202 pp.

Furth, Charlotte. *Ting Wen-chiang: Science and China's New Culture.* Cambridge, Mass., Harvard University Press, 1970. 307 pp.

Harrison, James P. *The Communists and Chinese Peasant Rebellions: A Study in the Rewriting of Chinese History.* London, Victor Gollancz, 1970. 363 pp.

Hinton, Harold C. *China's Turbulent Quest: An Analysis of China's Foreign Relations Since 1945.* New York, Macmillan, 1970. 340 pp.

Hinton, William. *Iron Oxen: A Documentary of Revolution in Chinese Farming.* London, Monthly Review Press, 1970. 225 pp.

Hsiang, Tso-liang. *Chinese communism in 1927: City vs. Countryside.* Hong Kong, Chinese University of Hong Kong, 1970. 197 pp.

Hsiung, James C. *Ideology and Practice: The Evolution of Chinese Communism.* New York, Praeger, 1970. 376 pp.

Hsü, Immanuel Chung-yüeh. *The Rise of Modern China.* New York, Oxford University Press, 1970. 830 pp.

Important Documents on the Great Proletarian Cultural Revolution in China. Peking, Foreign Languages Press, 1970. 323 pp.

Kennet, John. *The Rise of Communist China: With a Brief History of Japan.* Glasgow, Blackie & Son, 1970. 129 pp.

Kitagawa, Joseph M. (ed.). *Understanding Modern China.* Chicago, Quadrangle Books, 1970. 284 pp.

Lee, Chae-jin. *Communist China's Policy Toward Laos: A Case Study 1954-67.* Lawrence, University of Kansas Center for East Asian Studies, 1970. 161 pp.

Lewis, John Wilson (ed.). *Party Leadership and Revolutionary Power in China.* New York, Cambridge University Press, 1970. 422 pp.

Li, Cheng-chung. *The Chinese Communist War Tactics and Peace Strategy.* Taipei, World Anti-Communist League, 1970. 103 pp.

Li, Dun-jen. *The Road to Communism: China since 1912.* New York, Van Nostrand-Reinhold, 1970. 403 pp.

Li, Tien-min. *Chou En-lai.* Taipei, Institute of International Relations, 1970. 426 pp.

Lifton, Robert Jay. *Die Unsterblichkeit des Revolutionärs: Mao Tse-tung und die chinesische Kulturrevolution.* München, List Verlag, 1970. 228 pp.

Meserve, Walter J., Jr., and Ruth I. (eds.). *Modern Drama from Communist China.* New York, New York University Press, 1970. 368 pp.

Meyer, Charles, and Allen, Ian (eds.). *Source Materials in Chinese History.* New York, Frederick Warne, 1970. 190 pp.

Pratt, Keith L. *Visitors to China: Eyewitness Accounts of Chinese History.* New York, Praeger, 1970. 175 pp.

Price, Ronald Francis. *Education in Communist China.* New York, Praeger, 1970. 308 pp.

Prybyla, Jan S. *The Political Economy of Communist China.* Scranton, Pa., International Textbook, 1970. 605 pp.

Schwartz, Benjamin Isadore. *Communism & China: Ideology in Flux.* New York, Atheneum, 1970. 254 pp.

Spence, Jonathan D. *To Change China: Western Advisers in China, 1620-1960.* Boston, Little, Brown and Co., 1970. 335 pp.

Trager, Frank N., and Henderson, William (eds.). *Communist China, 1949-1969: A Twenty-Year Appraisal.* New York, New York University Press, 1970. 356 pp.

Tuan, Yi-fu. *China.* Chicago, Aldine, 1970. 224 pp.

U.S. Department of State. Bureau of Intelligence and Research. *Directory of Chinese Communist Officials: Party, Provincial, Municipal and Military.* Washington, U.S. Government Printing Office, 1970. 251 pp.

Vallette-Henery, Martine (comp. and trans.). *De la révolution littéraire a là littérature révolutionnaire: récits chinois, 1918-42.* Paris, Editions de l'Herne, 1970. 333 pp.

Van Ness, Peter. *Revolution and Chinese Foreign Policy: Peking's Support for Wars of National Liberation.* Berkeley, University of California Press, 1970. 266 pp.

Vogel, Ezra Feivel. *Canton Under Communism: Programs and Politics in a Provincial Capital, 1949-1968.* Cambridge, Mass., Harvard University Press, 1970. 448 pp.

Waller, D. *The Government and Politics of Communist China.* New York, Hillary House, 1970. 192 pp.

Wei, Chung-gi K. *The Kuomintang-Communist Struggle in China, 1922-1949.* The Hague, Martinus Nijhoff, 1970. 131 pp.

Wheelwright, E.L., and McFarlane, B. *Chinese Road to Socialism: Economics of the Cultural Revolution.* New York, Monthly Review Press, 1970. 256 pp.

Whitney, Joseph B.P. *China: Area, Administration, and Nation Building.* Chicago, University of Chicago Press, 1970. 198 pp.

Wong, Molly. *They Changed My China.* Nashville, Broadman, 1970. 127 pp.

Wu, Yuan-li, and Sheeks, Robert B. *The Organization and Support of Scientific Research and Development in Mainland China.* New York, Praeger, 1970. 592 pp.

Yu, George T. *China and Tanzania: A Study in Cooperative Interaction.* Berkeley, University of California Center for Chinese Studies, 1970. 100 pp.

India

Adhikari, G. (ed.). *Lenin and India.* New Delhi, People's Publishing House, 1970. 250 pp.

Ahmad, Muzaffar. *Myself and the Communist Party of India (1920-1929).* Calcutta, National Book Agency Private Limited, 1970.

Chattopadhyaya, Gautam. *Communism and Bengal's Freedom Movement, Volume I (1917-29).* 1970. No publisher. 188 pp.

Gupta, Ranajit Das. *Problems of Economic Transition: Indian Case Study.* Calcutta, National Publishers, 1970. 416 pp.

Loomis, Charles P., and Rytina, Joan Huber. *Marxist Theory and Indian Communism: A Sociological Interpretation.* East Lansing, Michigan State University Press, 1970. 148 pp.

Naik, J.A. *Soviet Policy Towards India: From Stalin to Brezhnev.* Delhi, Vikas Publications, 1970. 201 pp.

Sen, Mohit. *The Indian Revolution: Review and Perspective.* New Delhi, People's Publishing House, 1970.

Indonesia

Dahm, Bernhard. *History of Indonesia in the Twentieth Century.* New York, Praeger, 1970. 320 pp.

Feith, Herbert, and Castles, Lance. *Indonesian Political Thinking: 1945-1965.* Ithaca, N.Y., Cornell University Press, 1970. 505 pp.

Zainu'ddin, Ailsa Gwennyth. *A Short History of Indonesia.* New York, Praeger, 1970. 299 pp.

Japan

Béraud, Bernard. *La gauche révolutionnaire au Japon.* Paris, Editions du Seuil, 1970. 157 pp.

Olson, Lawrence Alexander. *Japan in Postwar Asia.* New York, Praeger, 1970. 292 pp.

Korea: Democratic People's Republic of Korea

Baik, Bong. *Kim Il-sung: Biography.* 3 volumes. Tokyo, Miraisha, 1969-1970.

Joy, Charles Turner. *How Communists Negotiate.* Santa Monica, Cal., Fidelis Publisher, 1970. 178 pp.

Kim, Byong Sik. *Modern Korea: The Socialist North, Revolutionary Perspectives in the South, and Unification.* New York, International Publishers, 1970. 319 pp.

Suh, Dae-Sook (ed.). *Documents of Korean Communism, 1918-1948.* Princeton, N.J., Princeton University Press, 1970. 591 pp.

Laos

Adams, Nina S., and McCoy, Alfred W. (eds.). *Laos: War and Revolution.* New York, Harper & Row, 1970. 482 pp.

Langer, Paul F., and Zasloff, Joseph. *North Vietnam and the Pathet Lao: Partners in the Struggle for Laos.* Cambridge, Mass., Harvard University Press, 1970. 262 pp.

Malaysia

Means, Gordon. *Malaysian Politics.* London, University of London Press, 1970. 447 pp.

Ryan, N.J. *The Making of Modern Malaysia and Singapore.* New York, Oxford University Press, 1970. 280 pp.

Mongolia
Petrov, Victor P. *Mongolia: A Profile.* New York, Praeger, 1970. 173 pp.

Nepal
Rose, Leo E., and Fisher, Margaret W. *The Politics of Nepal: Persistence and Change in an Asian Monarchy.* Ithaca, N.Y., Cornell University Press, 1970. 197 pp.

Pakistan
Ali, Tariq. *Pakistan: Military Rule or People's Power?* London, Jonathan Cape, 1970. 270 pp.

Philippines
Pomeroy, William J. *American Neo-colonialism: Its Emergence in the Philippines and Asia.* New York, International Publishers, 1970. 255 pp.

Roosevelt, Nicholas. *The Philippines: A Treasure and a Problem.* New York, Praeger, 1970. 315 pp.

Thailand
Poole, Peter A. *The Vietnamese in Thailand: A Historical Perspective.* Ithaca, N.Y., Cornell University Press, 1970. 180 pp.

Weatherbee, Donald E. *United Front in Thailand: A Documentary Analysis.* Columbia, University of South Carolina, Institute of International Studies, 1970. 103 pp.

Wilson, David A. *The United States and the Future of Thailand.* New York, Praeger, 1970. 182 pp.

Vietnam
Brandon, Henry. *Anatomy of Error: The Secret History of the Vietnam War.* London, Deutsch, 1970. 178 pp.

Chung, Ly Qui (ed.). *Between Two Fires: The Unheard Voices of Vietnam.* New York, Praeger, 1970. 144 pp.

Figueres, Leo, and Fourniau, Charles. *Ho Chi Minh, Notre Camarade.* Paris, Editions sociales, 1970. 267 pp.

Gheddo, Piero. *The Cross and the Bo-Tree: Catholics and Buddhists in Vietnam.* New York, Sheid and Ward, 1970. 368 pp.

Giap, General Vo Nguyen. *Banner of People's War, The Party's Military Line.* New York, Praeger, 1970. 118 pp.

Hosmer, Stephen T. *Viet Cong Repression and Its Implications for the Future.* Lexington, Mass., Heath Lexington Books, 1970. 176 pp.

French, W. *Patterns for Victory.* New York, Exposition Press, 1970. 170 pp.

Joint Development Group. *The Postwar Development of the Republic of Vietnam: Policies and Programs.* New York, Praeger, 1970. 552 pp.

Kang, Pilwon. *The Road to Victory in Vietnam.* New York, Exposition Press, 1970. 78 pp.

Keesings Research Report. *South Vietnam: A Political History, 1954-1970.* New York, Scribner's, 1970. 168 pp.

McAlister, John T., Jr., and Mus, Paul. *The Vietnamese and Their Revolution.* New York, Harper & Row, 1970. 173 pp.

Our President Ho Chi Minh. Hanoi, Foreign Languages Publishing House, 1970. 207 pp.

Shaplen, Robert. *The Road from War: Vietnam 1965-1970.* New York, Harper & Row, 1970. 368 pp.

Sansom, Robert L. *The Economics of Insurgency in the Mekong Delta of Vietnam.* Cambridge, Mass., M.I.T. Press, 1970. 283 pp.

Stetler, Russell (ed.). *The Military Art of People's War: Selected Writings of General Vo Nguyen Giap.* New York, Monthly Review Press, 1970. 320 pp.

Woodis, Jack (ed.). *Ho Chi Minh: Selected Articles and Speeches.* New York, International Publishers Co., Inc., 1970. 176 pp.

INDEX

INDEX OF PERSONS

811